RESEARCH METHODS

FOR

SOCIAL WORKERS

AN INTRODUCTION

12

Credits appear on pages 763–764 and represent an extension of the copyright page.
Pair Bond Publications
652 Wynding Oaks
Kalamazoo, Michigan 49006
(269) 353-7100
www.PairBondPublications.com

RESEARCH METHODS
FOR
SOCIAL WORKERS

AN INTRODUCTION

12

Richard M. Grinnell, Jr.
Western Michigan University

Margaret Williams
University of Calgary

Yvonne A. Unrau
Western Michigan University

Preface

TIME FLIES FAST. The first edition of this book was published nearly 30 years ago. And, from the get-go, we've always intended it to be used by beginning social work students as their first introduction to basic social work research methodology. As in the previous editions, we've wanted to create an inexpensive, "student-friendly" introduction to social work research methods imbedded within the scientific method of inquiry—the most commonly used framework to generate relevant social work knowledge.

BOOK'S PHILOSOPHY

THE THREE OF US have been teaching social work research methods for decades. Given our teaching experience—and with the changing demographics of our ever-increasing first-generation university student population—we asked ourselves a simple question: "What research methodology can *realistically* be taught to these beginning social work students in a typical one-semester social work research methods course?" The answer to our question is contained within the chapters that follow.

- **Competency 4:** Engage in Practice-Informed Research and Research-Informed Practice

- **Competency 9:** Evaluate Practice with Individuals, Families, Groups, Organizations, and Communities

— **Newly updated content has been added** to this edition in an effort to keep information current, while retaining the material that has stood the test of time. In fact, this book is 214 pages longer than the previous edition.

— **Two new chapters have been added:**

- Chapter 3: Writing Literature Reviews

- Chapter 8: The Mixed-Methods Research Approach

— **The glossary contains 26 new entries.**

— **Evidence-based practice content has been added throughout the entire book.**

— **Three research roles are emphasized throughout the book.** As contained in all chapter openings, we stress that for students to become successful evidence-based practitioners they have an ethical obligation to integrate at least one of the three research roles into their daily practice activities:

  1. Research consumer

  2. Research partner—either as a co-researcher or research participant

  3. Creator and disseminator of research (or knowledge)

— **Critical thinking/application/integration exercises have been added.** The numerous exercises at the end of each chapter provide great springboards for classroom discussion.

— **Numerous instructor resources are available within the book's website** (www. PairBondPublications.com).

The creative use of our book is highly encouraged. We only provide the minimal course content that we feel should be taught to beginning social work students. It's up to the instructor to add to our foundation through the use of the book's website and/or their own personal material, additional readings, videos, group assignments, guest lectures, and so forth.

KEEPING STUDENTS IN MIND

FIRST AND FOREMOST, students will appreciate the book's relevant social work content and practicality.

On content . . . Students will:

1. Easily follow what's being presented,

2. Comprehend all the concepts,

3. Clearly understand the logic of how the research process unfolds, and

4. Appreciate how the research enterprise helps them to become competent professional social workers.

On practicality . . . The overall usefulness of this edition has been improved via direct student feedback. Students told us they wanted:

1. *Rounded corners* and *more physical flexibility.* They believed this would make it easier to get the book in and out of their backpacks.

2. *Larger typeface.* As one student openly put it, "I don't want to have to squint when reading a textbook—especially a research book and all."

3. *One-column format.* Many students believe that a two-column format make a book's content harder to follow than a one-column format—especially when tables, figures, graphs, and boxes are introduced.

4. *Extra blank space.* They simply wanted to write their classroom notes directly in the book rather than on separate notepads.

5. *An inexpensive book.* This book is the least expensive social work research methods book on the market today.

A Look to the Future

We hope graduating students will keep our book on their bookshelves and refer to it from time to time when they need to review a particular concept. If it helps them to expand their knowledge base and assists them in becoming evidence-based practitioners, our efforts will have been more than justified.

If our work also encourages them to use research findings in their future practices and to actually perform (or participate in) research studies in order to continue our pursuit of a stronger, better-knit theoretical base for contemporary social work practice, our task will be fully rewarded.

We hope that the apparent levity with which we have treated the social work research enterprise will be accepted in the same spirit as it was intended. Our goal was not to diminish research but to present the research process with warmth and humanness so that the students' first experience with it will be a positive one. After all, if wetting their big toes scares them, they will never learn to swim.

Richard M. Grinnell, Jr.

Margaret Williams

Yvonne A. Unrau

Contents in Brief

PART I The Contexts of Social Work Research

1 The Place of Research in Social Work   2

2 Formulating Research Questions   62

3 Writing Literature Reviews   100

4 Research Ethics   124

5 Culturally Competent Research   172

PART II Approaches to Knowledge Development

6 The Quantitative Research Approach   206

7 The Qualitative Research Approach   250

8 The Mixed-Methods Research Approach   278

PART III   Measuring Variables

9 Measurement   304

10 Measuring Instruments   342

PART IV   Sampling and Research Designs

11 Sampling   370

12 Single-Subject Designs   398

13 Group Designs   438

PART V   Collecting Data

14 Collecting Quantitative Data   498

15 Collecting Qualitative Data   528

16 Selecting a Data-Collection Method   554

PART VI   Analyzing Data

17 Analyzing Quantitative Data   592

18 Analyzing Qualitative Data   624

PART VII   Research Proposals and Reports

19 Quantitative Proposals and Reports   658

20 Qualitative Proposals and Reports   694

Glossary   732

Credits   763

References and Further Reading   765

Index   773

Contents in Detail

PART I
The Contexts of Social Work Research

CHAPTER 1: THE PLACE OF RESEARCH IN SOCIAL WORK 2

TOWARD ACCOUNTABILITY 5

Council on Social Work Education

National Association of Social Workers

This Book's Objectives

WAYS OF KNOWING 9

Authority

Questioning the Accuracy of Authority Figures

Tradition

Sorry, That's the Way It's Done Around Here
The Need to "Fit In"

Experience

Beliefs and Intuition

Professional Ethical Concerns

The Scientific Method

Phases of the Scientific Method
It Doesn't Exist If It Can't Be Observed and Measured
Nothing Is Absolutely Certain Forever
Example of the Scientific Inquiry Process
The Purpose of Social Work Research

APPROACHES TO THE SCIENTIFIC METHOD 25

The Quantitative Approach

The Qualitative Approach

The Mixed-Methods Approach

Selecting a Research Approach

PURE AND APPLIED RESEARCH STUDIES 33

Pure Research Studies

Applied Research Studies

RESEARCH AND PRACTICE 36

RESEARCH ROLES 38

The Research Consumer

The Creator and Disseminator of Knowledge

The Contributing Partner

Integrating the Three Research Roles

CHARACTERISTICS OF RESEARCHERS 42

Value Awareness

Skeptical Curiosity

Sharing

Honesty

GOT ATTITUDE? 45

EVIDENCE-BASED PRACTICE 46

COMMITTING TO LIFELONG LEARNING 51

DEFINITION OF SOCIAL WORK RESEARCH 53

SUMMARY 54

CHAPTER 2: FORMULATING RESEARCH QUESTIONS 62

FACTORS AFFECTING QUESTIONS 64

The Social Work Profession

Pure Research Questions
Applied Research Questions
Social Problems Must Be Changeable

The Social Work Agency

The Researcher

Value Systems of the Researchers

The Social Work Practitioner

Ethical and Cultural Considerations

Political and Social Considerations

THE KNOWLEDGE-LEVEL CONTINUUM 80

Exploratory Research Studies

Descriptive Research Studies

Explanatory Research Studies

CLASSIFICATIONS OF QUESTIONS 87

Existence Questions

Composition Questions

Relationship Questions

Descriptive-Comparative Questions

Causality Questions

Causality-Comparative Questions

Causality-Comparative Interaction Questions

CRITERIA FOR GOOD QUESTIONS 92

Relevant

Researchable

Feasible

Ethical and Culturally Sensitive

SUMMARY 94

CHAPTER 3: WRITING LITERATURE REVIEWS 100

WHAT IS A LITERATURE REVIEW? 102

THE LOGIC OF DOING LITERATURE REVIEWS 104

Helps to Bring Clarity and Focus to the Research Question

Helps to Identify Gaps in the Literature

Helps to Prevent the Duplication of Knowledge

Helps to Broaden the Knowledge Base

Helps to Contextualize the Research Project

Helps to Improve a Study's Methodology

Helps to Assist in Identifying Opposing Views

WHERE & HOW TO SEARCH FOR INFORMATION 108

The Internet

STORING AND MANAGING INFORMATION 109

READING FOR A LITERATURE REVIEW 110

Preview

Overview

Inview

Developing a Theoretical Framework

Writing and Organizing a Literature Review

CRITERIA OF A GOOD LITERATURE REVIEW 117

SUMMARY 118

CHAPTER 4: RESEARCH ETHICS 124

USING CLIENTS AS RESEARCH PARTICIPANTS 126

OBTAINING INFORMED CONSENT 128

Bribery, Deception, and Other Forms of Coercion
Ingredients of an Informed Consent Form

ANONYMITY VERSUS CONFIDENTIALITY 140

Ensuring Confidentiality

DESIGNING THE STUDY IN AN ETHICAL MANNER 141

Step 2: Develop the Research Question

Refine the Research Question Through the Literature
Evaluate the Literature

Step 5: Select a Research Approach

Step 6: Specify How Variables Are Measured

Be Aware of Cultural Issues

Step 7: Select a Sample

Recruitment

Step 8: Select a Research Design

Beneficence
Equipoise, or the Uncertainty Principle
Deception

Step 9: Select a Data-Collection Method

How Data Are Collected
Who's Going to Collect the Data?
Frequency and Timing of Data Collection

Step 10: Analyze the Data

Step 11: Write and Disseminate the Research Report

ETHICS AND OUR SOCIAL SERVICE PROGRAMS 161

Misuses of Research Results

Justifying Decisions Already Made
Safeguarding Public Relations
Appraising Staff Performance

Fulfilling Funding Requirements

SUMMARY 165

CHAPTER 5: CULTURALLY COMPETENT RESEARCH 172

OUR VILLAGE 175

Working with Stakeholders or Research Teams

THE IMPACT OF CULTURE 178

Bridging the Culture Gap

Cultural Awareness

Ethnocentrism

Enculturation

Intercultural Communication

Nonverbal Communication

Verbal Communication

CULTURAL FRAMEWORKS 184

Orientation to Data

Decision Making

Individualism

Tradition

Pace of Life

CULTURALLY COMPETENT RESEARCHERS 190

Cultural Awareness

Intercultural Communication Skills

Specific Knowledge about the Culture

Appropriately Adapting Research Studies

Working with Stakeholders

Adapting Processes

Providing Meaningful Products

SUMMARY 196

PART II
Approaches to Knowledge Development

CHAPTER 6: THE QUANTITATIVE RESEARCH APPRAOCH   206

WHAT IS THE POSITIVISTIC WAY OF THINKING?   208

Striving Toward Measurability

Striving Toward Objectivity

Striving Toward Reducing Uncertainty

Striving Toward Duplication

Striving Toward the Use of Standardized Procedures

STEPS OF THE RESEARCH APPROACH   213

Step 1: Identifying the Problem

Step 2: Selecting Specific Variables

Step 2a: Determining What Others Have Found

Step 2b: Refining the General Problem Area

Step 2c: Developing Concepts

Step 2d: Identifying Variables Within Concepts

Step 2e: Defining Attributes of Variables

Step 2f: Defining Independent and Dependent Variables

Step 2g: Constructing a Hypothesis

Step 2h: Evaluating the Hypothesis

Step 3: Designing the Study

Step 3a: Measuring Variables

Step 3b: Deciding on a Sample and Research Design

Step 3c: Addressing Ethical and Cultural Issues

Step 4: Collecting the Data

Step 5: Analyzing the Data

Descriptive Statistics

Inferential Statistics

Step 6: Interpreting the Findings

  Step 6a: Comparing Your Results with Other Findings
  Step 6b: Specifying the Study's Limitations

Step 7: Presenting/Disseminating the Study's Findings

AN EXTENDED EXAMPLE   236

What's the Problem?

Formulating Initial Impressions

Determining What Others Have Found

Refining the General Problem Area

Measuring the Variables

Selecting a Sample

Addressing Ethical and Cultural Issues

Collecting the Data

Analyzing the Data

Interpreting the Data

Comparing Results with Findings from Previous Studies

Specifying the Study's Limitations

Writing and Disseminating the Study's Results

SUMMARY   244

CHAPTER 7: THE QUALITATIVE RESEARCH APPROACH   250

WHAT IS THE INTERPRETIVE WAY OF THINKING?   252

One Reality Versus Many

  Changing Realities

Subjects Versus Research Participants

Researchers' Values

Commonalities of All Qualitative Research Studies

PHASES OF THE QUALITATIVE APPROACH   256

Phases 1 and 2: Problem Identification and Question Formulation

Phase 3a: Designing the Research Study

Phase 3b: Collecting the Data

Phases 3c and 3d: Analyzing and Interpreting the Data

Numbers Versus Words

Data ≠ Information

Phases 4 and 5: Presentation and Dissemination of Findings

COMPARING RESEARCH APPROACHES   265

USING BOTH APPROACHES IN A SINGLE STUDY   267

What Do You Really Want to Know?

Example of Using Both Approaches in a Single Study

ADVANTAGES AND DISADVANTAGES   271

SUMMARY   273

CHAPTER 8: THE MIXED-METHODS RESEARCH APPROACH   278

POPULARITY OF THE APPROACH   280

An Intuitive Research Method

An Accessible Approach to Scientific Inquiry

DEFINITION   282

RESEARCH PROBLEMS AND MIXED METHODS   284

One Data Source May Be Insufficient

Example

Explain a Study's Initial Results

Example

Generalize Exploratory Findings

Example

Enhance a Study with a Second Research Approach

Example

How Best to Employ a Theoretical Stance

Example

Understand a Research Objective Through Multiple Phases

Example

ADVANTAGES **292**

CHALLENGES **294**

    Skills of the Researcher

        Quantitative Skills

        Qualitative Skills

        Solid Grounding in Mixed-Methods Research

    Time and Resources

CONVINCING OTHERS **296**

FINDING MIXED-METHODS RESEARCH STUDIES **297**

SUMMARY **298**

PART III
Measuring Variables

CHAPTER 9: MEASUREMENT **304**

LEVELS OF MEASUREMENT **306**

    Nominal Measurement

    Ordinal Measurement

    Interval Measurement

    Ratio Measurement

DESCRIBING VARIABLES BY MEASURING THEM **312**

    Correspondence

    Standardization

    Quantification

    Duplication

CRITERIA FOR SELECTING AN INSTRUMENT **316**

    Utility

    Sensitivity to Small Changes

Nonreactivity

Reliability

Test-Retest Method

Alternate-Form Method

Split-Half Method

Observer Reliability (Reliability of the Process

Validity

Content Validity

Criterion Validity

Face Validity

Construct Validity

RELIABILITY AND VALIDITY REVISITED   328

MEASUREMENT ERRORS   330

Constant Errors

Random Errors

IMPROVING VALIDITY AND RELIABILITY   334

SUMMARY   335

CHAPTER 10: MEASURING INSTRUMENTS   342

QUESTIONS TO ASK BEFORE MEASURING   344

Why Do We Want to Make the Measurement?

What Do We Want to Measure?

Who Will Make the Measurement?

What Format Do We Require?

Where Will the Measurement Be Made?

When Will the Measurement Be Made?

TYPES OF MEASURING INSTRUMENTS   351

Journals or Diaries

Logs

Inventories

Checklists

Summative Instruments

STANDARDIZED MEASURING INSTRUMENTS 356

Evaluating Standardized Measuring Instruments

Advantages and Disadvantages

Locating Standardized Measuring Instruments

Commercial or Professional Publishers

Professional Books and Journals

SUMMARY 361

Part IV
Sampling and Research Designs

CHAPTER 11: SAMPLING 370

POPULATIONS AND SAMPLING FRAMES 373

Sampling Frames

SAMPLING PROCEDURES 374

Probability Sampling

Simple Random Sampling

Systematic Random Sampling

Stratified Random Sampling

Cluster Random Sampling

Nonprobability Sampling

Availability Sampling

Purposive Sampling

Quota Sampling

Snowball Sampling

SAMPLE SIZE 385

Lessons about Sample Quality

ADVANTAGES AND DISADVANTAGES 391

SUMMARY **391**

CHAPTER **12**: SINGLE-SUBJECT DESIGNS **398**

WHAT ARE SINGLE-SUBJECT DESIGNS? **400**

THE RESEARCH PROCESS **402**

UNIT OF ANALYSIS **402**

REQUIREMENTS **404**

Setting Measurable Client Objectives

Target Problems

Selecting Valid and Reliable Outcome Measures

Graphically Displaying the Resulting Data

EXPLORATORY DESIGNS **409**

A Design

B Design

BB₁ Design

BC Design

DESCRIPTIVE DESIGNS **417**

AB Design

ABC and *ABCD* Designs

EXPLANATORY DESIGNS **419**

Reversal Designs

ABA and ABAB Designs

BAB Design

BCBC Design

Multiple-Baseline Designs

More Than One Case

More Than One Setting

More Than One Problem

RETROSPECTIVE BASELINES **428**

ETHICAL ISSUES **429**

SUMMARY 431

CHAPTER 13: GROUP DESIGNS 438

KNOWLEDGE LEVELS 440

CHARACTERISTICS OF "IDEAL" EXPERIMENTS 441

Controlling the Time Order of Variables

Manipulating the Independent Variable

Establishing Relationships between Variables

Controlling Rival Hypotheses

Holding Extraneous Variables Constant

Using Correlated Variation

Using Analysis of Covariance

Using a Control Group

Randomly Assigning Research Participants to Groups

Matched-Pairs Method

CLASSIFYING GROUP RESEARCH DESIGNS 451

ONE-GROUP DESIGNS 452

One-Group Posttest-Only Design

Cross-Sectional Survey Design

Longitudinal Designs

Trend Studies

Cohort Studies

Panel Studies

One-Group Pretest-Posttest Design

INTERNAL VALIDITY 468

History

Maturation

Testing Effects

Instrumentation Error

Statistical Regression

Differential Selection of Research Participants

Mortality

Reactive Effects of Research Participants

Interaction Effects

Relations between Experimental and Control Groups

Diffusion of Treatments

Compensatory Equalization

Compensatory Rivalry

Demoralization

TWO-GROUP DESIGNS 478

Comparison Group Pretest-Posttest Design

Comparison Group Posttest-Only Design

Classical Experimental Design

Randomized Posttest-Only Control Group Design

EXTERNAL VALIDITY 485

Selection-Treatment Interaction

Specificity of Variables

Multiple-Treatment Interference

Researcher Bias

SUMMARY 487

PART V
Collecting Data

CHAPTER 14: COLLECTING QUANTITATIVE DATA 498

DATA COLLECTION METHODS AND SOURCES 500

TYPES OF DATA 501

SURVEY QUESTIONNAIRES 503

Establishing Data Collection Procedures

Recording Survey Data

Establishing Reliability and Validity

Advantages and Disadvantages

STRUCTURED OBSERVATIONS   508

Establishing Data Collection Procedures

Recording Structured Observational Data

Establishing Reliability and Validity

Advantages and Disadvantages

SECONDARY DATA   513

Establishing Data Collection Procedures

Recording Secondary Data

Establishing Reliability and Validity

Advantages and Disadvantages

EXISTING STATISTICS   517

Example of Using Existing Statistics

Establishing Data Collection Procedures

Recording Existing Statistical Data

Establishing Reliability and Validity

Advantages and Disadvantages

SUMMARY   521

CHAPTER 15: COLLECTING QUALITATIVE DATA   528

NARRATIVE INTERVIEWING   532

Establishing Data Collection Procedures

Recording Narrative Data

Trustworthiness and Truth-Value of Narrative Data

Advantages and Disadvantages

PARTICIPANT OBSERVATION   537

Establishing Procedures to Collect Data

Recording Participant Observational Data

Trustworthiness and Truth-value

Advantages and Disadvantages

SECONDARY CONTENT DATA 541

Establishing Procedures
Recording
Establishing the Trustworthiness and Truth-Value
Advantages and Disadvantages

HISTORICAL DATA 543

Establishing Procedures to Collect Data
Recording
Establishing the Trustworthiness and Truth-Value
Advantages and Disadvantages

SUMMARY 546

CHAPTER 16: SELECTING A DATA-COLLECTION METHOD 554

DATA COLLECTION VIA THE RESEARCH PROCESS 556

Selecting a Research Topic and Research Question
Designing the Research Study and Collecting the Data
Analyzing and Interpreting the Data
   Example
Presentation and Dissemination of Findings

SELECTING A DATA-COLLECTION METHOD 562

Size
Scope
Program Participation
Worker Cooperation
Intrusion into the Lives of Research Participants
Resources
Time
Data-Collection Methods Used In Previous Studies

EXAMPLE: SELECTING A METHOD 578

TRYING OUT THE METHOD 579

IMPLEMENTATION AND EVALUATION

Implementation

Evaluation

SUMMARY 582

PART VI
Analyzing Data

CHAPTER 17: ANALYZING QUANTITATIVE DATA 592

ENTERING DATA INTO COMPUTERS 595

DESCRIPTIVE STATISTICS 596

Frequency Distributions

Measures of Central Tendency

Mode

Median

Mean

Measures of Variability

Range

Standard Deviation

INFERENTIAL STATISTICS 607

Statistics That Determine Associations

Chi-Square

Correlation

Statistics That Determine Differences

Dependent t-Tests

Independent t-Tests

One-Way Analysis of Variance

SUMMARY 617

CHAPTER 18: ANALYZING QUALITATIVE DATA   624

PURPOSE OF QUALITATIVE DATA ANALYSIS   627

Checking Your Biases at the Door

PHASE 1: PLANNING THE ANALYSIS   629

Step 1: Transcribing the Data

Task 1a: Deciding What Computer Program to Use, If Any
Task 1b: Deciding Who Will Transcribe the Data

Step 2: Establishing General Rules for the Analysis

Task 2a: Previewing the Data
Task 2b: Keeping a Journal

PHASE 2: DOING THE ANALYSIS   634

Step 3: Doing First-Level Coding

Task 3a: Identifying Meaning Units
Task 3b: Creating Categories
Task 3c: Assigning Codes to Categories
Task 3d: Refining and Reorganizing Categories

Step 4: Doing Second-Level Coding

Task 4a: Comparing Categories

PHASE 3: LOOKING FOR MEANING   641

Step 5: Interpreting Data and Building Theory

Task 5a: Developing Conceptual Classifications Systems
Task 5b: Presenting Themes or Theory

Step 6: Assessing the Trustworthiness of the Results

Task 6a: Establishing Our Own Credibility
Task 6b: Establishing the Dependability of the Data
Task 6c: Establishing Our Control of Biases

EVALUATING YOUR DATA ANALYSIS PLAN   648

SUMMARY   651

PART VII
Research Proposals and Reports

CHAPTER 19: QUANTITATIVE PROPOSALS AND REPORTS 658

WRITING QUANTITATIVE RESEARCH PROPOSALS 661

Part 1: Research Topic

Part 2: Literature Review (

Part 3: Conceptual Framework

Part 4: Research Question or Hypothesis

Part 5: Methodology

Part 5a: Research Design

Part 5b: Operational Definitions

Part 5c: Population and Sample

Part 5d: Data Collection

Part 5e: Data Analysis

Part 6: Limitations

Part 7: Administration

WRITING QUANTITATIVE RESEARCH REPORTS 675

Part 1: Problem

Part 2: Method

Part 3: Findings

Part 4: Discussion

Limitations

SUMMARY 688

CHAPTER 20: QUALITATIVE PROPOSALS AND REPORTS 694

WRITING QUALITATIVE RESEARCH PROPOSALS 697

Purpose of Writing a Proposal

Intended Audience

Content and Writing Style

ORGANIZING THE RESEARCH PROPOSAL   700

Part 1: Research Topic

Part 2: Literature Review

Part 3: Conceptual Framework

Part 4: Questions and Hypotheses

Part 5: Operational Definitions

Part 6: Research Design

Part 7: Population and Sample

Part 8: Data Collection

Part 9: Data Analysis

Part 10: Limitations

Part 11: Administration

EVALUATING RESEARCH PROPOSALS   719

WRITING QUALITATIVE RESEARCH REPORTS   721

Abstract

Introduction

Method

Analysis and Findings

Discussion

References

SUMMARY   726

GLOSSARY   732

CREDITS   763

REFERENCES AND FURTHER READINGS   765

INDEX   773

PART I

The Contexts of Social Work Research

CHAPTER 1: The Place of Research in Social Work **2**

CHAPTER 2: Formulating Research Questions **62**

CHAPTER 3: Writing Literature Reviews **100**

CHAPTER 4: Research Ethics **124**

CHAPTER 5: Culturally Competent Research **172**

1

CHAPTER

COMPETENCY 1: Demonstrate Ethical and Professional Behavior

You will learn that in order to be a successful evidence-based practitioner you have an ethical obligation to integrate three research roles into your daily practice activities as discussed in Chapter 1: (1) research consumer, (2) research partner—either as a co-researcher or research participant, and (3) creator and disseminator of research (or knowledge).

This entire chapter pertains to these three professional roles in that you'll learn that one of the best ways to help you become an ethical and professional evidence-based social work practitioner is knowing how our profession's knowledge base is best generated through "objective" research studies; that is, you have an ethical obligation to fully understand and appreciate how objective social work research studies can produce reliable and valid "practice implications" for our profession.

COMPETENCY 4: Engage in Practice-Informed Research and Research-Informed Practice

Competency 4 also pertains to the entire chapter because you have to:

1. Evaluate the degree of objectivity that a social work research study has obtained, given the needs of the study's specific population or research participants (**research consumer**—research-informed practice);

2. Participate in a research study—either as a co-researcher or research participant (**research partner**—practice-informed research). See 1 above and 3 below; and

3. Know how to design a research study that is as objective as possible before you actually start the study (**creator and disseminator of research**—practice-informed research).

You also need to utilize evidence-based practice recommendations whenever possible; that is, you need to integrate (1) the best available research-based evidence with (2) your clinical expertise and (3) your client's values.

All of the above implies you'll need to know how objective a research study actually was that produced the research-based evidence. In short, you need to ask and then answer a simple question: How seriously should I take the findings of any specific research study given the level of its objectivity?

COMPETENCY 9: Evaluate Practice with Individuals, Families, Groups, Organizations, and Communities

You will learn that the only way you can legitimately evaluate the effectiveness of your day-to-day practice activities (in addition to the social work program where you work) is by knowing how the entire research process unfolds and, more important, how the "research" process is the same as the social work "practice" process.

The Place of Research in Social Work

CHAPTER 1	Step 1. Understanding the Research Process
CHAPTER 2	Step 2. Developing Research Questions
CHAPTER 3	Step 3. Reviewing the Literature
CHAPTERS 4 & 5	Step 4. Being Aware of Ethical and Cultural Issues
CHAPTERS 6–8	Step 5. Selecting a Research Approach
CHAPTERS 9 & 10	Step 6. Specifying How Variables Are Measured
CHAPTER 11	Step 7. Selecting a Sample
CHAPTERS 12 & 13	Step 8. Selecting a Research Design
CHAPTERS 14–16	Step 9. Selecting a Data-Collection Method
CHAPTERS 17 & 18	Step 10. Analyzing the Data
CHAPTERS 19 & 20	Step 11. Writing the Research Report

MADAME CLEO IS AN ASTROLOGICAL CONSULTANT. She advertises widely on television promising that her astounding insights into love, business, health, sex, and relationships will help her viewers to achieve more fulfilling and gratifying lives. "Ha!" you think, "I bet she can't do this for me! I bet she's just out for the money! But if she could only tell me . . . How do I know if she's for real or I'm just getting taken for a ride?"

There's a parallel here between the clients who receive social services and you, the future social worker. Most people who we help—in common with all those people who are never seen by social workers—would like more fulfilling and rewarding lives.

Like Madame Cleo's naïve clientele, who get suckered into calling her on the phone, many of our clients also have personal issues, money issues, relationship issues, or health issues. Unlike Madame Cleo, however, who only has to be accountable to her bank account, we, as professionals, are required to be accountable to society and must be able to provide answers to four basic accountability questions:

1. How **do I know** if I have helped my clients?
2. How **do my clients know** that I have helped them?

3. How **does our profession know** that we, as a collective group of social workers, have helped our clients?

4. How **do the funding bodies** that fund our programs (which employ us) know how effectively their dollars are being spent?

TOWARD ACCOUNTABILITY

WHAT IS THE ROLE that research plays in answering the previous four accountability questions? Briefly, a significant one! That's the position of both the Council on Social Work Education (CSWE) and the National Association of Social Workers (NASW).

These two prestigious national accountability organizations have a tremendous amount of jurisdiction in terms of what curriculum content is required to be taught in all accredited social work programs in the United States (CSWE) and how the students, after they graduate, practice their craft (NASW).

COUNCIL ON SOCIAL WORK EDUCATION

THE CSWE IS THE OFFICIAL educational organization that sets minimum curriculum standards for bachelor of social work (BSW) and master of social work (MSW) programs throughout the United States. This accreditation organization firmly believes that all social work students should know the basic principles of how the scientific method of inquiry process can actually be useful for all social workers to know. So do your professors.

For example, the latest version of the CSWE's *Educational Policy and Accreditation Standards* (2015) contains two very general "research-type" policy competency statements that all social work students must follow. These two competencies are outlined in Box 1.1 on the following two pages.

With these two CSWE "research-type" competency statements in mind, you'll need to know basic research methodology so that you can be in compliance with them; that is, it's extremely difficult—if not impossible—for you to meet the CSWE's two policy statements without understanding the contents of this book.

BOX 1.1	The CSWE's Competencies 4 and 9

COMPETENCY 4: Engage in Practice-informed Research and Research-informed Practice

Social workers understand quantitative and qualitative research methods and their respective roles in advancing a science of social work and in evaluating their practice. Social workers know the principles of logic, scientific inquiry, and culturally informed and ethical approaches to building knowledge. Social workers understand that evidence that informs practice derives from multi-disciplinary sources and multiple ways of knowing. They also understand the processes for translating research findings into effective practice. Social workers:

— use practice experience and theory to inform scientific inquiry and research;

— apply critical thinking to engage in analysis of quantitative and qualitative research methods and research findings; and

— use and translate research evidence to inform and improve practice, policy, and service delivery.

COMPETENCY 9: Evaluate Practice with Individuals, Families, Groups, Organizations, and Communities

Social workers understand that evaluation is an ongoing component of the dynamic and interactive process of social work practice with, and on behalf of, diverse individuals, families, groups, organizations, and communities. Social workers recognize the importance of evaluating processes and outcomes to advance practice, policy, and service delivery effectiveness. Social workers understand theories of human behavior and the social environment, and critically evaluate and apply this knowledge in evaluating outcomes. Social workers understand qualitative and quantitative methods for evaluating outcomes and practice effectiveness.

Social workers:

— select and use appropriate methods for evaluation of outcomes;

— apply knowledge of human behavior and the social environment, person-in-environment, and other multidisciplinary theoretical frameworks in the evaluation of outcomes; and

— critically analyze, monitor, and evaluate intervention and program processes and outcomes; and apply evaluation findings to improve practice effectiveness at the micro, mezzo, and macro levels.

Now that we know that the CSWE has a great deal to say about our "research competencies," let's turn our attention to the second professional organization that we have to be accountable to—the NASW.

NATIONAL ASSOCIATION OF SOCIAL WORKERS

JUST LIKE THE CSWE, the NASW is a parallel practice organization that works to enhance the professional growth and development of social workers. Like the CSWE for social work students, the NASW (2017) also believes that practicing social workers should know the basic ethical principles of research and evaluation as outlined in Box 1.2 on the following page. Do the other "non-research" social work courses that you are taking address any of these principles?

THIS BOOK'S OBJECTIVES

THIS BOOK PROVIDES you with the beginning social work research content you'll need to comply with the research standards set out by the CSWE (e.g., Box 1.1) and NASW (e.g., Box 1.2). Unlike Madame Cleo, however, social work students and practitioners alike are expected to have a solid research knowledge base to guide and support their interventions. This knowledge base is generally derived from your social work education.

BOX 1.2	The NASW's Basic "Research and Evaluation Principles"

— Social workers should monitor and evaluate policies, the implementation of programs, and practice interventions.

— Social workers should promote and facilitate evaluation and research to contribute to the development of knowledge.

— Social workers should critically examine and keep current with emerging knowledge relevant to social work and fully use evaluation and research evidence in their professional practice.

— Social workers should report evaluation and research findings accurately. They should not fabricate or falsify results and should take steps to correct any errors later found in published data using standard publication methods.

— Social workers engaged in evaluation or research should be alert to and avoid conflicts of interest and dual relationships with participants, should inform participants when a real or potential conflict of interest arises, and should take steps to resolve the issue in a manner that makes participants' interests primary.

— Social workers should educate themselves, their students, and their colleagues about responsible research practices.

Of course, we, as a profession, tend to have more credibility than astrological consultants like Madame Cleo. We have graduated from accredited social work programs (CSWE) and have solid recognized practice qualifications (NASW).

You are expected to have not only good intentions but also the skills and knowledge to convert your good intentions into desired practical results that will help your clients.

It all boils down to the fact that we have to be accountable to society, and to do so means that we need to acquire the knowledge and skills to help our clients in an effective and efficient manner. Much of this knowledge comes from the results of research studies that are disseminated through our professional literature.

WAYS OF KNOWING

THE PREVIOUS DISCUSSION focused on the need for our profession to become more accountable by increasing our knowledge base in reference to the types of interventions that work best with various client systems (e.g., individual, family, group, community, organization). This should automatically lead to the question, "Where do I acquire the necessary knowledge base to help my clients?" The answer is simple: You will acquire it through five highly interrelated sources, collectively known as "the ways of knowing," which are:

1. Authority
2. Tradition
3. Experience
4. Beliefs and intuition
5. The scientific method

All five of these "ways of knowing" heavily overlap with one another, but it greatly simplifies things to discuss them separately.

AUTHORITY

THE FIRST WAY you "know" something is that someone in an authority position—like your research instructor—told you so; that is, some things you "know" because someone in authority told you they were true. Had you lived in Galileo's time, for example, you would have "known" that there were seven heavenly bodies: the sun, the moon, and five planets. Since seven was a sacred number in the seventeenth century, the correctness of this belief was self-evident and was proclaimed by professors of philosophy. Let's not forget that the earth was also flat at the time!

But Galileo peeked through his telescope in 1610 and saw four satellites circling Jupiter. Nevertheless, it was clear to those in authority that Galileo was wrong. Not only was he wrong, he had blasphemed against the accepted order.

They denounced Galileo and his telescope and continued to comfortably believe in the sacredness of the number seven.

But the authorities could have looked through Galileo's telescope! They could have seen for themselves that the number of heavenly bodies had risen to eleven! In fact, they refused to look because it wasn't worth their while to look: They "knew" they were right.

They had to be right because, in Galileo's time, the primary source of "how you knew something" was by authority—not by reason, and certainly not by observation. Today, this may seem a bit strange, and we may feel a trifle smug about the fact that, in our time, we also rely on our own observations *in addition* to authority.

QUESTIONING THE ACCURACY OF AUTHORITY FIGURES

YOU HAVE LITTLE CHOICE but to rely on authority figures in your quest for knowledge. You wouldn't progress very fast in your social work program if you felt it necessary to personally verify everything your professors said. Similarly, practicing social workers simply lack the time to evaluate the credibility of the research studies that produced the practice recommendations in the first place; they have no choice but to trust statements made by "esteemed" researchers— the authority figures—who conducted the research studies and declared their findings to be "true."

EXPERTS CAN BE WRONG. Yes, experts can indeed be wrong and the consequences can sometimes be disastrous. A few decades ago, for example, authority figures in family therapy believed that children who were schizophrenic came from parents who had poor parenting skills. Acting rationally—for the moment, that is—researchers emphasized such causative factors as parental discord, excessive familial interdependency, and mothers whose overprotective and domineering behaviors did not allow their children to develop individual identities.

In accordance with these "research findings," many social workers assumed that all families who had children with schizophrenia were dysfunctional. With these research findings in mind, many social workers focused their interventions on changing the family system. However, they often inadvertently instilled guilt into the parents and increased tensions rather than helping the parents to cope with their children's unfortunate situations.

However, recent research studies now show that schizophrenia is caused largely by genetic and other biological factors, not by bad parenting as once believed. According to these *current* findings, the most effective social work intervention is to support the family system by providing a nonstressful environment. This is what social workers currently do, again relying on current authority figures.

More than likely the authorities are correct this time. But they are not quite as exact today as they will be tomorrow when our knowledge of schizophrenia and good parenting has progressed a little bit more. So what are we to do when we need to trust the experts but the experts might be wrong? Put simply, we need to ascertain the integrity of the research studies that produced the findings and practice recommendations in the first place—simple as that.

More specifically, we must be able to distinguish the good research studies from the bad and, quite frankly, the awful ones. One of the main purposes of this book is to enable you, the future social worker, to adequately evaluate the quality of research studies that produced research findings.

You need to decide for yourself which good research findings you will clutch to your heart and use to help your clients, and which findings you will disregard because they were generated from poorly designed studies. Remember, not every research study is a good one. Also remember that there are many good ones that generate relevant and high-quality knowledge that we can use with our clients. Simply put, good research studies will have creditable evidence to substantiate their practice recommendations.

WHERE DOES THIS "CREDIBLE EVIDENCE" (OR DATA) COME FROM? We always need to ask, "Where did the evidence (or data) come from that was used to substantiate the study's findings?" The kind of evidence on which a practice recommendation is based upon must always be evaluated in terms of the overall quality of the research study that produced it paying particular attention to the data source(s) that was used to make the recommendation in the first place.

Using television media (especially Faux News) as a data source is always of a questionable value. For example, we obtain knowledge by watching television shows and movies in addition to reading newspapers, journals, and magazine articles.

Using the media as a data source is always of questionable value. For example, we obtain knowledge by watching television shows and movies in addition to reading newspapers, journals, and magazine articles. These forms of communication provide rich information (right and wrong) about the social life of individuals and society in general. Most people, for example, who have had no contact with criminals learn about crime by these forms of communication, and as we know all too well, the media can easily perpetuate the myths of any given culture (Neuman, 2012):

> "The media show that most people who receive welfare are African American (most are actually non-African American), that most people who are mentally ill are violent and dangerous (only a small percentage actually are), and that most people who are elderly are senile and in nursing homes (a tiny minority are).
>
> Television repeatedly shows low-income, inner-city African American youth using illegal drugs. Eventually, most people "know" that urban African Americans use illegal drugs at a much higher rate than other groups in the United States, even though this notion is false."

In addition to the above myths, Bruce Thyer and Monica Pignotti (2015) have beautifully put together a list of additional myths that Lilenfeld, Lynn, Ruscio, and Beyerstein (2010) outlined in their book titled, *50 Great Myths of Popular Psychology* (2010):

— Old age is typically associated with increased dissatisfaction and senility.

— When dying, people pass through a universal series of psychological stages.

— Human memory works like a tape recorder or video camera, and accurately records the events we've experienced.

— Most students learn best when teaching styles are matched to their learning styles.

— Low self-esteem is a major cause of psychological problems.

— Most people who were sexually abused in childhood develop severe personality disturbances in adulthood.

— Psychiatric labels cause harm by stigmatizing people.

— Only deeply depressed people commit suicide.

— Adult children of alcoholics display a distinctive pattern of symptoms.

— There has recently been a massive epidemic of infantile autism.

— Expert judgment and intuition are the best means of making clinical decisions.

— Abstinence is the only realistic goal for alcoholics.

— All effective psychotherapies force people to confront the "root" causes of their problems in childhood.

TRADITION

THE SECOND WAY of adding to your social work knowledge base is simply through tradition. Obviously, authority and tradition are highly related to one another. For example, some things you "know" because your mother "knew" them and her mother before her, and they are a part of your cultural tradition. Your mother was also an authority figure who learned her bits and pieces through tradition *and* authority.

More often than not, people tend to accept cultural beliefs without much question. They may doubt some of them and test others for themselves, but for the most part they behave and believe as tradition dictates. To be sure, such conformity is useful, as our society could not function if each custom and belief was reexamined by each individual in every generation.

On the other hand, unquestioning acceptance of traditional dictates easily leads to stagnation and to the perpetuation of wrongs. It would be unfortunate, for example, if women were never allowed to vote because women had never traditionally voted, or if racial segregation and slavery were perpetuated because traditionally that's just the way it was.

And let's not forget that interracial marriages were at one time illegal. Some traditional beliefs are based on the dictates of authority carried on through time, such as opposition to same-sex marriages. The origins of other beliefs are lost in history.

SORRY, THAT'S THE WAY IT'S DONE AROUND HERE

EVEN IN SOCIAL SERVICE PROGRAMS, whose history is relatively brief, things tend to be done in certain ways because they have always been done in those ways. When you first enter a social service program as a practicum student, for example, your colleagues will show you how the program runs.

You may be given a manual detailing your program's policies and proce- dures, which contains everything from staff holidays and locking up client files at night, to standard interviewing techniques with children who have been physically and emotionally abused. Informally, you will be told other things such as how much it costs to join the coffee club, whom to ask when you want a favor, whom to phone for certain kinds of information, what form to complete to be put on the waiting list for a parking space, and what form to fill out to order more forms.

In addition to this practical information, you may also receive advice about how to help your future clients. Your colleagues may offer you a few of their opinions about the most effective treatment intervention strategies that are used in your practicum setting.

If your practicum setting is a child sexual abuse treatment program, for ex- ample, it may be suggested to you that the nonoffending mother of a child who has been sexually abused herself does not need to address her own sexual abuse history in therapy in order to empathize with and protect her daughter. Such a view would support the belief that the best interventive approach is a learning one, perhaps helping the mother learn better communication skills with her daughter.

Conversely, the suggestion may be that the mother's personal exploration into her psyche (whatever that is) is essential, so the intervention should be of a psychodynamic nature. Whatever the suggestion, it's likely that you, as a begin- ning social work student, will accept it, along with the information about the coffee club.

THE NEED TO "FIT IN"

TO BE SURE, you will want to fit in and become a valued member of the team. If the nonoffending mother is the first client you have really been responsible for, you may also be privately relieved that the intervention decision has been made for you. You may believe that your colleagues have more professional experience than you and surely should know best.

In all likelihood, they probably do know best. However, they also were once beginning social work students like yourself, and they probably formed their professional opinions in the same way you are currently forming yours. They too once trusted their supervisors' knowledge bases and their experiences (to be discussed below). In other words, much of what you will initially be told is based upon the way your practicum site has traditionally worked. This should not be a surprise to you.

This might be a good moment to use your newfound library skills (Chapter 3) to evaluate the literature on the best way to intervene with children who have been sexually abused. But if you actually happen to find a different and more effective way to intervene, you may quickly discover that your colleagues are unreceptive or even hostile. They "know" what they do already works with their clients—they "know it works" because it has traditionally worked for years.

Thus, on the one hand, tradition as a way of knowing is extremely useful in that it simply allows you to learn from the achievements and mistakes of those who have done your job before you. You don't have to reinvent the wheel, as you've been given a head start. On the other hand, tradition can become way too comfortable. It can blind you to better ways of doing things. Tradition dies hard, very hard indeed.

EXPERIENCE

THE THIRD WAY of acquiring your knowledge base is through plain old-fashioned experience. You "know" that buttered bread falls when you drop it—buttered side down, of course. You "know" that knives cut and fire burns. You "know," as you gain experience in social work, that certain interventional approaches tend to work better than others with certain types of clients in certain types of situations. Such experience is of enormous benefit to your clients.

Experience is a great way to "know" things. Use it when you can. However, as with anything else, experience has its advantages and disadvantages. Experience in one area, for example, can blind you to the issues in another. Health planners from mental health backgrounds, for example, may see mental illness as the most compelling community health problem simply because of their experiences with the mentally ill.

Mental health issues may therefore command more dollars and attention than other public health issues that are equally deserving such as homelessness, poverty, and child abuse. Being aware of your own biases will allow you to make the most of your own experience while taking due account of the experiences of others.

BELIEFS AND INTUITION

AT THIS POINT, it's useful to differentiate among knowledge, beliefs, and intuition. Like everything else in life, they heavily interact with each other. Knowledge is an accepted body of facts or ideas mainly acquired through the use of the scientific method. We now know that the earth is round, for example, because we have been into space and observed it from above.

A few centuries ago, we would have *known* that the earth is flat because someone in authority said it is or because tradition had always held it to be flat—very flat indeed. Thus, knowledge is never final or certain. It's always changing as new facts come to our attention and new theories explaining the facts are developed, tested, and accepted or rejected.

Beliefs (or faith), on the other hand, are a body of ideas that are acquired mainly through the reliance on tradition and/or authority. These represent a way of thinking about something that has not been proven by the scientific method, and thus they are unscientific opinions, or ideas, at best.

Belief systems have remarkable staying power. Various beliefs about life after death, for example, have been held since the beginning of time by large numbers of people, and they will doubtless continue to be held, without much change, because there's nothing to change them.

More recently, the belief that one acquires worth through work has become strongly held in North American society. This belief holds that the harder you work, the more virtue you acquire by doing the work. At the same time, it's believed that people will avoid work if at all possible—presumably because they value ease over virtue—so many of the social service programs we have in place are designed to punish our clients' "idleness" and reward their "productivity."

Intuition is a natural ability or power that makes it possible to know something without any proof or evidence. It's a feeling that guides a person to act a certain way without fully understanding why. It can be described in a number of ways: revelation through insight, conviction without reason, or immediate apprehension without rational thought. In short, you "know" something without having a clue of how you know it. It has been suggested that intuition springs from a rational process at the subconscious level.

With the preceding discussion in mind professional ethical concerns dictate that we should never rely *solely* on our beliefs and intuition when working with clients (Grinnell, 1985, 1995; Grinnell & Siegel, 1988). Take careful note of the word *solely.* Unfortunately, like tradition, beliefs and intuition also die hard.

PROFESSIONAL ETHICAL CONCERNS

LET'S USE AN EXAMPLE to illustrate a professional ethical concern about using beliefs and intuition in your daily practices. Suppose one day Jane goes to her family physician for a medical checkup because she has been feeling tired and depressed. After talking with her for a few minutes, the physician says, "My intuition tells me that you have high blood pressure," and then proceeds to give Jane hypertension medication. Following the physician's advice, she takes the medication for a few months and begins to feel better. Because she's now feeling better, Jane phones the physician and asks if it's okay to stop taking the medication. The physician says yes.

At no time did the physician take Jane's blood pressure, either to confirm the initial diagnostic intuitive hunch or to determine the effects of the medication later. Hence, it was entirely possible that she was taking a drug for which she had no need, or a drug that could actually harm her; alternatively, she may be stopping a medication that has indeed been helping her. The point here is that the physician made crucial decisions about beginning and ending an intervention (treatment) without gathering and evaluating all the necessary data.

Ethical social workers do not treat clients the way this physician did. Just as the wrong medication has the potential to harm, so does the wrong social work intervention. In the past, some studies have shown that the recipients of social work services have fared worse or no better than those who did not receive our services. Thus, we always have a responsibility to evaluate the effect of our interventions.

We must fully realize that we have no business intervening in other people's lives simply on the assumption that our good intentions will lead to good client outcomes. Although we may mean well, our good intentions alone do not ensure that we really "help" our clients.

We have a moral obligation to utilize solid research findings—even more so when the clients have not asked for our services. Truly professional social workers never rely *solely* on their good intentions, intuitions, experiences, uninformed opinions, and subjective judgments. They also use the results of research findings that were derived from good research studies in an effort to guide their interventions. And, more important, these findings must have been derived from the use of the scientific method of inquiry, which now brings our discussion to the fifth and final way of knowing—the scientific method.

THE SCIENTIFIC METHOD

WE HAVE NOW COME TO THE FIFTH and final way of knowing. This way of acquiring knowledge is through the use of the scientific method—sometimes called the *problem-solving process*, the *research method*, or the *research process*. The scientific method is the newest way of knowing when compared with the other four.

The scientific method is a way of knowing that is based on observable and/or measureable facts and objectivity. Simply put, it's a method of knowing that can be shared and objectively critiqued by others. It's the use of careful thought and the systematic use of sound data-gathering and analytical procedures that makes a research study more easily verifiable and replicable by other folks than the other four ways of knowing (Maschi & Youdin, 2012).

Aristotle, for example, believed that women had fewer teeth than men. Although he was twice married and the number of teeth possessed by women and men was a contentious issue in his day (believe it or not), it never occurred to him to ask either of his two wives to open their mouths so he could observe and count the number of teeth each had.

He could have then simply compared the number of teeth each of his wives had with the number of teeth he had. Simply put, Aristotle didn't use the scientific method to determine if woman had fewer teeth than men. This is a solution that would easily occur to anyone born in the twenty-first century because we're accustomed to evaluating our assumptions in the light of our observations.

The social work profession—and modern society—is enamored with knowledge development through the use of the scientific method. Acquiring knowledge through the use of research findings that were derived from this method of knowing is the most objective way of knowing something. Lawrence Neuman (2012) nicely sums up what it's all about:

> The scientific method is not one single thing; it refers to the ideas, rules, techniques, and approaches that the scientific community uses. The method arises from a loose consensus within the community of scientists. It includes a way of looking at the world that places a high value on professionalism, craftsmanship, ethical integrity, creativity, rigorous standards, and diligence.
>
> It also includes strong professional norms such as honesty and uprightness in doing a research study, great candor and openness about how one conducted a study, and a focus on the merits of the research study itself and not on any characteristics of individuals who conducted the study.

PHASES OF THE SCIENTIFIC METHOD

AS WE KNOW BY NOW, obtaining knowledge that was obtained by the scientific method is one of the most objective ways of obtaining any kind of knowledge. It's a process that contains four phases. On a very general level, and in the simplest of terms, the scientific method is a process as illustrated in Figure 1.1 on the following page.

It begins with the first phase: some kind of an observation and/or measurement. Suppose, for example, we find in the garage an unidentified bag of seeds, and we don't know what kind of seeds they are. We plant a random seed from the bag into the ground, and it grows into a petunia.

This might be a coincidence, but if we plant thirty-seven more seeds from the same bag, and all of them grow into petunias, we might assume that all the seeds in our bag have something to do with the petunias. We have now reached the second phase in the scientific method; we have made an assumption based on our observations.

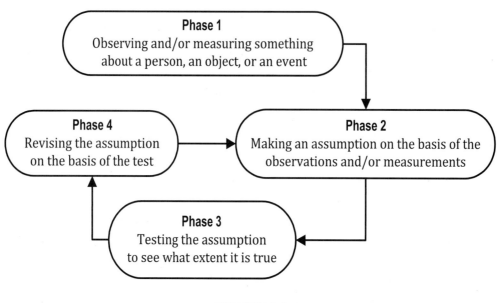

FIGURE 1.1

Phases of the Scientific Inquiry Process

The third phase is to test our assumption. This is done by planting yet another seed (the thirty-eighth) in the same way as before. If it too, becomes a petunia, we will be more certain that all the seeds in our bag will grow into petunias. On the other hand, if the thirty-eighth seed grows into a cabbage, we will begin to wonder if our original assumption—that the bag contains all petunia seeds—was wrong, which is the fourth phase of the scientific method.

It's possible, of course, that we are quite mad and we only imagined those petunias in the first place. We would be more certain of the real existence of those petunias if someone else had seen them as well. The more people who observed them the surer we would become.

It Doesn't Exist If It Can't Be Observed and Measured

The scientific inquiry process holds that, in most cases, something exists *only* if we can observe and measure it. To guard against objects that are "seen" without existing, such as cool pools of water observed by people dying of thirst in deserts, the scientific method has taken the premise one step farther: A thing exists if, and only if, we can measure it. The cool pools of water that we observed, for example, probably could not be measured by a thermometer and a depth gauge.

NOTHING IS ABSOLUTELY CERTAIN FOREVER

Things that have always occurred in sequence, such as summer and fall, probably will continue to occur in sequence. In all likelihood, rivers will flow downhill, water will freeze at zero degrees centigrade, and crops will grow if planted in the spring.

But nothing is certain; nothing is absolute. It's a matter of slowly acquiring knowledge by making observations and measurements, deriving assumptions from those observations and measurements, and testing the assumptions by making more observations and measurements. Even the best-tested assumption is held to be true only until another observation comes along to disprove it.

Nothing is forever. It's all a matter of probabilities. Let's say you have lived your whole life all alone in a log cabin in the middle of a large forest. You have never ventured as far as a hundred yards from your cabin and have had no access to the outside world whatsoever—yup, no Internet either, Gasp! You have observed for your entire life that all the ducks that flew over your land were white.

You have never seen a differently colored duck. Thus, you assume, and rightfully so, that all ducks are white. You would only have to see one nonwhite duck to disprove your white-duck assumption. Nothing is certain, no matter how long you "objectively observed" it.

EXAMPLE OF THE SCIENTIFIC INQUIRY PROCESS

Suppose, for a moment, you're interested in determining whether the strength of a child's attachment to his/her mother affects the child's social skills. In order to test your assumption (hypothesis, if you will), you must now decide on what you mean by "child" (say, under 6 years of age), and you need to find some young children and their mothers.

PHASE 1: OBSERVING AND/OR MEASURING. Next, you need to decide what you mean by "attachment," and you need to observe how attached the children are to their mothers. Because you need to measure your observations, you will also need to come up with some system whereby certain observed behaviors mean "strong attachment," other behaviors mean "medium attachment," and still other behaviors mean "weak attachment."

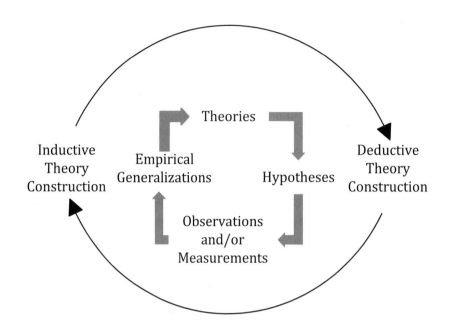

FIGURE 1.2

Inductive / Deductive Cycle of Theory Construction

Then you need to decide what you mean by "social skills," and you now need to observe and measure the children's social skills. All of these definitions, observations, and measurements constitute Phase 1 of the scientific inquiry process (see Figure 1.1 on page 20).

PHASE 2: ASSUMING. On the basis of your Phase 1 data, you might formulate an assumption, hunch, or hypothesis to the effect (for instance) that children who have higher attachments with their mothers will have higher social skills than children who have lower attachments to their mothers.

This is Phase 2 of the scientific inquiry process and involves inductive logic (see Figure 1.2 above). When using inductive logic, you simply begin with detailed observations and/or measurements of the world obtained in Phase 1 and move toward more abstract generalizations and ideas. If your assumption is correct, you can use it to predict that a particular child with a strong attachment to her mother will also demonstrate strong social skills. This is an example of deductive logic—you are deducing from the general to the particular.

PHASE 3: TESTING. In Phase 3, you set about testing your assumption, observing and measuring the attachment levels and social skills of as many other children as you can manage. Data from this phase may confirm or cast doubt upon your assumption. The data might also cause you to realize that "attachment" is not as simple a concept as you had first imagined. It's not just a matter of the strength of the attachment; rather, the type of the attachment is also a factor (e.g., secure, insecure, disorganized).

If you have tested enough children from diverse cultural backgrounds, you might also wonder if your assumption holds up better in some cultures than it does in others. Is it more relevant, say, for children raised in nuclear families than for children raised in more communal environments such as a First Nations reserve or an Israeli kibbutz?

PHASE 4: REVISING. These considerations in Phase 3 will lead you to Phase 4, in which you revise your conjecture in the light of your observations (inductive logic) and begin to test your revised hunch all over again (deductive logic). Hopefully, this will not be a lonely effort on your part.

Other researchers interested in attachment will also examine your assumption and the evidence you formulated it from, and conduct their own studies to see how right you really were. This combined work, conducted with honesty, skepticism, sharing, and freedom from entrenched beliefs, simply allows our knowledge base in the area of attachment to increase.

THE PURPOSE OF SOCIAL WORK RESEARCH

WHAT'S THE PURPOSE of social work research anyhow? Allan Rubin and Earl Babbie (2017) have provided us with four non-mutually exclusive purposes. You need to remember that social work research studies do not always fall neatly into one of the four categories and usually have more than one purpose. Box 1.3 briefly considers each purpose.

1. Exploration
2. Description
3. Explanation
4. Evaluation

BOX 1.3	**Four Purposes of Social Work Research**

1. **EXPLORATION.** Much of social work research is conducted to explore a topic—to provide a beginning familiarity with it. This purpose is typical when a researcher is examining a new interest, when the subject of study is relatively new or unstudied, or when a researcher seeks to test the feasibility of undertaking a more careful study. For example, suppose your first job as a social worker is to develop services for the frail [older adults] in a predominantly ethnic minority community about which you know very little.

   You want to conduct a community-wide survey to assess the precise extent of the need for and likely utilization of alternative services that you are contemplating developing. Before mounting a large-scale study geared to producing conclusive findings, you'd be well advised to begin with a smaller, more flexible exploratory study that will help you plan a larger and more careful study in a culturally-sensitive manner.

2. **DESCRIPTION.** Many social work studies seek a second purpose: to *describe situations and events.* The researcher observes and then describes what was observed. Because scientific observation is careful and deliberate, scientific descriptions are typically more accurate and precise than casual descriptions. For example, a researcher might assess the needs of a community by conducting a survey of community residents.

3. **EXPLANATION.** The third general purpose of social work research is to explain things. Reporting why some cities have higher child abuse rates than others is a case of explanation, but simply reporting the different child abuse rates is description. Researchers have an explanatory purpose if they wish to know why battered women repeatedly return to live with their batterers, rather than simply describing how often they do.

4. **EVALUATION.** A fourth purpose of social work research is to evaluate social policies, programs, and interventions. The evaluative purpose of social work research actually encompasses all three of the preceding purposes: exploration, description, and explanation. A number of questions might be asked in order to understand whether a social policy, program, or intervention is effective or not. For example, in order to determine if there is a need for social work services within a particular community, one might

> explore what services are needed by administering a survey to a sample of community citizens.

APPROACHES TO THE SCIENTIFIC METHOD

NOW THAT WE KNOW how the scientific method works, we'll turn our attention to how we actually go about using the three complementary research approaches it contains:

1. The quantitative (positivistic) research approach
2. The qualitative (interpretive) research approach
3. The mixed-methods research approach (combines quantitative and qualitative approaches into one study)

Their unique characteristics and contributions to our knowledge base are examined in Chapters 6, 7, and 8 respectively. Which approach is to be taken is determined by the research question or hypothesis, and/or by the philosophical inclination of the researcher. All three approaches complement each other and are equally important in the generation and testing of social work knowledge.

All three research approaches strive to generate valid and reliable research findings that are relevant to our profession. All three generally follow the four phases of the scientific method as outlined in Figure 1.1 on page 20, but they do so in their own particular way, as outlined in Table 1.1 on pages 26–29.

On a general level, quantitative research studies rely on the quantification of collecting and analyzing data and sometimes use statistics to test hypotheses established *prior to* actually carrying out the study. On the other hand, qualitative research studies rely on qualitative and descriptive methods of data collection and generate hypotheses and generalizations *during* the research study.

A mixed-methods research study gathers quantitative and qualitative data within a single study. It then *purposively and systematically integrates* the two types of data in an effort to strengthen the findings from the study. Notice the words *purposively and systematically integrates.*

TABLE 1.1

The Three Complementary Research Approaches Within the Scientific Method

Differences with respect to:	Quantitative Research Approach — Chapter 6 —	Qualitative Research Approach — Chapter 7 —	Mixed-Methods Research Approach — Chapter 8 —
Approaches to reality	One objective reality is unchanged during the course of the study.	Many subjective "realities" are changed during the course of the study and is clearly acknowledged within the research report.	Acknowledges and embraces the differences between unchanged and changed realities during the study. Integrates how the two different views of reality mesh with each other in order to strengthen a study's findings.
Underpinning philosophy	Rationalism: We acquire knowledge because of our capacity to reason.	Empiricism: We acquire knowledge from our sensory experiences.	Knowledge is gained through our capacity to reason *and* from our sensory experiences.
Main purpose	Quantifies the extent of variation in a phenomenon, situation, or issue. Seeks to explain, predict, or test existing hypotheses.	Describe a variation within a phenomenon, situation, or issue. Provides a deeper meaning of particular human experiences and generates deeper observations that are not easily quantifiable. May seek to generate future hypotheses.	Integrates both quantitative and qualitative data into a single study in an effort to increase our understanding of the phenomenon being studied.

Approach to inquiry	Structured, rigid, predetermined methodology. Deductive logic is usually applied.	Subjective, unstructured, flexible, open methodology. Inductive logic is usually applied.	Can be structured, unstructured, or both. Integrates results generated from the deductive portion of the study with the inductive portion when feasible.
Researcher's dominant value base	Researcher puts aside own values. Reliability and objectivity (value-free) are paramount within a quantitative study.	Researcher recognizes own values and does not claim to be value-free.	Dominant value of one or both.
Role of research subject / participant	Passive (as research subject)	Active (as research participant)	Recognizes, embraces, and integrates the quantitative and qualitative findings that are generated via the research subjects/participants.
Sample size	Many research subjects are involved with an emphasis on greater sample sizes whenever possible.	Few research participants are involved	Larger sample size for some aspects of the study and smaller for other aspects depending upon the study's purpose

Cost	Generally, the least expensive of the three research approaches	Generally, more expensive than a quantitative approach but cheaper than a mixed-methods approach	Generally, the most expensive of the three research approaches
Measurement of variables	Data are obtained by structured observations and measurements with an emphasis on using standardized measuring instruments whenever possible	Data are obtained by observations and asking questions with an emphasis on describing the variables studied. More often than not, the researcher *is* the measuring instrument	Acknowledges and clearly describes how the study's quantitative and qualitative variables are measured. Provides a qualitative meaning behind quantitative findings.
Analysis of data	Data are *quantitative* in nature. Uses statistical procedures depending on the study's purpose.	Data are *qualitative* in nature. Research participants' responses, narratives, or observational data are used to identify and describe main themes within the data obtained.	Acknowledges how the study's quantitative and qualitative variables are analyzed.
Communication of findings	Organization is usually *analytical* in nature, drawing inferences and conclusions, and testing magnitude and strength of the relationships between and among variables.	Organization is usually *descriptive* and narrative in nature.	Similar to a quantitative or qualitative research report. However, generally speaking, qualitative and mixed-methods research reports are much longer than quantitative reports.

Generalizability of findings	High	Limited	Appreciates and clearly delineates the strengths and limitations of a study's findings when it comes to generalizing its results to a larger population.

THE QUANTITATIVE APPROACH (CHAPTER 6)

A GARDEN-VARIETY quantitative research study follows the general steps of the scientific method in a more-or-less straight forward manner as outlined in Figure 1.3 on the following page:

Step 1: A problem area is chosen and a relevant researchable question or specific hypothesis is specified.

Step 2: Relevant variables within the research question or hypothesis are delineated.

Step 3: A plan is developed for measuring the variables within the research question or hypothesis.

Steps 4-5: Relevant data are collected for each variable and then analyzed to determine what they mean.

Step 6: On the basis of the data generated, conclusions are drawn regarding the research question or hypothesis.

Step 7: A report is written giving the study's findings, conclusions, and recommendations.

The study may then be evaluated by others and perhaps replicated (or repeated) to support or repudiate the application of the study's findings. In general, quantitative research studies are usually deductive (see Figure 1.2 on page 22) in nature and attempt to draw large and representative samples of people so that their findings can be generalized to larger populations (Engel & Schutt, 2016).

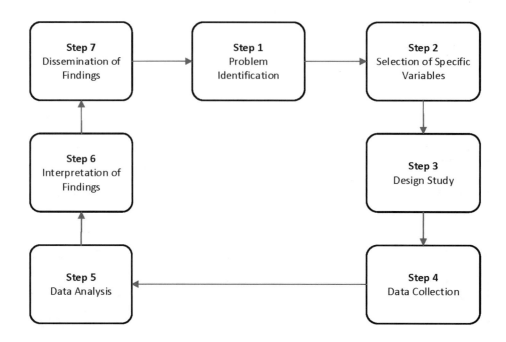

FIGURE 1.3

Generic Steps of the Quantitative (Positivistic) Research Approach

THE QUALITATIVE APPROACH (CHAPTER 7)

MEANINGFUL PROBLEM AREAS also drive qualitative research studies. However, their direct relationship to the scientific method is somewhat different than in the quantitative approach. In a quantitative study, conceptual clarity about the research question (or hypothesis) more often than not precedes the collection and analysis of data.

In contrast to the quantitative approach, researchers doing qualitative studies do not use the data-collection and analysis process simply to answer questions (or to test hypotheses). It's used first to discover what the most important questions are, and then to refine and answer questions (or test hypotheses) that are increasingly more specific. The process involves moving back and forth between data and their interpretation, between answers and questions and the development of social work theory.

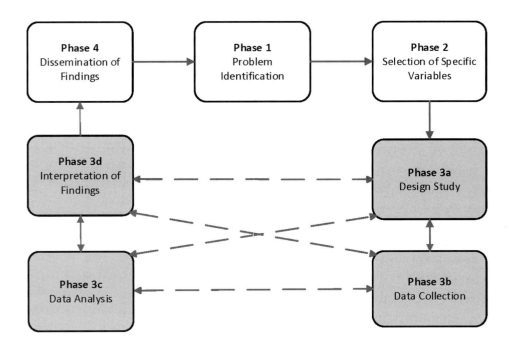

FIGURE 1.4

Generic Phases of the Qualitative (Interpretive) Research Approach

Using a holistic attitude, the qualitative research approach explores the richness, depth, and complexity of phenomena being studied. Using an inductive process (see Figure 1.2), qualitative methods generate narrative data from information-rich cases. Qualitative inductive methods emphasize the deeper meanings of the research participants' experiences. Note that the quantitative research approach has steps (Figure 1.3) and the qualitative approach has phases (Figure 1.4).

Figure 1.4 above shows how the qualitative research approach unfolds. Note how Phases 3a–d heavily interact with one another (see dashed arrows among the four phases). In Chapter 7 we will discuss in more detail how to do a qualitative research study.

THE MIXED-METHODS APPROACH (CHAPTER 8)

WITH A LITTLE FORETHOUGHT you can *integrate* both quantitative and qualitative data in a single study. When this is done a new "third research approach" naturally emerges—not surprisingly called the *mixed-methods research approach.* It capitalizes on the advantages that both research approaches bring to the research enterprise.

SELECTING A RESEARCH APPROACH

PUNCH (2009) suggests you ask yourself a series of questions before finally selecting on one of the three research approaches to answer your research question:

— What exactly am I trying to find out? Different questions require different methods to answer them.

— What kind of focus on my topic do I want to achieve? Do I want to study this phenomenon or situation in detail? Or am I mainly interested in making standardized and systematic comparisons and in accounting for variance?

— How have other researchers dealt with this topic? To what extent do I wish to align my project with this literature?

— What practical considerations should sway my choice? For instance, how long might my study take, and do I have the resources to study it this way? Can I get access to the single case I want to study in depth? Are samples and data readily available?

— Will I learn more about this topic using a quantitative, a qualitative, or a mixed-methods research approach? What will be the knowledge payoff of each research approach?

— What seems to work best for me? Am I committed to a particular research approach, which implies a particular methodology? Do I know what good quantitative, qualitative and mixed-methods research studies look like?

PURE AND APPLIED RESEARCH STUDIES

ACCORDING TO Rick Grinnell, Mike Rothery, and Ray Thomlison (1993), research studies can be loosely classified into pure or applied.

PURE RESEARCH STUDIES

PURE RESEARCH STUDIES are motivated primarily by a researcher's curiosity. The questions they address are considered important because they can produce results that improve our ability to describe or explain phenomena. Successfully answering a pure research question advances theory.

Social workers with a sociological background may be interested, for example, in the organizational patterns that evolve in a social system such as the John Wilson Elementary School when an intruder threatens children (see Box 1.4).

A few pure research questions that could be formulated from Box 1.4 on the following two pages could be:

— What are the specific processes whereby the teachers formulate a coherent response to the threat?

— How are parents, often relatively marginal members of the school community, drawn into more central positions and made effective partners in the effort to maintain a defense?

— What differentiates this school, where the children reportedly cope with danger while maintaining good morale, from other schools where similar stress would have more debilitating effects?

Social workers with a psychological background also would be interested in responses to stress, but from a different perspective. If their focus is on the development of personality, they may attempt to identify traits that allow some children to cope more effectively with danger than others. If they focus on the perpetrators, they may try to learn what it actually is about such people that could explain why they behave in ways that are disgusting to most other people.

All of these potential research questions are motivated by a desire to increase or improve the knowledge base of our profession. The questions have a theoretical relevance, and the purpose in seeking to answer them is to advance basic knowledge about how social systems organize themselves or how personality develops.

BOX 1.4	Another Kidnap Has Parents Nervous

INNISFAIL—Anxious parents are uniting to protect their kids after the fifth child abduction incident since June in this normally peaceful town.

And teachers are on red alert for strangers.

The drastic precautions have been forced on them by the latest kidnap bid—the attempted abduction last Friday of a seven-year-old girl inside the town's only elementary school.

As John Wilson Elementary School ended its day Tuesday, the parking lot was jammed with parents, big brothers, big sisters, friends, and neighbors.

"Now, everybody's coming to the school to pick up their kids—or other people's kids. Even parents that never used to come and get their kids are walking them to school every day now," said Jeanette Clark, waiting for her daughter.

"We have to make sure every child gets home safely now.

"This last abduction was really serious because the guy went right into the school," she said.

The culprit, described as a 50-year-old white male with brown hair and a moustache, walked into the school, grabbed the girl, who was just coming out of the bathroom, and demanded, "Come with me."

But the girl bit his arm and ran for help.

Laurie Moore, mother of a Grade 3 girl, said she and her friends with children are emphasizing "stay away from strangers" warnings.

"I tell my daughter not to talk to anyone, and if anyone comes near her she has to scream and run. It really is sad that we all have to go through this," she said.

School Principal Bill Hoppins has created a volunteer program where parents can help each other by supervising kids on the playground during the morning.

Tim Belbin, whose daughter attends Grade 2, said he's willing to offer his time to watch his and other children.

"I find this all really disturbing . . . really scary."

The abduction attempt has also prompted teachers to supervise all the students in their classes as they leave the school grounds and make sure they can identify all adults in the area.

"If we don't know them, we have to go up and ask them, even if they don't like it," said Hoppins.

And Hoppins said that when students are absent without a parental notification, their homes are called immediately. "There have been a number of precautions taken here since the last abduction attempt. And we are working together with the parents.

APPLIED RESEARCH STUDIES

THE ADVANTAGE OF APPLIED RESEARCH over pure research is pointed up in a defense of "useful" rather than "useless" facts presented by Sherlock Holmes to his companion, Dr. Watson, in Conan Doyle's story *A Study in Scarlet*:

> "You see," he explained, "I consider that a man's brain originally is like a little empty attic, and you have to stock it with such furniture as you choose. ... It's a mistake to think that the little room has elastic walls and can distend to any extent. ... There comes a time when for every addition of knowledge you forget something that you knew before. It's of the highest importance, therefore, not to have useless facts elbowing out the useful ones."
>
> "But the Solar System!" I protested.
>
> "What the deuce is it to me?" he interrupted impatiently: "You say that we go around the sun. If we went around the moon it would not make a pennyworth of difference to me or to my work." (Doyle, 1901/1955, p. 11)

A social worker with professional responsibilities for knowing how to be helpful in circumstances like those at Innisfail's elementary school may have some sympathy for Holmes's position. Theory about the dynamics of social organizations or the development of personality is fine—for those who have time to invest in such issues.

For an applied researcher, there is reason to be interested in the young girl who bit her assailant and ran for help, for example. How did she know so clearly what to do that she could handle the attack with such competence? Can anything be learned from her history that would help parents or teachers prepare other children to be equally effective should the need arise?

A researcher could also be interested in how the principal of the school handled the situation. Can generalizable guidelines be extracted from the principal's approach to mobilizing teachers and parents? Should other professionals be informed about what the principal did to enable the children to keep their spirits up while at the same time alerting them to the danger?

Many practicing social workers would be interested in the long-term effects of this kind of experience on the children. Some children will certainly be more deeply affected than others, and it's important to know how they are affected and what kinds of attention to their emotional needs will help them cope adaptively with the experience and its aftermath. These questions are motivated in part by curiosity, as pure research questions are, but there is another need operating as well, and that is mastery.

In sum, the goal of pure research studies is to develop theory and expand our profession's knowledge base, and the goal of applied research studies is to develop solutions for problems and applications in practice. The distinction between theoretical results and practical results marks the principal difference between pure and applied research studies.

RESEARCH AND PRACTICE

BELIEVE IT OR NOT, social work research and practice have much in common. In fact, they have more commonalities than differences in that they are both problem-solving processes. As can be seen in Figure 1.5, there are parallels between social work research and social work practice (Duehn, 1985).

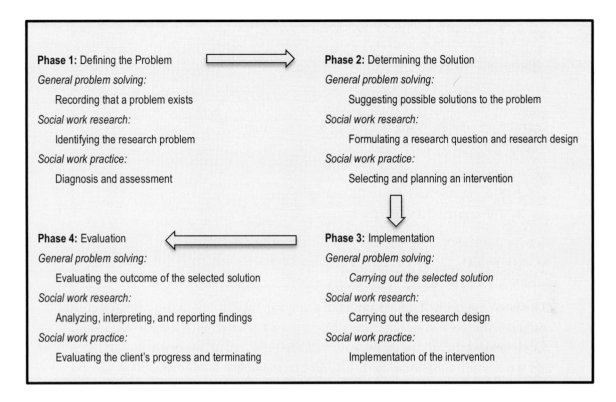

FIGURE 1.5

Parallels among General Problem Solving, Research, and Practice

All social work activities, both practice and research, are organized around one central assumption: There is a preferred order of thinking and action that, when rigorously followed, will increase the likelihood of achieving our objectives.

Social work practitioners and researchers base their conclusions on careful observation, systematic trial, and intelligent analysis. Both observe, reflect, conclude, try, monitor results, and continuously reapply the same problem-solving process until the problem at hand is addressed.

Bruce Friedmann (2007), via Figure 1.6 on page 39, provides us with a very simple pictorial example of how the research process is nothing more than the application of the problem-solving model that you learned in your introductory social work practice courses.

Research Roles

WE HAVE LOOKED at the reasons why social workers need to use research findings that were derived by the scientific method. Since there are many different ways of actually engaging within the scientific method, it's useful to look at the three highly interrelated "research roles" that social workers might play:

1. The research consumer
2. The creator and disseminator of research (or knowledge)
3. The contributing partner

THE RESEARCH CONSUMER

THE FIRST SOCIAL WORK RESEARCH ROLE you can take is that of the research consumer. If you go to your doctor to discuss your arthritis, for example, you would surely expect the doctor to be aware of the most recent advances in the management and treatment of arthritis. All professionals, in all disciplines, are expected by their clients to keep up with the latest developments in their fields.

They do this by attending conferences, reading books and journals, and paying attention to the results derived from research studies. In other words, these professionals—which includes you as a social worker—are research consumers, and, as previously noted, they need to know enough about the scientific method to consume research studies wisely, separating the nutritious wheat from the dubious chaff.

THE CREATOR AND DISSEMINATOR OF RESEARCH

YOU MAY BE CERTAIN that you will never yourself conduct a research study. "Never ever!" you say—but then you find that you are the only staff person in a small voluntary social service program that desperately requires a needs assessment if the program is to serve its clients and keep its funding base. You look up "needs assessment" in forgotten research texts, and you sweat, and stumble through them because someone has to do the study and there's no one there but you. You will now take the role of creator and disseminator of knowledge—which means you'll be doing a research study.

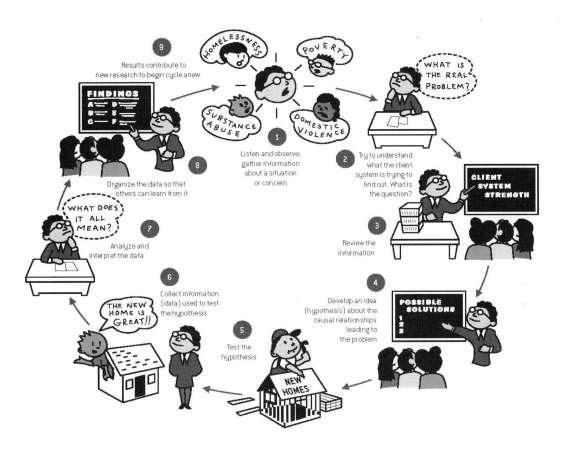

FIGURE 1.6

Research as a Problem-Solving Process (an expansion of Figure 1.5)

This may seem like an unlikely scenario, but in fact many social service programs are very small and are run on a wing and a prayer by a few paid staff and a large volunteer contingent. They rise and flourish for a time and die, and death is often hastened along by their inability to demonstrate, in "objective" research terms, how much good they are doing on their clients' behalf, how little it's costing, and what the dreadful social consequences would be if they weren't there to do it.

You may escape being the sole social worker in a program that needs research know-how. But even if you are a mere cog in an immense machine of interlocking social workers, the time may come when you want to try a new intervention. Most social workers implement interventions in some way or another, but more often than not, many of them don't:

1. Carry out their interventions in any meaningful structured way;

2. Write down exactly what the interventions were (perhaps an intervention for raising Jody's self-esteem);

3. Provide a rationale as to why they needed them in the first place (nothing else was working with Jody);

4. Specify how they evaluated them (Jody's self-esteem was measured before and after implementing the intervention); or

5. Communicate to others how effective the interventions actually were (Jody's self-esteem score rose significantly from X to Y and was still at its higher level three months later).

They simply don't tell anyone else they did it, except for a few murmurs, rapidly forgotten, to a colleague over coffee. One consequence of this is that other Jody-types, who might benefit from the same intervention, never have the opportunity to do so because their social workers didn't know that it existed. Another consequence is that the social service program cannot use this newly founded intervention as evidence of its effectiveness to place before its funders such as the United Way.

THE CONTRIBUTING PARTNER

IN REALITY, MANY SOCIAL SERVICE PROGRAMS conduct some kind of research studies from time to time, particularly evaluative studies. Many more agree to host studies conducted by researchers external to the program such as university professors and graduate students. You'll become a contributing partner in a research study when you agree to participate in the endeavor in one way or another.

Social work research studies rarely take place in a laboratory, but instead they're usually conducted in field settings. Data may be taken from the program's clients and/or their case files and may be collected in the program or in the clients' homes. Since social workers are usually employed by social service programs, they are often drawn into the program's research activities by default.

Such activities are normally conducted by a team, consisting of researchers and program staff members. The solitary social work researcher, like the solitary mad scientist, is very much a thing of the past. Staff members who contribute to research studies may have specific skills to offer that they never imagined were related to "research".

One worker, for example, may be particularly acute and accurate when it comes to observing client behaviors. A second may work well as a liaison between the clients and the researcher or between one program and another. Some social workers are cooperative in research endeavors and others are less so, depending on their attitudes toward knowledge development through the use of the scientific method.

Those of us who know the most about scientific methods tend to be the most cooperative and also the most useful. Hence, the greater the number of social workers who understand research principles, the more likely it is that relevant studies will be successfully completed and that our knowledge base will be increased.

INTEGRATING THE THREE RESEARCH ROLES

JUST ABOUT EVERYTHING IN LIFE is interdependent on everything else. Chaos theory comes readily to mind concerning the idea of interdependence. The same holds true with the three research roles noted earlier—they are not independent of one another. They must be integrated if research is to accomplish its goals of increasing our profession's knowledge base and improving the effectiveness of our interventions with clients.

The issue is not whether we should consume research findings, produce and disseminate research results, or become contributing partners in research studies. Rather, it's whether we can engage the full spectrum of available knowledge and skills in the continual improvement of our practices. Social workers who adopt only one or two of the three research roles are shortchanging themselves and their clients (Reid & Smith, 1989):

> "If research is to be used to full advantage to advance the goals
> of social work, the profession needs to develop a climate in
> which both doing and consuming research are normal
> professional activities. By this we do not mean that all social
> workers should necessarily do research or that all practice should
> be based on the results of research, but rather that an ability to
> carry out studies at some level and the facility in using

scientifically based knowledge should be an integral part of the
skills that social workers have and use."

There are economic as well as ethical reasons for integrating the three research roles into our daily activities. For example, it was once believed that
throwing money haphazardly at social problems would solve them. This simply
didn't work then and it doesn't work now. Today, funding sources demand valid
and reliable data, or evidence, that social service programs are accomplishing
their intended goals and objectives.

Anecdotal case studies alone are lame if they are not accompanied by valid
and reliable data of the program's effectiveness. In the competitive scramble of
social service programs for limited funds, the programs that can demonstrate
their effectiveness and efficiency will prevail. Hence, learning how to integrate
the three research roles into our daily practices is a matter of survival in our
profession.

Expanding our research/practice base is also a way of enabling our profession to assert its place in the community of human service professionals. It's a
way of carving out a niche of respectability, of challenging the insidious stereotype that, although social workers have their hearts in the right place, they're
uninformed and ineffective in addition to being overly optimistic.

Any profession (and especially ours) that bases its credibility on faith or
ideology alone will have a hard time surviving. Although a research base to our
profession will not guarantee us public acceptance, the absence of such a base
and the lack of vigorous research efforts to expand it will—in the long run—
undoubtedly erode our credibility (Grinnell & Siegel, 1988).

CHARACTERISTICS OF RESEARCHERS

WE NOW TURN OUR ATTENTION to the characteristics that all social work researchers should have. By now you should be familiar with how our profession
can become more accountable by increasing your understanding of how you—
as a future social worker—actually know something. And, more importantly,
you should have an adequate appreciation of how the use of the scientific method generates more objective knowledge for our profession than the other four
ways of knowing.

When researchers use the scientific method to generate knowledge, via research findings, they must personally possess four important characteristics embedded within the method itself. More specifically, researchers must:

1. Be aware of their own values,
2. Be skeptics,
3. Share their findings with others, and
4. Be honest.

Let's discuss each characteristic one at a time, even though they are all highly intertwined and comingled with one another.

VALUE AWARENESS

LIKE A JUDGE (and not Judge Judy!), you must be aware of and be able to set aside your values when you do a research study. Value awareness means that you must know your own values and your research study must not be affected by them; that is, you must be unbiased and impartial to the highest degree as humanly possible. This means that you, as a mortal social work researcher, should be able to put aside your personal values both when you are conducting research studies and when you are evaluating the results obtained by other researchers.

If your personal value system dictates, for example, that health care should be publicly funded and equally available to everyone, you should still be able to use the scientific method to acquire knowledge about the advantages and disadvantages of a privatized system. If the evidence from your own or someone else's study shows that privatized health care is superior in some respects to the system you believe is best, you should be able to weigh this evidence objectively, even though it may conflict with your personal value system.

SKEPTICAL CURIOSITY

NOW THAT YOU ARE VALUELESS, you must also become insatiably curious. We now know that knowledge acquired using the scientific method is never certain. Scientific "truth" remains true only until new evidence comes along to show that it's not true, or only partly true.

Skeptical curiosity means that all research findings derived from the scientific method should be—and, most important, must be—questioned. Wherever possible, new studies should be conducted by different researchers to see if the same results are obtained again. In other words, research studies (whenever possible) should be replicated.

Replication of the same study, with the same results, by another researcher makes it less likely that the results of the first study were affected by bias, dishonesty, or just plain error. Thus, the findings are more likely to be "true" in the sense that they are more likely to reflect a reality external to the researchers.

We will come back to this business of external reality later on. For now, it's enough to say that the continual replication of research studies is a routine practice in the physical sciences, but it's far rarer in the social sciences, especially in the social work profession, for two main reasons. First, it's much more difficult to replicate a study of people than a study of physical objects. Second, researchers in the social sciences have a harder time finding money to do research studies than researchers in the physical sciences.

SHARING

LIKE YOUR MOTHER SAID, you must share your stuff with others. Sharing means that the results of your research study and the methods used to conduct it must be available to everyone so that your study's findings can be critiqued and the study replicated. It's worth noting that sharing findings from a research study is a modern value. It wasn't that long ago that illiteracy among peasants and women was valued by those who were neither.

Knowledge has always been a weapon as well as a tool. Those who know little may be less likely to question the wisdom and authority of those who are above them in the social hierarchy. Public education is thus an enormously powerful social force that allows people to access and question the evidence, or data, upon which their leaders make decisions on their behalf.

HONESTY

NOT ONLY MUST YOU BE VALUELESS, be a skeptic, have a curious nature, and share your research findings with others, you must also be honest in what you share. Honesty means, of course, that you are not supposed to fiddle with the results obtained from your study. This may sound fairly straightforward, but, in fact, the results of research studies are rarely as clear-cut as we would like them to be.

Quite often, and in the most respectable of social work research centers and in-stitutes, social policies are formulated on the basis of whether one wiggle on a graph is slightly longer than the corresponding woggle.

If *dishonesty* means a deliberate intention to deceive, then probably very few researchers are dishonest. If it means that researchers allow their value systems and their preconceived ideas to influence their data-collection methods, their data analyses, and their interpretations of the data, then there are probably a few guilty ones among us. In this sense, the term *honesty* includes an obligation, on the part of researchers, to be explicit about what their values and ideas are.

They need to be sufficiently self-aware to both identify their value systems and perceive the effects of these upon their own work; and then they need to be sufficiently honest to make an explicit statement about where they stand so that others can evaluate the conclusions drawn from their research studies.

GOT ATTITUDE?

THE RESEARCH METHOD, or "the scientific method to inquiry," if you will, refers to the many ideas, rules, techniques, and approaches that we—the research com-munity—use. The research attitude, on the other hand, is simply a way that we view the world. It's an attitude that highly values craftsmanship, with pride in creativity, high-quality standards, and hard work. These traits must be incorpo-rated into all three research approaches to knowledge building (i.e., quantitative approach, qualitative approach, mixed-methods approach) in order for the find-ings generated from research studies to be appropriately utilized within our profession's knowledge base. As Fred Grinnell (1992) states:

> Most people learn about the "scientific method" rather than
> about the "scientific attitude." While the "scientific method" is
> an ideal construct, the "scientific attitude" is the way people
> have of looking at the world. Doing science includes many
> methods: what makes them scientific is their acceptance by the
> scientific collective. (p. 125)

EVIDENCE-BASED PRACTICE

EVIDENCE-BASED PRACTICE is often described as a process in which practitioners integrate information about client needs and values with knowledge of research findings on effective interventions (Gambrill, 2003; Gambrill, 2006; Sackett, Straus, Richardson, Rosenberg, & Haynes, 2000).

Eileen Gambrill (2006) outlines the following five-step process in conducting evidence-based practice, which was originally articulated by Sackett et al. (2000) and eloquently stated by John Wodarski and Laura Hopson, (2014):

1. **Construct well-structured answerable questions that will guide practice decisions.** Creating specific questions based on information provided during the assessment process will help practitioners and clients define the primary presenting problem and choose an appropriate intervention strategy. An example of a well-structured answerable question is:

   > Will my client's anxiety symptoms be reduced by participation in weekly cognitive behavioral therapy sessions?

2. **Find the best available evidence with which to answer these questions.** Clinicians have access to a number of online resources for finding information on evidence-based practices. Many federal funders of social service programs provide a list of the interventions they consider to be evidence based. Such lists are available through the National Registry of Effective Programs and Practices, the National Institute of Drug Abuse, the Office of Juvenile Justice and Delinquency Prevention, the Centers for Disease Control and Prevention, and other federal organizations. University libraries typically provide online access to current research articles for students, but practitioners who are not affiliated with a university are unlikely to have access to these resources.

3. **Apply critical thinking in analyzing the evidence for its validity, impact on client outcomes, and applicability for**

practice settings. Although practitioners are limited in the amount of time they can devote to reading research articles, it's important to examine studies for the size of the effect on client outcomes. Practitioners also need the skills to evaluate whether something other than the intervention evaluated may be responsible for their outcomes. This information is invaluable in determining whether the researcher's conclusions are justified and the intervention is likely to be helpful to your client.

4. **Use this critical analysis of the research to guide practice decisions.** This includes deciding whether the intervention is relevant for your client and his or her presenting problem given the existing research support and considering client values and preferences.

5. **Evaluate the effectiveness of the intervention with your unique clients within your practice settings.** Even interventions with solid research support need to be evaluated with your clients. The client populations, settings, and clinicians participating in research studies may differ from those in your setting, and the intervention may affect your clients differently. Therefore, systematically measuring your clients' progress toward achieving their desired outcomes is important even when the intervention has been shown to be effective with other clients.

Ed Mullen, Jennifer Bellamy and Sarah Bledsoe (2018), among others, believe that the evidence-based practice framework will help social workers to operate efficiently and effectively by using the technology recently developed within our new global information age. This age has already empowered us to make more rational and informed decisions about the service options we have at our disposal.

It can enhance our ability, for example, to successfully navigate the mass of information that is now readily available through the Internet and other forms of media in an attempt to make our intervention choices mindfully without being overwhelmed or misled.

Evidence-based practice improves the flow of information back and forth from researchers, practitioners, and clients alike. This makes social workers better equipped to help a client system to make informed choices in the selection of the final interventions utilized.

Within this framework, social work practitioners join with their clients and provide them with both empirical and practical knowledge about various treatment options. Although the final treatment decisions are made in the context of the best available evidence, clients' values and preferences ultimately drive the process.

In short, what evidence is found is then integrated with client circumstances and preferences—again drawing on clinical expertise to integrate data from the various sources. In essence, research evidence supports and guides—but does not drive—the evidence-based process. A few good examples (via Box 1.5) of how you can use the evidence-based practice process when you graduate from your social work program are nicely summed up by Bonnie Yegidis, Bob Weinbach, and Laura Myers (2018).

BOX 1.5	Steps of the Evidence-Based Practice Process

THE FIVE-STEP process of evidence-based practice (EBP) is briefly illustrated below (Strauss et al., 2005):

Step 1. Convert your need for information about the causes of the problem, and for possible interventions, into an answerable question;

Step 2. Track down the best evidence with which to answer that question;

Step 3. Critically appraise that evidence for its validity, impact, and applicability;

Step 4. Integrate the critical appraisal with your clinical expertise and the client's unique values and circumstances; and

Step 5. Evaluate your effectiveness and efficiency in carrying out Steps 1 to 4 and seek ways to improve your practice. (pp. 3–4)

A considerable amount of literature, both within and outside the field of social work, is available that focuses on each of these five steps. An excellent resource for understanding EBP is the *Social Workers' Desk Reference* (Corcoran & Roberts, 2015). Gambrill and Gibbs (2009) describe effective ways to develop well-structured questions (related to Step 1 of EBP). These questions typically contain four parts:

P—the **population** of clients,

 I—the **intervention** of concern,

C—what the intervention may be **compared** to, and

O—hoped for **outcomes.**

Three simple examples of PICO questions include:

1. How do persons with obsessive-compulsive disorder fare after being treated with exposure therapy and response prevention, compared to similar clients who are not treated at all?

2. How do clients receiving TANF benefits who also receive a job-finding club intervention fare compared to TANF recipients who did not receive this intervention?

3. Are people with alcoholism who regularly attend AA meetings more abstinent than similar individuals who do not attend AA meetings?

STEP 1: ASK AN ANSWERABLE QUESTION

The idea is when a social worker meets a client with a problem, one of the outcomes of the assessment process will be to formulate one or more answerable questions, which might have a bearing on what intervention(s) options are presented to that particular client. However, not all answerable questions bear on the topic of choosing interventions. Similar questions may be created to evaluate assessment methods, as in the following two questions:

1. Do children who are assessed for potential sexual abuse through the use of anatomically correct dolls more accurately report actual episodes of abuse compared to similar children who are assessed without the use of such dolls?

2. Does the use of the genogram to assess clients result in a more accurate understanding of the client's background than standard clinical interviews?

Other questions may be focused on issues such as the etiology of certain conditions, the cost benefits of certain interventions, or questions related to the potentially harmful effects of a possible treatment intervention(s) such as rebirthing therapy or facilitated communication.

STEP 2: TRACK DOWN EVIDENCE TO ANSWER QUESTION IN STEP 1

Once one or more answerable questions have been formulated, the next step is to track down credible information that may help answer it (see Chapter 3). This process is addressed in Rubin and Parrish (2009) and may involve searching electronic databases, locating credible practice guidelines, or finding systematic reviews bearing on the relevant topic.

Among the higher or more credible forms of evidence that EBP particularly seeks to locate are randomized controlled trials (see Montgomery & Mayo-Wilson, 2009), meta-analyses (Corcoran & Littell, 2009), systematic reviews (Littell & Corcoran, 2009), and practice guidelines (Howard, Perron, Vaughn, 2009).

STEP 3: APPRAISE EVIDENCE FOUND IN STEP 2

The third step, critically appraising studies for EBP, is the focus of Bronson's (2009) study. Here, social workers brings to bear their skills in reading and appraising research, paying attention to issues of internal and external validity, relevance, sampling, statistical analysis, and so forth.

STEP 4: INTEGRATE EVIDENCE FOUND IN STEP 3

The fourth step in EBP is integrating the information found from diverse sources with your clinical expertise and the client's unique values and preferences. Of course, your professional ethical standards are also a crucial consideration, as are available resources. This important topic is discussed by Gambrill (2009).

STEP 5: EVALUATE YOUR OWN EFFECTIVENESS AND EFFICIENCY

The fifth step involves self-evaluating your own effectiveness and efficiency. This requires your ability to not only conduct EBP but also evaluate the outcomes with your client, which is actually the point of the entire exercise. Thyer and Myers's works (i.e., 2007, 2009) are good resources to use in this regard. Portions of the preceding description of EBP are based on Thyer and Myers (2010).

In the twenty-first century there still remain obstacles to the use of—and objections to—EBP (Rosen, 2003). However, most of the obstacles can be overcome and many of the objections reflect a misunderstanding of EBP. EBP is not intended to dictate to social workers what decisions they should make, only to get them to use all of the available data (including their practice expertise, professional values, and their knowledge of individual clients and their values and preferences) in making them.

While EBP can result in cost savings for health insurance providers and other third parties alike, that's not its purpose—its purpose is to offer services and programs with the greatest potential for client success. Besides, what's wrong with cost cutting, as long as our clients are the ultimate beneficiaries?

While there are still problems for which effective interventions have not been identified through research, these gaps do not negate the need for social work practitioners to know how to conduct research studies, locate and critically evaluate the research findings of others, and—when available—to use these findings as important components of their practice decision making.

Describing how the evidence-based practice process works is way beyond the scope of this introductory research methods book. Nevertheless you need to know the contents in this book in order for you to have a meaningful appreciation of its applicability and relevance to contemporary social work practice.

COMMITTING TO LIFELONG LEARNING

AS YOU KNOW BY NOW, a research base within our profession will not guarantee its public acceptance, but there is no doubt that the absence of such a base and the lack of vigorous research efforts to expand it will, in the long run, erode our credibility and be harmful to our clients. In order to be sure that this doesn't happen, you'll need to a become lifelong learner after your graduate with your social work degree.

Lifelong learning is nothing more than for you to continue to learn new and exciting stuff after your graduate—it means that your learning doesn't stop when you walk across the stage at graduation. Judy Krysik and Jerry Finn

(2018) provide some fantastic tips on how to become lifelong learners. The expectations for producing and using research in professional social work practice are clear. The question that remains is: How?

> Entry-level social work jobs can be demanding, leaving little time for consultation, research, or even reflection. A social worker is more likely to use research if the employing agency or organization has a culture that supports it and if the worker is committed to making it happen. Will you commit yourself to a career of lifelong learning? If so, your very first step is to develop an action plan to make it happen. Here are a few ideas that you might consider adopting. (p. 19)

— Join the National Association of Social Workers.

— Choose a professional social work conference that is relevant to your practice area, and make a commitment to attend every year.

— Ask your manager or supervisor to subscribe to a professional journal(s).

— Join a Listserv dedicated to critiquing knowledge in your area of practice.

— Join your local library, and spend at least one day a month in professional development reading about the latest research in your area.

— Initiate a brown-bag lunch session at your workplace at which you and your colleagues discuss research.

— Attend research-based training and workshops whenever possible.

— Continue your formal education by taking courses online or at a university or college.

— Make a presentation to share your research findings at a conference.

— Evaluate your day-to-day practices; that is, evaluate if you are effective with your clients.

— Collaborate with others to evaluate the services provided by your agency or organization.

— Seek employment in agencies and organizations whose culture supports using research and evaluating practice.

DEFINITION OF SOCIAL WORK RESEARCH

SO FAR, WE HAVE DISCUSSED the various ways of obtaining knowledge and briefly looked at the characteristics and phases of the scientific method. Armed with this knowledge, we now need a definition of research, which is composed of two syllables, *re* and *search*.

Dictionaries define the former syllable as a prefix meaning "again, anew, or over again," and the latter as a verb meaning "to examine closely and carefully, to test and try, or to probe" (Duehn, 1985). Together, these syllables form a noun that describes a careful and systematic study in some field of knowledge, undertaken to establish facts or principles. Social work research therefore can be defined as follows:

> Social work research is a systematic and objective inquiry that utilizes the scientific method to solve human problems and creates new knowledge that is generally applicable to the social work profession.

We obtain much of our knowledge base from the findings derived from research studies that utilize the scientific method. However, all research studies have built-in biases and limitations that create errors and keep us from being absolutely certain about the studies' outcomes.

This book helps you to understand these limitations and to take them into account in the interpretation of research findings, and helps you to avoid making errors or obtaining wrong answers. One of the principal products of a research study is obtaining systematic and objective data—via the scientific method—about reality as it genuinely is, unbiased and error-free.

SUMMARY

THIS CHAPTER BRIEFLY DISCUSSED how we need to become more accountable to society and how we can use the five "ways of knowing" to accomplish this goal. We then discussed the three main research approaches to the scientific method and compared their similarities and differences. The chapter then went on to outline how pure and applied research studies can be used in the research enterprise.

The chapter then discussed how social work research and practice used the same problem-solving process and delineated how you can easily participate in one or more of the three research roles that are open to you. The evidence-based practice process was introduced with the understanding that social workers have an ethical obligation to use treatment interventions that have been shown to be effective whenever possible.

We then presented the four characteristics that all social work researchers must possess when they produce knowledge using the scientific method followed by a definition of social work research. The chapter then went on to presenting a few tips for you to consider in becoming a lifelong learner in your quest to become a competent contemporary social work practitioner. Given all of the above the chapter ended with a definition of social work research.

In sum, this chapter explored the place of research in social work and advocated that our practices be based on valid and reliable research findings that were derived from the scientific method. The following chapter builds upon this one in that it discusses how researchers choose what problems to research in the first place.

	Study Questions for Chapter 1
	Essay — Discussion
1	Before you entered your social work program and before you read this chapter, how did you think our profession obtained its knowledge base? Provide as many examples as you can to justify your response.
2	1. In your own words, list the two main CSWE "research-related" competencies that you are expected to master as a social work practitioner (Box 1.1 on pages 6 and 7). 2. Now discuss how you plan to integrate each competency into your daily social work activities when you graduate and become a professional social worker. You need to formulate a plan for how you are going to do this. Provide as many examples as you can to justify your position.
3	1. In your own words, list the six NASW research-related principles that you are expected to master as a social work practitioner (Box 1.2 on page 8). 2. Now discuss how you plan to integrate each principle into your daily social work activities when you graduate and become a professional social worker. You need to formulate a plan for how you are going to do this. Provide as many examples as you can to justify your position.
4	1. List the five ways we obtain our knowledge base. 2. Now discuss how you plan to use each one when you graduate and become a professional social worker. Provide an example for each one of the five ways of knowing.
5	What are the main differences among knowledge, experience, tradition, beliefs, and intuition? Provide as many social work examples as you can to justify your response.
6	What is *professional judgment*? Provide as many social work examples as you can to justify your response.
7	Discuss why a professional judgment on your part, no matter how uncertain you may be, is far more beneficial to your client than just using your intuition.

8	1. What is the *scientific method*? 2. How is this method of knowing more "objective" than the other four ways of knowing? Provide as many social work examples as you can to justify your response.
9	Take a look at Figure 1.1 on page 20. Describe the phases of the scientific inquiry process in your own words using one common social work example throughout your discussion.
10	1. What is inductive logic (Figure 1.2)? 2. What is deductive logic (Figure 1.2)? 3. Compare the two forms of logic using one social work research example of your choice.
11	1. List and discuss the four characteristics that social work researchers must possess. 2. Identify any of the characteristics that surprised you. 3. Identify one characteristic that you think you may have trouble with as a future social work researcher and delineate the ways you could grow in this area.
12	In reference to Question 11, what additional characteristics do you feel social work *researchers* should have?
13	In reference to Question 11, do you feel that line-level social work *practitioners* should also possess these four characteristics? If so, which ones?
14	Look at Table 1.1 on pages 26–29. In *your own words* compare and contrast the quantitative (positivistic), the qualitative (interpretive), and the mixed-methods research approaches to knowledge development in relation to each one of the 12 rows in the table. Provide social work examples throughout your discussion.
15	1. What is the difference between pure and applied research studies? 2. When would you use each of them? Provide as many examples as you can to justify your response.

16	**Background:** Review our definition of social work research on page 53. 1. After reading Chapter 1, formulate your own definition of social work research. 2. Use Google to find five other definitions of *social work research.* 3. Compare and contrast the ones you found with your own. 4. What are their commonalities? What are their differences? 5. **Now the hard part:** Revise your own definition of *social work research* (1 above) by integrating our definition of *social work research* and the 5 definitions you found on the Internet. Don't be shy, go for it! 6. Present your revised definition to the rest of the class. What were their comments? 7. Did they help you refine your revised definition even further?
17	Review Figures 1.5 (page 37) and 1.6 (page 39) for a moment. In your own words describe how the social work research process is the same as the social work practice process. Use a social work example throughout your discussion. Also discuss how you think the two processes are not the same.
18	Review the evidence-based practice process on pages 46–51. 1. At this point in your research course (and in the book for that matter), discuss what knowledge and skills you think you'll need to carry out all five steps embedded within the evidence-based process. 2. Where do you plan on obtaining the knowledge and skill set you have just identified above to become an evidence-based practitioner? 3. Quickly skim through the rest of the chapters in this book. At this point do you see any chapters that may be helpful to you when you become an evidence-based practitioner? If so, which chapters stick out the most to you, and why? Which ones don't, and why?
19	List the three research roles you can take as a professional social work practitioner. Now discuss how you could be in each role as a social worker upon graduation. Use specific social work examples throughout your discussion.
20	Why is making a commitment to lifelong learning so important? Provide as many social work examples as you can to justify your response.

	Critical Thinking — Application — Integration
21	**YOU'RE NOW A RESEARCHER** Pretend for the moment you want to do a research study that describes the barriers that first-generation ethnic minority social work students face when they enter your social work program. 1. List the five ways that you can "know" what the barriers are. 2. What are the advantages and disadvantages of each way of "knowing"? Provide as many examples as you can to illustrate your points. 3. At this point in the book, and using the "most objective way of knowing," describe how you would go about answering this simple research question: What barriers do first-generation ethnic minority social work students face when they enter my social work program?
22	**PRACTICE VS. RESEARCH** **Practice:** Pretend for the moment you're employed as a social worker in your university's student counseling center. A first-generation ethnic minority student comes into your office where she tells you she feels lonely and isolated and wants to go home and drop out of school. 1. Using this chapter as a guide—and in particular Figures 1.5 and 1.6—describe the steps you would go through to help your client with her problems. Be specific and back up all your statements with specific examples. **Research:** Let's suppose that now you want to do a research study that tries to find out what factors are involved that make first-generation ethnic minority students at your university feel lonely and isolated. 2. Using this chapter as a guide—and in particular Figures 1.5 and 1.6—describe the steps you would go through to answer your research question: Why do first-generation ethnic minority students feel isolated? Be specific and back up all your statements with specific examples. **NOTE:** This exercise should help you to realize that social work practitioners and researchers use the identical problem-solving process as illustrated in Figures 1.5 and 1.6.

23	**THE SCIENTIFIC METHOD AND THE PRACTITIONER** **Scenario 1:** Make an argument that to be an effective evidence-based social work practitioner **you must know** how the scientific method of inquiry process advances our profession's knowledge base. Provide clear and explicit **practice-related** social work examples to illustrate your main points. **Scenario 2:** Make an argument that **you do not have to know** how the scientific method of inquiry process advances our profession's knowledge base to be an effective evidence-based social work practitioner. Provide clear and explicit **practice-related** social work examples to illustrate your main points. **Time to Choose:** Which one of the above two scenarios do you feel is more consistent with the concept of the contemporary evidence-based social work practice process as illustrated on pages 46–51? Why? Provide relevant social work examples to illustrate your main points.
24	**THE SCIENTIFIC METHOD AND THE RESEARCHER** **Scenario 1:** Make an argument that to be a competent social work researcher **you must know** how the scientific method of inquiry process advances our profession's knowledge base. Provide clear and explicit **research-related** social work examples to illustrate your main points. **Scenario 2:** Make an argument that **you do not have to know** how the scientific method of inquiry process advances our profession's knowledge base to be a competent social work researcher. Provide clear and explicit **research-related** social work examples to illustrate your main points. **Time to Choose:** Which one of the above two scenarios do you feel is more consistent with the place of research in social work? Why? Provide relevant social work examples to illustrate your main points.
25	**TIME TO PUT ON YOUR CRITICAL THINKING HAT** 1. Discuss the similarities and differences between your responses to Questions 23 and 24. 2. What are your thoughts on the belief that you need to know how the scientific method of inquiry process advances our profession's knowledge base whether you're a social work *practitioner* (Question 23) or a social work *researcher* (Question 24)? **NOTE:** This exercise should help you to understand that the skills you draw upon to help answer client practice problems are same skills you'll need to answer research problems as well.

26	**RESEARCH AND YOUR PROFESSIONAL DEVELOPMENT** 1. Review the three social work research-related roles you can take when you graduate—CSWE Competency 1 at the beginning of this chapter (page 2) and on pages 38–42. Thoroughly discuss how you feel this chapter will help you to perform one or more research-related roles when you graduate. Which one of the three roles do you believe this chapter helped you with the most? Why? Discuss in detail and provide an example to illustrate your main points. 2. Review CSWE Competency 4 at the beginning of this chapter (page 2). Thoroughly discuss how you feel this chapter will help you to become a practice-informed researcher and a research-informed practitioner. Discuss in detail and provide an example to illustrate your main points. 3. Review the evidence-based practice process as illustrated on pages 46–51. Thoroughly discuss how this chapter helps you to develop the skills you'll need for implementing one or more steps of the evidence-based practice process. Now discuss which step(s) you feel this chapter will help you with the most. Why? Be very specific and use relevant social work examples to illustrate your main points throughout your discussion. **NOTE:** This exercise should help you to understand that the skills you draw upon to become an ethical researcher are the same skills you will need in practice situations as well. In short, you can use this chapter to help you become more "ethically aware" in your day-to-day practice activities with all your client systems.
27	**MOVING AHEAD BY LOOKING BACK** At this point in your research methods course, how comfortable are you with discussing the place of research in social work with your field instructor, with your practice instructor, with your research instructor, with your supervisor at work, with the director of your social work program, or with your classmates? Discuss in detail.

2

CHAPTER

COMPETENCY 1: Demonstrate Ethical and Professional Behavior

You will learn that in order to be a successful evidence-based practitioner you have an ethical obligation to integrate three research roles into your daily practice activities as discussed in Chapter 1: (1) research consumer, (2) research partner—either as a co-researcher or research participant, and (3) creator and disseminator of research (or knowledge).

This entire chapter pertains to these three professional roles as you'll learn that one of the best ways to become an ethical and professional evidence-based social work practitioner is knowing how to apply four basic criteria in the assessment of a research question (or hypothesis) for relevancy, practicality, and usefulness to real-life social work practice, education, or policy.

COMPETENCY 4: Engage in Practice-Informed Research and Research-Informed Practice

Competency 4 also pertains to the entire chapter because you have to:

1. Evaluate the degree to which a research study adhered to the basic principles of formulating social work research questions (or hypotheses), given the study's specific population or research participants. You will learn that the only way you can legitimately evaluate the effectiveness of your day-to-day practice activities (in addition to the social work program where you work) is not only knowing how research questions (or hypotheses) are formulated in the first place, but also becoming fully aware of what they are trying to accomplish: to explore, to describe, or to explain (**research consumer**—research-informed practice);

2. Participate in a research study—either as a co-researcher or research participant (**research partner**—practice-informed research). See 1 above and 3 below; and

3. Know how to formulate meaningful, relevant, and useful research questions (or hypotheses) before you actually begin a research study (**creator and disseminator of research**—practice-informed research).

You'll also need to utilize evidence-based practice recommendations whenever possible; that is, you'll need to integrate (1) the best available research-based evidence with (2) your clinical expertise and (3) your client's values.

All of the above implies you'll need to know how a research study formulated its final research question (or hypothesis) that produced the research-based evidence. In short, you need to ask and then answer a simple question: How seriously should I take the findings of any specific research study given the overall creditability and usefulness of its research question (or hypothesis)?

COMPETENCY 9: Evaluate Practice with Individuals, Families, Groups, Organizations, and Communities

See Competencies 1 and 4.

2

CHAPTER

Formulating Research Questions

CHAPTER 1	**Step 1.**	Understanding the Research Process
CHAPTER 2	**Step 2.**	Developing Research Questions
CHAPTER 3	**Step 3.**	Reviewing the Literature
CHAPTERS 4 & 5	**Step 4.**	Being Aware of Ethical and Cultural Issues
CHAPTERS 6–8	**Step 5.**	Selecting a Research Approach
CHAPTERS 9 & 10	**Step 6.**	Specifying How Variables Are Measured
CHAPTER 11	**Step 7.**	Selecting a Sample
CHAPTERS 12 & 13	**Step 8.**	Selecting a Research Design
CHAPTERS 14–16	**Step 9.**	Selecting a Data-Collection Method
CHAPTERS 17 & 18	**Step 10.**	Analyzing the Data
CHAPTERS 19 & 20	**Step 11.**	Writing the Research Report

THE LAST CHAPTER DISCUSSED how we go about knowing something and placed a considerable emphasis on the fact that knowing something derived from the scientific method of inquiry is more objective, if you will, than knowing that same thing through authority, tradition, experience, in addition to beliefs and intuition.

In this chapter we discuss how research questions are formulated that can be answered through using any one of the three research approaches within the scientific method—quantitative, qualitative, or both (also known as *mixed-methods*). Before you can even begin to start formulating a research question, however, you need to fully appreciate the direct and indirect factors that affect its construction—the topic that follows.

FACTORS AFFECTING RESEARCH QUESTIONS

THERE ARE SIX highly overlapping factors that indirectly or directly affect the formulation of a social work research question (Grinnell & Williams, 1990; Williams, Grinnell, & Tutty, 1997). For the sake of clarity, these factors are presented separately, although in reality they always act in combination. The six factors are:

1. The social work profession
2. The social work agency
3. The researcher
4. The social work practitioner
5. Ethical and cultural considerations
6. Political and social considerations

THE SOCIAL WORK PROFESSION

THE FIRST FACTOR THAT AFFECTS how social work research questions are formulated is our very own profession. Doing a research study that answers a research question in a social work practice setting is enormously different from doing one in a scientific laboratory or in an artificial setting. Many social work research questions are geared toward our clients who often participate in our research projects.

They have special needs that we must take into consideration if we use them as research participants; that is, those folks who we will collect data from that will answer our research question. Many of these considerations fall into the "ethics" category and will be fully discussed in Chapter 4.

PURE RESEARCH QUESTIONS

AS WE KNOW from the previous chapter, we welcome pure research questions with open arms that are geared toward increasing our knowledge base. Identifying a body of social work knowledge, as distinct from sociological or psychological knowledge, is often a difficult task. Our profession has always been something of a poor relation among the social sciences, borrowing bits of information from psychology, anthropology, and sociology, pieces from political science and economics, and never finding much that can be classified as distinctly and uniquely social work.

However, we are hardly in a position to complain about this. The knowledge garnered from social psychology is obtained largely from research questions that were answered from studies undertaken by psychologists. Similarly, the knowledge we borrow from anthropology, sociology, political science, and economics is gathered by people in these fields.

As can be seen in Box 2.1, it seems only reasonable that the knowledge specific to our field should be obtained by social workers who formulate their own research questions and conduct subsequent research studies that answer them in their particular areas of expertise.

BOX 2.1	Where Do Research Questions Come From?

SO HOW DO RESEARCHERS come up with the idea for a research question? Probably one of the most common sources of research ideas is the experience of practical problems in our field. Many researchers are directly engaged in social, health, or human service program implementation and come up with their ideas based on what they see happening around them. Others aren't directly involved in service contexts, but work with (or survey) people who are in order to learn what needs to be better understood.

Many of the ideas would strike the outsider as silly or worse. For instance, in health services areas, there is great interest in the problem of back injuries among nursing staff. It's not necessarily the thing that comes first to mind when we think about the health care field, but if you reflect on it for a minute longer, it should be obvious that nurses and nursing staff do an awful lot of lifting in performing their jobs. They lift and push heavy equipment, and they lift and push oftentimes heavy patients.

If five or ten out of every hundred nurses were to strain their backs on average over the period of one year, the costs would be enormous—and that's pretty much what's happening. Even minor injuries can result in increased absenteeism; major ones can result in lost jobs and expensive medical bills.

The nursing industry figures that this is a problem that amounts to tens of millions of dollars annually in increased health care costs. The health care industry has developed a number of approaches, many of them educational, to try to reduce the scope and cost of the problem. So, even though it might seem silly at first, many of these practical problems that arise in practice can lead to extensive research efforts.

THE LITERATURE

Another source for research ideas is the literature (to be discussed shortly). Certainly, many researchers get ideas for research by reading the literature and thinking of ways to extend or refine previous research studies. One type of literature that acts as a source of good research ideas is the requests for proposals (RFPs) that are published by government agencies. These RFPs describe some problem that the agency would like researchers to address—they are virtually handing the researcher an idea!

Typically, the RFP describes the problem that needs to be addressed, the contexts in which it operates, the approach they would like you to take to investigate to address the problem, and the amount they would be willing to pay for such a study. Clearly, there's nothing like potential research funding to get researchers to focus on a particular research topic.

And let's not forget the fact that many researchers simply think up their research topics on their own. Of course, no one lives in a vacuum, so we would expect that the ideas you come up with on your own are influenced by your background, culture, education, and experiences.

APPLIED RESEARCH QUESTIONS

OUR PROFESSION ALSO APPRECIATES answers that were derived from applied research questions that can be used to enhance our daily practice activities. As we have established in the previous chapter, if we are to remain involved in the well being of our clients, we must become more active in assessing the effectiveness and efficiency of our interventions.

The social problem of domestic violence, for example, will not be solved by indiscriminate funding of emergency shelters for women who have been battered, by treatment for men who have been abusive toward their partners, by services for children who have been victimized, or by higher education for all and sundry.

Good research questions are needed both to determine the most effective ways of helping people and to evaluate the usefulness of our social service programs currently being funded. Evaluation of existing social service programs is no longer the rather laissez-faire affair that it once was.

As recently as the 1970s, it would have been enough for a program's director to convince a funding body that the program it was funding was meeting its goal, keeping within its budget, and generally providing a useful service to the community, without having to produce detailed objective data to that effect.

Today, funders want "objective data" derived from research studies that determine if the agency's goals are being met at the least possible cost. They want the results of evaluative studies, performed according to accepted research methods. They simply want proof.

The demand for evaluation is so pervasive that if we do not evaluate our own programs, the evaluations will often be conducted for us by professional evaluators, hired by the folks who fund us in the first place. Until recently, all evaluations of social work programs were carried out by non–social workers who were skilled in such techniques as planning, programing, and budget systems (PPBS) but who knew very little about social work values and practices.

Few of our programs are cost-efficient in the way that businesses must be in order to survive. The purpose of a business is to make a profit; the purpose of a social work program is to salvage human lives. Because of this distinction, social work administrators objected to the use of business cost-efficiency criteria to measure the worth of human services. They questioned the meaning of the word "efficient" in the human context: Did it mean efficient in terms of time, money, labor, suffering, human rights, or something else?

Eventually, we began to conduct evaluative studies and tried to reach a compromise between PPBS efficiency and client needs. The prestige of our profession has benefitted from the fact that we are now empowered to evaluate our own programs in light of our own value systems. Clients have also benefitted, since their needs are not now sacrificed arbitrarily to costs. These gains are lost, however, if the agency's staff ignores evaluations until they are imposed upon them from outside the agency.

In sum, it would benefit of both social workers and their clients if we were to take more responsibility for formulating research questions and conducting subsequent research studies that answer them on our own programs. This would provide us with the authority to advocate for clients, to be heard by other professionals with regard to clients, to maintain control over programs serving clients, and to bring about needed change. In this present age of accountability, there is no doubt that a profession that strives for status must be accountable.

To some degree it's a question of "the more accountability the more status," because accountability is status. It symbolizes power. It's apparent, therefore, that if our profession wishes to crawl up the status ladder, its driving force must be accountability. The way to achieve accountability is by answering well-formulated and well-thought-out research questions.

However, we must never forget that accountability is not all a facade. As we know from the previous chapter, the scientific method—as one of the five ways of knowing—is not just a path to authority and status. It also allows us to determine how best to serve our clients, how to determine the effectiveness of our services, and how to improve the services we offer.

Today, funders want "objective data" derived from research studies that determine if the agency's goals are being met at the least possible cost.

SOCIAL PROBLEMS MUST BE CHANGEABLE

WE STRONGLY INVITE RESEARCH QUESTIONS that will solve social problems. However, the problems must be changeable—and have a solution to boot. We have already talked about what motivates social workers to do research studies in the last chapter. Your supervisor may want you to, or you might have to for the sake of your clients, or you could be just interested in something. Sometimes the research question is mostly already there, and it only remains for you to word it more precisely so that it can become researchable.

Perhaps, for example, your social service program provides substance abuse treatment to First Nations adolescents, and it wants to know whether the spirituality component it has recently introduced makes the treatment more effective. At other times, you begin more generally with a broad topic area—poverty, for example—and then you will need to decide what particular aspects of your general topic area you want to address before you can formulate a sound research question.

Simply put, social work research topics—and the research questions they generate—deal with social problems. A social problem is something we wish we didn't have. We do not define a social problem in the first place unless we believe that change both ought to and probably can occur.

This may not sound particularly profound, but consider for a moment what it is that causes some social circumstances and not others to be defined as "problems." In our day, poverty is seen as a social problem. In earlier times, poverty certainly existed, but it was not considered a problem in the sense that we felt we ought to do something about it. The attitude was very much that the poor are always with us—they always have been, they probably always will be, and that's just the way life is.

Knowing that our profession is the first factor that affects research questions, we now turn our attention to the second, the social work agency where the practitioners work.

THE SOCIAL WORK AGENCY

THE SECOND FACTOR affecting research questions is the social work agency—the place where we work. This factor heavily overlaps with the previous one—the social work profession itself. Most of us are employed by a social work program housed within an agency. A child protection agency, for example, may run an investigation program whose sole purpose is to investigate alleged cases of child abuse and neglect.

The same agency may provide in-home support services to families who have abused or neglected their children—a second program. The agency may run a survivor-witness program for children and nonoffending parents who have to appear in court—a third program.

Social work research topics—and the research questions they generate—deal with social problems.

Research studies that answer research questions are usually conducted within the confines of a program. The word "confines" is used advisedly since no study can be undertaken without the support, or at least the toleration, of the program's director. Some program directors are supportive of research studies, while others shiver at the merest mention, but all of them have some things in common. The first of these is that they all worry about money.

Program directors of social work agencies have very little money. They worry that in the coming year they may have even less money—that their funding will be cut or even terminated, their clients will suffer, and their staff will be unemployed. They worry that all these disasters will follow in the wake of an evaluative research study. People doing research studies often have access to client files and to clients.

We sometimes talk to staff and examine agency procedures. We are in an excellent position to embarrass everyone by breaching client confidentiality, making inappropriate statements at the wrong times to the wrong people, and writing reports that comment on the program's weaknesses but disregard its strengths.

All programs, like all people, have flaws. Few are efficient in the business sense and most are open to doubt concerning their effectiveness. Program directors know this. They work to improve programs, serving their clients as best they can with limited resources and knowledge that is patchy at best—because the knowledge has not been gained and the research studies necessary to gain it have not been undertaken.

> Research studies that answer research questions are usually conducted within the confines of a program.

It's not surprising, then, that program directors find themselves torn with regard to the place of the research enterprise in our profession. They understand that increased knowledge, via answering research questions, is necessary in order to serve clients better, but sometimes they wish that the knowledge could be gathered somewhere else: not through their programs, not with their client files, not using their scarce resources, and not taking up the time of their staff. They correctly argue that resources given to research studies are resources taken away from client services.

They may think, privately, that research reports are useful only to those engaged in the studies in the first place. There is an upside to all of this gloom, however. It's possible that the research report might reflect the program in a good light, delighting its funders and improving its standing in the public eye. In addition, the study might reveal a genuinely practical way in which the program could improve its services to its clients or do what it does more efficiently.

Many program directors will therefore give permission for research studies to be conducted, provided that the person(s) doing the study is of good standing in the social work community, the proposed study meets the staff's approval, and agreements are entered into concerning confidentiality and the use of the program's staff and financial resources.

Larger agencies often have special committees to evaluate research requests (to be discussed in Chapter 4). Few, if any, of our programs are designed with the notion that someday the program will be engaged in the research process.

In some programs, client files have become more ordered with the advent of the computer, but frequently data are difficult both to find and to interpret. The entries in client files may be made by different workers at different times, in writing ranging from copperplate to scrawl, with different viewpoints on the people and events involved, and sometimes with vital data missing.

Policies and procedures manuals, long outdated, may bear little relationship to the policies currently in place and the procedures actually undertaken. When this occurs, we must often become dependent upon the goodwill of staff to provide guidance and explanations, even when the original plan was just a quiet session with client files.

A researcher's positive relationships with program staff cannot be overemphasized. If you don't possess sound social skills you'll never be given permission to do a research study within a social work agency.

THE RESEARCHER

THE THIRD FACTOR affecting the formulation of research questions is the person actually doing the study—you, the researcher. To illustrate how social work researchers are motivated to come up with specific research questions, two articles from Canadian newspapers will be used as examples (Grinnell, Rothery, & Thomlison, 1993).

As you know, the article reproduced in Box 1.1 in the previous chapter is concerned with the attempted abduction of a child in an elementary school at Innisfail, Alberta, and the article in Box 2.2 in this chapter remarks on the unusual lack of stereotyping of Native Indians in a Canadian television program. The two articles can easily be applied equally to the problems of child abuse and racism throughout the world.

What motivates social workers to pose research questions? One way to answer this question is by examining possible reactions to the articles reproduced in Boxes 1.1 and 2.2. Readers will have different reactions to the story about the kidnapped child (Box 1.1).

BOX 2.2	Show Ignores Native Stereotypes

Gibsons, B.C. (CP)—Native actress Marianne Jones had to fight to keep from laughing when a script once called for her to utter the line: "Him shot six times."

"It was really a difficult thing to say," recalls Jones, who now plays Laurel on CBC's *Beachcombers*.

That, she says, is typical of the way natives are portrayed on TV and films.

And that, she says, is what's different about *Beachcombers*.

"It's one of the only shows that portrays native people on a day-to-day basis," says Jones.

"No other series has that sort of exposure. When you think of how many native people there are in the country, it's amazing that there isn't more."

Television's portrayal of natives touches a nerve in Jones.

The striking actress with shoulder-length raven hair cherishes her Haida heritage. She identifies her birthplace as "Haida Gwaii—that's the Queen Charlotte Islands, the real name."

The four natives in *Beachcombers* are depicted as people rather than stereotypes.

"I've done a lot of other shows and they sort of want to put you in a slot: You're a noble savage, you know, the Hollywood stereotypes that have been perpetuated forever."

She admits that natives are struggling with their identity these days; wrestling with tradition and the attractions of the 20th century.

"We're all weighing the traditional life, the spirituality, against being human . . . We're living today."

"Everybody has a fridge, so to speak," she adds with a raspy laugh.

Jones is doing her part by venturing into video production, starting with a documentary on a Haida artist.

"For a long time, native people have not been allowed or able to define their own images."

"We need to take control to get rid of those Hollywood stereotypes, and to change native people on television to real people."

Parents of young children, for example, may feel fear and anxiety about the safety of their children because they may be reminded that in their communities there are those who could harm them. They and others may experience anger toward those who victimize children and a desire to see them caught, restrained, or punished. They may feel concern for the abducted seven-year-old, mixed with feelings of relief that she was returned to her family.

A researcher's positive relationships with program staff cannot be overemphasized.

An adult who was victimized as a child, for example, may be likely to have more complex and strong emotional reactions than a person who was not victimized as a child. Teachers, social workers, and police officers whose jobs entail responsibility for such situations may experience professional curiosity.

With the second article (Box 2.2), a reader may react with admiration for Marianne Jones, who has overcome the barriers imposed by racism to establish herself in a difficult career. Those of you who are members of a minority group may well applaud more enthusiastically than those of you who are not; you may even share her success in some way.

An administrator in a school system that serves minority students may sense an opportunity—a chance to answer a meaningful research question into what images of minorities are perpetuated through the educational system and what impact this has on the students. Some readers may have little or no reaction, however. If nothing in their past history or current involvements is linked to the issues of child abuse (Box 1.1) or racism (Box 2.2), they may merely glance at the articles and pass them over quickly.

A great variety of responses to these two news items is possible, each shaped by the reader's history and circumstances. It is in reactions such as these that research questions are born. We may be drawn into projects simply because they are there—support is available to conduct a particular study, or our careers will benefit from seizing the opportunities.

Nevertheless, a research question would not be formulated without someone, somewhere, sometime, confronting a situation or event and finding it relevant. Potential researchers begin with the sense (often vaguely formulated) that there is more to be known about a problem area; a question exists that is important enough to justify investing time and other resources in the search for an answer.

The most important thing to know before doing any research study is what implications the study's findings might produce that will advance the knowledge base of social work practice, and/or education, and/or policy.

VALUE SYSTEMS OF THE RESEARCHERS

AT EVERY STAGE IN THE RESEARCH PROCESS, there are decisions to be made based on the knowledge and value systems of the person formulating the research question and conducting the research study. If we are investigating poverty, for example, and believe that poverty results from character flaws in the poor, we might study treatment interventions designed to overcome those flaws.

On the other hand, if we believe that ghettos are a factor, we might prefer to focus on environmental causes. In short, the research questions we finally select are determined by our own value systems as well as by the social and political realities of the hour.

Another factor in our study of poverty is how we define "poor." What annual income should a person earn in order to be categorized as poor? We may decide that "poor," in the context of our study, means an annual income of less than $20,000, and that we do not need to talk to anyone who earns more than that. If we decide that the upper limit should be $30,000, we are automatically including many more people as potential participants for our study. Thus, the data collected about "the poor" will depend largely on who is defined as "poor."

> If you don't possess sound social skills you'll never be given permission to do a research study within a social work agency.

Our final report will probably include recommendations for change based on our study's findings—which is based on our research question of course. These recommendations, too, will depend on our personal value systems, modified by social, political, and economic realities.

It may be our private opinion that welfare recipients should be given only the absolute minimum of resources necessary to sustain life in order to motivate them to find work. On the other hand, we may believe that a decent standard of living is every human being's birthright. Whatever our opinion, it's likely that we will clothe it in suitable phraseology and incorporate it somehow into our recommendations.

The opinions and attitudes of social workers in regard to research practices play a vital part in the formulation of research questions.

Personal value systems are particularly evident in program evaluations. Our programs are often labeled as ineffective, not as a result of poor goal achievement, but because there is disagreement about the goal itself. Is a drug prevention program "successful" if it reduces drug use among its clients, or must clients abstain altogether before success can be claimed? Then there is the question of how much success constitutes "success."

Is a job placement program worth funding if it finds jobs for only 50 percent of its clients? Should an in-home support program be continued if the child is removed from the home in 30 percent of the cases? Next, there is the matter of what types of clients are the most deserving. Should limited resources be used to counsel people dying of cancer, or would the money be better spent on those who are newly diagnosed? Is it worthwhile to provide long-term treatment for one family whose potential for change is small, while other families with more potential linger on the waiting list? These types of value-based questions are endless.

THE SOCIAL WORK PRACTITIONER

SOCIAL WORKERS' BELIEFS AND ATTITUDES also affect how research questions are formulated that will be answered in agency settings. Some social workers, for example, refuse to have an observer present at an interview with a client on the grounds that the client will be unable to speak freely and the social worker–client relationship will be disrupted.

This difficulty can be resolved in facilities with one-way mirrors; but, if no such mirror exists, a person wishing to answer a research question that determines the effectiveness and efficiency of a treatment intervention, for example, may not be able to watch the intervention in a practical, clinical setting.

An alternative to the physical presence of the person doing the study is a video recorder. A few social workers—whose belief in disruption leads them to be disrupted—also object to video recorders, although experience has shown that most clients ignore video recorders after the first few curious glances. Indeed, some social workers seem to believe that there is a sort of an aura surrounding practice relationships that is shattered by such devices.

To the extent that video recorders, paper-and-pencil questionnaires, and computer question-and-answer programs are shunned out of hand, the effectiveness of the intervention can never be objectively established. To a degree, it's true that the act of measuring alters what it measures, but often the change is neither great nor long-lasting.

The opinions and attitudes of social workers in regard to research practices thus play a vital part in the formulation of research questions. It's not just our attitude that makes a difference; it's the attitudes of everyone involved in the study.

ETHICAL AND CULTURAL CONSIDERATIONS

THE FIFTH IMPORTANT FACTOR affecting the formulation of social work research questions is ethical and cultural considerations. Physical scientists are by no means exempt from ethical considerations. Consider Robert Oppenheimer and other atomic scientists, who learned too late that their scientific findings about splitting the atom were used to create an atomic bomb—a purpose the scientists themselves opposed.

A physical scientist who wishes to run tests on water samples, for example, does not have to consider the feelings of the water samples or worry about harming them. No large dilemma is presented if one of the water samples must be sacrificed to the cause of knowledge building.

For people engaged in social work research studies, however, the ethical issues are far more pervasive and complex. A fundamental principle of formulating a social work research question is that any increase in our knowledge base, while much desired, must never be obtained at the expense of human beings. Since many of our research questions revolve directly around human beings, safeguards must be put in place to ensure that our research participants are never harmed, either physically or psychologically.

An American committee known as the National Commission for the Protection of Human Subjects of Biomedical and Behavioral Research is only one of several professional organizations and lay groups that focus on protecting the rights of research participants. Most research participants, however, have never heard of any of them.

Clients participating in studies do not put their trust in committees; they trust the individual practitioners who involve them in the studies. It's therefore incumbent upon all of us to be familiar with ethical principles so that our clients' trust will never be betrayed.

Essentially, there are three precautionary ethical measures that must be taken before beginning any research study that will answer any research question. These are:

1. Obtaining the participant's informed consent
2. Designing the study in an ethical manner
3. Ensuring that others will be properly told about the study's findings.

All three of these concerns are discussed in detail in Chapter 4 on research ethics.

POLITICAL AND SOCIAL CONSIDERATIONS

THE LAST FACTOR that affects social work research questions is political and social considerations. Ethics and politics are interrelated, but a useful distinction exists in that ethics has to do with the methods employed in answering the research question, whereas politics is concerned with the practical costs and uses of the study's findings.

Consider, for example, the area of race relations. Most social researchers in the 1960s supported the cause of African-American equality in America. In 1969, Arthur Jensen, a Harvard psychologist, examined data on racial differences in IQ test results and concluded that genetic differences between African Americans and Caucasians accounted for the lower IQ scores of African Americans. Jensen was labeled a racist, and such was the furor surrounding his study that other people were reluctant to pursue any line of inquiry involving comparisons between Caucasians and African Americans.

Consequently, a needed investigation into the higher rate of mortality seen in African-American women with breast cancer compared to similarly afflicted Caucasian women was not conducted. The study may have revealed racial differences in genetic predispositions to breast tumors, and the National Cancer Institute, at that time, was understandably reluctant to use the word "genetic" in connection with African Americans. It's not infrequently the case that sensitivity about vulnerable populations leads to avoidance of research studies that might benefit those groups.

Politics plays an important role not only in what research studies are funded or conducted but also in what findings are published. Contrary opinions or unpopular opinions are no longer punished, as they were in Galileo's day, by the Inquisitional Tribunal or the rack, but they are still punished.

Punishment may be delivered in the form of articles and books that are never published, invitations to present research papers that are never offered, academic appointments that are never given—and research proposals that are never funded.

Finding the answer to a research question can be an extremely expensive endeavor. If a funding body cannot be found to support the research project, the study may never be conducted. Funding bodies tend either to be governments or to be influenced by government policies and a person doing a research study is as interested as anyone else in money, recognition, and professional advancement. It's therefore often the case that funded studies follow directions consistent with the prevailing political climate.

> Clients participating in research studies do not put their trust in committees; they trust the individual practitioners who involve them in the studies.

Studies under one administration may inquire into ways of improving social services and discovering better designs for public housing. Under another administration, attention may shift to the efficiency of existing programs, as measured through program evaluations.

It's important to remember, though, that not all research studies are expensive, and many can be conducted without the aid of government money. No large amounts of extra funding are needed to integrate evaluation into the normal routine of clinical practice. Program evaluations do not cost large amounts of money when conducted by program staff themselves.

In sum, social work research questions are affected not only by the personal biases of the person conducting the study that answer the questions, but also by prevailing beliefs on such sensitive issues as race, gender, poverty, disability, sexual orientation, violence, and so forth. Government positions both shape and are shaped by these beliefs, leading to support of some research questions but not of others.

Legitimate inquiry is sometimes restricted by fear that data uncovered on one of these sensitive issues will be misinterpreted or misused, thereby bringing harm to vulnerable client groups.

THE KNOWLEDGE-LEVEL CONTINUUM

ONCE YOUR RESEARCH QUESTION is formulated it then must be answered. We will now turn our attention to how the three research approaches answer various types of research questions. All research studies fall anywhere along the knowledge-level continuum depending on how much is already known about the research question under investigation (Figure 2.1).

The mixed-method research approach can easily be used at all three knowledge levels—especially at the exploratory and descriptive levels. However, at the explanatory level, the findings from a quantitative study are given first priority and then can be supplemented with qualitative data that provide meaning to the findings.

The mixed-methods research approach can be used at all three knowledge levels: exploratory, descriptive, and explanatory.

How much is known about the research question determines the purpose of the study. If you didn't know anything, for example, you will merely want to explore the research area, gathering basic data. Studies like this, conducted for the purpose of exploration are known, logically enough, as *exploratory studies* and fall at the bottom of the knowledge-level continuum as can be seen in Figure 2.1 on the following page.

Exploratory research questions usually adopt a qualitative, or interpretive, research approach. However, they can also adopt a quantitative, or positivistic, approach as well, in which case they would be classified as mixed-methods— assuming of course that the findings from both approaches are truly *integrated* into the study's overall research design. One again, note the word *integrated.*

When you have gained some knowledge of the research topic area through exploratory studies, the next task is to describe a specific aspect of the topic area in greater detail, using words (qualitative) and/or numbers (quantitative). These studies, whose purpose is description, are known as *descriptive studies* and fall in the middle of the knowledge-level continuum as presented in Figure 2.1.

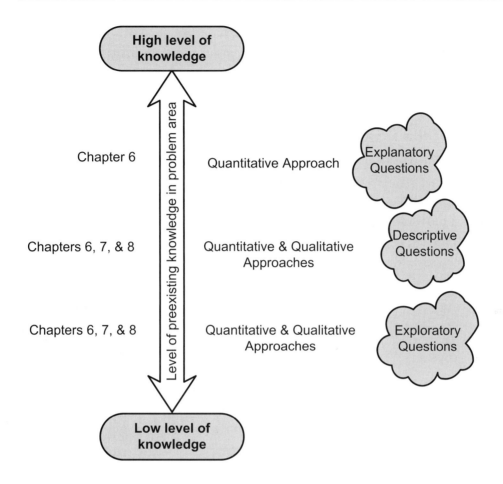

FIGURE 2.1

The Knowledge-Level Continuum, Predominate Approaches to the Scientific Method, and Types of Questions Answered

They can adopt a quantitative and/or qualitative research approach. After descriptive studies have provided a substantial knowledge base in the research topic area, you will be in a position to ask very specific and more complex research questions—causality questions. These kinds of studies are known as *explanatory studies.*

The division of the knowledge continuum into three parts—exploratory, descriptive, and explanatory—is a useful way of categorizing research studies in terms of their purpose, the kinds of questions they can answer, and the research approach(es) they can take in answering the questions.

How much is known about the research question determines the purpose of the study.

However, as in all categorization systems, the three divisions are totally arbitrary and some social work research studies defy categorization, falling nastily somewhere between exploratory and descriptive, or between descriptive and explanatory. This defiance is only to be expected since the knowledge-level continuum is essentially that—a continuum, not a neat collection of categories.

In a nutshell, research studies can be loosely classified into three generic categories:

EXPLORATORY RESEARCH STUDIES

EXPLORATORY STUDIES are most useful when the research topic area is relatively new. In the United States during the 1970s, for example, the development of new drugs to control the symptoms of mental illness, together with new federal funding for small, community-based mental health centers, resulted in a massive discharge of people from large state-based mental health institutions.

Some folks applauded this move as restoring the civil liberties of the mentally ill. Others were concerned that current community facilities would prove inadequate to meet the needs of the people being discharged and their families. Social workers active in the 1970s were eager to explore the situation, both with an eye on influencing social policy and in order to develop programs to meet the perceived needs of this group of people.

The topic area here is very broad. What are the consequences of a massive discharge of people who are psychiatrically challenged and were recently institutionalized? Many different questions pertaining to the topic can be asked.

Where are these people living now? Alone? In halfway houses? With their families? On the street? Are they receiving proper medication and nutrition? What income do they have? How do they spend their time? What stresses do they suffer? What impact have they had on their family members and the communities in which they now reside? What services are available to them? How do they feel about being discharged?

No single study can answer all these questions. It's a matter of devising a sieve-like procedure where the first sieve with the biggest holes identifies general themes. Each general theme is then put through successively finer sieves until more specific research questions can be asked.

Let's take a closer look at Figure 2.2 for a minute. You might begin to explore the consequences of the massive discharge by gathering together a group of these discharged people and asking them a basic qualitatively oriented exploratory question: What have been your experiences since you were discharged? (What are the components that make up the discharge experience?) The question will be answered using qualitative data. Individual answers via words—not numbers—will generate common themes.

At this point, you might feel a need for numbers. How many of them are living where? How many times have they moved on average? What percentage of those who moved in with their families stayed there? These are quantitatively oriented descriptive questions, aimed at describing, or providing an accurate profile of this group of people.

You are now moving up the knowledge continuum in Figure 2.1 from the exploratory to the descriptive category, but before we go there; let's summarize the general goals of exploratory research studies (Neuman, 2012):

— Become familiar with the basic facts, people, and concerns involved.

— Develop a well-grounded mental picture of what is occurring.

— Generate many ideas and develop tentative theories and conjectures.

— Determine the feasibility of doing additional research.

— Formulate questions and refine issues for more systematic inquiry.

— Develop techniques and a sense of direction for future research.

DESCRIPTIVE RESEARCH STUDIES

AT THE DESCRIPTIVE LEVEL, suppose you have decided to focus your research questions on those people who moved in with their families. You have an idea, based on your previous qualitatively oriented exploratory study, that there might be a relationship between the length of time spent in the institution and whether or not this group of people moved in with their families after discharge.

You would like to confirm or refute this relationship by using a much larger group of respondents than you used in your exploratory study (Figure 2.2). Another important tentative relationship that emerged at the exploratory level was the relationship between staying in the family home and the level of acceptance shown by the family.

You would like to know if this relationship holds with a larger group. You would also like to know if there is a real difference between accepting and rejecting families: Is Group A different from Group B? And what factors contribute to acceptance or rejection of the discharged family member?

Eventually, you would like to know if there is anything social workers can do to facilitate acceptance, but you don't have enough data yet to be able to usefully ask that question. In general, the goals of descriptive research studies are as follows (Neuman, 2012):

— Provide an accurate profile of a group.

— Describe a process, mechanism, or relationship.

— Give a verbal or numerical picture (e.g., percentages).

— Find information to stimulate new explanations.

— Create a set of categories or classify types.

— Clarify a sequence, set of stages, or steps.

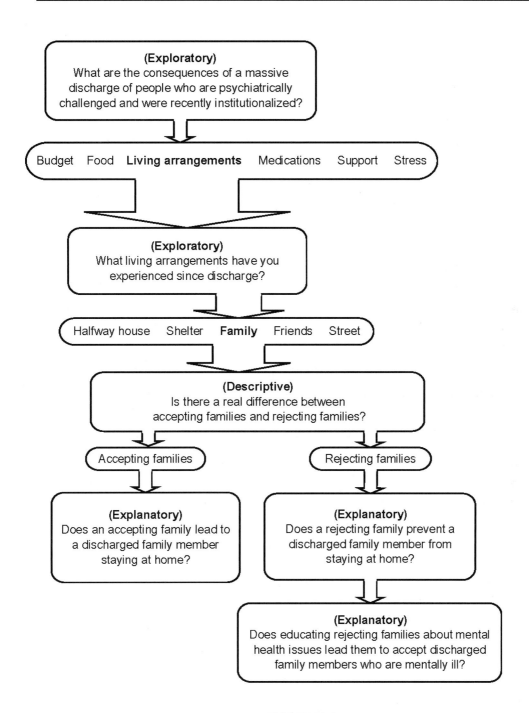

FIGURE 2.2

Example of a Simple Sieving Procedure

EXPLANATORY RESEARCH STUDIES

SUPPOSE YOU HAVE LEARNED from your descriptive studies that there are real differences between accepting and rejecting families and that these differences seem to have a major impact on whether or not the discharged person stays at home. Now you would like to ask two related explanatory, or causality, questions:

Explanatory research questions:

1. Does an accepting family lead to a discharged family member to stay at home?

2. Does a rejecting family prevent a discharged family member from staying at home?

In both cases, the answers will probably be yes, to some extent. Perhaps 30% of staying at home is explained by an accepting family and the other 70% remains to be explained by other factors: the severity of the discharged person's symptoms, for example, or the degree of acceptance shown by community members outside the family.

Now you might want to know whether acceptance on the part of the family carries more weight in the staying-at-home decision than acceptance on the part of the community. The answer to this question will provide a direction for possible intervention strategies: You will know whether to focus your attention on individual families or on entire communities.

Suppose you decide, for example, on the basis of your own and other explanatory studies, to focus on the families, and the intervention that you choose for increasing their acceptance is education about mental illness. In order to evaluate the effectiveness of your intervention, you will eventually need to ask another explanatory question:

Explanatory research question:
Does educating rejecting families about mental health issues lead them to accept discharged family members who are mentally ill?

With the answer to this question, you have concluded your sieving procedures, as outlined in Figure 2.2, moving from a broad exploratory question about discharge experiences to a tested intervention designed to serve the discharged people and their families. In general, these are the goals of explanatory research studies (Neuman, 2012):

— Determine the accuracy of a principle or theory.

— Find out which competing explanation is better.

— Link different issues or topics under a common general statement.

— Build and elaborate a theory so it becomes more complete.

— Extend a theory or principle into new areas or issues.

— Provide evidence to support or refute an explanation.

CLASSIFICATIONS OF QUESTIONS

FIGURES 2.1–2.3 show how research questions can be placed on a continuum from simple (exploratory studies) to complex (explanatory studies). Not surprisingly we need to ask simple questions first. When we have the answers to these simple questions, we then proceed to ask more complex ones. We are thus moving from "little knowledge about our research question" to "more knowledge about our research question."

Figure 2.3 on page 90 presents the knowledge continuum (from high to low—middle arrow), seven general classifications that research questions can take (left side), and the research approach (right side) that is most appropriate to answer each question classification. Once again, the mixed-method approach can be used at all seven levels depending on the goals of the studies. On a general level, there are seven types of questions that research studies can answer:

1. Existence
2. Composition
3. Relationship
4. Descriptive-comparative
5. Causality

6. Causality-comparative
7. Causality-comparative interaction

EXISTENCE QUESTIONS

SUPPOSE FOR A MOMENT you have an assumption that there is an association between low self-esteem in women and spousal abuse. You are going to study this topic—over a number of studies—starting at the beginning. The beginning, at the bottom of the knowledge continuum, is an existence question: in fact, two *existence questions* since your assumption involves two concepts: (1) self-esteem and (2) spousal abuse.

First, knowing nothing whatsoever about either self-esteem or spouse abuse, let alone whether there is an association between them, you want to know if self-esteem and spousal abuse actually exist in the first place. Self-esteem and spouse abuse arsse concepts—they are nothing more than ideas, human inventions if you like—that have become very familiar to social workers, and it's tempting just to say, "Of course they exist! I know they exist."

But there must have been a time when self-esteem was no more than a vague idea among students of human nature that some people seem to feel better about themselves than other people do. It would then have been just a matter of contacting Ms. Smith—and Ms. Jones, and Ms. Tasmania—and asking them, "Do you feel good about yourself?"

This qualitative study, sometimes referred to as interpretive—and many others like it, conducted by different researchers over time—would have provided an indication that yes indeed, some people do feel better about themselves than other people do. Self-esteem, if that is what you want to call (or label) the feeling, does in fact exist. The same process can be done to determine if spouse abuse exists. However, spouse abuse can be more easily observed and measured than self-esteem.

COMPOSITION QUESTIONS

THE SECOND QUESTION—"What is it that makes you feel good about yourself?"—is a simple attempt to find out what particular personal attributes contribute to self-esteem. That is, it answers the *composition question* next on the knowledge continuum. Qualitative studies exploring this dimension may have discovered that people who feel good about themselves in general also specifically feel that they are liked by others; that they are competent, intelligent, caring, and physically attractive; and that they have a host of other attributes that together make up the concept "self-esteem."

Thus, qualitative studies provide *descriptive* or *qualitative* data indicating that self-esteem exists and what it is. Similarly, they indicate that women are in fact sometimes abused by their partners and what particular forms such abuse can take.

RELATIONSHIP QUESTIONS

GOING UP ONE MORE NOTCH on the list, you next come to *relationship questions.* What, if any, is the relationship between women's self-esteem and spousal abuse? Here, you might begin with another qualitative study, trying to determine, on an individual basis, whether there seems to be any connection between having low self-esteem and being abused.

If there does seem to be enough evidence to theorize that such a relationship may exist, you might then use the quantitative research approach to see if the relationship holds for a larger number of women rather than just the small number you interviewed in your qualitative study.

DESCRIPTIVE-COMPARATIVE QUESTIONS

NEXT ON THE CONTINUUM you come to *descriptive-comparative questions:* Is Group A different from Group B? Here you might go in a number of different directions: You might wonder, for example, whether there is any difference in self-esteem levels between women in heterosexual relationships and women in lesbian relationships.

Does self-esteem differ between First Nations women and non–First Nations women? Do women with different sexual orientations or from different cultural groups also differ in how often they are abused, or how severely, or in what particular way?

Because you are asking about differences between social groups, which involve large numbers of people, you will need quantitative methods to address these questions. These will be discussed in Chapter 6.

FIGURE 2.3

Types of Research Questions, the Knowledge-Level Continuum, and PREDOMINATE Research Approaches That Answer the Research Questions (an expansion of Figure 2.1)

CAUSALITY QUESTIONS

THIRD FROM THE TOP of the continuum are the *causality* questions. Does low self-esteem actually cause women to be abused? Or, for that matter, does being abused cause low self-esteem? Most complex behaviors don't have single causes. Being abused might certainly contribute to having low self-esteem, but it's highly unlikely to be the sole cause.

Similarly, it's unlikely that having low self-esteem leads inevitably to being abused. Positivistic studies here, with their use of impressive statistics, can tell us what percentage of the abuse can be explained by low self-esteem and what percentage remains to be explained by other factors.

CAUSALITY-COMPARATIVE QUESTIONS

IF FACTORS OTHER THAN low self-esteem that cause abuse, it would be nice to know what they are and how much weight they have. Perhaps heavy drinking on the part of the abuser is a factor. Perhaps poverty is, or the battering suffered by the abuser as a child. Once these possible factors have been explored, using the same process you used in your exploration of self-esteem and spousal abuse, quantitative methods can again tell us what percentage of abuse is explained by each factor.

If low self-esteem accounts for only two percent, say, and heavy drinking accounts for eight percent, you will have answered the *causality-comparative question.* You will know, on the average, that heavy drinking on the abuser's part has more effect on spousal abuse than does the woman's self-esteem level.

The mixed-methods research approach can be used at all seven types of research questions as illustrated in Figure 2.3.

CAUSALITY-COMPARATIVE INTERACTION QUESTIONS

AT THE TIP-TOP OF THE CONTINUUM are the *causality-comparative interaction questions.* They ask whether your research findings only hold up under certain conditions. For example, if it's true that heavy drinking contributes more to spousal abuse than does the woman's level of self-esteem, perhaps that is only true for couples who are living in poverty. Or, it's only true for couples with children, or it's only true if the abuser was himself abused.

This final type of question, again answered through quantitative methods, reflects the highest aim of social work research—explanation. If we are to give our clients the best possible service, we need to know about causes and effects. What action or attribute on the part of whom causes how much of what effect, and under what conditions? What type of treatment will cause the most change in a particular type of client in a particular situation?

CRITERIA FOR GOOD QUESTIONS

FROM THE PRECEDING DISCUSSION you now know how research questions spring to life and how they can be classified. Your research question now needs to be evaluated. Every research question must be:

1. Relevant
2. Researchable
3. Feasible
4. Ethical and culturally sensitive

If it doesn't pass muster on all four criteria, it's worthless and must be discarded like an old pair of sneakers or your iPhone 9.

RELEVANT

RELEVANCE IS ONE OF THOSE THINGS, like efficiency, that is never absolute: The same research question may be less or more relevant depending on who is defining what is meant by "relevant" in what particular context. A research question about Chinese pottery, for example, might be relevant to researchers who are interested in Chinese potters or to archaeologists but may be less relevant to social workers.

To social workers, relevant research questions are those whose answers will have an impact on our social policies, and/or theories, and/or practices, and/or educational content. Within this framework, the degree of relevance of any particular study is usually decided by the organization that funds it, the program that houses it, and the research team who undertakes it.

RESEARCHABLE

SOME VERY INTERESTING QUESTIONS cannot be answered through the research process, either because of the nature of the question or because of the difficulties inherent in collecting the necessary data. For example, research studies cannot answer the question "Does God exist?" or "Is abortion wrong?" With respect to the latter, we may be able to collect evidence related to the effects of experiencing or being denied an abortion, but we cannot answer the underlying moral question.

In general, questions concerning faith or moral decisions are outside the province of research. Then there is the matter of technical difficulties inherent in the research question itself. For example, Aristotle believed that children would be healthier if conceived when the wind was from the north.

We are as interested in the health of children as Aristotle was, but, even supposing that we accepted the direction of the wind at conception as a possible contributing factor to healthier children, the question would not be researchable because of the practical difficulties associated with determining the direction of the wind at conception in a large enough number of cases. Researchability, then, has to do with whether the research question is appropriate for scientific inquiry and whether it's possible to collect valid and reliable data that would be needed to answer the question.

FEASIBLE

FEASIBILITY CARRIES the "collection of the necessary data" issue one step farther in that it has to be feasible. Feasibility means just that—whether your research project is feasible to carry out. Perhaps it's possible to collect data about the direction of the wind at conception (windsocks attached to every home combined with careful recordkeeping), but it's not possible for you to do it, given your limited resources and your inability to influence homebuilding and protection of privacy standards. The question about the relationship between the wind and the health of children might therefore be researchable, but it's not feasible as far as you are concerned.

Your available resources have a profound effect on the scope of the research study you are able to mount and thus on the questions you are able to answer. In other words, given all these things, could you practically do what you have planned?

ETHICAL AND CULTURALLY SENSITIVE

THERE IS A POTENTIAL FOR HARM not just in the way the study is conducted but in the way the research question is phrased. Researchers are in a wonderful position to offend just about everyone if they fail to pay attention to the cultural, gender, and sexual orientation aspects of their research questions. Not only might they offend people, but they might cause harm, not just to research participants but to entire groups of people.

We will discuss ethics in depth in Chapter 4, and in Chapter 5 we will address the cultural considerations that must be taken into account when doing research studies. For now, just remember that your research question must be ethical and culturally sensitive in addition to being relevant, researchable, and feasible.

SUMMARY

THIS CHAPTER STARTED OUT discussing the six factors that affect formulating social work research questions: the social work profession, the social work agency, the researcher, the social work practitioner, ethical and cultural considerations, and political and social considerations. We then went on to present the three main forms that research studies can take: exploratory, descriptive, and explanatory. Next, we talked about how research studies can be classified via the research questions they address. Finally, we presented the four considerations that all research questions must contain: relevance; researchability; feasibility; ethical acceptability and cultural sensitivity.

Study Questions for Chapter 2	
Essay — Discussion	
1	Before you entered your social work program and before you read this chapter, how did you think our profession formulated research questions? Provide as many examples as you can to justify your response.
2	List each of the factors that affect social work research studies. Discuss how they are highly related to one another using one common social work example throughout your discussion.
3	What social work research question would you like answered? Why? Discuss how it was influenced by each of the factors presented in the book.
4	Discuss what the knowledge-level continuum is all about. Provide specific social work examples for each one of the three levels.
5	Select a general social work problem area such as homelessness, depression, anxiety, addiction, domestic violence, child abuse, or truancy. Now formulate a research question within your problem area for each one of the three knowledge levels: exploratory, descriptive, and explanatory.
6	With Question 5 in mind, list all three research questions. Then list and discuss how each of your three research questions will be influenced by each of the six factors that affect the formulation of research problems.
7	With Questions 5 and 6 in mind, evaluate each of your three research questions with the four criteria found in the book.
8	With Questions 5, 6, and 7 in mind, formulate a social work research question for each of the seven classifications that research studies can fall under (Figure 2.3 on page 90). Be sure to use your general problem area as you did with Questions 5, 6, and 7.

9	What is the sieving procedure all about, as illustrated in Figure 2.2 on page 85? Provide a social work example throughout your discussion to illustrate your main points.

Critical Thinking — Application — Integration

10	**RESEARCH QUESTIONS AND THE REAL WORLD OF RESEARCH** Locate any published social work research article that contains a social work problem area or population that you're interested in. Be sure the study tried to answer a research question of some kind. 1. What was the study's research question? 2. Was the research question clearly stated? Discuss in detail. 3. What was the knowledge level of the research question? 4. Where on Figures 2.1 and 2.3 did the research question fall? Provide a rationale for your selection. 5. Using the contents within this chapter, discuss all of the six factors that must have affected the researcher's formulation of the final research question. Provide hypothetical examples throughout your discussion. 6. Evaluate the study's research question on each one of the four criteria presented in this book.
11	**RESEARCH QUESTIONS AND THE RESEARCHER** **Scenario 1:** Make an argument that to be a competent social work researcher **you must know** how to formulate relevant, useful, and ethical social work research questions. Provide a clear and explicit **research-related** social work example to illustrate your main points. **Scenario 2:** Make an argument that **you do not have to know** how to formulate relevant, useful, and ethical social work research questions to be a competent social work researcher. Provide a clear and explicit **research-related** social work example to illustrate your main points. **Time to Choose:** Which of the above two scenarios do you feel is more consistent with the place of research in social work? Why? Provide relevant social work examples to illustrate your main points.

12	**RESEARCH QUESTIONS AND THE PRACTITIONER** **Scenario 1:** Make an argument that to be an effective evidence-based social work practitioner **you must know** how to formulate relevant, useful, and ethical social work research questions. Provide a clear and explicit **practice-related** social work example to illustrate your main points. **Scenario 2:** Make an argument that **you do not have to know** how to formulate relevant, useful, and ethical social work research questions to be an effective evidence-based social work practitioner. Provide a clear and explicit **practice-related** social work example to illustrate your main points. **Time to Choose:** Which of the above two scenarios do you feel is more consistent with the concept of the contemporary evidence-based social work practice process as illustrated on pages 46–51? Why? Provide relevant social work examples to illustrate your main points.
13	**TIME TO PUT ON YOUR CRITICAL THINKING HAT** 1. Discuss the similarities and differences between your responses to Questions 11 and 12. 2. What are your thoughts on the belief that you'll need to know how to formulate relevant, useful, and ethical social work research questions whether you're a social work *practitioner* (Question 12) or a social work *researcher* (Question 11)?

14	**RESEARCH AND YOUR PROFESSIONAL DEVELOPMENT** Review the three social work research-related roles you can take when you graduate—CSWE Competency 1 at the beginning of this chapter on page 62 (also discussed in Chapter 1 on pages 38–42). 1. Thoroughly discuss how you feel this chapter will help you to perform one or more research-related roles when you graduate. Which one of the three roles do you believe this chapter helped you with the most? Why? Discuss in detail and provide an example to illustrate your main points. 2. Review CSWE Competency 4 at the beginning of this chapter on page 62. Thoroughly discuss how you feel this chapter will help you to become a practice-informed researcher and a research-informed practitioner. Discuss in detail and provide an example to illustrate your main points. 3. Review the evidence-based practice process as illustrated on pages 46–51. Thoroughly discuss how this chapter helps you to develop the skills you'll need for implementing one or more steps of the evidence-based practice process. 4. Discuss which step(s) you feel this chapter will help you with the most. Why? Be very specific and use relevant social work examples to illustrate your main points throughout your discussion. **NOTE:** This exercise should help you to realize that you can use "research roles" to help you become an evidence-based social work practitioner.
15	**MOVING AHEAD BY LOOKING BACK** At this point in your research methods course, how comfortable are you with discussing the place of research in social work with your field instructor, with your practice instructor, with your research instructor, with your supervisor at work, with the director of your social work program, or with your classmates? Discuss in detail.

3

CHAPTER

COMPETENCY 1: Demonstrate Ethical and Professional Behavior

You will learn that in order to be a successful evidence-based practitioner you have an ethical obligation to integrate three research roles into your daily practice activities as discussed in Chapter 1: (1) research consumer, (2) research partner—either as a co-researcher or research participant, and (3) creator and disseminator of research (or knowledge).

This entire chapter pertains to these three professional roles as you'll learn that one of the best ways to become an ethical and professional evidence-based social work practitioner is knowing how the existing literature is utilized to formulate relevant, useful, and meaningful research *and* practice questions. More importantly, you'll learn that you must use the existing literature in every step of the research process and practice process as well (see Figure 1.5 on page 37).

COMPETENCY 4: Engage in Practice-Informed Research and Research-Informed Practice

Competency 4 also pertains to the entire chapter because you have to:

1. Evaluate the degree to which a social work research study appropriately utilized the literature in reference to the formulation of the study's research question or hypothesis (**research consumer**—research-informed practice);

2. Participate in a research study—either as a co-researcher or research participant (**research partner**—practice-informed research). See 1 above and 3 below; and

3. Know how to actually find, evaluate, and use the literature when formulating a meaningful, relevant, and useful research question (or hypothesis) before you actually do a research study (**creator and disseminator of research**—practice-informed research).

You also need to utilize evidence-based practice recommendations whenever possible; that is, you need to integrate (1) the best available research-based evidence with (2) your clinical expertise and (3) your client's values.

All of the above implies you'll need to evaluate the degree to which a research study used the literature to formulate its research question (or hypothesis) that led to its research-based evidence. In short, you need to ask and then answer a simple question: How seriously should I take the findings of any specific research study given its overall creditability in relation to how well it utilized the existing literature within every step of the research process?

COMPETENCY 9: Evaluate Practice with Individuals, Families, Groups, Organizations, and Communities

See Competencies 1 and 4.

Writing Literature Reviews

CHAPTER 1	**Step 1.** Understanding the Research Process
CHAPTER 2	**Step 2.** Developing Research Questions
CHAPTER 3	**Step 3.** Reviewing the Literature
CHAPTERS 4 & 5	**Step 4.** Being Aware of Ethical and Cultural Issues
CHAPTERS 6–8	**Step 5.** Selecting a Research Approach
CHAPTERS 9 & 10	**Step 6.** Specifying How Variables Are Measured
CHAPTER 11	**Step 7.** Selecting a Sample
CHAPTERS 12 & 13	**Step 8.** Selecting a Research Design
CHAPTERS 14–16	**Step 9.** Selecting a Data-Collection Method
CHAPTERS 17 & 18	**Step 10.** Analyzing the Data
CHAPTERS 19 & 20	**Step 11.** Writing the Research Report

ALL SOCIAL WORK RESEARCH STUDIES must draw upon the literature in just about every step of the research process. Yours is no exception. A literature review is an essential early step in refining your research question or writing a research proposal.

This chapter demystifies the literature review process by focusing on what it is, how it's perceived by social work students, why you are required to undertake a literature review when doing a research study (or writing a research proposal), how to go about doing a literature review, and finally what the characteristics of a good literature review may look like.

WHAT IS A LITERATURE REVIEW?

Doing a research study can be seen as an entry into an academic conversation that has been going on in professional social work journals and books. Just as you would do when joining any other conversation, you'll first listen to what the conversation is about, figure out what the main issues of debate are, and determine who is responding to whom—and in what way.

The literature review section of your research study or proposal is a way of reporting to your reader on the academic conversation in which you are planning to participate. In the simplest of forms, a literature review generally involves the search for and documentation of primary (original) sources of scholarship, rather than secondary sources, which are reports of other people's work. Cooper and Hedges (1994) describe the literature review as,

> A literature review reports on primary or original scholarship. The primary reports used in a literature review may be verbal, but in the vast majority of cases they are written documents. The types of scholarship may be empirical, theoretical, critical/analytical, or methodological in nature. Second, a literature review seeks to describe, summarize, evaluate, clarify, and/or integrate the content of primary reports.

This should give you some idea of what a literature review may involve. Reviewing the literature is a continuous process. It begins before a specific research question has been finalized, and it continues until the final report is finished. To summarize:

1. The literature review draws mainly on primary sources.
2. It can have a variety of purposes:

   - to help you identify a suitable topic for study

   - to help you identify relevant literature for your study

   - to help you get an idea of what the main debates are on your topic area

   - to help you understand the issues involved

   - to help inform your own ideas about your research problem area

   - to gain familiarity with the accepted research approaches and methods in our profession

   - to become a critical co-conversant in the "academic conversation"

3. It's a continuous process, which begins before a research question is finalized and continues to the end.

4. It's a well-written, coherent product, appropriate to the
purpose for which you need it.

Now that you have some idea of what a literature review is, the question
that must be looked at more closely concerns the reasons for engaging in a
literature review: Why is it regarded as an essential part of your research
study?

THE LOGIC OF DOING LITERATURE REVIEWS

A LITERATURE REVIEW IS BASED upon the assumption that doing a research
study is not something that happens in isolation. It's something that is done
and developed by a community of academic researchers. (Think of the academic conversation analogy: You can't have a conversation all on your own!)
This means that knowledge development is seen to be a cumulative activity,
and you can learn from what other researchers and writers have done before
you.

What you are researching in the present must be built upon the
knowledge of what has been researched in the past. Researchers read previous studies to compare, replicate, or criticize the findings of other writers.
When you are participating in the academic conversation—by doing a research study or writing a research proposal—you are responding to issues
raised, drawing links between what various authors have said, showing
where there might be some contradictions, or raising some considerations
that haven't been addressed before.

But you can do this only if you know what the conversation has been and is
about, so you must know what the past and current debates are in the literature.
Ranjit Kumar (1994) has put together a useful list of seven overlapping purposes of a literature review:

1. It helps to bring clarity and focus to the research question.
2. It helps to identify gaps.
3. It prevents the duplication of knowledge.
4. It helps to broaden the knowledge base.
5. It helps to contextualize the research project.
6. It helps to improve a study's methodology.
7. It assists in identifying opposing views.

HELPS TO BRING CLARITY AND FOCUS TO THE RESEARCH QUESTION

YOU CANNOT UNDERTAKE a literature review unless you know what you want to find out. On the other hand, a literature review is also necessary in helping you to shape and narrow your research question. This is because reviewing the literature helps you to better understand your subject area, and thus helps you to conceptualize your research question much more clearly and precisely.

A literature review helps you to understand the relationship between your research question and the body of existing knowledge in that area. In other words, the literature contributes to your understanding of *why* your research question is a problem. When you do a literature review, you can identify more information and ideas that might be directly relevant to your study.

HELPS TO IDENTIFY GAPS IN THE LITERATURE

TO IDENTIFY THE OBVIOUS gaps in your general problem area, you have to know the literature. In doing a literature review, you become aware of what has already been done and what remains to be done in your study's area. Be careful of claiming that there are gaps in the knowledge when you have not done a thorough review of the literature.

HELPS TO PREVENT THE DUPLICATION OF KNOWLEDGE

YOU MAY FEEL EXCITED about a particular idea—your research question that was derived from a general problem area—and believe that you are the only person to have had this idea. More often than not, after you read the existing literature, you will quickly discover that your research question has indeed been thought of before.

A good literature review helps you to avoid reinventing the wheel. In other words, it can keep you from merely answering research questions that were previously answered by other researchers before you. Of course, planning to replicate studies (a legitimate form of research) or aiming to study an issue for which there is no definitive answer (e.g., the link between mind and brain) is not merely duplicating research studies. You are contributing to the body of knowledge by either validating previous studies or contributing some new insights on a longstanding issue. Very few research studies produce a definitive answer to a research question.

Thus, don't think because your research question has been previously written about that the final answer also has been discovered. A literature review is also useful to get to know what has worked—and what has not—in terms of scientific methodology so that you can avoid making the same mistakes as others may have made.

HELPS TO BROADEN THE KNOWLEDGE BASE

YOU SHOULD READ WIDELY in the subject area in which you intend to conduct your research study. It's important that you know what other researchers have found, who the authors considered to be movers and shakers are, what the seminal works are in your research study's problem area, what the key issues and crucial questions are, and what theories have been put forward in the relevant body of knowledge.

You will also be able to see how others have defined concepts that you will be using, and what the widely accepted definitions (or interpretations) are. You will be in a better position to work out interpretations of your key concepts that suit your study's purposes from this existing knowledge base.

Our profession has, over the years, developed basic research practices and conventions. Consult the literature to familiarize yourself with the acceptable research conventions and approaches adopted in the research literature. When you undertake a degree in social work, you are supposed to be an expert in your concentration area, or at least an apprentice who demonstrates mastery in your area of study. The more you know, the better the position you are in to study your topic.

HELPS TO CONTEXTUALIZE THE RESEARCH PROJECT

YOU MUST PROVIDE A SIGNPOST to let your readers know where your research question and your methodological research approach that will answer the question are coming from. This signposting allows readers to see which theories and principles have been influential in shaping your approach to your research study or research proposal. As has already been indicated, the literature review enables you to build a platform based on existing knowledge from which you can carry on and explain what your contribution will be to the field when your research study is finished.

The literature review can put your study into historical and other perspectives, and can provide an intellectual context for your work. This enables you to position your study in relation to what others have written. Context reviews help you to (1) place your project in the larger picture, (2) establish links between your topic and the existing body of knowledge, (3) establish the relevance and significance of your research question, and (4) establish the possible implications of your position.

HELPS TO IMPROVE A STUDY'S METHODOLOGY

GOING THROUGH THE EXISTING LITERATURE helps you to acquaint yourself with the various scientific methodologies that others have used to answer research questions similar to those you are investigating. You can see what has worked and what has not worked for others who were using similar procedures and methods, and what problems they faced.

In learning about the scientific methodologies that others have used, you will be better able to select a methodology that is capable of giving you reliable and valid answers to your research question and that is appropriate for the problem area in which you are studying (Kumar, 1994).

HELPS TO ASSIST IN IDENTIFYING OPPOSING VIEWS

A LITERATURE REVIEW helps identify differences between your study and previous studies. The idea that your research study builds on earlier work does not necessarily imply that it extends, flows from, or approves of earlier work found in the literature. Indeed, your work might be highly critical of earlier work and even seek to discredit it.

However, even if you are critical of a particular theory or methods of conducting a research study, you will still need to review the literature to argue the weaknesses of the previous studies and the benefits of the alternative approach that you have chosen. In a nutshell, you cannot justifiably reject or criticize something if you don't clearly understand (and demonstrate to your readers that you clearly understand) what it is you are rejecting or criticizing.

WHERE & HOW TO SEARCH FOR INFORMATION

YOU NEED TO KNOW how to use the computers in your university or college library and how to use indexes and abstracts. You can organize searches based on subjects, themes, or keywords. Find out who your subject librarians are and make friends with them. Interlibrary loans are extremely useful and provide an efficient service.

When searching electronic databases and the shelves of the library, it's important to establish the credibility of the source you find. Is it an academically acknowledged database? Are the entries still relevant? The date of the publication is important. For empirical studies, you should concentrate on the latest publications and work backward from these as they become outdated.

Remember, researchers build on the work of those who have gone before them (just as you need to do in your own study). With theoretical articles, it's not as important to have the most current articles as you might be drawing on classic texts that are more dated. The quickest way of getting an overview of the trends in the debates is to look at the professional journals in your problem area.

You will eventually get an idea of what will make a successful study in your study's problem area. You can compare the studies you find and any publications that come from them with what you intend to do in your study. More important authors tend to be quoted more frequently, and you will be able to tell who the highly regarded authors are in your study's problem area simply by perusing the literature.

THE INTERNET

The Internet is a terrific tool for obtaining information. However, you need to know your way around it if you want to avoid drawing on inappropriate sites. Most professional journals are now available in electronic form online, and you should check which of these are available at your university or college. Although some journals are available in this form, it should not be seen as an alternative to searching the print versions of journals and books in your university or college library. This is because some of the literature is still only available in printed form.

The Internet is also useful for "gray material," which is information such as government policy documents, speeches, press releases, and so forth. The advantage of the Internet is its immediacy of access, and the information is often very recent. But you must be careful of what you find on the Internet because anyone can write anything there—so unless you know that a site is an academically acknowledged one, you can't be sure of the credibility of information you find there.

STORING AND MANAGING INFORMATION

IN SEARCHING THE LITERATURE, it's very important to develop some sort of filing system—either as hard copy or on a computer. Remember to store all details so that you don't have to go back to the original sources. This can be a very annoying task, but outstanding or incomplete references must be tracked down when you write your final research report or develop your research proposal. Details on the following should be kept and arranged alphabetically:

— Author(s) (surname and initial)

— Title of the book (if a chapter in an edited collection is used, note the chapter title as well)

— Journal title (and title of article)

— Relevant pages

— Journal volume

— Month of publication

— Year of publication

— Publisher

— Library where information is found

— How the item relates to your research project

It's important to keep these sources accurately and consistently. You can either write the details of each reference separately on a blank index card (on sale in any stationery store), which you will file alphabetically, or you can use one of the many inexpensive software programs such as EndNote (www. endnote.com) to enter your references. We suggest using software programs.

READING FOR A LITERATURE REVIEW

THERE IS NO SHORTCUT to doing a good research study. You must read—period, full stop. There is simply no way around it. But there are different ways of reading. The process of reading has three different aspects:

— **Preview,** in which you do a broad and superficial sweep of the literature

— **Overview,** in which you slightly engage with the material

— **Inview,** in which you read very carefully for understanding of the material

PREVIEW

LOTS OF INFORMATION from books, journals, and the Internet is available to you as a university or college student. You can waste hundreds of hours reading irrelevant information and, in this way, procrastinate about getting down to writing. You need to become skilled at selecting the right sources for your purposes.

To do so, you need to be able to preview books and journal articles quickly by looking at the title, date of publication, author, organization responsible for publication, and the table of contents:

— **The title.** From the title, you can predict whether some of the information for your research question may be covered.

— **Date of publication.** Is the book or journal article fairly current and up to date?

— **Author(s)/organization/publisher.** Are they reputable? Have you heard of them before? Is there any information on them? Are they attached to a credible institution?

— **Table of contents/subheadings**. Will some of the necessary information for your research question be covered? Will it be directly relevant to your topic, or will it just give you a broad overview? Which chapter(s) or sections of the book look relevant to your research study?

In the preview stage, to locate literature it helps if you jot down your research question, what you know about it, what you would like to know about it, any questions you have about it, and the value it may have for your literature review.

OVERVIEW

ONCE YOU HAVE SELECTED a book or journal article you want to read, the best way to begin to understand it is to get a sense of how the whole book or journal article (or sections of it) is structured. You can do this by overviewing the work. This will give you a sense of its whole framework (or structure) so that when you read it in detail you will be able to fit what you read into the whole context of the work.

Not only will the overview help you to find information quickly, it will assist your understanding as you read. In doing a survey or overview, you should concentrate on headings, subheadings, introductions, conclusions, the opening and closing sentences of sections, graphs, tables, and any summaries that the piece provides.

INVIEW

THE *INVIEW* INVOLVES a detailed and careful reading of the subject matter, ensuring that you understand the concepts and follow the argument. Take clear and detailed notes of everything you read. Keep your research question in mind, and don't record pages of information that aren't directly and meaningfully relevant to your study's research question.

You could keep summaries of your readings in a particular file or in a software program. Don't forget, at the same time, to record all the necessary details of the reference. In your summaries, you might include what the main issues and arguments are, a critical comment, and how the content relates to your proposed research study.

You should read broadly and deeply in your field of study before beginning to write a literature review. This helps you to locate your study in a wider theoretical landscape. Then read deeply in the narrower field of your research question so that you have a detailed account of the existing literature as it relates to your study's problem area.

After reading in an intensive way, you need to make notes of your own, draw a conceptual map, and respond—this is how you begin to prepare an argument for your literature review. Select a suitable structure in terms of which to organize the literature, and use subheadings.

> **You should read broadly and deeply in your field of study before beginning to write a literature review.**

You could begin your inview of the literature by finding an introductory book or key articles that introduce the main concepts and theoretical language in the problem area that you are going to study. Try to identify the concepts that you don't understand, and discuss these with your fellow students and instructor.

You should develop a conceptual map and try to fit new readings into this map. Pull together themes and issues that belong together. Once you have developed a map, a rough structure of your draft framework, keep slotting in information under the headings and subheadings that you develop. Kumar (1994) suggests the following four points:

1. Note the theories put forward, the criticisms of these and their basis, and the methodologies adopted (e.g., study design, sample size and its characteristics, measurement procedures) and the criticisms of them.

2. Examine to what extent the findings can be generalized to other situations.

3. Notice where significant differences of opinion exist among researchers, and give your view about the validity of these differences.

4. Ascertain the areas in which little or nothing is known—the gaps that exist in the body of knowledge.

DEVELOPING A THEORETICAL FRAMEWORK

STUDENTS STRUGGLE with developing theoretical frameworks. A possible reason for this is that no correct and clear-cut theoretical framework exists. The question about which framework in your subject area is most appropriate is itself a question of debate within the literature.

Nevertheless, the theoretical framework is where you highlight the main thrust of the academic conversation you are entering. Note the similarities and differences between themes and theories, agreements and disagreements among authors, and the bearing that these have on your research topic. Use these as a basis for developing the theoretical framework that is best suited to the purpose of your study.

A theoretical framework sets up key concepts, interpretations, approaches, claims, foundations, principles, and other items that will influence the design of your structure, and how you will sort the information and analyze the findings of your study. Unless you review the literature in relation to this framework, you won't be able to develop a focus in your literature search. In other words, the theoretical framework provides you with a guide as you read (Kumar, 1994).

You must first go through the literature to develop this framework, and then have the framework in hand while you go through the literature. A good idea is to go through some of the literature to develop this framework, then use this skeleton framework to guide your readings further. As you read more, you may change the framework, but if you don't have some structure, you will be bogged down in a lot of unnecessary readings and note taking that aren't directly relevant to your study.

The theoretical framework is the basis of your research problem. Of course, competing theoretical frameworks are put forward to explain the issue you will be researching, so you will need to discuss—based on the arguments put forward by other authors—why this particular framework is appropriate for your purposes.

WRITING AND ORGANIZING A LITERATURE REVIEW

YOUR WRITING SHOULD BE SIGNPOSTED at every point; that is, you should say what you are going to do, then do it, then say what you have done. You will need to do and redo things—the process of research and writing is messy and doubles back on itself. Only in the end does it appear as seamless and linear.

Even the best authors have reworked their text many, many times before it was finally printed. Coherence only emerges over time. Unfortunately, there are no shortcuts. In the literature review, you should present an exposition (a clear and coherent summary with a particular purpose) of the issue you are studying, which you then use as the base for an argument. Rather than just stating facts, use an argument to convince the reader that your particular interpretation is true.

You can use the findings of other authors to support your claims. You should have a central argument (the main point you want to put forward), then use each paragraph to develop a part of the main argument. You must state the argument early on and sum it up in the conclusion. All your points should link to your main argument. You can organize your literature review in one of the following four ways:

1. **By date of study.** Here, you would start with older studies and work toward the latest. This is the least ordered of the literature reviews.

2. **By school of thought/theory.** This is a review of the theoretical positions of scholars. You could organize it from oldest to most recent, or you could start with approaches or definitions that you feel to be inappropriate or that have been discredited by recent scholarship. You would follow this with a discussion of those points that would form the frame of reference for your study.

3. **By themes that have emerged from the literature.** The headings and subheadings should be based on the literature and should be precise, should be descriptive of the contents, and should follow a logical progression. Substantiations and contradictions should be clearly referenced. Your arguments should be conceptually clear, highlighting the reasons for and against and referring to the main findings, gaps, and issues.

4. **By research approach.** You can, for example, compare past positivistic approaches (Chapter 6) interpretive approaches (Chapter 7) and mixed-methods approaches (Chapter 8) in

your study's problem area and show how they produced different results, if any.

Try to answer the following five questions:

1. What do you consider to be the most important theories and perspectives to arise from the literature? How have these affected your understanding of your topic?

2. How does your research question link with the state of knowledge as reflected in the literature?

> Even the best authors have reworked their text many, many times before it was finally printed.

3. What questions are raised by the literature that your research study addresses?

4. Has anyone ever done this before? What partial answers to your research question have been found before? How did previous researchers go about asking such questions? What methodological issues are raised by the literature in question?

5. In what way is your topic valid, important, and doable? How will your research study add to the literature?

If you're still undecided on how to construct your literature review, here is a suggestion on how to get started. Go back to your research proposal and list the ten keywords (or phrases) you have noted as capturing the main concepts of your study. Jot them down in a column. Then, for each concept jotted down, ask yourself, "What does the literature say about this?"

Next to each one, identify three or four readings that address this concept. Make clear and honest summaries of each reading. Then critically engage with your summaries, noting the trends, similarities, differences, gaps, and implications.

Rewrite this draft into flowing text. Do this for each listed concept (the concept can be a subheading), and you'll have the first draft of your literature review. You should keep a log or a journal of information that you gathered during your whole writing process. You need to ignore references that aren't relevant any more and pare the references down if needed.

BOX 3.1	Literature Review Tips

ONE OF THE MOST IMPORTANT EARLY STEPS in a research project is conducting the literature review. This is also one of the most humbling experiences you're likely to have. Why? Because you're likely to find out that just about any worthwhile idea you will have has been thought of before, at least to some degree. Every time I teach a research methods course, I have at least one student come to me complaining that they couldn't find anything in the literature that was related to their topic. And nearly every time they have said that, I was able to show them that was only true because they had looked for articles that were exactly the same as their research topic.

A literature review is designed to identify related research, to set the current research project within a conceptual and theoretical context. When looked at that way, there is almost no topic that is so new or unique that we can't locate relevant and informative related research. Below are two tips for conducting the literature review.

TIP 1: **Concentrate your efforts on the scientific literature.** Try to determine what the most credible research journals are in your topic area and start with those. Put the greatest emphasis on research journals that use a blind review system. In a blind review, authors submit potential articles to a journal editor, who in turn asks several reviewers to provide a critical review of the paper. The paper is sent to these reviewers with no identification of the author so that there will be no personal bias (either for or against the author). Based on the reviewers' recommendations, the editor can accept the article for publication, reject it, or recommend that the author revise and resubmit it. Articles in journals with blind review processes can be expected to have a fairly high level of credibility.

TIP 2: **Do your review early in the research process.** You are likely to learn a lot during the literature review that will help you in making the trade-offs you'll need to face. After all, previous researchers also had to face trade-off decisions.

WHAT SHOULD YOU LOOK FOR IN THE LITERATURE REVIEW?

— You might be able to find a study that is quite similar to the one you are thinking of doing. Because all credible research studies have to review the literature themselves, you can check their literature review to get a quick-start on your own.

— Prior research will help ensure that you have included all the major relevant constructs in your study. You may find that other, similar studies have routinely looked at an outcome that you might not have included. If you did your study without that construct, it would not be judged credible because it ignored a major construct.

— The literature review will help you to find and select appropriate measuring instruments. You will readily see what measurement instruments researchers have been using in contexts similar to yours.

— The review will help you to anticipate common problems in your research context. You can use the prior experiences of others to avoid common pitfalls.

CRITERIA OF A GOOD LITERATURE REVIEW

YOUR LITERATURE REVIEW MUST COVER the main aspects of your study and be fair in its treatment of authors. The literature review should do justice to an author's arguments before critiquing them. (You can't agree or disagree with something if you don't have a clear idea of what it is you're agreeing or disagreeing with!) It should be topical.

The review shouldn't be confined to Internet sources. It should be well organized around your research questions and key concepts rather than just a summary of what you have read. Take note of the authority of authors and the reliability and validity of the research methods they used to answer their research questions.

There's a delicate balance between discussing what others have said and found, and developing your own voice. You are neither just listing what others have said, nor are you merely "telling your own story." You need to demonstrate that you have an informed voice. So don't quote too many studies or begin with "Smith (20xx) found that . . ." as it shifts the focus of your own argument onto that of others.

It's better to develop a theme and then cite the work of relevant authors to reinforce your argument. Don't be tempted to report everything you know—be selective about what you report. Every reference you use must build on the evidence you are presenting to support your case. Using your own words to describe difficult concepts will help convince yourself and others that you really understand the material.

SUMMARY

THIS CHAPTER PRESENTED a brief discussion on how the professional literature can be used to formulate research questions. Your literature review should be specific, current, of historical interest, coherent, interesting, and well organized around your research question and key concepts rather than being a mere summary of what you have read. It should be a critical discussion of relevant information from different sources.

Do you remember that your research question must be ethical? Well, the next chapter describes how ethics plays a significant role not only in formulating research questions but also during the entire research process itself.

	Study Questions for Chapter 3
	Essay — Discussion
1	Before you entered your social work program, and before you read this chapter, how knowledgeable were you in relation to the roles that a literature review played when formulating a research question? Discuss fully.
2	Discuss how a literature review can be thought of as an academic conversation. Use one common social work example throughout your discussion.
3	What are primary sources of scholarship? Provide a social work example.
4	What are secondary sources of scholarship? Provide a social work example.
5	Discuss why a literature review should use primary sources of scholarship rather than secondary ones. Provide a social work example.
6	List the seven main purposes of literature reviews. Provide a social work example for each purpose.
7	Discuss how the literature can be used in all eleven steps of the research process (page 101). Use one common social work example throughout your discussion.
8	Discuss in detail how a literature review can help you to bring clarity and focus to your research question. Provide an example in your discussion.
9	Discuss in detail how a literature review can help you to identify gaps in the literature. Provide an example in your discussion.
10	Discuss in detail how a literature review can help you to avoid doing a research study that has already been done before. Provide an example in your discussion.

11	Discuss in detail how a literature review can help you to broaden your knowledge base. Provide an example in your discussion.
12	Discuss in detail how a literature review can help you to put your research project into context. Provide an example in your discussion.
13	Discuss in detail how a literature review can help you to improve your research study's methodology. Provide an example in your discussion.
14	Discuss in detail how a literature review can help you to identify both opposing views and any differences between your proposed study and previous studies. Provide an example in your discussion.
15	Discuss how you plan to file what you find in the literature; that is, what information are you going to collect about each source you find and how are you going to catalog what you find?
16	Discuss the concept of *preview*. Discuss how you would go about *previewing* the literature for a social work topic of your choice.
17	Given your topic above, discuss how you would go about *overviewing* the literature.
18	With the same topic above, discuss how you would go about *inviewing* the literature.
19	What is a theoretical framework? How is it useful to you as a social work researcher? As a social work practitioner? Provide an example in your discussion.
20	List and then discuss each of the four ways a literature review can be organized. Provide one common social work example throughout your discussion.
21	List the common mistakes you can make when doing a literature view. Now discuss in detail how you plan to avoid making each mistake.

	Critical Thinking — Application — Integration
22	**APPLICATION OF LITERATURE REVIEWS** Locate any published social work research article that contains a social work problem area or population that you're interested in. Be sure the study tried to answer a research question of some kind. 1. How was the literature review organized: by date of study, by school of thought/theory, or by themes that have emerged from the literature? 2. Did the research study develop a theoretical framework? If so, what was it? 3. How did the study's literature review help bring clarity and focus to the research question? Provide specific examples from the article. 4. How did the study's literature review help identify any gaps in the existing literature? Provide specific examples from the article. 5. How did the study's literature review prevent the duplication of knowledge? Provide specific examples from the article. 6. How did the study's literature review help to broaden our profession's knowledge base? Provide specific examples from the article. 7. How did the study's literature review help to contextualize the entire research project? Provide specific examples from the article. 8. How did the study use the literature to help improve its overall methodology? Provide specific examples from the article. 9. How did the study use the literature to assist in identifying any opposing views? Provide specific examples from the article.
23	**LITERATURE REVIEWS AND THE RESEARCHER** **Scenario 1:** Make an argument that to be a competent social work researcher **you must know** how to effectively find and use the existing literature when engaging in a research study. Provide a clear and explicit **research-related** social work example to illustrate your main points. **Scenario 2:** Make an argument that **you do not have to know** how to effectively find and use the existing literature when engaging in a research study to be a competent social work researcher. Provide a clear and explicit **research-related** social work example to illustrate your main points. **Time to Choose:** Which one of the above two scenarios do you feel is more consistent with the place of research in social work? Why?

24	**LITERATURE REVIEWS AND THE PRACTITIONER** **Scenario 1:** Make an argument that to be an effective evidence-based social work practitioner **you must know** how to effectively find and use the existing literature to help you with obtaining more information on various practice interventions. Provide a clear and explicit **practice-related** social work example to illustrate your main points. **Scenario 2:** Make an argument that **you do not have to know** how to effectively find and use the existing literature to help you with obtaining more information on various practice interventions to be an effective evidence-based social work practitioner. Provide a clear and explicit **practice-related** social work example to illustrate your main points. **Time to Choose:** Which one of the above two senarios do you feel is more consistent with the concept of the contemporary evidence-based social work practice process as illustrated on pages 46–51? Why? Provide relevant social work examples to illustrate your main points.
25	**TIME TO PUT ON YOUR CRITICAL THINKING HAT** 1. Discuss the similarities and differences between your responses to Questions 23 and 24. 2. What are your thoughts on the belief that you'll need to know how to effectively find and use the existing literature whether you're a social work *practitioner* (Question 24) or a social work *researcher* (Question 23)?

LITERATURE REVIEWS AND YOUR PROFESSIONAL DEVELOPMENT

Review the three social work research-related roles you can take when you graduate—CSWE Competency 1 at the beginning of this chapter on page 100 (also discussed in Chapter 1 on pages 38–42).

26

1. Thoroughly discuss how you feel this chapter will help you to perform one or more research-related roles when you graduate. Which one of the three roles do you believe this chapter helped you with the most? Why? Discuss in detail and provide an example to illustrate your main points.

2. Review CSWE Competency 4 at the beginning of this chapter on page 100. Thoroughly discuss how you feel this chapter will help you to become a practice-informed researcher and a research-informed practitioner. Discuss in detail and provide an example to illustrate your main points.

3. Review the evidence-based practice process as illustrated on pages 46–51. Thoroughly discuss how this chapter helps you to develop the skills you'll need for implementing one or more steps of the evidence-based practice process.

4. Discuss which step(s) you feel this chapter will help you with the most. Why? Be very specific and use relevant social work examples to illustrate your main points throughout your discussion.

NOTE: This exercise should help you to realize that you can use "research roles" to help you become an evidence-based social work practitioner.

27

MOVING AHEAD BY LOOKING BACK

At this point in your research methods course, how comfortable are you with discussing the place of research in social work with your field instructor, with your practice instructor, with your research instructor, with your supervisor at work, with the director of your social work program, or with your classmates?

4

CHAPTER

COMPETENCY 1: Demonstrate Ethical and Professional Behavior

You will learn that in order to be a successful evidence-based practitioner you have an ethical obligation to integrate three research roles into your daily practice activities as discussed in Chapter 1: (1) research consumer, (2) research partner—either as a co-researcher or research participant, and (3) creator and disseminator of research (or knowledge).

This entire chapter pertains to these three professional roles when it comes to becoming an ethically sensitive social work practitioner (**research consumer**) and an ethically sensitive social work researcher (**research partner** and **creator and disseminator of research**).

COMPETENCY 4: Engage in Practice-Informed Research and Research-Informed Practice

Competency 4 also pertains to the entire chapter because you have to:

1. Evaluate the degree to which a social work research study was ethically sensitive, given the needs of the study's specific population or research participants (**research consumer**—research-informed practice);

2. Participate in a research study—either as a co-researcher or research participant (**research partner**—practice-informed research). See 1 above and 3 below; and

3. Know how to become an ethically sensitive social work researcher before you actually do a research study (**creator and disseminator of research**—practice-informed research).

You also need to utilize evidence-based practice recommendations whenever possible; that is, you need to integrate (1) the best available research-based evidence with (2) your clinical expertise and (3) your client's values.

All of the above implies you'll need to know how a research study addressed the various ethical issues that produced its ethically-sensitive research-based evidence. In short, you need to ask and then answer a simple question: How seriously should I take the findings of any specific research study given how well it addressed the various ethical issues throughout the entire research process?

COMPETENCY 9: Evaluate Practice with Individuals, Families, Groups, Organizations, and Communities

See Competencies 1 and 4.

4

C H A P T E R

Research Ethics

CHAPTER 1	**Step 1.** Understanding the Research Process
CHAPTER 2	**Step 2.** Developing Research Questions
CHAPTER 3	**Step 3.** Reviewing the Literature
CHAPTERS 4 & 5	**Step 4.** Being Aware of Ethical and Cultural Issues
CHAPTERS 6–8	**Step 5.** Selecting a Research Approach
CHAPTERS 9 & 10	**Step 6.** Specifying How Variables Are Measured
CHAPTER 11	**Step 7.** Selecting a Sample
CHAPTERS 12 & 13	**Step 8.** Selecting a Research Design
CHAPTERS 14–16	**Step 9.** Selecting a Data-Collection Method
CHAPTERS 17 & 18	**Step 10.** Analyzing the Data
CHAPTERS 19 & 20	**Step 11.** Writing the Research Report

THE FIRST CHAPTER OF THIS BOOK DISCUSSED the five ways of acquiring knowledge and stressed how you should obtain your knowledge from findings that were derived from the scientific method whenever possible. We also indicated that you should never ignore the other four ways of knowing. Remember, professional judgments are always based on utilizing all five ways of knowing.

Chapter 2 presented how to formulate social work research questions that can be answered by using the scientific method. As you know, we presented four criteria that you must apply when evaluating any question you want to research—and one of the four criteria was ethics, the purpose of this chapter.

USING CLIENTS AS RESEARCH PARTICIPANTS

MANY SOCIAL WORK RESEARCH STUDIES use clients as research participants, sometimes inappropriately called *subjects*. When using clients within our research studies, we need to be extremely careful not to violate any of their ethical rights. Sounds simple, you say. Well, read on.

Consider Aristotle, for example. He believed that horses would become severely ill if they were bitten by pregnant shrewmice. He never tested his belief via the scientific method. If he wanted to he could have done a simple research study that arranged for a group of horses to be bitten by pregnant shrewmice (experimental group) and a group of horses that would not be bitten (control group). He then could have compared the illness rate of the horses in the experimental group to the illness rate of the horses in the control group.

If he did this simple study, however, he would have had to solve the resulting ethical dilemma. Was he justified in subjecting a few horses to the discomfort of being bitten by pregnant shrewmice just to gain enough knowledge to help all horses in the future?

Now suppose the horses were people. To social workers, the answer is apparent: No, we are not justified! Increasing the sum of knowledge is a worthy aim, but the client, or research participant, must not be harmed in the process. We are not in the business of committing lesser evils for the sake of greater goods.

Not harming our clients, by commission or omission, is a cardinal rule of the research process and imposes a major limitation. There are a number of bodies devoted to ensuring that harm does not occur. All universities, for example, have ethics committees, or institutional review boards (IRBs), and many large social service programs do as well.

There are also various professional associations and lay groups that focus on protecting research participants. However, it's likely that the participants in your research study will never have heard of any of these bodies. They will do what you ask them to do either because they trust you or because they think they have no other choice but to participate.

> The responsibility of not hurting any of your research participants is squarely on your shoulders.

The responsibility of not hurting any of your research participants is squarely on your shoulders. We will now turn our attention of obtaining their informed consent to participate in your research study, with an eye to doing no harm to them whatsoever. You must always remember that their safety comes first and your research project second.

OBTAINING INFORMED CONSENT

BEFORE YOU INVOLVE ANY HUMAN BEING in a research study, you must obtain the person's informed consent. The key word here is *informed.* The word "informed" means that all of your potential research participants must fully understand what is going to happen in the course of your study, why it's going to happen, and what its effect will be on them.

If the person is psychiatrically challenged, mentally delayed, or in any other way incapable of full understanding, your study must be fully and adequately explained to someone else—perhaps a parent, guardian, social worker, spouse, or someone to whom the participant's welfare is important.

> It's extremely important for potential participants to know that they are not signing away their rights when they sign a consent form.

All written communications must be couched in simple language that all potential participants will understand. Some researchers, particularly academics, have a tendency to confuse obscurity with profundity. They use technical terms so firmly embedded in convoluted sentence structures that the meaning falters and disappears altogether at the second comma.

It's clear that no research participant may be bribed, threatened, deceived, or in any way coerced into participating in your study. Questions must be encouraged, both initially and throughout the course of the study. People who believe they understand may have misinterpreted your explanation or understood it only in part.

They may say they understand when they do not, in an effort to avoid appearing foolish. They may even sign documents they do not understand to confirm their supposed understanding, and it's your responsibility to ensure that their understanding is real and complete.

It's extremely important for potential participants to know that they are not signing away their rights when they sign a consent form. They may decide at any time to withdraw from the study *without penalty*, without so much as a reproachful glance. When completed, the study's results must also be made available to them.

BRIBERY, DECEPTION, AND OTHER FORMS OF COERCION

IT GOES WITHOUT SAYING that consent must never be obtained through bribery, threats, deception, or any form of coercion. You may feel insulted that such a possibility would even be mentioned in a text addressed to social workers, but consider what constitutes bribery. For example, if you offer $100 to the chief executive officer of an agency to persuade her to take part in your study, this is bribery.

If you want to know how your research participants *really* behave when no one else is looking, you will have to deceive them into believing that they are *not* being watched. You might think you can do this using an interview room with a one-way mirror, or you might pretend to be an ordinary member of a group when you are, in fact, a glint-eyed observer. Neither of these behaviors is ethically acceptable.

The only conditions under which deception might be countenanced—and it's a very large *might*—are when the data to be obtained are vitally important and there is no other way to get them. If you can persuade the various ethics committees that review your research proposal that both these conditions exist, you *might* be given permission to carry out the study.

> Consent must never be obtained through bribery, threats, deception, or any form of coercion.

Even then, you would have to be sure that the deception was thoroughly explained to all the participants when the study was over and that arrangements had been made—free counseling, for example—to counter any harm they might have suffered.

Last, but not least, there are threats. No researcher would ever persuade potential participants to cooperate by threatening that, if they do not, worse things will befall them. But a *perceived* threat, even if not intended, can have the same effect. For example, a woman awaiting an abortion may agree to provide private information about herself and her partner because she believes that, if she does not, she will be denied the abortion. It's of no use to tell her that this is not true; she may simply feel she is not in a position to take any chances.

There are captive populations in prisons, schools, and institutions who may agree out of sheer boredom to take part in a research study. Or they may participate in return for certain privileges or because they fear some reprisal. There may be people who agree because family members pressure them into it, or they want to please their social workers, or they need some service or payment that they believe depends on their cooperation. Often, situations like these cannot be changed, but at least you can be aware of them and do your best to deal with them in an ethical and straightforward manner.

INGREDIENTS OF AN INFORMED CONSENT FORM

A WRITTEN CONSENT FORM should be only part of the process of informing research participants of their roles in the study and their rights as volunteers. As we have said before, it must give potential participants a basic description of the purpose of the study, the study's procedures, and their rights as voluntary participants. A consent form must provide in plain and simple language sixteen ingredients:

1. That participants are being asked to participate in a research study

2. That their participation is voluntary, and that they may discontinue participation at any time without penalty or loss of benefits to which they are otherwise entitled (e.g., in their standing as a patient, student, or employee)

3. The names of the investigators and their affiliations

4. The purposes of the research study, simply explained

5. What the study's procedures will be

6. The expected duration of their participation

7. Any reasonably foreseeable risks or discomforts

8. Any safeguards to minimize the risks

9. Any benefits to the participants or to others that may reasonably be expected from the research study. (in most cases, the study is not being performed for the benefit of the participants but for the potential benefit of others. This broader social benefit to the public should be made explicit.)

10. In cases where an incentive is offered, a description of the incentive and of how and under what conditions it is to be obtained

11. Appropriate alternative procedures or courses of treatment, if applicable

12. The extent, if any, to which confidentiality of records identifying the participants will be maintained (not an issue unless participants can be identified)

13. Any restrictions on confidentiality. (for example, if any of the information gained during the study might have to be disclosed as required by law, as in instances of child abuse, absolute confidentiality cannot be ensured.)

14. What monetary compensation or medical or psychological treatment will be provided for any research-related injury (if more than minimal risk)

15. Contact information for questions about the study (name, office address, and phone contacts for the researcher, faculty advisor, and irb staff). Do not include home phone numbers.

16. That the researcher will keep one copy of the signed consent form and give another signed copy to the participants

Using the preceding points, Box 4.1 provides an example of an actual consent letter written to the social workers that were the legal guardians of foster care adolescents in a residential treatment facility. The letter was written to "persuade" the social workers to have their clients (foster care adolescents) participate in a research study.

In this study, the adolescents' biological parents were not involved because the adolescents were wards of the state. If a social worker agreed to have his adolescents participate in the study, then the adolescents would be given assent forms to sign (Box 4.2).

In a nutshell, consent forms need to be signed by adults or legal guardians, and assent forms must be signed by non-adults—children and adolescents. If your study is going to use children and/or adolescents as research participants, you will have to obtain the consent of at least one of their parents or legal guardians (via consent forms) in addition to your research participants' consent (via assent forms). In this case you will have to write two forms, one for the adolescents' legal guardians (consent form) and one for the adolescents (assent form). Writing consent and assent forms takes an astronomical amount of time—never underestimate the time factor.

BOX 4.1	**Example of a Consent Form**

NOTE: This consent form was given to social workers that were the legal guardians of the foster youth (clients) whom we wanted to participate in our workshop. We asked the workers whether they would agree to have their clients participate in our workshop BEFORE we could ask the youth whether they wanted to participate.

If a worker agreed via this consent form that we could contact his clients, we then asked the youths via an assent form (Box 4.2) whether they wanted to participate. If a worker did not agree to have her clients participate in our workshop, we did not ask those youths to participate.

(LETTERHEAD)

You are invited to have your clients participate in Chatham-Kent Children's Services (CKCS) Help-Seeking Project for Adolescents in Out-of-Home Placement. The project is funded by the Provincial Centre of Excellence for Child and Youth Mental Health. The primary person in charge of the project is Mike Stephens, Chief Executive Officer of CKCS.

This handout describes our project and will help you decide if you want to have your clients participate. You are 100% free to choose whether or not you will have your clients take part in the study. Before you decide, however, you need to know what will be expected of them if you agree to have them participate and the risks and benefits of their participation. Please take time to read this handout.

There are no negative consequences for either you or your clients in reference to your decision as to their potential participation. Your clients can drop out of the study at any time. The services they receive from CKCS will not be affected by your decision to have them participate in this project.

If you agree to have your clients take part in the project they will be asked to sign a separate assent form. The assent form is a shorter version of this consent form and contains important information about the project. When they sign the assent form, they give their "consent," which means that they agree to participate in the project.

What's the Project About Anyway?

The main purpose of our project is to find out whether a workshop on help-seeking for youth living in out-of-home placement at CKCS will help them become more skilled at asking for help when personal or emotional problems arise. We don't yet know whether our help-seeking workshop works. So we have designed a project that will involve about 120 youth, ages 12 years and older, who are living at CKCS.

Half of the youth who participate in the project will attend a special workshop, and the other half will not. The workshop will give them information and ideas about how to seek help when personal or emotional problems arise. We will then compare the help-seeking skills of those youth who attended the workshop with those who did not in order to learn whether the workshop was helpful.

As you can see below, they will be assigned, by chance, to a group who attend the workshop, or to a group who do not attend. That is, they may or may not attend the workshop even though they agree to participate in the project (via an assent form). If we learn that the workshop is helpful in the way we expect, then all youth that did not get to attend the workshop will be offered a chance to attend it at a later date, as long as they are still living at CKCS.

In total, about 120 youth will participate in the project. Everyone will be asked to complete a set of questionnaires at four different times: this week, 5 weeks from now, 10 weeks from now, and 5 months from now. Step by step, this is what will happen if you agree to have your clients participate in the project AND they have also agreed.

1. They will be contacted twice by telephone. Sometime this week, and then again 5 months from now, a CKCS staff member will call them by telephone and ask them questions. The phone interview takes about 30 minutes and includes questions about common emotional and behavioral problems experienced by teenagers. They do not have to answer any questions they don't want to.

2. They will be asked to come to CKCS four times over the next 5 months and to complete four other surveys. These surveys are completed at the CKCS computer lab using a special computer program. Sitting at their own computers and wearing headphones, they will see each question appear on the computer screen and hear the question being read through the headphones.

3. They will answer the questions by clicking the computer mouse. The computer surveys should take about 30 to 40 minutes to complete each time. As we said above, they do not have to answer any questions that they don't want to. They will be paid for their participation. They will receive $10 the first time they answer the survey questions, $15 the second time, $20 the third time, and $30 the fourth time.

4. Snacks also will be provided at each meeting, and bus fare to CKCS will be available if they need it. In addition to the above surveys, a project staff member will review their CKCS case files for information such as their placements, services they have received, and family contacts.

5. By chance, half of the youth participating in the project will be invited to attend a 2- to 3-hour workshop that will include six youths at a time. The workshop will take place at CKCS and be run by a CKCS staff member. The purpose of the workshop is to give them additional information about how they can best get help for their personal or emotional problems while living in a CKCS placement.

6. If they leave CKCS within 5 weeks of the start of the project, their participation in the project will automatically end.

HOW WILL THEIR PRIVACY BE PROTECTED?

Confidentiality describes what we do to keep information gathered about your clients completely private. In order to protect their privacy in this project:

1. We use numbers instead of names (or other identifiers) on all the data we obtain so that no one can connect the data with you or them.

2. The data collected for this project will be sent to researchers at Western Michigan University. Once again, the data will not include anything that would individually identify you or them. The researchers and their staff have been trained in protecting everyone's confidentiality.

3. No CKCS staff member will have access to the data that your clients provide as part of this project. None of the data collected from your clients will be shared with you (their Children's Service Worker and legal guardian), their foster parents or caregivers, or any other workers at CKCS. The data collected will only be used for this project.

4. All data will be stored in a safe, locked area. The computers for this project are protected by a firewall system and passwords.

5. All the adolescents' answers will be kept absolutely private unless a staff member thinks they might be in danger of hurting themselves. For example, if an adolescent tells us that he or she is using illegal drugs, or is thinking of harming him or herself or someone else, project staff are obligated to inform you because you are his or her legal guardian and CKCS Children's Service Worker.

6. The information from the project will be used to write papers, make presentations, and work with other education or research centers to improve out-of-home services for youth. Please remember that their names, or any information that could identify them, will never be used. We will evaluate the survey answers "as a group" and not for any one individual. They will not be identified (for example, by name or social security number) in any reports or publications of this project.

WILL THEIR INFORMATION BE SHARED WITH OTHERS?

Yes. As we have said before, if we know or think we know that one of your clients is being abused, under law we must take action to protect that person. We also must report if we hear that an individual intends to harm himself or herself or someone else. We will inform you immediately if this is the case.

WHAT ARE THEIR RIGHTS AS A PARTICIPANT IN OUR PROJECT?

As participants in our project, your clients have certain rights that protect them from potential harm. After you, as their legal guardian, have provided your consent to have them participate in the project (via signing this form), their specific rights are as follows:

1. It is up to them to decide if they want to be in our project. That means their participation is completely voluntary.

2. They have the right to change their mind at any time about being in the project. If they decide to leave the project, there will be no penalty of any kind.

3. They have the right to refuse to answer any question(s). Some questions might be personal or sensitive to them. These questions are important to our project, and we would like them to answer the questions honestly. However, if there are questions they do not want to answer, they may skip them and move on to other questions.

4. They will be given copies of this project description (your consent form). If they want to participate in our project, they will also sign an assent form.

5. Their assent forms will also be explained verbally to them. If they have any difficulty in reading these forms, a staff person will read them to your client.

6. At any time they can ask any staff member questions about our project. They may also call collect Mike Stephens (x-xxx-xxx-xxxx, extension xxx).

7. If they would like to contact someone outside the project staff with questions or concerns, they can call Yvonne Unrau at xxx-xxx-xxxx or Rick Grinnell at xxx-xxx-xxxx, who are the two Western Michigan University researchers involved with the project. They may also contact the Chair of the Human Subjects Institutional Review Board (xxx-xxx-xxxx) or the Vice President for Research (xxx-xxx-xxxx) at Western

Michigan University if questions or problems arise during the course of the study. They may call collect.

RISKS ASSOCIATED WITH PARTICIPATING IN THIS PROJECT

There are very few risks in this project. The adolescents may, however, feel a little embarrassed or uncomfortable because of the personal nature of some questions on the surveys or due to certain project activities such as role-plays in the workshop. Remember, they do not have to answer any questions or take part in any activities at any time.

WHAT ARE THE BENEFITS TO THEM?

Many people find it helpful to think and talk about personal information about themselves and their families. Being in the project gives them a chance to do this. The project may improve our knowledge about how youth in care can better seek help when they need it. The information gained may help us understand more about how parents, foster parents, and CKCS can work together to help teenagers who are placed in foster or group care.

This information might be used to prevent problems for teenagers in the future and to help those that are having trouble. As a participant, they will be part of a valuable project that might help other people in the future. Please sign below to show that you have reviewed this project description, that you consent to have your clients participate, and that you have had all your questions answered.

_____

Social worker's signature (as legal guardian) and date

BOX 4.2	Example of an Assent Form

NOTE: This assent form was given to the foster youth after their respective social workers had provided us with permission to contact them via a consent form (Box 4.1).

(LETTERHEAD)

I have been invited to be part of a study entitled "Chatham-Kent Children's Services (CKCS) Help-Seeking Project for Adolescents in Out-of-Home Placement."

The main purpose of the study is to see whether a workshop and additional support given to youth living at CKCS will make them more skilled at asking for help with personal or emotional problems. In this study:

1. I will be phoned by a CKCS staff member twice over 20 weeks and be asked to answer questions on the phone. This will take about 15 minutes each time.

2. I will be invited to come to CKCS four times over the next 20 weeks to answer questions from four other survey questionnaires about my help-seeking behaviors using a special computer program at CKCS.

3. After the first testing, CKCS will pay me $10 (or equivalent).

4. After the second testing point, CKCS will pay me $15 (or equivalent).

5. After the third testing point, CKCS will pay me $20 (or equivalent).

6. After the fourth (and final) time, CKCS will pay me $30 (or equivalent).

7. CKCS will provide food snacks at each testing time.

8. A project staff member will look at my case file to obtain basic information about me such as my age, sex, time in care, etc.

9. My name will not be recorded; instead of recording my name, a number code will be used.

10. I also may be invited to participate in a 2- to 3-hour workshop with a small group of about five other youth in care. The workshop will take place at CKCS and will be run by a CKCS mental health worker and possibly someone who formerly lived in an out-of-home placement.

11. At the workshop, I will get information and ideas about asking for help related to personal or emotional problems that are common with teenagers.

12. If I don't want to participate at this time, the service I receive from CKCS will not be affected.

13. Even if I agree today to participate by signing this form, I can change my mind at any time and withdraw from the study, and there will be no effect on the service I receive from CKCS.

14. If I choose to complete any or all of the questionnaires for the study, then my scores will be sent to researchers at Western Michigan University in Kalamazoo, Michigan.

15. As mentioned previously, my name will not be on any of the surveys that are sent to Michigan. The researchers will use a code number instead of my name. The researchers will keep a list of names and code numbers that will be destroyed once the researchers have looked at all the questionnaires.

16. All my answers will be kept private, which means even my Children's Service Worker or caregivers won't know what I say unless project staff members think I might be in danger of hurting myself or others. Then project staff will need to tell my Children's Service Worker.

17. My signature below indicates that I have agreed to be interviewed by phone and take the surveys on the computer.

YOUR SIGNATURE ALSO INDICATES THAT YOU AGREE:

1. to have your case file at CKCS reviewed for information it contains.

2. to be assigned to participate in a special help-seeking workshop for this project, if selected.

3. to allow CKCS to give the researchers your survey results and case file information (your name will not be sent to the researchers).

4. that you have had a chance to ask any questions you may have.

_____

Print your name on above line.

_____ (Date: _____)

Sign your name on the above line and put in today's date.

ANONYMITY VERSUS CONFIDENTIALITY

A PROMISE OF PARTICULAR CONCERN to many research participants is that of anonymity. A current illegal drug user may be afraid of being identified. Folks receiving social services may be concerned whether anyone else might learn that they are receiving them. Also, there is often some confusion between the terms "anonymity" and "confidentiality."

Some research studies are designed so that no one, not even the person doing the study, knows which research participant gave what response. An example is a mailed survey form bearing no identifying marks whatsoever and asking the respondent not to provide a name. In a study like this, the respondent is *anonymous.*

It's more often the case, however, that we do in fact know how a particular participant responded and have agreed not to divulge the information to anyone else. In such cases, the information is considered *confidential.* Part of our explanation to a potential research participant must include a clear statement of what information will be shared and with whom it will be shared (e.g., Boxes 4.1 and 4.2).

ENSURING CONFIDENTIALITY

THE FIRST STEP IN THE PROCESS for ensuring confidentiality is often to assign a code number to each participant. The researcher and her assistants alone know that Ms. Smith, for example, is number 132. All data concerning Ms. Smith are then combined with data from all the other participants to produce summary aggregated results that do not identify Ms. Smith in any way. No one reading the final research report or any publication stemming from it will know that Ms. Smith took part in the study at all.

Sometimes, complete confidentiality cannot be guaranteed.

Sometimes, however, complete confidentiality cannot be guaranteed. In a study undertaken in a small community, for example, direct quotes from an interview with "a" social worker may narrow the field to three because there are only three social workers there. Then the flavor of the quote may narrow it again to Mr. Jones, who said the same thing in church last Sunday. If there is any risk that Mr. Jones might be recognized as the source of the quote, this possibility must be clearly acknowledged in the letter of consent that Mr. Jones is asked to sign.

Although the ideal is to obtain written consent from the potential participant before the study begins, it's not always possible to obtain the consent in writing. In a telephone interview, for example, the information that would have been contained in a letter of consent is usually read to the participant, and oral consent is obtained.

If a number of participants are to be interviewed by telephone, the same information, set out in exactly the same way, must be read to them all. A mailed questionnaire is sent out with an accompanying introductory letter. This letter contains a statement that filling out the questionnaire and sending it back constitutes consent.

DESIGNING A STUDY IN AN ETHICAL MANNER

ONCE YOU HAVE OBTAINED INFORMED CONSENT from your research participants, you then need to actually carry out your research study in an ethical manner. During every step in any proposed social work research study, you will be called upon to make numerous ethical decisions. There are eight overlapping steps that we need to take when conducting any research study.

This section covers eight—out of the eleven—steps of the research process and discusses the ethical issues we need to address for each one. Each step overlaps with the other steps. Thus, it's totally impractical to discuss ethical issues that need to be addressed within each step in a complete vacuum, isolated from the other steps; that is, all steps are influenced by the ethical decisions made in the other steps, as depicted at the beginning of this chapter (see page 125):

— **Step 2:** Develop the research question
— **Step 5:** Select a research approach
— **Step 6:** Specify how variables are measured
— **Step 7:** Select a sample
— **Step 8:** Select a research design
— **Step 9:** Select a data-collection method
— **Step 10:** Analyze the data
— **Step 11:** Write and disseminate the research report

STEP 2: DEVELOP THE RESEARCH QUESTION

AS WE KNOW FROM CHAPTER 2, we must address a simple question: What is the purpose of our research study in the first place? Will it increase our understanding of the problem we are investigating? Is it likely to benefit individuals (or groups) in need?

The National Association of Social Worker's *Code of Ethics* (2017) contains an ethical standard that requires social work students to be educated in research methodology.

Sometimes a research study can *directly benefit* those who participate in it—that is, the research participants themselves. In addition, it may *indirectly benefit* others who share the same or a similar condition or problem but are not actually participating in the study; that is, they are not directly involved in the study as research participants.

If the study does not directly or indirectly benefit its participants, then it must contribute to our professional social work knowledge base. If the research question posed already has been answered, however, what's the argument for answering it again?

The researcher may believe it's important to replicate clinical findings and/or generalize the study's findings to other populations, or to simply replicate the study using a more rigorous and creditable research design, which in turn would produce more trustworthy findings.

Research training is another acceptable reason for conducting a research study that may not directly benefit its participants. In many universities and research institutions alike, providing opportunities for students to learn how to conduct research studies is an important function.

The National Association of Social Worker's *Code of Ethics* (2017) also contains an ethical standard that requires students to be educated in research methodology. In cases where there may be little direct or indirect benefit to the research participants, the level of risk posed by their participation in research studies should be minimal; that is, there should be little to no chance that their participation in the research studies could harm them in any way.

REFINE THE RESEARCH QUESTION THROUGH THE LITERATURE

AFTER IDENTIFYING A RESEARCH QUESTION, the next goal is to refine it further by surveying the relevant literature, as discussed in the previous chapter. This involves a thorough review of the theory and other research studies related to the research question.

It's important to base any research inquiry on a solid understanding of what came before: "What do we already know about the potential research question under investigation?" Critical to refining the initial research question *is asking an answerable question.* For example,

---

Question:
What social work intervention(s) will decrease gang-related "tagging" (graffiti) on public school grounds?

As we know from Chapter 2, once we have a question that can be answered, such as this one, we can then refine it a bit more. This part of the research process is roughly analogous to the assessment phase in clinical social work practice. Once the client's presenting problem (the research question) is posed, we then proceed to identify the parameters of the problem and explore its impact on the client's functioning.

As newer and more specific client information is drawn out during the assessment phase of social work practice, we then refine and increase the clarity and precision of the original problem statement. This process in clinical assessment is called *targeting.* Basing our choice of intervention on conclusions drawn quickly and imprecisely about the target problem compromises ethical practice.

EVALUATE THE LITERATURE

WHAT IS *ACCEPTABLE* KNOWLEDGE? Is all information found on Google "good"? Is one search engine or bibliographic resource superior to another in the value of the information it generates? And what impact do the answers to these questions have on the services we provide to our clients? Even many elementary schools now inform their students that Wikipedia is *not* an acceptable reference source to be used in an academic paper.

Using search engines to find treatments for depression, for example, yields numerous links to psychotropic medication before psychosocial treatments are even cited. Indeed, information on how to commit suicide exists side by side with scholarly papers on factors related to preventing suicide!

Evaluating sources of knowledge was much easier (however inefficient) before the advent of the Internet. Professional journals and books, along with professional consensus, were considered the building blocks of our profession's knowledge base. These were available by subscription and in bookstores; most of us had to go to libraries or buy books to access this information. The Internet has broadened and extended our information sources beyond expectation and, at the same time, has made it much more difficult to critically assess the information found there.

Today, credible sources of practice information are available on the Internet, such as the Cochrane Collaboration (www.cochrane.org) and the Campbell Collaboration (www.campbellcollaboration.org). These organizations' Web sites include both systematic reviews and meta-analyses covering the assessment and treatment of health, mental health, and social welfare problems.

It's important to base any research inquiry on a solid understanding of what came before.

Evidence-based practice guidelines represent the best of scholarly consensus and are available for mental health, substance abuse, and other areas of social work practice. What's the best kind of evidence to inform our day-to-day practice? An evidence credibility hierarchy continuum exists that stretches from lowest to highest.

It starts with anecdotal case reports (lowest) and moves up to randomized clinical trials (highest). This hierarchy is helpful in guiding our choice of what intervention to use in solving a client's problem. The most robust type of evidence to support a particular intervention for a particular client problem is the most ethical one to use.

STEP 5: SELECT A RESEARCH APPROACH

AS WE REFINE OUR RESEARCH QUESTION in Step 2, the research approach finally used will become much clearer. Figure 2.2 on page 85 provides a diagram of how research questions are refined. Certain questions can be better answered by a quantitative (positivistic) approach, a qualitative (interpretive) approach, or a mixed-methods approach. All three of these interconnected approaches are discussed in Chapters 6, 7, and 8 respectively.

Our literature review, discussed in Chapter 3, will probably suggest what approach may be the most appropriate for our particular topic area and the intended population (research participants) we wish to explore. Sometimes our own biases about research approaches or the biases of the larger research community influence us as we select a research approach.

For example, some researchers do not have a high regard for qualitative approaches, whereas others have a strong preference for them. As we know from the preceding chapters, a research approach should not be dictated by this kind of sophomoric thinking. As we noted at the outset of this section, our selected research approach—and the ethical issues contained within it—should strive to reduce, not introduce, bias.

All too often, a randomized clinical trial is held up as the gold standard of scientific inquiry. In certain fields of inquiry, a rich history of research and development exists, and a social work intervention might be ready for a randomized experimental study like those discussed in Chapter 13.

> We have a responsibility to our research participants to select a research approach that will produce useful, reliable, and valid findings.

But what about an intervention that has not yet been described as a detailed proceduralized or manualized treatment? In this case, it's unethical to choose a randomized control research design because the intervention is clearly not ready to be tested. We have a responsibility to our research participants—as well as to the larger professional community—to select a research approach that will produce useful, reliable, and valid findings.

STEP 6: SPECIFY HOW VARIABLES ARE MEASURED

MANY OF THE GUIDELINES for specifying the measurement of variables (covered in Chapters 9 and 10) are helpful in avoiding the potential ethical pitfalls in Step 6. For example, we need to avoid measurement methods and instruments with obvious biases, such as the biases related to gender, age, sexual orientation, and culture. If we are studying the sexual habits of men and women, for example, the language of the questions we formulate should not assume that all the research participants are heterosexual.

We must strive to explain our study's procedures in terms that can be easily understood by prospective participants.

In fact, our *Code of Ethics* stresses the need for us to understand and respect the full extent of social diversity found within our client systems. This understanding and respect for individual differences must be reflected in the selection and measurement of the variables we wish to study.

In selecting the variables to study, we also need to base our selection on the literature and not conduct a fishing expedition in which every variable imaginable is included in the study in an effort to search for something of significance.

Having specific research questions and hypotheses guiding each phase of the study is not just good research practice, it's also good ethical practice. In a nutshell, research participants should not be asked to provide a wealth of information that may or may not address the central question(s) of the research study.

BE AWARE OF CULTURAL ISSUES

AS WE WILL SEE IN THE NEXT CHAPTER, a study that fails to take into account cultural issues is unlikely to produce valid and reliable findings. Cultural issues must be considered at every step of the research process, from developing the research question to disseminating the study's findings. As we know from our social work practice classes, perceptions and definitions of child sexual abuse are socially constructed and are shaped by specific cultural, social, and historical perspectives.

Thus, we must take into account how our potential study's participants perceive and understand child sexual abuse, in addition to the cultural customs about discussing such a sensitive topic. These cultural contexts influence how the research questions are asked, how study participants are recruited, and how data are collected and finally analyzed.

We may find that little or no information is available on the social problem being addressed in the culture of the population in which we are interested. In this case, we need to consult representatives from the group we are studying for advice and guidance. *Focus groups* with these individuals will help to clarify many potential issues.

Pilot testing the measuring procedures using people from the group of interest is absolutely essential in an effort to avoid any misunderstandings, the possibility of offending our study's participants, and, ultimately, the production of data that are not reliable and valid.

EXAMPLES OF CULTURAL ISSUE AWARENESS. A proposed research study of the experiences of political refugees to the United States from former Soviet Bloc countries may be a relatively novel area of inquiry, with limited advice available in the professional literature. Thus, in designing a research questionnaire, we would likely find that talking to the immigrants and the social service staff who works with refugees will be the most helpful in understanding the challenges faced by this particular population.

Another example of an extremely important topic under the general area of cultural issues is that of language. If the data collection method(s), such as those discussed in Chapters 14–16, involve gathering data directly from our research participants, then we need to be sensitive to issues related to language.

Even when collecting data from participants who speak the same language as the social worker, we must be sensitive to regional dialects, the age of the respondents, and the like. When doing research studies with adolescents or "Millennials," for example, you have to consider the trade-off between using Standard English, slang, Web speak, or other types of communication they commonly use.

As we know from earlier in this chapter, when obtaining informed consent from potential research participants, we must strive to explain our study's procedures in terms that can be easily understood by prospective participants. Our *Code of Ethics* and the next chapter clearly address the importance of considering cultural issues when designing a research study. We are reminded to respect the cultural and ethnic backgrounds of the people with whom we work.

This includes recognizing the strengths that exist in all cultures—which is critical when designing research questions and hypotheses, selecting variables to be studied, and conducting all other steps of the research process itself. Thus, the above-mentioned study of political refugees needs to consider their strengths as well as their challenges and difficulties.

STEP 7: SELECT A SAMPLE

HOW WE SELECT RESEARCH PARTICIPANTS for potential participation in our research studies is a very important ingredient of the research process. Although sampling methods are primarily driven by the study's purpose, sampling decisions also are influenced by our own personal values and sometimes by convenience. Ethical concerns include whether the potential research participants are representative of the target population we really want to study.

In other words, is this the group most affected by the problem we are trying to answer via the research study? As we will see in Chapter 11 on sampling, it's important to ask whether the group is diverse enough to represent those who are affected by the problem.

Research studies with samples lacking in cultural diversity may limit generalization to the broader population under study, and they also compromise social work ethical tenets that address social justice and increased inclusion. Intentionally or inadvertently excluding certain individuals or groups from participating in a research study can markedly affect the data gathered and the conclusions drawn about the phenomena under study.

For instance, a research study of immigrants that excludes non–English-speaking individuals, nonreaders, and agency clients who come in before or after regular hours for the convenience of the researchers introduces several types of sampling biases that will directly affect the generalizability of study's results. This example also ignores the mandate that all social workers must engage in culturally competent practice and research that respects client diversity.

RECRUITMENT

HOW POTENTIAL RESEARCH PARTICIPANTS are recruited also requires an ethical lens. Assessing all possible ways that a potential research participant might feel undue influence to participate—such as a personal appeal, a financial incentive, the status of being part of a special group, other tangible or intangible benefits, or just plain-old fear of repercussions—can be a daunting task, to say the least.

Who is actually recruiting the participants? Does the gatekeeper—or the process of the recruitment effort itself—exert pressure, subtle or direct, to participate or not to participate? Social workers hold an ethical obligation to examine the fairness or *equity* of recruitment strategies within target populations and the representativeness (or diversity) of the sample finally selected to be included in the study.

As we know from earlier portions of this chapter, our *Code of Ethics* includes standards that mandate that we obtain potential research participants without threatening to penalize anyone who refuses to participate—and without offering inappropriate rewards for their participation. Just as clients have the right to self-determination in social work practice, so too do participants who volunteer for research projects.

> Just as clients have the right to self-determination in social work practice, so too do participants who volunteer for research projects.

Take a look at Boxes 4.1 and 4.2, which provide examples of consent (Box 4.1) and assent (Box 4.2) forms. Do you see any possibility that the foster youth were unduly influenced to participate and/or would not receive services if they did not participate? Why or why not? And speaking of ethical recruitment, take a look at Box 4.3 on pages 150–151.

STEP 8: SELECT A RESEARCH DESIGN

THE RESEARCH DESIGN that is finally chosen also warrants examination from an ethical perspective. In intervention or evaluation research, in which participants are randomized to either an intervention group or a control group, concerns often arise about withholding treatment or providing a less potent intervention for control group members.

The ability to randomly assign research participants to groups significantly strengthens arguments about whether a particular intervention is responsible for the change (if any) that has occurred for the individuals in the intervention group.

This decision, however, must be weighed against the reality of the participant's life or problem situation. Clients can be randomly assigned to two groups: one group receives the intervention (experimental group), and the other group does not receive it (control group). If the experimental group does better than the control group after the study is completed, the control group would then receive the same intervention that the experimental group received earlier.

Because the control group receives the intervention at a later date, there are no ethical violations present in this particular research design when implemented correctly. However, a delay must always be weighed against the benefit, as some delays may be detrimental or even fatal.

BOX 4.3	**Heart's in the Right Place but Head Isn't**

LET'S BEGIN OUR VENTURE into recruiting research participants from an ethical perspective with a short vignette that illustrates how a beginning graduate-level social work student, Margaret, wanted to recruit clients (research participants) for a research study.

In her field practicum, Margaret is helping her professor recruit families for a research study that is aimed at providing an intervention to improve the parenting skills of pregnant and parenting teenagers. She recruits potential research participants at the local public social services office (her practicum setting), where the pregnant teenagers meet weekly with their child protection workers.

According to the research study's recruitment protocol, recruitment takes place via colorful flyers handed out to clients by the receptionist as they enter the agency. The clients are asked by the receptionist to talk with Margaret to get further information on an "important" study in which they may wish to participate.

One day, Margaret notices a young pregnant teenager crying in the waiting room and asks her if she can do anything to help. Listening to her story, Margaret unwittingly finds herself strongly encouraging the teenager to participate in the research project (a new intervention, yet to be tested) by telling her how much the intervention would improve her parenting skills.

She also suggests that her participation in the research study would reflect favorably on the child protection worker's evaluation of the teen. At this point, do you see anything wrong with Margaret's behaviors?

Margaret responded to the client's sad story with encouragement that she believed to be in the client's best interests—participating in the research study. Margaret increases the client's motivation to participate by telling her it will improve her parenting skills.

In addition, Margaret asserts that the client's participation would favorably impact the child protection worker's assessment of the teen. Although Margaret's intentions may be understandable to the novice, she has in fact violated the ethical principles of both practice and research in one brief three-minute conversation. More specifically, and in no particular order, Margaret:

1. Assumed she understood the client's problem without conducting an adequate assessment.

2. Did not fully disclose the purpose of the research study.

3. Exerted coercive influence over the client to participate by telling her the intervention will work for her without actually knowing if it would.

4. Suggested that the client's participation in the study would favorably affect the agency's perception of her.

5. Did not realize that the young woman may have felt that she had to participate in the research study to receive the services she was asking for by coming into the agency in the first place.

6. Did not tell the client that she may be randomly assigned to a control group (those who do not receive the treatment) and, thus, may receive no intervention whatsoever (at this time, that is).

7. Did not obtain the consent of the teen's parents or legal guardian.

Oh, by the way, this incident actually happened!

The diagram below illustrates the kind of study that was used with the foster care adolescents described in Boxes 4.1 and 4.2. The experimental group received the social work intervention or workshop (top arrow), and the control group did not (bottom arrow).

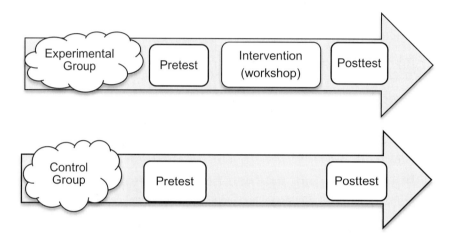

One important fact that we may lose sight of is that a new, untested intervention may not necessarily be better than no treatment at all. It is, as they say, an "empirical question" and deserves testing. What is clear is that individuals applying for social work services have the right to receive the best known evidence-based interventions at that time.

In other words, it's unethical to withhold an intervention that has already been demonstrated to be effective. Protecting clients from deprivation of services and ensuring that they have access to the best interventions is also a mandate of our *Code of Ethics.*

Individuals applying for experimental or innovative services of any type have the right to know the availability of alternative forms of interventions and the risks and benefits of each intervention. Exploring the use of different kinds of control conditions and determining which is best, both for the clients and for answering the research question, is an important ethical task.

BENEFICENCE

CENTRAL TO THE CONSIDERATION of the ethical issues in experimental designs is the question of *beneficence.* Researchers and the IRBs that guide them must consider how to maximize the benefit and minimize harm to participants when considering how best to test the effectiveness of a social work intervention. The possibility of other viable treatment methods must be considered as well, as opposed to offering no treatment. Again, our *Code of Ethics* mandates that we must protect both clients and research participants from deprivation of access to evidence-based services.

EQUIPOISE, OR THE UNCERTAINTY PRINCIPLE

HIGHLY RELATED TO PROVIDING the most effective services as possible is the concept of *equipoise,* also called the *uncertainty principle.* This principle maintains that research studies that randomize their research participants to different treatment groups should be conducted only if there is a true uncertainty about which of the treatment alternatives is most likely to benefit them. Some questions are easy to answer, but some pose serious dilemmas to the researcher.

For instance, if an intervention being tested is known to be superior to an alternative inferior intervention, it's unethical to assign individuals to the inferior intervention. Similarly, an experimental research study that contains two interventions is unethical if a third intervention exists that is known to be more effective, unless the researchers have questions about the efficacy of the effective intervention for a particular subgroup of clients.

> It's unethical to withhold an intervention that has already been demonstrated to be effective.

All too often, however, beneficence and equipoise raise challenging questions for social work researchers, especially those working in fields where there are relatively few data to support the effectiveness of alternative interventions. Moreover, if the usual intervention (sometimes called "TAU," treatment as usual) has little or no evidence to support its effectiveness, can it be considered an appropriate comparison treatment?

DECEPTION

DECEPTION IS ANOTHER ASPECT of a study's research design that requires ethical forethought. Let's consider an example to illustrate this point. José wanted to study racial/ethnic bias in employment practices in family service agencies in Chicago. He mailed numerous fake application letters to all family service agencies in Chicago that had current openings for full-time clinicians. Each letter contained the exact same qualifications, but he would change his name to reflect four different groups of people: African-American, Latino, Asian, or Irish heritage.

In short, everything was the same except his name. José planned to simply count the number of interview requests he received, broken down by each group. Sounds harmless, you say? Read on.

In no way in his cover letter for employment did José indicate he was conducting a research study. To José's surprise, all of Chicago's executive directors of family service agencies met at a local conference and started talking about good job candidates they were going to follow up on. José's name came up several times in the conversation.

The executive directors soon became angry when they found out they had been duped by José. Several of them had not interviewed other qualified individuals because they were holding slots open to interview José when time permitted.

José, his school, his dean, and the federal government all became involved in addressing the consequences of his unethical use of deception. José's actions ignored a key concept of our *Code of Ethics*: Whether acting as a practitioner or a researcher, social workers are mandated to act with integrity and in a trustworthy manner.

Generally, it's good practice to avoid deception whenever possible. Although it sounds reasonable to say that good social work researchers should *never* lie to their potential research participants or provide them with less than a full disclosure about the methods of their studies, in reality this is not always desirable. For example, a social worker assessing bias toward developmentally delayed clients by staff employed at correctional institutions understandably initially might not want to disclose the entire purpose of the study because it might affect how the custodial staff responds.

We need to ask the ethical question: Is deception absolutely necessary to carry out the study? In other words, is deception necessary to prevent participants from trying to respond in a contrived and/or socially desirable manner?

Next, we need to ask whether there is a possibility that the deception will harm our research participants, in either the short or long term. If the deception causes or encourages participants to react in ways they might not otherwise, or allows them to make choices at odds with their personal views of themselves (e.g., a decision-making study that allows a participant to lie, cheat, or steal), learning later about their behavior might be psychologically distressing.

Our *Code of Ethics* mandates not only that we protect our research participants from mental distress but also that we protect our clients from all harm to the fullest extent possible. The majority of deception that is approved in research studies is of minimal risk to research participants and is far less dramatic than José's study of racial/ethnic bias in hiring practices.

For example, Jennifer would have been wiser if she had used *more* deception in her study that monitored children's seat belt use on school buses. Climbing onto a school bus after the young children had boarded, she announced, "I am doing a research study for your principal, and I'm counting the number of safe and smart children on this bus who buckle up!"

In this one simple very honest sentence she immediately gave away the purpose of her study, which resulted in an immediate flurry of seat belt buckling—thus defeating her ability to get an accurate and realistic count of those children who would not have buckled up if it weren't for her disclosure of the study. On another topic: Do you think Jennifer needed permission from the children's parents to do her simple head count? Why or why not? After all, the children were minors.

DEBRIEFING. One of the ways in which we can appropriately counteract the use of deception is by using debriefing procedures after the study is over. *Debriefing* involves explaining the true purpose of the research study to the participants after the study is completed, along with *why* the deception was necessary in the first place. If there is a concern about psychological distress as a result of having been deceived by the study, for example, then participants must be offered adequate means of addressing this distress.

In some cases of minimal-risk research involving deception, debriefing participants about the true nature of the study and their responses may cause greater distress than not fully understanding their actions in the study.

Also, experienced mental health professionals and IRBs might disagree on whether distressing self-knowledge can be mitigated effectively and how this should best be done, or even whether a study should be conducted in view of the psychological risks to potential participants. One possible way that our *Code of Ethics* offers to mitigate the situation is to offer participants "appropriate supportive services" after the study.

STEP 9: SELECT A DATA-COLLECTION METHOD

STEP 9 OF THE RESEARCH PROCESS, data collection, contains the following three ethical issues that surround the data-collection process.

1. How data are collected
2. Who's going to collect the data
3. Frequency and timing of data collection

HOW DATA ARE COLLECTED

AS WE WILL SEE IN CHAPTER 16, a researcher's choice of how to collect the data that best answer the research question can introduce unintended bias, coercing some and potentially excluding other desired participants. Awareness is the key to understanding the ethical implications of data collection.

EXAMPLE 1. Aiesha wants to do a follow-up study with juveniles released from custody in her state's detention facilities. She conducts a phone survey during the hours she's at work (standard business hours) and calls the youths' "home" phone numbers.

Aiesha is unaware that she is missing the youths who (1) do not have phones (2) have phones but simply do not answer them (3) do not hang out at home during the day (4) operate primarily from cell phones and (5) she is possibly inadvertently informing housemates who answer that the person being called was formerly detained.

EXAMPLE 2. One of Aiesha's colleagues, Barbara, is using an "anonymous" Internet-based survey to examine the educational aspirations of young adults. As part of her study, she asks participants about their recreational drug use and about any knowledge they might have about their parents' recreational use of illegal substances.

Although she does not ask for names or other identifying information, it's possible to trace respondents by their computers' Internet protocol (IP) addresses. Barbara forgot that all researchers must protect their participants' identities, just as practitioners must protect clients' privacy, according to our *Code of Ethics*.

Further, although the youths have consented to participate via completion of the Internet survey itself, Barbara also was gathering data about the youths' parents. The parents have *not* consented to have their children give Barbara data about them.

Collecting data about parental substance abuse via their children without the parents' consent is not a good idea to say the least. A situation similar to this one resulted in the temporary shutdown of all federal research at one eastern university after a very irate parent contacted the U.S. Department of Health and Human Services' Office for Human Research Protection.

WHO'S GOING TO COLLECT THE DATA?

WHO IS ACTUALLY GOING TO COLLECT the data that will answer the research question constitutes yet another ethical decision to be made. Anyone in a position of power or authority over the participant, such as teachers, social workers, health-care officials, administrators—anyone who can either supply or deny the resources that research participants need—introduces the potential for undue influence.

Coercion can easily result in less-than-willing participation. It also may influence the quality of the data collected because the participants may respond differently than they normally would if they believe that individuals who have authority over them may see their responses.

Paper and pencil surveys about anger and urges to act impulsively that are completed by clients arrested for interpersonal violence are an example. Our *Code of Ethics* also asserts that the presence of coercion violates the tenets of voluntary participation in both practice and research activities.

FREQUENCY AND TIMING OF DATA COLLECTION

FINALLY, THE CHOICE we make about the frequency and timing of data-collection activities also may raise privacy issues. Some research designs call for collecting data at additional intervals after the main part of the study has been completed with all research participants. In situations such as these, the consent and/or assent letter(s) (e.g., Boxes 4.1 and 4.2) must inform potential research participants that they will be contacted in the future.

STEP 10: ANALYZE THE DATA

DATA ANALYSIS AND DRAWING CONCLUSIONS from the data, unfortunately, represent one step in the research process that many social workers most often wish to outsource or turn over to others. Those of us who are not research oriented are often unfamiliar with data analysis beyond basic statistics and may avoid reading the results section of journal articles, skipping ahead to the discussion section and assuming that the author will review what is most important.

We rely heavily on the peer review process in professional publications for assurance that appropriate methods of data analysis are used. However, does this excuse us from not knowing statistics? Some have suggested that ethical data analysis begins with our moral responsibility to *understand* the analyses that data undergo before we make use of the research results.

Ethical problems in data analysis are rooted, broadly speaking, in the research environment. Don't be more invested in supporting your theories than in testing them! The researcher's personal attachment to specific theories and the importance of obtaining statistical significance so that the research results can be published or receive other indicators of peer approval are real parts of the research environment.

Our common understanding of research "success" is based on the outcomes of the study—that is, whether the study's findings support the researcher's hypotheses. Hearing a researcher say the project did not "turn out," generally means that the results did not support the researcher's theories.

The following are a few guidelines related to data analysis:

— Present research findings and results openly and honestly.
   Do not omit contradictory findings.

— Untrue or deceptive statements should be avoided in
   research reports.

— Clearly delineate the limits and boundaries of inference used. This may include subjects sampled for participation or levels of experimental variables.

— Provide complete and clear documentation, including how the data were gleaned (edited), the statistical procedures used, and the assumptions made about the data.

— The role of data analyst ideally is neutral so that statistical procedures may be applied without concern for a favorable outcome.

Social workers wishing to employ ethical analysis strategies should incorporate these five principles into their work. Much more will be said about analyzing quantitative data in Chapter 17 and qualitative data in Chapter 18.

STEP 11: WRITE AND DISSEMINATE THE RESEARCH REPORT

THE FINAL STEP, writing and disseminating the research report, is fraught with potential ethical dilemmas. To begin, all too often we neglect to write a report and disseminate the findings of our research studies. Somehow we get caught up in our busy schedules and the need to move on to the next project, and we fail to attend to this crucial last step. Not reporting findings is a disservice to everyone who participated in and funded the study.

Moreover, our *Code of Ethics* calls for us to facilitate informed participation in the general community for shaping public social policy and human service institutions, as well as to engage in social and political action ourselves. Depending on the nature of the research study, the findings might be important in advocating for social justice for our constituents, such as providing equal access to benefits and resources that will meet their basic needs and allow them to realize their full potential.

In addition to reporting to the community at large, we have a responsibility to report our findings to our research participants and our community that is supposed to benefit from our study's findings. In particular, if our recruitment process involved promising to make a report available to potential study participants, it's critical that we share our findings with them in clear, understandable language.

There are a host of methods for disseminating research findings, including research summaries, journal articles, books, press releases, flyers, posters, brochures, letters of thanks to study participants, study newsletters, local conferences, and seminars. Social workers need to consider the goal of the reporting and the needs of the target audience in selecting a distribution method.

For a broader audience, we need to find ways to make the content comprehensible and interesting. We need to be good storytellers when communicating research findings while taking care not to distort them. As we will see in the following chapter, we must also find culturally sensitive ways to report our study's findings to both our research participants and communities, when appropriate.

Our *Code of Ethics* also provides a thorough discussion of the importance of protecting clients' right to privacy. Providing feedback to our participants while still maintaining their confidentiality can be challenging in certain situations. To illustrate, our research participants may have been in domestic violence shelters, mental health institutions, or juvenile justice placements and then were returned home or released to more open settings. Simply obtaining a current address is often difficult, but even when the address is obtained, involuntary clients often do not want others to know that they have received social services.

Hence, participants may not wish to receive a research report, which in some way labels them as affiliated with a particular agency or service. A cover letter thanking a woman for her involvement in an interpersonal violence study can "out" her and may even create a dangerous situation. Incarcerated youth, who were once eager to see the results of a study they participated in, may feel awkward and embarrassed 18 months later when the report arrives mailed to their homes.

Another ethical dilemma that we sometimes face arises when there's a conflict between the participants' agency, policymakers, advocacy groups, and/or the group that funded the study and the researcher. If stakeholders are displeased with certain findings, or with the way in which the researcher has interpreted them, this can seriously complicate the dissemination of the findings. Our *Code of Ethics* highlights our responsibility to report accurately our evaluation and research findings—and, it should go without saying, not to fabricate the results.

To the extent possible, we should come to some general agreement in the early stages of planning our research study about how these issues will be resolved. In fact, our *Code of Ethics* cautions us to identify potential conflicts of interest, inform the participants when a real or potential conflict of interest develops, and place primary importance on the participants' interests in resolving any conflicts of interest.

Often, the sharing of findings will be a delicate matter. Agency staff may be reluctant to hear, for example, that their program may be less effective than they had thought. If they were not engaged in the research process in the first place and they know little about the research methods, they may be tempted to dismiss the findings and block any attempt on the part of the researcher to discuss recommendations for improvement. Thus, findings must be presented carefully, to the right people, in the right order, and at the right time.

Practitioners wrestle every day with a similar problem. Mr. Yen might not want to be told that his daughter is still threatening to run away despite all those parenting classes and family therapy sessions he attended. His daughter might not want him to know. His wife might not want him to know either, in case this bit of data spurs him to inappropriate disciplinary steps. The social worker must decide whom to tell, as well as how, when, and how much. The same holds true when doing research studies.

ETHICS AND OUR SOCIAL SERVICE PROGRAMS

WE NOTED IN CHAPTER 1 that one thing all agency administrators have in common is worry. They worry about how effectively they are serving their clients and how they can demonstrate their effectiveness to funders. They worry about offending people. They worry about whether they will be seen to be doing the right thing, with the right people, in the right place, and at the right time. All these worries have ethical and political overtones.

Take effective service to clients, for example. There is nothing absolute about *effectiveness*. The same service may be deemed to be effective or ineffective depending on how effectiveness is defined and who does the defining. For instance, the aim of a drug rehabilitation program might be to ensure that every client who comes through its doors will absolutely and positively abstain 100% from using any type of drug forevermore.

This aim, though worthy, is probably impossible to achieve. The program's actual achievement—in terms of the percentage of clients who completely abstained, partially abstained, or did not abstain from using a particular drug over a particular period—will be seen as successful or not depending on the political climate.

If marijuana is currently viewed as a gateway to hell, for example, the program's lack of success in curtailing its use will be judged more harshly than in a more tolerant climate. If a more immediate concern is gas sniffing among First Nations children, the program is likely to be judged on how well it's dealing with solvent abuse. Effectiveness thus tends to be defined and evaluated with respect to the external political and social issues of the hour.

There are also the internal politics of the program to be considered. Staff members will each have their individual views about which of the many issues facing the program should be given priority, how scarce resources should be used, which treatment modality is best, what the reporting structure ought to be, and, in general, who ought to do what, where, how, and when. These inevitable tensions affect the research climate within the program.

Most social service programs will be less or more receptive to research endeavors at different times, depending on their internal political situations and their current level of staff morale. When staff are feeling overworked, underpaid, and unappreciated, they will be less inclined to cooperate with research efforts, but, at the same time, this is the moment when they might benefit most from an evaluative study designed to improve client service delivery or to optimize the organizational structure.

Conversely, when morale is low due to conflicts with administrators, an evaluative study might just serve to exacerbate the conflicts. Researchers, like all social workers, have the potential to help or to harm. If they are to help, they must be sensitive to internal and external political considerations so that they can conduct a useful study in the right way, in the right place, at the right time.

MISUSES OF RESEARCH RESULTS

IT MIGHT BE WORTHWHILE here to consider the misuses of research results. A study that sets out to be useful can turn out to be harmful if the results are used in an unethical way. There are four primary ways in which research results may be misused within social service programs:

1. To justify decisions already made
2. To safeguard public relations
3. To appraise the performance of staff
4. To fulfill funding requirements

JUSTIFYING DECISIONS ALREADY MADE

WE SAID EARLIER that a common aim among agency administrators is to avoid offending people. In our opinion, there is no one on earth who is more politically correct than an agency's executive director. Indeed, in the present political climate where services to clients are increasingly community based, programs make it a priority to establish and maintain good relationships with community stakeholders. There are usually a large number of stakeholder groups, each with its own agenda, so maintaining good relationships with all of them requires a great deal of tact.

For example, mindful of the needs of its client group, the agency might propose to build a hospice for AIDS patients in a nearby residential area. The homeowners in the area object. In company with other public-spirited citizens, they approve of hospices for AIDS patients—and rehabilitation programs for young offenders, and homes for pregnant adolescents—but they don't want them in their own backyards. Sound familiar?

The agency, trapped between its duty to its clients and its duty to its neighbors, will go through the normal processes of convening meetings, establishing committees, collecting comments, and issuing reports. It's also quite likely that a research study will be commissioned into the advisability of building the hospice as proposed.

Again, the researchers need to be sensitive to the political currents both within and outside the agency setting. Probably some stakeholders have already decided that they want the hospice built and are looking to the research report to confirm this opinion. Other stakeholders will not want the hospice built in their neighborhood and also expect that the research report will support their position. Trapped, like the agency, between a rock and a hard place, the researchers will need to consider very carefully the uses that are likely to be made of their research results.

If the results will be used solely to justify a decision that has already been made on other grounds, then it's unethical to undertake the study. On the other hand, if it's possible that an objective, bias-free appraisal of the advantages and disadvantages of building the hospice will actually sway the decision, then the study should be done. The researchers must decide whether to undertake the study based on their judgment of the ethical and political factors involved.

SAFEGUARDING PUBLIC RELATIONS

ANOTHER OF THE WORRIES SHARED BY AGENCY ADMINISTRATORS is negative publicity. Perhaps a worker in a group home has been indicted for the sexual abuse of residents, or a foster parent has abused a child. These kinds of incidents inevitably attract intense media scrutiny, and it's tempting for administrators to immediately commission an evaluative study to investigate the problem, declining to comment until the research results become available.

Now, there's nothing wrong with an evaluative study. It may, indeed, be the best way to determine why the problem occurred and what can be done to prevent it from occurring again in the future. But if the sole purpose of the study is to delay comment until the furor has died down, then it's simply not ethical for a researcher to undertake the study. Neither is it ethical if there is an unspoken expectation that the researcher will discover only what the foster care program wants.

If parts of the report are taken out of context in order to show the program in a good light, or if the results are distorted to avoid public embarrassment, then the integrity of the study will obviously be compromised. In such a situation, the researcher will be at fault as well.

It used to be the case that researchers were not held responsible for the uses made of their study results and recommendations. Their jobs were merely to produce them. Now, however, it's considered essential for researchers to do the best they can to ensure that results are used in an ethical way.

APPRAISING STAFF PERFORMANCE

THE THIRD POSSIBLE MISUSE of research results is for performance appraisals. Again, there is nothing wrong with a performance appraisal. Most workers are required to undergo an annual evaluation of how well they performed during the previous year. However, a performance appraisal and a research study are two separate things.

For example, consider a research study designed to document overall client progress within a program by aggregating (or adding up) the progress made by the clients of each individual social worker. Before they are aggregated, the study results have the potential to demonstrate that the clients of one social worker made more progress overall than the clients of another. And this, in turn, may be taken to indicate that one social worker is more competent than the other.

In a study of this kind, it's unethical for researchers to release results before they have been aggregated—that is, before they are in a form that will protect the confidentiality of the social workers that participated in the study. In the event that they are prematurely released, it's certainly not ethical for administrators to use the information to appraise a particular social worker. Nevertheless, there have been instances when research results have been used for political purposes, to promote or undermine a specific worker or program, so researchers need to be wary of this.

FULFILLING FUNDING REQUIREMENTS

MOST EVALUATION STUDIES are used, at least in part, to demonstrate accountability to funders. Indeed, almost all social service programs, particularly new or pilot projects, are funded with the stipulation that they should be evaluated. It's not unethical, therefore, to use evaluation research to fulfill funding requirements. But it is unethical to use evaluation research solely to fulfill funding requirements without any real intention of using the information gathered to improve the program.

SUMMARY

THIS CHAPTER BRIEFLY looked at a few of the ethical factors that affect the social work research enterprise. You now know how research is used in social work (Chapter 1), how to formulate research questions through the literature (Chapters 2 and 3), and how to behave in an ethical manner when doing a research study (this chapter). You're now an ethical researcher who can formulate good social work research questions, but you need to be a culturally sensitive one as well—the topic of the next chapter.

	Study Questions for Chapter 4
	Essay — Discussion
1	List and discuss in detail the ethical issues that are involved in the early stages of doing a research or evaluation study. Provide one common social work example throughout your entire discussion.
2	1. What is informed consent? 2. Discuss why this is important in a research study. Provide examples.
3	1. What are consent forms? 2. Why are consent forms necessary when conducting a research study? 3. What are their ingredients? Provide as many examples as you can to justify your response. 4. Are there any other topics that you think should be included in a consent form that this chapter didn't cover? If so, what are they?
4	1. What are assent forms? 2. Why are assent forms necessary when conducting a research study? 3. What are their ingredients? Provide as many examples as you can to justify your response. 4. Are there any other topics that you think should be included in an assent form that this chapter didn't cover? If so, what are they?

5	What are the main differences between a consent form and an assent form? Discuss in detail.
6	1. What are bribery and deception? 2. When can you ethically bribe or deceive a research participant? Provide examples to illustrate your points.
7	What is the difference between anonymity and confidentiality? Provide as many examples as you can to justify your response.
8	Discuss the ethical issues that may arise in *Step 2* of the research process. Discuss them in detail and apply a social work example throughout.
9	Discuss the ethical issues that may arise in *Step 5* of the research process. Discuss them in detail and apply a social work example throughout.
10	Discuss the ethical issues that may arise in *Step 6* of the research process. Discuss them in detail and apply a social work example.
11	Discuss the ethical issues that may arise in *Step 7* of the research process. Discuss them in detail and apply a social work example throughout.
12	Discuss the ethical issues that may arise in *Step 8* of the research process. Discuss them in detail and apply a social work example.
13	Discuss the ethical issues that may arise in *Step 9* of the research process. Discuss them in detail and apply a social work example.
14	Discuss the ethical issues that may arise in *Step 10* of the research process. Discuss them in detail and apply a social work example throughout.

15	Discuss the ethical issues that may arise in *Step 11* of the research process. Discuss them in detail and apply a social work example throughout.
16	Discuss the ethical issues that surround the misuse of research results in relation to *justifying decisions already made.* Provide a social work example throughout your discussion.
17	Discuss the ethical issues that surround the misuse of research results in relation to *public relations.* Provide a social work example throughout your discussion.
18	Discuss the ethical issues that surround the misuse of research results in relation to *performance appraisals.* Provide a social work example throughout your discussion.
19	Discuss the ethical issues that surround the misuse of research results in relation to *fulfilling funding requirements.* Provide a social work example throughout your discussion.
20	1. In groups of four, create a hypothetical research study that would require the participation of social work clients. 2. Decide on the study's purpose and the research methodology. 3. Discuss how you would protect the participants from harm, ensure confidentiality, provide adequate information about the study, and encourage their voluntary participation. 4. Draft an informed consent statement. Read the statement to the class. (Use information from the entire chapter.)

Critical Thinking — Application — Integration

| 21 | **YOU'RE NOW AN ETHICAL RESEARCHER**
Background: Pretend for the moment you want to do a research study that describes the barriers that first-generation ethnic minority social work students face when they enter your social work program. |

1. Discuss how you will go about explicitly examining the theoretical framework that is the foundation of your research study with an ethical lens. Provide as many examples as you can to illustrate your points.

2. Discuss the ethical issues that you will have to deal with for each one of the eight steps of the research process that are discussed in this chapter (i.e., Steps 2, 5, 6, 7, 8, 9, 10, and 11). Be very specific and detail how you will address each ethical issue that you have identified within each step.

22

PRACTICE VS. RESEARCH

Practice: Pretend for the moment you're employed as a social worker in your university's student counseling center. A first-generation ethnic minority student comes into your office where she tells you she feels lonely and isolated and wants to go home and drop out of school.

1. Using this chapter as a guide, describe in detail how you would use the chapter's contents to help you establish a worker/client relationship with her when it comes to becoming an ethically sensitive **practitioner.**

Research: Let's suppose that now you want to do a research study that will try to find out what factors are involved that make first-generation ethnic minority students at your university feel lonely and isolated.

2. Using this chapter as a guide, describe in detail how you would use the chapter's contents to help you in your research study when it comes to becoming an ethically sensitive social work **researcher.**

NOTE: This exercise should help you to realize that social work practitioners and researchers have to be ethically accountable when working with clients (practice) and research participants (research) alike.

23

ETHICS AND THE PRACTITIONER

Scenario 1: Make an argument that to be an effective evidence-based social work practitioner **you must be** ethically sensitive to your clients' needs. Provide a clear and explicit **practice-related** social work example to illustrate your main points.

Scenario 2: Make an argument that **you do not have to be** ethically sensitive to be an effective evidence-based practitioner. Provide a clear and explicit **practice-related** social work example to illustrate your main points.

Time to Choose: Which one of the above two scenarios do you feel is more consistent with the concept of the contemporary evidence-based social work practice process as illustrated on pages 46–51? Why? Provide relevant social work examples to illustrate your main points.

24	**ETHICS AND THE RESEARCHER** **Scenario 1:** Make an argument that to be an effective social work researcher **you must be** ethically sensitive to your study's population. Provide a clear and explicit **research-related** social work example to illustrate your main points. **Scenario 2:** Make an argument that to be an effective social work researcher **you do not have to be** ethically sensitive to your study's population. Provide a clear and explicit **research-related** social work example to illustrate your main points. **Time to Choose:** Which of the above two scenarios do you feel is more consistent with the place of research in social work? Why? Provide relevant social work examples to illustrate your main points.
25	**TIME TO PUT ON YOUR CRITICAL THINKING HAT** 1. Discuss the similarities and differences between your responses to Questions 23 and 24. 2. What are your thoughts on the belief that you will need to function in an ethical manner whether you're a social work *practitioner* (Question 23) or a social work *researcher* (Question 24)? **NOTE:** This exercise should help you to understand that the skills you draw upon to become an ethical researcher are the same skills you will need in practice situations as well. In short, you can use this chapter to help you become more ethically aware in your day-to-day practice activities with all your client systems.

26	**ETHICS AND YOUR PROFESSIONAL DEVELOPMENT** 1. Review the three social work research-related roles you can take when you graduate—CSWE Competency 1 at the beginning of this chapter on page 124 (also discussed in Chapter 1 on pages 38–42). Thoroughly discuss how you feel this chapter will help you to perform one or more research-related roles when you graduate. Which one of the three roles do you believe this chapter helped you with the most? Why? Discuss in detail and provide an example to illustrate your main points. 2. Review CSWE Competency 4 at the beginning of this chapter on page 124. Thoroughly discuss how you feel this chapter will help you to become a practice-informed researcher and a research-informed practitioner. Discuss in detail and provide an example to illustrate your main points. 3. Review the evidence-based practice process as illustrated on pages 46–51. Thoroughly discuss how this chapter helps you to develop the skills you'll need for implementing one or more steps of the evidence-based practice process. 4. Discuss which step(s) you feel this chapter will help you with the most. Why? Be very specific and use relevant social work examples to illustrate your main points throughout your discussion. **NOTE:** This exercise should help you to understand that the skills you draw upon to become an ethical researcher are the same skills you will need in practice situations as well. In short, you can use this chapter to help you become more "ethically aware" in your day-to-day practice activities with all your client systems.
27	**MOVING AHEAD BY LOOKING BACK** At this point in your research methods course, how comfortable are you with discussing the place of research in social work with your field instructor, with your practice instructor, with your research instructor, with your supervisor at work, with the director of your social work program, or with your classmates? Discuss in detail.

5

CHAPTER

COMPETENCY 1: Demonstrate Ethical and Professional Behavior

You will learn that in order to be a successful evidence-based practitioner you have an ethical obligation to integrate three research roles into your daily practice activities as discussed in Chapter 1: (1) research consumer, (2) research partner—either as a co-researcher or research participant, and (3) creator and disseminator of research (or knowledge).

This entire chapter pertains to these three professional roles when it comes to becoming a culturally competent practitioner (**research consumer**) and a culturally competent researcher (**research partner** and **creator and disseminator of research**).

COMPETENCY 4: Engage in Practice-Informed Research and Research-Informed Practice

Competency 4 also pertains to the entire chapter because you have to:

1. Evaluate the overall degree to which a social work research study was culturally sensitive, given the needs of the study's specific population or research participants (**research consumer**—research-informed practice);

2. Participate in a research study—either as a co-researcher or research participant (**research partner**—practice-informed research). See 1 above and 3 below; and

3. Know how to become a culturally competent social work researcher before you actually do a research study (**creator and disseminator of research**—practice-informed research).

You also need to utilize evidence-based practice recommendations whenever possible; that is, you need to integrate (1) the best available research-based evidence with (2) your clinical expertise and (3) your client's values.

All of the above implies you'll need to know how to assess the overall cultural competency level of a research study that produced its culturally competent research-based evidence. In short, you'll need to ask and then answer a simple question: How seriously should I take the findings of any specific research study given how well it addressed the various cultural competency issues throughout the entire research process?

COMPETENCY 9: Evaluate Practice with Individuals, Families, Groups, Organizations, and Communities
See Competencies 1 and 4.

5

Culturally Competent Research

CHAPTER 1   **Step 1.** Understanding the Research Process

CHAPTER 2   **Step 2.** Developing Research Questions

CHAPTER 3   **Step 3.** Reviewing the Literature

CHAPTERS 4 & 5   **Step 4.** Being Aware of Ethical and Cultural Issues

CHAPTERS 6–8   **Step 5.** Selecting a Research Approach

CHAPTERS 9 & 10   **Step 6.** Specifying How Variables Are Measured

CHAPTER 11   **Step 7.** Selecting a Sample

CHAPTERS 12 & 13   **Step 8.** Selecting a Research Design

CHAPTERS 14–16   **Step 9.** Selecting a Data-Collection Method

CHAPTERS 17 & 18   **Step 10.** Analyzing the Data

CHAPTERS 19 & 20   **Step 11.** Writing the Research Report

YOU NOW KNOW HOW THE RESEARCH PROCESS IS USED in our profession (Chapter 1), how to formulate research problems through the literature (Chapters 2 and 3), and how to abide by ethical principles when doing research studies (Chapter 4). Using the four previous chapters as background, this chapter explores basic culture issues that also need to be taken into account when doing a social work research study. As you know from reading the previous chapter on ethics, many cultural and ethical issues are highly intertwined.

This chapter is a logical extension of the previous one in that we provide a brief overview of culture and cultural competence, followed by a discussion of key issues in culturally competent research practices. As the issues are discussed, we make use of examples of worldview perceptions, communications, and behaviors that may be characteristic of particular cultures. These are intended only as examples of cultural patterns and not to suggest that any characteristics describe all members of the group.

We fully recognize that cultures are not monolithic and that a variety of cultural patterns may exist within broadly defined cultural groups. The descriptions provided within this chapter are for illustrative purposes only and are not meant to be stereotypical of the members of any culture.

We also know that each individual is unique, and we recognize that within any culture a wide range of individual perceptions, communications, and behaviors may exist. In social work research, as in any other human interactive process, there is no substitute for meeting each person with openness and acceptance, regardless of cultural background.

OUR VILLAGE

OUR VILLAGE HAS GROWN to encompass the world. Faster means of transportation (e.g., air travel) and communication (e.g., Internet, social media), the expansion of trade, and the human desire to seek a better life have created societies that no longer find their roots in one cultural tradition or their voice in one common language. Rather, migration trends and globalization activities have laid the foundations for complex, culturally diverse societies with representation from several racial, ethnic, and cultural groups.

Diversity is reflected throughout our society: in schools, in the workplace, and within all types of formal and informal organizations. Social service organizations are no exception; there is increasing diversity both among staff and also among service recipients. Of course, diversity also has an impact on social work research; the challenge for researchers is to work effectively in culturally diverse settings.

> In social work research, as in any other human interactive process, there is no substitute for meeting each person with openness and acceptance, regardless of cultural backaround.

WORKING WITH STAKEHOLDERS OR RESEARCH TEAMS

AS IS MADE CLEAR THROUGHOUT THIS BOOK, doing a research study is more than the technical practice of formulating research questions, organizing and implementing data collection activities, analyzing data, and reporting findings. Although these are important research activities, researchers also need to work effectively with a variety of stakeholders or research teams in a wide range of organizations. The tasks include working with research teams to clarify expectations, identify interests, reconcile differences, and win cooperation.

You must therefore be adept at establishing interpersonal and working relationships in addition to bringing technical expertise to the research process. When working with different cultural groups or in different cultural settings, you must be culturally competent and also have the ability to adapt the technical aspects of the research procedures so that they are appropriate for your specific research setting and research participants alike. To achieve community involvement with a lens toward culturally sensitivity, the following questions should be considered when forming a research team that will guide you through your study:

— What history (e.g., prior practice and research, knowledge of group and/or community) does the research team have with the racial/ethnic group members included in your study?

— What efforts have been made to ensure the inclusion of the perspective of racial/ethnic group members in the design, conduct, and analysis of the study?

— What is the race/ethnicity of the research team, including the principal investigator, consultants, data collectors, and coders?

— Have potential biases of research team members been recognized?

— What efforts have been made to counter potential biases of the research team in working with racial/ethnic minority groups?

It's not necessary for the researcher to be a member of the racial/ethnic group being studied, but achieving culturally competent research knowledge of the community is crucial. Cross-cultural research is strengthened when researchers study the beliefs, values, and social structures that form the context of the participants' worldview and when they incorporate that knowledge into the design and conduct of their studies.

BOX 5.1	**Some Important Things to Consider When Doing Cross-Cultural Research**

— How ethnic and cultural groups are defined has been a source of confusion and, often, inaccurate representation of cultural and ethnic groups in research.

— Many factors have adversely influenced cultural research. These include racism, homophobia, and gender bias. Research with cultural groups tends to be pathology-based as a result of the cultural biases toward some groups.

— The monolithic perspective—the assumption that cultural groups are homogenous—has hampered research with cultural groups. Overgeneralizations related to the monolithic perspective have led to increased stigma and stereotyping of some ethnic groups.

— Within- and between-group comparisons are difficult when examining ethnic groups. Inadequate definitions of populations render much of what we consider ethnic research marginally useful.

— The role of socioeconomic factors and ethnic group functioning has not received sufficient attention in research. Members of ethnic and cultural groups experience more economic and social disadvantage than European Americans.

— Obtaining adequate samples remains problematic in cultural and ethnic research. Mistrust of investigators, lack of meaningful incentives for participants, fear of negative reception by researchers, and economic hardship create participant barriers in cultural and ethnic research.

— Faulty research methodology and design has further blurred perception of ethnic groups. Research methods emphasizing the strengths of ethnic groups are rare.

— The use of standardized instruments when evaluating diverse groups is also problematic. Sometimes findings are invalid because measurement instruments have not been normed for use with ethnic and cultural groups.

— Publication in mainstream journals can be difficult. Research that challenges widely held views of cultural groups may be rejected by major journals. Much of the best cultural research is published in second- and third-tier journals. This limits the dissemination of important works.

— Academic institutions need to refine cultural education. While there have been some advances, the language used to describe cultural groups and the scope of educational material require expansion and refinement.

— Ethical considerations are also important. Participant rights, such as confidentiality and informed consent, are vital if we are to increase ethnic participation in research. The introduction of Internet technology to research also requires strict adherence to ethical guidelines.

— Increasing ethnic participation in research is a continuing struggle. However, when a strengths-based approach is used, there is greater likelihood that members of ethnic groups will participate.

— Ethnic research should have, as its primary concern, an agenda of improving the social, political, emotional, and economic conditions for members of ethnic communities. To improve the lives of ethnic groups, research must address the social, political, and economic factors that create and maintain disadvantage for some ethnic groups.

THE IMPACT OF CULTURE

CULTURE IS MANY THINGS: a set of customs, traditions, and beliefs, and a worldview. It's socially defined and passed on from generation to generation (Porter & Samovar, 2006; Thomas & Inkson, 2009). Culture is manifested in the perceptions through which we view our surroundings and the patterns of language and behavior through which we interact with others. Culture exists at two levels:

— **Micro-level.** Micro-level culture is found with individuals and is reflected in their personal values, beliefs, communication styles, and behaviors.

— **Macro-level.** Macro-level culture exists within organizations, institutions, and communities; it's manifested in mandates, policies, and practices.

Fundamentally, culture acts as a filter through which people view, perceive, and evaluate the world around them. At the same time, it also provides a framework within which people process information, think, communicate, and behave. Because different cultures establish different frameworks for perceiving and judging as well as for thinking and acting, misperceptions, miscommunications, and conflicts are not only possible but also likely. Where people are unaware of how culture filters thinking, actions, perceptions, and judgments, the likelihood for misunderstanding is even greater.

The Japanese, for example, have traditionally used bowing as a form of greeting, but in North America handshakes are prevalent; in certain European countries, hugging and kissing are customary. It's easy to see that what is meant as a friendly gesture in one culture may be viewed as an intrusion in another. In a meeting, for example, a statement that is meant as a hypothetical example in one culture may be viewed as a firm commitment in another.

Unless you sit at the table and know the rules the group operates by, you could develop a research study that misses the point. You need to start off with a model that is culturally informed in order to come up with data and meaningful recommendations that will be helpful and relevant to the community you are working in.

In North America, for example, there is considerable emphasis on the "bottom line," which may translate to outcomes in a positivistic research study. Thus, social work evaluations are often concerned with assessing the outcomes of a social service program. In some cultures, however, the fact that a program has been created and now operates and provides employment for community members may be viewed as at least as important as the actual results of the social services it delivers.

BRIDGING THE CULTURE GAP

UNDER THE PRINCIPLE "RESPECT FOR PEOPLE," as set out by the American Evaluation Association (2004), researchers are expected to be aware of—and respect differences among—people and to be mindful of the implications of cultural differences on the research or evaluation processes. Social work researchers thus need:

1. A clear understanding of the impact of culture on human and social processes generally and on evaluation processes specifically (Cultural awareness)

2. Skills in cross-cultural communication to ensure that they can effectively interact with people from diverse backgrounds (Intercultural communication)

CULTURAL AWARENESS

AS THE PREVIOUS DISCUSSION MAKES CLEAR, culture provides a powerful organizing framework that filters perceptions and communications and also shapes behaviors and interactions. To practice effectively in different cultural settings, researchers need a general awareness of the role that culture plays in shaping our perceptions, ideas, and behaviors.

Further, we need fundamental attitudes of respect for difference, a willingness to learn about other cultures, and a genuine belief that cultural differences are a source of strength and enrichment rather than an obstacle to be overcome. In particular, social work researchers need cultural awareness: they need to be on guard that their perceptions, communications, and actions are not unduly influenced by ethnocentrism, enculturation, and stereotyping—processes that act as barriers to effective communication and relationships. The term *cultural awareness* contains two overlapping concepts:

1. Ethnocentrism
2. Enculturation

ETHNOCENTRISM

BECAUSE OUR OWN HISTORY is inevitably based in our own culture, and because we generally continue to be immersed in that culture, a natural human tendency is to judge others and other cultures by the standards of our own beliefs and values. This is known as *ethnocentrism,* and it leads to defining the world in our own terms. Thus, we might tend to view as normal that which is typical in our own culture; the different practices, structures, or patterns that may be typical in other cultures are likely then to be viewed as "abnormal" or even problematic (Neuliep, 2000).

> Ethnocentrism is defining the world in our own terms.

Among some social groups, for example, child rearing is viewed as a community responsibility, with extended family and other community members taking an active role when necessary. This is seldom typical in urban North American culture, where high mobility often places families in communities without extended family or other support networks.

Thus, in a large urban setting, an appropriate outcome for family support programs may be that the family remains intact, but in communities located in rural or remote areas or on Native American reservations, a more appropriate outcome might be that suitable caregiving arrangements are identified within the family's kinship or community network. An ethnocentric researcher might unwittingly apply mainstream North American values to a Native American family support program, which would clearly result in a distortion in the evaluation process.

ENCULTURATION

***ENCULTURATION* IS A CLOSE COUSIN TO ETHNOCENTRISM.** It's a related process, which refers to the fact that, as children, we learn to behave in ways that are appropriate to our culture. We also come to adopt a variety of core beliefs about human nature, human experience, and human behavior.

This process teaches us how to behave, interact, and even think. Of course, other cultural groups will have different ways of thinking, behaving, and interacting. In some Asian cultures, for example, people value discussion, negotiation, and relationship, whereas in North America, people tend to be more direct and task-oriented (Hall, 1983). Similarly, some cultures such as the Swiss and Germans emphasize promptness,

> Enculturation refers to the fact that, as children, we learn to behave in ways that are appropriate to our culture.

whereas in some Southern U.S. cultures, a meeting is seldom expected to start at the appointed time, but only after everyone has arrived (Lewis, 1997).

The differences in behavior patterns and interactions are real; however, it's important for researchers to recognize that others' patterns are as legitimate and appropriate as their own. When we are unable to do this, stereotyping may occur, resulting in misunderstanding and misjudgment.

For example, a social work researcher may become frustrated because it's difficult to start meetings on time in a community or because it's not possible to keep to a tight schedule, and she may begin to stereotype the group she is working with as uninterested, uncooperative, and disorganized. Obviously, such stereotypes will have the effect of creating additional barriers to communications and interactions and will hinder the research process.

INTERCULTURAL COMMUNICATION

AWARENESS OF THE IMPACT OF CULTURE is important, but effective relationships depend on the actual communications. Because social work research is as much a relationship process as a technical matter, effective communication is always important, particularly so in communication across cultures.

There are many models of intercultural communication. One of the more useful ones is offered by Porter and Samovar (2006). In this model, perceptions are regarded as the gateway to communication; they are the means by which people select, evaluate, and organize information about the world around them.

Perceptions, of course, depend in large part upon an individual's worldview, which is, in part, formed as a result of his or her cultural experiences. Perceptions help us select, organize, and interpret a variety of external stimuli, including the communications that others direct toward us.

After we process the communications that are directed toward us, we usually respond. Different cultures support different communication patterns and styles, and thus our response is also shaped and formed, at least in part, by our cultural background. Communications, then, are inextricably bound with culture. The opportunity for misunderstanding, ever present in any communication, is even greater when individuals from different cultural backgrounds interact.

Intercultural communication takes place at both the nonverbal and verbal levels. Anyone who interacts with members of another culture needs an understanding of both nonverbal and verbal communication patterns typical in that culture. We will briefly look at communication at each of these levels:

1. Nonverbal communication
2. Verbal communication

NONVERBAL COMMUNICATION

AN IMPORTANT PART OF HUMAN COMMUNICATION takes place nonverbally. Facial expressions, time, use of space, and gestures convey much information and are deeply based in culture. Without an understanding of the meaning of nonverbal communication symbols used by a culture, it's all too easy to misinterpret signs.

A hand gesture that has virtually no meaning in one culture can easily be a vulgar symbol in another culture. For example, the OK sign, widely used in North America, is a circle formed by the thumb and the first finger; this sign is considered to be offensive and unacceptable in Brazil, and to mean money in Japan (Morrison, Conway, & Borden, 1994).

One's physical position in relation to another person may result in an inadvertent message of disinterest or aggression. North Americans usually feel comfortable standing at a distance of about two and a half to four feet from others. However, members of some cultures, among them Arabic societies, prefer to stand much closer when engaged in conversations (Hall, 1983). Researchers who position themselves at a North American distance may be perceived as cold, aloof, and uninterested by members of such cultures.

Similarly, the use of eye contact carries culturally specific meaning. In European-based cultures, eye contact is used extensively to demonstrate interest and to confirm that one is listening. Many other cultures, however, do not use eye contact extensively and may perceive it as disrespectful and even threatening. For example, prolonged eye contact in Japanese is considered to be rude (Samovar, Porter, & Stefani, 1998).

VERBAL COMMUNICATION

ON THE VERBAL LEVEL, words also derive much of their meaning through culture. As language is the primary means through which a culture communicates its values and beliefs, the same words may have different meanings within different cultures.

For example, the Japanese use the word *hai,* meaning "yes," to indicate that they have heard what was said and are thinking about a response. Because, in many circumstances, it's considered impolite to openly express disagreement, *hai* is used even when the listener actually disagrees with what is being said (Koyama, 1992). Thus, the meaning assigned to "yes" is quite different than that commonly understood by North Americans, who consider "yes" to mean that the listener is in agreement.

The social work research process uses an extensive transmission of information through communications. Thus, it's vital that verbal communications be accurate and effective. Without an understanding of intercultural communication generally and an ability to understand the specific patterns used by the group with whom the researcher is dealing, communication problems may arise and derail the research process.

CULTURAL FRAMEWORKS

AS WE HAVE SEEN, culture often defines a group's values and beliefs, and creates its communication patterns. In addition, culture also provides frameworks for other complex structures and processes. Different cultural groups have different methods of gathering data and of making decisions. An understanding of these patterns is essential to ensure that data collection and analytical processes are appropriate and final research reports are practical and relevant. We will now briefly discuss the following cultural frameworks:

1. Orientation to data
2. Decision making
3. Individualism
4. Tradition
5. Pace of life (and concepts of time)

ORIENTATION TO DATA

SOME CULTURES THRIVE on "hard data" and greatly value processes, such as research studies, that produce data that can then be considered and acted upon (Lewis, 1997; Thomas & Inkson, 2009). These cultures, which include the North American mainstream culture, are considered data oriented.

On the other hand, some cultures such as Middle Eastern and Latin American cultures are viewed as "dialogue oriented," in that they pay more attention to relationships and process than to data (Lewis, 1997). These groups tend to view statistics and data with some suspicion and regard them as only part of a picture. Such cultures consider relationships and context to be more important than numbers.

DECISION MAKING

IN MANY WESTERN CULTURES, logic and rationality are highly valued and used extensively in making decisions about important matters (Hoefstede, 1997; Lewis, 1997). The quantitative (positivistic) research approach (Chapter 6) is an example of this style of "scientific" thinking. However, some cultures are less impressed by "hard science" and prefer a softer, more personal approach to knowledge development, often called the qualitative (interpretive) research approach (Chapter 7).

When researchers prepare a report for people whose culture supports a scientific orientation to thinking, quantitative data with statistical analyses are quite appropriate; however, if the users are people who come from a culture that prefers more subjective and intuitive approaches to decision making, a report organized around the presentation of strictly quantitative results can easily become useless and/or incomprehensible.

INDIVIDUALISM

ALTHOUGH MOST CULTURES support both individualistic and collectivistic tendencies, there is in every culture a bias toward one or the other (Hoefstede, 1997). In individualistic cultures, such as the mainstream North American culture, people work toward individual goals and achievement.

In collectivistic cultures, people are group oriented; loyalty, relation-ships, and overall community development are valued while individual goals are downplayed. In such cultures, the family, organizations with which peo-ple are affiliated (including the workplace), and the community are particu-larly important.

BOX 5.2	Guiding Principles for Multicultural Evaluation

INCLUSION IN DESIGN AND IMPLEMENTATION

— Multicultural evaluation is not imposed on diverse communities; communities understand and support the rationale for the research and agree with the methods used to answer key evaluation questions.

— Diverse beneficiary stakeholders are actively involved in all phases of the evaluation, including problem definition, development of research questions, methods chosen, data collection, analysis, and reporting.

— To the extent possible, multicultural evaluation empowers diverse communities to do self-evaluation through intentional capacity building in evaluation.

ACKNOWLEDGMENT/INFUSION OF MULTIPLE WORLDVIEWS

— Evaluators in multicultural evaluations have a genuine respect for the communities being studied and seek a deep understanding of different cultural contexts, practices, and paradigms of thinking.

— "Expert" knowledge does not exclusively reside with the evaluator; the grantee and/or community being studied is assumed to know best their issues, strengths, and challenges.

— The diversity of communities studied is represented in multicultural evaluation staffing and expertise whenever possible.

APPROPRIATE MEASURES OF SUCCESS

— Measures of success in multicultural evaluations are discussed and/or collaboratively developed with those being evaluated.

— Data-collection instruments and outcome measures are tested for multicultural validity across populations that may not speak English, may be less literate, or may be from a different culture.

— Multicultural evaluation data-collection methods and instruments accommodate different cultural contexts and consider alternative or nontraditional ways of collecting data.

CULTURAL AND SYSTEMS ANALYSIS

— Multicultural evaluations take into account how historical and current social systems, institutions, and societal norms contribute to power and outcome disparities across different racial and ethnic communities.

— Multicultural evaluations incorporate and trace the impacts of factors related to racial, cultural, gender, religious, economic, and other differences.

— Multicultural evaluation questions take a multiple-level approach to understanding root causes and impact at the individual, interpersonal, institutional, cultural, system, and policy level rather than focusing the analysis solely on individual behavior.

RELEVANCE TO DIVERSE COMMUNITIES

— Multicultural evaluations inform community decision-making and program design.

— Findings from multicultural evaluations are co-owned with diverse communities and shared in culturally appropriate ways.

Keeping in perspective an organization's cultural view on individualism versus collectivism is important in understanding the behaviors, interactions, work processes, and structures that may be found in the course of a research or evaluation study. What may appear from an individualistic perspective to be an unwieldy work processes involving too many people may, in fact, be explained by a culture-based desire not to leave anyone out and to create as wide a network of involvement as possible.

TRADITION

SOME CULTURES ARE MORE TRADITIONAL and value the status quo and conformity while others encourage innovation and view change as necessary if progress is to be made (Dodd, 1998). Change-oriented cultures such as mainstream North American society encourage experimentation, risk taking, and innovation. They consider change to be an opportunity to improve.

In other cultures, such as some traditional Asian cultures, values are centered on tradition and continuity. The young are expected to give way to the wishes of the older generation, and new ideas are not encouraged because they might disrupt the structure of society.

You should readily recognize that the research process, as a change- and improvement-oriented activity, is grounded in Western cultural values. As such, the concept of "research" itself may seem alien to those steeped in more traditional cultures. After all, research and evaluations are concerned with identifying areas for improvement, which therefore implies change, but traditional cultures value stability and continuity.

Inevitably, social work researchers will sometimes work with organizations that are based in a tradition-oriented culture. In such circumstances, we need to be sensitive to the fact that there may not exist a common understanding even about the basic premises of the research processes.

PACE OF LIFE

IN NORTH AMERICA, especially in larger cities, we live our lives at an accelerated pace. Our schedules are jammed with many activities; agendas are overloaded, and there is an expectation that everything is a priority and must be done immediately. Time is viewed as linear and rigid; we live with the sense that if we miss an event it's forever gone. In such cultures, which are called *monochronic,* people tend to organize their lives by the clock (Hall, 1983).

Clearly, in such cultures it's important to be on time for meetings, to meet deadlines, and to stay on schedule (Cooper, Calloway-Thomas, & Simonds, 2007; Samovar, Porter, & Stefani, 1998). In a sense, time is so central that members of the culture are hardly aware of its importance, but all things, including personal relationships, take second place to successful time management.

On the other hand, in polychronic cultures life is lived at a slower pace; activities grind to a halt on weekends, during rest times, and during festivals and important celebrations. Slower-paced cultures—for example, those in Latin America, the Middle East, and Indonesia—tend to be less aware of time and hold less of a concept of it as a commodity that must be managed.

Time may be seen as circular and flexible; the Indonesians even refer to it as "rubber time" (Harris & Moran, 1996). In polychronic cultures, time is not nearly as important an organizing force in people's lives as it is in monochronic cultures; if the scheduled start time passes without the event taking place, people are not unduly disturbed as another appropriate start time can be set.

"Time is money" could not have arisen as a central idea in these cultures, which focus on relationships and interactions. Time management and business come second in such cultures (Hall, 1983); rather, it's vital to establish a personal relationship before conducting business.

Obviously, researchers need to have a good understanding of the concept of time that is held within the setting where they conduct their work. Tight schedules that provide few opportunities for cementing working relationships and that disregard widely observed rest periods, holidays, and celebrations are obviously unrealistic and will be unsuitable in polychronic cultures. Attempting to impose such a schedule will be regarded as thoughtless and will impede rather than facilitate the research process.

Further, in assessing the achievement of milestones and other accomplishments, we need to take into account the concept of time and the pace of life prevalent in the particular culture. In setting up a new social service program, for example, planning, procedure, policy development, initial staffing, and other preparatory activities may be accomplished in a much briefer period of time in one setting than in another. Both the concepts of time and the pace of life might be, in fact, equally appropriate when the cultural orientation toward time is taken into account.

CULTURALLY COMPETENT RESEARCHERS

ALTHOUGH SOME RESEARCHERS come from minority backgrounds, many do bring a mainstream North American cultural orientation to their work. This orientation will result in part from their own cultural background and in part from their formation and education as researchers.

The methods of social work research are, to a large degree, based in a Western or North American cultural tradition. Inevitably, researchers will bring their own culturally based beliefs, values, and perspectives as well as their culturally based toolkit to their work.

More and more research studies are conducted in settings that are culturally different from mainstream North American culture. Research studies are conducted on reservations, at women's shelters, in organizations serving immigrants, and at agencies that grew from the needs and aspirations of minority communities and reflect the cultures of those communities.

Those of us, who undertake a research study in a culturally different setting, or among people from different cultural backgrounds, require the skills to effectively conduct the work and to make the research process more meaningful within those settings. The essential competencies for a researcher to be culturally sensitive are:

1. Cultural awareness
2. Intercultural communication skills
3. Specific knowledge about the culture in which we hope to work
4. An ability to appropriately adapt evaluation methods and processes

CULTURAL AWARENESS

TO BE EFFECTIVE IN INTERCULTURAL WORK, social work researchers need a degree of cultural awareness that provides them with an understanding of the impact of culture on all human values, attitudes, and behaviors as well as interactions and processes. They need to understand how culture filters communications and how the research process itself is a culture-based activity. Further, we should have an understanding of concepts such as ethnocentrism, enculturation, and stereotyping—all of which may subtly, or not so subtly, raise barriers to effective communication and relationships.

In addition, we need to bring attitudes of openness and acceptance to our work as well as a genuine belief that cultural differences need not pose barriers but rather can strengthen and enrich the research process. Researchers who wish to practice in diverse settings also need a high degree of self-awareness as well as an understanding of their own cultural values and experiences, and the impact of these values and experiences on their communication patterns, relationships, and professional work.

Cultural awareness increases through contact with other cultures and through experiencing differences. Traveling, working in culturally different settings, and living in diverse communities are ways that you can develop your awareness and attitudes.

INTERCULTURAL COMMUNICATION SKILLS

THE ABILITY TO APPROACH OTHERS with openness and acceptance is foundational to effective communication, regardless of setting; in intercultural communication, it's particularly important. However, effective intercultural communication also requires specific knowledge of the other culture and its communication symbols.

As we now know, the meaning of nonverbal or verbal symbols is culturally defined. It's therefore important to know the meaning of common nonverbal and verbal communication symbols to ensure accuracy in both the transmission and the reception of messages.

Social work researchers can prepare for their work by reading novels set in the culture, watching high-quality movies, and perusing books and guides that describe prevailing communication patterns. The use of cultural guides, discussed in the following section, is also helpful in learning to understand the meaning of common communication symbols.

SPECIFIC KNOWLEDGE ABOUT THE CULTURE

IN THE PREVIOUS SECTION, the importance of developing specific understandings about prevailing communication patterns in a specific culture was discussed. However, a researcher who wishes to be effective in a culturally different setting must understand more than communication patterns. Specific knowledge about various details of the culture is important to ensure that effective relationships can be established, that the work is planned in a realistic manner, and that the resulting products will have utility.

Among other things, it's important to have some sense of the history of the group who comprise the culture in which the research study will be conducted. On Native American reservations, for example, the history of oppression and dislocation is vitally important and has framed their values, attitudes, and beliefs. Among certain immigrant groups, escape from oppression is a dominant theme, and an emphasis on newly found freedoms and opportunities frames these individualistic and achievement-oriented cultures.

Beyond history, the specific values, beliefs, and perspectives that shape individuals' and groups' perceptions and communications are vital to understand, as are the cultural structures, processes, and frameworks that are characteristic of the group. For example, in working with Native American groups on reservations, it's customary to include elders on advisory committees and to listen with respect to the ideas and opinions that they express.

Concepts of time have been discussed previously; it's sufficient to say that the scheduled starting time for meetings may or may not be firmly fixed, depending on the setting. Meetings on reservations may begin with a prayer to the Creator rather than a review of the agenda as is the case in most Western-oriented institutions.

There are numerous other details about a culture that are important to understand if we wish work successfully in any research setting. For example, one of the authors of this book conducted an evaluation on a reservation and had the opportunity to observe restorative justice circles in action. The program had been conceived carefully with extensive use of traditional symbols. One of these symbols was the circle itself, which symbolized a teepee; a convention had developed over time that participants entered and left the circle in one particular place, which symbolized the entry to the teepee.

Entering or leaving the circle in any other place was regarded as the equivalent of walking through the walls of the teepee. Of course, a social work researcher coming from the outside would not have been aware of this and would inevitably have committed a cultural faux pas. Happily, the researcher's team included a member from the community itself, who served as a cultural guide and briefed the researcher on the meaning of the cultural symbols involved as well as the appropriate behaviors.

In general, specific cultural knowledge can be obtained through the same methods as suggested for understanding the specifics of communication patterns: travel, reading guidebooks and histories by writers from the culture, and watching movies. Engaging collaborators from within the cultural group, even if not from within the organization itself, is perhaps the most effective way of learning about values, beliefs, traditions, behavior patterns, and the detailed texture of another culture.

APPROPRIATELY ADAPTING RESEARCH STUDIES

DEVELOPING CULTURAL AWARENESS, intercultural communication skills, and specific knowledge of the culture of the group with which researchers are involved is foundational to conducting effective research studies. The final set of skills involves adapting the research process so that it will be appropriate and meaningful within the culture of the organization where the study is being conducted. Adapting research studies involves:

1. Working with stakeholders
2. Ensuring that the work processes are appropriate
3. Ensuring that the products are meaningful

WORKING WITH STAKEHOLDERS

AS DISCUSSED THROUGHOUT THIS BOOK, a variety of groups—including funders, staff members, program participants, and community members—may have an interest in how a social work research study is done and, consequently, in the final results. Different groups of stakeholders are likely to have different interests, and this will particularly be true in the case of conducting evaluations in settings with culturally different stakeholders.

Generally, funders represent powerful institutions such as governments and foundations within mainstream society. They will therefore articulate their interests from a North American or Western cultural perspective. For example, funders for a social service program will likely be interested in data that shed light on the extent to which the program is delivering the services that had been contracted and with what effect. Further, they will prefer to have the data packaged as a formal report, replete with quantitative data and statistics as well as specific recommendations for improvement.

On the other hand, if the setting is based in a different culture, staff members, service recipients, and community members may be more interested in understanding the role that the program is playing within the community. If they come from a dialogue-oriented culture, they may be interested in descriptions of the service process and the service recipients' stories about their experiences with the service and its impact on their families. They will be looking not so much to receive data for the purpose of making changes but rather to develop a broader and deeper understanding of the program and its place in the community.

Researchers need to work at understanding each stakeholder group's perspectives, expectations, and interests and to realize that these may be fundamentally different from one another. A culturally competent researcher must be committed to accommodating the different perspectives and interests of the diverse stakeholders within the research process.

ADAPTING PROCESSES

A PROGRAM EVALUATION, for example, always involves obtaining the cooperation of staff members and other stakeholder groups in carrying out the required research procedures—particularly for the data collection system. The effectiveness of such a system depends on staff members carrying out their assigned roles in the research process in a knowledgeable and consistent manner. It's therefore very important that the work processes be designed so that they are congruent with the culture within the organization.

For example, we need to take into account the cultural meaning of time in the organization. If the organization is polychronic and operates at a relatively relaxed pace, the scheduling of research activities such as data collection must take this into account. A schedule that is appropriate in an organization that operates from a monochronic cultural perspective may be totally unfeasible within a polychronic culture. Attempting to impose such a schedule will likely create tensions and stresses: at best, it may result in an inconsistent implementation of the research activities; at worst, the entire research study may be discredited and collapse.

It's thus important that we design work processes in a manner that is congruent with the cultural meaning of time. Scheduling should take into account the concept of time and orientation to time so as not to impose a burden that would be regarded by the culture as unduly stressful or inappropriate. The process should ensure that holidays, community celebrations, and festivals are taken into account when setting schedules.

Similarly, data collection activities need to take into account both the cultural orientation of the staff members who are likely to collect the data and the research recipients who are likely to provide the data. In dialogue-oriented cultures, the collection of highly quantitative data involving the use of standardized measures, rating scales, and structured surveys may be inappropriate and result in inconsistent data collection at best.

At worst, research participants and staff members will go through the motions of providing and collecting data without really understanding why the data are needed or how they are to be used. The reliability and validity of such data, of course, are likely to be low, compromising the entire research effort.

Data collection protocols and procedures need to take into account whether research participants are oriented to "data" or "dialogue" and should be designed to be as meaningful and culturally appropriate as possible. In dialogue-oriented cultures, it may not be entirely possible or advisable to avoid the collection of quantitative data, but such data collection methods should be used sparingly. Ample explanations and support should also be provided to research participants so that they can find meaning in these tasks and carry them out effectively.

PROVIDING MEANINGFUL PRODUCTS

ULTIMATELY, RESEARCH STUDIES are undertaken to generate information products that stakeholders will find useful. It's particularly important that the final products be appropriate to the culture of stakeholders. As discussed earlier, funders are likely to find reports useful when they address the extent to which the social service program meets its contractual obligations for providing services and describe the outcomes of those services. Further, funders will look for quantitative data and statistical analyses that support the findings of the report. Managers who regularly deal with funders may also favor reports of this type.

However, other stakeholder groups may not find such products useful or understandable. This will be especially the case if stakeholders come from cultural backgrounds that are dialogue oriented. Reports with descriptions, stories, illustrations, and even pictures are likely to prove more meaningful to such stakeholders.

Culturally competent researchers should accommodate all stakeholder groups who have a legitimate interest in the results derived from a research study. Tailoring final reports to funders' needs alone is a poor practice and is unlikely to result in meaningful program change. Program development necessarily comes from the inside and is based primarily on the initiative of the managers and staff.

The final products from a research study should support the efforts of managers and staff to develop the program by providing data that are meaningful, practical, and useful. It's usually the case that positivistic (Chapter 6) and interpretive (Chapter 7) approaches can be combined within a single study (Chapter 8). Although matters that interest funders are likely to be more suited to quantitative data collection and analyses, increased understanding can result from including descriptively oriented material that focuses on contextual matters.

Statistics describing the demographic makeup of clients, for example, can be supplemented by providing more detailed descriptions of a few selected clients. Often this can be accomplished by providing people with the opportunity to tell their stories in their words.

SUMMARY

ARMED WITH ALL THE ETHICS KNOWLEDGE you gained from the last chapter and combined with this one, you should now have a sound grasp of how to do ethical and culturally competent research studies. Conducting an ethical and culturally sensitive social work research study is an extremely complex endeavor, and undertaking research that involves stakeholders from different cultural backgrounds adds considerable complexity.

Study Questions for Chapter 5	
Essay — Discussion	
1	Before you entered your social work program, and before you read this chapter, how knowledgeable were you in relation to the various issues that need to be addressed when using minorities and disadvantaged groups as research participants? Discuss fully.
2	Discuss in detail why it's important to know the cultural make-up of your stakeholders who are on your research team. How does this affect the research process? Provide as many examples as you can to justify your response.
3	List and discuss the specific "social work" skills you think you will need when working with your stakeholders or research group. Provide examples to illustrate your points.
4	Discuss how social work research can be affected by culture at both the micro level (e.g., research participants, researchers) and at the macro level (e.g., your organization, institutions, the greater community). What culturally type of barriers exist at these levels and how would you work through them? Provide as many examples as you can to justify your response.
5	Discuss how your biases as a social work researcher can affect the research process in relation to *ethnocentrism*. Provide as many examples as you can to justify your response.
6	Discuss how your biases as a social work researcher can affect the research process in relation to *enculturation*. Provide as many examples as you can to justify your response.
7	List and discuss in detail the issues you will need to consider to actually become a culturally competent social work researcher. In your own words, define a culturally-competent researcher. Use a common social work example throughout your discussion.

8	When doing a social work research study, discuss the practical strategies we can use to produce an accurate portrayal and understanding of minorities and disadvantaged groups. Use a common social work example throughout your discussion.
9	Discuss in detail how you will become a competent social work researcher in relation to "intercultural communication skills." Use a common social work example throughout your discussion.
10	Discuss in detail how you will become a competent social work researcher in relation to "specific knowledge about the culture in which you hope to study." Use a common social work example throughout your discussion.
11	Discuss in detail how you will become a competent social work researcher in relation to "your ability to appropriately adapt evaluation methods and processes." Use a common social work example throughout your discussion.
12	Discuss how you will go about developing specific cultural knowledge about your research participants. Provide as many examples as you can to illustrate your points.
13	Discuss how you will go about explicitly examining the theoretical framework that is the foundation of your research study with a cultural lens. Provide as many examples as you can to illustrate your points.
14	Discuss how you will go about defining and measuring "ethnicity" in a meaningful manner. Why is this important? Provide as many examples as you can to illustrate your points.
15	Discuss how you will go about choosing measuring instruments that are appropriate for all the ethnic groups in your study. Why is this important? Provide as many examples as you can to illustrate your points.
16	Discuss how you will go about making sure that you will interpret your study's results to accurately reflect the lives of your research participants. Why is this important? Provide as many examples as you can to illustrate your points.

17	Discuss how you will precisely define the population of your research participants. Why is this important? Provide as many examples as you can to illustrate your points.
18	Discuss how you will go about developing meaningful collaborations with your research participants. Why is this important? Provide as many examples as you can to illustrate your points.
19	Discuss how you will go about encouraging buy-in with all of your stakeholders. Why is this important? Provide as many examples as you can to illustrate your points.
20	Discuss how you will go about providing timely feedback of your study's results in a clear and useful format conveyed through culturally appropriate methods. Why is this important? Provide as many examples as you can to illustrate your points.
21	Discuss how you will avoid deficit model interpretations. Why is this important? Provide as many examples as you can to illustrate your points.

Critical Thinking — Application — Integration

22	**YOU'RE NOW A CULTURALLY COMPETENT RESEARCHER** **Background:** Pretend for the moment you want to do a research study that describes the barriers that first-generation ethnic minority social work students face when they enter your social work program. 1. Discuss how you will go about explicitly examining the theoretical framework that is the foundation of your research study with a cultural lens. Provide as many examples as you can to illustrate your points. 2. Discuss how you will go about defining and measuring "ethnicity" in a meaningful manner. Why is this important? Provide as many examples as you can to illustrate your points. 3. Discuss how you will go about choosing measuring instruments that are appropriate for all the ethnic groups in your study. Why is this important? Provide as many examples as you can to illustrate your points. 4. Discuss how you will go about making sure that you will interpret your study's results to accurately reflect the lives of your research participants. Why is this important? Provide as many examples as you can to illustrate

your points.

5. Discuss how you will precisely define the population of your research participants. Why is this important? Provide as many examples as you can to illustrate your points.

6. Discuss how you will go about *developing meaningful collaborations* with your research participants. Why is this important? Provide as many examples as you can to illustrate your points.

7. Discuss how you will go about *encouraging buy-in* with all of your stakeholders. Why is this important? Provide as many examples as you can to illustrate your points.

8. Discuss how you will go about providing *timely feedback* of your study's results in a clear and useful format conveyed through culturally appropriate methods. Why is this important? Provide as many examples as you can to illustrate your points.

9. Discuss how you will avoid *deficit model interpretations.* Why is this important? Provide as many examples as you can to illustrate your points.

23

PRACTICE VS. RESEARCH

Background: Pretend for the moment you're employed as a social worker in your university's student counseling center. A first-generation ethnic minority student comes into your office where she tells you she feels lonely and isolated and wants to go home and drop out of school. Ah, you say, thinking about the preceding exercise (i.e., Number 22).

1. **Practice:** Using this chapter as a guide, describe in detail how you would use the chapter's contents to help you establish a **worker/client relationship** with her.

2. **Research:** Let's suppose that now you want to do a research study that will try to find out what factors are involved that make first-generation ethnic minority students at your university feel lonely and isolated. Using this chapter as a guide, describe in detail how you would use the chapter's contents to help you in your **research study**.

NOTE: This exercise should help you to realize that social work practitioners and researchers have to be culturally competent when working with clients (practice) and research participants (research) alike.

24	**CULTURAL COMPETENCY AND THE PRACTITIONER** **Scenario 1:** Make an argument that to be an effective evidence-based social work practitioner **you must be** culturally competent. Provide a clear and explicit **practice-related** social work example to illustrate your main points. **Scenario 2:** Make an argument that **you do not have to be** culturally competent to be an effective evidence-based practitioner. Provide a clear and explicit **practice-related** social work example to illustrate your main points. **Time to Choose:** Which one of the above two scenarios do you feel is more consistent with the concept of the contemporary evidence-based social work practice process as illustrated in Chapter 1 on pages 46–51? Why? Provide relevant social work examples to illustrate your main points.
25	**CULTURAL COMPETENCY AND THE RESEARCHER** **Scenario 1:** Make an argument that **you must be** culturally competent to be an effective social work researcher. Provide a clear and explicit **research-related** social work example to illustrate your main points. **Scenario 2:** Make an argument that **you do not have to be** culturally competent to be an effective social work researcher. Provide a clear and explicit **research-related** social work example to illustrate your main points. **Time to Choose:** Which one of the above two scenarios do you feel is more consistent with the place of research in social work? Why? Provide relevant social work examples to illustrate your main points.
26	**TIME TO PUT ON YOUR CRITICAL THINKING HAT** 1. Discuss the similarities and differences between your responses to Questions 24 and 25. 2. What are your thoughts on the belief that you will need to be culturally competent whether you're a social work *practitioner* (Question 24) or a social work *researcher* (Question 25)?

27	**CULTURAL COMPETENCE AND YOUR PROFESSIONAL DEVELOPMENT** 1. Review the three social work research-related roles you can take when you graduate—CSWE Competency 1 at the beginning of this chapter on page 172 (also discussed in Chapter 1 on pages 38–42). Thoroughly discuss how you feel this chapter will help you to perform one or more research-related roles when you graduate. Which one of the three roles do you believe this chapter helped you with the most? Why? Discuss in detail and provide an example to illustrate your main points. 2. Review CSWE Competency 4 at the beginning of this chapter on page 172. Thoroughly discuss how you feel this chapter will help you to become a practice-informed researcher and a research-informed practitioner. Discuss in detail and provide an example to illustrate your main points. 3. Review the evidence-based practice process as illustrated on pages 46–51. Thoroughly discuss how this chapter helps you to develop the skills you'll need for implementing one or more steps of the evidence-based practice process. 4. Discuss which step(s) you feel this chapter will help you with the most. Why? Be very specific and use relevant social work examples to illustrate your main points throughout your discussion. **NOTE:** This exercise should help you to understand that the knowledge and skills you draw upon to become culturally competent in research situations are the same in practice situations as well. In short, you can use this chapter to help you become more culturally competent in your day-to-day practice activities with all your client systems.
28	**MOVING AHEAD BY LOOKING BACK** At this point in your research methods course, how comfortable are you with discussing the place of research in social work with your field instructor, with your practice instructor, with your research instructor, with your supervisor at work, with the director of your social work program, or with your classmates? Discuss in detail.

PART II

Approaches to Knowledge Development

CHAPTER 6: The Quantitative Research Approach **206**

CHAPTER 7: The Qualitative Research Approach **250**

CHAPTER 8: The Mixed-Methods Research Approach **278**

6

CHAPTER

2015 EPAS COMPETENCIES

COMPETENCY 1: Demonstrate Ethical and Professional Behavior

You will learn that in order to be a successful evidence-based practitioner you have an ethical obligation to integrate three research roles into your daily practice activities as discussed in Chapter 1: (1) research consumer, (2) research partner—either as a co-researcher or research participant, and (3) creator and disseminator of research (or knowledge).

This entire chapter pertains to these three professional roles because an ethical and professional evidence-based social work practitioner must understand and appreciate the advantages and disadvantages that are embedded within all three research approaches to knowledge development that produce social work practice recommendations: quantitative (this chapter), qualitative (Chapter 7), and mixed-methods (Chapter 8).

COMPETENCY 4: Engage in Practice-Informed Research and Research-Informed Practice

Competency 4 also pertains to the entire chapter because you have to:

1. Evaluate the overall value of the practice recommendations that a quantitative (positivistic) research study puts forward by assessing how closely the study followed the quantitative research approach that was used to formulate the study's findings and practice recommendations (**research consumer**—research-informed practice);

2. Participate in a research study—either as a co-researcher or research participant (**research partner**—practice-informed research). See 1 above and 3 below; and

3. Understand and appreciate the advantages and disadvantages of using the quantitative research approach to knowledge building before you actually do a quantitative research study (**creator and disseminator of research**—practice-informed research).

You'll also need to utilize evidence-based practice recommendations whenever possible; that is, you need to integrate (1) the best available research-based evidence with (2) your clinical expertise and (3) your client's values.

All of the above implies you'll need to know how to assess the overall rigor of a quantitatively based research study that produced its quantitative research-based evidence. In short, you need to ask and then answer a simple question: How seriously should I take the findings of any specific quantitatively oriented research study given how well the study followed the *positivist way of thinking?*

COMPETENCY 9: Evaluate Practice with Individuals, Families, Groups, Organizations, and Communities

See Competencies 1 and 4.

6

The Quantitative Research Approach

CHAPTER 1	**Step 1.** Understanding the Research Process
CHAPTER 2	**Step 2.** Developing Research Questions
CHAPTER 3	**Step 3.** Reviewing the Literature
CHAPTERS 4 & 5	**Step 4.** Being Aware of Ethical and Cultural Issues
CHAPTERS 6–8	**Step 5.** Selecting a Research Approach
CHAPTERS 9 & 10	**Step 6.** Specifying How Variables Are Measured
CHAPTER 11	**Step 7.** Selecting a Sample
CHAPTERS 12 & 13	**Step 8.** Selecting a Research Design
CHAPTERS 14–16	**Step 9.** Selecting a Data-Collection Method
CHAPTERS 17 & 18	**Step 10.** Analyzing the Data
CHAPTERS 19 & 20	**Step 11.** Writing the Research Report

PREVIOUS CHAPTERS HAVE DISCUSSED how social work knowledge is best generated through the use of the scientific method which contains three research approaches. Knowledge gained from employing any of these approaches is much more objective than knowledge derived from the other four ways of "knowing" (i.e., authority, tradition, experience, in addition to beliefs and intuition). Before we discuss the quantitative approach to knowledge development, however, you'll need to thoroughly understand and appreciate how this approach is embedded within the positivist way of thinking.

WHAT IS THE POSITIVISTIC WAY OF THINKING?

OUR DISCUSSION ON HOW POSITIVISTS think has been adapted and modified from Grinnell and Williams (1990), Krysik and Grinnell (1997), Williams, Tutty, and Grinnell (1995), Williams, Unrau, and Grinnell (1998), and Unrau, Grinnell, and Williams (2008). In a nutshell, the positivist way of thinking strives to accomplish five basic interwoven goals:

1. Measurability

2. Objectivity

3. Reducing uncertainty

4. Duplication

5. Use of standardized procedures

STRIVING TOWARD MEASURABILITY

THE POSITIVIST WAY OF THINKING tries to study only those things that can be objectively measured. That is, knowledge gained through this belief is based on *objective measurements* of the real world, not on someone's opinions, beliefs, hunches, intuitions, or past experiences. Conversely, and as you know from Chapter 1, knowledge gained through tradition or authority may rely more on people's experiences, opinions, and beliefs than through the use of the scientific method of inquiry, which as you know relies heavily on the measurement of variables.

Concepts that cannot be measured or even seen—such as the id, ego, or superego—are not amenable to a positivistic-oriented research study but rather rely on tradition and authority. In short, a positivistic principle would be that the things you believe to exist must be able to be measured.

However, at this point in our discussion, it's useful to remember that researchers doing studies within a positivistic framework believe that practically everything in life is measurable. In fact, some say that a thing—or a variable, if you will—doesn't exist unless it can be measured. What's your opinion on this statement?

STRIVING TOWARD OBJECTIVITY

THE SECOND IDEAL OF THE POSITIVISTIC BELIEF is that research studies must be as objective as possible. The variables that are being observed and/or measured must not be affected in any way by the person doing the observing or measuring. Physical scientists have observed inanimate matter for centuries, confident in the belief that objects do not change as a result of being observed.

In the sub-world of the atom, however, physicists are beginning to learn what social workers have always known: Things *do* change when they are observed. People think, feel, and behave very differently as a result of being observed. Not only do they change, they change in different ways depending on who's doing the observing and/or measuring.

There is yet another problem. Some observed behaviors, for example, are open to interpretation by the folks doing the observing. To illustrate this point, let's take a simple example of a client you are seeing, named Ron, who is severely withdrawn. He may behave in one way in your office in individual treatment sessions and in quite another way when his mother joins the interviews.

You may think that Ron is unduly silent, while his mother remarks on how much he's talking. If his mother wants him to talk, perhaps as a sign that he is emerging from his withdrawal, she may perceive him to be talking more than he really is.

All folks doing research studies with the positivistic framework go to great lengths to ensure that their own hopes, fears, beliefs, and biases do not affect their research results, and that the biases of others do not affect them either. Nevertheless, as discussed in later chapters, complete objectivity is rarely possible in social work research despite the many strategies that have been developed over the years to achieve it.

Suppose, for example, that a social worker is trying to help a mother interact more positively with her child. The worker, together with a colleague, may first observe the child and mother in a playroom setting, recording how many times the mother makes eye contact with the child, hugs the child, criticizes the child, makes encouraging comments, and so forth on a 3-point scale: discouraging, neutral, or encouraging. The social worker may perceive a remark that the mother has made to the child as "neutral," while the colleague thinks it was "encouraging."

As you will see throughout this book, in such a situation it's impossible to resolve the disagreement. If there were six objective observers, for example, five opting for neutral and only one for encouraging, the sole "encouraging observer" is more likely to be wrong than the other five, and it's very likely that the mother's remark was neutral.

As you know from Chapter 1, as more people agree on what they have observed, the less likely it becomes that the observation was distorted by bias, and the more likely it is that the agreement reached is "objectively true." As should be obvious by now, objectivity is largely a matter of agreement. There are some things, usually physical phenomena, about which most people agree. Most people agree, for example, that objects fall when dropped, water turns to steam at a certain temperature, and sea water contains salt.

However, there are other things—mostly to do with values, attitudes, and feelings—about which agreement is far rarer. An argument about whether Beethoven is a better composer than Willie Nelson, for example, cannot be objectively resolved.

Neither can a dispute about the rightness of capital punishment, euthanasia, same-sex marriages, or abortion. It's not surprising, therefore, that physical researchers, who work with physical phenomena, are able to be more objective than social work researchers, who work with human beings.

STRIVING TOWARD REDUCING UNCERTAINTY

POSITIVISTIC-ORIENTED RESEARCH STUDIES try to totally rule out uncertainty. However, since all observations and/or measurements in the social sciences are made by human beings, personal bias cannot be entirely eliminated, and there's always the possibility that an observation and/or measurement is in error, no matter how many people agree about what they saw or measured.

There is also the possibility that the conclusions drawn from even an accurate observation or measurement will be wrong. A huge number of people may agree, for example, that an object in the sky is a UFO when in fact it's a meteor. Even if they agree that it's a meteor, they may come to the conclusion—probably erroneously—that the meteor is a warning from angry extraterrestrials.

In the twentieth century, most people do not believe that natural phenomena have anything to do with extraterrestrial beings. They prefer the explanations that modern researchers have proposed. Nevertheless, no researcher would say—or at least be quoted as saying—that meteors and extraterrestrial beings are not related for certain.

When utilizing the scientific method of knowledge development, nothing is certain. Even the best-tested theory is only tentative and accepted as true until newly discovered evidence shows it to be untrue or only partly true. All knowledge gained through the scientific method is thus provisional. Everything currently accepted as true is true only with varying degrees of probability.

STRIVING TOWARD DUPLICATION

POSITIVISTIC RESEARCHERS try to do research studies in such a way that their studies can be duplicated by other researchers. Suppose, for a moment, you are running a twelve-week intervention program to help fathers who have abused their children to manage their anger without resorting to physical violence. You have put a great deal of effort into designing your program, and believe that your intervention (the program) is more effective than other interventions that are geared toward anger management.

You develop a method of measuring the degree to which the fathers in your group have learned to dissipate their anger in nondamaging ways, and you find that, indeed, the group of fathers shows marked improvement. Improvement shown by one group of fathers, however, is not convincing evidence for the effectiveness of your intervention.

Perhaps your measurements were in error and the improvement was not as great as you hoped for. Perhaps the improvement was a coincidence, and the fathers' behaviors changed because they had joined health clubs and each had vented his fury on a punching bag. To be more certain, you duplicate your intervention and measuring procedures with a second group of fathers. In other words, you replicate your study.

After you have used the same procedures with a number of groups and obtained similar results each time, you might expect that other social workers will eagerly adopt your anger-management intervention. But, as presented in the previous chapters, tradition dies hard. Other social workers have a vested interest in their interventions, and they may suggest that you found the results you did only because you *wanted* to find them.

To counter any suggestion of bias, you ask another, independent social worker to use your same anger-management intervention and measuring methods with other groups of fathers. If the results are the same as before, your colleagues in the field of anger management may choose to adopt your intervention method.

Whatever your colleagues decide, you are excited about your newfound intervention. You wonder if your methods would work as well with women as they do with men, with adolescents as well as with adults, with Native Americans, Asians, or African Americans as well as with Caucasians, with mixed groups, larger groups, or groups in different settings. In fact, you have identified a lifetime project, since you will have to apply your intervention and measuring procedures repeatedly to all these different groups of people.

STRIVING TOWARD THE USE OF STANDARDIZED PROCEDURES

FINALLY, A TRUE-TO-THE-BONE positivistic researcher tries to use well accepted "research-type" standardized procedures. For a positivistic-oriented research study to be creditable, and before others can accept its results, they must be satisfied that your study was conducted according to accepted scientific standardized procedures. The allegation that your work lacks objectivity is only one of the criticisms they might bring.

In addition, they might suggest that the group of fathers you worked with was not typical of abusive fathers in general, and that your results are not therefore applicable to other groups of abusive fathers. It might be alleged that you did not make proper measurements, or you measured the wrong variables, or you did not take enough measurements, or you did not analyze your data correctly, and so on.

To negate these kinds of criticisms, over the years social work researchers have agreed on a set of standard procedures and techniques that are thought most likely to produce "true and unbiased" knowledge—which is what this book is all about. Certain steps must be performed in a certain order. Foreseeable errors must be guarded against.

Ethical behavior with research participants and colleagues must be maintained, as discussed in detail in Chapter 4. These procedures must be followed if your study is both to generate usable results and to be accepted as useful by other social workers.

STEPS OF THE RESEARCH APPROACH

WE NOW TURN OUR ATTENTION to the seven general sequential steps (in a more-or-less straightforward manner) that all quantitative studies follow, as illustrated in Figure 6.1 on the following page. This seven-step figure has been shortened from the generic eleven-step research process as depicted at the beginning of the chapter on page 207.

FIGURE 6.1

Steps of the Quantitative (Positivistic) Research Approach

The most important thing to remember at this point is that all the steps in Figure 6.1 are highly intertwined to various degrees and it's difficult, if not impossible, to describe a single step in isolation from the remaining six steps. However, for the sake of simplicity, we'll describe each step in a sequential manner.

These steps yield a very useful format for obtaining knowledge in our profession. The quantitative research approach is a tried and tested method of scientific inquiry. In a nutshell, most of the critical decisions to be made in a quantitative research study occur *before* the study is ever started. This means that the researcher is well aware (or should be aware!) of all the study's limitations before the study actually begins.

It's possible, therefore, for a researcher to decide that a quantitative study has simply way too many limitations and to conclude that it should not be performed. Regardless of whether a proposed study is ever carried out, the process always begins with choosing a research topic and focusing the research question (the topic of Chapter 2).

STEP 1: IDENTIFYING THE PROBLEM

AS CAN BE SEEN IN FIGURE 6.1 ON THE PREVIOUS PAGE, the first step of the quantitative approach to knowledge development is to identify a general problem area to study and then to refine this general area into a research question that can be answered or a hypothesis that can be tested

Quantitative studies are usually deductive processes; that is, they usually begin with a broad and general query about a general social problem then pare it down to a specific research question or hypothesis. For instance, your general research problem may have started out with a curiosity about racial discrimination within public social service agencies. Your general problem area could be written simply as:

> **General problem area:**
> Racial discrimination within public social service agencies

STEP 2: SELECTING SPECIFIC VARIABLES

YOU MAY HAVE NOTICED through your professional practice as a medical social worker in a local hospital, for example, that many of the patients within your hospital are from ethnic minority backgrounds who have the following three characteristics, or variables, if you will:

1. High unemployment rates
2. A large proportion of their members living under the poverty level
3. Low levels of educational attainment

You believe that these three conditions alone should increase the likelihood that they will use the hospital's social service department where you work. Conversely, and at the same time, you have also observed that there are more ethnic majorities than minorities who are seen in your hospital's social service department. Where the research study actually takes place is called the *research setting*. So your research setting for this study is the hospital where you're employed.

Your personal observations may then lead you to question whether discrimination against ethnic minorities exists in terms of their access to your hospital's social service department. You can easily test the possibility of such a relationship by using the quantitative research approach.

As should be evident by now, Steps 1 and 2 are highly intertwined and comingled, and they usually take place at the same time. Step 2 within the quantitative research process has eight sub-steps:

— **Step 2a:** Determining what others have found

— **Step 2b:** Refining the general problem area

— **Step 2c:** Developing concepts

— **Step 2d:** Identifying variables within concepts

— **Step 2e:** Defining attributes of variables

— **Step 2f:** Defining independent and dependent variables

— **Step 2g:** Constructing a hypothesis

— **Step 2h:** Evaluating the hypothesis

STEP 2A: DETERMINING WHAT OTHERS HAVE FOUND

THE NEXT PHASE in focusing your research question is visiting the library and using the Internet to review the literature related to your two concepts:

1. Racial discrimination within social services (Concept 1)
2. Access to social service (Concept 2)

You will want to read the literature related to your two main concepts within the general research question: racial discrimination within social service agencies and access to them. You will want to learn about how various theories explain both of your main concepts in order to arrive at a meaningful research question. It may be, for example, that many ethnic minority cultures are unlikely to ask strangers for help with life's personal difficulties.

STEP 2B: REFINING THE GENERAL PROBLEM AREA

FURTHERMORE, you may learn that most social service programs are organized using bureaucratic structures, which require potential clients to talk to several strangers (e.g., telephone receptionist, waiting-room clerk, intake worker) before they are able to access social services.

Given that you know, via the literature, that ethnic minorities do not like talking with strangers about their personal problems, and that social services are set up for people to deal with a series of strangers, you could develop a very simple quantitative research question:

> **Quantitative research question:**
> Do patients who come from ethnic minority backgrounds have difficulty accessing my hospital's social service department?

STEP 2C: DEVELOPING CONCEPTS

YOU HAVE MADE THE GENERAL BROAD GENERAL PROBLEM AREA of racial discrimination more specific by narrowing it down to a person's ethnicity. At this point, you have yet to refine your second concept in your research question, access to your hospital's social services. This will be done later on. For now, let's review the concept of concepts.

CONCEPTS. What are *concepts* anyway? Concepts are nothing more than ideas. When you speak of a client's ethnic background, for example, you have in mind the concept of *ethnicity*. When you use the word *ethnicity*, you are referring to the underlying idea that certain groups of people can be differentiated from other groups in terms of physical characteristics, customs, beliefs, language, and so on.

Take a female patient in your hospital, for example, who has just been referred to your social service department. She is a *patient* in the hospital, she is a *woman,* and she is now also your *client.* If she's married, she's a *wife.* If she has children, she's a *mother.* She may be a *homeowner,* a *committee member,* an *Asian,* and a *Catholic.* She may even be *hostile, demanding,* or *compassionate.*

All of these characteristics are concepts. They are simply ideas that all members of a society share—to a greater or lesser degree, of course. Some concepts are perceived the same way by all of us. On the other hand, some concepts give rise to huge disagreements. The concept of being a mother, for example, involves the concept of children and, specifically, the concept of having given birth to a child. Today, however, most people would agree that giving birth to a child is only one way of defining a mother.

The idea of motherhood in Western society involves more than simply giving birth. Also involved in motherhood are the concepts of loving the child, caring for the child's physical needs, offering the child emotional support, advocating for the child with others, accepting legal and financial responsibility for the child, and being there for the child in all circumstances and at all times. Some of us could easily argue that a woman who does all of these things is a mother, whether she has given birth or not.

Others would say that the biological mother is the only real mother, even if she abandoned her child at birth. Like many other qualities of interest to social workers, ethnicity is a highly complex concept with many possible dimensions. Intelligence is another such concept, as are alienation, morale, conformity, and a host of others.

STEP 2D: IDENTIFYING VARIABLES WITHIN CONCEPTS

YOU CAN NOW BREAK DOWN your global concept, the ethnicity of patients who seek out your hospital's social service department, into a variable by breaking down ethnicity into different ethnic groups. Some patients will belong to one ethnic group, some to another, some to a third, and so on. In other words, these people *vary* with respect to which ethnic group they belong to. Any concept that can vary, logically enough, is called a variable, so your variable's name is *ethnic group.*

STEP 2E: DEFINING ATTRIBUTES OF VARIABLES

YOU NOW HAVE GONE from your general concept of ethnicity to a variable, ethnic group. Finally, you need to think about which particular ethnic groups will be useful for your study. Perhaps you know that Asians are patients within your hospital, as are Caucasians, Latinos, African Americans, and Native Americans. This gives you five attributes for your ethnic group variable:

> **Attributes for ethnic group variable:**
> 1. Asian
> 2. Caucasian
> 3. Latino
> 4. African American
> 5. Native American

During your quantitative study you will ask all of the hospital's patients which one of the five ethnic groups they belong to; or perhaps these data will be recorded on the hospital's intake forms, and you will not need to ask them at all.

In any case, the resulting data will be in the form of numbers or percentages for each attribute. You will have succeeded in measuring the variable *ethnic group* by describing it in terms of five attributes. You will note that these five categories only provide one possible description. You could also have included Pacific Islanders, for example, if there were any receiving medical treatment in your hospital, and then you would have had six attributes of your ethnic group variable instead of only five:

> **Attributes for ethnic group variable:**
> 1. Asian
> 2. Caucasian
> 3. Latino
> 4. African American
> 5. Native American
> 6. **Pacific Islanders**

If you were afraid that not all clients receiving medical treatment would fit into one of your six categories, then you could include a seventh miscellaneous category, *other,* to be sure you had accounted for everyone:

Attributes for ethnic group variable:

1. Asian

2. Caucasian

3. Latino

4. African American

5. Native American

6. Pacific Islanders

7. **Other**

By reviewing the literature and your knowledge of your social service unit, you have more or less devised a direction for your study in relation to your ethnicity concept. From the general problem area of racial discrimination, you have come up with a concept (ethnicity), a variable (ethnic group), and seven attributes for your variable as illustrated in Box 6.1 on the following page.

As you know, ethnicity is not the only concept of interest in your study. There is also *access to social work services,* which is the idea that some people, or groups of people, are able to access social work services more readily than other people or groups.

You might think of access simply in terms of how many of the patients receiving medical treatment within your hospital actually saw a social worker. Clients will vary with respect to whether they saw a social worker, so you have the variable, *saw social worker,* and two attributes of that variable:

Saw a social worker?

Yes, the client saw a social worker

No, the client did not see a social worker

BOX 6.1	From General Problem Area to Attributes

General Problem Area: Racial discrimination

Concept: Ethnicity

Variable: Ethnic group

Attributes: Asian

Caucasian

Latino

African American

Native American

Pacific Islander

Others

You could, for example, ask each patient upon leaving the hospital a very simple question:

Question:

Did you see a social worker while you were in the hospital?

1. Yes

2. No

If you wish to explore access in more depth, you might be interested in the factors affecting access. For example, perhaps your review of the literature has led you to believe that some ethnic groups tend to receive fewer referrals to social work services than other groups. If this is the case in your hospital, clients will vary with respect to whether they received a referral, and you immediately have a second variable—*referral*—and two attributes of that variable:

> **Was the patient referred?**
>
> **Yes,** the patient was referred
>
> **No,** the patient was not referred

Once again, this variable can take the form of a very simple question:

> **Question:**
>
> When you were a patient within the hospital, were you at anytime referred to the hospital's social service department?
>
> **1.** Yes
>
> **2.** No

However, there is more to accessing hospital social work services than just being referred. Perhaps, according to the literature, certain ethnic groups are more likely to follow up on a referral than other groups because of cultural beliefs around the appropriateness of asking non-family members for help. In that case, you have a third variable, *follow-up of referral,* with two attributes of its own:

> **Did the client follow-up on the referral?**
>
> **Yes,** the client followed up
>
> **No,** the client did not follow up

This also can be put into a question form:

> **Question:**
>
> If you were referred to social work services while you were a patient in the hospital, did you follow up on the referral and actually see a social worker?
>
> **1.** Yes
>
> **2.** No

In addition, those who do try to follow up on referrals may meet circumstances within the referral process that are more intimidating for some than for others. Perhaps they are obliged to fill out a large number of forms or tell their stories to many unfamiliar people before they actually succeed in getting an appointment with a social worker.

If this is the case, they *vary* with respect to how intimidating they find the process, which gives you a fourth variable, *feelings of intimidation around the referral process.* The attributes here are not so immediately apparent, but you might decide on just three:

> **Feelings of intimidation:**
> - Not at all intimidated
> - Somewhat intimidated
> - Very intimidated

This also can be put into the form of a simple question that you would ask all patients who were referred to social services:

> **Simple research question:**
>
> How intimidated were you when you were referred to the social service department?

By reviewing the literature and your knowledge of your hospital's social service department, you have more or less devised a direction for your study in relation to your access concept. You have come up with a concept, four variables, and attributes for each one of the four variables (see Box 6.2):

BOX 6.2	**From Concepts to Variables to Attributes**

Concept: Access to social work services

First Variable: Saw social worker?

Attributes: Yes

No

Second Variable: Referral?

Attributes: Yes

No

Third Variable: Follow-up of referral?

Attributes: Yes

No

Fourth Variable: Feeling of intimidation surrounding the referral process

Attributes: Not at all intimidated

Somewhat intimidated

Very intimidated

STEP 2F: DEFINING INDEPENDENT AND DEPENDENT VARIABLES

A SIMPLE QUANTITATIVE RESEARCH study may choose to focus on the relationship between only two variables, which is called a *bivariate relationship*. The study tries to answer, in general terms: Does variable *X* affect variable *Y*? Or, how does variable *X* affect variable *Y?* This would be a great time for you to review Figure 2.3 on page 90.

If one variable affects the other, the variable that does the affecting is called an *independent variable*, symbolized by *X*. The variable that is affected is called the *dependent variable*, symbolized by *Y.* If enough is known about the topic, and you have a good idea of what the effect will be, the question may be phrased, If X occurs, will Y result? If variable X affects variable Y, whatever happens to Y will depend on X.

NO INDEPENDENT OR DEPENDENT VARIABLES. Some quantitative research studies are not concerned with the effect that one variable might have on another. Perhaps it's not yet known whether two variables are even associated, and it's far too soon to postulate what the relationship between them might be. For example, your study might try to ascertain the answer to a simple question:

Question:

How intimidated were you when you were referred to the social service department?

1. Not at all intimidated

2. Somewhat intimidated

3. Very intimidated

In the above simple question, there is no independent variable, nor is there a dependent variable. There is only one variable: the degree of intimidation felt by one group of people, members of the ethnic minority. You could even include members of the ethnic majority as well and ask this question:

Simple research question:

How intimidated do ALL patients feel when they are referred to my hospital's social service department?

STEP 2G: CONSTRUCTING A HYPOTHESIS

THERE ARE MANY TYPES of hypotheses, but we will only briefly discuss two:

1. Nondirectional
2. Directional

NONDIRECTIONAL HYPOTHESES. A nondirectional hypothesis (also called a two-tailed hypothesis) is simply a statement that says you expect to find a relationship between two or more variables. You're not willing, however, to stick your neck out as to the specific relationship between them. A nondirectional hypothesis for each one of your access variables could be, for example:

- **Nondirectional Research Hypothesis 1**: Saw a Social Worker

  Ethnic minorities and ethnic majorities see hospital social workers differentially.

- **Nondirectional Research Hypothesis 2:** Referral

  Ethnic minorities and ethnic majorities are referred to the hospital's social service department differentially.

- **Nondirectional Research Hypothesis 3:** Follow-up

  Ethnic minorities and ethnic majorities vary to the degree they follow up on referrals.

- **Nondirectional Research Hypothesis 4:** Intimidation

  Ethnic minorities and ethnic majorities differ in terms of how intimidated they were about the referral process.

DIRECTIONAL HYPOTHESES. Unlike a nondirectional hypothesis, a directional hypothesis (also called a one-tailed hypothesis) specifically indicates the predicted direction of the relationship between two variables. The direction stated is based on an existing body of knowledge related to the research question.

You may have found out through the literature (in addition to your own observations), for example, that you have enough evidence to suggest the following directional research hypotheses:

- **Directional Research Hypothesis 1:** Saw a Social Worker

  Ethnic majorities see hospital social workers more often than ethnic minorities.

- **Directional Research Hypothesis 2:** Referral

  Ethnic majorities are referred to the hospital's social service department more often than ethnic minorities.

- **Directional Research Hypothesis 3:** Follow-up

  Ethnic majorities follow up with social service referrals more often than ethnic minorities.

- **Directional Research Hypothesis 4:** Intimidation

  Ethnic minorities are more intimidated by the referral process than ethnic majorities.

As you shall see in this book, many research questions have at least one independent variable and one dependent variable. You could easily design your quantitative study to have one independent variable, ethnicity (i.e., ethnic minority or ethnic majority), and one dependent variable, difficulty in accessing social services (i.e., yes or no). You could easily organize your variables in this way because you are expecting that a person's ethnicity is somehow related to his/her difficulty in accessing social services.

It would be absurd to say the opposite—which the degrees of difficulty that people have in accessing social services influences their ethnicity. You could write your directional hypothesis as follows:

Directional hypothesis:

Ethnic minorities have more difficulty than ethnic majorities in accessing my hospital's social service department

---

Having set out your hypothesis in this way, you can plainly see that your research design will compare two groups of folks (ethnic minorities and ethnic majorities) in terms of whether or not (yes or no) each group had difficulty accessing your hospital's social service department. Your research design is the blueprint for the study. It's a basic guide to deciding how, where, and when data will be collected.

STEP 2H: EVALUATING THE HYPOTHESIS

YOU MUST NOW EVALUATE your hypothesis. Our discussion on how to evaluate hypotheses has been adapted and modified from Grinnell and Williams

(1990), Williams, Tutty, and Grinnell (1995), and Williams, Unrau, and Grinnell (1998). Hypotheses have to contain five ingredients; that is, they must be:

1. Relevant
2. Complete
3. Specific
4. Testable
5. Ethically and culturally sensitive

RELEVANCE. It's hardly necessary to stress that a useful hypothesis is one that contributes to the profession's knowledge base. Nevertheless, some social work problem areas are so complex that people may become sidetracked while reading the professional literature and end up developing very interesting hypotheses that are totally unrelated to the original problem area they had wanted to investigate.

They needlessly run down a bunch of rabbit holes. The relevancy criterion is a reminder that the hypothesis must be directly related to the research question, which in turn must be directly related to the study's general problem area.

COMPLETENESS. A hypothesis should be a complete statement that expresses your intended meaning in its entirety. The reader should not be left with the impression that some word or phrase is missing, such as:

An incomplete hypothesis:
Moral values are declining

Other examples would include a whole range of comparative statements without a reference point. The statement "Males are more aggressive," for example, may be assumed to mean "Men are more aggressive than women," but someone investigating the social life of animals may have meant "Male humans are more aggressive than male gorillas."

SPECIFICITY. A hypothesis must be unambiguous. The reader should be able to understand what each variable contained in the hypothesis means and what relationship, if any, is hypothesized to exist between them. Consider, for example, this hypothesis:

A poorly worded hypothesis:
Bad timed family therapy affects success.

"Badly timed family therapy" may mean that therapy is offered too soon or too late for the family to benefit; or that the social worker or family are late for therapy sessions; or that sessions are too long or too short to be effective. Similarly, "success" may mean that the family's problems are resolved as determined by objective measurement, or it may mean that the family or the social worker is satisfied with the therapy, or any combination of these.

With regard to the relationship between the two variables, the reader may assume that you are hypothesizing a negative correlation; that is, the *more* badly timed the therapy, the *less* success will be achieved. On the other hand, perhaps you are only hypothesizing an association, that bad timing will invariably coexist with lack of success. Be that as it may, the reader should not be left to guess at what you mean by a hypothesis. If you are trying to be both complete and specific, you may hypothesize, for example:

A properly worded hypothesis:
Family therapy that is undertaken *after* the male perpetrator has accepted responsibility for the sexual abuse of his child is more likely to succeed in reuniting the family than family therapy undertaken *before* the male perpetrator has accepted responsibility for the sexual abuse.

This hypothesis is complete and specific. It leaves the reader in no doubt as to what you mean, but it's also somewhat wordy and clumsy. One of the difficulties in writing a good hypothesis is that specific statements need more words than unspecific or ambiguous statements.

POTENTIAL FOR TESTING. The fourth criterion for judging whether a hypothesis is good and useful is the ease with which its truth can be verified. Some statements cannot be verified at all with currently available measurement techniques. "Telepathic communication exists between identical twins" is one such statement.

A hypothesis of sufficient importance will often generate new data-gathering techniques, which will enable it to be eventually tested. Nevertheless, as a rule it's best to limit hypotheses to statements that can be tested immediately by currently available measurement methods.

ETHICALLY AND CULTURALLY SENSITIVE. Well, if we have to explain this criterion you don't belong in social work. Read Chapter 4 on ethics and Chapter 5 on cultural competence to review all of the ethical and cultural issues that must be dealt with in a research study—especially when it comes to formulating research questions and hypotheses.

STEP 3: DESIGNING THE STUDY

AFTER ALL OF THE NECESSARY WORK has been done in relation to formulating your research question and/or hypothesis, you need to state how your study is going to unfold; that is, you now need to describe how you are going to measure your variables and select your research sample. Like Step 2, Step 3 also has sub-steps:

— **Step 3a:** Measuring variables

— **Step 3b:** Deciding on a sample

— **Step 3c:** Addressing ethical and cultural issues

STEP 3A: MEASURING VARIABLES

ALL OF YOUR VARIABLES must be able to be objectively measured. This means that you must precisely record the variable's frequency, duration, and/or magnitude (intensity). Think about your ethnic minority variable for a minute. As noted earlier, you could simply operationalize this variable into two categories, ethnic minority and ethnic majorities:

Question:

Are you a member of an ethnic minority?

1. Yes

2. No

Here you are simply measuring the presence (ethnic minority) or absence (ethnic majority) of a trait for each research participant within your study. You also need to measure the variable of difficulty in accessing the hospital's social service department. One again, you could have measured this variable in a number of ways. You are measuring it by asking each person a simple question:

Question:

Did you have difficulty in accessing our hospital's social service department?

1. Yes

2. No

STEP 3B: DECIDING ON A SAMPLE AND RESEARCH DESIGN

SAMPLING IS NOTHING MORE than selecting units (e.g., people, organizations) from a specific population of interest so that by studying the sample you can generalize your results back to the population from which the sample was drawn. You will be analyzing the data from your sample to determine if your research question has been answered or your hypothesis has been confirmed.

How you go about selecting your sample, administering the measuring instruments, and analyzing your data is loosely referred to as your general research design. Much more will be said about sampling in Chapter 11 and research designs in Chapters 12 and 13.

STEP 3C: ADDRESSING ETHICAL AND CULTURAL ISSUES

IT GOES WITHOUT SAYING that you must review all the ethical and cultural issues in every step of your proposed research study before you collect one speck of data. The main two questions you need to ask yourself at this point are:

1. Is my proposed research study *ethical* (Chapter 4)?
2. Is my proposed research study *culturally sensitive* (Chapter 5)?

STEP 4: COLLECTING THE DATA

ONLY AFTER YOU DECIDE that your study is ethical and culturally sensitive can you start to collect your data. Data collection is where the rubber hits the road. The data you collect must reflect a condition in the *real* world and should not be biased by the person collecting the data in any way.

In your quantitative study, the research participants produce the data—not you, the researcher. That is, you only record the data that each participant individually provides (probably through a questionnaire of some type) for both of your variables:

1. "Ethnic minority" or "ethnic majority" for the ethnicity variable
2. "Yes" or "No" for the access to social service variable

Your data-collection procedures must be able to be duplicated by others. In other words, they must be sufficiently clear and straightforward that other researchers could use them in their research studies.

Data collection is a critical step in the research process because it's the link between theory and practice. Your research study always begins with an idea that is molded by a conceptual framework, which uses preexisting knowledge about your study's problem area.

Once your research question has been refined to a researchable level, data are sought from a selected source(s) and gathered using a data-collection method. The data collected are then used to support or supplant your original study's conceptions about the research problem under investigation.

STEP 5: ANALYZING THE DATA

ONCE YOU HAVE COLLECTED your data via the previous step, you need to analyze them. You asked your research participants to fill out a simple two-question questionnaire that only asked two questions:

Question 1:

Are you a member of an ethnic minority?

1. Yes

2. No

Question 2:

Did you have difficulty in accessing our hospital's social service department?

1. Yes

2. No

There are two major types of quantitative data analysis:

1. Descriptive statistics

2. Inferential statistics

DESCRIPTIVE STATISTICS

AS PRESENTED IN CHAPTER 17, *descriptive statistics* describe your study's sample or population. Consider your ethnicity variable for a moment. You can easily describe your research participants in relation to their ethnicity by stating how many of them fell into each attribute of the variable. Suppose, for example, that 40 percent of your sample is in the ethnic minority category and the remaining 60 percent are in the ethnic majority category as shown:

> **Attributes:**
>
> Ethnic minority.....40%
>
> Ethnic majority.....60%

These two percentages will give you a picture of what your sample looks like in relation to ethnicity. A different picture could be produced where 10 percent of your sample are members of ethnic minorities and 90 percent are not:

> **Attributes:**
>
> Ethnic minority.....10%
>
> Ethnic majority.....90%

The above describes only one variable—ethnicity. A more detailed picture is given when data for two variables are displayed at the same time (e.g., Table 6.1). Suppose, for example, that 70 percent of your research participants who are members of ethnic minorities reported that they had difficulty in accessing your hospital's social services, compared with 20 percent of those who are in the ethnic majority (See Table 6.1 on the following page).

Other descriptive information about your research participants could include variables such as average age, percentages of males and females, average income, and so on. Much more will be said about descriptive statistics in Chapter 17 when we discuss how to analyze quantitative data (data that are in the form of numbers).

INFERENTIAL STATISTICS

INFERENTIAL STATISTICS DETERMINE the probability that a relationship between the two variables within your sample also exists within the population from which it was drawn. Suppose in your quantitative study, for example, you

TABLE 6.1
Difficulty in Accessing Social Services

	Having Difficulty?	
Ethnicity	Yes	No
Ethnic Minority	70%	30%
Ethnic Majority	20%	80%

find a statistically significant relationship between your research participant's ethnicity and whether they accessed social services within your hospital setting.

The use of inferential statistics will permit you to say whether or not the relationship detected in your study's sample exists in the larger population from which it was drawn. Much more will also be said about inferential statistics in Chapter 17.

STEP 6: INTERPRETING THE FINDINGS

ONCE YOUR DATA have been analyzed and put into a visual display, they need to be interpreted; that is, what do they mean—in words? You could come up with the following simple interpretation after looking at Table 6.1 above:

> Members of ethnic minorities had more difficulty in accessing
> social services than members of ethnic majorities.

STEP 6A: COMPARING YOUR RESULTS WITH OTHER FINDINGS

YOUR FINDINGS NOW need to be compared with what other studies have found. This is the time to review the literature once again, as discussed in Chapter 3. At this point, you need to state how your study's findings are either consistent with or inconsistent with other findings from similar studies.

STEP 6B: SPECIFYING THE STUDY'S LIMITATIONS

AT THIS POINT, you need to state the limitations of your study. You will need to state how well your study addressed all the threats to internal and external validities, as discussed in Chapter 13.

STEP 7: PRESENTING/DISSEMINATING THE STUDY'S FINDINGS

QUANTITATIVE FINDINGS are easily summarized in tables, figures, and graphs. When data are disseminated to laypeople, we usually rely on straightforward graphs and charts to illustrate our findings. As discussed in Chapter 17, presentation of statistical findings is typically reserved for professional journals.

AN EXTENDED EXAMPLE

LET'S FORGET about racial discrimination and access to social services within your hospital for a moment and focus on poverty, domestic violence, substance abuse, and homelessness.

WHAT'S THE PROBLEM?

LET'S PRETEND FOR A MOMENT that you're a social worker in a large social service agency. Agency intake data from the past three years reveal that many of your clients experience similar social issues. More specifically, most clients seeking services from your agency regularly present with one or more of the following four problems:

1. Poverty
2. Domestic violence
3. Substance abuse
4. Homelessness

Your agency's executive director establishes a "Practice Informed by Research" Committee that is charged with the following mandate:

> **Mandate:**
>
> To design a research study involving agency clientele so that workers at the agency will be better informed about the complex relationship between the issues of poverty, domestic violence, substance abuse, and homelessness

You are asked to chair this committee. Gladly, you accept and begin leading your committee through the remaining steps of the research process, as outlined in Figure 6.1 on page 214.

FORMULATING INITIAL IMPRESSIONS

AS COMMITTEE CHAIR, your first step is to invite open discussion with your committee members about what they "know" about each of the four presenting problems, or issues, and the relationship between them.

Drawing upon the task-group facilitation skills you learned in one of your social work practice classes, you help your committee members tease out the source(s) of their collective wisdom (or knowledge) as a group.

As a group you discuss possible relationships among the presenting problems and try to determine whether your answers are based on authority, tradition, experience, intuition, or the scientific method. During these discussions, the committee members learn some very important things, such as (1) how much of their present knowledge is based on empirical knowledge versus other ways of knowing; (2) the biases, values, or beliefs that are active among committee members; and (3) how the scientific method can be used to expand everyone's knowledge base. Six possible questions you could formulate are as follows:

1. Is poverty related to domestic violence?
2. Is poverty related to substance abuse?
3. Is poverty related to homelessness?
4. Is domestic violence related to substance abuse?
5. Is domestic violence related to homelessness?
6. Is substance abuse related to homelessness?

DETERMINING WHAT OTHERS HAVE FOUND

GIVEN YOUR SUPERB SKILLS as a group facilitator, you have energized your committee members and stimulated their curiosity such that they are eager to read the latest research about poverty, domestic violence, substance abuse, and homelessness. Each committee member accepts a task to search the literature for articles and information about the relationship between one or more of the four presenting problems of interest.

Committee members search a variety of sources such as professional journals, credible websites, and books. Using quality criteria to evaluate the evidence of information gathered, the committee synthesizes the knowledge gathered from these empirical sources. If so desired, the committee might endeavor to systematically assess the literature gathered through meta-analyses. Below are two general questions that you need to address in relation to your problem area:

1. What does the available literature have to say about poverty, domestic violence, substance abuse, and homelessness?

2. Has it been established that any two or more of these variables are, in fact, related? And if so, what is the relationship between or among them?

With a synthesis of the literature gathered, your committee will be in an excellent position to make an informed statement about up-to-date knowledge on the relationship between poverty, domestic violence, substance abuse, and homelessness.

REFINING THE GENERAL PROBLEM AREA

BY THIS POINT, the excitement of your committee members has waned. As it turns out, the task of reviewing the literature has been more onerous than anticipated because the number of research studies investigating poverty, domestic violence, substance abuse, and homelessness is overwhelming. For example, when searching for studies on domestic violence, committee members had to define "partner" in domestic violence and decide whether the research studies to be reviewed would include gay and lesbian partners as well as heterosexual partners. Moreover, applying criteria to evaluate individual studies was not as straightforward as initially thought.

But your committee has trudged through and found relevant empirical articles. To recharge the committee and keep the momentum of the research process going, you work with committee members to set priorities for the remainder of your work together. In short, you need to decide what research question(s)—exploratory, descriptive, or explanatory—will be the focus of your investigation. You also need to decide which research design is best suited to investigating the proposed research question.

The committee now decides to focus on the descriptive relationship between only two presenting problem areas—domestic violence and substance abuse. One of the many oversimplified examples from the preceding four highly interrelated variables (i.e., poverty, domestic violence, substance abuse, homelessness) might be:

Hypothesis: Relationship between two variables

Clients with substance abuse problems will also have domestic violence issues.

MEASURING THE VARIABLES

YOU NEED NOW TO REVIEW with your committee members the work you have accomplished in the previous steps. Planning thus far has largely been a conceptual exercise. However, when you start to define and decide how to measure your variables, you soon realize that the tasks become much more specific. With respect to measurement, committee members must develop a way to measure the two presenting problems (i.e., substance abuse and domestic violence) that will be studied and find measuring instruments for each variable.

Find out how other researchers measured their variables. If you feel that the variables were measured properly in previous studies, then you can use the same method to measure your variables, too. There is no need to reinvent the wheel if the previous measurements are valid and reliable. Your committee believes that the previous studies measured the two variables well, so you decide also to use them in your study. Thus you decide that your two variables will be measured as follows:

1. Substance abuse: *Substance Abuse Questionnaire* (SAQ)
2. Domestic violence: *Domestic Violence Inventory* (DVI)

SELECTING A SAMPLE

WITH A CLEAR RESEARCH HYPOTHESIS (i.e., *Clients with substance abuse problems will also have domestic violence issues*), a solid understanding of other research studies, and the selection of measuring instruments for key variables, your next step for the committee is to decide on the sampling procedures that will be used in the study. At this point, research and practice knowledge come together to help you ascertain which parameters for the sample will be most meaningful.

For example, it turns out that intake data show that most (but not all) clients presenting with either substance abuse or domestic violence problems at intake report that they have been living together for more than one year. The intake data show that only a handful of coupled clients are in new relationships of less than one year. Consequently, this characteristic of agency clients becomes a criterion to define the population, and consequently the sample, to be studied.

Once all of the sampling criteria are established, the committee must decide which particular sampling method to use. The aim is to select a sample that is representative (e.g., similar in age, race, marital status, and service history) of *all* clients who fit the eligibility criteria. Much more will be said about sampling in Chapter 11.

After reviewing the literature and evaluating all of the logistics in relation to administering the measuring instruments, the committee members decide to administer them as follows:

Protocol for administering the measuring instruments to a sample:

The SAQ and DVI will be administered to all partners living together for more than one year who are receiving social services from XYZ agency from July 1, 2018, to June 30, 2019. Both measuring instruments will be administered by the intake worker during the client's second visit to the agency.

ADDRESSING ETHICAL AND CULTURAL ISSUES

AS AN ETHICAL SOCIAL WORK PRACTITIONER who adheres to the NASW *Code of Ethics*, you are aware that not one speck of data for the study will be collected until proper procedures have been developed and independently reviewed. After reading Chapters 4 and 5 of this text and Section 5 of the NASW *Code of Ethics*, the committee gets to work on developing proper consent forms and research protocols as well as obtaining all necessary ethics approvals. Remember that you must:

— Write the research participant consent form and/or assent form

— Obtain written permission from your agency

— Obtain written approvals from appropriate institutional review boards (IRBs)

COLLECTING THE DATA

AT THIS POINT in the quantitative research process your study should be ethically and culturally sound. As discussed in Chapter 4, you can only collect data after you have obtained written consent and/or assent from your research participants. Data collection is a step that indicates the study is underway.

There are many different methods of data collection available, and each has particular advantages and disadvantages. Continuing with our example, data collection involves administering the SAQ and DVI instruments to sampled partners who have been living together for more than one year.

Once the study is underway, the protocols established for data collection should be carried out precisely so as to avoid errors. Moreover, data-collection procedures should not be changed. If changes are necessary, then they must be approved by the ethical oversight bodies involved *before* those changes are implemented.

Your committee's focus at this point is only to monitor that the study is being carried out as planned and to use research principles to troubleshoot any problems that arise.

ANALYZING THE DATA

GATHERING AND ANALYZING YOUR DATA is an exciting process because this is when you and your committee will get the answer to your hypothesis. Your committee members ensure that the data are properly entered into an appropriate computer program and analyzed. Chapter 17 discusses quantitative data analysis in detail. Your quantitative data analysis could be as simple as the following:

Data analysis:

— There were a total of 200 couples in the study; 150 had domestic violence issues, and 50 did not.

— Of the 150 couples who had domestic violence issues, 85% of them had at least one partner also experiencing substance abuse issues.

INTERPRETING THE DATA

GETTING AN ANSWER to your hypothesis and deciding on the usefulness of the answer are two separate steps. The committee will go beyond the reported "facts," as stated above, and make a conclusive statement such as:

Conclusion from the data analysis:

Substance abuse and domestic violence are co-occurring problems for most clients served by the agency. Thus, social work practitioners must be skilled in treating both presenting problems.

COMPARING RESULTS WITH FINDINGS FROM PREVIOUS STUDIES

AS COMMITTEE CHAIR, you know that every research study is only a single piece in the puzzle of knowledge development. Consequently, you ask the committee to consider the findings of your study in the context of the other research studies that you reviewed, as well as any new studies published while your study was being done.

By contrasting your findings with what others have found, your committee builds on the existing knowledge base. Simply put, your findings need to be compared with what others have found. For example,

---

Comparing your study's findings with findings from other studies:

— The findings from this study are consistent with the findings from other studies; that is, domestic violence and substance abuse issues are highly related to one another.

— This study adds new knowledge by finding this relationship for couples that have been living together for more than one year.

SPECIFYING THE STUDY'S LIMITATIONS

NO RESEARCH STUDY is perfect, and that includes yours. Many study limitations are predetermined by the particular research design that was used. For example, threats to internal and external validity are limitations commonly discussed in research reports and journal articles (Chapter 13).

Acknowledging your study's limitations can be a humbling experience. While you may be better informed at the conclusion of your study, completing one research study is not enough to alleviate your clients' struggles and suffering. The limitation section of your research report could read:

Limitations of our study:

— The limitations of this descriptive research design do not permit any inference of causation. We will never know if substance abuse causes domestic violence, or if domestic violence causes substance abuse.

— Also we will never know how poverty and homelessness play a role in domestic violence and substance abuse since these two variables were not included in the study.

WRITING AND DISSEMINATING THE STUDY'S RESULTS

A FINAL, IMPORTANT STEP in the research process is sharing the new knowledge learned in your study. In the academic world, dissemination most often refers to publication of the study in a peer-reviewed journal. While some practitioners also publish in peer-reviewed journals, dissemination in the practice world more commonly refers to sharing findings at conferences or local meetings.

The idea of dissemination is to make your study's results available to others who are working in the same area—whether as practitioners, researchers, policy makers, or educators. As committee chair you want to share your study's results with others in your agency.

The knowledge gained might be used to develop new procedures in the agency (e.g., intake, training, or referrals). Whatever the route of dissemination, the aim is to complete your research study with the highest level of integrity so that your results will be most useful to others.

Even with all the limitations of your study's research design, some data are better than none; that is, no matter how many threats to internal and external validity exist (Chapter 13), as long as the study's procedures and limitations are clearly spelled out in the final report, your study's findings will be useful to others.

SUMMARY

THIS CHAPTER BEGAN with a brief discussion on how the positivistic way of thinking can answer many of the research questions we can ask in addition to testing our hypotheses. We then delineated the generic steps that are taken when doing a quantitatively oriented study. The following chapter is a logical extension of this one in that it presents how the qualitative approach can answer our research questions as well.

	Study Questions for Chapter 6
	Essay — Discussion
1	Before you entered your social work program, and before you read this chapter, how did you think the quantitative research approach contributed to our profession's knowledge base? Discuss fully.
2	Discuss why the quantitative research approach is useful to knowledge generation. Discuss in detail using a social work example to illustrate your points.
3	In your own words, define the quantitative research approach. Provide a social work example to illustrate your points.
4	What is the positivistic way of thinking? Discuss in detail. Provide a social work example to illustrate your points.
5	Discuss why the quantitative research approach to knowledge generation places such a heavy emphasis on the *measurability of variables* within research studies. Discuss in detail using a social work example to illustrate your points.
6	Discuss why the quantitative research approach to knowledge generation places such a heavy emphasis on *objectivity* within research studies. Discuss in detail using a social work example to illustrate your points.
7	Discuss why the quantitative research approach to knowledge generation places such a heavy emphasis on *trying to reduce uncertainty* within research studies. Discuss in detail using a social work example to illustrate your points.
8	Discuss why the quantitative research approach to knowledge generation places such a heavy emphasis on the *duplication of research studies.* Discuss in detail using a social work example to illustrate your points.

9	In your own words, describe the quantitative research process by using one common social work example throughout your discussion.
10	What are concepts? Provide a few social work examples of them.
11	What are variables? Provide a few social work examples of them.
12	What are the main difference between concepts and variables? Provide social work examples to illustrate your points.
13	What are attributes of variables? Provide social work examples to illustrate your points.
14	What are independent variables? What are dependent variables? What are the main differences between them? Provide social work examples to illustrate your points.
15	What are nondirectional hypotheses? Provide a few social work examples.
16	What are directional hypotheses? Provide a few social work examples.
17	What are the differences between nondirectional and directional hypotheses? Provide a common example in your answer.

Critical Thinking — Application — Integration

	THE QUANTITATIVE RESEARCH APPROACH AND THE RESEARCHER
	Scenario 1: Make an argument that to be a competent social work researcher **you must know** the fundamental principles of the quantitative (positivistic) research approach in addition to its advantages and disadvantages. Provide clear and explicit **research-related** social work examples to illustrate your main points.
18	**Scenario 2:** Make an argument that **you do not have to know** the fundamental principles of the quantitative (positivistic) research approach in addition to its advantages and disadvantages to be a competent social work researcher. Provide clear and explicit **research-related** social work examples

to illustrate your main points.

Time to Choose: Which one of the above two scenarios do you feel is more consistent with the place of research in social work? Why? Provide relevant social work examples to illustrate your main points.

| 19 | **THE QUANTITATIVE RESEARCH APPROACH AND THE PRACTITIONER**

Scenario 1: Make an argument that to be an effective evidence-based social work practitioner **you must know** the fundamental principles of the quantitative (positivistic) research approach in addition to its advantages and disadvantages. Provide clear and explicit **practice-related** social work examples to illustrate your main points.

Scenario 2: Make an argument that **you do not have to know** the fundamental principles of the quantitative (positivistic) research approach in addition to its advantages and disadvantages whatsoever to be an effective evidence-based social work practitioner. Provide clear and explicit **practice-related** social work examples to illustrate your main points.

Time to Choose: Which one of the above two scenarios do you feel is more consistent with the concept of the contemporary evidence-based social work practice process as illustrated on pages 46–51? Why? Provide relevant social work examples to illustrate your main points. |
| 20 | **TIME TO PUT ON YOUR CRITICAL THINKING HAT**

1. Discuss the similarities and differences between your responses to Questions 18 and 19.

2. What are your thoughts on the belief that you'll need to know the fundamental principles of the quantitative (positivistic) research approach in addition to its advantages and disadvantages to be an effective evidence-based social work *practitioner* (Question 19) or a social work *researcher* (Question 18)? |

21

APPLICATION OF THE QUANTITATIVE RESEARCH APPROACH

Locate a published quantitatively oriented social work research article that contains a social work problem area or population that you're interested in. We suggest you locate a quantitatively oriented research study in Bruce Thyer's journal *Research on Social Work Practice* (Sage Publications). Hands down, this is the best journal to find good quantitatively oriented social work research studies. Use your newfound article when discussing the exercises that follow in addition to Figure 6.1 on page 214.

Step 1 (page 215 and all of Chapter 2): Discuss how the author identified the general problem area (Step 1 of the quantitative research approach). Do you have a clear understanding of the study's problem area? Could the author have been clearer? Justify your response by citing specific examples within the article's problem area that could have been clearer.

Step 2 (pages 215–230): Describe in your own words how the author probably followed the eight sub-steps in Step 2 of the quantitative research approach. Due to journal space limitations, most authors do not describe the process they used within each of the eight sub-steps. Nevertheless, all researchers who do quantitative studies have to go through each sub-step in one way or another.

Now the fun part: Describe what you believe this "one way or another" was for each one of the eight sub-steps; that is, what do you think was going though the author's mind when addressing each sub-step? What specific questions within this step do you think the author should have asked—and answered—for the study to be successful?

Step 3 (pages 230–232): Hypothetically describe how the author could have addressed the three sub-steps in Step 3. What specific questions within this step do you think the author should have asked—and answered—for the study to be successful?

Step 4 (page 232): Once again, get inside the author's head and discuss what she must have been thinking about when deciding on a data collection method for the study. What specific questions within this step do you think the author should have asked—and answered—for the study to be successful?

Step 5 (pages 233–235): You guessed it—it's time to do the same task as above only in relation to data analysis.

Step 6 (page 236): Yup, once again, but this time pay particular attention to the how the author compared the results of her study with other studies.

Step 7 (page 236): Nothing to do here since the author published the study you found at the beginning of this exercise—which is Step 7 of the quantitative research approach, dissemination of findings.

22	**QUANTITATIVE RESEARCH AND YOUR PROFESSIONAL DEVELOPMENT** 1. Review the three social work research-related roles you can take when you graduate—CSWE Competency 1 at the beginning of this chapter on page 206 (also discussed in Chapter 1 on pages 38–42). Thoroughly discuss how you feel this chapter will help you to perform one or more research-related roles when you graduate. Which one of the three roles do you believe this chapter helped you with the most? Why? Discuss in detail and provide an example to illustrate your main points. 2. Review CSWE Competency 4 at the beginning of this chapter on page 206. Thoroughly discuss how you feel this chapter will help you to become a practice-informed researcher and a research-informed practitioner. Discuss in detail and provide an example to illustrate your main points. 3. Review the evidence-based practice process as illustrated on pages 46–51. Thoroughly discuss how this chapter helps you to develop the skills you'll need for implementing one or more steps of the evidence-based practice process. 4. Discuss which step(s) you feel this chapter will help you with the most. Why? Be very specific and use relevant social work examples to illustrate your main points throughout your discussion. **NOTE:** This exercise should help you to realize that you can use "research roles" to help you become an evidence-based social work practitioner.
23	**MOVING AHEAD BY LOOKING BACK** At this point in your research methods course, how comfortable are you with discussing the place of research in social work with your field instructor, with your practice instructor, with your research instructor, with your supervisor at work, with the director of your social work program, or with your classmates? Discuss in detail.

7

CHAPTER

COMPETENCY 1: Demonstrate Ethical and Professional Behavior

You will learn that in order to be a successful evidence-based practitioner you have an ethical obligation to integrate three research roles into your daily practice activities as discussed in Chapter 1: (1) research consumer, (2) research partner—either as a co-researcher or research participant, and (3) creator and disseminator of research (or knowledge).

This entire chapter pertains to these three professional roles because an ethical and professional evidence-based social work practitioner must understand and appreciate the advantages and disadvantages that are embedded within all three research approaches to knowledge development that produce social work practice recommendations: quantitative (Chapter 6), qualitative (this chapter), and mixed methods (Chapter 8).

COMPETENCY 4: Engage in Practice-Informed Research and Research-Informed Practice

Competency 4 also pertains to the entire chapter because you have to:

1. Evaluate the overall value of the practice recommendations that a qualitative (interpretive) research study puts forward by evaluating the kinds of qualitative evidence that it used to formulate its findings and practice recommendations (**research consumer**—research-informed practice);

2. Participate in a research study—either as a co-researcher or research participant (**research partner**—practice-informed research). See 1 above and 3 below; and

3. Understand and appreciate the advantages and disadvantages of using the qualitative research approach to knowledge building before you actually do a qualitative research study (**creator and disseminator of research**—practice-informed research).

You'll also need to utilize evidence-based practice recommendations whenever possible; that is, you need to integrate (1) the best available research-based evidence with (2) your clinical expertise and (3) your client's values.

All of the above implies you'll need to know how to assess the overall rigor of a qualitatively based research study that produced its qualitative research-based evidence. In short, you need to ask and then answer a simple question: How seriously should I take the findings of any specific qualitatively oriented research study given how well the study followed the *interpretive way of thinking?*

COMPETENCY 9: Evaluate Practice with Individuals, Families, Groups, Organizations, and Communities

See Competencies 1 and 4.

The Qualitative Research Approach

CHAPTER 1   **Step 1.** Understanding the Research Process

CHAPTER 2   **Step 2.** Developing Research Questions

CHAPTER 3   **Step 3.** Reviewing the Literature

CHAPTERS 4 & 5   **Step 4.** Being Aware of Ethical and Cultural Issues

CHAPTERS 6–8   **Step 5.** Selecting a Research Approach

CHAPTERS 9 & 10   **Step 6.** Specifying How Variables Are Measured

CHAPTER 11   **Step 7.** Selecting a Sample

CHAPTERS 12 & 13   **Step 8.** Selecting a Research Design

CHAPTERS 14–16   **Step 9.** Selecting a Data-Collection Method

CHAPTERS 17 & 18   **Step 10.** Analyzing the Data

CHAPTERS 19 & 20   **Step 11.** Writing the Research Report

THE PREVIOUS CHAPTER PRESENTED a brief discussion on how social work knowledge is generated via the quantitative research approach, sometimes called the *positivistic research approach*. As you know, this approach provides us with quantitative data—that is, data that contain numbers. This chapter is a logical extension of the last one in that we now focus on the qualitative research approach, sometimes called the *interpretive research approach*. This approach provides us with qualitative data—that is, data that contain words, diagrams, illustrations, pictures, and stories.

As we know, the quantitative approach to knowledge development is embedded within the positivistic way of thinking about or viewing the world. In direct contrast to the quantitative approach, the qualitative approach to knowledge development is embedded within the interpretive way of thinking about or viewing the world. We will now turn our attention to the interpretive way of thinking.

WHAT IS THE INTERPRETIVE WAY OF THINKING?

THE QUALITATIVE RESEARCH APPROACH is the second research approach embedded within the scientific method of inquiry. It basically discards the quantitative notion that there is only one "external reality" waiting to be discovered. Instead, it's based on the interpretive perspective that takes the position that "reality" is defined by the research participants' interpretations of their own realities. In sum, the *subjective* reality is studied via by qualitative research approach rather than the *objective* one studied by the quantitative approach.

As you will see in Chapters 14–16, the differences between the philosophy of the quantitative and qualitative research approaches naturally lead to different data collection methods and analyses. Subjective reality, for example, cannot be easily explored through quantitatively oriented data-collection methods such as mailed surveys, structured observations, and analyses of existing statistics. However, there are a few good qualitatively oriented ways we can use to determine our research participant's subjective reality: interviewing, participant observations, secondary text data, and historical data.

> The differences between the philosophy of the quantitative and qualitative research approaches naturally lead to different data collection methods and analyses.

ONE REALITY VERSUS MANY

FROM THE QUANTITATIVE STANDPOINT, if you do not accept the idea of a single reality—which is not changed by being observed and/or measured, and from which you, the researcher, are "detached" from the study—then you are not a "real researcher" doing a "real research study." Thus, your study's findings are not considered to be of much use by those who strictly follow the positivistic approach.

But many of these researchers whose views were not thought to be valid were women and/or came from diverse minority groups. Some feminists, for example, have argued that there is not only one reality—there are many realities. They contend that men and women experience the world differently and so they both exist in different realities, constructed by them from their own perceptions.

CHANGING REALITIES

AS DISCUSSED IN CHAPTER 4, people from various cultural groups view "their worlds" from their individual perspectives, beliefs, and traditions, which means they will experience their own realities. As for the idea that reality is not changed by being observed and/or measured, some feminists have argued that a relationship of some kind is always formed between the researcher and the research participant (subject), resulting in yet another mutual reality constructed between the two of them. In any study involving human research participants, there will thus be at least three realities:

1. The researcher's reality
2. The research participant's reality
3. The mutual reality they (researcher and research participant) both create and share

Moreover, all three realities are constantly changing as the study proceeds and as further interactions occur. The quantitative notion of a single unchanged and unchanging reality, some feminists have argued, was typically a male idea, probably due to the fact that men view human relationships as less important than do women.

This is a low blow that will quite properly be resented by the many men who do in fact ascribe importance to relationships. But, that aside, perhaps the problem lies less with *phenomenalism* (a single unchanged reality as opposed to multiple changing realities) than it does with *scientism* (the idea that the physical and social sciences can be approached in the same way).

SUBJECTS VERSUS RESEARCH PARTICIPANTS

HAVING DEALT with what data are (don't ever write "data *is*"), let's go back to the implications of collecting data about people's subjective realities. Because it's the research participant's reality you want to explore, the research participant is a very important data source.

The quantitative approach may seem like it tends to relegate the research participant to the status of an object or subject. In a study of cesarean births at a hospital during a certain period, for example, Ms. Smith will not be viewed as an individual within the quantitative approach to knowledge development, but only as the seventeenth woman who experienced such a birth during that period. Details of her medical history may be gathered without any reference to Ms. Smith as a separate person with her own hopes, fears, failings, and strengths.

Conversely, a qualitative lens to cesarean births will focus on Ms. Smith's individual experiences. What was *her* experience? What did it mean to *her*? How did *she* interpret it in the context of *her own* reality?

Compared with the quantitative approach where research participants (subjects) are more passive than active, the qualitative approach actively engages the research participants to vigorously engage and guide the studies as they go along. So, at the risk of sounding overly simplistic, think of it this way: The quantitative approach gathers numbers from passive subjects whereas the qualitative approach gathers words from active research participants.

RESEARCHERS' VALUES

IN ORDER TO DISCOVER the truth of Ms. Smith's reality, however, you must be clear about the nature of your own reality. In Chapter 1 we talked about *value awareness* as one of the characteristics that you must have if you're going to do a quantitatively oriented research study; that is, you need to put aside your own values when you are conducting it or when you are evaluating the results obtained by other researchers. This is sometimes called *disinterestedness.*

Researchers who are *disinterested* are ones who are able to accept evidence, or data, that run against their own values. From a hardline positivistic perspective, this putting aside of values seems more akin to sweeping them under the carpet and pretending they don't exist. Researchers engaged in quantitative studies will deny that their own values are important. They claim their values have nothing to do with the study. In a nutshell, their values cease to exist.

> Qualitative researchers are not only a part of their own realities; they are a part of the mutual reality that is constructed through their interactions with their research participants.

Qualitative researchers take a very different view. Their values are not only a part of their own realities, they are a part of the mutual reality that is constructed through their interactions with their research participants. Qualitative researchers must therefore acknowledge and thoroughly explore their values so that the mutual shaping of realities resulting from the interaction with their research participants may be more completely and honestly understood.

The term *value awareness,* while important to both research approaches, is thus understood in different ways. To quantitative researchers, it means putting values aside so they don't affect the study. To qualitative researchers, it means an immersion in values so that their inevitable effect is understood and their research participants' realities emerge more clearly.

COMMONALITIES OF ALL QUALITATIVE RESEARCH STUDIES

LESLIE TUTTY, MIKE ROTHERY, AND RICK GRINNELL (1996) present a few characteristics that most qualitative research studies have in common:

1. They are conducted primarily in the natural settings where the research participants carry out their daily business in a "non-research" atmosphere.

2. Variables cannot be controlled and experimentally manipulated (though changes in variables and their effect on other variables can certainly be observed).

3. The questions to be asked are not always completely conceptualized at the outset (although they can be).

4. The data collected are heavily influenced by the experiences and priorities of the research participants, rather than being collected by predetermined and/or highly structured and/or standardized measurement instruments.

5. Meanings are drawn from the data (and presented to others) using processes that are more natural and familiar than those used within the quantitative method. The data need not be reduced to numbers and statistically analyzed although counting and statistics can be employed if they are thought useful.

PHASES OF THE QUALITATIVE APPROACH

LIKE QUANTITATIVE RESEARCHERS, qualitative researchers make a major commitment in terms of time, money, and resources when they undertake research studies. As can be seen in Figure 6.1 on page 214, a quantitative study has basic sequential steps that must be followed to produce useful quantitative data.

On the other hand, as can be seen in Figure 7.1 on the following page, a qualitative study does not have these specific steps—the activities are more phases than steps, as many of the phases highly interact with one another as the study progresses from one phase to the next. Look at how Phases 3a through 3d interact between and among one another. In short, they all are done at the same time. See **bold arrows** between dashed phases that show how Phases 3a–3d highly interact with one another.

One of the major differences between the two research approaches is how they utilize the literature. In a quantitative study, the literature is utilized the most within the first three steps of the research process. In a qualitative study, the literature is heavily utilized in all of the phases. The qualitative research approach is akin to exploring a social problem maze that has multiple entry points and paths.

You have no way of knowing whether the maze will lead you to a place of importance or not, but you enter into it out of your own curiosity and, perhaps, even conviction. You enter the maze without a map or a guide; you have only yourself to rely on and your notebook to record important events, observations, conversations, and impressions along the way.

You will begin your journey of qualitative inquiry by stepping into one entrance and forging ahead. You move cautiously forward, using all of your senses in an effort to pinpoint your location and what surrounds you at any one time.

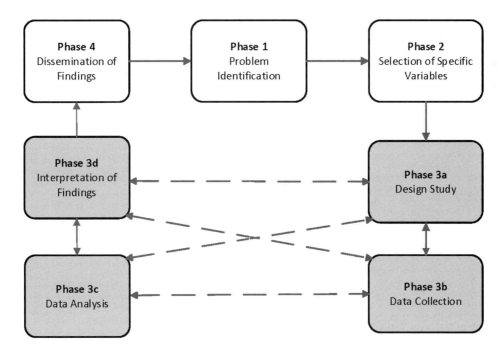

FIGURE 7.1

Generic Phases of the Qualitative (Interpretive) Research Approach

You may enter into dead-end rooms within the maze and have to backtrack. You may also encounter paths that you did not think possible. In some cases, you may even find a secret passageway that links you to a completely different maze.

PHASES 1 AND 2: PROBLEM IDENTIFICATION AND QUESTION FORMULATION

QUALITATIVE STUDIES ARE GENERALLY INDUCTIVE and require you to reason in such a way that you move from a part to a whole or from a particular instance to a general conclusion (see Figure 7.1). Let's return to the research problem introduced in the last chapter—racial discrimination within the social services. You begin the qualitative research process, once again, from your observations and/or hunches—ethnic minorities have the highest incidence of unemployment, poverty, and low education, but more Caucasians than ethnic minorities seek assistance from social services.

One of the major differences between the quantitative and qualitative research approaches is how they utilize the literature.

You can focus your qualitative research question by identifying the key concepts in your question. These key concepts set the parameters of your research study—they represent the outside boundaries of your maze. As in the quantitative research approach, you would want to review the literature related to your key concepts, but your literature review would have a very different purpose.

Rather than pinpointing exact variables to study, you review the literature to see how your key concepts have been generally described and defined by previous researchers. You might learn whether your maze will have rounded or perpendicular corners, or whether it will have multiple levels.

The knowledge you glean from the literature search assists you with ways of thinking that you hope will help you move through the maze and arrive at a meaningful understanding of the problem it represents. However, you must also be prepared to abandon what you think you know and accept new experiences as you proceed.

Let's revisit your research question:

> **Research question:**
> Do ethnic minorities have difficulty in accessing social services?

In your literature review, you would want to focus on definitions and theories related to discrimination within the social services. In the quantitative research approach, you reviewed the literature to search for meaningful variables that could be measured. In the qualitative approach, however, you do not want to rely on the literature to define your key variables. Rather, you will rely upon the qualitative research process itself to identify key variables and how they relate to one another. Remember, the identification and refinement of these variables will be coming from your research participants.

On rare occasions, hypotheses can be used in a qualitative research study. They can focus your research question even further. A hypothesis in a qualitative study is less likely to be outright accepted or rejected, as is the case in a quantitative study. Rather, it's a working hypothesis and is refined over time as new data are collected.

Your hypothesis is changed throughout the qualitative research process based on the reasoning of the researcher, not on any statistical test. All of this leads us to ask the question, "What do qualitative researchers actually do when they carry out a research study?" Neuman (2012) has outlined ten activities that the qualitative researcher engage in when carrying out a study:

1. Observes ordinary events and activities as they happen in natural settings, in addition to any unusual occurrences

2. Is directly involved with the people being studied and personally experiences the process of daily social life in the field

3. Acquires an insider's point of view while maintaining the analytic perspective or distance of an outsider

4. Uses a variety of techniques and social skills in a flexible manner as the situation demands

5. Produces data in the form of extensive written notes, as well as diagrams, maps, or pictures to provide detailed descriptions

6. Sees events holistically (e.g., as a whole unit, not in pieces) and individually in their social context

7. Understands and develops empathy for members in a field setting, and does not just record "cold" objective facts

8. Notices both explicit and tacit aspects of culture

9. Observes ongoing social processes without upsetting, disrupting, or imposing an outside point of view

10. Is capable of coping with high levels of personal stress, uncertainty, ethical dilemmas, and ambiguity

PHASE 3A: DESIGNING THE RESEARCH STUDY

YOU CAN ENTER INTO A QUALITATIVE RESEARCH STUDY with general research questions or working hypotheses but you are far less concerned about homing in on specific variables. Because qualitative research studies are inductive processes, you do not want to constrain yourself with preconceived ideas about how your concepts or variables will relate to one another.

Thus, while you will have a list of key concepts, and perhaps loosely defined variables, you want to remain open to the possibilities of how they are defined by your research participants and any relationships that your research participants may draw. In short, your research participants will refine the variables as your study progresses

A qualitative study is aimed at obtaining an in-depth understanding of a few cases rather than a general understanding of many cases or people. Thus, more often than not, the number of research participants in a qualitative study is much smaller than in a quantitative one. As discussed in Chapter 11, you will probably want to use a purposeful sampling strategy to select your research participants. This process selects the "best-fitting" people to provide data for your study.

The qualitative research approach is about studying a social phenomenon within its natural context. As such, the *case study* is a major qualitative research design. A case can be a person, a group, a community, an organization, or an event. You can study many different types of social phenomena within any one of these cases. Any case study design can be guided by different qualitative research methods.

PHASE 3B: COLLECTING THE DATA

QUALITATIVE RESEARCHERS are the principal instruments of data collection. This means that data collected are somehow "processed" through the person collecting them. Interviewing, for example, is a common data-collection method that produces text data (see Chapter 15). Data collection in the interview is interactive, so you can check out your understanding and interpretation of your participants' responses as you go along. To collect meaningful text data, you want to be immersed into the context or setting of the study.

You want to have some understanding, for example, of what it's like to be a client of a social service agency before you talk to clients about their experiences of discrimination, if any, within the social services. If you do not have a grasp of the setting in which you are about to participate, then you run the risk of misinterpreting what your research participants tell you.

> The qualitative research approach is about studying a social phenomenon within its natural context.

Given that your general research question evolves in a qualitative study, the data collection process is particularly vulnerable to the biases of the data collector. There are three principles to guide you in your data collection efforts:

First, make every effort to be aware of your own biases. In fact, your own notes on reactions and biases to what you are studying will be used as sources of data later on, when you interpret the data (Chapter 18).

Second, data collection is a two-way street. The research participants tell you their stories, and you tell them your understanding or interpretation of their stories. It's a process of checks and balances.

Third, qualitative data collection typically involves multiple data sources and multiple data-collection methods. In your study, you may see clients, line-level social workers, and supervisors as potential data sources. You may collect data from each of these groups using interviews, observation, and existing documentation (data-collection methods).

PHASES 3C AND 3D: ANALYZING AND INTERPRETING THE DATA

COLLECTING, ANALYZING, AND INTERPRETING QUALITATIVE DATA are highly intermingled. Let's say that, in your first round of data collection, you interview a number of ethnic minority clients about their perceptions of racial discrimination in the social services. Suppose they consistently tell you that to be a client of social services, they must give up many of their cultural values. You could then develop more specific research questions for a second round of interviews in an effort to gain a deeper understanding of the relationship between cultural values and being a social service client.

Overall, the process of analyzing qualitative data is an iterative one. This means that you must read and reread the volumes of data that you have collected. You will look for patterns and themes that help to capture how your research participants are experiencing the problem you are studying.

The ultimate goal is to interpret data in a way that reveals the true expressions of your research participants. You want to explain meaning according to the beliefs and experiences of those who provided the data. The aim is for you to "walk the walk" and "talk the talk" of your research participants and not to impose "outside" meaning to the data they provided. Much more will be said about analyzing and interpreting qualitative data in Chapter 18.

NUMBERS VERSUS WORDS

THE QUALITATIVE APPROACH to knowledge development says that the only real way to find out about the subjective reality of our research participants is to ask them, and the answer will come back in words, not in numbers. In a nutshell, qualitative research approaches produce qualitative data in the form of text. Quantitative research methods produce quantitative data in the form of numbers.

DATA ≠ INFORMATION

LET'S PAUSE FOR A MOMENT to discuss what is meant by data. The word "data" is plural; the singular is "datum" (from the Latin *dare*, "to give"). A datum is thus something that is given, either from a quantitative observation and/or measurement or from a qualitative discussion with Ms. Smith about her experiences in giving birth at her home.

A number of observations and/or measurements with the quantitative approach, or a number of discussions with the qualitative approach constitute data. Data are not the same thing as information, although the two words are often used interchangeably. The most important thing to remember at this point is that both approaches to the research method produce data; they simply produce different kinds of data.

Information is something you hope to get from the data once you have analyzed them—whether they are numbers or words. You might, for example, collect data about the home-birthing experiences of a number of women, and your analysis might reveal commonalties between them: perhaps all the women felt that their partners had played a more meaningful role in the birthing process at home than would have been possible in a hospital setting.

The enhanced role of the partner is *information* that you, as the researcher, have derived from the interview *data*. In other words, data are pieces of evidence, in the form of words (qualitative data) or numbers (quantitative data), that you put together to give you information—which is what the scientific research method is all about.

> Information is something you hope to get from the data once you have analyzed them—whether they are numbers or words.

So, in a nutshell, *information* is how you interpret the data. For example, if it's 86 degrees Fahrenheit outside, this is a fact measured by a thermometer. Someone who lives in Arizona may interpret this fact by saying it's "mild," while someone in Alaska may say it's "very hot." The interpretation of facts depends on one's individual reality. Information is nothing more than the subjective interpretation of objective facts.

PHASES 4 AND 5: PRESENTATION AND DISSEMINATION OF FINDINGS

QUALITATIVE RESEARCH REPORTS are generally lengthier than quantitative ones. This is because it's not possible to strip the context of a qualitative study and present only its findings. The knowledge gained from a qualitative endeavor is nested within the context from which it was derived. Furthermore, text data are more awkward and clumsy to summarize than numerical data.

Unlike quantitative studies, you cannot rely on a simple figure or table to indicate a finding. Instead, you display text, usually in the form of quotes or summary notes, to support your conclusions. Much more will be said about the presentation and dissemination of the findings derived from qualitative research studies in Chapters 18 and 20.

TABLE 7.1

Philosophical Differences Between the Quantitative and Qualitative Research Approaches Investigating the Identical Problem Area—Racial Discrimination within the Public Social Service System

Philosophical Concept	Research Approach	
	Quantitative (Positivistic) — Chapter 6 —	**Qualitative (Interpretive)** — Chapter 7 —
Perceptions of Reality	Ethnic minorities share similar experiences within the public social service system. These experiences can be described objectively; that is, a single reality exists outside any one person.	Individual and ethnic group experiences within the public social service system are unique. Their experiences can only be described subjectively; that is, a single and unique reality exists within each person.
Ways of "Knowing"	The experience of ethnic minorities within public social services can be revealed by closely examining specific parts of their experiences. Scientific principles, rules, and tests of sound reasoning are used to guide the research process.	The experience of ethnic minorities within public social services is revealed by capturing the whole experiences of a few cases. Parts of their experiences are considered only in relation to the whole of them. Sources of knowledge are illustrated through stories, diagrams, and pictures that are shared by the people with their unique life experiences.

Value Bases	The researchers suspend all their values related to ethnic minorities and social services from the steps taken within the research study. The research participant "deposits" data, which are screened, organized, and analyzed by the researchers who do not attribute any personal meaning to the research participants or to the data they provide.	The researcher *is* the research process, and any personal values, beliefs, and experiences of the researcher will influence the research process. The researcher learns from the research participants, and their interaction is mutual.
Applications	Research results are generalized to the population from which the sample was drawn (e.g., other minority groups, other social service programs). The research findings tell us the *average* experience that ethnic minorities have within the public social service system.	Research results tell a story of a few individuals' or one group's experience within the public social service system. The research findings provide an in-depth understanding of a few people. The life context of each research participant is key to understanding the stories he/she tells.

COMPARING RESEARCH APPROACHES

BY COMPARING THE PHILOSOPHICAL UNDERPINNINGS of quantitative and qualitative research approaches you can more fully appreciate their important differences. Each approach offers you a unique method of studying a social work–related problem and the same research problem can be studied using either approach.

Suppose for a moment that you are interested in a broad social problem such as racial discrimination. In particular, let's say you are interested in studying the social problem of racial discrimination within public social service programs. Let's now look at the major differences, via their philosophical concepts, between the two approaches and see how a general research problem, racial discrimination, could be studied under both approaches.

Table 7.1, on pages 264 and 265, compares how the two different research approaches could be used to examine the identical general problem area—racial discrimination within the public social service system.

So far we have been focusing on the differences between the two research approaches, but they also have many similarities. First, they both use careful and diligent research processes in an effort to discover and interpret knowledge. They both are guided by systematic procedures and orderly plans.

Second, both research approaches can be used to study any particular social problem. The quantitative approach is more effective than the qualitative approach in reaching a specific and precise understanding of one aspect (or part) of an already well-defined social problem. The quantitative approach seeks to answer research questions that ask about quantity, such as:

— Are women more depressed than men?

— Does the use of child sexual abuse investigation teams reduce the number of times an alleged victim is questioned by professionals?

— Is the degree of aggression related to the severity of crimes committed among inmates?

A qualitative research approach, on the other hand, aims to answer research questions that provide you with a more comprehensive understanding of a social problem from an intensive study of a few people. This approach is usually conducted within the context of the research participants' natural environments (Rubin & Babbie, 2017). Research questions for which the qualitative research approach would be appropriate might include:

— How do women experience depression as compared with men?

— How do professionals on child sexual abuse investigation teams work together to make decisions?

— How do federal inmates describe their own aggression in relation to the crimes they have committed?

As you will see throughout this book, both approaches can be used to study the same social problem—with different research questions, of course. Whichever approach is used clearly has an impact on the type of findings produced to answer a research question or to test a hypothesis.

USING BOTH APPROACHES IN A SINGLE STUDY

GIVEN THE SEEMINGLY CONTRADICTORY philosophical beliefs associated with the two research approaches, it's difficult to imagine how they could exist together in a single research study. Thus, many research studies use only one approach. The reason may, in part, relate to philosophy, but practical considerations of cost, time, and resources are also factors.

It's not unusual, however, to see quantitative data used within a qualitative study or qualitative data in a quantitative one. If you are using a quantitative approach, you could still ask research participants a few open-ended questions to more fully explain their experiences. In this instance, your quantitative research report would contain some pieces of qualitative data to help bring meaning to the study's quantitative findings.

Let's say you want to conduct a qualitative research study to examine your research question about discrimination within the public social service system. Surely you would want to identify how many research participants were included, as well as important defining characteristics such as their average age, the number who had difficulty accessing social services, or the number who were satisfied with the services they received.

While it's possible to incorporate qualitative research activities into a quantitative study (and quantitative research activities into a qualitative one), the dominant approach you select must be guided by your purpose for conducting the study in the first place. Ultimately, all research studies are about the pursuit of knowledge, but what kind of knowledge you are after is totally up to you—the social work researcher.

BOX 7.1	**Formulating Qualitative Research Questions**

QUALITATIVE ANALYSIS SEEKS to capture the richness of people's experiences in their own terms. Understanding and meaning emerge from in-depth analysis of detailed descriptions and verbatim quotations. The following example, one nurse's responses to a closed- and open-ended question on a survey, illustrates what is meant by depth, detail, and meaning. The first question was from a closed-ended question on a survey questionnaire:

QUANTITATIVE CLOSED-ENDED QUESTION:

Accountability, as practiced in our primary health care system, creates an undesirable atmosphere of anxiety among nurses. Check one below:

✓ 1. Strongly agree
   2. Agree
   3. Disagree
   4. Strongly disagree

As you can see above one nurse marked "strongly agree" to the above question. Now compare this response (1) to her response to the following open-ended question:

QUALITATIVE OPEN-ENDED QUESTION:

Please add any personal comments you'd like to make about any part of the primary health care system's accountability approach.

HER RESPONSE:

"Fear" is the word for "accountability" as applied in our system. Accountability is a political ploy to maintain power and control us. The disappointment in our system is incredible. You wouldn't believe the new layers of administration that have been created just to keep this system going. Come down and visit us in hell sometime.

These two responses illustrate one kind of difference that can exist between qualitative data derived from responses to open-ended questions and quantitative measurement. Quantitative measures are succinct and easily aggregated for analysis; they are systematic, standardized, and easily presented in a short space.

By contrast, qualitative responses are longer and more detailed; analysis is difficult because responses are neither systematic nor standardized. The open-ended response permits us to understand the world as seen by the respondent.

Direct quotations are a basic source of raw data in interpretive studies. They reveal the respondent's level of emotion, thoughts, experiences, and basic perceptions.

It's important to keep in mind that the purposes and functions of qualitative and quantitative data on questionnaires are different, yet complementary. The statistics from standardized items make summaries, comparisons, and generalizations quite easy and precise, whereas the narrative comments from open-ended questions are typically meant to provide a forum for explanations, meanings, and new ideas.

WHAT DO YOU REALLY WANT TO KNOW?

AS MENTIONED PREVIOUSLY, both research approaches have their advantages and disadvantages, and both shine in different phases within the research method. Which approach you select for a particular study depends not on whether you are a positivist or an interpretivist but on what particular research question your study is trying to answer. Are you looking for descriptions or explanations? If the former, a qualitative study will be spot on; if the latter, a quantitative one will do the trick.

Human nature being what it is, we are always looking, in the end, for explanation. We want to know not only what reality is like but also what its interconnections are and what we can do to change it to make our lives more comfortable and safer. However, first things first: Description comes before explanation. Before you can know whether poverty is related to child abuse, for example, you must be able to describe both poverty and child abuse as fully as possible. Similarly, if you want to know whether low self-esteem in women contributes to spousal abuse, you must know what self-esteem is and what constitutes abuse.

By now, because you are a social worker interested in people and not numbers, you may be ready to throw the whole quantitative research approach out the window. But let's be sure that you don't throw out the baby with the bath water. Social work values dictate that you must make room for different approaches to knowledge development, different opinions, and differing views on what reality really is. Believe us, the two different approaches each have value in their own way, depending on what kind of data (quantitative and/or qualitative) you hope to gain from a particular research study.

EXAMPLE OF USING BOTH APPROACHES IN A SINGLE STUDY

SUPPOSE, FOR EXAMPLE, you believe that cesarean operations are being conducted too often and unnecessarily for the convenience of obstetricians rather than for the benefit of mothers and their babies. To confirm or refute this hunch (it has yet to be proven), you would need data on the number of cesarean births in a particular time frame, and on how many of them were justified on the basis of medical need. Numbers would be required—quantitative data.

Which research approach you select for a particular study depends not on whether you are a positivist or an interpretivist but on what particular research question your study is trying to answer.

The questions about how many and how often could not be answered solely by descriptions of Ms. Smith's individual experiences. On the other hand, Ms. Smith's experiences would certainly lend richness to the part of your study that asked how far the hospital's services took the well being of mothers into account.

Many of the best research studies use quantitative and qualitative methods within the same study (topic of next chapter). It's important to remember that the former provides the necessary numerical data while the latter provides the human depth that allows for a richer understanding of the numbers in their particular context.

Sometimes, therefore, depending on the research question (assumption) to be answered, Ms. Smith will be seen as no more than a number. At other times, her individuality will be of paramount importance. If she is seen as a number, for example, her role will be passive. She will be one of a large number of persons.

On the other hand, if she is seen as an individual, her part in the research study will be far more active. It's *her* reality that you are now exploring. She will be front and center in a research study that is driven by her and not the researcher. Even the language will change. She is no longer a subject—or possibly an object—but a full and equal *participant*, along with the researcher.

Box 7.1 provides an interesting example of how one researcher asked both open- and closed-ended questions in a mail survey. The closed-ended questions could be considered quantitative, while the open-ended one could be considered qualitative.

ADVANTAGES AND DISADVANTAGES

ACCORDING TO COLORADO STATE UNIVERSITY'S WRITING CENTER (2011), qualitative research has several advantages and disadvantages.

The **advantages** of the qualitative method are as follows:

1. Accounts for the complexity of group behaviors

2. It reveals interrelationships among multifaceted dimensions of group interactions

3. It provides context for behaviors

4. It reveals qualities of group experience in a way that other forms of research cannot

5. It helps determine questions and types of follow-up research

6. It reveals descriptions of behaviors in context by stepping outside the group

7. It allows qualitative researchers to identify recurring patterns of behavior that participants may be unable to recognize

Qualitative research expands the range of knowledge and understanding of the world beyond ourselves. It often helps us see why something is the way it is, rather than just presenting a phenomenon. For instance, a quantitative study may find that students who are taught composition using a process method receive higher grades on papers than students taught using a product method.

However, a qualitative study of composition instructors could reveal why many of them still use the product method even though they are aware of the benefits of the process method.

The **disadvantages** of the qualitative method are as follows:

1. Researcher bias can bias the design of a study

2. Researcher bias can enter into data collection

3. Sources or subjects may not all be equally credible

4. Some subjects may be previously influenced and affect the outcome of the study

5. Background information may be missing

6. The study group may not be representative of the larger population

7. Analysis of observations can be biased

8. Any group that is studied is altered to some degree by the very presence of the researcher. Therefore, any data collected are somewhat skewed

9. It takes time to build trust with participants that facilitates full and honest self-representation. Short-term observational studies are at a particular disadvantage where trust building is concerned

10. The quality of the data alone is problematic. Ethnographic research is time-consuming, potentially expensive, and requires a well trained researcher

11. Too few data can lead to false assumptions about behavior patterns. Conversely, a large quantity of data may not be effectively processed

12. The data collector's first impressions can bias data collection

13. Narrative inquiries do not lend themselves well to replicability and are not generalizable

14. Narrative inquiries are considered unreliable by experimentalists. However, ethnographies can be assessed and compared for certain variables to yield testable explanations;

this is as close as ethnographic research gets to being empirical in nature

15. Qualitative research is neither prescriptive nor definite. While it provides significant data about groups or cultures and prompts new research questions, narrative studies do not attempt to answer questions, nor are they predictive of future behaviors

SUMMARY

THIS CHAPTER BRIEFLY DISCUSSED the qualitative research approach to knowledge building and also highlighted a few differences and similarities between the quantitative approach. These two complementary and respected research approaches differ in terms of their philosophical principles, but they both generate useful knowledge for our profession. They simply complement each other by providing different kinds of data, quantitative and qualitative.

The most important thing to remember is that the research question determines which research approach(es) is(are) utilized to answer the question. The question always guides the research approach that will answer it, so a chosen predetermined research approach should never guide the formulation of the question.

The following chapter describes in detail how you can combine both approaches in a single research study, but the most important thing to remember about the next chapter is that you must *purposely and systematically integrate* both quantitative and qualitative data into a single study in an effort to increase our understanding of the phenomenon being studied. In other words, both approaches have to complement the overall purpose of the study.

	Study Questions for Chapter 7
	Essay — Discussion
1	1. Discuss the qualitative (interpretive—this chapter) way of thinking. 2. Now discuss the quantitative (positivistic—Chapter 6) way of thinking. 3. Compare and contrast the two ways of thinking using one common social work example throughout your discussion.
2	1. What kind of data do positivistic research studies produce? 2. What kind of data do interpretive research studies produce? 3. Provide specific social work examples for each research approach.
3	1. How many realities do positivistic researchers believe to exist? 2. How many realities do interpretive researchers believe to exist? 3. Compare and contrast their differential perceptions of realities. Use as many social work examples that you can think of to illustrate your points.
4	Discuss the differential roles that research participants play within quantitative and qualitative research studies. Provide examples to illustrate your points.
5	Discuss the differences between data and information. Use a social work example throughout your discussion.
6	Discuss the term "value awareness" in reference to quantitative and qualitative studies. Provide social work examples to illustrate your points.
7	List, discuss, and provide social work examples of the commonalities in all qualitative research studies.
8	List, discuss, and provide specific social work examples of all the phases within the qualitative research approach.

9	Provide one common social work example when comparing both research approaches in reference to their *philosophical differences.*
10	Provide one common social work example when comparing both research approaches in reference to their *differential perceptions of reality.*
11	Provide one common social work example when comparing both research approaches in reference to their *differential perceptions on ways of knowing.*
12	Provide one common social work example when comparing both research approaches in reference to their *differential value bases.*
13	Provide one common social work example when comparing both research approaches in reference to their *applications to social work practice.*
14	List, discuss, and provide specific social work examples of the two research approaches in reference to their *similarities.*
15	Discuss in detail how you would go about combining both research approaches in a single social work study.

Critical Thinking — Application — Integration

16	**APPLICATION OF THE QUALITATIVE RESEARCH APPROACH** Locate a published qualitatively oriented social work research article that contains a social work problem area or population that you're interested in. We suggest you locate a qualitatively oriented research study in Karen Staller and Karen Broadhurst's journal *Qualitative Social Work* (Sage Publications). Hands down, this is the best journal to find good qualitative social work research studies. Use your newfound article when discussing the exercises that follow in addition to Figure 7.1 on page 257. **First—Phases 1 and 2** (pages 258–260): Using the book's content when discussing this phase in relation to *problem identification and question formulation,* list and discuss the specific questions you think the author should have asked—and answered—for the study to be successful. **Second—Phase 3a** (page 260): Using the book's content when discussing this phase in relation to *designing the research study,* list and then discuss the

specific questions you think the author should have asked—and answered—for the study to be successful.

Third—Phase 3b (page 261): Using the book's content when discussing this phase in relation to *collecting data,* list and discuss the specific questions you think the author should have asked—and answered—for the study to be successful.

Fourth—Phase 3c and 3d (pages 262–263): Using the book's content when discussing this phase in relation to *analyzing and interpreting qualitative data,* list and discuss the specific questions you think the author should have asked—and answered—for the study to be successful.

Fifth—Phases 4 and 5 (page 263–264): Using the book's content when discussing this phase in relation to *disseminating the study's findings,* list and discuss the specific questions you think the author should have asked—and answered—for the study to be successful.

THE QUALITATIVE RESEARCH APPROACH AND THE RESEARCHER

Scenario 1: Make an argument that to be a competent social work researcher **you must know** the fundamental principles of the qualitative (interpretive) research approach in addition to its advantages and disadvantages. Provide a clear and explicit **research-related** social work example to illustrate your main points.

17

Scenario 2: Make an argument that **you do not have to know** the fundamental principles of the qualitative (interpretive) research approach in addition to its advantages and disadvantages to be a competent social work researcher. Provide a clear and explicit **research-related** social work example to illustrate your main points.

Time to Choose: Which one of the above two scenarios do you feel is more consistent with the place of research in social work? Why? Provide relevant social work examples to illustrate your main points.

THE QUALITATIVE RESEARCH APPROACH AND THE PRACTITIONER

Scenario 1: Make an argument that to be an effective evidence-based social work practitioner **you must know** the fundamental principles of the qualitative (interpretive) research approach in addition to its advantages and disadvantages. Provide clear and explicit **practice-related** social work examples to illustrate your main points.

18

Scenario 2: Make an argument that **you do not have to know** the fundamental principles of the qualitative (interpretive) research approach in addition to its advantages and disadvantages to be an effective evidence-based social work practitioner. Provide clear and explicit **practice-related** social work examples to illustrate your main points.

Time to Choose: Which one of the above two scenarios do you feel is more consistent with the concept of the contemporary evidence-based social work practice process as illustrated on pages 46–51? Why? Provide relevant social work examples to illustrate your main points.

19	**TIME TO PUT ON YOUR CRITICAL THINKING HAT** **1.** Discuss the similarities and differences between your responses to Questions 17 and 18. **2.** What are your thoughts on the belief that you'll need to know the fundamental principles of the qualitative (interpretive) research approach in addition to its advantages and disadvantages to be an effective evidence-based social work *practitioner* (Question 18) or a social work *researcher* (Question 17)?
20	**QUALITATIVE RESEARCH AND YOUR PROFESSIONAL DEVELOPMENT** **1.** Review the three social work research-related roles you can take when you graduate—CSWE Competency 1 at the beginning of this chapter on page 250 (also discussed in Chapter 1 on pages 38–42). Thoroughly discuss how you feel this chapter will help you to perform one or more research-related roles when you graduate. Which one of the three roles do you believe this chapter helped you with the most? Why? Discuss in detail and provide an example to illustrate your main points. **2.** Review CSWE Competency 4 at the beginning of this chapter on page 250. Thoroughly discuss how you feel this chapter will help you to become a practice-informed researcher and a research-informed practitioner. Discuss in detail and provide examples to illustrate your main points. **3.** Review the evidence-based practice process as illustrated on pages 46–51. Thoroughly discuss how this chapter helps you to develop the skills you'll need for implementing one or more steps of the evidence-based practice process. **4.** Discuss which step(s) you feel this chapter will help you with the most. Why? Be very specific and use relevant social work examples to illustrate your main points throughout your discussion. **NOTE:** This exercise should help you to realize that you can use "research roles" to help you become an evidence-based social work practitioner.

8

CHAPTER

COMPETENCY 1: Demonstrate Ethical and Professional Behavior

You will learn that in order to be a successful evidence-based practitioner you have an ethical obligation to integrate three research roles into your daily practice activities as discussed in Chapter 1: (1) research consumer, (2) research partner—either as a co-researcher or research participant, and (3) creator and disseminator of research (or knowledge).

This entire chapter pertains to these three professional roles because an ethical and professional evidence-based social work practitioner must understand and appreciate the advantages and disadvantages that are embedded within all three research approaches to knowledge development that produce social work practice recommendations: quantitative (Chapter 6), qualitative (Chapter 7), and mixed-methods (this chapter).

COMPETENCY 4: Engage in Practice-Informed Research and Research-Informed Practice

Competency 4 also pertains to the entire chapter because you have to:

1. Evaluate the overall value of the practice recommendations that a mixed method research study puts forward by evaluating the kinds of mixed method evidence that it used to formulate its findings and practice recommendations (**research consumer**—research-informed practice);

2. Participate in a research study—either as a co-researcher or research participant (**research partner**—practice-informed research). See 1 above and 3 below; and

3. Understand and appreciate the advantages and disadvantages of using the mixed methods research approach to knowledge building before you actually do a mixed methods research study (**creator and disseminator of research**—practice-informed research).

You'll also need to utilize evidence-based practice recommendations whenever possible; that is, you need to integrate (1) the best available research-based evidence with (2) your clinical expertise and (3) your client's values

All of the above implies you'll need to know how to assess the overall rigor of a mixed methods research study that produced its mixed methods research-based evidence. In short, you need to ask and then answer a simple question: How seriously should I take the findings of any specific mixed methods research study given how well the study followed the *positivist and interpretive ways of knowing?*

COMPETENCY 9: Evaluate Practice with Individuals, Families, Groups, Organizations, and Communities

See Competencies 1 and 4.

8

The Mixed-Methods Research Approach

CHAPTER 1   **Step 1.** Understanding the Research Process

CHAPTER 2   **Step 2.** Developing Research Questions

CHAPTER 3   **Step 3.** Reviewing the Literature

CHAPTERS 4 & 5   **Step 4.** Being Aware of Ethical and Cultural Issues

CHAPTERS 6–8   **Step 5.** Selecting a Research Approach

CHAPTERS 9 & 10 **Step 6.** Specifying How Variables Are Measured

CHAPTER 11   **Step 7.** Selecting a Sample

CHAPTERS 12 & 13 **Step 8.** Selecting a Research Design

CHAPTERS 14–16   **Step 9.** Selecting a Data-Collection Method

CHAPTERS 17 & 18 **Step 10.** Analyzing the Data

CHAPTERS 19 & 20 **Step 11.** Writing the Research Report

CHAPTER **1** PRESENTED A BRIEF RATIONALE of why we should use, whenever possible, the scientific method of inquiry to answer our research questions or to test our hypotheses. As presented in Table 1.1 on pages 26–29, the scientific method contains three types of research approaches to answer our research questions or to test our hypotheses—the quantitative approach (sometimes called *positivistic*) and the qualitative approach (sometimes called *interpretive*).

With a little forethought you can easily combine both research approaches in a single study. When this is done the research approach is called the *mixed-methods* research approach. Mixed-methods research studies involve carefully integrating both the quantitative and qualitative approaches into a single study.

POPULARITY OF THE APPROACH

WHY ARE RESEARCHERS drawn to the mixed-methods research approach? Its popularity can be easily documented through journal articles, conference proceedings, books, and the formation of special interest groups (Creswell, 2010; Plano Clark, 2010). The mixed-methods research approach has been called:

— The "third methodological movement" following the developments of the first quantitative (positivistic) and then qualitative (interpretive) research approach (Tashakkori & Teddlie, 2003a, p. 5),

— The "third research paradigm" (Johnson & Onwuegbuzie, 2004, p. 15), and

— "A new star in the social science sky" (Mayring, 2007, p. 1).

AN INTUITIVE RESEARCH METHOD

WHY DOES THIS APPROACH MERIT SUCH SUPERLATIVES? One answer is that it's an intuitive way of doing a research study that we use in our everyday lives. Consider for a moment *An Inconvenient Truth*, the award-winning documentary on global warming featuring the former U.S. Vice President and Nobel Prize winner Al Gore.

In Gore's documentary, he narrated both the statistical trends (quantitative) and the stories (qualitative) of his personal journey related to the changing climate and global warming. His documentary brings together both quantitative data (derived from the positivistic point of view) and qualitative data (derived from the interpretive point of view) to tell a single story.

Also, listen closely to CNN's broadcast reports about President Trump, immigration, hurricanes, tornadoes, Russia, China, North Korea, global warming, tidal waves, forest fires, gun laws, voting rights, budget hearings, or financial bailouts. The "trends" uncovered using quantitative data-collection techniques (e.g., standard measuring instruments such as thermometers for global warming topics) are supported by the individual stories collected using qualitative techniques (e.g., qualitative interviews, subjective observations).

Or listen to commentators at sporting events. There's often a play-by-play commentator who describes the somewhat linear unfolding of the game (a positivistic perspective, if you will) and then the additional commentary by the "color" announcer who tells us about the individual stories and highlights of the personnel on the playing field (from an interpretive point of view, if you will). Again, both quantitative and qualitative data come together in these broadcasts.

In these instances, we see mixed-methods thinking in ways that Greene (2007) called the "multiple ways of seeing and hearing." These multiple ways are visible in everyday life, and the mixed-methods research approach becomes a natural outlet for many, but not all, research studies.

AN ACCESSIBLE APPROACH TO SCIENTIFIC INQUIRY

But other factors also contribute to the ever-growing interest in mixed-methods research. We now fully recognize it as an accessible approach to the scientific inquiry process (see Figure 1.1 on page 20). Many researchers have research questions (or problems) that can best be answered using mixed-methods approaches, and they see the value of using them (as well as the challenges they pose).

Understanding the nature of the mixed-methods research approach is an important first step to actually using it in a research study. Thus, this chapter reviews several preliminary considerations necessary before you can design a mixed-methods study. We are assuming you have mastered the content in the previous seven chapters.

DEFINITION

A DEFINITION for the mixed-methods research approach must incorporate many diverse viewpoints. It has six core characteristics:

1. **Collects, analyzes, and justifies the use of both quantitative and qualitative data (based on the research question of course).**

   Example: A researcher collects quantitative data via standardized measuring instruments (e.g., Chapter 10) and qualitative data via interviews with focus groups (Chapter 15) in order to see if the two types of data show similar results but from different perspectives. See the study on developing a health-promotion perspective for older driver safety in the occupational science area by Classen et al. (2007).

2. **Mixes, integrates, or links quantitative and qualitative data by (1) combining or merging them, (2) having one build on the other, or (3) embedding one within the other.**

   Example: A researcher collects data using quantitative-types of experimental procedures (Chapter 13) and follows up with qualitative-types of interviews (Chapter 15) with a few individuals who participated in the research study to help explain their scores on the experimental outcomes. See the study of college students' copy-and-paste note-taking by Igo, Kiewra, & Bruning (2008).

3. **Gives priority to one or both forms of data.**

   Example: A researcher explores how individuals describe a topic by starting with face-to-face qualitative interviews (Chapter 15), analyzing the qualitative data (Chapter 17), and using the findings to develop a mailed survey instrument (Chapter 14). This instrument is then administered to a sample from a population (Chapter 11) to see if the qualitative findings can be generalized to a population. See the study of lifestyle behaviors of Japanese college women by Tashiro (2002) and the psychological study of the tendency to perceive the self as significant to others in young adults' romantic relationships by Mak and Marshall (2004).

4. **Uses these procedures in a single study or in multiple phases of a program of study**.

   Example: A researcher conducts an experiment (Chapter 13) in which quantitatively oriented measuring instruments (Chapter 10) are used to assess the impact of a treatment intervention on an outcome variable. Before the experiment begins, however, the researcher collects qualitative data to help design the treatment intervention itself or to design better strategies to recruit participants (Chapter 14) to the study. See the study of physical activity and diet for families in one community by Brett, Heimendinger, Boender, Morin, & Marshall (2002).

5. **Frames these procedures within philosophical worldviews and theoretical lenses.**

   Example: A researcher seeks to change our understanding of some issues facing women (Chapter 2). The researcher gathers data through qualitatively oriented focus groups

(Chapter 15) in order to explore the meaning of the issues for women (Chapter 18).

The larger framework of change guides the researcher and informs all aspects of the study, including the issues being studied, data collection, and the call for reform at the end of the study. See the study exploring student–athlete culture and understanding specific rape myths by McMahon (2007).

6. **Combines the procedures into specific research designs that direct the plan for conducting the study.**

Example: A researcher seeks to evaluate a social service program that has been implemented in the community (Chapter 13). The first step is to collect and analyze qualitative data via face-to-face interviews (Chapters 15 and 18) to determine what questions need to be addressed (Chapter 2). Then a measuring instrument is designed (Chapters 9 and 10) to measure the impact of the program. This instrument is then used to compare certain outcomes both before and after the program has been implemented (Chapter 13).

From this comparison, follow-up individual face-to-face interviews are conducted to determine why the program did or did not work. This multiphase mixed-methods study is often found in long-term evaluation projects. See the study of the long-term impacts of qualitative programs at a historical site by Farmer & Knapp (2008).

Box 8.1 on the following two pages provides an example of how the mixed-methods approach can be used in a single study on domestic violence.

RESEARCH PROBLEMS AND MIXED METHODS

THE AUTHORS OF THE PRECEDING EXAMPLES crafted their studies as mixed-methods projects based on their assumption that mixed methods could best answer their research questions. When preparing a research study employing the mixed-methods approach, we need to provide a justification for its use. Not all research questions justify the use of a mixed-methods approach, just as not all situations justify the use of either the quantitative or the qualitative approach.

BOX 8.1	**The Mixed-Methods Research Approach to Understanding Domestic Violence**

SUPPOSE YOU'RE INTERESTED in studying domestic violence and want to conduct a research study with the following six sub-objectives:

1. To determine the prevalence of domestic violence in your community
2. To understand the nature and extent of domestic violence in your community
3. To find out what it means for a woman and a man to live in a household with domestic violence
4. To understand why, in spite of domestic violence, some victims—men as well as women—continue to live in the relationship
5. To describe the types of social work services that are available to victims of domestic violence in your community
6. To establish the socioeconomic demographic profile of people who are consumers of your services

To achieve the above six sub-objectives, your overall study needs to be carried out by using the quantitative and qualitative research approaches at the same time. For example:

1. **Sub-objective 1** may be best studied through data-collection methods that are usually associated with the quantitative (positivistic) research approach—that is, counting the number of households with domestic violence episodes using a predetermined and accepted set of criteria. This approach will provide numerical data.
2. For **sub-objective 2,** you will need to use data-collection and analysis methods from *both* research approaches. The nature of domestic violence

can best be explored through traditional qualitative (interpretive) data-collection methods such as in-depth personal interviews, focus groups, narratives, participant observation, and oral histories. The extent of domestic violence is probably best answered through traditional quantitative (positivistic) data-collection methods such as mailed and telephone surveys and analyses of agency records.

3. **Sub-objective 3** can best be explored using qualitative data-collection methods such as in-depth interviews, group interviews with victims, narratives, oral histories, and case studies, as no quantitative method will give you more accurate data on what it means for a victim to live in a house with domestic violence.

4. The reasons for living in the relationship in spite of violence **(sub-objective 4)** can be investigated through a number of data-collection methods belonging to both research approaches. You can collect data through one method only or through a number of them.

5. Similarly, "types of service" **(sub-objective 5)** can best be studied through an interpretive data-collection approach such as in-depth interviews with social workers and their clients alike.

6. The "profile of consumers" **(sub-objective 6)** may be answered by using traditional quantitative data-collection methods such as mailed survey questionnaires or highly structured interview schedules.

There might be times, however, when the qualitative approach is indeed the best approach to use, such as when we wish to explore a problem, honor the voices of our research participants, map the complexity of the situation, or convey multiple perspectives from our research participants. At other times, the quantitative research approach might be best, because we may seek to understand the relationship among variables or to determine if one group performs better on an outcome variable than another group.

We should never minimize, however, the importance of choosing either a quantitative approach or a qualitative one when it's fully merited by the research question under investigation. Instead of thinking about fitting different methods to specific content topics, for example, we suggest thinking about fitting methods to different types of research problems. For example, we may find that a mailed survey best fits a quantitative approach because of the need to understand the views of a large number of participants within an entire population.

An experiment may also work best when we need to determine whether a treatment works better than a control condition. Likewise, ethnography may best fit a qualitative approach because of the need to understand how culture-sharing groups work.

What situations, then, warrant an approach that thoughtfully and systematically combines quantitative and qualitative research methodologies—a mixed-methods inquiry? Research problems suited for mixed-methods research approaches are those in which:

1. One data source may be insufficient
2. Results need to be explained
3. Exploratory findings need to be generalized
4. A second method is needed to enhance a primary method
5. A theoretical stance needs to be employed
6. An overall research objective can be best addressed with multiple phases or projects

ONE DATA SOURCE MAY BE INSUFFICIENT

QUALITATIVE DATA can provide a *detailed* understanding of a problem while quantitative data can provide a more *general* understanding of a problem. This qualitative understanding arises out of studying a few individuals and exploring their perspectives in great depth whereas the quantitative understanding arises from examining a large number of people and assessing responses to a few variables. The limitations of one approach can be offset by the strengths of the other, and the combination of quantitative and qualitative data provide a more complete understanding of the research problem than either approach by itself.

There are several ways in which one data source (who generated the data) may be inadequate. One type of data may not tell the complete story, or we may lack confidence in the ability of one type of data to fully answer the research question. The results from the quantitative and qualitative data may be contradictory, which could not be known by collecting only one type of data.

Further, the type of evidence gathered from one level in an organization might differ from evidence obtained from other levels. These are all situations in which using only one approach to address the research problem would be insufficient. A mixed-methods design best fits this kind of scenario.

EXAMPLE

WHEN KNODEL AND SAENGTIENCHAI (2005) studied the role that older-aged parents play in the care and support of adult sons and daughters with HIV and AIDS and AIDS orphans in Thailand, they collected both quantitative survey data and qualitative open-ended interview data. They explained that they used both forms of data to understand the problem because quantitative data alone would be inadequate:

> The issues (in the interviews) covered were similar to the AIDS
> parents survey, but the conversational nature of the interview
> and the fact it allowed open-ended responses provided
> parents the opportunity to elaborate on the issues and the
> circumstances affecting them. (p. 670)

EXPLAIN A STUDY'S INITIAL RESULTS

SOMETIMES THE RESULTS of a study may provide an incomplete understanding of a research problem and further explanation is needed. In this case, a mixed-methods study is used with the second database helping to explain the first database. A typical situation is when the meaning of quantitative results requires an explanation.

Quantitative results can easily provide general explanations for the relationships among variables, but the more detailed understanding of what the statistical tests or effect sizes actually mean is lacking. Qualitative data and results can help build that understanding.

EXAMPLE

WEINE ET AL. (2005) conducted a mixed-methods study investigating family factors and processes involved in Bosnian refugees participating in multiple-family support and education groups in Chicago. The first quantitative phase of their study addressed the factors that predicted engagement in the groups, while the second qualitative phase consisted of interviews with family members to assess the family processes involved in engagement as multiple-family groups. The researchers' rationale for using a mixed-methods design to study this situation was as follows:

Quantitative analysis addressed the factors that predicted engagement. In order to better understand the processes by which families experience engagement, we conducted a qualitative content analysis to gain additional insight. (p. 560)

GENERALIZE EXPLORATORY FINDINGS

IN SOME RESEARCH PROJECTS, the investigators may not know the questions that need to be asked, the variables that need to be measured, and the theories that may guide the study. These unknowns may be due to the specific remote population being studied (e.g., Native Americans in Alaska) or the novelty of the research topic.

In these situations, it's best to explore *qualitatively* to learn what questions, variables, theories, and so forth need to be studied and then follow up with a *quantitative* study to generalize and test what was learned from the exploration. A mixed-methods project is ideal in these situations. In a nutshell, we can easily begin a study with a qualitative phase in order to explore and then follow up with a quantitative phase to test whether the qualitative results generalize.

EXAMPLE

KUTNER, STEINER, CORBETT, JAHNIGEN, AND BARTON (1999) studied issues important to terminally ill patients. Their study began with qualitative data generated via one-on-one interviews, and this information was used to develop a quantitative measuring instrument that was administered to a second sample of terminally ill patients to test whether the identified issues varied by demographic characteristics:

The use of initial open-ended interviews to explore the important issues allowed us to formulate relevant questions and discover what were truly concerns to this population. (p. 1350)

ENHANCE A STUDY WITH A SECOND RESEARCH APPROACH

IN SOME SITUATIONS, a second research approach can be added to the study to provide an enhanced understanding of some phase of the research project. For example, we can enhance a quantitative design (e.g., experiment, correlational study) by adding qualitative data or by adding quantitative data to a qualitative design (e.g., grounded theory, case study). In both of these cases, a second approach is embedded, or nested, within a primary approach. The embedding of qualitative data within a quantitative study is typical.

EXAMPLE

DONOVAN ET AL. (2002) conducted an experimental trial comparing the outcomes for three groups of men with prostate cancer who were receiving different treatment procedures. They began their study, however, with a qualitative component in which they interviewed the men to determine how best to recruit them into the study (e.g., how best to organize and present the information) because all the men had received abnormal results and sought the best treatment.

Toward the end of their article they reflected on the value of this preliminary, smaller, qualitative component used to design procedures for recruiting individuals to the study:

> We showed that the integration of qualitative research methods allowed us to understand the recruitment process and elucidate the changes necessary to the content and delivery of information to maximize recruitment and ensure effective and efficient conduct of the study. (p. 768)

HOW BEST TO EMPLOY A THEORETICAL STANCE

A SITUATION MAY EXIST in which a theoretical perspective provides a framework for the need to gather both quantitative and qualitative data in a mixed-methods study. The data might be gathered at the same time or in a sequence, with one form of data building on the other. The theoretical perspective could seek to bring about change or simply provide a lens through which the entire study might be viewed.

EXAMPLE

FRIES (2009) CONDUCTED a study using Bourdieu's reflexive sociology ("the interplay of objective social structure with subjective agency in social behavior," p. 327) as a theoretical lens for gathering both quantitative and qualitative data in the use of complementary and alternative medicine. He gathered survey and interview data in the first phase, analyzed statistical population health data in the second phase, and analyzed interview data in the third phase. Fries concluded that:

> This study has presented a case study from the sociology of alternative medicine to show how reflexive sociology might provide a theoretical basis for mixed-methods research oriented toward understanding the interplay of structure and agency in social behavior. (p. 345)

UNDERSTAND A RESEARCH OBJECTIVE THROUGH MULTIPLE RESEARCH PHASES

IN RESEARCH PROJECTS that span several years and have many components, such as program evaluation studies and multiyear health investigations, we may need to connect several studies to reach an overall objective. These studies may involve projects that gather both quantitative and qualitative data simultaneously or sequentially. These types of studies are called multiphase or multiproject mixed-methods studies and often involve teams of researchers working together over many phases of the project.

EXAMPLE

AMES, DUKE, MOORE, AND CUNRADI (2009) conducted a multiphase study of the drinking patterns of young U.S. Navy recruits during their first three years of military service. They conducted a study over a five-year period and gathered data to develop a measuring instrument in one phase, to modify their model in another phase, and to analyze their data through a final phase. The researchers presented a figure depicting the phases of their study over the five years and introduced the implementation sequence in this way:

The complexity of the resulting research design, consisting of both longitudinal survey data collection with a highly mobile population coupled with qualitative interviewing in diverse settings, required the formation of a methodologically diverse research team and a clear delineation of the temporal sequence by which qualitative and quantitative findings would be used to inform and enrich one another. (p. 130)

The preceding scenarios illustrate situations in which the mixed-methods approach fits the problems under study. They also begin to lay the groundwork for understanding the designs of mixed-methods approaches and the reasons the authors cite for undertaking them. Although in each example we cite only a single reason for using the mixed-methods approach, many authors cite multiple reasons, and we recommend that aspiring (and experienced) researchers begin to take note of the rationales that authors provide for using mixed-methods approaches.

ADVANTAGES

UNDERSTANDING THE NATURE of the mixed-methods research approach involves more than knowing its definition and when it should be used. We also need to know the advantages of using it so that we can convince others of its value.

Mixed-methods research provides strengths that offset the weaknesses of both the quantitative and qualitative approaches. This has been the historical argument for mixed-methods research for more than thirty years (e.g., Jick, 1979). One might argue that the quantitative approach is weak in understanding the context or setting in which people talk, and the voices of research participants are not directly heard in a quantitative study. Further, quantitative researchers remain in the background, and their biases and interpretations are seldom discussed.

The qualitative research approach makes up for these weaknesses, but it is seen as deficient because of the personal interpretations made by the researchers and the ensuing bias that is generated, and the difficulty in generalizing findings to a large group because of the limited number of participants studied. The quantitative approach does not have these weaknesses. Thus, the strengths of one approach make up for the weaknesses of the other.

Mixed-methods research provides more evidence for studying a research problem than either the quantitative *or* the qualitative approach alone. Researchers are able to use all the data-collection tools available rather than only the strategies typically associated with either the positivistic (quantitative) or the interpretive (qualitative) research traditions. In a nutshell, mixed-methods approaches help answer questions that cannot be answered solely by the quantitative or the qualitative approach alone.

For example, "Do participant views from interviews and from standardized measuring instruments converge or diverge?" is a mixed-methods question. Others would be, "In what ways do qualitative interviews explain the quantitative results of a study?" (using qualitative data to explain the quantitative results) and "How can a treatment be adapted to work with a particular sample in an experiment?" (exploring qualitatively before an experiment begins). To answer these questions, neither a quantitative nor a qualitative approach by itself would provide a satisfactory answer.

Mixed-methods provides a bridge across the sometimes adversarial divide between quantitative and qualitative researchers. We are social, behavioral, and human sciences researchers first, and divisions between quantitative and qualitative research only serve to narrow the approaches and the opportunities for collaboration.

The mixed-methods approach encourages the use of multiple worldviews or paradigms (i.e., beliefs, values) rather than those typically associated with either the positivistic tradition or the interpretive tradition. It also encourages us to think about a paradigm that might encompass all of the quantitative and qualitative approaches, such as pragmatism.

Mixed-methods approaches are practical in the sense that researchers are free to use all methods possible to address various research problems. They are also practical because individuals tend to solve problems using both numbers and words, combine inductive and deductive thinking, and employ skills in observing people as well as recording behavior. It's natural, then, for individuals to employ mixed-methods approaches as preferred modes for understanding the real social world.

CHALLENGES

THE MIXED-METHODS RESEARCH APPROACH is not the answer for every research-er or for every research situation or problem. Some studies are best done using either quantitative or qualitative methods alone. The mixed-methods approach requires certain skills, time, and resources for extensive data collection and analysis. Researchers may need to explain why they used a mixed-methods de-sign so that our scholarly community will accept the study.

There are two major issues that need to be addressed *before* doing a mixed-methods research study:

1. Skills of the researcher
2. Time and resources

SKILLS OF THE RESEARCHER

THE MIXED-METHODS RESEARCH APPROACH is realistic for a research study if the researcher has the requisite skills. We strongly recommend that researchers first gain experience with both the quantitative approach (Chapter 6) and the qualitative approach (Chapter 7) *separately* before undertaking a mixed-methods study. At a minimum, we should be acquainted with both quantitative and qualitative data collection (Chapters 14–16) and analysis (Chapters 17 and 18) procedures.

QUANTITATIVE SKILLS

MIXED-METHODS RESEARCHERS should be familiar with common methods of collecting quantitative data, such as using standardized measurement instru-ments and closed-ended attitudinal scales. You will need an awareness of the logic of hypothesis testing and the ability to use and interpret statistical anal-yses, including common descriptive and inferential procedures available in sta-tistical software packages. Finally, you will need to understand essential issues of rigor in quantitative research studies, including reliability, validity, experi-mental control, and generalizability. Quantitative data analysis is discussed in-depth in Chapter 17.

QUALITATIVE SKILLS

A SIMILAR SET OF QUALITATIVE RESEARCH SKILLS is necessary. You should be able to identify the central phenomenon of your study; to pose qualitative, meaning-oriented research questions; and to consider research participants as the experts. You should be familiar with common methods of collecting qualitative data, such as semistructured interviews using open-ended questions (Chapter 15) and qualitative observations.

You'll also need basic skills in analyzing qualitative text data, including coding text and developing themes and descriptions based on these codes, and should be acquainted with various qualitative data-analysis software packages. Finally, it's important that you understand essential issues of persuasiveness in qualitative research, including credibility, trustworthiness, and common validation strategies. Qualitative data analysis is discussed in depth in Chapter 18.

SOLID GROUNDING IN MIXED-METHODS RESEARCH

FINALLY, THOSE UNDERTAKING THIS APPROACH to answer a research question should have a solid grounding in mixed-methods research. This requires reading the literature on mixed-methods that has accumulated since the late 1980s and noting the best procedures and the latest techniques for conducting a good inquiry. It may also mean taking courses in mixed-methods research, which are beginning to appear both online and in residence on many campuses. It may mean apprenticing with someone familiar with doing mixed-methods studies who can provide an understanding of the skills involved in conducting this form of scientific inquiry.

TIME AND RESOURCES

EVEN WHEN YOU HAVE THESE BASIC quantitative and qualitative research skills, you should ask yourself if a mixed-methods approach is feasible, given your timeframe and resources. These are important issues to consider early in the planning stage. Your study may require extensive time, resources, and effort. You'll need to consider the following three questions:

1. Is there sufficient time to collect and analyze two different types of data?

2. Are there sufficient resources from which to collect and analyze both types of data?

3. Do I have the skills to complete this study?

In answering these questions, you'll need to consider how long it will take to gain approval for your study, to gain access to your research participants, and to complete the data collection and analysis. You will also need to keep in mind that qualitative data collection and analysis often require more time than that needed for quantitative data. The length of time required for a mixed-methods study also depends on whether your study will be using a one-phase, two-phase, or multiphase design.

You'll also need to think about the expenses that will be part of your study. These expenses may include, for example, printing costs for measuring instruments, recording and transcription costs for interviews, cost for data analyses, and costs for computer software programs.

Because of the increased demands associated with mixed-methods designs, you should consider working in a team. Teams bring together individuals with diverse methodological and content expertise and involve more personnel in the mixed-methods project. Working within a team setting, however, can be challenging and can easily increase the costs associated with your research project.

In addition, individuals with the necessary skills need to be located, and team leaders need to create and maintain a successful collaboration among all team members. However, the diversity of a team may be a strength because the members will represent different specialties and content areas.

CONVINCING OTHERS

MIXED-METHODS RESEARCH STUDIES are relatively new in terms of the methodologies available to social work researchers. As such, others may not be convinced of or understand the value of their use. Some may see it as a "new" approach. Others may feel that they do not have time to learn this new approach, and some may object to the use of mixed methods on philosophical grounds regarding the mixing of different philosophical positions (See Table 1.1 on pages 26–29). Still others might be so entrenched in their own methods and approaches to research that they might not be open to the possibility of their being another approach to knowledge generation.

One way to help convince others of the utility of the mixed-methods approach is to locate exemplary mixed-methods studies in the literature on a topic or in a content area and share these studies with others in an effort to educate them. These studies can be selected from prestigious journals with national and international reputations.

FINDING MIXED-METHODS RESEARCH STUDIES

HOW DO YOU FIND THESE MIXED-METHODS STUDIES? They can be difficult to locate in the literature because only recently have researchers begun to use the term "mixed-methods" in their titles or in their articles. Also, some disciplines may use different terms for naming this research approach. Based on our extensive work with the literature, we have developed a short list of terms that you can use to search for mixed-methods studies within electronic databases and journal archives. These four terms are:

1. mixed method* (where * is a wildcard that will allow hits for

   "mixed method," "mixed-methods," and "mixed methodology"),

2. quantitative AND qualitative,

3. multimethod, and

4. survey AND interview.

Note that the second search term uses the logic operator AND (i.e., quantitative AND qualitative). This requires that both words appear in the document so it will satisfy the search criteria. If you find too many articles try limiting your search so that the terms must appear within the abstract or restricting it to recent years. If not enough articles result, try searching for combinations of common data-collection techniques, such as "survey AND interview."

By using these strategies, you may locate a few good examples of mixed-methods studies that illustrate the core characteristics introduced in this chapter. Sharing these examples with stakeholders can be helpful when convincing them of the utility and feasibility of a mixed-methods approach.

SUMMARY

THIS CHAPTER PRESENTED A BRIEF INTRODUCTION on how a mixed-methods research study can be used to answer social work problems. It assumes that the reader has a solid understanding of the previous two chapters which discussed the quantitative and qualitative research approaches respectively.

Study Questions for Chapter 8	
Essay — Discussion	
1	1. Discuss the qualitative (interpretive) way of thinking. 2. Discuss the quantitative (positivistic) way of thinking. 3. Discuss the rationale of why a research study—if at all possible—should contain both research approaches in a single research study. Use one common social work example throughout your discussion to illustrate your main points.
2	Before you entered your social work program, and before you read this chapter, how did you think the mixed-methods research approach contributed to our profession's knowledge base?
3	There are six general types of social work research studies for which a mixed-methods research approach is better to use than only a quantitative research approach or only a qualitative research approach. 1. List all six types of studies. 2. Now provide a hypothetical social work example in relation to how a mixed-methods research approach is better suited for *each type of study* than using either *only* a quantitative approach or *only* a qualitative approach.
4	List the advantages of using a mixed-methods research approach to knowledge generation. Now provide a social work example for each advantage.

5	List the disadvantages of using a mixed-methods research approach to knowledge generation. Now provide a social work example for each disadvantage.
6	Doing a mixed-methods research study requires specific skills, time, and resources. List and thoroughly discuss each one. Provide a social work example of each in your discussion.
7	Discuss why the mixed-methods research approach is an "accessible approach" to scientific inquiry. Provide as many social work examples as you can to illustrate your main points.
8	Provide your own definition of the mixed-methods research approach to knowledge development.
9	List each one of the six core components of the mixed-methods research approach. Now choose a social problem, such as delinquency, homelessness, depression, or anxiety, and provide an example of how it can be "researched" with the use of the mixed-methods approach.
10	Discuss why it is *not* advisable to select one of the three research approaches before formulating your research question.
11	With the above question in mind, discuss why you need to formulate your research question before you select a research approach to answer it. Provide as many social work examples as you can to illustrate your main points.
12	Let's say you want to do a research study on the teaching effectiveness of the social work instructors at your school of social work. How would you go about doing strictly a quantitative study? A qualitative one? Now, how would you combine both approaches to form a mixed-methods study? See Box 7.1 on pages 268–269 for some hints how this can be done.
13	With respect to the above question, list the specific skills you would need to do a quantitative study, a qualitative study, and a mixed-methods study. Do you have them? If not, how will you get them?
14	In your own words discuss why the mixed-methods research approach to knowledge development within our profession has become so popular. Provide as many social work examples as you can to illustrate your main points.

15	Discuss why the mixed-methods research approach is an "intuitive" research method. Provide as many social work examples as you can to illustrate your main points.

Critical Thinking — Application — Integration

16	**APPLICATION OF THE MIXED-METHODS RESEARCH APPROACH** 1. Locate a published mixed-methods social work research article that contains a social work problem area or population that you're interested in. — For research studies that are *predominately qualitative* in nature check out Karen Staller and Karen Broadhurst's journal *Qualitative Social Work* (Sage Publications). Hands down, this is the best journal to find good qualitative social work research studies. — For research studies that are *predominately quantitative* in nature check out Bruce Thyer's journal *Research on Social Work Practice* (Sage Publications) for possible articles to use for this exercise. Hands down, this is the best journal to find good quantitatively oriented social work research studies. 2. Discuss the quantitative component of the article. What content in Chapter 6 did the author use when carrying out the quantitative component? 3. Discuss the qualitative component of the article. What content in Chapter 7 did the author use when carrying out the qualitative component? 4. Using this chapter as a guide discuss exactly how the author used the "mixed-methods" research approach. 5. Discuss the article's quantitative findings and its qualitative findings. What did you learn from the findings? How do you plan on using these findings in your day-to-day practice activities? 6. Do you feel the article's qualitative component actually enhanced the overall usefulness of the quantitative findings? If so, how? If not, why not? Discuss in detail. 7. Do you feel the article's quantitative component actually enhanced the overall usefulness of the qualitative findings? If so, how? If not, why not?

17	**THE MIXED-METHODS RESEARCH APPROACH AND THE RESEARCHER** **Scenario 1:** Make an argument that to be a competent social work researcher **you must know** the fundamental principles of the mixed-methods research approach in addition to its advantages and disadvantages. Provide a clear and explicit **research-related** social work example to illustrate your main points. **Scenario 2:** Make an argument that **you do not have to know** the fundamental principles of the mixed-methods research approach in addition to its advantages and disadvantages to be a competent social work researcher. Provide a clear and explicit **research-related** social work example to illustrate your main points. **Time to Choose:** Which one of the above two scenarios do you feel is more consistent with the place of research in social work? Why? Provide relevant social work examples to illustrate your main points.
18	**THE MIXED-METHODS RESEARCH APPROACH AND THE PRACTITIONER** **Scenario 1:** Make an argument that to be an effective evidence-based social work practitioner **you must know** the fundamental principles of the mixed-methods research approach in addition to its advantages and disadvantages. Provide a clear and explicit **practice-related** social work example to illustrate your main points. **Scenario 2:** Make an argument that **you do not have to know** the fundamental principles of the mixed-methods research approach in addition to its advantages and disadvantages whatsoever to be an effective evidence-based social work practitioner. Provide a clear and explicit **practice-related** social work example to illustrate your main points. **Time to Choose:** Which one of the above two scenarios do you feel is more consistent with the concept of the contemporary evidence-based social work practice process as illustrated on pages 46–51? Why? Provide relevant social work examples to illustrate your main points.
19	**TIME TO PUT ON YOUR CRITICAL THINKING HAT** 1. Discuss the similarities and differences between your responses to Questions 17 and 18. 2. What are your thoughts on the belief that you'll need to know the fundamental principles of the mixed-methods research approach in addition to its advantages and disadvantages to be an effective evidence-based social work *practitioner* (Question 18) or a social work *researcher* (Question 17)?

20	**MIXED-METHODS RESEARCH AND YOUR PROFESSIONAL DEVELOPMENT** 1. Review the three social work research-related roles you can take when you graduate—CSWE Competency 1 at the beginning of this chapter on page 278 (also discussed in Chapter 1 on pages 38–42). Thoroughly discuss how you feel this chapter will help you to perform one or more research-related roles when you graduate. Which one of the three roles do you believe this chapter helped you with the most? Why? Discuss in detail and provide an example to illustrate your main points. 2. Review CSWE Competency 4 at the beginning of this chapter on page 278. Thoroughly discuss how you feel this chapter will help you to become a practice-informed researcher and a research-informed practitioner. Discuss in detail and provide an example to illustrate your main points. 3. Review the evidence-based practice process as illustrated on pages 46–51. Thoroughly discuss how this chapter helps you to develop the skills you'll need for implementing one or more steps of the evidence-based practice process. 4. Discuss which step(s) you feel this chapter will help you with the most. Why? Be very specific and use relevant social work examples to illustrate your main points throughout your discussion. **NOTE:** This exercise should help you to realize that you can use "research roles" to help you become an evidence-based social work practitioner.
21	**MOVING AHEAD BY LOOKING BACK** At this point in your research methods course, how comfortable are you with discussing the place of research in social work with your field instructor, with your practice instructor, with your research instructor, with your supervisor at work, with the director of your social work program, or with your classmates? Discuss in detail.

Measuring Variables

CHAPTER 9: Measurement **304**

CHAPTER 10: Measuring Instruments **342**

9

CHAPTER

COMPETENCY 1: Demonstrate Ethical and Professional Behavior

You will learn that in order to be a successful evidence-based practitioner you have an ethical obligation to integrate three research roles into your daily practice activities as discussed in Chapter 1: (1) research consumer, (2) research partner—either as a co-researcher or research participant, and (3) creator and disseminator of research (or knowledge).

This entire chapter pertains to these three professional roles when it comes to the process of determining the validity and reliability of measuring instruments that are used not only within social work practice settings (**research consumer**) but also in research situations (**research partner** and **creator and disseminator of research**).

COMPETENCY 4: Engage in Practice-Informed Research and Research-Informed Practice

Competency 4 also pertains to the entire chapter because you have to:

1. Evaluate the criteria the authors of research studies used in relation to the selection of their measuring instruments. You'll also need to know the advantages, the disadvantages, and the specific criteria that apply to evaluating measuring instruments (**research consumer**—research-informed practice);

2. Participate in a research study—either as a co-researcher or research participant (**research partner**—practice-informed research). See 1 above and 3 below; and

3. Know how to determine the validity and reliability of measuring instruments that will measure the variables in your research study (**creator and disseminator of research**—practice-informed research).

You also need to utilize evidence-based practice recommendations whenever possible; that is, you need to integrate (1) the best available research-based evidence with (2) your clinical expertise and (3) your client's values.

All of the above implies you'll need to know how to assess the overall strengths and limitations of the measuring instrument(s) used in a research study that produced its research-based evidence. In short, you need to ask and then answer a simple question: How seriously should I take the findings of any specific research study given the reliability and validity of the measuring instrument(s) the study utilized?

COMPETENCY 9: Evaluate Practice with Individuals, Families, Groups, Organizations, and Communities

You will learn that measuring your practice *effectiveness* implies that you're competent in measuring the outcomes of your interventions with your various client systems. See Competencies 1 & 4.

9

CHAPTER

Measurement

CHAPTER 1	**Step 1.** Understanding the Research Process
CHAPTER 2	**Step 2.** Developing Research Questions
CHAPTER 3	**Step 3.** Reviewing the Literature
CHAPTERS 4 & 5	**Step 4.** Being Aware of Ethical and Cultural Issues
CHAPTERS 6–8	**Step 5.** Selecting a Research Approach
CHAPTERS 9 & 10	**Step 6.** Specifying How Variables Are Measured
CHAPTER 11	**Step 7.** Selecting a Sample
CHAPTERS 12 & 13	**Step 8.** Selecting a Research Design
CHAPTERS 14–16	**Step 9.** Selecting a Data-Collection Method
CHAPTERS 17 & 18	**Step 10.** Analyzing the Data
CHAPTERS 19 & 20	**Step 11.** Writing the Research Report

THE MEASUREMENT OF VARIABLES IS THE CORNERSTONE of all social work positivistic research studies. Shining and formidable measuring instruments may come to mind, measuring things to several decimal places. The less scientifically inclined might merely picture rulers, but, in any case, measurement for most of us means reducing something to numbers. As we know, these "somethings" are called variables, and all variables can take on different measurement levels.

LEVELS OF MEASUREMENT

OUR DISCUSSION OF MEASUREMENT LEVELS has been adapted and modified from Williams, Tutty, and Grinnell (1995). As we know from Chapter 6, the characteristics that describe a variable are known as its *attributes*. The variable *gender*, for example, can have two attributes—*male* and *female*—because gender in humans can be thought of as only containing two attributes: male and female.

However, our current and evolving notion of gender is changing drastically where male and female have been expanded to include many more attributes than the traditional two. In fact, Facebook now allows users to self-identify as something other than either male or female. It has 56 different categories for gender—not just the customary two.

The variable *ethnicity* has a number of possible attributes: *African American, Native American*, *Asian, Latino American,* and *Caucasian* are just five examples of the many attributes of the variable ethnicity. A point to note here is that the attributes of gender differ in kind from one another—male is different from female—and, in the same way, the attributes of ethnicity are also different from one another.

Now consider the variable *income*. Income can only be described in terms of amounts of money: $15,000 per year, $288.46 per week, and so forth. In whatever terms a person's income is actually described, it still comes down to a number. Because every number has its own category, as we mentioned before, the variable income can generate as many categories as there are numbers, up to the number covering the research participant who earns the most.

These numbers are all attributes of income, and they are all different, but they are not different in *kind*, as male and female are, or Native American and Latino; they are only different in *quantity*. In other words, the attributes of income differ in that they represent more or less of the same thing whereas the attributes of gender differ in that they represent different kinds of things.

Income will, therefore, be measured in a different way from gender. When we want to measure income, for example, we will be looking for categories (attributes) that are *lower* or *higher* than each other; on the other hand, when we measure gender, we will be looking for categories (attributes) that *are different in kind* from each other.

Mathematically, there is not much we can do with categories that are different in kind. We cannot subtract Latinos from Caucasians, for example, whereas we can quite easily subtract one person's annual income from another and come up with a meaningful difference. As far as mathematical computations are concerned, we are obliged to work at a lower level of complexity when we measure variables like ethnicity than when we measure variables like income.

Depending on the nature of their attributes, all variables can be measured at one (or more) of four measurement levels:

1. Nominal
2. Ordinal
3. Interval
4. Ratio

NOMINAL MEASUREMENT

NOMINAL MEASUREMENT IS THE LOWEST LEVEL OF MEASUREMENT and is used to measure variables whose attributes are different in kind. As we have seen, gender is one variable measured at a nominal level, and ethnicity is another. *Place of birth* is a third, because "born in California," for example, is different from "born in Chicago," and we cannot add "born in California" to "born in Chicago," or subtract them or divide them, or do anything statistically interesting with them at all.

ORDINAL MEASUREMENT

ORDINAL MEASUREMENT IS A HIGHER LEVEL OF MEASUREMENT than nominal and is used to measure those variables whose attributes can be rank ordered: for example, socioeconomic status, sexism, racism, client satisfaction, and the like. If we intend to measure *client satisfaction*, we must first develop a list of all the possible attributes of client satisfaction; that is, we must think of all the possible categories into which answers about client satisfaction might be placed.

Some clients will be *very satisfied*—one category, at the high end of the satisfaction continuum; some will be *not at all satisfied*—a separate category, at the low end of the continuum; and others will be *generally satisfied, moderately satisfied*, or *somewhat satisfied*—three more categories, at differing points on the continuum, as illustrated:

1. Not at all satisfied
2. Somewhat satisfied
3. Moderately satisfied
4. Generally satisfied
5. Very satisfied

The above is a 5-point scale with a brief description of the degree of satisfaction represented by a number (i.e., 1, 2, 3, 4, 5). Of course, we may choose to express the anchors in different words, substituting *extremely sat-isfied* for *very satisfied*, or *fairly satisfied* for *generally satisfied*. We may select a 3-point scale instead, limiting the choices to *very satisfied*, *moderately satis-fied,* and *not at all satisfied*; or we may even use a 10-point scale if we believe that our respondents will be able to rate their satisfaction with that degree of accuracy.

Whichever particular method is selected, some sort of scale is the only measurement option available because there is no other way to categorize client satisfaction except in terms of more satisfaction or less satisfaction. As we did with nominal measurement, we might assign numbers to each of the points on the scale. If we used the 5-point scale as illustrated on the previous page, we might assign:

5 to very satisfied
4 to generally satisfied
3 to moderately satisfied
2 to somewhat satisfied
1 to not at all satisfied

Here, the numbers do have some mathematical meaning. Five (*very satis-fied*) is in fact better than 4 (*generally satisfied*), 4 is better than 3, 3 is better than 2, and 2 is better than 1. The numbers, however, say nothing about *how much better* any category is than any other. We cannot assume that the dif-ference in satisfaction between *very* and *generally* is the same as the differ-ence between *generally* and *moderately*.

In short, we cannot assume that the intervals between the anchored points on the scale are all the same length. Most definitely, we cannot assume that a client who rates a service at 4 (*generally satisfied*) is twice as satisfied as a client who rates the service at 2 (*somewhat satisfied*).

In fact, we cannot attempt any mathematical manipulation at all. We cannot add the numbers 1, 2, 3, 4, and 5, nor can we subtract, multiply, or divide them. As its name might suggest, all we can know from ordinal meas-urement is the order of the categories.

INTERVAL MEASUREMENT

SOME VARIABLES, SUCH AS CLIENT SATISFACTION, have attributes that can be rank-ordered—from *very satisfied* to *not at all satisfied*, as we have just discussed. As we saw, however, these attributes cannot be assumed to be the same distance apart if they are placed on a scale; and, in any case, the distance they are apart has no real meaning. No one can measure the distance between *very satisfied* and *moderately satisfied*; we only know that the one is better than the other.

Conversely, for some variables, the distance, or interval, separating their attributes *does* have meaning, and these variables can be measured at the interval level. An example in physical science would is the Fahrenheit or Celsius temperature scales. The difference between 80 degrees and 90 degrees is the same as the difference between 40 and 50 degrees. Eighty degrees is not twice as hot as 40 degrees; nor does zero degrees mean no heat at all.

In social work, interval measures are most commonly used in connection with standardized measuring instruments, as presented in Chapter 10. When we look at a standardized intelligence test, for example, we can say that the difference between IQ scores of 100 and 110 is the same as the difference between IQ scores of 95 and 105, based on the scores obtained by the many thousands of people who have taken the test over the years. As with the temperature scales, a person with an IQ score of 120 is not twice as intelligent as a person with a score of 60, nor does a score of 0 mean no intelligence at all.

RATIO MEASUREMENT

THE HIGHEST LEVEL OF MEASUREMENT, ratio measurement, is used to measure variables whose attributes are based on a true zero point. It may not be possible to have zero intelligence, but it's certainly possible to have zero children or zero money. Whenever a question about a particular variable might elicit the answer "none" or "never," that variable can be measured at the ratio level.

The question "How many times have you seen your social worker?" might be answered "Never." Other variables commonly measured at the ratio level include length of residence in a given place, age, number of times married, number of organizations belonged to, number of antisocial behaviors, number of case reviews, number of training sessions, number of supervisory meetings, and so forth. With a ratio level of measurement, we can meaningfully interpret the comparison between two scores.

A person who is 40 years of age, for example, is twice as old as a person who is 20 and half as old as a person who is 80. Children aged 2 and 5, respectively, are the same distance apart as children aged 6 and 9. Data resulting from ratio measurement can be added, subtracted, multiplied, and divided. Averages can be calculated, and other statistical analyses can be performed.

It's useful to note that although some variables *can* be measured at a higher level, they may not need to be. The variable *income*, for example, can be measured at a ratio level because it's possible to have a zero income, but, for the purposes of a particular study, we may not need to know the actual incomes of our research participants, only the range within which their incomes fall.

A person who is asked how much he or she earns may be reluctant to give a figure ("mind your own business" is a perfectly legitimate response) but may not object to checking one of a number of income categories, choosing, for example, between:

1. less than $5,000 per year
2. $5,001 to $15,000 per year
3. $15,001 to $25,000 per year
4. $25,001 to $35,000 per year
5. more than $35,000 per year

Categorizing income in this way reduces the measurement from the ratio level to the ordinal level. It will now be possible to know only that a person checking Category 1 earns less than a person checking Category 2, and so on. We will not know *how much* less or more one person earns than another and we will not be able to perform statistical tasks such as calculating average incomes, but we will be able to say, for example, that 50 percent of our sample falls into Category 1, 30 percent into Category 2, 15 percent into Category 3, and 5 percent into Category 4. If we are conducting a study to see how many people fall in each income range, this may be all we need to know.

In the same way, we might not want to know the actual ages of our sample, only the range in which they fall. For some studies, it might be enough to measure age at a nominal level—to inquire, for example, whether people were born during the Depression, or whether they were born before or after 1990. When studying variables that can be measured at any level, the measurement level chosen depends on what kind of data are needed, and this in turn is determined by why the data are needed, which in turn is determined by our research question.

DESCRIBING VARIABLES BY MEASURING THEM

THE PURPOSE OF MEASURING A VARIABLE is to describe it as completely and accurately as possible. Often, the most complete and accurate possible description of a variable involves not only numbers but also words.

When doing any research study—quantitative (Chapter 6), qualitative (Chapter 7), or mixed-methods (Chapter 8)—we need to describe the variables as accurately and completely as possible for four reasons:

1. Correspondence
2. Standardization
3. Quantification
4. Duplication

CORRESPONDENCE

CORRESPONDENCE MEANS MAKING A LINK between what we measure and/or observe and the theories we have developed to explain what we have measured and/or observed. For example, the concept of attachment theory can easily explain the different behaviors (variables) of small children when they are separated from—or reunited with—their mothers.

Measuring and recording children's behaviors in this context provide a link between the abstract and the concrete—between attachment (an unspecific and nonmeasurable concept) and its indicators, or variables, such as a child's behaviors (a more specific and more measurable variable).

STANDARDIZATION

VARIABLES CAN BE COMPLEX, and the more complex they are the more likely it is that people will interpret the exact same variable in different ways. Like concepts, a single variable can at times mean different things to different people, even when using the same words.

"Self-esteem," for example, can mean different things to different people. However, the perceptions linked to self-esteem (that is, the empirical indicators of self-esteem) may be drawn together in the form of a measuring instrument, as they are in Hudson's *Index of Self-Esteem* (see Figure 9.1 on the following page).

You may or may not agree that all of the 25 items, or questions, contained in Hudson's *Index of Self-Esteem* together reflect what you mean by self-esteem—but at least you know what Hudson meant, and so does everyone else who is using his measuring instrument. By constructing this instrument, Hudson has *standardized* a complex variable so that everyone using his instrument will mean the same thing by the variable and measure it in the same way.

Moreover, if two or more different researchers use his instrument with the same research participants, they ought to get approximately the same results. The use of the word "approximately" here means that we must allow for a bit of error—something discussed at the end of this chapter.

QUANTIFICATION

QUANTIFICATION MEANS NOTHING MORE than defining the level of a variable in terms of a single number, or score. The use of Hudson's *Index of Self-Esteem*, for example, results in a single number, or score, obtained by following the scoring instructions. Reducing a complex variable such as self-esteem to a single number has disadvantages in that the richness of the variable can never be completely captured in this way.

However, it also has advantages in that numbers can be used in statistics to search for meaningful relationships between one variable and another. For example, you might hypothesize that there is a relationship between two variables: self-esteem and marital satisfaction.

Hudson has *quantified* self-esteem, allowing the self-esteem of any research participant to be represented by a single number. He has also done this for the variable of marital satisfaction. Because both variables have been broken-down to two numbers, you can use statistical methods (discussed in Chapter 17) to see whether the relationship you hypothesized actually does exist.

Name:_____ Today's Date:_____

This questionnaire is designed to measure how you see yourself. It is not a test, so there are no right or wrong answers. Please answer each item as carefully and as accurately as you can by placing a number beside each item as follows:

- **1** = None of the time
- **2** = Very rarely
- **3** = A little of the time
- **4** = Some of the time
- **5** = A good part of the time
- **6** = Most of the time
- **7** = All of the time

1. ___ I feel that people would not like me if they really knew me well.
2. ___ I feel that others get along much better than I do.
3. ___ I feel that I am a beautiful person.
4. ___ When I am with others I feel they are glad I am with them.
5. ___ I feel that people really like to talk with me.
6. ___ I feel that I am a very competent person.
7. ___ I think I make a good impression on others.
8. ___ I feel that I need more self-confidence.
9. ___ When I am with strangers I am very nervous.
10. ___ I think that I am a dull person.
11. ___ I feel ugly.
12. ___ I feel that others have more fun than I do.
13. ___ I feel that I bore people.
14. ___ I think my friends find me interesting.
15. ___ I think I have a good sense of humor.
16. ___ I feel very self-conscious when I am with strangers.
17. ___ I feel that if I could be more like other people I would have it made.
18. ___ I feel that people have a good time when they are with me.
19. ___ I feel like a wallflower when I go out.
20. ___ I feel I get pushed around more than others.
21. ___ I think I am a rather nice person.
22. ___ I feel that people really like me very much.
23. ___ I feel that I am a likeable person.
24. ___ I am afraid I will appear foolish to others.
25. ___ My friends think very highly of me.

FIGURE 9.1

Hudson's *Index of Self-Esteem*

AUTHOR: Walter W. Hudson

PURPOSE: To measure problems with self-esteem.

DESCRIPTION: The *ISE* is a 25-item scale designed to measure the degree, severity, or magnitude of a problem a client has with self-esteem. Self-esteem is considered as the evaluative component of self-concept. The *ISE* is written in very simple language, is easily administered, and is easily scored. Because problems with self-esteem are often central to social and psychological difficulties, this instrument has a wide range of utility for a number of clinical problems.

The *ISE* has a cutting score of 30 (+ or −5), with scores above 30 indicating the respondent has a clinically significant problem and scores below 30 indicating the individual has no such problem. Another advantage of the *ISE* is that it is one of nine scales of the *Clinical Measurement Package* (Hudson, 1982), all of which are administered and scored the same way.

NORMS: This scale was derived from tests of 1,745 respondents, including single and married individuals, clinical and nonclinical populations, college students and nonstudents. Respondents included Caucasians, Japanese, and Chinese Americans, and a smaller number of members of other ethnic groups. Not recommended for use with children under the age of 12.

SCORING: For a detailed description on how to score the *ISE,* see: Bloom, Fischer, and Orme (2009) or go to: www.walmyr.com.

RELIABILITY: The *ISE* has a mean alpha of .93, indicating excellent internal consistency, and an excellent (low) S.E.M. of 3.70. The *ISE* also has excellent stability with a two-hour test-retest correlation of .92.

VALIDITY: The *ISE* has good know-groups validity, significantly distinguishing between clients judged by clinicians to have problems in the area of self-esteem and those known not to. Further, the *ISE* has very good construct validity, correlating well with a range of other measures with which it should correlate highly, e.g., depression, happiness, sense of identity, and scores on the *Generalized Contentment Scale* (depression).

PRIMARY REFERENCE: Hudson, W.W. (1982). *The clinical measurement package: A field manual.* Chicago: Dorsey

FIGURE 9.1a

Basic Information about Hudson's *Index of Self-Esteem*

DUPLICATION

IN THE PHYSICAL SCIENCES, experiments are routinely replicated. For example, if you put a test-tube containing 25 ounces of a solution into an oven to see what is left when the liquid evaporates, you may use five test-tubes containing 25 ounces each, not just one. Then, you will have five identical samples of solution evaporated at the same time under the same conditions, and you will be much more certain of your results than if you had just evaporated one sample. The word *replication* means doing the same thing more than once at the same time.

In our profession, we can rarely replicate research studies, but we can *duplicate* them. That is, a second researcher can attempt to confirm a first researcher's results by doing the same thing again later on, as much as is practically possible under the same conditions. Duplication increases certainty, and it's only possible if the variables being studied have been *standardized* and *quantified*.

For example, you could duplicate another researcher's work on attachment only if you measured attachment in the same way. If you used different child behaviors to indicate attachment and you assigned different values to mean, say, weak attachment or strong attachment, you may have done a useful study, but it would not be a duplicate of the first.

CRITERIA FOR SELECTING AN INSTRUMENT

NOW THAT YOU KNOW why you need to measure variables, let's go on to look at *how* you measure them in the first place. To measure a variable, you need a measuring instrument to measure it with—much more about this topic in the following chapter. Most of the measuring instruments used in social work are paper and pencil instruments like Figure 9.1.

Many other people besides Hudson have come up with ways of measuring self-esteem, and if you want to measure self-esteem in your study, you will have to choose between the various measuring instruments that are available. The same embarrassment of riches applies to most of the other variables you might want to measure.

Remember that a variable is something that varies between research participants. Participants will vary, for example, with respect to their levels of self-esteem. What you need are some criteria to help you decide which instrument is best for measuring a particular variable in any given particular situation. There are five criteria that will help you to do this:

1. Utility
2. Sensitivity to small changes
3. Nonreactivity
4. Reliability
5. Validity

UTILITY

IN ORDER TO COMPLETE Hudson's *Index of Self-Esteem* (Figure 9.1), for example, a research participant must preferably be able to read. Even if you, as the researcher, read the items to the participants, they must be able to relate a number between 1 and 7 (where 1 = none of the time, and 7 = all of the time) to each of the 25 items, or questions.

Further, they must know what a "wallflower" is before they can answer Item 19. If the research participants in your study cannot do this for a variety of reasons, then no matter how wonderful Hudson's *Index of Self-Esteem* might be in other respects, it's not useful to you in your particular study.

Hudson's *Index of Self-Esteem* may take only a few minutes to complete, but other instruments can take far longer. The Minnesota Multiphase Personality Inventory (the MMPI), for example, can take three hours or more to complete, and some people may not have the attention span or the motivation to complete the task. In sum, a measuring instrument is not useful if your research participants are unable or unwilling to complete it for whatever reasons. If they do complete it, however, you then have to score it.

The simple measuring instrument contained in Figure 9.1 is relatively quick and simple to score, but other instruments are far more complex and time consuming. Usually, the simple instruments—quick to complete and easy to score—are less accurate than the more demanding instruments, and you will have to decide how far you are prepared to sacrifice accuracy for utility.

The main consideration here is what you are going to do with the measurements once you have obtained them. If you are doing an assessment that might affect a client's life in terms of treatment intervention, referral, placement, and so on, accuracy is paramount, and you will need the most accurate instrument (probably the longest and most complex) that the client can tolerate.

On the other hand, if you are doing an exploratory research study where the result will be a tentative suggestion that some variable may be related to another, a little inaccuracy in measurement is not the end of the world, and utility might be more important.

SENSITIVITY TO SMALL CHANGES

SUPPOSE THAT ONE OF YOUR PRACTICE OBJECTIVES with your 8-year-old client Johnny is to help him stop wetting his bed during the night. One obvious indicator of the variable—bedwetting—is a wet bed. Thus, you hastily decide that you will measure Johnny's bedwetting behavior by having his mother tell you when Johnny has—or has not—wet his bed during the week. That is, Did he or did he not wet his bed at least once during the week?

However, if Johnny has reduced the number of his bed-wetting incidents from five per week to only once per week, you will not know whether your intervention was working well because just the one bedwetting incident per week was enough to officially count as "wetting the bed." In other words, the way you chose to measure Johnny's bedwetting behavior was sensitive to the large difference between wetting and not wetting in a given week, but insensitive to the smaller difference between wetting once and wetting more than once in a given week.

In order to be able to congratulate Johnny on small improvements, and of course to track his progress over time, you will have to devise a more sensitive measuring instrument, such as one that measures the number of times Johnny wets his bed per week. Often, an instrument that is more sensitive will also be less convenient to use, and you will have to balance sensitivity against utility.

NONREACTIVITY

A *REACTIVE* MEASURING INSTRUMENT is nothing more than an instrument that changes the behavior or feeling of a person that it was supposed to measure. For instance, you might have decided, in the example of Johnny, to use a device that rings a loud bell every time Johnny has a bedwetting accident.

His mother would then leap from sleep, make a check mark on the form you had provided, and fall back into a tormented doze. This would be a sensitive measure—though intrusive and thus less useful. However, it might also cause Johnny to reduce his bedwetting behavior, in accordance with behavior theory.

Clinically, this would be a good thing—unless he developed bell phobia—but it's important to make a clear distinction between an *instrument* that is designed to *measure* a behavior and an *intervention* that is designed to *change* it. If the bell wakes up Johnny so that he can go to the bathroom and thus finally eliminate his bedwetting behavior, the bell is a wonderful *intervention*. It's not a good measuring instrument, however, as it has changed the very behavior it was supposed to measure. A change in behavior resulting from the use of a measuring instrument is known as a *reactive effect*.

The ideal, then, is a *nonreactive* measuring instrument that has no effect on the variable being measured. If you want to know, for example, whether a particular intervention is effective in raising self-esteem in girls who have been sexually abused, you will need to be sure that any measured increase in self-esteem is due to the intervention and *not* to the measuring instrument you happen to be using. If you fail to make a distinction between the measuring instrument and the intervention, you will end up with no clear idea at all about what is causing what.

Sometimes, you might be tempted to use a measuring instrument as a clinical tool. If your client responded to Hudson's *Index of Self-Esteem* Item 13 (Figure 9.1) that she felt she was boring people all of the time, you might want to discuss with her the particular conversational gambits she feels are so boring in order to help her change them. This is perfectly legitimate so long as you realize that, by so doing, you have turned a measuring instrument into part of an intervention.

RELIABILITY

A GOOD MEASURING INSTRUMENT IS RELIABLE in that it gives the same score over and over again provided that the measurement is made under the same conditions and nothing about the research participant has changed. A reliable measuring instrument is obviously necessary because, if you are trying to track the increase in a client's self-esteem, for example, you need to be sure that the changes you see over time are due to changes in the client, not to inaccuracies in the measuring instrument.

Researchers are responsible for ensuring that the measuring instruments they use are reliable. Hence, it's worth looking briefly at the four main methods used to establish the reliability of a measuring instrument:

1. Test-retest method
2. Alternate-form method
3. Split-half method
4. Observer reliability

TEST-RETEST METHOD

THE TEST-RETEST METHOD of establishing reliability involves administering the same measuring instrument to the same group of people on two separate occasions. The two sets of results are then compared to see how similar they are; that is, how well they *correlate*. We will discuss *correlation* more fully in Chapter 17. For now, it's enough to say that correlation in this context can range from 0 to 1, where 0 means no correlation at all between the two sets of scores and 1 means a perfect correlation.

Generally, a correlation of 0.8 means that the instrument is reasonably reliable and 0.9 is very good. Note that there is a heading RELIABILITY in Figure 9.1a, which means that Hudson's *Index of Self-Esteem* has "excellent stability with a two-hour test-retest correlation of 0.92." The "two-hour" bit means, of course, that the two administrations of the instrument took place two hours apart.

The problem with completing the same instrument twice is that the answers given on the first occasion may affect the answers given on the second. This is known as a *testing effect.* For example, Ms. Smith might remember what she wrote the first time and write something different just to enliven the proceedings. She may be less anxious, or more bored or irritated the second time, just because there was a first time, and these states might affect her answers.

Obviously, the greater the testing effects, the less reliable the instrument. Moreover, the closer together the tests, the more likely testing effects become because Ms. Smith is more likely to remember the first occasion. Hence, if the instrument is reliable over an interval of two hours and you want to administer it to your study participants on occasions a day or a month apart, it should be even more reliable with respect to testing effects.

People may change their answers on a second occasion for reasons other than testing effects: they are having a good day or a bad day; or they have a cold; or there is a loud pneumatic drill just outside the window.

However, a word of caution is in order. Sometimes clients complete the same measuring instrument every few weeks for a year or more as a way of monitoring their progress over time. The more often an instrument is completed, the more likely it is to generate testing effects. Hence, social service programs that use instruments in this way need to be sure that the instruments they use are still reliable under the conditions in which they are to be used.

ALTERNATE-FORM METHOD

THE SECOND METHOD of establishing the reliability of a measuring instrument is the alternate-form method. As the same suggests, an alternate form of an instrument is a second instrument that is as similar as possible to the original except that the wording of the items contained in the second instrument has changed. Administering the original form and then the alternate form reduces testing effects because the respondent is less likely to base the second set of answers on the first.

However, it's time-consuming to develop different but equivalent instruments, and they must still be tested for reliability using the test-retest method, both together as a pair, and separately as two distinct instruments.

SPLIT-HALF METHOD

THE SPLIT-HALF METHOD involves splitting one instrument in half so that it becomes two shorter instruments. Usually, all the even-numbered items, or questions, are used to make one instrument while the odd-numbered items make up the other. The point of doing this is to ensure that the original instrument is internally consistent; that is, it's homogeneous, or the same all the way through, with no longer or more difficult items appearing at the beginning or the end.

When the two halves are compared using the test-retest method, they should ideally yield the same score. If they did give the same score when one half was administered to a respondent on one occasion and the second half to the same respondent on a different occasion, they would have a perfect correlation of 1. Again, a correlation of 0.8 is thought to be good and a correlation of 0.9 very good. Figure 9.1a, under the RELIABILITY section, shows that Hudson's *Index of Self-Esteem* has an internal consistency of 0.93.

OBSERVER RELIABILITY (RELIABILITY OF THE PROCESS)

SOMETIMES, BEHAVIORS ARE MEASURED by observing how often they occur, or how long they last, or how severe they are. The results are then recorded on a straightforward, simple form. Nevertheless, this is not as easy as it sounds because the behavior, or variable, being measured must first be very carefully defined and people observing the same behavior may have different opinions as to how severe the behavior was, or how long it lasted, or whether it occurred at all.

The level of agreement or correlation between trained observers thus provides a way of establishing the reliability of the process used to measure the behavior. Once we have established the reliability of the process, we can use the same method to assess the reliability of other observers as part of their training. The level of agreement between observers is known as *inter-rater reliability*.

VALIDITY

A MEASURING INSTRUMENT IS VALID if it measures what it's supposed to measure—and measures it accurately. If you want to measure the variable assertiveness, for example, you don't want to mistakenly measure aggression instead. There are several kinds of validity—in fact, we should really refer to the *validities* of an instrument—and we will look at the following four:

1. Content validity
2. Criterion validity
3. Face validity
4. Construct validity

BOX 9.1	Major Types of Reliability
TEST-RETEST METHOD	Does an individual respond to a measuring instrument in the same general way when the instrument is administered twice?
ALTERNATE-FORMS METHOD	When two forms of an instrument that are equivalent in their degree of validity are given to the same individual, is there a strong convergence in how that person responds?
SPLIT-HALF METHOD	Are the scores on one half of the measuring instrument similar to those obtained on the other half?
OBSERVER RELIABILITY	Is there an agreement between the observers who are measuring the same variable?

CONTENT VALIDITY

THINK FOR A MOMENT about the variable self-esteem. In order to measure it accurately, you must first know what it is; that is, you must identify all the indicators (questions contained in the measuring instrument) that make up self-esteem, such as feeling that people like you, feeling that you are competent, and so on—and on and on and on . . . It's probably impossible to identify *all* the indicators that contribute to self-esteem.

It's even less likely that everyone (or even most people) will agree with all the indicators identified by someone else. Arguments may arise over whether "feeling worthless," for example, is really an indicator of low self-esteem or whether it has more to do with depression, which is a separate variable altogether.

Furthermore, even if agreement could be reached, a measuring instrument like Hudson's *Index of Self-Esteem* would have to include at least one item, or question, for *every* agreed-upon indicator. If just one was missed— for example, "sense of humor"—then the instrument would not be accurately measuring self-esteem.

Because it did not include all the possible content, or indicators, related to self-esteem, it would not be *content valid*. Hudson's *Index of Self-Esteem*, then, is not perfectly content valid because it's not possible to cover every indicator related to self-esteem in just 25 items. Longer instruments have a better chance of being content valid (perhaps one could do it in 25 *pages* of items), but, in general, perfect content validity cannot be achieved in any measuring instrument of a practical length. Content validity is a matter of "more or less" rather than "yes or no," and moreover it is strictly a matter of opinion.

For example, experts differ about the degree to which various instruments are content valid. It's therefore necessary to find some way of *validating* an instrument to determine how well it is, in fact, accurately measuring what it's supposed to measure. One such way is through a determination of the instrument's *criterion validity.*

CRITERION VALIDITY

AN INSTRUMENT HAS CRITERION VALIDITY if it gives the same result as a second instrument that is designed to measure the same variable. A client might complete Hudson's *Index of Self-Esteem*, for example, and achieve a score indicating high self-esteem. If the same client then completes a second instrument also designed to measure self-esteem and again achieves a good score, it's very likely that both instruments are, in fact, measuring self-esteem. Not only do they have good criterion validity in that they compare well with each other, but probably each instrument also has good content validity.

If the same client does not achieve similar scores on the two instruments, however, then neither of them are criterion valid, probably one is not content valid, and both will have to be compared with a third instrument to resolve the difficulty. There are two categories of criterion validity:

1. Concurrent validity
2. Predictive validity

CONCURRENT VALIDITY. Concurrent validity mainly deals with the present. For example, suppose you have an instrument—say, a reading test—designed to distinguish between children who need remedial reading services and children who do not. To validate the measuring instrument, you ask the classroom teacher which children she thinks need remedial reading services. If the teacher and your instrument both come up with the same list of children, your instrument has criterion validity. If not, you will need to find another comparison: a different reading test or the opinion of another teacher.

In short, concurrent validity refers to the ability of a measuring instrument to predict accurately an individual's *current* status. An example of an instrument with concurrent validity is a psychopathology scale that is capable of distinguishing between adolescents who are *currently* in need of psychiatric treatment and those who are not.

PREDICTIVE VALIDITY. Predictive validity deals with the future. Perhaps you have an instrument (say a set of criteria) designed to predict which students will achieve high grades in their social work programs. If the students your instrument identified had indeed achieved high grades by the end of their BSW programs and the others had not, your instrument would have *predictive* validity.

Thus, predictive validity denotes an instrument's ability to predict future performance or status from present performance or status. An instrument has predictive validity if it can distinguish between individuals who will *differ at some point in the future*.

In sum, concurrent and predictive validity are concerned with prediction, and both make use of some external criterion that is purportedly a valid and reliable measure of the variable being studied. What differentiates the two is time. Concurrent validity predicts current performance or status, and predictive validity predicts future performance or status.

Moreover, concurrent validity involves administering an instrument and comparing its scores with an external criterion at approximately the same time, or concurrently. In contrast, predictive validity entails comparative measurement at two different (present and future) points in time.

The major concern of criterion validity, however, is not whether an instrument is valid for concurrent or future discriminations. Rather, the concern is with the use of a second measure as an independent criterion to check the validity of the first measure (Kyte & Bostwick, 1981).

FACE VALIDITY

FACE VALIDITY, IN FACT, HAS NOTHING TO DO WITH what an instrument actually measures but only with what it *appears* to measure to the one who is completing it. Strictly speaking, it's not a form of validity. For example, suppose that you are taking a course on social work administration. You have a lazy instructor who has taken your final exam from a course he taught for business students last semester.

The exam, in fact, quite adequately tests your knowledge of administration theory, but it does not seem relevant to you because the language it uses relates to the business world not to social work situations.

You might not do very well on this exam because, although it has content validity (it adequately tests your knowledge), it does not have face validity (an appearance of relevance to the respondent). The moral here is that a measuring instrument should not only *be* content valid, to the greatest extent possible, but also should *appear* content valid to the person who completes it.

CONSTRUCT VALIDITY

WHAT SETS CONSTRUCT VALIDITY APART from content and criterion validity is its preoccupation with theory, explanatory constructs, and the testing of hypothesized relationships between and among variables. Construct validity is very difficult to understand because it involves determining the degree to which an instrument successfully measures a theoretical concept. The difficulty derives in part from the abstract nature of concepts.

As you know, a concept is a characteristic or trait that does not exist as an isolated, observable dimension of behavior. It cannot be seen, felt, or heard, and it cannot be measured directly—its existence must be inferred from the evidence at hand.

Thus, the concept "hostility" may be inferred from observations of presumably hostile or aggressive acts; the concept "anxiety" may be inferred from test scores, galvanic skin responses, observations of anxious behaviors, and so on. Other typical concepts of concern to us are motivation, social class, delinquency, prejudice, and organizational conflict.

Construct validity is evaluated by determining the degree to which certain explanatory concepts account for variance, or individual differences, in the scores of an instrument. Put another way, it's concerned with the meaning of the instrument—that is, what it is measuring, and how and why it operates the way it does.

To assess the construct validity of the Rorschach inkblot test, for example, we would try to determine the factors, or concepts, that account for differences in responses on the test. Attempts might be made to determine whether the test measures emotional stability, sociability, or self-control and whether it also measures aggressiveness. The question would be: What proportion of the total test variance is accounted for by the concepts of emotional stability, sociability, self-control, and aggressiveness?

With construct validity, there is usually more interest in the property, or concept, being measured than in the instrument itself. Thus, it involves validation not only of the instrument but also of the theory underlying it. To establish construct validity, the meaning of the concept must be understood, and the propositions the theory makes about the relationships between this and other concepts must be identified.

We try to discover what predictions can be made on the basis of these propositions and whether the measurements obtained from the instrument will be consistent with those predictions. If the predictions are not supported, there is no clear-cut guide as to whether the shortcoming is in the instrument or in the theory.

Suppose a study is conducted to test the hypothesis that self-referred clients are more likely to have favorable attitudes toward treatment than those who come to the agency on some other basis. If the findings do not support the predicted relationship between self-referral and attitude toward treatment, should it be concluded that the measure is not valid or that the hypothesis is incorrect?

In such a situation, the concept of attitude toward treatment and the network of propositions that led to this prediction should be reexamined. Then the concept might be refined with more detailed hypotheses about its relationship to other concepts, and changes might be made in the instrument.

Construct validation makes use of data from a variety of sources. It is a painstaking building process much like theory construction—an attempt to ferret out the dimensions that an instrument is tapping and thereby to validate the theory underlying the instrument.

BOX 9.2	Major Types of Validity
CONTENT VALIDITY	Does the measuring instrument adequately measure the major dimensions of the variable under consideration?
(FACE VALIDITY)	Does the measuring instrument appear to measure the subject matter under consideration? Not really a form of validity.
CRITERION VALIDITY	Does the individual's measuring instrument score predict the probable behavior on a second variable (criterion-related measure)?
CONSTRUCT VALIDITY	Does the measuring instrument appear to measure the general construct (element) it purports to measure

RELIABILITY AND VALIDITY REVISITED

BEFORE WE LEAVE RELIABILITY AND VALIDITY, we should say something about the relationship between them. If an instrument is not reliable, it cannot be valid. That is, if the same person completes it a number of times under the same conditions and it gives different results each time, it cannot be measuring anything accurately.

However, if an instrument *is* reliable, that does not necessarily mean it's valid. It could be reliably and consistently measuring something other than what it's supposed to measure, in the same way that people can be reliably late or watches can be reliably slow. The relationship between validity and reliability can be illustrated with a simple analogy. Suppose that you are firing five rounds from a rifle at three different targets, as illustrated in Figure 9.2 below:

— **In Figure 9.2a,** the bullet holes are scattered, representing a measuring instrument that is neither reliable nor valid.

— **In Figure 9.2b,** you have adjusted your sights, and now all the bullet holes are in the same place but not in the center as you intended. This represents a measuring instrument that is reliable but not valid.

— **In Figure 9.2c,** all the shots have hit the bull's eye: the instrument is both reliable and valid.

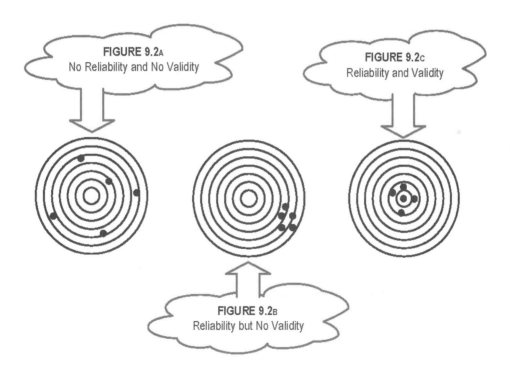

FIGURE 9.2
Targets Illustrating the Validity / Reliability Relationship

MEASUREMENT ERRORS

NO MATTER HOW GOOD the reliability and validity of a measuring instrument, no measurement is entirely without error. You can make two errors when you measure variables. Your measurements can contain:

1. Constant errors
2. Random errors

CONSTANT ERRORS

CONSTANT ERRORS, AS THE NAME SUGGESTS, are those errors that stay constant throughout the research study. They stay constant because they come from an unvarying source. That source may be the measuring instruments used, the research participants, or the researchers themselves. Because we have already spent some time discussing the limitations of measuring instruments, we will focus this discussion on errors caused by the researchers and their research participants.

Research participants, with all the best will in the world, may still have personal styles that lead to error in research results. If they are being interviewed, for example, they may exhibit *acquiescence* (a tendency to agree with everything the researcher says, no matter what it is), or *social desirability* (a tendency to say anything that they think makes them look good), or *deviation* (a tendency to seek unusual responses).

If they are filling out a self-administered instrument, such as Hudson's *Index of Self-Esteem*, they may show *error of central tendency*, always choosing the number in the middle and avoiding commitment to either of the ends. Moreover, they have personal characteristics with respect to gender, age, ethnic background, and knowledge of the English language that remain constant throughout the study and may affect their answers.

Researchers also have personal styles and characteristics. Interviewers can affect the answers they receive by the way they ask the questions, by the way they dress, by their accent, mannerisms, gender, age, ethnic background, or even by their hairstyles. According to Gerald Bostwick and Nancy Kyte (1981), observers who are watching and rating research participants' behavior can commit various sins in a constant fashion, for example:

— **Contrast error**—to rate others as opposite to oneself with respect to a particular characteristic

— **Halo effect**—to think that a participant is altogether wonderful or terrible because of one good or bad trait. Or to think that the trait being observed must be good or bad because the participant is altogether wonderful or terrible

— **Error of leniency**—to always give a good report

— **Error of severity**—to always give a bad report

— **Error of central tendency**—observers, like participants, can choose always to stay comfortably in the middle of a rating scale and avoid both ends

Because these errors are constant throughout the study, they are sometimes recognized, and steps can be taken to deal with them. A different interviewer or observer might be found, for example, or allowances might be made for a particular participant's characteristics or style.

RANDOM ERRORS

RANDOM ERRORS THAT ARE NOT CONSTANT are difficult to find and make allowances for. Random errors spring out of the dark, wreak temporary havoc, and go back into hiding. It has been suggested that eventually they cancel each other out, and indeed they might. They might not as well, but there is little researchers can do about them except to be aware that they exist. According to Nancy Kyte and Gerald Bostwick (1981) there are three types of random error:

1. **Transient qualities of the research participant**—things such as fatigue or boredom, or any temporary personal state that will affect the participant's responses

2. **Situational factors**—the weather, the pneumatic drill outside the window, or anything else in the environment that will affect the participant's responses

3. **Administrative factors**—anything relating to the way the instrument is administered, or the interview conducted, or the observation made. These include transient qualities of the researcher (or whoever collects the data) as well as accidents like reading out the wrong set of instructions.

BOX 9.3	Culturally Sensitive Measurement

INSTRUMENT BIAS

Researchers have debated measurement issues with racial/ethnic minorities for decades. Prominent among the debates has been the issue of testing the intelligence of ethnic minority children. Some researchers have argued that scores on standardized intelligence tests are underestimates of these children's actual abilities. The primary concern pertains to the standardization of the measuring instruments themselves.

It has been suggested that the samples used to standardize the instruments did not include enough ethnic minority children to provide the valid interpretation of the instruments' scores when they were used with ethnic minority children. Also, to do well on intelligence tests, ethnic minority children must demonstrate proficiency with the European American culture.

On the other hand, there is no such requirement for European American children to demonstrate proficiency with ethnic minority cultures. By default, the European American culture is deemed "superior" to the ethnic minority culture.

MEASUREMENT SENSITIVITY

The lack of sensitivity of measuring instruments with ethnic minority populations has been well documented. However, these instruments continue to be used with populations for which they were not designed. The question of validity is apparent. As we know from this chapter, validity addresses the extent to which a measuring instrument achieves what it claims to measure.

In many cases, we have no means to determine the validity of measuring instruments or procedures with ethnic minorities because ethnic minorities were not included in the development of instruments or procedures. Nevertheless, researchers have attempted to interpret results using culturally insensitive instruments. This undoubtedly has led to the misrepresentation and misunderstanding of ethnic minorities.

IMPORTANCE OF VARIABLES MEASURED

Of equal concern to the quality of measurement is whether or not the variables being measured are similarly important to all cultures and ethnic groups. The assumption that all groups value variables equally is another potential misuse of measurement and could assert the superiority of one group's values and beliefs over those of another. For example, when spirituality, a variable, is studied, it may be of greater importance for Native Americans than for other groups. For a group who values spirituality, attainment of material possessions may be of lesser importance than spirituality. We know that there are often competing values in research. Thus, we need to study those variables that are important to each group—not only important to the researcher—and attempt to further our understanding of the importance placed on their valued beliefs, and lifestyles.

LANGUAGE

Language also creates measurement issues. Some ethnic minorities lack facility with the English language, yet they are assessed with measuring instruments that assume English is their primary language. There have been some efforts to translate measuring instruments into other languages, but few studies have been conducted regarding the equivalency of the translations from the original instruments to the newly translated ones. The results of translated versions may be different from those with the English versions.

Translators and interpreters also have been used to bridge the language barriers with ethnic minority populations. Some suggest that the presence of interpreters and translators influences the participants' responses. The extent to which interpreters and translators influence the research participants' responses remains a contentious issue.

OBSERVATIONS

Qualitative studies using observational data collection methods are subject to misinterpretation as well. In observing nonverbal communication such as body language, for example, a researcher can easily misinterpret research participants' behaviors. In some Native American cultures, for example, a subordinate making direct eye contact with a person in authority would be deemed disrespectful. But in European American culture, direct eye contact indicates respect. In this case, unfamiliarity with the culture could easily lead a researcher to incorrectly interpret the eye-contact behavior.

In short, measuring instruments and procedures remain problematic with research studies that focus on ethnic minorities. The validity of studies using instruments insensitive to ethnic minorities has created erroneous and conflicting reports. Refinement of the instruments (and their protocols) is necessary to improve the understanding of ethnic minorities with respect to their own values, beliefs, and behaviors.

IMPROVING VALIDITY AND RELIABILITY

WHEN A MEASURING INSTRUMENT does not achieve acceptable levels of validity and reliability—that is, when much error occurs—researchers often attempt to redesign the instrument so that it's more valid and reliable. Below are six techniques for improving a measuring instrument's reliability and validity (Monette, Sullivan, & DeJong, 2011):

1. **Be clearer on what you are measuring.** Often, validity and reliability are compromised because the researcher is not sufficiently clear and precise about the nature of the variables being measured and their possible indicators. Rethinking the variables helps in revising the instrument to make it more valid.

2. **Provide better training for those who will apply the measuring instruments.** This is especially useful when a measuring instrument is used to assess research participants' feelings or attitudes. Previous research studies show that people who apply an instrument can be intentionally and unintentionally biased, and thus intentionally and/or unintentionally produce error.

3. **Obtain the research participants' personal reactions about the measuring instrument.** Those under study may have some insight regarding why the verbal reports,

observations, or archival reports are not producing accurate measures of their behaviors, feelings, or knowledge levels. They may, for example, comment that the wording of questions is ambiguous or that members of their subculture interpret some words differently than the researcher intended.

4. **Obtain higher measurement levels of a variable.** This does not guarantee greater validity and reliability, but a higher level of measurement can produce a more reliable measuring instrument in some cases. So when the researcher has some options in terms of how to measure a variable, it's worth considering a higher level of measurement (e.g., nominal to ordinal, ordinal to interval).

5. **Use more indicators of a variable.** This also does not guarantee enhanced reliability and validity, but a summated measuring instrument that has many questions, or items, can produce a more valid measure than one with fewer items. Thus, the more items, the higher the reliability and validity.

6. **Conduct an item-by-item assessment.** If the measuring instrument consists of a number of questions, or items, perhaps only one or two of them are the problem. Deleting them may improve the instrument's validity and reliability.

SUMMARY

MEASUREMENT SERVES AS A BRIDGE between theory and reality. Our variables within a positivistic study must be operationalized in such a way that they can be measured. The measuring instrument we select will depend on why we need to make the measurement and under what circumstances it will be administered. Provided that a number of instruments can be found that seem to meet our needs, the next step is to evaluate them.

Measurement error refers to variations in an instrument's score that cannot be attributed to the variable being measured. Basically, all measurement errors can be categorized as constant errors or random errors. The next chapter is a logical extension of this one as it presents the many different types of measuring instruments that are available for our use.

	Study Questions for Chapter 9
	Essay — Discussion
1	Before you entered your social work program, and before you read this chapter, how knowledgeable were you about measurement validity and reliability? Discuss fully.
2	The measurement of variables has four basic functions. List each function and then discuss why each one is important for social work *researchers* and *practitioners* to know. Provide social work examples throughout your discussion to illustrate your main points.
3	What is measurement *validity*? What is measurement *reliability*? Discuss the main differences between the two concepts and provide social work examples throughout your discussion to illustrate your main points.
4	In your own words describe *content validity* and provide social work examples throughout your discussion to illustrate your main points.
5	In your own words describe *face validity* and provide social work examples throughout your discussion to illustrate your main points.
6	In your own words describe *criterion validity* and provide social work examples throughout your discussion to illustrate your main points.
7	In your own words describe *concurrent and predictive validity* and provide social work examples throughout your discussion to illustrate your main points.
8	In your own words describe *construct validity* and provide social work examples throughout your discussion to illustrate your main points.
9	In your own words describe *convergent-discriminant validation* and provide social work examples throughout your discussion to illustrate your main points.

10	In reference to the reliability of a measuring instrument, discuss the concept of *stability*. Provide social work examples throughout your discussion to illustrate your main points.
11	In reference to the reliability of a measuring instrument, discuss the concept of *equivalence*. Provide social work examples throughout your discussion to illustrate your main points.
12	In reference to the reliability of a measuring instrument, discuss the concept of *homogeneity*. Provide social work examples throughout your discussion to illustrate your main points.
13	In reference to the reliability of a measuring instrument, describe the *test-retest method* and provide social work examples throughout your discussion to illustrate your main points.
14	In reference to the reliability of a measuring instrument, describe the *effects of testing* and provide social work examples throughout your discussion to illustrate your main points.
15	In reference to the reliability of a measuring instrument, describe the *alternate-forms method* and provide social work examples throughout your discussion to illustrate your main points.
16	In reference to the reliability of a measuring instrument, describe the *split-half method* and provide social work examples throughout your discussion to illustrate your main points.
17	What is *measurement error*? Why is it important to know? Provide social work examples throughout your discussion to illustrate your main points.
18	In reference to measurement error, describe *constant errors* and provide social work examples throughout your discussion to illustrate your main points.
19	In reference to measurement error, describe *random errors* and provide social work examples throughout your discussion to illustrate your main points.
20	List and discuss each one of the three measurement errors that can occur due to the personal styles of respondents. Provide social work examples throughout your discussion to illustrate your main points.

21	List and discuss each one of the five measurement errors that can occur due to the reactions of observers. Provide social work examples throughout your discussion to illustrate your main points.

Critical Thinking — Application — Integration

22	**MEASUREMENT AND THE PRACTITIONER** **Scenario 1:** Make an argument that to be an effective evidence-based social work practitioner **you must know** how to assess the reliability and validity of measuring instruments that are used in social work research studies. Provide a clear and explicit **practice-related** social work example to illustrate your main points. **Scenario 2:** Make an argument that **you do not have to know** how to assess the validity and reliability of measuring instruments that are used in social work research studies to be an effective evidence-based practitioner. Provide a clear and explicit **practice-related** social work example to illustrate your main points. **Scenario 3:** Make an argument that as a social work practitioner you need to know how to assess the reliability and validity of measuring instruments that are used in research studies AND how to assess the reliability and validity of measuring instruments that are used in social work practice situations. **Time to Choose:** Which one of the above three scenarios do you feel is more consistent with the concept of the contemporary evidence-based social work practice process as illustrated on pages 46–51 ? Why? Provide relevant social work examples to illustrate your main points.
23	**MEASUREMENT AND THE RESEARCHER** **Scenario 1:** Make an argument that to be a competent social work researcher **you must know** how to assess the reliability and validity of measuring instruments. Provide a clear and explicit **research-related** social work example to illustrate your main points. **Scenario 2:** Make an argument that **you do not have to know** how to assess the reliability and validity of measuring instruments to be a competent social work researcher. Provide a clear and explicit **research-related** social work example to illustrate your main points. **Time to Choose:** Which one of the above two scenarios do you feel is more consistent with the place of research in social work? Why? Provide relevant social work examples to illustrate your main points.

24	**TIME TO PUT ON YOUR CRITICAL THINKING HAT** 1. Discuss the similarities and differences between your responses to Questions 23 and 24. 2. What are your thoughts on the belief that you will need to know how to assess the validity and reliability of measuring instruments whether you're a social work *practitioner* (Question 22) or a social work *researcher* (Question 23)?
25	**APPLICATION OF VALIDITY AND RELIABILITY** Locate a published quantitative social work-related journal article that utilized a measuring instrument of some kind. We suggest you locate a quantitatively oriented research study in Bruce Thyer's journal *Research on Social Work Practice* (Sage Publications). Hands down, this is the best journal to find good quantitatively oriented social work research studies. 1. What is the name of the measuring instrument used, and what variable did it measure? 2. Did the author of the study provide information on the instrument's reliability and validity? If so, what types of reliability and validity were reported? 3. Did the author mention anything about the instrument's cultural sensitivity (Chapter 5)? If so, what was discussed? 4. Do you feel the measuring instrument really measures the variable it purports to measure? If so, why? If not, why not?
26	**MIXED-METHODS RESEARCH (CHAPTER 8)** Pretend for the moment that you wish to do a **quantitatively** oriented research study (Chapter 6) to determine whether BSW-level social workers burn out quicker than MSW-level social workers. You also wish to add a **qualitative** component (Chapter 7) to your study in an effort to add more meat to your study's quantitative findings and recommendations. 1. Using what you have learned so far in your research methods course, delineate how you would do your mixed-methods study, highlighting the specific measuring instrument that you have chosen to measure burnout and how you would collect additional relevant qualitative data for your study that would enhance your quantitative findings and recommendations (Think Box 7.1 on pages 268–269). **NOTE:** You're going to have to locate a measuring instrument that measures "burnout."

MEASUREMENT AND YOUR PROFESSIONAL DEVELOPMENT

1. Review the three social work research-related roles you can take when you graduate—CSWE Competency 1 at the beginning of this chapter on page 304 (also discussed in Chapter 1 on pages 38–42). Thoroughly discuss how you feel this chapter will help you to perform one or more research-related roles when you graduate. Which one of the three roles do you believe this chapter helped you with the most? Why? Discuss in detail and provide an example to illustrate your main points.

2. Review CSWE Competency 4 at the beginning of this chapter on page 304. Thoroughly discuss how you feel this chapter will help you to become a practice-informed researcher and a research-informed practitioner. Discuss in detail and provide an example to illustrate your main points.

3. Review the evidence-based practice process as illustrated on pages 46–51. Thoroughly discuss how this chapter helps you to develop the skills you'll need for implementing one or more steps of the evidence-based practice process.

4. Discuss which step(s) you feel this chapter will help you with the most. Why? Be very specific and use relevant social work examples to illustrate your main points throughout your discussion.

NOTE: This exercise should help you to understand that measuring instruments that are used in "research studies" are also used in "practice situations." In short, you can use this chapter to help you assess the reliability and validity of the measuring instruments that you are going to use in your day-to-day practice activities for all of your client systems.

MOVING AHEAD BY LOOKING BACK

At this point in your research methods course, how comfortable are you with discussing the place of research in social work with your field instructor, with your practice instructor, with your research instructor, with your supervisor at work, with the director of your social work program, or with your classmates? Discuss in detail.

10

CHAPTER

2015 EPAS COMPETENCIES

COMPETENCY 1: Demonstrate Ethical and Professional Behavior

You will learn that in order to be a successful evidence-based practitioner you have an ethical obligation to integrate three research roles into your daily practice activities as discussed in Chapter 1: (1) research consumer, (2) research partner—either as a co-researcher or research participant, and (3) creator and disseminator of research (or knowledge).

This entire chapter pertains to these three professional roles when it comes to selecting, implementing, and evaluating the various measuring instruments that are used in social work practice (**research consumer**) and research studies (**research partner** and **creator and disseminator of research**).

COMPETENCY 4: Engage in Practice-Informed Research and Research-Informed Practice

Competency 4 also pertains to the entire chapter because you have to:

1. Evaluate the author's rationale for why a specific measuring instrument(s) was used to measure the variables within the research study. You'll also need to know the advantages, the disadvantages, and the specific criteria that apply to evaluating measuring instruments—especially standardized measuring instruments (**research consumer**—research-informed practice);

2. Participate in a research study—either as a co-researcher or research participant (**research partner**—practice-informed research). See 1 above and 3 below; and

3. Know how to find, evaluate, and select appropriate measuring instruments to measure the variables in your research study (**creator and disseminator of research**—practice-informed research).

You also need to utilize evidence-based practice recommendations whenever possible; that is, you need to integrate (1) the best available research-based evidence with (2) your clinical expertise and (3) your client's values.

All of the above implies you'll need to know how to assess the strengths and limitations of the various measuring instruments (and methods of their use) that were used in a research study that produced its research-based evidence. In short, you need to ask and then answer a simple question: How seriously should I take the findings of any specific research study given the degree of reliability and validity of the study's measuring instrument(s)?

COMPETENCY 9: Evaluate Practice with Individuals, Families, Groups, Organizations, and Communities

You will learn that to determine your practice effectiveness, you will need to know how to select appropriate instruments to measure the outcomes (evaluation) of your practices with your various client systems. See Competencies 1 and 4.

Measuring Instruments

CHAPTER 1	Step 1. Understanding the Research Process
CHAPTER 2	Step 2. Developing Research Questions
CHAPTER 3	Step 3. Reviewing the Literature
CHAPTERS 4 & 5	Step 4. Being Aware of Ethical and Cultural Issues
CHAPTERS 6–8	Step 5. Selecting a Research Approach
CHAPTERS 9 & 10	Step 6. Specifying How Variables Are Measured
CHAPTER 11	Step 7. Selecting a Sample
CHAPTERS 12 & 13	Step 8. Selecting a Research Design
CHAPTERS 14–16	Step 9. Selecting a Data-Collection Method
CHAPTERS 17 & 18	Step 10. Analyzing the Data
CHAPTERS 19 & 20	Step 11. Writing the Research Report

AS WE KNOW FROM THE PREVIOUS CHAPTERS IN THIS BOOK, on a very general level, variables refine concepts, and attributes refine variables. For example, the concept "ethnicity" can be refined more specifically in terms of the existence of ethnic groups. "Ethnic group" is a variable because research participants will *vary* with respect to which ethnic group they belong to. "Ethnic group" can be refined further, via its attributes. The ethnic groups that people can belong to—Asian, Caucasian, Latino, and so on—constitute the attributes of the variable "ethnic group."

All of this refinement stuff boils down to measurement, as pure and simple as that. As we saw in the last chapter, we need to measure the variables in our research study. One easy way to measure them is through measuring instruments that are as valid and reliable as possible. Before we select a measuring instrument to measure them, however, we need to ask ourselves a few basic questions.

QUESTIONS TO ASK BEFORE MEASURING

WHAT WE WANT is some method of making a selection from the huge array of measuring instruments that exist. There are six questions we can ask ourselves to help us make our choice. When we have answered them, we will be able to distinguish the kind of instrument we need from the kind we do not need; hopefully, this will eliminate a large number of all those instruments lying in wait in the library and on the Internet. The six questions are:

1. Why do we want to make the measurement?
2. What do we want to measure?
3. Who will make the measurement?
4. What format do we require?
5. Where will the measurement be made?
6. When will the measurement be made?

Let's take an extremely simple and offbeat example to illustrate how the use of measuring instruments can be used. Let's say we want to know whether there is a relationship between the two variables: depression and sleep patterns.

WHY DO WE WANT TO MAKE THE MEASUREMENT?

THE FIRST QUESTION IS *Why do we want to make the measurement?* At first glance, this does not seem too difficult to answer. We just want to measure depression and sleep patterns with some type of measuring instruments—one for depression and one for sleep patterns—in order to study the relationship between the two variables, if any. But things are not quite as simple as they appear. You just cannot select an instrument in a willy-nilly fashion. The selection of a measuring instrument must be rationally made.

The point of making this selection is to discover how accurate we need the instrument to be. If our measurement is going to affect someone's life, for example, it has to be as accurate as we can possibly make it. We might be doing an assessment that will be used in making decisions about treatment interventions, referrals, placements, and so forth. On the other hand, if our measurement will not affect anyone's life directly, we can afford to be a little less rigid in our requirements. How much less rigid depends on what we are doing.

If this is to be a beginning research study (e.g., exploratory) in a relatively unexplored field, the result will only be a tentative suggestion that some variable is possibly related to some other variable—for instance, sleep patterns are related to depression. A little inaccuracy in measurement in this case is not the end of the world.

When a little more is known in our subject area (e.g., descriptive, explanatory), we might be able to formulate and test a more specific hypothesis; for example, depressed people spend less time in delta-wave NREM sleep than nondepressed people. In this case, we obviously should be able to measure sleep patterns accurately enough to distinguish between delta-wave NREM sleep and other kinds of sleep.

All in all, how accurate our measurement needs to be depends on our purpose. Because we are only doing a beginning study, we can afford to be relatively inaccurate. In general, the higher our research question is on the knowledge level continuum (Figure 2.3 on page 90), the more accurate our measurements of our variables need to be.

In short, measuring instruments that measure the variables within causality-comparative interaction questions (the highest level of research questions) need to be more accurate than instruments that are used to measure existence questions (the lowest level of research questions). We have now answered the first question: *Why do we want to make the measurement?*

WHAT DO WE WANT TO MEASURE?

THE SECOND QUESTION IS *What do we want to measure?* We know the answer to that one also: we simply want to measure two variables, depression and sleep patterns. But here again, it's not as simple as it may seem. Not only are measuring instruments more accurate or less accurate, they can be *wideband* or *narrowband*. *Wideband* instruments measure a broad trait or characteristic. A trait is pretty much the same thing as a characteristic, and it means some aspect of character such as bravery, gaiety, or depression.

Logically enough, *narrowband* instruments measure just a particular aspect of a particular trait. A narrowband instrument, for example, might tell us how depressed Uncle Fred feels about his daughter moving to Moose Jaw, but it will not give us an overall picture of Uncle Fred's depression. Thus, a wideband instrument will give an overall picture of Uncle Fred's depression, but it will not tell us how he feels about his daughter moving to Moose Jaw.

In our particular study, we are not interested too much in how Uncle Fred feels about his daughter moving to Moose Jaw. If he's one of our research participants, we just want to know about his overall depression level so that we can relate it to his sleep patterns. We need a wideband instrument then, which does not have to be absolutely smack-on 100% accurate.

WHO WILL MAKE THE MEASUREMENT?

THE THIRD QUESTION ASKS, *Who will make the measurement?* We will—that seems obvious enough. However, it's not always social workers who complete the measuring instruments. More often than not, our research participants complete them. In our study, it will be the people who participate in our study who will fill out the instrument to measure their depression levels. Sometimes family members complete the measuring instruments, or teachers, specially trained outside observers, or the staff members in an institution.

The point is that different kinds of people require different kinds of measuring instruments. An instrument that could be completed easily and accurately by a trained social worker might prove too difficult for Uncle Fred, who has arthritis and cataracts and a reading level of around the fourth grade. In our simple research study, we will have to be sure the instrument we finally select is easy for our research participants to understand. So far, then, to measure the depression levels of our research participants, we need a wideband instrument, easy to complete, and not necessarily smack-on accurate.

WHAT FORMAT DO WE REQUIRE?

THE FOURTH QUESTION IS *What format do we require?* A format is the way our questions will look on the page. They may appear as:

A simple **inventory**, such as:

List below the things that make you feel depressed.

1.
2.
3.
4.
5.

Or a **checklist,** such as:

> Check below all the things that you sometimes feel.
>
> _____   My mother gets on my nerves.
>
> _____   My father does not understand me.
>
> _____   I do not get along very well with my sister.
>
> _____   I think I hate my family sometimes.

Or a **scale,** such as:

> How satisfied are you with your life? (Circle one number below.)
>
> **1.** Very unsatisfied
>
> **2.** Somewhat satisfied
>
> **3.** Satisfied
>
> **4.** More than satisfied
>
> **5.** Very satisfied

More often than not, measuring instruments contain a number of items, or questions, that when totaled yield more accurate results than just asking one question. These measuring instruments are called summative scales and will be discussed more thoroughly later in this chapter.

After careful thought, we decide that a wideband, easy-to-complete, not-smack-on-accurate summative scale would do the job. However, we have not finished yet. Instruments may be unidimensional or multidimensional. A unidimensional instrument only measures one variable—for example, self esteem (e.g., Figure 9.1 on page 314).

By contrast, a multidimensional instrument measures a number of variables at the same time. A multidimensional instrument is nothing more than a number of unidimensional instruments stuck together. Most often these are called subscales. For example, Figure 10.1 is a multidimensional instrument that contains three subscales, or three unidimensional instruments:

1. Relevance of received social services (Items 1–11)
2. The extent to which the services reduced the problem (Items 12–21)
3. The extent to which services enhanced the client's self-esteem and contributed to a sense of power and integrity (Items 22–34)

Because our study is rather simplistic, we only need two unidimensional instruments—one for depression and one for sleep patterns.

WHERE WILL THE MEASUREMENT BE MADE?

QUESTION FIVE ASKS, *Where will the measurement be made?* Well, probably in our good friend's sleep laboratory. At first glance, it may seem that it does not matter where the measurement is made, but in fact it matters a great deal. For example, we might have a child who throws temper tantrums mostly in school. In this case, measurements dealing with temper tantrums should obviously be made at school.

We can see that an instrument that is to be completed in a railway station might differ from an instrument that is to be used in the comparative serenity of our office. It should be shorter, say, and simpler, and possibly printed on paper that glows in the dark so that if it gets torn out of our hands, we can chase after it more easily. We decide that our research participants will probably be equally depressed everywhere, more or less, and that the measurements will take place in our friend's sleep laboratory.

WHEN WILL THE MEASUREMENT BE MADE?

OUR LAST QUESTION, question six, is *When will the measurement be made?* Probably sometime in August, if it all goes well, that is. But no, the month of the year is not what is meant by *when. When* refers to the time or times during the study when a measurement is made.

SOCIAL SERVICE SATISFACTION SCALE

Using the scale from one to five described below, please indicate at the left of each item the number that comes closest to how you feel.

1 Strongly agree

2 Agree

3 Undecided

4 Disagree

5 Strongly disagree

1. ___ The social worker took my problems very seriously.
2. ___ If I had been the worker, I would have dealt with my problems in the same way.
3. ___ The worker I had could never understand anyone like me.
4. ___ Overall the agency has been very helpful to me.
5. ___ If friends of mine had similar problems I would tell them to go to the agency.
6. ___ The social worker asks a lot of embarrassing questions.
7. ___ I can always count on the worker to help if I'm in trouble.
8. ___ The agency will help me as much as it can.
9. ___ I don't think the agency has the power to really help me.
10. ___ The social worker tries hard but usually isn't too helpful.
11. ___ The problem the agency helped me with is one of the most important in my life.
12. ___ Things have gotten better since I've been going to the agency.
13. ___ Since I've been using the agency my life is more messed up than ever.
14. ___ The agency is always available when I need it.
15. ___ I got from the agency exactly what I wanted.
16. ___ The social worker loves to talk but won't really do anything for me.
17. ___ Sometimes I just tell the social worker what I think she wants to hear.
18. ___ The social worker is usually in a hurry when I see her.
19. ___ No one should have any trouble getting some help from this agency.
20. ___ The worker sometimes says things I don't understand.
21. ___ The social worker is always explaining things carefully.
22. ___ I never looked forward to my visits to the agency.
23. ___ I hope I'll never have to go back to the agency for help.
24. ___ Every time I talk to my worker I feel relieved.
25. ___ I can tell the social worker the truth without worrying.
26. ___ I usually feel nervous when I talk to my worker.
27. ___ The social worker is always looking for lies in what I tell her.
28. ___ It takes a lot of courage to go to the agency.
29. ___ When I enter the agency I feel very small and insignificant.
30. ___ The agency is very demanding.
31. ___ The social worker will sometimes lie to me.
32. ___ Generally the social worker is an honest person.
33. ___ I have the feeling that the worker talks to other people about me.
34. ___ I always feel well treated when I leave the agency.

FIGURE 10.1

Reid-Gundlach Social Service Satisfaction Scale

As will be seen in Chapters 11 and 12, there are certain research designs in which we measure a client's problem, do something to change the problem, and then measure the problem again to see if we have changed it. This involves two measurements, the first and second measurements of the problem. In research jargon, we represent these measurements as Os (O stands for Observation). Whatever we do to change the problem—usually a social work intervention—is represented by X.

In short, in research designs we represent the dependent variables by Os, and the independent variables by Xs. If our research design is such that we make an initial measurement of the dependent variable (O_1), introduce an independent variable (X), and then measure the same dependent variable again (O_2), our design would look like: $O_1 \, X \, O_2$.

To sum up the selection of the two measuring instruments we are going to use in our study—one for depression and one for sleep patterns—we need to find instruments that are (1) wideband, (2) unidimensional, (3) summative, (4) do not necessarily have to be smack-on accurate, and (5) easy to complete in a sleep laboratory.

TYPES OF MEASURING INSTRUMENTS

THE TYPE OF MEASURING INSTRUMENT you choose to measure your variables within your research study depends on your research situation—the question you are asking, the kind of data you need, the research participants you have selected, and the time and money you have available.

Every measuring instrument you consider must be evaluated in terms of the five criteria discussed in the previous chapter; that is, it must be useful, sensitive, nonreactive, reliable, and valid. In general, there are many different types of measuring instruments. We will only discuss five:

1. Journals or diaries
2. Logs
3. Inventories
4. Checklists
5. Summative instruments

JOURNALS OR DIARIES

JOURNALS OR DIARIES are a useful means of data collection when you are undertaking an interpretive study. They are usually not used as data collection methods within positivistic studies. Perhaps in your interpretive study you are asking the question "What are women's experiences of home birth?" and you want your research participants to keep a record of their experiences from early pregnancy to after delivery.

With respect to the five criteria mentioned in the previous chapter, a journal is *valid* in this context to the extent that it completely and accurately describes the relevant experiences and omits the irrelevant experiences. This can only be achieved if the women keeping them have reasonable language skills, can stick pretty much to the point (will they include a three-page description their cats or their geraniums?), and are willing to complete their journals on a regular basis.

A word is in order here about *retrospective data*—that is, data based on someone's memory of what occurred in the past. There is some truth to the idea that we invent our memories. At least, we might embellish or distort them, and a description is much more liable to be accurate if it's written immediately after the event it describes rather than days or weeks later.

The journal is *reliable* insofar as the same experience evokes the same written response. Over time, women may tire of describing again an experience almost identical to the one they had last week, and they may omit it (affecting validity), or change it a little to make it more interesting (again affecting validity), or try to write it in a different way (affecting reliability).

Utility very much depends on whether the woman likes to write and is prepared to continue with what may become an onerous task. Another aspect of utility relates to your own role as researcher. Will you have the time required to go through each journal and perform the kind of qualitative analysis as outlined in Chapter 18?

Sensitivity has to do with the amount of detail included in the journal. To some degree, this reflects completeness and is a validity issue, but small changes in women's experiences as the pregnancy progresses cannot be tracked unless the experiences are each described in some detail.

Journals are usually very reactive. Indeed, they are often used as therapeutic tools simply because the act of writing encourages the writer to reflect on what has been written, thus achieving deeper insights which may lead to behavior and/or affective changes. Reactivity is not desirable in a measuring instrument.

On the other hand, an interpretive study seeks to uncover not just the experiences themselves but the meaning attached to them by the research participants, and meaning may emerge more clearly if the participants are encouraged to reflect. Researchers themselves keep journals while conducting interpretive studies. Journal keeping by the researcher is discussed in Chapter 18 on qualitative data analyses.

LOGS

YOU HAVE PROBABLY USED LOGS in your field placement, so we will not discuss their use in depth. When used in research situations, they are nothing more than a structured kind of journal, where the research participant is asked to record in note form the events related to particular experiences or behaviors.

Each note usually includes headings: the event itself, when and where the event happened, and who was there. A log may be more valid than a journal in that the headings prompt the participant to include only relevant information with no discursive wanderings into cats or geraniums.

The log may be more reliable because it's more likely that a similar experience will be recorded in a similar way. It may be more useful because it takes less time for the participant to complete and less time for the researcher to analyze. It's usually less sensitive to small changes because it includes less detail, and it may be somewhat less reactive depending on the extent to which it leads to reflection and change.

INVENTORIES

AN INVENTORY IS A LIST made by the research participants. For example, the following is an inventory designed to measure depression:

> List below the things that make you feel depressed.
>
> 1.
> 2.
> 3.
> 4.

This is valid to the degree that the list is complete, and sensitive in that the addition or omission of items over time is indicative of change. It's useful if the participant is prepared to complete it carefully and truthfully, and it's probably fairly reactive in that it provokes thought. Inventories are commonly used in interpretive studies.

CHECKLISTS

A CHECKLIST IS A LIST PREPARED BY THE RESEARCHER. For example, a checklist designed to measure depression would include more items than shown but would follow this format:

> Check below all the things that you have felt during the past week.
> _____   A wish to be alone
> _____   Sadness
> _____   Powerlessness
> _____   Anxiety

With respect to the five evaluative criteria presented in the previous chapter, the same considerations apply to a checklist as to an inventory except that content validity may be compromised if the researcher does not include all the possibilities that are relevant to the participant in the context of the study.

SUMMATIVE INSTRUMENTS

ON A GENERAL LEVEL, inventories and checklists ask for yes or no answers. In other words, they are *dichotomous* in that research participants can only respond in one of two ways: *yes,* this occurred, or *no,* this did not occur.

Summative measuring instruments provide a greater range of responses, usually asking how frequently or to what degree a particular item, or question, applies. For example, the depression checklist shown above on the previous page may be presented in the form of a summated instrument, as follows:

Indicate how often you have experienced the following feelings by circling the appropriate number.

	Never	Rarely	Sometimes	Often
A wish to be alone	1	2	3	4
Sadness	1	2	3	4
Powerlessness	1	2	3	4
Anxiety	1	2	3	4

The words "never" and "often" are known as *anchors* and serve to describe the meanings attached to their respective values. Participants circle a number for each item and the scores are summed, or totaled. With only the four items shown (an actual depression scale would contain many more), the lowest possible score is 4, and the highest possible score is 16.

This instrument is an example of a *summative instrument.* A summative measuring instrument is any instrument that allows the researcher to derive a sum or total score from a number of items, or questions. Most, but not all, summated measuring instruments are designed so that low scores indicate a low level of the variable being measured (depression, in this case) and high scores indicate a high level. Figures 9.1 on page 314 and 10.1 on page 350 are excellent examples of summative instruments.

When doing a positivistic study, summative measuring instruments should be used whenever possible as they are more valid and reliable than the other four types. However, you must always take into account your research question or hypothesis and from this question or hypothesis determine what type of instrument will be the best one to measure your variables.

STANDARDIZED MEASURING INSTRUMENTS

STANDARDIZED MEASURING INSTRUMENTS are used widely in social work because they have usually been extensively tested and they come complete with information on the results of that testing. Figure 9.1, via Figure 9.1a, is an excellent example of a summative standardized measuring instrument in that it provides information about itself in six areas:

1. Purpose
2. Description
3. Norms
4. Scoring
5. Reliability
6. Validity

Purpose is a simple statement of what the instrument is designed to measure. *Description* provides particular features of the instrument, including its length and often its *clinical cutting score*. The clinical cutting score is different for every instrument (if it has one, that is) and is the score that differentiates the respondents with a clinically significant problem from the respondents with no such problem.

In Hudson's *Index of Self-Esteem* (Figure 9.1 on page 314), for example, people who score above 30 (±5 for error) have a clinically significant problem with self-esteem, and people who score less than 30 do not.

The section on *norms* tells you who the instrument was validated on. The *Index of Self-Esteem*, for example (see NORMS in Figure 9.1a on page 315), was tested on 1,745 respondents, including single and married individuals, clinical and nonclinical populations, college students and nonstudents, Caucasians, Japanese, and Chinese Americans, and a smaller number of other ethnic groups.

It's important to know this because people with different characteristics tend to respond differently to the sort of items contained in Hudson's *Index of Self-Esteem*. For instance, a woman from a culture that values modesty might be unwilling to answer that she feels she is a beautiful person all of the time (Item 3). She might not know what a wallflower is (Item 19), and she might be very eager to assert that she feels self-conscious with strangers (Item 16) because she thinks that women ought to feel that way.

It's therefore very important to use any measuring instrument *only* with people who have the same characteristics as the people who participated in testing the instrument. As another example, instruments used with children must have been developed using children.

Scoring gives instructions about how to score the instrument. *Reliability* and *validity* were already discussed in the previous chapter. Summated standardized instruments are usually reliable, valid, sensitive, and nonreactive. It's therefore very tempting to believe that they must be useful, whatever the research situation. More often than not, they *are* useful—provided that what the instrument measures and what the researcher *wants* to measure are the same thing.

If you want to measure family coping, for example, and come across a wonderful standardized instrument designed to measure family cohesion, you must resist the temptation to convince yourself that family cohesion is what you really wanted to measure in the first place. Just remember that the variable being measured selects the instrument, the instrument doesn't select the variable.

EVALUATING STANDARDIZED MEASURING INSTRUMENTS

THERE ARE SEVERAL CRITERIA that must be considered when it comes time to evaluating standardized measuring instruments Catheleen Jordan, Cynthia Franklin, and Kevin Corcoran (2018) present four of them:

1. **THE SAMPLE FROM WHICH DATA WERE DRAWN**

    a. Are the samples representative of pertinent populations?

    b. Are the sample sizes sufficiently large?

    c. Are the samples homogeneous?

    d. Are the subsamples pertinent to respondents' demographics?

    e. Are the data obtained from the samples up to date?

2. **THE VALIDITY OF THE INSTRUMENT**

   a. Is the content domain clearly and specifically defined?

   b. Was there a logical procedure for including the items?

   c. Is the criterion measure relevant to the instrument?

   d. Was the criterion measure reliable and valid?

   e. Is the theoretical construct clearly and correctly stated?

   f. Do the scores converge with other relevant measures?

   g. Do the scores discriminate from irrelevant variables?

   h. Are there cross-validation studies that conform to these concerns?

3. **THE RELIABILITY OF THE INSTRUMENT**

   a. Is there sufficient evidence of internal consistency?

   b. Is there equivalence between various forms?

   c. Is there stability over a relevant time interval?

4. **THE PRACTICALITY OF APPLICATION**

   a. Is the instrument an appropriate length?

   b. Is the content socially acceptable to respondents?

   c. Is the instrument feasible to complete?

   d. Is the instrument relatively direct?

   e. Does the instrument have utility?

   f. Is the instrument relatively nonreactive?

   g. Is the instrument sensitive to measuring change?

   h. Is the instrument feasible to score?

ADVANTAGES AND DISADVANTAGES

LIKE EVERYTHING IN LIFE, there are advantages and disadvantages to standardized measuring instruments. Judy Krysik and Jerry Finn (2018) briefly describe them as follows:

ADVANTAGES

1. Standardized instruments are readily available and easy to access.

2. The development work has already been done.

3. They have established reliability and validity estimates.

4. Norms may be available for comparison.

5. Most are easy to complete and score.

6. In many instances, they are available free of charge.

7. They may be available in different languages.

8. They specify age range and reading level.

9. Time required for administration has been determined.

DISADVANTAGES

1. The norms may not apply to the target population.

2. The language may be difficult.

3. The tone might not fit with the philosophy of the program, for example, deficit based versus strength based.

4. The target population may not understand the translation.

5. The scoring procedure may be overly complex.

6. The instrument may not be affordable.

7. Special qualifications or training might be required for use.

8. The instrument may be too long or time consuming to administer.

LOCATING STANDARDIZED MEASURING INSTRUMENTS

ONCE YOU DECIDE that you want to measure a variable through the use of a standardized instrument, the next consideration is to find it. The two general sources for locating such instruments are:

1. Commercial or professional publishers
2. Professional books and journals

COMMERCIAL OR PROFESSIONAL PUBLISHERS

NUMEROUS COMMERCIAL AND PROFESSIONAL PUBLISHING COMPANIES specialize in the production and sale of standardized measuring instruments for use in the social services. They can be easily found on the Internet. The cost of instruments purchased from a publisher varies considerably, depending on the instrument, the number of copies needed, and the publisher.

The instruments generally are well developed, and their psychometric properties are supported by the results of several research studies. Often manuals that include the normative data for the instrument accompany them. As well, publishers are expected to comply with professional standards such as those established by the American Psychological Association. These standards apply to claims made about the instrument's rationale, development, psychometric properties, administration, and interpretation of results.

Standards for the use of some instruments have been developed to protect the interests of clients. Consequently, purchasers of instruments may be required to have certain qualifications, such as possession of an advanced degree in a relevant field. A few publishers require membership in particular professional organizations.

Most publishers will, however, accept an order from a social work student if a qualified person, such as an instructor, who will supervise the use of the instrument, cosigns it.

PROFESSIONAL BOOKS AND JOURNALS

STANDARDIZED MEASURING INSTRUMENTS are most commonly described in human service journals. The instruments usually are supported by evidence of their validity and reliability, although they often require cross-validation and normative data from more representative samples and sub-samples. More often than not, however, the complete instrument cannot be seen in the articles that describe them. However, they usually contain a few items that can be found in the actual instrument.

Locating instruments in journals or books is not easy. Of the two most common methods, computer searches of databanks and manual searches of the literature, the former is faster, unbelievably more thorough, and easier to use. Unfortunately, financial support for the development of comprehensive databanks has been limited and intermittent.

Another disadvantage is that many articles on instruments are not referenced with the appropriate indicators for computer retrieval. These limitations are being overcome by the changing technology of computers and information retrieval systems.

Several services now allow for a complex breakdown of measurement need. Databanks that include references from over 1,300 journals, updated monthly, are now available from a division of *Psychological Abstracts Information Services* and from *Bibliographic Retrieval Services*.

Nevertheless, most social workers will probably rely on manual searches of references such as *Psychological Abstracts*. Although the reference indices will be the same as those in the databanks accessible by computer, the literature search can be supplemented with appropriate seminal (original) reference volumes.

SUMMARY

AS YOU KNOW, Chapter 9 discussed measurement in general. This chapter was a logical continuation of it in that we presented a few ways variables could be measured via measuring instruments. We discussed six basic questions you need to ask yourself before selecting a measuring instrument that will measure your variables within your research question or hypothesis.

We then went on to discuss the five basic types of measuring instruments that you can choose from. The last part of the chapter discussed standardized measuring instruments, highlighted how to evaluate them, and presented their advantages and disadvantages, along with a brief discussion on how to find them.

	Study Questions for Chapter 10
	Essay — Discussion
1	Before you entered your social work program, and before you read this chapter, how knowledgeable were you about the various types of standardized measuring instruments? Discuss in detail.
2	In your own words describe *measuring instruments*. What's so "standardized" about them anyway? Provide social work examples throughout your discussion to illustrate your main points.
3	List and discuss the main advantages of using standardized measuring instruments in social work research and practice. Provide social work examples throughout your discussion to illustrate your main points.
4	What are *journal or diaries*? How can they be used in social work research and practice? Provide social work examples throughout your discussion to illustrate your main points.
5	What are *logs*? How can they be used in social work research and practice? Provide social work examples throughout your discussion to illustrate your main points.
6	What are *inventories*? How can they be used in social work research and practice? Provide social work examples throughout your discussion to illustrate your main points.
7	What are *checklists*? How can they be used in social work research and practice? Provide social work examples throughout your discussion to illustrate your main points.

8	What are *summative instruments*? How can they be used in social work research and practice? Provide social work examples throughout your discussion to illustrate your main points.
9	When selecting an instrument to measure a variable of some kind, you need to ask and answer six questions. List each question and discuss why the answer is important for you to know either as a social work *researcher* or as a social work *practitioner*. Provide social work examples throughout your discussion to illustrate your main points.
10	When choosing a standardized measuring instrument from the hundreds that exist, you need to ask and answer four questions. List each question and discuss why the answer is important for you to know either as a social work *researcher* or as a social work *practitioner*. Provide social work examples throughout your discussion to illustrate your main points.
11	What are nonstandardized measuring instruments? In what research or practice situations would it be appropriate to use them? Provide social work examples throughout your discussion to illustrate your main points.
12	List and then discuss each one of the nine advantages of using standardized measuring instruments either in *research* situations or *practice* situations? Provide social work examples throughout your discussion to illustrate your main points.
13	List and then discuss each one of the eight disadvantages of using standardized measuring instruments either in *research* situations or *practice* situations? Provide social work examples throughout your discussion to illustrate your main points.

14	1. List the six questions that need to be answered before selecting a measuring instrument. 2. Now pretend you're going to find a measuring instrument that measures the interviewing skills of social work students. Answer each of the six questions in relation to finding such an instrument, keeping in mind who is going to complete the instrument—which is probably you. 3. Could your field instructor also fill it out? Why or why not? 4. How about your instructor who taught you interviewing skills? 5. How about your clients that you saw in your field placement?
15	1. Locate a summative measuring instrument that measures a variable of interest to you. 2. Evaluate the instrument on the four global criteria that are presented in this book, paying particular attention to all of their sub-criteria. Provide a social work example for each sub-criterion.
16	Discuss the two main sources for locating measuring instruments. Provide social work examples to illustrate your points.
17	1. Go to the website www.walmyr.com and click on the sample scales tab, then find the short-form scales option. 2. From the numerous variables that come up, pick an instrument that measures a variable you're interested in. 3. Now, with the help of Google, find three other measuring instruments that claim they measure the same variable as the one you picked out from www.walmyr.com. 4. Compare and contrast their features such as scoring, format, and end results. Discuss what you learned from this exercise.
18	Select a standardized measuring instrument that measures a variable of your choice. Discuss how valid and reliable it is via the contents of Chapter 9.
19	Select a standardized measuring instrument that measures a variable of your choice. Using Chapter 9 as a guide, discuss the level of measurement the instrument produces. Justify your response via the use of examples.

	Critical Thinking — Application — Integration
	MEASURING INSTRUMENTS AND THE PRACTITIONER
	Scenario 1: Make an argument that to be an effective evidence-based social work practitioner **you must know** how to find, select, and use measuring instruments. Provide a clear and explicit **practice-related** social work example to illustrate your main points.
20	**Scenario 2:** Make an argument that **you do not have to know** how to find, select, and use measuring instruments to be an effective evidence-based practitioner. Provide a clear and explicit **practice-related** social work example to illustrate your main points.
	Time to Choose: Which one of the above two scenarios do you feel is more consistent with the concept of the contemporary evidence-based social work practice process as illustrated on pages 46–51? Why? Provide relevant social work examples to illustrate your main points.
	MEASURING INSTRUMENTS AND THE RESEARCHER
	Scenario 1: Make an argument that to be a competent social work researcher **you must know** how to find, select, and use measuring instruments. Provide a clear and explicit **research-related** social work example to illustrate your main points.
21	**Scenario 2:** Make an argument that **you do not have to know** how to find, select, and use measuring instruments to be a competent social work researcher. Provide a clear and explicit **research-related** social work example to illustrate your main points.
	Time to Choose: Which one of the above two scenarios do you feel is more consistent with the place of research in social work? Why? Provide relevant social work examples to illustrate your main points.
	TIME TO PUT ON YOUR CRITICAL THINKING HAT
22	**1.** Discuss the similarities and differences between your responses to Questions 20 and 21.
	2. What are your thoughts on the belief that you will need to find, select, and use measuring instruments whether you're a social work *practitioner* (Question 20) or a social work *researcher* (Question 21)?

23	**APPLICATION OF MEASURING INSTRUMENTS** Locate a published quantitative social work-related journal article that utilized a measuring instrument of some kind. We suggest you locate a quantitatively oriented research study in Bruce Thyer's journal *Research on Social Work Practice* (Sage Publications). Hands down, this is the best journal to find good quantitatively oriented social work research studies. 1. What was the name of the measuring instrument? 2. What variable did it measure? 3. Did the author of the study provide information on the instrument's reliability and validity? If so, what types of reliability and validity were reported? 4. Did the author mention anything about the instrument's cultural sensitivity (Chapter 5)? If so, what was discussed? 5. Do you feel the measuring instrument really measures the variable it purports to measure? If so, why? If not, why not?
24	**MIXED-METHODS RESEARCH (CHAPTER 8)** Pretend for the moment that you wish to do a **quantitatively** oriented research study (Chapter 6) to determine the factors of why social workers burn out on the job so quickly. You also wish to add a **qualitative** component (Chapter 7) to your study in an effort to add more meat to your study's quantitative findings and recommendations. 1. Using what you have learned so far in your research methods course, delineate how you would do your mixed-methods study (Chapter 8), highlighting the specific measuring instrument that you have chosen to measure burnout (for your quantitative component) and how you would collect additional relevant qualitative data for your study that would enhance your study's quantitative findings and recommendations (Think Box 7.1 on pages 268–269). **NOTE:** You're going to have to locate a measuring instrument that measures "burnout" for your quantitative component.

MEASURING INSTRUMENTS AND YOUR PROFESSIONAL DEVELOPMENT

1. Review the three social work research-related roles you can take when you graduate—CSWE Competency 1 at the beginning of this chapter on page 342. This concept is also discussed in Chapter 1 on pages 38–42. Thoroughly discuss how you feel this chapter will help you to perform one or more research-related roles when you graduate. Which one of the three roles do you believe this chapter helped you with the most? Why? Discuss in detail and provide examples to illustrate your main points.

2. Review CSWE Competency 4 at the beginning of this chapter on page 342. Thoroughly discuss how you feel this chapter will help you to become a practice-informed researcher and a research-informed practitioner. Discuss in detail and provide examples to illustrate your main points.

25

3. Review the evidence-based practice process as illustrated on pages 46–51. Thoroughly discuss how this chapter helps you to develop the skills you'll need for implementing one or more steps of the evidence-based practice process.

4. Discuss which step(s) you feel this chapter will help you with the most. Why? Be very specific and use relevant social work examples to illustrate your main points throughout your discussion.

NOTE: This exercise should help you to understand that measuring instruments that are used in "research studies" are also used in "practice situations." In short, you can use this chapter to help you find, assess, and use measuring instruments in your day-to-day practice activities.

26	**BEFORE AND AFTER** ***Part 1 (before):*** Before enrolling in your current research methods course, and before you read this chapter on measuring instruments, how did you think social work practitioners measured their effectiveness with their various client systems? What measurement methods did you feel they used before you read this chapter? Do you feel the methods were ethical? If so, how? If not, why not? ***Part 2 (after):*** After reading this chapter discuss any new types of measuring instruments you learned about that you did not know about before reading it. List each new type you learned about (e.g., journals, diaries, logs, inventories, checklists, or summative) and provide a hypothetical social work "practice" situation and a hypothetical "research" situation that demonstrates the use of your newfound method(s). **NOTE:** This exercise should help you to understand that measuring instruments that are used in "research studies" are the same that are used in "practice situations." In short, you can use this chapter to help you find, assess, and use measuring instruments in your day-to-day practice activities for all of your client systems.
27	**MOVING AHEAD BY LOOKING BACK** At this point in your research methods course, how comfortable are you with discussing the place of research in social work with your field instructor, with your practice instructor, with your research instructor, with your supervisor at work, with the director of your social work program, or with your classmates? Discuss in detail.

PART IV

Sampling and Research Designs

CHAPTER 11: Sampling **370**

CHAPTER 12: Single-Subject Designs **398**

CHAPTER 13: Group Designs **438**

11

CHAPTER

2015 EPAS COMPETENCIES

COMPETENCY 1: Demonstrate Ethical and Professional Behavior

You will learn that in order to be a successful evidence-based practitioner you have an ethical obligation to integrate three research roles into your daily practice activities as discussed in Chapter 1: (1) research consumer, (2) research partner—either as a co-researcher or research participant, and (3) creator and disseminator of research (or knowledge).

This entire chapter pertains to these three professional research-related roles when it comes to selecting, implementing, and evaluating the various sampling methods that can be used in social work research studies.

COMPETENCY 4: Engage in Practice-Informed Research and Research-Informed Practice

Competency 4 also pertains to the entire chapter because you have to:

1. Evaluate the appropriateness of the sampling method(s) utilized in a published research study (**research consumer**—research-informed practice);

2. Participate in a research study—either as a co-researcher or research participant (**research partner**—practice-informed research). See 1 above and 3 below; and

3. Know the advantages and disadvantages of the various sampling methods, in addition to knowing how to implement them, when you actually conduct a research study (**creator and disseminator of research**—practice-informed research).

You also need to utilize evidence-based practice recommendations whenever possible; that is, you need to integrate (1) the best available research-based evidence with (2) your clinical expertise and (3) your client's values.

All of the above implies you'll need to know how to assess the strengths and limitations of the various sampling methods that were used in a research study that produced its research-based evidence. In short, you need to ask and then answer a simple question: How seriously should I take the findings of any specific research study given the appropriateness of the study's sampling method?

COMPETENCY 9: Evaluate Practice with Individuals, Families, Groups, Organizations, and Communities

You will learn that to design an evaluation of any kind, you will need to choose appropriate sampling methods to evaluate a single client system (Chapter 12) or an entire social service program (Chapter 13). See Competencies 1 and 4.

Sampling

CHAPTER 1	**Step 1.**	Understanding the Research Process
CHAPTER 2	**Step 2.**	Developing Research Questions
CHAPTER 3	**Step 3.**	Reviewing the Literature
CHAPTERS 4 & 5	**Step 4.**	Being Aware of Ethical and Cultural Issues
CHAPTERS 6–8	**Step 5.**	Selecting a Research Approach
CHAPTERS 9 & 10	**Step 6.**	Specifying How Variables Are Measured
CHAPTER 11	**Step 7.**	Selecting a Sample
CHAPTERS 12 & 13	**Step 8.**	Selecting a Research Design
CHAPTERS 14–16	**Step 9.**	Selecting a Data-Collection Method
CHAPTERS 17 & 18	**Step 10.**	Analyzing the Data
CHAPTERS 19 & 20	**Step 11.**	Writing the Research Report

THE LAST CHAPTER DISCUSSED measuring instruments—how to select them, where to find them, and how to evaluate them. This chapter discusses who will complete them. In short, we discuss how to select the actual people, or research participants, who you will administer the measuring instruments to.

Let's continue with the previous example we used in the last chapter where we are trying to discover whether there is a relationship between two variables—depression and sleep patterns. At this point, it's obviously necessary to find a few people so we can measure their depression levels (Variable 1) and sleep patterns (Variable 2).

One way of doing this is to phone our trusty social worker friend, Ken, who works with people who are depressed and ask if he will please find us some clients, or research participants, who do not mind sleeping in a laboratory once a week with wires attached to their heads. "Certainly," says Ken crisply. "How many do you want?" "Er . . ." we say, "how many have you got?"

"Oh, lots," says Ken with cheer. "Now, do you want them young or old, male or female, rich or poor, acute or chronic, severely or mildly depressed . . . ?" He adds, "Oh, and by the way, all of them are refugees from Outer Ganglinshan." We decide that we need to think about this some more. Suppose that the sleep patterns of Outer Ganglinshanians who are depressed are different from the sleep patterns of Bostonians who are depressed.

Suppose even further that men who are depressed have different sleep patterns from women who are depressed, or adolescents who are depressed from seniors who are depressed, or Anabaptists who are depressed from Theosophists who are depressed. The list of possibilities is endless.

One solution, of course, would be to assemble all the people who are depressed in the Western Hemisphere in the hope that Anabaptists and Theosophists and so forth are properly represented.

This leaves out the Eastern Hemisphere, but we have to eliminate something because our sleep laboratory has only ten beds. There is another difficulty, too. Not only are we restricted to ten sleeping people, but also on our limited budget we will be hard pressed to pay them bus fare from their homes to our laboratory.

> A population is the totality of persons or objects with which our research study is concerned.

This being the case, we have to forget about the Western Hemisphere and concentrate on the area served by the city transit, within which there are probably very few Anabaptists who are depressed and no Theosophists at all to speak of.

How are we going to select ten people from this small area and still be fair to the Theosophist population? The answer is simple: we do this through the use of sampling frames.

POPULATIONS AND SAMPLING FRAMES

A *POPULATION* IS THE TOTALITY OF PERSONS or objects with which our research study is concerned. If, for example, we are interested in all the people who are depressed in the Western Hemisphere, then our population is all the people who are depressed in the Western Hemisphere.

If we decide to restrict our study to all the people who are depressed in the area served by city transit, then our population is all the people who are depressed in the area served by city transit. However we decide to define our population, the results of our study will apply only to that population from which our sample was drawn. Thus, we cannot do our study on folks within the confines of city transit and then apply the results to the whole of the Western Hemisphere.

SAMPLING FRAMES

WHEN OUR POPULATION HAS BEEN DEFINED, the next step is to make a list of all the people (or other units such as case files) included in that population.

A sampling frame is composed of all the individual people (or units) you have selected from the population.

Such a list is called a *sampling frame.* For example, if our population is to be all the people who are depressed in the area served by city transit, then we must create a list, or sampling frame, of all the people who are depressed in the area served by city transit. Obtaining a sampling frame is often one of the hardest parts of a research study.

We probably will not be able to generate a list of all the people who are depressed in the area served by city transit because there is not a single person or social service program that knows about all of them. It might be better to restrict our study to all the depressed people treated by Ken—or some other source of people who are depressed that will provide us with a list.

Suppose, then, that we have decided to restrict our study to all the people who are depressed treated by Ken. We may think that "all the people who are depressed treated by Ken" is a reasonable definition of our population. But a population has to be defined exactly. "All the people who are depressed treated by Ken" is possibly not very exact, especially when we consider that Ken has been treating them for over twenty years.

The ones treated eighteen and nineteen years ago have doubtless disappeared by now over the far horizon; indeed, the fates of those treated a mere year ago might be equally veiled in mystery. Perhaps we should redefine our population as "all the people who are depressed treated by Ken over the last three months," or better yet as "all the people who are depressed treated by Ken from January 1 to March 31."

SAMPLING PROCEDURES

IF WE CAN MAKE A THREE-MONTH LIST of all the people who are depressed treated by Ken from January 1 to March 31, we have our sampling frame. The next thing is to use it to select our sample. This process is called *sampling,* and the people (or other units such as case files) picked from a sampling frame make up a *sample.* There are two main ways of selecting samples:

1. Probability sampling
2. Nonprobability sampling

PROBABILITY SAMPLING

THE FIRST MAIN CATEGORY OF SAMPLING PROCEDURES is probability sampling. This method of sampling is used more often in positivistic studies than in interpretive ones. A *probability sample* is one in which all the people (or units in the sampling frame) have the same known probability of being selected for the sample. By probability, we mean chance, such as the probability of winning a lottery. The selection is based on some form of random procedure of which there are four main types:

1. Simple random sampling (requires a sampling frame)
2. Systematic random sampling (requires a sampling frame)
3. Stratified random sampling (requires a sampling frame)
4. Cluster random sampling (does not require a sampling frame)

SIMPLE RANDOM SAMPLING

THE FIRST TYPE OF PROBABILITY SAMPLING is simple random sampling. Suppose now that there are 100 names in our sampling frame; that is, Ken has seen 100 different clients who are depressed from January 1 to March 31.

We assign each one of these clients a number; the first one on the list will be 001, the second 002, and so on until 100 is reached. Then we take a book of random numbers, open the book at random, and pick a digit on the page also at random. The first half page of such a table is shown in Table 11.1.

Suppose the digit we happen to pick on is 1, the second digit in the number in the sixth row from the bottom in the second column from the left. (That whole number is **81864** and is highlighted in **bold**.) The two digits immediately to the right of 1 are 8 and 6; thus, we have 186. We take three digits in total because 100, the highest number on our sampling frame has three digits. The number 186 is more than 100, so we ignore it.

TABLE 11.1

Partial Page of a Random Numbers Table

02584	75844	50162	44269	76402	33228	96152	76777
66791	44653	90947	61934	79627	81621	74744	98758
44306	88222	30967	57776	90533	01276	30525	66914
01471	15131	38577	03362	54825	27705	60680	97083
65995	81864	19184	61585	19111	08641	47653	27267
45567	79547	89025	70767	25307	33151	00375	17564
27340	30215	28376	47390	11039	39458	67489	48547
02584	75844	56012	44269	76402	33228	96152	76777
66791	44653	90497	61934	79627	81621	74744	98758
44306	80722	30317	57776	90533	01276	30525	66914
65995	**81864**	19184	61585	19131	08641	47653	27267
45567	79547	89025	70767	25307	33151	00375	17564
27340	30215	23456	47390	11039	39458	67489	48547
02471	10721	30577	03362	54825	27705	60680	97083
60791	40453	90227	61934	79627	81621	74744	98758
43316	87212	36967	57576	90533	01276	30525	66914

Going down the column, 954 is also more than 100, so we ignore it also. The next one, 021, is less than 100, so we can say that we have selected number 021 on our sampling frame to take part in our study. After 072 and 045 there are no more numbers less than 100 in the second column (middle three digits), so we go to the third column (middle three digits). Here we discover seven more people (i.e., 016, 094, 096, 049, 031, 057, 022).

We go down the columns; picking out numbers, until it occurs to us that we do not really know how many numbers should be selected. Our sleep laboratory has accommodation for ten, but then if we do a different ten each night of the week, that is seventy people. With Sundays off, to keep us sane, we have sixty. If we keep union hours, we are looking at closer to thirty-five. There has to be a better way than union hours to figure out our sample size. So, before looking at sample size, we should examine three more probability sampling procedures.

SYSTEMATIC RANDOM SAMPLING

THE SECOND TYPE OF PROBABILITY SAMPLING is systematic random sampling. Here, the size of our sampling frame is divided by the desired sample size to give us our *sampling interval.* To state it more simply, if we only want half the sampling frame to be in our sample, we select every other person. If only a third of the sampling frame is needed to be in our sample, we pick every third person; for a quarter, every fourth person; for a fifth, every fifth person; and so on.

The problem with this approach is that we need to know the exact size of our sampling frame in order to do it. We will not really know what our sample size ought to be until later in this chapter. At this point, we can only make a guess. Let's assume that we will work at our sleep lab every weeknight. Ten sleepers every night for five nights gives us a sample size of five nights times ten sleepers which equals fifty.

The idea of a sampling interval can be expressed mathematically in the following way. Suppose that the size of our sampling frame is 100 and we have set our sample size—the number of people taking part in our study—at fifty. Then, dividing the former by the latter (100/50 = 2) provides the size of the sampling interval, which in this case is two.

If our sample was only going to be one-fourth of the size of our sampling frame (instead of one-half), our sampling interval would be four instead of two. We might start at the fourth person on our sampling frame and pick out, as well, the eighth, twelfth, sixteenth persons, and so on.

The problem with this method is that everyone does not have the same chance of being selected. If we are selecting every other person, starting with the second person, we select the fourth, sixth, and so on. But this means that the third and the fifth never get a chance to be chosen. This procedure introduces a potential bias that calls for caution.

Suppose, for example, we have applied for a credit card and the credit card company examines our bank account every thirtieth day. Suppose, further, that the thirtieth day falls regularly on the day after we have paid this month's rent and on the day before we receive last month's paycheck. In other words, our bank account, while miserable at all times, is particularly low every thirtieth day. This is hardly fair because we never get a chance to show the company how rich we are on days other than the thirtieth.

If we do not have to worry about this sort of bias, then a systematic sample is largely the same as a simple random sample. The selection is just a bit easier because we do not have to bother with random numbers as presented in Table 11.1.

STRATIFIED RANDOM SAMPLING

THE THIRD TYPE OF PROBABILITY SAMPLING is stratified random sampling. If, for example, our study of depression and sleeping patterns is also concerned with religious affiliation, we can look at our sampling frame and count how many of them are Christians, Jews, Muslims, Buddhists, Hindus, Theosophists, and so forth. Suppose that, in our population of 100, we found 40 Jews, 19 Christians, 10 Muslims, 10 Buddhists, 10 Hindus, 10 Sikhs, and 1 lone Theosophist.

Now, we can sample our religious categories, or strata, either proportionally or disproportionally. If we sample our sampling frame proportionally, we will choose, say, one-tenth of each category to make up our sample; that is, we will randomly select 4 Jews, 1.9 Christians, 1 Muslim, 1 Buddhist, 1 Hindu, 1 Sikh, and 0.1 of a Theosophist. This comprises a total sample of 10, as illustrated in Table 11.2 below.

TABLE 11.2
Stratified Random Sample Example (Sampling Frame = 100 people)

Category	Number	1/10 Proportionate Sample	Number and (Disproportionate Sampling Fractions) for a Sample of 1 per Category
Jews	40	4.0	1 (1/40)
Christians	19	1.9	1 (1/19)
Muslims	10	1.0	1 (1/10)
Buddhists	10	1.0	1 (1/10
Hindus	10	1.0	1 (1/10)
Sikhs	10	1.0	1 (1/10)
Theosophists	1	.1	1 (1)
Totals . . .	100	10.0	7

However; the 1.9 Christians and the 0.1 of a Theosophist present a difficulty. In this case, it is necessary to sample disproportionately. For example, it may be preferable to choose one member of each religious affiliation for a total sample of seven. In this case, the sampling fraction is not the same for each category; it is 1/40 for Jews, 1/19 for Christians, 1/10 for Muslims, Buddhists, Hindus, and Sikhs, and 1 for Theosophists. A total sample of only seven is not a good idea for reasons that will be discussed shortly.

Our sampling frame is divided into religious categories only if we believe that religious affiliation will affect either depression or sleep patterns—that is, if we really believe that Buddhists who are depressed have different sleep patterns than Muslims who are depressed, everything else being equal.

However, we must admit that we do not believe this. There is nothing in the literature or our past experience to indicate anything of the sort. And anyway, our friend's clients who are depressed, from whom our sample will be drawn, will not include anything so interesting as Buddhists and Muslims. Probably the best we can hope for is a few odd sects and the town atheist.

This method, though, could be used to look at the sleep patterns of different age groups. Our sampling frame could be divided quite sensibly into eight categories: those aged 10 to 20, 21 to 30, and 31 to 40 years, and so on until we reach 81 to 90 years. We might then sample proportionately by randomly selecting one-tenth of the people in each category.

Or we might sample disproportionately by selecting, say, six people from each category, regardless of the number of people in the category. It might be preferable to sample disproportionately, for example, because there are a small number of people in the 71 to 80 and 81 to 90 categories, but it is our belief that advanced age significantly affects sleep patterns. Therefore, we want to include in our sample more than the one or two elderly people who would be included if we took one-tenth of each category.

Categorizing people in terms of age is fairly straightforward. They have only one age, and they usually know what it is. Other types of categories, though, are more complex. Psychological labels, for instance, can be uncertain such that people fall into more than one category and the categories themselves are not homogeneous; that is, the categories are not made up of people who are all alike.

There's no point in using stratified random sampling unless the categories are both homogeneous and different from each other. In theory, the more homogeneous the categories are, the fewer people will be needed from each category to make up our sample. Suppose, for example, we had invented robots that were designed to perform various tasks. Those robots designed to be electricians were all identical, and so were all the plumbers, doctors, lawyers, and so forth. Of course, each kind of robot was different from every other kind.

If we then wanted to make some comparison between all lawyer and all doctor robots, we would only need one of each because same-kind robots are all the same; or, in other words, the robot categories are completely homogeneous. People categories are never completely homogeneous, but the more homogeneous they are, the fewer we need from each category to make comparisons. The fewer we need, the less our study will cost.

However, we must take care not to spend the money we save in this manner on the process of categorization. If people already are in categories, as they might be in a hospital, very good. If they are easy to categorize—say, by age—that's very good, too. If they are not already categorized and are difficult to categorize, it might be more appropriate to use another sampling method.

There is one more point to be considered. The more variables we are looking at, the harder it is to create homogeneous strata. It is easy enough, for example, to categorize people as Buddhists or Hindus, or as aged between 21 and 30 or 31 and 40. It is not nearly so easy if they have to be, say, between 21 and 30 *and* Buddhist.

CLUSTER RANDOM SAMPLING

THE FOURTH TYPE OF PROBABILITY SAMPLING is cluster random sampling. This is useful if there is difficulty creating a sampling frame. Suppose, for a moment, we want to survey all the people in the area served by city transit (the population) to see whether they are satisfied with the transit system. We do not have a list of every person in this specific population so we can't construct a sampling frame. There is a list, however, of all the communities in the city served by the transit system, and we can use this list as an alternative sampling frame.

First, we randomly select a community, or cluster, and survey every person living there. We will be certain what this community thinks about the transit system as we talked to every member of it. But there is still the possibility that this community, in which there are a large number of families with children, has a different opinion from that of a second community, which consists largely of senior citizens.

Perhaps we ought to survey the second community as well. Then there is a third community inhabited largely by penniless writers, artists, and social work students who might have yet a different opinion. Each community is reasonably homogeneous; that is, the people within each individual community are very much like each other. But the communities themselves are totally unlike; that is, they are heterogeneous with respect to each other.

One of the problems here is that we may not be able to afford to survey everyone in the three clusters. But we could compromise. Perhaps we could survey not every street in each cluster but only some streets taken at random—and not every house on our chosen streets, but only some houses, also taken at random. This way, we survey more clusters but fewer people in each cluster.

The only difficulty here is that, because we are not surveying everyone in the community, we might happen to select people who do not give us a true picture of that community. In a community of people with small children, for example, we might randomly select a couple who does not have children and does not intend to, and whose home was demolished, moreover, to make way for the transit line. Such untypical people introduce an error into our results that is due to our sampling procedure and is therefore called *sampling error.*

We will now turn our attention to the second, and last, category of sampling procedures—nonprobability sampling.

NONPROBABILITY SAMPLING

IN NONPROBABILITY SAMPLING, not all the people in the sampling frame have the same probability of being included in the sample, and for each one of them the probability of inclusion is unknown. This form of sampling is often used in qualitative (or interpretive) studies where their purpose is just to collect as much valid and reliable data as possible. There are four types of nonprobability sampling procedures:

1. Availability sampling
2. Purposive sampling
3. Quota sampling
4. Snowball sampling

AVAILABILITY SAMPLING

THE FIRST TYPE OF NONPROBABILITY SAMPLING is availability sampling. It is also called *accidental sampling* and *convenience sampling*. It's the simplest of the four nonprobability sampling procedures. As its name suggests, it involves selecting for our sample the first people or units who make themselves available to us. We might survey people, for example, who pass us in a shopping mall.

Or we might base our study on the caseload of a particular social worker. Or we might just seize upon the first fifty of Ken's clients who are depressed who agree to sleep in our lab with wires attached to their heads. In fact, Ken himself was selected by availability—he was a friend of ours, and he was available. There was nothing random about selecting Ken whatsoever. Not very scientific to say the least, but very practical indeed.

PURPOSIVE SAMPLING

THE SECOND TYPE OF NONPROBABILITY SAMPLING is purposive sampling. This type is used when we want to purposely choose a particular sample. For example, if we are testing a questionnaire that must be comprehensible to less well-educated people while not offending the intelligence of better-educated people, we might present it both to doctoral candidates and to people who left school cheerfully as soon as they could.

In other words, we purposely choose the doctoral candidates and the happy school leavers to be in our two subsamples. There is nothing random about it. In the same way, if we know from previous studies that there is more family violence in the city than in the country, we might restrict our sample to those families who live in cities. Purposive sampling is very useful in qualitative (or interpretive) research studies.

QUOTA SAMPLING

THE THIRD TYPE OF NONPROBABILITY SAMPLING is quota sampling. In this type of sampling, we decide, on the basis of theory, that we should include in our sample so many of a certain type of person. Suppose we wanted to relate the sleep patterns of people who are depressed to body weight and age.

TABLE 11.3
Quota Sampling Matrix of Body Weight by Age

	Body Weight	
Age	Obese	Nonobese
Young	*Category A* Obese / Young	*Category B* Nonobese / Young
Old	*Category C* Obese / Old	*Category D* Nonobese / Old

We might decide to look at extremes; for example, obese and young, nonobese and young, obese and old, and nonobese and old. This gives us four categories (i.e., *A, B, C,* and *D*) as illustrated in Table 11.3 above. We might want, for example, fifteen people in each category, or for some reason we might need more elderly people than young. In this case, we may decide on ten people in each of categories A and B and twenty people in each of categories *C* and *D*.

Whatever quotas we decide on, we only have to find enough people to fill them who satisfy the two conditions of weight and age. We might discover all the obese people at a weight loss clinic, for example, or all the young, nonobese ones at a support group for anorexics. It doesn't matter where or how we find them so long as we do.

SNOWBALL SAMPLING

THE FOURTH TYPE OF NONPROBABILITY SAMPLING is snowball sampling. If a follow-up study is to be conducted on a self-help group that broke up two years ago, for example, we might find one member of the group and ask that member to help us locate other members. The other members will then find other members and so on until the whole group has been located.

The process is a bit like telling one person a secret, with strict instructions not to tell it to anyone else. Like purposive sampling, snowball sampling is commonly used in qualitative research studies.

BOX 11.1	**Cultural Sensitivity and Sampling**

SAMPLING—how we select people to participate in research studies—has been and remains problematic in culturally based studies. In some cases, it is very difficult to define the population to be studied, let alone draw a representative sample from the population. For example, sexual orientation remains ill defined, thereby rendering studies with this population somewhat limited. Given the limited precision with which we define groups, convenience sampling (studying those who are available) is prominent in cultural and ethnic research. Convenience samples can be problematic for a variety of reasons.

It is certain that convenience samples will be biased. For example, the literature on African Americans is focused primarily upon poor and disadvantaged individuals and families. Many poor and disadvantaged African Americans appear at public agencies to seek some type of assistance. While seeking assistance, they may participate in research studies or provide data that then are used to make inferences about all African Americans in general.

However, are we certain that data collected from poor and disadvantaged African Americans are applicable to African Americans who are not similarly disadvantaged? Probably not. Nevertheless, generalizations based upon skewed samples have been made with respect to all African Americans.

A similar predicament exists in terms of sexual orientation. The emergence of AIDS and HIV has brought much attention to gays. Sexual activity and other behaviors associated with contracting and transmitting the HIV were scrutinized. Some researchers concluded that some gays have many sexual partners and use illicit substances. This may be true for some, but not all.

Recent efforts by gays to gain legal recognition of same-sex unions and marriages suggest that some gays prefer long-term relationships over casual sexual encounters. Overgeneralizations, based upon research samples of gays with AIDS and their substance-abuse behaviors, have hindered understanding of gays and their relationships.

Research studies that have focused on women's issues are also subject to sampling errors. As mentioned previously, research samples composed of single mothers in poverty have been used to make generalizations for all women. Convenience samples drawn from women living under poverty conditions are insufficient when addressing the needs of women who may not be in poverty.

It's nearly impossible to replicate a research study that uses a convenience sample. As we know, one of the benchmarks of the scientific method is its ability to replicate research studies. Research studies that use convenience samples, however, are susceptible to local and geographic influences. The extent of the generalization of their findings is compromised because of the susceptibility to regional influences.

While convenience samples may be better than no samples at all, recognition of the limitations of convenience samples must be observed when interpreting a study's findings. The dangers of overgeneralizations made from samples that are too small or inadequate can have far-reaching negative consequences for the populations being studied.

In a perfect world (and where would that be?), probabilistic sampling techniques are preferable to nonprobabilistic ones. Inadequate definitions of specific population parameters (or sampling frame) of minority and ethnic populations increase the difficulty associated with adequate sample selections. Sampling remains an area requiring further refinement if we are to improve research efforts with women and with ethnic and cultural groups.

SAMPLE SIZE

BEFORE OUR SAMPLE CAN BE SELECTED, we obviously have to decide on how many people are needed to take part in our study; in other words, we have to decide on our sample size. The correct sample size depends on both our population and research question.

If we are dealing with a limited population, for example, such as the victims of some rare disease, we might include the whole population in our study. Then we would not take a sample. Usually, however, the population is large enough that we do need to take a sample, the general rule being the larger the sample, the better.

As far as a minimal sample size is concerned, experts differ. Some say that a sample of 30 will allow us to perform basic statistical procedures, while others would advise a minimum sample size of 100. In fact, sample size depends on how homogeneous our population is with respect to the variables we are studying.

Recalling all those categories of robot doctors, lawyers, and so forth considered a while back, if our population of robot doctors is all the same—that is, 100% homogeneous—we only need one robot doctor in our sample. On the other hand, if the factory messed up and our robot doctors have emerged with a wide range of medical skills, we will need a large sample to tell us anything about the medical skills of the entire robot doctor population. In this case, of course, medical skill is the variable we are studying.

Sample size must also be considered in relation to the number of categories required. If the sample size is too small, there may be only one or two people in a particular category—for example, 1.9 Christians and 0.1 of a Theosophist. This should be anticipated and the sample size adjusted. The situation can also be handled using the disproportionate stratified random sampling procedure. This procedure is the one where we selected one person from each religious category, thus neatly avoiding our 1.9 Christians and 0.1 of a Theosophist.

There are many formulas available for calculating sample size, but they are complicated and difficult to use. Usually, a sample size of one-tenth of the population is considered sufficient to provide reasonable control over sampling error. The same one-tenth convention also applies to categories of the population; we can include one-tenth of each category in our sample.

Now that you know that more confidence can be placed in the generalizability of statistics from larger samples when compared to smaller ones, you may be eager to work with random samples that are as large as possible. Unfortunately, researchers often cannot afford to sample a very large number of cases.

They therefore try to determine during the design phase of their studies how large a sample they must have to achieve their purposes. They have to consider the degree of confidence desired, the homogeneity of the population, the complexity of the analysis they plan, and the expected strength of the relationships they will measure. Russell Schutt (2008) presents four pointers when it comes to selecting sample sizes:

1. The less sampling error desired, the larger the sample size must be.

2. Samples of more homogeneous populations can be smaller than samples of more diverse populations. Stratified sampling uses prior information on the population to create more homogeneous population strata from which the sample can be selected, so the sample can be smaller than if simple random sampling were used.

3. If the only analysis planned for a survey sample is to describe the population in terms of a few variables, a smaller sample is required than if a more complex analysis involving sample subgroups is planned.

4. When the researchers will be testing hypotheses and expect to find very strong relationships between and among the variables, they will need smaller samples to detect these relationships than if they expect weaker relationships.

Researchers can make more precise estimates of the sample size required through a method termed *statistical power analysis*—a statistical/research design technique that is way beyond the scope of this book. Statistical power analysis requires a good advance estimate of the strength of the hypothesized relationship in the population. In addition, the math is complicated, so it helps to have some background in mathematics or to be able to consult a statistician.

You can obtain some general guidance about sample sizes from the current practices of social scientists. For professional studies of the national population in which only a simple description is desired, professional social science studies typically have used a sample size of between 1,000 and 1,500, with up to 2,500 being included if detailed analyses are planned.

Studies of local or regional populations often sample only a few hundred people, in part because these studies lack sufficient funding to draw larger samples. Of course, the sampling error in these smaller studies is considerably larger than in a typical national study (Schutt, 2008).

TABLE 11.4

Advantages and Disadvantages of Various Sampling Methods

Method	Description	Advantages	Disadvantages
Simple random	Random sample from whole population	Highly representative if all research participants participate; the ideal	Not possible without complete list of population members; potentially uneconomical to achieve; can be disruptive to isolate members from a group; time-scale may be too long, data/sample could change
Stratified random	Random sample from identifiable groups (strata), subgroups, etc.	Can ensure that specific groups are represented, even proportionally, in the sample(s) (e.g., by gender), by selecting individuals from strata list	More complex, requires greater effort than simple random; strata must be carefully defined
Cluster	Random samples of successive clusters of research participants (e.g., by institution) until small groups are chosen as units	Possible to select randomly when no single list of population members exists, but local lists do; data collected on groups may avoid introduction of confounding by isolating members	Clusters in a level must be equivalent and some natural ones are not for essential characteristics (e.g., geographic: numbers equal, but unemployment rates differ)

Stage	Combination of cluster (randomly selecting clusters) and random or stratified random sampling of individuals	Can make up probability sample by random at stages and within groups; possible to select random sample when population lists are very localized	Complex, combines limitations of cluster and stratified random sampling
Purposive	Hand-pick research participants on the basis of specific characteristics	Ensures balance of group sizes when multiple groups are to be selected	Samples are not easily defensible as being representative of populations due to potential subjectivity of researcher
Quota	Select research participants as they come to fill a quota by characteristics proportional to populations	Ensures selection of adequate numbers of research participants with appropriate characteristics	Not possible to prove that the sample is representative of designated population
Snowball	Research participants with desired traits or characteristics give names of further appropriate research participants	Possible to include members of groups where no lists or identifiable clusters even exist (e.g., drug abusers, criminals)	No way of knowing whether the sample is representative of the population from which it was drawn

	Either asking for volunteers, or the consequence of not all those selected finally participating, or a set of research participants who just happen to be available	Inexpensive way of ensuring sufficient number of research participants in a study	Can be highly unrepresentative
Accidental			

LESSONS ABOUT SAMPLE QUALITY

RAFAEL ENGLE AND RUSSELL SCHUTT (2010) provide four points that are implicit in the evaluation of samples:

1. We can't evaluate the quality of a sample if we don't know what population it is supposed to represent. If the population is unspecified because the researchers were never clear about just what population they were trying to sample, then we can safely conclude that the sample itself is no good.

2. We can't evaluate the quality of a sample if we don't know just how cases in the sample were selected from the population. If the method was specified, we then need to know whether cases were selected in a systematic fashion or on the basis of chance. In any case, we know that a haphazard method of sampling (e.g., availability sampling) undermines the generalizability of the findings.

3. Sample quality is determined by the sample actually obtained, not just by the sampling method itself. If many of the people selected for our sample are nonrespondents or people (or other entities) who do not participate in the study although they have been selected for the sample, the quality of our sample is undermined—even if we chose the sample in the best possible way.

4. We need to be aware that even researchers who obtain very good samples may talk about the implications of their findings

for some other groups that are larger than or just different from the population they actually sampled. For example, findings from a representative sample of students in one university often are discussed as if they tell us about ALL university students in general. And maybe they do; we just don't know.

ADVANTAGES AND DISADVANTAGES

THOMAS BLACK (1999), via Table 11.4 on pages 388–390, provides us with a brief list of the advantages and disadvantages of the various sampling techniques that can be used in all kinds of social work research studies.

SUMMARY

IN THE COURSE OF A RESEARCH STUDY, the entire population that we are interested in is usually too big to work with, and in any case we rarely have enough money to include everyone. For these reasons, it's necessary to draw a sample. The idea is that the sample represents the population from which it was drawn; that is, the sample is identical to the population with respect to every variable that we are interested in.

When the sample is truly representative of the population, we can generalize the results received from the sample back to the population from which it was drawn. However, no sample is ever *totally* representative of the population from which it was drawn.

	Study Questions for Chapter 11
	Essay — Discussion
1	In your own words discuss the concepts of populations and sampling frames. Provide a single social work example throughout your discussion.
2	List and then discuss the two sampling procedures. Provide as many social work examples as you can to illustrate your main points for each procedure.
3	List and then discuss the four probability sampling methods. Provide as many social work examples as you can to illustrate your main points for each sampling method.
4	List and then discuss the four nonprobability sampling methods. Provide as many social work examples as you can to illustrate your main points for each sampling method.
5	Discuss the concept of sample size. Provide a social work example throughout your discussion.
6	Take a look at Table 11.4 on pages 388–390. From this table, and in your own words, discuss the advantages and disadvantages of each of the eight types of sampling methods. Provide a social work example that highlights your main points for each method.
	Critical Thinking — Application — Integration
7	**SAMPLING METHODS AND THE PRACTITIONER** **Scenario 1:** Make an argument that to be an effective evidence-based social work practitioner **you must know** the advantages and disadvantages of the various sampling methods that are used in social work research studies (i.e., Table 11.4 on pages 388–390). Provide clear and explicit **practice-related** social work examples to illustrate your main points for each method. **Scenario 2:** Make an argument that **you do not have to know** the advantages and disadvantages of the various sampling methods (i.e., Table 11.4) that are used in social work research studies to be an effective evidence-based

practitioner. Provide clear and explicit **practice-related** social work examples to illustrate your main points for each method.

Time to Choose: Which one of the above two scenarios do you feel is more consistent with the concept of the contemporary evidence-based social work practice process as illustrated on pages 46–51? Why? Provide relevant social work examples to illustrate your main points.

8

SAMPLING METHODS AND THE RESEARCHER

Scenario 1: Make an argument that to be a competent social work researcher **you must know** the advantages and disadvantages of the various sampling methods that are used in social work research studies (i.e., Table 11.4). Provide clear and explicit **research-related** social work examples to illustrate your main points for each method.

Scenario 2: Make an argument that **you do not have to know** the advantages and disadvantages of the various sampling methods (i.e., Table 11.4) that are used in social work research studies to be a competent social work researcher. Provide clear and explicit **research-related** social work examples to illustrate your main points.

Time to Choose: Which one of the above two scenarios do you feel is more consistent with the place of research in social work? Why? Provide relevant social work examples to illustrate your main points.

9

TIME TO PUT ON YOUR CRITICAL THINKING HAT

1. Discuss the similarities and differences between your responses to Questions 7 and 8.

2. What are your thoughts on the belief that you'll need to know the advantages and disadvantages of sampling methods whether you're a social work *practitioner* (Question 7) or a social work *researcher* (Question 8)?

APPLICATION OF SAMPLING METHODS

Locate a published quantitative social work-related journal article of your choice. Be sure the study used a sampling method that this chapter describes. We suggest you locate a quantitatively oriented research study in Bruce Thyer's journal *Research on Social Work Practice* (Sage Publications). Hands down, this is the best journal to find good quantitatively oriented social work research studies.

10

1. What was the study's population?

2. What was the study's sampling frame—data source?

3. What was the study's sampling method(s) for each data source (e.g., research participants, client files, databanks)?

4. Would you have used a different sampling method to collect the data to answer the study's research question? If so, what method would you have used, and why?

5. With your knowledge of the various sampling methods that research studies can use, thoroughly discuss how you will use the material contained within this chapter when you begin to evaluate the appropriateness of a research study's sampling method(s) and discuss why you believe each criterion you select is important for your evaluation of the study's chosen method(s).

MIXED-METHODS RESEARCH (CHAPTER 8)

Pretend for the moment that you wish to do a **qualitatively** oriented research study (Chapter 7) to determine whether MSW-level social workers are "better" at interviewing their clients than BSW-level social workers. You also wish to add a quantitative component (Chapter 6).

11

1. Using what you have learned from Chapters 6–8 and this chapter, delineate how you would do your mixed-methods study, highlighting the specific sampling method(s) you have chosen for the quantitative component *and* the qualitative component.

2. What are the advantages and disadvantages of the method(s) you have selected? Use specific examples to illustrate your main points.

12	**RESEARCH AND YOUR PROFESSIONAL DEVELOPMENT** 1. Review the three social work research-related roles you can take when you graduate—CSWE Competency 1 at the beginning of this chapter on page 370. This concept is also discussed in Chapter 1 on pages 38–42. Thoroughly discuss how you feel this chapter will help you to perform one or more research-related roles when you graduate. Which one of the three roles do you believe this chapter helped you with the most? Why? Discuss in detail and provide an example to illustrate your main points. 2. Review CSWE Competency 4 at the beginning of this chapter on page 370. Thoroughly discuss how you feel this chapter will help you to become a practice-informed researcher and a research-informed practitioner. Discuss in detail and provide an example to illustrate your main points. 3. Review the evidence-based practice process as illustrated on pages 46–51. Thoroughly discuss how this chapter helps you to develop the skills you'll need for implementing one or more steps of the evidence-based practice process. 4. Discuss which step(s) you feel this chapter will help you with the most. Why? Be very specific and use relevant social work examples to illustrate your main points throughout your discussion.
13	**YOU'RE NOW A QUANTITATIVE RESEARCHER** Pretend for a moment that you want to do a **quantitative** research study (Chapter 6) that will assess the teaching effectiveness of the instructors who teach in your social work program. 1. What's your population? 2. What's your sampling frame? 3. What sampling method(s) are you going to use for selecting instructors from your sampling frame? 4. List and then discuss the advantages and disadvantages of the sampling method(s) you selected.

14	**YOU'RE NOW A QUALITATIVE RESEARCHER** Pretend for a moment that you want to do a **qualitative** research study (Chapter 7) that will assess the teaching effectiveness of the instructors who teach in your social work program. 1. What's your population? 2. What's your sampling frame? 3. What sampling method(s) are you going to use for selecting instructors from your sampling frame? 4. List and then discuss the advantages and disadvantages of the sampling method(s) you selected.
15	**YOU'RE NOW A MIXED-METHODS RESEARCHER** With the preceding two questions in mind (i.e., 13 & 14), discuss in detail how the two separate studies could be combined into one **mixed-methods study** (Chapter 8), paying particular attention to the different sampling methods you are going to use—for the quantitative component *and* the qualitative component.
16	**BEFORE AND AFTER** *Part 1 (before):* Before enrolling in your current research methods course, and before you read this chapter on sampling methods, how did you think social work researchers selected their samples (research participants) for their research studies? What sampling methods did you think they used before you read this chapter? Did you feel the sampling methods were ethical? If so, how? If not, why not? *Part 2 (after):* After reading this chapter discuss any new method(s) you learned about that you did not know about before reading it. List each new method you learned about and provide a hypothetical social work research study that demonstrates the use of your newfound method(s).
17	**MOVING AHEAD BY LOOKING BACK** At this point in your research methods course, how comfortable are you with discussing the place of research in social work with your field instructor, with your practice instructor, with your research instructor, with your supervisor at work, with the director of your social work program, or with your classmates? Discuss in detail.

12

CHAPTER

COMPETENCY 1: Demonstrate Ethical and Professional Behavior

You will learn that in order to be a successful evidence-based practitioner you have an ethical obligation to integrate three research roles into your daily practice activities as discussed in Chapter 1: (1) research consumer, (2) research partner—either as a co-researcher or research participant, and (3) creator and disseminator of research (or knowledge).

This entire chapter pertains to these three professional research-related roles when it comes to selecting, implementing, and evaluating the various single-subject designs that can be used in social work research and practice situations.

COMPETENCY 4: Engage in Practice-Informed Research and Research-Informed Practice

Given Competency 1 above, Competency 4 also pertains to the entire chapter because you have to:

1. Evaluate the appropriateness of the single-subject designs that were utilized in a published research study (**research consumer**—research-informed practice);

2. Participate in a single-subject research study either as a co-researcher or research participant (**research partner**—practice-informed research). See 1 above and 3 below; and

3. Know how to select and implement a single-subject design when you actually do a research study (**creator and disseminator of research**—practice-informed research).

You also need to utilize evidence-based practice recommendations whenever possible; that is, you need to integrate (1) the best available research-based evidence with (2) your clinical expertise and (3) your client's values.

All of the above implies you'll need to know how to assess the advantages and disadvantages of the single-subject design that was used in a research study that produced its research-based evidence. In short, you need to ask and then answer a simple question: How seriously should I take the findings of any specific single-subject research study given the specific design and data source(s) the study used?

COMPETENCY 9: Evaluate Practice with Individuals, Families, Groups, Organizations, and Communities

You will learn that you can easily evaluate the effectiveness of your day- to-day practice activities by using single-subject designs, whether your client is an individual, a family, a group, an organization, or a community. This competency pertains to the entire chapter. See Competencies 1 and 4.

Single-Subject Designs

CHAPTER 1   **Step 1.** Understanding the Research Process

CHAPTER 2   **Step 2.** Developing Research Questions

CHAPTER 3   **Step 3.** Reviewing the Literature

CHAPTERS 4 & 5   **Step 4.** Being Aware of Ethical and Cultural Issues

CHAPTERS 6–8   **Step 5.** Selecting a Research Approach

CHAPTERS 9 & 10   **Step 6.** Specifying How Variables Are Measured

CHAPTER 11   **Step 7.** Selecting a Sample

CHAPTERS 12 & 13   **Step 8.** Selecting a Research Design

CHAPTERS 14–16   **Step 9.** Selecting a Data-Collection Method

CHAPTERS 17 & 18   **Step 10.** Analyzing the Data

CHAPTERS 19 & 20   **Step 11.** Writing the Research Report

THE LAST CHAPTER DISCUSSED how we can select research participants for our research studies. This chapter is a logical extension of the previous one in that we now discuss simple research designs that will include our selected research participants. The simplest type of research designs—the topic of this chapter—is commonly referred to as single-subject designs. They are also called *single-case designs, single-system designs, N = 1, case-level designs, single-case experimentations,* and *idiographic research.*

WHAT ARE SINGLE-SUBJECT DESIGNS?

ON A VERY GENERAL LEVEL, single-subject designs are more "practice orientated" than group-level designs (discussed in the next chapter). That is, they are used more by social work "practitioners" than by social work "researchers."

Single-subject designs provide data about how well a treatment intervention is working so that alternative or complementary interventive strategies can be adopted if necessary. They can also indicate when a client's problem has been resolved. Single-subject designs are used to monitor client progress up to, and sometimes beyond, the point of termination.

They can also be used to evaluate the effectiveness of a social service program as a whole by aggregating or compiling the results obtained by numerous social workers serving their individual clients within the program. A family social service program might be evaluated, for example, by combining family outcomes on a number of families that have been seen by different social workers who work within the program.

According to Bloom, Fischer, and Orme (2009), the advantages of single-subject designs are as follows:

— They can be built into every social worker's practice with each and every case/situation without disruption of practice.

— They provide the tools for evaluating the effectiveness of our practice with each client, group, or system with which we work.

— They focus on individual clients or systems. If there is any variation in effect from one client or system to another, single-subject designs will be able to pick it up.

— They provide a continuous record of changes in the target problem over the entire course of intervention, not just pre- and posttest.

— They are practice-based and practitioner-oriented. Single-subject designs provide continuous assessment and outcome data to practitioners so that they can monitor progress and make changes in the nature of the intervention program if so indicated. Unlike traditional group designs—and the intervention programs they are used to evaluate—which ordinarily cannot be changed once the study has begun, single-subject designs are flexible; the worker can change the intervention and the design depending on the needs of the case.

— They can be used to test hypotheses or ideas regarding the relationship between specific intervention procedures and client changes, ruling out some alternative explanations and allowing an inference regarding causality: Was the intervention program responsible for the change in the target problem?

— They can be used to help the worker *assess* the case/situation, leading to selection of a more appropriate program of intervention by clarifying what seem to be the relevant factors involved in the problem.

— They essentially are theory-free; that is, they can be applied to the practice of any practitioner regardless of the worker's theoretical orientation or approach to practice.

— They are relatively easy to use and understand. They can be applied within the same time frame the social worker is currently using in seeing clients or others. In fact, the use of single-subject designs can actually enhance the worker's efficiency by saving time and energy in trying to record and evaluate the social worker's practice.

— They avoid the problem of outside researchers coming into an agency and imposing a study on the social workers. Single-subject designs are established and conducted by practitioners for their benefit and for the benefit of the client/systems.

— They provide a model for demonstrating our accountability to ourselves, our clients and consumers, our funding sources, and our communities. Systematic, consistent use of single-subject designs allows practitioners and agencies to collect a body of data about the effectiveness of practice that provides more or less objective information about the success of our practice.

THE RESEARCH PROCESS

ANY RESEARCH DESIGN—positivistic and interpretive alike—is nothing more than a plan for conducting the entire research study from beginning to end. They all try to answer the following basic questions:

— When, or over what period, should the research study be conducted?

— What variables need to be measured?

— How should the variables be measured?

— What other variables need to be accounted for or controlled?

— From whom should the data be collected?

— How should the data be collected?

— When should the data be collected?

— How should the data be analyzed?

— How should the results of the study be disseminated?

As you should know by now, these questions are highly commingled and are directly related to the research question we are trying to answer or the hypothesis we are testing. If you are exploring the concept of bereavement, for example, you will collect data from bereaved people and perhaps involved social workers, and you may also need to measure variables related to bereavement, such as grief, anger, depression, and levels of coping.

You might need to measure these variables over a period of months or years, and the way you measure them will suggest appropriate methods of how you will analyze your data. Decisions about how best to accomplish these steps depend on how much we already know about the bereavement process; that is, where your bereavement research questions fall on the knowledge level continuum as presented in Chapter 2.

UNIT OF ANALYSIS

SINGLE-SUBJECT DESIGNS are used to fulfill the major purpose of social work practice: to improve the situation of a client system—*an* individual client, *a* couple, *a* family, *a* group, *an* organization, or *a* community. Any of these client configurations can be studied with a single-subject design. In short, they are used to study *one* individual or *one* group intensively, as opposed to studies that use two or more groups of research participants.

Some single-subject designs are conducted in order to study one individual or case, some to study groups of people (including families, organizations, and communities), and some to study social artifacts (such things as birth practices or divorces). The individual, group, or artifact being studied is called the *unit of analysis*.

If you are exploring the advantages and disadvantages of home birth, for example, you might be asking questions from women who have experienced homebirth, but the thing you are studying—the *unit of analysis*—is the social artifact, home birth. Conversely, if you are a social work practitioner studying the impact of home birth on a particular client, the unit of analysis is the client or individual; and if you are studying the impact on a group of women, the unit of analysis is the group of women.

REQUIREMENTS

THE FOLLOWING DISCUSSION on the requirements of single-subject designs has been adapted and modified from three sources: Grinnell and Williams (1990); Williams, Tutty, and Grinnell (1995); and Williams, Unrau, and Grinnell (1998). In order to carry out a single-subject design:

1. The client's problem must be identified

2. The desired objective to be achieved must be decided upon

3. The intervention that is most likely to eliminate the client's problem must be selected

4. The intervention must be implemented

5. The client's progress must be continually monitored to see whether the client's problem has been resolved, or at least reduced

If practitioners are careful to organize, measure, and record what they do, via the above five points, single-subject designs will naturally take shape in the clients' files, and the results can be used to guide future interventive efforts. Only three things are required when doing a single-subject design:

1. Setting measurable client objectives
2. Selecting valid and reliable outcome measures
3. Graphically displaying the resulting data

SETTING MEASURABLE CLIENT OBJECTIVES

ONE OF THE FIRST TASKS a worker does when initially seeing a client is to establish the purpose of why they are together. Why has the client approached the worker? Or, in many nonvoluntary situations such as in probation and parole or child abuse situations, why has the worker approached the client? The two need to formulate objectives for their mutual working relationship.

TARGET PROBLEMS

A SPECIFIC, MEASURABLE, CLIENT-DESIRED OUTCOME OBJECTIVE is known as a *client target problem*. Client target problems are feelings, knowledge levels, or behaviors that need to be changed. Many times clients do not have just one target problem—they have many. They sometimes have a number of interrelated problems; even when there is only one that is more important than the rest, they may not know what it is. Nevertheless, they may be quite clear about the desired outcome of their involvement with social work services.

They may want to "fix" their lives so that "Johnny listens when I ask him to do something," or "My partner pays more attention to me," or "I feel better about myself at work." Unfortunately, many clients express their desired target problems in vague, ambiguous terms, possibly because they do not know themselves exactly what they want to change; they only know that something should be different. If a worker can establish (with the guidance of the client) what should be changed, why it should be changed, how it should be changed, and to what degree it should be changed, the solution to the problem will not be far away.

CLEARLY STATING THE TARGET PROBLEM. Consider Heather, for example, who wants her partner Ben to pay more attention to her. Heather may mean sexual attention, in which case the couple's sexual relations may be the target problem. On the other hand, Heather may mean that she and Ben do not socialize enough with friends, or that Ben brings work home from the office too often or has hobbies she does not share, or any of a host of things.

Establishing clearly what the desired change would look like is the first step in developing the target problem. Without this, the worker and client could wander around forever through the problem maze, never knowing what, if anything, needs to be solved. Desired change cannot occur if no one knows what change is desired. It is, therefore, very important that the target problem to be solved be precisely stated as early as possible in the client–social worker relationship.

Continuing with the example of Heather and Ben, and after a great deal of exploration, the worker agrees that Heather and Ben have many target problems to work on, such as improving their child-discipline strategies, improving their budgeting skills, improving their communication skills, and many other issues that, when dealt with, can lead to a successful marriage.

For now, however, they agree to work on one target problem: increasing the amount of time they spend together with friends. Heather may say that she wishes she and Ben could visit friends together more often. The target problem has now become a little more specific: it has narrowed from "increasing the amount of time they spend together with friends" to "Heather and Ben visiting friends more often." "Visiting friends more often with Ben," however, is still an ambiguous phrase. It may mean once a month or every night, and the achievement of the target problem's solution cannot be known until the meaning of "more often" has been clarified.

If Heather agrees that she would be happy to visit friends with Ben once a week, the ambiguous objective may be restated as a specific, measurable objective—"to visit friends with Ben once a week." The social worker may discover later that "friends" is also an ambiguous term. Heather may have meant "her friends," but Ben may have meant "his friends," and the social worker may have imagined that "the friends" were mutual.

The disagreement about who is to be regarded as a friend may not become evident until the worker has monitored their progress for a month or so and found that no improvement was occurring. In some cases, poor progress may be due to the selection of an inappropriate interventive strategy. In other cases, it may mean that the target problem itself is not as specific, complete, and clear as it should be. Before deciding that the interventive strategy needs to be changed, it is always necessary to clarify with the client exactly what it is that specifically needs to be achieved.

SELECTING VALID AND RELIABLE OUTCOME MEASURES

A TARGET PROBLEM MUST BE MEASUREABLE with valid and reliable measuring instruments as discussed in Chapters 9 and 10. Can Heather and Ben, who wanted to visit friends more often, be trusted to report truthfully on whether the friends were visited? Suppose she says they were not visited and he says they were? Social workers must always be very conscious of what measurement methods are both available and feasible when formulating a target problem with a client.

It may be quite possible for the social worker to telephone the friends and ask if they were visited; but if the worker is not prepared to get involved with Heather's and Ben's friends, this measurement method will not be feasible. If this is the case, and if Heather and/or Ben cannot be trusted to report accurately and truthfully, there is little point in setting the target problem.

Heather's and Ben's target problem can be easily observed and measured. However, quite often a client's target problem involves feelings, attitudes, knowledge levels, or events that are known only to the client and cannot be easily observed and/or measured.

Consider Bob, a client who comes to a social worker because he is depressed. The worker's efforts may be simply to lessen his target problem, depression, but how will the worker and/or Bob know when his depression has been alleviated or reduced?

Perhaps he will say that he feels better, or his partner may say that Bob cries less, or the worker may note that he spends less time in therapy staring at his feet. All these are indicators that his depression is lessening, but they are not very valid and reliable indicators. What is needed is a more "scientific method" of measuring depression. Fortunately, a number of paper-and-pencil standardized measuring instruments have been developed that can be filled out by the client in a relatively short period of time, can be easily scored, and can provide a fairly accurate picture of the client's condition.

One such widely used instrument that measures depression is Hudson's *General Contentment Scale* (*GCS*). Because higher scores indicate higher levels of depression, and lower scores indicate lower levels of depression, the target problem in Bob's case would be to reduce his score on the *GCS* to a level at which he can adequately function. People who are not depressed will still not score zero on the *GCS*.

Everyone occasionally feels blue (Item 2) or downhearted (Item 10). There is a clinical cutting score that differentiates a clinically significant problem level from a non-clinically significant problem level, and it will often be this score that the client aims to achieve.

If the target problem is "to reduce Bob's score on the *GCS* to or below the clinical cutting score of 30," the worker will know not only what the target problem is, but also precisely how Bob's success is to be measured. Usually, client success, sometimes referred to as client outcome, can be measured in a variety of ways. Bob's partner, Maria, for example, may be asked to record the frequency of his crying spells, and the target problem here may be to reduce the frequency of these spells to once a week or less.

Again, it would be important to further refine the term "crying spell" so that Maria knows exactly what it was she has to measure. Perhaps "crying spell" could be defined as ten minutes or more of continuous crying, and a gap of at least ten minutes without crying would define the difference between one "spell" and another.

There are now two independent and complementary indicators of Bob's level of depression: the *GCS* as rated by Bob, and the number of his ten-minute crying spells per day as rated by Maria. If future scores on both indicators display improvement (that is, they both go down), the worker can be reasonably certain that Bob's depression is lessening and the intervention is effective.

If the two indicators do not agree, however, the worker will need to find out why. Perhaps Bob wishes to appear more depressed than he really is, and this is an area that needs to be explored. Or perhaps Maria is not sufficiently concerned to keep an accurate recording of the number of Bob's ten-minute crying spells per day; and it may be Maria's attitude that has caused Bob's crying in the first place.

Accurate measurements made over time can do more than reveal the degree of a client's improvement. They can cast light on the problem itself and suggest new avenues to be explored, possibly resulting in the utilization of different interventive strategies.

Be that as it may, a client's target problem cannot be dealt with until it has been expressed in specific measurable indicators. These indicators cannot be said to be measurable until it has been decided how they will be measured. Specification of the target problem will, therefore, often include mention of an instrument that will be used to measure it. It will also include who is to do the measuring and under what circumstances.

It may be decided, for example, that Bob will rate himself on the *GCS* daily after dinner or once a week on Saturday morning, or that Maria will make a daily record of all crying spells that occurred in the late afternoon after he returned home from work. The physical record itself is very important, both as an aid to memory and to track Bob's progress. In a single-subject design, progress is usually monitored by displaying the measurements made in the form of graphs.

GRAPHICALLY DISPLAYING THE RESULTING DATA

AS WE KNOW FROM CHAPTER 9, the word *measurement* can be simply defined as the process of assigning a number or value to a variable. If the variable, or target problem, being considered is depression as measured by Hudson's *Generalized Contentment Scale* (*GCS*), and if Bob scores, say 62, then 62 is the number assigned to Bob's initial level of depression.

The worker will try to reduce his initial score of 62 to at least 30—the desired *minimum* score. The worker can then select and implement an intervention and ask Bob to complete the *GCS* again—say, once a week—until the score of 30 has been reached. Bob's depression levels can be plotted over time on a graph such as the ones displayed in this chapter.

EXPLORATORY DESIGNS

SUPPOSE YOU HAVE A CLIENT—Cecilia—whose underlying problem, you believe, is her high anxiety level. She will be the "subject" in your single-subject design. Before you go ahead with an intervention designed to decrease her social anxiety—an intervention Cecilia doesn't need if your belief is wrong—you will have to answer the simple question, "Does Cecilia really have a clinically significant problem with anxiety?" In other words, does the "anxiety problem" you think she has really exist in the first place?

In order to answer this question, you select a measuring instrument to measure her social anxiety level that is valid, reliable, sensitive, nonreactive, and useful in this particular situation. Say you choose the Interaction and Audience Anxiousness Scale (*IASS*).

FIGURE 12.1

A Design: Cecilia's Social Anxiety Scores for the First Seven Weeks
(Indicating that an intervention IS warranted)

On this particular measuring instrument, higher scores indicate higher social anxiety levels, and the minimal clinical cutting score is 40. Clinical cutting scores are usually displayed as dashed lines, as can be seen in Figure 12.1. You administer the *IASS* to Cecilia, and she scores 62 as shown in Figure 12.1 above:

Scores above the clinical cutting score indicate a clinically significant problem. You might think "Ah-ha! She has a problem since her score was 22 points higher than the "minimum clinical cutting score," and you rush forward with your intervention.

On the other hand, any social work intervention has the potential to harm as well as help (in the same way that any medication does), and you first want to be sure that this is a persisting problem and not just a reflection of Cecilia's high anxiety today. You might also want to be sure that her high anxiety problem will not go away by itself. Doctors usually do not treat conditions that resolve themselves, given time, and the same is true for social workers.

In order to see if Cecilia meets these three criteria for treatment—first, there really is a problem; second, the problem is persisting; and third, the problem is either stable at an unacceptable level or getting worse—you will need to administer the same measuring instrument two or three times more

FIGURE 12.1a

A Design: Cecilia's Social Anxiety Scores for the First Seven Weeks
(Indicating that an intervention IS NOT warranted)

at intervals of, say, a week. You might then graph your results as shown in Figure 12.1. This figure constitutes a baseline measure of Cecilia's social anxiety level over a seven-week period and is a very simple example of an *A* design.

There are four exploratory designs:

1. *A* design
2. *B* design
3. *BB₁* design
4. *BC* design

A DESIGN

AT THE RISK OF SOUNDING A BIT RIDICULOUS, we'll note that the letter *A* simply designates "a research study" where the intention is to establish, via measurement, a baseline for an individual client's problem. Perhaps "research study" is a grandiose term to describe a routine assessment, but the word *research* does mean *to look again,* and you are indeed looking again at Cecilia's potential problem in order to see whether her problem exists in the first place.

FIGURE 12.1b

A **Design: Cecilia's Social Anxiety Scores for the First Seven Weeks**
(Indicating that an intervention IS warranted)

Three data points are the minimum number needed to show any kind of trend, and some experts maintain that you need no less than seven. However, in a clinical situation the client's need for an intervention is the primary factor, and you will have to use your judgment to decide how long you ought to continue to gather baseline data before you intervene.

Figure 12.1 indicates a worsening problem, needing intervention, because the scores are generally getting higher as time goes on. Remember, higher scores mean higher levels of the problem. Had the scores been generally getting lower, the problem would have been improving by itself, and no intervention would be indicated as illustrated in Figure 12.1a.

If the scores fell more or less on a horizontal line, intervention would be indicated so long as the line was above the clinical cutting score (Figure 12.1b) but not if the line was below it as illustrated in Figure 12.1c.

B DESIGN

THE SECOND TYPE OF EXPLORATORY SINGLE-SUBJECT RESEARCH DESIGNS is the *B* design. As we have seen, an *A* design answers the question "Does the problem exist?" The *A* design also answers another type of exploratory question: "Does the problem exist at different levels over time?" In other words, "Is the problem changing *by itself?*"

FIGURE 12.1c

A **Design: Cecilia's Social Anxiety Scores for the First Seven Weeks**
(Indicating that an intervention IS NOT warranted)

A *B* design also addresses the question "Is the problem changing?" but here we want to know whether the problem is changing *while an intervention is being applied*. Bob is Cecilia's friend and has also come to you complaining that he experiences a great deal of anxiety in social situations.

He is nervous when he speaks to his boss or when he meets people for the first time, and the prospect of giving public presentations at work appalls him. You decide that you will measure Bob's anxiety level using the same standardized measuring instrument as you did with Cecilia (Interaction and Audience Anxiousness Scale, *IASS*). As you know about this particular standardized measuring instrument, higher scores indicate higher anxiety levels, and the clinical cutting score for the *IASS* is 40.

Bob, like Cecilia, scores 62. This one score is more of a base point rather than a baseline, but you decide that it would be inappropriate to collect baseline data over time in Bob's case as he is experiencing a great deal of discomfort at work, is highly nervous in your presence (you are a stranger, after all), and probably will not be able to bring himself to seek help in the future if he does not receive some kind of intervention now.

FIGURE 12.2
B Design: Bob's Social Anxiety Scores for the First Seven Weeks

You therefore begin your intervention, engaging Bob to the extent that he returns the following week, when you administer the *IASS* again. Now he scores 52. In the third week, he scores 49, as shown in Figure 12.2. Figure 12.2 is a simple example of a *B* design, in which you track change in the problem level at the same time as you are intervening. You do not know, from this graph, whether your intervention *caused* the change you see. Anything else could have caused it.

Perhaps Bob is having a weekly massage to reduce muscle tension, or his boss has been fired, or the public presentation that he was supposed to do has been postponed. Therefore, you cannot use the *B* design to answer explanatory research questions that come quite high on the knowledge continuum (refer to Figure 2.1 on page 81).

On the other hand, you might make the clinical decision that it is worth trying a variation on your intervention: you might apply it more *frequently* by having Bob come twice a week instead of once, or you might apply it more *intensively* by increasing the amount of time Bob is expected to spend each evening on relaxation exercises. You can graph the changes that occur while you are applying the variation, as shown in Figure 12.3.

FIGURE 12.3

BB₁ Design: Bob's Social Anxiety Scores for the *B* Phase and *B₁* Phase

BB₁ DESIGN

FIGURE 12.2 SHOWS that Bob's anxiety level has improved but it has not fallen below the clinical cutting score. Moreover, it does not look as though it will because it has been relatively stable for the last three weeks. It may be that Bob is a naturally anxious person and no intervention, however inspired, will reduce his problem to below clinically significant levels.

Figure 12.3 shows two *phases:* the *B* phase and the *B₁* phase, separated by the vertical dotted line that runs between weeks 7 and 8. Week 7 marks the end of your original intervention, designated by the *B* intervention, and all the scores obtained by Bob while you were applying the *B* intervention constitute the *B* phase.

If it seems odd to call the first intervention *B* instead of *A*, remember that *A* has been used already to designate baseline scores. Week 8 marks the beginning of the variation on your original intervention, designated *B₁*, and all the scores obtained by Bob while you were applying the variation constitute the *B₁* phase. The *B* and *B₁* phases together constitute the *BB₁* design.

When you look at the low scores Bob achieved in weeks 9–12, you might be tempted to think "Hallelujah! My specific intervention *did* work. All Bob needed was a bit more of it." However, the same considerations apply to the *BB₁* design as apply to the *B* design. You simply cannot be sure that there is

FIGURE 12.4

BC Design: Bob's Social Anxiety Scores for the *B* Phase and *C* Phase

any relationship between your intervention and Bob's decreased anxiety, far less that one was the cause of the other.

BC DESIGN

THE LAST EXPLORATORY SINGLE-SUBJECT RESEARCH DESIGN is the *BC* design. Let's go back in time to the point where you decided that it was worth trying a variation on your *B* intervention with Bob. Suppose you had decided instead to try an entirely different intervention, designated as *C* because it is a *different* intervention, following immediately after *B*.

Now you implement the *C* intervention, administering the *IASS* every week, graphing your results, and creating a *C* phase after the *B* phase as shown in Figure 12.4. Again, the *B* phase in Figure 12.4 is copied from Figure 12.2, and after the *C* intervention you see that Bob has succeeded in reducing his anxiety level to below the clinical cutting score of 40.

Repressing your hallelujahs, you realize that there is still no sure relationship between your intervention and Bob's success. Indeed, the waters are becoming more murky because even if your intervention was in fact related to Bob's success you would still not know whether it was the *C* intervention that did the trick, or a delayed reaction to *B,* or some combination of *B* and *C*.

FIGURE 12.5

AB Design: Cecilia's Self-Esteem Scores for the *A* Phase and *B* Phase

DESCRIPTIVE DESIGNS

THERE ARE TWO KINDS OF SINGLE-SUBJECT RESEARCH DESIGNS that center around answering descriptive research questions:

1. *AB* designs
2. *ABC* and *ABCD* designs

AB DESIGN

AN *AB* DESIGN is simply an *A*—or baseline phase—followed by a *B* or intervention phase. Returning to Cecilia, let's say she has a problem with low self-esteem and that you have already completed a four-week baseline phase with her, as shown in Figure 12.5, and that phase alone answered the two simple exploratory questions: "Does the problem exist?" and "Does the problem exist at different levels over time?" Now you implement a *B* intervention and find, to your pleasure, that Cecilia's self-esteem level approaches the clinical cutting score of 30 and falls below it at weeks 10–12.

What you really want to know, of course, is whether there is any relationship between your *B* intervention and Cecilia's success. You are now in a better position to hypothesize that there is because you know that Cecilia was not doing too well during the four weeks of the baseline phase and began to improve the week after you started your intervention (see Figure 12.5).

Something happened in week 5 to set Cecilia on the road to recovery, and it would be very coincidental if that something were not your intervention. However, coincidences do happen, and you cannot be 100% certain that your intervention *caused* the change you see unless you can eliminate all the other coincidental happenings that might have caused it.

Hence, the *AB* design cannot answer explanatory research questions, but the change between the baseline data (getting worse) and the intervention data (getting better) is enough to indicate that there may be some relationship between your intervention and Cecilia's improvement. The moral to the story is to *always collect baseline data if you can* because social work ethics requires you to be reasonably sure an intervention is effective before you try it again with another client.

ABC AND *ABCD* DESIGNS

AS WE HAVE DISCUSSED, you can always follow a *B* phase with a *C* phase if the *B* intervention did not achieve the desired result. An *A* phase followed by a *B* phase followed by a *C* phase constitutes an *ABC* design, and if there is a *D* intervention as well, you have an *ABCD* design. So long as there is a baseline, you can conclude fairly safely that there is a relationship between the results you see and the interventions you implemented.

However, if you have more than one intervention, you will not know which intervention—or combination of interventions—did the trick, and the more interventions you try the murkier the waters become.

Because a single intervention often comprises a package of practice techniques (e.g., active listening plus role play plus relaxation exercises), it is important to write down exactly what you did so that later on you will remember what the *B* or *C* or *D* interventions were.

EXPLANATORY DESIGNS

AS WE HAVE SEEN, if you want to show that a particular intervention caused an observed result, you must eliminate everything else that may have caused it; in other words, you must control for intervening variables. There are two types of single-subject designs that can answer causality, or explanatory research questions:

1. Reversal designs
2. Multiple-baseline designs.

REVERSAL DESIGNS

THE FIRST TYPE OF EXPLANATORY SINGLE-SUBJECT DESIGNS are the reversal designs. There are three kinds:

1. *ABA* and *ABAB* designs
2. *BAB* designs
3. *BCBC* designs

ABA AND *ABAB* DESIGNS

LOOK AT FIGURE 12.6, which illustrates Cecilia's success in getting her self-esteem score below the clinical cutting score in week 11 of the *B* intervention.

In week 12, you decide that you will withdraw your intervention related to Cecilia's self-esteem because she seems to be doing well, but you will continue to monitor her self-esteem levels to ensure that treatment gains are maintained.

Ongoing monitoring of problems that appear to be solved is something of a luxury in our profession. Too often our approach is crisis-oriented; follow-up tends to be ignored in the light of other, more pressing problems, and the result may well be a recurrence of the original problem because it had not been solved to the extent that the social worker thought.

FIGURE 12.6
ABA Design: Cecilia's Self-Esteem Scores

However, with Cecilia you follow up. In weeks 12 through 16, as shown in Figure 12.6, the score hovers at the clinical cutting score. Figure 12.6 illustrates an *ABA* design where the client's scores are displayed first without an intervention (the first *A* phase), then with an intervention (the *B* phase), then without an intervention again (the second *A* phase).

FIGURE 12.7
ABAB Design: Cecilia's Self-Esteem Scores

The scores are not as high in the second *A* phase as they were in the first *A* phase, and this is to be expected because some of the strategies Cecilia learned in the *B* phase should remain with her even though the intervention has stopped.

However, from a research point of view, the very fact that her scores increased again when you stopped the intervention makes it more certain that it was your intervention that caused the improvement you saw in the *B* phase. Cecilia's improvement when the intervention started might have been a coincidence, but it is unlikely that her regression when the intervention stopped was also a coincidence.

Your certainty with respect to causality will be increased even further if you reintroduce the *B* intervention in week 17 and Cecilia's score begins to drop again as it did in the first *B* phase.

Now you have implemented two *AB* designs one after the other with the same client to produce an *ABAB* design. This design is illustrated in Figure 12.7. It is sometimes called a *reversal* design or a *withdrawal* design. Causality is established with an *ABAB* design because the same intervention has been shown to work twice with the same client and you have baseline data to show the extent of the problem when there was no intervention.

BAB DESIGN

LET'S NOW RETURN TO BOB, with whom you implemented a *B* intervention to reduce his social anxiety as shown in Figure 12.2. When Bob's social anxiety level has fallen beneath the clinical cutting score, you might do the same thing with Bob as you did with Cecilia: withdraw the intervention and continue to monitor the problem, creating an *A* phase after the *B* phase. If the problem level worsens during the *A* phase, you intervene again in the same way as you did before, creating a second *B* phase and an overall design of *BAB*.

We have said that causality is established with an *ABAB* design because the same intervention has worked twice with the same client. We cannot say the same for a *BAB* design, however, as we do not really know that our intervention "worked" the first time. Because there was no initial baseline data (no first *A* phase), we cannot know whether the resolution of the problem on the first occasion had anything to do with the intervention.

The problem may have resolved itself or some external event (intervening variable) might have resolved it. Nor can we know the degree to which the problem changed during the first *B* phase (intervention) because there was no baseline data with which to compare the final result.

An indication of the amount of change can be obtained by comparing the first and last scores in the *B* phase, but the first score may have been an unreliable measure of Bob's problem. Bob may have felt less or more anxious that day than usual, and a baseline is necessary to compensate for such day-to-day fluctuations.

Because the effectiveness of the intervention on the first occasion is unknown, there can be no way of knowing whether the intervention was just as effective the second time it was implemented, or less or more effective. All we know is that the problem improved twice, after the same intervention, and this is probably enough to warrant using the intervention again with another client.

BCBC Design

A ***BCBC* DESIGN,** as the name suggests, is a *B* intervention followed by a *C* intervention implemented twice in succession. The point of doing this is to compare the effectiveness of two interventions—*B* and *C*. It is unlikely that a social worker would implement this design with a client because, if the problem improved sufficiently using *B*, you would not need *C*; if you did need *C*, you would hardly return to *B* whether or not *C* appeared to do the trick.

However, if the problem has nothing to do with a client's welfare but is concerned instead with a social work program's organizational efficiency, say, as affected by organizational structure, you might try one structure *B* followed by a different structure *C* and then do the same thing again in order to show that one structure really has proved more effective in increasing efficiency when implemented twice *under the same conditions.*

Multiple-Baseline Designs

The second type of explanatory single-subject designs are the multiple-baseline designs. Multiple-baseline designs are like *ABAB* designs in that the *AB* design is implemented more than once. However, whereas *ABAB* designs apply to one case with one problem in one setting, multiple-baseline designs can be used with:

1. More than one *case*
2. More than one *setting*
3. More than one *problem*

MORE THAN ONE CASE

SUPPOSE THAT, INSTEAD OF BOB with his social anxiety problem, you have three additional clients with anxiety problems, Breanne, Warren, and Alison. All three are residents in the same nursing home. You use the same measuring instrument to measure anxiety (the *IASS*) in all three cases, and you give all three clients the same intervention (*B* Phase).

However, you vary the number of weeks over which you collect baseline data (*A* Phase), allowing the baseline phase to last for six weeks in Breanne's case, eight weeks in Warren's case, and nine weeks for Alison. You plot your results as shown in Figure 12.8.

Breanne starts to show improvement in week 7, the week you began your intervention. Had that improvement been due to some intervening variable—for example, some anxiety-reducing change in the nursing home's routine—you would expect Warren and Alison to also show improvement.

The fact that their anxiety levels continue to be high indicates that it was your intervention, not some other factor that caused the improvement in Breanne. Causality is demonstrated again in week 9 when you begin to intervene with Warren, and Warren improves but Alison does not. Your triumph is complete when Alison, given the same intervention, begins to improve in week 10.

FIGURE 12.8

Multiple-Baseline Design across Clients:
Magnitude of Anxiety Levels for Three Clients

In a nutshell, a multiple-baseline design across clients is nothing more than stringing together a series of *AB* single-subject designs that use the same intervention and placing them on one graph. They can have differential baseline periods. This design simply determines whether one intervention will work with more than one client. Simple as that! We now turn our attention to see whether one intervention can work with one client in more than one setting.

MORE THAN ONE SETTING

ANOTHER WAY TO CONDUCT A MULTIPLE-BASELINE STUDY is with one client in a number of settings. Suppose that your objective is to reduce the number of a child's temper tantrums at home, in school, and at the daycare center where the child goes after school. The same intervention (*B* Phase) is offered by the parents at home, the teacher in school, and the worker at the daycare center.

They are also responsible for measuring the number of tantrums that occur each day. In our example, the baseline phase continues for different lengths of time in each of the three setting as shown in Figure 12.9. Once again, baselines do not have to be of equal lengths. If the child improves after the intervention begins in all three settings as shown in Figure 12.9, we may conclude that it was the intervention that caused the improvement in all three settings. A multiple-baseline design across settings simply determines whether one intervention will work with one client in multiple settings—in our example, at home, school, and daycare.

MORE THAN ONE PROBLEM

A THIRD WAY TO CONDUCT A MULTIPLE-BASELINE STUDY is to use the same intervention to tackle different target problems. Suppose that Joan is having trouble with her daughter, Anita. In addition, Joan is having trouble with her in-laws and with her boss at work.

After exploration, a worker may believe that all these troubles stem from her lack of assertiveness. Thus, the intervention would be assertiveness training. Progress with Anita might be measured by the number of times each day she is flagrantly disobedient.

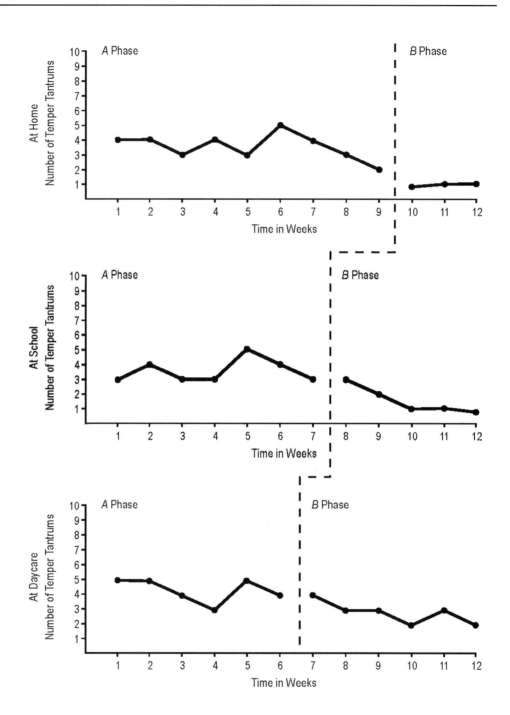

FIGURE 12.9

Multiple-Baseline Design across Settings:

Number of Temper Tantrums for One Client in Three Settings

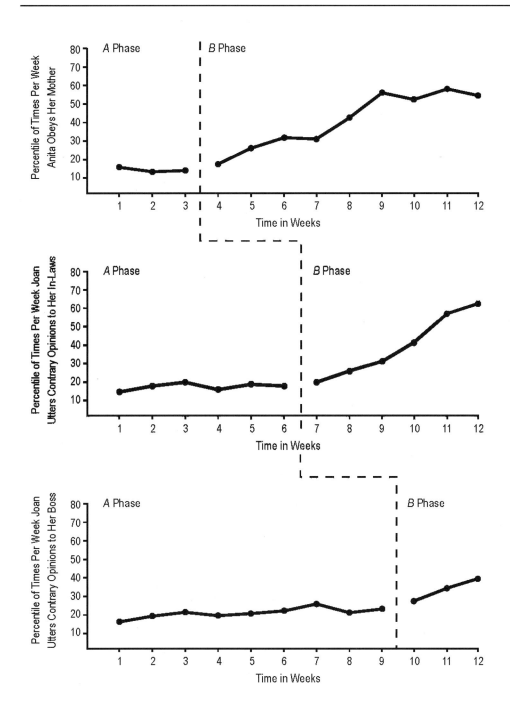

FIGURE 12.10

Multiple-Baseline Design across Client Problems:

Magnitude of Three Client Target Problem Areas for One Client

Progress can be measured with Joan's in-laws by the number of times she is able to utter a contrary opinion, and so on. Because the number of occasions on which Joan has an opportunity to be assertive will vary, these figures might best be expressed in percentiles. Figure 12.10 illustrates an example of a multiple-baseline design that was used to assess the effectiveness of Joan's assertiveness training in three problem areas.

Whether it is a reversal design or a multiple-baseline design, an *ABAB* explanatory design involves establishing a baseline level for the client's target problem. This will not be possible if the need for intervention is acute, and sometimes the very thought of an *A*-type design will have to be abandoned. It is sometimes possible, however, to construct a retrospective baseline; that is, to determine what the level of the problem was before an intervention is implemented.

RETROSPECTIVE BASELINES

THE BEST RETROSPECTIVE BASELINES are those that do not depend on the client's memory. If the target problem occurs rarely, memories may be accurate. For example, Tai, a teenager, and his family may remember quite well how many times he ran away from home during the past month. They may not remember nearly so well if the family members were asked how often he behaved defiantly. Depending on the target problem, it may be possible to construct a baseline from archival data, that is, from written records, such as school attendance sheets, probation orders, employment interview forms, and so forth.

Although establishing a baseline usually involves making at least three measurements before implementing an intervention, it is also acceptable to establish a baseline of zero, or no occurrences of a desired event. A target problem, for example, might focus upon the client's reluctance to enter a drug treatment program.

The baseline measurement would then be that the client did not go (zero occurrences), and the desired change would be that the client did go (one occurrence). A social worker who has successfully used the same tactics to persuade a number of clients to enter a drug treatment program has conducted a multiple-baseline design across clients.

As previously discussed, a usable baseline should show either that the client's problem level is stable or that it is growing worse. Sometimes an *A*-type design can be used even though the baseline indicates a slight improvement in the target problem. The justification must be that the intervention is expected to lead to an improvement that will exceed the anticipated improvement if the baseline trend continues.

Perhaps a child's temper tantrums are decreasing by one or two a week, for example, but the total number per week is still 18 to 20. If a worker thought the tantrums could be reduced to four or five a week, or they could be stopped altogether, the worker would be justified in implementing an intervention even though the client's target problem was improving slowly by itself.

In a similar way, a worker may be able to implement an *A*-type design if the client's baseline is unstable, provided that the intervention is expected to exceed the largest of the baseline fluctuations. Perhaps the child's temper tantrums are fluctuating between 12 and 20 per week in the baseline period, and it is hoped to bring them down to less than 10 per week.

Nevertheless, there are some occasions when a baseline cannot be established or is not usable, such as when a client's behaviors involve self-injurious ones. Also, sometimes the establishment of a baseline is totally inappropriate.

ETHICAL ISSUES

THERE ARE ALSO A FEW ETHICAL ISSUES we need to be aware of when using single-subject designs in practice and research situations. Rafael Engel and Russell Schutt (2010) discuss some of the ethical issues as follows:

> Like any form of research, single-subject designs require the informed consent of the participant. The structure of single-subject designs for research involves particularly unique conditions that must be discussed with potential participants. As we discussed in Chapter 4, all aspects of the research study, such as the purpose, measurement, confidentiality, and data collection, are a part of the information needed for informed consent. In particular, the need for repeated

baseline measurements and the possibility of premature withdrawal of treatment are particularly unique to single-subject design research.

Participants must understand that the onset of the intervention is likely to be delayed until either a baseline pattern emerges or some assigned time period elapses. Until this condition is met, a needed intervention may be withheld. Furthermore, the length of the baseline also depends on the type of design. In a multiple baseline design, the delay in the intervention may be substantial. The implications of this delay must be discussed as part of obtaining informed consent.

When a withdrawal or reversal design is used, there are additional considerations. The structure of such designs means that the intervention may be withdrawn just as the research participant is beginning to improve. The risks associated with prematurely ending treatment may be hard to predict.

If there is a carryover effect, the subject's condition may not worsen, but it is possible that the subject's condition or status may indeed worsen. Given this possibility, the use of an *ABAB* design as opposed to the *ABA* design is preferable for the purpose of research.

Obtaining informed consent may not be limited to the use of single-subject design for research purposes. As we noted in Chapter 1, the NASW *Code of Ethics* (2017) does not distinguish between the need for informed consent in research and the need for informed consent for practice evaluation. Specifically:

> 5.02(e) Social workers engaged in evaluation or research should obtain voluntary and written informed consent from participants, when appropriate, without any implied or actual deprivation or penalty for refusal to participate;

without undue inducement to participate; and with due regard for participants' well being, privacy, and dignity. Informed consent should include information about the nature, extent, and duration of the participation requested and disclosure of the risks and benefits of participation in research.

Others suggest that informed consent may not be necessary. For example, David Royse, Bruce Thyer, and Deb Padgett (2009) suggest that written informed consent is not necessarily for practice evaluation because the intent is not to provide generalized knowledge or publish the results. Even if written informed consent is not required when using these tools for practice evaluation and monitoring, social workers using these tools should be guided by practice ethics. According to the NASW *Code of Ethics*, social work practitioners should, as a part of their everyday practice with clients,

provide services to clients only in the context of a professional relationship based, when appropriate, on valid informed consent. Social workers should use clear and understandable language to inform clients of the purpose of the services, risks related to the services, limits to services because of the requirements of a third party payer, relevant costs, reasonable alternatives, clients' right to refuse or withdraw consent, and the time frame covered by the consent. (NASW, 2017, 1.03[a])

Therefore, if such techniques are going to be used as part of the overall intervention, clients should be aware of the procedures.

SUMMARY

THIS CHAPTER PRESENTED a brief overview of single-subject designs. We categorized them as exploratory, descriptive, and explanatory. No design is inherently inferior or superior to the others. Each has advantages and disadvantages in terms of time, cost, and the data that can be obtained. The following chapter presents another kind of research design, group designs.

Study Questions for Chapter 12

Essay — Discussion

1	In your own words, list and discuss the advantages of single-subject designs. Provide a single social work example throughout your discussion that illustrates your main points.
2	In your own words, list and then discuss the questions that single-subject designs can answer. Provide a single social work example throughout your discussion that illustrates your main points.
3	What is a unit of analysis? Discuss the various units of analysis that single-subject designs can be used for.
4	In your own words, list and discuss the three requirements of using single-subject designs. Provide a single social work example throughout your discussion that illustrates your main points.
5	Discuss the concept of *target problems*. Provide a single social work example throughout your discussion that illustrates your main points.
6	Discuss why single-subject designs need to have valid and reliable measuring instruments. Provide a single social work example throughout your discussion that illustrates your main points.
7	List and then discuss the four exploratory single-subject designs. Provide a social work example throughout your discussion that illustrates your main points for each of the four designs.
8	List and then discuss the two descriptive single-subject designs. Provide a social work example throughout your discussion that illustrates your main points for both designs.
9	List and then discuss the two explanatory single-subject designs. Provide a social work example throughout your discussion that illustrates your main points for both designs.

10	List and then discuss the three reversal single-subject designs. Provide a social work example throughout your discussion that illustrates your main points for each of the three designs.
11	List and then discuss the three multiple-baseline designs. Provide a social work example throughout your discussion that illustrates your main points for each of the three designs.
12	In your own words discuss the concept of retrospective baselines. Provide a social work example throughout your discussion that illustrates your main points.

Critical Thinking — Application — Integration

13	**YOU'RE A PRACTITIONER** Pretend for the moment you're employed as a social worker in your university's student counseling center. A student comes into your office complaining about his depression. You wish to determine the level of his depression and the effectiveness of your intervention **quantitatively.** 1. Using this chapter as a guide, describe in detail how you could use at least one of the four **exploratory** single-subject designs to monitor his depression levels and the effectiveness of your intervention. Create a graph like the ones displayed in the chapter. 2. Do the same for at least one of the two **descriptive** designs. 3. Do the same for at least one of the three **explanatory** designs. **NOTE:** This exercise should help you to realize that the single-subject designs used in "research studies" are the same that are used in "practice situations." In short, you can use this chapter to help you employ single-subject designs in your day-to-day practice activities for all of your client systems.

YOU'RE A RESEARCHER

Pretend that your school of social work wants to do a research study on determining the competency levels of its graduating students over a six-year period **after** it implements a new social work curriculum. The director of your school wants you to do a single-subject research design study to determine the competency levels of its students after they graduate over time.

1. List and then discuss the various single-subject designs you could use. List the advantages and disadvantages of each design, considering the research question.

2. From your list above, select one design that you think would be best to use. Provide a rationale for the selection.

3. What's the target problem?

4. What's the unit of analyses?

5. How are you going to collect the necessary data?

6. What data are you going to collect? Are the data reliable and valid? If so, why? If not, why not?

7. How are you going to display your study's findings?

8. Could you use retrospective baseline data? If so, why? If not, why not?

MIXED-METHODS RESEARCH/PRACTICE (CHAPTER 8)

With the preceding quantitatively oriented question in mind (Chapter 6), you also wish to add a qualitative component (Chapter 7) to your study in an effort to add more meat to your study's quantitatively oriented findings and recommendations.

1. Using what you have learned from Chapters 6–8 and this chapter outline, how you would do your mixed-methods study, highlighting the specific qualitative data collection methods (Chapter 15) you have chosen to use?

State specifically how the findings of your qualitative component could add to your study's quantitatively oriented findings and recommendations.

16	**SINGLE-SUBJECT DESIGNS AND THE RESEARCHER** **Scenario 1:** Make an argument that to be a competent social work researcher **you must know** the advantages and disadvantages of using single-subject designs. Provide clear and explicit **research-related** social work examples to illustrate your main points. **Scenario 2:** Make an argument that **you do not have to know** the advantages and disadvantages of single-subject designs to be a competent social work researcher. Provide clear and explicit **research-related** social work examples to illustrate your main points. **Time to Choose:** Which one of the above two scenarios do you feel is more consistent with the place of research in social work? Why? Provide relevant social work examples to illustrate your main points.
17	**SINGLE-SUBJECT DESIGNS AND THE PRACTITIONER** **Scenario 1:** Make an argument that to be an effective evidence-based social work practitioner **you must know** how to select and use single-subject designs for your day-to-day practice activities. Provide clear and explicit **practice-related** social work examples to illustrate your main points. **Scenario 2:** Make an argument that **you do not have to know** how to select and use single-subject designs for your day-to-day practice activities to be an effective evidence-based social work practitioner. Provide clear and explicit **practice-related** social work examples to illustrate your main points. **Time to Choose:** Which one of the above two scenarios do you feel is more consistent with the concept of the contemporary evidence-based social work practice process as illustrated on pages 46–51? Why? Provide relevant social work examples to illustrate your main points.
18	**TIME TO PUT ON YOUR CRITICAL THINKING HAT** 1. Discuss the similarities and differences between your responses to Questions 16 and 17. 2. What are your thoughts on the belief that you'll need to know the advantages and disadvantages of using single-subject designs whether you're a social work *practitioner* (Question 17) or a social work *researcher* (Question 16)?

19	**BEFORE AND AFTER** *Part 1 (before):* Before enrolling in your current research methods course, and before you read this chapter on single-subject designs, how did you think social work practitioners monitored their effectiveness with their various client systems? What methods did you think they used before you read this chapter? Did you feel the methods were ethical? If so, how? If not, why not? *Part 2 (after):* After reading this chapter discuss any new single-subject design(s) you learned about that you did not know about before reading it. List each new design you learned about and provide a hypothetical social work "practice" situation AND a hypothetical "research" situation that demonstrate the use of your newfound method(s). **NOTE:** This exercise should help you to realize that single-subject designs that are used in "research studies" are the same that are used in "practice situations." In short, you can use this chapter to help you employ single-subject designs in your day-to-day practice activities for all of your client systems.
20	**APPLICATION OF SINGLE-SUBJECT DESIGNS** Locate a published quantitative social work-related journal article that utilized a single-subject design. We suggest you locate a quantitatively oriented research study in Bruce Thyer's journal *Research on Social Work Practice* (Sage Publications). Hands down, this is the best journal to find good quantitatively oriented social work research studies. 1. What was the unit of analysis? 2. What was the study's target problem(s)? 3. What measuring instruments were used to measure the target problem(s)? Was the instrument reliable and valid? If so, how? If not, why not? 4. What specific single-subject design was used in the study? 5. How were the data collected; that is, what data gathering method was used in the study (e.g., surveys, observations, existing data)? 6. With your knowledge of the advantages and disadvantages of the various single-subject designs that research and practice studies can use, thoroughly discuss how you will use the material contained within this chapter when you begin to evaluate the appropriateness of the single-subject design that a research study has used and discuss why you believe each criterion you selected is important for your evaluation of the study's chosen design.

21	**SINGLE-SUBJECT DESIGNS AND YOUR PROFESSIONAL DEVELOPMENT** 1. Review the three social work research-related roles you can take when you graduate—CSWE Competency 1 at the beginning of this chapter on page 398. This concept is also discussed in Chapter 1 on pages 38–42. Thoroughly discuss how you feel this chapter will help you to perform one or more research-related roles when you graduate. Which one of the three roles do you believe this chapter helped you with the most? Why? Discuss in detail and provide an example to illustrate your main points. 2. Review CSWE Competency 4 at the beginning of this chapter on page 398. Thoroughly discuss how you feel this chapter will help you to become a practice-informed researcher and a research-informed practitioner. Discuss in detail and provide an example to illustrate your main points. 3. Review the evidence-based practice process as illustrated on pages 46–51. Thoroughly discuss how this chapter helps you to develop the skills you'll need for implementing one or more steps of the evidence-based practice process. 4. Discuss which step(s) you feel this chapter will help you with the most. Why? Be very specific and use relevant social work examples to illustrate your main points throughout your discussion. **NOTE:** This exercise should help you to realize that the single-subject designs that are used in "research studies" are the same that are used in "practice situations." In short, you can use this chapter to help you employ single-subject designs in your day-to-day practice activities for all of your client systems.
22	**MOVING AHEAD BY LOOKING BACK** At this point in your research methods course, how comfortable are you with discussing the place of research in social work with your field instructor, with your practice instructor, with your research instructor, with your supervisor at work, with the director of your social work program, or with your classmates? Discuss in detail.

13

CHAPTER

2015 EPAS COMPETENCIES

COMPETENCY 1: Demonstrate Ethical and Professional Behavior

You will learn that in order to be a successful evidence-based practitioner you have an ethical obligation to integrate three research roles into your daily practice activities as discussed in Chapter 1: (1) research consumer, (2) research partner—either as a co-researcher or research participant, and (3) creator and disseminator of research (or knowledge).

This entire chapter pertains to these three professional research-related roles when it comes to knowing the advantages and disadvantages of group research designs that social work researchers can use for quantitative (Chapter 6), qualitative (Chapter 7), and mixed-methods research studies (Chapter 8).

COMPETENCY 4: Engage in Practice-Informed Research and Research-Informed Practice

Competency 4 also pertains to the entire chapter because you have to:

1. Evaluate the internal and external validities of the group research design that was utilized in a research study (**research consumer**—research-informed practice);

2. Participate in a research study—either as a co-researcher or research participant (**research partner**—practice-informed research). See 1 above and 3 below; and

3. Know how to select the most appropriate group research design given your research question (or hypothesis) when you actually do a research study (**creator and disseminator of research**—practice-informed research).

You also need to utilize evidence-based practice recommendations whenever possible; that is, you need to integrate (1) the best available research-based evidence with (2) your clinical expertise and (3) your client's values.

All of the above implies you'll need to know how to assess the overall rigor (degree of internal and external validities) of the group research design that a research study used that produced its research-based evidence. In short, you need to ask and then answer a simple question: How seriously should I take the findings of any research study given how well it controlled for the internal and external validities that are inherent within the research design that the study used?

COMPETENCY 9: Evaluate Practice with Individuals, Families, Groups, Organizations, and Communities

See Competencies 1 and 4.

438

Group Designs

CHAPTER 1   **Step 1.** Understanding the Research Process

CHAPTER 2   **Step 2.** Developing Research Questions

CHAPTER 3   **Step 3.** Reviewing the Literature

CHAPTERS 4 & 5   **Step 4.** Being Aware of Ethical and Cultural Issues

CHAPTERS 6–8   **Step 5.** Selecting a Research Approach

CHAPTERS 9 & 10   **Step 6.** Specifying How Variables Are Measured

CHAPTER 11   **Step 7.** Selecting a Sample

CHAPTERS 12 & 13   **Step 8.** Selecting a Research Design

CHAPTERS 14–16   **Step 9.** Selecting a Data-Collection Method

CHAPTERS 17 & 18   **Step 10.** Analyzing the Data

CHAPTERS 19 & 20   **Step 11.** Writing the Research Report

NOW THAT YOU KNOW HOW TO USE SINGLE-SUBJECT DESIGNS we turn our attention to the various group-level designs that research studies can take. The two most important factors in determining what group design to use in a specific study are (1) what the research question is, and (2) how much knowledge about the problem area is available.

KNOWLEDGE LEVELS

IF THERE IS ALREADY A SUBSTANTIAL KNOWLEDGE BASE in your problem area, you will be in a position to address very specific research questions, the answers to which could add to the explanation of previously gathered data. If less is known about the problem area, your research questions will have to be of a more general, descriptive nature. If very little is known about the problem area, your questions will have to be even more general, at an exploratory level.

Research knowledge levels are arrayed along a continuum, from exploratory at the lowest end to explanatory at the highest (see Figures 2.1 on page 81 and 2.3 on page 90). Because research knowledge levels are viewed this way, the assignment of the level of knowledge accumulated in a problem area prior to a research study, as well as the level that might be attained by the research study, is totally arbitrary. There are, however, specific designs that can be used to provide us with knowledge at a certain level.

At the highest level are the *explanatory designs,* also called experimental designs or "ideal" experiments. These designs have the largest number of requirements (examined in the following section). They are best used in confirmatory research studies where the area under study is well developed, theories abound, and testable hypotheses can be formulated on the basis of previous work or existing theory. These designs seek to establish causal relationships between the independent and dependent variables.

In the middle range are the *descriptive designs*, sometimes referred to as quasi-experimental. A quasi-experiment resembles an "ideal" experiment in some aspects but lacks at least one of the necessary requirements.

At the lowest level are the *exploratory designs*, also called pre-experimental or nonexperimental, which explore only the research question or problem area. These designs do not produce statistically sound data or conclusive results, but they are not intended to. Their purpose is to build a foundation of general ideas and tentative theories, which can be explored later with more precise and hence more complex research designs and their corresponding data-gathering techniques.

The research designs that allow us to acquire knowledge at each of the three levels are described in a later section of this chapter. Before considering them, however, it's necessary to establish the characteristics that differentiate an "ideal" experiment, which leads to explanatory knowledge, from other studies that lead to the other two lower levels of knowledge (descriptive and exploratory).

CHARACTERISTICS OF "IDEAL" EXPERIMENTS

AN "IDEAL" EXPERIMENT is one in which a research study most closely approaches certainty about the relationship between the independent and dependent variables. The purpose of doing an "ideal" experiment is to determine whether it can be concluded from the study's findings that the independent variable is, or is not, the *only* cause of change in the dependent variable.

As pointed out in previous chapters, some social work research studies have no independent variable. An example would be a study that just wants to find out how many people in a certain community wish to establish a community-based halfway house for people who are addicted to drugs.

The concept of an "ideal" experiment is introduced with the word "ideal" in quotation marks because such an experiment is rarely achieved in social work research situations. On a general level, in order to achieve this high degree of certainty and qualify as an "ideal" experiment, an explanatory research design must meet six conditions:

1. The time order of the independent variable must be established.

2. The independent variable must be manipulated.

3. The relationship between the independent and dependent variables must be established.

4. The research design must control for rival hypotheses.

5. At least one control group should be used.

6. Random assignment procedures (and if possible, random sampling from a population) must be employed in assigning research participants (or objects) to groups.

CONTROLLING THE TIME ORDER OF VARIABLES

AS YOU KNOW FROM CHAPTER 6, in an "ideal" experiment the independent variable must precede the dependent variable in time. Time order is crucial if our research study is to show that one variable causes another, because something that occurs later cannot be the cause of something that occurred earlier.

Suppose we want to study the relationship between adolescent substance abuse and gang-related behavior. After some thought, we formulate a hypothesis:

> **Hypothesis:**
> Adolescent substance abuse causes gang-related behavior

In this hypothesis, the independent variable is adolescent substance abuse, and the dependent variable is gang-related behavior. The substance abuse must come *before* gang-related behavior because the hypothesis states that adolescent drug use causes gang-related behavior. We could also come up with the following hypothesis, however:

> **Hypothesis:**
> Adolescent gang-related behavior causes substance abuse

In this hypothesis, adolescent gang-related behavior is the independent variable, and substance abuse is the dependent variable. According to this hypothesis, gang-related behavior must come *before* the substance abuse.

MANIPULATING THE INDEPENDENT VARIABLE

MANIPULATION OF THE INDEPENDENT VARIABLE means that we must do something with the independent variable. In the general form of the hypothesis "if X occurs, then Y will result," the independent variable (X) must be manipulated in order to effect a variation in the dependent variable (Y). There are essentially three ways in which independent variables can be manipulated:

1. ***X* present versus *X* absent.** If the effectiveness of a specific treatment intervention is being evaluated, an experimental group and a control group could be used. The experimental group would be given the intervention (X) and the control group would not (no X).

2. **A small amount of X versus a larger amount of X.** If the effect of treatment time on client outcome is being studied, two experimental groups could be used, one of which would be treated for a longer period of time.

> **3.** *X versus something else.* If the effectiveness of two different treatment interventions is being studied, Intervention X_1 could be used with Experimental Group 1 and Intervention X_2 with Experimental Group 2.

Obviously, certain variables, such as the gender or race of our research participants, cannot be manipulated because they are fixed. They do not vary, so they are called constants, not variables, as was pointed out in Chapter 6. Other constants, such as socioeconomic status or IQ, may vary for research participants over their lifespans, but they are fixed quantities at the beginning of the study, probably will not change during the study, and are not subject to alteration by the one doing the study.

Any variable we can alter (such as treatment time) can be considered an independent variable. At least one independent variable must be manipulated in a research study if it's to be considered an "ideal" experiment.

ESTABLISHING RELATIONSHIPS BETWEEN VARIABLES

THE RELATIONSHIP BETWEEN the independent and the dependent variables must be established in order to infer a cause-and-effect relationship at the explanatory knowledge level. If the independent variable is considered to be the cause of the dependent variable, there must be some pattern in the relationship between these two variables. An example is the hypothesis "The more time clients spend in treatment (independent variable), the better their progress (dependent variable)."

CONTROLLING RIVAL HYPOTHESES

RIVAL HYPOTHESES MUST BE IDENTIFIED and eliminated in an "ideal" experiment. The logic of this requirement is extremely important, because this is what makes a cause-and-effect statement possible.

The prime question to ask when trying to identify a rival hypothesis is "What other extraneous variables might affect the dependent variable?" (What else might affect the client's outcome besides treatment time?) At the risk of sounding redundant, "What else besides *X* might affect *Y?*"

Perhaps the client's motivation for treatment, in addition to the time spent in treatment, might affect the client's outcome. If so, motivation for treatment is an extraneous variable that could be used as the independent variable in the rival hypothesis "The higher the clients' motivation for treatment, the better their progress."

Perhaps the social worker's attitude toward the client might have an effect on the client's outcome, or the client might win the state lottery and ascend abruptly from depression to ecstasy. These extraneous variables could potentially be independent variables in other rival hypotheses. They must all be considered and eliminated before it can be said with reasonable certainty that a client's outcome resulted from the length of treatment time and not from any other extraneous variables.

Control over rival hypotheses refers to efforts on our part to identify and, if at all possible, to eliminate the extraneous variables in these alternative hypotheses. Of the many ways to deal with rival hypotheses, three of the most frequently used are:

1. Holding extraneous variables constant
2. Using correlated variation
3. Using analysis of covariance

HOLDING EXTRANEOUS VARIABLES CONSTANT

THE MOST DIRECT WAY to deal with a rival hypothesis is to keep constant the critical extraneous variables that might affect the dependent variable. As we know, a constant cannot affect—or be affected—by any other variable. If an extraneous variable can be made into a constant, then it cannot affect either the study's real independent variable or the dependent variable.

Let's take an overly simple example to illustrate this point. Suppose a social worker who is providing a treatment intervention called cognitive behavioral therapy (CBT) to anxious clients wants to relate client outcome to length of treatment time. However, a consulting psychiatrist who has them on antidepressant medication is also seeing all her clients.

Because medication may also affect her clients' outcomes (i.e., anxiety levels), it can be considered another independent variable that could be used in a rival hypothesis. However, because her study included her clients who all were taking medication for some time before the treatment intervention began, and who continue to take the same medicine in the same way throughout treatment, then medication can be considered a constant (in this study, anyway).

Any change in the clients' anxiety levels after the CBT intervention will, therefore, be a result of the intervention with the help of the medication. Holding it constant has eliminated the extraneous variable of medication, which might form a rival hypothesis. In short, this study started out with one independent variable, the CBT intervention, then added the variable of medication to it, so the final independent variable = CBT intervention + medication.

This is all very well in theory. In reality, however, a client's drug regime is usually controlled by the psychiatrist and may well be altered at any time. Even if the regimen is not altered, the effects of the drugs might not become apparent until the study is under way.

In addition, the client's level of anxiety might be affected by a host of other extraneous variables over which the social worker has no control at all: for example, living arrangements, relationships with other people, the condition of the stock market, the election of an unhinged president, or an unexpected visit from an IRS agent.

These kinds of pragmatic difficulties tend to occur frequently in social work practice and research. It's often impossible to identify all rival hypotheses, let alone eliminate them by keeping them constant.

USING CORRELATED VARIATION

RIVAL HYPOTHESES CAN ALSO BE CONTROLLED with correlated variation of the independent variables. Suppose, for example, that we are concerned that income has an effect on a client's compulsive behavior. The client's income, which in this case is subject to variation due to seasonal employment, is identified as an independent variable. The client's living conditions—a hotel room rented by the week—are then identified as the second independent variable that might well affect the client's level of compulsive behavior.

These two variables, however, are correlated, because living conditions are highly dependent on income. Correlated variation exists if one potential independent variable can be correlated with another; then only one of them has to be dealt with in the research study.

USING ANALYSIS OF COVARIANCE

IN CONDUCTING AN "IDEAL" EXPERIMENT, we must always aim to use two or more groups that are as equivalent as possible on all important variables. Sometimes this goal is not feasible, however. Perhaps we are obliged to use existing groups that are not as equivalent as we would like.

Or perhaps during the course of the study we discover inequivalencies between the groups that were not apparent at the beginning. A statistical method called *analysis of covariance* can be used to compensate for these differences. The mathematics of the method are far beyond the scope of this text, but an explanation can be found in most statistics texts.

USING A CONTROL GROUP

AN "IDEAL" EXPERIMENT should use at least one control group in addition to the experimental group. The experimental group may receive an intervention that is withheld from the control group, or equivalent groups may receive different interventions or no interventions at all.

A social worker who initiates a treatment intervention is often interested in knowing what would have happened had the intervention not been used or had some different intervention been substituted. Would members of a support group for alcoholics have recovered anyway, without the social worker's efforts? Would they have recovered faster or more completely had family counseling been used instead of the support group approach?

The answer to these questions will never be known if only the support group is studied. But what if another group of alcoholics is included in the research design? In a typical design with a control group, two equivalent groups, 1 and 2, would be formed, and both would be administered the same pretest to determine the initial level of the dependent variable (e.g., degree of alcoholism).

Then an intervention would be initiated with Group 1 but not with Group 2. The group treated—Group 1, or the experimental group—would receive the independent variable (the intervention). The group not treated—Group 2, or the control group—would not receive it. This can be easily diagramed, as illustrated:

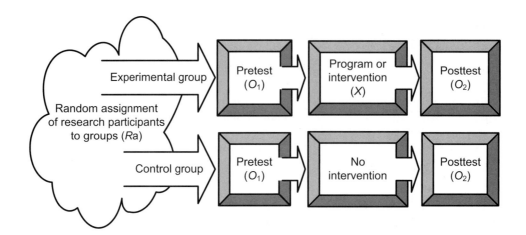

R_a = Random assignment to a group (i.e., experimental or control)
O_1 = First measurement of the dependent variable
X = Independent variable, or intervention
O_2 = Second measurement of the dependent variable

At the conclusion of the intervention, both groups would be given a posttest (the same measure as the pretest). Both the pretest and the posttest consist of the use of some sort of data-gathering procedure, such as a survey or self-report measure, to measure the dependent variable before and after the introduction of the independent variable. There are many types of group research designs, and there are many ways to graphically display them. In general, group designs can be written in symbols.

The R_a in this design indicates that the research participants were randomly assigned to each group. The symbol X, which, as usual, stands for the independent variable, indicates that an intervention is to be given to the experimental group *after* the pretest (O_1) and *before* the posttest (O_2).

The absence of X for the control group indicates that the intervention is not to be given to the control group. This design is called a classical experimental design (see Figure 13.9 on page 482) because it comes closest to having all the characteristics necessary for an "ideal" experiment.

RANDOMLY ASSIGNING RESEARCH PARTICIPANTS TO GROUPS

ONCE A SAMPLE HAS BEEN SELECTED (see Chapter 9), the individuals (or objects or events) in it are randomly assigned to either an experimental or a control group in order to insure that the two groups are equivalent as much as possible. This procedure is known as *random assignment* or *randomization.* In random assignment, the word "equivalent" means equal in terms of the variables that are important to the study, such as the clients' motivation for treatment, or problem severity.

If the effect of treatment time on client outcome is being studied, for example, the research design might use one experimental group that is treated for a comparatively longer time, a second experimental group that is treated for a shorter time, and a control group that is not treated at all.

If we are concerned that the clients' motivation for treatment might also affect their outcomes, the research participants can be assigned so that all the groups are equivalent (on the average) in terms of their motivation for treatment.

The process of random sampling from a population followed by random assignment of the sample to groups can be illustrated per below diagram. Let's say that the research design calls for a sample size of one-tenth of the population. From a population of 10,000, therefore, a random sampling procedure is used to select a sample of 1,000 individuals.

Then random assignment procedures are used to place the sample of 1,000 into two equivalent groups of 500 individuals each. In theory, Group A will be equivalent to Group B, which will be equivalent to the random sample, which will be equivalent to the population in respect to all important variables contained within the research sample.

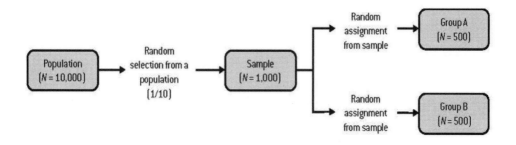

MATCHED-PAIRS METHOD

ANOTHER, MORE DELIBERATE METHOD of assigning research participants or other units to groups, a subset of randomization, involves matching. Suppose a new training program for teaching parenting skills to foster mothers is being evaluated. A standardized measuring instrument that measures parenting skill level (the dependent variable) is administered to 10 foster mothers. The scores can range from 100 (excellent parenting skills) to 0 (poor parenting skills).

The 10 women would then be matched in pairs according to their parenting skill level; the two most skilled foster mothers would be matched (Pair 1), then the next two (Pair 2), and so on. One person in the first pair would then be randomly assigned to the experimental group and the other placed in the control group.

It doesn't make any difference to which group the first research participant is randomly assigned so long as there is an equal chance that she will go to either the control group or the experimental group. In this example, the first person is randomly chosen to go to the experimental group, as illustrated:

Rank Order of Parenting Skills Scores (in parentheses)

First Pair

– (99) Randomly assigned to the experimental group

– (98) Assigned to the control group

Second Pair

– (97) Assigned to the control group

– (96) Assigned to the experimental group

Third Pair

– (95) Assigned to the experimental group

– (94) Assigned to the control group

Fourth Pair

– (93) Assigned to the control group

– (92) Assigned to the experimental group

Fifth Pair

– (91) Assigned to the experimental group

– (90) Assigned to the control group

As can be seen, the foster parent with the highest score (99) is randomly assigned to the experimental group, and this person's "match," with a score of 98, is assigned to the control group. This process is reversed with the next matched pair, where the first person is assigned to the control group and the match is assigned to the experimental group.

If the assignment of research participants according to scores is not reversed for every other pair, one group will be higher than the other on the variable being matched. To illustrate this point, suppose the first participant (highest score) in each match is always assigned to the experimental group. The experimental group's average score would be 95 (99 + 97 + 95 + 93 + 91 = 475/5 = 95), and the control group's average score would be 94 (98 + 96 + 94 + 92 + 90 = 470/5 = 94).

If every other matched pair is reversed, however, as in the example, the average scores of the two groups are closer together: 94.6 for the experimental group (99 + 96 + 95 + 92 + 91 = 473/5 = 94.6) and 94.4 for the control group (98 + 97 + 94 + 93 + 90 = 472/5 = 94.4). In short, 94.6 and 94.4 (difference of 0.2) are closer together than 95 and 94 (difference of 1).

CLASSIFYING GROUP RESEARCH DESIGNS

GROUP RESEARCH DESIGNS can be classified into as many different types of classification systems as there are folks who are willing to classify them. We are going to classify them into:

1. One-group research designs
2. Two-group research designs

The main difference between the two classifications is that the one-group designs don't compare their research participants with another group; they simply don't have another group of participants to compare to. On the other hand, the two-group designs do just that: they compare one group of research participants against another group—usually to ascertain whether a particular group (experimental group) has more positive outcomes on a dependent variable then the other group (control or comparison group).

Let's begin our discussion with the simplest of all research designs—those that use only one group of research participants.

ONE-GROUP DESIGNS

ONE-GROUP DESIGNS MEASURE (1) the participants' success with an intervention (program objective) after they leave a program, and (2) any nonprogram objective at any time. One-group designs are exceptionally useful for providing a framework for gathering data—especially for needs assessments and process evaluations. In fact, two-group designs are rarely used in needs assessments and process evaluations. There are numerous types of one-group research designs, but we present only the four basic ones:

1. One-group posttest-only design (Figure 13.1a)
2. Cross-sectional survey design (Figure 13.2a)
3. Longitudinal designs
   - Trend studies (Figure 13.3a, Box 13.1)
   - Cohort studies (Figure 13.4a, Box 13.2)
   - Panel studies (Figure 13.5a, Box 13.3)
4. One-group pretest-posttest design (Figure 13.6)

ONE-GROUP POSTTEST-ONLY DESIGN

THE ONE-GROUP POSTTEST-ONLY DESIGN is sometimes called the *one-shot case study* or *cross-sectional case study design*. Suppose in a particular small community there are numerous parents who are abusive toward their children. The city decides to hire a school social worker, Antonia, to implement a social service program that is supposed to reduce the number of parents who abuse their children.

She creates a 12-week child abuse prevention program (the intervention) and offers it to parents who have children in her school who wish to participate on a voluntary basis. A simple research study is then conducted to answer the rather simplistic question, "Did the parents who completed the program stop abusing their children?" The answer to this question will determine the success of her program, or intervention.

There are many different ways in which her program can be evaluated. For now, and to make matters as simple as possible, we are going to evaluate it by simply calculating the percentage of parents who said they stopped abusing their children after they attended the 12-week program—the program's objective.

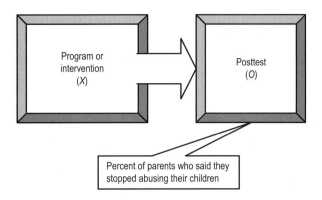

FIGURE 13.1a
One-Group Posttest-Only Design

At the simplest level, the program could be evaluated with a one-group posttest-only design. The basic elements of this design (Figure 13.1a) can be written in symbols such as:

X = Child Abuse Prevention Program, or the intervention

O = First and only measurement of the program objective

All that this design provides is a single measure (O) of what happens when one group of people is subjected to one intervention or experience (X). It's safe to assume that all the members within the program had physically abused their children before they enrolled, because people who do not have this problem would not have enrolled in such a program.

But even if the value of O indicates that some of the parents did stop being violent with their children after the program, it cannot be determined whether they quit *solely* because of the intervention or because something else may have caused the parents to quit.

Such somethings are called a rival hypotheses, or alternative explanations. Perhaps a law was recently passed that made it mandatory for the police to arrest folks who behave violently toward their children, or perhaps the local television station started to report such incidents on the nightly news, complete with pictures of the abusive parents.

These or other extraneous variables might have been more important in persuading the parents to cease their abusive behavior toward their children than their voluntary participation in Antonia's program. All we will know from this design is the number and percentage of the folks who self-reported that they stopped hurting their children after they successfully completed Antonia's 12-week program.

Figure 13.1b below presents the results from a simple survey question (illustrated below) that Antonia included in a mailed survey that was completed by her past participants:

> **Survey question:**
> Do you continue to abuse your children?
> **1.** Yes, I stopped
> **2.** No, I did not stop

Notice that 85% of the parents reported they do not abuse their children after they completed Antonia's program. So Antonia could place the results of her survey question in a simple pie chart such as Figure 13.1b. And yes, we are fully aware of the problems with parents self-reporting whether or not they continue to abuse their children, but for now just go along with us. The one-group posttest-only design is also used a lot in process evaluations when it comes to the collection of client satisfaction data.

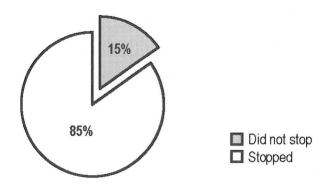

FIGURE 13.1b

Percentage of Parents Who Stopped Physically Abusing Their Children after Leaving Antonia's Program (from Figure 13.1a)

Cross-Sectional Survey Design

Let's take another example of a design that *does not* have an intervention of some kind called a cross-sectional survey design. In doing a cross-sectional survey, we survey *only once* a cross section of some particular population.

In addition to running her child abuse prevention program for abusive parents, Antonia also wants to start a child abuse educational program for all the children in her school.

Before Antonia starts the program, she wants to know what parents think about the idea—kind of like a mini-needs assessment. She may send out questionnaires to all the parents, or she may decide to telephone every second parent, or every fifth or tenth, depending on how much time and money she has. She asks one simple question in her mini-needs assessment survey:

Survey question:
Do you support our school offering a child abuse educational program that your child could enroll in on a voluntary basis and with your consent?
1. Yes
2. No

The results of her simple survey constitute a single measurement, or observation, of the parents' opinions of her proposed educational program (the one for the children) and may be written as shown below:

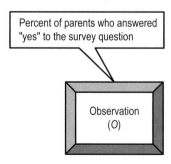

FIGURE 13.2a

Antonia's Cross-Sectional Survey Design

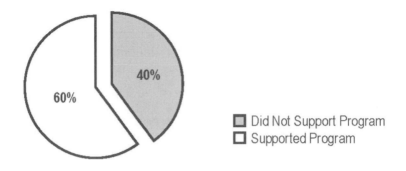

FIGURE 13.2b

**Percentage of Parents Who Supported a Voluntary Child Abuse
Educational Program (from Figure 13.2a)**

The symbol O in Figure 13.2a on the previous page represents the entire cross-sectional survey design because such a design involves making only a single observation, or measurement, at one time period. Note that there is no X, because there is really no intervention.

Antonia wants only to ascertain the parents' attitudes toward her proposed program—nothing more, nothing less. This type of design is used a lot in needs assessment studies. Data that are derived from such a design can be displayed in a simple pie chart as in Figure 13.2b above. Notice that 60% of the parents supported their children attending a voluntary child abuse educational program.

LONGITUDINAL DESIGNS

THE LONGITUDINAL DESIGN provides for multiple measurements (Os) of the program objective—or some other variable of interest—over time, not just at one point in time. Notice that the two previous designs—the one-group post-test-only design and the cross-sectional survey design—measured a variable only once. In contrast, longitudinal designs measure variables more than one time, thus the name *longitudinal.* They can be broken down into three general types:

1. Trend studies
2. Cohort studies
3. Panel studies

TREND STUDIES

A TREND STUDY TAKES DIFFERENT SAMPLES of people who share a similar characteristic at different points in time. Antonia may want to know whether parents of second-graders at her school are becoming more receptive to the idea of the school offering their children a child abuse prevention education program. Her population of interest is simply the parents who have children in the second grade.

Remember, a trend study samples different groups of people at different points in time from the same population of interest. So, to answer her question, she may survey a sample of the parents of second-graders this year (Sample 1), a sample of the parents of the new complement of second-graders next year (Sample 2), and so on (Sample 3) until she thinks she has sufficient data to answer her question. Each year the parents surveyed will be different, but they will all be parents of second-graders—her population of interest. In this case:

O_1 = First measurement of a variable in Sample 1 (year 2016)
O_2 = Second measurement of the same variable in Sample 2 (year 2017)
O_3 = Third measurement of the same variable in Sample 3 (year 2018)

Antonia will be able to determine whether parents, as a group, are becoming more receptive to the idea of introducing child abuse prevention material to their children as early as second grade. In other words, she will be able to measure any attitudinal trend that is, or is not, occurring. The design can be written as shown in Figure 13.3a, and the data from Antonia's study could be displayed in a simple bar graph like Figure 13.3b. Notice that the percentage of parents desiring such a program is going up over time.

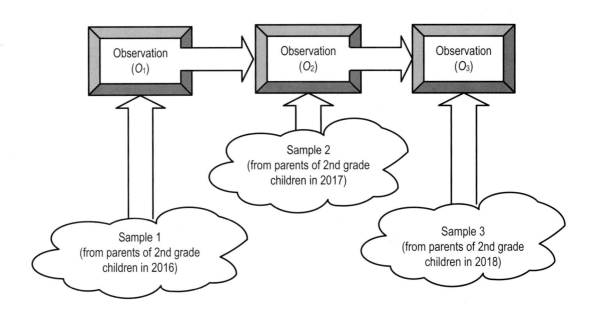

FIGURE 13.3a

Antonia's Trend Study

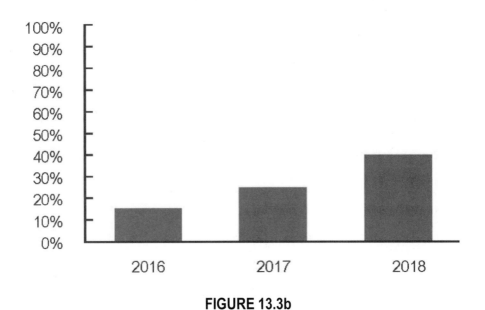

FIGURE 13.3b

Displaying Data for a Trend Study (from Figure 13.3a above): Percentage of Parents Who Support a Prevention Educational Program by Year

BOX 13.1	Trend Studies in a Nutshell

THE TREND STUDY is probably the most common of the longitudinal studies. A trend study samples different groups of people at different points in time from the same population. For example, trend studies are often used with public opinion polls.

Suppose that 2 months before a year-long gun control campaign, a sample of adults is drawn: Of these adults, 64% report that they're in favor of strict gun control regulation, and 34% report that they are not. A year later, a different sample drawn from the same population shows a change: 75% report that they're in favor of gun control, and 25% report that they are not. This is a sample example of a trend study.

Trend studies provide information about net changes at an aggregate level. In the example, we know that in the period under consideration the gun control program gained 11 percentage points (75 − 64 = 11) more support. However, we do not know how many people changed their positions (from con to pro *or* from pro to con), nor do we know how many stayed with their original choice. To determine both the gross change and the net change, a panel study would be necessary, as presented in Box 13.3.

CHARACTERISTICS

— Data are collected from the population at more than one point in time. (This does not always mean that the same subjects are used to collect data at more than one point in time, but that the subjects are selected from the population for data at more than one point in time.)

— There is no experimental manipulation of variables, or more specifically, the investigator has no control over the independent variable.

— This kind of study involves data collection only. No intervention is made by the investigator other than the choice of method or instrument to collect data.

— In analyzing the data, the investigator draws conclusions and may attempt to find correlations between variables. Therefore, trend studies are uniquely appropriate for assessing change over time.

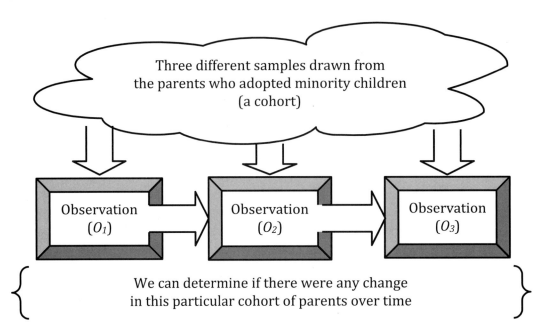

FIGURE 13.4a
Antonia's Cohort Study

COHORT STUDIES

A COHORT STUDY TAKES PLACE when research participants have a certain condition and/or receive a particular treatment and are sampled over time. For example, AIDS survivors, sexual abuse survivors, or parents of children can easily be followed over time. Unlike a trend study, which does not follow a particular cohort of individuals over time, a cohort study does just that: It follows a particular cohort of people who have shared a similar experience.

Antonia might select, for example, one particular group of parents who have adopted minority children, and measure their attitudes toward child abuse prevention education in successive years. Again, the design can be written as shown in Figure 13.4a, and the data could be presented in a format in a simple graph such as Figure 13.4b, where:

O_1 = First measurement of a variable for a **sample** of individuals within a given cohort

O_2 = Second measurement of the variable for a **different sample** of individuals within the same cohort **1 year later**

O_3 = Third measurement of the variable for a **different sample** of individuals within the same cohort **after 2 years**

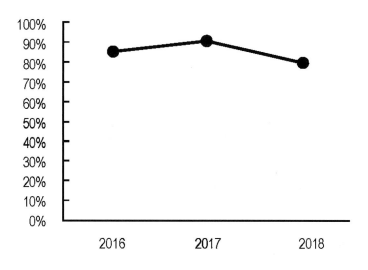

FIGURE 13.4b

**Displaying Data for a Cohort Study (from Figure 13.4a):
Percentage of Parents with Minority Children Who Support a
Prevention Educational Program by Year**

BOX 13.2	Cohort Studies in a Nutshell

A COHORT STUDY is a study in which subjects who presently have a certain condition and/or receive a particular treatment are followed over time and compared with another group who are not affected by the condition under investigation. For research purposes, a cohort is any group of individuals who are linked in some way or who have experienced the same significant life event within a given period.

There are many kinds of cohorts, including birth (e.g., all those who born between 1970 and 1975), disease, education, employment, family formation, and so on. Any study in which there are measures of some characteristic of one or more cohorts at two or more points in time is a cohort analysis.

In some cases, cohort studies are preferred to randomized experimental designs. For instance, because a randomized controlled study to test the effects of smoking on health would be unethical, a reasonable alternative would be a study that identifies two groups, a group of people who smoke and a group of people who do not, and follows them forward through time to see what health problems they develop.

In general, a cohort analysis attempts to identify cohort effects: Are changes in the dependent variable (health problems in this example) due to aging, or are they present because the sample members belongs to the same cohort (smoking versus nonsmoking)?

In other words, cohort studies are about the life histories of sections of populations and the individuals they comprise. They can tell us what circumstances in early life are associated with the population's characteristics in later life—what encourages the development in particular directions and what appears to impede it. We can study such developmental changes across any stage of life in any life domain: education, employment, housing, family formation, citizenship, or health.

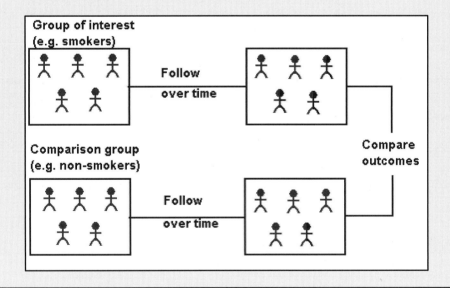

PANEL STUDIES

IN A PANEL STUDY, the *same individuals* are followed over a period of time. Antonia might select one random sample of parents, for example, and measure their attitudes toward child abuse prevention education in successive

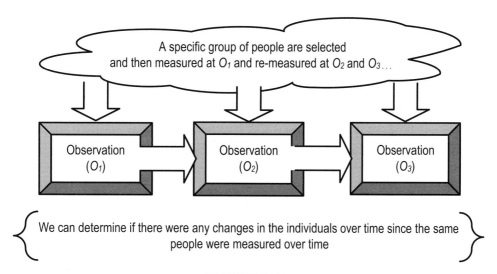

FIGURE 13.5a
Antonia's Panel Study

years. Unlike trend and cohort studies, panel studies can reveal both net change and gross change in the program objective for the *same individuals.* Additionally panel studies can reveal shifting attitudes and patterns of behavior that might go unnoticed with other research approaches.

For example, Bob is measured once at Time 1, then again at Time 2, and so forth. We would do this for each individual in the study. Again, the design can be illustrated as in Figure 13.5a, and hypothetical data could be displayed in a simple graph as in Figure 13.5b.

Figure 13.5b presents the results of the percentages of the same parents who want to have a child abuse prevention education program in their children's school, as measured over a three-year period from 2016 to 2018, where:

O_1 = First measurement of attitudes toward child abuse prevention education for a sample of individuals

O_2 = Second measurement of attitudes toward child abuse prevention education for the **same individuals 1 year later**

O_3 = Third measurement of attitudes toward child abuse prevention education for the **same individuals after 2 years**

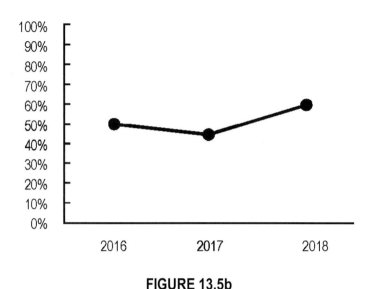

FIGURE 13.5b

Displaying Data for a Panel Study (from Figure 13.5a):
Percentage of Parents Who Support a Prevention Educational
Program by Year

ONE-GROUP PRETEST-POSTTEST DESIGN

THE ONE-GROUP PRETEST-POSTTEST DESIGN is also referred to as a before-and-after design because it includes a pretest of the program objective, and the pretest results are compared with the posttest results. This is the first design we've discussed that uses a pretest of some kind. It's written as shown in Figure 13.6 and hypothetical data could be displayed as in Table 13.1 where:

O_1 = First measurement of the program objective
X = Program, or the intervention (see Box 13.4 on page 467)
O_2 = Second measurement of the program objective

The pretest-posttest design, in which a pretest precedes the introduction of the intervention and a posttest follows it, can be used to determine, on a general level, how the intervention affects a particular group. The design is used often in social work decision-making. The differences between O_1 and O_2, on which these decisions are based, could be due to many other internal validity factors (to be discussed in the next section) rather than to the intervention.

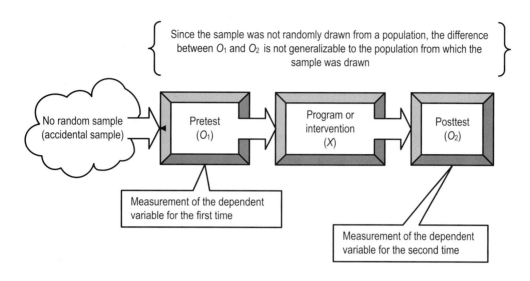

FIGURE 13.6
One-Group Pretest-Posttest Design

Let's take another indicator of how Antonia's child abuse prevention program could be evaluated. Besides counting the number of parents who stopped physically abusing their children as the only indicator of her program's success, she could have a second outcome indicator such as a reduction in the parents' risk for abusive and neglectful parenting behaviors.

TABLE 13.1
Displaying Data for a One-Group Pretest-Posttest Design (from Figure 13.6)

	Pretest Average (O_1)	Posttest Average (O_2)	Difference Average $(O_2 - O_1)$
Intervention Group	50	80	30

BOX 13.3	Panel Studies in a Nutshell

PANEL STUDIES measure the same sample of respondents at different points in time. Unlike trend studies, panel studies can reveal both net change and gross change in the dependent variable for the same people. Additionally, panel studies can reveal shifting attitudes and patterns of behavior that might go unnoticed with other research approaches.

Depending on the purpose of the study, researchers can use either a continuous panel, consisting of members who report specific attitudes or behavior patterns on a regular basis, or an interval panel, whose members agree to complete a certain number of measurement instruments only when the information is needed. In general, panel studies provide data suitable for sophisticated statistical analysis and might enable researchers to predict cause-effect relationships.

Panel data are particularly useful in predicting long-term or cumulative effects which are normally hard to analyze in a one-shot case study (or cross-sectional study). For example, in the early 80's, the National Broadcasting Company supported a panel study in order to investigate the causal influence of violent TV viewing on aggression among young people.

In brief, the methodology in the study involved collecting data on aggression, TV viewing, and a host of sociological variables from children in several metropolitan cities in the US. About 1,200 boys participated in the study and the variables were measured six times for 3 year study period.

The researchers sought to determine whether TV viewing at an earlier time added to the predictability of aggression at a later time. After looking at all the results, the investigators concluded that there was no consistent statistically significant relationship between watching violent TV programs and later acts of aggression.

An instrument that measures their attitudes toward physical punishment of children could easily measure this program objective. Let's say that Antonia had the parents complete the instrument *before* participating in the child abuse prevention program (O_1) and *after* completing it (O_2). In this example all kinds of things could have happened between O_1 and O_2 to affect the participants' behaviors and feelings—such as the television station's deciding to publicize the names of parents who are abusive to their children.

Just the experience of taking the pretest could motivate some participants to stop being abusive toward their children. Maturation (the children are growing up and are becoming less difficult to discipline) could also affect the results between the pretest and posttest measurements.

These issues are referred to as alternative explanations and rival hypotheses and can make most of us question the results of just about any outcome evaluation. The easiest way you can control for all this messy stuff is by using two groups of participants, which eliminates many of the threats to internal validity.

BOX 13.4	Treatment: A Variable or a Constant?

FOR INSTRUCTIONAL PURPOSES, group designs are displayed using symbols where *X* is the independent variable (treatment) and *O* is the measure of the dependent variable. This presentation is accurate when studies are designed with two or more groups. When one-group designs are used, however, this interpretation does not hold.

In one-group designs, the treatment, or program, cannot truly vary because all research participants have experienced the same event; that is, they all have experienced the program. Without a comparison or control group, treatment is considered a constant because it's a quality shared by all members in the research study. In short, time is the independent variable.

There does not necessarily have to be an independent variable in a study, however; we may just want to measure some variable in a particular population such as the number of people who receive a certain type of social service intervention over a 10-year period. In this situation, there is no independent or dependent variable.

INTERNAL VALIDITY

INTERNAL VALIDITY IS A TERM we use to assess the "approximate certainty" about inferences regarding cause-and-effect or causal relationships. Thus, internal validity is predominantly relevant only to the research designs that try to establish causal relationships between the independent and dependent variables. In any causal study we should be able to conclude from our findings that the intervention is, or is not, the only cause of change in the dependent variable, or outcome variable, or program objective.

If our explanatory study does not have internal validity, such a conclusion is not possible, and the study's findings can be misleading. Internal validity is concerned with one of the requirements for an "ideal" research study—the control of rival hypotheses, or alternative explanations for what might bring about a change in the program objective.

In short, the higher the internal validity, the greater the extent to which rival hypotheses (or alternative explanations) can be controlled; the lower the internal validity, the less they can be controlled. We will discuss only ten threats to internal validity, which are:

1. History
2. Maturation
3. Testing effects
4. Instrumentation error
5. Statistical regression
6. Differential selection of research participants
7. Mortality
8. Reactive effects of research participants
9. Interaction effects
10. Relations between experimental and control groups

HISTORY

THE FIRST THREAT TO INTERNAL VALIDITY, history, refers to any outside event, either public or private, that may affect the program objective and that was not taken into account in our design. Many times, it refers to events that occur between the first and second measurement of the program objective (the pretest and the posttest).

If events occur that have the potential to alter the second measurement, there is no way of knowing how much (if any) of the observed change in the program's objective is a function of the intervention and how much is attributable to these events.

Suppose, for example, we are investigating the effects of an educational program on racial tolerance. We may decide to measure the program objective (decreasing racial tolerance in the community) before introducing the intervention, the educational program. The educational program is then implemented and is represented by X.

Finally, racial tolerance is measured again, after the program has run its course. This final measurement yields a posttest score, represented by O_2. As you know, the one-group pretest-posttest study design is presented in Figure 13.6 on page 465.

The difference between the values O_2 and O_1 represents the difference in the degree of racial tolerance in the community before and after the educational program. If the study is internally valid, $O_2 - O_1$ will yield a crude measure of the effect of the educational program on racial tolerance, and this is what we were trying to discover.

Now suppose that before the posttest could be administered, a colossal terrorist attack occurs in the United States, such as the type that occurred in New York on September 11, 2001.

It may be fair to say that terrorism can be expected to have a negative effect on racial tolerance, and the posttest scores may, therefore, show a lower level of tolerance than if the terrorist act had not occurred. The effect, $O_2 - O_1$, will now be the combined effects of the educational program *and* the terrorist act, not the effect of the program alone, as we initially intended.

Terrorism is an extraneous variable that we could not have anticipated and did not control for when we designed the study. Other examples might include an earthquake, an election of a rogue president, illness, divorce, marriage, or a racially divisive incident like the 2012 shooting of Trayvon Martin in Florida—any event, public or private, that could affect the dependent variable, or program objective. Any such variable that is unanticipated and uncontrolled for is an example of history.

However, the effects of history are controlled for with the use of a control group; that is, the control group would theoretically have experienced the act of terrorism exactly like the experimental group. Thus, both groups would have been exposed to the extraneous terrorism variable and this would make it a constant in the research design.

So, whenever a control or comparison group is used in a study, it's usually safe to say that the effects of history have been controlled for (not history itself, of course, as this is reserved for the person up above). The most important thing to remember as a mortal is that you cannot control history—history marches on with or without you. You can however, control for the *effects* of history by adding a control or comparison group to your research design.

MATURATION

MATURATION, THE SECOND THREAT TO INTERNAL VALIDITY, is history's first cousin. It refers to changes, both physical and psychological, that take place in our research participants over time and can affect the dependent variable, or program objective. Suppose that we are evaluating an intervention strategy designed to improve the behavior of adolescents who engage in delinquent behavior. Because the behavior of adolescents changes naturally as they mature, any observed change may have resulted as much from their natural development as from the intervention strategy.

> Maturation is a threat to internal validity that refers to the aging effects or developmental changes that influence the dependent variable.

Maturation refers not only to physical or mental growth, however. Over time, people grow older, more or less anxious, more or less bored, and more or less motivated to take part in a study. All these factors and many more can affect the way in which people respond when the program objective is measured a second or third time.

Like history as previously discussed, the *effects* of maturation can indeed be controlled for with the use of a control or comparison group. Like history, you cannot control maturation; you can only control for the *effects* of maturation by using control or comparison groups in your research designs.

TESTING EFFECTS

TESTING EFFECTS is sometimes referred to as *initial measurement effect.* Thus, the pretests that are the starting point for many research designs are another potential threat to internal validity. One of the most utilized designs involves three steps: (1) measuring some program objective, such as learning behaviors in school or attitudes toward work; (2) initiating a program to change that variable; and then (3) measuring the program objective again at the conclusion of the program. As you know, this design is known as the one-group pretest-posttest design and is illustrated in Figure 13.6 on page 465.

The testing effect is the effect that taking a pretest might have on posttest scores. Suppose that Roberto, a research participant, takes a pretest to measure his initial level of racial tolerance before being exposed to a racial tolerance educational program. He might remember some of the questions on the pretest, think about them later, and change his views on racial issues before taking part in the educational program. After the program, his posttest score will reveal his changed opinions, and we may incorrectly assume that the program was *solely* responsible, whereas the true cause was his experience with the pretest *and* the intervention.

Sometimes a pretest induces anxiety in a research participant so that Roberto receives a worse score on the posttest than he should have; or boredom caused by having to respond to the same questions a second time may be a factor. To avoid the testing effect, we may wish to use a design that does not require a pretest.

> Testing effects are a threat to internal validity that refers to the principle that taking pretests will affect posttest scores.

If a pretest is essential, we then must consider the length of time between the pretest and posttest measurements. A pretest is far more likely to affect the posttest when the time between the two is short. The nature of the pretest is another factor. Measuring instruments that deal with factual matters, such as knowledge levels, may have large testing effects because the questions tend to be more easily recalled.

INSTRUMENTATION ERROR

THE FOURTH THREAT TO INTERNAL VALIDITY is instrumentation error. This is simply a list of all the troubles that can afflict the measurement process. The instrument may be unreliable or invalid, as presented in Chapters 7 and 8. A mechanical instrument, such as an electroencephalogram (EEG), may malfunction. Occasionally, the term *instrumentation error* is used to refer to an observer whose observations are inconsistent or to measuring instruments that are valid and reliable in themselves but have not been administered properly.

Administration, with respect to a measuring instrument, means the circumstances under which the measuring instrument is made: where, when, how, and by whom. A mother being asked about her attitudes toward her children, for example, may respond in one way in the social worker's office and in a different way at home while her children are screaming around her feet.

Instrumentation error is a threat to internal validity that refers to the weaknesses of a measuring instrument itself, such as invalidity, unreliability, improper administration, or mechanical breakdowns.

A mother's verbal response may differ from her written response, or she may respond differently in the morning than she would in the evening, or differently alone than she would in a group. These variations in situational responses do not indicate a true change in the feelings, attitudes, or behaviors being measured but are only examples of instrumentation error.

STATISTICAL REGRESSION

THE FIFTH THREAT TO INTERNAL VALIDITY, statistical regression, refers to the tendency of extremely low and extremely high scores to regress, or move toward the average score for everyone in the study. Suppose an instructor makes her class take a multiple-choice exam and the average score is 50.

Now suppose that the instructor separates the low scorers from the high scorers and tries to even out the level of the class by giving the low scorers special instruction. To determine whether the special instruction has been effective, the entire class then takes another multiple-choice exam. The result of the exam is that the low scorers (as a group) do better than they did the first time, and the high scorers (as a group) do worse. The instructor believes that this has occurred because the low scorers received special instruction and the high scorers did not.

According to the logic of statistical regression, however, both the average score of the low scorers and the average score of the high scorers would move toward the total average score for both groups (i.e., 50). Even without any special instruction, and still in their state of ignorance, the low scorers (as a group) would be expected to have a higher average score than they did before. Likewise, the high scorers (as a group) would be expected to have a lower average score than they did before.

> Statistical regression is a threat to internal validity that refers to the tendency for extreme scores at pretest to become less extreme at posttest.

It would be easy for the research instructor to assume that the low scores had increased because of the special instruction and the high scores had decreased because of the lack of it. This is not necessarily so, however; the instruction may have had nothing to do with it. It may all be due to statistical regression where the high group goes down and the low group goes up.

DIFFERENTIAL SELECTION OF RESEARCH PARTICIPANTS

THE SIXTH THREAT TO INTERNAL VALIDITY is differential selection of research participants. To some extent, the participants selected for a study are different from one another to begin with. "Ideal" research designs, however, require random sampling from a population (if at all possible) and random assignment to groups. This ensures that the results of a study will be generalizable to the larger population from which they were drawn (thus addressing threats to external validity, to be discussed later).

> Differential selection is a threat to internal validity that refers to the potential lack of equivalency among preformed groups of research participants.

This threat, however, is present when we are working with preformed groups or groups that already exist, such as classes of students, self-help groups, or community groups. It's probable those different preformed groups will not be equivalent with respect to relevant variables and that these initial differences will invalidate the results of the posttest.

A child abuse prevention educational program for children in schools might be evaluated by comparing the prevention skills of one group of children who have taken the educational program with the skills of a second group who have not. To make a valid comparison, the two groups must be as similar as possible with respect to age, gender, intelligence, socioeconomic status, and anything else that might affect the acquisition of child abuse prevention skills.

We would have to make every effort to form or select equivalent groups, but the groups are sometimes not as equivalent as might be hoped—especially if we are obliged to work with preformed groups, such as classes of students or community groups. If the two groups were different before the intervention was introduced, there is not much point in comparing them at the end.

Accordingly, preformed groups should be avoided whenever possible. If it's not feasible to do this, rigorous pretesting must be done to determine in what ways the groups are (or are not) equivalent and we must compensate for differences by using statistical methods.

MORTALITY

THE SEVENTH THREAT TO INTERNAL VALIDITY is mortality, which simply means that research participants may drop out before the end of the study. Their absence will probably have a significant effect on the study's findings because people who drop out are likely to be different in some ways from those participants who stay to the end. People who drop out may be less motivated to participate in the intervention than are people who stay in, for example.

Mortality is a threat to internal validity that refers to the loss of research participants through normal attrition over time in research designs that require pretests and posttests.

Because dropouts often have such characteristics in common, it cannot be assumed that the attrition occurred in a random manner. If considerably more people drop out of one group than out of the other, the result will be two groups that are no longer equivalent and cannot be usefully compared. We cannot know at the beginning of the study how many people will drop out, but we can watch to see how many do. Mortality is never problematic if dropout rates are 5% or less *and* if the dropout rates are similar for the both groups.

REACTIVE EFFECTS OF RESEARCH PARTICIPANTS

THE EIGHTH THREAT TO INTERNAL VALIDITY is reactive effects. Changes in the behaviors or feelings of research participants may be caused by their reaction to the novelty of the situation or to the knowledge that they are participating in a study.

The classic example of reactive effects was found in a series of studies carried out at the Hawthorne plant of the Western Electric Company, in Chicago, many years ago. Researchers were investigating the relationship between working conditions and productivity. When they increased the level of lighting in one section of the plant, productivity increased; a further increase in the lighting was followed by an additional increase in productivity.

When the lighting was then decreased, however, production levels did not fall accordingly but continued to rise. The conclusion was that the workers were increasing their productivity not because of the lighting level but because of the attention they were receiving as research participants in the study.

The term *Hawthorne effect* is still used to describe any situation in which the research participants' behaviors are influenced not by the intervention but by the knowledge that they are taking part in a research project. Another example of such a reactive effect is the placebo given to patients, which produces beneficial results because the patients believe its medication.

> Reactive effects are a threat to internal validity that refers to a process in which change in the dependent variable is induced by the research procedures themselves.

Ensuring that all participants in a study, in both the experimental and the control groups, appear to be treated equally can control reactive effects. If one group is to be shown an educational film, for example, the other group should also be shown a film—some film carefully chosen to bear no relation-ship to the variable being investigated. If the study involves a change in the participants' routine, this in itself may be enough to change behavior, and care must be taken to continue the study until novelty has ceased to be a fac-tor.

INTERACTION EFFECTS

INTERACTION AMONG THE VARIOUS THREATS to internal validity can have an ef-fect of its own. Any of the factors already described as threats may interact with one another, but the most common interactive effect involves differen-tial selection and maturation.

Let's say we are studying two preformed groups of clients who are being treated for depression. The intention was for these groups to be equivalent, in terms of both their motivation for treatment and their levels of depres-sion. It turns out that Group A is more generally depressed than Group B, however.

Interaction effects are a threat to internal validity that refer to the effects produced by the combination of two or more threats to internal validity.

Whereas both groups may grow less motivated over time, it's likely that Group A, whose members were more depressed to begin with, will lose motivation more com-pletely and more quickly than Group B. Nonequivalent preformed groups thus grow even less equivalent over time as a result of the interaction between differen-tial selection and maturation.

RELATIONS BETWEEN EXPERIMENTAL AND CONTROL GROUPS

THE FINAL GROUP OF THREATS to internal validity has to do with the effects that may happen when using two or more groups of research participants. These effects include:

1. Diffusion of treatments
2. Compensatory equalization
3. Compensatory rivalry
4. Demoralization

DIFFUSION OF TREATMENTS

DIFFUSION, OR IMITATION, of treatments may occur when members of the experimental and control groups talk to each other about the study. Suppose a study is designed to present a new relaxation exercise to the experimental group and nothing at all to the control group. There is always the possibility that one of the participants in the experimental group will explain the exercise to a friend who happens to be in the control group. The friend explains it to another friend, and so on. This might be beneficial for the control group, but it undermines the study's findings.

COMPENSATORY EQUALIZATION

COMPENSATORY EQUALIZATION OF TREATMENT occurs when the person doing the study and/or the staff member administering the intervention to the experimental group feels sorry for people in the control group who are not receiving it and attempts to compensate them. A social worker might take a control group member aside and covertly demonstrate the relaxation exercise, for example.

On the other hand, if our study has been ethically designed, there should be no need for guilt on the part of the social worker because some people are not being taught to relax. They can be taught to relax when our study is over as pointed out in Chapter 4 on ethics.

COMPENSATORY RIVALRY

COMPENSATORY RIVALRY IS AN EFFECT that occurs when the control group becomes motivated to compete with the experimental group. For example, a control group in a program to encourage parental involvement in school activities might get wind that something is up and make a determined effort to participate, too, on the basis that "anything they can do, we can do better." There is no direct communication between the groups, as there is in the diffusion of treatment effect, only rumors and suggestions of rumors. However, rumors are often enough to threaten the internal validity of a study.

DEMORALIZATION

IN DIRECT CONTRAST WITH COMPENSATORY RIVALRY, demoralization refers to feelings of deprivation among the control group that may cause them to give up and drop out of the study, in which case this effect would be referred to as *mortality*. The people in the control group may also get angry.

Now that you have a sound understanding of internal validity, we turn our attention to two-group designs that have to minimize as many threats to internal validity as possible if they are to support cause-and-effect statements such as "my intervention *caused* my clients to get better."

TWO-GROUP DESIGNS

EXCEPT FOR THE ONE-GROUP PRETEST-POSTTEST DESIGN, one-group designs do not intend to determine cause-effect relationships. Thus, they are not concerned with internal validity issues. Two-group designs on the other hand help us produce data for coming a bit closer to proving cause-and-effect relationships; so now internal validity issues come readily into play. There are many two-group designs, but we will discuss only four of them.

1. Comparison group pretest-posttest design (Figure 13.7)
2. Comparison group posttest-only design (Figure 13.8)
3. Classical experimental design (Figure 13.9)
4. Randomized posttest-only control group design (Figure 13.10)

COMPARISON GROUP PRETEST-POSTTEST DESIGN

THE COMPARISON GROUP PRETEST-POSTTEST DESIGN simply elaborates on the one-group pretest-posttest design by adding a comparison group. This second group receives both the pretest (O_1) and the posttest (O_2) at the same time as the experimental group, but it does not receive the intervention. Also, random assignment to groups is never done in this design.

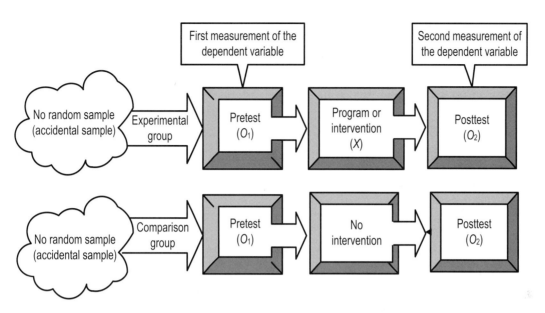

FIGURE 13.7
Comparison Group Pretest-Posttest Design

This design is written as shown in Figure 13.7 above, and hypothetical data could look like those displayed in Table 13.2 on the following page, where:

O_1 = First measurement of the program objective
X = The program, or intervention
O_2 = Second measurement of the program objective

The experimental and comparison groups formed under this design will probably not be equivalent because members are not randomly assigned to the two groups (notice the 10-point difference at pretest). The pretest scores, however, will indicate the extent of their differences. If the differences are not statistically significant but are still large enough to affect the posttest, the statistical technique of analysis of covariance can be used to compensate for this.

So long as the groups are at least somewhat equivalent at pretest, this design controls for nearly all of the threats to internal validity. But because random assignment to groups was not used, many of the external validity threats remain (to be discussed at the end of chapter).

TABLE 13.2

Displaying Data for a Comparison Group Pretest-Posttest Design
(from Figure 13.7 on page 479)

	Pretest Average (O_1)	Posttest Average (O_2)	Difference Average $(O_2 - O_1)$
Intervention Group	50	80	30
Comparison Group	60	70	10
Difference			20

COMPARISON GROUP POSTTEST-ONLY DESIGN

THE COMPARISON GROUP POSTTEST-ONLY DESIGN improves on the one-group posttest-only design by introducing a comparison group that does not receive the intervention but is subject to the same posttest as those who do (the comparison group). The basic elements of the comparison group posttest-only design are as shown in Figure 13.8, and hypothetical data could be displayed as in Table 13.3, where:

X = The program, or intervention

O_1 = First and only measurement of the program objective

In Antonia's child abuse prevention program, if the January, April, and August sections are scheduled but the August sessions are canceled for some reason, those who would have been participants in that section could be used as a comparison group. If the values of O_1 on the measuring instrument were similar for the experimental and comparison groups, it could be concluded that the program was of little use because those who had experienced it (those who had received X) were not much better or worse off than those who had not.

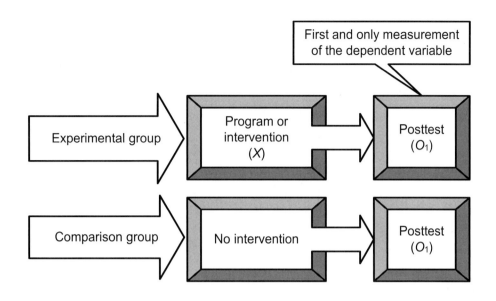

FIGURE 13.8
Comparison Group Posttest-Only Design

A problem with drawing this conclusion, however, is that there is no evidence that the groups were equivalent to begin with. Selection, mortality, and the interaction of selection and other threats to internal validity are thus the major difficulties with this design. The use of a comparison group, however, controls for the effects of history, maturation, and testing.

TABLE 13.3

Displaying Data for a Randomized Posttest-Only Comparison Group Design (from Figure 13.8 above)

	Posttest Average
Intervention Group	80
Comparison Group	70
Difference	10

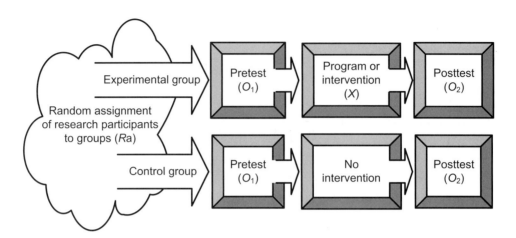

FIGURE 13.9

Classical Experimental Design

CLASSICAL EXPERIMENTAL DESIGN

THE CLASSICAL EXPERIMENTAL DESIGN is the basis for all the experimental designs. It involves an experimental group and a control group, both created by a random assignment method (and, if possible, by random selection from a population).

Both groups take a pretest (O_1) at the same time, after which the intervention (X) is given only to the experimental group; then both groups take the posttest (O_2) at the same time.

The classical experimental design is shown in Figure 13.9 above, and the typical way to present the data is displayed in Table 13.4 on the following page. Because the experimental and control groups are randomly assigned, they are equivalent with respect to all important variables. This group equivalence in the design helps control for many of the threats to internal validity because both groups will be affected by them in the same way, where:

R_a = Random assignment to a group

O_1 = First measurement of the program objective

X = The program, or intervention

O_2 = Second measurement of the program objective

RANDOMIZED POSTTEST-ONLY CONTROL GROUP DESIGN

THE RANDOMIZED POSTTEST-ONLY CONTROL GROUP DESIGN is identical to the comparison group posttest-only design, except that the participants are randomly assigned to two groups. This design, therefore, has a control group rather than a comparison group.

This design usually involves only two groups, one experimental and one control. There are no pretests. The experimental group receives the intervention and takes the posttest; the control group only takes the posttest. This design can be written as shown in Figure 13.10, and data generated from this design can be presented as in Table 13.5.

In addition to measuring change in a group or groups, a pretest also helps to ensure equivalence between the control and the experimental groups. As you know, this design does not have a pretest. The groups have been randomly assigned, however, as indicated by R, and this, in itself, is theoretically enough to ensure equivalence without the need for a confirmatory pretest.

This design is useful in situations where it's not possible to conduct a pretest or where a pretest would be expected to strongly influence the results of the posttest because of the effects of testing. This design also controls for many of the threats to internal validity (previously discussed) and external validity (discussed in the following section).

TABLE 13.4
Displaying Data for a Classical Experimental Design (from Figure 13.9)

	Pretest Average (O_1)	Posttest Average (O_2)	Difference Average ($O_2 - O_1$)
Intervention Group	50	80	30
Control Group	50	70	20
Difference			10

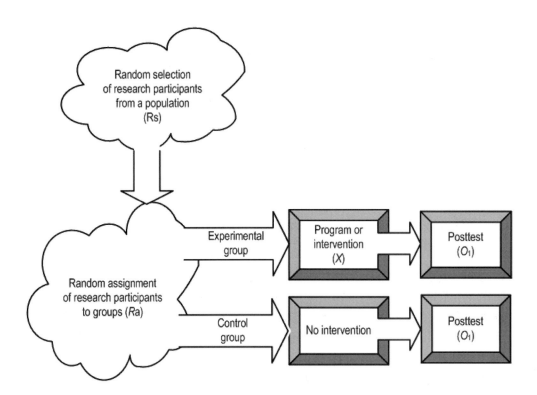

FIGURE 13.10

Randomized Posttest-Only Control Group Design

TABLE 13.5

**Displaying Data for a Randomized
Posttest-Only Control Group Design
(from Figure 13.10 above)**

	Posttest Average
Intervention Group	80
Control Group	50
Difference	30

EXTERNAL VALIDITY

EXTERNAL VALIDITY IS THE DEGREE to which the results of a specific study are generalizable to another population, to another setting, and to another time. There are many threats to internal validity, but we will only discuss four of them:

1. Selection-treatment interaction
2. Specificity of variables
3. Multiple-treatment interference
4. Researcher bias

SELECTION-TREATMENT INTERACTION

THE FIRST THREAT to external validity is selection-treatment interaction. This threat commonly occurs when a design cannot provide for random selection of participants from a population. Suppose we wanted to study the effectiveness of a family service agency staff, for example.

If our research proposal was turned down by fifty agencies before it was accepted by the fifty-first, it's very likely that the accepting agency differs in certain important aspects from the other fifty. It may accept the proposal because its social workers are more highly motivated, more secure, more satisfied with their jobs, or more interested in the practical application of the study than are the average agency staff member.

As a result, we would be assessing the research participants on the very factors for which they were unwittingly (and by default) selected—motivation, job satisfaction, and so on. The study may be internally valid, but because it will not be possible to generalize the results to other family service agencies it will have little external validity.

SPECIFICITY OF VARIABLES

SPECIFICITY OF VARIABLES has to do with the fact that a research project conducted with a specific group of people at a specific time and in a specific setting may not always be generalizable to other people at different times and in different settings.

For example, a measuring instrument used to measure the social support levels of upper-socioeconomic-level Caucasian suburban children does not provide an equally accurate measure of social support when it's applied to lower-socioeconomic-level children of racial minorities in the inner city.

MULTIPLE-TREATMENT INTERFERENCE

THE THIRD THREAT TO EXTERNAL VALIDITY, multiple-treatment interference, occurs when a research participant is given two or more interventions in succession, so the results of the first intervention may affect the results of the second. A client who attends treatment sessions, for example, may not seem to benefit from one therapeutic technique, so another is tried. In fact, the client may have benefited from the first technique, but the benefit may not become apparent until the second technique has been tried.

As a result, the effects of both techniques become commingled, or the results may be erroneously ascribed to the second technique alone. Because of this threat, interventions should be given separately if possible. If the research design does not allow this, sufficient time should be allowed to elapse between the two interventions in an effort to minimize the possibility of multiple-treatment interference.

In addition, your research participants may be getting help in other places besides the program you are evaluating. They may, for example, being offered help by other caseworkers, probation officers, various self-help groups, hospitals, clinics, friends, clergy, and even their mothers and fathers in addition to the odd social work practicum student or two. All these other helping sources will affect the results of your study.

RESEARCHER BIAS

THE FINAL THREAT TO EXTERNAL VALIDITY is researcher bias. Researchers, like people in general, tend to see what they want to see or expect to see. Unconsciously and without any thought of deceit, they may manipulate a study so that the actual results agree with the anticipated results. A practitioner may favor an intervention so strongly that the study is structured to support it, or the results may be interpreted favorably. The phrase "If I didn't believe it, I wouldn't have seen it" readily comes to mind.

If we know which individuals are in the experimental group and which are in the control group, this knowledge alone might affect the study's results. Students whom an instructor believes to be bright, for example, often are given higher grades than their performance warrants, whereas students believed to be dull are given lower grades. The way to control for researcher bias is to perform a double-blind experiment in which neither the research participants nor the evaluator knows who's in the experimental or control groups. The use of standardized measuring instruments to measure the dependent variables also helps control for researcher bias.

SUMMARY

RESEARCH DESIGNS COVER THE ENTIRE RANGE of research questions and provide data that can be used to gain knowledge for our profession. No single design is inherently inferior or superior to the others. Each has advantages and disadvantages. Those of us who are familiar with them will be well equipped to select the one that is most appropriate to a particular evaluative effort.

Study Questions for Chapter 13

Essay — Discussion

1	Before you entered your social work program, and before you read this chapter, how knowledgeable were you about using group research designs within social work research studies? Discuss fully.
2	What are knowledge levels? Why should we know them? Provide social work examples throughout your discussion to illustrate your main points.
3	What are "ideal" experiments"? List each of the six conditions necessary for an "ideal" experiment to occur. For each condition, discuss its underlying premise and provide a social work example throughout your discussion to illustrate your main points.
4	What is the *matched pairs* method of assignment to groups? Provide social work examples throughout your discussion to illustrate your main points.
5	What are *group research designs*? Provide social work examples throughout your discussion to illustrate your main points.
6	What are *one-group research designs*? Provide social work examples throughout your discussion to illustrate your main points.
7	What are *one-group posttest-only designs*? Describe in detail how they work and what they are supposed to accomplish. Provide social work examples throughout your discussion to illustrate your main points.
8	What are *cross-sectional survey designs*? Describe in detail how they work and what they are supposed to accomplish. Provide social work examples throughout your discussion to illustrate your main points.

9	What are *longitudinal designs*? Describe in detail how they work and what they are supposed to accomplish. Provide social work examples throughout your discussion to illustrate your main points.
10	What are *trend studies*? Describe in detail how they work and what they are supposed to accomplish. Provide social work examples throughout your discussion to illustrate your main points.
11	What are *cohort studies*? Describe in detail how they work and what they are supposed to accomplish. Provide social work examples throughout your discussion to illustrate your main points.
12	What are *panel studies*? Describe in detail how they work and what they are supposed to accomplish. Provide social work examples throughout your discussion to illustrate your main points.
13	What are *one-group pretest-posttest designs*? Describe in detail how they work and what they are supposed to accomplish. Provide social work examples throughout your discussion to illustrate your main points.
14	What are *interrupted time-series designs*? Describe in detail how they work and what they are supposed to accomplish. Provide social work examples throughout your discussion to illustrate your main points.
15	What is internal validity? Why do we need to know the internal validity of a research study? Provide social work examples throughout your discussion to illustrate your main points.
16	List the ten threats to a research study's internal validity. Discuss what each threat means to you as a beginning social work researcher. Use social work examples to illustrate your main points.
17	What are *two-group research designs*? Provide social work examples throughout your discussion to illustrate your main points.

18	What are *comparison group pretest-posttest designs*? Describe in detail how they work and what they are supposed to accomplish. Provide social work examples throughout your discussion to illustrate your main points.
19	What are *comparison group posttest-only designs*? Describe in detail how they work and what they are supposed to accomplish. Provide social work examples throughout your discussion to illustrate your main points.
20	What are *classical experimental designs*? Describe in detail how they work and what they are supposed to accomplish. Provide social work examples throughout your discussion to illustrate your main points.
21	What are *randomized posttest-only control group designs?* Describe in detail how they work and what they are supposed to accomplish. Provide social work examples throughout your discussion to illustrate your main points.
22	What is external validity? Why do we need to know the external validity of a research study?
23	List the four threats to a research study's external validity. Discuss what each threat means to you as a beginning social work researcher. Use social work examples to illustrate your main points.

Critical Thinking — Application — Integration

24	**GROUP RESEARCH DESIGNS AND THE RESEARCHER** **Scenario 1:** Make an argument that to be a competent social work researcher **you must know** how to select and use group research designs in addition to knowing each design's advantages and disadvantages. Provide clear and explicit **research-related** social work examples to illustrate your main points. **Scenario 2:** Make an argument that **you do not have to know** how to select and use group research designs in addition to knowing each design's advantages and disadvantages to be a competent social work researcher. Provide clear and explicit **research-related** social work examples to illustrate

your main points.

Time to Choose: Which one of the two preceding scenarios do you feel is more consistent with the place of research in social work? Why? Provide relevant social work examples to illustrate your main points.

25	**GROUP RESEARCH DESIGNS AND THE PRACTITIONER** **Scenario 1:** Make an argument that to be an effective evidence-based social work practitioner **you must know** how to select and use group research designs to evaluate the effectiveness of your interventions. Provide a clear and explicit **practice-related** social work example to illustrate your main points. **Scenario 2:** Make an argument that **you do not have to know** how to select and use group research designs to evaluate the effectiveness of your interventions to be an effective evidence-based social work practitioner. Provide clear and explicit **practice-related** social work examples to illustrate your main points. **Time to Choose:** Which one of the above two scenarios do you feel is more consistent with the concept of the contemporary evidence-based social work practice process as illustrated on pages 46–51? Why? Provide relevant social work examples to illustrate your main points.
26	**TIME TO PUT ON YOUR CRITICAL THINKING HAT** 1. Discuss the similarities and differences between your responses to Questions 24 and 25. 2. What are your thoughts on the belief that you'll need to know the advantages and disadvantages of group research designs whether you're a social work *practitioner* (Question 25) or a social work *researcher* (Question 24)?

APPLICATION OF GROUP RESEARCH DESIGNS

Locate a published quantitatively oriented social work journal article that utilized any one of the group research designs presented in this chapter. We suggest you locate a quantitatively oriented research study in Bruce Thyer's journal *Research on Social Work Practice* (Sage Publications). Hands down, this is the best journal to find good quantitatively oriented social work research studies.

1. What was the study's sample or population—data source(s)?

2. What was the study's dependent variable?

3. What was the study's independent variable?

4. What was the study's primary data collection method?

5. What measuring instrument was used to measure the dependent variable? Was it reliable and valid? If so, how? If not, why not?

6. What specific group research design was used in the study?

7. What internal and external validity factors did the research design control for? Discuss in detail. Provide specific examples from the research study to illustrate your main points.

8. What internal and external validity factors did the research design not control for? Discuss in detail. Provide specific examples from the research study to illustrate your main points.

9. With your knowledge of the advantages and disadvantages of the various group research designs that researchers and practitioners alike can use, thoroughly discuss how you will use the material contained within this chapter when you begin to evaluate the appropriateness of any research study's overall internal and external validities. Discuss why you believe each criterion you selected is important for your evaluation of the study's chosen design.

27

GROUP RESEARCH DESIGNS AND YOUR PROFESSIONAL DEVELOPMENT

1. Review the three social work research-related roles you can take when you graduate—CSWE Competency 1 at the beginning of this chapter on page 438. This concept is also discussed in Chapter 1 on pages 38–42. Thoroughly discuss how you feel this chapter will help you to perform one or more research-related roles when you graduate. Which one of the three roles do you believe this chapter helped you with the most? Why? Discuss in detail and provide an example to illustrate your main points.

2. Review CSWE Competency 4 at the beginning of this chapter (page 438). Thoroughly discuss how you feel this chapter will help you to become a practice-informed researcher and a research-informed practitioner. Discuss in detail and provide an example to illustrate your main points.

28

3. Review the evidence-based practice process as illustrated on pages 46–51. Thoroughly discuss how this chapter helps you to develop the skills you'll need for implementing one or more steps of the evidence-based practice process.

4. Discuss which step(s) you feel this chapter will help you with the most. Why? Be very specific and use relevant social work examples to illustrate your main points throughout your discussion.

NOTE: This exercise should help you to realize that the group research designs that are used in "research studies" are the same that are used in "practice situations." In short, you can use this chapter to help you employ group research designs to evaluate your effectiveness with all of your client systems.

YOU'RE NOW A RESEARCHER

Pretend that your school of social work wants to do a research study to determine if the school's curriculum **increased** the interviewing skills of its graduating students. Your school's director is putting you in charge of designing a quantitatively oriented group research design to determine if the school is really **100%** responsible for increasing the interviewing skills of its student body. (Hint: Notice the word *increased* and the value *100%*.)

1. List and then discuss the various group research designs that you could use.

2. Select one that you think will be the best to answer your research question. Why did you pick this specific research design?

3. Are you going to randomly assign students to groups? If so, what's the purpose?

4. Are you going to use a one-group research design or a two-group design? Why? Justify your position.

5. What are the independent and dependent variables?

6. What internal and external validates did your selected research design control for—and more importantly *not* control for?

7. What's the unit of analysis?

8. Are you going to use standardized measuring instruments? If so, which ones?

9. How are you going to actually collect the data?

10. What specific data are you going to collect?

11. How are you going to display the data once they have been collected and analyzed?

12. Could you use retrospective baseline data? If so, why?

29

30	**MIXED-METHODS RESEARCH/PRACTICE (CHAPTER 8)** With your quantitatively oriented research question in mind (from Question 29), you also wish to add a qualitative component to your study in an effort to add more meat to your study's quantitatively oriented findings and recommendations. This would be a great time to review Chapters 6–8. 1. Using what you have learned so far in this course, clearly and thoroughly discuss how you would do your mixed-methods research study, highlighting the specific qualitative data collection methods you have chosen to use (Chapter 15). 2. State specifically what the findings of your qualitative component could add to your study's quantitative findings and recommendations. Think Box 7.1!
31	**BEFORE AND AFTER** *Part 1 (before):* Before enrolling in your current research methods course, and before you read this chapter on group research designs, how did you think social work practitioners monitored their effectiveness with their various client systems? What methods did you think they used before you read this chapter? Do you feel the methods were ethical? If so, how? If not, why not? *Part 2 (after):* After reading this chapter discuss any new group research design(s) you learned about that you did not know about before reading it. List each new design you learned about and provide a hypothetical social work **practice** situation where you could use each one of your newfound designs. **NOTE:** This exercise should help you to realize that group research designs that are used in "research studies" are the same that are used in "practice situations." In short, you can use this chapter to help you employ group research designs in your day-to-day practice activities for all of your client systems.
32	**MOVING AHEAD BY LOOKING BACK** At this point in your research methods course, how comfortable are you with discussing the place of research in social work with your field instructor, with your practice instructor, with your research instructor, with your supervisor at work, with the director of your social work program, or with your classmates? Discuss in detail.

PART V

Collecting Data

CHAPTER 14: Collecting Quantitative Data **498**

CHAPTER 15: Collecting Qualitative Data **528**

CHAPTER 16: Selecting a Data-Collection Method **554**

14

CHAPTER

2015 EPAS COMPETENCIES

COMPETENCY 1: Demonstrate Ethical and Professional Behavior

You will learn that in order to be a successful evidence-based practitioner you have an ethical obligation to integrate three research roles into your daily practice activities as discussed in Chapter 1: (1) research consumer, (2) research partner—either as a co-researcher or research participant, and (3) creator and disseminator of research (or knowledge).

This entire chapter pertains to these three professional research-related roles when it comes to knowing the advantages and disadvantages of the quantitative data gathering methods that social work researchers and practitioners can use.

COMPETENCY 4: Engage in Practice-Informed Research and Research-Informed Practice

Competency 4 also pertains to the entire chapter because you have to:

1. Evaluate the appropriateness of the quantitative data collection method(s) and data source(s) utilized in a research study (**research consumer**—research-informed practice);

2. Participate in a research study—either as a co-researcher or research participant (**research partner**—practice-informed research). See 1 above and 3 below; and

3. Know how to select the most appropriate quantitative data collection method(s) and data source(s) when you actually do a research study (**creator and disseminator of research**—practice-informed research).

You also need to utilize evidence-based practice recommendations whenever possible; that is, you need to integrate (1) the best available research-based evidence with (2) your clinical expertise and (3) your client's values.

All of the above implies you'll need to know how to assess the strengths and limitations of the quantitative data collection method(s) used in a research study that produced its research-based evidence. In short, you need to ask and then answer a simple question: How seriously should I take the findings of any specific quantitative research study given the overall suitability of the quantitative data collection method(s) and data source(s) the study utilized?

COMPETENCY 9: Evaluate Practice with Individuals, Families, Groups, Organizations, and Communities

See Competencies 1 and 4.

Collecting Quantitative Data

CHAPTER 1   **Step 1.** Understanding the Research Process

CHAPTER 2   **Step 2.** Developing Research Questions

CHAPTER 3   **Step 3.** Reviewing the Literature

CHAPTERS 4 & 5   **Step 4.** Being Aware of Ethical and Cultural Issues

CHAPTERS 6–8   **Step 5.** Selecting a Research Approach

CHAPTERS 9 & 10   **Step 6.** Specifying How Variables Are Measured

CHAPTER 11   **Step 7.** Selecting a Sample

CHAPTERS 12 & 13   **Step 8.** Selecting a Research Design

CHAPTERS 14–16   **Step 9.** Selecting a Data-Collection Method

CHAPTERS 17 & 18   **Step 10.** Analyzing the Data

CHAPTERS 19 & 20   **Step 11.** Writing the Research Report

DATA COLLECTION IS THE VERY HEARTBEAT of all research studies—positivistic or interpretive alike. Our goal is to collect good data—qualitative data (i.e., words) for interpretive studies and quantitative data (i.e., numbers) for positivistic studies—with a steady rhythm and in a systematic manner. When data collection becomes erratic or stops prematurely, all research studies are in grave danger.

With that in mind, this chapter briefly presents a variety of data collection methods that can produce data for quantitative research studies. Likewise, the next chapter presents various data collection options that can be used with qualitative studies.

DATA COLLECTION METHODS AND SOURCES

THERE IS A CRITICAL DISTINCTION BETWEEN a data collection method and a data source. This distinction must be clearly understood before we collect any data whatsoever. A *data collection method* consists of a detailed plan of procedures that aims to gather data for a specific purpose—that is, to answer a research question or to test a hypothesis.

Any data collection method can tap into a variety of *data sources*. The primary source of data in most social work research studies is people. Rarely do we use machines (e.g., biofeedback) to monitor change in people's attitudes, knowledge, or behaviors. Rather, we tend to collect data about people from the people themselves.

Data collected directly from people can be firsthand or secondhand data. Firsthand data are obtained from people who are closest to the problem we are studying. Single mothers participating in a parent support group, for example, can easily provide firsthand data to describe their own stresses as single mothers.

Secondhand data may come from people who are indirectly connected to the primary problem (i.e., stress of single mothers) we are studying. A parent support group facilitator, for example, can record secondhand observations of "stress" behaviors displayed by parents in the parent support group. The facilitator can also collect data from family members. Grandparents, for example, can provide data that reflect their perceptions of how "stressed out" their granddaughters may be (Unrau, 2011).

Regardless of the data collection method or the data source, *all* data are eventually collected, analyzed, and interpreted as part of the research process. We will discuss shortly the basic data collection methods that commonly produce quantitative data for positivistic studies. Before we do this, however, we need to understand the various types of data.

> Any data collection method can tap into a variety of data sources.

TYPES OF DATA

WHAT EXACTLY ARE DATA? They are recorded units of information that are used as the basis for reasoning, calculation, and discussion (a single unit of information is called a *datum*). We can collect *original data* and/or *existing data*. The distinction between the two is a simple one. We collect original data (for the first time) during the course of our study to fulfill a specific purpose: to answer our research question or test our hypothesis. Unlike original data, we can use existing data that have been previously collected and stored, either manually or in a computer, before our study was even fully conceptualized.

We can also distinguish between types of data by the research approach used. In a positivistic study, for example, we analyze *numerical data* using mathematical computations and calculations (Chapter 17). On the other hand, an interpretive study typically analyzes words or *text data* (Chapter 18).

A single research study can easily incorporate both quantitative and qualitative types of data.

We analyze text data by reading and re-reading; our task is to look for common and differentiating characteristics and themes within the words. A single research study can easily incorporate both quantitative and qualitative types of data. In fact, interpretive and positivistic data collection methods can produce complimentary data.

As you know, quantitative data are used in research studies that utilize the positivistic research approach. The previous chapters discussed how this approach aims to reduce research topics into concepts and clearly defined variables. One of the major steps in a positivistic study is "focusing the question," which requires that we develop operational definitions for all the variables in our study. Let's revisit our two-variable research question that has been used throughout this book:

Research question:

Do people who come from ethnic minority backgrounds have difficulty in accessing social services?

As we know, a positivistic research study requires that we operationally define "ethnicity" and "difficulty in accessing social services" in such a way that we can measure each variable. We could easily measure both of our study's variables using two categories each:

Variable 1: Ethnicity

What is your ethnicity? *(Circle one category below.)*

1. Ethnic Minority
2. Ethnic Majority

Variable 2: Accessing services

Did you have difficulty in accessing any form of social services over the last 12-month period? (*Circle one category below.*)

1. Yes

2. No

In Chapter 6, however, we learned that our two variables (i.e., ethnicity and difficulty in accessing social services) could be operationally defined in a variety of ways. Let's consider the two-variable research question for the various data collection methods that are most often associated with producing quantitative data:

1. Survey questionnaires
2. Structured observations
3. Secondary data
4. Existing statistics

SURVEY QUESTIONNAIRES

SURVEY RESEARCH OR SURVEYS in themselves are a method for researching social problems. The aim of a survey is to collect data from a population, or a sample of research participants, in order to describe them as a group. One form that a survey can take is a questionnaire, which is a carefully selected set of questions that relate to the variables in our research question.

When data are collected using survey questionnaires, we get our research participants' perceptions about the variable being measured. Think about a survey questionnaire that you have filled out recently—a marketing survey, a consumer satisfaction questionnaire, or a teaching evaluation of your instructor. Your answers reflected your perceptions and were probably different from the perceptions of others who answered the same survey.

> The aim of a survey is to collect data from a population, or a sample of research participants, in order to describe them as a group.

A survey questionnaire is one data collection method that we can use to collect data in order to answer our two-variable research question. It would have to include items that measure our two variables—ethnicity and difficulty in accessing social services. We would ask clients within our study to "self-report" what they perceive their ethnicity to be and whether they have experienced difficulty in accessing social services over the last 12-month period.

There are two basic types of survey questionnaires. Nonstandardized survey questionnaires are one type. The two questions we posed are a very basic example of a nonstandardized survey questionnaire. The two-question survey is nonstandardized because the items have not been tested for reliability or validity.

There are two basic types of survey questionnaires: nonstandardized, and standardized.

We have no way of knowing whether our research participants will respond to our two questions in a uniform way. At best, we can comment on our survey questionnaire's face validity; that is, do its items "look" like they are measuring the variables we are interested in? Nonstandardized questionnaires are often developed when standardized questionnaires are not available or suited to our specific research question.

As you know from Chapter 10, most standardized survey questionnaires are scientifically constructed to measure one specific variable. Let's say we have searched the library and computer databases for a standardized survey questionnaire that measures our dependent variable, difficulty in accessing social services.

Suppose the closest standardized questionnaire we find is the *Reid-Gundlach Social Service Satisfaction Scale (R-GSSSS)*, which contains 34-items and measures clients' satisfaction with social services they have received (see Figure 10.1 on page 350). Clients would read each item and rate how much they agree with each item. A 7-point scale is used:

1. None of the time
2. Very rarely
3. A little of the time
4. Some of the time
5. A good part of the time
6. Most of the time
7. All of the time

The *R-GSSSS* specifically measures satisfaction with social services, a concept that closely relates to our access variable but is not an exact measure of it. In other words, satisfaction with social services is not the same as difficulty in accessing social services, but it could be used as a proxy measure to answer our research question.

Because it is a proxy measure, we would be making a humongous leap to say that the clients who are most dissatisfied with the social services are the same clients that will have the most difficulty in accessing new social services. This is a very huge leap, to say the least.

How we proceed in collecting survey questionnaire data varies depending upon whether we collect them via the mail, telephone interviews, or face-to-face interviews. When a questionnaire is sent through the mail, our research participants must also be provided with sufficient instructions to self-administer the questionnaire. This means that they must have all the necessary instructions to successfully complete the survey questionnaire alone.

When telephone or face-to-face interviews are used, the interviewer is available to assist the research participant with any difficulties in completing the questionnaire. Regardless of how our questionnaires are administered, there are some basic procedures that we can use to increase the likelihood of obtaining accurate and complete data.

ESTABLISHING DATA COLLECTION PROCEDURES

THERE ARE BASIC PROCEDURES that must be considered before any survey questionnaire is administered to potential research participants. First, it's essential that straightforward and simple instructions accompany the questionnaire. Our objective is to have each research participant complete the questionnaire in exactly the same way, which means they must have the same understanding of each question.

Suppose for a moment that we ask one of our two questions posed earlier: "Did you have difficulty in accessing any form of social services over the last 12-month period?" It's clear that we want our research participants to answer our question with respect to the past 12 months and not any other time frame.

A second procedure that must be established is how informed consent will be obtained from the research participants (see Chapter 4). This is a task that can be accomplished by writing a cover letter explaining the purpose of

the research study and questionnaire, who the researchers are, that participation is entirely voluntary, how the data will be used, and the steps taken to
guarantee confidentiality. A cover letter is usually sent out with mailed questionnaires, read aloud over the telephone, or presented in face-to-face interviews.

To decrease the likelihood of any misunderstanding, elementary language should be used in the cover letter (the same as in the questionnaire).
It may even be possible to have the cover letter (and questionnaire) translated into our research participants' native language(s).

In our study, we are asking about ethnicity, which suggests that English
could be a second language for many of our research participants. Depending on the geographic area in which we are conducting our study, we may
wish to translate our cover letter and questionnaire into the dominant language of the geographic area.

If our survey questionnaire is to be administered over the telephone or
face-to-face by an interviewer, training of interviewers will be a necessary
third procedure. In the same way that we want research participants to have
the same understanding of the questionnaire's items, we want interviewers
to handle potential queries in a consistent manner. Interviewers must be
trained to ask the questions within our questionnaire in such a way that they
do not influence the research participants' answers.

Basically, interviewers should refrain from discussing individual questions with research participants, from varying their tone of voice when asking the questions, and from commenting on the research participants' answers. The interviewer's task is to keep the research participant focused on
answering the questions at hand, to answer questions for clarification, and
to record the answers.

To save on time and resources, it may be possible to administer survey
questionnaires in a group format. This usually means that we meet a group
of research participants in their own environment. Suppose, for example, we
were specifically interested in the accessibility of social services among Native people. We would need to travel to the reserve, then administer our
questionnaire at a central location on the reserve that's convenient for our
research participants.

RECORDING SURVEY DATA

THE DATA WE GATHER FROM QUESTIONNAIRES usually are in numerical form. Our question that asks whether clients had difficulty accessing any form of social services over the last 12 months will produce a number of "yes" responses and a number of "no" responses.

We can add up the total sum of responses for each category and calculate the number of clients who had difficulty accessing social services broken down by ethnicity (i.e., ethnic minority and ethnic majority).

ESTABLISHING RELIABILITY AND VALIDITY

RELIABILITY AND VALIDITY are critical to determining the credibility of any data collection instrument. Standardized questionnaires have associated with them values of both. Reliability values tell us how confident we can be in using our questionnaire over two or more time periods, across different people, and across different places. Validity values give us information about how good our questionnaire is at measuring what it purports to measure. The validity value for the *R-GSSSS*, for example, is reasonably high at 0.95 (the highest possible value is 1.0).

Reports on the *R-GSSSS* also note that the standardized questionnaire is useful for measuring differences in race. Specifically, African Americans and Mexican Americans are reported to predictably have lower scores. We can also assess the face validity of the *R-GSSSS* by simply looking at the 34 items contained within it (see Figure 10.1 on page 350).

To save on time and resources, it may be possible to administer survey questionnaires in a group format.

A quick glance tells us that the items reflect the "idea" of client satisfaction with social services. When using unstandardized questionnaires, we do not have the luxury of reporting reliability or validity. In this instance, we must ensure that our questionnaire, at the very least, has face validity.

ADVANTAGES AND DISADVANTAGES

OVERALL, THE MAJOR ADVANTAGE of survey questionnaires is that they offer a relatively inexpensive way to collect new data. In addition, they can easily reach a large number of people, provide specific data, collect data efficiently, and be input into a computer easily. An additional advantage of standardized questionnaires is that the data they generate can be compared with the data collected in other studies that used the same standardized questionnaire.

The overall major disadvantages of survey questionnaires include: (1) research participants must be literate, (2) surveys usually get a low response rate, (3) the research participants must have a mailing address or telephone to be reached, (4) in-depth or open-end responses are missed, and (5) simple questions are utilized to provide answers to complex research questions.

STRUCTURED OBSERVATIONS

"STRUCTURED OBSERVATION" is a self-explanatory data collection method. A trained observer records the interaction of others in a specific place over an agreed upon amount of time using specific procedures and measurements. Structured observation aims to observe the natural interactions between and among people that occur either in natural or in artificial settings (Polster & Collins, 2018).

If we want to observe how people of different ethnic backgrounds interact with their social worker, for example, we could set up structured observations at the social worker's offices (natural environment), or we could set up interviews to be observed from behind one-way mirrors (artificial setting).

The data collected from structured observation reflect the trained observers' perceptions of the interactions. That is, the observers do not interact with the people they are observing. They simply watch the interactions and record the presence or absence of certain behaviors.

Observers could, for example, count the number of times clients (comparing ethnic minority and ethnic majority groups) mention a barrier or obstacle to accessing a social service, or monitor whether social workers engage in behaviors that specifically assist clients in accessing new services. These observations, of course, would take place during "normal" meetings between social workers and their clients.

Structured observation requires that the variables being measured are specifically defined. We must "micro-define" our variables. In our two-variable research question, for example, we have already operationally defined "ethnic" as having two categories: ethnic minority and non–ethnic minority. In measuring our difficulty in accessing social services variable, we could measure it by the number of social services referred by a social worker in a 60-minute interview.

We could then compare the results of our difficulty in accessing social services variable across our two ethnicity groups. Would we find that social workers are more or less likely to offer social service referrals to clients who are from an ethnic minority or a non–ethnic minority group?

There are three general types of recording that can be used with structured observation. Observations can be measured for frequency (e.g., count a behavior every time it occurs), for duration (e.g., how long does the behavior last each time it occurs), and for magnitude (e.g., the varying intensity of a behavior such as mild, moderate, or severe).

Whether we use frequency, duration, or magnitude (or some combination), depends on the picture we want to develop to answer our research question. Do we want to describe difficulty in accessing social services by how many times services are offered to clients (frequency), by how much time social workers spend explaining how services can be accessed (duration), or by the degree of sincerity that the workers display when offering service referrals (magnitude)?

When we record the presence or absence of behaviors during an interaction between and among people, our observations can be structured in such a way as to help the observers record the behaviors accurately. Suppose for a moment, social worker interviews with clients take an average of one hour. We could set recording intervals at every minute so that we have 60 recording intervals in one hour.

> The data collected from structured observation reflect the trained observers' perceptions of the interactions.

The observers would sit with a stopwatch and record whether the social workers offered any social services to their clients in the first minute, the second minute, and each minute thereafter until the interviews end. Interval recording assists the observers in making continuous observations throughout the interaction. Spot-check recording is another way to schedule observation recordings.

Unlike interval recording which is continuous, spot-check recording is a way to record intermittent observations. It may be possible to observe and record the presence or absence of a behavior for one minute every five minutes, for example.

ESTABLISHING DATA COLLECTION PROCEDURES

THE PROCEDURES ESTABLISHED FOR STRUCTURED OBSERVATION are firmly decided upon before actual observations take place. That is, the observers are specifically trained to watch for the presence or absence of specific behaviors and the recording method is set. The types of data to be recorded are selected (i.e., frequency, duration, or magnitude), and the nature of the recording is decided (i.e., continuous, interval, or spot-check).

Observers and not the persons engaging in the behaviors generally record data. As such, it's essential that observers be trained to "see" behaviors in a reliable way. Imagine that you are one of the observers and your main task is to record magnitude ratings of the degree of sincerity that social workers display when they offer social service referrals. You must decide whether the social workers' gestures are mildly, moderately, or extremely sincere. How would you know to rate a behavior that you observed as "mildly sincere" versus "moderately sincere"?

Training of observers requires that all variables be unequivocally clear.

Training of observers requires that all variables be unequivocally clear. Thus, observers are usually trained using mock trials. They are selected for their ability to collect data according to the rules of the research study, not for their unique views or creative observations.

In a nutshell, the observers are an instrument for data collection, and an effort is made to calibrate all instruments of the research study in the same way. To allow for several different observers to view the same situation, we may choose to videotape interactions.

A decision must also be made about who will be the best observers. Should only professionally trained outside observers be selected? This would include people who are completely unfamiliar with the context of the study but are skilled observers. How about indigenous observers—people who are familiar with the nature of the interaction to be observed?

In our example, indigenous observers could include people such as other social workers, social work supervisors, other clients, or staff from other social service offices. Who we choose to observe may depend upon availability, expense, or how important we feel it is for the observers to be familiar or unfamiliar with the situation being observed. Measurement that reflects cultural variables, for example, may require indigenous observers.

RECORDING STRUCTURED OBSERVATIONAL DATA

THE RECORDING INSTRUMENT FOR STRUCTURED OBSERVATION generally takes the form of a grid or checklist. The behaviors being observed and the method of recording are identified. The simplest recording form to construct is one that records frequency. The recording form would simply identify the period of observation and the number of times a specific behavior occurs:

Observation Period	Frequency
3:00 P.M. to 4:00 P.M.	✓✓✓✓

For duration recording, it's necessary to add the duration in minutes at each occurrence of the behavior:

Observation Period	Frequency and (Duration, in minutes)
3:00 P.M. to 4:00 P.M.	1 (5), 2 (11), 3 (15)

For magnitude recording, we record the time of occurrence and give a corresponding rating for the behavior. To simplify recording, the magnitude ratings are generally coded by assigning a number to each category. For example:

1 = Mildly sincere

2 = Moderately sincere

3 = Extremely sincere

Observation Time	Magnitude
3:17 P.M.	1
3:25 P.M.	1
3:29 P.M.	2

ESTABLISHING RELIABILITY AND VALIDITY

AS WE KNOW FROM CHAPTERS 9 AND 10, validity refers to whether we are measuring what we think we are measuring. In other words, are we really measuring or observing "difficulty in accessing social services"? Validity, in this instance, should make us think about whether our criteria for observation (i.e., how we operationalized our variable) are reasonable representations of the variable.

Reliability, on the other hand, can be assessed in more concrete ways. Once we have established an operational definition for each variable and the procedures for observation and recording, we can test their reliability. A simple method for determining reliability is to use two independent raters who observe the exact same situation.

How well do their recordings match? Do the two observers produce the same frequencies? The same duration periods? The same magnitude ratings? Do they agree 100 percent or only 50 percent?

One hundred percent agreement suggests that the measure is a reliable one, compared to 50 percent, which suggests we should go back to the drawing board to come up with more precise operational definitions for both variables or more exact recording procedures.

ADVANTAGES AND DISADVANTAGES

STRUCTURED OBSERVATION helps us to collect precise, valid, and reliable data within complex interactions. We are able to tease out important behaviors that are direct (or indirect) measures of the variable we are interested in. The data produced are objective observations of behaviors and thus are not tainted by our individual self-perceptions.

Think back to the survey questionnaire method of data collection that we discussed at the beginning of this chapter. The data collected using a survey questionnaire reflect the research participants' own perceptions. Structured observation, on the other hand, gives a factual account of what actually took place. It can explain one component of a social interaction with objectivity, precision, and detail.

The major disadvantage of structured observation is the time and resources needed to train skilled observers. Think about the amount of time it would take, for example, to get you and, say, two other observers to agree on what constitutes "mild," "moderate," or "extremely" sincere behavior of social workers.

Another disadvantage of structured observation is that it's a microscopic approach to dealing with complex social interactions. By focusing on one or two specific details (variables) of an interaction, we may miss out on many other important aspects of the interactions.

SECONDARY DATA

WHEN EXISTING DATA ARE USED to answer a newly developed research question (or to test a hypothesis), the data are considered secondary. In other words, the data are being used for some purpose other than the original one for which they were collected. Unlike survey questionnaires or structured observation mentioned previously, collecting secondary data is unobtrusive.

Because data already exist, it's not necessary to ask people questions (as in survey questionnaires) or to be observed (as in structured observations). Furthermore, secondary data can exist in numerical form (quantitative) or text form (qualitative). Our discussion in this section focuses on existing quantitative data.

> Unlike survey questionnaires or structured observation collecting secondary data is unobtrusive.

Let's go back to our two-variable research question that asks about the relationship between clients' ethnicity and whether they have difficulty in accessing social services. So far, we have discussed data collection methods within a social service context and have focused on the interaction between social workers and their clients. Within a social service program there are many client records that could provide meaningful data to answer our simple research question. It's likely, for example, that client intake forms collect data about clients' ethnicity.

We can be assured that an ethnicity question on an existing client intake form was not thought up to answer our specific research question. Rather, the program likely had other reasons for collecting the data, such as needing to report the percentage of clients who come from an ethnic minority that they have seen in a given fiscal period.

The social service program may also have records that contain data that we could use for our difficulty in accessing social services variable. Social workers, for example, may be required to record each service referral made for each client. By reading each client file, we would be able to count the number of service referrals made for each client.

Secondary data can also be accessed from existing data bases around the world. Census databases are a common example. With the advances of computer technology, databases are becoming easier to access. The Inter-University Consortium for Political and Social Research (ICPSR) is the largest data archive in the world; it holds more than 17,000 files of data from more than 130 countries.

We could use the ICPSR data, for example, to compare the accessibility of social services for clients from different ethnic groups across various countries. Of course, we could only do this if meaningful data already exist within the database to answer our research question.

ESTABLISHING DATA COLLECTION PROCEDURES

GIVEN THAT SECONDARY DATA ALREADY EXIST, there is no need to collect them. Rather, our focus shifts to evaluating the dataset's worth with respect to answering our research question. The presence of datasets has an important influence on how we formulate our research questions or test our hypotheses. When original data are collected, we design our research study and tailor our data collection procedures to gather the "best" data possible. When data exist, we can only develop a research question that is as good as the data that we have available.

Because secondary data influence how we formulate our research questions, we must firmly settle on a research question before analyzing them. Datasets can have a vertigo effect, leaving us feeling dizzy about the relationships between and among variables contained within them. It may be that we begin with a general research question, such as our two-variable question about ethnicity and difficulty in accessing social services, and move to a more specific hypothesis.

Suppose our existing dataset contained data about client ethnicity (e.g., Asians, African Americans, Caucasians, Native Americans) and data about difficulty in accessing social services (e.g., yes or no). We could return to the literature for studies that might help us formulate a directional (one-tailed) hypothesis.

> **Secondary data can also be accessed from existing databases around the world.**

A directional hypothesis would suggest that one or more of these four ethnic groups would have more (or less) difficulty accessing social services than the remaining groups. If no such literature exists, however, we would pose a nondirectional (two-tailed) hypothesis, which indicates that we have no basis to suggest that one of the four ethnic groups would have more or less difficulty accessing social services than any of the others.

Another influence of an existing dataset is on how we operationally define the variables in our study. Simply put, our study's variables will have already been operationally defined for us. The definition used to collect the original data will be the definition we use in our study as well.

It's possible to create a new variable by recasting one or more of the original variables in an existing dataset. For instance, suppose we are interested to know whether our clients are parents. Existing program records, however, only list the number of children in each family.

We could recast these data by categorizing those clients who have one or more children versus those who have no children, thus creating a two-category variable. Clients with one or more children would be categorized as "parents" versus clients without any children who would be classified as "not parents."

One final consideration for using existing secondary data is that of informed consent. Just because data exist does not mean that we have free rein to use them in future studies. It may be that clients have provided information on intake forms because they believed it was necessary to do so in order to receive services (see Chapter 4 on ethics).

RECORDING SECONDARY DATA

RECORDING SECONDARY DATABASES are a simple matter because data have already been collected, organized, and checked for accuracy. Our task is to work with them and determine the best possible procedures for data analyses. One feature of existing databases is that they generally include a large number of cases and variables. Thus, some advanced knowledge of statistical software packages is required to extract the variables of interest and conduct the data analyses.

ESTABLISHING RELIABILITY AND VALIDITY

ONCE OUR RESEARCH QUESTION IS FORMULATED and our variables have been operationally defined, it's important to establish the dataset's credibility. We must remember that all datasets are not created equal, particularly with respect to their validity and reliability. Most importantly, we want to check out the data source. If ethnic status is recorded on a social service program's client intake form, for example, we would want to know how the data were obtained.

All datasets are not created equal, particularly with respect to their validity and reliability.

The data would be considered unreliable and even invalid if the workers simply looked at their clients and checked one of several ethnicity categories. A more reliable and valid procedure would be if they asked their clients what ethnic category they come from and at the same time showed them the categories to be selected. Datasets that are accompanied by clear data collection procedures are generally more valid and reliable than those datasets that are not.

ADVANTAGES AND DISADVANTAGES

THE ADVANCEMENT OF COMPUTER TECHNOLOGY increases the likelihood that secondary data will be used more often in future social work research studies. It's a reasonably inexpensive way to gather and analyze data to answer a research question or to test a hypothesis.

Given that datasets are developing around the world, researchers can fairly easily compare datasets from different countries and across different time spans. Datasets are at our fingertips, provided that we have a research question or hypothesis to match. One major disadvantage of using an existing dataset is that our research question is limited by the possibilities of the dataset. We must make the best use of the data available to us, with the understanding that the "best" may not be good enough to answer our research question or test our hypothesis.

EXISTING STATISTICS

EXISTING STATISTICS ARE A SPECIAL FORM of secondary data. They *exist* in a variety of places. A unique feature of existing statistics is that they exist only in numerical form. We might have statistics, for example, that report 20 percent of clients served by social services were Native, 30 percent were Hispanic, and 50 percent were Caucasian.

The following provides an example of how Fran, a clinical director of a private social service agency, used existing statistics for her research question. One difference between existing statistics and secondary data is that statistics summarize data in aggregate form. The below example is from Jackie Sieppert, Steve McMurtry, & Bob McClelland (2011).

EXAMPLE OF USING EXISTING STATISTICS

FRAN IS CLINICAL DIRECTOR of a private, nonprofit agency that provides foster care, group-home care, and residential treatment for children in a small city in Arizona. She has noticed that there is a higher number of ethnic minority children in her agency's caseload than would be expected based on the proportion of ethnic minority children in the general population. She decides to do a study of this issue using existing statistics already gathered by various sources as her data collection method.

Fran first talks with the information specialist at the local library, asking for help to conduct a computer search through the library's existing databases. The search reveals a series of reports, titled Characteristics of Children in Substitute and Adoptive Care, that were sponsored by the American Public Welfare Association and that provide several years of data reported by states on their populations of children in various kinds of foster and adoptive care.

She also locates an annual publication produced by the Children's Defense Fund, and this provides a variety of background data on the well-being of children in the United States. Next, Fran checks in the library's government documents section. She locates recent census data on the distribution of persons under the age of 18 across different ethnic groups in her county.

Fran now quickly turns to state-level resources, where a quick check of government listings in the telephone book reveals two agencies that appear likely to have relevant data. One is the Foster Care Review Board, which is composed of citizen volunteers who assist juvenile courts by reviewing the progress of children in foster care statewide.

A call to the Board reveals that they produce an annual report that lists a variety of statistics. These include the number of foster children in the state, where they are placed, and how long they have been in care.

Fran also learns that the Board's annual reports from previous years contain similar data, thus a visit to the Board's office provides her with the historical data needed to identify trends in the statistics she is using. Finally, she discovers that two years earlier the Board produced a special issue of its annual report that was dedicated to the topic of ethnic minority children in foster care, and this issue offers additional statistics not normally recorded in most annual reports.

Another state agency is the Administration for Children, Youth, and Families, a division of the state's social services department. A call to the division connects her with a staff member who informs her that a special review of foster children was conducted by the agency only a few months before. Data from this review confirm her perception that minority children are overrepresented in foster care in the state, and it provides a range of other data that may be helpful in determining the causes of this problem.

From these sources Fran now has the data she needs to paint a detailed picture of minority foster children at the national and state levels. She also has the ability to examine the problem in terms of both point-in-time circumstances and longitudinal trends, and the latter suggest that the problem of overrepresentation has grown worse. There is also evidence to indicate that the problem is more severe in her state than nationally.

Finally, corollary data on related variables, together with the more inten-sive work done in the special studies by the Foster Care Review Board and the Administration for Children, Youth, and Families, gives Fran a basis for beginning to understand the causes of the problem and the type of research study that must be done to investigate solutions.

In the same way that secondary data are used for a purpose other than what was originally stated, so it is for existing statistics. With existing statis-tics, however, we are one step further removed from the original data. A sta-tistic, for example, can be computed from 3,000 cases or from 30 cases—each produces only a single value.

There are two main types of statistics for us to be concerned with. The first is descriptive statistics, which simply describe the sample or population being studied. Statistics used for descriptive purposes include things like percentages, percentiles, means, standard deviations, medians, ranges, and so on.

The second type of statistics—inferential statistics—includes test statis-tics such as chi-square, *t*-test, analysis of variance (ANOVA), regression, and correlation. Do not panic; we will give an introductory discussion on statis-tics in Chapter 17. For now, we need only to know that descriptive statistics tell us about the characteristics of a sample or a population. Inferential sta-tistics tell us about the likelihood of a relationship between and among vari-ables within a population.

When using existing statistics as our "data" we proceed in much the same way as when we use secondary data. Both are unobtrusive methods of data collection in that no persons will be asked to provide data about them-selves—the data already exist and have been used to calculate a statistic. Therefore, we must establish their credibility.

ESTABLISHING DATA COLLECTION PROCEDURES

USING EXISTING STATISTICS in a research study influences our research ques-tion (and hypotheses) to a greater degree than when using secondary data. If existing statistics are to assist in developing a research question, then ad-vanced knowledge of statistics is required. We would need to understand the purpose of each statistic, the assumptions behind it, and how it was calculat-ed.

We would not want to gather existing statistics without also collecting information about how the original data (used to calculate our existing statistics) were collected and analyzed. This information is important to assessing the credibility of the statistics that we would use for our research study.

RECORDING EXISTING STATISTICAL DATA

RECORDING EXISTING STATISTICS IS DIFFERENT from recording secondary data. In the case of secondary data, the data are already in a recorded form. When working with existing statistics, it's usually necessary to extract the statistics from their original sources and reconfigure them in a way that permits us to conduct an appropriate data analysis. It may be, for example, that we need to extract percentage figures from a paragraph within a published article, or mean and standard deviation scores from an already existing table in a research report.

ESTABLISHING RELIABILITY AND VALIDITY

CHECKING THE RELIABILITY AND VALIDITY of existing statistics requires us to look for a few basic things. First, we want to be sure that the studies or reports from which we are extracting the statistics use comparable conceptual and operational definitions. If we are to compare statistical results about the accessibility of social services to clients who are from different ethnic groups across two different studies, we want to be certain that both studies had reasonably similar operational definitions for the two variables that we are interested in.

We can also examine previously conducted studies for their own assessment of their validity and reliability. Were sound procedures used to collect the original data? Were the original data analyzed in an appropriate way? What were the limitations of each study? By asking these types of questions about previous studies, we can get clues as to the credibility of the statistics that we are about to use in our own research study.

ADVANTAGES AND DISADVANTAGES

THE ADVANTAGES OF USING EXISTING STATISTICS are many. Given that existing data are used, via the form of statistics, it's a relatively inexpensive approach and is unobtrusive. By using existing statistics, we can push the knowledge envelope of what we already know and ask more complex research questions. The use of existing statistics also provides us with the opportunity to compare the results of several research studies in an empirical way.

One disadvantage of using existing statistics is that we are not provided with data for individual cases. We can only answer research questions and test hypotheses about groups of people. Because data are already presented in a summary (i.e., statistical) form, it's difficult to assess how the data were collected and analyzed. Because the data have been handled by different individuals, there is an increased chance that human error has occurred somewhere along the way.

SUMMARY

IN THIS CHAPTER we have described different methods for collecting quantitative data. We have demonstrated that one research question can be answered using any data collection method. Different data collection methods produce different types of data. Data collection methods that are more commonly associated with quantitative or numerical data are survey questionnaires, structured observation, secondary data, and existing statistics.

In the next chapter, we will look at the various data collection methods that can be used to collect qualitative data.

	Study Questions for Chapter 14
	Essay — Discussion
1	In your own words discuss the differences between a data collection method and a data source. Provide a single social work example throughout your discussion to illustrate your main points.
2	What are survey questionnaires? Discuss the advantages and disadvantages of using them as a data collection method. Provide social work examples throughout your discussion to illustrate your main points.
3	What are structured observations? Discuss the advantages and disadvantages of using them as a data collection method. Provide social work examples throughout your discussion to illustrate your main points.
4	What are secondary data? Discuss the advantages and disadvantages of using them as a data collection method. Provide social work examples throughout your discussion to illustrate your main points.
5	What are existing statistics? Discuss the advantages and disadvantages of using them as a data collection method. Provide social work examples throughout your discussion to illustrate your main points.
	Critical Thinking — Application — Integration
6	**RESEARCH VS. PRACTICE** Pretend for the moment you're employed as a social worker in your university's student counseling center. A student comes into your office complaining about his depression. 1. Using this chapter as a guide, describe in detail how you could use some of the quantitative data gathering techniques discussed in this chapter to assess the degree of his depression. **NOTE:** This exercise should help you to realize that the quantitative data collection methods social work researchers use are the same as those practitioners use, and vice versa (see Figure 1.5 on page 37). In short, you can

use Chapters 14–16 to help you gather data for your day-to-day practice activities for all of your client systems.

QUANTITATIVE DATA COLLECTION AND THE RESEARCHER

Scenario 1: Make an argument that to be a competent social work researcher **you must know** the advantages and disadvantages of the various quantitative data collection methods. Provide clear and explicit **research-related** social work examples to illustrate your main points.

Scenario 2: Make an argument that **you do not have to know** the advantages and disadvantages of the various quantitative data collection methods to be a competent social work researcher. Provide clear and explicit **research-related** social work examples to illustrate your main points.

Time to Choose: Which one of the above two scenarios do you feel is more consistent with the place of research in social work? Why? Provide relevant social work examples to illustrate your main points.

QUANTITATIVE DATA COLLECTION AND THE PRACTITIONER

Scenario 1: Make an argument that to be an effective evidence-based social work practitioner **you must know** the advantages and disadvantages of the various quantitative data collection methods. Provide clear and explicit **practice-related** social work examples to illustrate your main points.

Scenario 2: Make an argument that **you do not have to know** the advantages and disadvantages of the various quantitative data collection methods to be an effective evidence-based practitioner. Provide clear and explicit **practice-related** social work examples to illustrate your main points.

Time to Choose: Which one of the above two scenarios do you feel is more consistent with the concept of the contemporary evidence-based social work practice process as illustrated on pages 46–51? Why? Provide relevant social work examples to illustrate your main points.

9	**TIME TO PUT ON YOUR CRITICAL THINKING HAT** **1.** Discuss the similarities and differences between your responses to Questions 7 and 8. **2.** What are your thoughts on the belief that you need to know the advantages and disadvantages of the various quantitative data collection methods whether you're a social work *practitioner* (Question 8) or a social work *researcher* (Question 7)? **NOTE:** This exercise should help you to realize that the quantitative data collection methods that social work researchers use are the same as practitioners use, and vice versa (see Figure 1.5 on page 37). In short, you can use Chapters 14–16 to help you gather data for your day-to-day practice activities for all of your client systems.
10	**YOU'RE NOW A RESEARCHER** Pretend for a moment that you want to do a quantitative research study to assess the interviewing skills of your fellow social work students. This would be an excellent time to review Chapter 6. **1.** List and then discuss the various quantitative data collection methods that you could use. **2.** What are the advantages and disadvantages of each one? Discuss fully. **3.** What data would each method produce for your data source(s)? Discuss fully.
11	**MOVING AHEAD BY LOOKING BACK** At this point in your research methods course, how comfortable are you with discussing the place of research in social work with your field instructor, with your practice instructor, with your research instructor, with your supervisor at work, with the director of your social work program, or with your classmates? Discuss in detail.

12	**YOU'RE NOW A DATA SOURCE** Pretend that your school of social work wants to do a quantitative research study on determining the competency levels of its graduating students—which includes you, a graduating student. 1. List and then discuss the various quantitative data collection methods that your school could use. 2. From a data-source's perspective (you), what quantitative data collection method(s) do you think would be best for your school to use with you. Why? 3. What data could you provide the school that would be reliable and valid in relation to its research question? Justify your response and use examples to illustrate your main points. 4. What qualitative data collection methods (next chapter) could your school use to supplement its quantitative findings and recommendations (Chapter 14)? Think Box 7.1 on pages 268–269.
13	**APPLICATION OF QUANTITATIVE DATA COLLECTION METHODS** Locate a published quantitative social work-related journal article of your choice. Be sure the author collected quantitative data and the article is reporting the results from a quantitative research study. We suggest you locate a quantitatively oriented research study in Bruce Thyer's journal *Research on Social Work Practice* (Sage Publications). Hands down, this is the best journal to find good quantitatively oriented social work research studies. 1. What was the study's data source(s)? 2. What quantitative data collection method(s) was used for each data source(s)? 3. With your knowledge of the various quantitative data collection methods that research studies can use, thoroughly discuss how you will use the material contained within this chapter when you begin to evaluate the appropriateness of the research study's quantitative data collection method(s) and discuss why you believe each criterion you selected is important for your evaluation of the study's chosen method(s). 4. Would you have used a different quantitative method to collect the data to answer the study's research question? If so, what method would you have used, and why?

14	**MIXED-METHODS RESEARCH (CHAPTER 8)** Pretend for the moment that you wish to do a **qualitatively** oriented research study (Chapter 7) to determine if MSW-level social workers are "better" at interviewing their clients than BSW-level social workers. You also wish to add a quantitative component (Chapter 6) to your study. 1. Using what you have learned so far in your research methods course, delineate how you would do your mixed-methods research study, highlighting the specific quantitative data collection method(s) you have chosen. 2. State specifically what the findings of your quantitative component could add to the study's qualitative findings and practice recommendations.
15	**QUANTITATIVE DATA COLLECTION AND YOUR PROFESSIONAL DEVELOPMENT** 1. Review the three social work research-related roles you can take when you graduate—CSWE Competency 1 at the beginning of this chapter on page 498. This concept was also discussed in Chapter 1 on pages 38–42. Thoroughly discuss how you feel this chapter will help you to perform one or more research-related roles when you graduate. 2. Which one of the three roles do you believe this chapter helped you with the most? Why? Discuss in detail and provide an example to illustrate your main points. 3. Review CSWE Competency 4 at the beginning of this chapter on page 498). Thoroughly discuss how you feel this chapter will help you to become a practice-informed researcher and a research-informed practitioner. Discuss in detail and provide an example to illustrate your main points. 4. Review the evidence-based practice process as illustrated on pages 46–51. Thoroughly discuss how this chapter helps you to develop the skills you'll need for implementing one or more steps of the evidence-based practice process. 5. Discuss which step(s) you feel this chapter will help you with the most. Why? Be very specific and use relevant social work examples to illustrate your main points throughout your discussion. **NOTE:** This exercise should help you to realize that you can use all kinds of quantitative data collection methods to help you become an evidence-based social work practitioner.

15

CHAPTER

COMPETENCY 1: Demonstrate Ethical and Professional Behavior

You will learn that in order to be a successful evidence-based practitioner you have an ethical obligation to integrate three research roles into your daily practice activities as discussed in Chapter 1: (1) research consumer, (2) research partner—either as a co-researcher or research participant, and (3) creator and disseminator of research (or knowledge).

This entire chapter pertains to these three professional research-related roles when it comes to knowing the advantages and disadvantages of the qualitative data gathering methods that social work researchers and practitioners can use.

COMPETENCY 4: Engage in Practice-Informed Research and Research-Informed Practice

Competency 4 also pertains to the entire chapter because you have to:

1. Evaluate the appropriateness of the qualitative data collection method(s) and data source(s) utilized in a research study (**research consumer**—research-informed practice);

2. Participate in a research study—either as a co-researcher or research participant (**research partner**—practice-informed research). See 1 above and 3 below; and

3. Know how to select the most appropriate qualitative data collection method(s) and data source(s) when you actually do a research study (**creator and disseminator of research**—practice-informed research).

You also need to utilize evidence-based practice recommendations whenever possible; that is, you need to integrate (1) the best available research-based evidence with (2) your clinical expertise and (3) your client's values.

All of the above implies you'll need to know how to assess the strengths and limitations of the qualitative data collection method that was used in a research study that produced its research-based evidence. In short, you need to ask and then answer a simple question: How seriously should I take the findings of any specific qualitative research study given the overall suitability of the qualitative data collection method(s) and data source(s) the study utilized?

COMPETENCY 9: Evaluate Practice with Individuals, Families, Groups, Organizations, and Communities
See Competencies 1 and 4.

15
CHAPTER

Collecting Qualitative Data

CHAPTER 1	**Step 1.** Understanding the Research Process
CHAPTER 2	**Step 2.** Developing Research Questions
CHAPTER 3	**Step 3.** Reviewing the Literature
CHAPTERS 4 & 5	**Step 4.** Being Aware of Ethical and Cultural Issues
CHAPTERS 6–8	**Step 5.** Selecting a Research Approach
CHAPTERS 9 & 10	**Step 6.** Specifying How Variables Are Measured
CHAPTER 11	**Step 7.** Selecting a Sample
CHAPTERS 12 & 13	**Step 8.** Selecting a Research Design
CHAPTERS 14–16	**Step 9.** Selecting a Data-Collection Method
CHAPTERS 17 & 18	**Step 10.** Analyzing the Data
CHAPTERS 19 & 20	**Step 11.** Writing the Research Report

AS WE KNOW FROM THE LAST CHAPTER, all research studies require data—regardless of whether a positivistic or interpretive approach is used. We have already discussed that quantitative data are represented numerically, and qualitative data are usually expressed using words.

A second key difference between these two types of data is that qualitative data are collected to "build" a story or understanding of a concept or variable, compared to quantitative data, which narrows in on a select few variables. A third difference worth noting is that qualitative data are generally "bulkier" than quantitative data. As we will see, a single word, a sentence, or even an entire page of text can represent qualitative data.

The exact point in time when data are collected in the research process is another difference between quantitative and qualitative data. We have stressed that quantitative data collection can *only occur* once variables have been completely operationally defined—in fact, the reliability and validity of our measurements depend on it.

Qualitative data, on the other hand, can be collected during many different steps in the research process. We may collect data near the beginning of our study to help us focus our research question and identify key variables to be explored later on in the research process. Qualitative data collected in later steps in our study can be used to check out any assumptions we may have and any new ideas that emerge (see Chapter 7).

When collecting quantitative data, the rules for data collection are tried and tested *before* collecting any data—procedures can be outlined in a checklist format, where the data collector checks off each procedure as it's completed. For qualitative data, however, explicit procedures of data collection are not necessarily known before the data collection process starts. Rather, the procedures used are documented *as they happen*. It's only after data collection is complete that a detailed description of the procedure can be articulated.

This is not to say that in qualitative data collection we can willy-nilly change our minds or that anything goes. Research is still research, which means that a systematic approach to inquiry is used. The big difference for interpretive research is that the systematic nature of data collection applies to how we record and monitor the data collection process.

Any changes in data collection (e.g., change in questions, research participants, or literature review) are based on data already collected. More will be explained about how qualitative data collection procedures are monitored in Chapter 18. For now, let's return to our research question from the preceding chapter.

Research question:
Do people who come from ethnic minority backgrounds have difficulty in accessing social services?

We have already discussed in the last chapter four different methods of collecting quantitative data to answer the above research question. Now we will turn to four data collection methods that are more commonly associated with producing qualitative data to answer the same research question:

1. Narrative interviewing
2. Participant observation
3. Secondary content data
4. Historical data

NARRATIVE INTERVIEWING

WE HAVE SEEN IN THE PREVIOUS CHAPTER how interviewing is used to collect quantitative data via survey questionnaires, in which interviewers are trained to ask questions of research participants in a uniform way and interaction between interviewers and their research participants is minimized. Interviewing for qualitative data, on the other hand, has a completely different tone (Tutty, Rothery, & Grinnell, 1996).

The aim of narrative interviewing is to have research participants tell stories in their own words. Their stories usually begin when we ask our identified research question. For example, we could begin an interview by saying, "Could you tell me about your experiences as a Native client in terms of accessing social services?"

Qualitative interviewers are not bound by strict rules and procedures. Rather, they make every effort to engage research participants in meaningful discussions. In fact, the purpose is to have research participants tell their own stories in their own ways. The direction the interviews take may deviate from the original research problem being investigated depending on what research participants choose to tell interviewers. Data collected in one research interview can be used to develop or revise further research questions in subsequent research interviews.

> The purpose of narrative interviewing is to have research participants tell their own stories in their own ways.

The narrative interview is commonly used in case study research where numerous interviews are usually conducted to learn more about a "case," which could be defined as a person, a group of people, an event, or an organization. The narrative interview is also a basic component of other research pursuits, such as feminist research and participatory action research (Gochros, 2018).

ESTABLISHING DATA COLLECTION PROCEDURES

DATA COLLECTION AND DATA ANALYSIS are intertwined in an interpretive research study. Thus, the steps we take in collecting data from a narrative interview will evolve with our study. Nevertheless, we must be clear about our starting point and the procedures that we will use to "check and balance" the decisions we make along the way. One of the aims of an interpretive research approach is to tell a story about a problem without the cobwebs of existing theories, labels, and interpretations.

As such, we may choose to limit the amount of literature we review before proceeding with data collection. The amount of literature we review is guided by the interpretive research approach we use. A grounded theory approach, for example, suggests that we review some literature at the beginning of our study in order to help frame our research question. We would then review more literature later on, taking direction from the new data that we collect.

It's necessary for us to decide when and how to approach potential research participants before data collection occurs. Think about our simple research question for a moment—Do clients who come from an ethnic minority have difficulty in accessing social services? Who would we interview first? Would we interview someone receiving multiple social services or someone not receiving any? Is there a particular ethnic group that we would want represented in our early interviews?

Remember that the data we collect in our beginning interviews will directly influence how we proceed in later interviews. It's possible for the professional literature, or our expert knowledge, to point us to a particular starting place. Regardless of where we begin, it's critical for us to document our early steps in the data collection process. The notes we take will be used later on to recall the steps we took, and more importantly, why we took them.

> The data we collect in our beginning interviews will directly influence how we proceed in later interviews.

Let's say, for example, that our interest in our research question stems from the fact that many ethnic minority people we know in our personal lives (not our professional lives) have complained about access to social services. We may choose to begin interviewing with an individual we already know.

On the other hand, we may decide after a cursory review of the literature that most of the existing research on our research problem is based on interviews with people who, in fact, are receiving services. We may then choose to begin interviewing clients who are from an ethnic minority and who are *not* currently receiving any social services but are named on social service client lists.

We must also establish how the interview will be structured. Interviewing for qualitative data can range from informal casual conversations to more formal guided discussions. An informal interview is unplanned. The interviewer begins, for example, by asking Native clients a general question, such as the one presented earlier—could you tell me about your experiences in accessing social services?

The discussion that would follow would be based on the natural and spontaneous interaction between the interviewer and the research participant. The interviewer has no way of knowing at the outset what direction the interview will take or where it will end.

A guided interview, on the other hand, has more structure. The exact amount of structure varies from one guided interview to another. In any case, the interviewer has an interview schedule, which essentially amounts to an outline of questions and/or concepts, to guide the interview with the research participant.

Interviewing for qualitative data can range from informal casual conversations to more formal guided discussions.

A loosely structured interview schedule may simply identify key concepts or ideas to include in the interview at the appropriate time. In our study, for example, we might want the interviewer to specifically ask each research participant about language barriers and social isolation, if these concepts do not naturally emerge in the interviews. A highly structured interview schedule would list each question to be asked during the interviews. The interviewer would read the question out to the research participants and record their answers.

RECORDING NARRATIVE DATA

THE MOST RELIABLE WAY TO RECORD INTERVIEW DATA is through the use of audiotape. Videotape is also a possibility, but many people are uncomfortable with being filmed. The audiotape is an excellent record of an interview because it gives us verbatim statements made by our research participants. The tone, pace, and "atmosphere" of the interview can be recalled by simply replaying the tape.

To prepare data for analysis, however, it's necessary to transcribe every word of the interview. As we will see in Chapter 18, the transcription provides text data, which will be read (and reread) and analyzed. Because audio data are transformed into text data, verbatim statements are used. In addition, any pauses, sighs, and gestures are noted in the text. The following is an example of an excerpt of text data based on our question asked earlier:

> **Research Participant Number 6:** Being a Native in social ser-
> vices, huh . . . well, it's not so good, eh people don't know . . .
> they don't see the reserve or the kids playing . . . even when
> they see they don't see. The kids you know, they could have
> some help, especially the older ones (sighs and pauses for a
> few seconds). My oldest you know, he's 12 and he goes to
> school in the city. He comes home and doesn't know what to
> do. He gets into trouble. Then the social services people
> come with their briefcases and tell you what to do (voice
> gets softer). They put in stupid programs and the kids don't
> want to go you know, they just want to play, get into trouble
> stuff (laughs) . . .

> **Interviewer:** Hmmm. And how would you describe your own
> experiences with social services?

Because the interviewing approach to data collection is based on the interaction of the interviewer and the research participant, both parts of the discussion are included in the transcript. But data collection and recording do not stop here. The interviewer must also keep notes on the interview to record impressions, thoughts, perspectives, and any data that will shed light on the transcript during analysis. An example of the interviewer's notes from the above excerpt is:

> **September 12 (Research Participant Number 6):** I was feeling
> somewhat frustrated because the research participant kept
> talking about his children. I felt compelled to get him to talk
> about his own experiences but that seemed sooooo much
> less important to him.

As we will see in Chapter 18, the verbatim transcript and the interviewer's notes are key pieces of data that will be jointly considered when text data are analyzed.

TRUSTWORTHINESS AND TRUTH-VALUE OF NARRATIVE DATA

REGARDLESS OF THE TYPE OF INTERVIEW or the data recording strategy that we select, we must have some way to assess the credibility of the data we collect. With quantitative data, we do this by determining the reliability and validity of the data—usually by calculating a numerical value. In contrast, with qualitative data we are less likely to generate numerical values and more likely to document our own personal observations and procedures.

An important question to assess the trustworthiness and truth-value of the text data (and our interpretation of it) is whether we understand what our research participants were telling us from their points of view. Two common ways to check the credibility of interview data are triangulation and member checking. These procedures will be discussed in more detail in Chapter 18.

Regablardless of the type of interview or the data recording strategy that we select, we must have some way to assess the credibility of the data we collect.

Briefly, triangulation involves comparing data from multiple perspectives. It may be that we interview several people (i.e., data sources) on one topic, or even that we compare quantitative and qualitative data for the same variable. Member checking simply involves getting feedback from our research participants about our interpretation of what they said.

ADVANTAGES AND DISADVANTAGES

THE MAJOR ADVANTAGE OF NARRATIVE INTERVIEWING is the richness of data that are generated. Narrative interviewing allows us to remain open to learning new information or new perspectives about old ideas. Because the interviewer is usually the same person who is the researcher, there is a genuine interest expressed in the interviews.

The major disadvantage associated with narrative interviewing is that it's time consuming. Not only does it take time to conduct the interviews, but considerable time also must be allotted for transcribing the text data. Narrative interviews produce reams and reams of text, which make it difficult to conduct an analysis. Researchers can tire easily and are subject to imposing their own biases and perspectives on what the research participants say.

PARTICIPANT OBSERVATION

PARTICIPANT OBSERVATION is a way for us to be a part of something and study it at the same time. This method of data collection requires us to establish and maintain ongoing relationships with research participants in the field setting. We not only listen, observe, and record data, but also participate in events and activities as they happen. Our role in participant observation can be described on a continuum (see Figure 15.1 above), with one end emphasizing the *participant role* and the other end emphasizing the *observer role*.

> There are four participant observation roles you can take when collecting data for your qualitative study.

An "observer-participant" has the dominant role of observation whereas the "participant-observer" is predominantly a participant. Suppose we were to use participant observation as a data collection method for our study. An example of an observer-participant is a researcher who joins a group of people, say Natives living on their reserve, for events related to our research study. We may travel with a community social worker, for example, and par-

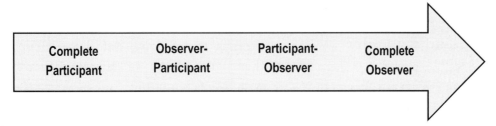

FIGURE 15.1

Continuum of Participant Observation

ticipate in community meetings on the reserve to discuss access to social services.

An example of a participant-observer could be when a social worker has the dual responsibility of conducting the meeting and observing the interactions of community members. A participant-observer could also be identified within his or her unique community.

A Native resident of the reserve, for example, could participate in the meeting as a resident and as an observer. In any case, participant observation always requires that one person assumes a dual role. For ethical reasons, the role must be made explicit to all persons participating in the research study. Whether the researcher is a social worker or a Native resident of the reserve, he or she must declare his or her dual role before the community meeting (i.e., data collection) gets under way.

ESTABLISHING PROCEDURES TO COLLECT DATA

GIVEN THE DUAL ROLE OF RESEARCHERS in participant observation, formulating steps for data collection can be tricky. It's essential for the researcher to keep a balance between "participation" and "observation." Suppose our Native resident who is a participant-observer gets so immersed in the issues of the community meeting that she forgets to look around or ask others questions related to the research study.

An important consideration for a participant observation study is how to gain access to the group of people being studied.

Someone who completely participates will not be very effective in noting important detail with respect to how other people participated in the meeting. On the other hand, if our Native researcher leans too far into her observation role, others might see her as an outsider and express their views differently than if they believed she had a vested interest within the community.

An important consideration for a participant observation study is how to gain access to the group of people being studied. Imagine who might be welcomed into a community meeting on a Native reserve and who might be rejected. Chances are that the Native people on a reserve would be more accepting of a Native person, a person known to them, or a person whom they trust as compared to a non-Native person, a stranger, or a person whom they know but do not trust.

In participant observation we would need to understand the culture of the reserve in order to know who to seek permission from. In participant observation, entry and access is a process more analogous to peeling away the layers of an onion than it is to opening a door. Forming relationships with people is a critical part of data collection.

The more meaningful relationships we can establish, the more meaningful data we will collect. This is not to say, however, that we somehow trade relationship tokens for pieces of information. Rather, research participants should feel a partnership with the researcher that is characterized by mutual interest, reciprocity, trust, and cooperation.

RECORDING PARTICIPANT OBSERVATIONAL DATA

THE DATA GENERATED from participant observation come from observing, interviewing, using existing documents and artifacts, and reflecting on personal experiences. Below are a few examples:

Observation (September 12, 9:30AM Meeting Start Time):
When the social worker announced the purpose of the meeting was to discuss access to social services for people living on the reserve, there was a lot of agreement from a crowd of 42 people. Some cheered, some nodded their heads, and others made comments like, "it's about time."

Research participant's verbatim comment (September 12, 10:15AM): "Native people don't use social services because they are not offered on the reserve."

Existing document: A report entitled *"The Social Service Needs of a Reserve Community"* reports that there have been three failed attempts by state social workers to keep a program up and running on the reserve. Worker turnover is identified as the main contributing factor of program failures.

Researcher's personal note (September 12, 10:44AM): I feel amazed at the amount of positive energy in the room. I can sense peoples' frustrations (including my own), yet I am in awe of the hopeful and positive outlook everyone has to want to develop something that works for our community. I am proud to be a part of this initiative to improve services in the community.

Overall, participant observers produce "participant observational" data through the use of detailed and rich notes. Several strategies can be used for documenting notes. We can take notes on an ongoing basis, for example, by being careful to observe the time and context for all written entries. A more efficient method, however, would be to carry your trusty smartphone, which gives you the flexibility to state a thought, to record a conversation, and to make summary comments about what you observe and hear.

Collecting data on an ongoing basis is preferable because it increases the likelihood of producing accurate notes in addition to remembering key events. In some instances, however, participation in a process that prevents us from recording any data, which leaves us to record our notes after the event we are participating in has ended.

TRUSTWORTHINESS AND TRUTH-VALUE

GIVEN THAT MULTIPLE DATA SOURCES ARE POSSIBLE in participant observation, it's possible to check the credibility of the data through triangulation. By reviewing the four data recording examples on the previous page, we can be reasonably confident that there is agreement about the state of social services on the reserve. The four separate data entries seem to agree that social services on the reserve are inadequate in terms of the community's needs.

> Collecting data on an ongoing basis is preferable because it increases the likelihood of producing accurate notes in addition to remembering key events.

The flexibility of participant observation allows us to seek out opportunities to check out our personal assumptions and ideas. After hearing the general response of Native community members at the beginning of the meeting, for example, we may choose to ask related questions to specific individuals. We can also check our perceptions along the way by sharing our own thoughts, asking people to comment on data summaries, or asking people how well they think two data sources fit together.

ADVANTAGES AND DISADVANTAGES

A MAJOR ADVANTAGE OF PARTICIPANT OBSERVATION is that we can collect multiple sources of data and check the credibility of the data as we go. Because of the participant role, any observations made are grounded within the context in which they were generated. A "complete participant" is more likely to pick up subtle messages, for example, than would be a "complete observer."

The disadvantages of participant observation are related to time considerations. As with narrative interviewing, a considerable amount of time must be allotted to data recording and transcription. The researcher also runs the risk of becoming too immersed as a participant or too distant as an observer—both are situations that will compromise the data collected.

SECONDARY CONTENT DATA

SECONDARY CONTENT DATA are existing text data. In the same way that existing quantitative data can be used to answer newly developed research questions, so can existing qualitative (or content) data. In this case, the text data were recorded at some other time and for some other purpose than the research question that we have posed. Let's return to our research question— Do clients who come from an ethnic minority have difficulty in accessing social services?

With the use of content data, we could answer our question using context data that already exist. It may be, for example, that social workers are mandated to record any discussion they had about barriers to accessing social services for their clients on their client files. Case notes, for example, may read "client does not have reliable transportation" or "client has expressed a strong wish for a worker who has the same ethnic background."

Content data can be firsthand or secondhand.

These types of comments can be counted and categorized according to meaningful themes. In this instance, we are zeroing in on text data for specific examples of recorded behaviors, much like the microscopic approach of structured observation.

We must be aware that content data can be firsthand or secondhand. In our example, firsthand data would be generated when the social workers document their own behaviors in relation to offering services to their clients. When social workers record their own impressions about how their clients respond to offers of services, secondhand data are produced (LeCroy & Solomon, 2011).

ESTABLISHING PROCEDURES

CONTENT DATA ARE RESTRICTED to what is available. That is, if 68 client files exist, then we have exactly 68 client files to work from. We do not have the luxury of collecting more data. Like secondary quantitative data, we are in a position only to compile the existing data, not to collect new data.

It's possible, however, that content data are available from several sources. Client journals may be on file, or perhaps the agency recently conducted an open-ended client satisfaction survey, which has handwritten responses to satisfaction-type questions from clients.

A major consideration of content data is whether a sufficient amount exists to adequately answer our research question. If there are not enough data, we do not want to spend precious time reading and analyzing them. We must also remember that we are reading and reviewing text data for a purpose that they were not originally intended for.

Content data
exist in text form.

Suppose, for example, you kept a daily journal of your personal experience in your research course. Would you write down the same thoughts if you knew your journal would be private compared with if you were to share your writings with your research instructor? The original intent of writing is essential to remember because it provides the context in which the writing occurred.

Because we are examining confidential client case files, we must establish a coding procedure to ensure that our clients' confidentiality and anonymity are maintained. In fact, it's not at all necessary for us, as researchers, to know the names of the client files we are reading. Given our research question, we need only to have access to those portions of clients' files that contain information about client ethnicity and the difficulty clients have in accessing social services.

RECORDING

AS WE KNOW, content data exist in text form. If they exist in handwritten form, it's necessary to type them out into transcript form. It's useful to make several copies of the transcripts to facilitate data analysis. More will be said about preparing transcripts in Chapter 18.

ESTABLISHING THE TRUSTWORTHINESS AND TRUTH-VALUE

CLEARLY, FIRSTHAND DATA are more credible than secondhand data when dealing with existing text data. Because the data are secondary, questions of credibility center more around data analysis than data collection. In our example, it may be possible to triangulate data by comparing the files of different workers or by comparing different client files with the same worker. It also may be possible to member check (Chapter 18) if workers are available and consent to it.

ADVANTAGES AND DISADVANTAGES

A MAJOR ADVANTAGE of content data is that they already exist. Thus, time and money are saved in the data collection process. The task of the researcher is simply to compile data that are readily available and accessible. The disadvantages of content data are that they are limited in scope. The data were recorded for some other purpose and may omit important detail that would be needed to answer our research question.

HISTORICAL DATA

HISTORICAL DATA ARE COLLECTED in an effort to study the past (Stuart, 2011). Like the participant-observation method to data collection, historical data can come from different data sources. Data collection can be obtrusive, as in the case of interviewing people about past or historical events, or unobtrusive, as in the case when existing documents (primarily content data) are compiled. When our purpose is to study history, however, special cases of content data and interviewing are required.

Suppose we recast our research question to ask, "Did clients who come from an ethnic minority have difficulty accessing social services from 1947 to 1965?" Phrased this way, our question directs us to understand *what has been* rather than *what is*.

When collecting historical data, it's important to sort out firsthand data from secondhand data.

In order for us to answer our new research question, we would need to dig up remains from the past that could help us to describe the relationship, if any, between ethnicity and difficulty in accessing social services for our specified time period. We would search for documents such as related reports, memos, letters, transcriptions, client records, and documentaries, all dating back to the time period. Many libraries store this information in their archives.

We could also interview people (e.g., social workers and clients) who were part of social services between 1947 and 1965. People from the past might include clients, workers, supervisors, volunteers, funders, or ministers. The purpose of our interviews would be to have people remember the past—that is, to describe factual events from their memories. We are less interested in people's opinions about the past than we are about what "really" happened.

When collecting historical data, it's important to sort out firsthand data from secondhand data. Firsthand data, of course, are more highly valued because the data are less likely to be distorted or altered. Diaries, autobiographies, letters, home videos, photographs, and organizational minutes are all examples of firsthand data. Secondhand data, on the other hand, include documents like biographies, books, and articles.

ESTABLISHING PROCEDURES TO COLLECT DATA

IT'S PROBABLY MORE ACCURATE to say that we retrieve historical data than it is to say that we collect it. The data already exist, in long-forgotten written documents, dusty videotapes, or peoples' memories. Our task is to resurface a sufficient amount of data so that we can describe, and sometimes explain, what happened (Stuart, 2011).

One of the first considerations for conducting a historical research study is to be sure that the variable being investigated is one that existed in the past. Suppose, for example, we had a specific interest in the relationship among three variables: client ethnicity, difficulty in accessing social services, and computer technology.

More specifically, let us say that we were interested in knowing about the relationship among these three variables, if any, for our specified time period, 1947 to 1965. It would be impossible to determine the relationship among these three variables from a historical perspective because computers were not (or were rarely) used in the social services from 1947 to 1965. Thus, there would be no past to describe or explain—at least not where computers are concerned.

Once we have established that our research question is relevant, we can delineate a list of possible data sources and the types of data that each can produce. The total list of data sources and types must be assessed to determine whether, in fact, sufficient data exist to answer our research question. It's possible, however, that data do exist but they are not accessible. Client records, for example, may be secured. Documents may be out of circulation, thus requiring a researcher to travel to where the data are stored.

RECORDING

DESPITE THE FACT that historical data, in many cases, already exist, it's usually necessary to reproduce the data. When interviews are used, interview notes are recorded and the interviews are transcribed as we have discussed in other interpretive data collection methods. When past documents are used, they ought to be duplicated to create working copies. Original documents should be protected and preserved so that they can be made available to other interested researchers.

ESTABLISHING THE TRUSTWORTHINESS AND TRUTH-VALUE

ASSESSING THE TRUSTWORTHINESS and truth-value of historical data, in many ways, is the process of data analysis. Do different people recall similar facts? Do independent events from the past tell the same story? Much effort goes into triangulating pieces of data. The more corroboration we have among our data, the stronger our resulting conclusions will be.

When reconstructing the past, our conclusions can only be as good as the data we base them on. Are the data authentic? How much of our data are firsthand compared to secondhand? Do we have sufficient data to describe the entire time period of interest? Perhaps we might have to cut back a few years; or if other data emerge, perhaps we can expand our time period.

ADVANTAGES AND DISADVANTAGES

HISTORICAL DATA are unique and used for a specific purpose—to describe and explain the past. It's the only way for us to research history. When secondary data are readily available and accessible, the cost is minimized. When interviews are used, they provide us with an opportunity to probe further into the past and our area of interest.

The disadvantages of historical data are that they are not always easily available or accessible. There is also a risk of researcher bias such as when a letter or document is analyzed out of context. The past cannot be reconstructed, for example, if we impose present-day views, standards, and ideas.

SUMMARY

IN THIS CHAPTER we discussed different methods to collect qualitative data. With the previous chapter in mind we now know that that one research question can be answered using any data collection method—quantitative or qualitative. Different data collection methods produce different types of data. Data collection methods that are more commonly associated with qualitative or text data are narrative interviewing, participant observation, secondary content data, and historical data.

Study Questions for Chapter 15

	Essay — Discussion
1	In your own words describe qualitative data in detail. Provide social work examples throughout your discussion to illustrate your main points.
2	What is narrative interviewing? Discuss in detail how you can use narrative interviewing as a qualitative data gathering method in social work research situations. Provide social work examples throughout your discussion to illustrate your main points.
3	Discuss how you would record narrative data for a hypothetical social work research study. Provide social work examples throughout your discussion to illustrate your main points.
4	Discuss how you would assess the trustworthiness and truth-value of narrative data. Provide social work examples throughout your discussion to illustrate your main points.
5	Discuss the advantages and disadvantages of using narrative interviewing as a qualitative data gathering method. Provide social work examples throughout your discussion to illustrate your main points.
6	What is participant observation? Discuss in detail how you can use participant observation as a qualitative data gathering method in social work research situations. Provide social work examples throughout your discussion to illustrate your main points.
7	Discuss how you would record participant observational data for a hypothetical social work research study.
8	Discuss how you would assess the trustworthiness and truth-value of participant observational data. Provide social work examples throughout your discussion to illustrate your main points.
9	Discuss the advantages and disadvantages of using participant observational data as a qualitative data gathering method. Provide social work examples throughout your discussion to illustrate your main points.

10	What are secondary content data? Discuss in detail how you can use secondary content data as a qualitative data gathering method in social work research situations. Provide social work examples throughout your discussion to illustrate your main points.
11	Discuss how you would record secondary content data for a hypothetical social work research study. Provide social work examples throughout your discussion to illustrate your main points.
12	Discuss how you would assess the trustworthiness and truth-value of secondary content data. Provide social work examples throughout your discussion to illustrate your main points.
13	Discuss the advantages and disadvantages of using secondary content data as a qualitative data gathering method. Provide social work examples throughout your discussion to illustrate your main points.
14	What are historical data? Discuss in detail how you can use historical data as a qualitative data gathering method in social work research situations. Provide social work examples throughout your discussion to illustrate your main points.
15	Discuss how you would record historical data for a hypothetical social work research study. Provide social work examples throughout your discussion to illustrate your main points.
16	Discuss how you would assess the trustworthiness and truth-value of historical data. Provide social work examples throughout your discussion to illustrate your main points.
17	Discuss the advantages and disadvantages of using historical data as a qualitative data gathering method. Provide social work examples throughout your discussion to illustrate your main points.

Critical Thinking — Application — Integration

18	**RESEARCH VS. PRACTICE** Pretend for the moment you're employed as a social worker in your university's student counseling center. A student comes into your office complaining about his depression. Using this chapter as a guide, describe in detail how you could use some of the qualitative data gathering techniques discussed in this chapter

to assess the degree of his depression.

NOTE: This exercise should help you to realize that the qualitative data collection methods that social work researchers use are the same as practitioners use, and vice versa (see Figure 1.5 on page 37). In short, you can use Chapters 14–16 to help you gather data for your day-to-day practice activities for all of your client systems.

QUALITATIVE DATA COLLECTION AND THE PRACTITIONER

Scenario 1: Make an argument that to be an effective evidence-based social work practitioner **you must know** the advantages and disadvantages of the various qualitative data collection methods that are used in social work research studies. Provide clear and explicit **practice-related** social work examples to illustrate your main points.

19

Scenario 2: Make an argument that **you do not have to know** the advantages and disadvantages of the various qualitative data collection methods that are used in social work research studies to be an effective evidence-based practitioner. Provide clear and explicit **practice-related** social work examples to illustrate your main points.

Time to Choose: Which one of the above two scenarios do you feel is more consistent with the concept of the contemporary evidence-based social work practice process as illustrated ion pages 46–51? Why? Provide relevant social work examples to illustrate your main points.

QUALITATIVE DATA COLLECTION AND THE RESEARCHER

Scenario 1: Make an argument that to be a competent social work researcher **you must know** the advantages and disadvantages of the various qualitative data collection methods. Provide clear and explicit **research-related** social work examples to illustrate your main points.

20

Scenario 2: Make an argument that **you do not have to know** the advantages and disadvantages of the various qualitative data collection methods to be a competent social work researcher. Provide clear and explicit **research-related** social work examples to illustrate your main points.

Time to Choose: Which one of the above two scenarios do you feel is more consistent with the place of research in social work? Why? Provide relevant social work examples to illustrate your main points.

21	**TIME TO PUT ON YOUR CRITICAL THINKING HAT** 1. Discuss the similarities and differences between your responses to Questions 19 and 20. 2. What are your thoughts on the belief that you need to know the advantages and disadvantages of the various qualitative data collection methods whether you're a social work *practitioner* (Question 19) or a social work *researcher* (Question 20)? **NOTE:** This exercise should help you to realize that the qualitative data collection methods that social work researchers use are the same as practitioners use, and vice versa (see Figure 1.5 on page 37). In short, you can use Chapters 14–16 to help you gather data for your day-to-day practice activities for all of your client systems.
22	**YOU'RE NOW A RESEARCHER** Pretend for a moment that you want to do a qualitative research study to assess the interviewing skills of your fellow social work students. This would be an excellent time to review Chapter 7. 1. List and then discuss the various qualitative data collection methods that you could use. 2. What are the advantages and disadvantages of each one? 3. What kinds of data would each method produce for your data source(s)? Discuss fully.
23	**YOU'RE NOW A DATA SOURCE** Pretend that your school of social work wants to do a qualitative research study on determining the competency levels of its graduating students—which includes you, a graduating student. 1. List and then discuss the various qualitative data collection methods that your school could use. 2. From a data-source's perspective (you), what qualitative data collection method(s) do you think would be best for your school to use with you. Why? 3. What data could you provide the school that would be reliable and valid? Justify your response and use examples to illustrate your main points. 4. What quantitative data collection methods could your school use to supplement its qualitative findings (Chapter 14)? Think Box 7.1 on pages 268–269.

APPLICATION OF QUALITATIVE DATA COLLECTION METHODS

Locate a published qualitative social work-related journal article of your choice. Be sure the author collected qualitative data and the article is reporting the results from a qualitative research study. We suggest you locate a qualitatively oriented research study in Karen Staller and Karen Broadhurst's journal *Qualitative Social Work* (Sage Publications). Hands down, this is the best journal to find good qualitative social work research studies.

1. What was the study's data source(s)?

2. What was the study's qualitative data collection method(s) for each data source?

3. With your knowledge of the various qualitative data collection methods that research studies can use, thoroughly discuss how you will use the material contained within this chapter when you begin to evaluate the appropriateness of the research study's qualitative data collection method(s) and discuss why you believe each criterion you selected is important for your evaluation of the study's chosen method(s).

4. Would you have used a different qualitative method to collect the data to answer the study's research question? If so, what method would you have used, and why?

A MIXED-METHODS RESEARCH QUESTION (CHAPTER 8)

Pretend for the moment that you wish to do a **quantitatively** oriented research study (Chapter 6) to determine if MSW-level social workers are "better" at interviewing their clients than BSW-level social workers. You also wish to add a qualitative component (Chapter 7) to your study in an effort to add more meat to your study's findings.

1. Using what you have learned from Chapters 6–8, 14, and 15, delineate how you would do your mixed-methods study, highlighting the specific qualitative data collection method(s) you have chosen.

2. State specifically what the findings of your qualitative component could add to the study and how your qualitative component would provide more meat to your study's quantitative findings and practice recommendations.

26	**QUALITATIVE DATA COLLECTION AND YOUR PROFESSIONAL DEVELOPMENT** 1. Review the three social work research-related roles you can take when you graduate—CSWE Competency 1 at the beginning of this chapter on page 528. Thoroughly discuss how you feel this chapter will help you to perform one or more research-related roles when you graduate. Which one of the three roles do you believe this chapter helped you with the most? Why? Discuss in detail and provide an example to illustrate your main points. 2. Review CSWE Competency 4 at the beginning of this chapter on page 528. Thoroughly discuss how you feel this chapter will help you to become a practice-informed researcher and a research-informed practitioner. Discuss in detail and provide an example to illustrate your main points. 3. Review the evidence-based practice process as illustrated on pages 46–51. Thoroughly discuss how this chapter helps you to develop the skills you'll need for implementing one or more steps of the evidence-based practice process. 4. Discuss which step(s) you feel this chapter will help you with the most. Why? Be very specific and use relevant social work examples to illustrate your main points throughout your discussion. **NOTE:** This exercise should help you to realize that you can use all kinds of qualitative data collection methods to help you become an evidence-based social work practitioner.
27	**MOVING AHEAD BY LOOKING BACK** At this point in your research methods course, how comfortable are you with discussing the place of research in social work with your field instructor, with your practice instructor, with your research instructor, with your supervisor at work, with the director of your social work program, or with your classmates? Discuss in detail.

16

CHAPTER

2015 EPAS COMPETENCIES

COMPETENCY 1: Demonstrate Ethical and Professional Behavior

You will learn that in order to be a successful evidence-based practitioner you have an ethical obligation to integrate three research roles into your daily practice activities as discussed in Chapter 1: (1) research consumer, (2) research partner—either as a co-researcher or research participant, and (3) creator and disseminator of research (or knowledge).

This entire chapter pertains to these three professional research-related roles when it comes to applying eight criteria that must be addressed when selecting and evaluating various data collection method(s) and data source(s) that social work researchers and practitioners can use.

COMPETENCY 4: Engage in Practice-Informed Research and Research-Informed Practice

Competency 4 also pertains to the entire chapter because you have to:

1. Evaluate the appropriateness of the data collection method(s) and data source(s) utilized in a research study (**research consumer**—research-informed practice);

2. Participate in a research study—either as a co-researcher or research participant (**research partner**—practice-informed research). See 1 above and 3 below; and

3. Know how to select the most appropriate data collection method(s) and data source(s) when you actually do a research study (**creator and disseminator of research**—practice-informed research).

You also need to utilize evidence-based practice recommendations whenever possible; that is, you need to integrate (1) the best available research-based evidence with (2) your clinical expertise and (3) your client's values.

All of the above implies you'll need to know how to assess the strengths and limitations of the data collection method(s) and data source(s) used in a research study that produced its research-based evidence. In short, you need to ask and then answer a simple question: How seriously should I take the findings of any specific research study given the overall appropriateness of the data collection method(s) and data source(s) the study utilized?

COMPETENCY 9: Evaluate Practice with Individuals, Families, Groups, Organizations, and Communities
See Competencies 1 and 4.

Selecting a Data Collection Method

CHAPTER 1	**Step 1.**	Understanding the Research Process
CHAPTER 2	**Step 2.**	Developing Research Questions
CHAPTER 3	**Step 3.**	Reviewing the Literature
CHAPTERS 4 & 5	**Step 4.**	Being Aware of Ethical and Cultural Issues
CHAPTERS 6–8	**Step 5.**	Selecting a Research Approach
CHAPTERS 9 & 10	**Step 6.**	Specifying How Variables Are Measured
CHAPTER 11	**Step 7.**	Selecting a Sample
CHAPTERS 12 & 13	**Step 8.**	Selecting a Research Design
CHAPTERS 14–16	**Step 9.**	Selecting a Data-Collection Method
CHAPTERS 17 & 18	**Step 10.**	Analyzing the Data
CHAPTERS 19 & 20	**Step 11.**	Writing the Research Report

Ⅰ N THE LAST TWO CHAPTERS we discussed eight methods of data collection, which were divided by the type of data that each is most likely to produce—quantitative data (Chapter 14) or qualitative data (Chapter 15). This chapter examines the data-collection process from the vantage point of choosing the most appropriate data-collection method and data source for any given research question or hypothesis.

DATA COLLECTION VIA THE RESEARCH PROCESS

DATA COLLECTION IS A CRITICAL STEP in the research process because it's the link between theory and practice. Our research study always begins with an idea that is molded by a conceptual framework, which uses preexisting knowledge about our study's problem area. Once our research problem and question have been refined to a researchable level, data are sought from a selected source(s) and gathered using a data-collection method. The data

> **Note:** This would be an ideal time to review the previous two chapters before reading further in addition to Chapters 6–8. In a nutshell, this chapter will be meaningless to you if you haven't read the previous ones.

collected are then used to support or supplant our original study's conceptions about our research problem under investigation (Unrau, 2011).

The role of data collection in connecting theory and practice is understood when looking at the entire research process. As we have seen in previous chapters of this book, choosing a data-collection method and data source follows the steps of selecting a research topic area, focusing the topic into a research question, and designing the research study.

> One factor that affects how our research question is answered depends upon how we conceptualize and measure the variables within it.

Data collection comes before the steps of analyzing the data and writing the research report. Although data collection is presented in this text as a distinct phase of the research process, in reality it cannot be tackled separately or in isolation.

All steps of the research process must be considered if we hope to come up with the best strategy to gather the most relevant, reliable, and valid data to answer a research question or to test a hypothesis. This section discusses the role of data collection in relation to the other steps of the generic research process as outlined in Chapters 6–8.

SELECTING A RESEARCH TOPIC AND RESEARCH QUESTION

OUR SPECIFIC RESEARCH QUESTION identifies the general problem area and the population to be studied. It tells us what we want to collect data about and alerts us to potential data sources. It does not necessarily specify the exact manner in which our data will be gathered, however. Let's return to our research question:

Research question:
Do people who come from ethnic minority backgrounds have difficulty in accessing social services?

Our research question identifies a problem area (difficulty in accessing social services for people who are ethnic minorities) and a population (social service clients). It does not state how the question will be answered. We have seen in the last two chapters that our research question, in fact, could be answered using various data-collection methods. One factor that affects how our question is answered depends upon how we conceptualize and measure the variables within it. As we know, "accessing social services" could be measured in a variety of ways.

Another factor that affects how a research question is answered (or a hypothesis is tested) is the *source* of the data—that is, who or what is providing them. If we want to get firsthand data about the accessibility of social services, for example, we could target the clients as a potential data source. If such firsthand data sources were not a viable option, secondhand data sources could be sought.

Social workers, for example, can be asked for their perceptions of how accessible social services are to their clients who come from ethnic minorities. In other instances, secondhand data can be gleaned from existing reports (secondary data or content data) written about clients (or client records) that monitor client progress and social worker–client interactions.

> The research design flows from the research question, which flows from the problem area.

By listing all possible data-collection methods and data sources that could provide sound data to answer a research question, we develop a fuller understanding of our initial research problem. It also encourages us to think about our research problem from different perspectives, via the different data sources.

Because social work problems are complex, data collection is strengthened when two or more data sources are used. For example, if social workers (Source 1) and clients (Source 2) were to each report their perceptions of service accessibility in a similar way, then we could be more confident that the data (from both of these sources) accurately reflect the problem being investigated.

DESIGNING THE RESEARCH STUDY AND COLLECTING DATA

AS WE KNOW, the research design flows from the research question, which flows from the problem area. A research design organizes our research question into a framework that sets the parameters and conditions of the study. As mentioned, the research question directs *what* data are collected and *who* data could be collected from. In a positivistic study, the research design re-fines the *what* question by operationalizing variables and the *who* question by developing a sampling strategy.

In an interpretive study, however, the research design identifies the starting point for data collection and how such procedures will be monitored and recorded along the way. In both research approaches, the research design also dictates (more or less) *when*, *where,* and *how* data will be collected.

The research design outlines how many data collection points our study will have and specifies the data sources. Each discrete data gathering activity constitutes a data collection point and defines *when* data are to be collected. Thus, using a one-group posttest-only design (i.e., Figure 13.1a on page 453), we will collect data only once from a single group of research participants. On the other hand, if a classical experimental design is used (i.e., Figure 13.9 on page 482), data will be collected at two separate times with two different groups of research participants—for a total of four discrete data collection points.

Where the data are collected is also important to consider. If our research question is too narrow and begs for a broader issue that encompasses individuals living in various geographic locations, then mailed survey questionnaires would be more feasible than face-to-face interviews. If our research question focuses on a specific population where all research participants live in the same geographic location, it may be possible to use direct observations or individual or group interviews.

> We must always consider which method of data collection will lead to the most valid and reliable data to answer a research question or to test a hypothesis.

Because most social work studies are applied, the setting of our study usually involves clients in their natural environments where there is little control over extraneous variables. If we want to measure the clients' perceptions about their difficulty in accessing social services, for example, do we observe clients in agency waiting rooms, observe how they interact with their social workers, or have them complete a survey questionnaire of some kind? In short, we must always consider which method(s) of data collection will lead to the most valid and reliable data to answer a research question or to test a hypothesis.

The combination of potential data-collection methods and potential data sources is another important consideration. A research study can have one data collection source and still use multiple data-collection methods. Our program's clients (Data Source 1) in our study, for example, can fill out a standardized questionnaire that measures their perceptions of how accessible social services are (Data-collection Method 1) in addition to participating in face-to-face interviews (Data-collection Method 2).

In the same vein, another study can have multiple data sources and one data-collection method. In this case, we can collect data about difficulty in accessing social services through observation recordings by social workers (Data Source 1), administrators (Data Source 2), or other citizens (Data Source 3).

The combination of data-collection methods should not be too taxing on any research participant or any system, such as the social service program itself. That is, data collection should not interfere greatly with the day-to-day activities of the persons providing (or responsible for collecting) the data. In some studies, there is no research design per se (e.g., Figure 13.2a on page 455). Instead, we can use existing data to answer our research question.

Such is the case when secondary or content data are used. When the data already exist, we put more effort into ensuring that the research question is a good fit with the data at hand. Regardless of what data-collection method is used, once the data are collected, they are subject to analysis.

ANALYZING AND INTERPRETING THE DATA

COLLECTING DATA IS A RESOURCE-INTENSIVE ENDEAVOR that can be expensive and time consuming—for both quantitative and qualitative research studies. The truth of this statement is realized in the data analysis step of our research study. Without a great deal of forethought about what data to collect, data can be thrown out because they cannot be organized or analyzed in any meaningful way.

In short, data analyses should always be considered when choosing a data-collection method and data source because the analysis phase must summarize, synthesize, and ultimately organize the data in an effort to have as clear-cut an answer as possible to our research question. When too much (or too little) data are collected, we can easily become bogged down (or stalled) by difficult decisions that could have been avoided with a little fore-thought.

After thinking through our research problem and research question and selecting a viable data collection and data source, it's worthwhile to list out the details of the type of data that will be produced. Specifically, we must think about how the data will be used in our data analysis. This exercise provides a clearer idea of the type of results we can expect.

EXAMPLE

THE MAIN VARIABLE in our research question is difficulty in accessing social services. Suppose the social worker decides to collect data about this variable by giving clients (data source) a brief standardized questionnaire (data-collection method) to measure their perceptions. Many standardized questionnaires contain several subscales that, when combined, give a quantitative measure of a larger concept.

The *R-GSSSS* introduced in Chapter 10 (Figure 10.1), for example, is made up of three subscales: (1) relevance, (2) impact, and (3) gratification. Thus, the *R-GSSSS* has four scores associated with it: (1) a relevance score, (2) an impact score, (3) a gratification score, and (4) a total score—which is a measure of satisfaction. With three separate subscales, we can choose to use any one subscale (one variable), all three subscales (three variables), or a total score (one variable).

> Data analyses should always be considered when choosing a data collection method and data source.

Alternatively, if data about difficulty in accessing social services were to be collected using two different data sources such as social worker (Data Source 1) and client (Data Source 2) observations, we must think about how the two data sources fit together; that is, will data from the two sources be treated as two separate variables? If so, will one variable be weighted differently in our analysis than the other? Thinking about how the data will be summarized helps us to expose any frivolous data—that is, data that are not suitable to answering our research question.

Besides collecting data about our study's variables, we must also develop a strategy to collect demographic data about the people who participate in our study. Typical demographic variables include age, gender, education level, and family income. However, we must always remember not to collect data that we will not use.

In sum, it's simply unethical to collect data we never intend to use. Demographic data provide a context for our study. Some data-collection methods, such as standardized questionnaires, include these types of data. Often, however, we are responsible for obtaining them as part of the data-collection process.

PRESENTATION AND DISSEMINATION OF FINDINGS

IT'S USEFUL TO THINK ABOUT OUR FINAL RESEARCH REPORT when choosing a data-collection method and data source as it forces us to visualize how our study's findings will ultimately be presented (see Chapters 19 and 20). It identifies both who the audience of the study will be and who the people interested in our findings are. Knowing who will read our research report and how it will be disseminated helps us to take more of an objective stance toward our study. In short, we can take a third-person look at what our study will finally look like.

Such objectivity helps us to think about our data-collection method(s) and data source(s) with a critical eye. Will consumers of our research study agree that the clients in fact were the best data-collection source(s)? Were the data-collection method(s) and analysis(es) sound? These are some of the practical questions that bring scrutiny to the data-collection process.

SELECTING A DATA-COLLECTION METHOD

THINKING THROUGH THE STEPS in the research process from the vantage point of collecting data permits us to refine the conceptualization of our study and the place of data collection within it. It also sets the context within which our data will be gathered. Clearly, there are many viable data-collection methods and data sources that can be used to answer any research question (See Table 16.1 on pages 564–572). Nevertheless, there are eight practical criteria that ultimately refine the final data-collection method(s) and data source(s) to fit the conditions of any given research study. These are:

1. Size
2. Scope
3. Program participation
4. Worker cooperation
5. Intrusion into the lives of research participants
6. Resources
7. Time
8. Data-collection methods used in previous studies

SIZE

THE SIZE OF OUR RESEARCH STUDY reflects just how many people, places, or systems are represented in it. Yes, size does indeed matter. As with any planning activity, the more people involved, the more complicated the process and the more difficult it is to arrive at a mutual agreement.

Decisions about which data-collection method and which data source to use can be stalled when several people, levels, or systems are involved. This is because individuals have different interests and opinions. Imagine if our research question about whether ethnicity is related to difficulty in accessing social services were examined on a larger scale such that all social service programs in the country were included.

Our study's complexity is dramatically increased because of such factors as the increased number of programs, clients, funders, government representatives, and social workers involved. The biases within each of these stakeholder groups make it much more difficult to agree upon the best data-collection method(s) and data source(s) for our study.

Our study's sample size is also a consideration. This is particularly true for positivistic studies, which aim to have a sample that is representative of the population of interest. With respect to sample size, this means that we should strive for a reasonable representation of the sampling frame.

When small-scale studies are conducted, such as a program evaluation in one social work program, the total number of people in the sampling frame may be in the hundreds or fewer. Thus, randomly selecting clients poses no real problem.

TABLE 16.1

Advantages and Disadvantages of Selected Social Work Research and Social Work Practice Data-Collection Methods

Method	Description	Advantages	Disadvantages
Questionnaire (General)	A paper and pencil method for obtaining responses to statements or questions by using a form on which participants provide opinions or factual information	Is a relatively inexpensive, quick way to collect large amounts of data from large samples in short amounts of time Is convenient for respondents to complete Can result in more honest responses via anonymity Allows use of readily available questionnaires is well suited for answering questions related to "What?" "Where?" and "How many?	Limited ability to know whether you are actually measuring what you intend to measure Limited ability to discover measurement errors Limited length and breadth of questions No opportunity to probe or obtain clarification Reliance on self-report Reliance on participants' ability to recall behaviors and events Limited capability to measure different kinds of outcomes Not well suited to answering questions related to "How?" and "Why?" Difficult to administer with low-literacy groups

One-to-One Interview (General)	An interaction between two people in which information is gathered relative to respondent's knowledge, thoughts, and feelings about different topics	Allows greater depth than a questionnaire Provides data that are deeper, richer, and have more context Allows interviewer to establish rapport with respondent Allows interviewer to clarify questions Is a good method for working with low-literacy respondents Has higher response and completion rates Allows for observation of nonverbal gestures	Need for extensive time and personnel Need for highly trained, skilled interviewers Limited number of people can be included Open to interviewer bias Prone to respondents giving answers they believe are expected or socially desirable No anonymity Potentially invasive for personal questions
One-to-One Interview (Unstructured)	An interaction between two people in which the totally free response pattern allows respondents to express ideas in their own way and time	Can elicit personal information Can gather relevant unanticipated data Permits interviewer to probe for more information	Need for great interviewer skill More prone to bias in response interpretation Time-consuming data analysis
One-to-One Interview (Semi-structured)	An interaction between two people with limited free response, building around a set of basic questions from which the interviewer may branch off	Combines efficiency of structured interview with ability to probe and investigate interesting responses	No true exploratory research permitted Predetermined questions limit ability to probe further

One-to-One Interview (Structured)	An interaction between two people with predetermined questions, often with structured responses	Is easy to administer Does not require as much training of interviewer	Less ability to probe for additional information No clarification of ambiguous responses
Focus Group	Interviews with groups of people (anywhere from 4 to 12) selected because they share certain characteristics relevant to the questions of study, in which the interviewer encourages discussion and expression of differing opinions and viewpoints	Studies participants in natural, real-life atmosphere Allows for exploration of unanticipated issues as they are discussed Increases sample size in interpretive studies Saves time and money Stimulates new ideas among participants Gains additional information from observation of group process Promotes greater spontaneity and candor	Less interviewer control than in a one-to-one interview Sometimes difficult to analyze data Context of comments must be considered Need for highly trained observer-moderators No isolation of individual's train of thought throughout
Phone Interview	One-to-one conversation over the phone	May lower costs May promote greater candor via anonymity	Phones not always available Unlisted numbers present sampling bias No opportunity to observe nonverbal gestures

| Participant Observation (General) | Evaluator measures behaviors, interactions, and processes by directly watching participants | Gathers spontaneous data

Codes behaviors in a natural setting such as a lunch room or a hallway

Provides a check against distorted perceptions of participants

Works well with a homogeneous group

Is a good technique to combine with other methods

Is well suited for study of body language (kinesics) and study of people's use of personal space and its relationship to culture (proxemics) | Need for highly trained observer

Recording of behaviors and events potentially from memory

Difficult quantification and summary of data

Difficult to maintain objectives. Very time-consuming and expensive |
| Participant Observation (Participant as Observer) | Evaluator's role as observer is known to the group being studied, but that role is secondary to his or her role as a participant | Retains benefits of participant without ethical issues at stake for evaluator | Observer difficulty in maintaining two distinct roles

Potential for resentment among other participants of observer's role

Observer presence can change nature of the interactions being observed |

Participant Observation (Observer as Participant)	Evaluator's role as observer is known to the group being studied, and his or her primary role is to assess the program	Allows evaluator to be more focused on observation role while still maintaining connection to other participants	Evaluator clearly an outsider Observer presence can change nature of the interactions being observed
Participant Observation (Complete Observer)	Evaluator is a silent observer with no formal role as participant; evaluator may also be hidden from the group, or his or her presence may be unnoticed and unobtrusive in a completely public setting	Permits more objective observations Does not distract evaluator with a participant role Does not interfere in any way with the group's process when evaluator is hidden	Observer presence, if known, can inhibit or change interactions of participants Use of hidden observer raises ethical questions

Document Analysis	Unobtrusive measure using analysis of diaries, logs, letters, and formal policy statements to learn about values and beliefs of participants in a setting or group, or about processes involved in a program and their impact. Examples: class reviews, letters to teachers, letters from parents, or letters from former students	Reduces problems of memory relating to when, where, with whom (diaries) Provides access to thoughts and feelings that may not otherwise be accessible Can be less threatening to participants Allows collection and analysis of data on evaluator's own schedule Is relatively inexpensive	Quality of data variation among subjects Use of diaries potentially causing change in subject behaviors Not well suited for low-literacy groups Potentially very selective data No opportunities for clarification of data
Archival Data	Analysis of archival data from a society, community, or organization. Examples: birth rates, census data, contraceptive purchase data, or logs of number of visits to hospitals for STIs	Is more accurate than self-report	Not all data available or fully reported Difficult to match geographical or individual data

Historical Data	Analysis of historical data as a method of discovering from records and personal accounts what happened in the past; especially useful for establishing a baseline or background of a program or participants before measuring outcomes	Provides baseline data that can help with interpretation of outcome findings Helps answer questions about why a program is or is not successful in meeting its goals Provides a picture of the broader context within which a program is operating	Potentially difficult to obtain data Data that may be incomplete, missing, or inaccurate Reliance on selective memory of events and behaviors by participants Accuracy difficult to verify

| Secondary Analysis | Analysis of data that already exist (not the collection of new or original data) | Is considerably cheaper and faster than doing original studies

Offers benefit of research from some of the top scholars in the field, which for the most part ensures quality data

Has advantages of putting less strain on limited funds and time, and providing samples drawn from larger populations

Provides flexibility: you might only extract a few figures from a table, or you might use the data in a subsidiary role in your research or even in a central role

Is readily available via a network of data archives in which survey data files are collected and distributed | With national population survey data, difficulty in finding relevant data for well-defined minority subgroups

Potential for irresponsible analyses: variables and data can be manipulated and transformed in ways that lessen validity of the original research

Large data files and difficult statistical packages, particularly with large samples |

Online Surveys	Questionnaires administered online through available online resources. Example: SurveyMonkey.com	Saves money by delivering questionnaires online rather than paying for postage or for interviewers	Population and sample limited to those with access to a computer and online network
		Facilitates changes to questionnaires and the copying and sorting of data	Difficulty in guaranteeing anonymity and confidentiality of data
		Can be delivered to recipients in seconds rather than in days as with traditional mail	Initial difficulties in constructing formats for computer questionnaires
		Allows sending invitations and receiving responses in a very short time, thus allowing faster participation level estimates as well	Need to provide respondents with additional instruction and orientation for the computer system
		Has higher response rates on private networks in contrast with paper surveys or interviews	Potential for computer glitches impeding collection
		Obtains more honest answers in contrast with paper surveys or interviews	Response rates not necessarily higher. (Research has shown that e-mail response rates are higher, but those rates applied only during the first few days; thereafter, the rates were not significantly higher.)
		Allows participants to answer in minutes or hours, and permits global coverage	

On the other hand, when large-scale studies are conducted, such as when the federal government chooses to examine a social service program that involves hundreds of thousands of people, sampling can become more problematic. If our sample is in the hundreds, it's unlikely that we would be able to successfully observe or interview all participants to collect data for our study. Rather, a more efficient manner of data collection—say a mailed survey—may be more appropriate.

SCOPE

THE SCOPE OF OUR RESEARCH STUDY is the second matter to consider when selecting a data-collection method. Scope refers to how much of our *problem area* will be covered. If in our research question, for example, we are interested in gathering data on other client-related variables such as language ability, degree of social isolation, and level of assertiveness, then three different aspects of our problem area will be covered.

In short, we need to consider whether one method of data collection and one data source can be used to collect all the data. It could be that client records, for example, are used to collect data about clients' language abilities, interviews with clients are conducted to collect data about social isolation, and observation methods are used to gather data about clients' assertiveness levels.

PROGRAM PARTICIPATION

MANY SOCIAL WORK RESEARCH EFFORTS are conducted in actual real-life program settings. Thus, it's essential that we gain the support of program personnel to conduct our study. Program factors that can impact the choice of our data-collection methods and data sources include variables such as the program's clarity in its mandate to serve clients, its philosophical stance toward clients, and its flexibility in client record keeping.

— **First,** if a program is not able to clearly articulate a client service delivery plan, it will be difficult to distinguish between clinical activity and research activity, and to determine when the two overlap.

— **Second,** some programs tend to base themselves on strong beliefs about a client population, which affect who can have access to clients and in what manner. A child sexual abuse investigation program, for example, may be designed specifically to avoid the problem of using multiple interviewers and multiple interviews of children in the investigation of an allegation of sexual abuse. As a result, the program would be hesitant for us to conduct interviews with the children to gather data for research purposes.

— **Third,** to save time and energy there is often considerable overlap between program client records and research data collection. The degree of willingness of a program to adapt to new record-keeping techniques will affect how we might go about collecting certain types of data.

WORKER COOPERATION

ON A GENERAL LEVEL, programs have fewer resources than they need and more clients than they can handle. Such conditions naturally lead their administrators and social workers to place intervention activity as a top priority (versus research activity). When our research study has social workers collecting data as a part of their day-to-day activities, it's highly likely that they will view data collection as additional paperwork and not as a means to expedite decision-making in their work.

Program workers will be affected by our study whether they are involved in the data collection process or not.

Getting cooperation of social workers within a program is a priority in any research study that relies directly or indirectly on their meaningful participation. Program workers will be affected by our study whether they are involved in the data-collection process or not. They may be asked to schedule additional interviews with families or adjust their intervention plans to ensure that data collection occurs at the optimal time.

Given the fiscal constraints faced by programs, the workers themselves often participate as data collectors. They may end up using new client recording forms or administering questionnaires. Whatever the level of their participation, it's important for us to strive to achieve a maximum level of their cooperation.

There are three factors to consider when trying achieving the maximum cooperation from workers.

— **First,** we should make every effort to work effectively and efficiently with the program's staff. Cooperation is more likely to be achieved when workers participate in the development of our study plan from the beginning. Thus, it's worthwhile to take time to explain the purpose of our study and its intended outcomes at an early stage in the study. Furthermore, administrators and front-line workers alike can provide valuable information about which data-collection method(s) may work best.

— **Second,** we must be sensitive to the workloads of the program's staff. Data-collection methods and sources should be designed to enhance the work of professionals. Client recording forms, for example, can be designed to provide focus for supervision meetings as well as summarize facts and worker impressions about a case.

— **Third,** a mechanism ought to be set up by which workers receive feedback based on the data they have collected. When a mechanism for feedback is put in place, for example, workers are more likely to show interest in the data-collection activity. When data are reported back to the program's staff before the completion of our study, however, we must ensure that the data will not bias later measurements (if any).

INTRUSION INTO THE LIVES OF RESEARCH PARTICIPANTS

WHEN CLIENTS ARE USED AS A DATA SOURCE, client self-determination takes precedence over research activity. As we know, clients have every right to refuse participation in a research study and cannot be denied services because they are unwilling to participate. It's unethical, for example, when a member of a group-based treatment intervention has not consented to participate in the study but participant observation is used as the data-collection method.

As we know from Chapter 4, this is unethical because group members may end up being observed as part of the group dynamic in the data-collection process even though they refused to give their prior consent. The data-collection method(s) we finally select must be flexible enough to allow our study to continue even with the possibility that some clients will not participate.

Ethnic and cultural consideration must also be given to the type of data-collection method used. One-on-one interviewing with Syrian refugees, for example, may be extremely terrifying for them, given the interrogation they may have experienced in their own country.

Moreover, if we, as data collectors, have different ethnic backgrounds than our research participants, it's important to ensure that interpretation of the data (e.g., their behaviors, events, or expressions) are accurate from the *clients'* perspectives—not our own!

We must also recognize the cultural biases of standardized measuring instruments because most are based on testing with Caucasian groups. The problems here are twofold.

— **First,** we cannot be sure whether the concept that the instrument is measuring is expressed the same way in different cultures. For instance, a standardized self-report instrument that measures family functioning may include an item such as "We have flexible rules in our household that promote individual differences," which would likely be viewed positively by North American cultures but negatively by many Asian cultures.

— **Second,** because standardized measuring instruments are written in English, research participants must have a good grasp of English to ensure that the data collected from them are valid and reliable. Another consideration comes into play when particular populations have been the subjects of a considerable amount of research study already.

Many aboriginal people living on reserves, for example, have been subjected to government surveys, task force inquiries, independent research projects, and perhaps even to the curiosities of social work students in their practicum settings.

When a population has been extensively researched, it's even more important that we consider how the data-collection method will affect those people participating in the study. Has the data-collection method been used previously? If so, what was the nature of the data collected? Could the data be collected using less intrusive methods?

RESOURCES

THERE ARE VARIOUS COSTS associated with collecting data in any given research study. Materials and supplies, equipment rental, transportation costs, and training for data collectors are just a few things to consider when choosing a data-collection method. In addition, once the data are collected, additional expenses can arise when the data are entered into a computer or transcribed.

An efficient data-collection method is one that collects credible data to answer a research question or test a hypothesis while requiring the least amount of time and money. In our example, to ask clients about their perceptions about the difficulty in accessing social services via an open-ended interview may offer rich data, but we take the risk that clients will not fully answer our questions in the time allotted for the interview.

> An efficient data collection method is one that collects credible data to answer a research question or test a hypothesis while requiring the least amount of time and money.

On the other hand, having them complete a self-report questionnaire about access to social services is a quicker and less costly way to collect data, but it gives little sense about how well the clients understood the questions being asked of them or whether the data obtained reflect their true perceptions.

TIME

TIME IS A CONSIDERATION when our study has a fixed completion date. Time constraints may be self- or externally imposed. Self-imposed time constraints are personal matters we need to consider. Is our research project a part of a thesis or dissertation? What are our personal time commitments?

Externally imposed time restrictions are set by someone other than the person who is doing the study. For instance, our research study may be limited by the fiscal year of a social service program and/or funding source. Other external pressures may be political, such as an administrator who wants research results for a funding proposal or to present at a conference.

DATA-COLLECTION METHODS USED IN PREVIOUS STUDIES

HAVING REVIEWED THE PROFESSIONAL LITERATURE on our problem, we need to be well aware of other data-collection methods that have been used in similar studies. We can evaluate earlier studies strengths and weaknesses of their data-collection methods and thereby make a more informed decision as to the best data-collection strategy to use in our specific situation.

Further, we need to look for diversity when evaluating other data-collection approaches; that is, we can triangulate results from separate studies that used different data-collection methods and data sources.

EXAMPLE: SELECTING A METHOD

AS SHOULD BE EVIDENT BY NOW, choosing a data-collection method and data source for a research study is not a simple task as illustrated in Table 16.2 on page 580. There are numerous conceptual and practical factors that must be thought through if we hope to arrive at the best possible approach to gathering data. How do we appraise all the factors to be considered in picking the best approach?

Table 16.2 is an example of a grid that can be used to assist us in making an informed decision about which data-collection method is best. The first section of the grid highlights the eight general criteria for selecting a data-collection method discussed earlier. The bottom section provides five additional criteria that were related to a specific research study we did a few years back. Can you guess what our study was all about just by looking at the five additional criteria we used to select our data-collection method(s)?

The grid can be used as a decision-making tool by subjectively rating how well each data-collection method measures up to the criteria listed in the left column of Table 16.2. We mark a "+" if the data-collection method has a favorable rating and a "−" if it has an unfavorable one. When a particular criterion is neutral, in which case it has no positive or negative effect, then a zero is indicated.

Once each data-collection method has been assessed on all the criteria, we can simply add the number of pluses and minuses to arrive at a plus or minus total for each method. This information can be used to help us make an informed decision about the best data-collection method, given all the issues raised. Based on Table 16.2, where only five data-collection methods are illustrated, the survey was the most appealing for our study.

Trying Out the Method

Data collection is a particularly vulnerable time for a research study because it's the point where talk turns into action. So far, all the considerations that have been weighed in the selection of a data-collection method have been in theory. All people involved in our research endeavor have conveyed their suggestions and doubts on the entire process.

Once general agreement has been reached about which data-collection method(s) and data source(s) to use, it's time to test the waters. Trying out a data-collection method can occur informally by simply testing it out with available and willing research participants or, at the very least, with anyone who has not been involved with the planning of the study.

The purpose of this trial run is to ensure that those who are going to provide data understand the questions and procedures in the way that they were intended. Table 16.3 on page 581 illustrates an example of how a simple data-collection plan can be formulated before a study actually begins. It then can be followed to guide the data-collection process as the study gets underway.

Data-collection methods might also be tested more formally, such as when a pilot study is conducted. A pilot study involves carrying out all aspects of the data-collection plan on a mini-scale. That is, a small portion of our study's actual sample is selected and run through all steps of the data-collection process.

In a pilot study, we are interested in the process of the data collection as well as the content. In short, we want to know whether our chosen data-collection method produces the expected data. Are there any unanticipated barriers to gathering the desired data? How do research participants respond to our data-collection procedures?

TABLE 16.2

Decision-Making Grid for Choosing a Data-Collection Method

Criteria	Surveys	Structured Observations	Secondary Analyses	Content Analysis	Interviewing
General Criteria for All Research Studies					
1. Size	+	0	+	+	+
2. Scope	+	—	—	—	—
3. Program participation	+	0	+	+	—
4. Worker cooperation	+	—	+	+	—
5. Intrusion into Clients' lives	—	—	+	+	—
6. Resources	+	—	+	+	0
7. Time	+	—	+	+	0
8. Previous research	+	0	—	—	+
Criteria for Our Specific Study					
1. Student availability	+	+	0	0	+
2. Student reading level	+	0	0	0	0
3. School preference	+	—	—	0	—
4. School year end	—	—	+	+	—
5. Access to existing records	0	0	+	+	0
Totals …	8	— 6	5	6	— 3

TABLE 16.3

Example of a Data-Collection Plan for Two Variables That Are Measured Three Times

a	b	c	d	e	f	g
Variable	**Indicator**	**Who** provides the data	**How** data are gathered	**When** data are gathered	**Where** data are gathered	**Who** collects the data
Self-esteem	*Rosenberg Self-Esteem Scale*	Client	1. Self-administered 2. Self-administered 3. Self-administered	1. Intake 2. Exit interview 3. 3 months after intervention	1. Waiting room 2. Office 3. Client's home	1. Receptionist 2. Social Worker 3. Case-aide
Social support systems	*Perceived Social Support Scale*	Client	1. Self-administered 2. Self-administered 3. Self-administered	1. Intake 2. Last day of intervention 3. 1 month after intervention	1. Waiting room 2. In therapy session 3. Group interview in coffee shop	1. Case-aide 2. Research assistant 3. Researcher

a = This column is where you list specifically what variable(s) you are going to use to measure.

b = This column is where you list specifically how you are going to measure each variable in column *a*. For example, the indicators for self-esteem and social support can be measured by many different means. In our example, we chose one standardized measuring instrument for each variable: the *Rosenberg Self-Esteem Scale* for our self-esteem variable and the *Scale of Perceived Social Support* for our social support variable.

c = This column is where you list specifically who is going to provide the data, via the use of your selected measuring instrument, or indicator (*b*). In a nutshell, this person, called a data source, is the one who is going to provide the data for the measuring instrument. Once again, a measuring instrument can be completed by a variety of different data sources.

d = This column is where you list specifically how the measuring instrument is going to be administered. Not only can you use a variety of indicators (*b*) to measure a variable (*a*), but you also have a variety of options for how to administer them (*d*). For example, you can read the items or questions on the measuring instrument to your clients, or you can have your clients fill out the instrument themselves. You can also have clients complete them individually with no one around or in group settings such as parks, waiting rooms, and coffee shops.

e = This column is where you state the exact time frame in which the measuring instrument is going to be completed. Once again, there are many options available. For example, clients could complete measuring instruments at home on Friday nights before bedtime or at the beginning of your interview.

f = This column, which is highly related to the previous column (*e*), is where you list the specific location where the measuring instrument will be completed. For example, you can have your clients complete the *Rosenberg Self-Esteem Scale* in your program's waiting room, at home, or in your office.

g = This column is where you list specifically who is going to collect the data via the measuring instrument when it's completed. After the data source (*c*) has provided the data for the measuring instrument (*b*), who's going to collect the completed instrument for analysis? And, more importantly, who is going to collate all the data into a databank for further analyses?

IMPLEMENTATION AND EVALUATION

THE DATA COLLECTION STEP of a research study can go smoothly if we act pro-actively. That is, we should guide and monitor the entire data-collection process according to the procedures and steps that were set out in the planning stage of our study and were tested in the pilot study (see Table 16.3 on page 581).

IMPLEMENTATION

THE MAIN GUIDING PRINCIPLE to implementing the selected data-collection method is that a systematic approach to data collection must be used. This means that the steps to gathering data should be methodically detailed so that there is no question about the tasks of the person(s) collecting the data—the data collector(s).

> It must be very clear from the beginning who is responsible for collecting the data.

This is true whether using a positivistic or interpretive research approach. As we know, the difference between these two research approaches is that the structure of the data-collection process within an interpretive research study (Chapter 7) is documented as the study progresses. By contrast, in a positivistic research study (Chapter 6) the data-collection process is decided at the study's outset and provides much less flexibility after the study is under way.

It must be very clear from the beginning who is responsible for collecting the data. When we take on the task, there is reasonable assurance that the data collection will remain objective and be guided by our research interests. Data collection left to only one person may be a formidable task. We must determine the amount of resources available to decide what data-collection method is most realistic. Regardless of the study size, we must attempt to establish clear roles and boundaries with those involved in the data-collection process.

The clearer our research study is articulated, the less difficulty there will be in moving through all the steps of the study. In particular, it is critical to identify who will and will not be involved in the data-collection process. To further avoid mix-ups and complications, specific tasks must be spelled out for all persons involved in our study. Where will the data be stored? Who will collect them? How will the data-collection process be monitored?

In many social work research studies, frontline social workers are involved in data-collection activities as part of their day-to-day activities. They typically gather intake and referral data, write assessment notes, and even use standardized questionnaires as part of their assessments. Data collection in programs can easily be designed to serve the dual purposes of research *and* intervention inquiry.

Thus, it's important to establish data-collection protocols to avoid problems of biased data. As mentioned, everyone in a research study must agree *when* data will be collected, *where*, and in *what* manner. Agreement is more likely to occur when we have fully informed and involved everyone participating in our study (see Table 16.3 on page 581).

EVALUATION

THE PROCESS OF SELECTING a chosen data-collection method is not complete without evaluating it. Evaluation occurs at two levels. First, the strengths and weaknesses of a data-collection method(s) and data source(s) are evaluated, given the research context in which our study takes place.

If, for example, data are gathered by a referring social worker about clients presenting problems, it must be acknowledged that the obtained data offer a limited (or restricted) point of view about the clients' problems. The strength of this approach may be that it was the only means for collecting the data.

> A good strategy for monitoring the implementation of a data collection method is to keep a journal of the data collection process.

A second level of evaluation is monitoring the implementation of the data-collection process itself. When data are gathered using several methods (or several sources), it's beneficial to develop a checklist of what data have been collected for each research participant. Developing a strategy for monitoring the data-collection process is especially important when the data must be collected in a timely fashion.

If pretest data are needed before a client enters a treatment program, for example, the data collection must be complete before admission occurs. Once a client has entered the program, opportunity to collect pretest data is lost.

Another strategy for monitoring evaluation is to keep a journal of the data-collection process. The journal records any questions or queries that arise in the data collection step. We may find, for example, that several research participants completing a questionnaire have difficulty understanding one particular question.

In addition, sometimes research participants have poor reading skills and require assistance with completion of some self-report standardized questionnaires. Documenting these idiosyncratic incidents accumulates important information by which to comment on our data's validity and reliability (overall credibility).

SUMMARY

THERE ARE MANY POSSIBLE DATA COLLECTION METHODS and data sources that can be used in any given research situation. We must weigh the pros and cons of both within the context of a particular research study to arrive at the best data collection method and data source. This process involves both conceptual and practical considerations.

Now that we know how to collect quantitative and qualitative data for any given research study, we will turn our attention to analyzing them. Thus, Chapter 17 presents how to analyze quantitative data, and Chapter 18 discusses how to analyze qualitative data.

	Study Questions for Chapter 16
	Essay — Discussion
1	What is a data source? What is a data-collection method? Discuss the differences between a data source and data-collection method. Provide social work examples throughout your discussion to illustrate your main points.
2	Discuss how data are collected and utilized within quantitative research studies (Chapter 6), within qualitative research studies (Chapter 7), and within mixed-methods research studies (Chapter 8). Provide social work examples throughout your discussion to illustrate your main points.
3	First, list all eight criteria that need to be addressed when selecting a data-collection method. Second, for each criterion, discuss how this single criterion can influence the selection of a data-collection method. Provide social work examples throughout your discussion to illustrate your main points.
4	What is meant by "trying out the selected data-collection method"? Provide social work examples throughout your discussion to illustrate your main points.
5	Take a look at Table 16.1 on pages 564–572. It contains 16 different types of data-collection methods. Provide an example of how you could use each one within a hypothetical social work research study of your choice. You can use the same study for more than one type if you wish, or you can use different hypothetical studies to illustrate how you could use each type.
6	Formulate a directional hypothesis (Chapter 6) that will be tested by an experimental design (i.e., Figure 13.9 on page 482). 1. List the various data sources that you can use to test your hypothesis. 2. List the various data-collection methods that you can use for each data source (see Table 16.1 on pages 564–572 in addition to Chapters 14 and 15). 3. Discuss the strengths and limitations of each data source and each data-collection method. 4. Which data source(s) and data-collection method(s) are the best ones to use in your study? Why? Defend your position using Tables 16.2 and 16.3 as guides.

7	With Question 6 in mind, create your version of Table 16.3 on page 581 in relation to your hypothesis, highlighting your selected dependent variable(s) [column *a*] and data source(s) [column *c*]
8	Take a look at Table 16.1 on pages 564–572. What other data-collection methods do you feel are not contained in the table? What are their advantages and disadvantages? Provide a social work example throughout your discussion to illustrate your main points.
9	Take a look at Table 16.2 on page 580. What other general criteria do you believe are relevant when it comes to selecting a data-collection method? What are their advantages and disadvantages? Provide a social work example throughout your discussion to illustrate your main points.

Critical Thinking — Application — Integration

10	**RESEARCH VS. PRACTICE** Pretend for the moment you're employed as a social worker in your university's student counseling center. A student comes into your office complaining about her high anxiety levels. 1. Using this chapter (and the previous two) as a guide, describe in detail how you would use the two concepts of "data sources" and "data gathering methods" to help her. (See the title of Table 16.1 on pages 564–572.) 2. Construct a table like Table 16.3 to guide your data-collection process. Remember, your dependent variable is anxiety (column *a* in Table 16.3 on page 581). **NOTE:** This exercise should help you to realize that "research techniques" and "practice techniques" can be the same, as discussed in Chapter 1 (see Figure 1.5 on page 37). In short, you can use Chapters 14–16 to help you gather data for your day-to-day practice activities for all of your client systems.

11	**DATA COLLECTION AND THE PRACTITIONER** **Scenario 1:** Make an argument that to be an effective evidence-based social work practitioner **you must know** the advantages and disadvantages of the various data-collection methods that are used in social work research studies. Provide a clear and explicit **practice-related** social work example to illustrate your main points. **Scenario 2:** Make an argument that **you do not have to know** the advantages and disadvantages of the various data-collection methods that are used in social work research studies to be an effective evidence-based practitioner. Provide a clear and explicit **practice-related** social work example to illustrate your main points. **Time to Choose:** Which one of the above two scenarios do you feel is more consistent with the concept of the contemporary evidence-based social work practice process as illustrated on pages 46–51? Why? Provide relevant social work examples to illustrate your main points.
12	**DATA COLLECTION AND THE RESEARCHER** **Scenario 1:** Make an argument that to be a competent social work researcher **you must know** the advantages and disadvantages of the various data-collection methods that are used in social work research studies. Provide a clear and explicit **research-related** social work example to illustrate your main points. **Scenario 2:** Make an argument that **you do not have to know** the advantages and disadvantages of the various data-collection methods that are used in social work research studies to be a competent social work researcher. Provide a clear and explicit **research-related** social work example to illustrate your main points. **Time to Choose:** Which one of the above two scenarios do you feel is more consistent with the place of research in social work? Why? Provide relevant social work examples to illustrate your main points.

13	**TIME TO PUT ON YOUR CRITICAL THINKING HAT** **1.** Discuss the similarities and differences between your responses to Questions 11 and 12. **2.** What are your thoughts on the belief that social work researchers and practitioners use the same kind of data-collection methods? For example, take a look at Table 16.1 on pages 564–572 for a moment. What data-collection methods do you feel researchers use that practitioners don't? And what data-collection methods do practitioners use that researchers don't? Justify your responses and use social work examples to illustrate your main points. **NOTE:** This exercise should help you to realize that "research data-gathering techniques" and "practice data-gathering techniques" are the same whether you're a researcher or practitioner.
14	**APPLICATION OF DATA COLLECTION METHODS** Locate a published social work quantitatively oriented article of your choice. Be sure the research study used a data-collection method to gather data from a data source(s). **1.** What was its data source(s)? **2.** What was its data-collection method(s) for each data source? **3.** With your knowledge of the various data-collection methods that research studies can use, thoroughly discuss how you will use the material contained within this chapter when you begin to evaluate the appropriateness of the research study's data-collection method(s) and discuss why you believe each criterion you selected is important for your evaluation of the study's chosen method(s). **4.** Would you have used a different method to collect the data to answer the study's research question (or to test its hypothesis)? If so, what method would you have used, and why? **5.** Do you believe you have the knowledge and skills to actually implement a quantitative research study such as the one you found? Why or why not? What specific knowledge and skills do you feel you lack? Discuss *where, when,* and *how* you plan on obtaining the necessary knowledge and skills.

15	**MIXED-METHODS RESEARCH (CHAPTER 8):** Pretend for the moment that you wish to do a **quantitatively** oriented research study (Chapter 6) to determine if MSW social workers are "better" at interviewing their clients than BSW social workers. You also wish to add a **qualitative** component (Chapter 7) to your study in an effort to add more meat to your study's quantitatively oriented findings and recommendations. Using what you have learned from Chapters 6–8 and 14–16, delineate how you would do your mixed-methods study (Chapter 8), highlighting the specific data-collection methods and data sources you have chosen (see Table 16.1 on pages 564–572).
16	**DATA COLLECTION AND YOUR PROFESSIONAL DEVELOPMENT** 1. Review the three social work research-related roles you can take when you graduate—CSWE Competency 1 at the beginning of this chapter on page 554. This concept was also discussed in Chapter 1 on pages 38–43. Thoroughly discuss how you feel this chapter will help you to perform one or more research-related roles when you graduate. Which one of the three roles do you believe this chapter helped you with the most? Why? Discuss in detail and provide an example to illustrate your main points. 2. Review CSWE Competency 4 at the beginning of this chapter on page 554. Thoroughly discuss how you feel this chapter will help you to become a practice-informed researcher and a research-informed practitioner. Discuss in detail and provide an example to illustrate your main points. 3. Review the evidence-based practice process as illustrated on pages 46–51. Thoroughly discuss how this chapter helps you to develop the skills you'll need for implementing one or more steps of the evidence-based practice process. 4. Discuss which step(s) you feel this chapter will help you with the most. Why? Be very specific and use relevant social work examples to illustrate your main points throughout your discussion. **NOTE:** This exercise should help you to realize that you can use "research data-gathering techniques" to help you become an evidence-based social work practitioner.

17	YOU'RE NOW A RESEARCHER 1. Pretend for a moment that you're a student on a committee whose main task is to construct a table like Table 16.3 on page 581 in reference to the teaching effectiveness of the teachers in your school of social work. Use as many data sources and data-collection methods you can think of when it comes to measuring the teaching effectiveness of your school's instructors. 2. Provide a detailed rational of why you chose each data source (e.g., you, mom, dad, sisters, brothers, student peers, school administrators, other instructors in your school, your practicum instructor, university personnel files, your current clients) and why you chose a specific data-collection method for each data source (see Table 16.1 on pages 564–572 for various data collection methods). **Now the hard part:** Discuss what each data source would bring to the party. That is, what valid and reliable data would each source contribute to the overall findings of your study? Be creative. Think outside the box. Take a chance.
18	BEFORE AND AFTER *Part 1 (before):* Before enrolling in your current research methods course, and before you read the previous two chapters and this chapter on data collection, how did you think social work researchers selected their data-collection methods? What data-collection methods did you think they used before you read these three chapters? Do you feel the data-collection methods were ethical? If so, how? If not, why not? *Part 2 (after):* After reading this chapter and the previous two chapters on collecting data, discuss any new data-collection method you learned about that you did not know about before reading the three chapters. List each new method you learned about and provide a hypothetical social work research study that demonstrates the use of your newfound method(s).
19	MOVING AHEAD BY LOOKING BACK At this point in your research methods course, how comfortable are you with discussing the place of research in social work with your field instructor, with your practice instructor, with your research instructor, with your supervisor at work, with the director of your social work program, or with your classmates? Discuss in detail.

Analyzing Data

CHAPTER 17: Analyzing Quantitative Data **592**

CHAPTER 18: Analyzing Qualitative Data **624**

17

CHAPTER

COMPETENCY 1: Demonstrate Ethical and Professional Behavior

You will learn that in order to be a successful evidence-based practitioner you have an ethical obligation to integrate three research roles into your daily practice activities as discussed in Chapter 1: (1) research consumer, (2) research partner—either as a co-researcher or research participant, and (3) creator and disseminator of research (or knowledge).

This entire chapter pertains to these three professional research-related roles when it comes to collecting, displaying, and analyzing quantitative data.

COMPETENCY 4: Engage in Practice-Informed Research and Research-Informed Practice

Competency 4 also pertains to the entire chapter because you have to:

1. Evaluate the appropriateness of the quantitative data analysis that was utilized in a quantitative research study (**research consumer**—research-informed practice);

2. Participate in a quantitative research study—either as a co-researcher or research participant (**research partner**—practice-informed research). See 1 above and 3 below; and

3. Know how to collect, display, and interpret quantitative data before you actually do a quantitative research study (**creator and disseminator of research**—practice-informed research).

You'll also need to utilize evidence-based practice recommendations whenever possible; that is, you need to integrate (1) the best available research-based evidence with (2) your clinical expertise and (3) your client's values.

All of the above implies you'll need to evaluate the strengths and limitations of the research-based quantitative evidence a study produced. In short, you need to ask and then answer a simple question: How seriously should I take the findings and recommendations of any quantitative research study given the level of rigor the author used in analyzing the quantitative data?

COMPETENCY 9: Evaluate Practice with Individuals, Families, Groups, Organizations, and Communities

See Competencies 1 and 4.

Analyzing Quantitative Data

CHAPTER 1	**Step 1.**	Understanding the Research Process
CHAPTER 2	**Step 2.**	Developing Research Questions
CHAPTER 3	**Step 3.**	Reviewing the Literature
CHAPTERS 4 & 5	**Step 4.**	Being Aware of Ethical and Cultural Issues
CHAPTERS 6–8	**Step 5.**	Selecting a Research Approach
CHAPTERS 9 & 10	**Step 6.**	Specifying How Variables Are Measured
CHAPTER 11	**Step 7.**	Selecting a Sample
CHAPTERS 12 & 13	**Step 8.**	Selecting a Research Design
CHAPTERS 14–16	**Step 9.**	Selecting a Data-Collection Method
CHAPTERS 17 & 18	**Step 10.**	Analyzing the Data
CHAPTERS 19 & 20	**Step 11.**	Writing the Research Report

AFTER QUANTITATIVE DATA ARE COLLECTED THEY NEED TO BE ANALYZED—the purpose of this chapter. To be honest, a thorough understanding of quantitative statistical methods is far beyond the scope of this book and would necessitate more in-depth study, through taking one or more statistics courses. Instead, we briefly describe a select group of basic statistical analytical methods that are used frequently in many quantitative *and* qualitative social work research studies. Our emphasis is not on providing and calculating formulas, but rather on helping the reader to understand the underlying rationale for their use.

We present two basic groups of statistical procedures. The first group is called *descriptive statistics*; these procedures simply describe and summarize one or more variables for a sample or population. They provide information about only the group included in the study. The second group is called *inferential statistics*; these procedures determine if we can generalize findings derived from a sample to the population from which the sample was drawn. In other words, knowing what we know about a particular sample, can we infer that the rest of the population is similar to the sample that we have studied?

Before you read further, we encourage you to reread Chapter 9 on levels of measurement. It's extremely important for you to have a sound understanding of the four levels of measurement before you dive into statistics.

ENTERING DATA INTO COMPUTERS

THE USE OF COMPUTERS has revolutionized the analysis of quantitative and qualitative data. Where previous generations of researchers had to rely on hand-cranked adding machines to calculate every small step in a data analysis, today we can enter raw scores into a personal computer and with few complications direct the computer program to execute just about any statistical test imaginable.

Seconds later, the results are available. While the process is truly miraculous, the risk is that, even though we have conducted the correct statistical analysis, we may not understand what the results mean, a factor that will almost certainly affect how we interpret the data.

We can code data from all four levels of measurement into a computer for any given data analysis (see Chapter 9). The coding of nominal data is perhaps the most complex, because we have to create categories that correspond to certain possible responses for a variable.

One type of nominal-level data that is often gathered from research participants is *place of birth.* If, for the purposes of our study, we were interested in whether our research participants were born in either Canada or the United States, we would assign only three categories to *place of birth:*

1. Canada
2. United States
9. Other

The *other* category (9) appears routinely at the end of lists of categories and acts as a catchall, to cover any category that may have been omitted.

When entering nominal-level data into a computer, because we do not want to enter *Canada* every time the response on the questionnaire is Canada, we may assign it the code number 1 so that all we have to enter is 1. Similarly, the United States may be assigned the number 2, and "other" may be assigned the number 9.

These numbers have no mathematical meaning. We are not saying that Canada is better than the United States because it comes first, or that the United States is twice as good as Canada because the number assigned to it is twice as high. We are merely using numbers as a shorthand device to record *qualitative* differences: differences in *kind,* not in amount.

Most coding for ordinal-, interval-, and ratio-level data is simply a matter of entering the final score, or number, from the measuring instrument that was used to measure the variable directly into the computer. If a person scored a 45 on a standardized measuring instrument, for example, the number 45 would be entered into the computer.

Although almost all data entered into computers are in the form of numbers, we need to know at what level of measurement the data exist so that we can choose the appropriate statistic(s) to describe and compare the variables.

As you know from Chapter 9 about the four different measurement levels, let's turn to the first group of statistics that can be helpful for the analyses of data—descriptive statistics. This would is an excellent time to review Chapter 9 as this chapter assumes you know Chapter 9's content inside and out.

DESCRIPTIVE STATISTICS

DESCRIPTIVE STATISTICS are commonly used in most quantitative and qualitative research studies. They describe and summarize a variable(s) of interest and portray how that particular variable is distributed in the sample, or population. Before looking at descriptive statistics, however, let's examine a social work research example that will be used throughout this chapter.

Thea Black is a social worker who works in a treatment foster care program. Her program focuses on children who have behavioral problems who are placed with "treatment" foster care parents. These parents are supposed to have parenting skills that will help them provide the children's special needs.

Thus, Thea's program also teaches parenting skills to these treatment foster care parents. She assumes that newly recruited foster parents are not likely to know much about parenting children who have behavioral problems. Therefore, she believes that they would benefit from a training program that teaches these skills in order to help them to deal effectively with the special needs of these children who will soon be living with them.

Thea hopes that her parenting skills training program will increase the knowledge about parental management skills for the parents who attend.

She assumes that with such training the foster parents will be in a better position to support and provide clear limits for their foster children.

After offering the training program for several months, Thea became curious about whether the foster care providers who attended the program were, indeed, lacking in knowledge of parental management skills as she first believed (her tentative hypothesis).

She was fortunate to find a valid and reliable standardized instrument that measures the knowledge of such parenting skills, the Parenting Skills Scale (*PSS*). Thea decided to find out for herself how much the newly recruited parents knew about parenting skills—clearly a descriptive research question.

At the beginning of one of her training sessions (*before* they were exposed to her skills training program), she handed out the *PSS,* asking the twenty individuals in attendance to complete it and also to include data about their gender, years of education, and whether they had ever participated in a parenting skills training program before. All of these variables could be potentially extraneous ones that might influence the level of knowledge of parenting skills of the twenty participants.

For each foster care parent, Thea calculated the *PSS* score, called a *raw score* because it has not been sorted or analyzed in any way. The total score possible on the *PSS* is 100, with higher scores indicating greater knowledge of parenting skills. The scores for the *PSS* scale, as well as the other data collected from the twenty parents, are listed in Table 17.1 on the following page.

At this point, Thea stopped to consider how she could best utilize the data that she had collected. She had data at three different levels of measurement. At the nominal level, Thea had collected data on gender (3rd column), and whether the parents had any previous parenting skills training (4th column). Each of these variables can be categorized into two responses.

The scores on the *PSS* (2nd column) are ordinal because, although the data are sequenced from highest to lowest, the differences between units cannot be placed on an equally spaced continuum. Nevertheless, many measures in the social sciences are treated as if they are at an interval level, even though equal distances between scale points cannot be proved. This assumption is important because it allows for the use of inferential statistics on such data.

TABLE 17.1

Data Collection for Four Variables from Foster Care Providers

Number	PSS Score	Gender	Previous Training	Years of Education
01	95	Male	No	12
02	93	Female	Yes	12
03	93	Male	No	08
04	93	Female	No	12
05	90	Male	Yes	12
06	90	Female	No	12
07	84	Male	No	14
08	84	Female	No	18
09	82	Male	No	10
10	82	Female	No	12
11	80	Male	No	12
12	80	Female	No	11
13	79	Male	No	12
14	79	Female	Yes	12
15	79	Female	No	16
16	79	Male	No	12
17	79	Female	No	11
18	72	Female	No	14
19	71	Male	No	15
20	55	Female	Yes	12

Finally, the data on years of formal education (5th column) that were collected by Thea are clearly at the ratio level of measurement, because there are equally distributed points and the scale has an absolute zero.

In sum, it seemed to Thea that the data could be used in at least two ways. First, the data collected about each variable could be described to provide a picture of the characteristics of the group of foster care parents. This would call for descriptive statistics. Second, she might look for relationships between some of the variables about which she had collected data, procedures that would utilize inferential statistics. For now let us begin by looking at how the first type of descriptive statistic can be used with Thea's dataset.

FREQUENCY DISTRIBUTIONS

ONE OF THE SIMPLEST PROCEDURES that Thea can employ is to develop a frequency distribution of her data. Constructing a frequency distribution involves counting the occurrences of each value, or category, of the variable and ordering them in some fashion. This *absolute* or *simple frequency distribution* allows us to see quickly how certain values of a variable are distributed in our sample.

The *mode*, or the most commonly occurring score, can be easily spotted in a simple frequency distribution (see Table 17.2). In this example, the mode is 79, a score obtained by five parents on the *PSS* scale. The highest and the lowest scores are also quickly identifiable. The top score was 95, while the foster care parent who performed the least well on the *PSS* scored 55.

There are several other ways to present frequency data. A commonly used method that can be easily integrated into a simple frequency distribution table is the *cumulative frequency distribution*, shown in Table 17.3 on the following page.

In Thea's dataset, the highest *PSS* score, 95, was obtained by only one individual. The group of individuals who scored 93 or above on the *PSS* measure includes four foster care parents. If we want to know how many scored 80 or above, if we look at the number across from 80 in the cumulative frequency column, we can quickly see that 12 of the parents scored 80 or better.

TABLE 17.2
Frequency Distribution
(from Table 17.1)

PSS Score	Absolute Frequency
95	1
93	3
90	2
84	2
82	2
80	2
79	5
72	1
71	1
55	1

Other tables use percentages rather than frequencies, sometimes referred to as *percentage distributions*, shown in the far-right column in Table 17.3. Each of these numbers represents the percentage of participants who obtained each *PSS* value. Five individuals, for example, scored 79 on the *PSS*.

TABLE 17.3

Cumulative Frequency and Percentage Distribution of Parental Skill Scores (from Table 17.1)

PSS Score	Absolute	Cumulative	Percentage Distribution
95	1	1	5
93	3	4	15
90	2	6	10
84	2	8	10
82	2	10	10
80	2	12	10
79	5	17	25
72	1	18	5
71	1	19	5
55	1	20	5
Totals . . .	20		100

Since there were a total of 20 foster care parents, 5 out of the 20, or one-quarter of the total, obtained a score of 79. This corresponds to 25 percent of the participants.

Finally, *grouped frequency distributions* are used to simplify a table by grouping the variable into equal-sized ranges, as shown in Table 17.4. Both absolute and cumulative frequencies and percentages can also be displayed using this format. Each is calculated in the same way that was previously described for nongrouped data, and the interpretation is identical.

Looking at the absolute frequency column, for example, we can quickly identify the fact that seven of the foster care parents scored in the 70–79 range on the *PSS*. By looking at the cumulative frequency column, we can see that 12 of 20 parents scored 80 or better on the *PSS*. Further, from the absolute percentage column, it's clear that 30 percent of the foster parents scored in the 80–89 range on the knowledge of parenting skills scale.

Note that each of the other variables in Thea's dataset could also be displayed in frequency distributions. Displaying years of education in a fre-

TABLE 17.4
Grouped Frequency Distribution of Parental Skill Scores
(from Table 17.1)

PSS Score	Absolute	Cumulative	Absolute Percentage
90 - 100	6	6	30
80 - 89	6	12	30
70 - 79	7	19	35
60 - 69	0	19	0
50 - 59	1	20	5
Totals . . .	20		100

quency distribution, for example, would provide a snapshot of how this variable is distributed in Thea's sample of foster care parents. However, with two category nominal variables, such as gender (male, female) and previous parenting skills training (yes, no), cumulative frequencies become less meaningful, and the data are better described as percentages.

Thea noted that 55 percent of the foster care parents who attended the training workshop were women (obviously the other 45 percent were men) and that 20 percent of the parents had already received some form of parenting skills training (while a further 80 percent had not been trained).

MEASURES OF CENTRAL TENDENCY

WE CAN ALSO DISPLAY THE VALUES obtained on the *PSS* in the form of a graph. A *frequency polygon* is one of the simplest ways of charting frequencies. The graph in Figure 17.1 displays the data that we had previously put in Table 17.2. The *PSS* score is plotted in terms of how many of the foster care parents obtained each score. As can be seen from Table 17.2 and Figure 17.1, most of the scores fall between 79 and 93. The one extremely low score of 55 is also quickly noticeable in such a graph because it's so far removed from the rest of the values.

A frequency polygon allows us to make a quick analysis of how closely the distribution fits the shape of a normal curve. A *normal curve*, also known

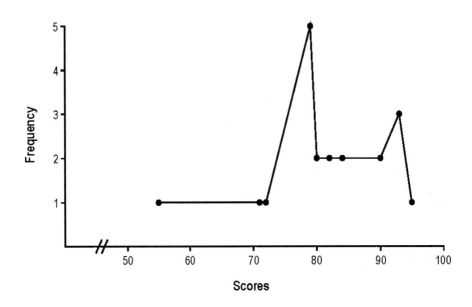

FIGURE 17.1

Frequency Polygon of Parental Scores (from Table 17.2)

as a *bell-shaped distribution* or a *normal distribution*, is a frequency polygon in which the greatest number of responses fall in the middle of the distribution and fewer scores appear at the extremes of either very high or very low scores (see Figure 17.2).

Many variables in the social sciences are assumed to be distributed in the shape of a normal curve. Low intelligence, for example, is thought to be relatively rare as compared to the number of individuals with average intelligence. On the other end of the continuum, extremely gifted individuals are also relatively uncommon.

Of course, not all variables are distributed in the shape of a normal curve. Some are such that a large number of people do very well (as Thea found in her sample of foster care parents and their parenting skill levels). Other variables, such as juggling ability, for example, would be charted showing a fairly substantial number of people performing poorly.

Frequency distributions of still other variables would show that some people do well, and some people do poorly, but not many fall in between. What is important to remember about distributions is that, although all dif-

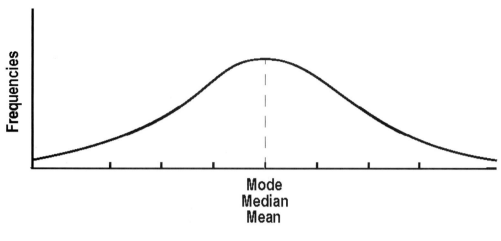

FIGURE 17.2
The Normal Distribution

ferent sorts are possible, most statistical procedures assume that there is a normal distribution of the variable in question in the population.

When looking at how variables are distributed in samples and populations it's common to use measures of *central tendency*, such as the mode, median, and mean, which help us to identify where the typical or the average score can be found. These measures are used so often because not only do they provide a useful summary of the data, they also provide a common denominator for comparing groups to each other. They are:

1. Mode
2. Median
3. Mean

MODE

AS MENTIONED EARLIER, the mode is the score, or value, that occurs the most often—the value with the highest frequency. In Thea's dataset of parental skills scores the mode is 79, with five foster care parents obtaining this value. The mode is particularly useful for nominal level data. Knowing what score occurred the most often, however, provides little information about the other scores and how they are distributed in the sample or population.

Because the mode is the least precise of all the measures of central tendency, the median and the mean are better descriptors of ordinal level data and above. We now turn our attention to the second measure of central tendency, the median.

MEDIAN

THE MEDIAN IS THE SCORE that divides a distribution into two equal parts or portions. In order to do this, we must rank-order the scores, so at least an ordinal level of measurement is required. In Thea's sample of 20 *PSS* scores, the median would be the score above which the top ten scores lie and below which the bottom ten fall. As can be seen in Table 17.2, the top ten scores finish at 82, and the bottom ten scores start at 80. In this example, the median is 81, since it falls between 82 and 80.

MEAN

THE MEAN IS THE MOST SOPHISTICATED measure of central tendency and is useful for interval or ratio levels of measurement. It's also one of the most commonly utilized statistics. A mean is calculated by summing the individual values and dividing by the total number of values. The mean of Thea's sample is 95 + 93 + 93 + 93 + 90 + 90 + ... 72 + 71 + 55/20 = 81.95. In this example, the obtained mean of 82 (we rounded off for the sake of clarity) is larger than the mode of 79 or the median of 81.

The mean is one of the previously mentioned statistical procedures that assumes that a variable will be distributed normally throughout a population. If this is not an accurate assumption, then the median might be a better descriptor. The mean is also best used with relatively large sample sizes where extreme scores (such as the lowest score of 55 in Thea's sample) have less influence.

MEASURES OF VARIABILITY

WHILE MEASURES OF CENTRAL TENDENCY PROVIDE valuable information about a set of scores, we are also interested in knowing how the scores scatter themselves around the center. A mean does not give a sense of how widely distributed the scores may be. This is provided by measures of variability such as the range and the standard deviation. There are many types of variability. We will only discuss two:

1. Range
2. Standard deviation

RANGE

THE RANGE IS SIMPLY THE DISTANCE between the minimum and the maximum score. The larger the range, the greater the amount of variation of scores in the distribution. The range is calculated by subtracting the lowest score from the highest. In Thea's sample, the range is 40 (95 – 55). The range does not assume equal interval data. It is, like the mean, sensitive to deviant values because it depends on only the two extreme scores.

We could have a group of four scores ranging from 10 to 20: 10, 14, 19, and 20, for example. The range of this sample would be 10 (20 – 10). If one additional score that was substantially different from the first set of four scores was included, this would change the range dramatically. In this example, if a fifth score of 45 was added, the range of the sample would become 35 (45 – 10), a number that would suggest quite a different picture of the variability of the scores.

STANDARD DEVIATION

THE STANDARD DEVIATION is the most utilized indicator of dispersion. It provides a picture of how the scores distribute themselves around the mean. Used in combination with the mean, the standard deviation provides a great deal of information about the sample or population without our ever needing to see the raw scores. In a normal distribution of scores (as described previously) there are six standard deviations: three below the mean and three above, as is shown in Figure 17.3.

In this perfect model we always know that 34.13 percent of the scores of the sample fall within 1 standard deviation above the mean, and another 34.13 percent fall within 1 standard deviation below the mean. Thus, a total of 68.26 percent, or about two-thirds of the scores, is between +1 standard deviation and –1 standard deviation from the mean.

This leaves almost one-third of the scores to fall farther away from the mean, with 15.87 percent (50% to 34.13%) above +1 standard deviation, and 15.87 percent (50% to 34.13%) below 1 standard deviation.

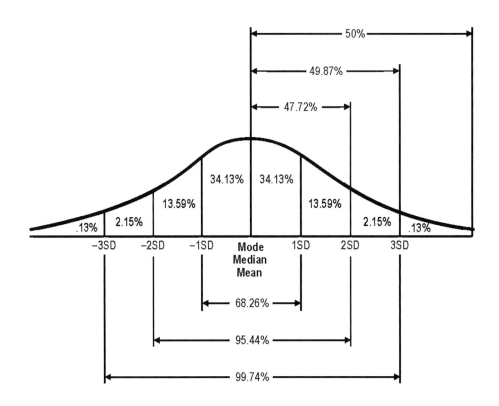

FIGURE 17.3
Proportions of the Normal Curve

In total, when we look at the proportion of scores that fall between +2 and −2 standard deviations, 95.44 percent of scores can be expected to be found within these parameters. Furthermore, 99.74 percent of the scores fall between +3 standard deviations and −3 standard deviations about the mean. Thus, finding scores that fall beyond 3 standard deviations above and below the mean should be a rare occurrence.

The standard deviation has the advantage, like the mean, of taking all values into consideration in its computation. Also similar to the mean, it's utilized with interval or ratio levels of measurement and assumes a normal distribution of scores.

Several different samples of scores could have the same mean, but the variation around the mean, as provided by the standard deviation, could be quite different, as is shown in Figure 17.4a. Two different distributions could have unequal means and equal standard deviations, as in Figure 17.4b, or unequal means and unequal standard deviations, as in Figure 17.4c.

The standard deviation of the scores of Thea's foster care parents was calculated to be 10. Again, assuming that the variable of knowledge about parenting skills is normally distributed in the population of foster care parents, the results of the *PSS* scores from the sample of parents about whom we are making inferences can be shown in a distribution like Figure 17.5.

As can also be seen in Figure 17.5, the score that would include 2 standard deviations, 102, is beyond the total possible score of 100 on the test. This is because the distribution of the scores in Thea's sample of parents does not entirely fit a normal distribution. The one extremely low score of 55 (see Table 17.1) obtained by one foster care parent would have affected the mean as well as the standard deviation.

INFERENTIAL STATISTICS

THE GOAL OF INFERENTIAL STATISTICAL TESTS is to rule out chance as the explanation for finding either associations between variables or differences between variables in our samples. Because we can rarely study an entire population, we are almost always dealing with samples drawn from that population. The danger is that we might make conclusions about a particular population based on a sample that is uncharacteristic of the population it's supposed to represent.

For example, perhaps the group of foster parents in Thea's training session happened to have an unusually high level of knowledge of parenting skills. If she assumed that all the rest of the foster parents that she might train in the future were as knowledgeable, she would be overestimating their knowledge, a factor that could have a negative impact on the way she conducts her training program.

To counteract the possibility that the sample is uncharacteristic of the general population, statistical tests take a conservative position as to whether we can conclude that there are relationships between the variables within our sample. The guidelines to indicate the likelihood that we have indeed found a relationship or difference that fits the population of interest are called *probability levels*.

The convention in most social science research is that variables are significantly associated or groups are significantly different if we are relatively certain that in 19 samples out of 20 (or 95 times out of 100) from a particu-

(a) Equal means, unequal standard deviations

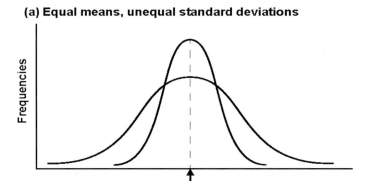

(b) Unequal means, equal standard deviations

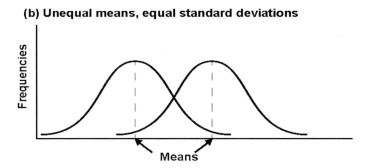

(c) Unequal means, unequal standard deviations

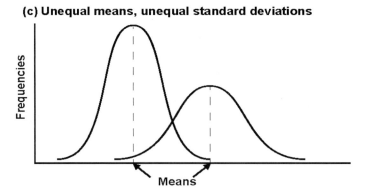

FIGURE 17.4

Variations in the Normal Distribution

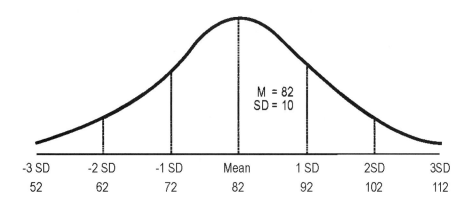

FIGURE 17.5
Distribution of Parental Skills Scores

lar population, we would find the same relationship. This corresponds to a probability level of .05, written as ($p < .05$).

Probability levels are usually provided along with the results of the statistical test to demonstrate how confident we are that the results actually indicate statistically significant differences. If a probability level is greater than .05 (e.g., .06, .10), this indicates that we did not find a statistically significant difference.

STATISTICS THAT DETERMINE ASSOCIATIONS

THERE ARE MANY STATISTICS that can determine whether there is an association between two variables. We will briefly discuss two:

1. Chi-square
2. Correlation

CHI-SQUARE

THE CHI-SQUARE TEST REQUIRES measurements of variables at only the nominal or ordinal level. Thus, it's very useful because much data in social work are gathered at these two levels of measurement. In general, the chi-square test looks at whether specific values of one variable tend to be associated with specific values of another.

In short, we use it to determine whether two variables are related. It cannot be used to determine whether one variable *caused* another, however. In thinking about the foster care parents who were in her training program, Thea was aware that women are more typically responsible for caring for their own children than men. Even if they are not mothers themselves, they are often in professions such as teaching and social work where they are caretakers.

Thus, she wondered whether there might be a relationship between gender and previous training in parenting skills, such that women were less likely to have taken such training because they already felt confident in their knowledge of parenting skills.

As a result, her one-tailed hypothesis was that fewer women than men would have previously taken parenting skills training courses. Thea could examine this possibility with her 20 foster care parents using a chi-square test. In terms of gender, Thea had data from the nine (45%) men and 11 (55%) women. Of the total group, four (20%) had previous training in foster care training, while 16 (80%) had not.

As shown in Table 17.5, the first task was for Thea to count the number of men and women who had previous training and the number of men and women who did not have previous training. She put these data in one of the four categories in Table 17.5. The actual numbers are called *observed frequencies*. It's helpful to transform these raw data into (percentages), making comparisons between categories much easier.

We can, however, still not tell simply by looking at the observed frequencies whether there is a statistically significant relationship between gender (male or female) and previous training (yes or no). To do this, the next step is to look at how much the observed frequencies differ from what we would expect to see if, in fact, if there was no relationship. These are called *expected frequencies*. Without going through all the calculations, the chi-square table would now look like Table 17.6 for Thea's dataset.

Because the probability level of the obtained chi-square value in Table 17.6 is greater than .05, Thea did not find any statistical relationship between gender and previous training in parenting skills. Thus, statistically speaking, men were no more likely than women to have received previous training in parenting skills; her research hypothesis was not supported by the data.

TABLE 17.5

Frequencies (and percentages) of Gender by Previous Training (from Table 17.1)

	Previous Training?		
Gender	Yes	No	Total
Male	1 (11)	8 (89)	9
Female	3 (27)	8 (73)	11
Totals . . .	4 (20)	16 (80)	20 (100)

CORRELATION

TESTS OF CORRELATION investigate the strength of the relationship between two variables. As with the chi-square test, correlation cannot be used to imply causation, only association. Correlation is applicable to data at the interval and ratio levels of measurement. Correlational values are always decimalized numbers, never exceeding ±1.00.

The size of the obtained correlation value indicates the strength of the association, or relationship, between the two variables. The closer a correlation is to zero, the less likely it is that a relationship exists between the two variables. The plus and minus signs indicate the direction of the relationship. Either high positive (close to +1.00) or high negative numbers (close −1.00) signify strong relationships.

In most positive correlations, though, the scores vary similarly, either increasing or

TABLE 17.6

Chi-Square Table for Gender by Previous Training (from Table 17.5)

	Previous Training?	
Gender	Yes	No
Male		
Observed	1.0	8.0
Expected	1.8	7.2
Female		
Observed	3.0	8.0
Expected	2.2	8.8

Note: $X^2 = 0.8$; $df = 1$; $p > .05$

decreasing. Thus, as parenting skills increase, so does self-esteem, for example. A negative correlation, in contrast, simply means that as one variable increases the other decreases. An example would be that as parenting skills increase the stresses experienced by foster parents decrease.

Thea may wonder whether there is a relationship between the foster parents' years of education and score on the *PSS* knowledge test. She might reason that the more years of education completed, the more likely the parents would have greater knowledge about parenting skills.

To investigate the one-tailed hypothesis that years of education are positively related to knowledge of parenting skills, Thea can correlate the *PSS* scores with each person's number of years of formal education using one of the most common correlational tests, Pearson's *r*.

The obtained correlation between *PSS* score and years of education in this example is $r = -.10$ ($p > .05$). It was in the opposite direction of what she predicted. This negative correlation is close to zero, and its probability level is greater than .05. Thus, in Thea's sample, the parents' *PSS* scores are not related to their educational levels.

If the resulting correlation coefficient (*r*) had been positive and statistically significant ($p < .05$), it would have indicated that as the knowledge levels of the parents increased so would their years of formal education. If the correlation coefficient had been statistically significant but negative, this would be interpreted as showing that as years of formal education increased, knowledge scores decreased.

If a correlational analysis is misinterpreted, it's likely to be the case that the researcher implied causation rather than simply identifying an association between the two variables. If Thea were to have found a statistically significant positive correlation between knowledge and education levels and had explained this to mean that the high knowledge scores were a result of higher education levels, she would have interpreted the statistic incorrectly.

STATISTICS THAT DETERMINE DIFFERENCES

TWO COMMONLY USED STATISTICAL PROCEDURES, *t*-tests and analysis of variance (ANOVA), examine the means and variances of two or more separate groups of scores to determine whether they are statistically different from one another. *T*-tests are used with only two groups of scores, whereas ANOVA is used when there are more than two groups. Both are characterized by having a dependent variable at the interval or ratio level of measurement, and an independent, or grouping, variable at either the nominal or ordinal level of measurement. Several assumptions underlie the use of both *t*-tests and ANOVAs.

First, it's assumed that the dependent variable is normally distributed in the population from which the samples were drawn. Second, it's assumed that the variance of the scores of the dependent variable in the different groups is roughly the same. This assumption is called *homogeneity of variance*. Third, it's assumed that the samples are randomly drawn from the population.

Nevertheless, as mentioned in Chapter 13 on group research designs, it's a common occurrence in social work that we can neither randomly select from a population nor randomly assign individuals to either the experimental or the control group. In many cases this is because we are dealing with already preformed groups, such as Thea's foster care parents.

Breaking the assumption of randomization, however, presents a serious drawback to the interpretation of the research findings, which must be noted in the limitations and the interpretations section of the final research report. One possible difficulty that might result from nonrandomization is that the sample may be uncharacteristic of the larger population in some manner.

It's important, therefore, that the results not be used inferentially; that is, the findings must not be generalized to the general population. The design of the research study is thus reduced to a descriptive level, being relevant to only those individuals included in the sample.

DEPENDENT *T*-TESTS

DEPENDENT *T*-TESTS ARE USED to compare two groups of scores from the same individuals. The most frequent example in social work research is looking at how a group of individuals change from before they receive a social work intervention (pre) to afterward (post). Thea may have decided that although she knew the knowledge levels of the foster care parents before receiving training was interesting, it did not give her any idea about whether her program helped the parents to improve their skill levels.

In other words her research question became "After being involved in the program, did parents know more about parenting skills than before they started?" Her hypothesis was that knowledge of parenting skills would improve after participation in her training program.

Thea managed to contact all the foster care parents in the original group (Group A) one week after they had graduated from the program and asked them to fill out the *PSS* knowledge questionnaire once again. Because it was the same group of people who were responding twice to the same questionnaire, the dependent *t*-test was appropriate.

Using the same set of scores collected by Thea previously as the pretest, the mean *PSS* was 82, with a standard deviation of 10. The mean score of the foster care parents after they completed the program was calculated as 86, with a standard deviation of 8.

A *t*-value of 3.9 was obtained, significant at the .05 level, indicating that the levels of parenting skills significantly increased after the foster care parents participated in the skills training program. The results suggest that the average parenting skills of this particular group of foster care parents significantly improved (from 82 to 86) after they had participated in Thea's program.

INDEPENDENT *T*-TESTS

INDEPENDENT *T*-TESTS are used for two groups of scores that have no relationship to each other. If Thea had *PSS* scores from one group of foster care parents and then collected more *PSS* scores from a second group of foster care parents, for example, these two groups would be considered independent, and the independent *t*-test would be the appropriate statistical analysis to determine whether there was a statistically significant difference between the means of the two groups' *PSS* scores.

Thea decided to compare the average *PSS* score for the first group of foster care parents (Group A) with the average *PSS* score of parents in her next training program (Group B). This would allow her to see whether the first group (Group A) had been unusually talented or conversely were less well versed in parenting skills than the second group (Group B). Her hypothesis was that there would be no differences in the level of knowledge of parenting skills between the two groups.

Because Thea had *PSS* scores from two different groups of participants (Groups A and B), the correct statistical test to identify whether there are any statistical differences between the means of the two groups is the independent *t*-test. Let's use the same set of numbers that we previously used in the example of the dependent *t*-test in this analysis, this time considering the posttest *PSS* scores as the scores of the second group of foster care parents.

As can be seen from Figure 17.6, the mean *PSS* of Group A was 82 and the standard deviation was 10. Group B scored an average of 86 on the *PSS*, with a standard deviation of 8. Although the means of the two groups are four points apart, the standard deviations in the distribution of each are fairly large, so there is considerable overlap between the two groups. This would suggest that statistically significant differences will not be found.

The obtained *t*-value to establish whether this four-point difference (86 − 82) between the means for two groups is statistically significant was calculated to be $t = 1.6$ with a $p > .05$. The two groups were thus not statistically different from one another, and Thea's hypothesis was supported.

Note, however, that Thea's foster care parents were not randomly assigned to each group, thus breaking one of the assumptions of the *t*-test. As discussed earlier, this is a serious limitation to the interpretation of the study's results. We must be especially careful not to generalize the findings beyond the groups included in the study.

Also note that in the previous example, when using the same set of numbers but a dependent *t*-test, we found a statistically significant difference. This is because the dependent *t*-test analysis is more robust than the independent *t*-test, because having the same participant fill out the questionnaire twice, under two different conditions, controls for many extraneous variables, such as individual differences, that could negatively influence an analysis of independent samples.

ONE-WAY ANALYSIS OF VARIANCE

A ONE-WAY ANOVA IS THE EXTENSION of an independent *t*-test that uses three or more groups. Each set of scores is from a different group of participants. For example, Thea might use the scores on the *PSS* test from the first group of foster care parents from whom she collected data before they participated in her program, but she might also collect data from a second and a third group of parents before they received the training. The test for significance of an ANOVA is called an *F*-test.

We could actually use an ANOVA procedure on only two groups, and the result would be identical to the *t*-test. Unlike the *t*-test, however, obtaining a

FIGURE 17.6

Frequency Distributions of *PSS* Scores from Two Groups of Foster Care Providers

significant *F*-value in a one-way ANOVA does not complete the analysis. Because ANOVA looks at differences between three or more groups, a significant *F*-value only tells us that there is a statistically significant difference among the groups. It does not tell us between which ones. To identify this, we need to do a *post-hoc* test.

A variety is available, such as Duncan's multiple range, Tukey's honestly significant difference test, and Newman-Keuls, and they are provided automatically by most computer statistics programs.

But one caution applies: a post-hoc test should be used *only after finding a significant F-value,* because some of the post-hoc tests are more sensitive than the *F*-test and so might find significance when the *F*-test does not. Generally, we should use the most conservative test first, in this case the *F*-test.

In the example of Thea's program, let's say that she collected data on a total of three different groups of foster care parents. The first group of foster care parents scored an average of 82 on the *PSS* (standard deviation 10). The second group scored an average of 86 (standard deviation 8), and the mean score of the third group was 88 with a standard deviation of 7.

The obtained *F*-value for the one-way ANOVA is 2.63, with a *p* > .05. Thus, we must conclude that there are no statistically significant differences between the means of the groups (i.e., 82, 86, and 88). Because the *F*-value was not significant, we would not conduct any post-hoc tests. This finding would be interesting to Thea because it suggests that all three groups of foster care parents started out with approximately the same knowledge levels, on average, before receiving training.

SUMMARY

THIS CHAPTER PROVIDED A BEGINNING look at the rationale behind some of the most commonly used statistical procedures, both those that describe samples and those that analyze data from a sample in order to make inferences about the larger population. The level of measurement of the data is key to the kind of statistical procedures that can be used.

Descriptive statistics are used with data from all levels of measurement. The mode is the most appropriate measure of central tendency for measurements of this level. It's only when we have data from interval and ratio levels that we can utilize inferential statistics—those that extend the statistical conclusions made about a sample by applying them to the larger population.

Descriptive measures of central tendency, such as the mode, median, and mean of a sample or population, all provide different kinds of information, each of which is applicable only to some levels of measurement. In addition to knowing the middle or average of a distribution of scores as provided by measures of central tendency, it's useful to know the value of the standard deviation, which shows us how far away from the mean the scores are distributed.

It's assumed that many variables studied in social work can be found in a normal distribution in the total population. Consequently many descriptive and inferential statistics assume such a distribution for their tests to be valid.

Study Questions for Chapter 17
Essay — Discussion

1	Before you entered your social work program, and before you read this chapter, how knowledgeable were you about the methods of analyzing quantitative data? Discuss fully.
2	What are quantitative data? Provide social work examples throughout your discussion to illustrate your main points.
3	What are the four levels of measurement for quantitative data? Provide an example of each and discuss how it can be used in a social work *research* situation and a social work *practice* situation.
4	Discuss the purposes of using descriptive statistics to analyze quantitative data. Provide social work examples throughout your discussion to illustrate your main points.
5	What are *frequency distributions*? Provide social work examples throughout your discussion to illustrate your main points.
6	What are *measures of central tendency*? Provide social work examples throughout your discussion to illustrate your main points.
7	What are *modes*? Provide social work examples throughout your discussion to illustrate your main points.
8	What are *medians*? Provide social work examples throughout your discussion to illustrate your main points.
9	What are *means*? Provide social work examples throughout your discussion to illustrate your main points.

10	Locate a quantitatively oriented journal article that used one or more of the three measures of central tendency. Were the statistics meaningful to you? If so, why? If not, why not?
11	What are *measures of variability*? Provide social work examples throughout your discussion to illustrate your main points.
12	What are *ranges*? Provide social work examples throughout your discussion to illustrate your main points.
13	What are *standard deviations*? Provide social work examples throughout your discussion to illustrate your main points.
14	Locate a quantitatively oriented journal article that used standard deviations in its data analysis. Was it meaningful to you? If so, why? If not, why not?
15	Discuss the main purpose of using *inferential statistics* to analyze quantitative data. Provide social work examples throughout your discussion to illustrate your main points.
16	Discuss how the *chi-square test* can be used to determine if there is an association between two variables.
17	Locate a quantitatively oriented journal article that used the chi-square test in its data analysis. Was it meaningful to you? If so, why? If not, why not?
18	Discuss how *tests of correlation* can be used to determine the strength of the relationships between two variables. Provide social work examples throughout your discussion to illustrate your main points.
19	Discuss how the *dependent t-test* can be used to determine if there is a relationship between two variables. Provide social work examples throughout your discussion to illustrate your main points.
20	Discuss how the *independent t-test* can be used to determine if there is a relationship between two variables. Provide social work examples throughout your discussion to illustrate your main points.

21	What's the main difference between an independent *t*-test and an analysis of variance? Provide social work examples throughout your discussion to illustrate your main points.
22	Discuss how a *one-way analysis of variance* can be used to determine if there are any significant differences between the means of three or more groups. Provide social work examples throughout your discussion to illustrate your main points.

Critical Thinking — Application — Integration

23	**APPLICATION OF DESCRIPTIVE STATISTICS** Locate a published social work-related journal article of your choice that contains one or more of the descriptive statistics covered in this chapter. Be sure the article analyzes quantitative data of some kind. We suggest you locate a quantitatively oriented research study in Bruce Thyer's journal *Research on Social Work Practice* (Sage Publications). Hands down, this is the best journal to find good quantitatively oriented social work research studies. 1. In relation to the study's findings, which descriptive statistic(s) did it use? 2. With your knowledge of descriptive statistics, thoroughly discuss how you will use the material contained within this chapter when you begin to evaluate the appropriateness of the descriptive statistic(s) the study utilized, and discuss why you believe each criterion you selected is important for your evaluation of the study's chosen descriptive statistic(s). 3. Do you believe you have the knowledge and skills to actually implement a quantitative research study such as the one you found? Why or why not? What specific knowledge and skills do you feel you lack? Discuss *where, when,* and *how* you plan on obtaining the necessary knowledge and skills.

APPLICATION OF INFERENTIAL STATISTICS

Locate a published social work-related journal article of your choice that contains one or more of the inferential statistics covered in this chapter. Be sure the article analyzes quantitative data of some kind. We suggest you locate a quantitatively oriented research study in Bruce Thyer's journal *Research on Social Work Practice* (Sage Publications). Hands down, this is the best journal to find good quantitatively oriented social work research studies.

1. In relation to the study's findings, which inferential statistic(s) did it use?

2. With your knowledge of inferential statistics, thoroughly discuss how you will use the material contained within this chapter when you begin to evaluate the appropriateness of the inferential statistic(s) the study utilized, and discuss why you believe each criterion you selected is important for your evaluation of the study's chosen inferential statistic(s).

3. Discuss how each one of the inferential statistics the study utilized was beneficial to your understanding of the study's findings.

4. Do you believe you have the knowledge and skills to actually implement a quantitative research study such as the one you found? Why or why not? What specific knowledge and skills do you feel you lack? Discuss *where, when,* and *how* you plan on obtaining the necessary knowledge and skills.

QUANTITATIVE DATA ANALYSIS AND THE SOCIAL WORK PRACTITIONER

Scenario 1: Make an argument that to be an effective evidence-based social work practitioner **you must know** how quantitative data are analyzed. Provide a clear and explicit **practice-related** social work example to illustrate your main points.

Scenario 2: Make an argument that **you do not have to know** how quantitative data are analyzed to be an effective evidence-based practitioner. Provide a clear and explicit **practice-related** social work example to illustrate your main points.

Time to Choose: Which one of the above two scenarios do you feel is more consistent with the concept of the contemporary evidence-based social work practice process as illustrated on pages 46–51? Why? Provide relevant social work examples to illustrate your main points.

24

25

26	QUANTITATIVE DATA ANALYSIS AND THE SOCIAL WORK RESEARCHER **Scenario 1:** Make an argument that to be a competent social work researcher **you must know** how quantitative data are analyzed. Provide a clear and explicit **research-related** social work example to illustrate your main points. **Scenario 2:** Make an argument that **you do not have to know** how quantitative data are analyzed to be a competent social work researcher. Provide a clear and explicit **research-related** social work example to illustrate your main points. **Time to Choose:** Which one of the above three scenarios do you feel is more consistent with the place of research in social work? Why? Provide relevant social work examples to illustrate your main points.
27	**Critical Thinking Question** 1. Discuss the similarities and differences between your responses to Questions 25 and 26. 2. What are your thoughts on the belief that you need to know how to do quantitative data analyses whether you're a social work *practitioner* (Question 25) or a social work *researcher* (Question 26)?

QUANTITATIVE DATA ANALYSIS AND YOUR PROFESSIONAL DEVELOPMENT

28

1. Review the three social work research-related roles you can take when you graduate—CSWE Competency 1 at the beginning of this chapter on page 592. This concept was also discussed in Chapter 1 on pages 38–42. Thoroughly discuss how you feel this chapter will help you to perform one or more research-related roles when you graduate. Which one of the three roles do you believe this chapter helped you with the most? Why? Discuss in detail and provide an example to illustrate your main points.

2. Review CSWE Competency 4 at the beginning of this chapter on page 592. Thoroughly discuss how you feel this chapter will help you to become a practice-informed researcher and a research-informed practitioner. Discuss in detail and provide an example to illustrate your main points.

3. Review the evidence-based practice process as illustrated on pages 46–51. Thoroughly discuss how this chapter helps you to develop the skills you'll need for implementing one or more steps of the evidence-based practice process.

4. Discuss which step(s) you feel this chapter will help you with the most. Why? Be very specific and use relevant social work examples to illustrate your main points throughout your discussion.

NOTE: This exercise should help you to realize that you can use "research techniques" to help you become an evidence-based social work practitioner.

LOOKING AHEAD BY THINKING BACK

29

At this point in your research methods course, how comfortable are you with discussing the place of research in social work with your field instructor, with your practice instructor, with your research instructor, with your supervisor at work, with the director of your social work program, or with your classmates? Discuss in detail.

18

CHAPTER

2015 EPAS COMPETENCIES

COMPETENCY 1: Demonstrate Ethical and Professional Behavior

You will learn that in order to be a successful evidence-based practitioner you have an ethical obligation to integrate three research roles into your daily practice activities as discussed in Chapter 1: (1) research consumer, (2) research partner—either as a co-researcher or research participant, and (3) creator and disseminator of research (or knowledge).

This entire chapter pertains to these three professional research-related roles when it comes to collecting, displaying, and analyzing qualitative data.

COMPETENCY 4: Engage in Practice-Informed Research and Research-Informed Practice

Competency 4 also pertains to the entire chapter because you have to:

1. Evaluate the thoroughness of the qualitative data analysis that was used in a qualitative research study (**research consumer**—research-informed practice);

2. Participate in a qualitative research study—either as a co-researcher or research participant (**research partner**—practice-informed research). See 1 above and 3 below; and

3. Know how to collect, display, and interpret qualitative data before you actually do a qualitative research study (**creator and disseminator of research**—practice-informed research).

You'll also need to utilize evidence-based practice recommendations whenever possible; that is, you need to integrate (1) the best available research-based evidence with (2) your clinical expertise and (3) your client's values.

All of the above implies you'll need to evaluate the strengths and limitations of the research-based qualitative evidence the study produced. In short, you need to ask and then answer a simple question: How seriously should I take the findings and recommendations of any qualitative research study given the level of rigor the author used in analyzing the qualitative data?

COMPETENCY 9: Evaluate Practice with Individuals, Families, Groups, Organizations, and Communities
See Competencies 1 and 4.

Analyzing Qualitative Data

CHAPTER 1	**Step 1.**	Understanding the Research Process
CHAPTER 2	**Step 2.**	Developing Research Questions
CHAPTER 3	**Step 3.**	Reviewing the Literature
CHAPTERS 4 & 5	**Step 4.**	Being Aware of Ethical and Cultural Issues
CHAPTERS 6–8	**Step 5.**	Selecting a Research Approach
CHAPTERS 9 & 10	**Step 6.**	Specifying How Variables Are Measured
CHAPTER 11	**Step 7.**	Selecting a Sample
CHAPTERS 12 & 13	**Step 8.**	Selecting a Research Design
CHAPTERS 14–16	**Step 9.**	Selecting a Data-Collection Method
CHAPTERS 17 & 18	**Step 10.**	Analyzing the Data
CHAPTERS 19 & 20	**Step 11.**	Writing the Research Report

THE LAST CHAPTER discussed the methods of analyzing quantitative data that are derived from positivistic research studies. In this chapter, we turn to the analysis of qualitative data that are derived from interpretive research studies—that is, data collected in the form of words (i.e., text data), most often from interviews, open-ended items on questionnaires, or personal logs.

To be honest, a thorough understanding of qualitative data analysis methods is far beyond the scope of this book. Such comprehension necessitates more in-depth study through taking one or more qualitative data analysis courses.

Unlike numbers, which are used in quantitative analyses, words give us descriptions or opinions from the unique point of view of the person who spoke or wrote the words. Like everything else in life, text data have both disadvantages and advantages.

The disadvantages are that words tend to be open to different interpretations and cannot be collected from large numbers of people at a time because the process of collection and analysis is much more time consuming than is the case for numerical data. The major advantage is that the material is very rich, containing multiple facets, and may provide us with a deeper understanding of the underlying meaning than would be possible if we just collected numbers (Tutty, Rothery, & Grinnell, 1996).

PURPOSE OF QUALITATIVE DATA ANALYSIS

USUALLY, WE NEED THE DEEPER UNDERSTANDING provided by qualitative data when we know very little about the problem or situation we are investigating and are not yet in a position to formulate theories about it for testing. In other words, we are at the exploratory end of the knowledge continuum, seeking to form patterns out of individual experiences so that we can develop more general theories.

The primary purpose of a qualitative data analysis is to sift and sort the masses of words we have collected from our research participants in such a way that we can derive patterns related to our research question—to identify the similarities and differences presented by individuals and the possible links between them.

> Qualitative data analyses analyze the meaning of words (or text data), not numbers.

Suppose for a moment that we are investigating postnatal depression among women. We may be interested in what the symptoms are, how new mothers experience them, and how they feel their depression affects their relationship with their newborns. We may also be interested in whether the women who experience postnatal depression are similar in any way with respect to various characteristics such as age, ethnic background, desire for the baby, partner or family support, socioeconomic status, medical history, and so on.

Indeed, we may have structured our interviews to collect specific data related to these kinds of variables. If we did, then we have already theorized that these characteristics or variables are related to postnatal depression, and we may, even subconsciously, look for patterns in the data that will confirm our theories.

> Unlike numbers, which are used in quantitative analyses, words give us descriptions or opinions from the unique point of view of the person who spoke or wrote the words.

There's nothing really evil about this. Researchers are human beings with a normal human tendency to make connections between events on the frailest of evidence, and it's a very rare researcher who starts on a research study with no preconceived notions at all.

Checking Your Biases at the Door

The important thing is to be aware of our human frailties with respect to drawing unwarranted conclusions, and to organize our data collection and analysis so that these frailties are minimized as far as possible. A look at some of the assumptions underlying qualitative (interpretive) research might help us to accomplish this:

— We're assuming that the goal of interpretive research (Chapter 7) is to reach an in-depth understanding of each of our research participants with respect to the research question, including experiences that are unique to them. We will not achieve this goal if we do not allow participants to express their uniqueness during data collection. Neither will we achieve it if we ignore the uniqueness during data analysis because we were hoping to uncover patterns and this is an anomaly that does not quite fit.

— It's also easy to ignore uniqueness if it does not fit with the findings of other researchers. An exploratory topic tends to reveal little in the way of previous research, but there is usually some, and it's tempting to disregard a unique experience if it seems to contravene what others have found.

— Information is always provided in some context. In the case of a research study, the context is the way in which the information was elicited (e.g., the phrasing of a question). In an interview, the context is the relationship between the interviewer and the interviewee.

— Preconceptions on the part of the interviewer tend to elicit responses that fit with the preconceptions. Thus, it's important in analysis not to look at just the response but at the emotional atmosphere surrounding the response and the question that was responded to.

There are three major phases involved in a basic qualitative data analysis. They are:

— **Phase 1:** We must plan how we will do the analysis. This involves describing exactly how we will transcribe spoken or written data into a usable form and what rules we will use to fit the pieces of data together in a meaningful way.

— **Phase 2:** We must do the analysis that will follow the general rules we set out at the beginning and perhaps revise these rules along the way if we come across some data to which our rules cannot be sensibly applied. It's important to note though that whatever rules we finally decide on must be applied to all our data. Changing our mind about rules will mean going back over the material we have worked on already; indeed, qualitative analysis is usually a back-and-forth sort of process, involving many re-readings and re-workings as new insights appear and we begin to question our initial theories or assumptions.

— **Phase 3:** We need to draw meaning from our analysis; that is, to identify relationships between the major themes that have emerged and to build theories around these for testing in the future.

The remainder of this chapter will describe the three phases of doing a qualitative data analysis briefly mentioned above. We will now turn attention to the first phase—Planning the Analysis.

PHASE 1: PLANNING THE ANALYSIS

THERE ARE TWO STEPS involved in planning a qualitative analysis:

— **Step 1:** Transcribing the data
— **Step 2:** Establishing general rules for the analysis

STEP 1: TRANSCRIBING THE DATA

TRANSCRIBING OUR DATA itself involves two tasks:

— **Task 1a:** Deciding what computer program to use (if any)
— **Task 1b:** Deciding who will transcribe the data

TASK 1A: DECIDING WHAT COMPUTER PROGRAM TO USE, IF ANY

IF RESPONSES ARE WRITTEN, as in open-ended items on a questionnaire or personal logs, transcription may be a matter of typing the responses, either just for easier reading or with the aim of using a computer program to assist with the analysis. A few researchers, distrustful of computers, prefer to use a traditional cut-and-paste method, physically cutting the manuscript and grouping the cut sections together with other related sections.

A computer need not be used for transcription in this case. A simple out-dated typewriter would do, or even legible handwriting. Some researchers trust the computer just sufficiently to allow it to move selected passages together with other selected passages to electronically form a group of related data.

The majority of word-processing programs can accomplish this. An increasing number of researchers, however, use computer programs that have been developed specifically to assist with the analysis of qualitative data. A few familiar names are ETHNOGRAPH, HYPERQUAL, ATLAS.ti, NUD*IST, and NVivo.

Your personal biases must always be acknowledged and dealt with when doing a qualitative data analysis.

New programs are always coming onto the market, so it's wise to consult colleagues or computer companies about which programs might be most helpful for a particular project. It's important to note that no computer program can do the analysis for us. The most it can do is free up time for us to spend on considering the meaning of our data in Phase 3.

TASK 1B: DECIDING WHO WILL TRANSCRIBE THE DATA

SOME RESEARCHERS ARE FORTUNATE enough to have a research or administrative assistant to help them in the transcription process. If this is the case, it's necessary to lay down guidelines right at the beginning about how the material should be transcribed. If an interview has been audio taped or video-taped, for example, the questions should be included in the transcript as well as the answers.

Nonverbal communications such as pauses, laughing or crying, and voice tone should be included in brackets so that the emotional context of the interview is captured as far as possible in the transcript. Those fortunate re-searchers with assistants are nevertheless well advised to transcribe at least the first few interviews themselves so that assistants can see what ought to be included.

Another concern is how to format the transcript so that it's easy to read and analyze. It's a good idea to leave a margin of at least two inches along the right side so that we can write notes and codes alongside the corresponding text. It's also a good idea to number each line of the transcript so that we can readily identify each segment of data.

Computer programs designed to assist in qualitative analysis will auto-matically do this. For example, suppose we worked in a foster care agency and we were asking foster parents who had resigned from the agency in the past year why they had resigned. A few lines from one of our interviews might be transcribed like this:

1. Sue (angrily): His behavior was just too much and nobody from the agency told
2. us that he'd set fires before and was probably going to burn our house down. I
3. suppose they thought that if they'd told us that we wouldn't have taken him but
4. I do feel that we were set up from the beginning (sounding very upset). And when
5. we called the agency, there was only an answering machine and it was a whole
6. day before the social worker called us back.
7. Interviewer: That's dreadful.

Reading these lines after the transcript is completed might immediately set us thinking about how foster parents' reasons for resigning could be sep-arated into categories. One category might be the foster child's behavior (much worse than the foster parents had been led to expect).

Or this might be two categories: (1) the child's behavior and (2) the dis-crepancy between the actual behavior and the expected behavior. Another category might be negative feelings toward the agency, with two subcatego-ries: the feeling of having been set up, and the perceived lack of support in a time of crisis. It might not take long at all for these tentative categories to harden into certainties.

Having read the first six lines from one interview, we now feel we know why foster parents resign, and it only remains to confirm the reasons we have found by picking out similar sentiments from our interviews with other foster parents. Job completed!

Actually, we've barely begun. Since we cannot—and do not wish to—stop our minds from jumping ahead in this fashion, we must find some way to organize our thoughts such that our intuitive leaps do not blind us to different and perhaps contradictory insights yielded by other interviews. There are two techniques that might help us to do this: previewing the data, and keeping a journal. Both these techniques will also help us to establish general rules for our analysis—the second and last step in the planning stage.

STEP 2: ESTABLISHING GENERAL RULES FOR THE ANALYSIS

ESTABLISHING GENERAL RULES for the analysis ensures that our efforts are systematic and the same rules are applied to all our data. We use rules to decide how we could fit together pieces of data in a meaningful way and how these groups of data could be categorized and coded (to be discussed shortly).

For example, what criteria or rule do we use to decide whether a child's worsened behavior after a visit with the biological parents should be categorized under "child's behaviors" or under "relationships with biological parents"? Although we clarify and refine the rules throughout the study, by the time we have finished we should have a set of rules that have been consistently applied to every piece of data. We start to think about what rules might apply during the previewing task.

There are two basic tasks that take place when establishing rules for a qualitative data analysis:

— **Task 2a:** Previewing the data
— **Task 2b:** Keeping a journal

TASK 2A: PREVIEWING THE DATA

THE PROCESS OF TRANSCRIPTION might be ongoing throughout the study, with each interview transcribed as soon as it's completed, or transcription might not begin until all the data have been assembled. Whichever method is used, it's important to read all the transcripts before beginning to formally identify categories.

It's also important to give all the transcripts and all parts of the transcripts the same amount of attention. We may be in peak form at the beginning of the day while reading the first few pages of the first transcript, for example, but by the end of the day and by the end of the third transcript, this initial peak has waned to weary impatience.

We would be better advised to read only for as long as we remain interested in the material. This will obviously mean that the process of previewing the data extends over a longer period; qualitative data analysis takes time—lots and lots of time—in addition to lots of patience.

It's a lengthy process of discovery, whose pace cannot be forced. If we are rereading material, it sometimes helps to read the last third of an interview at moments of high energy instead of the first third. That way, we will not lose valuable insights from later sections of the interview transcript.

TASK 2B: KEEPING A JOURNAL

SOME PEOPLE LOVE journals, and others hate them, but the interpretive researcher cannot afford to be without one. The journal should be started at the same time as the study is started. It should include notes on the planned method and any changes in the plan, with dates and reasons. For example, perhaps the plan was to interview all the foster parents who had resigned from the agency during the last year, but some of them would not agree to be interviewed.

> Qualitative researchers use journals that detail the entire research process.

We may believe that those who agreed differed in some important respects from those who refused. They were more satisfied with the agency perhaps. If this were the case, the data from our more satisfied sample might lead us to faulty conclusions, possibly causing us to place more emphasis on personal reasons for resignation such as failing health or family circumstances, and less on agency-related reasons such as poor information-sharing or support.

Whatever the difficulties we encounter and the assumptions we make, our journal should keep an accurate record of them as we move along in the data analysis. Because the work we do must be open to scrutiny by others, it's essential to keep a record of all our activities and the feelings and reasoning behind them.

When the data-collection stage begins, the journal can be used to record personal reactions to the interview situation. For example, we might feel more personal empathy with one foster parent than with another and be tempted to give more weight to the remarks of the parent with whom we sympathized. An unconscious overreliance on one research participant or one subset of research participants will hopefully reveal itself as we read through our journal entries later during the course of the analysis.

Journals are used to record the researcher's personal reactions to interviews.

When we begin to categorize and code the data, we can use the journal to keep notes about the process, writing down the general rules, revisions to the rules, and questions or comments with respect to how particular pieces of data might be categorized. Let's now turn our attention to actually analyzing qualitative data.

PHASE 2: DOING THE ANALYSIS

ONCE ALL THE DATA have been previewed we can start on coding them. There are two levels of coding:

— **Step 3:** First-level coding, which deals with the concrete ideas evident in the transcript.

— **Step 4:** Second-level coding, which looks for and interprets the more abstract meanings underlying these concrete ideas.

STEP 3: DOING FIRST-LEVEL CODING

THERE ARE FOUR TASKS in first-level coding:
— **Task 3a:** Identifying meaning units
— **Task 3b:** Creating categories
— **Task 3c:** Assigning codes to categories
— **Task 3d:** Refining and reorganizing categories

TASK 3A: IDENTIFYING MEANING UNITS

A **MEANING UNIT** is a piece of data, which we consider to be meaningful by itself. It might be a word, a partial or complete sentence, or a paragraph or more. For example, let's look once again at the interview segment presented earlier on page 631:

1. <u>Sue (angrily): His behavior was just too much and nobody from the agency told</u>

2. *us that he'd set fires before and was probably going to burn our house down. I*

3. *suppose they thought that if they'd told us that we wouldn't have taken him but*

4. **I do feel that we were set up from the beginning (sounding very upset). And when**

5. ***we called the agency, there was only an answering machine and it was a whole***

6. ***day before the social worker called us back.***

7. Interviewer: That's dreadful.

In the above segment we might easily identify four meaning units. The first unit (<u>underlined,</u> line 1) relates to the child's behavior. The second unit (*italics,* lines 2 and 3) relates to lack of information provided by the agency. The third (**bold,** line 4) relates to feeling set up by the agency. The fourth unit (***bold italics,*** lines 5 and 6) relates to poor support on the part of the agency. Of course, different researchers might identify different meaning units or label the same units differently.

For example, lines 4, 5, and 6 might be identified as relating to agency response style rather than poor support and might involve two distinct meaning units, "response method" and "response time." Similarly, the partial sentence in line 2, *"he'd set fires before,"* might be viewed as a separate meaning unit relating to the child's past rather than present behavior.

The first run-through to identify meaning units will always be somewhat tentative and subject to change. If we are not sure whether to break a large meaning unit into smaller ones, it may be preferable to leave it as a whole. We can always break it down later in the analysis, and breaking down large units tends to be easier than combining smaller ones, especially once second-level coding begins.

> A meaning unit is a piece of data, which we consider to be meaningful all by itself.

TASK 3B: CREATING CATEGORIES

ONCE WE HAVE IDENTIFIED meaning units in the transcript, our next task is to consider which of them fit together into categories. Perhaps we should have a category labeled "child's behavior" into which we put all meaning units related to the child's behavior, including the second meaning unit identified above, "nobody from the agency told us that he'd set fires before and was probably going to burn our house down."

Or perhaps we should have two categories, "child's present behavior" and "child's past behavior," in which case the second meaning unit might belong in the latter category. Or perhaps we feel that the vital words are "nobody told us," and this second meaning unit really belongs in a different category labeled "provision of information by agency." All other meaning units to do with foster parents being given information by the agency would then belong in this same category even though they had nothing to do with the child's behavior.

Qualitative researchers need to keep the number of categories in their analyses to a manageable number.

Because these kinds of decisions are often difficult to make, it's a good idea to note in our journal how we made the decisions we did and what alternatives we considered at the time. What rules did we use to decide whether a particular meaning unit was similar to—or different from—another meaning unit? How did we define our categories in order to decide whether a group of similar meaning units should be placed in one category or in another?

As we continue to examine new meaning units, we will use these rules to decide whether each new unit is similar to existing units and belongs in an existing category or whether it's different from existing units and needs a new separate category. The number of categories will therefore expand every time we identify meaning units that are different in important ways from those we have already categorized.

Since too many categories will make the final analysis very difficult, we should try to keep the number within manageable limits. This may mean revising our initial rules about how categories are defined and what criteria are used to decide whether meaning units are similar enough to be grouped together. Of course, any change in rules should be noted in our journal, together with the rationale for the change.

The complexity of our categorization scheme also needs to be considered. One meaning unit may, in fact, fall into more than one category, or a group of meaning units may overlap with another group. Large, inclusive categories may consist of a number of smaller, more exclusive subcategories. For example, as we saw, the meaning unit *"nobody from the agency told us that he'd set fires before and was probably going to burn our house down"* has to do both with lack of information provided by the agency and with the child's past behavior.

Sometimes meaning units cannot be clearly placed into any category and fall into the category of "miscellaneous." When we are tired, most everything may seem to be "miscellaneous," but miscellaneous units should make up no more than 10 percent of the total data set. More than that suggests that there is a problem with the original categorization scheme.

The real purpose of a miscellaneous category is to prevent our throwing out meaning units that, at first glance, appear to be irrelevant. Such throwing out is risky because at some point we may decide that our whole categorization scheme needs massive revision and we must start the whole process again from scratch.

TASK 3C: ASSIGNING CODES TO CATEGORIES

CODES ARE SIMPLY a shorthand form of the category name. They typically take the form of strings of letters and/or symbols. Codes used in *The Ethnograph,* for example, may be up to ten letters long and can also include symbols. Codes are usually displayed in the margins (often the right margin) of the transcribed text.

If we had a category labeled "child's behavior," we might simply code this CB where the C stands for the foster child and the B stands for behavior. If we want to distinguish between past and present behavior, we might use the codes CPASTB and CPRESB, respectively.

If there is a category relating to the behavior of the foster parents' own children (perhaps this has worsened since the foster child moved in), we might use the codes FPCPASTB and FPCPRESB, respectively, where the FPC stands for the foster parents' child.

> Codes are shorthand forms for labeling categories.

In fact, we might make it a rule that codes starting with C, FP, FPC, and A stand for things to do with the foster child, the foster parents, the foster parents' children, and the agency, respectively. Then AINF>FP might mean information provided by the agency to the foster parents, and AINF<FP might mean information provided by the foster parents to the agency.

It's a good idea to keep the codes as short as possible in the beginning because they tend to become longer as the analysis grows more complex. However, there are many different ways to assign codes and so long as the code is clearly related to the category, it doesn't really matter which system is used.

TASK 3D: REFINING AND REORGANIZING CATEGORIES

BEFORE MOVING ON from first-level coding, we need to make a final sweep through the data to ensure that our analysis reflects what our research participants have said. We should consider the logic underlying the rules we made for grouping meaning units and defining categories.

We may, for example, be confused about why we created some categories, or feel uncertain about why a particular meaning unit was put into a particular category. We might find that some categories are too complex and need to be split into smaller categories; or some categories are poorly defined; or some of the categories that we expected to emerge from the data are missing altogether.

We might, for example, have expected that some foster parents would resign because of poor health, but there is no category coded FPHEA. Investigation reveals that foster parents did indeed mention their poor health but they always ascribed it to the strain of dealing with the foster child or the foster child's biological parents or the agency.

Hence, the meaning units including poor health have been categorized under "foster child's present behavior (CPRESB)" or "relationships with agency (AREL)" or "relationships with biological parents (BPREL)" and have not been broken down finely enough to isolate poor health as a separate category. We may wish to create such a category, or we may prefer to note its absence in our journal together with other categories that are incomplete or in some way unsatisfactory.

This is a good time to ask a colleague to analyze one or two of our interviews using the rules we have devised. In this way, we can check that the categories themselves and the rules that define them make sense. If our colleague organizes meaning units in a significantly different way, for example, our categorization scheme may need to be substantially revised.

It's probably time to stop first-level coding when all our meaning units fit easily into our current categorization scheme and there are no more units that require the creation of new categories. If interviews are continuing during first-level coding, we will probably find the data becoming repetitive; yielding no new piece of information that cannot be fitted into the present scheme.

Now that we're done first-level coding, it's time to turn our attention to the final step in Phase 1—second level coding.

STEP 4: DOING SECOND-LEVEL CODING

THE NEXT MAJOR STEP in the data analysis process is second-level coding. As noted earlier, this is more abstract and involves interpreting what the first-level categories mean. During first-level coding, we derived meaning units from interviews with individuals, and we derived categories by comparing the meaning units to see which were similar enough to be grouped together.

During second-level coding we will compare the categories themselves to uncover possible relationships between or among them. The point of doing this is to identify themes based on patterns that repeatedly occur among our categories.

TASK 4A: COMPARING CATEGORIES

A COMPARISON OF CATEGORIES in any interpretive study will probably yield many different types of relationships. Coleman and Unrau (2011) have suggested that the following three types of relationships are among those most commonly found:

1. **A temporal relationship.** One category may be found to often precede another. For example, foster children whose own parents are abusive might initially behave well because they are happy to be living away from the abuse. Later, however, they may push for a return to their families of origin, and their response to the foster parents may become less positive.

2. **A causal relationship.** One category may be perceived to be the cause of another. For example, foster parents may believe that the child's bad behavior after every visit with the biological parent was the cause of their own negative attitudes toward the biological parent. However, it's always risky to assume that one category caused another when, in fact, the opposite may be true. Perhaps the foster parents started off with a negative attitude toward the child's biological parents, the child was more than usually angry about this after visits home, and the child demonstrated rage by behaving badly.

3. **One category may be contained within another category.** At this stage of the analysis, we may decide that two categories that we had thought to be separate are in fact linked. For example, foster parents may have said that they were never introduced to the child's biological parents by the agency, and we have categorized this separately from their statement that the agency was not entirely truthful with them about the child's past behavior. Now we realize that these are both examples of lack of information provided to the foster parent by the agency.

A comparison of categories in any qualitative study will probably yield many different types of relationships.

Furthermore, foster parents complained that they were not invited to agency meetings in which the child's progress was reviewed. Lack of information and non-attendance at meetings might combine to form a theme related to the agency's attitude toward the foster parents. The theme might be that the agency does not appear to accept the foster parents as equal partners in the task of helping the child.

When we have identified themes based on patterns among our categories, we code these themes in the same way as we coded our categories. If one of our themes is that the agency does not view foster parents as equal partners, for example, we might code this as A<FP-PART. Once themes have been identified and coded, the process of second-level coding is complete.

PHASE 3: LOOKING FOR MEANING

DRAWING MEANING from our data is perhaps the most rewarding step of a qualitative data analysis. It involves two important steps:

— **Step 5:** Interpreting data and building theory
— **Step 6:** Assessing the trustworthiness of the results

STEP 5: INTERPRETING DATA AND BUILDING THEORY

THIS STEP INVOLVES TWO TASKS:

— **Task 5a:** Developing conceptual classifications systems
— **Task 5b:** Presenting themes or theory

TASK 5A: DEVELOPING CONCEPTUAL CLASSIFICATIONS SYSTEMS

THE ULTIMATE GOAL of an interpretive research study is to identify any relationships between the major themes that emerge from the data set. During first-level coding, we used meaning units to form categories. During second-level coding, we used categories to form themes.

Now we will use themes to build theories. In order to do this, we must understand the interconnections between themes and categories. There are several strategies that might be useful in helping us to identify these connections. Miles and Huberman (1994) have suggested the following strategies for extracting meaning from a qualitative dataset:

— **Draw a cluster diagram.** This form of diagram helps us to think about how themes and categories may or may not be related to one another. Draw and label circles for each theme and arrange them in relation to each other. Some of the circles will overlap, others will stand-alone. The circles of the themes of more importance will be larger, in comparison to themes and categories that are not as relevant to our conclusions. The process of thinking about what weight to give the themes, how they interact, and how important they will be in the final scheme will be valuable in helping us to think about the meaning of our study.

— **Make a matrix.** Matrix displays may be helpful for noting relations between categories or themes. Designing a two-dimensional matrix involves writing a list of categories along the left side of a piece of paper and then another list of categories across the top.

For example, along the side, we might write categories related to the theme of the degree of partnership between the agency and the foster parents. One such category might be whether the foster parents were invited to agency meetings held to discuss the child's progress. Then, along the top we might write categories related to the theme of foster parents' attitudes toward the agency.

One category here might be whether foster parents felt their opinions about the child were listened to by the agency. Where two categories intersect on the matrix, we could note with a plus sign (+) those indicators of partnership or lack of partnership that positively affect parents' attitudes. Conversely, we would mark with a minus sign (–) those that seem to have a negative effect. Such a matrix gives us a sense of to what degree and in what ways foster parents' attitudes toward the agency are molded by the agency's view of foster parents as partners.

— **Count the number of times a meaning unit or category appears.** Although numbers are typically associated with quantitative studies, it's acceptable to use numbers in qualitative work in order to document how many of the participants expressed a particular theme. We might be interested, for example, in finding out how many participants experienced specific problems related to lack of agency support. We would write the code names for the foster parents interviewed down the left side of a piece of paper and the list of problems across the top.

To fill in the chart, we would simply place a check mark beside each foster parent's code name if she or he experienced that particular problem. Numbers will help protect our analysis against bias that occurs when intense but rare examples of problems are presented.

For example, many foster parents may have felt that they were not given sufficient information about the child's past behavior, but only one may have felt that the agency deliberately set her up. Although, we will certainly not discount this foster parent's experience, we might prefer to view it as an extreme example of the results of poor information sharing.

— **Create a metaphor.** Developing metaphors that convey the essence of our findings is another mechanism for extracting meaning. One example of a metaphor concerning battered women is "the cycle of violence," which effectively describes the tension building between couples until the husband beats his wife, followed by a calm, loving phase until the tension builds again.

— **Look for missing links.** If two categories or themes seem to be related but not directly so, it may be that a third variable connects the two.

— **Note contradictory evidence.** It's only natural to want to focus on evidence that supports our ideas. Because of this human tendency, it's particularly important to also identify themes and categories that raise questions about our conclusions. All contradictory evidence must be accounted for when we come to derive theories pertaining to our study area, for example, theories about why foster parents resign.

TASK 5B: PRESENTING THEMES OR THEORY

SOMETIMES IT'S SUFFICIENT to conclude an interpretive study merely by describing the major themes that emerged from the data. For example, we may have used the experiences of individual foster parents to derive reasons for resignation common to the majority of foster parents we studied.

When categorized, such reasons might relate to inadequate training; poor support from the agency; failure on the agency's part to treat the foster parents as partners; negative attitudes on the part of the foster parents' friends and extended family; unrealistic expectations on the part of the foster parents with respect to the foster child's progress and behavior; poor relations between the biological and foster parents; the perceived negative influence of the foster child on the foster parents' own children; marital discord attributed to stress; failing health attributed to stress; and so on.

We might think it sufficient in our conclusions to present and describe these categories, together with recommendations for improvement. On the other hand, we might wish to formulate questions to be answered in future studies. What would change if agencies were to view foster parents as partners rather than as clients? If we think we know what would change, we might want to formulate more specific questions. For example,

Are agencies that view foster parents as partners more likely to provide foster parents with full information regarding the child's background than agencies that do not view foster parents as partners?

Or we might want to reword the above general question to form a specific hypothesis:

Agencies that view foster parents as partners are more likely to provide foster parents with full information regarding the child's background than agencies that do not view parents as partners.

In order to arrive at this hypothesis, we have essentially formulated a theory about how two of our concepts are related. We could carry this further by adding other concepts to the chain of relationships and formulating additional hypotheses:

Foster parents who have full information about the child's background are less likely to have unrealistic expectations about the child's behavior and progress than foster parents who do not have full information about the child's background.

And,

Foster parents who have unrealistic expectations about the child's behavior and progress are more likely to experience marital discord (due to the fostering process) than foster parents who do not have unrealistic expectations.

Indeed, we might weave all the various woes our study has uncovered into an elaborate pattern of threads, beginning with the agency's reluctance to view foster parents as partners and ending with the foster parents' resignations. In our excitement, we might come to believe that we have solved the entire problem of resigning foster parents. We could naively come up with:

If agencies would only change their attitudes with respect to foster parents' status and behave in accordance with this change in attitude, then all foster parents would continue to be foster parents until removed by death.

It's at this point that we need to focus on the second stage of our search for meaning: assessing the trustworthiness of our results.

STEP 6: ASSESSING THE TRUSTWORTHINESS OF THE RESULTS

THERE ARE THREE MAJOR REASONS why disgruntled agencies, as well as other actors, may not agree that our results are as trustworthy as we believe. They can be broken into three tasks:

— **Task 6a:** Establishing our own creditability
— **Task 6b:** Establishing the dependability of the data
— **Task 6c:** Establishing our control of biases and preconceptions

TASK 6A: ESTABLISHING OUR OWN CREDIBILITY

BECAUSE AN INTERPRETIVE STUDY depends so much on human judgment, it's necessary to demonstrate that our own personal judgment is to be trusted. Part of this relates to our training and experience. Another important part is the record we made in our journal detailing the procedures we followed, the decisions we made and why we made them, and the thought processes that led to our conclusions. If we can demonstrate that we were qualified to undertake this study and we carried it out meticulously, others are far more likely to take into account our conclusions.

TASK 6B: ESTABLISHING THE DEPENDABILITY OF THE DATA

IF WE HAVE BEEN CONSISTENT in such things as interview procedures and developing rules for coding, and if we have obtained dependable data through a rigorous, recorded process, then another researcher should be able to follow the same process, make the same decisions, and arrive at essentially the same conclusions. Also, if we ourselves redo part of the analysis at a later date, the outcome should be very similar to that produced in the original analysis.

In order to ensure that others and we could duplicate our work, Coleman and Unrau (2011) have suggested we need to pay attention to the following standard issues:

— **The context of the interviews.** Some data-collection situations yield more credible data than others, and we may choose to weight our interviews accordingly. Some authors claim, for example, that data collected later in the study are more dependable than data collected at the beginning because our interviewing style is likely to be more relaxed and less intrusive. In addition, data obtained firsthand are considered to be more dependable than secondhand data, which are obtained through a third party. Similarly, data offered voluntarily are thought to be stronger than data obtained through intensive questioning, and data obtained from research participants in their natural environments (e.g., home or neighborhood coffee shop) are to be more trusted than data provided by research participants in a foreign or sterile environment (e.g., researcher's office or an interviewing room).

— **Triangulation.** Triangulation is commonly used to establish the trustworthiness of qualitative data. There are several different kinds of triangulation, but the essence of the method lies in a comparison of several perspectives. For example, we might collect data from the agency about what information was provided to foster parents in order to compare the agency's perspective with what foster parents said. With respect to data analysis, we might ask a colleague to use our rules to see if he or she makes the same decisions about meaning units, categories, and themes. The hope is that different perspectives will confirm each other, adding weight to the credibility of our analysis.

— **Member checking.** Obtaining feedback from research participants is a credibility technique that is unique to interpretive studies. While such feedback should be an ongoing part of the study (e.g., interview transcripts may be presented to research participants for comment), it's particularly useful when our analysis has been completed, our interpretations made, and our conclusions drawn.

Research participants may not agree with our interpretation or conclusions, and may differ among each other. If this is the case, we need to decide whether to exclude the interpretations to which they object, or whether to leave them in, merely recording the dissenting opinions and our position in relation to them.

TASK 6C: ESTABLISHING OUR CONTROL OF BIASES

SINCE ALL HUMAN BEINGS inevitably have biases and preconceptions about most everything; one way to demonstrate that we are in control of ours is to list them. Such a list is useful to both ourselves and others when we want to check that our conclusions have emerged from the data rather than from our established beliefs.

Also useful is our journal where we documented our attempts to keep ourselves open to what our research participants had to say. As Heather Coleman and Yvonne Unrau (2011) point out, we may want to consider the following points in relation to bias:

— Our personal belief systems may affect our interpretation of the data. Member checking has already been mentioned as a way to safeguard against this.

— We might draw conclusions before the data are analyzed or before we have decided about the trustworthiness of the data collected. Such conclusions tend to set to a cement-like hardness and are likely to persist despite all future indications that they were wrong.

— We might censor, ignore, or dismiss certain parts of the data. This may occur as a result of data overload or because the data contradict an established way of thinking.

— We might make unwarranted or unsupported causal statements based on impressions rather than on solid analysis. Even when our statements are based on solid analysis, it's a good idea to actively hunt for any evidence that might contradict them. If we can demonstrate that we have genuinely searched for (but failed to find) negative evidence, looking for outliers and using extreme cases, our conclusions will be more credible.

— We might be too opinionated and reduce our conclusions to a limited number of choices or alternatives.

— We might unthinkingly give certain people or events more credibility than others. Perhaps we have relied too much on information that was easily accessible or we have given too much weight to research participants we personally liked. If we detect such a bias, we can interview more people, deliberately searching for atypical events and research participants who differ markedly from those we have already interviewed. Hopefully, these new data will provide a balance with the data originally collected.

Once we have assessed the trustworthiness of our results, it only remains to write the report describing our methods and findings.

EVALUATING YOUR DATA ANALYSIS PLAN

THE BEST WAY TO ACTUALLY EVALUATIVE the quality of your qualitative data analysis plan is to evaluate your entire research study from the get-go. In short, your data analysis can only be as good as the study's research design that was used to obtain the data in the first place.

It's simply impossible to evaluate your study's data analysis plan in total isolation from your study's methodology. In this spirit, Jim Raines (2011) has provided a nice list of 32 questions that you should ask yourself before ever embarking on a qualitative research study.

Potential Introduction and Literature Review Issues

1. Are your philosophical assumptions and values well identified?

2. Are the databases you searched sufficient to the research question you are trying to answer?

3. Is your literature review relevant to both your research problem and population?

4. Is the literature that you reviewed current?

5. Do you use headings and subheadings to organize your ideas?

6. Do you identify any differences in findings from previous research studies?

7. Does your literature review support the purpose of your study?

Potential Research Question, Conceptual Definitions, Rationale, and Ethical Issues

8. Is your research question crystal clear?

9. Does your research question include all the major concepts that are in your study?

10. Are your conceptual definitions multidimensional?

11. Will your definitions evolve as participants provide their perspectives?

12. Do you have a logical rationale for doing a qualitative study in the first place?

13. Is there a good fit between your research question and your data-collection method?

14. Does your research study demonstrate your value awareness?

15. How do you plan on using informed consent procedures?

16. Does your study advance the common good of your research participants?

Potential Data Collection Procedures and Rigor Issues

17. Do you explain the reasons for the type of sampling method you will use?

18. How do you plan on reporting your subjectivity?

19. How do you plan on addressing the issue of bias by you and your research participants?

20. What strategies are you going to use to improve the credibility of your study's findings?

21. What strategies are you going to use to improve the transferability of your study's findings?

22. What strategies are you going to use to improve the dependability of your study's findings?

23. What strategies are you going to use to improve the confirmability of your study's findings?

Potential Data Analysis Procedures and Discussion Issues

24. What strategies are you going to use to increase the accuracy of your study's transcriptions?

25. What is your specific plan for analyzing the data?

26. How do you plan on developing categories for first-level coding?

27. How to you plan on establishing relationships between categories clarified during second-level coding?

28. How to you plan on developing themes and theories within your data analyses?

29. How do you plan on addressing your study's limitations from an interpretive perspective?

30. How do you plan on integrating your study's results with the previous literature?

31. How do you plan on developing implications for social work theory, practice, or policy?

32. Do you plan on making recommendations for future research studies?

SUMMARY

THIS CHAPTER HAS PRESENTED a brief systematic and purposeful approach to data analysis for a qualitative research study. The major steps of a data analysis include transcript preparation, planning the analysis, first-level coding, second-level coding, interpretation and theory building, and assessing the trustworthiness of the results. Although these steps have been presented in a linear fashion, any real qualitative analysis will involve moving back and forth between them in order to produce rich and meaningful findings.

Study Questions for Chapter 18

Essay — Discussion

1	Before you entered your social work program, and before you read this chapter, how knowledgeable were you about methods for analyzing qualitative data? Discuss fully.
2	What are qualitative data? Provide social work examples throughout your discussion to illustrate your main points.
3	What is the main difference between quantitative data and qualitative data? Provide social work examples throughout your discussion to illustrate your main points.
4	In your own words describe what qualitative data analysis is all about. Provide social work examples throughout your discussion to illustrate your main points.
5	List the two steps that are involved in establishing an initial framework for a qualitative data analysis. Describe the overall purpose of each step using social work examples throughout your discussion.
6	Step 1 requires you to put your qualitative data in transcript form and includes five tasks. Describe each task and use the same social work example throughout your discussion.
7	Step 2 requires you to establish a concrete plan for carrying out your qualitative data analysis and includes two tasks. Describe each task, using your example from the previous question.
8	List the two steps involved in coding your qualitative dataset. Describe its purpose using social work examples throughout your discussion.

9	Step 3 requires you to do first-level coding with your qualitative data. Describe in detail the purpose of first-level coding and provide social work examples throughout your discussion to illustrate your main points.
10	Step 3 contains five tasks. Describe each one using social work examples to illustrate your main points.
11	Step 4 requires you to do second-level coding with your qualitative data. Describe in detail the purpose of second-level coding and provide social work examples throughout your discussion to illustrate your main points.
12	Step 4 contains two tasks. Describe each one using social work examples to illustrate your main points.
13	List the two steps that are used to look for meaning and relationships within your qualitative dataset. Describe the purpose of each using social work examples throughout your discussion.
14	Step 5 requires you to interpret your qualitative data. Describe in detail the purpose of qualitative data interpretation and provide social work examples throughout your discussion to illustrate your main points.
15	Step 5 contains two tasks. Describe each one using social work examples to illustrate your main points.
16	Step 6 requires you to assess the trustworthiness of your study's results. Why is this necessary? Provide social work examples throughout your discussion to illustrate your main points.
17	Step 6 contains three tasks. Describe each one using social work examples throughout your discussion to illustrate your main points.

Critical Thinking — Application — Integration

| 18 | **APPLICATION OF QUALITATIVE DATA ANALYSIS**

Locate a published qualitatively oriented social work-related journal article of your choice. Be sure the article analyzes qualitative data of some kind. We |

suggest you locate a qualitatively oriented research study in Karen Staller and Karen Broadhurst's journal *Qualitative Social Work* (Sage Publications). Hands down, this is the best journal to find good qualitative social work research studies.

1. With your knowledge of qualitative analysis, thoroughly discuss how you will use the material contained within this chapter when you begin to evaluate the overall trustworthiness of the study's results, paying particular attention to data analysis.

2. Did the study use triangulation and member checking? If so, do you think this added to the overall credibility of the data analysis? Provide specific examples to illustrate your main points.

3. Did the author include a "quantitative" component (**mixed-methods research** as discussed in Chapter 8)? If so, what did it contain? What did the quantitative component add to the qualitative findings?

4. Do you believe you have the knowledge and skills to actually implement a qualitative research study such as the one you found? Why or why not? What specific knowledge and skills do you feel you lack? Discuss *where, when,* and *how* you plan on obtaining the necessary knowledge and skills.

19

QUALITATIVE DATA ANALYSIS AND THE PRACTITIONER

Scenario 1: Make an argument that to be an effective evidence-based social work practitioner **you must know** how to analyze qualitative data. Provide a clear and explicit **practice-related** social work example to illustrate your main points.

Scenario 2: Make an argument that to be an effective evidence-based social work practitioner **you must know** how to analyze quantitative AND qualitative data (**mixed-methods research** as discussed in Chapter 8). Provide a clear and explicit **practice-related** social work example to illustrate your main points.

Scenario 3: Make an argument that **you do not have to know** how to analyze any kind of data whatsoever to be an effective evidence-based practitioner. Provide a clear and explicit **practice-related** social work example to illustrate your main points.

Time to Choose: Which one of the above three scenarios do you feel is more consistent with the concept of the contemporary evidence-based social work practice process as illustrated on pages 46–51? Why? Provide relevant social work examples to illustrate your main points.

20	**QUALITATIVE DATA ANALYSIS AND THE RESEARCHER** **Scenario 1:** Make an argument that to be a competent social work researcher **you must know** how to analyze qualitative data. Provide a clear and explicit **research-related** social work example to illustrate your main points. **Scenario 2:** Make an argument that to be a competent social work researcher **you must know** how to analyze qualitative AND quantitative data (**mixed-methods research** as discussed in Chapter 8). Provide a clear and explicit **research-related** social work example to illustrate your main points. **Scenario 3:** Make an argument that **you do not have to know** how to analyze any data whatsoever to be a competent social work researcher. Provide a clear and explicit **research-related** social work example to illustrate your main points. **Time to Choose:** Which one of the above three scenarios do you feel is more consistent with the place of research in social work? Why? Provide relevant social work examples to illustrate your main points.
21	**TIME TO PUT ON YOUR CRITICAL THINKING HAT** 1. Discuss the similarities and differences between your responses to Questions 19 and 20. 2. What are your thoughts on the belief that analyzing qualitative data for a research study (Question 20) is very similar to analyzing qualitative data from client interviews (Question 19)?

22	**QUALITATIVE DATA ANALYSIS AND YOUR PROFESSIONAL DEVELOPMENT** 1. Review the three social work research-related roles you can take when you graduate—CSWE Competency 1 at the beginning of this chapter on page 624. This concept was also discussed in Chapter 1 on pages 38–42. Thoroughly discuss how you feel this chapter will help you to perform one or more research-related roles when you graduate. Which one of the three roles do you believe this chapter helped you with the most? Why? Discuss in detail and provide an example to illustrate your main points. 2. Review CSWE Competency 4 at the beginning of this chapter on page 624. Thoroughly discuss how you feel this chapter will help you to become a practice-informed researcher and a research-informed practitioner. Discuss in detail and provide an example to illustrate your main points. 3. Review the evidence-based practice process as illustrated on pages 46–51. Thoroughly discuss how this chapter helps you to develop the skills you'll need for implementing one or more steps of the evidence-based practice process. 4. Discuss which step(s) you feel this chapter will help you with the most. Why? Be very specific and use relevant social work examples to illustrate your main points throughout your discussion. **NOTE:** This exercise should help you to realize that you can use "research techniques" to help you become an evidence-based social work practitioner.
23	**LOOKING AHEAD BY THINKING BACK** At this point in your research methods course, how comfortable are you with discussing the place of research in social work with your field instructor, with your practice instructor, with your research instructor, with your supervisor at work, with the director of your social work program, or with your classmates? Discuss in detail.

VII

Research Proposals and Reports

CHAPTER 19: Quantitative Proposals and Reports **658**

CHAPTER 20: Qualitative Proposals and Reports **694**

19

CHAPTER

COMPETENCY 1: Demonstrate Ethical and Professional Behavior

You will learn that in order to be a successful evidence-based practitioner you have an ethical obligation to integrate three research roles into your daily practice activities as discussed in Chapter 1: (1) research consumer, (2) research partner—either as a co-researcher or research participant, and (3) creator and disseminator of research (or knowledge).

In reference to numbers 2 and 3 above, this means you need to write quantitative research proposals to advance our profession's knowledge base (practice-informed research) and write reports for possible publication based on your study's results (research-informed practice). This entire chapter is devoted to this topic.

You do not have to have the skills to write quantitative research proposals and reports to be a research consumer.

COMPETENCY 4: Engage in Practice-Informed Research and Research-Informed Practice

Competency 4 also pertains to the entire chapter because you have to:

1. Be competent in writing quantitative research proposals that seek funds to carry out your proposed research studies (**research partner** in addition to **creator and disseminator of research**—practice-informed research);

2. Be competent in writing quantitative research reports based on quantitative research studies (**research partner** in addition to **creator and disseminator of research**—practice-informed research).

COMPETENCY 9: Evaluate Practice with Individuals, Families, Groups, Organizations, and Communities

See Competencies 1 and 4.

19

Quantitative Proposals and Reports

CHAPTER 1   **Step 1.** Understanding the Research Process

CHAPTER 2   **Step 2.** Developing Research Questions

CHAPTER 3   **Step 3.** Reviewing the Literature

CHAPTERS 4 & 5   **Step 4.** Being Aware of Ethical and Cultural Issues

CHAPTERS 6–8   **Step 5.** Selecting a Research Approach

CHAPTERS 9 & 10   **Step 6.** Specifying How Variables Are Measured

CHAPTER 11   **Step 7.** Selecting a Sample

CHAPTERS 12 & 13   **Step 8.** Selecting a Research Design

CHAPTERS 14–16   **Step 9.** Selecting a Data-Collection Method

CHAPTERS 17 & 18   **Step 10.** Analyzing the Data

CHAPTERS 19 & 20   **Step 11.** Writing the Research Report

THIS CHAPTER DISCUSSES both how to write a quantitative (or positivistic) research proposal, which is done *before* the study begins, and how to write its corresponding research report, which is done *after* the study is completed. We present them together because a research proposal describes what is *proposed* to be done, while a research report describes what actually *has been* done.

As will be emphasized throughout the chapter, there is so much overlap between the two that a majority of the material written for a research proposal can be easily used in writing the final research report.

This chapter incorporates most of the contents of the preceding chapters, so it's really a summary of the entire research process (and this book) up to report writing. We will use an example of Lula Wilson, a social work practitioner who works at a local domestic violence shelter. On a very general level, she wants to do a quantitative research study on the problems children experience that have witnessed domestic violence.

Note: Authors who write quantitative research proposals must fully understand and appreciate the content contained in the previous 18 chapters since most of the content is used in writing quantitative research proposals. This would be an ideal time to review previous chapters before reading further. This chapter will be meaningless to you if you have not read the previous chapters—especially Chapters 6, 14, and 17.

Writing Quantitative Research Proposals

When writing any research proposal, we must always keep in mind the purposes for its development and be aware of politically sensitive research topics (see Chapters 4 & 5). These are, primarily, to get permission to do the study and, second, perhaps to obtain some funds with which to do it.

There's also a third purpose—to persuade the people who will review the proposal that its author, Lula, is competent to carry out the intended study. Finally, the fourth purpose of a proposal is to force Lula to write down exactly *what* is going to be studied, *why* it's going to be studied, *who's* going to do the study, and *how* it's going to be studied.

In doing this, she may think of aspects of the study that had not occurred to her before. For example, she may look at the first draft of her proposal and realize that some essential details were forgotten—for instance, that the research participants who are going to fill out self-report standardized measuring instruments must be able to read.

The intended readers of the proposal determine how it will be written. It's important to remember that the reviewers will probably have many proposals to evaluate at once. Some proposals will need to be turned down because there will not be sufficient funds, space, or staff time, to accept all of them.

Thus, proposal reviewers are faced with some difficult decisions on which ones to accept and which ones to reject. People who review research proposals often do so on a voluntary basis.

> A majority of the material written for a quantitative research proposal can be easily used in writing the final research report.

With the above in mind, the proposal should be written so that it is easy to read, easy to follow, easy to understand, clearly organized, and brief. It must not ramble or go off into anecdotes about how Lula became interested in the subject in the first place. Rather, Lula's proposal must describe her proposed research study simply, clearly, and concisely. These are very hard tasks and require a lot of rewriting—and we mean *a lot of rewriting!*

Now that we know the underlying rationale for the proposal, the next step is to consider what content it should include. This depends to some extent on who will be reviewing it. If the proposal is submitted to an academic committee, for example, it will often include more of a literature review and more details of the study's research design than if it were submitted to a local social work funding organization such as United Way. Some funding bodies specify exactly what they want included and in what order; others leave it to the author's discretion.

The simplest and most logical way to write the proposal is in the same order that a research study is conducted. For example, when a research study is done, a general topic area is decided upon. This is followed by a literature review in an attempt to narrow the broad research area into more specific research questions or hypotheses.

We will now go back and look at how each step of the quantitative research approach (see Figure 6.1 on page 214) leads to the writing of a parallel section in a research proposal. Let's turn to the first task of proposal writing, specifying the research topic.

PART 1: RESEARCH TOPIC (CHAPTER 2)

THE FIRST STEP IN BEGINNING any research study is to decide what the study will be about. The first task in writing a proposal, therefore, is to describe, in general terms, what *exactly* is going to be studied. Lula may describe, for example, her proposed study's general problem area as:

General problem area:
Problems experienced by children who witness domestic violence

---

Lula needs to convince the proposal reviewers that the general problem area is a good one to study. This task is accomplished by outlining the significance of Lula's proposed study in three specific social work areas: (1) its practical significance, (2) its theoretical significance, and (3) its social policy significance. Depending on to whom the proposal is submitted, Lula may go into detail about these three areas or describe them briefly.

It may be known, for example, that the funding organization that will review the proposal is mostly interested in improving the effectiveness of individual social workers in their day-to-day practice activities. If this is the case, the reviewers will more likely be interested in the practical significance of Lula's proposed study than its theoretical and/or policy significance.

Therefore, Lula's proposal would neither go into detail about how her proposed study might generate new social work theory, nor elaborate on the changes in social policy that might follow directly from the study's results.

Since Lula is going to submit her proposal to the women's emergency shelter where she works, she would be smart in obtaining informal input from her agency's executive director at this stage in writing the proposal. Informal advice at an early stage is astronomically important to proposal writers. In sum, Part 1 of the proposal describes *what* is going to be studied and *why* it should be studied.

> Part 1 of a research proposal describes what is going to be studied and why it should be studied.

PART 2: LITERATURE REVIEW (CHAPTER 3)

THE SECOND PART OF A PROPOSAL contains the literature review. This is not simply a list of all the books and journal articles that vaguely touch on the general problem area mentioned in Part 1 (i.e., problems experienced by children who witness domestic violence). When a research study is done, it is mainly trying to add another piece to a jigsaw puzzle already begun by other researchers. The purpose her literature review, then, will be to show how her proposed study fits into "the whole."

The trouble is that it might be a very big whole. There easily could be literally hundreds of articles and books filled with previous research studies on the Lula's general topic area. If Lula tries to list every one of these, the reviewers of the proposal, probably her colleagues who work with her at the shelter, will very quickly lose interest and patience somewhere in the middle of Part 2.

> The literature review has many purposes and is an extremely important component of a research proposal.

Her literature review has to be selective—listing enough material to show that she is thoroughly familiar with her topic area, but not enough to induce stupor in the reviewers. This is a delicate balance. She should include findings from recent research studies along with any classical ones.

On the other side of the coin, another possibility is that previous research studies on Lula's general topic area may be limited. In this case, all available material is included. However, her proposal can also branch out into material that is partially related or describes a parallel topic area.

Lula might find a research article, for example, that claims that children whose parents are contemplating divorce have low social interaction skills. This does not bear directly on the matter of problems children have who witnessed domestic violence (the general problem area previously mentioned). However, since marital separation can be a result of domestic violence, it might be indirectly relevant. In short, a literature review serves four overlapping purposes:

— **First,** it shows the reviewers that Lula understands the most current and central issues related to the general topic area that she proposes to study.

— **Second,** it points out in what ways her proposed study is the same as, or different from, other similar studies.

— **Third,** it describes how the results of her proposed study will contribute to answering her research question.

— **Fourth,** it introduces and conceptually defines all the variables that will be examined throughout the study.

At this stage, Lula does not operationally define her study's variables—that is, in such a way that allows their measurement. They are only abstractly defined. For example, if Lula is going to study the social interaction skills of children who witness domestic violence, her proposal so far introduces only the concepts of:

1. Children
2. Domestic violence
3. Children witnessing domestic violence
4. Children's social interaction skills

PART 3: CONCEPTUAL FRAMEWORK (CHAPTER 3)

A CONCEPTUAL FRAMEWORK takes the variables that have been mentioned in Part 2, illustrates their possible relationship to one another, and discusses why the relationship exists the way she proposes they do and not in some other, equally possible way. The author's suppositions might be based on past professional experience.

For example, Lula has observed numerous children who accompanied their mothers to women's emergency shelters. She has made subjective observations of these children over the past two years and finally wishes to test out two hunches objectively.

— **First,** Lula believes that children who have witnessed domestic violence seem to have lower social interaction skills than children who have not witnessed domestic violence.

— **Second,** Lula believes that of the children who have been a witness to domestic violence, boys seem to have lower social interaction skills than girls.

However, the above two hunches are based on only two-year *subjective* observations, which need to be *objectively* tested—the purpose of her study.

As we know, ideally, Lula's hunches should be integrated with existing theory or findings derived from previous research studies. In any case, Lula should discuss these assumptions and the reasons for believing them as the basis for the variables that are included in her proposed study.

> A conceptual framework clearly discusses how the variables in a proposed research study relate to one another.

PART 4: RESEARCH QUESTION OR HYPOTHESIS (CHAPTER 2)

GIVEN THE FIRST THREE PARTS of Lula's proposal so far, we can easily see that she wants to see if children who have witnessed domestic violence have lower social interaction skills than those children who have not witnessed it. And of the children who have witnessed domestic violence, she wants to determine whether boys have lower social interaction skills than girls.

It must be remembered that the two areas her study proposes to explore have been delineated out of her past experiences and have not been formulated on existing theory or previous research findings. From Lula's general problem area, she formulated two related research hypotheses as follows:

> **Research hypothesis 1:**
> Children who have witnessed domestic violence will have lower social interaction skills than children who have not witnessed such abuse.
>
> **Research hypothesis 2:**
> Of those children who have witnessed domestic violence, boys will have lower social interaction skills than girls.

PART 5: METHODOLOGY

PART 5 OF A RESEARCH PROPOSAL, often commonly called the "methodology" section of a research proposal contains five highly interdependent sub-parts:

— **Part 5a:** Research design (Chapter 13)
— **Part 5b:** Operational definitions (Chapters 9 and 10)
— **Part 5c:** Population and sample (Chapter 11)
— **Part 5d:** Data collection (Chapters 14 and 16)
— **Part 5e:** Data analysis (Chapter 17)

PART 5A: RESEARCH DESIGN (CHAPTER 13)

IN RELATION TO RESEARCH HYPOTHESIS 1, Lula's study would use the children who accompanied their mothers to the women's emergency shelter. These children would then be broken down into two mutually exclusive groups:

— Those children who witnessed domestic violence
— Those children who did not witness it

As presented in Chapter 13, a very simple comparison two group pre-test-posttest research design could be used to test Research Hypothesis 1 (see Figure 13.7 on page 479). One group would be those children who witnessed domestic violence and the second group would be those children who did not witness it. The average social interaction skills between the two groups can then be compared.

In relation to Research Hypothesis 2, within the group of children who have witnessed domestic violence, the children's social interaction skills between the boys and girls can be compared. This simple procedure would test Research Hypothesis 2.

Once again, as presented in Chapter 13, a simple comparison two-group research design could be used to test Research Hypothesis 2. One group would consist of the boys and the other group would consist of the girls.

In Lula's study, there are two separate mini-research studies running at the same time— Research Hypotheses 1 and 2. All Lula wants to do is to see if there is a relationship between the social interaction skills of children who have and have not

> The *research design* section of a research proposal must be clearly linked to the research question to be answered or the hypothesis to be tested.

witnessed domestic violence (Research Hypothesis 1). In addition, for those children who have witnessed domestic violence, she wants to see if boys have lower social interaction skills than girls (Research Hypothesis 2).

PART 5B: OPERATIONAL DEFINITIONS (CHAPTERS 9 & 10)

AS MENTIONED, VARIABLES ARE ABSTRACTLY AND CONCEPTUALLY DEFINED in the conceptual framework part of the proposal (Part 3). Part 5b provides operational definitions of them; that is, they must be defined in ways in which they can be measurable. Let's take Lula's first simple research hypothesis previously mentioned.

In this hypothesis there are four main variables that must be operationalized before Lula's study can begin:

1. Children
2. Domestic violence
3. Children witnessing domestic violence
4. Children's social interaction skills

Each variable must be measured in such a way that there is no ambiguity as to what they mean. Let's start off by operationally defining "children."

VARIABLE 1: CHILDREN. For example, what constitutes a child? How old must the child be? Does the child have to be in a certain age range, for example between the ages of 5–10? Does the child have to be a biological product of either the mother or the father? Can the child be a stepchild? Can the child be adopted? Does the child have to live full-time at home?

Since Lula's study is extremely basic, she may wish to define a child operationally in such a way that permits the largest number of children to be included in her study. She would, however, turn to the literature to find out how other researchers have operationally defined "children," and she would use this operational definition if it made sense to her.

Operational definitions define how the variables are going to be measured.

However, in a simple study such as this one, a child could be operationally defined as "any person who is considered to be a child as determined by the mother." This is a very vague operational definition, at best, but it's more practical than constructing one such as, "a person between the ages of 5–17 who has resided full-time with the biological mother for the last 12-month period."

If such a complex operational definition was utilized, Lula would have to provide answers to questions as: Why the ages of 5–17, why not 4–18? What is the specific reason for this age range? Why must the child live at home full-time, why not part-time? Why must the mother be the biological mother, why not a non-biological mother? What about biological fathers? Why must the child have had to live at home for the past 12 months, why not two years, four years?

In short, Lula's operational definition of a child must make sense and be based on a rational or theoretical basis. For now, Lula is going to make matters simple: A child in her study will be operationally defined as any child whose mother validates their relationship. This simple operational definition makes the most practical sense to Lula.

VARIABLE 2: DOMESTIC VIOLENCE. Let's now turn to Lula's second variable—domestic violence. What is it? Does the male partner have to shove, push, or threaten his partner? How would a child, as operationally defined above, know when it occurs? Does a husband yelling at his wife imply domestic violence? If so, does it have to last a long time? If it does, what is a long time? Is

Lula interested in the frequency, duration, or magnitude of yelling—or all three?

A specific operational definition of domestic violence has to be established in order for the study to be of any value. Like most variables, there are as many operational definitions of domestic violence as there are people willing to define it.

For now, Lula is going to continue to make her simple study simple by operationally defining domestic violence as, "women who say they have been physically abused by their partners." Lula can simply ask each woman who enters the shelter if she believes she has been physically abused by her partner.

The data provided by the women will be "yes" or "no." Lula could have looked at the frequency, duration, or magnitude of such abuse, but for this study, the variable is a dichotomous one: Either domestic violence occurred, or it did not occur—as reported by the women. Questions regarding its frequency (how many times it occurred), its duration (how long each episode lasted), and its magnitude (the intensity of each episode) are not asked.

> Operational definitions of all variables must make sense, be realistic, and have a theoretical basis if at all possible.

VARIABLE 3: CHILDREN WITNESSING DOMESTIC VIOLENCE. The third variable in Lula's hypothesis is the child (or children) who witnesses domestic violence. Now that operational definitions of a "child" and "domestic violence" have been formulated, how will she know that a child has witnessed such an abuse? Each child could be asked directly, or a standardized checklist of possible verbal and physical abuses that a child might have witnessed can be given to the child, who is then asked how many times such abuse has been observed.

Obviously, the child would have to know what constitutes domestic violence to recognize it. In addition, the child would have to be old enough to respond to such requests, and the operational definition that is used for domestic violence must be consistent with the age of the child. For example, the child must be able to communicate to someone that domestic violence has in fact occurred—not to mention the question of whether the child could recognize it in the first place.

In Lula's continuing struggle to keep her study as simple as possible, she operationally defines "a child witnessing domestic violence" by asking the mothers who come to the women's emergency shelter if their child(ren) witnessed the physical abuse.

Lula is interested only in the women who come to the shelter as a result of being physically abused by their partners. Women who come to the shelter for other reasons are not included in her study. It must be kept in mind that Lula's study is focusing only upon physical abuse and not emotional, financial, or mental abuse.

So far, Lula's study is rather simple in terms of operational definitions. Up to this point she is studying mothers who bring their child(ren) with them to one women's emergency shelter. She simply asks the mother if the person(s) with her is her child(ren), which operationally defines "child."

The mother is asked if she believes her partner physically abused her, which defines "domestic violence." The mother is also asked if the child(ren) who is(are) accompanying her to the shelter saw the physical abuse occur, which operationally defines "children witnessing domestic violence."

VARIABLE 4: CHILDREN'S SOCIAL INTERACTION SKILLS. Let's now turn to Lula's fourth and final variable in her hypothesis—the children's social interaction skills. How will they be measured? What constitutes the social interaction skills of a child? They could be measured in a variety of ways through direct observations of parents, social work practitioners, social work researchers, social work practicum students, teachers, neighbors, and even members from the children's peer group.

They could also be measured by standardized measuring instruments such as the ones discussed in Chapters 9 and 10. Lula decides to use one of the many standardized measuring instruments that measure social interaction skills of children, named the *Social Interaction Skills of Children Assessment Instrument* (*SISOCAI*).

All in all, Part 5b of a proposal provides operational definitions of the variables that were abstractly defined in Part 3. It should be noted that the four variables that have been operationally defined should be defined from the available literature, if appropriate. (This procedure makes a study's results generalizable from one research situation to another.).

However, there might be times when this is not possible. Lula's proposal must specify what data gathering instruments are going to be used, including their validity and reliability, as presented in Chapters 9 and 10.

In summary, let's review how Lula intends to operationally define her four key variables:

1. **Child.** Any person who the mother claims is her child.

2. **Domestic Violence.** Asking the mother if her partner physically abused her.

3. **Child Witnessing Domestic Violence.** Asking the mother if the child(ren) who accompanied her to the shelter witnessed the abuse.

4. **Children's Social Interaction Skills.** The SISOCAI score for each child in the study.

The first three operational definitions are rather rudimentary, at best. There are many more sophisticated ways of operationally defining them. However, alternative definitions will not be explored, because Lula wants to keep her research proposal as uncomplicated as possible as she knows that the shelter does not want a study that would intrude too heavily into its day-to-day operations.

On a very general level, the more complex the operational definitions of variables used in a research study, the more the study will intrude on the research participants' lives—in addition to the agency's day-to-day operations.

PART 5C: POPULATION AND SAMPLE (CHAPTER 11)

THIS PART OF THE PROPOSAL presents a detailed description of who will be studied. Lula's research study will use the children who accompanied their mothers to one women's emergency shelter who wish to voluntarily participate, and whose mothers agree that their children can be included in the study (see Chapter 4 on research ethics). Each child will then each go into one of two distinct groups: those who have witnessed domestic violence, and those who have not (according to the mothers, that is).

All research proposals must clearly state who is going to participate in the research study; that is, who's going to be included in the study's sample.

Lula's study could have used a comparison group of children from the same local community who have never witnessed domestic violence and have never been to a women's emergency shelter. However, Lula chose to use only those children who accompanied their mothers to the shelter where she works.

There is no question of random selection from some population, and it's not possible to generalize the study's findings to any general population of children who have and have not witnessed domestic violence. The results of Lula's study will apply only to the children who participated in it.

PART 5D: DATA COLLECTION (CHAPTERS 14 & 16)

THIS PART PRESENTS a detailed account of how the data are going to be collected—that is, the specific data collection method(s) that will be used. As we know, data can be collected using interviews (individual or group), surveys (mail or telephone), direct observations, participant observations, secondary analyses, and content analyses.

Lula is going to collect data on the dependent variable by having her research assistant complete the *SISOCAI* for each identified child during a one-half hour interview one day after the mother enters the shelter with her child(ren). Those mothers who do not bring their children with them will not be included in Lula's study.

All research proposals must clearly state the study's data-collection plan on how data for each variable is to be collected; that is, *who* is going to collect them, and *when and where* will they be collected?

In addition to the children, their mothers are also going to be interviewed to some small degree. Lula will ask each mother if she believes her partner physically assaulted her. These responses will then be used to operationally define "domestic violence."

Each mother will also provide data on whether or not her child(ren) who accompanied her to the shelter saw the abuse occur. The mothers' responses will then operationally define whether or not the child(ren) witnessed domestic violence.

Finally, this section should discuss ethical and cultural issues involved in the data collection process (Chapters 4 & 5). Chapters 14–16 in this book present various data collection methods that can be used in research studies. These chapters should be reread thoroughly before writing Part 5d of a research proposal.

PART 5E: DATA ANALYSIS (CHAPTER 17)

THIS PART DESCRIBES THE WAY THE DATA WILL BE ANALYZED, including the statistical procedures to be used, if any. Having clearly specified the research design in Part 5a, this part specifies exactly what statistical test(s) will be used to answer the research questions or test the hypotheses.

The *SISOCAI* produces interval-level data, and a child's social interaction skill score on this particular instrument can range from 0–100, where higher scores mean better social skills than lower scores. Since there are two groups of children that are being used to test both research hypotheses, and the dependent variable (*SISOCAI*) is at the interval-level of measurement, an independent *t*-test would be used to test both research hypotheses.

PART 6: LIMITATIONS

THERE ARE LIMITATIONS IN EVERY RESEARCH STUDY, often due to problems that cannot be eliminated entirely—even though steps can be taken to reduce them. Lula's study is certainly no exception. Limitations inherent in a study might relate to the validity and reliability of the measuring instruments, or to the generalizability of the study's findings. Sometimes the data that were needed could not be collected for some reason. In addition, this part should mention all extraneous variables that have not been controlled for.

For example, Lula may not have been able to control for all the factors that affect the children's social interaction skills. Although she believes that having witnessed domestic violence leads to lower social skills for boys as compared to girls, it may not be possible to collect reliable and valid data about whether the children saw or did not see an abuse occur. In Lula's study, she is going to simply ask the mothers, so in this case, she has to take the mothers' word for it.

She could ask the children, however. This would produce another set of limitations in and of itself. For example, it would be difficult for Lula to ascertain whether a child did or did not see a form of domestic violence as perceived by the child. It may be hard for a child to tell what type of abuse occurred.

All proposed research studies have limitation of some kind such as representative samples, measurement issues, and data collection and analyses challenges.

Also the frequency, duration, and magnitude of a particular form of domestic violence may be hard for the child to recall. All of these limitations, and a host of others, must be delineated in this part of the proposal. In addition, asking children if they saw the abuse occur might prove to be a traumatic experience for them.

Some limitations will not be discovered until the study is well underway. However, many problems can be anticipated and these should be included in the proposal, together with the specific steps that are intended to minimize them.

PART 7: ADMINISTRATION

THE FINAL PART OF A RESEARCH PROPOSAL contains the organization and resources necessary to carry out the study. First, Lula has to find a base of operations (e.g., desk, telephone). She has to think about who is going to take on the overall administrative responsibility for the study.

How many individuals will be needed? What should their qualifications be? What will be their responsibilities? To whom are they responsible? What is the chain of command? Finally, Lula has to think about things such as a computer, stationery, telephone, travel, and parking expenses.

When all of the details have been put together, an organizational chart can be produced that shows what will be done, by whom, where, and in what order. The next step is to develop a time frame. By what date should each anticipated step be completed?

Optimism about completion dates should be avoided, particularly when it comes to allowing time to analyze the data and writing the final report (to be discussed shortly). Both of these activities always take far longer than anticipated, and it's important that they be properly done—which takes more time than originally planned.

When the organizational chart and time frame have been established, the final step is to prepare a budget. Lula has to figure out how much each aspect of the study—such as office space, the research assistant's time, staff time, and participants' time, if any—will cost.

We have now examined seven parts that should be included when writing a research proposal. Not all proposals are organized in precisely this way; sometimes different headings are used or information is put in a different part of the proposal.

For example, in some proposals, previous studies are discussed in the conceptual framework section rather than in the literature review. Much depends on for whom the proposal is being written and on the author's personal writing style.

Most, if not all, of the content that has been used to write the various parts of a research proposal can be used to write the final research report. Let's now turn to that discussion.

WRITING QUANTITATIVE RESEARCH REPORTS

A RESEARCH REPORT IS A WAY OF DESCRIBING the completed study to other people. The findings can be reported by way of an oral presentation, a book, or a published paper. The report may be addressed solely to colleagues at work or to a worldwide audience. It may be written simply, so that everyone can understand it, or it may be so highly technical that it can only be understood by a few.

The most common way of sharing a study's findings with other professionals is to publish a report in a professional journal. Most journal reports run about 25 double-spaced, typewritten pages, including figures, tables, and references. As we know, proposals are written with the proposal reviewers in mind. Similarly, a research report is written with its readers in mind.

Two versions of the same study can be written: a technical one, and a nontechnical one.

However, some of the readers who read research reports will want to know the technical details of how the study's results were achieved, and others will only want to know how the study's results are relevant to social work practice, without the inclusion of the technical details. There are a number of ways to deal with this situation.

First, a technical report can be written for those who can understand it, without worrying too much about those who cannot. In addition, a second report can be written that skims over the technical aspects of the study and concentrates mostly on the practical application of the study's findings.

Thus, two versions of the same study can be written: a technical one, and a nontechnical one. The thought of writing two reports where one would suffice will not appeal to very many of us, however. Usually, we try to compensate for this by including those technical aspects of the study that are necessary to an understanding of the study's findings. This is essential, because readers will not be able to evaluate the study's findings without knowing how they were arrived at.

All research reports must have some practical, theoretical, or policy significance; that is, they should contribute to social work policy, practice, or education.

However, life can be made easier for nontechnical audiences by including some explanation of the technical aspects and, in addition, paying close attention to the practical application of the study's results. In this way, we will probably succeed in addressing the needs of both audiences—those who want all the technical details and those who want none.

A report can be organized in many different ways depending on the intended audience and the author's personal style. Often, however, the same common-sense sequence is followed when the basic problem solving method was discussed at the beginning of this book. In order to solve a problem, the problem must be specified, ways of solving it must be explored, a solution to solve the problem must be tried, and an evaluation must take place to see if the solution worked.

In general, this is the way to solve practice and research problems. It's also the order in which a research report is written. First, a research problem is defined. Then, the method used to solve it is discussed. Next, the findings are presented. Finally, the significance of the findings to the social work profession is discussed.

PART 1: PROBLEM

PROBABLY THE BEST WAY TO BEGIN a research report is to explain simply what the research problem is. Lula might say, for example, that the study's purpose was to ascertain if children who have witnessed domestic violence have lower social interaction skills than children who have not witnessed such abuse.

In addition, the study wanted to find out, of those children who have witnessed domestic violence, if boys have lower social interaction skills than girls. But why would anyone want to know about that? How would the knowledge derived from Lula's study help social workers?

Thinking back to her proposal, this question was asked and answered once before. In the first part of her proposal, when the research topic was set out, the significance of the study was discussed in the areas of practice, theory, and social policy. This material can be used, suitably paraphrased, in Part 1 of the final report.

One thing that should be remembered, though, is that a research report written for a journal is not, relatively speaking, very long. A lot of information must be included in less than 25 pages, and the author cannot afford to use too much space explaining to readers why this particular study was chosen. Sometimes, the significance of the study will be apparent and there is no room to belabor what is already obvious.

In Part 2 of the proposal, a literature review, was done in which Lula's proposed study was compared to other similar studies, highlighting similarities and differences. Also, key variables were conceptually defined. In her final report, she can use both the literature review and her conceptually defined variables that she presented in her proposal.

> Research proposals can answer research questions and/or test hypotheses.

The literature review might have to be cut back if space is at a premium, but the abstract and conceptual definitions of all key variables must be included. In Part 3 of her proposal, she presented a conceptual framework. This can be used in Part 1 of the final report, where Lula must state the relationships between the variables she is studying.

In Part 4 of the research proposal, a research question to be answered or hypothesis to be tested was stated. In the final report, we started out with that, so now we have come full circle. By using the various parts of the proposal for the first part of the research report, we have managed to considerably cut down writing time.

In fact, Part 1 of a research report is nothing more than a cut-and-paste job of the first four parts of the research proposal. Actually, if the first four parts of the research proposal were done correctly, there should be very little original writing within Part 1 of a research report.

One of the most important things to remember when writing Part 1 of a report is that the study's findings have to have some form of utilization potential for social workers, or the report would not be worth writing in the first place. More specifically, the report must have some practical, theoretical, or policy significance. Part 1 of a research report tells why the study's findings would be useful to the social work profession. This is mentioned briefly but is picked up later in Part 4.

Joel Fischer (1981) has provided us with 15 points we need to consider when evaluating the Problem section a published research report:

1. Adequacy of the literature review

2. Clarity of the problem area and research question under investigation

3. Clarity of the statement of the hypothesis

4. Clarity of the specification of the independent variable

5. Clarity of the specification of the dependent variable

6. Clarity of the definitions for major concepts

7. Clarity of the operational definitions

8. Reasonableness of assumption of relationship between the independent and dependent variables

9. Number of independent variables tested

10. Specification of independent variables in rival hypotheses

11. Adequacy in the control of independent variables in rival hypotheses

12. Clarity of the researcher's orientation

13. Clarity of the study's purpose

14. Clarity of the study's auspices

15. Reasonableness of the author's assumptions

PART 2: METHOD

PART 2 OF A REPORT CONTAINS THE METHOD(S) used to answer the research problem. This section usually includes descriptions of the study's research design, a description of the research participants who were a part of the study (study's sample), and a detailed description of the data gathering procedures (who, what, when, how), and presents the operational definition of all variables.

Once again, sections of the original research proposal can be used. For example, in Part 5b of the proposal, key variables were operationally defined; that is, they were defined in a way that would allow them to be measured. When and how the measurements would occur were also presented in Part 5d. This material can be used again in the final report.

Part 5a of the proposal described the study's research design. This section of the proposal was used—about half way through—to link the parts of the study together into a whole. Since a research design encompasses the entire research process from conceptualizing the problem to disseminating the findings, Lula could take this opportunity to give a brief picture of the entire process.

This part presents *who* would be studied (the research participants, or sample), *what* data would be gathered, *how* the data would be gathered, *when* the data would be gathered, and *what* would be done with the data once obtained (analysis).

In the final report, there is not a lot of space to provide this information in detail. Instead, a clear description of how the data were obtained from the measuring instruments must be presented. For example, Lula could state in this part of the report, that "a research assistant rated each child on the *SISOCAI* during a one-half hour interview one day after the mother entered the shelter."

Joel Fischer (1981) has provided us with 35 points we need to consider when evaluating the Methods section a published research report:

1. Clarity of the specification of the kinds of changes desired

2. Appropriateness of the outcome measures

3. Degree of validity of the outcome measures

4. Degree of reliability of the outcome measures

5. Degree of use of a variety of outcome measures

6. Clarity about how data were collected

7. Clarity about who collects data

8. Degree of avoidance of error in process of data collection

9. Clarity of the statement of the research design

10. Adequacy of the research design (re: purpose)

11. Clarity and adequacy of time between pretest and posttest

12. Appropriateness in the use of control group(s)

13. Appropriateness in the use of random assignment procedures

14. Appropriateness in the use of matching procedures

15. Experimental and control group equivalency at pretest

16. Degree of control for effects of history

17. Degree of control for effects of maturation

18. Degree of control for effects of testing

19. Degree of control for effects of instrumentation

20. Degree of control for statistical regression

21. Degree of control for differential selection of clients

22. Degree of control for differential mortality

23. Degree of control for temporal bias

24. Degree of control for integrity of treatment

25. Ability to distinguish causal variable

26. Degree of control for interaction effects

27. Overall degree of success in maximizing internal validity

28. Adequacy of sample size

29. Degree of accuracy in defining the population

30. Degree of adequacy in the representativeness of the sample

31. Degree of control for reactive effects of testing

32. Degree of control for interaction between selection and experimental variable

33. Degree of control for special effects of experimental arrangements

34. Degree of control for multiple treatment interference

35. Overall degree of success in maximizing external validity

PART 3: FINDINGS

PART 3 OF A REPORT PRESENTS THE STUDY'S FINDINGS. Unfortunately, Lula's original proposal will not be of much help here because she did not know what she would find when it was written—only what she hoped to find.

One way to begin Part 3 of a report is to prepare whatever figures, tables, or other data displays that are going to be used. For now, let us take Lula's research Hypothesis 1 as an example of how to write up a study's findings.

TABLE 19.1

Means and Standard Deviations of Social Interaction Skills of Children Who Did and Did Not Witness Domestic Violence (*N* = 80)

Witness?	Mean	Standard Deviation	*n*
Yes	45	11	40
No	75	9	40
Average...	60		

Let's suppose that there were 80 children who accompanied their mothers to the shelter. All of the mothers claimed their partners physically abused them. Lula's research assistant rated the 80 children's social skills, via the *SISOCAI*, one day after they accompanied their mothers to the shelter. Thus, there are 80 *SISOCAI* scores. What is she going to do with all that data?

The goal of tables and figures is to organize the data in such a way that the reader takes them in at a glance and says, "Ah! Well, it's obvious that the children who witnessed domestic violence had lower *SISOCAI* scores than the children who did not see such abuse."

As can be seen from Table 19.1 the average *SISOCAI* score for all of the 80 children is 60. These 80 children would then be broken down into two subgroups: those who witnessed domestic violence, and those who did not—according to their mothers, that is.

For the sake of simplicity let us say there were 40 children in each subgroup. In the first subgroup, the average *SISOCAI* score for the 40 children is 45; in the second subgroup, the average *SISOCAI* score for the 40 children is 75. Table 19.1 allows the reader to quickly compare the average *SISOCAI* score for each one of the two subgroups (i.e., yes = 45; no = 75).

The reader can see, at a glance, that there is a 30-point difference between the two average *SISOCAI* scores (75 – 45 = 30). The children who witnessed domestic violence scored 30 points lower, on the average, on the *SISOCAI* than those children who did not witnesses domestic violence.

Thus, by glancing at Table 19.1, Lula's Research Hypothesis 1 is supported in that children who witness domestic violence had lower social interaction skills than children who did not witness it.

However, it is still not known from Table 19.1 whether the 30-point difference between the two average *SISOCAI* scores is large enough to be statistically significant. The appropriate statistical procedure for this design is the independent *t*-test, as described in Chapter 17. The results of the *t*-test could also be included under Table 19.1, or they could be described in the findings section:

"The result of an independent *t*-test between the SISOCAI scores of children who witnessed domestic violence as compared to those children who did not witness it was statistically significant ($t = 3.56$, *df* = 78, $p < .05$). Thus, children who witnessed domestic violence had statistically significant lower social interaction skills, on the average, than children who did not witness such abuse."

Table 19.2 presents the study's findings for Lula's second research hypothesis. This table uses the data from the 40 children who witnessed domestic violence (from Table 19.1). As can be seen from Tables 19.1 and 19.2, the average social skill score for the 40 children who witnessed domestic violence is 45.

TABLE 19.2

Means and Standard Deviations of Social Interaction Skills of Boys and Girls Who Witnessed Domestic Violence (from Table 19.1, *N* = 40)

Gender	Mean	Standard Deviation	*n*
Boys	35	12	20
Girls	55	13	20
Average . . .	45		

Table 19.2 further breaks down these 40 children into two subgroups: boys and girls. Out of the 40 children who witnessed domestic violence, 20 were boys and 20 were girls. As can be seen from Table 19.2, boys had an average social skill score of 35 as compared with the average score for girls of 55. Thus, the boys scored, on the average, 20 points lower than the girls. So far, Lula's second research hypothesis is supported.

However, it is still not known from Table 19.2 whether the 20-point difference between the two average *SISOCAI* scores is large enough to be statistically significant. The appropriate statistical procedure for this design is the independent *t*-test, as described in Chapter 17. The results of the *t*-test could be included under Table 19.2, or they could be described in the findings section as follows:

> "The result of an independent *t*-test between the SISOCAI scores for boys and girls who witnessed domestic violence was statistically significant ($t = 2.56$, $df = 38$, $p < .05$). Thus, boys had statistically significant lower social interaction skills, on the average, than girls."

Once a table (or figure) is constructed, the next thing that has to be done is to describe in words what it means. Data displays should be self-explanatory if done correctly. It is a waste of precious space to repeat in the text something that is perfectly apparent from a table or figure.

At this point, Lula has to decide whether she is going to go into a lengthy discussion of her findings in this part of the report or whether she is going to reserve the discussion for the next part. Which option is chosen often depends on what there is to discuss. Sometimes it is more sensible to combine the findings with the discussion, pointing out the significance of what has been found as she goes along. Joel Fischer (1981) has provided us with six points we need to consider when evaluating the Findings section a published research report:

1. Adequacy of the manipulation of the independent variable
2. Appropriateness in the use of follow up measures
3. Adequacy of data to provide evidence for testing of hypotheses
4. Clarity in reporting statistics
5. Appropriateness in the use of statistical controls
6. Appropriateness of statistics utilized

PART 4: DISCUSSION

THE FINAL PART OF A REPORT presents a discussion of the study's findings. Care should be taken not to merely repeat the study's findings that were already presented in Part 3. It can be tempting to repeat one finding in order to remind the reader about it preliminary to a discussion, and then another finding, and then a third . . . and, before we know it, we have written the whole of the findings section all over again and called it a discussion. What's needed here is control and judgment—a delicate balance between not reminding the reader at all and saying everything twice.

On the other hand, Lula might be tempted to ignore her findings altogether, particularly if she did not find what she expected. If the findings did not support her hypothesis, she may have a strong urge to express her viewpoint anyway, using persuasive prose to make up for the lack of objective evidence. This temptation must be resisted at all costs.

The term "discussion" relates to what she found, not to what she thinks she ought to have found, or to what she might have found under slightly different circumstances. Perhaps she did manage to find a relationship between the variables in both of her hypotheses.

However, to her dismay, she may have found that the relationship was the opposite of what she predicted. For example, suppose her data indicated that children who witnessed domestic violence had higher social interaction skills than children who did not witness it (this is the opposite of what she predicted).

LIMITATIONS

THIS UNEXPECTED RESULT MUST BE DISCUSSED, shedding whatever light on the surprising finding. Any relationship between two variables is worthy of discussion, particularly if they seem atypical or if they are not quite what was anticipated.

A common limitation in social work research has to do with not being able to randomly select research participants from a specific population. Whenever we cannot randomly select research participants the sample cannot be considered to be truly representative of the population in question, and we cannot generalize the study's results back to the population of children who witnessed or did not witness domestic violence in the community. The simplest way to deal with this limitation is to state it directly.

Another major limitation in this study is that we will never know the social interaction skills of children who did not accompany their mothers to the shelter. The social skills of children who stay home may somehow be quite different from those children who accompanied their mothers.

In fact, there are a host of other limitations in this simple study, including the simple fact that, in reference to Research Hypothesis 2, boys who did not see domestic violence may also have lower social interaction skills than girls—this was never tested in Lula's study.

Nevertheless, we should also bear in mind the fact that few social work studies are based on truly representative random samples. In Lula's study, however, she still managed to collect some interesting data.

All social work researchers would like to be able to generalize their findings beyond the specific research setting and sample. From a research perspective (not a practice perspective), Lula is not really interested in the specific children in this particular study. She's more interested in children who witness domestic violence in general.

Technically, the results of her study cannot be generalized to other populations of children who witness domestic violence, but she can suggest that she might find similar results with other children who accompany their mothers to similar women's shelters. She can imply and can recommend further studies into the topic area.

Sometimes we can find support for our suggestions in the results of previous studies that were not conclusive either, but that also managed to produce recommendations. It might even be a good idea to extract these studies from the literature review section in Part 1 of the report and resurrect them in the discussion section.

On occasion, the results of a study will not agree with the results of previous studies. In this case, we should give whatever explanations seem reasonable for the disagreement and make some suggestions whereby the discrepancy can be resolved. Perhaps another research study should be undertaken that would examine the same or different variables.

Perhaps, next time, a different research design should be used or the research hypothesis should be reformulated. Perhaps other operational definitions could be used. Suggestions for future studies should always be specific, not just a vague statement to the effect that more research studies need to be done in this area.

In some cases, recommendations can be made for changes in social work programs, interventions, or policies based on the results of a study. These recommendations are usually contained in reports addressed to people who have the power to make the suggested changes. When changes are suggested, the author has to display some knowledge about the policy or program and the possible consequences of implementing the suggested changes.

Finally, a report is concluded with a summary of the study's findings. This is particularly important in longer reports or when a study's findings and discussion sections are lengthy or complex. Sometimes, indeed, people reading a long report read only the summary and a few sections of the study that interests them.

Joel Fischer (1981) has provided us with 14 points we need to consider when evaluating the Discussion section a published research report:

1. Degree to which data support the hypothesis

2. Extent to which the conclusions are consistent with the data

3. Degree of uniformity between tables and text

4. Degree of researcher bias

5. Clarity as to cause of changes in dependent variable

6. Degree to which rival hypotheses were avoided in the design

7. Degree to which potential rival hypotheses were dealt with

8. Degree of control for threats to internal validity

9. Reasonableness of opinions about implications

10. Clarity as to meaning of change(s)

11. Adequacy in relating findings to previous literature

12. Adequacy of conclusions for generalizing beyond data

13. Extent that the research design accomplishes the study's purpose

14. Appropriateness in the handling of unexpected consequences

SUMMARY

THE PURPOSE OF WRITING a research proposal is fourfold. A research proposal is necessary, first, to obtain permission to carry out the study and, second, to secure the funds with which to do it. Third, researchers need to convince the proposal reviewers that they are competent enough to do the study. Fourth, we need to think over precisely what we want to study, why we want to study it, what methods we should use, and what difficulties we are likely to encounter.

A proposal should be well organized and easy to read so that reviewers have a clear picture of each step of the study. The information included in most proposals can be set out under seven general headings, or parts.

Using a majority of the material from the research proposal, a research report is written that can be broken down into four general headings, or parts: problem, method, findings, and discussion. The four parts of a research report parallel the seven parts of the research proposal. This is not surprising, since both the report and the proposal are describing the same study.

Study Questions for Chapter 19
Essay — Discussion

1	In your own words, describe what a quantitative research proposal is all about. Use social work examples to illustrate your main points.
2	List and thoroughly discuss the four main purposes of a social work research proposal. Provide a social work example that illustrates each purpose.
3	Online, search for "How to write a research proposal." Locate at least five links on the subject. What are their similarities and differences? Did any of them contain content that this chapter should have included? If so, what content?
4	In groups of four, write a brief 4-page research proposal that tests this hypothesis: MSW graduates make better social workers than BSW graduates. Be sure to include all seven components of a research proposal. Hint: You're going to have to operationally define "better" along with "MSW graduates," "BSW graduates," and "social worker."
5	In the same group of four, pretend you actually implemented your proposal (Question 4). Make up fake data that supports your hypothesis. Now use these fake data to write a simple research report that includes all four parts described in this chapter.
6	This chapter provided 15 points to consider when evaluating the *Problem section* of a research report. Discuss if you believe your research report (Question 5) adequately addressed each point. If so, why? If not, why not?
7	This chapter provided 35 points to consider when evaluating the *Method section* of a research report. Discuss whether you believe your research report (Question 5) adequately addressed each point. If so, why? If not, why not?
8	This chapter provided 6 points to consider when evaluating the *Findings section* of a research report. Discuss whether you believe your research report (Question 5) adequately addressed each point. If so, why? If not, why not?

9	This chapter provided 14 points to consider when evaluating the *Discussion section* of a research report. Discuss if you believe your research report (Question 5) adequately addressed each point. If so, why? If not, why not?
10	Discuss how quantitative research proposals utilize all the contents in this book. Provide one simple example from each one of the preceding 18 chapters that could be included in a research proposal. You should have 18 points in total—one for each chapter.
11	If you currently have a practicum ask your field instructor for copies of any quantitatively oriented research proposals they may have in their filing cabinets. Select one proposal and critique it using the contents of this chapter—and the entire book for that matter.

Critical Thinking — Application — Integration

12	**APPLICATION OF QUANTITATIVE RESEARCH PROPOSALS** Locate a published quantitatively oriented social work research article that contains a social work problem area or population that you're interested in. We suggest you locate a quantitatively oriented research study in Bruce Thyer's journal *Research on Social Work Practice* (Sage Publications). Hands down, this is the best journal to find good quantitatively oriented social work research studies. 1. Using the contents of this chapter, write a brief 5-page hypothetical quantitative research proposal that the author could have written for the quantitative research study. 2. Compare your quantitative proposal with those generated by your classmates who used the same research study. What did you learn from comparing your proposal with others? 3. Did the research study also contain a "qualitative" component (**mixed-methods research** as discussed in Chapter 8)? If so, what did it contain? How did this "qualitative" component add more meat to the quantitative findings? **NOTE:** You're working backward here. That is, you're reconstructing what a hypothetical quantitatively oriented research proposal could have looked like given the contents of the actual published research study. Remember, research proposals contain statements about what we *will do* (future tense); research reports contain statements about what we *have done* (past tense).

QUANTITATIVE RESEARCH PROPOSALS AND THE PRACTITIONER

Scenario 1: Make an argument that to be an effective evidence-based social work practitioner **you must know** how to write quantitatively based research proposals and reports. Provide a clear and explicit **practice-related** social work example to illustrate your main points.

Scenario 2: Make an argument that to be an effective evidence-based social work practitioner **you must know** how to write quantitatively AND qualitatively based research proposals and reports (**mixed-methods research** as discussed in Chapter 8). Provide a clear and explicit **practice-related** social work example to illustrate your main points.

Scenario 3: Make an argument that **you do not have to know** how to write any kind of research proposal or report to be an effective evidence-based social work practitioner. Provide a clear and explicit **practice-related** social work example to illustrate your main points.

Time to Choose: Which one of the above three scenarios do you feel is more consistent with the concept of the contemporary evidence-based social work practice process as illustrated on pages 46–51? Why? Provide relevant social work examples to illustrate your main points.

13	

QUANTITATIVE RESEARCH PROPOSALS AND THE RESEARCHER

Scenario 1: Make an argument that to be a competent social work researcher **you must know** how to write quantitatively based research proposals and reports. Provide a clear and explicit **research-related** social work example to illustrate your main points.

Scenario 2: Make an argument that to be a competent social work researcher **you must know** how to write quantitatively AND qualitatively based research proposals and reports (**mixed-methods research** as discussed in Chapter 8). Provide a clear and explicit **research-related** social work example to illustrate your main points.

Scenario 3: Make an argument that **you do not have to know** how to write any kind of research proposal or report to be a competent social work researcher. Provide a clear and explicit **research-related** social work example to illustrate your main points.

Time to Choose: Which one of the above three scenarios do you feel is more consistent with the place of research in social work? Why? Provide relevant social work examples to illustrate your main points.

14	

15	**TIME TO PUT ON YOUR CRITICAL THINKING HAT** **1.** Discuss the similarities and differences between your responses to Questions 13 and 14. **2.** What are your thoughts on the belief that you need to know how to write **quantitatively** based research proposals whether you're a social work *practitioner* (Question 13) or a social work *researcher* (Question 14)? **3.** What are your thoughts on the belief that you need to know how to write **qualitatively** based research proposals whether you're a social work *practitioner* (Question 13) or a social work *researcher* (Question 14)?
16	**QUANTITATIVE RESEARCH PROPOSALS AND YOUR PROFESSIONAL DEVELOPMENT** **1.** Review the three social work research-related roles you can take when you graduate—CSWE Competency 1 at the beginning of this chapter on page 658. This concept was also discussed in Chapter 1 on pages 38–42. Thoroughly discuss how you feel this chapter will help you to perform one or more research-related roles when you graduate. Which one of the three roles do you believe this chapter helped you with the most? Why? Discuss in detail and provide an example to illustrate your main points. **2.** Review CSWE Competency 4 at the beginning of this chapter on page 658. Thoroughly discuss how you feel this chapter will help you to become a practice-informed researcher and a research-informed practitioner. Discuss in detail and provide an example to illustrate your main points. **3.** Review the evidence-based practice process as illustrated on pages 46–51. Thoroughly discuss how this chapter helps you to develop the skills you'll need for implementing one or more steps of the evidence-based practice process. **4.** Discuss which step(s) you feel this chapter will help you with the most. Why? Be very specific and use relevant social work examples to illustrate your main points throughout your discussion. **NOTE:** This exercise should help you to realize that you can use "research roles" to help you become an evidence-based social work practitioner.

20

CHAPTER

2015 EPAS COMPETENCIES

COMPETENCY 1: Demonstrate Ethical and Professional Behavior

You will learn that in order to be a successful evidence-based practitioner you have an ethical obligation to integrate three research roles into your daily practice activities as discussed in Chapter 1: (1) research consumer, (2) research partner—either as a co-researcher or research participant, and (3) creator and disseminator of research (or knowledge).

In reference to numbers 2 and 3 above, this means you need to write qualitative research proposals to advance our profession's knowledge base (practice-informed research) and write reports for possible publication based on your study's results (research-informed practice). This entire chapter is devoted to this topic.

You do not have to have the skills to write qualitative research proposals and reports to be a research consumer.

COMPETENCY 4: Engage in Practice-Informed Research and Research-Informed Practice

Competency 4 also pertains to the entire chapter because you have to:

1. Be competent in writing qualitative research proposals that seek funds to carry out your proposed research studies (**research partner** in addition to **creator and disseminator of research**—practice-informed research);

2. Be competent in writing qualitative research reports based on qualitative research studies (**research partner** in addition to **creator and disseminator of research**—practice-informed research).

COMPETENCY 9: Evaluate Practice with Individuals, Families, Groups, Organizations, and Communities

See Competencies 1 and 4.

Qualitative Proposals and Reports

CHAPTER 1   **Step 1.** Understanding the Research Process

CHAPTER 2   **Step 2.** Developing Research Questions

CHAPTER 3   **Step 3.** Reviewing the Literature

CHAPTERS 4 & 5   **Step 4.** Being Aware of Ethical and Cultural Issues

CHAPTERS 6–8   **Step 5.** Selecting a Research Approach

CHAPTERS 9 & 10   **Step 6.** Specifying How Variables Are Measured

CHAPTER 11   **Step 7.** Selecting a Sample

CHAPTERS 12 & 13   **Step 8.** Selecting a Research Design

CHAPTERS 14–16   **Step 9.** Selecting a Data-Collection Method

CHAPTERS 17 & 18   **Step 10.** Analyzing the Data

CHAPTERS 19 & 20   **Step 11.** Writing the Research Report

LIKE QUANTITATIVE (POSITIVISTIC) RESEARCH PROPOSALS AND REPORTS presented in the previous chapter, qualitative (interpretive) research proposals and their corresponding reports are also similar to one another. If we explain clearly what we intend to do when we write our proposal, for example, and we actually carry out our study as we originally planned, then writing our research report is largely a matter of changing "we will do" (as in the proposal) to "we did" (as in the report). This is true for everything but describing our study's findings in the research report.

As we will see, there's a good deal of similarity between quantitative and qualitative research proposals and reports. After all, the research process follows a logical progression whether or not it's quantitative or qualitative. We need to know from the very beginning of our research study *what* we

---

Note: Authors who write qualitative research proposals must fully understand and appreciate the content contained in the previous 19 chapters since most of the content is used in writing qualitative research proposals. This would be an ideal time to review previous chapters before reading further. This chapter will be meaningless to you if you have not read the previous chapters—especially Chapters 7, 15, and 18.

want to study, *why* we want to study it, *what* methods we will use to study it, *how* long our research study will take, and *how* much it will cost.

In addition, we need to know *what* data will be collected, from *whom*, in *what* way, and *how* they will be analyzed. For the sake of continuity, this chapter—on qualitative proposals and reports—uses roughly the same format that was used in the last chapter that described quantitative proposals and reports.

We will once again use the same example: Lula Wilson, a social work practitioner who wants to do a qualitative research study on children and their mothers in the women's emergency shelter where she works. Lula did a quantitative proposal in the previous chapter—now she wants to do a qualitative one.

> Just like in quantitative research proposals, a majority of the material written for qualitative ones can be easily used in writing the final research report.

WRITING QUALITATIVE RESEARCH PROPOSALS

BEFORE WE BEGIN TO WRITE the very first word of any research proposal we need to know why we want to write it and who will read it. As we have seen from the last chapter, knowing the purpose and our intended audience helps us to make important decisions about what we should include, in what order, and what writing style to use.

PURPOSE OF WRITING A PROPOSAL

THERE ARE THREE GENERAL PURPOSES for writing a research proposal, no matter what is being proposed.

1. We need to obtain permission to do the study.
2. We need to obtain funding for the study.
3. We need to write down exactly what we intend to study, why, and how.

As we know from Chapter 4, obtaining permission to do our study is often a matter of resolving ethical and informed consent issues to the satisfaction of various ethics committees.

Most universities and colleges have ethics committees, which decide whether our proposed study is designed in such a way that the interests of its research participants are ethically addressed. Many social services agencies throughout the world have their own ethics committees, which vet all proposed research endeavors that involve their clients and staff.

If Lula is associated in any way with a university, for example, and if her women's emergency shelter has its own ethics committee, she will have to obtain permission from both ethics committees before she can begin her study. Even if no ethics committees are involved, Lula will have to discuss her proposed study with her supervisor, who would probably have to obtain official permission from the shelter's Board of Directors.

All research studies require some level of funding. Even if Lula is prepared to do all the work on her own time using her own clients, there will still be direct and indirect costs such as photocopying, travel, phone, faxing, and postage. If Lula wants her shelter to cover these costs, she must include a budget in her proposal and get the budget approved before she begins her study. If it's a larger study, necessitating money from a funding body, then Lula must tailor her research proposal to meet the requirements of the particular funding body to which she is applying.

Most funding bodies have application forms that ask the applicant to supply the study's details under specific headings. Usually, funding bodies also want to know how qualified the particular applicant is to undertake the proposed study. In other words, Lula will have to convince the funding body that she personally has the experience and educational qualifications necessary to obtain meaningful and trustworthy results from her proposed study.

After permission and funding, the third purpose of writing a proposal is to force Lula to clarify her thoughts a bit more. In the process of describing her proposed study in sufficient detail in an attempt to convince others of its importance, Lula may think of aspects of her study that she has not thought of before. She may realize, for example, that she has little experience with interviewing children, and someone who has more experience with interviewing children may be in a better position to interview them.

INTENDED AUDIENCE

MOST RESEARCH PROPOSALS ARE REVIEWED BY BUSY PEOPLE who have a great deal of other work and probably a number of proposals to review. Thus, Lula's proposal should be as short as she can possibly make it. It should concisely describe her proposed study, its budget, and time frame in a way that is easy to read, to follow, and to understand.

Many proposals have to be rejected because there is insufficient funding or facilities to support them all, and those that are rejected are not necessarily the least worthy in terms of their importance. They are, however, often the least worthy in terms of how well they were organized and written. Lula will therefore be well advised to keep her proposal simple, clear, and brief.

CONTENT AND WRITING STYLE

A PROPOSAL'S CONTENT AND WRITING STYLE will largely depend on who's going to review it. As already noted, some funding bodies stipulate on their application forms what and how much they want included, and in what format and order. If there is no such stipulation, it's simplest and most logical to write the research proposal in the order that the study will be conducted; that is, the order followed in this chapter.

How much to include under what heading depends on the intended audience: A research proposal submitted to an academic committee, for example, often requires more of a literature review than a proposal submitted to a funding organization.

> Just as in quantitative research proposals, authors need to write qualitative ones in the same order that their research studies unfold.

Style similarly depends on the recipient. In most cases, it's safest to write formally, using the third person. As we know, however, qualitative research studies are often more subjective than qualitative ones, their terminology is different, their underlying assumptions are different, and the researcher's own thoughts and feelings are an important component.

It may therefore be appropriate to acknowledge the interpretive nature of the study by using a more personal writing style. As will be the case in writing the final research report, the style used depends on the proposal's intended audience and the author's personal judgment.

ORGANIZING THE RESEARCH PROPOSAL

AS PREVIOUSLY NOTED, if the proposal's recipients have provided no guidance as to how its contents should be organized, it's simplest to present the proposed study in the order in which it would be conducted.

PART 1: RESEARCH TOPIC (CHAPTER 2)

THIS FIRST SECTION OF A RESEARCH PROPOSAL does nothing more than introduces the study to its readers. It examines the nature of the research question being explored and its significance, both to social work in general and to the recipient of the proposal in particular. As with quantitative studies, a qualitative one should have practical significance, theoretical significance, or significance with respect to social policy; or it may touch on all three areas.

The author's task is to explain what research question is being asked and why the answer to this question will be of benefit, paying particular attention to the interests of the proposal's reviewers. Lula may write, for example, about the general topic area in her study as follows:

> **General topic area:**
> The problems experienced by children who witness their mothers being physically abused by their fathers

As with quantitative research studies, qualitative ones should have practical significance, theoretical significance, or significance with respect to social policy; or it may touch on all three areas.

The results of such a study—knowing what these problems are—might generate new social work theory or might lead to changes in social policy. If Lula is going to submit her proposal to the women's emergency shelter where she works, however, her fellow social workers are more likely to be interested in how an understanding of the children's problems might help them to address the children's needs on a very practical level. Lula will therefore emphasize the practical significance of her study.

PART 2: LITERATURE REVIEW (CHAPTER 3)

AS WITH QUANTITATIVE RESEARCH STUDIES, there are four purposes in carrying out a literature review for qualitative studies:

1. **To assure the reviewers that Lula understands the current issues related to her research topic.**

2. **To point out ways in which her study is similar to, or different from, other studies that have been previously conducted.** Because many qualitative studies deal with topics about which little is known, Lula may not find many studies that have explored children's experiences with respect to their witnessing domestic violence. Such a paucity of information will support Lula's contention that her study needs to be conducted.

3. **To fit Lula's study into the jigsaw puzzle of present knowledge.** Even if there is little knowledge in the area, there will still be some, and Lula's task is to explain how her study will fit with what is known already and will help to fill the knowledge gaps.

4. **To introduce and conceptualize the variables that will be used throughout the study.** Lulu's proposal, for example, will include such concepts as children, domestic violence (or partner abuse, marital abuse, wife abuse, whichever term is preferred) and children witnessing domestic violence.

PART 3: CONCEPTUAL FRAMEWORK (CHAPTERS 3, 7, & 15)

AS WE KNOW, in quantitative research studies, the conceptual framework identifies the possible relationships between and among concepts to one another. Identifying the ways that concepts might be connected lays the groundwork for developing a research question or research hypothesis. In the last chapter, for example, Lula formulated the research hypothesis as follows:

> **Research hypothesis:**
> Children who have witnessed domestic violence will have lower social interaction skills than children who have not witnessed such violence.

That is, her conceptual framework included the idea that a particular concept—children's social interaction skills—was directly related to another concept—whether the children witnessed the abuse or not.

In qualitative studies, the level of knowledge in the topic area will probably be too low to allow such possible connections between and among concepts to be investigated. Children's poor social interaction skills may indeed be one of the problems experienced by children who witness their mothers being physically abused by their fathers, but Lula does not know that yet. Her research question at this stage is simply, "What problems do these children experience?"

Relationships between and among concepts can still be hypothesized, however, even at an exploratory level, and even if the hypothesized relationships will not be tested during the course of the study. People reading a qualitative study, for example, are usually more interested in where the study took place and whether the influence of the clinical setting (i.e., the shelter) was appropriately acknowledged in the data analysis.

A conceptual framework identifies the possible relationships between and among concepts to one another.

Lula must therefore take into account the possibility that the problems experienced by the children in her study may have been due to the study's setting (i.e., the shelter) and not so much from their witnessing the abuse. If she conceptualizes this possibility early, she may decide to interview the children's mothers, asking them not only to identify their children's problems but also to describe each problem before and after coming into the shelter.

Similarly, she may want to explore the possibility that the children's problems may have been related to the children being abused themselves and not just to their witnessing their mothers being physically abused by their fathers.

PART 4: QUESTIONS AND HYPOTHESES (CHAPTERS 2 & 18)

A **QUALITATIVE RESEARCH STUDY** rarely tests a research hypothesis. It's very important, however, that the questions to be answered during the course of a qualitative study be clearly formulated before it begins. Lula could formulate quite specific research questions, such as:

— What types of problems do children who have witnessed domestic violence experience?

— Does the type of abuse witnessed (e.g., hitting, yelling) affect the type of problems experienced by the children?

— Does the intensity of the abuse—witnessed by the children— affect the problems they experience?

— Does the frequency (e.g., daily, weekly) of the abuse—witnessed by the children—affect the problems they experience?

— Does the duration (e.g., over months, years) of the abuse— witnessed by the children—affect the problems they experience?

— Does the child's gender affect the types of problems they experience?

— Does the child's age affect the types of problems they experience?

— Do the child's problems, as perceived by the mother, affect the mother's decision to leave the abusive relationship?

— Do the child's problems, as perceived by the mother, affect the mother's decision about whether to return to the abusive relationship?

> Qualitative research studies rarely test hypotheses.

If Lula is going to formulate specific research questions, she will probably need to use a fairly structured interview schedule when she collects interview data from the mothers and their children. On the other hand, she may prefer to formulate just a few more general questions, such as:

— What types of problems do children who have witnessed domestic violence experience?

— What effects do these problems have on the children?

In this case, she would use an unstructured interview schedule, which would allow the mothers and children to guide the interviews themselves, relating what is important to them in their own way. Lula's decision about whether to formulate specific or general research questions depends on the level of knowledge about the study's topic area.

If enough knowledge is available to enable her to formulate specific research questions, she will probably do that. If not, one of the purposes of her study would be to gain enough knowledge to allow specific research questions to be formulated in the future.

PART 5: OPERATIONAL DEFINITIONS (CHAPTERS 7 & 18)

AS WE KNOW, operationally defining a variable in a quantitative (positivistic) research study means defining all variables in such a way that they can be measured. In the last chapter, for example, Lula operationally defined the level of a child's social interaction skills in terms of the child's score derived from a standardized measuring instrument (*SISOCIA*). The idea behind operationally defining a variable in this way is that both its definition and its measurement are consistent and objective.

On a general level, most qualitative research studies do not have elaborate and sophisticated operational definitions of the variables they wish to study.

Lula did not define "children's social interaction skills" herself (except insofar as she selected the measuring instrument), and she did not ask the children or their mothers what they perceived "children's social interaction skills" to be. Similarly, the measured result for each child (a numerical score) did not depend on anyone's personal perception on how well, or how badly, the child interacted socially with others.

Conversely, in qualitative studies, we are not as interested in objectively defining or measuring our concepts as we are when doing quantitative studies. Indeed, we actively encourage our research participants to provide us with their own, subjective definitions, since we are trying to understand their problems as they perceive them to be.

Similarly, we measure the extent, or effect, of a problem in terms of the research participants' subjective viewpoints. Hence, Lula will not have to worry about how to operationally define "a child" or "a child's problem," and she will not have to decide whether "a child witnessing domestic violence" means seeing it, or hearing it, or merely being aware that it's occurring.

Lula might want to collect data about the ages of the children in her study, whether they are the biological children of their mothers, and whether or not they live full time at home, but none of these data will be used to exclude any child from the study on the grounds that the child is too old or too young, or otherwise does not fit Lula's operational definition of "a child."

Lula does not have an elaborate and complicated operational definition of a child. In her qualitative study, "a child" is simply operationally defined as "any person whom the mother considers to be her child." Similarly, "a problem" is whatever the mother and/or child considers to be problematic. "Domestic violence" is defined as whatever the research participants think it is; and children have "witnessed domestic violence" if they and/or their mothers believe that they have.

It might be as well here to put in a word about measurement. The word "measurement" is often associated with numbers, and hence with positivistic studies. To "measure" something, however, only means to describe it as accurately and completely as possible.

If we cannot describe it with numbers, we may still be able to describe it with words, and this qualitative type of measurement is just as valid as a positivistic numerical measurement. Hence, Lula is measuring the problems experienced by children when she encourages the mothers and their children to describe those problems as accurately and completely as they can—in words, not numbers.

In quantitative studies, efforts are made to mitigate the effects of researcher bias through objective measurement. In qualitative studies, however, the use of measurement is to capture the subjective experiences of the research participants. Thus, it's vital for Lula to be aware of the effects of her own feelings upon the research participants she will be interviewing.

Any prior assumptions she has made and any position she might hold must be clearly outlined at the beginning of her study so that the reader of her proposal can evaluate the degree to which her study's potential findings would reflect the research participants' opinions rather than Lula's opinions.

Similarly, it's important to record the interests and possible biases of the organization that is funding the study in addition to the agency where the study actually takes place. Would certain findings be more welcome to the funding body or the agency than other findings? Is the researcher under any pressure to emphasize certain aspects of the study's results to the detriment of other aspects? Again, the reader of a research proposal must be able to evaluate the degree to which the proposed study's auspices would potentially affect the study's findings.

A clear statement of the study's purpose might deflect critics who argue that the proposed study did not fulfill other purposes that the critics, themselves, may perceive as more important. Lula's research study might have a practical purpose, for example, where it would be in tune with the interests of the staff who work within the women's emergency shelter that would provide both funding for the study and access to its clients.

Lula simply wants to know what the children's problems are so that the shelter can better meet the needs of the children and their mothers. She is not overly interested in adding to social work theory or changing social policy, although her study's results may indeed have implications in both of these areas.

She is less likely to be criticized for not placing sufficient emphasis on theory and policy in her discussion if she has clearly stated from the beginning that her proposed study's purpose is to inform day-to-day practice activities within her specific shelter.

PART 6: RESEARCH DESIGN (CHAPTERS 7, 12, 15, & 18)

WE NOW COME TO THE *HOW* OF THE STUDY. This section includes information about what data will be collected, in what way and from whom, and how they will be analyzed. While writing about these matters, there will be many opportunities to address issues related to the study's *trustworthiness*. Paying attention to four major concerns provides evidence of a study's trustworthiness:

1. **Credibility,** or truth value

2. **Transferability,** or applicability

3. **Dependability,** or consistency

4. **Confirmability,** or neutrality

These four concerns are roughly equivalent to the positivistic concepts of internal validity and external validity as outlined in Chapter 13. The first issue related to trustworthiness is credibility (akin to internal validity), which is particularly important and is built on the following six aspects of a qualitative study:

1. **Triangulation of data sources**—collecting data about the same thing from a number of different data sources; also engagement with research participants over a long period of time.

2. **Consulting with colleagues**—consulting with them about ethical and legal matters, and about the methods chosen to select the sample of research participants and to collect and analyze the data.

3. **Negative case analysis**—ensuring that information from all data sources is included in the data analysis, even when information from one data source seems to contradict themes or conclusions common to other data sources.

> The concept of *transferability* as used in qualitative research studies is like the concept of *external validity* in quantitative ones.

4. **Referential adequacy**—keeping a complete and accurate record of all personal interviews and observations, such as videotapes, audiotapes, case notes, and transcriptions.

5. **Member checks**—asking research participants to provide feedback on the information collected from the researcher and the conclusions drawn by the researcher.

The second issue related to trustworthiness is transferability (akin to external validity, or generalizability), which is addressed through a rich description of the study's clinical setting and the research participants. Findings from a qualitative research study are usually not generalized beyond the setting in which the study took place.

The findings may be applicable, however, to similar client populations: women and children in similar women's emergency shelters elsewhere, for example. Readers can only judge to what degree a study's findings may be applicable to their own clientele when the researcher provides a detailed description of the study's research participants in addition to their special needs and circumstances.

The third issue is dependability (akin to reliability), which relates to efforts to maintain consistency throughout the study. Were all interviews conducted in the same setting, according to the same format, and recorded in the same way? Were all research participants asked to provide feedback on the data collected, or only some? During data analysis, were rules concerning categorization and coding consistently applied?

Aspects of the study related to credibility, as previously described, may be used to demonstrate dependability as well: for example, referential adequacy, providing evidence of consistent interviewing procedures, and providing evidence that all research participants were asked for their feedback.

The last issue, confirmability (akin to objectivity), has to do with Lula's awareness of her own role in influencing the data provided by the research participants and the conclusions she drew from the data. All qualitative researchers should keep journals in which they record their own thoughts and feelings about the study's research participants and about their interviews and observations.

Lula should note in her journal, for example, why she made the decisions she did about methodological matters, such as sampling procedures, and data collection and analysis techniques. While conducting the data analysis, she will record decisions and concerns about organizing and interpreting the data she collected.

These journal entries disclose the degree of impartiality she brought to the entire research process; where she was not impartial, it discloses her awareness, or lack thereof, about her own assumptions and biases. With respect to dependability (discussed previously), it provides a record of how consistent her decision-making was and how consistently she conducted her interviews and analyzed her data.

PART 7: POPULATION AND SAMPLE (CHAPTERS 7, 11, & 15)

IN THIS PART OF THE PROPOSAL, Lula provides only a general description of who her research participants will be, together with a rationale for selecting these and not others. In qualitative studies, there is no attempt to select a random sample. Indeed, the sample often consists of all those persons available to be studied who fit broad criteria. Lula could draw her sample of research participants, for example, from all those women who are residents in her women's emergency shelter at a specific time.

Because Lula's study involves the effects on children who witnessed domestic violence, she will need to exclude from her sample all women who do not have children *and* all women who say that their children did not witness the abuse. Lula may personally believe that no child whose mother is being abused can remain unaware of that abuse, and the definition of "witnessing" for her may include a child's awareness as well as seeing or hearing.

In addition, it would be interesting to explore conflicting perceptions between the mothers and their children, when the children believe that they have witnessed domestic violence and their mothers believe that they have not. Lula is unlikely, however, to elicit information about the effects of witnessing domestic violence from women who do not believe that their children witnessed it; nor are these women likely to give Lula permission to interview their children on the subject.

> On a general level, qualitative studies mainly use purposive sampling and snowball sampling techniques when it comes to selecting their research participants.

Lula may decide to include women who do not have their children with them at the shelter. Whether she does so will depend on a number of factors. First, how many women can she interview, given her own and the women's time constraints? This will depend on how long she expects each interview to take, which, in turn, depends on such factors as the structure and depth of the interview.

In addition, she must consider the time required for transcribing and analyzing each interview in its entirety. If the number of women who have their children at the shelter is equal to, or larger than, the number of women Lula can reasonably interview, then she will exclude women whose children are not present.

If the number is smaller, she may consider including these women, but that decision as well will depend on a number of factors. Uppermost in the mind of any qualitative researcher is the notion of the study's trustworthiness.

As discussed earlier, one way of establishing the trustworthiness of data is to collect data about the same variable from a number of different data sources. Data on the problems experienced by children, for example, may be collected from three data sources:

1. The children themselves
2. Their mothers
3. Shelter staff who have observed the children

Such a triangulation of data sources allows assessment of the trustworthiness of the data obtained from any one given source. If children are not present at the shelter, then data on their problems can be obtained only from their mothers, and there will be no way to check on the "accuracy" of the data they provide.

Another way to establish trustworthiness is to ask each research participant to comment on the data gathered and the conclusions that the researcher drew from the data. Lula might want to submit the transcript of each interview to the research participant concerned to make sure that she has adequately captured what the participant was trying to say.

Ethical and cultural considerations need to be addressed when selecting samples for qualitative research studies.

Then, she might want to discuss her findings with the other research participants to see if they believe that she has interpreted what they said correctly and has drawn conclusions that seem reasonable to them as well. None of this will be possible if the research participants have left the emergency shelter and disappeared before Lula has transcribed and analyzed her data.

She might, therefore, want to restrict her sample of women to those who are likely to remain in her shelter for a number of weeks or who will go on to a halfway house or some other traceable address. Of course, if she does this, she will lose data from women whose very transience might affect their children's problems and the way those problems are perceived.

Lula must also consider whether to interview the children and, if so, children in what age groups. She may not be skilled in interviewing young children and may feel that children under school age cannot be meaningfully interviewed at all.

If there are enough women in the shelter who have older children present, she may consider restricting her sample of research participants to women whose children are, say, 10 years old or older. She will have to justify selecting age 10 instead of 8 or 12, for example, and she will lose data pertaining to the problems experienced by any excluded children.

With this in mind, she may consider enlisting the assistance of a colleague who is more skilled at eliciting information from younger children—through data collection methods such as drama, art, or play—than she is. But now she has to think about how such interview data would be analyzed and how she would integrate them with the data collected through her own personal interviews with the mothers.

The child's gender may be another consideration. Perhaps Lula has an idea that girls tend to display more internalizing problem behaviors—such as withdrawal and depression—than boys. And Lula may believe that boys tend to display more externalizing behaviors—such as hostility and aggression—than girls. She might therefore want to ensure that her study contains approximately equal numbers of girls and boys.

If she purposefully drew her sample of research participants in this way, she would have to explain that she expected to find more internalizing behaviors in girls and more externalizing behaviors in boys. This would constitute a research hypothesis, which would need to be included in the Questions and Hypotheses section and justified through the literature review. Or perhaps Lula would phrase it as a research question, simply asking whether the gender of the child was related to the type of problem behavior he or she exhibited.

Similarly, Lula might have an idea that the types of problem behaviors exhibited by children depend on their ethnic background. If she were able to conduct only a small number of interviews, for example, she might purposefully select women and children from different ethnic backgrounds to make up her sample of research participants (called *purposive sampling*, see Chapter 11). Here again, she would have to justify her choice, including a relevant research question and addressing the matter in the literature review.

Lula thus has a number of factors to consider in deciding whom to include as research participants in her study. The main consideration, however, is always the willingness of the research participant to take part in the study.

Like most social work populations, women in emergency shelters are an extremely vulnerable group, and it's vital to ensure that they feel freely able to refuse to participate in the study, knowing that their refusal will in no way affect the quality of the services they receive.

Similarly, the social workers within Lula's women's emergency shelter must also feel able to refuse, knowing that their refusal will not affect the terms of their employment. It's quite likely that Lula will not have the luxury of selecting her research participants in terms of the age, gender, or ethnic background of the children.

More probably, Lula will just interview those women who agree to be interviewed and who also give permission for her, or a colleague, to interview their children as well. The children will not be in a position to sign an assent form, as their mothers and the social workers will do, but it's still extremely important to ensure that they understand their rights with respect to refusing to take part in the study or withdrawing from it at any time. (see Chapter 4).

PART 8: DATA COLLECTION (CHAPTERS 2, 7, 15, & 18)

THIS PART OF A QUALITATIVE RESEARCH PROPOSAL provides a detailed account of how the data are going to be collected, together with a justification for using the data collection method selected rather than some other method. Lula could use focus groups, for example, rather than unstructured interviews to collect data from the women.

She could decide not to interview children, but instead to observe the children's behaviors herself, without involving a colleague or other social workers. If she does involve the shelter's social workers, she might decide just to interview them and ask how they define the children's problem behaviors and what problem behaviors they have observed in the children under study.

On the other hand, she might ask them first to define children's problem behaviors, then to purposefully observe certain children with respect to these behaviors, and finally to report their observations back to her. Whatever she decides, she must first justify her decisions and then clearly describe the methods to be used. She should state, for example, that the abused women, the shelter's workers, and the children aged 10 or over will be interviewed by her, if that is what she has decided to do.

She should also specify where these interviews would take place, how long approximately each is expected to last, and to what degree the content will be guided by an interview schedule. She should also specify the time frame within which all the interviews will be completed and how the interviews will be recorded. Videotaping, audio taping, and taking notes during the interview all have their advantages and disadvantages, which need to be discussed.

If a colleague is to work with the younger children, for example, details of the methods used to elicit interview data from these children must be given. In addition, the colleague's credentials must be included at the beginning of the proposal, since this colleague is now a co-researcher and her experience and qualifications will affect the trustworthiness of the study's findings.

Ethical considerations that were not covered in the discussion about selecting research participants should also be addressed in this section. Should Lula obtain completed consent forms from the mothers and assent forms from their children, for example, before she asks the shelter's social workers to observe the children or to discuss their behaviors with her?

Should she share the social worker's comments with the mothers and their children and tell the social workers beforehand that this is to be done? Should she share data obtained from the children with their mothers or make it clear that such data will not be shared?

> There are many data-collection methods that can be used in qualitative studies. However, interviewing is probably the most utilized.

Social workers might not be so honest in their comments if they know that the data will be shared: and neither might the children. In addition, children who know they are being observed might not behave as they otherwise would.

These are old dilemmas that always affect data collection methods, and Lula must specify what dilemmas she may encounter and how she plans to resolve them. It's as well to state how the mothers, children, and social workers are to be approached, and precisely what they are going to be told about her study and their own part in it. Samples of consent forms (for the mothers) and assent forms (for the children) should be included as two appendixes at the end of the proposal.

Lula's journal is also a form of data. It will include little in the way of data collected from her research participants, but it will include Lula's reactions to these data and a chronology of her study's process. Lula might therefore want to state in her proposal that she will keep a journal to record notes on the decisions she is going to make during every stage of her study, with particular reference to the study's trustworthiness.

PART 9: DATA ANALYSIS (CHAPTERS 2, 7, 15, &18)

THIS PART OF A QUALITATIVE RESEARCH PROPOSAL describes the way the data will be analyzed. There are usually no statistical procedures to be discussed, as there may be in a quantitative study, but there are a number of other matters. As presented in Chapter 18, a decision must be made about whether to use a software computer program to aid in the data analysis and, if so, which one.

Then Lula must decide who will transcribe the interviews and how the transcripts should be formatted. She must establish a plan for her data analysis, including some plan for making journal entries.

> Qualitative research studies usually do not try to establish causality between and among variables.

She might want to add in her proposal that after she has analyzed the data using first- and second-level coding methods and after she has drawn conclusions, she will assess the trustworthiness of her study's findings. She will do this by documenting what she is going to do to establish credibility, transferability, dependability (consistency), and confirmability (control of biases and preconceptions).

PART 10: LIMITATIONS (CHAPTERS 2, 7, 11, 15, & 18)

ALL RESEARCH STUDIES HAVE LIMITATIONS. Some might even suggest that one of the main limitations of a qualitative study is that it's not a quantitative one, but this is simply not true. Every study is judged on how well it fulfills its own purpose, and one of the purposes of a qualitative study is usually to understand the experiences of the research participants in-depth, including experiences that are unique to them.

The purpose of Lula's study is to gain a better understanding of the problems experienced by children who have witnessed domestic violence, from the different perspectives of the mothers, their children, and the shelter's social workers, so that the needs of these children can be better identified and met.

A discussion of a study's limitations should include only factors that impede the fulfillment of this purpose. Lula's study, for example, is not limited because she did not operationally define the concepts "domestic violence" and "children witnessing domestic violence."

Part of her study's purpose is to find out how the mothers and their children themselves define "domestic violence;" that is, to find out what it was that the children in her study actually witnessed, and what they and their mothers think that "witnessing" includes.

From an ideal standpoint, Lula's study is limited with respect to its transferability (generalizability, in positivistic terms). It would have been ideal if she could have constructed a sampling frame of all the children in the world who had witnessed domestic violence, taken a random sample, and interviewed all these children and their mothers in depth.

Quantitative researchers sometimes restrict their studies to manageable samples (research participants) and then generalize from the samples to the populations from which they were drawn. It's a limitation, however, if their samples did not adequately represent their populations, thus restricting the ability to generalize from the samples to their populations.

It's not considered a limitation, however, that interpretive studies do not use larger populations in the first place. Similarly, Lula does not need to apologize for having chosen to work only with those women and their children who were residents in her particular women's emergency shelter at the time she wanted to conduct her study.

On the other hand, some of these women whose children had witnessed domestic violence may have refused to participate, and that would be a limitation to Lula's study: those women may have felt particularly traumatized by their children's involvement, to the point where they felt unable to discuss it. By losing them, Lula would lose a different and valuable perspective.

> Generally speaking, qualitative research studies have fewer research participants than those in quantitative ones.

Another limitation to Lula's study is that many of the children who have witnessed domestic violence may have been abused themselves. It may be impossible for the mothers and/or children to distinguish between the effects of being abused themselves and the effects of witnessing the abuse.

The only way Lula could deal with this is to divide her population of children who have witnessed abuse into two groups: those who have been abused, according to their mothers, and those who have not.

Of course, it might be argued that witnessing domestic violence constitutes emotional abuse. If Lula subscribes to this view, she might wish to ask the mothers specifically whether their children have been physically or sexually abused, since all the children in her sample will have been emotionally abused according to her own definition.

Nevertheless, in practical terms, Lula can form her two groups of children merely by including a question about physical or sexual abuse during her interviews with them and with their mothers. If Lula identifies this limitation early on while she is conceptualizing her study, she can include the two groups in her study's research design, mentioning the question about domestic violence in the data collection section, and noting, in the data analysis section, that she will accord each group a separate category.

Thus, her study's limitation will have ceased to be a limitation and will have become an integral part of her study. This is one of the purposes of a research design, of course: to identify and address a study's potential limitations so that they can be eliminated or at least alleviated to the greatest possible extent before the study actually starts.

Essentially, what Lula has done in thinking about children who have been abused themselves is to identify a confounding or intervening variable that might interfere with the relationship between their witnessing domestic violence and their experiencing problems, if any, due to witnessing it.

Writing the final research report based off of a qualitative research study takes a tremendous amount of time, skill, and patience.

Inevitably, there will be a host of other confounding variables because no one can tell for certain whether children's particular problematic behaviors are due to witnessing domestic violence or to some other factor(s). Lula will be able to conclude only that children who witnessed domestic violence experienced certain problems, not that the problems were caused by witnessing the violence in the first place.

Failure to establish causality, however, is only a limitation if the establishment of causality was one of the purposes of the study. In this case, it was not; and indeed the kind of rigorous research design needed to establish causality is usually inappropriate in a qualitative study.

Lula may find that her sample of children is not diverse enough in terms of age, gender, or ethnic background to allow her to draw conclusions about the effects of these variables on their problem behaviors. Again, this is a study limitation only if she has stated her intention to draw such a conclusion. The major limitation that Lula is likely to encounter in her study is related to the issue of credibility or truth value (internal validity, in positivistic terms).

How will she know whether the mothers and their children were truthful in relating their experiences or whether their remarks were geared more toward pleasing her or making themselves appear more socially desirable?

And if their remarks were based on memories of previous abusive behaviors, how far were those memories reliable? These are common dilemmas in both research and clinical interviews. One way to handle them is through triangulation: obtaining data on a variable from more than one data source.

Another way is to constantly reflect on the quality of the data being obtained throughout the interview process and to record the results of these reflections in the researcher's journal. The following are examples of the kinds of questions Lula might ask herself while she is pursuing her reflections:

1. Is the interviewee withholding something—If so, what should I do about it?

2. What impact might my race, age, social status, gender, or beliefs have on my interviewee? What difference might it make that I work at the women's emergency shelter?

3. Did what the interviewee said ring true—or did she want to please me, or look good, or protect someone else, or save herself embarrassment? Why am I feeling so stressed after this interview? Am I getting the kinds of data that are relevant for my study?

These questions might improve the quality of the data obtained by making Lula more aware of possible sources of error. Even if they do not, Lula will have shown that she has recognized her study's limitations and will take the necessary steps to deal with each limitation.

PART 11: ADMINISTRATION

THE FINAL PART OF A RESEARCH PROPOSAL deals with the organization and resources necessary to carry out the proposed study. Lula might want to separate her role as a researcher from her role as one of the shelter's social workers, for example, by equipping herself with a desk and computer in a room other than that which she usually uses.

If "researcher space" is not a problem, Lula will still need to think about where she should base her operations: where she will write up her notes, analyze her data, and keep the records of her interviews. Then she has to think about administrative responsibilities.

Will she take on the overall responsibility for her study herself or will that fall to her supervisor? What will be the responsibilities of her colleague and the shelter's social workers? To whom will they report? What is the chain of command?

When Lula has put together the details of who does what, in what order, and who is responsible to whom, she will be in a position to consider a time frame. How long will each task take and by what date ought it to be completed? It's very easy to underestimate the amount of time needed to analyze qualitative data and to feed the information back to the research participants for their comments (member checking).

It's also easy to underestimate the time needed to write the final report. Neither of these tasks should be skimped, and it's very important to allow adequate time to complete them thoroughly—more time, that is, than the researcher believes will be necessary at the beginning of the qualitative study.

Finally, Lula must consider a budget. If she has to purchase a software computer program to help her analyze her interview data, who will pay for it? Who will cover the costs related to transcribing the data and preparing and disseminating the final report? How much money should she allocate to each of these areas? How much should she ask for overall?

When she has decided on all this, Lula will have completed her research proposal. As discussed, not all proposals are organized in this way, but all essentially contain the information that has been discussed in the preceding sections. This same information can be used to write the final research report.

EVALUATING RESEARCH PROPOSALS

AFTER YOU HAVE COMPETED all 11 parts of your qualitative research proposal, you need to evaluate its overall rigor. Thankfully, Jim Raines (2011) has provided us with a list of 32 questions that you need to ask and answer after you have completed the first draft. If you cannot fully and adequately answer all of the 32 questions that follow you should not undertake the study.

1. Are the databases you searched sufficient to the research question you are trying to answer?

2. Are your philosophical assumptions and values well identified?

3. Is your literature review relevant to both your research problem and population?

4. Is the literature that you reviewed current at the time it was written?

5. Do you use headings and subheadings to organize your ideas?

6. Do you identify any differences in findings from previous research studies?

7. Does your literature review support the purpose of your study?

8. Is your research question crystal clear?

9. Does your research question include all of the major concepts that are in your study?

10. Are your conceptual definitions multidimensional?

11. Will your definitions evolve as participants provide their perspectives?

12. Do you have a logical rationale for doing a qualitative study in the first place?

13. Is there a good fit between your research question and your data-collection method?

14. Does your research study demonstrate your value awareness?

15. How do you plan on using informed consent procedures?

16. Does your study advance the common good of your research participants?

17. Do you explain the reasons for the type of sampling method you will use?

18. How do you plan on reporting your subjectivity?

19. How do you plan on addressing the issue of bias by you and your research participants?

20. What strategies are you going to use to improve the credibility of your study's findings?

21. What strategies are you going to use to improve the transferability of your study's findings?

22. What strategies are you going to use to improve the dependability of your study's findings?

23. What strategies are you going to use to improve the confirmability of your study's findings?

24. What strategies are you going to use to increase the accuracy of your study's transcriptions?

25. What is your specific plan for analyzing the data?

26. How to you plan on developing categories for first-level coding?

27. How to you plan on establishing relationships between categories clarified during second-level coding?

28. How to you plan on developing themes and theories within your data analyses?

29. How do you plan on addressing your study's limitations from a qualitative perspective?

30. How do you plan on integrating your study's results with the previous literature?

31. How do you plan on developing implications for social work theory, practice, or policy?

32. Do you plan on making recommendations for future research studies?

WRITING QUALITATIVE RESEARCH REPORTS

AS WITH A POSITIVISTIC RESEARCH REPORT, a qualitative one is a way of describing the research study to other people. How it's written and to some degree what it contains depend on the audience it's written for. Lula may want to present her study's findings, for example, only to the board of directors and staff of the women's emergency shelter where she works.

In this case, it will be unnecessary to describe the clinical setting (i.e., the shelter) in detail since the audience is already familiar with it. This very familiarity will also mean that Lula must take extra care to protect the identities of her research participants because personal knowledge of the women and children concerned will make it easier for her audience to identify them.

Lula will probably want to submit a written report—particularly if the shelter funded her study—but she may also want to give an oral presentation. As she imagines herself speaking the words she has written, she may find that she wants to organize the material differently or use a different style than she would if she were preparing a written report. Perhaps she will use less formal language, or include more detail about her own thoughts and feelings, or shorten the direct quotes made by the research participants.

> Qualitative research studies usually generate longer research reports than quantitative ones.

Other possible outlets for her work include books, book chapters, journal articles, and presentations at conferences. Again, depending on the audience, she might write quite simply or she might include a wealth of technical detail, perhaps describing at length the methods she used to categorize and code her interview data.

In order to avoid writing a number of reports on the same study aimed at different audiences, she might choose to include in the main body of the report just sufficient technical detail to establish the study's trustworthiness, while putting additional technical material in appendixes for those readers who are interested. Whatever approach she chooses, it's important to remember that qualitative research studies are based on a different set of assumptions than quantitative ones.

As we know by now, the goal of a qualitative study is to understand the experiences of the study's research participants in depth, and the personal feelings of the researcher cannot be divorced from this understanding. It's therefore often appropriate to report a qualitative study using a more personal style, including both quotes from interviews with the research participants and the researcher's own reflections on the material. The aim is to produce a credible and compelling account that will be taken seriously by the reader.

The material itself can be organized in a number of ways, depending on whether or not it's to be presented in book form or more concisely in the form of a journal article. An article usually contains six parts:

1. An abstract
2. An introduction
3. A discussion of methodology
4. A presentation of the analysis and findings
5. A conclusion, or discussion of the significance of the study's findings
6. A list of references

ABSTRACT

AN ABSTRACT IS A SHORT STATEMENT—often about 200 words—that summarizes the purpose of the study, its methodology, its findings, and its conclusions. Journal readers often decide on the basis of the abstract whether they are sufficiently interested in the topic to want to read further.

Thus, the abstract must provide just enough information to enable readers to assess the relevance of the study to their own work. A statement of the study's research question, with enough context to make it meaningful, is usually followed by a brief description of the study's methodology that was used to answer the research question.

Lula might say, for example, that she interviewed eight women and eleven children who were residents in a women's emergency shelter in a small town in Alberta, Canada, plus three of the shelter's social workers. She might go on to identify the problems experienced by the children who had witnessed domestic violence, stating that these problems were derived from analyses of interview data. Finally, she would outline the practical implications from the study for social work practice, resulting from a greater understanding of the children's problems.

INTRODUCTION

THE MAIN BODY OF THE REPORT begins with the introduction. It describes the *what* and *why* components of the study, which Lula has already written about in the first five parts of her research proposal. If she goes back to what she wrote before, she will see that she has already identified her research question and put it into the context of previous work through a literature review. She has discussed why she thinks this question needs to be answered, clarified her own orientation and assumptions, and commented on the interests of the women's emergency shelter or other funding organizations.

In addition, she has identified the variables relevant to her study and placed them within an appropriate framework. In short, she has already gathered the material needed for her introduction, and all that remains is to ensure that it's written in an appropriate style.

METHOD (CHAPTERS 2, 7, 11, 15, & 18)

AFTER THE *WHAT* AND THE *WHY* COMPONENTS of the study comes the *how*. In the methods section, Lula describes how she selected her sample of research participants and how she collected her data. She must provide a justification for why she chose a particular sampling and data collection method(s).

Again, if she looks back at her research proposal, she will see that she has already written about this in Parts 6, 7, and 8: research design, population and sample, and data collection, respectively. As before, she can use this same material, merely ensuring that it's written in a coherent style.

ANALYSIS AND FINDINGS (CHAPTERS 2, 7, 11, 15, & 18)

MATERIALS ON DATA ANALYSIS AND FINDINGS are often presented together. Descriptive profiles of research participants and direct quotes from their interviews are used to answer the research question being explored. In her proposal, Lula has already written the part on data analysis in her research proposal, which stated what computer programs she was going to use (if any) and what first- and second-level coding methods she proposes to use.

In her research report, however, she would want to identify and provide examples of the meaning units she derived from the first-level coding process. One segment from one of her interviews might have gone as follows:

1. **Pam (sounding upset): The poor kid was never the same after that. The**

2. **first time, you know, it was just a slap on the butt that she might even**

3. **have mistaken for affection, but that second time he slammed me right**

4. **against the wall and he was still hitting my face after I landed. (pause) No**

5. mistaking that one, is there, even for a four-year old? (longer pause) No, well,

6. I guess I'm kidding myself about that first time. She knew all right. *She was*

7. *an outgoing sort of kid before, always out in the yard with friends,* but then

8. she stopped going out, and she'd follow me around, kind of, as if she was

9. afraid to let me out of her sight.

Lula may have identified three meaning units in this data segment. The first (in **bold**, lines 1–4) relates to what might and might not constitute domestic violence in the mind of a 4-year-old child. The second (in *italics*, lines 6 and 7) relates to the child's behavior before witnessing the abuse; and the third (underlined, lines 7–9) relates to the child's behavior after witnessing the abuse. In her report, Lula might want to identify and briefly describe the meaning units she derived from all her interviews, occasionally illustrating a unit with a direct quote to provide context and meaning.

As discussed in Chapter 18, Lula's next task in the analysis is to identify categories, assign each meaning unit to a category, and assign codes to the categories. A description of these categories will also come next in her report. She may have found, for example, that a number of mothers interpreted their child's behavior after witnessing domestic violence as indicative of fear for the mother's safety.

Instead of one large category "child's behavior after witnessing domestic violence," Lula may have chosen instead to create a number of smaller categories reflecting distinct types of behavior. One of these was "after witnessing domestic violence, child demonstrates fear for mother's safety," and Lula coded it as *CAWFMSAF,* where *C* stands for "the child," *AW* stands for "after witnessing domestic violence," and *FMSAF* stands for "fear for mother's safety."

Depending on the number and depth of the interviews conducted, Lula may have a very large number of meaning units, and may have gone through an intricate process of refining and reorganizing in order to come up with appropriate categories. In a book, there will be room to describe all this, together with Lula's own reflections on the process; but in a journal article, running to perhaps twenty-five pages overall, Lula will have to be selective about what parts of the process she describes and how much detail she provides.

Although meaning units and categories are certainly a major part of Lula's findings, the majority of readers will be more interested in the next part of the analysis: comparing and contrasting the categories to discover the relationships between and among them in order to develop tentative themes or theories.

By doing this, Lula may have been able to finally identify the problems most commonly experienced by children who have witnessed domestic violence. She may even have been able to put the children's problems in an order of importance as perceived by the mothers and their children.

In addition, she may have been able to add depth by describing the emotions related to the children's problems: perhaps guilt, on the mother's part, or anger toward the father, or a growing determination not to return to the abusive relationship. These themes will constitute the larger part of Lula's analysis and findings section, and it's to these themes that she will return in her discussion.

DISCUSSION (CHAPTERS 2, 7, 11, 15, & 18)

THIS PART OF THE RESEARCH REPORT presents a discussion of the study's findings. Here, Lula will point out the significance of her study's findings as they relate to the original purpose. If the purpose of her study was to inform practice by enabling the shelter's social workers to better understand the needs of children who have witnessed domestic violence, then Lula must provide a link between the children's problems and their needs resulting from those problems. She must also point out exactly how the shelter's social workers' practice might be informed.

If she has found from her study, for example, that children who witnessed domestic violence tend to experience more fear for their mothers' safety than children who had not witnessed the abuse, then a related need might be to keep the mother always within sight.

Social workers within the shelter who understand this need might be more willing to tolerate children underfoot in the shelter's kitchen, for example, and might be less likely to tell Mary to "give Mom a moment's peace and go and play with Sue." These kinds of connections should be made for each theme that Lula identified in her study.

The final part of a research report often has to do with suggestions for future research studies. During the process of filling knowledge gaps by summarizing the study's findings, Lula will doubtless find other knowledge gaps that she believes ought to be filled. She might frame new research questions relating to these gaps; or she might even feel that she has sufficient knowledge to enable her to formulate research hypotheses for testing in future research studies.

REFERENCES

FINALLY, BOTH QUANTITATIVE AND QUALITATIVE RESEARCHERS are expected to provide a list of references that will enable the reader to locate the materials used for documentation within the report. If the manuscript is accepted for publication, the journal will certainly ask for any revisions it considers appropriate with regard to its style. It's important to note that quotes from a study's research participants do not have to be referenced, and adequate steps should always be taken to conceal their identities.

SUMMARY

THE PURPOSES OF WRITING A RESEARCH PROPOSAL are threefold: to obtain permission to do the study, to obtain funding for the study, and to encourage the author to think carefully through what he or she wants to study and what difficulties are likely to be encountered.

The proposal itself should be clear, brief, and easy to read. Although proposals may be differently organized depending on who is to receive them, the information included in most proposals may be logically set out under general headings identified in this chapter.

The information contained under most of these headings can also be used to write the research report. Because the proposal outlines *what will be done* and the research report describes *what was done*, the proposal and the report should parallel each other closely, unless the implementation of the study differed widely from what was planned.

	Study Questions for Chapter 20
	Essay — Discussion
1	In your own words, describe what a qualitative research proposal is all about. Use social work examples to illustrate your main points.
2	Review the previous chapter, Chapter 19, on writing quantitative research proposals and reports. Discuss the similarities and differences between quantitative research **proposals** (Chapter 19) and qualitative research **proposals** (this chapter). Use social work examples to illustrate your main points.
3	Review the previous chapter, Chapter 19, on writing quantitative research proposals and reports. Discuss the similarities and differences between quantitative research **reports** (Chapter 19) and qualitative research **reports** (this chapter). Use social work examples to illustrate your main points.
4	In groups of four, write a brief 4-page qualitative research proposal that is geared toward shedding light on social work students' perceptions of their preparedness to enter the social work profession after they graduate.
5	In the same group of four, pretend you actually implemented your proposal (Question 4). Make up fake data. Now use these fake data to write a simple qualitative research report.
6	This chapter provided 32 points to consider when evaluating a qualitative research proposal. Discuss whether you believe your research proposal (Question 4) adequately addressed each point. If so, how? If not, why not?
7	If you currently have a practicum, ask your field instructor for copies of any qualitative research proposals they might have in their filing cabinets. Select one proposal and critique it using the contents of this chapter—and the entire book, for that matter.
8	Discuss how qualitative research proposals and reports utilize all the contents in this book. Provide one simple example from each one of the preceding 19 chapters that could be included in a qualitative research proposal. You should have 19 points in total—one for each chapter.

	Critical Thinking — Application — Integration

APPLICATION OF QUALITATIVE RESEARCH PROPOSALS

Locate a published qualitatively oriented social work research article that contains a social work problem area or population that you're interested in. We suggest you locate a qualitatively oriented research study in Karen Staller and Karen Broadhurst's journal *Qualitative Social Work* (Sage Publications). Hands down, this is the best journal to find good qualitative social work research studies.

1. Using the contents of this chapter, write a brief 5-page hypothetical qualitative research proposal the author could have written for the qualitative research study.

2. Compare your qualitative proposal with those of your classmates who used the same research study. What did you learn from comparing your proposal with others?

9

3. Did the research study also contain a "quantitative" component (**mixed-methods research** as discussed in Chapter 8)? If so, what did it contain? How did this "quantitative" component add to the study's overall findings and practice implications?

4. Do you believe you have the knowledge and skills to actually implement a qualitative research study such as the one you found? Why or why not? What specific knowledge and skills do you feel you lack? Discuss *where, when,* and *how* you plan on obtaining the necessary knowledge and skills.

NOTE: You're working backward. That is, you're reconstructing what a hypothetical research proposal could have looked like given the contents of the actual published research study. Remember, research proposals contain statements about what we *will do* (future tense); research reports contain statements about what we *have done* (past tense).

10	**RESEARCH PROPOSALS AND THE RESEARCHER** **Scenario 1:** Make an argument that to be a competent social work researcher **you must know** how to write qualitatively based research proposals and reports. Provide clear and explicit **research-related** social work examples to illustrate your main points. **Scenario 2:** Make an argument that to be a competent social work researcher **you must know** how to write qualitatively AND quantitatively based research proposals and reports (**mixed-methods research** as discussed in Chapter 8). Provide clear and explicit **research-related** social work examples to illustrate your main points. **Scenario 3:** Make an argument that **you do not have to know** how to write any kind of research proposals or reports whatsoever to be a competent social work researcher. Provide clear and explicit **research-related** social work examples to illustrate your main points. **Time to Choose:** Which one of the above three scenarios do you feel is more consistent with the place of research in social work? Why? Provide relevant social work examples to illustrate your main points.
11	**RESEARCH PROPOSALS AND THE PRACTITIONER** **Scenario 1:** Make an argument that to be an effective evidence-based social work practitioner **you must know** how to write quantitatively based research proposals and reports. Provide a clear and explicit **practice-related** social work example to illustrate your main points. **Scenario 2:** Make an argument that to be an effective evidence-based social work practitioner **you must know** how to write quantitatively AND qualitatively based research proposals and reports (**mixed-methods research** as discussed in Chapter 8). Provide a clear and explicit **practice-related** social work example to illustrate your main points. **Scenario 3:** Make an argument that **you do not have to know** how to write any kind of research proposals or reports whatsoever to be an effective evidence-based social work practitioner. Provide a clear and explicit **practice-related** social work example to illustrate your main points. **Time to Choose:** Which one of the above three scenarios do you feel is more consistent with the concept of the contemporary evidence-based social work practice process as illustrated in Box 1.5 on pages 49–52? Why? Provide relevant social work examples to illustrate your main points.

12	**TIME TO PUT ON YOUR CRITICAL THINKING HAT** 1. Discuss the similarities and differences between your responses to Questions 10 and 11. 2. What are your thoughts on the belief that you'll need to know how to write qualitatively based research proposals whether you're a social work *practitioner* (Question 11) or a social work *researcher* (Question 10)?
13	**RESEARCH AND YOUR PROFESSIONAL DEVELOPMENT** 1. Review the three social work research-related roles you can take when you graduate—CSWE Competency 1 at the beginning of this chapter on page 702. This concept was also discussed in Chapter 1 on pages 38–43. Thoroughly discuss how you feel this chapter will help you to perform one or more research-related roles when you graduate. Which one of the three roles do you believe this chapter helped you with the most? Why? Discuss in detail and provide an example to illustrate your main points. 2. Review CSWE Competency 4 at the beginning of this chapter on page 702. Thoroughly discuss how you feel this chapter will help you to become a practice-informed researcher and a research-informed practitioner. Discuss in detail and provide an example to illustrate your main points. 3. Review the evidence-based practice process as illustrated on pages 46–51. Thoroughly discuss how this chapter helps you to develop the skills you'll need for implementing one or more steps of the evidence-based practice process. 4. Discuss which step(s) you feel this chapter will help you with the most. Why? Be very specific and use relevant social work examples to illustrate your main points throughout your discussion. **NOTE:** This exercise should help you to realize that you can use "research roles" to help you become an evidence-based social work practitioner.
14	**MOVING AHEAD BY LOOKING BACK** At this point in your research methods course, how comfortable are you with discussing the place of research in social work with your field instructor, with your practice instructor, with your research instructor, with your supervisor at work, with the director of your social work program, or with your classmates? Discuss in detail.

Glossary

Abstracting indexing services:
Providers of specialized reference tools that make it possible to find information quickly and easily, usually through subject headings and/or author approaches.

Abstracts: Reference materials consisting of citations and brief descriptive summaries from positivist and interpretive research studies.

Accountability: A system of responsibility in which program administrators account for all program activities by answering to the demands of a program's stakeholders and by justifying the program's expenditures to the satisfaction of its stakeholders.

Aggregated case-level evaluation designs: The collection of a number of case-level evaluations to determine the degree to which a program objective has been met.

Aggregate-level data: Derived from micro-level data, aggregate-level data are grouped so that the characteristics of individual units of analysis are no longer identifiable; for example, the variable "gross national income" is an aggregation of data about individual incomes.

Alternate-forms method: A method for establishing reliability of a measuring instrument by administering, in succession, equivalent forms of the same instrument to the same group of research participants.

Alternative hypothesis: See *Rival hypothesis*.

Analytical memos: Notes made by the researcher in reference to interpretive data that raise questions or make comments about meaning units and categories identified in a transcript.

Analytic generalization: The type of generalizability associated with case studies the research findings of case studies are not assumed to fit another case no matter how apparently similar; rather, research findings are tested to see if they do in fact fit; used as working hypotheses to test practice principles.

Annual report: A detailed account or statement describing a program's processes and results over a given year, usually produced at the end of a fiscal year.

Antecedent variable: A variable that precedes the introduction of one or more dependent variables.

Antiquarianism: An interest in past events without reference to their importance or significance for the present; the reverse of presentism.

***A* phase:** In case-level evaluation designs, a phase (*A* phase) in which the baseline measurement of the target problem is established before the intervention (*B* phase) is implemented.

Applied research approach: A search for practical and applied research results that can be used in actual social work practice situations; complementary to the pure research approach.

Area probability sampling: A form of cluster sampling that uses a three-stage process to provide the means to carry out a research study when no comprehensive list of the population can be compiled.

Assessment-related case study: A type of case study that generates knowledge about specific clients and their situations; focuses on the perspectives of the study's participants.

Audit trail: The documentation of critical steps in an interpretive research study that allows for an independent reviewer to examine and verify the steps in the research process and the conclusions of the research study.

Authority: The reliance on authority figures to tell us what is true; one of the six ways of knowing.

Availability sampling: See *Convenience sampling*.

Axes: Straight horizontal and vertical lines in a graph upon which values of a measurement, or the corresponding frequencies, are plotted.

Back-translation: The process of translating an original document into a second language, then having an independent translator conduct a subsequent translation of the first translation back into the language of origin; the second translation is then compared with the original document for equivalency.

Baseline: A period of time, usually three or four data collection periods, in which the level of the client's target problem is measured while no intervention is carried out; designated as the *A* phase in single-system designs (case-level designs).

Between research methods approach: Triangulation by using different research methods available in *both* the interpretive and the positivist research approaches in a single research study.

Bias: Not neutral; an inclination to some form of prejudice or preconceived position.

Biased sample: A sample unintentionally selected in such a way that some members of the population are more likely than others to be picked for sample membership.

Binomial effect size display (BESD): A technique for interpreting the r value in a meta-analysis by converting it into a 2 × 2 table displaying magnitude of effect.

Biography: Tells the story of one individual's life, often suggesting what the person's influence was on social, political, or intellectual developments of the times.

***B* phase:** In case-level evaluation designs, the intervention phase, which may, or may not, include simultaneous measurements.

Case: The basic unit of social work practice, whether it be an individual, a couple, a family, an agency, a community, a county, a state, or a country.

Case-level evaluation designs: Designs in which data are collected about a single-client system—an individual, group, or community—in order to evaluate the outcome of an intervention for the client system; a form of appraisal that monitors change for individual clients; also called *single-system research designs*.

Case study: Using research approaches to investigate a research question or hypothesis relating to a specific case; used to develop theory and test hypotheses; an in-depth form of research in which data are gathered and analyzed about an individual unit of analysis, person, city, event, or society. It allows more intensive analysis of specific details; the disadvantage is that it is hard to use the results to generalize to other cases.

Categories: Groupings of related meaning units that are given one name; used to organize, summarize, and interpret qualitative data. Categories in an interpretive study can change throughout the data-analysis process, and the number of categories in a given study depends upon the breadth and depth the researcher aims for in the analysis.

Category: In an interpretive data analysis, an aggregate of meaning units that share a common feature.

Category saturation: The point in a qualitative data analysis when all identified meaning units fit easily into the existing categorization scheme and no new categories emerge; the point at which first-level coding ends.

Causality: A relationship of cause and effect; the effect will invariably occur when the cause is present.

Causal relationship: A relationship between two variables for which we can state that the presence of, or absence of, one variable determines the presence of, or absence of, the other variable.

CD-ROM sources: Computerized retrieval systems that allow searching for indexes and abstracts stored on compact computer discs (CDs).

Census data: Data from the survey of an entire population in contrast to a survey of a sample.

Citation: A brief identification of a reference that includes name of author(s), title, source, page numbers, and year of publication.

Classic experimental design: An explanatory research design with randomly assigned experimental and control groups in which the dependent variable is measured before and after the treatment (the independent variable) for both groups, but only the experimental group receives the treatment (the dependent variable).

Client system: An individual client, a couple, a family, a group, an organization, or a community that can be studied with case- and program-level evaluation designs and with positivist and interpretive research approaches.

Closed-ended questions: Items in a measuring instrument that require respondents to select one of several response categories provided; also known as *fixed- alternative questions.*

Cluster diagram: An illustration of a conceptual classification scheme in which the researcher draws and labels circles for each theme that emerges from the data; the circles are organized in a way to depict the relationships between themes.

Cluster sampling: A multistage probability sampling procedure in which the population is divided into groups (or clusters); the groups, rather than the individuals, are selected for inclusion in the sample.

Code: The label assigned to a category or theme in a qualitative data analysis; shortened versions of the actual category or theme label; used as markers in a qualitative data analysis; usually no longer than eight characters in length and can use a combination of letters, symbols, and numbers.

Codebook: A device used to organize qualitative data by applying labels and descriptions that draw distinctions between different parts of the data that have been collected.

Coding: (1) In data analysis, translating data from respondents onto a form that can be read by a computer. (2) In interpretive research, marking the text with codes for content categories.

Coding frame: A specific framework that delineates what data are to be coded and how they are to be coded in order to prepare them for analyses.

Coding sheets: In a literature review, a sheet used to record for each research study the complete reference, research design, measuring instrument(s), population and sample, outcomes, and **other significant features of the study.**

Cohort study: A longitudinal survey design that uses successive random samples to monitor how the characteristics of a specific group of people, who share certain characteristics or experiences (cohorts), change over time.

Collaterals: Professionals or staff members who serve as indigenous observers in the data collection **process.**

Collective biographies: Studies of the characteristics of groups of people who lived during a past **period and had some major factor in common.**

Collectivist culture: Societies that stress interdependence and seek the welfare and survival of the group above that of the individual; collectivist cultures are characterized by a readiness to be influenced by others, preference for conformity, and cooperation in relationships.

Comparative rating scale: A rating scale in which respondents are asked to compare an individual person, concept, or situation with others.

Comparative research design: The study of more than one event, group, or society to isolate explanatory factors. There are two basic strategies in comparative research: (1) the study of elements that differ in many ways but that have some major factor in common, and (2) the study of elements that are highly similar but different in some important aspect, such as modern industrialized nations that have different health insurance systems.

Comparison group: A nonexperimental group to which research participants have not been randomly assigned for purposes of comparison with the experimental group. Not to be confused with control group.

Comparison group posttest-only design: A descriptive research design with two groups, experimental and comparison, in which the dependent variable is measured once for both groups, and only the experimental group receives the treatment (the independent variable).

Comparison group pretest-posttest design: A descriptive research design with two groups, experimental and comparison, in which the dependent variable is measured before and after the treatment for both groups, but only the experimental group receives the treatment.

Compensation: Attempts by researchers to compensate for the lack of treatment for control group members by administering it to them; a threat to internal validity.

Compensatory rivalry: Motivation of control group members to compete with experimental group members; a threat to internal validity.

Completeness: One of the four criteria for evaluating research hypotheses.

Complete observer: A term describing one of four possible research roles on a continuum of participant observation research; the complete observer acts simply as an observer and does not participate in the events at hand.

Complete participant: The complete participant is at the far end of the continuum from the complete observer in participant observation research; this research role is characterized by total involvement.

Comprehensive qualitative review: A nonstatistical synthesis of representative research studies relevant to a research problem, question, or hypothesis.

Computerized retrieval systems: Systems in which abstracts, indexes, and subject bibliographies are incorporated in computerized databases to facilitate information retrieval.

Concept: An understanding, an idea, or a mental image; a way of viewing and categorizing objects, processes, relations, and events.

Conceptual classification system: The strategy for conceiving how units of qualitative data relate to each other; the method used to depict patterns that emerge from the various coding levels in qualitative data.

Conceptual framework: A frame of reference that serves to guide a research study and is developed from theories, findings from a variety of other research studies, and the author's personal experiences and values.

Conceptualization: The process of selecting the specific concepts to include in positivist and interpretive research studies.

Conceptual validity: See *Construct validity*.

Concurrent validity: A form of criterion validity that is concerned with the ability of a measuring instrument to predict accurately an individual's status by comparing concurrent ratings (or scores) on one or more measuring instruments.

Confidentiality: An ethical consideration in research whereby anonymity of research participants is safeguarded by ensuring that raw data are not seen by anyone other than the research team and that data presented have no identifying marks.

Confounding variable: A variable operating in a specific situation in such a way that its effects cannot be separated; the effects of an extraneous variable thus confound the interpretation of a research study's findings.

Consistency: Holding steadfast to the same principles and procedures in the qualitative data-analysis process.

Constant: A concept that does not vary and does not change; a characteristic that has the same value for all research participants or events in a research study.

Constant comparison: A technique used to categorize qualitative data; it begins after the complete set of data has been examined and meaning units identified; each unit is classified as similar or different from the others; similar meaning units are lumped into the same category and classified by the same code.

Constant error: Systematic error in measurement; error due to factors that consistently or systematically affect the variable being measured and that are concerned with the relatively stable qualities of respondents to a measuring instrument.

Construct: See *Concept*.

Constructivism: Associated with the interpretive research approach. It's based on the understanding or meaning of phenomena that are formed through research participants and their subjective views.

Construct validity: The degree to which a measuring instrument successfully measures a theoretical construct; the degree to which explanatory concepts account for variance in the scores of an instrument; also referred to as *conceptual validity* in meta-analyses.

Content analysis: A data-collection method in which communications are analyzed in a systematic, objective, and quantitative manner to produce new data.

Content validity: The extent to which the content of a measuring instrument reflects the concept that is being measured and in fact measures that concept and not another.

Contextual detail: The particulars of the environment in which the case (or unit of analysis) is embedded; provides a basis for understanding and interpreting case study data and results.

Contradictory evidence: Identifying themes and categories that raise questions about the conclusions reached at the end of qualitative data analysis; outliers or extreme cases that are inconsistent or contradict the conclusions drawn from qualitative data; also called *negative evidence*.

Contributing partner: A social work role in which the social worker joins forces with others who perform different roles in positivist and interpretive research studies.

Control group: A group of randomly assigned research participants in a research study who do not receive the experimental treatment and are used for comparison purposes. Not to be confused with *comparison group*.

Control variable: A variable, other than the independent variable(s) of primary interest, whose effects we can determine; an intervening variable that has been controlled for in the study's research design.

Convenience sampling: A nonprobability sampling procedure that relies on the closest and most available research participants to constitute a sample.

Convergent validity: The degree to which different measures of a construct yield similar results, or converge.

Correlated variables: Variables whose values are associated; values of one variable tend to be associated in a systematic way with values in the others.

Cost-benefit analysis: An analytical procedure that not only determines the costs of the program itself but also considers the monetary benefits of the program's effects.

Cost-effectiveness analysis: An analytical procedure that assesses the costs of the program itself; the monetary benefits of the program's effects are not assessed.

Cover letter: A letter to respondents or research participants that is written under the official letterhead of the sponsoring organization and describes the research study and its purpose.

Credibility: The trustworthiness of both the steps taken in qualitative data analysis and the conclusions reached.

Criterion validity: The degree to which the scores obtained on a measuring instrument are comparable with scores from an external criterion believed to measure the same concept.

Criterion variable: The variable whose values are predicted from measurements of the predictor variable.

Cross-cultural comparisons: Research studies that include culture as a major variable; studies that compare two or more diverse cultural groups.

Cross-sectional research design: A survey research design in which data are collected to indicate characteristics of a sample or population at a particular moment in time.

Cross-tabulation table: A simple table showing the joint frequency distribution of two or more nominal-level variables.

Cultural encapsulation: The assumption that differences between groups represent some deficit or pathology.

Culturally equivalent: Similarity in the meaning of a construct between two cultures.

Cultural relativity: The belief that human thought and action can be judged only from the perspective of the culture out of which they have grown.

Cut-and-paste method: A method of analyzing qualitative data whereby the researcher cuts segments of the transcript and sorts these cuttings into relevant groupings; it can be done manually or with computer assistance.

Data: The numbers, words, or scores, generated by positivist and interpretive research studies. The word *data* is plural.

Data analyses: The process of turning data into information; the process of reviewing, summarizing, and organizing isolated facts (data) such that they formulate a meaningful response to a research question.

Data archive: A place where many datasets are stored and from which data can be accessed.

Data coding: Translating data from one language or format into another, usually to make it readable for a computer.

Data-collection method: Procedures specifying techniques to be employed, measuring instruments to be used, and activities to be conducted in implementing a positivist or interpretive research study.

Dataset: A collection of related data items, such as the answers given by respondents to all the questions in a survey.

Data source: The provider of the data, whether it be primary (the original source) or secondary (an intermediary between the research participant and the researcher analyzing the data).

Datum: Singular of *data*.

Deduction: A conclusion about a specific case(s) based on the assumption that it shares a characteristic with an entire class of similar cases.

Deductive reasoning: Forming a theory, making a deduction from the theory, and testing this deduction, or hypothesis, against reality; in research, applied to theory in order to arrive at a hypothesis that can be tested; a method of reasoning whereby a conclusion about specific cases is reached based on the assumption that they share characteristics with an entire class of similar cases.

Demand needs: When needs are defined by only those individuals who indicate that they feel or perceive the need themselves.

Demographic data: Vital and social facts that describe a sample or a population.

Demoralization: Feelings of deprivation among control group members that may cause them to drop out of a research study; a threat to internal validity.

Dependability: The soundness of both the steps taken in a qualitative data analysis and the conclusions reached.

Dependent events: Events that influence the probability of occurrence of each other.

Dependent variable: A variable that is dependent on, or caused by, another variable; an outcome variable, which is not manipulated directly but is measured to determine if the independent variable has had an effect.

Derived scores: Raw scores of research participants, or groups, converted in such a way that meaningful comparisons with other individuals, or groups, are possible.

Descriptive research: Research studies undertaken to increase precision in the definition of knowledge in a problem area where less is known than at the explanatory level; situated in the middle of the knowledge continuum.

Descriptive statistics: Methods used for summarizing and describing data in a clear and precise manner.

Design bias: Any effect that systematically distorts the outcome of a research study so that the study's results are not representative of the phenomenon under investigation.

Determinism: A contention in positivist research studies that only an event that is true over time and place and that will occur independent of beliefs about it (a predetermined event) permits the generalization of a study's findings; one of the four main limitations of the positivist research approach.

Deterministic causation: When a particular effect appears, the associated cause is always present; no other variables influence the relationship between cause and effect; the link between an independent variable that brings about the occurrence of the dependent variable every time.

Dichotomous variable: A variable that can take on only one of two values.

Differential scale: A questionnaire-type scale in which respondents are asked to consider questions representing different positions along a continuum and to select those with which they agree.

Differential selection: A potential lack of equivalency among preformed groups of research participants; a threat to internal validity.

Diffusion of treatments: Problems that may occur when experimental and control group members talk to each other about a research study; a threat to internal validity.

***d* index:** A measure of effect size in a meta-analysis.

Directional hypothesis: See *One-tailed hypotheses.*

Directional test: See *One-tailed hypotheses.*

Direct observation: An obtrusive data-collection method in which the focus is entirely on the behaviors of a group, or persons, being observed.

Direct observation notes: These are the first level of field notes, usually chronologically organized; they contain a detailed description of what was seen and heard and may also include summary notes made after an interview.

Direct relationship: A relationship between two variables such that high values of one variable are found with high values of the second variable.

Discriminant validity: The degree to which a construct can be empirically differentiated or discriminated from other constructs.

Divergent validity: The extent to which a measuring instrument differs from other instruments that measure unrelated constructs.

Double-barreled question: A question in a measuring instrument that contains two questions in one, usually joined by an *and* or an *or.*

Duration recording: A method of data collection that includes direct observation of the target problem and recording of the length of time each occurrence lasts within a specified observation period.

Ecological fallacy: An error of reasoning committed by coming to conclusions about individuals based only on data about groups.

Edge coding: Adding a series of blank lines on the right side of the response category in a measuring instrument to aid in processing the data.

Effect size: In meta-analysis, the most widely used measure of the dependent variable; the effect size statistic provides a measure of the magnitude of the relationship found between the variables of interest and allows for the computation of summary statistics that apply to the analysis of all the studies considered as a whole.

Embedded design: This is a mixed-methods design in which the researcher collects and analyzes quantitative and qualitative data within a traditional quantitative or qualitative design to enhance the overall design in some way.

Emergent mixed-methods designs: These are found in mixed-methods studies where the use of mixed methods arises due to issues that develop while conducting the research.

Empirical: Knowledge derived from the six ways of knowing.

Error of central tendency: A measurement error due to the tendency of observers to rate respondents in the middle of a variable's value range, rather than consistently too high or too low.

Error of measurement: See *Measurement error*.

Ethical research project: The systematic inquiry into a problem area in an effort to discover new knowledge or test existing ideas; the research study is conducted in accordance with professional standards.

Ethics in research: Positivist and interpretive data that are collected and analyzed with careful attention to their accuracy, fidelity to logic, and respect for the feelings and rights of research participants; one of the four criteria for evaluating research problem areas and formulating research questions out of the problem areas.

Ethnicity: A term that implies a common ancestry and cultural heritage and encompasses customs, values, beliefs, and behaviors.

Ethnocentricity: Assumptions about normal behavior that are based on one's own cultural framework without taking cultural relativity into account; the failure to acknowledge alternative worldviews.

Ethnograph: A computer program designed for qualitative data analyses.

Ethnographic: A form of content analysis used to document and explain the communication of meaning, as well as to verify theoretical relationships; any of several methods of describing social or cultural life based on direct, systematic observation, such as becoming a participant in a social system.

Ethnography: The systematic study of human cultures and the similarities and dissimilarities between them.

Ethnomethodology: Pioneered by Harold Garfinkel, this method of research focuses on the commonsense understanding of social life held by ordinary people (the ethos), usually as discovered through participant observation; often the observer's own methods of making sense of the situation become the object of investigation.

Evaluation: A form of appraisal using valid and reliable research methods; there are numerous types of evaluations geared to produce data that in turn produce information that helps in the decision-making process; data from evaluations are used to develop quality programs and services.

Evaluative research designs: Case- and program-level research designs that apply various research designs and data-collection methods to find out if an intervention (or treatment) worked at the case level and if the social work program worked at the program level.

Existing documents: Physical records left over from the past.

Existing statistics: Previously calculated numerical summaries of data that exist in the public domain.

Experience and intuition: Learning what is true through personal past experiences and intuition; two of the six ways of knowing.

Experiment: A research study in which we have control over the levels of the independent variable and over the assignment of research participants, or objects, to different experimental conditions.

Experimental designs: (1) Explanatory research designs or "ideal experiments." (2) Case-level research designs that examine the question, "Did the client system improve because of social work intervention?"

Experimental group: In an experimental research design, the group of research participants exposed to the manipulation of the independent variable; also referred to as a *treatment group*.

Explanatory research: "Ideal" research studies undertaken to infer cause-and-effect and directional relationships in areas where a number of substantial research findings are already in place; situated at the top end of the knowledge continuum.

Exploratory research: Research studies undertaken to gather data in areas of inquiry where very little is already known; situated at the lowest end of the knowledge continuum. See *Nonexperimental design*.

External evaluation: An evaluation that is conducted by someone who does not have any connection with the program; usually an evaluation that is requested by the agency's funding sources; this type of evaluation complements an in-house evaluation.

External validity: The extent to which the findings of a research study can be generalized outside the specific research situation.

Extraneous variables: See *Rival hypothesis*.

Face validity: The degree to which a measurement has self-evident meaning and measures what it appears to measure.

Feasibility: One of the four criteria for evaluating research problem areas and formulating research questions out of the problem areas.

Feedback: When data and information are returned to the persons who originally provided or collected them; used for informed decision making at the case and program levels; a basic principle underlying the design of evaluations.

Field notes: A record, usually written, of events observed by a researcher. The notes are taken as the study proceeds and later are used for analyses.

Field research: Research conducted in a real-life setting, not in a laboratory. The researcher neither creates nor manipulates anything within the study, but observes it.

Field-tested: The pilot of an instrument or research method in conditions equivalent to those that will be encountered in the research study.

File drawer problem: (1) In literature searches or reviews, the difficulty in locating studies that have not been published or are not easily retrievable. (2) In meta-analyses, errors in effect size due to reliance on published articles showing statistical significance.

First-hand data: Data obtained from people who directly experience the problem being studied.

First-level coding: A process of identifying meaning units in a transcript, organizing the meaning units into categories, and assigning names to the categories.

Flexibility: The degree to which the design and procedures of a research study can be changed to adapt to contextual demands of the research setting.

Focus group interview: A group of people brought together to talk about their lives and experiences in free-flowing, open-ended discussions that usually focus on a single topic.

Formative evaluation: A type of evaluation that focuses on obtaining data that are helpful in planning the program and in improving its implementation and performance.

Frequency recording: A method of data collection by direct observations in which each occurrence of the target problem is recorded during a specified observation period.

Fugitive data: Informal information found outside regular publishing channels.

Gaining access: A term used in interpretive research to describe the process of engagement and relationship development between the researcher and the research participants.

Generalizable explanation evaluation model: An evaluation model whose proponents believe that many solutions are possible for any one social problem and that the effects of programs will differ under different conditions.

Generalizing results: Extending or applying the findings of a research study to individuals or situations not directly involved in the original research study; the ability to extend or apply the findings of a research study to subjects or situations that were not directly investigated.

Goal Attainment Scale (GAS): A modified measurement scale used to evaluate case or program outcomes.

Government documents: Documents issued by local, state, and federal governments; they include reports of legislative committee hearings and investigations, studies commissioned by legislative commissions and executive agencies, statistical compilations such as the census, the regular and special reports of executive agencies, and much more.

Grand tour questions: Queries in which research participants are asked to provide wide-ranging background information; mainly used in interpretive research studies.

Graphic rating scale: A rating scale that describes an attribute on a continuum from one extreme to the other, with points of the continuum ordered in equal intervals and then assigned values.

Grounded theory: A final outcome of the interpretive research process that is reached when the insights are grounded on observations and the conclusions seem to be firm.

Group evaluation designs: Evaluation designs that are conducted with groups of cases for the purpose of assessing to what degree program objectives have been achieved.

Group research designs: Research designs conducted with two or more groups of cases, or research participants, for the purpose of answering research questions or testing hypotheses.

Halo effect: A measurement error due to the tendency of an observer to be influenced by a favorable trait of a research participant.

Hawthorne effect: Effects on research participants' behaviors or attitudes attributable to their knowledge that they are taking part in a research study; a reactive effect; a threat to external validity.

Heterogeneity of respondents: The extent to which a research participant differs from other research participants.

Heuristic: A theory used to stimulate creative thought and scientific activity.

Historical research: The process by which we study the past; a method of inquiry that attempts to explain past events based on surviving artifacts.

History in research design: The possibility that events not accounted for in a research design may alter the second and subsequent measurements of the dependent variable; a threat to internal validity.

Homogeneity of respondents: The extent to which a research participant is similar to other research participants.

Hypothesis: A theory-based prediction of the expected results of a research study; a tentative explanation that a relationship between or among variables exists.

Hypothetico-deductive method: A hypothesis-testing approach that a hypothesis is derived on the deductions based from a theory.

Ideographic research: Research studies that focus on unique individuals or situations.

Implementation of a program: The action of carrying out a program in the way that it was designed.

Independent variable: A variable that is not dependent on another variable but is believed to cause or determine changes in the dependent variable; an antecedent variable that is directly manipulated to assess its effect on the dependent variable.

Index: A group of individual measures that, when combined, are meant to indicate some more general characteristic.

Indigenous observers: People who are naturally a part of the research participants' environment and who perform the data-collection function; includes relevant others (e.g., family members, peers) and collaterals (e.g., social workers, staff members).

Indirect measures: A substitute variable, or a collection of representative variables, used when there is no direct measurement of the variable of interest; also called a *proxy variable*.

Individualism: A way of living that stresses independence, personal rather than group objectives, competition, and power in relationships; achievement measured through success of the individual as opposed to the group.

Individual synthesis: Analysis of published studies related to the subject under study.

Inductive reasoning: A method of reasoning whereby a conclusion is reached by building on specific observations of events, things, or processes to make inferences or more general statements; applied to data collection and research results to make generalizations to see if they fit a theory.

Inferential statistics: Statistical methods that make it possible to draw tentative conclusions about the population based on observations of a sample selected from that population and, furthermore, to make a probability statement about those conclusions to aid in their **evaluation.**

Information anxiety: A feeling attributable to a lack of understanding of information, being overwhelmed by the amount of information to be accessed and understood, or not knowing if certain information exists.

Informed consent: Signed statements obtained from research participants prior to the initiation of the research study to inform them about what their participation entails and that they are free to decline participation.

In-house evaluation: An evaluation that is conducted by someone who works within a program; usually an evaluation for the purpose of promoting better client services; also known as an *internal evaluation*. This type of evaluation complements an external evaluation.

Institutional review boards (IRBs): Boards set up by institutions to protect research participants and to ensure that ethical issues are recognized and responded to in a study's research design.

Instrumentation: Weaknesses of a measuring instrument, such as invalidity, unreliability, improper administration, or mechanical breakdowns; a threat to internal validity.

Interview protocol: A form used in qualitative research to collect qualitative data. On the form are questions to be asked during an interview and space for recording data gathered during the interview. This protocol also provides space to record essential data such as the time, day, and place of the interview.

Integration: Combining evaluation and day-to-day practice activities to develop a complete approach to client service delivery; a basic principle underlying the design of evaluations.

Interaction effects: Effects produced by the combination of two or more threats to internal validity.

Internal consistency: The extent to which the scores on two comparable halves of the same measuring instrument are similar; inter-item consistency.

Internal validity: The extent to which it can be demonstrated that the independent variable within a research study is the only cause of change in the dependent variable; overall soundness of the experimental procedures and measuring instruments.

Interpretive research approach: Research studies that focus on the facts of nature as they occur under natural conditions and emphasize qualitative description and generalization; a process of discovery sensitive to holistic and ecological issues; a research approach that is complementary to the positivist research approach.

Interobserver reliability: The stability or consistency of observations made by two or more observers at one point in time.

Interpretive notes: Notes on the researcher's interpretations of events that are kept separate from the record of the facts noted as direct observations.

Interquartile range: A number that measures the variability of a data set; the distance between the 75th and 25th percentiles.

Interrater reliability: The degree to which two or more independent observers, coders, or judges produce consistent results.

Interrupted time-series design: An explanatory research design in which there is only one group of research participants and the dependent variable is measured repeatedly before and after treatment; used in case- and program-evaluation designs.

Interval level of measurement: The level of measurement with an arbitrarily chosen zero point that classifies its values on an equally spaced continuum.

Interval recording: A method of data collection that involves a continuous direct observation of an individual during specified observation periods divided into equal time intervals.

Intervening variable: See *Rival hypothesis*.

Interview data: Isolated facts that are gathered when research participants respond to carefully constructed research questions; data in the form of words, recorded by transcription.

Interviewing: A conversation with a purpose.

Interview schedule: A measuring instrument used to collect data in face-to-face and telephone interviews.

Intraobserver reliability: The stability of observations made by a single observer at several points in time.

Intrusion into lives of research participants: The understanding that specific data-collection methods can have negative consequences for research participants; a criterion for selecting a data-collection method.

Itemized rating scales: A measuring instrument that presents a series of statements that respondents or observers rank in different positions on a specific attribute.

Journal: A written record of the process of an interpretive research study. Journal entries are made on an ongoing basis throughout the study and include study procedures as well as the researcher's reactions to emerging issues and concerns during the data-analysis process.

Key informants: A subpopulation of research participants who seem to know much more about "the situation" than other research participants.

Knowledge base: A body of knowledge and skills specific to a certain discipline.

Knowledge creator and disseminator: A social work role in which the social worker actually carries out and disseminates the results of a positivist and/or interpretive research study to generate knowledge for our profession.

Knowledge-level continuum: The range of knowledge levels, from exploratory to descriptive to explanatory, at which research studies can be conducted.

Latent content: In a content analysis, the true meaning, depth, or intensity of a variable, or concept, under study.

Levels of measurement: The degree to which characteristics of a dataset can be modeled mathematically; the higher the level of measurement, the more statistical methods that are applicable.

Limited review: An existing literature synthesis that summarizes in narrative form the findings and implications of a few research studies.

Literature review: See *Literature search* and *Review of the literature*.

Literature search: Scanning books and journals for basic, up-to-date research articles on studies relevant to a research question or hypothesis; should be sufficiently thorough to maximize the chance of including all relevant sources. See *Review of the literature*.

Logical consistency: The requirement that all the steps within a positivist research study must be logically related to one another.

Logical positivism: A philosophy of science holding that the scientific method of inquiry is the only source of certain knowledge; in research, focuses on testing hypotheses deduced from theory.

Logistics: In evaluation, refers to getting research participants to do what they are supposed to do, getting research instruments distributed and returned; in general, the activities that ensure that procedural tasks of a research or evaluation study are carried out.

Longitudinal case study: An exploratory research design in which there is only one group of research participants and the dependent variable is measured more than once.

Longitudinal design: A survey research design in which a measuring instrument is administered to a sample of research participants repeatedly over time; used to detect dynamic processes such as opinion change.

Magnitude recording: A direct-observation method of soliciting and recording data on the amount, level, or degree of the target problem during each occurrence.

Management information system (MIS): System in which computer technology is used to process, store, retrieve, and analyze data collected routinely in such processes as social service delivery.

Manifest content: Content of a communication that is obvious and clearly evident.

Manipulable solution evaluation model: An evaluation model whose proponents believe that the greatest priority is to serve the public interest, not the interests of stakeholders, who have vested interests in the program being evaluated; closely resembles an outcome evaluation.

Matching: A random assignment technique that assigns research participants to two or more groups so that the experimental and control groups are approximately equivalent in terms of pretest scores or other characteristics, or so that all differences except the experimental condition are eliminated.

Maturation: Unplanned change in research participants due to mental, physical, or other processes operating over time; a threat to internal validity.

Meaning units: In a qualitative data analysis, a discrete segment of a transcript that can stand alone as a single idea; can consist of a single word, a partial or complete sentence, a paragraph, or more; used as the basic building blocks for developing categories.

Measurement: The assignment of labels or numerals to the properties or attributes of observations, events, or objects according to specific rules.

Measurement error: Any variation in measurement that cannot be attributed to the variable being measured; variability in responses produced by individual differences and other extraneous variables.

Measuring instrument: Any instrument used to measure a variable.

Media myths: The content of television shows, movies, and newspaper and magazine articles; one of the six ways of knowing.

Member checking: A process of obtaining feedback and comments from research participants on interpretations and conclusions made from the qualitative data they provided; asking research participants to confirm or refute the conclusions made.

Merging: A mixing strategy in which quantitative and qualitative results are brought together through a combined analysis.

Meta-analysis: A research method in which mathematical procedures are applied to the positivist findings of studies located in a literature search to produce new summary statistics and to describe the findings for a meta-analysis.

Methodology: The procedures and rules that detail how a single research study is conducted.

Micro-level data: Data derived from individual units of analysis, whether these data sources are individuals, families, corporations, etc.; for example, age and years of formal schooling are two variables requiring micro-level data.

Missing data: Data not available for a research participant about whom other data are available, such as when a respondent fails to answer one of the questions in a survey.

Missing links: When two categories or themes seem to be related, but not directly so, it may be that a third variable connects the two.

Mixed-methods case study: This is a variant of the embedded design in which the researcher collects both qualitative and quantitative data within a case study.

Mixed-methods research questions: These are questions in a mixed-methods study that address the mixing or integration of quantitative and qualitative data.

Mixed research model: A model combining aspects of interpretive and positivist research approaches within all (or many) of the methodological steps contained within a single research study.

Monitoring approach to evaluation: Evaluation that aims to provide ongoing feedback so that a program can be improved while it is still under way; it contributes to the continuous development and improvement of a human service program; this approach complements the project approach to evaluation.

Mortality: Loss of research participants through normal attrition over time in an experimental design that requires retesting; a threat to internal validity.

Multicultural research: Representation of diverse cultural factors in the subjects of study; such diversity variables may include religion, race, ethnicity, language preference, gender, etc.

Multigroup posttest-only design: An exploratory research design in which there is more than one group of research participants and the dependent variable is measured only once for each group.

Multiple-baseline design: A case-level evaluation design with more than one baseline period and intervention phase, which allows causal inferences to be made regarding the relationship between a treatment intervention and its effect on clients' target problems and which helps control for extraneous variables. See *Interrupted time-series design*.

Multiple-group design: An experimental research design with one control group and several experimental groups.

Multiple-treatment interference: Effects of the results of a first treatment on the results of second and subsequent treatments; a threat to external validity.

Multistage probability sampling: Probability sampling procedures used when a comprehensive list of the population does not exist and it is not possible to construct one.

Multivariate: (1) A relationship involving two or more variables. (2) A hypothesis stating an assertion about two or more variables and how they relate to one another.

Multivariate analysis: A statistical analysis of the relationship among three or more variables.

Narrowband measuring instrument: Measuring instruments that focus on a single variable or a few variables.

Nationality: A term that refers to country of origin.

Naturalist: A person who studies the facts of nature as they occur under natural conditions.

Needs assessment: Program-level evaluation activities that aim to assess the feasibility for establishing or continuing a particular social service program; an evaluation that aims to assess the need for a human service by verifying that a social problem exists within a specific client population to an extent that warrants services.

Negative case sampling: Purposefully selecting research participants based on the fact that they have different characteristics than previous cases.

Nominal level of measurement: The level of measurement that classifies variables by assigning names or categories that are mutually exclusive and exhaustive.

Nondirectional test: See *Two-tailed hypotheses*.

Nonexperimental design: A research design at the exploratory, or lowest, level of the knowledge continuum; also called *pre-experimental*.

Nonoccurrence data: In the structured-observation method of data collection, a recording of only those time intervals in which the target problem did not occur.

Nonparametric tests: Refers to statistical tests of hypotheses about population probability distributions, but not about specific parameters of the distributions.

Nonprobability sampling: Sampling procedures in which all of the persons, events, or objects in the sampling frame have an unknown, and usually different, probability of being included in a sample.

Nonreactive: Methods of research that do not allow the research participants to know that they are being studied; thus, they do not alter their responses for the benefit of the researcher.

Nonresponse: The rate of nonresponse in survey research is calculated by dividing the total number of respondents by the total number in the sample, minus any units verified as ineligible.

Nonsampling errors: Errors in a research study's results that are not due to the sampling procedures.

Norm: In measurement, an average or set group standard of achievement that can be used to interpret individual scores; normative data describing statistical properties of a measuring instrument such as means and standard deviations.

Normalization group: The population sample to which a measuring instrument under development is administered to establish norms; also called the *norm group*.

Normative needs: When needs are defined by comparing the objective living conditions of a target population with what society—or, at least, that segment of society concerned with helping the target population—deems acceptable or desirable from a humanitarian standpoint.

Null hypothesis: A statement concerning one or more parameters that is subjected to a statistical test; a statement that there is no relationship between the two variables of interest.

Numbers: The basic data unit of analysis used in positivist research studies.

Objectivity: A research stance in which a study is carried out and its data are examined and interpreted without distortion by personal feelings or biases.

Observer: One of four roles on a continuum of participation in participant observation research; the level of involvement of the observer participant is lower than of the complete participant and higher than of the participant observer.

Obtrusive data-collection methods: Direct data-collection methods that can influence the variables under study or the responses of research participants; data-collection methods that produce reactive effects.

Occurrence data: In the structured-observation method of data collection, a recording of the first occurrence of the target problem during each time interval.

One-group posttest-only design: An exploratory research design in which the dependent variable is measured only once.

One-group pretest-posttest design: A descriptive research design in which the dependent variable is measured twice—before and after treatment.

One-stage probability sampling: Probability sampling procedures in which the selection of a sample that is drawn from a specific population is completed in a single process.

One-tailed hypotheses: Statements that predict specific relationships between independent and dependent variables.

Online sources: Computerized literary retrieval systems that provide printouts of indexes and abstracts.

Open-ended questions: Unstructured questions in which the response categories are not specified or detailed.

Operational definition: Explicit specification of a variable in such a way that its measurement is possible.

Operationalization: The process of developing operational definitions of the variables that are contained within the concepts of a positivist and/or interpretive research study.

Ordinal level of measurement: The level of measurement that classifies variables by rank-ordering them from high to low or from most to least.

Outcome: The effect of the manipulation of the independent variable on the dependent variable; the end product of a treatment intervention.

Outcome measure: The criterion or basis for measuring effects of the independent variable or change in the dependent variable.

Outcome-oriented case study: A type of case study that investigates whether client outcomes were in fact achieved.

Outside observers: Trained observers who are not a part of the research participants' environment and who are brought in to record data.

Paired observations: An observation involving two variables, where the intent is to examine the relationship between them.

Panel research study: A longitudinal survey design in which the same group of research participants (the panel) is followed over time by surveying them on successive occasions.

Parametric tests: Statistical methods for estimating parameters or testing hypotheses about population parameters.

Participant observation: An obtrusive data-collection method in which the researcher, or the observer, participates in the life of those being observed; both an obtrusive data-collection method and a research approach, this method is characterized by the one doing the study undertaking roles that involve establishing and maintaining ongoing relationships with research participants who are often in the field settings, and observing and participating with the research participants over time.

Participant observer: The participant observer is one of four roles on a continuum of participation in participant observation research; the level of involvement of the participant observer is higher than of the complete observer and lower than of the observer participant.

Permanent product recording: A method of data collection in which the occurrence of the target problem is determined by observing the permanent product or record of the target problem.

Pilot study: See *Pretest* (2).

Population: An entire set, or universe, of people, objects, or events of concern to a research study, from which a sample is drawn.

Positivism: See *Positivist research approach*.

Positivist research approach: A research approach to discover relationships and facts that are generalizable; research that is "independent" of subjective beliefs, feelings, wishes, and values; a research approach that is complementary to the interpretive research approach.

Posttest: Measurement of the dependent variable after the introduction of the independent variable.

Potential for testing: One of the four criteria for evaluating research hypotheses.

Practitioner/researcher: A social worker who guides practice through the use of research findings; collects data throughout an intervention using research methods, skills, and tools; and disseminates practice findings.

Pragmatists: Researchers who believe that both interpretive and positivist research approaches can be integrated in a single research study.

Predictive validity: A form of criterion validity that is concerned with the ability of a measuring instrument to predict future performance or status on the basis of present performance or status.

Predictor variable: The variable that, it is believed, allows us to improve our ability to predict values of the criterion variable.

Preexposure: Tasks to be carried out in advance of a research study to sensitize the researcher to the culture of interest; these tasks may include participation in cultural experiences, intercultural sharing, case studies, ethnic literature reviews, value statement exercises, etc.

Preliminary plan for data analysis: A strategy for analyzing qualitative data that is outlined in the beginning stages of an interpretive research study; the plan has two general steps: (1) previewing the data, and (2) outlining what to record in the researcher's journal.

Presentism: Applying current thinking and concepts to interpretations of past events or intentions.

Pretest: (1) Measurement of the dependent variable prior to the introduction of the independent variable. (2) Administration of a measuring instrument to a group of people who will not be included in the study to determine difficulties the research participants may have in answering questions and the general impression given by the instrument; also called a *pilot study*.

Pretest-treatment interaction: Effects that a pretest has on the responses of research participants to the introduction of the independent variable or the experimental treatment; a threat to external validity.

Previous research: Research studies that have already been completed and published and that provide information about data-collection methods used to investigate research questions that are similar to our own; a criterion for selecting a data-collection method.

Primary data: Data in its original form, as collected from the research participants. A primary data source is one that puts as few intermediaries as possible between the production and the study of the data.

Primary language: The preferred language of the research participants.

Primary reference source: A report of a research study by the person who conducted the study, usually an article in a professional journal.

Probability sampling: Sampling procedures in which every member of the designated population has a known probability of being selected for the sample.

Problem area: In social work research, a general expressed difficulty about which something researchable is unknown; not to be confused with *research question*.

Problem-solving process: A generic method with specified phases for solving problems; also described as the *scientific method*.

Process-oriented case study: A type of case study that illuminates the micro-steps of intervention that lead to client outcomes; describes how programs and interventions work and gives insight into the "black box" of intervention.

Professional standards: Rules for making judgments about evaluation activity that are established by a group of persons who have advanced education and usually have the same occupation.

Program: An organized set of political, administrative, and clinical activities that function to fulfill some social purpose.

Program development: The constant effort to improve program services to better achieve outcomes; a basic principle underlying the design of evaluations.

Program efficiency: Assessment of a program's outcome in relation to the costs of obtaining the outcome.

Program evaluation: A form of appraisal, using valid and reliable research methods, that examines the processes or outcomes of an organization that exists to fulfill some social purpose.

Program goal: A statement defining the intent of a program that cannot be directly evaluated; it can, however, be evaluated indirectly by the program's objectives, which are derived from the program goal; not to be confused with *program objectives*.

Program-level evaluation: A form of appraisal that monitors change for groups of clients and organizational performance.

Program objectives: A statement that clearly and exactly specifies the expected change, or intended result, for individuals receiving program services; qualities of well-chosen objectives are meaningfulness, specificity, measurability, and directionality; not to be confused with *program goal*.

Program participation: The philosophy and structure of a program that will support or supplant the successful implementation of a research study within an existing social service program; a criterion for selecting a data-collection method.

Program process: The coordination of administrative and clinical activities that are designed to achieve a program's goal.

Program results: A report on how effective a program is at meeting its stated objectives.

Project approach to evaluation: Evaluation that aims to assess a completed or finished program. This approach complements the monitoring approach.

Proxy: An indirect measure of a variable that a researcher wants to study; often used when the variable of inquiry is difficult to measure or observe directly.

Pure research approach: A search for theoretical results that can be used to develop theory and expand our profession's knowledge bases; complementary to the applied research approach.

Purists: Researchers who believe that interpretive and positivist research approaches should never be mixed.

Purpose statement: A declaration of words that clearly describes a research study's intent.

Purposive sampling: A nonprobability sampling procedure in which research participants with particular characteristics are purposely selected for inclusion in a research sample; also known as *judgmental* or *theoretical sampling*.

Qualitative data: Data that measure a quality or kind. When referring to variables, qualitative is another term for categorical or nominal variable values; when speaking of kinds of research, qualitative refers to studies of subjects that are hard to quantify.

Quantification: In measurement, the reduction of data to numerical form in order to analyze them by way of mathematical or statistical techniques.

Qualitative validity: Assessing whether the information obtained through the qualitative data collection is accurate through such strategies as member checking, triangulation of evidence, searching for disconfirming evidence, and asking others to examine the data.

Quantitative data: Data that measure a quantity or amount.

Qualitative data analysis: Process that involves coding the dataset, dividing the text into small units (phrases, sentences, or paragraphs), assigning a label to each unit, and then grouping the codes into themes.

Quantitative data analysis: Process that involves analyzing the data based on the type of questions or hypotheses and using the appropriate statistical test to address the questions or hypotheses.

Quasi-experiment: A research design at the descriptive level of the knowledge continuum that resembles an "ideal" experiment but does not allow for random selection or assignment of research participants to groups and often does not control for rival hypotheses.

Questionnaire-type scale: A type of measuring instrument in which multiple responses are usually combined to form a single overall score for a respondent.

Quota sampling: A nonprobability sampling procedure in which the relevant characteristics of the sample are identified, the proportion of these characteristics in the population is determined, and research participants are selected from each category until the predetermined proportion (quota) has been achieved.

Race: A variable based on physical attributes that can be subdivided into the Caucasoid, Negroid, and Mongoloid races.

Random assignment: The process of assigning individuals to experimental or control groups so that the groups are equivalent; also referred to as *randomization*.

Random error: Variable error in measurement; error due to unknown or uncontrolled factors that affect the variable being measured and the process of measurement in an inconsistent fashion.

Randomized cross-sectional survey design: A descriptive research design in which there is only one group, the dependent variable is measured only once, the research participants are randomly selected from the population, and there is no independent variable.

Randomized longitudinal survey design: A descriptive research design in which there is only one group, the dependent variable is measured more than once, and research participants are randomly selected from the population before each treatment.

Randomized one-group posttest-only design: A descriptive research design in which there is only one group, the dependent variable is measured only once, and research participants are randomly selected from the population.

Randomized posttest-only control group design: An explanatory research design in which there are two or more randomly assigned groups, the control group does not receive treatment, and the experimental groups receive different treatments.

Random numbers table: A computer-generated or published table of numbers in which each number has an equal chance of appearing in each position in the table.

Random sampling: An unbiased selection process conducted so that all members of a population have an equal chance of being selected to participate in a research study.

Rank-order scale: A comparative rating scale in which the rater is asked to rank specific individuals in relation to one another on some characteristic.

Rating scale: A type of measuring instrument in which responses are rated on a continuum or in an ordered set of categories, with numerical values assigned to each point or category.

Ratio level of measurement: The level of measurement that has a nonarbitrary, fixed zero point and classifies the values of a variable on an equally spaced continuum.

Raw scores: Scores derived from administration of a measuring instrument to research participants or groups.

Reactive effect: (1) An effect on outcome measures due to the research participants' awareness that they are being observed or interviewed; a threat to external and internal validity. (2) Alteration of the variables being measured or the respondents' performance on the measuring instrument due to administration of the instrument.

Reactivity: The belief that things being observed or measured are affected by the fact that they are being observed or measured; one of the four main limitations of the positivist research approach.

Reassessment: A step in a qualitative data analysis in which the researcher interrupts the data-analysis process to reaffirm the rules used to decide which meaning units are placed within different categories.

Recoding: Developing and applying new variable value labels to a variable that has previously been coded. Usually, recoding is done to make variables from one or more datasets comparable.

Reductionism: In the positivist research approach, the operationalization of concepts by reducing them to common measurable variables; one of the four main limitations of the positivist research approach.

Relevancy: One of the four criteria for evaluating research problem areas and formulating research questions out of the problem areas.

Reliability: (1) The degree of accuracy, precision, or consistency in results of a measuring instrument, including the ability to produce the same results when the same variable is measured more than once or repeated applications of the same test on the same individual produce the same measurement. (2) The degree to which individual differences on scores or in data are due either to true differences or to errors in measurement.

Replication: Repetition of the same research procedures by a second researcher for the purpose of determining if earlier results can be confirmed.

Researchability: The extent to which a research problem is in fact researchable and the problem can be resolved through the consideration of data derived from a research study; one of the four criteria for evaluating research problem areas and formulating research questions out of the problem areas.

Research attitude: A way that we view the world. It is an attitude that highly values craftsmanship, with pride in creativity, high-quality standards, and hard work.

Research consumer: A social work role reflecting the ethical obligation to base interventions on the most up-to-date research knowledge available.

Research design: The entire plan of a positivist and/or interpretive research study from problem conceptualization to the dissemination of findings.

Researcher bias: The tendency of researchers to find the results they expect to find; a threat to external validity.

Research hypothesis: A statement about a study's research question that predicts the existence of a particular relationship between the independent and dependent variables; can be used in both the positivist and interpretive approaches to research.

Research method: The use of positivist and interpretive research approaches to find out what is true; one of the ways of knowing.

Research participants: People utilized in research studies; also called *subjects* or *cases*.

Research question: A specific research question that is formulated directly out of the general research problem area; answered by the interpretive and/or positivist research approach; not to be confused with *problem area*.

Resources: The costs associated with collecting data in any given research study; includes materials and supplies, equipment rental, transportation, training staff, and staff time; a criterion for selecting a data-collection method.

Response categories: Possible responses assigned to each question in a standardized measuring instrument, with a lower value generally indicating a low level of the variable being measured and a larger value indicating a higher level.

Response rate: The total number of responses obtained from potential research participants to a measuring instrument divided by the total number of responses requested, usually expressed in the form of a percentage.

Response set: Personal style; the tendency of research participants to respond to a measuring instrument in a particular way, regardless of the questions asked, or the tendency of observers or interviewers to react in certain ways; a source of constant error.

Review of the literature: (1) A search of the professional literature to provide background knowledge of what has already been examined or tested in a specific problem area. (2) Use of any information source, such as a computerized database, to locate existing data or information on a research problem, question, or hypothesis.

Rival hypothesis: A hypothesis that is a plausible alternative to the research hypothesis and might explain the results as well or better; a hypothesis involving extraneous or intervening variables other than the independent variable in the research hypothesis; also referred to as an *alternative hypothesis*.

Rules of correspondence: A characteristic of measurement stipulating that numerals or symbols are assigned to properties of individuals, objects, or events according to specified rules.

Sample: A subset of a population of individuals, objects, or events chosen to participate in or to be considered in a research study.

Sampling error: (1) The degree of difference that can be expected between the sample and the population from which it was drawn. (2) A mistake in a research study's results that is due to sampling procedures.

Sampling frame: A listing of units (people, objects, or events) in a population from which a sample is drawn.

Sampling plan: A method of selecting members of a population for inclusion in a research study, using procedures that make it possible to draw inferences about the population from the sample statistics.

Sampling theory: The logic of using methods to ensure that a sample and a population are similar in all relevant characteristics.

Scale: A measuring instrument composed of several items that are logically or empirically structured to measure a construct.

Scattergram: A graphic representation of the relationship between two interval- or ratio-level variables.

Science: Knowledge that has been obtained and tested through use of positivist and interpretive research studies.

Scientific community: A group that shares the same general norms for both research activity and acceptance of scientific findings and explanations.

Scientific determinism: See *Determinism*.

Scientific method: A generic method with specified steps for solving problems; the principles and procedures used in the systematic pursuit of knowledge.

Scope of a study: The extent to which a problem area is covered in a single research study; a criterion for selecting a data-collection method.

Score: A numerical value assigned to an observation; also called *data*.

Search statement: A statement developed by the researcher prior to a literature search that contains terms that can be combined to elicit specific data.

Secondary analysis: An unobtrusive data-collection method in which available data that predate the formulation of a research study are used to answer the research question or test the hypothesis.

Secondary data: Data that predate the formulation of the research study and that are used to answer the research question or test the hypothesis.

Secondary data sources: A data source that provides non-original, second-hand data.

Secondary reference source: A source related to a primary source or sources, such as a critique of a particular source item or a literature review, bibliography, or commentary on several items.

Second-hand data: Data obtained from people who are indirectly connected to the problem being studied.

Selection-treatment interaction: The relationship between the manner of selecting research participants and their response to the independent variable; a threat to external validity.

Self-anchored scales: A rating scale in which research participants rate themselves on a continuum of values, according to their own referents for each point.

Self-disclosure: Shared communication about oneself, including one's behaviors, beliefs, and attitudes.

Semantic differential scale: A modified measurement scale in which research participants rate their perceptions of the variable under study along three dimensions—evaluation, potency, and activity.

Sequential triangulation: When two distinct and separate phases of a research study are conducted and the results of the first phase are considered essential for planning the second phase; research questions in Phase 1 are answered before research questions in Phase 2 are formulated.

Service recipients: People who use human services—individuals, couples, families, groups, organizations, and communities; also known as *clients* or *consumers*; a stakeholder group in evaluation.

Simple random sampling: A one-stage probability sampling procedure in which members of a population are selected one at a time, without a chance of being selected again, until the desired sample size is obtained.

Simultaneous triangulation: When the results of a positivist and interpretive research question are answered at the same time; results to the interpretive research questions, for example, are reported separately and do not necessarily relate to, or confirm, the results from the positivist phase.

Situationalists: Researchers who assert that certain research approaches (interpretive or positivist) are appropriate for specific situations.

Situation-specific variable: A variable that may be observable only in certain environments and under certain circumstances, or with particular people.

Size of a study: The number of people, places, or systems that are included in a single research study; a criterion for selecting a data-collection method.

Snowball sampling: A nonprobability sampling procedure in which individuals selected for inclusion in a sample are asked to identify other individuals from the population who might be included; useful to locate people with divergent points of view.

Social desirability: (1) A response set in which research participants tend to answer questions in a way that they perceive as giving favorable impressions of themselves. (2) The inclination of data providers to report data that present a socially desirable impression of themselves or their reference groups; also referred to as *impression management.*

Socially acceptable response: Bias in an answer that comes from research participants trying to answer questions as they think a "good" person should, rather than in a way that reveals what they actually believe or feel.

Social work research: Scientific inquiry in which interpretive and positivist research approaches are used to answer research questions and create new, generally applicable knowledge in the field of social work.

Socioeconomic variables: Any one of several measures of social rank, usually including income, education, and occupational prestige; abbreviated "SES."

Solomon four-group design: An explanatory research design with four randomly assigned groups, two experimental and two control; the dependent variable is measured before and after treatment for one experimental and one control group, but only after treatment for the other two groups, and only experimental groups receive the treatment.

Specificity: One of the four criteria for evaluating research hypotheses.

Split-half method: A method for establishing the reliability of a measuring instrument by dividing it into comparable halves and comparing the scores between the two halves.

Spot-check recording: A method of data collection that involves direct observation of the target problem at specified intervals rather than on a continuous basis.

Stakeholder: A person or group of people having a direct or indirect interest in the results of an evaluation.

Stakeholder service evaluation model: Proponents of this evaluation model believe that program evaluations will be more likely to be utilized, and thus have a greater impact on social problems, when they are tailored to the needs of stakeholders; in this model, the purpose of program evaluation is not to generalize findings to other sites, but rather to restrict the evaluation effort to a particular program.

Standardized measuring instrument: A professionally developed measuring instrument that provides for uniform administration and scoring and generates normative data against which later results can be evaluated.

Statistics: The branch of mathematics concerned with the collection and analysis of data using statistical techniques.

Stratified random sampling: A one-stage probability sampling procedure in which a population is divided into two or more strata to be sampled separately, using simple random or systematic random sampling techniques.

Structured interview schedule: A complete list of questions to be asked and spaces for recording the answers; the interview schedule is used by interviewers when questioning respondents.

Structured observation: A data-collection method in which people are observed in their natural environments using specified methods and measurement procedures. See *Direct observation*.

Subscale: A component of a scale that measures some part or aspect of a major construct; also composed of several items that are logically or empirically structured.

Summated scale: A questionnaire-type scale in which research participants are asked to indicate the degree of their agreement or disagreement with a series of questions.

Summative evaluation: A type of evaluation that examines the ultimate success of a program and assists with decisions about whether a program should be continued or chosen in the first place among program options.

Survey research: A data-collection method that uses survey-type instruments to obtain opinions or answers from a population or sample of research participants in order to describe or study them as a group.

Synthesis: Undertaking the search for meaning in our sources of information at every step of the research process; combining parts such as data, concepts, and theories to arrive at a higher level of understanding.

Systematic: Methodical; used to refer to how the steps of a research study are arranged.

Systematic random sampling: A one-stage probability sampling procedure in which every person at a designated interval in a specific population is selected to be included in a research study's sample.

Systematic error: Measurement error that is consistent, not random.

Target population: The group about which a researcher wants to draw conclusions; another term for a population about which one aims to make inferences.

Target problem: (1) In case-level evaluation designs, the problem social workers seek to solve for their clients. (2) A measurable behavior, feeling, or cognition that is either a problem in itself or symptomatic of some other problem.

Temporal research design: A research study that includes time as a major variable; the purpose of this design is to investigate change in the distribution of a variable or in relationships among variables over time; there are three types of temporal research designs: cohort, panel, and trend.

Temporal stability: Consistency of responses to a measuring instrument over time; reliability of an instrument across forms and across administrations.

Testing effect: The effect that taking a pretest might have on posttest scores; a threat to internal validity.

Test-retest reliability: Reliability of a measuring instrument established through repeated administration to the same group of individuals.

Thematic notes: In observational research, a record of emerging ideas, hypotheses, theories, and conjectures. They provide a place for the researcher to speculate and identify themes, link ideas and events, and articulate thoughts as they emerge in the field setting.

Theme: In a qualitative data analysis, a concept or idea that describes a single category or a grouping of categories; an abstract interpretation of qualitative data.

Theoretical framework: A frame of reference that serves to guide a research study and is developed from theories, findings from a variety of other studies, and the researcher's personal experiences.

Theoretical sampling: See *Purposive sampling*.

Theory: A reasoned set of propositions, derived from and supported by established data, that serves to explain a group of phenomena; a conjectural explanation that may, or may not, be supported by data generated from interpretive and positivist research studies.

Time orientation: An important cultural factor that considers whether one is more focused on the future, the present, or the past. For instance, individuals who are "present- oriented" would not be as preoccupied with advance planning as those who are "future-oriented."

Time-series design: See *Interrupted time-series design*.

Tradition: Traditional cultural beliefs that we accept without question as true; one of the ways of knowing.

Transcript: An electronic, written, printed, or typed copy of interview data or any other written material that have been gathered for an interpretive research study.

Transition statements: Sentences used to indicate a change in direction or focus of questions in a measuring instrument.

Treatment group: See *Experimental group*.

Trend study: A longitudinal study design in which data from surveys carried out at periodic intervals on samples drawn from a particular population are used to reveal trends over time.

Triangulation: The idea of combining different research methods in all steps associated with a single research study; assumes that any bias inherent in one particular method will be neutralized when used in conjunction with other research methods; seeks convergence of a study's results; using more than one research method and source of data to study the same phenomenon and to enhance validity. There are several types of triangulation, but the essence of the term is that multiple perspectives are compared. It can involve multiple data sources or multiple data analyzers; the hope is that the different perspectives will confirm each other, adding weight to the credibility and dependability of qualitative data analysis.

Triangulation of analysts: Using multiple data analysts to code a single segment of a transcript and comparing the amount of agreement between them; a method used to verify coding of qualitative data.

Two-phase research model: A model combining interpretive and positivist research approaches in a single study where each approach is conducted as a separate and distinct phase of the study.

Two-tailed hypotheses: Statements that *do not* predict specific relationships between independent and dependent variables.

Unit of analysis: A specific research participant (person, object, or event) or the sample or population relevant to the research question; the persons or things being studied. Units of analysis in research are often persons, but may be groups, political parties, newspaper editorials, unions, hospitals, schools, etc. A particular unit of analysis from which data are gathered is called a *case*.

Univariate: A hypothesis or research design involving a single variable.

Universe: See *Population*.

Unobtrusive methods: Data-collection methods that do not influence the variable under study or the responses of research participants; methods that avoid reactive effects.

Unstructured interviews: A series of questions that allow flexibility for both the research participant and the interviewer to make changes during the process.

Validity: (1) The extent to which a measuring instrument measures the variable it is supposed to measure and measures it accurately. (2) The degree to which an instrument is able to do what it is intended to do, in terms of both experimental procedures and measuring instruments (internal validity) and generalizability of results (external validity). (3) The degree to which scores on a measuring instrument correlate with measures of performance on some other criterion.

Variable: A concept with characteristics that can take on different values.

Verbatim recording: Recording interview data word for word and including significant gestures, pauses, and expressions of persons in the interview.

Wideband measuring instrument: An instrument that measures more than one variable.

Within-methods research approach: Triangulation by using different research methods available in either the interpretive or the positivist research approaches in a single research study.

Words: The basic data unit of analysis used in interpretive research studies.

Worker cooperation: The actions and attitudes of program personnel when carrying out a research study within an existing program; a criterion for selecting a data-collection method.

Working hypothesis: An assertion about a relationship between two or more variables that may not be true but is plausible and worth examining.

Credits

Boxes: 1.4: From *Calgary Herald*, "Another kidnap bid has parents nervous," September 6, 1991, p. 6; 2.1 & 3.1: From William M.K. Trochim, *Research Methods Knowledge Base*. Retrieved July 22, 2010 at: www.socialresearch methods.net; 2.2: From *Calgary Herald*, "Show ignores Native stereotype," September 6, 1991, Section B, p. 6; 7.1: From Silverman, D. (2010). *Qualitative research* (3rd ed.). Thousand Oaks, CA: Sage; 8.1: Adapted and modified from Kumar, R. (1994). *Research methodology: A step-by-step guide for beginners.* White Plains, NY: Longman; 9.1 & 9.2: From Kyte, N.S., & Bostwick, G.J., Jr. (1981). Measurement. In R.M. Grinnell, Jr. (Ed.), *Social work research and evaluation.* Itasca, IL: F.E. Peacock Publishers; 5.2, 9.3, & 11.1: From McKinney, R. (2011). Research with minority and disadvantaged groups. In R.M. Grinnell, Jr., & Y.A. Unrau (Eds.). *Social work research and evaluation: Foundations of evidence-based practice* (10th ed.). New York: Oxford University Press; and, 13.1–13.3: From *Web Center for Social Research Methods*. Retrieved on July 22, 2017 at: www.socialresearch methods.net.

Figures: 1.5: From Duehn, W.D. (1985). Practice and research. In R.M. Grinnell, Jr. (Ed.), *Social work research and evaluation* (2nd ed.). Itasca, IL: F.E. Peacock; 9.1 & 9.1a: From Walter W. Hudson. Copyright © 1993 by WALMYR Publishing Company; 9.2: From Kyte, N.S., & Bostwick, G.J., Jr. (1981). Measurement. In R.M. Grinnell, Jr. (Ed.), *Social work research and evaluation.* Itasca, IL: F.E. Peacock Publishers; 10.1: From Reid, P.N., & Gundlach, J.H. (1983). A scale for the measurement of consumer satisfaction with social services, *Journal of Social Service Research*, 7, 37–54; 12.8–12.10 (and related text): From Polster, R., & Lynch, M. (1981). Single-subject designs. In R.M. Grinnell, Jr. (Ed.), *Social work research and evaluation*. Itasca: IL: F.E. Peacock Publishers; and 17.3 & 17.4: From Beless, D.W. (1981). Univariate analysis. In R.M. Grinnell, Jr. (Ed.), *Social work research and evaluation.* Itasca, IL: F.E. Peacock Publishers.

Tables: 16.1: From, Debra W. Haffner and Eva S. Goldfarb. "But does it work? Improving evaluations of sexuality education," SIECUS Report, vol. 25, no. 6 (August/September, 1997).

Chapters: 3: by Vivienne Bozalek and Nelleke Bak; 4: (pages 141–161) by Andre Ivanoff and Betty Blythe; 5: by Carol Ing; 8: Adopted and modified from Creswell, J.W., & Plano Clark, V.L. (2007). *Designing and conducting mixed-methods research.* Thousand Oaks, CA: Sage. Reprinted with permission; and 17 & 19: Adapted and modified from Williams, M., Tutty, L.M., & Grinnell, R.M., Jr. (1995). *Research in social work: An introduction* (2nd ed.). Itasca, IL: F.E. Peacock. Reprinted with permission.

References and Further Readings

Ames, G.M., Duke, M.R., Moore, R.S., & Cunradi, C.B. (2009). The impact of occupational culture on drinking behavior of young adults in the U.S. Navy. *Journal of Mixed Methods Research, 3*, 129–150.

Black, T.R. (1999). *Doing quantitative research in the social sciences: An integrated approach to research design, measurement, and statistics*. Thousand Oaks, CA: Sage.

Bloom, M., Fischer, J., & Orme, J. (2009). *Evaluating practice: Guidelines for the accountable professional* (6th ed.). Englewood Cliffs, NJ: Prentice-Hall.

Bostwick, G.J., Jr., & Kyte, N.S. (1981). Measurement. In R.M. Grinnell, Jr. (Ed.), *Social work research and evaluation* (pp. 181–195). Itasca, IL: F.E. Peacock.

Brett, J.A., Heimendinger, J., Boender, C., Morin, C., & Marshall, J.A. (2002). Using ethnography to improve intervention design. *American Journal of Health Promotion, 16(6),* 331-340.

Bronson, D.E. (2009). Critically appraising studies for evidence-based practice. In A. R. Roberts (Ed.). *Social worker's desk reference* (2nd ed., pp. 1137–1141). New York. Oxford University Press.

Calgary Herald: "Another kidnap bid has parents nervous," September 6, 1991, p. 1.

Calgary Herald: "Show ignores Native stereotype," September 6, 1991, Section B, p. 6.

Classen, S., Lopez, D. D. S., Winter, S., Awadz, K.D., Ferree, N., & Garvan, C.W. (2007). Population-based health promotion perspective for older driver safety: Conceptual framework to intervention plan. *Clinical Intervention in Aging, 2,* 677–693.

Coleman, H., & Unrau, Y. (2011). Qualitative data analysis. In R.M. Grinnell, Jr., & Y.A. Unrau (Eds.), *Social work research and evaluation: Foundations of evidence-based practice* (9th ed., pp. 447–464). New York: Oxford University Press.

Colorado State University's Writing Center (2011). http://writing.colostate.edu.

Cooper, H., & Hedges, L.V. (1994). *The handbook of research synthesis*. New York: Russell Sage Foundation.

Cooper, J., Calloway-Thomas, C., & Simonds, C.J. (2007). Non-verbal communication. In P.J. Cooper, C. Calloway-Thomas, & C.J. Simonds (Eds.), *Intercultural communication: A text with readings* (pp. 132–142). Boston: Pearson.

Corcoran, J., & Littell, J.H. (2009). Meta-analysis and evidence-based practice. In A. R. Roberts (Ed.). *Social worker's desk reference* (2nd ed., pp. 1149–1152). New York. Oxford University Press.

Corcoran, K., & Hozack, N. (2010). Locating assessment instruments. In B. Thyer (Ed.). *The handbook of social work research methods* (2nd. ed.). Thousand Oaks, CA: Sage.

Corcoran, K., & Roberts, A.R. (Eds.). (2015). *Social workers' desk reference* (3rd ed.). New York: Oxford University Press.

Council on Social Work Education (2015). *Baccalaureate and masters curriculum policy statements*. Alexandria, VA: Author.

Creswell, J.W. (2010). *Designing and conducting mixed-methods research* (2nd ed.). Thousand Oaks, CA: Sage.

Creswell, J.W., & Plano Clark, V.L. (2007). *Designing and conducting mixed methods research.* Thousand Oaks, CA: Sage.

Donovan, J., Mills, N., Smith, M., Brindle, L., Jacoby, A., Peters, T, et al. (2002). Improving design and conduct of randomized trials by embedding them in qualitative research: ProectT (Prostate Testing for Cancer and Treatment) study. *British Medical Journal, 325,* 766–769.

Doyle, C. (1901/1955). *A treasury of Sherlock Holmes.* Garden City, NY: Hanover House.

Duehn, W.D. (1985). Practice and research. In R.M. Grinnell, Jr. (Ed.), *Social work research and evaluation* (2nd ed., pp. 19–48). Itasca, IL: F.E. Peacock.

Engel, R., & Schutt, K. (2016). *The practice of research in social work* (4th ed.) Thousand Oaks, CA: Sage.

Farmer, J., & Knapp, D. (2008). Interpretation programs at a historic preservation site: A mixed methods study of long-term impact. *Journal of Mixed Methods Research, 2,* 340–361.

Fischer, J. (1981). A framework for evaluating empirical research reports. In R.M. Grinnell, Jr. (Ed*.), Social work research and evaluation* (pp. 347–366). Itasca, IL: F.E. Peacock.

Fischer, J., & Corcoran, K. (2007). *Measures for clinical practice* (3rd ed.). *Volume 1: Couples, families, and children.* Volume 2: *Adults.* New York: Oxford University Press.

Friedmann, B. (2007). *The research tool kit: Putting it all together* (2nd ed.). Belmont, CA: Wadsworth.

Fries, C. J. (2009). Bourdieu's reflexive sociology as a theoretical basis for mixed methods research: An application to complementary and alternative medicine. *Journal of Mixed Methods Research, 3,* 326–348.

Gambrill, E. (2003). Evidence-based practice: Sea change or emperor's new clothes. *Journal of Social Work Education, 39*, 3–23.

Gambrill, E. (2006). Evidence-based practice and policy: Choices ahead. *Research on Social Work Practice, 16*, 338–357.

Gambrill, E. (2009). Integrating information from diverse sources in evidence-based practice. In A. R. Roberts (Ed.). *Social worker's desk reference* (2nd ed., pp. 1120–1126). New York. Oxford University Press.

Gambrill, E., & Gibbs, L. (2009). Developing well-structured questions for evidence-informed practice. In A. R. Roberts (Ed.). *Social worker's desk reference* (2nd ed., pp. 1120–1126). New York. Oxford University Press.

Gochros, H.L. (2018). Qualitative interviewing. In R.M. Grinnell, Jr., & Y.A. Unrau (Eds.), *Social work research and evaluation: Foundations of evidence-based practice* (11th ed.). New York: Oxford University Press.

Greene, J.C. (2007). *Mixed methods in social inquiry.* San Francisco: Jossey-Bass.

Greene, J.C., Caracelli, V.J., & Graham, W.F. (1989). Toward a conceptual framework for mixed-method evaluation designs. *Educational Evaluation and Policy Analysis, 11(3),* 255-274.

Grinnell, F. (1992). *The scientific attitude* (2nd ed.). Boulder, CO: Westview Press.

Grinnell, R.M., Jr. (1981). Becoming a knowledge-based social worker. In R.M. Grinnell, Jr. (Ed.), *Social work research and evaluation* (pp. 1–8). Itasca, IL: F.E. Peacock.

Grinnell, R.M., Jr. (1985). Becoming a practitioner/researcher. In R.M. Grinnell, Jr. (Ed.), *Social work research and evaluation* (5th ed., pp. 3–24). Itasca, IL: F.E. Peacock.

Grinnell, R.M., Jr. (1993). Group research designs. In R.M. Grinnell, Jr. (Ed.), *Social work research and evaluation* (4th ed., pp. 118–153). Itasca, IL: F.E. Peacock.

Grinnell, R.M., Jr. (1995). The generation of knowledge. In R.M. Grinnell, Jr. (Ed.), *Social work research and evaluation* (2nd ed., pp. 1–15). Itasca, IL: F.E. Peacock.

Grinnell, R.M., Jr. (1997a). The generation of knowledge. In R.M. Grinnell, Jr. (Ed.), *Social work research and evaluation: Quantitative and qualitative approaches* (5th ed., pp. 3–24). Itasca, IL: F.E. Peacock.

Grinnell, R.M., Jr. (1997b). Preface. In R.M. Grinnell, Jr. (Ed.), *Social work research and evaluation: Quantitative and qualitative approaches* (5th ed., pp. xvii–xxvi). Itasca, IL: F.E. Peacock.

Grinnell, R.M., Jr., & Siegel, D.H. (1988). The place of research in social work. In R.M. Grinnell, Jr. (Ed.), *Social work research and evaluation* (3rd ed., pp. 9–24). Itasca, IL: F.E. Peacock.

Grinnell, R.M., Jr., & Stothers, M. (1988). Research designs. In R.M. Grinnell, Jr. (Ed.), *Social work research and evaluation* (3rd ed., pp. 199–239). Itasca, IL: F.E. Peacock.

Grinnell, R.M., Jr., & Unrau, Y.A. (Eds.) (2018). *Social work research and evaluation: Foundations of evidence-based practice* (11th ed.). New York: Oxford University Press.

Grinnell, R.M., Jr., & Williams, M. (1990). *Research in social work: A primer.* Itasca, IL: F.E. Peacock.

Grinnell, R.M., Jr., Rothery, M., & Thomlison, R.J. (1993). Research in social work. In R.M. Grinnell, Jr. (Ed.), *Social work research and evaluation* (4th ed., pp. 2–16). Itasca, IL: F.E. Peacock.

Grinnell, R.M., Jr., Williams, M., & Tutty, L.M. (1997). Case-level evaluation. In R.M. Grinnell, Jr. (Ed.), *Social work research and evaluation: Quantitative and qualitative approaches* (5th ed., pp. 529–559). Itasca, IL: F.E. Peacock.

Hall, E.T. (1983). *The dance of life: Other dimensions of time.* New York: Doubleday.

Harris, P.R., & Moran, T. (1996). *Managing cultural differences: Leadership strategies for a new world business* (4th ed.). London: Gulf.

Howard, M.O., Perron, B. E., Vaughn, M.G. (2009). Practice-guidelines and evidence-based practice. In A. R. Roberts (Eds.). *Social worker's desk reference* (2nd ed., pp. 1157–1162). New York. Oxford University Press.

Hudson, W.W. (1982). *The clinical measurement package: A field manual.* Chicago: Dorsey.

Igo, L.B., Kiewra, K.A., & Bruning, R. (2008). Individual differences and intervention flaws: A sequential explanatory study of college students' copy-and-paste note taking. *Journal of Mixed Methods Research, 2,* 149–168.

Ivanoff, A., & Blythe, B. (2018). Research ethics. In R.M. Grinnell, Jr., & Y.A. Unrau (Eds.). *Social work research and evaluation: Foundations of evidence-based practice* (11th ed.). New York: Oxford University Press.

Jick, T.D. (1979). Mixing qualitative and quantitative methods: Triangulation in action. *Administrative Science Quarterly, 24,* 602–611.

Johnson, R.B., & Onwuegbuzie, A.J. (2004). Mixed methods research: A research paradigm whose time has come. *Educational Researcher, 33(7),* 14-26.

Jordan, C., Franklin, C., & Corcoran, K. (2018). Standardized measuring instruments. In R.M. Grinnell, Jr., & Y. Unrau (Eds.), *Social work research and evaluation: Foundations of evidence-based practice* (11th ed.). New York: Oxford University Press.

Knodel, J., & Saengtienchai, C. (2005). Older-aged parents: The final safety net for adult sons and daughters with AIDS in Thailand. *Journal of Family Issues, 26,* 665–698.

Koyama, T. (1992). *Japan: A handbook in intercultural communication.* Sydney: National Center for English Language and Teaching and Research.

Krysik, J., & Finn, J. (2018). *Research for effective social work practice* (4th ed.). New York: Routledge.

Krysik, J., & Grinnell, R.M., Jr. (1997). Quantitative approaches to the generation of knowledge. In R.M. Grinnell, Jr., & Y.A. Unrau (Eds.), *Social work research and evaluation: Quantitative and qualitative approaches* (5th ed., pp. 67–105). Itasca, IL: F.E. Peacock.

Kumar, R. (1994). *Research methodology: A step-by-step guide for beginners.* White Plains, NY: Longman.

Kutner, J.S., Steiner J.F., Corbett, K.K., Jahnigen, D. W., & Barton, PL. (1999). Information needs in terminal illness. *Social Science and Medicine, 48,* 1341–1352.

Lewis, R.D. (1997). *When cultures collide: Managing successfully across cultures.* London: Nicholas Brealey.

Lilienfeld, S.O., Lynn, S.J., Ruscio, J., & Beyerstein, B.L. (2010). *50 great myths of popular psychology.* West Sussex, UK: Wiley-Blackwell.

Littell, J.H., & Corcoran, J. (2009). Systematic reviews and evidence-based practice. In A. R. Roberts (Ed.). *Social worker's desk reference* (2nd ed., pp. 1152–1156). New York. Oxford University Press.

Mak, L., & Marshall, S.K. (2004). Perceived mattering in young adults' romantic relationships. *Journal of Social and Personal Relationships, 24,* 469–486.

Maschi, T., & Youdin, R. (2012). *Social worker as researcher: Integrating research with advocacy.* Boston: Pearson.

Mayring, P. (2007). Introduction: Arguments for mixed methodology. In P. Mayring, G. L. Huber, L. Gurtler, & M. Kiegelmann (Eds.), *Mixed methodology in psychological research* (pp. 1-4). Rotterdam/Taipei: Sense Publishers.

McMahon, S. (2007). Understanding community-specific rape myths: Exploring student athlete culture. *Affilia, 22,* 357–370.

Miles, M.B., & Huberman, A.M. (1994). *Qualitative data analysis: An expanded sourcebook.* Thousand Oaks, CA: Sage.

Monette, D.R., Sullivan, T.J., & DeJong, C.R. (2011). *Applied social research: A tool for the human services.* (8th ed.). Belmont, CA: Brooks/Cole.

Montgomery, P., & Mayo-Wilson, E. (2009). Randomized controlled trials and evidence-based practice. In A. R. Roberts (Ed.). *Social worker's desk reference* (2nd ed., pp. 1142–1148). New York. Oxford University Press.

Mullen, E.J., Bellamy, J.L., & Bledsoe, S.E. (2018). Evidence-based practice. In R.M. Grinnell, Jr., & Y.A. Unrau (Eds.). *Social work research and evaluation: Foundations of evidence-based practice* (11th ed.). New York: Oxford University Press.

National Association of Social Workers. (2017). *Code of ethics.* Silver Spring, MD: Author.

Neuman, W.L. (2012). *Basics of social research: Qualitative and quantitate approaches* (3rd ed.). Boston: Pearson.

Plano Clark, V.L. (2005). *Cross-disciplinary analysis of the use of mixed methods in physics education research, counseling psychology, and primary care.* Doctoral dissertation, University of Nebraska at Lincoln, 2005. Dissertation Abstracts International, 66, 02A.

Plano Clark, V.L. (2010). The adoption and practice of mixed methods: U.S. trends in federally funded health-related research. *Qualitative Inquiry.* Prepublished April 15, 2010, DOI:10.1177/1077800410364609

Plano Clark, V.L. (2010). The adoption and practice of mixed methods: U.S. trends in federally funded health-related research. *Qualitative Inquiry.* DOI:10.1177/1077800410364609

Plano Clark, V.L., & Badiee, M. (2010). Research questions in mixed methods research. In A. Tashakkori & C. Teddlie (Eds.), *SAGE Handbook of mixed methods in social & behavioral research* (2nd ed.). Thousand Oaks, CA: Sage.

Plano Clark, V.L., & Creswell, J.W. (2010). *Understanding research: A consumer's guide.* Upper Saddle River, NJ: Pearson Education.

Plano Clark, V.L., & Galt, K. (2009, April). *Using a mixed methods approach to strengthen instrument development and validation.* Paper presented at the annual meeting of the American Pharmacists Association, San Antonio, TX.

Plano Clark, V.L., & Wang, S.C. (2010). Adapting mixed methods research to multicultural counseling. In J. G. Ponterotto, J. M. Casas, L. A. Suzuki, & C. M. Alexander (Eds.), *Handbook of multicultural counseling* (3rd ed., pp. 427–438). Thousand Oaks, CA: Sage.

Plano Clark, V.L., Huddleston-Casas, C.A., Churchill, S.L., Green, D.0., & Garrett, A.L. (2008). Mixed methods approaches in family science research. *Journal of Family Issues, 29,* 1543–1566.

Polster, R.A., & Collins, D. (2018). Structured observation. In R.M. Grinnell, Jr., & Y.A. Unrau (Eds.), *Social work research and evaluation: Foundations of evidence-based practice* (11th ed.). New York: Oxford University Press.

Porter, R.E., & Samovar, L.A. (2006). Understanding intercultural communication: An overview. In L.A. Samovar, R.E. Porter, & E.R. McDaniel (Eds.), *Intercultural communication: A reader* (11th ed., pp. 6–16). Belmont, CA: Wadsworth.

Punch. K.F. (2009). *Introduction to research methods in education.* Thousand Oaks, CA: Sage.

Raines, J.C. (2011). Evaluating qualitative research studies. In R.M. Grinnell, Jr., & Y.A. Unrau (Eds.), *Social work research and evaluation: Foundations of evidence-based practice* (9th ed., pp. 488–503). New York: Oxford University Press.

Reid, W.J., & Smith, A.D. (1989). *Research in social work* (2nd ed.). New York: Columbia University Press.

Rosen, A. (2003). Evidence-based social work practice: Challenges and promise. *Social Work Research, 27,* 197–208.

Royse, D., Thyer, B., & Padgett, D. (2009). *Program evaluation: An introduction.* Belmont, CA: Wadsworth.

Rubin, A., & Babbie, E. (2017). *Research methods for social work* (9th ed.). New York: Cengage.

Rubin, A., & Parrish, D. (2009). Locating credible studies for evidence-based practice. In A. R. Roberts (Ed.). *Social worker's desk reference* (2nd ed., pp. 1127–1136). New York. Oxford University Press.

Sackett, D.L., Rosenberg, W.M.C., Muir Gray, J.A., Haynes, R.B., & Richardson, W.S. (1996). Evidence-based medicine: What it is and what it isn't: It's about integrating individual clinical expertise and the best external evidence. *British Medical Journal, 31,* 71–72.

Sackett, D.L., Straus, S.E., Richardson, W.S., Rosenberg, W., & Haynes, R.B. (2000). *Evidence based medicine: How to practice and teach EBM* (2nd ed.). New York: Churchill Living.

Samovar, L.A., Porter, R.E., & Stefani, L.A. (1998). *Communication between cultures.* Belmont, CA: Wadsworth.

Sayre, K. (2002). *Guidelines and best practices for culturally-competent evaluations.* Denver, CO: The Colorado Trust.

Schutt, R. (2008). *Investigating the social world: The process and practice of research* (6th ed.). Thousand Oaks, CA: Pine Forge Press.

Sieppert, J.D., McMurtry, S.L., & McClelland, R.W. (2011). Utilizing existing statistics. In R.M. Grinnell, Jr., & Y.A. Unrau (Eds.), *Social work research and evaluation: Foundations of evidence-based practice* (9th ed., pp. 389–401). New York: Oxford University Press.

Straus, S.E., Richardson, W.S., Glasziou, P., & Haynes, R.B. (2005). *Evidence-based medicine: How to practice and teach EBM* (3rd ed.). New York: Elsevier/Churchill Livingstone.

Stuart, P. (2011). Historical research. In R.M. Grinnell, Jr., & Y.A. Unrau (Eds.), *Social work research and evaluation: Foundations of evidence-based practice* (9th ed., pp. 402–412). New York: Oxford University Press.

Tashakkori, A., & Creswell, J.W. (2007). Exploring the nature of research questions in mixed methods research [Editorial]. *Journal of Mixed Methods Research, 1(3),* 207-2 11.

Tashakkori, A., & Teddlie, C. (1998). *Mixed methodology: Combining qualitative and quantitative approaches.* Thousand Oaks, CA: Sage.

Tashakkori, A., & Teddlie, C. (Eds.). (2003). *Handbook of mixed methods in social & behavioral research.* Thousand Oaks, CA: Sage.

Tashiro, J. (2002). Exploring health promoting lifestyle behaviors of Japanese college women: Perceptions, practices, and issues. *Health Care for Women International, 23,* 59-70.

Thomas, D.C., & Inkson, K. (2009). *Cultural intelligence: Living and working globally* (2nd ed.). San Francisco: Berrett-Koehler.

Thyer, B.A., & Myers, L.L. (2007). *A social worker's guide to evaluating practice outcomes.* Alexandria VA: Council on Social Work Education.

Thyer, B.A., & Myers, L.L. (2009). *N* = 1 experiments and their role in evidence-based practice. In A. R. Roberts (Ed.). *Social worker's desk reference* (2nd ed., pp. 1176–1182). New York. Oxford University Press.

Thyer B.A., & Myers, L.L. (2010). Cultural diversity and social work practice: An evidenced-based approach. In B.A. Thyer, J.S. Wodarski, L. Myers, & D.F. Harrison (Eds.). *Human diversity and social work practice: An evidenced-based approach* (3rd ed., pp. 3–28). Springfield, IL: Charles C. Thomas.

Thyer, B.A, & Pignotti, M.G. (2015). *Science and pseudoscience in social work practice.* New York: Springer.

Tutty, L.M., Grinnell, R.M., & Williams, M. (1997). Research problems and questions. In R.M. Grinnell, Jr. (Ed.), *Social work research and evaluation: Quantitative and qualitative approaches* (5th ed., pp. 49–66). Itasca, IL: F.E. Peacock.

Tutty, L.M., Rothery, M.L., & Grinnell, R.M., Jr. (Eds.). (1996). *Qualitative research for social workers: Phases, steps, and tasks.* Boston: Allyn & Bacon.

Unrau, Y.A. (2011). Selecting a data collection method and data source. In R.M. Grinnell, Jr., & Y.A. Unrau (Eds.), *Social work research and evaluation: Foundations of evidence-based practice* (9th ed., pp. 413–426). New York: Oxford University Press.

Weinbach, R.W., & Grinnell, R.M., Jr. (2015). *Statistics for social workers* (9th ed.). New York: Pearson.

Weine, S., Knafi, K., Feetham, S., Kulauzovic, Y, Klebic, A., Sclove, S., et al. (2005). A mixed methods study of refugee families engaging in multiple-family groups. *Family Relations, 54,* 558-568.

Weine, S., Knafi, K., Feetham, S., Kulauzovic, Y, Klebic, A., Sclove, S., et al. (2005). A mixed methods study of refugee families engaging in multiple-family groups. *Family Relations, 54,* 558–568.

Williams, M., Grinnell, R.M., Jr., & Tutty, L.M. (1997). Research contexts. In R.M. Grinnell, Jr. (Ed.), *Social work research and evaluation: Quantitative and qualitative approaches* (5th ed., pp. 25–45). Itasca, IL: F.E. Peacock.

Williams, M., Tutty, L.M., & Grinnell, R.M., Jr. (1995). *Research in social work: An introduction* (2nd ed.). Itasca, IL: F.E. Peacock.

Williams, M., Unrau, Y.A., & Grinnell, R.M., Jr. (1998). *Introduction to social work research* (3rd ed.). Itasca, IL: F.E. Peacock.

Wodarski, J.S., Hopson, L. M. (2012). *Research methods for evidence-based practice.* Thousand Oaks, CA: Sage.

Yegidis, B.L., Weinbach, R.W., & Myers, L.L. (2018). *Research methods for social workers* (8th ed.). New York: Pearson.

Index

A design, 411–412
AB design, 417–418
ABA design, 419–421
ABAB design, 419–421
ABC design, 418
ABCD design, 418
Abstract section, within qualitative research reports, 722–723
Accountability, toward, 5–9
Adapting processes, 190–191
Adapting research studies, 189
Administration section:
    within qualitative research proposals, 717–719
    within quantitative research proposals, 674–675
Advantages of the qualitative research approach, 271
Alternate-form method, as a form of reliability, 321
Analysis and findings section, within qualitative research reports, 723–725
Analysis of covariance, 447

Analysis of data, 233–235
Analyzing data, 560–562
Anonymity, promising, 140–141
ANOVA, 612–613
Applicability, within qualitative research proposals, 706–709
Applied research:
    questions, 67–70
    studies, 35–36
Archival data, as a data-collection method, 569
Assent form, 138–139
Assigning codes to categories for qualitative data, 637–638
Attitude of researchers, 45–46
Attributes of variables, 218–224
Audience, of qualitative research proposals, 698–699
Authority, as a way of knowing, 9–13
Availability sampling, 382

B design, 412–414
BAB design, 421–422
BB₁ design, 415–416

BC design, 416

Beliefs, as a way of knowing, 16–18

Biases, researcher, 628–629

Bribery, use of, 129–130

Category creation for qualitative data, 636–637

Causality-comparative interaction research questions, 91

Causality-comparative research questions, 91

Central tendency, measures of, 601–603

Checklist, 348, 354

Chi-square, 609–611

Classification of research questions, 87–91

Cluster random sampling, 380–381

Coercion, use of, 129–130

Cohort studies, 460–462

Collecting data, 232

Communication:

intercultural, 180–181

nonverbal, 181

Comparison group:

posttest-only design, 480–482

pretest-posttest design, 478–480

Compensatory equalization, as a threat to internal validity, 477

Compensatory rivalry, as a threat to internal validity, 477

Competencies, CSWE, 5–7

Composition research questions, 88–89

Concepts, development of, 217–218

Conceptual classification systems for qualitative data, 641–643

Conceptual frameworks:

within qualitative research proposals, 701–702

within quantitative research proposals, 664–665

Concurrent validity, 325

Confidentiality, promising, 140–141

Confirmability, within qualitative research proposals, 706–709

Consent form, 130–137

Consistency, within qualitative research proposals, 706–709

Constant errors, 330–331

Construct validity, 326–328

Content validity, 323–324

Contributing partner, 40–41

Control groups, using, 447–448

Correlated variation, 446

Correlation, 611–612

Correspondence, as used in measurement, 312

Creator and disseminator of knowledge, 38–40

Credibility, within qualitative research proposals, 706–708

Criteria of a good literature review, 117–118

Criterion validity, 324–326

Cross-sectional survey design, 455–456

CSWE competencies, 5–7

Cultural awareness, 187

Cultural:

considerations in research, 77–78

frameworks, 182186

issues, 241

sensitivity and sampling, 384–385

Culturally competent research, 172–203

Culturally-sensitive research questions, 93–94

Culture gap, bridging, 178–182

Data analysis section:

within qualitative research proposals, 714

within quantitative research proposals, 673

Data collection method, selection of, 554–589

Data collection section, within qualitative research proposals, 712–713

Data collection, 232, 241:

qualitative, 528–552

quantitative, 448–526

within quantitative research proposals, 672–673

Data source, insufficient, 287–288

Data sources, 500–501

Data, analysis of, 233–235

Data, analyzing:

qualitative, 624–656

quantitative, 592–623

Data:

entering into computers, 595–596

secondary, 513–516

types of, 501–503

Deception, use of, 129–130

Decision making, 183

Demoralization, as a threat to internal validity, 478

Dependability, within qualitative research proposals, 706–709

Dependent *t*-tests, 613–614

Dependent variables, creating, 224–227

Descriptive research:

    descriptive-comparative research questions, 89

    designs, 417–418

    research studies, 84–85

    statistics, 233–234, 596–606

Developing concepts, 217–218

Diaries, 352–353

Differential selection of research participants, as a threat to internal validity, 473–474

Diffusion of treatments, as a threat to internal validity, 477

Directional hypotheses, 226–227

Disadvantages of the qualitative research approach, 272–273

Discussion section:

within qualitative research reports, 725–726

within quantitative research reports, 685

Disseminating findings, 244

Document analysis, as a data-collection method, 568

Duplication, as used in measurement,

Enculturation, 179–180

Errors:

    constant, 330–331

    random, 331–334

Ethical considerations in research, 77–78, 124–171, 241

Ethically-sensitive research questions, 93–94

Ethnocentrism, 179

Evidence-based practice process, 46–51

Existence research questions, 86

Existing statistics, 517–521

Experience, as a way of knowing, 15–16

Experiments, ideal, 441–451

Explanatory research designs, 86–87, 419–428

Exploratory research designs, 82–84, 409–416

External validity, 485–488

Extraneous variables, 445–446

Face validity, 326

Feasibility of research questions, 93

Findings sections, within quantitative research reports, 681–684

Findings, interpreting research, 235

First-level coding for qualitative data, 634–639

Focus groups, as a data-collection method, 566

Frequency distribution, 599–600

Funding requirements, fulfilling, 165

General problem area, refining, 217, 238–239

Historical data, 543–546, 569

History, as a threat to internal validity, 468–470

Honesty, 45

Hudson's *Index of Self-Esteem,* 314–315

Hypotheses:

    directional, 226–227

    evaluation of, 227–230

    nondirectional., 226–227

    within qualitative research proposals, 703–704

    within quantitative research proposals, 665

Ideal experiments, 441–451

Identifying meaning units for qualitative data, 635

Impact of culture on research studies, 176–177

Impressions, formulating, 237

Independent *t*-tests, 614–615

Independent variables:

    creating, 224–227

    manipulation of, 443–444

Individualism, 183184

Inferential statistics, 234–235, 607–617

Informed consent, obtaining, 128–139

Initial impressions, formulating, 237

Instrumentation error, as a threat to internal validity, 472

Instruments, measuring, 342–368

Interaction effects, as a threat to internal validity, 476

Intercultural communication skills, 180–181, 187–188

Internal validity, 468–478

Internet, as used in literature reviews, 108–109

Interpreting data, 560–562

Interpretive way of thinking, 252–256
Interval measurement, 309–310
Interviewing, narrative, 532–537
Introduction section, within qualitative research reports, 723
Intuition, as a way of knowing, 16–19
Intuitive research methods, 281
Inventories, 353–354
Inventory, example, 347
Inview, as used in literature reviews, 111–112

Journals, 352–353
Justifying decisions already made, 163–164

Knowing, ways of, 9–25
Knowledge levels, 440–441
Knowledge-development, approaches to, 205–302
Knowledge-level continuum, 80–87

Lifelong learning, 52–53
Limitations section:
    within qualitative research proposals, 714–717
    within quantitative research proposals, 673–674
    within quantitative research reports, 685–687
Literature reviews:
Logic of, 104–107
    within qualitative research proposals, 701
    within quantitative research proposals, 663–664
    writing, 102–123
Logs, 353
Longitudinal designs, 456–464

Managing information in literature reviews, 109–110
Matched-pairs method, 449–451
Maturation, as a threat to internal validity, 470
Mean, 604
Measurement error, 330–334
Measurement, 20–21,304–341
Measurement, levels of, 306–311
Measures of central tendency, 601–603
Measures of variability, 604–607
Measuring instruments, 342–368

Measuring objectives, 405–409
Median, 604
Member checks, within qualitative research proposals, 707
Methods section:
    within qualitative research reports, 723
    within quantitative research reports, 679–681
Methodology, within quantitative research proposals, 666–673
Mixed-methods research approach, 32, 278–301:
    advantages, 292–293
    challenges, 294–296
    definition, 282–284
    finding studies, 297
Mode, 603–604
Mortality, as a threat to internal validity, 474–475
Multiple-baseline designs, 422–428
Multiple-treatment interference, as a threat to external validity, 487

Narrative interviewing, 532–537
NASW principles, 7–9
Negative case analysis, within qualitative research proposals, 707
Neutrality, within qualitative research proposals, 706–709
Nominal measurement, 308
Nondirectional hypotheses, 226–227
Nonprobability sampling, 381–385
Nonreactivity, as a criterion for selection of a measuring instrument, 318–319
Nonverbal communication, 181
Normal curve, 606
Normal distribution, variations of, 608

Observation, participant, 537–541
Observations, 20–21, 508–513
Observer reliability, as a form of reliability, 322
One-group posttest-only design, 452–454
One-group pretest-posttest design, 464–467
One-group research designs, 452–478
One-tailed hypotheses, 226–227
One-to-one interviews:
    (general), as a data-collection method, 565

(semi-structured), as a data-collection method, 565

(structured), as a data-collection method, 556

(unstructured), as a data-collection method, 565

One-way analysis of variance, 615–617

Online surveys, as a data-collection method, 571

Operational definitions:
    within qualitative research proposals, 704–706
    within quantitative research proposals, 667–671

Ordinal measurement, 308–309

Organizing a literature review, 113–117

Orientation to data, 183

Overview, as used in literature reviews, 111

Pace of life, 185–186

Panel studies, 462–464

Participant observation, 537–541

Phases of the qualitative research process, 256–265

Phone interviews, as a data-collection method, 566

Political considerations in research 78–80

Population section:
    defining, 373
    within qualitative research proposals, 708–712
    within quantitative research proposals, 671–672

Positivistic way of thinking, 208–213

Predictive validity, 325–326

Presentation of findings, 562

Pretest-treatment interaction, as a threat to external validity, 485

Preview, as used in literature reviews, 110–111

Principles, NASW, 7–9

Probability sampling, 375–381

Problem section, within quantitative research reports, 677–679

Problem-solving process, 39

Providing meaningful products, 191–192

Public relations, 164

Pure research questions, 33–35, 65–67

Purposive sampling, 382

Qualitative research approach, 30–31, 213–244, 250–277, 268–269

Qualitative research reports, writing, 721–726

Quantification, as used in measurement, 313

Quantitative data, collection of, 448–526

Quantitative research approach, 29–30, 206–249

Quantitative research proposals, development of, 658–692

Quantitative research reports, 658–692

Questionnaires, as a data-collection method, 564

Questionnaires, survey, 503–508

Questions, within qualitative research proposals, 703–704

Quota sampling, 382–383

Random assignment, 448–451

Random errors, 331–334

Randomized posttest-only control group design, 483–484

Range, 605

Ratio measurement, 310–311

Reactive effects of research participants, as a threat to internal validity, 475–476

Reactive effects, as a threat to external validity, 486

Reality, perceptions of, 253–254

References section, within qualitative research reports, 726

Referential adequacy, within qualitative research proposals, 707

Reid-Gundlach *Social Service-Satisfaction Scale*, 350

Relations between experimental and control groups, as a threat to internal validity, 476–478

Relationship research questions, 89

Relevancy of research questions, 92

Reliability of outcome measures, 406–409

Reliability, 319–322

Reliability, as a criterion for selection of a measuring instrument, 319–320

Reliability, improving, 334–335

Research approaches, comparison of, 32, 265–267

Research consumer, 38
Research designs:
  within qualitative research proposals, 706–708
  within quantitative research proposals, 666–667
Research ethics, 124–171
Research findings:
  interpreting, 235
  presentation of, 562
Research participants, 126–127, 254–255
Research process, 402–403
Research questions:
  applied, 65–67
  criteria for, 92–94
  formulation of, 64–98
  pure, 65–67
  within quantitative research proposals, 665
Research reports:
  quantitative, 658–692
  writing, 675–687
Research roles, integration of, 41–42
Research studies:
  applied, 35–36
  designing in an ethical manner, 141–160
  pure, 33–35
  subjects, 254–255
Research topic:
  selection of, 557–558
  within qualitative research proposals, 700
  within quantitative research proposals, 662–663
Researchability of research questions, 92–93
Researcher bias, as a threat to external validity, 487
Researchers, characteristics of, 42–45
Researchers:
  attitudes, 45–46
  culturally competent, 186–194
  values, 255–256
Retrospective baselines, 428–429
Reversal designs, 419–422
Rival hypotheses, 444–445
Rules for qualitative data analysis, 632–634

Sample:
  deciding on a, 231

quality, 390–391
  sample section, within qualitative research proposals, 708–712
  selection, 240
  size, 385–387
  within quantitative research proposals, 671–672
Sampling frames, 374
Scale, 348
Scientific method:
  approaches to, 25–32
  as a way of knowing, 18–25
  phase of, 19–20
Searching for information, 108
Second-level coding for qualitative data, 639–640
Secondary analysis, as a data-collection method, 570
Secondary content data, 541–543
Secondary data, 513–516
Selection-treatment interaction, as a threat to external validity, 485–486
Sensitivity to small changes, as a criterion for selection of a measuring instrument, 318
Sharing, 44
Simple inventory, 347
Simple random sampling, 375–376
Single-subject designs, 398–437
Skeptical curiosity, 43–44
Snowball sampling, 383
Social considerations in research 78–80
Social service programs, ethics of, 161–165
Social work practice process, 36–37
Social work research process, 36–37
Social work research:
  definition of, 53–54
  purpose of, 23–25
Specificity of variables, as a threat to external validity, 486
Split-half method, as a form of reliability, 321
Staff performance, appraising, 164–165
Stakeholders, working with, 175–176, 189–190
Standard deviation, 605607
Standardization, as used in measurement, 312–313
Standardized measuring instruments, 356–359

Statistical regression, as a threat to internal validity, 472–473

Statistics, existing, 517–521

Storing information in literature reviews, 109–110

Stratified random sampling, 378–380

Striving toward duplication, 212–213

Striving toward objectivity, 209–210

Striving toward reducing uncertainty, 211

Structured observations, 508–513

Summative instruments, 355–356

Survey questionnaires, 503–508

Systematic random sampling, 377–378

t-tests:

    dependent, 613–614

    independent, 614–615

Target problems, 405–406

Test-retest method as a form of reliability, 320

Testing effects, as a threat to internal validity, 471

Time-order of variables, 442–443

Tradition, as a way of knowing, 13–15

Transcribing qualitative data, 629–632

Transferability, within qualitative research proposals, 706–709

Trend studies, 457–459

Triangulation of data sources, within qualitative research proposals, 707

Trustworthiness of qualitative data, 641–648

Truth-value, within qualitative research proposals, 706–709

Two-group designs, 478–484

Two-tailed hypotheses, 226–227

Types of data, 501–503

Unit of analysis, 403–404

Utility, as a criterion for selection of a measuring instrument, 317–318

Validity, 322–329

Validity, improving, 334–335

Value awareness, 43

Value systems, the researcher, 75–76

Variables:

    dependent, 224–227

    independent, 224–227

    measurement of, 230–231, 239–240

    relationships between, 444

    selection, of, 215–216

    time order of, 442–443

    within concepts, finding, 218

Ways of knowing, 9–25

A History of the Jews
in the Modern World

A History of the Jews in the Modern World

in the Modern World

———❖———

Howard M. Sachar

Alfred A. Knopf
New York
2005

THIS IS A BORZOI BOOK
PUBLISHED BY ALFRED A. KNOPF

Copyright © 2005 by Daniel A. Sachar

All rights reserved. Published in the United States by Alfred
A. Knopf, a division of Random House, Inc., New York,
and in Canada by Random House of Canada Limited, Toronto.
www.aaknopf.com
Portions of this book were originally published in *The Course of Modern Jewish
History* in 1958 by World Pub. Co. Cleveland, and revised edition in 1990
by Vintage Books, a division of Random House, Inc., New York.
Knopf, Borzoi Books, and the colophon are registered trademarks
of Random House, Inc.

Library of Congress Cataloging-in-Publication Data
Sachar, Howard Morley, [date].
A history of the Jews in the modern world / Howard M. Sachar.— 1st ed.
p.   cm.
"This is a Borzoi Book"—CIP galley
Includes bibliographical references and index.
ISBN 0-375-41497-5
1. Jews—History—17th century.   2. Jews—History—18th century.
3. Jews—History—1789–1945.   4. Jews—History—1945–   I. Title.
DS124.S18 2005
909'.04924—dc22   2004048814

Printed in the United States of America
First Edition

For Talia

Contents

Foreword   xi

I	*The Jew as Non-European*	3
II	*A Glimmering of Dawn in the West*	18
III	*An Ambivalent Emancipation in the West*	34
IV	*Incarceration: The Jews of Tsarist Russia*	51
V	*The Triumph of Emancipation in the West*	73
VI	*Jews in an Emancipated Economy*	100
VII	*The Impact of Western Culture on Jewish Life*	120
VIII	*A Sephardic-Oriental Diaspora*	138
IX	*The Rise of Jewish Life in America*	155
X	*False Dawn in the East: Alexander II and the Era of "Enlightenment"*	175
XI	*Russian Twilight: The Era of Pogroms and May Laws*	193
XII	*A Migration of East European Jewry: 1881–1914*	207
XIII	*The Onset of Modern Antisemitism*	222
XIV	*The Mutation of Racism*	242
XV	*The Rise of Zionism*	255
XVI	*The Evolution of Jewish Radicalism: Tsarist Russia*	284
XVII	*Socialist "Internationalism" in Western Europe: The Trauma of World War I*	310
XVIII	*The Triumph of Bolshevism*	323
XIX	*The Balfour Declaration and the Jewish National Home*	344
XX	*The Legacy of Progressivism: Immigrant Jewry in the United States*	370
XXI	*Successor States and Minority Guarantees: 1919–1939*	399

XXII	*The Triumph of East European Fascism*	418
XXIII	*A Final Symbiosis of Jewish and Western Culture*	444
XXIV	*A Climactic Onslaught of Postwar Antisemitism*	469
XXV	*The Triumph of Nazism*	492
XXVI	*The Quest for Sanctuary: 1933–1939*	514
XXVII	*The Holocaust of European Jewry*	527
XXVIII	*The* Final Solution *and the Struggle for Jewish Survival*	551
XXIX	*The Birth of Israel*	572
XXX	*Eastern Jewry in the Postwar: A Failed Convalescence*	595
XXXI	*A Precarious Revival in Western Europe*	629
XXXII	*The Jews of British Commonwealth*	648
XXXIII	*A Latin Israel in the Southern Hemisphere*	668
XXXIV	*The Efflorescence of American-Jewish Community*	685
XXXV	*The Jewish State and World Jewry*	702
XXXVI	*Israel, the United States, and the Struggle for Soviet Jewry*	717
	Afterword	736
	Bibliography	745
	Index	787

A Note About Style

Although proper names have been rendered for the most part in their native spellings, readers will note occasional asymmetries. This is by design, in an effort to avoid confusion, or at least irritation. Who remembers Prussia's King Frederick II (the Great) as Friedrich II? Conversely, who encounters Imperial Germany's Kaiser Wilhelm II as William II? Or Austria's beloved Emperor Franz Josef as Francis Joseph? Native spellings have been used for a majority of Russian names, yet it would similarly be counterproductive to list Tsar Nicholas as Tsar Nikolai, Tsar Alexander as Tsar Aleksandr, Alexander Kerensky as Aleksandr Kerenski, or Leon Trotsky as Lev Trotski.

By the same token, the Hebrew (or Yiddish) "chet," pronounced from the back of the palate, often is transliterated as "ch," as in the Hebrew proper name Chaim. While "Chaim" actually has been left intact, due to universal reader familiarity with Chaim Weizmann, the "chet" otherwise is spelled with an "h." This simplifies usage for such terms as Hasidim, Halutzim, and Hovevei Zion.

In short, the rule of thumb in nomenclature has been to select familiarity over consistency.

Foreword

During the past half-century, the scholarship devoted to modern Jewish history has grown exponentially. Indeed, few peoples of such limited numbers have evoked a comparable effulgence of research and publication. There is logic in the seeming imbalance. Notwithstanding their modest demography, the Jews have functioned not simply as the anvil for the hammers of other, larger, and more powerful nations. They have generated a formidable musculature in their own right. Whether in economics, politics, culture, diplomacy, or even warfare, their role over the past three centuries looms strikingly out of proportion to their attenuated critical mass.

In chronicling the modern fate and fortune of the Jews, I have made every effort to give appropriate attention to the rise of Zionism and the Jewish National Home in Palestine. Nevertheless, the reader will observe that the State of Israel is not discussed in this volume, except in its relationship specifically to Jews living beyond Israel's frontiers. The omission is deliberate. The history of an independent nation deserves independent treatment.

A predecessor of this volume, *The Course of Modern Jewish History*, was published in 1958. While the "matrix" of that earlier work resembles the structure of this one, the similarity ends there. I venture to hope that my authorial judgment over the ensuing decades, like the discipline of Jewish historiography itself, has matured sufficiently to profit from the extensive research and self-sacrifice of others. It requires only a glance at the enclosed bibliography to grasp the magnitude of my debt to authorities in the field. Some of my fellow historians have read draft chapters of this book and have generously offered their corrections and suggestions. I am most grateful to Professor Michael Berkowitz of University College, London, for his commentary on material relating to antisemitism. At my own institution, George Washington University, colleagues deserving of warm thanks are Professor Muriel Atkin, for chapters relating to Tsarist Russia and the Soviet Union; Professor R. Emmett Kennedy, for issues relating to France; Professor Andrew Zimmerman, for chapters dealing with Germany; Professor Robert Paul Churchill, for material relating to modern European philosophy; and, assuredly not least, Professor Marc Saperstein, for chapters ranging from Jewish intellectual and religious developments to the Holocaust.

Mr. Michael Whine, director of England's Community Security Trust, has been an indispensable source of information on the circumstances of contemporary Anglo-Jewry, even as Rabbi Andrew Baker, director of International Jewish Affairs for the American Jewish Committee, has graciously facilitated my contacts with agencies and institutions in Jewish communities worldwide. Special mention here must also be made of Dr. David Ettinger, social science research director at the George Washington University Library, for help in tracking down foreign titles; and of Ms. Ann Kort, who volunteered her extensive editorial experience to proofread my manuscript. I include herewith the author's customary exoneration of others' responsibility for the book's errors.

It is no longer possible to thank the many scores of individuals who contributed to my earlier publishing efforts, and in the process enriched the "database" and influenced many of the conclusions of this one. Nevertheless, ongoing relationships deserve ongoing acknowledgment and gratitude: to Ms. Jane Garrett of Alfred A. Knopf, my friend and forbearing editor of over thirty-six years; and to my co-researcher and intellectual muse of more than forty-one years, Eliana Steimatzky Sachar, my wife.

HMS
Kensington, Maryland
June 7, 2004

A History of the Jews
in the Modern World

I

The Jew as Non-European

A TREMULOUS MINORITY

In the eighteenth century, a majestic silhouette of battlements and spires greeted the traveler who made his way down the valley of the lower Main River. It was the profile of Frankfurt, one of the four remaining free cities of the Holy Roman Empire, and one of the German world's three most important commercial entrepôts. Frankfurt's cobblestoned streets teemed with movement, with shouting hucksters, bawling cattle driven in for sale and slaughter, rattling vegetable carts pushed along to market, paunchy burghers and weather-beaten farmers arguing the cost and quality of produce. But as the traveler continued down the main Sachsenhäuser Bridge into the city's principal business center, pausing occasionally to sample the wares in shops and pavilions, stalls and warehouses, he found his way barred by the Börheimertor, a large wooden gate demarcating still another townlet within the larger urban area, a ganglion of twisting alleys, ramshackle storefronts and cramped apartment structures. The gate's solitary entrance, guarded by an armed warden, suggested that a prison community may have been locked inside. The notion was not entirely far-fetched. The little enclosure was the *Judengasse*, the ghetto of the Jews.

The ghetto of Frankfurt-am-Main, and comparable enclaves in scores of other towns and cities throughout West-Central Europe, evinced a central fact of Jewish life well into the Modern Era. This was the Jews' indeterminate status as non-Europeans. It is fair to speculate, then, whether the Jews were foreigners or interlopers. Were they voluntary immigrants newly arrived from other lands or continents? Or had they been transported to Europe as captives, as African slaves had been imported to the New World? None of these descriptions would have been apt. The Jews were neither recent slaves nor recent immigrants. Most, rather, were descended from ancestors who had lived on European soil for many hundreds of years, in some instances as far back as the Roman Empire. In the German world, their settlement traced back at least to the eleventh century, and in Frankfurt itself to the twelfth century, when some two hundred Jews took up residence in the squalid little encincture beyond the Börheimertor. Even this initial settlement in Frankfurt was intermittently curtailed. In the fourteenth century, the city's inhabitants, and those of other German communities, were ravaged by the bubonic plague. Afterward, it became the custom to attribute the "Black Death" to the Jews, the "wizards," the "devils," who had survived the epidemic in inexplicably greater numbers than their neighbors (possibly owing to Judaic hygienic regulations). In their fear and rage, local populations in ensuing years hurled themselves into a succession of anti-Jewish massacres. Those Jews who escaped Christian mobs fled eastward, most of them ultimately to settle in Polish and other Slavic territories (p. 9ff.).

In the sixteenth century, small numbers of Jews ventured a return to Central Europe. Their reception was not congenial—not in an age of religious turmoil. This time, they encountered the animus of Protestant Reformers and Catholic Counter-Reformers alike. The obloquy that attached to their presence was revealed in an obscene sixteenth-century graffito carved into Frankfurt's ghetto wall. It revealed a trio of Jews debasing themselves around a sow. As one Jew suckled at the animal's teats, another (in rabbinical garb) lifted the *Judensau's* tail, allowing the third (also a rabbi) to drink the animal's excrement. Several feet higher on the ghetto wall an even more repellent carving appeared, this one of a dead baby, its body punctured by countless miniature knife wounds, and beneath its corpse an array of nine daggers. The caption read, "On Maundy Thursday in the year 1475, the little child Simon, aged two, was killed by the Jews." The inscription alluded to the death of Simon of Trent, allegedly a victim of Jewish "ritual murder." In Frankfurt, these graphic expressions of Jew-hatred dated back at least to the fourteenth century, and in France to the twelfth century, when the myth first became current that Jews were enjoined by their religion to slay Christian maidens and children, whose blood was presumed necessary for the Passover festival. Thus diabolized, most Jews would not risk setting foot in Central Europe until the latter seventeenth century. Only then, with religious passions largely exhausted following the carnage of the Thirty Years' War, did Habsburg Emperor Ferdinand III allow substantial numbers of Jews to resettle in Prague and Budapest and in such imperial "free" cities as Frankfurt; and other German princes also then relaxed their bans on Jews.

Nevertheless, throughout the Habsburg Empire and the German principalities alike, numerous towns, districts, and duchies continued to exclude Jews. Some municipalities admitted Jews, some did not. Even in Leipzig, where Jews played an important role in the city's great fairs, it was not until 1713 that a single Jewish family was permitted to settle permanently, and forty more years passed before a second one was admitted. Official policy was continually in flux. Vienna's tiny nucleus of Jews was expelled in 1670. Although several Jewish families were readmitted five years later, it was not until 1748 that Jews were allowed to form an organized community in the Austrian capital. Even where the various governments of Central and Western Europe allowed a certain incremental Jewish resettlement, their reasons were narrowly pragmatic. Barred from access to the feudal land system of Europe, Jews over the centuries had generated a compensatory vocational experience in trade and moneylending. Determined to exploit this Jewish talent for producing liquid wealth, substantial numbers of rulers were willing intermittently to protect "their" Jews as dependable sources of taxes and loans. Thus, Habsburg Emperor Ferdinand II, although a militant early-seventeenth-century defender of the Counter-Reformation, was unwilling to dispense with Jewish funds for his military campaigns. Neither would Protestant kings and dukes. It was strictly as a quid pro quo for their money, therefore, that Jewish communities were allowed to revive in a succession of Protestant and Catholic dominions. By the mid-1700s, the Jewish demography in Central and Western Europe may have approached 300,000–400,000. These included approximately 165,000 in the German states; 35,000 in Habsburg Bohemia, Moravia, as well as in the city of Vienna; 80,000 in Hungary; 40,000 in France; 80,000 in the Dutch and Belgian Netherlands; and 8,000 in England.

A People in Quarantine

For the privilege of return, however, the Jews paid a price that transcended loans and taxes. Responding to the demands of clergy and of local guild members, state and local governments limited Jews to vocations disdained by gentiles. For this reason, perhaps as many as three-fourths of the Jews in Central and Western Europe were limited to the precarious occupations of retail peddling, hawking, and "street-banking," that is, moneylending. Some Jews managed to earn enough to establish small shops. Most did not. In their struggle for a livelihood, they generated a sizable underclass of beggars, fencers, pimps, even robbers, thereby creating a self-fulfilling gentile scenario of Jews, one that would be endlessly invoked by Jew-haters throughout the late eighteenth and nineteenth centuries.

These constraints must be judged in the context of their time, of course. If Jews possessed fewer rights than did their urban Christian neighbors, they also bore fewer obligations and enjoyed more privileges than did Europe's peasant masses. Even in comparatively prosperous Western Europe, most villagers remained bound to the soil. In 1689 a French commentator, Jean de La Bruyère, described his nation's peasantry as "savage-looking beings . . . black, livid, and sunburnt. . . . They seem capable of articulation and, when they stand erect, they display human lineaments. They are in fact men. [Yet] they retire at night into their dens, where they live on black bread, water and roots." As late as the eighteenth century, French and German peasants were encumbered by a wide variety of tailles, tithes, decimes, and quitrents, obliged to pay tolls and dues at bridges and fairs, to labor on the king's roads, to serve in militias, to purchase their staples from royal monopolies. In contrast, the Jews were better off. Although burdened with arbitrary restrictions and taxes that often were little short of crippling, they were spared the obligation of feudal military service. They could move reasonably freely from place to place. They were allowed in effect to govern themselves (pp. 8–9). These were not trivial privileges.

Nevertheless, even in a Europe not lacking in afflictions and injustices, there remained constraints on Jewish life that eventually became insupportable. One of these was the ghetto. These walled slum-shanty neighborhoods effectively barred Jews from all but the narrowest, commercial—daytime— interaction with the gentile citizenry. It had not always been so. The first Spanish and Italian ghettos of the late medieval era actually had been requested by the Jews themselves as private, self-governing "territories." Beyond trading hours, after all, what need or desire could Jews have had for contact with the hostile Christian world? Who would have imagined in those earlier years, when populations were small and plague-decimated, that in time the ghetto would become dangerously overcrowded? By the mid-sixteenth century, however, the ghetto more commonly was imposed from above as a kind of holding pen, and not merely as a convenient reflection of corporate autonomy. It was the era of the Counter-Reformation, and if the Church could not evict infidels altogether from the local terrain, it was seized of the need at least to segregate them beyond the pale of society. In the case of the Jews, moreover, who absorbed much of the punishment well-armed Protestant nations were able to escape, the grotesquerie of a badge, a gabardine, or a peaked hat was apparently no longer enough to warn Christians off. A more thoroughgoing quarantine was deemed necessary. To that end, Pope Paul IV decreed the first "official" ghetto in Rome in 1555. Other Catholic sovereigns followed Paul's example. Soon the German Protestant duchies, craving their own religious uniformity, issued the fiats that similarly ghettoized the Jewries of northern Europe.

With hardly an exception, the ghetto was assigned to the most squalid section of the city. Thus, Pope Paul IV ordered the Roman ghetto to be located on the malarial left bank of the Tiber River. As late as the nineteenth century this congested enclave was described by an Italian writer as "a formless heap of hovels and dirty cottages, ill-kept, in which a population of nearly four thousand souls vegetates, when half that number could with difficulty live there. The conglomeration of human beings, wretched for the most part, render this hideous dwelling place nauseous and deadly." So were they all.

In eighteenth-century Frankfurt, the Judengasse was barely a quarter-mile square, and no fewer than 3,000 people were impacted there. Denied space for new dwellings, the Jews were obliged to enlarge existing buildings—occasionally to the height of four stories. Little wonder that many ghettos became firetraps. The Frankfurt Judengasse endured at least three major conflagrations, in 1711, 1721, and 1774. Even in the best of times, moreover, the ghettos' sheer congestion and squalor were notorious. A traveler in 1794 observed that "most of the people among the Frankfurt Jews, even those who are in the blooming years of their life, look like the talking dead. . . . Their deathly pallor sets them apart from all the other inhabitants. . . ." The young Goethe described the Judengasse as a "hellish slum."

Except for the express purpose of business, Jews were forbidden to leave their enclosure. After nightfall, on Sundays and Christian holidays, the gates were locked and Jews were shut off from the outside world altogether. Even in daylight hours, when Jews were permitted to conduct their business in the surrounding community, they were barred from parks, inns, coffeehouses, from the better promenades, even from the immediate vicinity of cathedrals. Although Jews were allowed to travel, they had to pay heavily for a special *Leibzoll,* a "body tax," for the privilege of entering a neighboring community. Thus, in Mainz, the duties levied by local customs officials were classified as "Honey, Hops, Wood, Jews, Chalk, Cheese, Charcoal." A Jew was required to pay three gulden to enter Munich and forty kreuzer a day to remain there. At the Leipzig fair, Jews were under orders to wear yellow badges to mark their identity. In 1710, a Hamburg municipal ordinance forbade Jews to build a synagogue, to attend private services in numbers exceeding ten families, to marry or "hold commerce" with Christian women, to appear in public on any occasion when crowds of people assembled. In 1750, Frederick II of Prussia divided the kingdom's Jewry into six classes. The most important encompassed the Jewish majority, who remained entirely ghettoized. Other categories included a small minority of *Schutzjuden,* that is, of specially protected or privileged Jews, who, in return for a substantial fee, were given temporary travel and domicile rights; and "generally privileged" Jews, a minuscule group of industrialists and financiers, temporarily valuable to the king, who were accorded full privileges of residence and occupation, including the right to purchase land and build homes wherever they chose, and to pass these rights on to their children. With few exceptions, the Jews were obliged to live quietly and unobtrusively—"still und ruhig leben."

More galling yet were the unnatural restrictions imposed on Jewish family life. Even "generally privileged" Jews were strictly limited in the number of children they were permitted to settle with them. "In order that in the future all deception, cheating and secret and forbidden increase of the number of families may be more carefully avoided," Frederick II's charter declared (in cognizance of the Jewish underclass), "no Jew shall be allowed to marry, nor will he receive permission [the official *matrikel*] to settle in additional numbers, nor will he be believed, until a careful investigation has been made by the War and Domains Offices." In the Frankfurt Judengasse, the Jews were limited to twelve weddings a year, and to none for couples who had not reached the marital age of twenty-five, specifically decreed for Jews.

A HERMETIC SOCIETY

The Judengasse signified more than Jewish isolation. It also attested to Jewish self-government. Since the early Middle Ages, corporativism, the division of society into separate and self-ruling corporations, was the institution that allowed a ruler to delegate governing responsibilities to barons, dukes, townships, guilds, even universities, in the expectation that they would perform administrative duties that he, the king, could not afford to perform himself. Under this system, each corporate group functioned within its own delimited sphere of rights and responsibilities. The imperial free city of Frankfurt, the separate little Jewish "city" within Frankfurt, were merely evidence of this corporative reality. By the eighteenth century, as royal and baronial regimes augmented their civil services, the need for such an autonomous division of society had largely atrophied. But like so many other anachronisms of the *ancien régime*, corporativism lingered on well into the Age of Absolutism.

It was logical, therefore, for Europe's Jews also to be organized on the basis of corporate autonomy. Under this rubric, Jews operated their own public services, maintained their own streets and sewers, their own schools, hospitals, and public baths, regulated their own trade and markets. Similarly, all legal disputes between Jews were resolved within the Jewish community, in Jewish courts before Jewish judges who administered Jewish laws based on Talmudic precepts. It was a complex accumulation of responsibilities, and inevitably it mandated a Jewish "government." Known as a *kehillah* (or *kahal* in Poland), such a governing body functioned in cities as diverse as Frankfurt, Hamburg, Altona, and Fürth; in Habsburg Vienna, Prague, and Pest. In rural areas, where Jewish populations were too small to sustain individual communal bodies, regional *kehillot* were established.

Ostensibly elective, the kehillah by and large reflected the influence of heavyweight taxpayers. Indeed, with few exceptions, these communal governing boards were dominated by a tight clique of affluent patricians, known as *parnassim*—in effect, as communal elders. The parnassim were invested with far-reaching powers. They appointed the judges, rabbis, and other kehillah officials. They also appointed the tax assessors and auditors. It was this latter function, moreover, that generated not merely revenue but a painful burden for West European Jewry. Jewish townsmen were obliged, in the first place, to pay considerable sums to fund the expenses of Jewish communal life. But, in addition, as the price of their toleration, they were required to deliver over substantial collective assizes to the royal, baronial, and municipal treasuries. Responsibility for assessing and collecting this cumulation of taxes was left to the parnassim, few of whom evinced any meaningful sense of noblesse oblige. Like the gentile governments that served as their models, Jewish governing oligarchies tended increasingly to shunt the yoke of taxation on to the common people. By the late eighteenth century, it was specifically this fiscal burden, not only doubly heavy but inequitably distributed, that was becoming all but insupportable for Europe's most tremulous minority.

When American slaves in the antebellum South gave vent to their emotions in folk songs, their lyrics alluded to green pastures, to golden slippers, to spirits of departed ancestors promenading in heaven, garbed in robes that invariably were white. The Jews, too, compensated for the humiliation and squalor of ghettoization by embellishing the charms and allurements of freedom and nature. Witness a modern traveler's description of a seventeenth-century synagogue in Bechhofen, Germany:

> A shewbread table is the center of attention on the north wall, and a lighted menorah on the south. The Ark [of the Torah] is richly carved and the wall about it sown with inscriptions, foliage, and symbolic lions, trees, trumpets, and harvest fruits. The timbers of the barrel vault are alive with birds and beasts—unicorn, horse, lion, hare, fox, elephant and squirrel—the One Hundred and Fourth Psalm set to line and color. Two trumpeting lions flanked by Jerusalem and again by harvest fruits share the drum of the west walls; and beneath them are paneled inscriptions, appropriately near the doorway, the saying from the Talmud: "Since Jerusalem has fallen, closed are all the gates of heaven save one, the gate of tears."

A Reorientation to the East

If our eighteenth-century traveler had been transplanted from Germany to Poland, he would have encountered a marked contrast of external surroundings. Wandering through the mud-caked Polish plain, he would have noted few bustling municipalities such as Frankfurt. Ramshackle villages were the rule here. Moreover, if few cities of Western dimensions could be found in this sprawling hinterland, neither could Western-style ghettos. In their place, hamlets and often entire towns appeared to be almost exclusively Jewish. The sheer breadth of this Jewish presence signified a shift in the Jews' geographic dispersion, one that had begun as far back as the late fourteenth century. It was the bitterest era of the Jewish experience since the loss of their ancient homeland. South of the Pyrenees, thousands of Jews were beginning to flee the Christian *reconquista* of their Iberian diaspora, most of them to seek refuge in North Africa (p. 148). At the same time, gentile populations in Western Europe, blaming "infidel devils" for the ravages of the bubonic plague, were launching the chain reaction of massacres that drove *Ashkenazic* (German and French) Jews eastward—also by the tens of thousands.

For these Ashkenazim, the likeliest sanctuary was to be found in the Commonwealth of Poland. A mighty federation of Polish, Lithuanian, Ukrainian, and Belorussian nations, Poland already comprised the largest empire in Eastern Europe. Its rulers now were prepared to make room for still other settlers. With their feudal economy continually in need of replenishment, the Polish kings were not slow in discerning advantage in a Jewish presence. Here an experienced and literate mercantile people would fill a vacuum in trade and banking, in the administration of royal and aristocratic estates, in the assessment and collection of taxes. As it became known, therefore, that Poland was offering sanctuary, Jews began moving eastward in growing velocity. Three centuries later, they would number some 800,000 in the Polish Commonwealth's population of approximately 12.7 million. In this new and open terrain, Jews preserved and developed their own religious and cultural traditions even more freely than in the German-speaking world (although their vernacular, ironically, remained the medieval German they had brought with them from Central Europe).

Jewish settlement was densest in eastern and southern Poland, especially in the Ukrainian and Belorussian areas that had been annexed in the sixteenth century. Here a dozen Polish *szlachta*—feudal magnates—owned most of the land, with the rural population subsisting as their tenants. It was specifically in these colonized sectors that the need was greatest for a mercantile class. The Jews fulfilled the role with alacrity. Diffused principally in smaller towns and villages, where they often comprised a majority of the local inhabitants, they served the landowning gentry as estate and business managers, as rent and tax collectors from the Ukrainian and Polish peasantry. It was Jews who ran the aristocrats' mills, supervised their forests and the marketing of their timber, the sale of their farm produce and cattle, and operated and occasionally subleased their local distilleries and taverns. This vibrant Jewish middle class was not yet typical of Polish Jewry at large, most of whom maintained their Central European vocations of petty trade and small handicrafts. Nevertheless, Jewish economic circumstances in Poland appeared far more promising than in the West. So did their opportunities of domicile. Although Jews in the larger Polish towns tended to be restricted to clearly defined quarters, the amplitude they enjoyed to live and work as they chose was far superior to their cramped and marginal subsistence in the West.

In Poland, as far back as the fourteenth century, the first privilege the Jews themselves requested and received was to operate their own kahals (kehillot). From the outset, the competence of these governing institutions was fully as broad-ranging as in the West. It embraced market and other commercial activities, the maintenance of the Jews' streets, sewage, synagogues, ritual baths, and the care of the Jews' own poor and ill. As always, these services were funded by Jewish taxes, assessed and levied by Jewish parnassim, enforced by Jewish judges. Yet, far more than in the extensively urbanized Jewish communities of the West, local kahals in Poland were dominated by wider, regional kahals. Linked together under the Va'ad (Committee) of Four Lands, this network encompassed Jewish settlements extending through four major provinces of the Polish Commonwealth: Great Poland, Little Poland, Lithuania, and Volhynia. It was the Va'ad of Four Lands that arbitrated fiscal, social, and welfare issues among the Jews, and determined annual tax quotas among them.

Those quotas were in every respect as substantial as in the West. Beyond Jewish communal assessments, the taxes included the usual general payments due royal or baronial treasuries, and often were supplemented by ad hoc imposts for the care of state dignitaries or local garrisons. The charges continued to rise, moreover, often to quadruple, by the late seventeenth century. Eventually, regional kahals were compelled to borrow to meet these surcharges. For Jewish families, the escalating fiscal burden became more oppressive yet when kahal officials, often working closely with the Polish magnates, began shifting a number of the heaviest taxes to less well connected rural Jewish communities. Here, too, as in the West, class tensions became seriously inflamed. All the more so as they became entangled with others of Polish Jewry's mounting burden of afflictions.

UKRAINIAN HORROR AND SPIRITUAL CRISIS

The gravest of these crises was growing gentile resentment at the Jewish presence. In contrast to Western Europe, this animus did not initially take the form of religious diabolization. In Poland, after all, Jews interacted with the local population at almost every level, and were a familiar and routine presence. Rather, it was the Jewish economic role that came to loom largest in the consciousness of peasants and townsmen alike. Gentile rancor became particularly intense in the Ukrainian provinces. By the seventeenth century, among this overwhelmingly agricultural population, it was intolerable that the Jews, a people more alien even than the Roman Catholic Poles, should be compounding Ukrainian servitude by collecting rents and taxes on behalf of the Polish oppressors.

In the spring of 1648, popular rage was channeled into military action. The catalyst was Bohdan Chmielnicki, son of a minor Ukrainian noble. Mobilizing the support of neighboring federations of Cossacks and Crimean Tatars, Chmielnicki launched an explosive uprising against Poles and Jews alike, a campaign that indiscriminately slaughtered Polish landlords, Catholic priests, Ukrainian Uniate Christians, as well as Jewish estate agents, tax collectors, tavern-owners, small merchants and their families—men, women, and children. As the Polish administration collapsed, Jews living in outlying rural areas decamped for such barricaded towns as Tulchin, Nemirov, Ostrog, Tarnopol, and Dubnow. But flight availed them little. Chmielnicki's legions were unstoppable, flooding over southeastern Poland, reaching the very gates of Lvov. Here again, Poles and Jews were seized, slain, and often hanged together with pigs.

In the early 1650s, border elements of Russians that were allied with Chmielnicki poured into eastern Lithuania and Belorussia, sacking Mohilev, Vitebsk, and Minsk, pillaging and burning Vilna. Once again, Jews by the thousands were massacred. By 1654, the Polish army managed to reorganize itself and suppress the rebellion. Yet, by then, it appeared that as many as 50,000 Jews had been murdered. In later decades, in the course of recurrent Ukrainian outbreaks, 75,000 additional Jews may have perished. Eventually, by the end of the century, the Poles succeeded in regaining control over the larger, eastern sector of Ukraine. Only then did the surviving Jewish population begin to recover, even to regain a measure of its demographic mass. But the economic and psychological scars of the Chmielnicki era would not easily be healed.

There were longer-ranging psychological consequences. By the eighteenth century, as Jews in Ukraine and Poland sensed the fragility of their position, they turned for consolation to a neo-mystical alternative. It was a continent-wide phenomenon. In Western Europe, where the Thirty Years' War had reduced hundreds of thousands of Germans to eating grass in the streets, the austere pieties of Lutheranism offered only meager emotional solace. A warm gust of evangelicalism proved far more effective. In eighteenth-century England, the shock of agricultural enclosures and early industrialization accounted for a Methodist insurrection against Anglican "sensibility." Throughout the Continent, even as far away as Russia, little sects of millenarians—Shakers, Baptists, Dunkers, Dukhobors, among others—made their appearance to emphasize new birth, personal discourse with the Holy Spirit, even ecstatic trances. In Ottoman Turkey, a hallucinatory version of Sufist euphorianism projected its influence as far afield as the Caucasus and southern Ukraine.

In some measure, the circumstances that gave rise to Christian and Moslem theosophy were reflected in Jewish life, and generated parallel mystical-evangelical movements. The best known of these was Hasidism (literally, "righteousness," or "piety"). It was in eighteenth-century Ukraine, many decades after the Chmielnicki horror had crested, that the Jewish future once again appeared precarious. This time the crisis was political, and lay in the Polish kingdom's all-enveloping political and economic catatonia (p. 15). In confronting the new challenge, Talmudic Judaism offered insufficient emotional anchorage. Other, more soul-satisfying alternatives were urgently needed.

In fact, there existed earlier precedents for an intensely mystical version of religiosity. One was the Kabbalistic apocalypticism that swelled up in response to the Jewish exodus from Spain and Portugal between the fourteenth and sixteenth centuries. In Eastern and Southern Europe, too, immediately following the Chmielnicki massacres, tens of thousands of Polish and Ukrainian Jews had been deranged into a kind of prayerful expectancy that a messiah would arise to lead them back to the Holy Land. Charlatans were not lacking to capitalize on this hysteria. Thus, Shabbtai Zvi, a Jew of Smyrna, and Jacob Frank, a Podolian Jew, made bombastic claims to the messiahship, and evoked a near-hysterical response throughout the entire European Jewish world. Although these men dissipated their followings by opportunistically apostatizing—to Islam in the case of Shabbtai Zvi, to Christianity in the case of Frank—the frenzied apocalypticism they had aroused was not to ebb so easily.

Within the framework of traditional Judaism itself, as it happened, a more "respectable" version of mysticism began to make its appearance. By the early eighteenth century, its principal exponents were itinerant lay preachers who traveled from town to town in Eastern Europe proclaiming the importance of fasting and penitence, threatening a demon-filled hell for the impure, and a physical heaven for the appropriately repentant. Several of these preachers moved beyond eschatology to a kind of pragmatic religious sociology. By laying their emphasis upon faith rather than learning, they exploited the resentment nourished by the Jewish poor against the Jewish middle class, and specifically against the oligarchy that dominated Jewish communal affairs, both in and out of kahal government. It was the members of this privileged group, after all, who enjoyed the leisure for study. Flaunting their superior Talmudic education over the Jewish common people, the affluent minority transformed its economic eminence into a symbol of both cultural and social aristocracy. For their part, the Jewish masses in their resentment became susceptible to any preachers who could restore their sense of dignity and self-worth. In the eighteenth century, the most charismatic of these evangelists appeared in the person of Israel Ben-Eliezer of Miedzyboz, soon to be known as the Baal Shem-Tov—the "Master of the Good Name."

Knowledge of the man's origins is imprecise. It is believed that he was born in or around 1700, in Miedzyboz, a middle-sized, largely Jewish town in the Polish province of Podolia. Kabbalism was a major force here. It was from Podolia, shortly after his marriage at the age of fifteen, that the ungainly and pockmarked Israel Ben-Eliezer traveled to the Carpathian Mountains, where he earned his livelihood as a ditchdigger. Even as he labored, however, the youth's work frequently was interrupted by visions and long spells of mystical introspection. Convinced that his "revelations" were divinely inspired, Israel, the "Baal Shem-Tov," returned to Podolia, where he began preaching an unsophisticated brand of religious fundamentalism. Although the youth borrowed liberally from earlier versions of Kabbalism, his parables, the "legends of the Baal Shem-Tov," were entirely his own, and he expounded them with passion. It was through these simple folktales and homilies that the Baal Shem-Tov emphasized the importance of worshipping God through prayer rather than through "mere" study. The supplications of the impoverished and illiterate were of enduring value, he insisted, if they were deeply felt and honestly expressed. In a critical departure from his evangelical predecessors, moreover, the Baal Shem-Tov argued that love of God was best expressed through joy and ecstatic flights of the soul, rather than through asceticism and mortification.

The young man's message swept with torrential speed and power through the dense Jewish populations of southern Poland, and most specifically through the traumatized Ukrainian provinces. Thus, after the Master himself died, in 1760, his disciples traveled to all corners of the Eastern world to develop an impressive network of Hasidic conventicles, all led by charismatic preachers, some of whom would found "dynasties" to be carried on by their sons and sons-in-law. However much traditional rabbis, the defenders of Talmudic Judaism, protested against this revivalist "heresy," even issuing a ban of excommunication against its practitioners, the movement was seized by an apparently irresistible momentum. Among its most compelling attractions were its sheer simplicity, even its crudity, its fiercely joyous revivalist prayer meetings, its genial toleration of dancing and drinking.

By the turn of the century, Hasidism had become irretrievably ensconced in the regions of densest Jewish habitation, even beyond the Polish Ukraine, in Moldavia, in Hungary, and in other regions that—not coincidentally— were exposed to the Sufist mysticism then taking root in the neighboring Ottoman world. For the Jews, the movement's joyous brand of fundamentalism offered an indispensable, even a narcotic, compensation for the increasingly grim vicissitudes of their lives in Eastern Europe. Yet, by the same token, Hasidism throughout the late eighteenth and early nineteenth centuries would also devolve into an unregenerate defender of pietistic obscurantism, and eventually into the single most formidable adversary of humanistic enlightenment among the Jews of Eastern Europe (pp. 16, 72).

THE LAST YEARS OF THE POLISH "SANCTUARY"

In the sixteenth century, the Kingdom of Poland–Grand Duchy of Lithuania was the most powerful state in Eastern Europe. Two centuries later, it had become the weakest. A decisive factor in this transformation was the overweening economic and political influence acquired by Poland's landed nobility, and their shameless use of the *liberum veto,* the right even of a single delegate in the Sejm, the nation's parliament, to block any legislation threatening his personal estate or prerogatives. By the mid-1700s, entire sessions of the Sejm were left functionally paralyzed as a consequence of the magnates' arrogance and rapacity. It was a stance, in turn, that blocked the king from asserting his executive responsibilities, and over time reduced him to little more than a royal figurehead.

The crisis of a dysfunctional government affected not merely Poland's economic and political viability but its very national survival. In 1772, king and Sejm alike were helpless to defend their country against the intimidation of powerful neighboring enemies. Ultimately, they offered little more than token resistance as Russia, Austria, and Prussia annexed major sectors of Polish territory. In all, the nation lost almost one-third of its land and more than one-third of its population. It was the sheer magnitude of the amputation, however, that appeared at least briefly to spur the magnates to contrition, and into a serious commitment to political reform. During the celebrated "Aristocrats' Republic" of 1788–92, the nobility canceled the liberum veto, allowing the king once again to assert effective executive power, and even authorizing a Western-style cabinet of ministers.

Sadly, the genuflection to political modernization came too late. The Russian Empire was not prepared to tolerate a reformed and functional regime along its borders. Preemptively, in 1793, the tsarist government dispatched still another army into Poland and carved out for itself an even larger segment of the country, adding Lithuania and much of western Ukraine to its earlier acquisition of Belorussia and Latvia. The Prussians and Austrians also moved then, claiming additional sectors of remnant Poland for themselves, essentially in Posen and Galicia. Whereupon, in March 1794, the Polish national hero Thaddeus Kosciuszko organized a volunteer army and led it in a final, desperate uprising against the invaders. The revolt proved as hopeless as it was valiant. It was easily crushed. More tragically yet, as a coup de grâce, the three eastern powers in 1795 collaborated in a third and climactic partition of the attenuated Polish kingdom. Russia acquired Courland and the remainder of Lithuania; Prussia annexed the city of Warsaw and its surrounding appendage of central Poland; while Austria appropriated the balance of Little Poland, with its beauteous regional capital of Cracow. Henceforth, the Polish Commonwealth ceased to exist as an independent state.

These last decades of Polish expiration were fully as grim for the Jews as for the Poles. Their once favored status in the country had long been eroding. Decade by decade, the landowning *szlachta* had restricted their Jews' opportunities and privileges, including the privilege of urban domicile. Even in those towns and cities that remained open to Jews, the aristocracy chose to placate Poland's incipient middle class by restricting the Jews' former access to trading and professional guilds. Heavier poll taxes, too, were imposed on this minority people, and its earlier freedom to travel was circumscribed. More ominous yet, many of the more unscrupulous landowners encouraged peasants and town-dwellers alike to attribute their poverty and political impotence not to them, the landowners, but to the Jews. Exploiting folk superstitions, the magnates embellished traditional characterizations of Jews as desecrators of the Host, as ritual murderers of Christian women and children. The diversionary tactic served its purpose. Intermittent assaults then were directed exclusively at the Jews, particularly in Ukraine and Belorussia.

In their vulnerability, Jewish spokesmen repeatedly appealed to the Sejm for protection. The effort was not altogether futile. In the last years of the 1788–92 "Aristocrats' Republic," debates raged both in and out of the Sejm on the feasibility of "reforming" the Jews. In almost every detail, the controversy paralleled comparable Enlightenment debates on the Jews in Western Europe (p. 27). On the one hand, the very notion of full Jewish emancipation was as repugnant to Poland's incipient urban middle class as it was in the West. On the other hand, both King Stanislaus Augustus and progressive elements within the Sejm grasped that the nation's rehabilitation, its very survival, would require a more forbearing attitude to all Poland's races and nations. At first, it was the "liberals" who appeared to prevail. In 1792, acceding to committee recommendations, the Sejm prepared a law on the Jews. It offered them legal protection, including full rights of settlement in towns and villages, and admission to all merchant guilds. But the Jews for their part would be obliged to abandon their separate religious courts, their separate language, their medieval garb, and to accept strict limitations on their liquor traffic.

The Jews' reaction to this proposal was mixed. The enlightened and educated minority among them favored it. The Hasidic majority opposed it. The issue soon became moot, in any case. Even as the Polish legislators pondered their final decision on the bill, a Russian ultimatum late in 1792 ordered the Sejm to dissolve itself. And a year after that, Poland underwent its second and most draconian partition. In the twilight of the rump nation's existence, Jewish integration was the least of public concerns.

It is a sorely tried Jewry we encounter in Eastern Europe during the late eighteenth century, on the eve of *rozbier,* Poland's climactic partitions; and in

Western Europe, on the threshold of the French Revolution. In the East, between 850,000 and 900,000 Jews found themselves whipsawed between the autocracy of Polish gentry and Jewish kahal alike, by progressively heavier Polish intimidation and Jewish kahal extortion. In Western Europe, to be sure, ghetto Jews eked out only marginally improved livelihoods and were hardly less repugnant in the eyes of their Christian neighbors than in Poland. The essential difference between Polish Jewry and Western Jewry, therefore, was not to be found in their legal status. Both communities were quarantined as non-Europeans. Nor was the divergence related to their economic status. Both communities produced small middle-class elites, and drew their livelihoods and social roots from a much wider hinterland of petty traders. Both communities were governed by Jewish communal institutions whose officials often were as autocratic and rapacious as any in the Christian world. In all these respects, there was little to choose between Eastern and Western Jewry. Yet one significant disjunction was becoming at least faintly perceptible. In the East, the circumstances of Jewish life were steadily worsening. In the West, there were tentative prefigurations of better times to come.

II

A Glimmering of Dawn in the West

THE AGE OF MERCANTILISM

During the seventeenth and eighteenth centuries, life in Western Europe underwent a far-reaching economic revolution. The transformation began when the Continent's feudal-agricultural economy was inundated by vast new supplies of gold and silver from the mines of Peru and Mexico. As bullion was transmuted into negotiable currency, Europeans became increasingly dependent upon this specie for a rising standard of living. Money provided luxuries in food and dress for city-dwellers. For peasants in the field, money allowed a payoff of feudal obligations, the opportunity to own a plot of soil free and clear.

For the ruler, above all, money signified hired armies, civil servants, and financial independence of covetous nobility. So it was, during the Early Modern Era, that liquid wealth became the key to the governmental absolutism of such potentates as Friedrich Wilhelm, the Great Elector of Brandenburg, and Louis XIV, the "Sun King" of France. Moreover, in his quest for authoritarian independence, the typical sovereign of the Baroque Age viewed money as a commodity that dared not be shared with his dynastic rivals. Under this "mercantilist" strategy, each government set about developing a colonial reservoir of markets and raw materials ample enough to ensure a favorable net inflow of precious currency. Preoccupied with the accumulation of money, therefore, the typical West European ruler of the late seventeenth and early eighteenth centuries was less inclined to sustain his forebears' historic concern with issues of religion or religious heresy.

The Jews were among the earliest beneficiaries of the new economic pragmatism. Thus, in 1744, when Austria's Empress Maria Theresa impulsively ordered the banishment of Prague's tiny Jewish community, her ambassadors in Holland, England, and Denmark cautioned her (in response to Jewish entreaties) that expulsion of this talented mercantile people could adversely affect the Habsburg economy. Sobered by the warning, the empress agreed then not to "activate" the eviction decree. Few other rulers needed reminder of the function Jews had come to fulfill in state-building. In the century that had passed since the Thirty Years' War, as kings and dukes moved to rebuild their depleted treasuries, they had learned to appreciate the Jews' potential not only as traditional sources of tax revenues but, increasingly, as agents of mercantile growth.

The Dutch were among the earliest to exploit that potential. Winning their freedom from the Spanish Empire in 1609, nurturing their own vivid memories of Catholic oppression, the governing magnates of the Netherlands' United [Dutch] Provinces immediately proclaimed freedom of religion for all inhabitants. Doubtless they had in mind freedom essentially for Protestants of all denominations. Nevertheless, over the ensuing years, as tiny bands of *Sephardic* (Iberian) Jewish fugitives began arriving in the Netherlands, the government saw no reason to deny them entrance. With a few exceptions, the Jews were free to live wherever they chose, to practice their own rites and ceremonies, to engage in their livelihoods essentially without interference.

Soon, too, economic factors even more than religious ones produced a community of shared interest between Netherlanders and Jews. As the Dutch tightened their control over the outlet of the Rhine, Europe's largest inland transportation route, Amsterdam's emerging reputation as a deep-draft harbor accelerated the shift in continental traffic from the Mediterranean to the new Atlantic frontier. For the United Provinces, these logistical advantages were further enhanced by Protestant literacy and capitalist initiative. Within a very few years, therefore, the Dutch managed to preempt the lucrative carrying trade between Europe, the Middle East, and the West and East Indies. Ironically, they conducted the largest volume of that traffic with the empires of their perennial enemies, the Spaniards and the Portuguese. More ironically yet, it was in this commerce that the Jews had a unique role to play.

In earlier decades, Sephardic *conversos*—Iberian-Jewish converts to Catholicism—had been operating the principal import-export houses within the Spanish and Portuguese empires. Hereupon the (professing) Sephardic Jews of the Netherlands, who shared the same ethnic background, language, and commercial expertise, became the logical interlocutors with their *converso* kinsmen. The Netherlands government encouraged that relationship. In 1657, it directed its consuls and ambassadors abroad to extend Jewish traders the identical diplomatic protection accorded other Dutch citizens. Moreover, in their widening prosperity, Jews in the Netherlands soon formed an influential minority bloc within their nation's West and East Indies companies. Although most of the country's 5,000 or 6,000 Jews (by the end of the seventeenth century) were small merchants and artisans, their personal security and religious freedom were not surpassed anywhere else in Europe. Amsterdam's Jewish quarter, the Joodenbreestraat enclave along the bank of the Amstel

River, was notable for its extensive network of schools and communal offices. By 1675, the mighty Esnoga, Amsterdam's Great Synagogue, achieved renown as the largest Jewish house of worship in all of Europe, and as a model for the Bevis Marks Synagogue, the first openly recognized Jewish house of worship in London.

The synergy between Amsterdam's Jews and those of London was hardly oblique. As in many other West European nations, the England of Edward I had expelled its tiny Jewish population as far back as 1290. A handful of Jews had remained on secretly, but even as late as the seventeenth century their numbers did not exceed 100. Yet the fate of this tiny nucleus was about to change dramatically. In 1651, Parliament enacted the first in a series of Navigation Acts, designed to exclude Dutch vessels from Britain's extensive colonial carrying trade. The legislation posed an immediate threat to the Jews of Amsterdam, who had emerged as major players in the burgeoning Atlantic commerce. For them, the one logical route of continued access to that traffic would have been a physical presence in London. The notion was by no means far-fetched. The Puritan government of Oliver Cromwell, England's "Lord Protector," was not to be surpassed in its mercantilist aggressiveness by any other government in Europe. Thus, in 1655, when a delegation of Dutch Jews arrived in London to petition for readmission to England, Cromwell warmly endorsed their appeal. And when the House of Commons (fearing Jewish business competition) hesitated to confirm Cromwell's initiative, the Lord Protector acted on his own. He allowed handfuls of Dutch-Jewish traders to remain on "unofficially."

So did Cromwell's son, Richard, who succeeded his father as Lord Protector upon the latter's death in 1658. And so did the Restoration monarch, Charles II, who had dealt congenially with Jewish financiers while living in exile in Holland. In 1664, Charles assured the modest enclave of London Jews that they would enjoy "the same favour as formerly they have had, so long as they demean themselves peaceably & quietly with due obedience to [the king's] Lawes without scandall to his government." This they did ever after, participating quite openly and freely in British economic life. By 1700, their numbers reached 6,000. A century later, joined by additional thousands of Dutch, Central European, and North African Jews, their population in Britain approached 30,000.

Across the Channel, meanwhile, the Jews of Catholic France, totaling possibly as many as 35,000 in the early 1700s, had not yet achieved the same quasi-emancipated status of their kinsmen in Holland or England. The bulk of French Jewry was concentrated in the northeastern provinces of Alsace and Lorraine. Only recently annexed during Louis XIV's War of Devolution, Alsace-Lorraine was a German-speaking region, and its Jewish inhabitants suffered most of the residential and vocational constraints on Jews elsewhere in Western Europe. In southern France, however, there were important exceptions. In the fourteenth and fifteenth centuries, the Duchy of Provence had become an early sanctuary for Sephardic Jews fleeing Spanish persecution. Although King Louis XI promptly expelled this refugee population upon annexing Provence to France in 1481, a small group of *marranos,* nominally Christianized but in fact secretly practicing Jews, remained on. An important elite among this little Sephardic community, functioning as importers, exporters, and bankers, helped develop France's trade connections with the Middle East and the Caribbean. Some prospered so extensively that they dwelled in luxurious homes in Bordeaux and Saint-Esprit. By the early eighteenth century, numbering approximately 5,000, Provençal Sephardim hardly bothered to disguise their Jewish identity. In 1723, King Louis XV alluded specifically to the "Jews of the Portuguese Nation" when he confirmed them in their domicile and trading privileges.

AN AUGMENTED PRESENCE IN WESTERN EUROPE

Well into the Early Modern Era, to be sure, the largest numbers of Jews in the West remained confined by law and custom to their traditional ghetto neighborhoods. Few if any of them had been admitted to urban trade guilds. Nevertheless, in a period of mounting economic acquisitiveness, growing numbers of Jews throughout Western Europe managed to achieve a wider vocational leeway. As trade and manufacturing opened beyond traditional guild jurisdiction, Jews began moving into occupations substantially more diversified than moneylending and peddlery. In the German principalities and the Habsburg Empire alike, it was no longer a rarity for Jews to function as dealers in cattle, timber, and textiles. By the early eighteenth century, moreover, they had emerged as the Continent's preeminent distributors of such luxury materials as silks and satins. With goods supplied by their kinsmen in the Netherlands (who in turn traded extensively with *converso* kinsmen in the Indies and Latin America), West and Central European Jews also emerged as leading merchants in gold, silver, and precious gems.

The palpable economic value of these activities soon became evident to Europe's absolutist rulers. Frederick II of Prussia arguably was the most brilliant of the Enlightened Despots, a king who fancied himself as the patron saint of European rationalism. On the one hand, Frederick despised the Jews. In his *Political Testament,* he described them in 1752 as the most objectionable of all the nation's minorities, "avaricious, superstitious, backward." Yet, better than most of his royal colleagues, Frederick also understood the depth of the German world's economic backwardness. Industry was thinly dispersed and primitive. Commerce still was linked essentially to the rhythm of harvests and fairs. Grudgingly, then, the king was prepared to appoint Jews as court purveyors, as factory owners and managers of export houses. In 1763, Frederick allowed Jewish children to join their parents in residence beyond ghetto neighborhoods, provided these families established factories or "promote[d] the marketing of home products outside the countryside." Other princes followed the Prussian ruler's lead. In a widening succession of German states, Jews were granted privileged travel opportunities, rights of domicile outside the Judengassen, exemption from "Jew-taxes"—all as reward for establishing new industries and trade connections for their rulers.

The subtle improvement in Jewish economic status is well described in the diary entries of a Jewish woman, known only as "Glückel of Hameln," who lived between 1646 and 1724. During Glückel's years as a young woman in Hanover, her husband and brothers are seen earning their livelihoods as petty traders, trudging from door to door, buying and selling old gold. The wife of one of Glückel's Jewish neighbors sells feminine knickknacks at the Kiel fair. Other Jewish neighbors deal in ribbons, hardware, and cutlery, in small loans and in pawned, secondhand jewelry. Then, gradually, Glückel's relatives and friends enter the retail trade in cattle and textiles, in jewelry, liquor, and tobacco. The transition was characteristic. Over the years, Jews in larger numbers shared in the bulk purchase of commodities from Amsterdam, Danzig, and Poland, selling the goods afterward in the principal European fairs. By the late eighteenth century, Jews operated perhaps a fourth of all mercantile pavilions at the Leipzig fair, Europe's largest. By then, too, Jews were awarded contracts for the delivery of silver to government mints, for the sale of cash and bills of exchange on a scale that approached banking, for the manufacture of army uniforms and other military clothing.

It was this latter Jewish function, of provisioning their rulers' armies, that gave rise to a unique phenomenon in modern European history, the *Hofjude*, the "Court Jew." In their various wars, the dynasts of the Absolutist Age were in continual need of munitions, even of mercenary soldiers, from all parts of Europe. With few exceptions, the contractors were Jews. Dispersed throughout the Continent, Jewish businessmen over the years had developed extensive experience in mobilizing agents and subagents—usually fellow Jews—to seek out and acquire war surplus. Indeed, as early as the seventeenth century, many a Jewish commodity-dealer laid the basis of his fortune by the swift acquisition and sale of debris left on the battlefields of the Thirty Years' War.

An early example of these munitions-provisioners was Samuel Oppenheimer of Heidelberg (1630–1703), who emerged in the 1660s as military contractor to the Palatine Elector. Afterward, during the Hapsburg Empire's ongoing series of wars with France, Emperor Leopold I entrusted Oppenheimer with the task of supplying the entire Austrian army. It was a formidable challenge. Responding to it with alacrity, Oppenheimer dispatched his agents through the entirety of southern Germany to seek out grain, fodder, clothing, and gunpowder from other Jewish dealers. During the Turkish siege of Vienna in 1683, it was Oppenheimer again whose extensive resupply effort sustained the capital's defenders until the King of Poland came to their rescue. Similarly, Oppenheimer provisioned the empire's armies in their later Hungarian and Balkan campaigns. The man was well remunerated for his services. Yet, for a ghetto-bred Jew, no reward was more gratifying to Oppenheimer than his official titles of *Oberfaktor* (Supreme [Imperial] Supply Purveyor) and *Oberkriegsfaktor* (Supreme [Imperial] Military Supply Purveyor).

Numerous other Jewish army contractors operated on behalf of a wide range of German principalities, and most earned fortunes for their efforts. Possibly largest in scale, after Oppenheimer, were the Dutch Sephardim who provisioned the armies of Willem III of the Netherlands (later William III of England). During the long sequence of wars against Louis XIV, the contracting firm of Antonio Alvarez Machado and Jacob Pereira, and its network of subagents throughout Europe, emerged as "Providiteur Générale" of the entire Allied coalition. Early modern history is replete with the names of these Jewish suppliers. Yet Jews functioned as pioneer industrialists as well as contracting agents. In eighteenth-century Prussia, Levi Ulff established an army clothing factory at Charlottenberg. David Hirsch founded a military uniform factory in Berlin, and a velvet factory in Potsdam. Benjamin Elias Wulff operated a cotton and calico factory in Berlin's Tiergarten. Other Prussian-Jewish financiers constructed and managed cotton-cloth factories— all at a time when Christian merchants, even the few who possessed adequate capital, were fearful of so much as touching the virgin realm of industrial investment.

Jewish entrepreneurs supplied their rulers not only with munitions and factories, however, but with hard cash. Here lay their most decisive importance in the Age of Absolutism. The very laws that for years had barred Jews from merchant and craft guilds had forced them into the money trade. As early as the seventeenth century, even as the Netherlands in its wide-flung commerce with the mines of the New World grew into Europe's principal bullion and money market, Dutch Jews accordingly emerged as major players in the purchase and exchange of currencies on behalf of royal clients—in Protestant and Catholic Europe alike. Thus, a full century before the House of Rothschild achieved its renown, the banking House of López was operated by five Sephardic *conversos,* placed strategically in Lisbon, Toulouse, Bordeaux, Antwerp, and London.

It was not long, then, before Jews in German-speaking Europe achieved a comparable renown as court financiers. The most eminent of these was Samson Wertheimer. Based in Vienna, Wertheimer embarked on his career in the late seventeenth century as one of a number of small moneylenders for minor court nobility. It was during the War of the Spanish Succession, aggressively mobilizing a group of smaller Jewish bankers—Aaron Beer, Hirsch Kahn, Behrend Lehmann, among others—that Wertheimer developed the financial muscularity to lend millions of gulden to Emperor Leopold I and to the emperor's allies throughout Central Europe. Without these loans, and those of Samuel Oppenheimer, the Habsburg ruler almost certainly could not have waged his simultaneous wars against France and the Ottoman Empire.

Joseph Süss Oppenheimer has traditionally been regarded as the most flamboyant of these court financiers. Trained in banking by his wealthy uncle, Samuel Oppenheimer, the young man early on acquired a reputation for imaginative speculation as banker for the Landgrave of Hesse-Darmstadt. In 1732, while still in his thirties, Süss became court "factor" (moneylender), gemcollector, and private banker to Prince Karl Alexander of Württemberg. Indeed, he exploited his connections with such imagination and ruthlessness that he obtained almost complete control of the duchy's financial administration. In that capacity, Süss did not hesitate to pocket substantial bribes from businessmen in return for government contracts. Although envious Christian courtiers repeatedly drew Karl Alexander's attention to the malfeasance of this Jewish parvenu, the prince remained well satisfied with Süss's personal loyalty and the profits he produced. In 1737, however, Karl Alexander died, and Süss found himself without a protector. Soon afterward, a jury of nobles convicted him of fraud and embezzlement, as well as for the even less forgivable crime of "carnal relations" with Christian women. Süss perished on the gallows in 1738.

It was not the inducement of profits alone that motivated these Jewish factors and bankers. Above all else, they coveted their official titles of Hoffaktor or Hofagent, together with the rights and privileges that accorded to their positions, most notably the right to live outside the ghetto on a permanent basis, and not infrequently to attend court and mingle with the nobility. In 1791, the Berlin banker Daniel Itzig was granted a patent of naturalization that extended to him and his son "all rights possessed by the Christian citizens throughout the entire state of Prussia." Similar patents in the eighteenth century were granted to eleven other Jewish households. And what households they were! Behrend Lehmann's home in Cleves was virtually a palace. Süss Oppenheimer furnished his several homes, in Frankfurt, Stuttgart, and elsewhere, with costly objets d'art and paintings by Rubens, Teniers, Jordaens, and other Flemish masters, with precious china, rare engravings, gold vessels, and sumptuously bound books. Aristocrats in all but name, these Jewish birds of paradise entertained royalty, courtiers, and ambassadors in their homes and at the weddings of their children.

In their eminence, moreover, Court Jews often functioned as *shtadlanim*, that is, as intercessors, between the local Jewry and the ruler. It was through the good offices of powerful shtadlanim that Jews first won the en bloc privilege of settlement in Dresden, Leipzig, Kassel, Brunswick, and Breslau. Jewish "commoners" may have resented the ostentation and often dictatorial arrogance of these intercessors, of men like the Oppenheimers, Sinzheims, Wertheimers, and Lehmanns, but they also accepted and acknowledged the protection and influence these men exerted on their behalf. In truth, the pattern of obsequious Jewish dependence upon a few wealthy intercessors would endure in Jewish life well after political emancipation. It may actually have been the longest-lived of the Court Jews' role in modern Jewish history (pp. 111–13).

PREFIGURATIONS OF EMANCIPATION

There were other, more fundamental circumstances that laid the groundwork for an improvement in the Jewish condition. Mercantilist secularism and intellectual rationalism were preeminent among them. By the eighteenth century, religious fanaticism had all but exhausted itself in Western Europe. Physical assaults against Jews, as well as blood-libel accusations, were becoming much less common. So were mass expulsions. The sheer growth of Jewish demographic mass in West-Central Europe, reaching at least 600,000 souls by the mid-1700s, offered telling evidence of that new security.

In these same years, the despised underworld of hawkers, old-clothes peddlers, and ragpickers was giving way to incrementally more dignified livelihoods. The memoir literature of the Early Modern Era, from Samuel Pepys to Glückel of Hameln, makes reference to growing numbers of Jews working as wholesale merchants, as factory-owners, as private as well as public bankers. Vocational and residential opportunities were paralleled and augmented by improvements in juridical status. The Habsburg Emperor Joseph II was the first to countenance these changes as official policy. Although Joseph remained fully wedded to the tradition of "divine right," he was intent upon improving the welfare of his entire realm. Thus, in 1782, breaking with the pietistic rigidity of his late mother, Maria Theresa, Joseph issued a *Toleranzpatent* for the 6 million non-Catholics of his empire. They should be free, he proclaimed, to live and work on a basis of equality with all other citizens.

The pronunciamento in fact did not yet apply to Jews. But in October of that same year, Joseph issued a supplementary edict for the Jewry of Bohemia. In this province were to be found some 40,000 Jews, the largest Jewish population in the empire, except for recently annexed Polish Galicia. In its preamble, the decree observed that the government would be guided by the objective of making Jews "useful and serviceable to the State, principally through better education and the enlightenment of their youth, and by directing them to the sciences, the arts, and the crafts." To achieve that goal,

Jews in Bohemia henceforth would be allowed to move into nonrestricted neighborhoods, to enter any vocations of their choice, even to attend public schools and universities.

The benediction was by no means unqualified. In contrast to others of the empire's inhabitants, the Jews were not yet to be regarded as citizens, let alone eligible for government employment. Nor were they to be entirely spared the humiliation of Jew-taxes. To ensure their growing "usefulness" to the state, the Toleranzpatent obliged Jews to use the German language in all public documents, to Germanize their names and clothing, and above all to accept the jurisdiction of imperial courts in all civil and criminal matters. Nevertheless, the dispensation was significant. Late in the year, moreover, Joseph II extended his decree to Moravia, to Vienna and Lower Austria, and in 1783 to Hungary. In 1789, even Galicia, with its insular and impoverished Jewish population of some 212,000, fell within the ambit of the emperor's decree—although here local authorities managed in practice to obstruct many of its provisions. Notwithstanding its lingering inequities, Joseph II's legislative agenda for Habsburg Jewry unquestionably represented a giant step into the Modern Era.

For the largest numbers of Jews in West-Central Europe, therefore, the last decade of the eighteenth century brought an end to the worst of ghetto confinement, of vocational restrictions, and travel and "body" taxes. Even in the Prussia of Frederick II, where virtually none of the ghettos or special "Jew taxes" was yet eliminated, the practical realities of mercantilism were generating new categories of *Schutzjuden*. Beyond the inner circle of supply contractors, bankers, and financial advisers who achieved the status of Court Jews, growing numbers of other Jewish businessmen were proving their usefulness to the state through the industries they established, the munitions they provided, the valued commodities they imported. Their reward, as that of the Hofjuden, frequently was the dispensation of living outside ghetto walls, or traveling between cities without paying Jew-taxes, occasionally even of passing their special status down through their children. The numbers of these privileged Jews increased year by year, forming a significant Jewish middle class.

By the eighteenth century, moreover, a ruler's effort to centralize, to "rationalize" his government, entailed more than simply a curtailment of aristocratic prerogatives. It signified the demise of corporativism, the medieval legacy of provincial, baronial, municipal, or guild self-government. In this campaign, the fiscal and juridical autonomy of the Jewish kehillah also came under royal scrutiny. Thus, in Prussia, as early as 1730, King Friedrich Wilhelm I instituted a new Prussian Jewry Code that prohibited imposition of the *herem*, the rabbinical ban of excommunication, even where judgments were issued on purely Jewish religious matters. In other German states, the ambit of rabbinical jurisdiction was similarly being whittled away. So, too, were the taxation powers formerly reserved to the kehillot.

Altogether, in the eighteenth century, along with the impulsions of economic mercantilism and administrative centralization, the new motive force of secular enlightenment was challenging the certitudes of the ancien régime. The philosophes of Western Europe, popularizing the virtues of reason, encouraged a harshly uncompromising evaluation of society's anachronisms. The relics they targeted included the dysfunctional role of effete courtiers in determining public legislation, the engorged landholdings of a reactionary Church establishment, the recessive taxes and legal obligations inflicted on peasants in the field, and the gratuitous cruelties inflicted on convicts in prisons. It was perhaps inevitable, then, that the anomalous status of the Jews should also fall under scrutiny by the fashionable new "religion" of reason.

At first, Europe's rationalists approached the Jewish question with a certain ambivalence. Even among the Enlightenment's rather austere circle of intellectuals, distaste for Jews remained the norm. In one of his more "humanitarian" statements on the Jews, the incomparable Voltaire acknowledged simply that they should not be burned. Indeed, for most of the philosophes, the Jew was himself the very epitome of religious obscurantism and fanaticism. In his extensive article on the Jews in the *Encyclopedia,* Denis Diderot observed that the Talmud encouraged Jews "to steal the goods of Christians, to regard them as savage beasts, to push them over a precipice . . . and to utter every morning the most horrible imprecations against them." Voltaire acidly acknowledged his readiness "to sit down at one table and share a meal with a Turk, a Chinese, a Hindu, and . . . even a Jew, provided the Jew free himself first of his hateful Jewish superstitions and prejudices." How could a Jew, asked Johann Gottfried von Herder, expect humanitarian treatment as long as he remained obstinately loyal to his fanatical tribal law?

In the estimation of the early philosophes, no less invidious than the Jews' religious fanaticism was their implacable insularity. The Jews, declared Henri Grégoire, an Alsatian abbot who actually favored Jewish emancipation, "are scattered everywhere. They have struck roots, however, nowhere. . . . In London [a Jew] is not an Englishman, nor is he Dutch at The Hague, nor French in Metz. [The Jews] are a state within a state." It was a view shared even by committed rationalists. They shared, too, a common revulsion at Jewish economic activity, the still extensive Jewish predilection for hawking, peddling, and "usurious" moneylending. The philosophes' disdain in turn was closely linked to their suspicion of Jews on moral grounds. In dramas, novels, and polemical pamphlets of the Early Modern Era, the stock "Jew" character was a cheat, a thief, a coward, a sexual dissolute.

On the other hand, the very essence of the Enlightenment creed was the innate equality of all men. Embracing the Marquis de Condorcet's vision of "innate" human perfectibility, Europe's rationalists tended to agree that no people was "innately" incapable of that exalted status. In a "Letter to the Right Honourable Sir Thomas Chitty, Lord Mayor of London," an anonymous English merchant pleaded in 1753 for a more open policy toward non-Christians:

> In our conception of man [argued the writer], we should always accustom ourselves to look on the human race . . . as one and the same grand republic of which God is the common father. . . . We should not be limited to the love of our countries only, or the love of the Protestants only—this is a narrow, selfish, and contracted principle. The Englishman's heart should be more enlarged by an universal friendship and confidence between man and man and nation and nation.

Allusions to society's self-interest became an increasingly common feature of debates on the Jewish issue. In 1712, Joseph Addison wrote of the Jews: "They are dispersed through all the trading parts of the world, that they are become the instruments by which mankind are knit together by a general correspondence. They are the pegs and nails in a great building, which, though they are of but little value in themselves, are absolutely necessary to keep the whole frame together." As far back as 1690, the renowned contract theorist John Locke had developed the formula of a government entirely neutral in doctrinal matters, and the idea was further embellished sixty years later by the Baron de Montesquieu. The interplay of ideas and views, these men insisted, including religious views, would only serve to correct the abuses of society. "There is absolutely no such thing as a Christian commonwealth," wrote Locke. "Neither pagan, nor Mohammedan, nor Jew ought to be excluded from the civil rights of the commonwealth because of his religion."

The appeal to civil functionalism was perhaps best expressed by Christian Wilhelm von Dohm and the Abbé Grégoire. A councillor of the Prussian war ministry, Dohm in 1781 published a celebrated treatise, "On the Civil Improvement of the Jews" ("Über die bürgerliche Verbesserung der Juden"), which made the case for unlocking the talents of all and diverse peoples, and surely of the Jews, whose economic potential for society had barely been tapped. The pamphlet evoked much interest in rationalist circles, and appeared in translation in France in 1782 through the effort of the Count de Mirabeau. That same year, the Société des Arts et Sciences of Metz sponsored an essay competition—one of many in the Age of Enlightenment—on the proposition that "there are means of making the Jews happy and more useful in France." Nine essays were submitted, all but two of them treating the question sympathetically, and the prize was awarded to the Abbé Grégoire's essay on Jewish "regeneration" ("Essai sur la régéneration physique, morale et politique des juifs"). Like Dohm, Grégoire placed his emphasis on the self-interest of the state, and the Jews' potential value as an economic resource. To those, like Voltaire, Herder, and Diderot, who warned that the Jews were morally and culturally unprepared for citizenship, Dohm, Mirabeau, and Grégoire riposted vigorously. The sooner Jews were granted civil and religious equality, they insisted, the swifter "new Jews" would emerge, improved in their personal morality, business practices, and love of country.

A Paragon of Jewish Potentiality

But could the widening tolerationism of the eighteenth century be applied to the flesh-and-blood Jew, to the often uncouth denizen of the ghetto? A German writer, Christian Gellert, was optimistic. In his moralistic novel *The Life of the Swedish Countess von G*** (Das Leben der schwedischen Gräfin von G***)*, a noblewoman's "memoirs" describe a Polish Jew, his life saved by her husband, who afterward proves himself the most grateful and loyal of friends. The simplistic portrait was well received in Germany, and possibly influenced another contemporary writer, Gotthold Ephraim Lessing. A rather bohemian figure, Lessing as a young man enjoyed the company of actors, political radicals, and other "unrespectable" types. In later years, he would become a serious dramatist, the author of *Laokoon, Emilia Galotti,* and *Nathan der Weise.* In 1749, however, still a budding litterateur, Lessing ventilated his rather eccentric idealism in an unlikely one-act comedy, *Die Juden.* The play revolves about a gallant stranger who saves the purse and life of a wealthy baron by driving off a band of murderous highwaymen. Grateful, the baron is about to offer the mysterious benefactor his daughter's hand, until the stranger reveals himself to be a Jew. Although the marriage cannot take place, the baron in his gratitude declares: "O, how worthy of esteem the Jews would be if they were all like you!" "And how worthy of love the Christians would be," responds the Jew, "if they possessed all your qualities."

Lessing had not yet encountered Moses Mendelssohn (see below), but he was aware of more than a few "enlightened" and well-spoken Jews of his own generation. Some of these actually were studying at Austrian and German universities. Since the seventeenth century, in fact, Jews had been admitted to at least half of Western Europe's thirty universities. At the University of Halle alone between 1712 and 1780, nearly two hundred Jews received medical degrees. Jewish immersion in non-Jewish culture manifestly was not without precedent even before Lessing—or Mendelssohn—appeared on the scene of German history. Nevertheless, it is Mendelssohn who has appropriately been recognized as the principal catalyst of Jewish Enlightenment. Born in 1729, he was the son of an impoverished merchant family of Dessau, Prussia. Although as a youngster Mendelssohn received a conventionally Orthodox upbringing, he was much influenced in his adolescent years by an erudite local rabbi, David Hirsch Frankel, a man solidly versed in both secular and Jewish culture. When Frankel departed for Berlin to become chief rabbi of that city's modest Jewish community, the fourteen-year-old Mendelssohn followed on foot. Frankel then arranged lodgings for the youth in the garret of an affluent Berlin *Schutzjude*, Isaac Bernhard, where he earned his keep as a Hebrew tutor to Bernhard's children, and later as a bookkeeper in Bernhard's silk factory. It was similarly with the help of Bernhard and Frankel that Mendelssohn became acquainted with Western languages and literature, and began avidly studying them on his own. When Bernhard eventually took Mendelssohn into his silk factory as a bookkeeper, the young man found opportunity for an even more sustained intellectual exploration.

Physically, Mendelssohn was quite unprepossessing. His early years of impoverishment had afflicted him with rickets, leaving him with a conspicuously humped back. Yet the gentleness of his personal disposition and the elegance of his German expression fascinated and charmed those who made his acquaintance. One of these was Gotthold Lessing. The two met at the home of a mutual friend. Enthralled by the precocious young Jew, Lessing immediately took him under his wing and introduced him to his own literary milieu. By then, in the 1750s, a vibrant cultural ambience had developed in Berlin. Under the leadership of King Frederick II, the Prussian capital had become a major hub of German publishing, of fine arts, science, and education. Subsequently, Lessing was able to introduce Mendelssohn to numerous other writers and scholars, and these in turn encouraged the young man to try his wings as an author. It was with their help, in 1761, that Mendelssohn secured publication of his first collection of essays, *Philosophical Dialogues (Philosophische Gespräche)*.

The work was less than pathbreaking. It elaborated upon ideas fashionable at the time, those pioneered by the English deist Edward Herbert and by such precursors of natural theology as the Germans Christian Wolff and Gottfried Wilhelm Leibniz. Nevertheless, Mendelssohn's clarity of thought and stylistic precision almost immediately won him acceptance as one of Berlin's most renowned cultural icons. Other philosophical essays followed in quick succession. In 1763, one of these, "On Evidence in the Metaphysical Sciences" ("Abhandlung über die Evidenz in metaphysischen Wissenschaften"), was awarded the first prize of the Berlin Academy of Arts and Letters (the second prize went to Immanuel Kant). As comparably erudite religiophilosophic publications swiftly flowed from Mendelssohn's pen, ranging from *Phaedon* in 1767 to *Morning Hours (Morgenstunden)* in 1785, he found himself apotheosized as "the Jewish Socrates." As early as 1764, through the intercession at court of prominent friends, he was awarded the coveted status of *Schutzjude*, with the right to live outside the Jewish quarter and to travel freely in and out of Berlin. Married and a father by then, Mendelssohn in both his personal life and cultural eminence had achieved a fulfillment matched by few Jews of his era.

Nevertheless, even at the apogee of his reputation, "the Jewish Socrates" found himself preoccupied with his people's demeaning marginality. In 1774, journeying to Dresden to visit friends, he was astonished to learn that, as a Jew, he was ordered to pay the same 20 groschen "entrance fee" as an ox. Although the payment was refunded with apologies in his case, he brooded over the experience. "Sometimes in the evening I go for a stroll with my wife and children," he wrote later. " 'Father,' asks a child in his innocence, 'what is that boy calling after us? What have we done to them?' 'Yes, father,' says another, 'they always run after us in the street and call us: Jews! Jews! Is it such a disgrace among these people to be a Jew?' Alas, I cast down my eyes and I sigh within myself: 'Oh mankind, how could you have let it come to this?' " Yet the more Mendelssohn brooded about the circumstances of ghetto life, its backward educational system, its intellectual inbreeding, the more he was forced to acknowledge that the charge of obscurantism was not without justification. His people were unable so much as to speak the language of the host population. Their vernacular was Yiddish, a "jargon" that had been singled out by Voltaire and other critics as evidence of the Jews' cultural backwardness, and thus as a major obstacle to their emancipation. In his own life, Mendelssohn recognized the extent to which mastery of the German language and literature had served as the key to his cultural enrichment and social acceptance. It followed, then, that fluency in German was the indispensable key to the ghetto's "inner" locks. The "outer" locks would be opened later.

Mendelssohn was not alone in reaching this conclusion. During the 1770s, he had attracted around him a circle of cultivated young Jews, later to be dubbed *maskilim*, the Hebrew term for "enlightened ones." Whether as business or professional men, they shared Mendelssohn's vision of "self-liberation" from cultural ghettoization. One of these was Naphtali Herz Wessely, the Hamburg-born son of a wealthy *Hofjude*. With Mendelssohn, Wessely thought he knew where to begin the task of "self-liberation." Both men were aware that, in the sixteenth century, Martin Luther had translated the Latin Bible into German, and thereby had inspired the German people into achieving literacy in their own language. Mendelssohn and Wessely anticipated now that the identical goal could be achieved for German Jewry if the Torah, the core of the Hebrew Bible, were translated into modern German. It was also critical to provide the translation with a running commentary that would interpret the more primitive, anthropomorphic references in modern, rationalist terminology.

In 1773, therefore, under the two men's editorship, a team of young scholars set to work on the project. To help fund their efforts, Wessely exploited his family's connections and secured a major "start-up" grant from none other than the King of Denmark (for whom Wessely's father served as court purveyor); and later some five hundred—mainly Jewish—patrons agreed to underwrite the book's first edition. The project of translation and commentary required fully ten years. Upon its completion, however, in 1783, word of the monumental achievement spread rapidly, and with it growing orders for the volume. During the ensuing century, the Mendelssohn-Wessely Torah, expanded by other translator-commentators to encompass the entirety of the Old Testament, went through seventeen printings, and became a staple of virtually every literate Jewish home in Central Europe. They were German-speaking homes by then. In fostering Jewish "cultural liberation," Mendelssohn and Wessely's epic accomplishment proved fully as decisive for the Jews as the original Luther translation had been for a much wider audience two and a half centuries earlier. Altogether, Mendelssohn's pioneering vision ignited a quiet revolution in German-Jewish life.

There was an ironic aftermath to the great man's career, however, one that anticipated a dilemma that would confront German Jewry for at least two generations. In the years immediately following Mendelssohn's death in 1786, his disciples sustained the effort of transmitting secular information to the Jewish world. Initially, their vehicle was a Hebrew-language journal, *HaMe'assef (The Gatherer)*, which they eventually discarded once German became more widely disseminated among Jewish readers. The transformation actually was more than a linguistic one. The editors, among them Isaac Euchel, Mendel Breslau, Shalom HaCohen, even Naphtali Wessely, were not of the same mold as their master. They polemicized the virtues of secular humanism with such hectoring passion that, unwittingly, they compromised the values of Judaism itself.

The career of Solomon Maimon offered a poignant example of this ambivalence. Born in Sukoviboeg, Poland, in 1753, Maimon as a child was able to thread his way through the labyrinths of the Talmud with such phenomenal ease that the incredulous rabbis of his province offered to ordain him at the age of eleven. Upon refusing the honor, Maimon was married off (as an alternative reward) to a wellborn daughter of the town. At the age of fourteen, he became a father. Family responsibilities plainly were beyond his grasp. At the age of twenty-five, Maimon suddenly abandoned wife and son and trekked to the Prussian city of Königsberg, where he hoped to study medicine. Virtually penniless, he solicited handouts from the Königsberg Jewish community, but his uncouth demeanor did not ingratiate him with the kehillah. Neither did his chronic iconoclasm. Endlessly criticizing Orthodox Judaism as irrational and irrelevant, Maimon became a pariah to the locals. When he moved to Berlin and persisted in ventilating his heretical opinions, he was summarily expelled by the city's Jewish elders.

At this point, galled by the hostility he encountered everywhere among his own people, Maimon flirted briefly with the notion of apostatizing. But if he was too much a freethinker for Jews, he was hardly less so for Christians. Despondent, on the verge of starvation, rejected by Christian and Jew alike, Maimon made a bungling, unsuccessful attempt to drown himself. Eventually, he made his way back to Berlin. Here, briefly, his career took a turn for the better. In 1790 his first book, *Essay on Transcendental Philosophy (Versuch über die Transzendentalphilosophie)*, was praised by Kant. Lectures and tutoring came his way. For a while, Maimon even began to eat regularly. Soon other volumes followed. In one of them, a commentary on Maimonides' renowned medieval magnum opus, *Guide to the Perplexed (Moreh Nevuchim)*, Maimon achieved his own interpretive synthesis of rationalism and Judaism. The two, he observed (six centuries after Maimonides first established the thesis), were not necessarily contradictory. Here, at least, Maimon's stance evinced greater intellectual cogency than had Moses Mendelssohn's rather perfunctory defense of Orthodox Judaism as "revealed legislation."

Mendelssohn's cultural influence on German Jewry plainly far transcended that of the indecorous Maimon, whose rarest talent was for making himself hated. Even so, it was Maimon's career, not Mendelssohn's, that prefigured the Jewish cultural "eclectics" of a later generation, those who lived beyond the orbit of their own people but who failed to win acceptance in a non-Jewish milieu. The classicist Moses Hadas has incisively defined their crisis in suggesting that Maimon, who was buried in a heretic's grave outside the Jewish cemetery, was the first modern Jew (as Heinrich Heine doubtless was the best known) to prophesy correctly that neither the mass nor the Kaddish would be intoned at his funeral.

III

An Ambivalent Emancipation in the West

The French Revolution and the Jewish Question

Every student of history remembers the sequence of events. In 1789, the government of France faced bankruptcy. In May of that year, requiring financial advice, King Louis XVI convened an Estates-General, an assemblage of dignitaries whose two "upper" estates included senior members of the aristocracy and clergy, and whose third, "lower," estate included prominent representatives of the middle class. The distraught monarch received more advice than he bargained for. At the initiative of its bourgeois members, the Estates-General summarily convened a gathering of local assemblies. These were the delegates, in turn, who subsequently proclaimed themselves the National Assembly and promptly set about eradicating the traditional feudal privileges of Church and nobility. The Assembly's second objective was to write a constitution for France.

Although the process of formulation would consume more than two years, the constitution's prefix, "A Declaration of the Rights of Man," was completed as early as August 26, 1789, and proclaimed the right of all citizens, of whatever birth or station, to participate in the affairs of government. Acting on this epochal assertion, the delegates then set about eliminating those political and economic anachronisms that no longer withstood the scrutiny of reason. Preeminent among these was the barnacle of corporativism, including the privilege of aristocrats to impose tolls, taxes, juridical standards and regulations, to arrogate to themselves military and fiscal prerogatives and exemptions. All such "irrational" archaisms now were to be consigned to the dustbin of history. And so, presumably, was the autonomous corporation of the Jews, with its own parochial governing bodies, courts, and powers of collective assessment and taxation. Nevertheless, before the issue of Jewish self-rule could properly be addressed, a rather more far-reaching issue had to be confronted. This was the status of the Jews in France altogether.

On the eve of the Revolution, approximately 40,000 Jews lived in France, in a nation of some 28 million. Five or six thousand Jews of predominantly

Sephardic ancestry were ensconced in Bordeaux, Bayonne, Avignon, and neighboring towns in the country's southern regions. Tracing their roots in France back more than two centuries, the Sephardim enjoyed extensive latitude in their choice of economic activities, in their opportunities to purchase land and to build homes beyond the confines of their traditional "Jew quarters" (p. 22). Yet even these privileged veterans were limited in their activities and travels essentially to their districts of settlement. A much larger group of Jews, some 35,000 German-speaking Ashkenazim, lived in Alsace and Lorraine, northeastern border provinces that had been acquired by France during the wars of Louis XIV. Here, too, Jewish circumstances varied from town to town, but these tended to be far less congenial than those of their Sephardic coreligionists. In Strasbourg, the provincial capital of Alsace, Jews remained consigned to a literal ghetto. In smaller communities Jews were "encouraged" to live in slum areas, even obliged to pay Jew-taxes. Still unfamiliar with "respectable" livelihoods, thousands of Alsatian Jews continued to engage in peddlery, pawnbroking, and moneylending. Most of them remained quite poor, and distinctly repugnant to the surrounding population.

In 1786, responding to a succession of appeals from the local citizenry, King Louis XVI issued a decree barring Jewish moneylenders from reclaiming more than one-fifth of the debts owed them. The measure was an economic body blow to the entire Jewish economy. So ominous, in fact, were its implications, and so anguished were Jewish protests, that the government was persuaded finally to review the matter. Under the chairmanship of Minister Chrétien Malesherbes, a royal commission set about investigating the wider spectrum of Jewish grievances. For the first time, too, a number of Jewish communal leaders were allowed to offer their own testimony. The prospects of better treatment appeared favorable. Recently, the same commission had proposed the grant of equal citizenship to Protestants. Indeed, upon completing their discussions in May 1786, Malesherbes and his colleagues agreed to make the same recommendation for the Jews. But the suggestion remained dead on the paper. Conscious of Alsatian objections, King Louis vetoed it.

Nevertheless, the Malesherbes hearings took place at a time when Enlightenment figures were beginning to achieve a new consensus in favor of Jewish emancipation. In 1789, two of their most eminent spokesmen, the Count de Mirabeau and the Abbé Grégoire, sat in the newly convened National Assembly. Over the course of the summer discussions on the Declaration of the Rights of Man, both Mirabeau and Grégoire pressed vigorously for a specific reference to the Jews. As late as August, however, the best they could achieve was inclusion of a rather anodyne clause, that "no person shall be molested for his opinions, even such as are religious, provided that the manifestation of their opinions does not disturb the public order. . . ." Then, in the last week of September, anti-Jewish riots broke out in Alsace, instigated by local farmers in hock to Jewish moneylenders. The previous May, the Alsatians had ventilated their resentment against the Jews in a series of "cahiers de doléance," grievance petitions submitted to the Estates-General. No meaningful response was forthcoming then on the status of the Jews, one way or the other. But this time, responding to the unrest in Alsace, and to the intercession of Grégoire and the Count de Clermont-Tonnère, a liberal aristocrat, the Assembly decided to procrastinate no longer. It would evaluate the Jewish question in its wider dimensions. To that end, it invited an Alsatian-Jewish delegation to come to Paris to offer its own testimony. In October 1789, six Jewish representatives duly arrived at the capital to meet with Grégoire and a committee of legislators.

Leading the Jewish delegation was Berr Isaac Cerfberr. The son of a wealthy banker, Cerfberr himself owned a profitable tobacco company, and thus inherited his father's role as a "respectable" shtadlan to the French authorities. Before the committee, Cerfberr and his associates proved models of dignity in their appeal for freedom of residence, commerce, and marriage, and relief from all special Jew-taxes. The committee members reacted favorably. Upon their recommendation, the National Assembly agreed to place the question of Jewish civil rights on the agenda for December. But again, as in the case of the Malesherbes Commission, they were premature. During the intervening weeks, the Assembly members had before them not only the original "cahiers" of protest against Jewish usury, but new and wider complaints against Jewish avarice and separatism. Even non-Alsatian delegates vigorously supported these allegations. Thus, on December 24, 1789, when the Assembly approved its law granting Protestants equal rights with Catholics, it deferred equivalent action on the Jews.

The Sephardim of the south did not accept the decision passively. As veteran settlers in the country, boasting a sizable elite of respected merchants and bankers, and already enjoying substantial freedom of residence and vocation, they were mortified that their legal status should remain linked to that of the "boorish" Ashkenazim. Over the years, the Sephardim had repeatedly stressed this ethnic distinction. Thus, in 1763, stung by Voltaire's rancorous literary defamation of Jews, Isaac de Pinto of Bordeaux cited the numerous differences between "his" people and the "others." The Sephardim, insisted Pinto, generated wealth and culture; the Ashkenazim, usury and swindling. In 1777, Jacob Rodriguez of Bayonne published an open letter to the press, berating a gentile lawyer, Jean-Marie Goulleau, for stigmatizing the "Portuguese nation" in terms more appropriate for the Ashkenazim. Similarly, when Abraham Furtado and Salomon López-Dubec appeared before the Malesherbes Commission in 1786 to petition for Jewish rights, they appealed exclusively on behalf of their own "Portuguese Nation." The following year, yet another Sephardic delegation made the identical, selective, appeal to the Estates-

General, as did still another, before the National Assembly, in the winter of 1789–90. It was on this latter occasion that the appeal finally bore fruit. On January 28, 1790, following an extended debate, the Assembly voted to extend full civil rights to Jews of the "Portuguese, Spanish, and Avignonese nations." Profoundly relieved and gratified, the Sephardic delegates then returned home—to evince no further interest in the circumstances of their "low-born" coreligionists.

Cerfberr and his colleagues were unwilling to swallow the humiliation. Remaining in Paris, they forged on in their own campaign for emancipation. Months went by without result. But in the winter of 1790–91 they were offered a vital piece of information by a Parisian lawyer, Jacques Godard, himself a delegate to the National Assembly. The political balance of power in the Revolution was shifting to the populist Jacobin Party, Godard noted, and the focus of Jacobin power was increasingly to be found in the Commune of Paris, a collection of "representative citizens," bourgeoisie and workers alike. It was to the Commune, therefore, suggested Godard, that Jews should address their principal efforts. They did. On January 29, 1791, dressed in their uniforms as National Guardsmen and bearing certificates of "good behavior" from the Christian citizens of Paris, a Jewish delegation appeared before representatives of the Commune. Godard himself was present to plead the Jews' cause. Impressed, the Communards then sent word to their Jacobin colleagues in the National Assembly, endorsing the Jews' petition.

Even with this Jacobin support, the Assembly delegates moved cautiously, aware that the king's assent still was necessary. In April, they adopted a compromise resolution, placing the individual security and property of Jews under "protection of the law." In July, they took another incremental step, annulling all remaining Jew-taxes. Finally, on September 27, 1791, sensing the shift in the political climate, the Alsatian delegates dropped their opposition and joined with other Assembly members to issue a resolution of emancipation. Signed by King Louis XVI on November 13, the document in its key provisions read: "The National Assembly . . . cancels all adjournments, reservations and exceptions inserted in . . . decrees concerning individuals of the Jewish persuasion who shall take the civic oath, which oath will be regarded as a renunciation of all prohibitions and exceptions previously granted in their favor."

The phrase "in their favor" alluded to the "favor" of Jewish self-government. It was telling evidence that emancipation had not been granted simply as an act of enlightened humanitarianism. Rather, the dispensation fitted precisely into the ongoing eighteenth-century momentum toward administrative centralism. The highly acculturated Sephardim had accepted the trade-off between civil equality and self-government instantly and uncomplainingly. But their more parochial Ashkenazic cousins found the abdication of autonomy somewhat harder to swallow. On their behalf, Cerf-berr discreetly petitioned his contacts in the Assembly to grant the rabbinical courts special exemption. He got nowhere. Indeed, Clermont-Tonnère, the Abbé Grégoire's ally in the Jewish struggle and until then one of Cerfberr's most reliable interlocutors, issued a sharp reprimand:

> The Jews should be denied everything as a nation [he warned], but granted everything as individuals. They must disown their judges, they must have only ours. They must be refused legal protection for the maintenance of the supposed laws of their Jewish corporations. They must constitute neither a state, nor a political corps, nor an order. They must individually become citizens.

Duly chastened, Cerfberr and his associates then relinquished their lingering claims on communal autonomy.

There was enough to be grateful for. On September 27, upon learning of the Assembly's emancipation resolution, Cerfberr himself dispatched a letter of congratulation to the Jewish kehillah of Strasbourg. "God chose the noble French nation to reinstate us in our privileges," he wrote, "and bring us a new birth. . . . This nation asks no thanks, except that we show ourselves worthy citizens." In fulfillment of that goal, Cerfberr urged his fellow Jews to devote themselves to acculturation, to seize new educational opportunities, to "give signal proofs of [our] glowing patriotism." By and large, they did. Jews volunteered in extensive numbers for the National Guard and for the army, became lieutenants of the gendarmerie, made generous financial contributions to the revolutionary militia. In common with other Frenchmen, they also experienced the deprivations of the Robespierran Terror, when synagogues and churches alike were closed down, pillaged, and transformed into revolutionary "temples." And when the Terror finally crested, Jews shared the widespread relief of the French population at large as they prepared for lives of tranquillity as well as equality.

NAPOLEON APPRAISES THE JEWS

Even as the Terror receded, leaving in its wake the rubble of demolished Jewish institutions, a new question became urgent: Should Jews rebuild their former communal agencies or create new ones? During the ancien régime, heavily weighted by Jew taxes, the kehillot had gone deeply into debt to meet their collective fiscal obligations to the state. So had numerous Catholic and Protestant institutions, but the revolutionary government had taken over the latter's obligations and paid them off from public funds. Not so in the case of the Jews, who were presumed to be awash in money. They alone were held accountable for their communal debts. Until the emancipation, so the argument went, the Jews had been not simply a religious community, but in effect "foreigners," and thus as successors to "non-Frenchmen" they remained liable for their own, often quite substantial, communal fiscal obligations. Ironically, by adopting this rationale, the French government itself was inadvertently extending Jewish corporativism's tenuous lease on life.

Yet communal autonomy was not the only relic to persist in the aftermath of Jewish emancipation. Another was demographic and vocational inertia. Only a small minority of Jews appeared willing at first to venture beyond the cities and towns of Alsace-Lorraine. Fewer yet appeared interested in abandoning their traditional vocations in commerce and finance. Moreover, when the National Assembly during the early months of the Revolution confiscated and auctioned off the estates of émigré aristocrats, the farmers of Alsace managed to share in the purchasing frenzy by borrowing funds from Jewish moneylenders. As a result, no fewer than 40,000 farmers, substantial landowners by the turn of the century, found themselves heavily in debt to some 2,000 Jews. The consequence was predictable. It was an immediate revival of anti-Jewish unrest, of intermittent rioting and occasional pillaging of Jewish homes and shops.

The violence coincided with a developing political reaction in France: first with the right-wing Directory, which governed from 1795 to 1799; then, in 1799, with the rise of Napoleon Bonaparte as first consul and later, in 1804, as emperor. Throughout these transformations, Napoleon managed to preserve the spirit of fraternal nationalism, even the priceless revolutionary boon of equality before the law. But he scrapped the very notion of political liberty, and ruled France with an increasingly authoritarian hand. France's conservative and royalist elements, meanwhile, taking heart from the political shift rightward, intensified their propaganda campaign against the Revolution and its innovations. Not the least of these innovations was the emancipation of Protestants and Jews. Over the turn of the century, therefore, closet royalists shrewdly exploited public suspicions with ominous warnings that Jews and Protestants were buying up the countryside and desecrating churches. Louis Gabriel de Bonald, the "philosopher of royalism," took the lead in this campaign. He was joined by René de Chateaubriand and other defenders of the ancien régime, who trotted out the well-familiar prerevolutionary accusation that the Jews were a nation within a nation, an alien and unassimilable body—above all, usurers who were sucking the peasantry dry. For the Jews, a major preoccupation henceforth was Napoleon's reaction. Was the emperor paying heed to these accusations?

What little Napoleon knew of Jews was unfavorable. In January 1806, en route home from his recent military victory at Austerlitz, and passing through Alsace, he encountered the full force of local grievances against Jewish creditors. Afterward, meeting in Paris with his Council of State, he discussed the prospect of reimposing certain legal measures against this vexatious and apparently irredeemable "nation within a nation." His proposal was supported by the emperor's minister of "cults," Jean-Étienne-Marie Portalis, and by a fiery official of the ministry of the interior, Count Louis Mathieu Molé, whose hatred of Jews was compounded by a false but persistent rumor that his, Molé's, great-grandmother had been Jewish. At the Council's request, Molé in ensuing weeks formulated a lengthy report that proposed a moratorium on all debts owed the "detestable" Jewish creditors. Presented in late April, the suggestion appeared rather too draconian for the other councillors, who argued that the emperor's popularity rested upon his scrupulous protection of equality before the law, the Revolution's single most valued achievement. The meeting ended inconclusively. But in mid-May of 1806, the Council resumed its discussions, and this time the emperor was insistent that exceptional laws be adopted, for "the evil done by the Jews comes from the very temperament of this people." Two weeks later, Napoleon signed the series of decrees Molé had prepared for him. The most punitive of these measures suspended for one year Alsatian payment-obligations to Jewish creditors.

Yet the emperor had no intention merely of punishing the Jews, of reducing them to a sullen and uncooperative enclave. His instinct for wooing France's religious factions had always been sure and timely. Thus, he had assured Catholic friendship by his 1801 Concordat with the Vatican, restoring Catholicism as the Established Church of France in return for state control over all ecclesiastical appointments. Similarly, he had granted a "constitution" to French Protestants, conferring recognition on them as an "official" religious group—again, in return for the power of veto over their pastoral appointments. The wily ruler had few scruples even about flirting with Islam during his earlier military campaign in Egypt. He had solemnly mouthed quotations from the Koran, sported a fez, and managed eventually to win the muftis' *futwa* of approval for his impending offensive against the British and the Turks. "It was as a Catholic that I won the war in the Vendée," he observed to the Council of State in August 1801, "as a Moslem that I established myself in Egypt, and as an Ultramontane [supporter of the Italian papacy] that I won the confidence of the Italians. If I were governing Jews, I should rebuild the temple of Solomon."

And now, in May 1806, Napoleon made plain his determination to "govern" the Jews. In the second provision of the decree Molé had drafted for him, the emperor would balance his economic moratorium against Jewish creditors by summoning a formal assembly of Jewish "notables." These latter would offer their own views of the most effective methods for replacing "the shameful measures to which many [Jews] have resorted from generation to generation for many centuries." As Napoleon saw it, a conclave of this nature would evoke Jewish cooperation without incurring the stigma of counter-revolutionary illegality.

Napoleon Requalifies Emancipation

The Assembly of Jewish Notables was scheduled for July 6, 1806, in Paris. Prefects of the nation's *départements* would choose representatives from among rabbis, landholders, and other "respectable" Jewish personages, each appointee to represent not less than 1,000 and not more than 5,000 Jews. In this undertaking, it was hardly a simple matter for the prefects to accumulate the necessary demographic statistics, then to select appropriate delegates. Nevertheless, the mandate was fulfilled within six weeks, the data were gathered, the notables were appointed. Sephardic and Ashkenazic representatives alike would share in the proceedings. Among the latter, besides the estimable Cerfberr himself, three Cerfberr sons participated, as well as Cerfberr's brother-in-law, Rabbi David Sinzheim of Strasbourg. In all, eighty-two "notables" were appointed, each a man of property or prestige. At the last moment, they were joined by sixteen additional delegates selected from Napoleon's puppet Kingdom of Italy. All came at the expense of their own communities, and many were obliged to remain in Paris for over seven weeks (p. 44). Much of the extended time period was the result of internecine bickering between Cerfberr and Rabbi Abraham Furtado, leader of the Sephardic delegates, until the two eventually agreed to serve as joint chairmen.

The first session opened on July 26. In his opening address, Count Molé, one of three government commissioners appointed to supervise the assemblage, read off an official address from the emperor himself. After citing the usual list of anti-Jewish indictments—separatism, hostility to Christians, antisocial economic activities—Molé asked the Notables to resolve the manner in which the Jews might "reconcile [their] beliefs . . . with their duties as Frenchmen . . . [become] useful citizens, [and] . . . remedy the evil to which many of them apply themselves to the great detriment of our subjects." To that end, Molé—the emperor—posed twelve questions. These asked, in essence: Did Jewish law countenance polygamy? Intermarriage? Did Jews regard Frenchmen as brethren? As strangers? As legitimate targets for usury? Did Jews acknowledge France as their country? Were they prepared to defend it? Did Jews regard themselves bound by French law or by rabbinical law? Upon completing this love letter, Molé then appointed a committee to prepare a draft response that the Assembly should accept or reject. Cerfberr and Rabbi Furtado jointly presided.

On August 20, after three and a half weeks of intense discussions, the

Notables presented their collective response to Napoleon's questions. Rather to the commissioners' surprise, the document was a model of tact and conciliation. Of course the Jews regarded France as their country, it declared, and Frenchmen as their brothers. Of course the Jews were willing to defend France—"to the death." Of course decisions issued by rabbinical tribunals applied exclusively to "spiritual matters," not to secular ones. Of course the Jews were monogamous. The question of mixed marriages admittedly was more complex, for the rabbis were conscience-bound to oppose weddings outside the faith. Yet this issue was finessed, as well. The Bible, noted the response, forbade marriage with heathen peoples in ancient times. Plainly, the Christians of modern France did not fall into that category. As for usury, Jewish law was explicit that only a fair rate of interest might be charged Jews and non-Jews alike.

Although the commission reacted to the answers with skepticism, Napoleon apparently was prepared to accept them, even to endow them with a kind of numinous authenticity. On August 23, he revealed his scheme, and it proved hardly less than a bombshell for the Jews. It was the emperor's wish that the Assembly of Jewish Notables should now be superseded by a Great Sanhedrin, a modern-day version of the Jewish high tribunal of ancient Israel. In determining the membership of this inspired resurrection, the Assembly was instructed to select forty representatives from among its own delegates, and to invite thirty additional rabbis from throughout the French Empire to join the fifteen already in Paris. It was this convocation of eighty-five members, two-thirds of them rabbis, that would be transformed into the exalted Sanhedrin, a body that in turn would reconfirm, and thereby "sanctify," the Assembly's recent collective response. For their part, upon learning of Napoleon's proposal, French Jewry reacted in stunned astonishment, then in thrilled gratification. Indeed, as news of the emperor's envisaged Sanhedrin circulated throughout Europe, hosannas of joy were intoned in synagogues in France, Italy, Germany—even in far-off Russia (pp. 58–59). With one brilliant genuflection to this little people's religiohistoric traditions, Napoleon was emerging as a liberator, "a new Cyrus," as the great "white eagle" of Jewish folklore.

On February 4, 1807, all selections completed, the "Great Sanhedrin" was ceremonially drummed into the main conference room of the Hôtel de Ville, the City Hall of Paris. Addressing the assembled delegates, Molé this time explained that the original twelve questions, those posed earlier to the Assembly of Jewish Notables, were now to be confirmed by the Sanhedrin in forthright, unequivocal, and "sacerdotal" language. The emperor also expected the Sanhedrin to condemn the behavior of Alsace's moneylenders in the most solemn of "religious" terms, and to denounce Jewish moneylending altogether—unless the "usurers" themselves owned land, and thereby had a stake in the welfare of France. Hereupon the commissioners appointed Rabbi David Sinzheim as conference chairman. It was accordingly under Sinzheim's firm and dignified guidance, over the ensuing four and a half weeks of discussion, that the Sanhedrin produced its ratification of the Jewish Notables' earlier commitments.

Even more than the original responses, the new document was a model of forthrightness and lucidity. Once again, assurance was given that France alone would claim the political allegiance of the nation's Jews. The laws of Torah and Talmud were defined as exclusively religious, with the decisions of civil tribunals at all times to exercise priority over those of religious courts. It was this civil priority in turn that became the rationale for the Sanhedrin's response on intermarriage, for the rabbis disdained any longer to give "theological" justification for exogamous unions. At the same time, reaffirming the "love" they bore their fellow citizens, the delegates specifically encouraged the Jews of France to participate in all vocations and professions, and condemned moneylending at high rates of interest.

Presumably, the Jewish Notables' earlier commitments now had achieved "sacerdotal" validation. Thus, on March 7, the day before the Great Sanhedrin presented its responses and formally ended its proceedings, Rabbi Sinzheim delivered a short summary of its conclusions and proclaimed them as nothing less than a "social pact" between "the People of God and the People of France." His comments then were duly endorsed by Rabbi Furtado, on behalf of the Sephardic delegates. "France is our country," declaimed Furtado. "Jews, such today is your status. Your obligations are outlined. Your happiness is waiting."

The rhetoric was no mere florid verbalization. The Sanhedrin's renunciation of separate Jewish nationhood was an event of defining significance in Jewish history. It set the tone of Western Jewish life for at least a century to come. When the minister of cults, Jean-Étienne Portalis, wrote later that "the Jews ceased to be a people and remained only a religion," he discerned the Sanhedrin's implications perhaps more accurately than had the Jews themselves. The delegates may have intended only to reject the accusation of political separatism. But Jews in later generations, in the United States as well as in Western Europe, would transform the Sanhedrin's assurances into a virtual abdication of Jewish peoplehood in all but its narrowest religious connotations. The Twelve Answers would provide a rationale for "salon Jews" and *Kaiserjuden,* for Germans, Frenchmen, and Americans of the "Israelitisch" or "Mosaic" persuasion, for Jews eager to assume the protective coloration of their non-Jewish neighbors. The enduring significance of the Paris Sanhedrin, therefore, lay not only in that body's rejection of corporate Jewish autonomy, but in the sanction it provided for the rejection of Jewish civilization in its wider ethnic and cultural dimensions.

A COMMUNAL RECONSTRUCTION

As for the great "white eagle" of contemporary Jewish folklore, that popularized image of Napoleon bore scant resemblance to reality. The emperor's authentic attitude toward the Jews became rather clearer in March 1807, shortly after the Sanhedrin disbanded. The original Assembly of Jewish Notables, which had not expired but merely had been subsumed within its more august successor, was obliged to remain behind, at its own expense and at much personal inconvenience to its delegates. Molé and the other government commissioners wished the Notables to understand and to accept the emperor's new and very specific guidelines on the Jews. Those directives, published in their final version exactly one year later, on March 17, 1808, would take the form of three "organic" decrees.

In varying measure, each of the three directives reflected Napoleon's ineradicable distrust of the Jews. The first, to be known by Jews ever after as the "Infamous Decree," in practical fact reversed much of the National Assembly's original 1791 Act of Emancipation. As its preamble explained, the measure was designed "to weaken, if not destroy, the Jewish people's inclination to such a great number of practices which are contrary to civilization, and to the general order of society in all the countries of the world." To that end, Jews intent on taking up residence in Alsace-Lorraine for purposes of moneylending, retail shopkeeping, or old-clothes dealing, would now require special government permits—and these certificates would be tightly restricted. Even long-settled Jewish Alsatians and Lorrainers no longer were permitted to collect payment for sums lent in amounts beyond the value of their own real estate. Jews, it appeared, should be obliged to own a "stake" in the countryside. Inasmuch as the provision was made retroactive to loans outstanding, it instantly inflicted crippling losses on many hundreds of Jewish creditors. As to the future, "[n]o Jew who does not now own property in France can engage in such activity. . . ." By these restrictions, stated the decree, many départements would be spared the "disgrace of having become vassals to the Jews." The language presumably was softened by two qualifications. It was not to be applied to the more acculturated Sephardic Jews of the southern regions; and after ten years, the government could decide whether or not to prolong the restrictions to the Askenazim of the north.

The others of the emperor's March 1808 edicts, incorporated into an omnibus "Organic Regulation on the Mosaic Religion," dealt with the seemingly innocuous subject of Jewish religious organization. In his Concordat with the Vatican, Napoleon in 1801 had linked the Church's administrative hierarchy in France with the French state. That same year, Protestants also were given a government-sponsored imprimatur, with their religious leadership similarly placed under state-authorized "directories." Only the Jews remained beyond the ambit of an "official," "state-recognized" religion. But now, in March 1808, the government moved decisively to remedy that lacuna. In organizing the mechanics of the program, Molé and his fellow commissioners adopted the model they had used earlier with the Protestants. In each département possessing a Jewish population of at least 2,000, a *Consistoire Israélite* would be established, with the main synagogue to function as its administrative center. Initially, French Jewry would be allocated thirteen such *consistoires,* all to function under the supervision of the Consistoire Central Israélite in Paris. The number later would be enlarged to include the empire's German and Italian territories.

Each consistoire would operate under the practical direction of a board of Jewish "notables," usually two laymen and a rabbi. No distinction was made between Ashkenazic and Sephardic Jews. The two elements were obliged to work together, and thus the historic separation between the two communities gradually would be transcended. Whether Ashkenazic or Sephardic, however, the lay appointees would be selected exclusively from the more affluent classes. It soon became evident that the government's purpose was not only to secure men of "respectability," but men with deep pockets. In contrast to the administrative structure approved for Catholics and Protestants, the expenses of the Jewish consistoires, including salaries of rabbis, religious-school teachers, and of other communal functionaries, were to be borne not by the government treasury but by special taxes imposed on the Jews themselves— particularly on the more affluent Jews. Here, too, therefore, discrimination persisted long after official emancipation. And so it did, even more tellingly, in the special agenda Napoleon had in mind for the consistoires. That program comprised the second part of the Organic Regulation. It was to employ the moral force of the Jewish "establishment" as a corrective of Jewish behavior. Thus, consistorial officials were obliged to reprimand those Jews who were lapsing into "usury" and into other antisocial activities. They were obliged also to ensure that able-bodied Jewish youths presented themselves for military conscription. In short, the consistorial system was intended to function as a kind of police force over Jewish morals and mores.

Ironically, the consistoires proved a gratuitous innovation. In no sense were they needed to remind Jews of their civic duties. Well before the Great Sanhedrin and Napoleon's Organic Regulation, Jewish businessmen were beginning demonstrably, if less than spectacularly, to diversify their economic activities beyond moneylending and retail peddlery. Then and later, young Jews were serving in the army and on the empire's numerous battlefields. At Waterloo, fifty-two Jews were killed in action. Nevertheless, in Napoleon's lifetime and afterward, the Jews of France chose to overlook the emperor's devious blend of cosmetic egalitarianism and functional hostility. Over the decades, they preferred to sustain their idealized vision of "the white eagle," "the great liberator." And yet, in practical fact, the eagle's campaign of liberation was extended almost exclusively to other nations' Jews, to those who lived conveniently beyond the frontiers of France itself.

OTHER PEOPLE'S JEWS

Upon consolidating his power at home, Napoleon turned to the challenge of devouring his European neighbors. No army or combination of armies could stand in the emperor's way, for his strategic genius was combined with the fervor of the Revolution and the demographic resources of the largest state in Western Europe. By 1808, Napoleon had become master of the Continent. His brother Louis now governed in the Dutch Netherlands. A second brother, Jerome, ruled the Kingdom of Westphalia, the largest component of France's puppet Confederation of the Rhine. A third brother, Joseph, successively ruled the kingdoms of Naples and Spain. Tuscany was ruled by Elisa, the emperor's sister. Napoleon's stepson bore the title of Viceroy of Italy. Even the Grand Duchy of Warsaw, carved from Prussia, now operated under a French administration.

Throughout all these regions of the French Empire, local Jewish populations did indeed experience their first taste of authentic legal equality. In the case of the Netherlands, where Jews had been living in unchallenged personal security for two centuries, they had nevertheless remained barred from public office and from important merchant guilds. But in 1795, even before Napoleon appeared on the scene, a French revolutionary army overran the Netherlands and transformed the country into the puppet Batavian Republic. Within the year, Noël, the French ambassador-protector, installed the full panoply of revolutionary innovations, including administrative centralization and equality before the law. Among the beneficiaries of the new regime were some 45,000 Dutch Jews. Two years later, in 1798, a Jewish delegate to the "Batavian" National Assembly, Isaac da Costa Atias, was elected the body's president.

As in the case of the Dutch Netherlands, France's conquest of north-central Italy, in 1797, antedated the Napoleonic Empire. In ensuing years, to be sure, under Napoleon's hegemony, the peninsula was further resected, but the revolutionary precedents of equality before the law and freedom of economic opportunity remained unaltered. By the same token, no element in Italy welcomed these innovations more ecstatically than did the Jews, who had lived for centuries under the most unregenerately medieval dynasties in all of Western Europe. Numbering some 23,000, and divided essentially among Rome, Florence, Venice, Verona, and Ancona, Jews had endured ghettoized lives of dire poverty and squalor. Now, however, within a single

month of the French conquest, these same Jews were granted full and unqualified civil equality. Indeed, the transformation was so unexpected that few of
them ventured at first beyond the periphery of their former ghetto neighborhoods. In the brief interval of their emancipation, under Napoleon's satellite
Kingdom of Italy, only a small number of Jews managed to participate in
a scattering of municipal governments, although a somewhat larger group
enrolled in the National Guard and fought with Napoleon's armies on European battlefields.

Yet it was the German regions, encompassing Western Europe's single
densest Jewish population of between 325,000 and 350,000, where the trajectory of emancipation proved far more erratic. In thirty-six principalities and
four Hanseatic cities, France's puppet regimes moved with speed and efficiency to introduce the Code Napoléon and to proclaim equality before the
law for Jews and Christians alike. In the Kingdom of Westphalia, in the
duchies of Baden, Hesse-Nassau, and Mecklenburg, French engineers literally battered open the narrow entryways of Jewish shantytowns. Here, too,
however, a number of local Jewish communities reacted hesitantly to emancipation. They feared reprisal from their German neighbors.

A case in point was the Free City of Frankfurt, the site of the German
world's quintessential ghetto. Although the French did not directly occupy
this city-state, the neighboring presence of their army intimidated Frankfurt's
duke-primate in 1807 to offer his Jews a certain easement in their commercial
restrictions. Even this narrowly qualified "freedom," however, was withdrawn
a full two years before Napoleon's defeat, when the French emperor was too
heavily engaged elsewhere to bother with retribution. In Bavaria and Baden,
whose governments functioned by Napoleonic sufferance, a series of ordi-
nances authorized new residential and mercantile opportunities for Jews. But
in the face of glowering popular resentment, these limited concessions often
remained dead on the paper.

The Grand Duchy of Warsaw offered a particularly vivid example of governmental evasion. Amputated from Prussian-ruled Poland in 1807, and
transformed into a French appendage, this satellite regime was obliged forthwith to accept the Code Napoléon. It was a moment of epiphany for the
duchy's 180,000 to 200,000 Jews. Anticipating full emancipation, even joyously composing odes of praise for Napoleon, Warsaw's Jewish kahal immediately petitioned Warsaw's grand duke to activate their new civil status. But
the grand duke reacted cautiously. By then the provisions of Napoleon's 1808
"Infamous Decree" were becoming known, and with them the emperor's palpable distrust of Jews. In October of the same year, the duchy issued its own
version of the Infamous Decree, extending Jewish vocational and domicile
restrictions for a probationary ten-year period.

In these same years of French hegemony, the Habsburg Empire, largest of the Central European nations and the very epicenter of European Catholicism, managed to stave off political reform altogether. Habsburg Jewry, once the beneficiaries of Joseph II's celebrated Toleranzpatent, had lost many of its uncertain prerogatives after the emperor's death in 1790. In Vienna, a few dozen "tolerated" Jewish families achieved privileged status, but most still remained without access to "respectable" trades and professions, or rights of domicile beyond their Leopoldstadt ghetto enclave. In Habsburg Bohemia and Moravia, limitations on Jews remained even more inflexibly in force than in Austria. As late as 1814, fewer than 50,000 Jews lived in these two "Crown Lands." The 120,000 to 130,000 Jews of Hungary were confined mainly to the smaller towns and villages of the southeastern provinces. Only the 212,000 Jews of Habsburg Galicia remained comparatively unaffected by domicile restrictions. Except for the provincial capital of Lemberg (Lvov), where they lived essentially in their own quarters, village Jews—the majority—conducted their business freely with Poles and Ukrainians in the countryside. Nevertheless, even in this intermingled hinterland, Jews were barred from owning residential plots outside village limits. In not a single province throughout the entirety of the Habsburg Empire did Jews enjoy unrestricted domicile as a fundamental right.

EMANCIPATION AS STATE SURVIVALISM

Throughout most of the eighteenth century, prospects for an improvement of Jewish status in Prussia appeared equally uncertain. On the one hand, Frederick II's dislike of Jews, intense and unrequited, in every respect characterized that of the population at large. Moreover, by his conquest of Silesia in 1740, the king also acquired some 45,000 new Jews, raising Prussia's Jewish population to over 80,000. To isolate this unwelcome new infusion, Frederick tightened the limitations on Jewish domicile, vocations, and marriages. Yet the effort availed little. A sizable minority of Jewish business, indispensable to the monarchy, was steadily winning *Schutzjüdische* status for itself (p. 22). Then, as a consequence of the partitions of Poland, in 1772, 1793, and 1795, the number of Jews in Prussia rose to at least 135,000, by far the single largest Jewish enclave in Germany, and in Western Europe altogether. With a Jewry of such formidable dimensions, would a program of uncompromising quarantine really serve the king's needs any longer?

For Friedrich Wilhelm II, who succeeded his late uncle in 1786, the question soon became acutely relevant. Only a year later, in 1787, the Jews of Berlin petitioned the king to relax their harsh vocational and fiscal burdens. After some hesitation, Friedrich Wilhelm agreed to appoint a commission of inquiry. But two years went by before the commission issued its report, and the findings were negative. In 1795, the Jews petitioned once more. After a three-year wait, they were rebuffed yet again, this time with the observation that they would first have to undergo a "fundamental and general improvement." In 1806, however, a seismic event forced a major reappraisal of the monarchy's future. This was Napoleon's crushing military victory at Jena, a battle that all but annihilated the Prussian army. Indeed, the ensuing peace treaty all but annihilated Prussia as a state. It amputated many of the kingdom's former Rhineland possessions, as well as most of the eastern territories Prussia had annexed during the partitions of Poland.

It was at this juncture, facing the imminent danger of national extinction, that the government of Friedrich Wilhelm III (who had succeeded his father in 1797) grasped the urgent need to restructure the country's entire political and social system. To that end, between 1807 and 1808, under the leadership of Chancellor H. F. Karl von Stein, several critical innovations were enacted by the Diet and approved by the king. National military conscription was introduced. The army high command, formerly a privileged aristocracy, was reconstituted as a competitive quasi-meritocracy. In the civilian sector, too, urban corporations were rehabilitated as self-governing municipalities. Most of the feudal anachronisms in Prussia's landlord-tenant system were ended, transforming the peasantry into freeholders (albeit of barely viable plots).

During this formidable assault on the relics of Prussian corporativism the issue of the Jews no longer could be postponed. Chancellor Stein himself favored a gradual end to their anomalous status. The prospect of Jewish equality should no longer be frightening, he argued. After all, the Treaty of Tilsit already had shorn Prussia of its eastern provinces, those containing the largest number of impoverished and insular Polish Jews. If emancipation were granted, it would be extended to the smaller, "respectable," middle-class Jewish population of integral—remnant—Prussia. In 1808, Stein himself was dismissed from office, at the "recommendation" of Napoleon, who distrusted his efforts at national revival. By then, however, King Friedrich Wilhelm already had been well seized by the former chancellor's arguments. Thus, early in 1809 he commissioned State Minister Friedrich von Schrötter to explore a possible enlargement of Jewish rights. An unimaginative bureaucrat, Schrötter moved cautiously, still preferring to wait until the Jews themselves achieved a wider acculturation. But he was soon challenged on this approach. Minister of the Interior Wilhelm von Humboldt, a classical rationalist, favored the immediate award of civil equality to the Jews. By intermingling freely with the Prussian people, argued Humboldt, the Jews would more readily absorb Prussian "moral" values. Over the ensuing year and a half, these conflicting attitudes were debated rather inconclusively in the Diet and in ministerial circles.

Then, in the summer of 1810, Karl August von Hardenberg was appointed chancellor. No less ardent a disciple of the Enlightenment than Humboldt, with whom he worked closely, Hardenberg pressed for an early and unequivocal end to restrictions on Jews. Still another year and a half of tinkering followed. But finally, in December 1811, the chancellor felt able to submit his—now carefully refined—proposal to Friedrich Wilhelm. Upon adding a few minor modifications of his own, the king approved it, and the Diet then passed it. With the royal signature, the law accordingly was issued on March 11, 1812, as the Edict Concerning the Civil Status of Jews Within the Prussian State. By its terms, Jews would share in the civil rights of non-Jewish Prussians. They would be exempted henceforth from Jew-taxes and would be granted the right to settle freely in town or country and to marry without special royal permission. Like other Prussians, they would be allowed to vote in municipal and state elections.

As in France, rights brought attendant responsibilities. Jews now would be subject exclusively to state courts and their young men to military conscription. Most Jews in fact cordially welcomed these obligations as proof of their equality of status. Two lingering qualifications proved somewhat less congenial. Hardenberg had proposed that Jews should gradually become eligible to hold state office and to win promotion to officers' rankings in the military. The king vetoed both suggestions. Plainly, the edict of emancipation was even more grudging a benediction in Prussia than in France. In France, the government's single most notorious caveat, the Infamous Decree of 1808, gradually would be allowed to lapse (pp. 73–74). Not so in the Prussia of Friedrich Wilhelm III or of his successors. For this militaristic nation, Jewish civil rights was a dispensation intended exclusively for purposes of state survival, and in no sense for any high-flown ideal of rational humanitarianism. Whatever their ensuing contributions to the country's economic or cultural life, or their sacrifices on the battlefield, the Jews of Prussia, and later of Prussian-ruled Germany, would remain under a cloud of distrust for generations to come. The consequences would hardly be less tragic for the German psyche than for the Jewish.

IV

Incarceration: The Jews of Tsarist Russia

Russia's Polish Inheritance

Catherine II was thirty-three years old in 1762 when she ascended the throne of imperial Russia. A princess of the minor German principality of Anhalt-Zerbat, she had been dispatched to Russia at the age of fifteen to marry another minor German dynast, Peter of Holstein-Gottorp, who as a nephew of the Tsaritsa Elizabeth had been "co-opted" as the future tsar by the Russian Empire's still dominant nobility. Although Peter turned out to be a coarse and inattentive husband, the ingenue German princess accomplished more than survival at court. Earlier, Catherine had adopted the Russian Orthodox religion. Subsequently, to obtain a firm understanding of her new country, she mastered the Russian language and immersed herself in Russian literature. In 1762, moreover, when the Empress Elizabeth died and Peter was anointed the royal successor, it was Catherine who plotted with a group of intriguing magnates to depose him (although it is uncertain that she had anticipated his murder). Soon afterward, she herself ascended the throne as "Empress and Supreme Ruler of all the Russias."

In the ensuing years, Catherine fortified her position by her shrewd distribution of honors and rewards to key aides. Time also worked in her favor. She reigned over so long a period, until her death in 1796, that her rule achieved the legitimacy of longevity as well as of outstanding competence. It was Catherine, far more than her early-eighteenth-century predecessor, the tyrannical genius Peter I ("the Great"), who brought Western ideas into Russia, who licensed numerous publishing houses, established dozens of schools in provincial and district towns, fostered education for girls, and introduced the first teacher-training program in Russia. A self-proclaimed disciple of the French philosophes, the empress particularly admired the writings of the Baron de Montesquieu and acknowledged Montesquieu's *Spirit of the Laws* as the inspiration for her announced program of sweeping judicial reforms—an agenda that she never quite managed to enact.

But if Catherine the Great was enlightened, she was also a despot. The

French Revolution, occurring late in her reign, strengthened the empress's inclination toward political conservatism, and her decision to repudiate much of the cultural climate she herself had labored to foster. Intent on fortifying her autocracy, Catherine achieved that goal by lavishing grants of crown lands on the Russian gentry and thus drawing them into a self-interested alliance with the throne—a process that also vastly strengthened the institution of serfdom throughout the country, and with it the tribulations of millions of Russian peasants. Catherine's equally ruthless imperialism drew her into a series of victorious but costly wars against the Turks, as well as the spoliation of the foundering Polish Commonwealth, in 1772, 1793, and 1795 (pp. 15–16). It was the latter achievement that presented the empress with her most daunting challenge. Poland, more than any of her other acquisitions, encompassed a bewildering heterogeneity of fractious ethnic and religious communities. Besides Poles, these new elements included Ukrainians, Belorussians, Germans, Lithuanians, Estonians, Courlanders, Finns—and Jews.

In fact, long before its successive partitions of Poland, the Tsarist Empire encompassed small pockets of "indigenous" Jews. Their historic origins are shrouded in obscurity. Greek inscriptions near Odessa suggest that Jewish communities were established on the northern shore of the Black Sea as early as the first centuries of the Christian Era. From these borderlands of the Byzantine Empire, venturesome Jewish traders apparently explored much of the Russian interior, while Jews from Armenia and northern Persia penetrated the Asian terrain abutting the Caspian Sea. In the Early Middle Ages, Jewish émigrés from the more advanced countries of western Asia infiltrated the Caucasus region, thereby laying the foundations for communities of so-called Mountain Jews.

In all these non-European regions, the Jewish population increased significantly following each recurrent wave of Byzantine persecution. Between the seventh and tenth centuries, it was this fugitive Jewish nucleus that played a unique role in the rapidly expanding Khazar Empire, which covered a large segment of southern Russia, from the northern Caucasus and lower Volga River to the Crimean peninsula. After adopting Hebrew script from the Jews, the Khazarian ruler evidently chose to spurn both Islam and Byzantine Christianity in order to retain his neutrality between these two greater foreign civilizations. In their place, around 740, he adopted the third and least threatening monotheistic civilization, that of Judaism. Although Khazarian Judaism was by no means a pure variety, it was practiced widely. Neither did it disappear even after the Khazars ceased to exist as a distinct people.

As for European Russia, little is known of a Jewish presence during the early or late medieval centuries. The one exception was the Crimea, where Jewish traders established several independent communities that subsequently were augmented with descendants of the original Jewish settlers in

Khazaria. Otherwise, the prevailing xenophobia of both the Russian masses and their rulers kept Jews and other foreigners out of the European areas. Rare appearances of Jews seem to have exacerbated those ethnic tensions. Records tell of a certain Zecharia, a Kievian Jew, who settled in Novgorod in the fifteenth century and began engaging in religious propaganda. Apparently, he won over several Novgorod aristocrats and clerics, who repudiated the divinity of Jesus and insisted that the Messiah was still to come. From Novgorod, the heresy of Judaization spread also to Moscow. In 1479, following a visit to Novgorod, Tsar Ivan III personally brought back with him two Judaizing priests, whom he installed in two Moscow churches, and who in turn won over Ivan's daughter-in-law Yelena. Alarmed, the hierarchs of the Russian Orthodox Church between 1440 and 1505 condemned the Judaizing sect, in several instances publicly burning apostates at the stake and forcing others underground.

Similar repressive measures continued under Ivan's successor, Ivan IV ("the Terrible"). Ivan also rejected all advances by the kings of Poland to allow Polish-Jewish merchants to visit the Muscovite territories on business. The tsar's fear of heterodoxy was understandable. It was a time when Orthodox Russia was under a grave threat from Roman Catholic missionaries in the west and Islamic emissaries from the south. Although the Jews were far fewer in number, and lacking in military resources, they were feared for their high degree of literacy, while the Orthodox clergy, whose traditions harked back to Byzantium, envisaged Jews as the incarnation of a deicidal religion. The ban against them consequently remained intact, well into the eighteenth century.

By then, possibly, a stance of defensiveness against alien minorities or ideologies might have appeared gratuitous. Russia had emerged as the largest empire in the world, extending from the banks of the Vistula to the steppes of Siberia, from the Baltic to the Black Sea. Nevertheless, the tsarist domain remained steeped in medievalism, its people still clinging to the kind of atavistic religiosity that had begun to fade in the West. To the devoutly pietistic Russian, the Jew was not a mere cheapjack, not a contemptible old-clothes dealer, as in the West. The Jew was an infidel, the poisoner of the true faith, the killer of Christ. For the tsars, it appeared far better to ensure that the simple, devout Russian people not be contaminated by the devious race of Israel. Even the inspired barbarian Peter the Great, who imported thousands of non-Russians to help modernize his empire, refused to admit Jews. Two years after Peter's death, his widow, Catherine I, ordered the immediate expulsion even of the modest enclaves of Jews found in the western border provinces. "Henceforth they will not be admitted to Russia upon any pretext," she warned, "and a very close watch will be kept against them in all places." The exclusionist policy was maintained under the reigns of Peter II and Anna Ivanova. In 1742, upon learning that isolated communities of Jews somehow again had taken root in the border provinces, the Empress Elizabeth Petrovna issued a ukase proclaiming, firmly and decisively, that "[a]ll Jews . . . shall . . . be immediately deported, together with all their property, from our whole Empire. . . . They shall henceforth not be admitted . . . under any pretext and for any purpose, unless they be willing to adopt Christianity of the Greek persuasion." Such were the implacable anti-Jewish policies that Catherine II inherited upon coming to the throne. Whatever her own enlightened proclivities, Catherine as a newcomer, a former Protestant princess, was uninterested in offending Russia's powerful Church hierarchy. Thus, in the same year of her ascension, 1762, she permitted all foreigners to travel and settle in Russia, "krome Evreiev"—"except the Jews." The phrase would appear repeatedly in subsequent ukases and statutes.

Then in the ensuing three decades, with the partitions of Poland, the empire that had rejected a few thousand Jews suddenly found itself with at least 800,000 Jews on its hands. Exclusion no longer was a realistic option, no more than for millions of other non-Russians, whose faiths and ancient cultures in any case no longer could be fully absorbed into the Russian language and Russian Orthodox faith. With the first Polish partition of 1772, therefore, which brought with it an initial modest enclave of some 27,000 Jews, Catherine, in her renewed posture as enlightened despot, issued a manifesto welcoming all inhabitants, including Jews, as her new subjects, and promising to respect their former Polish "liberties." As a mercantilist, too, the empress was aware of the potential economic usefulness of Jews, and declared her willingnesss to let them exercise their commercial talents, even to share in the public life of their towns. But the promised toleration remained more theoretical than actual. All attempts by Jews to participate in municipal government were effectively blocked by their Russian neighbors, on the grounds that the Jews engaged in "parasitical," "exploitative" activities among the surrounding peasantry, especially through their control of the liquor trade.

The latter charge actually was well-founded. Accustomed in Poland to functioning as middlemen between aristocrats' estates and the countryside, Jews had become proficient in buying up and converting harvested grain and potato crops into mash, and mash into distilled spirits, which resisted the vicissitudes of the weather. The peasantry offered a sure and certain market for liquor, and the Jews exploited it fully. In turn, well apprised of the flourishing traffic, Catherine eventually agreed that the countryside required protection from the Jews. Initially, that safeguard took the form of punitive imperial and provincial taxes. But as subsequent partitions of Poland added hundreds of thousands of "foreign" Jews to the Tsarist Empire, Catherine sensed that comprehensive measures were required. In countenancing them, moreover, she embarked on a unique feat of social engineering. Its most salient feature was the decision to prohibit Jewish settlement in the interior, in the Great Russian hinterland.

To achieve this ethnic barrier, Catherine in a series of sweeping decrees issued in 1783, 1791, and 1794 limited the Jews' presence exclusively to their current terrain, that is, to the formerly Polish territories that even then were being sheared off by the ongoing partitions. Except for a few unsettled frontier areas in the south, no Jews henceforth were permitted to venture beyond this geographic enclave. It was an ample enclave, to be sure, for it encompassed not less than fifteen provinces in the northwestern and southwestern regions of European Russia, and included, in addition to ethnically Polish areas, the former Polish-ruled territories of Ukraine, Belorussia, Lithuania, Bessarabia, and "New" Russia. Indeed, it was only a century later, when Jews in these regions were driven in growing numbers from the countryside, that the vast enclosure began to acquire the characteristics of a geographic ghetto, to be known unofficially as the Pale of Settlement.

In the late eighteenth century, however, if Catherine's approach to the Jewish problem at best was uncertain and often contradictory, it was hardly more so than her other policies. Her facile Enlightenment promises of modern education, gender opportunity, and Montesquian liberalism soon came to be overshadowed by her augmented royal autocracy, her brutal spoliation of the Kingdom of Poland, her transformation of millions of peasants into landless serfs. Nor was the empress's ambivalence to end with her reign. She transmitted her crippled legacy to her descendants.

THE TWO FACES OF ALEXANDER I

Following her death in 1796, Catherine was succeeded by her son, Paul. An irascible tyrant, the new tsar reversed a number of his late mother's enlightened initiatives, specifically by imposing heavy-handed administrative controls on the empire's minority populations. Paul's single enduring accomplishment doubtless was worthy of note. Before a palace revolution in 1801 unseated and killed him, he managed to establish a more stable rule of succession, based on primogeniture. Thus, Paul was succeeded by his own son, the twenty-three-year-old Grand Duke Alexander, now to become Alexander I.

In contrast to his father, the new tsar was an impressive man—tall, gravely courteous, dignified. Much was expected of him by Russia's literate classes, for he enjoyed a vague reputation as a progressive. At his grandmother's insistence, an eminent Swiss rationalist, Frédéric-César de La Harpe, had been appointed his tutor. Indeed, the young tsar started off well, dabbling with the ideas of Enlightenment, encouraging the use of rationalist terminology in court. Moreover, his key advisers, the "Unofficial Committee," included four well-educated liberals: Prince Adam Czartoryski, Nicholas Novosiltsev, Count Paul Stroganov, and Count Victor Kochubei (soon to become minister of the interior). At their suggestion, Alexander abrogated the censorship, the ban on publishing houses, and restrictions on travel abroad. A certain limited social legislation also was introduced. The gentry were allowed voluntarily to emancipate their serfs (although few did). In the manner of his grandmother, Alexander gave high priority to education. Four new universities were established, forty-two secondary schools, and many scores of primary schools.

Nowhere did the tsar's good intentions register more palpably than on the status of the Jews. Upon ascending the throne, Alexander inherited a Jewish population that had grown to nearly 1 million. Fourteen years later, in 1815, with the annexation of the satellite Kingdom of Poland (p. 60), some 180,000 more Jews would be added to his realm. By then, this burgeoning minority people already was taking on the lineaments of a dense, apparently unassimilable Semitic archipelago in a Slavic sea. Living mainly in towns, the Jews zealously preserved their religious distinctiveness, their ethnic customs of diet and dress, their communal autonomy, their predilection for commerce. How were these people to be absorbed? How were they to be made loyal and useful Russian citizens? These were the issues that initially had been revisited after Catherine's death by Gabriel Derzhavin, a renowned poet and member of the imperial Senate, the tsar's advisory council.

In 1799, during the earlier reign of Paul I, Derzhavin had been sent off to Belorussia to examine that region's deteriorating economic conditions. In the process, he transcended his mandate to give special attention to the Jewish question. Relying on hearsay reports by the gentry and other locals, Derzhavin returned to St. Petersburg and formulated a report of exceptional harshness. In his own evaluation, the Jews were irredeemably corrupt. "Why the good Lord has put this dangerous people on the face of the earth," he speculated, "is a puzzle. . . . But if they have to be suffered, it is vital that they be made more useful to themselves and to the societies in which they are embedded." It was the poet-senator's recommendation, then, that the Jews, a "depraved, counterfeiting, liquor-dealing" element, be separated as far as possible from the "God-fearing, innocent, and naive Russian peasantry." With only a few exceptions—farmers, artisans, and large-scale merchants—the Jews should be moved to the frontier territories or driven from the empire altogether. He urged as well abolition of the Jews' communal kahal, censorship of their religious books, regular inspection of their homes, and Russianization of their names.

Derzhavin's report was submitted to the Senate in December 1800. Under the byzantine procedures of the tsarist government, the document was not seriously reviewed until November 1802, and by then under the aegis of

Alexander I, who had come to the throne the year before. The new tsar here-upon instructed his own committee, this one more progressive in outlook than its predecessor, to come up with its own recommendations. That it did, finally, in a report of September 1804. Unlike the Derzhavin Report, the new approach seemed at first to reflect classical Enlightenment ideals. "[I]t is more desirable and safe to lead the Jews to self-improvement," the report began, "by opening to them the roads that will lead them to happiness. . . . A minimum of restrictions, a maximum of liberties." Yet even this committee's proposals, as they were incorporated the following month in Tsar Alexander's "Statute Concerning the Organization of the Jews," soon were exposed as a mixed bag.

On the one hand, in the spirit of rationalism, the Jews were to be provided with every opportunity to acquire a secular education, to register their chil-dren either in Russian schools or in their own schools, provided instruction was given in Russian or in other modern European languages. Jewish kahals were to be stripped of their corporative-taxation powers and of their principal juridical powers, including, most specifically, use of the *herem,* the rabbinical ban of excommunication. Although the Jews would remain confined in their Pale of Settlement, they were free to buy or lease land, even were eligible for financial and tax inducements should they engage in "socially useful" voca-tions such as agriculture or industry. At the same time, as an inducement for Jews to abandon their "parasitic occupations," they were barred henceforth from producing or selling liquor in rural areas, and required to be registered in one of four "estates": merchant, townsman, craftsman, or "agriculturist."

Thus far, the statute, to be known ever after as the "Constitution of the Jews," appeared to be a reasonably progressive document, notwithstanding its contemptuous appraisal of the Jews as a people suffering from "moral and civil degradation." Jewish self-government, like corporativism in its wider sur-vival, was becoming an expendable anachronism. An open door for Jews in Russian-language schools would be entirely consonant with the spirit of the new age. Indeed, Jewish modernists afterward would express regret that their people had spurned the government's offer; for as late as 1840, Jewish parents had enrolled only forty-eight of their children in these institutions. Similarly, the ban on Jewish liquor-dealing in rural areas might have been interpreted as legitimate public policy. Even the effort to induce Jews into agriculture might have been taken seriously, all the more so when it was coupled with important financial incentives.

But on the other hand, it was also the "agricultural" paragraph that revealed the tsarist government's characteristically ambivalent blend of carrot and stick. Henceforth, the provision declared, only Jews of the "agricultural estate"—that is, practicing Jewish farmers—should be permitted to live in the Pale's rural areas. After a four-year transitional period, Jewish non-farmers and their families were to be banned from the countryside altogether. More than a shock, the provision was an incipient catastrophe, for it was in the countryside that the vast majority of the Pale's more than 1 million Jews lived. It was here, over the centuries, in their dense network of villages and hamlets, that they had functioned almost exclusively as middlemen between the agricultural hinterland and the towns. Now, within a grace period of a mere four years, they would be required to abandon their traditional commercial livelihoods and move exclusively into the Pale's towns and cities. No people could have been uprooted on such short notice without suffering economic ruination.

Once the "Constitution of the Jews" was published and became widely known, thousands of petitions and protests flooded into the government. They came not only from Jewish community leaders and private individuals but from Russian and Polish gentry. What would happen to the economy of the countryside, asked these landowners, if half a million Jewish merchants were driven out? Tsar Alexander remained unmoved. In December 1804, his government launched into a "preliminary" transplantation in the northwestern, Lithuanian, border regions. Here 60,000 Jewish families were summarily evicted and forced into the Pale's interior. "Jews pleaded for an extension of time," wrote one Russian observer. "They cried and groaned, but to no avail. They were driven mercilessly under a guard of peasants and, in some cases, of soldiers, [driven] like cattle into the towns and hamlets, and then on to open lots under the sky." Another writer, no friend of the Jews, also described the uprooting: "In the dead of winter half-naked Jews, driven from their [village] domiciles into the towns, were crowded together in quarters that gave them no breathing space, while others, ill-sheltered, were left exposed in the bitter cold . . . [to succumb] to disease and death."

ALEXANDER I IN WAR AND TRIUMPH

Ultimately, it was Napoleon Bonaparte who produced a moratorium on these expulsions. In the process of "reconstituting" the Sanhedrin and of eradicating ghettos in the regions of his conquests, the French emperor soon acquired mythic status among Jews in Eastern and Western Europe alike. In December 1805, moreover, Napoleon inflicted a shattering military defeat on the Austrians and Russians at Austerlitz. The ensuing Treaty of Pressburg left the French army as the dominating presence along Russia's frontiers. It was at this moment of his empire's acutest vulnerability, therefore, that Alexander's advisers warned that little would be gained by driving the Jews to desperation, and to possible collaboration with the French. The tsar concurred. He postponed the evictions.

A year and a half later, in February 1807, Napoleon's massive victory over the tsarist army at Eylau produced additional consequences for Russian Jewry. Under the terms of the ensuing Treaty of Tilsit, France acquired the territories Prussia had annexed during the eighteenth-century partitions of Poland. These now were to be transformed into the Grand Duchy of Warsaw, a French satellite regime. As elsewhere in the French Empire, the duchy's new constitution incorporated the Code Napoléon, with its guarantees of equality before the law for all citizens. In theory, the guarantees included the duchy's 180,000 Jews. In practical fact, the duchy's reactionary gentry managed to bar Jews from parliamentary and municipal elections, and from numerous trade and professional guilds. Nevertheless, as an emergent bourgeoisie, the city of Warsaw's 12,000 Jews, and tens of thousands of other Jews in the duchy's numerous towns and villages, discerned a certain hope in their future. They would soon find ways of achieving new economic and even cultural status for themselves (p. 71). For his part, Tsar Alexander could not have been unaware that similar expectations were likely to be kindled among his own vast Jewish population.

The issue of potential Russian-Jewish unrest became acutely relevant in 1812. In that year, Napoleon resumed his military offensive against the Tsarist Empire. This time his Grande Armée consisted of nearly half a million troops. Tsar Alexander, with his forces outnumbered, was compelled to adopt a strategy of retreat and scorched earth. Yet, in pulling back from the western regions, the Russian army was also evacuating terrain that included the Pale of Settlement, with its dense Jewish population. What then would be the reaction of this Jewry? Would they remain loyal to the tsar? Or, in gratitude to the "white eagle," would they help provision Napoleon's army?

The tsar's anxieties were misplaced. Napoleon's route of march passed through regions that were extensively inhabited by Hasidim. For these fundamentalists, the "white eagle" was not a liberator but a dangerous revolutionary atheist. Typical was the warning issued by the preeminent Hasidic dynast, Rabbi Zalman Schneur of Lyadi (Ukraine). It was in the Jews' self-interest, Zalman Schneur insisted, to resist all French appeals for collaboration. Whereas Napoleon was godless, the tsar was not. If the French were victorious, observed the rabbi, the Jews would be stripped "not merely of their worldly goods, but of Judaism itself." Other Hasidic leaders echoed Zalman Schneur's words almost verbatim. Whether their warnings reflected authentically spiritual considerations or fear of eventual tsarist retaliation, Napoleon received no meaningful help from the Jews during the entire period of his army's march and eventual ignominious retreat through Russia.

It was questionable whether Alexander was grateful. One possible indicator was his stance on the Jews at the postwar Congress of Vienna. Here it became clear that the tsar had not become an instant liberal. His people had spilled too much blood for him to countenance a Europe vulnerable once again to revolutionary passions and turmoil. Alexander in fact was periodically to be found on his knees, sobbing before a crucifix in the presence of Baroness Julie von Krüdener, a psychotic German pietist. Infused with a new spirit of evangelism, the tsar went so far as to persuade his monarchic colleagues to join him in a Holy Alliance dedicated to the preservation of monarchical conservatism in Europe. In this transformation from a youthful progressive to a middle-aged reactionary, Alexander was unlikely to evince solicitude on behalf of the Jews. At Vienna, he played along with his fellow statesmen in criticizing other, smaller countries for reimposing prewar restrictions on the Jews; but within his own realm that solicitude was distinctly absent.

It was a realm that included new territorial accessions. Indeed, at Vienna, the tsar's principal objective was to seize the Duchy of Warsaw for his empire. The Prussians and Austrians vigorously resisted this demand, and were supported by the British. Eventually, a compromise was reached. Alexander was awarded three-fifths of the duchy, which he promptly reconstituted and attached to his demesne as the quasi-autonomous Kingdom of Poland (subsequently to be known as Congress Poland), with himself as king. Deferring then to British pressure, Alexander promised to offer his new Polish subjects a reasonably progressive constitution. Yet the new constitution in practical fact brought little initial relief to the Jews. As in the predecessor Duchy of Warsaw, they remained barred from guilds, from new domiciles, from public office. Within his "integral" Russian Empire, meanwhile, Alexander tolerated no change whatever in Jewish status. The 1804 "Constitution of the Jews" remained in place, with its sword of Damocles hanging over "nonagriculturists." All other prewar constraints on Jewish domicile, vocations, and movement not only remained intact but were often tightened. In the prewar years, selected categories of Jews had been permitted to visit the Russian interior for business purposes. No longer. In 1825, new restrictions included a ban on Jewish settlement along a thirty-three-mile zone of the Pale's eastern border.

Nevertheless, even under these limitations, Russian Jews by and large still tended to regard themselves as more fortunate than their non-Jewish neighbors. The typical Russian peasant remained locked in servitude to his landlord. Illiterate, profoundly superstitious, often drunk, he lived in a rude hut, slept in his clothes, and fed his fire with animal dung. No Jew would dream of changing places with him. By the same token, if the Russian *muzhik* had his own reasons for seeking an improvement in his lot, the very notion of joining hands with the Jews was equally unthinkable. The Jews were an unidentifiable race. They were Antichrists who worshipped and blasphemed in a foreign language. When the peasant heard the Jews chanting in their synagogues, his instinctive reaction was to cross himself in gratitude for having been spared communion with the alien and sinister People of Israel.

NICHOLAS I: GOVERNMENT BY BARRACKS MASTER

In December 1825, Alexander I died. He left no heirs, and it appeared initially that his older brother, Constantine, would become his successor. But Constantine, who had married a Polish aristocrat not of royal blood, felt obliged to renounce his rights to the throne. The renunciation left Nicholas, the third brother, nineteen years younger than Alexander, as next in line. Nicholas presented none of the complexities that have fascinated Alexander's biographers. Stocky and muscular, with hard eyes and a perpetual thrust to his jaw, he was a military man to his very marrow. Unlike his late brother, who had been reared in the atmosphere of the eighteenth-century Enlightenment, the new tsar was brought up during the war against Napoleon and in a climate of growing reaction. He had married a German princess and maintained close ties with his father-in-law, the sternly conservative King Friedrich Wilhelm III of Prussia. He had also been discountenanced by a brief political revolt, the so-called Decembrist Uprising of 1825, in protest against his ascension to the throne. For Nicholas, therefore, the guiding impulsions of his own reign would be those of fervent piety, unquestioning obedience to duty, and unmitigated patriotism.

To translate these ideals into practical reality, Nicholas gave over to Count Victor Kochubei, the veteran minister of the interior, chairmanship of a committee charged with reevaluating and restructuring government operations. At the committee's recommendation, the Third Department of the Royal Chancery was assigned the task of investigating subversion, of seeking out ways to "guide" the lives and if possible the very thought of the Russian people. Whatever the diversity of the empire's individual religions and nations, they would somehow have to be brought under tight political and social control. The objective was particularly important in the case of the Jews.

For Nicholas, the Jews were a parasitical race, a people of deicide and heresy. More ominously yet, they were growing in numbers, achieving a demographic mass of at least 1.2 million by 1834. The tsar entirely agreed with Kochubei that Western Europe, then relaxing its constraints on the Jews, could not serve as a model for Russia, "because of the incomparably larger numbers of [Jews] among us." By contrast, Minister of Education Sergei Uvarov, widely regarded as the "ideologist" of the imperial court, cautioned that the objective of "social control" could best be achieved through a pragmatic, "rational" approach to the Jews. Faced with these mixed recommendations, uncertain how to proceed, Nicholas simply ordered his late father's

"Jewish committee," still functioning under its most recent chairman, Count Pavel Kiselev, to continue its work of reviewing and refining the full accumulation of existing or pending legislation on the Jews.

In the late 1820s and early 1830s, several of the features of that "legislation" were adapted in ways that were quite far-reaching. Not all of them were unreasonable, particularly the limitations imposed on Jewish marriage before the age of eighteen, and the ban on using the Yiddish language in public or official documents. But other measures were indeed gratuitous, even draconian. Thus, further to encourage Jews to abandon commerce, the government intensified its campaign to lure or harass Jewish non-farmers out of the Pale's rural areas. Few of these innovations were entirely new. Most still belonged to the category of "refinement." Yet one of Nicholas's earliest policy decisions was authentically original, and in fact proved to be the single most traumatic piece of "Jewish" legislation in modern Russian history. Adopted in 1827, this was the "Statute on the Recruitment of the Jews."

Until that year, Jews had been allowed to pay for the right of military exemption, a practice that extended back to the predecessor Polish Commonwealth. In maintaining this tradition, the tsarist government was influenced neither by benevolence nor even by financial considerations. For reasons both of suspect loyalty and of religious fanaticism, Jews simply were regarded as inferior military material. In 1827, however, Nicholas personally overruled these earlier exemptions. Believing fervently in the military life, he was persuaded that even a criminal or a coward could be trained to be a useful soldier. As for the Jews, how better to deal with such an intractable group than through the discipline of military service?

By law, all of the empire's male inhabitants were subject to conscription for a standard period of twenty-five years, although essentially on the basis of "militia" availability rather than for continual service. But under the 1827 statute, a distinction was to be made in the case of the Jews. Their draftable age was set at twelve. It was regarded as useful for Jewish conscripts in their tender years of earliest adolescence to serve first in special "cantonal"—in effect, Jewish—battalions, where they would receive an initial, "preliminary" indoctrination into the rigors of military life. It was significant that cantonal early conscription was applied as well to criminals, vagabonds, and diverse categories of illegitimate children. Thus, for the Jews, as for these other special categories, the cantonal battalions plainly were intended as a means of social and police control, a preliminary "amalgamation" into the obligations of Russian life.

To cosmeticize this objective, the government circulated "interpretive" literature throughout the Pale, emphasizing that Jewish conscripts would enjoy the fullest measure of religious freedom during their army service. Rabbis would be appointed as army chaplains. As the program developed, however, its "amalgamation" implications became rather clearer. In 1828, Tsar Nicholas issued a circular permitting army priests to baptize Jewish recruits even without prior authorization from their bishops. As a result, during the ensuing fifteen years, baptisms occurred at the rate of between 1,000 and 2,000 a year. The tsar actually was disappointed with these figures. In 1843 he ordered an increase in the number of priests assigned to Jewish cantonal battalions. As a result, from the moment Jewish youngsters were brought into camp, they were subjected to conversionary pressures. Harassed, beaten, jailed often on the flimsiest of pretexts, they were simultaneously assured that their punishment would be rescinded if they accepted baptism. The evidence suggests that as many as two-thirds of all Jewish cantonists eventually were baptized during their military service.

Conversionary pressures, however, were far transcended by the sheer physical and psychological horrors of child conscription. Under the terms of the 1827 statute, the Jews' own kahals were obliged to provide the lists of available recruits. Yet, in making their selections, these communal officials were aware that the marrying age in the Pale was extraordinarily low. Most Jewish males over the age of eighteen, and many over the age of fifteen, already were heads of families. Facing the brutal task of choosing between fathers or unmarried children, the kahal elders regretfully chose children—often at ages younger than twelve, and some as young as eight. In 1835, the famed political liberal Alexander Herzen encountered a group of these Jewish child-conscripts as he was changing trains at a depot several hundred miles inland from Moscow. He wrote later:

> It was one of the most awful sights I have ever seen, those poor, poor children. Boys of twelve or thirteen might have survived the trip, but [not] little fellows of eight and ten. . . . Pale, exhausted, with terrified faces, they stood in thick, clumsy, soldiers' overcoats . . . fixing helpless, pitiful eyes on the garrison soldiers who were roughly getting them into ranks. The white lips, the blue rings under their eyes bore witness to fever or congestion. And these sick children, without care or kindness, exposed to the raw wind that blows unobstructed from the Arctic Ocean, were going to their graves.

Understanding well the likely fate of their children, Jewish parents lived in mortal dread of conscription agents. Ironically, most of these notorious *khappers*—kidnappers—were Jews themselves, working under contract to the kahal. Lying in wait, they often burst in on Jewish homes at night to seize their intended prey. It was lucrative work. Apart from the salary they received from the kahal, the agents frequently released kidnapped children for ransom money and replaced them with others. They had learned that wealthier Jews would pay to ensure that their own children were bypassed for those of other, poorer families. Little wonder that an unbridgeable schism opened in Jewish society, with riots and attacks against the conscription agents and their kahal employers. Ultimately, the trauma inflicted by the cantonal conscription system would destroy the last remnants of the kahal's moral authority in the Pale.

A Reevaluation of Tsarist Tactics

Nicholas I's reign was not to be judged exclusively by its legacy of political and intellectual obscurantism. In the thirty years of his rule, the Russian Empire's agricultural sector gradually became more diversified, and significant grain surpluses began to provide a major share of Russia's developing foreign trade. Large quantities of government money went into the construction of new schools and higher technical institutes. A sunburst of Russian literature produced such giants as Pushkin, Krylov, Lermontov, Gogol, and Aksakov. In all other respects, however, Nicholas's tenure on the throne has quite properly been identified with implacable reaction. It was a policy he applied to foreign and domestic affairs alike. Doubtless the tsar was profoundly influenced by the 1825 Decembrist revolt, and even more by a military uprising in Congress Poland in 1830. A year of heavy fighting was needed before his army regained control of the satellite Polish kingdom. Soon afterward, Nicholas replaced the Polish constitution of 1825 with an "Organic Statute" that integrated the country more tightly into the Russian Empire.

It was in these same years of the 1830s and 1840s, moreover, that Nicholas set out to become in effect the policeman of Europe. In 1833, he reached agreement with the Prussian and Austrian governments to join forces in the event of future Polish unrest. In 1846, he helped the Austrians suppress an uprising in the "Free City" of Cracow. In 1848, he dispatched a 200,000-man army to crush a Hungarian uprising against Habsburg rule. As an integral feature of this reactionary "legitimism," Nicholas simultaneously embarked upon an intensive policy of Russification in his own western provinces of Lithuania, Belorussia, and Ukraine. Here the institutions of the Russian Orthodox Church were lavishly funded and enlarged at the expense of local ethnic churches and religious orders. The quasi-autonomy of the Duchy of Lithuania was repealed. And, by the same token, there was the perennial issue of the Jews to be revisited.

Years of vocational "persuasion" and intimidation seemingly had exerted little impact on this burgeoning minority population. Notwithstanding every tsarist strategy adopted for their "amalgamation," the Jews remained a cohesive mass, devoutly traditional in religion and sociology. The more they were abused, the more resistant they seemed to become to Nicholas's vision of a homogeneous empire. Plainly, a more "scientific" approach to this people had to be devised. In 1840, the tsar asked his trusted senior minister, the aged Pavel Kiselev, to come up with new and original ideas for coping with the Jewish problem. Kiselev then reconstituted his "Jewish committee," adding several new ministers and other senior officials, none of them an unregenerate reactionary. After four months of discussions, the committee produced a new omnibus memorandum, the so-called Kiselev Report. In its introduction, the document suggested that the "estrangement of the Jews from the civil order" could be ascribed to two principal factors. One was the administrative anomaly of the kahal, which separated Jews from governmental control. The second factor was the Talmud, whose teachings presumably encouraged Jewish insularity and fanaticism.

Although the committee's diagnosis was less than original, its prescription for change was distinctly mixed. On the one hand, it recommended that a five-year deadline be imposed on the Jews to become either farmers, artisans, or large-scale merchants (merchants of "high estate"). A Jew failing to establish his vocational "usefulness" within this period would be liable to a prolongation of his military service, then afterward to forcible retraining in one of the more "useful" occupations. Nicholas reacted well to the proposal. Indeed, he embellished it with a harshly punitive addendum of his own. In 1842, by tsarist decree, Jews living within thirty miles of the Austrian and Prussian borders were obliged to move from their villages and small towns into the larger towns and cities of the Pale's interior. Here again was a prescription for economic ruination. As many as 100,000 Jews might have been affected. But, in practical fact, no such mass evacuation ever was carried out. The intercession of Sir Moses Montefiore, a politically well-connected English Jew, gave the tsar pause at a time when he was seeking a closer diplomatic relationship with Britain (p. 97). More fundamentally, the Russian civil service was incapable of managing a demographic shift of these proportions.

Others of the Kiselev Committee's proposals, however, were both more original and seemingly easier of realization. One was to emulate the example of Western nations in drastically limiting the role of Jewish self-government. Far more than in the West, the kahal had come to function as a major obstacle to Jewish "amalgamation." Indeed, reacting to the proposal with enthusiasm, Nicholas superseded it by ordering the liquidation of the kahals altogether. The decree took effect in 1844. It had been long overdue. If Russia was ever to create a modern administration, all vestiges of corporativism would have to be discarded. From the Jewish viewpoint, too, the kahal's collaborative role in the military cantonist program had all but doomed its lingering influence.

EDUCATIONAL ENLIGHTENMENT: RUSSIAN JEWRY'S MISSED OPPORTUNITY

The Kiselev Committee won tsarist approval for yet another strategy of Jewish "amalgamation." This one endorsed the proposal of Count Sergei Uvarov, minister of education and public enlightenment. It was to launch an imaginative program of Jewish reeducation. Uvarov was fully committed to the notion that the Talmud and religious fanaticism lay at the heart of Jewish insularity. A veteran of government service, he had spent his formative years at Russia's embassies in Vienna and Paris, and was a member of several West European cultural academies. It was during that earlier period, too, that he had developed and refined his vision of a "legitimate" political system. It was to reflect a nation's most enduring characteristics, essentially its religion, patriotism, and national honor. In the 1830s, Uvarov had interpreted this objective for Russia as "Orthodoxy, Autocracy, Nationality." The credo was by no means a prescription for black reaction, however. As Uvarov wrote the tsar in 1837, the task of the ministry of education and enlightenment should be to blend Western-style enlightenment with the Russian "spirit."

Under this interpretation, Uvarov regarded it as no less his obligation to encourage "enlightenment" among the Jews. He had long maintained a special interest in the Jews, possibly as a consequence of his research into ancient civilizations and oriental cultures. He respected the Jews' "good qualities" and insisted that, "despite the mystical gibberish of their rabbis, [their] nation has displayed a splendid imaginativeness, which has lacked only judicious guidance." It was specifically this "guidance" that Uvarov was determined to provide. As early as 1838, even before winning formal endorsement from the government, the minister conferred with a number of Jewish leaders in Vilna to discuss his conception of a new educational program for Russian Jewry. In Vilna, a border community with close German connections and a strong anti-Hasidic tradition, a small group of *maskilim*—enlightened Jews—already had established several private schools offering secular as well as purely Jewish subjects.

Other such schools had been opened in Odessa, Kishinev, and Riga, cities that similarly maintained extensive trade and cultural ties with the West. The program's sponsors were an element with whom Uvarov was certain he could communicate. As he acknowledged now to his listeners in Vilna, it was quite understandable that even humanistic Jewish parents should remain suspicious of Russian schools. But would they not react more favorably if Jewish schools should themselves offer a program of combined secular and Jewish studies? Here the minister reminded his audience that he personally took an interest in Russian-Jewish scholars, and in the past had made it possible for them to study at Russian universities. "Give us a finger," he entreated the Vilna group, "and we shall stretch out our whole hand." The listeners reacted with caution, but seemingly without disapproval.

Turning then to the government, Uvarov in November 1838 made the identical case in a memorandum, "On the Education of the Jews." The logical approach to Jewish amalgamation, it insisted, was to reeducate a new Jewish generation in government-sponsored schools that adopted precisely the objectives and curriculum nurtured by humanistic Jews themselves. The Kiselev Committee agreed. So did the tsar. In late 1840, therefore, to help formulate his new educational policy, Uvarov set about organizing a series of joint committees of local Russian officials and Jewish maskilim. Six such committees were established, with those in Vilna and Odessa the most important. At the same time, aware of the still extensive reservoir of distrust among Jewish traditionalists, Uvarov maintained a low profile. His campaign for Jewish educational reform could be spearheaded more effectively by Jews themselves, and specifically by Western Jews who had pioneered similar experiments in their own countries. Here Uvarov believed that he knew where to turn. In January 1841 he invited Max Lilienthal, a progressive German rabbi, to visit him in St. Petersburg.

Munich-born, twenty-five years old, with a doctorate from Friedrich-Wilhelm University, Lilienthal during the previous two years had directed a small German-language Jewish school in Riga. Articulate and dynamic, Lilienthal in his palpable enthusiasm for a wider network of "enlightened" schools seemed a logical collaborator in the Uvarov program. The minister accordingly wasted little time in appointing Lilienthal director of the project—and thereby the first professing Jew ever to become an official member of a tsarist government. Over the ensuing weeks of January and February 1840, the two men worked intimately to devise a program likely to win the initial endorsement of prominent Jewish scholars elsewhere in Europe. They succeeded. Enthusiastic responses soon were forthcoming from such renowned figures as Leopold Zunz, Abraham Geiger, and Ludwig Philippson in Germany (pp. 130–34), and Samuel David Luzzatto in Italy. All vigorously supported the notion of secular education for Russia's parochial Jewry, and all promised help in securing qualified teachers for the anticipated schools. Eventually, they produced a list of some two hundred likely prospects.

With this commendation in hand, Lilienthal set off to make his case throughout the Pale. But in a majority of cities and towns he visited, the young educator encountered an unanticipated wall of opposition among the communal leadership. In his memoirs, Lilienthal recalled that, even in "enlightened" Vilna, the local rabbis now began to express grave reserve.

> "Doctor, you are a stranger here [they warned]. Do you know what you are undertaking? The course pursued against all religions except the Greek [Orthodox] proves clearly that the Government intends to have but one Church in the whole Empire. . . . We are sorry to state that we have no confidence in the new measures proposed by [Minister Uvarov], and that we look with gloomy foreboding into the future."

Some communities refused Lilienthal the courtesy of a hearing. In Minsk, bands of young Hasidim followed him down the street, shouting derisively, "Shaven one, get thee gone!" Later, when he attempted to address a public meeting in the same city, the audience became so unruly that the local fire department was summoned to disperse the crowd. In Vitebsk, members of the audience shouted that Lilienthal's eyes should be gouged out, his lips sewn shut. Police were summoned to protect him. Apprised of these indignities, Uvarov then arranged for thousands of circulars to be distributed in the Pale, warning that Lilienthal, as a government official, was entitled to "all the protection and privilege of the Imperial services," and that further unruly outbursts against him would produce serious consequences.

The warning had its effect. Throughout the remainder of 1841 and into the following year, Lilienthal crisscrossed the Pale, addressing every sizable Jewish community. This time audiences courteously heard him out, even agreed to nominate candidates for the "Jewish commission." In the hoary tradition of Russian sluggishness, the commission did not meet until August 1843, in St. Petersburg. Nevertheless, in December 1843, after a further series of lengthy discussions that were guided by Lilienthal and, intermittently, by Minister Uvarov himself, the commission reached agreement on an educational format. To be called Crown schools, the envisaged institutions would teach Jewish subjects for twenty-eight hours a week, while secular studies would be limited to fifteen hours a week. Jewish subjects would be taught by Jews, secular subjects by non-Jews. As a particularly compelling inducement for attendance, students attending Crown secondary schools would be exempted from military conscription for a period of ten years. Students winning exemplary marks in the Russian language and history would be exempted from conscription altogether. Additionally, two Crown rabbinical seminaries would be established, and operated exclusively by Jews. The Crown school agreement, requiring herculean patience and tact on Lilienthal's part, was a formidable achievement for a Western Jew, a comparative stranger to the Pale, not yet thirty years old. Once approved by the tsar in an imperial ukase of November 1844, the project seemed all but assured in its future success.

In October 1845, however, only eleven months after promulgation of the ukase, Lilienthal announced his resignation as director of the program. For many years afterward, the traditional explanation for this astonishing volte-face was the alleged discovery of a secret government agenda for the Crown schools. It was to convert Jewish students to Christianity. Lilienthal himself fostered this explanation. In his article for the *Allgemeine Zeitung des Juden-tums*, published in 1848, he insisted that "only when the Jews bow down to the Greek Cross will the Tsar be satisfied, irrespective of whether the converts be good or bad people." The rationale was factitious. Lilienthal's precipitous departure was impelled by careerism. He had become engaged to a Munich Jewish woman, Pepi Nettre. His prospective father-in-law, highly dubious of the entire Russian adventure, was continually dunning the young man to seek out a position with better financial prospects. And finally Lilienthal agreed. Sailing off with his bride to the United States, he eventually negotiated a well-paying rabbinical pulpit for himself in Cincinnati, Ohio.

Whatever his humiliation, Minister Uvarov would not be deterred from launching the Crown schools. He appointed a new director, Leon Mandel-shtam, a respected Russian-Jewish scholar and an ardent maskil. In the autumn of 1847, under Mandelshtam's energetic tutelage, and accompanied by much governmental fanfare, the first schools were opened, in Vilna and Odessa. By 1855, seventy-one such institutions were in operation, ministering to 3,500 students. Year after year, well into the 1860s, the quality of instruction was rigorously maintained, even approaching that of Western Europe. Nevertheless, it was also in the 1860s that the Crown school experiment began to founder. Despite the inducements of military exemption, the numbers of students began to decline, eventually languishing at an annual plateau of around 2,000. Years later, in 1873, Tsar Alexander II would put an end to the program altogether.

In their longer-term influence, the Crown schools were by no means an abject failure. Indeed, the very proof of their impact was the growing tendency of young Jews later to bypass the Crown institutions specifically for state gymnasia and universities, where their degrees would offer them still wider vocational opportunities. Meanwhile, even the limited number of Crown school graduates would play their own role in Jewish modernization. Several became instructors in the Crown schools, men like Abraham Gold-faden, Leo Pinsker, Israel Soloveichik, Lev Levanda, Aaron Liebermann— all eventually to emerge as prominent figures within the future *Haskalah* (enlightenment), Socialist, and Zionist movements (p. 187). It may only be speculated on the additional numbers of educated humanists Russian Jewry might have produced but for its implacable distrust of Minister Uvarov's intentions, and its no less unregenerate cultural parochialism.

PRAGMATIC EGALITARIANISM: THE TSAR'S MISSED OPPORTUNITY

In 1842, during one of his discussions with Lilienthal, the minister of education reminisced about his travels through Western Europe, and the favorable impression he had formed of the educated, public-spirited Jews he had encountered in Germany, Austria, and France—the kind he aspired to produce for Russia. "Believe me," Uvarov confessed, "if we had such Jews as I met in . . . Germany, we would treat them with the utmost distinction, but our Jews are entirely different." Yet the well-meaning Uvarov, and surely the grimly reactionary Nicholas I, failed to grasp that Russia's government also was entirely different from those in Western Europe. Was it not likely that a more consistent approach of encouragement and acceptance, rather than a baffling mélange of carrot and stick, would have produced a wider pool of humanistic, public-spirited Jews? Indeed, the tsar need not have traveled as far as Western Europe to discover the tangible advantages of a more relaxed and accommodating Jewish policy.

In 1815, the former Duchy of Warsaw was transformed into the Kingdom of Poland, to function quasi-autonomously under tsarist rule (p. 60). Congress Poland was far from a model of liberalism. Most of its old aristocratic privileges remained in place. But townsmen at least were moving up the social scale, sharing in elections to the Sejm, winning access to senior positions in government and military service. Even following the outbreak and subsequent failure of the 1830 national revolt, the inhabitants of Congress Poland continued to enjoy incrementally wider political and cultural opportunities than did their Russian counterparts. The circumstances of Polish Jewry were more anomalous yet. Very little may have changed in their legal status. The original, 1815 constitution stated clearly that only adherents of Christian denominations could enjoy political and most civil rights. As a consequence, Jews remained without citizenship, without the right to hold office, or to share in legislative elections of any kind.

Nevertheless, with Tsar Alexander I setting a more relaxed political tone in the early post-Napoleonic era, numerous Jews managed to bypass those restrictions, and continued to do so even in the early years of Nicholas I. Thus, the sheer economic growth of Congress Poland generated a quite substantial Jewish bourgeoisie. Among them were such prosperous bankers as Samuel Kronenberg and Alexander Cohen, import-export magnates like Isaac Rosen, Michael Ettinger-Rawski, and Alexander Wertheim. Few Poles could match the Jews' historic experience as textile manufacturers and distributors, as financiers and marketing intermediaries between town and countryside. Altogether, the region's urban economy was becoming thoroughly interpenetrated by this Jewish bourgeoisie. By 1830, as many as 100 affluent Jewish families were living in Warsaw's upper-middle-class neighborhoods, well beyond the city's traditional Jewish quarter; and by 1842, the number exceeded 1,000. Not least of all, middle-class Jews were providing their children with secular as well as Jewish education. By 1862, more than 7,000 Jewish children were enrolled in the nation's trade and commercial schools.

It was also from the 1820s on that a new Jewish cultural elite was gravitating into the liberal professions, into medicine, into the natural sciences, even into literature. Wealthy Jews also served increasingly as patrons of these cultural activities. In Warsaw, the single most influential intellectual journal was the *Biblioteka Warszawska.* Its two principal supporters were Leopold Kronenberg and Matthias Rosen. In 1843, Ludwik Natanson, age twenty-one, returned to Warsaw from his medical studies in Austria, and four years later began publishing Congress Poland's first medical journal. Ludwik's brother, Jakob, a chemist, was a prolific contributor of scientific articles to the *Great Polish Encyclopedia,* the nation's first such compilation. By no coincidence, that massive project was the accomplishment of Samuel Orgelbrand, owner of Warsaw's largest bookstore, who commissioned and completed the editing of the encyclopedia in 1840. Orgelbrand's bookstore and publishing house was one of fifteen such Jewish-owned institutions in Congress Poland. It was a synergy of cultures paralleled in the realm of Warsaw classical music, which was as overwhelmingly Jewish in performance as in patronage. The city's symphony orchestra was founded by Jews and its principal conductors were Jews. Altogether, the role of Jews in the cultural life of Congress Poland was perhaps best expressed by the Polish writer Jozef Kraszewski, who described Poland's natural sciences, medicine, and jurisprudence as the "Jewish sciences." Wherever he traveled in Warsaw, Kraszewski marveled, he encountered Jews who were either intellectuals themselves or the doyens of salons that functioned as showplaces for other intellectuals—Jews and Poles alike.

During the years since the late-eighteenth-century partitions of Poland, three Russian rulers—Catherine II, Alexander I, and Nicholas I—had made serious attempts to cope with a vast Jewish nation within their borders, to "amalgamate" that burgeoning minority presence into the empire's prevailing culture. Two of those monarchs entangled themselves in cross-purposes. Catherine and Alexander sought to lure Jews into Russian schools and into agriculture, and then impacted them into a vast geographical ghetto. Nicholas I at least moved closer to a strategy of consistency. Inheriting a Jewish policy that was a mixture of abuse and forbearance, he abandoned almost all pretext of benevolence. By destroying Jewish self-government, by dragging Jewish children to the baptismal font via the military barracks, the tsar presented Russian Jewry essentially with the alternatives of apostasy or strangulation. And when offered an imaginative program for acculturating the Jews through education, Nicholas forfeited that opportunity even more decisively than did the Jews themselves, by failing to link the Crown school program to the inducement of tangible economic and administrative rewards.

In the end, Jews remained Jews: stubborn, pietistic, clannish. The one and single prospect for luring this intensely ethnocentric minority into Russia's wider vocational and cultural landscape was to expand the functional equality of status already incrementally available to Jews—not to Jews in far-off Western Europe, but just across the provincial horizon, in Congress Poland. The prospect, and the opportunity, were ignored.

V

The Triumph of Emancipation in the West

A World Restored

In September 1814, the city of Vienna became the magnet for an unprecedented coruscation of visiting dignitaries. The gathering included the rulers
and state ministers of almost every nation in Europe, together with elaborate
retinues of lackeys and mistresses. Their arrival for an international congress
was Europe's most impressive diplomatic assemblage since the peace conference at Westphalia nearly two centuries earlier. Twenty-five years of political
upheaval and Napoleonic adventurism had left their world unrecognizable.
To achieve its reconstruction, the statesmen were agreed that in the Europe of
their lifetimes security and stability must prevail, at almost any cost.

The eminences in Vienna were not all archreactionaries. They acknowledged that the Holy Roman Empire could not be resuscitated, or the majority
of petty German dynasts returned to their thrones. But if Europe could not
be restored to its eighteenth-century "normalcy," some workable method
would have to be found to avoid the dangers of revolutionary anarchy. The
diplomats' thirst for quietude was entirely shared by populations that had
been exhausted and impoverished by the march and countermarch of mobs
and armies. Conservatism was Europe's prevailing mood, with its veneration
of tradition and the accumulated wisdom of ages gone by. It was a moment,
therefore, to repudiate such dangerous innovations as representative government, secularism, or egalitarianism.

Ironically, the reversion to political conservatism was least severe in France,
the original fount of revolutionary unrest. Although the Bourbon dynasty was
restored, Louis XVIII, the corpulent scion of the royal line, recognized that
equality before the law had emerged from the nation's indigenous social and
economic circumstances. It could not simply be legislated away. King Louis
consequently was prepared to accept a moderate, quasi-constitutional monarchy. The basic juridical gains of the Revolution survived, together with the
Code Napoléon. So, too, in large measure, did Jewish emancipation. Indeed,
in 1818, the Jews of France were liberated even from Napoleon's Infamous

Decree, the legislation that had inflicted gratuitous restraints upon Jewish economic activity. Thirteen years later, in 1831, under the successor Orleanist dynasty of King Louis-Philippe, the consistoires that had been established by Napoleon in 1808 were limited henceforth to the supervision of Jewish religious activities, and spared their former degrading function as monitors of Jewish business behavior, Jewish patriotism and military service. In turn, responding to assurances of enhanced security, French Jews ventured more rapidly than in past years to reconfigure their geographic and vocational identity. By then, nearly half their population—grown to approximately 60,000—had gravitated from their traditional northern and southern départements to Paris. Abandoning pawnbroking and other forms of lending, they moved increasingly into more conventional forms of retail and wholesale commerce, into small industry and the professions—into "respectability."

Yet, with the single exception of the Dutch Netherlands, where the restoration of the House of Orange in 1815 produced no change in the Jews' equality of citizenship, the juridical status of Jews elsewhere on the Continent was thrown seriously into question. In Italy, that status reflected the dismal political and social circumstances of the post-Napoleonic era altogether. The statesmen at Vienna expressed little interest in transforming Italy's ziggurat of separate principalities into a single, united country. Instead, Lombardy and Venetia were obliged to function as separate Habsburg puppet duchies. Modena, Parma, and Lucca similarly were allocated to Habsburg "viceroys." The Papal States were returned to the governance of their namesake, the Bishop of Rome; and the Bourbons were restored to their palace in Naples, once again to rule in the Kingdom of the Two Sicilies. Piedmont-Sardinia, ostensibly sovereign, remained dependent on the forbearance of Austria for its precarious independence.

As in the prerevolutionary era, therefore, the peninsula's approximately 20,000 Jews were dispersed essentially between Piedmont, Lombardy-Venetia, and Tuscany, in the north; and the "Romagna"—the Papal States—in the center. Many of the baneful anti-Jewish constraints and humiliations were restored, as well. Although the Austrian viceroy of Lombardy-Venetia was satisfied essentially to bar Jews from public office, from the liberal professions, and from the right to purchase land, Jews in Piedmont-Sardinia, Parma, and Modena were hustled back to their restricted neighborhoods, even subjected again to onerous Jew-taxes. Grimmest of all, however, was the fate of the Jews in the Papal States. Upon returning from his long exile during the years of Napoleon's puppet Kingdom of Italy, Pope Pius VII reestablished his former ecclesiastical regime down to its last medieval detail. Throughout the Romagna, Jews were confined to their former shantytowns, to peddling or petty retailing, and subjected to annual tributes.

In Rome itself, the city's 3,500 Jews were locked again in the most congested and squalid ghetto in all of Europe. And after Pius's death, in 1823, his successor, Leo XII, proved even more implacably reactionary. At the new pope's orders, Jewish attendance at papal sermons on Saturday afternoons and Christian holidays was made obligatory again. Jews also were required to possess special permits for travel outside the ghettos, even in daylight, or to hire Christian servants and wet nurses. From 1830 on, a new pope, Gregory XVI, permitted an incremental enlargement of the Roman ghetto and eased the laws on enforced sermon attendance and the employment of Christian servants. Yet, in every other respect, he maintained the grillwork of Jewish restrictions. The Jews, he reminded Prince Klemens von Metternich, the Austrian chancellor, who had interceded on their behalf at the request of the banker Salomon Rothschild, were "a nation of deicides and blasphemers of Christ, and sworn enemies of the Christian name."

Central Europe shared much of the fate of the Italian peninsula. On the one hand, the statesmen at Vienna were too pragmatic to seek a revival of the more than three hundred diverse principalities that had constituted the German world. Yet, in rejecting the appeal of German nationalists for a single, united German empire, they produced at best a ramshackle confederation of thirty-nine separate and sovereign political entities. The apparition was entirely the brainchild of Metternich, the Congress of Vienna's éminence grise. It ensured ongoing Austrian domination of German affairs. Further to eradicate the vestiges of Napoleon's rule, Metternich and his colleagues canceled the innovation of equality before the law, which the French emperor had institutionalized in his renowned Code Napoléon. More than any other decision taken at Vienna, it was repudiation of that corpus juris that apparently spelled finis to Jewish emancipation.

Not all Jews were prepared to accept that fate without protest. Rather, several of their most prominent bankers set about waging their own version of a rescue campaign. In that effort, the Rothschilds, the Itzigs, the Herzes, and the Arnsteins threw open their Vienna mansions to the visiting European statesmen, tendering them magnificent banquets and lavish gifts of jewelry. Nor did these financiers hesitate to single out Prussia's Karl August von Hardenberg and Wilhelm von Humboldt as their people's likeliest champions. These were the only statesmen in Germany, after all, to have taken the lead in voluntarily emancipating their own Jews (Karl von Stein, who as chancellor had seen through Jewish quasi-emancipation in 1812, was then living in Russia). "I am working with all my might to give the Jews civil rights," Humboldt wrote his wife in January 1815, "so that it will no longer be necessary . . . to go to Jewish homes."

In February 1815, as they labored with other diplomats on a constitution for a loose German confederation, Humboldt and Hardenberg explored ways of formulating a provision on the Jews. Version after version was drafted, revised, and discarded before the two men reached a workable compromise. Their projected statement, Article 16 of the Treaty of Vienna, assured the Jews of all "rights heretofore granted them in the several states." Almost at the last moment, however, on June 8, at the initiative of the mayor of Bremen, who in turn was responding to the protest of his city's gentile merchants, the wording of the article was revised. Reference now was made only to those rights that previously had been granted Jews "by" the several states. The consequences of the change, if subtle, eventually proved fatal. With the exception of Prussia and Baden, none of the individual German states had voluntarily granted the Jews civil rights during the Napoleonic era. French bayonets alone had prodded these governments into the concession. Nevertheless, for several weeks after Article 16 had been ratified, the Rothschilds and other Jewish intercessors exulted in their "victory." Only when the full implications of the revised language became evident did they sense that their "victory" was in fact a defeat.

The wording authentically reflected German popular sentiment during the early post-Congress years. In Bavaria, local populations reacted gleefully when the notorious *matrikel* law was reinstated, compelling Jews once again to secure this official document to establish domicile, or the right to marry, or to earn a livelihood in such typically "Jewish" vocations as wholesale food-marketing and cattle-dealing. Indeed, the return of the matrikel soon precipitated a major immigration of young Jewish men to the United States. Even in Prussia and Baden, the two German states that had voluntarily granted Jews civil rights during the Napoleonic era, Article 16 offered only minimal protection. In 1816–17, the Baden Diet issued legislation that distinguished between "full" citizens, with "full" political rights, and "protected residents." The Jews, of course, fell into the latter category. Prussia, encompassing between 140,000 and 150,000 Jews, turned out to be an even profounder disappointment. In 1816, King Friedrich Wilhelm III announced that the Jewish Emancipation Edict of 1812 would not apply to the "new provinces"—essentially Silesia, conquered from Austria in 1740, and Posen, acquired during the eighteenth-century partitions of Poland. The edict would be limited rather to the "old provinces" of Brandenburg, Saxony, Pomerania, and East and West Prussia; and in these restricted areas, too, distinction was made between citizens entitled to vote and a more limited minority entitled to hold public office. Thus, from 1816 on, only 28,000 Jews in the entirety of the Kingdom of Prussia enjoyed the rights of full citizenship. All others, as "protected residents," were confined to the larger towns, forbidden to marry before the age of twenty-four, and severely restricted in their choice of vocations.

Doubtless it was unrealistic for Jews to have anticipated emancipation in a post-Napoleonic Europe that as late as the 1820s seemed firmly wedded to romantic conservatism. For German nationalists, struggling to create a united empire, the Jew often became the incarnation of all the forces that blocked that effort. He was the cosmopolitan, the remnant of the Enlightenment, the parasite feeding upon the German organism. On every level of society now, voices were raised against the Jews. Professors and playwrights as well as street demagogues joined in the chorus. In 1819 the Burschenschaften, a league of university student societies devoted to a "Christian German Fatherland," helped organize the so-called Hep-Hep ("Down with the Jews") riots that swept from Frankfurt through numerous other German cities. Inflamed by the widening social disruptions of the early Industrial Revolution, these outbreaks continued for some four months, with the looting of Jewish homes and stores, even the burning of a number of synagogues. Jewish requests for protection served only to annoy municipal authorities. Thus, in 1830, Isaac Reutlinger of Karlsruhe alerted the police to an imminent anti-Jewish riot. When the violence occurred, the police accused Reutlinger of causing the riots himself. In 1848, Leo Oppenheimer of Heidelberg was heavily fined for his "exaggerated fearfulness" in appealing for police protection against anti-Jewish excesses.

Even more than the German regimes, Metternich and his colleagues in the Habsburg government appeared to be irretrievably committed to the status quo. Ironically, at the request of the Rothschilds, the Austrian chancellor was quite prepared to intervene on behalf of Jews in other lands (p. 75); but within the empire itself, restrictions survived intact. In Vienna and Prague, Jews were confined to slum neighborhoods. In Prague, as late as 1830, less than 10,000 "tolerated" Jews were permitted within the city limits. It was not uncommon in those years for police to awaken Jews at night, or to search passing omnibuses, or to descend upon synagogues, to require Jews to display their residence permits. As in the pre-Napoleonic era, Jews still were obliged to take separate and humiliating oaths in law courts, to pay special taxes even for legal residence and business permits.

LIBERALS, JEWS, AND THE EUROPEAN FREEDOM STRUGGLE

Except in France, however, the Jews of Western Europe were not alone in lamenting the demise of the Code Napoléon. During the 1820s, the Continent's emergent new middle class and many of its youthful student activists turned belatedly to the cause of political and national freedom. They had achieved little in allowing restoration governments to monopolize the cause of romantic self-fulfillment. Veneration of "Das Volk," after all, was as much an expression of the "General Will" as of medieval immobilism. By the third decade of the nineteenth century, these liberal and nationalist elements moved increasingly to the offensive.

For their part, the Jews grasped early on that their fate was linked to the triumph of political liberalism with all the certitude of a mathematical law. In the Italian peninsula, hundreds of Jews were active participants in Giuseppe Mazzini's Young Italy movement of the 1830s. One of these, Giuseppe Vitalevi, became Mazzini's closest lieutenant. Mazzini's political expedition into Savoy, in 1833, was financed by the Turin Jewish banking firm of Todros. During Mazzini's long exile in London, his most devoted British friends were the Rossellis, Sephardic businessmen; while the London home of Sara Levi Nathan for many years was the meeting place of émigré Italian revolutionaries. It was a loyalty that was warmly reciprocated. In 1847, Count Camillo di Cavour, the Piedmontese statesman who laid the diplomatic groundwork for Italian unification, made plain that his reformist program encompassed the cause of full Jewish emancipation. Few of his liberal nationalist colleagues expressed reservations. As the tiniest of the peninsula's minorities, Jews had always represented less a culture shock to their fellow Mediterraneans than to the Church hierarchy. Indeed, the Risorgimento, the struggle for Italian freedom and unity, was essentially an anticlerical movement. Nowhere else in Europe was the alliance between Jews and liberals more tightly knit than in Italy, or ultimately more productive.

In Hungary, the Jews' sheer demographic mass became an economic and political factor to be reckoned with. Following the issuance of Joseph II's Toleranzpatent, the immigration of Jews from Galicia raised Hungary's Jewish population to approximately 80,000 by 1787, to 130,000 by 1805, to 235,000 by 1840 (including the Jews of Slovakia and the South Slav regions). While most of these Galician newcomers were quite poor—Hasidim were prominent among them—Hungarian Jewry also generated a powerful economic elite of bankers, importers-exporters, and industrialists. From 1833 on, organizing themselves into the Hungarian-Jewish Council, the activists within this middle class began pressing for equality of legal status. Here they won the support of such Hungarian progressives as Count Istvan Szechenyi, an influential political reformist, of Baron Joseph Eotvos, a renowned Hungarian poet, and of Lajos Kossuth, a charismatic young nationalist orator and publicist. Writing for his party newspaper, *Pesti Hirlap,* Kossuth in 1844 affirmed that "the Jews of our fatherland must be considered no differently than all other inhabitants"—although he urged the Jews themselves to transcend their ethnic and religious clannishness.

By the 1840s, the Jews' struggle for civil rights, if still unconsummated throughout most of West-Central Europe, reflected their impressive trajectory of economic progress (p. 101). Throughout the German world, their image began gradually to change, and specifically among fellow middle-class elements. In Vienna, during these years, the barriers to Jewish settlement were slowly relaxed. Even as late as 1848, the city's Jews did not exceed 4,500, most of these still confined to the quasi-ghetto of the Leopoldstadt quarter.

Civil rights remained beyond their reach. But economic achievement gradually was lending this small core group the mantle of familiarity, if not yet of respectability.

At the same time, in the northern German states, the stock exchanges and chambers of commerce were selectively opening to Jews. Prussia as always remained the key to Jewish advancement. Here by the mid-1840s lived some 150,000 to 160,000 Jews, at least half the Jews in German-speaking Europe. Here, too, as the quintessence of German thoroughness, the Prussian government felt it useful to conduct detailed surveys on its Jewish residents. The evidence of Jewish embourgeoisement was becoming too palpable to ignore. In 1847, therefore, the Prussian Diet cautiously approved legislation authorizing Jews to hold lower-level government and academic positions. Elsewhere in Germany, some three hundred Jews were members of various municipal governments, half of these in the Prussian provinces of Posen and Upper Silesia. In professional life, a few dozen Jewish physicians were achieving a certain marginal deference in German society. By mid-century, Jews comprised 3 percent of the student body at Heidelberg University, and nearly 10 percent at the University of Breslau.

From Beneficiaries to Activists

It was also in the 1830s and 1840s that the Jews themselves adopted a more assertive stance in their own behalf. Although denied full access to political office, they found it possible to express their views as writers and publishers. Figures like Moses Hess, Heinrich Heine, Dagobert Oppenheim, and Joel Jacoby were emerging as highly respected political journalists. Trained initially as a physician, Jacoby belonged to the still limited circle of Jews who had studied at German universities—in his case, at Königsberg—and had intermingled there with German liberals. He was soon able to devote his best efforts to the cause of Jewish emancipation, although strictly within the larger struggle for German freedom and unification. "Just as I am both a Jew and a German," he wrote in one of his pamphlets, "so the Jew in me cannot become free without the German, and the German cannot be freed without the Jew. . . . We are languishing together in a great prison." Another Jewish activist, Ludwig Börne (born Loeb Baruch in the Frankfurt Judengasse three years before the French Revolution), lived to become one of Europe's most effective practitioners of incendiary journalism. An abrasive, uncompromising man, Börne in the "Letters from Paris" he produced for underground newspapers was characteristically acidulous in his indictment of Germany's agglomeration of reactionary governments. Even a two-year stint in prison for lèse-majesté did not temper his passionate republicanism, or his vigorous leadership of the Jung Deutschland circle of liberal intellectuals (p. 124).

In the pre-1848 era, however, it was Heinrich Heine who emerged as the most vibrant and widely read of these Jewish activists. Born in Düsseldorf in 1797, educated as a lawyer at the Universities of Bonn and Göttingen, widely traveled and profoundly erudite, Heine was well qualified to pass judgment on issues of both contemporary German politics and German culture. Characteristically, his first political tract, "Reisebilder," ostensibly a charming collection of German travel vignettes, emerged on careful reading as *aperçus* into the German political condition. Indeed, they were penetrating enough to send Heine packing for refuge in Paris. There he remained for twenty-five years, until his death in 1856, subsisting on an allowance provided by a wealthy uncle, writing prolifically, smuggling his articles back over the frontier in an edgy cat-and-mouse game with the German censors.

The precautions were not gratuitous. Heine's observations became increasingly pungent and uncompromising. For him, Germany's aristocracy was

> a handful of vulgar nobles who have learned nothing beyond horse-trading, card-sharping, drinking contests, and similar . . . rascally accomplishments. . . . They are indeed like thieves who pick one another's pockets while being led to the gallows. . . . What is the great task of our day? It is emancipation. Not simply the emancipation of the Irish, the Greeks, Frankfurt Jews, West Indian blacks, and all such oppressed peoples, but the emancipation of the whole world, and especially of Europe, which has now come of age, and is tearing itself loose from the apron-strings of the privileged classes. . . .

Heine came to be widely admired by the literate German *Mittelstand,* which passed his smuggled tracts from hand to hand and repeated his caustic insights with empathy and delight.

It was Gabriel Riesser, however, who evoked the widest resonance specifically among his fellow Jews. Born in Hamburg in 1806, Riesser as a young man earned a doctorate in law from Heidelberg. His summa cum laude credentials apparently were insufficient to win him a university teaching position, or even the right to practice law in his native Hamburg. Rather, as a Jew, he was obliged to earn his bread as a notary public, and even then only after 1840. In the depth of his outrage, Riesser devoted his principal efforts to the cause of Jewish emancipation. Whether in newspaper articles or public debate, he left his readers and listeners in no doubt that his views were unequivocally those of an identified Jew. He also made plain that the Jewish people were staking their claim for equal citizenship exclusively as a religious community. When Heinrich Paulus, a defender of the status quo, stigmatized the Jews as "Ausländer," foreigners who were incapable of understanding the

German "soul," Riesser's impassioned response precisely evoked the stance of the 1807 Sanhedrin:

> Where is the other state [he demanded] to which we owe loyalty? What other fatherland calls us to its defense? We have not emigrated to Germany. We were born here, and either we are Germans or we are men without a country. There is only one baptism that can consecrate a man to a nationality. That is the baptism of blood shed in a common battle for freedom and the fatherland.

Riesser's crusade was entirely frontal. He made a habit of patronizing cafés where Jews were not welcome, then suing the proprietors if he did not receive service. He founded the emancipationist periodical *Der Jude,* rejecting the fashionable German-Jewish euphemism "Israelite" or "German of the Mosaic persuasion." At much personal risk, attacking the political obscurantism of Prussia's King Friedrich Wilhelm IV, Riesser emerged by the 1840s as German Jewry's most admired political champion. It was his uncompromising aggressiveness that served as the model for Joel Jacoby, Andreas Gottschalk, Jakob de Jonge, Moses Hess, and scores of other German-Jewish political activists of his time. In the acuity and fortitude of their careers, they blended the quest for Jewish civil equality with the mission of European liberalism. The fusion became particularly significant in 1848, and after.

THE DAMASCUS AFFAIR AND EUROPEAN SELF-APPRAISAL

In early April 1840, newspapers throughout Europe began reporting a startling development that lately had taken place in Damascus, Syria. At nightfall on February 5, an Italian monk, Father Tomasso da Calangiano della Sardegna, failed to return to his Capuchin monastery upon completing his routine visits to parishioners in the Syrian capital. A middle-aged man, Father Tomasso had lived as a Capuchin missionary in Damascus for thirty-two years, and was much loved for his charitable work. The day after his disappearance, the Capuchins notified the French consul, Benoît Laurent-François, Count de Ratti-Menton. Ratti-Menton, a veteran of his country's diplomatic service, was the monks' logical first port of call. France traditionally had functioned as spokesman-protector of Roman Catholics in the Arab world. Immediately, Ratti-Menton pressed the local Syrian authorities to conduct an intensive search for the missing friar. The "results" he achieved were described in his sixteen-page report to the French foreign ministry.

The missing friar's colleagues explained that Father Tomasso had last been seen walking in the direction of the city's Jewish quarter. Suspicion then fell initially on a Jewish barber, wrote Ratti-Menton. Upon being detained and "queried," the barber confirmed local Arab rumors about Father Tomasso's fate. Allegedly, the friar had been called to the home of David Harari, a prominent Jewish businessman. There, several Jews, including the local rabbi, Moïse Antabi, seized and bound Father Tomasso, then slit his throat. "[The Jews] collected the blood in a large silver bowl," the report continued, "because it was to serve for their [Passover] holiday. They stripped the dead friar of his vestments . . . took his body to another room, cut it to pieces, and crushed its bones with an iron grinder. They put everything into a big coffee sack and threw it into a ditch. They then poured the blood into bottles, which they gave to the rabbi." In his account, Ratti-Menton explained that eleven Jewish suspects had been arrested and, after several days of interrogation (a process that later was disclosed to have caused the death of two prisoners and the blinding of another), all "confessed" to having participated in a rite to provide Christian blood for the matzo used in the Jews' Passover festival. Concluding his report, Ratti-Menton wrote that the Sherif of Damascus was expected to impose judgment and "the penalty on these people which I believe should be exemplary." The challenge to France, added the consul, as well as the outrageous assault on humanity represented by these "satanic sacrifices," required that the Jews of Damascus be subjected to a "salutary terror."

It was Realpolitik, not outrage, that induced Ratti-Menton to attribute the friar's apparent murder to Jewish rather than to Arab fanaticism. Nine years earlier, the province of Syria had been wrested from Ottoman control by Mehemet Ali, the khedive of Egypt. Nominally a servant of the Ottoman sultan, Mehemet Ali in practical fact had become a ruler in his own right. Moreover, in 1839, by military intimidation, the Egyptian khedive had extended his domain to the threshold of integral Turkey and was threatening to march on Constantinople. It was a development that evoked the keenest interest of the French government. Since the early nineteenth century, Britain had taken upon itself the role of patron-protector of the Ottoman Empire, which functioned as a useful barrier to Russian penetration into the eastern Mediterranean, Britain's "lifeline" to India. France, in turn, as Britain's perennial rival for empire, discerned in Mehemet Ali a potential counterweight to Turkish—and British—hegemony in the Near East. For this reason, no doubts should be raised about the "civilized" quality of Mehemet Ali's governance in Syria, his ability to provide monks and other Christians with every measure of personal security. Any violence perpetrated against European nationals should more expediently be attributed to Damascus's Jewish minority. Numbering barely 5,000 in a city of over 100,000, the Jews in their mysterious quasi-ghetto, and traditionally suspect in their "bloodthirsty" religious ceremonies, would fulfill the role of surrogates for Arab malfeasance.

At first, Ratti-Menton's tactic appeared to be vindicated. During the spring of 1840, as European newspapers reported the accusations against the imprisoned Jews, numerous discussions in public and private circles alike tended to accept at face value the Jews' alleged propensity for "ritual murder." But soon a different scenario began to emerge. Appeals from Jewish leaders in Damascus reached Jewish communal officials in the West. In graphic detail, they related the torture inflicted on the imprisoned Jewish suspects, the pall of terror that had descended upon the city's Jewish population. On March 25, one of these appeals reached Adolphe Crémieux, vice president of the Central Consistoire of "French Israélites." Crémieux was a man of considerable public stature. Born in Nîmes, the product of an acculturated Sephardic family, he had been trained as a lawyer, and from the 1830s on achieved a distinguished reputation as an advocate before the Court of Appeal in Paris. Indeed, in 1842, Crémieux would be elected to the Chamber of Deputies, and then go on to serve as minister of justice in the revolutionary government of 1848. A florid rhetorician with an instinct for the dramatic, Crémieux in the courtroom and in other public forums achieved his most vivid reputation defending victims of political and religious persecution. The fate of the Damascus Jews was precisely the issue to set his combative juices flowing.

As he set about requesting an interview with Adolphe Thiers, France's prime minister, Crémieux anticipated a sympathetic reception from a kindred spirit. Thiers, after all, presided over a liberal, constitutional government. Since the July 1830 Revolution, the new Orleanist monarchy had reaffirmed the principle of full Jewish equality. Yet, by the same token, Thiers over the years also revealed himself to be an ardent nationalist, even a protoimperialist, and in 1840 his overriding concern apparently was to retain Mehemet Ali as France's dependable client in the Levant. For this reason, the prime minister declined to receive Crémieux. Upon learning of this rebuff, James de Rothschild, the banking family's scion in Paris, immediately wrote his brother Salomon in Vienna that "there only remains for us to turn for help to . . . the press." Hereupon the Rothschilds and Crémieux launched into a vigorous letter-writing campaign to governments and newspapers worldwide. Initially, it was Jewish communal leaders who responded with particular vigor, organizing mass meetings in London, Paris, Hamburg, New York, Philadelphia, and other major centers of Western Jewish life. Thiers in turn reacted to these protest demonstrations in a tone of martyred aggrievement. Addressing the Chamber of Deputies on June 2, defending the role of Ratti-Menton in Damascus, the prime minister declaimed:

> [The Jews] . . . are more powerful in the world than they have pretensions to be. At this very moment they are putting forward their claims in every foreign chancellery . . . with an extraordinary vigor and with an ardor which can hardly be imagined. It requires courage for a minister to protect his agent under attack.

Crémieux actually had only begun his campaign. On June 4, he dispatched an appeal to London, to Sir Moses Montefiore, president of the Board of Deputies of British Jews (p. 97), to join with him and a delegation of France's Consistoire Central Israélite, in a visitation to Mehemet Ali in Alexandria. Montefiore agreed immediately and enthusiastically. He knew that he could depend upon the support of the British government, several of whose key figures already had expressed outrage at the Damascus atrocity. The most important of these eminences was Foreign Secretary Lord Palmerston, who even then was intent upon building an international coalition to force Mehemet Ali out of Ottoman Syria and who needed little encouragement to expose the Egyptian khedive as a threat to Mediterranean peace and stability. Indeed, Palmerston moved with characteristic vigor in directing British consuls in Alexandria, Damascus, and Constantinople to lend their fullest cooperation to the Jewish delegation. In mid-July of 1840, therefore, Crémieux, Montefiore, and their wives, as well as other officials of their respective Jewish organizations, sailed off for Egypt amid much public ceremony. Their initial reception was less auspicious, however. Reaching Alexandria in the blazing heat of a Mediterranean summer, the emissaries were unable to secure an audience with Mehemet Ali. The Egyptian khedive was heavily engaged in preparations for an invasion of Turkey—doubtless encouraged by the assurances of Thiers in Paris that France would "never sacrifice this man of genius." Thus, as the outbreak of war loomed in the Near East, the Jewish visitors found themselves entangled in a complex diplomatic web.

The human costs of that entanglement were experienced first and foremost by the eleven prisoners in Damascus. By August, four of them already had perished under torture, and the other seven were languishing on the brink of death. Nevertheless, unknown to the survivors, the Damascus Affair was beginning to evoke tremolos of concern well beyond the Jewish world, or British and French official circles. Although the Catholic press maintained a remorselessly anti-Jewish tone, government newspapers even in Catholic Austria tended increasingly to denigrate the "oft-refuted delusion," in the words of one journal, "that the Jews consume Christian blood." Here the moving force was Baron Salomon von Rothschild. At the banker's request, Prince Metternich ordered Austria's diplomatic representatives in the Near East to intercede with Mehemet Ali on behalf of the Jewish prisoners, at least to have them transported to Alexandria, where they could be "subjected to a strict and impartial investigation." The effect of Metternich's instructions was dramatic. Austria's ambassador in Constantinople, Bartolmäus von Stürmer, and its consul in Alexandria, Anton Laurin, promptly set about organizing a common front among the other European diplomats in Alexandria and Damascus. With the exception of the French, all endorsed the Austrian request—even the consuls of Spain and Tsarist Russia.

It was not only European pressure on behalf of the Damascus prisoners that gave Mehemet Ali pause. On August 16, led by Britain, the same European governments issued a stern warning to the Egyptian khedive, cautioning him to pull his forces away from the Turkish frontier on pain of international military intervention. At first, Mehemet Ali rejected the ultimatum, insisting that "France is ready to come to my aid and . . . has offered its intervention." But the khedive was wrong. On August 26, a British naval squadron intercepted and sank a convoy of Egyptian supply vessels en route to Syria. Not long afterward, contingents of Turkish and British troops landed on the Lebanese coast and Beirut was simultaneously bombarded by sea.

In France, the news touched off a furor of public indignation. Nevertheless, Thiers hesitated to be drawn into military action against Britain and possibly other European nations. At this point it dawned on Mehemet Ali that he had achieved nothing by allowing the fate of the Damascus Jews to enmesh him in a war of international opinion. August 28, 1840, became the turning point. On that day, Dr. Emile Gaetani, the khedive's private physician, and a Jew, removed a boil from Mehemet Ali's buttock. As he applied a dressing, Dr. Gaetani murmured to his royal patient that he, the khedive, would soon need all his strength, and "surely the voice of six million Jews raised in your favor would be of great importance." Mehemet Ali suddenly agreed. On September 6, he ordered the surviving prisoners released.

Early the next month, Montefiore, Crémieux, and their respective entourages departed—separately—for home. En route, Montefiore stopped off in Constantinople. Escorted by the British ambassador, he was received by Sultan Abd al-Mejjid I. Grateful to Britain for military support, the young ruler presented Montefiore with a handsomely bound *firman*, declaring that all notions of a Jewish blood ritual are "pure calumny," and promising that "the Jewish *millet* [nation] shall possess the same privileges as are granted to the numerous other millets who are subject to our authority." Thrilled, Montefiore in turn dispatched a message to London announcing that he, Montefiore, had won "the Magna Carta for the Jews in the Turkish dominions." Crémieux claimed essentially the same achievement for himself. The boasts were ludicrous. There would be no substantive change in the precarious status of Syrian Jewry (p. 151).

Exaggerated proclamations notwithstanding, the episode of 1840 was unquestionably a watershed of sorts for the Jews of nineteenth-century Europe. Never before had their emissaries evoked such an upsurge of spontaneous and collective Jewish action worldwide. Both Crémieux and Montefiore spoke as elected representatives of their fellow Jews, not as royally appointed shtadlanim. With the "power" of a united Jewry behind them, they felt correspondingly free to abandon obsequiousness as a tactic of communal policy and to engage in a forthright diplomacy of their own. To be sure, they succeeded mainly because the British government discerned usefulness in exploiting the Damascus Affair for purposes of Realpolitik. Yet the Jews themselves similarly were learning to exploit Realpolitik. If their leaders were not quite prepared to challenge their governments on lingering Jewish disabilities in Europe, at least by 1840 they no longer felt inhibited in seeking Western support on behalf of Jews in other, more backward realms. Even in the lingering twilight of the Metternichian era, the experience of mutual cooperation in the Damascus Affair registered affirmatively on the consciousness of Europeans and Jews alike. From then on, it appeared only a matter of time before the experience would be applied to the social landscape of Europe itself.

THE CHAIN REACTION OF 1848

In February 1848 the citizens of Paris lost patience with their colorless "umbrella king," the Orleanist Louis-Philippe. Although well disposed toward representative government, Louis-Philippe had been unsuccessful in his foreign policy, and his domestic program fell well short of authentic democracy. The mobs that sent him into exile were intent upon substituting a more vigorously egalitarian republic for a rather vapid constitutional monarchy. In France, the transition doubtless was of less than momentous importance. But its consequences in other lands were revolutionary. For the Italians, the upheaval in France was the spark needed to ignite a sequence of insurrections throughout their own peninsula. Charles Albert in Turin, Ferdinand II in Naples, Pius IX in Rome, the Grand Duke of Tuscany in Florence—all were intimidated into granting political representation to their subjects.

Almost inevitably, the revolutionary fever of 1848 spread to Austria, the very epicenter of European conservatism, and then eventually to the Habsburg provinces. In Vienna, the uprising forced the aging chancellor, Prince Metternich, into permanent exile; while the rather confused emperor, Ferdinand I, hurriedly consented to political reforms. In Bohemia and Hungary, citizen armies initially overpowered the imperial garrisons on their soil, then secured Ferdinand's promises of autonomy, of representative government, of peasant relief from feudal dues. In this new "golden era," moreover, with the time seemingly ripe for the establishment of an authentically united Germany, the leading political activists in each of the German principalities duly hurried off to Frankfurt to set about drafting a national constitution.

It was in this annus mirabilis of 1848 that the succession of upheavals ramified through the very heartland of West European Jewry. The German states alone encompassed more than 350,000 Jews, and there were at least another 100,000 in the German-speaking provinces of the Habsburg Empire. Together with the 340,000 Jews of (Greater) Hungary, France, and

Italy, at least 750,000 Jews lived in the areas roiled by political and nationalist unrest. In the years since the Congress of Vienna, these were also the Jews who had begun to make impressive progress toward economic integration. Politically, too, they were developing a sentience and skills not inferior to those of their non-Jewish neighbors (p. 101). Thus, in France, under the new Second Republic, the revolutionary cabinet included two Jews, the redoubtable Adolphe Crémieux as minister of justice, and Michel Goud-chaux as minister of finance. There was comparable Jewish participation in the Italian uprisings. Giuseppe Mazzini's veteran associate, Giuseppe Revere, edited the republican *Italia del Popolo* during the short-lived Milanese regime. He and two other Jews, Abraham Pesari and Salvatore Anau, were elected to that government's National Assembly. Daniele Manin, leader of the Venetian uprising, was a nonidentified half-Jew, but his cabinet included two profess-ing Jews, Leone Pincherle and Isaaco Pesaro Maurogonato. Jews also were substantially represented in the various Italian National Guard detachments.

It was in revolutionary Germany and Austria, however, that Jewish politi-cal figures began to achieve an unprecedented visibility as elected state representatives. The transition from passivity to activism was not universally smooth. In numerous rural localities, populist resentments led to anti-Jewish riots. But the revolutionary leadership for the most part welcomed Jews as comrades-in-arms. In the various congresses, assemblies, and committee meetings of the time, Jews suddenly emerged as a vibrant presence. In Berlin, Dr. Sigismund Stern was president of the city's first constitutional club. In Breslau, Moses Schreiber cofounded the German People's Union. In Mainz, Ludwig Bamberger founded the Democratic Party. For the first time, Jews were represented in the parliaments or constitutional assemblies of Prussia, Bavaria, Mecklenburg-Schwerin, Saxony-Anhalt, Hesse-Bamburg, Frank-furt, and Lübeck. In May 1848, when 830 delegates convened in Frankfurt as a "National German Parliament," the estimable Gabriel Riesser, one of nine Jewish members, was elected as the parliament's second vice president.

Jewish participation was not less vigorous in the revolutionary events sweeping the Habsburg Empire. In Vienna, in 1848, a dozen Jews were among the university students killed in the uprising's initial clash with the army. All the victims were buried in a common grave, and the mourners were addressed by rabbis and priests in a joint funeral service. In March 1848, Adolf Fischhof, a Jewish physician, was selected as Vienna's delegate to Austria's first popu-larly elected parliament; and in May he was selected as chairman of the Com-mittee of Public Safety, the parliament's executive organ. In ensuing weeks, as the revolution veered increasingly toward "radical" republicanism, Karl Chajzkes, Hermann Jellinek, and Karl Tausenau were among the Jews promi-nent in the left wing.

Throughout the empire's eastern and southern provinces, meanwhile, revolutionary elements tended to focus on their own nationalist agenda. Thus, in Hungary, Louis Kossuth set about mobilizing his followers in a campaign to wrest full independence from Vienna. It was specifically that effort, in turn, that became embroiled in complications on the issue of Hungary's minorities. The Magyar leadership rejected the very notion of ceding autonomy to the South Slavs. This was not a problem that should have affected the Jews, whose loyalties lay overwhelmingly with the Hungarian "elite." But almost from the moment that the Hungarian revolution began, in March 1848, it was accompanied by a series of anti-Jewish riots in the rural areas. Mortified, Kossuth hurried to Budapest's Grosswardein Synagogue to ask pardon of the Jews, and solemnly to pledge his commitment to full political equality (if not autonomy) for all Hungarians, Jews and non-Jews alike. The congregation was moved. Indeed, in June, it provided Kossuth's army with an 80,000 florin loan, then dispatched letters to other congregational boards, urging them to support the revolution. The appeal was widely heeded. Thirty thousand Jews enlisted in Kossuth's army, fully 11 percent of the force's total manpower.

In all its single-minded passion, was this Jewish revolutionary commitment to be requited for the Jews themselves? In much of Europe, apparently it was. The first act of the Venetian Republic, upon its establishment in March 1848, was to proclaim complete civil and political equality for citizens of all races and creeds. Jewish emancipation in Venetia was emulated in Lombardy, in Piedmont-Sardinia, in the smallest duchies of the Italian peninsula, even in the backward *mezzogiorno,* in the Kingdom of the Two Sicilies. When King Charles Albert of Piedmont-Sardinia launched his offensive into neighboring Italian principalities, he was emphatic in proclaiming freedom and equality no less than national unification as his rallying cry. By far the most telling evidence of Jewish emancipation, however, lay in the Papal States, where the newly established Roman Republic immediately and emphatically proclaimed the end of ghetto domicile, together with all other humiliating anti-Jewish restrictions.

In Germany, too, the new Prussian constitution of 1848 decreed equality before the law for all the nation's citizens, regardless of class or birth—a benediction that for the first time was applied to the tens of thousands of Polish Jews in Prussian Posen. Nor did the other newly "constitutionalized" German states, from Baden to Bavaria, from Anhalt-Dessau to Saxony, neglect to offer their Jews an identical panoply of freedoms. In May 1848, as the All-German Parliament convened in Frankfurt, its delegates promptly set about formulating a constitution for a united, authentically democratic kingdom. Thus, Article 146 of the draft constitution proclaimed that "enjoyment of civil and citizen rights will not be conditioned or limited by religious faith." Ironically, when the delegates recommended a separate provision, to correct "the peculiar condition of the Israelitisch race," it was Gabriel Riesser who objected.

The Jews were neither a separate race nor a separate nation, he insisted. They were "Germans of the Jewish faith," and consequently ought not to be "subjected" to more than a general statement of equal status. Riesser's declamation was unanimously embraced by other Jewish delegates. For them, the issue was one of principle. They preferred to secure their civil and religious rights as Germans, rather than specifically as Jews (although the legislators insisted upon incorporating the new law into the constitution).

THE REVOLUTION IMPLODES

It would soon become evident that the "universalist" approach to liberty and equality offered a less than ironclad guarantee of Jewish rights, and least of all in the Habsburg Empire, where racial heterogeneity posed a complicated challenge even to Austrian liberals. Since mid-March 1848, the nation's parliamentarians had been struggling to formulate a new democratic constitution. But as deliberations reached a climax in late April, nothing had been said about equality of race or creed, and surely not of Jewish equality. It was only months later, in January 1849, that the parliament formulated a provision, Article 51, declaring that "[a]ll ethnic groups in the Empire enjoy equality of rights. Every ethnic group has the inviolable right to cultivate its nationality and particularly its language." The article in fact was intended essentially as a grudging and belated genuflection to the empire's despised Slavic races. There was no assurance that it was intended to apply to religious minorities like the Jews.

The prospects for Jewish emancipation were comparably erratic in Hungary. Whatever Louis Kossuth's egalitarian instincts, these were by no means paralleled among his countrymen at large. Fearing a minority problem of their own, they hesitated to emancipate either Serbs, Croats, or Jews, peoples renowned and feared for the tenacity of their cultural heritages. Eventually, in July 1848, under pressure of a Serbian assault, the Hungarian Diet granted a qualified autonomist status to its Slavic nationalities, and in the same month introduced a bill affirming that "all Jews settled in Hungary . . . are declared equal with other citizens of this Fatherland. . . ." Yet, in the case of the Jews, the Diet's legislative committee procrastinated, citing the need for the Jews themselves first to achieve social and religious reforms among their own people. It was an old story. And as anti-Jewish riots continued throughout the Hungarian provinces, Kossuth in March 1849 sadly had to acknowledge to the Diet that Jewish emancipation "would be equivalent to throwing masses of this race [as victims] to the fury of their enemies." The issue of Jewish emancipation then was dropped.

Altogether, by the spring of 1848, the forces of conservatism were regrouping. In Italy, a powerful Austrian army shattered King Charles Albert's Piedmontese force at Custozza. Almost immediately, the constitutional regimes in other Italian principalities collapsed like tenpins; and in the Papal States, two French military divisions restored Pius IX to his pontifical throne. With the exception of Piedmont, Jews throughout the entirety of the Italian peninsula were "reinstated" in most of their old disabilities. In Rome, they were literally herded back into their ghetto. In Central Europe, too, the revolution eventually guttered out. Although economic progress clearly was gaining momentum in the German world, the *Mittelstand,* the emergent liberal middle class, would achieve its critical mass too late to save the revolutionary cause. Thus, in Prussia, King Friedrich Wilhelm IV's household cannon managed to scatter the crowds that had ruled Berlin's streets for months. In Bavaria, royalist forces regained control of their government. In March 1849, learning of the Prussian king's refusal to accept the crown of a united Germany, delegates at the Frankfurt parliamentary assembly began to disperse in confusion. In this darkening political climate, as the pendulum swung back to the right, hopes for Jewish emancipation rapidly faded. In Bavaria, even the Jewish matrikel was restored—for the second time (p. 76).

Finally, during the winter and spring of 1848–49, the Habsburg armies also managed their own counteroffensive and succeeded in trampling the revolutionary opposition underfoot. In December 1848, once Vienna was reoccupied, Emperor Ferdinand I, who had proved timorous and inept during the months of crisis, was persuaded to abdicate in favor of his nephew, the eighteen-year-old Franz Josef I. The new young ruler promptly vindicated the hopes of traditionalists by dismissing the revolutionary assembly, discarding the newly completed constitution, and systematically eradicating the last pockets of the uprising. Retribution took the form of imprisonments and occasional executions. Among the Jewish revolutionaries, Tausenau and Chajzkes managed to escape and live in exile. Jellinek was shot. Franz Josef then appealed to Nicholas I of Russia for help in suppressing the last of the national revolts, this one in Hungary. Eager to set an example for his own factious minorities, the "policeman of Europe" responded with alacrity. In June 1849 the tsar's infantry divisions swiftly overwhelmed the Magyars. In August, Kossuth's army surrendered.

The punishment inflicted on the Jews of Hungary was possibly the most vindictive in Europe. Scores of Jewish revolutionaries were executed. Rabbi Löw of Papa and Rabbi Schwab of Pest were imprisoned for sermonizing on behalf of Hungarian independence. In the case of the Jews alone, heavy fines were imposed on entire communities. Jews in the town of Gyor were obliged to pay 80,000 florins. In Pest, the local military commander required the Jews to furnish his troops with 30,000 uniforms. Moreover, by aligning themselves with Kossuth, Hungarian Jewry soon confronted an even longer-term risk to their collective security. This one came less from Austria than from the Slavic peoples who comprised Hungary's "underclass." Traditionally functioning as middlemen between townsmen and boyars, the Jews found themselves in the equivocal position of representing Magyar culture amid a predominantly Slavic hinterland. The suppurating resentment of this Slavic majority would remain a sword of Damocles over their heads for decades to come.

Brutal retributions notwithstanding, the 1848 revolutionary epoch was hardly without its longer-term value for European Jewry. It was the great testing ground for their political activity. Between 1789 and 1815, the Jews had secured their emancipation essentially as passive beneficiaries of the French National Assembly and Napoleon Bonaparte. In 1848, they themselves labored for their freedom—indeed, often as cutting-edge *engagés* in the wider struggle for liberal constitutionalism. "First comes the man," declared Rabbi Hirsch Mannheimer in a May 1848 sermon to his Cracow congregation, in Habsburg Poland, "then the citizen, and only then the Jew. No one must be able to accuse us of always thinking of ourselves first."

A Commitment under Consolidation

Jewish social marginality was by no means all-encompassing. Oases of progress were increasingly evident. In Austria, Bohemia, and Hungary, even in Galicia, domicile restrictions for Jews no longer were consistently enforced. In March 1849, only weeks after Emperor Franz Josef replaced the moribund revolutionary constitution with a more traditionally autocratic one of his own, he reassured members of a Viennese-Jewish delegation that they could ignore most of their former economic and residential bans. Two years later, the Habsburg government decreed that no one henceforth could be excluded from commerce and industry for reasons of birth, religion, or nationality. In Austria, as in the states of northern Germany, the 1850s and 1860s would open new educational opportunities for the nation's Jews, in middle schools and universities alike. Beyond all other factors, it was the sheer irresistible velocity of economic growth in Europe that was transforming the Jews' status.

As in the case of the 1840 Damascus Affair, moreover, acts of flagrant and gratuitous bigotry occasionally served as unintended catalysts for an accelerated emancipation. Among these episodes, the Mortara case of 1858 was by far the most grotesque. In the Papal States of central Italy lived some 15,000 Jews. Although the 8,000 Jews in Rome itself were confined again to their traditional ghetto, Jewish circumstances in other cities of the Romagna were somewhat more flexible. Thus, the 300 Jews of Bologna lived in reasonable security and comfort. Here Salomone David (Momolo) Mortara, a retailer of paper products, and his wife lived on terms of amity with their Bolognese gentile neighbors, and Christian servant girls helped them raise their eight children. On June 24, 1858, however, a contingent of papal carabinieri suddenly arrived at the Mortara apartment in the dawn hours. The police commander explained that they were acting at the orders of the local Inquisitor, Father Pier Gaetano Feletti, and were reluctantly obliged to take with them one of the Mortara children, Edgardo, age six. It had recently been learned, he continued, that several years earlier Edgardo had undergone baptism, and therefore he no longer could be raised in a Jewish household. The carabinieri then carried off the shrieking child.

As Mrs. Mortara collapsed in a dead faint, her husband, Momolo, rushed to the chambers of Father Feletti. The Inquisitor was "unavailable." Through a spokesman, however, Feletti revealed the circumstances of the abduction. Five years before, when Edgardo had become gravely ill, the family's eighteen-year-old servant girl, Anna Morisi, had secretly "baptized" the child by sprinkling water on him from a bucket and intoning a prayer (a process authorized under canon law). Anna afterward had left the Mortara household to return to her village; but, lately, to friends, she had divulged that earlier episode. The information only now had reached the Inquisitor, who immediately decreed that Edgardo must be placed in the custody of priests in Rome.

Rather than a flickering vestige of the Counter-Reformation, the abduction of Jewish children was a not uncommon occurrence in Italy, even as late as the nineteenth century. Over the years, in fact, Sabatino Scazzocchio, executive secretary of Rome's Jewish *cal* (kehillah), had developed much experience in negotiating on these matters with the Vatican. It was consequently to Scazzocchio in Rome that the frantic Momolo Mortara turned for help. After hearing out the terrified father, Scazzocchio immediately set out to meet with his traditional contacts at the Vatican. But this time, he could not secure an interview. It developed that the Vatican secretary of state, Cardinal Giacomo Antonelli, had himself confirmed the order for little Edgardo to be taken from his parents and to be consigned to the House of Catechumens. Here, by tradition, abducted Jews were confined for a transitional forty-day period, after which they usually emerged as committed Catholics. Scazzocchio—and the Mortaras—were informed that Edgardo was already joyously wearing the cross and attending mass. He would soon be allowed to receive visits from his parents "under appropriate chaperonage."

At this point, Scazzocchio decided to bypass the Vatican and appeal directly to liberal public opinion, both in and out of Italy. The response was not long in coming. Indeed, throughout the Jewish world, a firestorm erupted. Appealing for intercession with the Vatican, the Board of Deputies of British Jews dispatched letters of anguish and outrage, as did the Consistoire Israélite to France's Emperor Louis Napoleon and the Board of Delegates of American Israelites to the United States government. Mass meetings on behalf of Edgardo Mortara were organized by Jewish communities in virtually every major Western city, and addressed by prominent—non-Jewish—

political and religious leaders. Newspapers even in such Catholic nations as Austria, France, Bavaria, Belgium, and Italy expressed revulsion at the "heartless abduction of a small child" (in the words of a Belgian editorial). Government leaders then discreetly but persistently urged Pius IX to display moderation and human compassion. But the pontiff, with his own galled memories of liberal mistreatment in 1848, would not budge. A visit in April 1859 from the renowned Moses Montefiore, who arrived in Rome bearing letters from the British Foreign Office, was equally unavailing. The pope declined to receive Sir Moses, and it was left for Cardinal Antonelli to explain, once again, that "the laws of the Church prevented [Edgardo] from being given back to his parents." Only when the boy reached the age of eighteen could he decide his own course of action.

In June 1859, intent on breaking open the frozen map of the 1815 Treaty of Vienna, France's Emperor Louis Napoleon joined forces with King Victor Emmanuel II of Piedmont-Sardinia in a combined military offensive against the remaining Habsburg installations in northern Italy. By mid-1860, the entirety of the north-central Italian peninsula was in the hands of the Piedmontese House of Savoy, and was duly proclaimed the Kingdom of Italy. Within the former Papal States, only the city of Rome continued under the sovereign rule of the pope. The Franco-Italian military campaign in fact represented a serious disruption of the continental balance of power, one that in earlier years would have provoked a major diplomatic crisis. Not on this occasion. European forbearance was significantly influenced by a widely shared contempt for Pius IX. It was significant that the infuriated population of Bologna, as its first act of liberation in February 1860, jailed Father Feletti, the local Inquisitor, and placed him on trial for his role in the abduction of Edgardo Mortara. Feletti was exonerated on a legal technicality, but other prelates up and down the former Romagna were arrested and convicted on various offenses. The prestige of the Vatican manifestly had never fallen to lower estate in modern Europe. To his closest advisers, Pius IX acknowledged ruefully that "I have saved this Jewish soul, but I have paid for it with my papacy."

A decade later, in 1870, when the army of the Kingdom of Italy claimed the city of Rome as its capital, the pope was left with the Vatican alone as his political base. All remaining constraints were promptly removed from the city's Jews, who then became full and equal citizens of a constitutional state. Edgardo Mortara was now free to rejoin his family. But it was too late. During the preceding twelve years, Edgardo had ceased to be Edgardo. He had taken the name of Pius, and upon reaching the age of eighteen had become a devout novitiate of the Augustinian Order. Subsequently, he became so ardent a proselytizer that Pope Leo XIII awarded him the title of Apostolic Missionary. Conversant in six languages, Edgardo/Pius eventually was appointed a professor of theology at the Sapienza, the Vatican university. He died in 1940 at the Abbey of Bouhey, near Liège, shortly after the Nazi invasion of Belgium.

EMANCIPATION RECONFIRMED

For the Austrian government, the loss of its Italian provinces, then of its de facto protectorship over the papacy, convinced even the most traditionalist Habsburg official that major political reforms were needed if the heterogeneous empire were to survive. In 1867, therefore, a year after suffering the additional humiliation of military defeat at the hands of Prussia, Emperor Franz Josef procrastinated no longer. He authorized an *Ausgleich,* an imperial "rectification," that divided his realm into two parts. Under terms of the new constitution, Hungary, largest of the empire's non-German components, was granted full autonomy in its internal affairs. Moreover, basic rights of citizenship were extended to all Habsburg subject peoples, to Germans, Hungarians, and South Slavs, to Christians, Moslems, and Jews. From 1867 on, all citizens were to be equal before the law. For the Jews, all limitations on domicile, occupation, and officeholding were abolished, even in backward Galicia. Thus did emancipation come quietly, almost anticlimactically, for some 350,000 Habsburg Jews. In ensuing years, they would not be exceeded by any other of the empire's heterogeneity of peoples in their devotion to the royal dynasty or in their contributions to Austrian life.

Or to Hungarian life. Even before the Ausgleich, the Jews of this Central-East European realm gradually were achieving de facto economic and juridical protection. By 1860, the "Jewish oath" no longer was required in the nation's courts. Seven years later, a fully autonomous Hungarian parliament reconfirmed Vienna's imperial grant of equal Jewish rights and privileges. The Hungarian version read, quite simply: "The Israelite inhabitants of the country are declared entitled to the practice of all civil and political rights equally with the Christian inhabitants." And that was that. Henceforth, passionately availing themselves of their new economic and political opportunities, the quarter-million Jews of Greater Hungary played a more decisive role than any of the other religioethnic communities in the nation's ongoing industrialization and intellectual modernization.

In Germany, too, political modernization gradually regained much of its prerevolutionary momentum. In 1850, Prussia's King Friedrich Wilhelm IV agreed to a series of political reforms, if only to strengthen his realm against the overweening diplomatic influence of his dynasty's rivals, the Austrian Habsburgs. Not without reluctance, the king issued a constitution that was reasonably progressive for its time. The franchise was broadened, and the Prussian Diet was given rather more than consultative powers. Under the heavy throb of the Industrial Revolution, many of the aristocracy's quasi-feudal privileges were abrogated, even as selected categories of upper-middle-class Jews finally were granted the right to vote and to purchase land. The Prussian model soon was adopted by numerous other German principalities.

In July 1869, moreover, at the initiative of Prussian Chancellor Otto von Bismarck, the parliament of the newly established North German Confederation ended all limitations on citizenship "for religious reasons." Two years later, with the incorporation of Germany's southern, Catholic, states into a united empire, the law of emancipation was extended to the full plenum of Imperial Germany. The concessions actually evoked few dithyrambs among Germany's Jews. De facto emancipation had been a fact of their lives for over a decade. Nor did it escape them that social or cultural acceptance was hardly susceptible to legislation, no more than the appointment of Jews to senior political, diplomatic, or military ranks. From the late 1860s on, in any case, German Jews walked the streets as free men. No longer would urchins jeer them with the old eighteenth-century taunt: "Mach Mores, Jude!"—"Bow down, Jew!"

In France during the post-1815 decades, Jewish equality before the law survived essentially unchallenged, whether under the restored Bourbons, or the Orleanists, or the Second Empire of Louis Napoleon. A few vexations remained. Jews did not receive state funding for their consistoires, for their rabbinical salaries or religious schools, until 1831. The hated *More Judaïco*, the special "Jewish oath," was not abolished by the nation's high court until 1846. Otherwise, French Jews were free to live where they chose, to vote in all elections, to serve in the diplomatic and military officers corps. By the time the Third Republic was established, in 1870–71, Jewish numbers in France, which had reached 80,000 in 1869, had fallen to some 60,000, principally because of the loss of the dense Jewish population of Alsace-Lorraine after the Franco-Prussian War. Of those who remained, however, some two-thirds had taken up residence in Paris, where they were ensconced in the lower and middle ranks of the bourgeoisie. Notwithstanding its—briefly—shrunken demography, no Jewish population in Europe appeared more comfortably secure.

It was a self-assurance matched only by their coreligionists across the English Channel. By mid-century, at least three-quarters of England's still modest population of 40,000 Jews resided in London. Although the Rothschilds and a tiny minority of veteran financiers dominated the Jewish social and communal pyramid, most Jews were small businessmen, and a majority of these continued to live and work in the capital's rather shabby East End. They had long since taken for granted their equal status in British law courts and in the election booths. As early as the 1830s, moreover, Jews were beginning to run for municipal office, and their election as aldermen and even sheriffs in heavily Jewish districts was becoming a commonplace. In 1855, David

Salomons, an affluent banker, became the first Jewish Lord Mayor of the City of London (essentially the financial district within the far larger London Corporation). The single exception in this tranquil scene was the Jews' debarment from election to Parliament. Members of the House of Commons were obliged to take their oath of office "on the true faith of a member of the Church of England." For most Jews, however, the barrier was an irrelevance. Freedom to live in peace and to earn a livelihood were the rights that mattered.

The Jewish campaign to sit in Parliament nevertheless is usually dated from 1829. In that year Lord Wellington's Tory government approved a bill allowing Roman Catholics to sit in the Commons. Only Jews, and a minuscule group of Unitarians, remained beyond the privileged circle of legislators. The following year, therefore, the issue of Jewish debarment was raised by a parliamentary member, the renowned Whig historian Thomas Macaulay, who actually devoted his maiden speech in the House of Commons to a bill for revising the oath of membership on behalf of non-Christians. Neither the speech nor the bill evoked much interest. Virtually all the Tories and even numerous Whigs argued that the Jews were too few in number to be worth electing, and the presence of even one Jew in Parliament would destroy the "Christian character of the state." Nothing changed in Jewish political circumstances, not even two years later, when the First Reform Bill was passed, expanding the suffrage and apparently opening a new era for representative government in Britain. When the issue of Jewish political equality was raised again in 1834, it was buried again—essentially by indifference.

In any case, the issue of Jewish admission to the House of Commons was an abstraction. No Jew had been elected. In 1847, however, Lionel Rothschild, son of the renowned banker Nathan Mayer Rothschild (p. 103), was elected to represent the City of London. Rothschild duly presented himself at the opening of the Commons' next session, but was denied his seat for inability to take the required oath. Determined then to resolve a palpable legislative anachronism, Lord John Russell, prime minister of the Liberal-dominated government, reintroduced a bill that altered the oath's final clause to "so help me God." This time the measure passed—only to be vetoed again by the House of Lords, with its important contingent of Anglican bishops. In ensuing years, Lionel Rothschild would be elected three more times by his faithful London constituency. Each time the Commons voted to revise the oath, and four times the Upper House turned back the proposal. By 1858, however, the issue of Jewish political emancipation had become a nuisance and embarrassment to Parliament, and a source of ridicule in the country at large. At last, after Rothschild's fifth election, a compromise measure was adopted. Each chamber of Parliament would determine its own oath. In the Commons, the "so help me God" version won approval, and Lionel Rothschild finally took his seat, eleven years after his initial election. With the issue resolved, both Houses in 1866 adopted the Commons' oath. In 1885, Lionel's son Nathaniel was awarded a peerage, thereby becoming the first of many Jews to sit in the House of Lords.

"From Moses to Moses . . ."

It was not Lionel Rothschild, however, the pioneer of Anglo-Jewish emancipation, but Moses Montefiore, the defiant champion of Jewish rights abroad, who emerged as his people's authentic folk hero. Born in 1784 to an affluent Sephardic family, Montefiore was one of the first Jews to be admitted to the London stock exchange. Flourishing as a bullion broker, he was able to retire from active business by the age of forty to devote his energies and the bulk of his fortune to his fellow Jews. In that effort, no cause was dearer to Montefiore than restoration of a Jewish presence in the Holy Land. Throughout his long life he would make seven trips to Palestine, contributing funds for the establishment of farm villages, printing presses, flour mills, and other projects intended to nurture the country's minuscule Jewish settlement to economic self-sufficiency.

Between journeys to Palestine, Montefiore—since 1835 holding the title of president of the Board of Deputies of British Jews—was endlessly on the move in behalf of threatened Jewish communities elsewhere in the world. Although his most dramatic success was the release of the (surviving) Jewish prisoners of Damascus in 1840, no corner of the Diaspora was too remote for his personal intercession. In 1842, when Russia's Nicholas I announced that "state security" required the evacuation of some 100,000 Jews from their homes near the Austrian and Prussian borders, Montefiore embarked on an extended remonstrative campaign with the tsarist government. He climaxed the effort in 1846 by traveling to St. Petersburg, meeting with government officials, then with Tsar Nicholas himself, and eventually persuading the emperor to scale back the evacuation (p. 65). As in 1840, Montefiore once again was lionized by his fellow Jews as a king, a liberator, a new messiah.

The great man's forays were not always successful. His intervention with the Vatican to rescue the Mortara child failed. A visit to Rumania in 1867 produced little improvement for that country's much beleaguered Jewish population (p. 204). But Montefiore's effort in 1863 on behalf of Moroccan Jewry may have been the apotheosis of his career. Then seventy-nine years old, he set out from Gibraltar with his wife, Judith, on a daunting horse-and-carriage trek across 115 miles of Moroccan deserts and mountains. Upon reaching the capital city of Fez, where he was tendered a lavish reception by the sultan himself, Montefiore secured the Moroccan ruler's personal pledge of improved treatment of "his" Jews. Once again, the Jewish world was agog at Montefiore's amalgam of solicitude and tenacity. Little wonder that a common aphorism in the nineteenth century, as in the Middle Ages, declared: "From Moses to Moses, there is none unto Moses"—that is, from the original Moses the Lawgiver to Moses Maimonides the medieval physician-philosopher, and now to Moses Montefiore, no Jew could compare in stature.

The significance of Montefiore's career, however, may have been less his epic exertions in defense of his fellow Jews than the respect and consideration tendered him by the British establishment. As early as 1830, Montefiore was formally presented to King William IV by the Duke of Norfolk. In 1837, he was elected sheriff of Middlesex. That same year, Queen Victoria granted him a knighthood, with the word "Jerusalem" sewn on his personal pennant of baronetcy. In advance of Montefiore's initial visit to Palestine in 1827, and on each of his six later journeys there, the Foreign Office directed its consular officials along his scheduled route to extend him the utmost in diplomatic support. In 1840, before departing on his effort to liberate the Damascus Jews, the queen granted Montefiore an audience as a gesture of her personal concern for the success of his mission. And when at last the prisoners were released, Victoria solemnized Montefiore's triumph by authorizing embellishments to his baronet's coat of arms. In 1863, upon Montefiore's return from his exhausting journey on behalf of Moroccan Jewry, the Lord Mayor of London tendered him a public reception. The featured speaker was the redoubtable William E. Gladstone.

Four and a half years later, as prime minister, Gladstone offered Montefiore a peerage. The honor, which Sir Moses respectfully declined for reasons of age, had been suggested by the Earl of Shaftesbury, an obdurate Tory who years earlier had opposed the admission of Jews to the House of Commons. Now Shaftesbury had second thoughts, and in his contrition he proposed that

> [we] avail ourselves of the opportunity to show regard to God's ancient people. There is a noble member of the house of Israel, Sir Moses Montefiore, a man dignified by patriotism, charity, and self-sacrifice, on [whom] Her Majesty might graciously bestow the honour of the Peerage. It would be a glorious day for the House of Lords when that grand old Hebrew were enrolled on the lists of the hereditary legislators of England.

"A glorious day for the House of Lords." Britain in the 1860s was at the meridian of its wealth and power. Awestruck at their good fortune, the British people well understood that their island nation, lacking so much as grain to feed its population, had managed to dominate the markets of five continents and to plant the Union Jack on four of them. Surely, then, freedom was the indispensable attribute that endowed their country with its vitality and humanity, even as tolerance for other creeds and peoples sustained its vast eminence in international affairs. The climate of that pluralism required endless testing and reconfirmation. Who better than a Jew to serve as weathervane?

VI

Jews in an Emancipated Economy

DEMOGRAPHIC AND VOCATIONAL TRANSFORMATIONS

If our tourist friend of the first chapter had been transported from the mid-eighteenth century to the mid-nineteenth century, he would have had difficulty recognizing the countryside of Western Europe. The fields that once had been open and verdant now were becoming mottled with factories and grimed with the smoke of blast furnaces. A rural economy of farms and pastures, of handicrafts and artisanry, was beginning to give way to an economy based on coal, iron, and mass production.

A critical factor in this industrial transformation was the widening reservoir of inexpensive labor. Much of the surplus was the consequence of agricultural enclosures, as wealthy landlords simply evicted their tenants in anticipation of more profitable, large-scale farming. But demographic influences also helped launch the Industrial Revolution. For more than a thousand years, the population of Europe had grown slowly. From the eighteenth century on, however, under the impact of improved hygiene and technology, the Continent's human resources all but exploded, from 140 million to 260 million between 1750 and 1850, to nearly 500 million by 1914. In turn, the pressures of this human congestion imposed painful strains upon traditional family and village life. As tracts of land were divided and subdivided into dysfunctional miniplots, young people witnessed the shrinkage of their legacies and dowries. Few rural sons or daughters discerned a viable livelihood for themselves any longer at the family hearth. These were the circumstances that impelled the departure of village rustics, waves of migration that choked the slums of industrial cities and dramatically augmented the waiting cadres of factory labor. Accompanying these newcomers were others who formerly had comprised the very fabric of rural society, the smiths, millers, innkeepers, and priests. What need was there for them now? What need, moreover, for the petty trade of Jews?

As the legal barriers to their movement gradually eased, village Jews also found themselves swept up in the city-bound migration. As late as 1800, the

8,500 Jews of Prague comprised Europe's largest Jewish urban population west of the Tsarist Empire, followed by Hamburg and Munich, each with 6,400 Jews. By mid-century, however, Europe's urban Jewish population doubled and tripled. Prague by then encompassed 20,000 Jews; Vienna, 5,000; Berlin, 20,000; Hamburg and Frankfurt, 15,000 each; Breslau, 8,000; Paris, 24,000; Budapest, 60,000—and these figures would multiply still again by the end of the century. Gradually, changes in residence were translated into vocational alterations, as the inroads of the new commercial and industrial order encouraged Jews to shift from hawking and peddlery to retail shopkeeping, to wholesale distribution, to light industry, and increasingly to the professions.

Yet it was a much smaller Jewish minority, the bankers among them, who may have exerted the farthest-reaching impact on modern Europe's economic development. As in the seventeenth and eighteenth centuries, the most remunerative clients for Jewish moneylenders were governments. The Continent's revenue base had all but dried up in the ruination of the Napoleonic Wars, and taxation alone was inadequate to reduce its vast wartime deficits. State loans were floated only with great difficulty. Even in a relatively advanced nation such as Prussia, the number of individuals employed in banking and stock-brokerage amounted to less than 2,000, and few of these would so much as touch government bond issues. In Austria, the public treasury had never effectively been separated from the fledgling bank of issue, the Wiener Stadtbank, which possessed neither the resources nor the nerve to extend large-scale loans.

Here it was that nineteenth-century high finance remained substantially the prerogative of Jewish investment bankers. Their experience in dealing with portable funds was a venerable one (pp. 23–25). Indeed, a number of these men were lineal descendants of seventeenth- and eighteenth-century *Hofjuden,* and several of them administered the accumulated capital of three or four generations. Thus, in Berlin, between 1812 and 1815, of the thirty-two most highly rated banking houses, seventeen belonged to Jews, and seven to converted Jews. Not all of these Jewish financiers specialized in government loans, but nine of them did (as against none among non-Jews). The role of Frankfurt's Jewish bankers was even farther-reaching in public finance. At the beginning of the century, Frankfurt-am-Main was the domicile of a mere 600 Jewish families, most of these living in the city's squalid Judengasse. Among them, however, they owned the city's twelve largest banking houses. The figure actually was even more impressive than it seemed, inasmuch as Frankfurt in the eighteenth century was emerging as the German world's major financial center.

Located in the fertile Rhineland, Frankfurt adjoined the pulsing commercial route linking wealthy Holland, by way of the St. Gotthard Pass, with the historic trade emporium of Venice. It was the most heavily trafficked land highway in Europe, and Frankfurt in consequence burgeoned into its major entrepôt of commerce. As a result of the wide variety of currencies circulating through Europe in that age of mercantilism, much of Frankfurt's business related to banking, particularly to money-changing and bill-brokering— the purchase and sale of commercial IOUs. The vocation was a familiar one to Jews. In Frankfurt, their role in banking by the late 1700s already had become preeminent. Other Jewish banking families were establishing themselves elsewhere in Europe. These included the Warburgs in Hamburg, the Mendelssohns and Bleichröders in Berlin, the Oppenheimers of Cologne and Vienna, the Eskeleses and Arnsteins in Vienna, the Montagus, Goldsmids, and Hambros in London. But the pioneering era of Jewish state underwriting—the "Frankfurt Tradition"—has most commonly been identified with the members of a single legendary family.

"The Sixth Dynasty of Europe"

They were a classical product of the Frankfurt Judengasse. In 1751, Mayer Amschel Rothschild, recently orphaned, was apprenticed to the Oppenheimer family in Hanover, where he became proficient in the purchase and sale of rare coins and medals. A vigorous market existed for these baubles, especially among royalty and aristocrats. Thus, one of young Rothschild's most dependable clients was Wilhelm, prince of Hesse-Kassel. By 1769, relations between the two had become close enough for the prince to appoint Rothschild his *Hoffaktor*, his court agent. The arrangement established the basis of the young Jew's fortune, for Wilhelm himself was a prosperous bill-broker and coin dealer, and Mayer Amschel now served as his agent in both trades, and later as an agent for other European courts. By the turn of the century, Rothschild had become a wealthy man.

He was also a man who never forgot the source of his prosperity. In 1806, in the aftermath of the battle of Jena, when Prince Wilhelm made ready to flee Napoleon's occupying army, he gave over his personal estate to Rothschild's custody. Rothschild did more than guard the prince's fortune. He vastly enlarged it. Nine years earlier, in 1797, he had dispatched Nathan Mayer, the third of his five sons, to serve as the family's business representative in Manchester, England. In this urban heartland of the early Industrial Revolution, the portly, snub-nosed Nathan used his share of the family funds to set up a purchasing branch for British textiles. Negotiating directly with the manufacturers, he soon flourished handsomely on his own. Eventually, in 1803, Nathan moved to London, where he emulated his father by branching out into the trade in cotton, wheat, and weaponry. He also moved into banking. It was consequently to Nathan that Mayer Amschel Rothschild shipped most of Prince Wilhelm's liquid funds; and Nathan in turn used this estate as collateral for expanding the family's banking operations—thereby generating an even larger fortune both for the prince and for the Rothschilds.

In 1812, Mayer Amschel died, at the age of sixty-eight. His most enduring legacy by then was his earlier decision to encourage three of his five sons to install themselves in Paris, Manchester (and then London), as well as in Frankfurt. After his death, his two younger sons moved to Naples and Vienna. Each inherited a 20 percent share in the family banking business, and each shrewdly identified his future in the still underdeveloped market of government loans. Austria was a prime example. In the last years before the Napoleonic Wars, such local Jewish firms as Eskeles and Arnstein had become major financiers. By 1816, however, concerned by his growing dependence on Vienna's local Jewish banking community, Emperor Franz I turned instead to Salomon, one of the five Rothschild sons. As an inducement for the family's help, the emperor in 1822 accepted Chancellor Metternich's advice to appoint the entire Rothschild family to the "second-level nobility," with the title of barons (pp. 108–9).

Yet it was in London, where Nathan Mayer Rothschild had moved his base of operations, that the family's fortunes were most dramatically enlarged. During the Napoleonic Wars, it was Nathan who soon emerged as the principal conduit of government funds to Britain's armies on the Continent. The process began in 1811, when John Herries was appointed the nation's commissary in chief. On the advice of a mutual friend, Baron Limburger, a Leipzig tobacco merchant, Herries subsequently awarded Nathan the commission to transfer a substantial quantity of gold bullion to the army of General Arthur Wellesley (soon to become the Duke of Wellington), who was then engaged against Napoleon's forces in Spain. It was an inspired choice, for Nathan had devised a solution for transmitting these funds through enemy territory. Purchasing large quantities of gold in the bullion market, Nathan dispatched the ingots across the English Channel. Awaiting his packet boat at a French coastal inlet was his brother James. With his staff, James carried the bullion on to Paris. There it was secretly transmuted into bills of obligation to various Spanish bankers, allowing payments then to be disbursed to General Wellesley's troops in pesetas. Once perfected, other Rothschild transactions subsequently were conducted for the British government. Indeed, well before the wars ended, it was possible to discontinue the actual shipment of bullion. So respected was the House of Rothschild by then that its notes alone, transmitted through any of the family's branches, were honored by governments and private banks in local currency.

By 1814, John Herries was using Nathan Rothschild not only to pay Britain's troops on the Continent, but also to distribute Britain's massive financial subsidies to its coalition partners, among them Austria, Prussia, and Russia. Between 1812 and 1814, Britain paid out 42 million pounds to these allies, with most of the funds disbursed through local Rothschild agents. For his part, Nathan masterminded these enterprises on skill and nerve alone, without receiving a penny from the British government in advance. His promised commission of 2 percent depended entirely upon the success of the transfers. For the British government, the price doubtless was a modest one, but it was sufficient to make the Rothschilds immensely wealthy. The enterprise also helped train the family in the complexities of underwriting the debts of entire governments. Indeed, well before the triumph of the Allied coalition, the Rothschilds had begun to use their own funds in the purchase and sale of public bond issues. It was a risky business. Like exchange rates, bond values were highly sensitive to political and military developments. Nevertheless, between 1813 and 1815, maintaining a close watch on these contingencies, Nathan and his brothers bought up British bond issues and those of Britain's allies, and ultimately marketed them for substantial profits.

The most vivid example of the family's acuity may have been its reaction, in June 1814, to Napoleon's escape from Elba and his climactic encounter with the Allied armies at Waterloo. For the Rothschilds and other major owners of British bonds, nothing could have been more vital than intelligence on the outcome of that battle. If Napoleon won, their bonds would plummet in value. If he lost, bond values would rise. For thirty hours, the fate of Europe hung veiled in cannon smoke. On June 18, late in the afternoon, a Rothschild agent climbed into a packet boat at Ostend. In a pouch, he grasped a Dutch gazette still damp from the printer. By the dawn light of June 20, arriving at Folkestone harbor, he turned over the document to another waiting Rothschild employee. The latter then rushed back to London to confirm to Nathan Rothschild the thrilling news of the Allied victory at Waterloo— thereby allowing Nathan to luxuriate in the dramatic upsurge in value of his own great bloc of bonds.

In the highly speculative business of underwriting and selling public securities, it was crucial to secure intimate details on the issuing government's economic and political circumstances. Fortunately, the brothers Rothschild were well positioned to acquire that information from their numerous official and unofficial contacts. So it was, between 1815 and 1848, that the House of Rothschild entered the period of its most spectacular financial success. Inasmuch as few public loans were floated in this period without assurance of Rothschild support, the five brothers literally presided over the solvency of entire governments. By mid-century, their joint capital was estimated at the equivalent of $6 billion, significantly larger than the fortune achieved by any other banking family in history, whether the Fuggers of the Renaissance era or J. P. Morgan of the early twentieth century. No one in those decades considered grandiloquent the sobriquet widely attached to the House of Rothschild, "the sixth dynasty of Europe."

AN UNREQUITED INTERNATIONALISM

As the Rothschilds and other Jewish financiers enlarged upon their predecessors' historic role as Europe's pre-eminent underwriters of government loans, they well understood that their most important collateral was the stability of their borrowers. Thus, in the post–Congress of Vienna era, the Rothschilds shared with such conservative statesmen as Austria's Chancellor Metternich a vested interest in political quietude. Occasionally, as in England, they found qualified representative government palatable, but democracy they frankly distrusted. Thus, in 1831, when Louis-Philippe, France's new constitutional monarch, intimated his interest in fostering revolutionary governments in the Habsburg satellite provinces of Lombardy-Venetia, he evoked a stern Rothschild warning. "I informed His Majesty [King Louis-Philippe]," wrote James de Rothschild in Paris to his brother Salomon in Vienna, "that if he took Casimir Périer into his ministry, his credit would rise." Périer was a cautious financier, known to the Rothschilds for his distrust of military adventurism. Taking the hint, Louis-Philippe appointed Périer as his prime minister. All talk of intervention in northern Italy then ceased, and the French government protected its line of Rothschild credit. On other occasions, the Rothschilds waxed blunter yet. In 1839, King Leopold I of Belgium embarked on military preparations to wrest the provinces of Luxembourg and Limburg from the Dutch Netherlands. "The Belgian government," Salomon informed his brother James, "will not get a ha'penny from us. . . . Difficult though I found it to keep refusing, I shall feel compensated if Belgium yields and peace is restored." King Leopold yielded. Rothschild extended his loan.

There were other instances in which the Rothschilds flexed their muscles to ensure European peace: by withholding funds from Adolphe Thiers, France's belligerent premier, during the Mehemet Ali crisis of 1840 (pp. 81–82), and twice even from the Habsburg government when Vienna in the 1850s was on the verge of preemptive military action against Piedmont. "It is in the nature of things," Otto von Bismarck ruefully acknowledged in 1863, during his effort to finance Prussian rearmament, "that the [Rothschild] House should do everything possible to prevent war from breaking out. This fact shows how delicate one must be in dealing with the Rothschilds." The observation was prescient. The "House," like the majority of Jewish bankers, feared war, mobs, and populist "anarchy" even more than illiberal rule.

In the process of "internationalizing" their firms, moreover, Jewish bankers developed not only a vested interest in peace but a reliable source of information on European political issues. Early on, Mayer Amschel Rothschild sensed the vital importance of that intelligence. Beyond strategically locating his sons throughout the Continent, the founding father shrewdly negotiated a financial arrangement with the princely House of Thurn, hereditary post-master of the former Holy Roman Empire, to secure use of its renowned courier service. With this asset in hand, the family members were able swiftly and efficiently to share vital information with one another. In later decades, through flattery and discreet financial inducements, the brothers Rothschild also managed to obtain appointment as honorary consuls in their cities of residence, thereby positioning themselves even more reliably to garner and share their diplomatic insights for use on the stock exchange.

These contacts occasionally produced financial coups as dramatic as those Nathan achieved during the Napoleonic era. In the late 1860s, few officials of the British Board of Trade evinced much interest in the prospect of building a canal across the Isthmus of Suez. The slower Cape route around Africa appeared sufficient to ensure maritime access to India. Accordingly, when Ferdinand de Lesseps completed his construction of the Suez Canal in 1869, the British government stood by as the Canal Company's 400,000 stock shares were snapped up, variously, by the Ottoman sultan, the khedive of Egypt, and by private French financiers. But a few years later, in 1875, information leaked to Britain's Prime Minister Benjamin Disraeli that France's shareholders were collecting unanticipated dividends, and essentially from tolls paid by British shipping. As an investment alone, the waterway could be of much value to Britain. Its strategic usefulness as a foreshortened British shipping route to India was more important yet. Disraeli was intrigued, but could discern no way of obtaining a major bloc of shares for his government without engaging in competitive bidding.

Later that same year, however, Sir Henry Oppenheim, a Jewish publisher with important contacts in the Egyptian government, made a further discovery. Egypt's Khedive Ismail, whose lavish public expenditures had brought him to the verge of bankruptcy, was anxious to sell his own 200,000 shares, and for as paltry a sum as 4 million pounds sterling. The intelligence was transmitted to Disraeli, who sensed immediately the prospect of a major coup for Britain. But Parliament was not in session to vote the necessary funds. Whereupon, cognizant of the danger of waiting, the prime minister asked his close friend Lionel Rothschild (son of the late Nathan) for the necessary loan. Both men understood the risk. Parliament might decline to repurchase the stock. Nevertheless, Rothschild agreed on the spot. The purchase was consummated without delay, and the prime minister then dispatched to Queen Victoria the famous note: "It is just settled. You have it, Madam." When Parliament reconvened, it vindicated both Disraeli's faith and Rothschild's iron nerve by repurchasing the stock—at a decent profit for Rothschild. Once again, international connections had proved their indispensability.

Given the importance of these networks, it was hardly surprising that marriage arrangements among these Jewish Maecenases were negotiated as carefully as royal alliances. Louis Raphael Bischoffsheim, son of Raphael, founder of the immensely powerful House of Bischoffsheim (p. 114), dutifully married Amalia Goldschmidt, a sister of Benedict Goldschmidt, a prominent Frankfurt banker. Soon afterward, the House of Bischoffsheim was transformed into Bischoffsheim & Goldschmidt. In his Europe-wide financial transactions, Louis Raphael then acquired vital support from his nephew by marriage, Ludwig Bamberger, director of Bamberger & Co., and a future cofounder (in 1870) of the Deutsche Bank. Jonathan Bischoffsheim, Louis Raphael's brother and partner, settled in Brussels, marrying there into the opulent Hirsch family (p. 114). The marital chains extended further yet. In ensuing years, Benedict Goldschmidt, of Bischoffsheim & Goldschmidt, sired ten children. One child, Leopold Benedict, married Regina, a daughter of Jonathan Bischoffsheim. Another, Maximilian, married Minka Carolina, daughter of Baron Wilhelm Karl von Rothschild. Of the daughters of old Raphael Nathan Bischoffsheim, Amalia married the banker August Bamberger of Mainz, whose son, Heinrich, married the sister of Baron Moritz de Hirsch. A second daughter of Raphael Nathan Bischoffsheim, Clara, was the wife of L. Cahan d'Anvers, one of the directors of France's powerful Crédit Mobilier mortgage bank.

As for the widely dispersed Rothschilds, preference in marital alliances was given to family members of the various branches. Mayer Karl Rothschild of Naples married his cousin Louise, youngest daughter of Nathan Rothschild of London. Of the seven daughters produced by the marriage, Adele became the wife of Salomon, a son of the Paris James; Emma married Nathaniel, later to be anointed the first Lord Rothschild; Theresa married her cousin James Edward, grandson of the London Nathan. Charlotte, daughter of Karl von Rothschild, married Lionel Nathan (son of Nathan Mayer). By the late nineteenth century, there were no fewer than fifty-eight marriages among Rothschild cousins of various degrees.

Meanwhile, in the eyes of much of Christian Europe, it was specifically the widening entanglement of Rothschild marriages, and of many other Jewish bankers whose children married within the same concentric circles, that appeared to confirm suspicions of an international Jewish conspiracy. As Hannah Arendt famously observed:

> Where . . . was there better proof of the fantastic concept of a Jewish world government than in this one family, the Rothschilds, nationals of five different countries, prominent everywhere, in close cooperation with at least three different governments (French, Austrian, British), whose frequent conflicts never for a moment shook the solidarity of interests of their state bankers?

No propaganda could have created a symbol more effective for political purposes than the reality itself.

It was an irony that accusations of an international Jewish financial cabal should have gained their widest resonance just as the putative threat was ebbing. With the deaths of the original five Rothschild brothers, the close union among the family's branches was gradually altered. In part, the transformations reflected those of the Continent itself, as the nineteenth-century "Concert of Europe" gave way to an upsurge of competitive chauvinism. But they signified as well an immersion of the family's third and fourth generations into the mainstream of their various national cultures and aspirations.

The auguries of change were apparent initially in the disposition of Rothschild family property. In the days of Mayer Amschel, the five sons shared equally in the profit and loss of every transaction. By the 1860s, however, with each of the branches controlling its own private investments, they acted together only rarely, and by the time of the Franco-Prussian War, a decade later, the "House" of Rothschild legally and factually had devolved into individual national firms. Yet the process of decentralization reflected no less the acceptance of Rothschild grandchildren and great-grandchildren in the highest social circles of their countries, as philanthropists, as patrons of the arts and sciences, and finally as arbiters of social style and public comportment. In the years before 1914, the English, Austrian, French, and German family members all dutifully supported the foreign policies of their governments. And with the outbreak of the Great War, the young male Rothschilds all but vied with one another in their rush to enlist for military service. In 1917, when Evelyn de Rothschild, a scion of the British family, fell in battle on the Western front, the Sanhedrin's century-old Affirmation of National Identity achieved a certain poignant and elegiac reconfirmation.

AN ALLIANCE WITH POWER

As in the Early Modern Era of the *Hofjuden*, Jewish financiers preferred to negotiate less with private businessmen than with government officials, those with the likeliest access to tax income for repayment. The tradition lingered well into the nineteenth century. Like their predecessors, the Rothschilds and other Jewish bankers continued to deal principally with representatives of the highest state authority. By then, however, the recompense they anticipated lay not only in financial profit but in public recognition and honor. The quest for status assuredly influenced the close relationship that developed between the Rothschilds and the Metternichian government in Austria. Metternich's closest adviser, Friedrich von Gentz, became an intimate friend of Salomon Rothschild in Vienna. It was at Gentz's recommendation, in 1822, that Metternich arranged for Emperor Franz I to appoint Rothschild a baron, thereby making him the realm's first unbaptized Jew to ascend to the nobility (p. 103). In Prussia, during the post–Congress of Vienna era, Rothschild family "friends" included State Chancellor Karl August von Hardenberg and Wilhelm von Humboldt, the educational reformer and diplomat.

Altogether, in the German-speaking world of the 1830s and 1840s, the so-called Frankfurt Tradition, that is, the mutually profitable relationship between Jewish bankers and prominent government officials, extended through manifold echelons. By mid-century, even Prussia's unregenerately conservative Otto von Bismarck came to appreciate the kind of service he and his government might command from Jewish finance. Earlier, Bismarck had evinced a characteristic Junker disdain for Jews. In 1847, as Prussia's delegate to the Diet of the old German Confederation, he had opposed Jewish emancipation. Jews, he argued, should play no role in the public administration of Christian states. But in 1859, shortly before departing Berlin to take up his ambassadorship in Russia, Bismarck recognized the need for an experienced banker to handle his personal finances. Numerous of his fellow Junkers were boasting of "their" Jewish bankers, after all. He sought a recommendation from Baron Mayer Karl Rothschild, who lately had moved from Naples to Frankfurt to succeed his deceased and childless uncle, Amschel Mayer. Bismarck specified that his banker should be Jewish. In his reply, Mayer Karl suggested Gerson Bleichröder.

Born in Berlin in 1822, Bleichröder was the grandson of a *Schutzjude,* a "protected" Jew. His father, Samuel, initially had plied the Jewish vocation of a currency-changer before evolving into a merchant banker. The son, who in 1837 had been appointed a Rothschild agent in Berlin, flourished handsomely and soon became an important banker on his own account. In that role, Gerson Bleichröder was prepared to underwrite both public bond offerings and private industrial projects (p. 113). Meeting now with Bismarck in 1859, he impressed the Prussian statesman as both astute and *salonsfähig*—personally dignified. Soon agreement was reached for Bleichröder to manage Bismarck's private finances. From then on, Bleichröder collected Bismarck's salary and investment income alike, paid his debts, established accounts for him abroad, reinvested his income in government bonds and in private industrial ventures, and dramatically enlarged the Prussian statesman's estate.

Bismarck was gratified. In their correspondence, he increasingly shared political news with his trusted banker. At Bismarck's recommendation, King Wilhelm I in 1861 awarded Bleichröder the title of Kommerzienrat (Commercial Counselor), an honor that evoked additional medals and titles from other governments. The following year, Bismarck returned from St. Petersburg to become chancellor of Prussia and to embark upon his cherished dream of transforming his country into the nucleus of an enlarged German empire. Unlike the House of Rothschild, which feared disruptions in the balance of power, Bleichröder fully shared that vision. As far back as 1859, he had been one of the founders of the "Prussian Consortium," a syndicate of banks organized to help raise 30 million thalers for Prussian rearmament. Working closely now with Bismarck, Bleichröder became the chancellor's key adviser on the privatization of such Prussian state resources as its rich coal mines in the Ruhr. The money raised in these sales was never quite adequate to make up budgetary shortfalls. Nevertheless, on faith, Bismarck launched his war against Austria in 1866, and won it.

Four years later, the chancellor's vision approached fulfillment with the Prussian army's stunning military victory over France. Bleichröder's role again was central. In the aftermath of the triumph, the banker shuttled back and forth between Berlin and Paris to determine the amount of indemnities to be imposed on defeated France, then to guarantee financing both through his own bank and through the London Rothschilds as "backup" guarantors. No two men could have been closer in those years than Bleichröder and the German chancellor. Bismarck even secured the Jewish financier's discreet intervention in terminating a romantic relationship between his, Bismarck's, son Herbert and a divorced woman. Yet it was for his "state" services that Bleichröder in 1872 was awarded the title of baron.

Although Bleichröder was the first professing Jew in Germany to be raised to the "first order" of the nobility, it was the Austrian government's initial ennoblement of the brothers Rothschild that later allowed men like Bleichröder, Haber, Lehmann, Arnstein, and other Jewish bankers to flaunt the coveted "von" before their names. Thus, in Hungary, over the course of the nineteenth century, more than three hundred Jews were ennobled—fully 20 percent of the totality of ennoblements in this eastern Habsburg domain. Even in such "progressive" nations as France and England, Jewish financiers managed to remain close to the seats of political and social power. The Paris Rothschilds befriended the Count de Villèle, a premier under Louis XVIII's restoration government, then skillfully shifted their allegiance to Louis-Philippe in 1830, then survived the 1848 revolution—first by cultivating leading republicans and later by developing financial contacts with Emperor Louis Napoleon. By the time the Third Republic was ratified, in 1876, the French Rothschilds were sharing their social eminence with such Jewish banking families as Camondo, Cahan d'Anvers, Königswärter, Léonino, and d'Almeida, all of whom preened themselves in their exclusive Parisian faubourgs under titles bestowed during Louis Napoleon's Second Empire.

In England, Lionel de Rothschild, grandson of Mayer Amschel and son of Nathan, was elevated to a baronetcy, while the bankers Edward Speyer and Ernest Cassel similarly were honored with knighthoods. Lionel's magnificent London mansion and his famous country home in Gunnersbury Park were cynosures of mid-Victorian society. In the latter nineteenth century, everyone of consequence visited—princes, ambassadors, bishops, men of letters, rivals in the House of Commons who came to bury animosities in an atmosphere where the wit flowed as liberally as the wine. Lionel's son Nathaniel Mayer and the Prince of Wales had been friends since their Cambridge days. In 1881, the prince, the future Edward VII, struggled through a blizzard to reach the wedding of Leopold de Rothschild, Nathaniel Mayer's younger brother, at London's Central Synagogue. In 1885, Nathaniel Mayer would become the first English Jew to be elevated to the peerage (p. 97), thereby joining his continental cousins in the Rothschild "baronhood."

By the late nineteenth century, throughout the breadth of Europe, court circles were liberally sprinkled with Jewish nobility, the largest numbers of them bankers. If there was an irony in their ascendance, it lay in the medals and orders that compounded financial profits. These honorifics included the Order of Vladimir, from Russia's Jew-hating Nicholas I; from Spain, the Order of Isabella the Catholic, the queen who had expelled the Jews in 1492; the Order of Saint George from the malevolently anti-Jewish Pope Gregory XVI. In 1865, when Prussian Baron Becke, a friend of Bismarck's, contemplated seeking a loan from James de Rothschild, he conferred with Count Mülinen, an adviser to King Wilhelm I. "How would it be," suggested Mülinen, "if we gave him the Grand Cordon? It was the Cross of Stanislaus that made the Russian loan. Has he the Iron Cross, First Class? If not, can we let him hope for it . . . ?" But hope sprang eternal in the breasts of these financial arrivistes, whose notion of heaven not uncommonly was the *Almanach de Gotha.*

The Banker as Shtadlan

For Jewish banking eminences, in fact, more important even than royal approbation was their seigneurial responsibility for their own people. In the tradition of their *hofjüdische* predecessors, the Rothschilds and their colleagues were quite prepared to intercede for their fellow Jews at a moment's notice. In 1818, Amschel Mayer Rothschild rushed a dispatch to Chancellor Karl von Hardenberg, a veteran advocate of Jewish emancipation (pp. 49–50), to seek an end to Jewish inequities in Prussian Posen. The gentle Hardenberg then discussed the matter with King Friedrich Wilhelm III, and achieved a certain modest relaxation of Jew-taxes and vocational restrictions. That same year, three of the brothers Rothschild converged on the Congress of Aix-la-Chapelle to seek Metternich's help for Jews elsewhere in the German Confederation. Expressing his personal sympathy, Metternich promised to "investigate" the Jewish situation. On this occasion, the German Diet was unresponsive. But in 1837, again at the intercession of the Rothschilds, Metternich was somewhat more effective in securing an improvement of Jewish living conditions in the capital of Vienna.

In 1856, as a consequence of James de Rothschild's appeal to France's Emperor Louis Napoleon, the issue of Jewish persecution in Rumania was placed on the agenda of the Congress of Paris, at the end of the Crimean War. This time the effort was unavailing; Louis Napoleon's periodic queries of the Bucharest regime evoked only evasion or silence. But in later years, German pressure appeared likelier to exert a certain influence with the Rumanians. In 1866, the Prussian-born Karl of Hohenzollern-Sigmaringen was installed as Prince Carol of Rumania. Sensing a possible opening in this royal connection, the estimable Gerson von Bleichröder moved aggressively to champion the cause of Rumanian Jewry. In March 1872, freshly ennobled, Bleichröder reminded Bismarck of "the loathsome persecutions which the Jews living in Rumania have repeatedly suffered," and appealed to the chancellor's "well-known humanity" to join the protest of other European leaders on behalf of these victims. Bismarck was prepared to accommodate his faithful Bleichröder. Through the German consul in Bucharest, he discreetly reminded Prince Carol that the Jews "exercise a . . . considerable influence in the press, in politics, and in far-reaching circles." Nevertheless, the Rumanian government's response was characteristically evasive. The persecution of Jews continued.

In 1877, however, a crisis in the Balkans erupted in yet another war between Russia and Turkey. The Turks again were defeated, and in the ensuing diplomatic effort to bring order and stability to Southeastern Europe, the governments of the Great Powers agreed to dispatch their statesmen to an international congress, in Berlin. It was expected that the forthcoming conclave would establish the independence of several Balkan nations, Rumania among them. Here at last was a matchless opportunity for Jewish intercessors to seek a quid pro quo from Bucharest: full equality for the Jews in return for international recognition of Rumanian sovereignty. Again, Bleichröder emerged as the impresario of the diplomatic effort, recruiting Adolphe Crémieux, Moses Montefiore, the Rothschilds, and other Jewish luminaries to address a collective appeal to "the warm-hearted Prince Bismarck." And once more, in January 1878, the chancellor sent back word to Bleichröder, promising his fullest support. With this assurance in hand, Bleichröder promptly converted his office into a virtual headquarters of international Jewry and personally coordinated all Jewish contacts with the various European statesmen. Once it became known that Bismarck favored guarantees for the Jews, other diplomats added their endorsement. French Foreign Minister Waddington was among them. So was England's Prime Minister Disraeli, Austria's Foreign Minister Andrassy, and so, albeit grudgingly, was Russian

Foreign Minister Gorchakov. Elated, Bleichröder sent word to Crémieux: "We are on the eve of emancipation."

So it appeared. On July 1, at Bismarck's vigorous initiative, the congress duly incorporated into the Treaty of Berlin a key provision, Article 44, obliging the Rumanian government to extend equal political rights, including the right of naturalization, to all its inhabitants. The Rumanians signed—and little time passed before their "acquiescence" was exposed as a fraud. Indeed, as late as 1913, a grand total of 361 Jews (in a Jewish population of some 240,000) had been naturalized in Rumania. Yet Bucharest's campaign of sabotage could not have been anticipated on July 1, 1878. Rather, the moment was one of vast jubilation for Jews throughout Europe. That same night, flushed with triumph, Bleichröder entertained the European statesmen at his home for dinner. Except for Bismarck himself, who no longer attended private functions, they all came: Disraeli, Waddington, Andrassy, even Russia's Gorchakov—all the great and famous.

By then the richest man in Berlin, possibly in Germany, Bleichröder remained a parvenu and a snob to the end of his days. He had worked for his fellow Jews only as a collectivity, presiding over them as a self-ordained king. His diplomatic efforts on their behalf continued unremittingly, to be sure, as did his philanthropic benefactions. Yet, whenever he made his way along the Siegesalle, a fashionable Berlin avenue adjoining the Tiergarten, Bleichröder was careful to walk on the western rather than the eastern side, where most of the promenaders tended to be lower-middle-class Jews of East European background. The eastern side, he explained to his friend, "smelled too much of garlic." Bleichröder lived within an elegant enclave inhabited by other wealthy Jewish bankers, yet he rarely invited them, or any Jews, to his sumptuous receptions. He preferred the company of distinguished gentiles. Many of these in turn attended his funeral, when he died in 1893 at the age of seventy-one. The service was Jewish, and dignified. The newspapers carried long and respectful eulogies. Bleichröder would have been pleased. Doubtless he would have been less so had he known of Bismarck's terse reaction to his, Bleichröder's, extravagantly obsequious letter of gratitude following the Congress of Berlin: "Judendank"—"Jew thanks"—jotted the chancellor in the margin.

The Frankfurt Tradition Modified

As the preeminent underwriters of government bond offerings, the great Jewish bankers for many decades played only a limited role as financiers of private business. Nevertheless, as industrial expansion gained momentum throughout the nineteenth century, dynasties such as the Rothschilds, Bleichröders, and Hirsches began to exert a growing influence on the development of technology, and specifically of Europe's first railroads. In Austria, Salomon von Rothschild as early as 1838 financed the Kaiser-Ferdinand Nordbahn, linking Vienna with the salt mines of Galicia, with the coal basin of Märisch-Ostrau, and the steel mills of Witkowitz. In 1844, Salomon and his son Anselm established the powerful Creditananstalt banking consortium, modeled on the Parisian Crédit Mobilier (p. 116), which continued energetically financing Habsburg railroad construction. In France, too, in 1833, the Rothschilds underwrote construction of that nation's first railroad, the Paris-Saint-Germain line; even as the Königswärter banking firm subsequently underwrote a much wider network of rail lines traversing the breadth of France. In Germany during the 1860s and 1870s, Gerson von Bleichröder funded the immensely expensive, and immensely profitable, St. Gotthard Tunnel, opening up rail traffic from Central Europe to Italy.

Ultimately, the single most formidable European railroad achievement of the nineteenth century reflected the union of two powerful Jewish banking dynasties, the Bischoffsheims and the Hirsches. In the 1830s, Baron Jakob de Hirsch had served as private banker to King Ludwig I of Bavaria, who first ennobled the family. One of Jakob's sons, Josef, in conjunction with the Rothschilds and several other Jewish financiers, cofounded the East Bavarian Railroad. In the 1840s, Josef's son, Moritz, was apprenticed to the great banking house of Bischoffsheim & Goldschmidt, in Brussels. There he met and married Clara Bischoffsheim, daughter of Jonathan Raphael Bischoffsheim (p. 107), and was duly appointed a senior member of the firm. With a vast fortune on both sides of the family at his disposal, Moritz de Hirsch on his own soon emerged as the most imaginative and dynamic member of the combined banking operation.

Beyond all else, Moritz de Hirsch's genius lay in railroad development, a field that required as much diplomatic as financial skill. Thus, in 1865, he scored his first major coup by purchasing a controlling interest in the foundering Luxembourg Railroad, then persuading Louis Napoleon's government to open important route concessions for the line in France. At the same time, operating out of his own firm, Bischoffsheim & De Hirsch, the young financier was already embarked on the development of a series of light-rail feeder lines in Austria, Russia, and the Balkans. Amalgamating these routes into the larger trunk networks, Hirsch swiftly achieved a reputation as the greatest railroad entrepreneur of his era. Yet his most challenging project, the Trans-Balkan Railroad, still lay ahead, and it would keep him fully engaged for almost two decades.

The idea of a rail connection between Europe and Constantinople was not new. It was first proposed in the aftermath of the Crimean War, in 1856. Yet neither the Turks nor Europe's banking consortiums could agree upon the route or the financing of the network. By the late 1860s, however, Austrian officials displayed a growing interest in the scheme. A transportation network capable of linking Vienna with the Near East would offer a certain moral solace after the Hapsburg army's recent defeat in the Austro-Prussian War of 1866. More important, access to the Macedonian port of Salonika would provide Austria's predominantly land empire with a significant new maritime outlet to the Aegean. For these reasons, Austrian Foreign Minister von Beust actively supported Hirsch's effort to secure the concession from Turkey. The negotiations were successfully completed in April 1869. Under terms of the agreement, Hirsch would assume responsibility for constructing and operating a 2,500-kilometer (1,400-mile) rail network linking most of the principal towns of the Ottoman and Habsburg Balkans.

The project was a daunting one. Construction traversing the Balkan peninsula's formidable entanglement of mountains and ravines would depend upon the Ottoman government's ability to meet its payment obligations of up to 250,000 francs a kilometer. It soon became clear that most of the funding would have to be guaranteed in advance, and that the capital could only be raised through huge bond issues. In addressing that challenge, Hirsch successfully organized an underwriting syndicate of no fewer than eleven banks, most of them Jewish-owned, and then refloated seven new bond issues over the ensuing six years. In this fashion, with infinite patience and uncommon diplomatic skill, Hirsch managed to finance and orchestrate the huge construction project over the often bitter resistance of local Moslem populations, over intermittent political and military upheaval in the Balkan peninsula, periodic suspensions of Turkish payments, and numerous Turkish baksheesh "adjustments" (that would gain Hirsch his sobriquet as "Turkenhirsch"). In December 1888, almost miraculously, the railroad was completed in all its branch lines, and Constantinople effectively was connected with Vienna— and the West. Hirsch's entrepreneurial achievement was a staggering one, possibly matched in history only by Ferdinand de Lesseps's construction of the Suez Canal.

The project also made Hirsch one of the richest men in the world, and earned him accolades and decorations from nearly every country in Europe. Yet, by then, fame and wealth provided only bittersweet satisfaction. In 1887, he had been shattered by the death of his son, Lucien, at the age of thirty-one. Upon completing the Trans-Balkan project, the baron moved to Paris and announced his retirement. Henceforth, his main preoccupation was philanthropy. "My son I have lost," he explained, "but not my heir. Humanity is my heir." By the time of his own death, in 1896, Hirsch had given over 100 million francs to Jewish and non-Jewish causes alike, and his widow afterward would give away another 200 million, all in addition to Hirsch's massively funded ICA colonization foundation for the rescue and succor of Russian Jewry (p. 673).

Conceivably, "Turkenhirsch's" munificence surpassed even his financial genius. His time was past. By the latter nineteenth century, the insatiable industrial and reclamation needs of Western industrial economies required more capital than even these Jewish banking titans could generate. Innovations in finance capitalism were required. Of these, the most important was incorporation, allowing bank directors to tap the combined resources of thousands of small shareholders. The merchant investment bank soon became the joint-stock bank, its investors protected against undue loss by limited-liability legislation. Ironically, even the joint-stock bank was a Jewish innovation. It was pioneered in France by three Sephardic brothers, the Pereiras, who founded the Crédit Mobilier as a financial instrument that ultimately would be emulated by hundreds of other incorporated lending institutions. After 1871, the joint-stock bank began to flourish most impressively of all in the mighty new German Empire. By the same token, it was also in Germany that Jewish merchant banking underwent its most rapid demise. Indeed, in a united nation, Frankfurt itself lost its historic function as an exchange center for provincial currencies. The city's legendary gravitas terminated with a kind of poetic finality when Baron Wilhelm Karl von Rothschild died in 1901, and the Frankfurt House of Rothschild was liquidated.

It was not to be assumed that the Jews suddenly lost their importance in the world of finance. Descendants of such renowned banking families as Haber, Wassermann, Königswärter, Wertheimer, Oppenheimer, and Warburg either operated their own—modified, joint-stock—banks or served as directors of other institutions, among them the Deutsche Bank (the largest in Europe). As late as 1882, Jews comprised 43 percent of the proprietors or directors of Germany's ten largest banking and credit institutions. In Vienna, that same year, the proportion was estimated at 80 percent. In the Bohemian Crown lands and in the Habsburg port city of Trieste, banking was almost exclusively a Jewish vocation. If the tradition of Jewish banking eminence was fading, it was fading slowly and selectively.

By the 1890s, too, with all functional restraints on their mobility long since ended, Jews were moving far more rapidly into wider echelons of European economic life. In Prague, Budapest, Vienna, and other large Habsburg cities, Jews proved adaptable recruits to the new industrial age. The empire's fifteen largest textile factories were Jewish-owned. The chocolate industry, ready-made clothing, furniture manufacture, leather goods, and food processing were overwhelmingly the preserve of Austrian Jewry. In Hungary, the leading banking, commercial, and manufacturing companies were Jewish-owned. The Goldbergers of Obuda founded the largest textile-printing company in the empire. Henrik Levay established the Hungarian General Insurance Company, the largest in Hungary. Karoly Posner owned the largest paper-lithography-bookbinding company in the empire. In Germany, throughout these same late-nineteenth-century years, Jews were financing and organizing their own factories. As elsewhere, textiles were their best-known métier. Pioneering new techniques of dyeing and printing, Josef Liebermann (grandfather of the painter Max Liebermann) all but single-handedly drove English textile printers from the Continent. The Reichenherz family of Berlin operated textile factories employing 5,000 workers; while other Jewish entrepreneurs developed ancillary industries in thread, fabrics, ribbons, lace, and related clothing accessories. By the turn of the century, Jewish entrepreneurial ventures in textiles and clothing, and in shoe and furniture manufacturing, encompassed approximately half of all Jewish industrial enterprises in the Wilhelminian Empire.

Nevertheless, Jews in far greater proportions remained in the commercial sector of the middle class. Here, too, some of their enterprises were quite prepossessing. Thus, in Germany and Austria, as in the United States, Jews were the founding entrepreneurs of the department store, and their chains ultimately dominated the field in Europe altogether. Wholesale food and luxury items remained largely their preserve. Without question, the majority of Jewish businesses continued to be modest retail ventures. All the more so, as poorer communities of Jews from the eastern provinces flooded into such quasi-ghetto areas as Vienna's Leopoldstadt, Prague's Josefstadt, and Berlin's Wilhelmsdorf. Nevertheless, by the end of the century, most of these small-scale operations no longer were to be equated with the marginal hawking and huckstering vocations of earlier decades. To all appearances, Jews had established themselves as a "legitimate" subcommunity within the Continent's social firmament.

A PREFIGURATION OF ANTI-CAPITALISM

Legitimacy was not yet to be equated with approval. Throughout much of the nineteenth century, popular literature and theatrical performances in the German and Austrian empires remained merciless in their caricatures of the Rothschilds as "Jewish cash bags," or "Jews behind the throne." By the turn of the century, as the financial influence of the Rothschilds and other Jewish financiers actually began to wane, their "pernicious" role in the European economy would be singled out for harsher criticism, and for purposes rather more sinister than cultural or political derision (p. 228). Moreover, even in the heyday of the Frankfurt merchant-banking tradition, the symbiosis of Jews and finance capitalism became the target of a potent new intellectual assault. This one, ironically, was led by Jews themselves.

Ferdinand Lassalle was among the earliest of these iconoclasts. Born in 1825 in Breslau, the son of a prosperous silk-dealer, he was enrolled while still a teenager at a Leipzig commercial college in preparation for a business career. But in his second year of study, the twenty-year-old Lassalle met the forty-eight-year-old Heinrich Heine and soon became the famed writer's ideological disciple. Terming himself a "gladiator in the cause of human rights," Lassalle participated actively in the 1848 revolution in Prussia. Although he was arrested and convicted for incitement, and given a six-month sentence, the young idealist managed during his trial to launch a fiery attack on the judges and the government; and the subsequent publication of his remarks, in a pamphlet entitled *My Assize Comments (Meine Assisenrede)*, achieved wide circulation throughout the German world. By the time Lassalle was released, six months later, he had become something of a hero to Western Europe's youthful revolutionaries. Handsome as well as charismatic, he also developed a romantic liaison with a Countess von Hatzfeld, who subsequently underwrote his lifestyle as a society dandy and allowed him to cultivate his standing as a litterateur.

By mid-century, much of Lassalle's writing was devoted to the analysis of a new crisis in Europe's political economy. He was not the first to identify the emergent conflict between affluent employers and impoverished workers. In 1848, the Utopian Socialists in France had in effect fomented a class revolution within a political revolution. Yet Lassalle was among the earliest to discern in this unrest an opportunity, even an ethical mission, for the government to lift workers' "human consciousness" to a new level, by allying with the working classes against the "selfish" interests of the capitalist Mittelstand. Acting on this conviction, moreover (and on Countess von Hatzfeld's expense account), Lassalle in 1863 founded the General German Workers' Association.

The association's membership, consisting rather more of young intellectuals than of workers, responded passionately to this fire-breathing Jew. It hardly mattered to them that Lassalle never managed to translate his vision into a coherent political-economic ideology. They shared his conviction that the emancipation of workers could be achieved simply through universal suffrage and a pro-labor legislative agenda. Yet it was not Lassalle's unstructured utopianism that did him in. It was his succession of amorous affairs, climaxed by his courtship in 1863–64 of Helene von Dönniges, the Catholic daughter of a Bavarian diplomat. In September 1864, one of the "divine Helene's" gentile admirers provoked Lassalle into a duel, and in the ensuing exchange of shots Lassalle was killed, at the age of thirty-nine. So ended the career of a man whom Karl Marx described as "part Jew, part cavalier, part clown, part sentimentalist."

Except for his Jewish origins, the ponderous Marx would never have fitted that profile. Seven years older than Lassalle, he was born in 1818 in Trier, in the Catholic Rhineland. Although his career as journalist and ideologist, as "father" of the class revolution, has long since been integrated into historical vernacular (p. 310), Marx's Jewish associations were less widely publicized. He was the son of Hirsch Markus, a lawyer who converted to Lutheranism in 1817 in order to retain his Napoleonic-era status as a member of the bar. Markus's wife took this step eight years later, after the death of her father, Rabbi Isaac Pressburg. Their children then were baptized (and renamed "Marx") upon entering school. As a "Lutheran," Karl Marx experienced no difficulty in achieving a higher education at universities in Bonn, Berlin, and finally in Jena, where he earned a doctorate in philosophy. It was also in Jena, as an impecunious journalist-author, that the young Marx married the daughter of a Prussian aristocrat.

Earlier, as a student both in Berlin and Jena during the 1840s, Marx was decisively influenced by the philosophy of the late Georg W. F. Hegel, and afterward became one of Germany's innumerable "Young Hegelians." It was accordingly the Hegelian concept of the "dialectic" that would remain central in Marx's developing social philosophy (p. 286). And so, too, would Hegel's antipathy to Judaism, which the great thinker envisaged as a code of behavior rooted in an all-pervasive legalism, entirely devoid of any spiritual message whatever. Marx later expressed a comparable hostility in his article "On the Jewish Question" ("Zur Judenfrage"), published in the *Deutsch-Französischer Jahrbuch*, in 1844. While favoring the cause of equal Jewish rights, as an integral feature of a wider human emancipation, he was emphatic that the Jews as a religio-ethnic community had contributed nothing of worth to historical development. Their religion, he insisted, had become an antisocial element "which . . . will inevitably disintegrate." Worse yet, in Marx's description, "[t]he god of the Jews has been secularized and become the god of the world. Commerce is the true god of the Jew. . . . As soon as society succeeds in destroying the empirical essence of Judaism [that is], buying and selling . . . the Jew will become impossible. . . . [T]he social emancipation of Jewry is the emancipation of society from Judaism." Upon delivering himself of this ancestral burden, Marx would never again return to the Jewish question.

Society did it for him. As industrial capitalism gained momentum, it was a European irony and a Jewish tragedy that the Jew as putative financial wizard would become a bête noire in the gestating ideologies of political socialists and political reactionaries alike.

The Impact of Western Culture on Jewish Life

A Disorientation of Uncompleted Emancipation

In 1772, a Leipzig publisher issued a collection of poems by a Polish Jew, Issachar Falkensohn Behr. Written in the German language, the entire collection was titled, rather unimaginatively, *Poems of a Polish Jew.* After perusing Behr's verses, the mighty Goethe remarked: "It is extremely praiseworthy for a Polish Jew to give up business in order to learn German, to publish verses and devote himself to the Muses. But if he can be no more than a Christian *étudiant en belles lettres,* then he does wrong, I think, to make such a fuss about being a Jew." Goethe's observation doubtless was shared by many of his Jewish contemporaries. Well into the early nineteenth century, faced with the choice of "making a fuss" about their Jewishness or emulating their Christian neighbors, a significant minority of acculturated German Jews chose the latter alternative. More than acculturation, assimilation into the world of German Christendom appeared to be the only response to a still uncompleted emancipation.

In contrast to France or England, where the rights of citizenship came sooner rather than later, it was essentially in German-speaking Europe that Jews remained politically insecure well into the post-Napoleonic era, and their psychological balance remained correspondingly precarious. Although few Jews were susceptible to traditional methods of proselytization, economic opportunity and social acceptance were powerful inducements for relinquishment of the ancestral faith. Even the eccentric Solomon Maimon was tempted to follow this route, seeking baptism from a Lutheran pastor with the forthright explanation that apostasy offered the only hope of completing his education (p. 33). Over the turn of the nineteenth century, a small but vibrant minority of wellborn Jewish women also seemed to be drawn increasingly to the alternative of conversion and intermarriage. Unlike Jewish males, they were not in a position to compensate for social inferiority through economic power. Possibly, they were also more responsive to the emerging romantic movement, whose religious permutations often were emotionally more satisfying than those of Orthodox Judaism. Ironically, in Prussian social circles, Jewish salon hostesses exerted their own unique attraction for gentiles, even for those of the most distinguished background. Vivacious and witty, untrammeled by feudal traditions, they appeared more alert than aristocrats and their women to new literary and artistic developments. Statesmen and writers, intellectuals and vivants alike, found good food and stimulating conversation in their company.

But what conflicting emotions churned within the breasts of these exotic Jewish salonnières! Rachel Levin, born in Berlin in 1771, was among the most prominent of the hostesses. The daughter of a wealthy gem dealer, Rachel as a young woman found herself left with only a small share of her father's inheritance when he died. Nevertheless, subsisting on a modest allowance from her mother's family, and holding court at her self-styled "garret" on the Jägerstrasse, she managed through sheer force of intellect and temperament to attract to her soirées figures of every rank—princes, ambassadors, artists, scholars. Soon a veritable Rachel cult flourished around her. She was called "the most gifted woman in the universe," "a seeress with the influence of a Pythia," "the first modern woman of German culture."

Apparently none of these encomia brought Rachel emotional satisfaction. "How loathsomely degrading," she wrote a friend, "how offensive, insane, and lowly are my surroundings, which I cannot escape. One single defilement, a mere contact, sullies . . . my nobility." The "defilement" was her Jewish birth. "I imagine," she added, "that just as I was being thrust into this world a supernatural being plunged a dagger into my heart with these words: 'Now, have feeling, see the world as only a few can see it, be great and noble . . . but with one reservation: be a Jew!' " Eventually, in 1814, the forty-three-year-old Rachel married Karl August Varnhagen von Hense, son of a prominent Lutheran diplomatic family, and accepted baptism that same day. But conversion brought meager solace. As she confided afterward to friends, she was "bored to tears" as she had never been as a Jew. Her life was "one of constraint and ennui." Near its end, Rachel acknowledged to Varnhagen: "That which for such a long period of my life was my greatest shame, my bitterest suffering and misfortune—to have been born a Jew—I would not now have missed at any price."

Few other women of Rachel's station would have shared her belated contrition. In 1781, Marcus Herz was already thirty-two when he married Henriette de Lemos, the beauteous fifteen-year-old daughter of the chief physician of Berlin's Jewish Hospital. Herz, also a physician, enjoyed mingling with other scientists. Henriette preferred the company of writers and painters, and indulged that choice by transforming the family home into reputedly the most effervescent of all the renowned Berlin Jewish salons of the early nineteenth century. One of those who attended was young Wilhelm von Humboldt. He fell in love with Henriette. Nothing came of his ardor, but in later years, as a German statesman, his championship of Jewish emancipation (p. 49) almost certainly was influenced by his attendance upon Henriette at her soirées—a secret he confided to a friend in 1814. Ironically, Henriette by 1814 was herself virtually a Christian. Her religious transformation began as far back as 1796 when she met a young theologian, Friedrich Schleiermacher, who soon established himself as a perennial at the Herz receptions. The two became close friends. No routine literalist, Schleiermacher presented God as revealing Himself anew to each generation. Revelation, he insisted, was "true" religion, whereas Judaism, once a living faith, had long since expired in its own legalisms. Henriette evidently accepted Schleiermacher's formulation. In 1817, after her mother's death, she converted to Lutheranism, and remained quite fervent in her pieties for the rest of her long life.

Surely the most poignant example of the twilight world inhabited by fin-de-siècle Jews was the fate of Moses Mendelssohn's children. Mendelssohn's eldest daughter, Brendel, married Simon Veit, a Jewish banker. The couple's happiness was short-lived. High-strung and willful, "Dorothea," as she chose to call herself, became fatigued with the kindly but placid Veit and with his middle-class Jewish milieu. Her father had given her little training in Judaism. Soon after his death, she came to regard the ancestral religion as hardly more than a yoke in a loveless marriage. Moreover, like numerous other vibrant Jewish salon hostesses of her generation, Dorothea craved the life of romanticism, a movement that encouraged women to develop their own personalities independent of their husbands. Responding to that muse, she turned increasingly to the kind of bright, interesting men whom she had met in the soirées of Rachel Levin and Henriette Herz.

One of these was Friedrich Schlegel, seven years Dorothea's junior and a charismatic spokesman of the romantic movement. The relationship between the two quickly sparked fire. Within months, Dorothea resolved to divorce Veit, even to give him custody of their two surviving children. With the help of Schleiermacher and Henriette Herz, she won her freedom. In 1803, Dorothea and Schlegel married, and she converted to Lutheranism. Yet Protestantism for Dorothea was only a way station. The romantic circle to which she and Schlegel belonged was moving steadily rightward, and she moved with it, eventually finding in the pageantry of Roman Catholicism her "true Church." Undergoing a second conversion, Dorothea this time also brought her two sons (from Veit) to the baptismal font.

Dorothea's sister Henriette, youngest of Mendelssohn's daughters, was the least attractive. Short and slightly humpbacked like her father, she never married. In 1812, serving as a governess to the children of French Field Marshal Sebastiani, she became embittered with her spinster's life and joined Dorothea in the Catholic Church after their mother's death. Recha Mendelssohn, the middle daughter, was the only one of the three to remain a Jew. When Recha died in 1831, after years of illness and suffering, Dorothea noted sadly that her sister passed away without "alas, being a child of the Holy Church." Like Recha Mendelssohn, Moses Mendelssohn's son Josef, a banker, remained a Jew, the single one of three brothers to do so. Mendelssohn's second son, Abraham, also a banker, was rather more socially opportunistic. Although a committed agnostic, he had his own four children baptized, then added the suffix Bartholdy to his name, to distinguish his branch of the family from its forebears. Eventually, Abraham also had himself baptized, together with his wife, Leah Salomon. Little is known of Mendelssohn's third and youngest son, Nathan, except that he also converted.

COPING WITH A JEWISH IDENTITY

In the post-Napoleonic twilight years between marginalization and emancipation, escape from Jewish identity was by no means limited to salon hostesses or to figures on the periphery of Jewish life. The first wave of spontaneous, rather impulsive conversions may have crested with the grant of citizenship in Prussia in 1812, and in other states under Napoleon's heel; but a qualitatively different transformation occurred principally during the Metternichian era. For one thing, the new wave of conversions in Germany included far more men, possibly as many as 5,000 between 1800 and 1848. Some may have accepted baptism out of genuine spiritual conviction. Johann Emmanuel Veit went so far as to enter the Catholic priesthood and to become a famous preacher at St. Stephen's Cathedral in Vienna. Paulus (Selig) Cassel similarly became a renowned preacher in the Evangelical Church. August Neander, who had come under the influence of Schleiermacher's Christian romanticism, became a professor of theology at the University of Berlin and a noted Lutheran historian.

Otherwise, in early post-Napoleonic Europe, few Jewish apostates so much as pretended to be animated by ideological conviction. Their objective, quite undisguised, was civil equality. Such was the case of Loeb Baruch of Frankfurt (p. 79). Briefly liberated by Napoleon's army, Baruch after the Congress of Vienna was unprepared to return to his former status as an unemancipated Jew. In 1818 he was baptized and Germanized his name to Ludwig Börne. Almost immediately afterward, Börne produced his famous essay, "Für die Juden," the polemic in which he sought to defend Jewish rights, and thereby preclude the need for others to follow his own example. Centuries before, argued Börne, the Jews had given the world the ideal of universalism, and subsequently the Jewish nation itself was merged in universalism. If only the Jews were not continually being mistreated, they would assimilate all the more swiftly and disappear from the face of the earth.

Börne's colleagues were a group of politically progressive writers known to literary history as Jung Deutschland. Among their members, Karl Beck and Moritz Hartmann offered further insight into Jewish cultural ambivalences. Beck is hardly remembered today except as the poet whose "Lied von der Blauen Donau," set to music by Johann Strauss, became the "Blue Danube Waltz." Yet, in his poem "Das Junge Palästina," Beck affirmed in heartrending verses that his love for Germany was that of a spouse for his bride. Sadly, the bride did not respond. Like Börne, then, Beck concluded that Judaism had outlived its usefulness. Hopeful of finding warmth and understanding among others, he converted to Lutheranism. A similar approach was taken by Joel Jacoby. Born of Orthodox parents in Königsberg, in 1810, Jacoby ended his career in 1863 as a Catholic official in the Prussian propaganda service. Like Beck, he argued that the essence of Judaism had been transformed into Christianity, the more easily to be disseminated throughout the world. All that remained of the original Judaic creed was a fossil, to be revered essentially as a museum piece. "Thou has scattered us among all peoples and hast extinguished our radiance," Beck lamented. "Thou hast made our body immortal in history and we wander corpse-like among these blossoming mortals. . . . Lord, let us go hence! We are weak, we are tired, we yearn for the burial-vault. Other peoples are interred after completing the work of their days. Why not we?"

The case of Heinrich Heine (p. 80) was distinctly more complex. His apostasy was not to be confused with flight from Jewish identification. As a youth in Düsseldorf, growing up under French rule, Heine did not experience ghettoization. He attended German schools exclusively, and as a university student later in Bonn and Göttingen he associated by and large with non-Jews. It was only upon arriving in Berlin in 1821, intending to complete his studies, that Heine became acquainted with an intriguing group of Jewish classmates. Although culturally eclectic, they managed simultaneously to preserve their Jewish tradition. At this point, Heine began to reflect more seriously on his own heritage, even briefly to join the recently established Society for the Scientific Study of Jewish Culture (Verein für Kultur und Wissenschaft der Juden). But only three years later, at the age of twenty-seven, Heine underwent Lutheran baptism as "Christian Johann Heinrich Heine."

There was no mystery to the apparent volte-face. Heine frankly defined his baptism as a "ticket of admission to European culture," although it may also have been a ticket to better employment opportunities as a journalist. Either way, Heine never justified his apostasy on moral grounds. Indeed, the opposite was the case. When he learned afterward that Eduard Gans, his friend and early colleague in the Jewish Verein, also had apostatized, and actually had seemed enthusiastic about his new Christian faith, Heine produced a furious poem of castigation, "An Apostate" ("Einem Abtrünnigen"): "And so you crawled to the cross that you despise," wrote Heine, "to the cross that only a few weeks ago you thought of treading underfoot.... Yesterday a hero, and today already a scoundrel." Almost certainly the object of his contempt was not Gans alone.

With the passage of time, Heine even in the midst of his poetic creativity and his political pamphleteering experienced a nostalgic yearning for his ancestral religion. The cultural anomie gnawed at him with particular intensity in the 1840s and early 1850s, as he wasted away from syphilis (a not uncommon fate for those who had lived private lives as "Hellenes"). During the last eight years spent on his "mattress-grave," stricken as much by remorse as physical pain, Heine set about composing a romantic epic, *The Rabbi of Bachrach (Der Rabbiner von Bachrach)*. Yet his strength was not up to the task, and the work, never finished, was published in 1840 only in a fragmentary version. Instead, Heine managed to produce three long prose poems on Jewish themes. In the first and best known of these, "Princess Sabbath" ("Prinzessin Sabbat"), he elaborated upon the familiar German caricature of Moses Lump, or "Lümpchen," a bearded Jewish peddler of the Hamburg slums. In Heine's version, Lump is transformed on the Sabbath:

> But when Moses Lump comes home on Friday evening, he finds the seven-armed candelabrum lit, the table covered with a white cloth. He puts away his bundles and his worries and sits down with his unshapely wife and still more unlovely daughter. He eats with them fish cooked in a pleasant white garlic sauce and sings the most splendid songs of King David. He rejoices from the bottom of his heart at the exodus of the children of Israel from Egypt.... This man is happy. He does not have to torment himself with an education.... [H]e has his Sabbath lights.

By mid-century, Heine's *Judenschmerz* plainly had become as decisive an impulsion in his life as his political struggle for European liberation.

At the same time, amid the confusion and "soul malaise" of Jews seeking identity in an age of suspended emancipation, there were several who transcended even Heine in romanticizing their ancestry. Benjamin Disraeli offered a fascinating case study of this transposition. In his case, it was animated by political strategy. The son of a Jewish businessman who had chosen to have all his children baptized, Disraeli as a Tory member of Parliament worked his way up the "greasy pole" of British politics. In 1868, during the last illness of Prime Minister Lord Derby, he served a brief stint as Derby's interim replacement, and in 1874 finally won the prime ministry on his own. Over his ensuing six years in office, "Dizzy" (as both his political detractors and supporters dubbed him) shepherded through the House of Commons an unprecedented program of enlightened factory and welfare legislation. His achievements in foreign policy were more impressive yet. They were based on his idealized vision of the British Empire as a stronghold of peace and civilization. India was the pearl of that empire, and Disraeli's acquisition of controlling shares in the Suez Canal Company, in 1875, guaranteed Britain swift maritime access to the mighty Indian subcontinent (p. 106). A year later, Disraeli climaxed his imperial achievement by proclaiming Queen Victoria the Empress of India. Victoria, in turn, anointed Disraeli the Earl of Beaconsfield.

The achievements plainly were unprecedented for a man whose Jewish origins were imprinted as indelibly upon his features as upon his consciousness. It was Disraeli's genius to grasp that the inescapable actually might be politically exploitable. Early in his career he set about embellishing a compensatory version of his "aristocratic" Jewish descent. In an autobiographical note, he boasted that his Hebrew ancestors "assumed the name of d'Israeli, a name never borne before or since by any other family, in order that their race might be forever recognized." In the parliamentary election campaign of 1847, opposed by a member of the Duke of Cavendish's family, Disraeli boldly proclaimed his own pedigree as superior to that of the Cavendishes. "Fancy calling a fellow an adventurer," he mused on another occasion, reacting to an ethnic slur, "when his ancestors were probably on intimate terms with the Queen of Sheba."

Yet it was in his earlier career as a political novelist that Disraeli gave widest rein to his racial fantasies. *Alroy* was perhaps the most revealing example. Published in 1833, soon after Disraeli visited the Holy Land, it was based on an actual twelfth-century Jew, Menahem ben Solomon al-Ruhi, who lived in the Azerbaijani region of the Caucasus Mountains. The historical Alroy was believed to have rallied his fellow mountain Jews in revolt against their Moslem overlords, only to be treacherously murdered by his own father-in-law. Reworking the slender evidential record, Disraeli portrayed Alroy as "a son of the Prince of the Captivity" who mobilizes a Jewish army, overthrows the Moslem yoke, sweeps through the Holy Land and much of western Asia. Then, tragically, the gallant commander is overthrown in battle. Upon refusing to save his life by embracing Islam, he is executed. If the tale resembled numerous other lush oriental romances of the time, this one transparently identified Disraeli himself with the proud, "aristocratic" Jewishness of the legendary warrior chieftain. An identical racial bombast appears in Disraeli's "Young England" political satires: *Coningsby* (1844), *Sybil* (1845), and *Tancred* (1847). Turgid in plot and rhetoric, the novels abound in hyperbolic speculations on Jewish wisdom, genius, courage, vision. So did Disraeli's obiter dicta and conversations. For him, a central theme was the unique "racial" aristocracy of the Jews and thus, by intimation, of himself as a bearer of that ancestry and thereby an equal to any mandarin in the Tory Party.

It was in this overblown and improbable fashion that Disraeli actually managed to turn his Jewish birth to his political advantage. His displays of exoticism, strangeness, and mysteriousness appealed to the provincial, fog-bound British public. Politicians were awed by the magician (Carlyle dubbed him a "conjuror") who invested boring political transactions with an oriental flavor. Disraeli's achievements on behalf of the British Empire in Asia similarly were attributed to his instinctive "oriental" grasp of eastern politics. Working the credo of racial aristocracy overtime, the imaginative "Dizzy" eventually achieved renown not simply as Queen Victoria's first minister but as her trusted, even beloved, political confidant. With whom else, after all, would these two royalists of the blood feel comparably at ease?

A Reformulation of Judaism

The impact of Western culture was responsible for transformations not only in Jewish sociology but in Jewish religious practices. It was in Britain, ironically, the least obscurantist of European nations, that change was least dramatic. Part of the explanation lay in the very nature of Anglo-Jewish emancipation. The process had been less traumatic than in any major European nation. Notwithstanding the languid pace of their access to the House of Commons, the Jews were under little pressure to demonstrate their political reliability, and under none whatever to demonstrate the compatibility of the Jewish religion with Anglo-Saxon culture. It was not until 1819 that English replaced Ladino as the language of sermons in Bevis Marks Synagogue. Over the decades, tentative efforts at reform in ritual or ceremony were as modest in the synagogue as in the Church of England. A carefully modulated Orthodoxy functioned as the Jewish counterpart of Anglicanism. Like their British fellow citizens, Jews in England venerated a tradition that was not forcibly imposed. They were disinclined to tamper with it.

In France, too, doctrinal change initially was incremental, even tepid. As late as mid-century, most Jews were content to take their lead from the consistoires, and this mechanism of "ecclesiastical" control emulated the government itself in its noninterference in doctrinal matters. Ironically, the consistoires' initial mission was to enforce the anticlerical transformations of the revolutionary Napoleonic era; and salient among these changes was the redefined role of rabbis (and priests and ministers), who were limited henceforth to pastoral responsibilities. Thus, at the insistence of the laymen who dominated the consistoires, rabbis were obliged to deliver their sermons, to conduct marriage and funeral services, in the French language alone. As a measure of this "Gallicization," worship in the synagogues became increasingly decorous, and organ music was added. Over the years, prayers for the lost Jerusalem were dropped as incompatible with patriotism in France ("our only homeland"). Yet at no time did the consistoires, in their rigid centralism, so much as acknowledge that these periodic "adjustments" signified alteration of Judaism's fundamental tenets.

It was in the German-speaking world, rather, the largest reservoir of West-Central European Jewry, that the tremolos of religious change eventually would achieve institutional form. In 1808, under the rule of Jerome Bonaparte, Jews in the satellite Kingdom of Westphalia became subject to France's consistorial system, and to the declared consistorial objective of acculturation. In pursuit of that goal, Jerome Bonaparte appointed Israel Jacobson as Westphalian Jewry's consistorial president. Jacobson, a wealthy businessman of Seesen, had long advocated the "Occidentalization" of Jewish religious practices. To that end, adopting as his model the Lutheran Church, Jacobson and his fellow officials promptly set about "civilizing" congregational behavior, banning indecorous gossiping during religious services, the sale of synagogue honors, the endlessly embellished cantillation of increasingly incomprehensible Hebrew prayers. In his own synagogue in Seesen, Jacobson introduced an organ, as well as sermons in the German language to displace the Yiddishized German still extant among the majority of German Jews.

Following Napoleon's defeat at the battle of Leipzig in 1813, the Kingdom of Westphalia was dissolved, and with it the Jewish consistoire. At this point, moving to Hamburg, Jacobson promptly opened another synagogue, and pressed on determinedly with his agenda of Occidentalization. It was in this dynamic port city, moreover, with its 6,000 Jews, that Jacobson found several influential and affluent supporters for his program. One was David Friedländer, a former Berlin silk manufacturer who had been an early member of Moses Mendelssohn's enlightenment circle. Years before, at his own expense, Friedländer had established a Free School in Berlin, offering Jewish children instruction in both Jewish and secular subjects. It was the Free School and others that he helped organize throughout Prussia that became important nurseries of German culture. In the post-Napoleonic era, Friedländer assiduously maintained his enlightenment campaign in Berlin and Hamburg. Together with Jacobson he founded the New Israelite Temple Society, with the purpose of establishing still additional congregations to function on the identical modernist principles.

For both men, those principles far transcended mere decorum or aesthetics. Since Jews now were living in the modern world, Friedländer explained, they were only too eager to abandon obsolete and messianic prayers, like those invoking expectations of a return to Jerusalem. Synagogue services not only should be conducted in the German language, but emphasis in the liturgy and sermon should be shifted increasingly from ritual and ceremony to issues of ethical and moralistic behavior. Indeed, Judaism altogether should be stripped of its "legalistic Talmudisms" and its other accumulated Diaspora baggage. Samuel Holdheim and Gotthold Salomon, colleagues of Friedländer in the Berlin Reform Society, went even further, arguing that such venerated precepts as the Saturday Sabbath, separation of men and women in synagogue seating, the rite of circumcision—all should be discarded as anachronistic. The proposals were nothing if not revolutionary. It was hardly surprising that they should also have encountered indignant opposition among traditionalists. Retaliating, the Berlin kehillah actually persuaded the Prussian government to close down Friedländer's synagogue as a "nest of sectarianism." And Friedländer himself, exhausted by a lifetime devoted to Jewish enlightenment, apparently went over the line in his final years by advocating a "complete fusion" of Judaism and Christianity in a kind of universalistic creed.

Whether they realized it or not, these early-nineteenth-century reformers were responding to influences that transcended a mere quest for dignity in the synagogue or even modernization of religious ceremonial. One of these influences was German Protestantism. When Samuel Holdheim advocated a separation of religious and civil affairs, he was adopting the classical Protestant doctrine of the supremacy of state over church. The mixed seating of men and women in family pews similarly was a Protestant tradition, as was sermonizing in German. For Jewish reformers, these practices appeared equally appropriate for their own people. Indeed, as Hamburg's New Israelite Temple Society continued to grow, exceeding one hundred families by the early 1820s, including some of the most affluent and respected Jews in the city, its congregants enthusiastically embraced many of the reformers' innovations.

Of all the factors shaping the early Reform movement, however, the most decisive was the ongoing political debate over Jewish emancipation. To win back the equality of status they had briefly enjoyed during the Napoleonic era, large numbers of German Jews were seized of the need to provide incontrovertible evidence of their patriotism and acculturation. It was by no coincidence that the Hamburg reformers chose the anniversary of the Prussian victory over Napoleon at Leipzig as the dedication date for their congregation. It was equally fitting, they believed, to call their house of worship a temple, a term that historically had been reserved for the fallen sanctuary in Jerusalem. Several other temples were established, not only in Hamburg and Berlin but in Leipzig, Karlsruhe, and Stuttgart, all of their congregants fully committed to enlightenment, Occidentalization, acculturation—and patriotism.

THE RETURN TO HISTORY

Beyond these early experiments, however, Reform in the early post-Napoleonic years evoked only intermittent resonance among German Jews. Few of them gave much thought to substantive, doctrinal changes within the ancestral tradition. It was only in the 1830s, once Reform allied itself with the romantic movement, the great ideological engine of the nineteenth century, that more basic and enduring transformations could be achieved within Judaism itself.

For men like Johann Gottfried von Herder, Johann Gottlieb Fichte, or Ernst Moritz Arndt, the accumulated experience of past centuries, not "cosmopolitan rationalism," was the appropriate guide to modern social issues. It is recalled that the nationalist ideologues of the new industrial era, and the romantics who provided their raison d'être, laid their emphasis on their people's venerated traditions, on the color and pageantry, the emotions and achievements of their collective historic experience. The relevance of any institution or idea no longer was to be measured by its contemporary rationality or functionalism, but by its origin and history. "History," in the words of Friedrich von Schiller, "is the final court of appeal." In the 1820s and 1830s, therefore, responding to this injunction, and to the inspiration of men like Leopold von Ranke and Barthold Niebuhr, an army of trained researchers began to emerge from the Hegelian school prevalent in Germany's universities, ready and eager to apply the technique of rigorous scholarly investigation to the origins and development of contemporary institutions, to law, philosophy, government, literature—to religion.

As recently as the late eighteenth century, whatever meager information Jews knew of their postbiblical history they had acquired from the Talmud, from the prayer book, or simply from folklore. For most of them, the actual facts of the Jewish past remained cloaked in myth and misinformation. By the late 1700s and early 1800s, however, under the influence of the "new" German scholarship, a small group of university-trained Jews began to elevate the study of their people's history and literature from an undisciplined vocation to the respectability of an academic discipline. Leading this transformation was the single most commanding figure of Jewish learning in the nineteenth century, Leopold (Yom Tov Lippmann) Zunz.

Born in Detmold, Prussia, in 1794, Zunz was eight years old when his father died and his mother was obliged to send him to the Samson Freie Schule, a charity school established for Jewish orphans, in Wolfenbüttel. The institution was little more than a parochial *heder*, an Orthodox school. Nevertheless, on his own, the precocious youngster immersed himself in secular literature, and soon became obsessed with the study of history. In 1809, upon graduation, he became the first Jewish student to be admitted to the nearby Wolfenbüttel (secular) gymnasium, where he earned his tuition by giving private lessons in several European languages. Upon finishing his studies in 1815, Zunz moved to Berlin. Begging, borrowing, and tutoring, he managed to attend the city's recently opened Humboldt University (more generally to be known as the University of Berlin). Here Friedrich Karl von Savigny was making the case that law could only be understood as an organic development embracing a people's entire history and folklore. The philologist Friedrich August Wolf and the philosopher August Böckh similarly emphasized the organic-historic approach to their fields. Although Zunz ultimately received his doctorate from the University of Halle, it was at Berlin that the pattern was laid for his future career, for a calling that would be devoted single-mindedly to an "objective, scientific" reconstruction of the Jewish people's odyssey through history.

The effort was sustained at painful cost. Throughout his life, Zunz was engaged in a demeaning struggle for economic survival. Upon finishing university, he managed to earn an uncertain pittance as a lay preacher for several Reform congregations. During the mid-1820s, he directed a Sunday school. Intermittently, he returned to teaching and preaching at various congregations and parochial schools. Zunz lived to the uncommon age of ninety-two, but hardly a year of his life was free from virtual penury. It was the more remarkable, given the bitterness of his circumstances, that he became a river of creativity. Indeed, his first book, *Studies in Rabbinical Literature (Etwas über die rabbinische Literatur),* published in 1818, became the dividing line between the inbred *Lernen* of the ghetto and the true science of objective historical research. In the years that followed, a profusion of works flowed from his pen, ranging from essays on Spanish place-names in Hebrew writings to a biography of Rashi, the renowned medieval Talmudist, to encyclopedic compendia of Jewish historical statistics.

One of Zunz's earliest and most famous studies was his *History of Jewish Homiletics (Die gottesdienstliche Vorträge der Juden).* Produced in 1832 as a response to Orthodox protests against German-language sermons, Zunz's treatise offered historical evidence that preaching in the vernacular of the countries of Jewish domicile extended back to the earliest years of the Diaspora itself. In a later volume, *On History and Literature (Zur Geschichte und Literatur),* published in 1845, the chapter headings alone suggested the astonishing breadth of Zunz's scholarship. These included: Jewish literature in medieval France and Germany; Jewish publications and printers in Mantua; printing offices and annals of Hebrew typography in Prague; the Jewish poets of Provence; a history of the Jews of Sicily; a survey of Jewish numismatics.

In its erudition, the volume plumbed the reservoir of Jewish history as evidence that poetry, ethics, homilies, philosophy, folklore, printing, liturgy—all authenticated the extraordinary continuum of Jewish intellectual creativity.

As early as 1819, moreover, Zunz also found time to launch the Verein für Kultur und Wissenschaft der Juden, a society devoted to the "scientific" study of the Jewish people, and to their place in the history and literature of the non-Jewish world. Among those who joined Zunz in this ambitious venture was a group of some fifteen university graduates, among them Isaac Jost, Moses Moser, Eduard Gans, Isaac Auerbach, Joel Lis, Josef Hillmar, and later Moritz Steinschneider and Heinrich Graetz (see below). All shared Zunz's devotion to the mission of Jewish scholarship, although not all managed to sustain the master's inexhaustible scholarly tenacity and endurance. Indeed, most of them, including Gans and the young Heinrich Heine, became opportunistic converts to Christianity. But several others emerged as major figures in "the Science of Judaism."

One of these was Moritz Steinschneider. Born in 1816 in Habsburg Moravia, Steinschneider as a youth was the recipient of a conventional Jewish education. But soon afterward, with the awakening of his secular interests, the young man went on to earn a doctorate in philosophy and philology at the University of Berlin. Although in 1843 Steinschneider also received ordination as a rabbi, he evinced little interest in the pulpit. Instead, supporting himself as an instructor at Berlin's Jewish teachers' seminary, he gave himself over almost entirely to the calling of Jewish scholarship. The effort bore impressive fruit. By the age of twenty-eight, he had produced his first volume, a richly erudite survey of Jewish literature from medieval to modern times. A year later, he was called to Oxford to prepare the catalogue of Hebrew literature for the university's Bodleian Library. The assignment was destined to consume fully thirteen years of painstaking research, to fill 1,750 pages of double columns. To this day, the Bodleian's Hebrew Catalogue remains the single most important bibliographical reference ever produced in Jewish scholarship. Remarkably, Steinschneider also managed to produce similar, if more abbreviated, catalogues for a number of famous German libraries—all the while churning out scores of articles and several books of his own. Tributes to his scholarly genius took the form of honorary doctorates from several Western universities, including Columbia University in New York. The Prussian ministry of education bestowed the honorary title of professor on Steinschneider in 1894, at a time when Jews still were rarely offered full professorships in Germany.

While most of the giants of jüdische Wissenschaft published almost exclusively for a scholarly readership, one of them, Heinrich Graetz, took the trouble to address a more general audience. Born in 1817, the son of a butcher in Posen, Graetz underwent the kind of parochial Jewish education typical of this backward, formerly Polish province. At the same time, almost entirely on his own, he explored the German classics, tutored his way through a secular gymnasium, and eventually through the Universities of Breslau and Jena, securing a doctorate at the latter institution in 1845. After earning his bread for several years as a teacher in a series of Jewish schools, Graetz in 1854 finally secured the dignity of a faculty appointment at Breslau's newly founded Jewish Theological Seminary. It was in Breslau, between 1856 and 1873, that he produced his magnum opus, an eleven-volume *History of the Jews*. Graced by a felicitous literary style, the work was published in nine languages, and ultimately became the single most widely read work of Jewish scholarship of the nineteenth and early twentieth centuries.

Yet scholarship was but one facet of German-Jewish cultural modernization. Another was an upsurge of literary contributions on Jewish themes. By the mid-nineteenth century, an impressive spectrum of Jewish book clubs and cultural societies promoted this effort. One of its pioneering figures was a rabbi-journalist, Ludwig Philippson. A graduate of the University of Berlin and the occupant of a congregational pulpit in Magdeburg, Philippson himself published five Jewish historical novels. In 1837, he founded and edited the *Allgemeine Zeitung des Judentums,* a publication that would remain German Jewry's preeminent newspaper for the ensuing eighty-five years. Philippson's Institute for the Promotion of Jewish Literature (Institut zur Förderung der israelitischen Literatur) published some eighty Jewish novels and novellas, as well as a score of scholarly works. Among the latter was Graetz's epic multiplex history.

The Rise of "Historical Judaism"

During the mid-third of the nineteenth century, a younger generation of religious reformers appeared on the Jewish scene. Eagerly embracing the scholarly apparatus of jüdische Wissenschaft, the newcomers set about vigorously and systematically applying the Science of Judaism to the very ideology of the ancestral religion. Few of them were self-conscious *maskilim,* rationalist disciples of the great Moses Mendelssohn, in the manner of Friedländer and Jacobson's earlier generation. Indeed, most of them were ordained rabbis, and in an age of romantic historicism they well appreciated that austere rationalism would have pared away Judaism, ceremony by ceremony, doctrine by doctrine, until the residue left only the innermost kernel of prophetic ethics. Accordingly, their approach in the 1840s and 1850s was to substitute history for rationalism. History would decide the level of evolution Judaism had reached. History would determine the traditions that should be saved and those that were expendable.

Abraham Geiger was the driving force of this new historicism. Born in

Frankfurt in 1810, Geiger received a traditional Jewish schooling. Yet, like numerous other young Jews of his generation, he also became enamored of secular studies. Attending Heidelberg, he earned a doctorate in classical languages and ancient history. Not long afterward, ordained a rabbi, Geiger accepted a modest pulpit in Wiesbaden. Pastoral responsibilities were not his métier, however. His congregants understood and accepted that their young rabbi's passion lay in Jewish scholarship, specifically of the jüdische Wissenschaft school. Thus, at the age of twenty-six, Geiger founded an imposing publication, *The Scientific Journal for Jewish Theology (Der Wissenschaftliche Zeitschrift für jüdische Theologie)*. Recruiting contributions from such giants as Isaac Jost, Salomon Munk, and the mighty Zunz himself, and contributing formidable papers of his own, Geiger soon generated a respectable scholarly audience for his journal.

Indeed, Geiger's personal reputation as a creative savant, as well as a decorous innovator of mild liturgical reforms in his own Wiesbaden congregation, rapidly established him as something of a culture hero for other "progressive" Jews. It was on the basis of that reputation, in 1838, that he was invited to become associate rabbi of Breslau's largest synagogue. The capital of Prussian Silesia, Breslau by 1838 encompassed a substantial Jewish community of 6,500. Many of its members had begun to prosper, and to favor liberalism in politics and religion alike. Reflecting that orientation, the synagogue's board members had become impatient with their veteran incumbent rabbi, the unregenerately traditionalist Solomon Tiktin. Yet, hesitant to depose a man of senior years, they decided instead to "counterbalance" Tiktin by appointing Geiger as associate rabbi. The strategy was clumsy. In his outrage, Tiktin fought the Geiger appointment tooth and nail. There were lawsuits and counter-suits. By 1840, however, when the board cut off his salary, Tiktin had exhausted his recourses. He departed with his loyalists to establish his own, residual congregation; and Geiger then assumed his long-awaited pulpit— this time as senior rabbi.

If there were Jews in Breslau who expected Geiger to play the role of fiery iconoclast, they were soon disabused. The man's talent lay in approaching religion not as a rationalist reformer, but as a respecter of historical tradition. In his writings and sermons alike, Geiger steadfastly placed his emphasis upon the gradualism of Judaism's evolution. Nevertheless, it was this instinctive moderation, coupled with his distinguished intellectual reputation, that ultimately established Geiger as the figure likeliest to achieve a consensus for the modernization of Judaism. In the mid-1840s, he moved down that road by inaugurating a series of "synods" (on the Protestant model). The initial synod, convening in Brunswick in 1844, comprised both rabbis and lay congregational officials, all sharing a common proclivity for religious modernization. The synod was followed by two subsequent meetings, in Frankfurt in

1845, and Breslau in 1846. The number of participants never exceeded three dozen, but they represented a wide spectrum of reformist views, from the radicalism of Samuel Holdheim of Berlin to the cautious moderation of Dresden's Zacharias Frankel.

All the participants agreed that Judaism had evolved historically, and must continue to evolve. But if there was consensus on principles, it swiftly broke down on issues of practical application. Thus, at the initial, Brunswick colloquium, agreement was easily reached to dispense with all anthropomorphic characterizations of the Deity. Expendable, too, were prayers for restoration of the Temple of Jerusalem and the oath of loyalty to the state. The first was regarded as anachronistic, the latter as gratuitous. Primitive laws banning widows from remarrying were modified. Girls were allowed henceforth to participate in the ceremony of "confirmation." But serious disagreements arose on the issue of circumcision. Geiger and Holdheim viewed the rite as a "bloody practice," while others regarded the "Abrahamic Covenant" as the first of God's injunctions to the Jewish people. Neither could agreement be reached on the question of the Saturday Sabbath. Should the day of rest be shifted to Sunday for the convenience of worshippers? Here a decision would be influenced by interpretations of the Sabbath's actual purpose. Was the day sanctified at Sinai or merely representative of man's need for weekly rededication? Once more, as on the issue of Hebrew prayers in the liturgy (p. 136), no consensus was reached. Nor was it at the two ensuing synods.

By mid-century, even without consensus, Reform Judaism settled into a plateau in Germany. Manifestly, the plateau was functional, not doctrinal. If a growing minority of affluent and educated German Jews identified themselves with "progressivism," or "modernism," their congregations were hesitant to commit themselves "officially" on matters of religious ideology. One of the inhibitions was financial. Under the laws of Prussia and of several other German states, every "confessing" Jew was required to contribute to the maintenance of his community's principal congregation. If he wished to belong to an independent—that is, Reform—congregation, he was obliged to bear the burden of supporting them both. Yet, even more fundamentally, the typical German Jew was distracted by a movement that was in continuous search of a theology. He preferred to practice his version of Reform pragmatically, not to defend it ideologically.

These uncertainties notwithstanding, the effort to define a new, Reform version of Judaism fulfilled an important role for all of Western Jewry. It created a service that was dignified, simple, and decorous. By emancipating modern Jews from fundamentalist dogmas, it presented a new and presumably more respectable image of the Jew to a still skeptical German nation. Most decisively yet, a liberalized Judaism offered younger, educated Jews a religion solidly grounded in intellectual historicism, and spared them the choice of obscurantist literalism on the one hand or arid rationalism on the other.

AN ADAPTATION OF "HISTORICAL JUDAISM"

At the Frankfurt synod, as the "radicals" sought to limit the use of Hebrew in the liturgy to four or five crucial prayers, a substantial bloc of "moderates" reluctantly departed the conference. The man who led the walkout, Zacharias Frankel, was a Central European rabbi of distinguished reputation. Born in Prague in 1801, he was richly trained in both the Jewish and the secular traditions. After securing his rabbinical ordination, Frankel went on to earn a doctorate in classical philology at the University of Pest, before assuming the pulpit of the Great Synagogue of Dresden in 1836, where he held the title of Chief Rabbi of Saxony. It was during his tenure in Dresden that Frankel identified with the emerging new Reform experiment, and thereby fortified its prestige.

And yet, at the Frankfurt synod, it was Frankel whose reaction to the proposal of dispensing with Hebrew prayers opened a schism in the budding progressive movement. To his mind, the issue was not trivial. Rather, it widened his misgivings at the direction Reform was taking. For Samuel Holdheim and the "radicals," Judaism was a creed that had evolved from earliest times and was still in the process of evolution. Frankel viewed the matter differently. In his words, Judaism was not a creed. It was "the religion of the Jews," that is, the historic product of the Jewish mind and soul—and Hebrew was the language of that product. History was the palpable evidence not simply of Jewish anachronisms, argued Frankel, but of survivalist Jewish traditions. Under that interpretation, a rite or observance that had become deeply embedded in communal practice should not be summarily abrogated. At most, it should be cautiously reinterpreted until, very slowly, over a lengthy span of time, perhaps in the distant future, it ceased to be meaningful to the Jewish people.

Moreover, by the 1850s and 1860s, it was becoming evident that most of the Jews in German-speaking Europe tended to prefer the ritual and liturgy of a mildly conservative Judaism (or "positive-historical" Judaism, as Frankel called it). The compromise was in no sense an ideological one. It was entirely pragmatic, a stance well suited to a traditionally insecure people living in a conservative part of the world. In any case, by the end of the century the various branches of West European Judaism did not differ radically from one another. Most Jews had come to accept the value of a secular education. Even the typical synagogue religious school no longer resembled the parochial *heder* of the early nineteenth century. Rabbis by then were men of university training. Many had earned doctorates. All of them delivered their sermons in German, all of them intermingled German and Hebrew in their congregational prayer books, and the mixed seating of the sexes was increasingly the norm in German synagogues—or temples.

Whatever the nuances of ritual or ceremony among their various factions, it may well have been Abraham Geiger after all who emerged as the role model for a younger German-Jewish generation. More than an erudite intellectual or even a pioneering reformer, he was also a forthright champion of Jewish political and legal rights, and a patriot. From his pulpit, Geiger vigorously exhorted his congregants to participate in elections, to develop the musculature of good citizenship, to mobilize their gentile friends in the effort to assure full civil and political rights for Germans of all backgrounds. Thus, in 1863, on the twenty-fifth anniversary of his incumbency in Breslau, when tributes at the banquet in his honor were offered by Jews and non-Jews alike, Geiger characteristically responded with his toast to the German *Vaterland.* "Over and above everything else," he reminded his friends and colleagues, "I am a human being. It is only second to that, or in constant relation to it, that I am a German. And only lastly am I a Jew."

By 1874, the year of his death, Geiger shared a widely prevalent Western Jewish assumption that the history of the Jewish people as a nation had come to an end. Even among the great majority of Jews who maintained their Jewish communal loyalties and their "confessional" identification, the memory of Diaspora separatism and autonomy was fading rapidly. The largest numbers of German and French Jews now preferred to envision themselves as Germans or Frenchmen of the "Israelite" or "Mosaic" persuasion. The long shadow of the Napoleonic Sanhedrin reached across the century and occluded a memory that, for hundreds of thousands of modern Jews, was associated only with suffering and humiliation. Heinrich Heine on his mattress grave was writing of them, as well: "Over my head a strange tree gleams, filled with stars and birds whose white notes glimmer through its seven branches now that all is stilled. What? Friday night again, and all my songs forgotten?"

VIII

A Sephardic-Oriental Diaspora

FLIGHT TO THE OTTOMAN EMPIRE

The departure of between 150,000 and 200,000 Jews from *Sepharad*, the Iberian peninsula, began in 1391 and reached its denouement in the 1492 expulsion decree. The cumulative trauma represented the profoundest tragedy in the history of this little people since the loss of its original Jewish Commonwealth in 70 C.E. In the summer of 1492, a contemporary observer, the priest Andrés Bernáldes, described their climactic exodus:

> They went out from the lands of their birth, boys and adults, old men and children, on foot, or riding on donkeys or other beasts. . . . They went by the roads and fields with much labor and ill-fortune, some collapsing, others getting up, some dying, others giving birth, others falling ill, so that there was no Christian who was not sorry for them. . . . The rabbis were encouraging them and making the women and boys sing and beat drums and tambourines, to enliven the people. And so they went out of Castile.

On August 2 and 3, 1492, the last professing Jews on Spanish soil clambered aboard ship in Seville and El Puerto de Santa María. At the smaller, nearby harbor of Palos de la Frontéra, three small caravels were waiting to hoist sail. Their commander, Christopher Columbus, noted with interest the departing procession of refugee vessels, a "fleet of misery and woe," as he described it in his log. August 2, 1492, by coincidence was the ninth day of the Hebrew month of Av, the fast day commemorating the destruction of the Temple of Jerusalem, and the Children of Israel were setting out yet again into the featureless limbo of exile.

Their initial, instinctive destination was the Ottoman Empire, a realm that Moslem Turks had established over the previous two centuries in their ongoing conquest of Christian Byzantium. From bitter experience in their lives on Iberian soil, the Sephardic Jews had learned that toleration was likelier under

Moslem rule than under Christian. Indeed, the Turks had first given attention to the Jews well before the influx of refugee Sephardim. Shortly after his investiture of Constantinople in 1453, Sultan Mehmet II decided to gather up the 6,000 Romaniotes, the Greek-speaking Jews who had been living in Byzantine Asia Minor for a millennium, and to transplant them from their outlying communities to the capital, where they might serve as a commercial element in place of the Greeks. The Romaniotes soon would pay a collective price for this "blessing," mainly in the form of the sultan's recurrent collective fiscal extortions.

In later years, however, the arriving waves of Sephardim initially experienced the more benign face of Ottoman rule. Like their Romaniote predecessors, they were assured of physical protection. Sultan Bayezid II, who came to the imperial throne in 1481, grasped as astutely as had Mehmet II the value of a sophisticated commercial people, a race that shared the Turks' own distrust of the Christian world. For this reason, he encouraged the newcomers to settle both in Constantinople and in towns throughout Asia Minor and the Ottoman Balkans. Most of the newcomers were artisans or modest merchants. Some were peddlers. But an influx of later-arriving Portuguese Sephardim possessed a rather wider commercial experience. Within a few years, they proved their indispensability as assessors and collectors of taxes (on fish, fisheries, sheep, and candles), as minters of coins and as bankers. Not least of all, Jews almost immediately filled the vacuum of Ottoman medicine. From their midst came the empire's most respected physicians.

In the sixteenth and early seventeenth centuries, Sultans Selim I and Suleiman I added Syria and Egypt to their realm, then Belgrade and Buda. Sultan Murad IV added Baghdad and much of North Africa. The territorial breadth of these conquests at first significantly enhanced Ottoman-Jewish life. As in the Jews' earlier experience of Islamic grandeur, in Spanish Andalucía, a unified political entity provided them with broader opportunities of commerce. Indeed, a tangible consequence of their revived affluence was the dramatic increase in their numbers. In Asia Minor, the Jewish settlement in Constantinople numbered 8,000 by 1478, 18,000 by 1524, and possibly 25,000 by 1700, thus becoming the second-largest Jewish community in the world. In the Balkans, Salonika alone in 1700 encompassed a Jewish population of approximately 30,000. In the Arab world, Baghdad, whose Jewry had shrunk to fewer than 2,000 at the time of the Ottoman conquest in 1638, approached 15,000 by the mid-seventeenth century. Altogether, by then, the empire's Jewish population—in Turkey, the Arab Middle East, and the Balkans—was estimated at approximately 200,000.

A community this large in effect generated its own economic continuum. In 1555, a German visitor, Hans Dernschwam, who represented the Fugger banking house, noted that "[t]he Jews of Constantinople . . . have goldsmiths, lapidaries, painters, tailors, butchers, apothecaries, physicians, surgeons, cloth weavers . . . barbers, mirror makers, dyers . . . silk workers, gold washers . . . assayers, engravers." Beyond this talented pool of artisans, the Jews produced a far larger number of businessmen than did any other subjugated nation. Although most of their merchants remained modest shopkeepers, the classical Jewish roles of tax farmer, moneylender, and importer-exporter were established here early on. Nicholas de Nicolay, France's ambassador to Constantinople in 1557, was impressed that "[the Jews] have in their hands the most and greatest traffic and merchandise and ready money that is in the Levant. And likewise the . . . warehouses, the best furnished with all sorts of merchandise, which are in Constantinople, are those of the Jews."

In his magisterial economic history of Europe, Fernand Braudel describes a vast sixteenth-century Jewish trading network based in Constantinople, Izmir (Smyrna), Salonika, and Edirne. Each of these four cities in turn produced satellite Jewish communities. Sarajevo, Monastir, and Skopje linked Salonikan Jewry to the Adriatic and Venice. The Jewish settlements of Plovdiv (Plevna), Sofia, Nikopol, and Widden spanned the overland trade route from Constantinople via Edirne to the Danubian Basin, and then to Central Europe (p. 145). Wherever Ottoman Jews did business, they conducted their trade almost entirely with their fellow Sephardim. Speaking the same language, they also operated within the guidelines of their own commercial codes, resolved their own disputes within their own judicial system.

It is worth recalling that self-government was the norm for all the subject nations of the Ottoman Empire. In 1453, therefore, when Sultan Mehmet II authorized the appointment of a single leader to represent the Jews before his throne, this official—in later years usually the chief rabbi, the *haham bashi*—became a counterpart to the Greek patriarch and the Armenian metropolitan. Functioning as communal liaison for the Jews, he was the eminence responsible for their civic behavior and their collective tax payments. In this fashion, the Sephardic newcomers, like their kinsmen in Europe, maintained their own *cals* (kahals, kehillot, in Europe), their officially designated communities, with their own rabbinical courts, and their own tax-assessors and collectors. Communal autonomy was reflected as well in physical and social segregation. Each subject nation was strictly demarcated from the Turkish majority, and from one another. The Jews who arrived in Constantinople during the reign of Bayezid II were concentrated into the area along the southern shores of the Golden Horn, between the Greek quarter of Phanar and the walls of the city, in an area known as Balat. Comparably delimited Jewish quarters were established in the other major cities and towns of Turkey. But whether in Izmir, Bursa, or Edirne, the Jews were on their own. Indeed, so thoroughly were Jews (and some Christians) excluded from Turkish social and cultural life that they did not trouble themselves to master the

Turkish language until the late nineteenth century. The lacuna in every respect characterized the stratified mosaic of Ottoman society.

A specifically Jewish cultural life, on the other hand, was a much more fully developed phenomenon. For most of the sixteenth and early seventeenth centuries, the Jews in their growing numbers transformed their Ottoman enclave into the world center of Jewish scholarship. Constantinople's rabbinical seminaries, like those of Salonika, Safed, and Jerusalem, succeeded the once renowned academies of Córdoba, Toledo, and Girona. Hebrew prose, poetry, and liturgical epics also experienced a brief afterglow in the sixteenth- and seventeenth-century empire. The Ottoman-Jewish sunburst unquestionably was a mixed heritage. Even under such comparatively permissive sultans as Bayezid II, Selim I, Suleiman I, and Selim II, Jews were not allowed to forget their status as *dhimmi* (*dhinni*, in Turkish). Subjected to heavy taxes, they were forbidden to employ Turkish servants, to dress "immodestly," even to ride horses. Yet, whatever the inconvenience of these constraints, Ottoman Jews invariably were thankful, and usually obsequious, to their royal masters. The resplendent new empire had provided them with a revived breathing space.

TURKISH SUNSET

The six-decade reign of Suleiman the Great and the two Selims, ending in 1574, marked the apogee of the Ottoman golden age. Soon that glory would begin to fade, as Turkish military expansion in Europe foundered against stiffening Habsburg resistance. The army's conquest of the Arab Middle East and the North African littoral were impressive in scope, but counterproductive in the longer run. Vast and dispersed, the new territories seriously overextended the imperial administration. Additionally, an alteration of the historic maritime trade route, from the Mediterranean toward the Atlantic, began to threaten the Ottoman economy. With its customs stations bypassed and its coffers depleted, the Turkish government soon was reduced to accepting its funds wherever it could find them. At every level, it found them increasingly in bribes, whether dispersed among local officials, the royal harem, or the royal court itself. The Moslem religious establishment conceivably might have encouraged a spirit of moral integrity. By the mid-seventeenth century, however, Ottoman Islam had calcified, and its ideological fundamentalism in turn corrupted the empire's juridical and educational systems, and soon its entire popular culture. On the threshold of the Modern Era, the very nerve structure of the Ottoman realm appeared to be succumbing to political and social enervation.

Those years of imperial enfeeblement and religiocultural atrophy were somber ones for the Jews. In part, the diminution of their material and "moral" vitality reflected the palpable infirmity of the empire itself. Yet their malaise was exacerbated, as well, by a virtual cessation of Jewish immigration from Europe, the traditional reservoir of Sephardic artisans and merchants. In turn, Ottoman Greeks, favored by the solicitude and rising power of Christian Europe, began to preempt the Jews' mercantile position in the imperial economy. The vocational reversal of roles was accompanied by a widening Greek campaign of violence against Jewish neighborhoods in Constantinople, Izmir, and elsewhere in Asia Minor. Although the attacks frequently were linked to blood-libel accusations (p. 222), they were rooted even more fundamentally in economic competition.

Of graver concern yet, they exploited an emergent vacuum of royal protection. Fearful of offending the European Powers, the Ottoman government permitted Greeks and Armenians to supplant the Jews as tax- and customs-collectors, as imperial commercial agents and dragomans. In 1826, moreover, Sultan Mahmud II disbanded the chronically mutinous janissary corps, the empire's elite military caste. For nearly two centuries, Jews had functioned as the corps' quartermasters and textile suppliers. The loss of that unique connection soon proved devastating for the wider Jewish economy. With every passing year, Jews found themselves reduced to marginal livelihoods, as peddlers, house painters, porters, bootblacks, even ragpickers.

To some degree, the erosion of Jewish security and self-assurance also reflected Ottoman demographic as well as economic transformations. The incorporation of millions of Arabs over the seventeenth century for the first time gave the empire a Moslem majority. In ensuing decades, reflecting that new Islamic predominance, the government began enforcing dhinni laws against non-Moslems with a vigor not manifested since the conquest of Constantinople. This time, Jews suffered far more than Christians. Without European "brother" governments to intercede on their behalf, they were subjected once again to humiliating sumptuary regulations on clothing, to limitations on synagogue construction and repair, and confinement to painfully constricted residential quarters. By the early eighteenth century, letters from rabbis to colleagues in Europe provided despairing accounts of Moslem and Greek Christian derision and intimidation, of robberies, assaults, even killings. At a time when Jews in Western lands were inching toward emancipation, the status of their people in Constantinople was described by Charles MacFarlane, a British business agent, as "the last and most degraded of the Turkish *rayahs* [subject races] . . . loaded with the concurrent and utter contempt of Frank [European], Turk, and Armenian. . . . Throughout the Ottoman dominions, their pusillanimity is so excessive that they will flee before the uplifted hand of a child."

The collapse in the Jews' economic and political circumstances soon was reflected in their communal and cultural life. Well seized of Ottoman judicial

venality, Jews also learned to rely on baksheesh to overrule or evade the judgments of their own, Jewish courts. Bribery then began to infect the Jewish fiscal structure, and payoffs to communal assessors gradually shifted the tax
burden from the affluent to the poorer classes. At almost every level, the
debilitation of Ottoman public life in the seventeenth and eighteenth centuries exerted a concomitant influence on the Jews. As fundamentalism displaced moral austerity within the Islamic clerical hierarchy, so obscurantism
reigned increasingly uncontested among the Jews. Local rabbis functioned as
watchdogs less of communal morality than of social minutiae. Regulating
sabbaths and other holy days on an hour-by-hour basis, they monitored the
precise length of men's beards and the shape of their headgear, and forbade
women to appear in public unveiled. Schoolchildren learned their daily
lessons exclusively under blindered and despotic religious teachers. Nor, in
these years of malaise and cultural decrepitude, could Jews avoid exposure to
the more backward social customs and superstitions of their Moslem neighbors, to their incantations, conjurations, and talismans for protection against
physical afflictions and the omnipresent "evil eye" (p. 149). In the same measure, the Jews' family life became a microcosm of Near Eastern sociology.
They dwelt as extended families in communal courtyards, and were encouraged to intermarry with second or even first cousins, thus producing offspring
whose physiological and intellectual characteristics over the generations at
best were unlovely, at worst, dysfunctional.

Tanzimat: PROMISE AND NON-FULFILLMENT

Was there a glimmer of hope for revival? Much depended on the Turks themselves. In the early nineteenth century, with the European regions of its
empire beginning to crumble and its ramshackle administration faltering, the
Ottoman government embarked on a belated effort of Tanzimat—of political
reform and economic modernization. Launched by Sultan Mahmud II in
1826 with the destruction of the janissary corps (p. 142), the program gained
momentum under Mahmud's successor, Abd al-Majid I. One of Abd al-
Majid's most radical decrees, the 1839 "Rescript of the Rose Chamber,"
ordained nothing less than full legal equality for the empire's non-Moslem
communities.

Thus, over the mid-third of the century, a series of royal firmans officially
terminated dhinni poll taxes, reversed the inferior standing of non-Moslems
before state courts, and ended the humiliating restrictions imposed on their
clothing, housing, even their government employment. Military service was
opened to Moslems and non-Moslems alike (although both Jews and Christians tended to shun the "boon" of conscription, preferring to pay special taxes
as a kind of surrogate service). In the 1860s, following additional constitu-

tional improvements, several Jews were appointed to minor government positions, to district and municipal councils, and a few even to the (advisory) Council of State. During the reign of Abd al-Hamid II (1876–1909), a sultan otherwise notorious for brutality to Moslems and non-Moslems alike, occasional Jewish notables were awarded decorations and honorific titles. For the most part, however, the integration of Jews into Ottoman society remained at best tentative and superficial. Except for a small minority of bankers and merchants, the Jews' economic position continued its decline throughout the nineteenth century. Their cultural development languished. Under the supervision of the *haham bashi*, the chief rabbi, religion and education maintained a stance not only of intense pietism but, so it appeared, of incorrigible fundamentalism.

Nevertheless, it was in the realm of education that individual members of the Jewish community first ventured a cautious, modernizing initiative. By mid-century, a number of respected mercantile families began exploring ways of bypassing the parochial Jewish school system. Their original technique was to enroll their children in the developing network of Protestant and Catholic mission schools. These at least provided an important nucleus of secular subjects. So, increasingly, did local Greek and Armenian schools. To the incipient Jewish bourgeoisie, it was evident that their own educational system hardly dare offer less, if their children were to survive economically. Yet the decisive inspiration came from the West, and specifically from France. Since the 1860s, it was the powerful French-Jewish philanthropy, the Alliance Israélite Universelle, that accepted responsibility for educating Jews in the Near East and North Africa. By no coincidence, this was terrain regarded as legitimately within the French sphere of imperialist influence (p. 150). As Adolphe Crémieux and other leaders of the Alliance saw it, plain and simple French patriotism mandated an effort to "enlighten," in effect, to Gallicize, the unfortunate Sephardim.

Throughout the late nineteenth century, therefore, the Alliance opened a series of pilot schools, first in Constantinople, then in Izmir, Edirne, and several other middle-sized Turkish cities. The network widened in ensuing decades to include Syria, Egypt, the Balkans, and North Africa. Religious and Hebrew courses remained in the curriculum. But in the manner of the early Russian Crown schools, education now also included a core program of secular subjects, including "useful" languages. Instruction, too, was carried out in the "useful" language of French. Turkish was relegated to third place in these schools, after French and the Sephardic patois of Ladino (Hebrew came last). By the early twentieth century, the project had gained impressive momentum. In Turkey and the Balkans alone in 1908, some 40,000 students were enrolled in the Alliance network, all of them resonating to the model of France, the idealized heartland of commerce and prosperity—of "civilization." The struggle for Jewish renaissance was a poignant one, and all the more as it depended for its fulfillment upon a wider-ranging renaissance within the Ottoman Empire itself.

A Balkan Jerusalem

Even at the flood tide of Jewish departure from Spain and Portugal, in the fifteenth and sixteenth centuries, it was the Balkan peninsula, far more than Turkey itself (except for Constantinople), that became the principal sanctuary for Sephardic refugees. By 1550, some 20,000 Jews had settled in the Macedonian port of Salonika, where they soon comprised fully half the town's population. Beyond their Ladino language and Hispanicized folk mores, the newcomers brought with them their traditional mercantile and craft skills. Indeed, in Salonika as well as in several other Ottoman towns, in both Asia Minor and the Balkans, it was almost exclusively Sephardic weavers and dyers who developed the empire's textile industry.

Yet, more than handicrafts, business reigned as the queen of Jewish vocations in Salonika. With its superb harbor, the city had long since become a vital commercial entrepôt, the major relay station for trade between the eastern Mediterranean and Venice. Although Jews functioned as leading importers and exporters in both Salonika and Venice, in Salonika it was exclusively Jews who fulfilled this role. Here their warehouses dominated the harbor skyline, and Sephardic names (in the Hebrew alphabet) appeared on nearly every shop of note in the commercial districts. By the mid-seventeenth century, all businesses, Jewish and non-Jewish, were closed on Saturday and other Jewish holy days. Jews also lived where they worked. Their homes were near the port, in the *Francomahalla,* "the quarter of the Francos," where elite Jewish agents for European companies operated under the protection of the European consuls; and near the Hippodrome, on the edge of the Greek quarter, where scores of shops and ateliers similarly bore titles in Hebrew lettering. Moreover, in their affluence and communal vigor, Sephardic Jewry, with their dozens of synagogues, seminaries, schools, and printing presses, developed a cultural vibrancy second to none in the Diaspora—thereby earning for their community the sobriquet of a "university city." It was a Sephardic "city" continually renewed by the influx of fugitive conversos from Portugal and Italy. If the sixteenth and early seventeenth centuries were the golden age of Balkan Jewry, Salonika glowed in the vortex of that creativity.

But as the international trade routes shifted from the Mediterranean to the Atlantic during the seventeenth century, Salonikan Jewry began to share in the Ottoman Empire's collective economic and social lassitude. Here, too, the government's dhinni taxes became extortionate. Twice in the 1630s, Sultan Murad IV imposed a huge capital levy on the Jewish population. In ensuing decades, as a result, sheer social despair evoked protests, even occasional riots against the *cal*, the Jewish communal authority that assessed and collected these imposts. The Jews' frustration and hopelessness also evoked a compensatory upsurge of Kabbalism. In schools, seminaries, and private homes alike, study of the Bible and the Talmud was increasingly displaced by a fascinated obsession with mystery literature. In their passion to hasten the coming of the Redeemer, the faithful turned increasingly to the Kabbalistic nostrums of lengthy fasts and self-flagellation, and in the 1660s many became rapt followers of Shabbtai Zvi, a charismatic false messiah. Thus, over the years, as the Jews of Salonika devolved from wealthy capitalists to petty shopkeepers and artisans, then increasingly into a proletariat of fishermen, stevedores, carters, and porters, they, too, like their kinsmen in Constantinople, appeared to have lost their once renowned cultural vibrance.

The death knell was not quite ready to be sounded. In the mid- and late nineteenth century, tentative prefigurations of economic revival began to appear. In 1880, with Austrian funding, the harbor of Salonika was enlarged to provide wharfage for a more extensive maritime traffic. Eight years later, the city was connected to Baron de Hirsch's formidable new Trans-Balkan Railroad, linking it more efficiently with the commercial centers of the West. European technology and European ideas similarly began to make their way into the port community. Thus, by the early twentieth century, Salonikan Jewry, numbering approximately 90,000—still almost half the city's population—appeared to be regaining their preeminence in Salonika's commercial life, in shipping, import-export, tobacco manufacture and distribution, as well as in the more conventional retail enterprises. Once again, the rhythm of Salonikan life become attuned to its Jewish plurality.

As elsewhere in the Ottoman Empire, the establishment of a network of Alliance schools also fortified this reviving Jewish embourgeoisement. So did the growing number of young Salonikan Jews who journeyed directly to France for their higher education. "The century was drawing to a close," Leon Sciaky recalled in his *Farewell to Salonika* (1946). "Stealthily the West was creeping in, trying to lure the East with her wonders. She dangled before our dazzled eyes the witchery of her science and the miracle of her inventions. We caught a glimpse of her brilliance, and timidly listened to the song of the siren." Responding to that allure, the city's Jewish population by the early 1900s had embarked upon a modest cultural renaissance, generating a vigorous diversity of newspapers and journals, of drama, music, and political-party activities. The upsurge was expressive of a vibrant multilingual ethnicity in Hebrew, Ladino, and French (although still only rarely in Turkish or Greek).

IN A SLAVIC OCEAN

In the sixteenth and seventeenth centuries, the wave of Sephardim flowing into the Ottoman Balkans generated dynamic Jewish communities in the peninsula's Bulgarian-inhabited regions, in Sofia, Janina, Nikopol, Plovdiv (Plevna), and Yambol. As in Salonika and Constantinople, the newcomers applied their mercantile and handicraft skills, and trade and industry soon flourished in their hands. In Plovdiv, the production of woolens became virtually a Jewish monopoly, together with the city's leather, fur, and dying industries. By the same token, in their communal autonomy and supremacy, the Jews laid down their traditionally strict rules governing business affairs, and gentile merchants as always learned to accommodate to these regulations.

By the early nineteenth century, Jews in the Bulgarian regions numbered approximately 25,000 and comprised one-tenth of Sofia's and Plovdiv's populations. For the most part, their relations with their semiliterate Slavic neighbors were tolerable. Following the Russo-Turkish War of 1877–78, an occupying Russian army encouraged the Bulgars to vent their newly awakened nationalism in a series of anti-Jewish riots; but the violence subsided once the Russians departed in 1881. Afterward, Jews, Bulgars, Turks, Greeks, and others of Bulgaria's heterogeneity of peoples returned to their traditionally languid multiculturalism. Although the Jews for the most part were a lower-middle-class community, literacy among them was universal, if almost exclusively in Ladino and Hebrew. Even the poorest of Jewish children attended the network of their own schools—many of these now Alliance-funded. By the early twentieth century, Bulgaria's 43,000 Jews maintained over one hundred Ladino newspapers and journals, a wide skein of libraries, philanthropies, choral and drama groups, as well as "Israelite" economic syndicates, banks, and credit societies. Altogether, their settlement functioned as an ethnically vibrant Sephardic island within a Slavic ocean—and in later years would be unsurpassed in its Zionist loyalties.

It was an ethnic profile that characterized the largest numbers of Jews elsewhere in the Ottoman Balkans. Thus, as early as the sixteenth century, an extensive enclave of Sephardic refugees established itself in the provinces of Bosnia and Herzegovina, principally in Sarajevo, but also in the towns of Travnik, Banja Luka, and Mostar. Here, too, the newcomers brought their renowned skills of artisanry and entrepreneurialism, setting up workshops and offices in local commercial centers, developing residential neighborhoods around their own synagogues and self-governing cals. Their relations with the neighboring Slavs, Turks, Greeks, Armenians, and Gypsies were placid. By the late nineteenth century, the Jews of Sarajevo, numbering approximately 7,000 (12 percent of the city's population), had become a secure and respected minority community. If less than affluent by Western standards, they played as central a role in the economy of Bosnia-Herzegovina as did their fellow Sephardim elsewhere in the Balkans. In 1878, following Turkey's defeat in its latest war with Russia, Bosnia and Herzegovina were given over to Austrian "administration," and in 1908 the Austrians annexed the two provinces outright. The Jews' security remained unaffected.

So it did in neighboring Serbia. During the early seventeenth century, some 2,000 Sephardim took up residence virtually en bloc in the Dorcal quarter of Belgrade, a sprawling labyrinth of apartments and communal kitchens. Growing steadily over the ensuing decades, this congested Jewish enclave became in effect the nerve center of the town's international trade. It would survive in that role even following Serbia's emergence to independent statehood in 1878. Initially, the Jews were alarmed at the replacement of a benign (if corrupt) Ottoman administration by a fulminantly nationalist Slavic successor regime. They suffered a number of discriminatory taxes. These gradually eased, however. By 1912, numbering approximately 10,000, Serbian Jews shared with their non-Jewish neighbors an identical economic and political equality.

Their ethnic vitality also survived intact. Serbian Jewry's language and literature, their newspapers and journals, remained overwhelmingly Ladino. Their children attended their own network of schools, most of these characteristically supported by the Alliance. Altogether, throughout Constantinople and the Ottoman Balkans, the dense matrix of Sephardic Jews, numbering some 150,000 by 1912—at least half the Jewish population of the Ottoman Empire in its entirety—sustained as vigorous a Jewish identity as that in any corner of the Diaspora, not excluding the mighty Jewish hinterland of tsarist Russia.

The Maghreb

Beyond the frontiers of Europe, the largest demographic reservoir of Jews in the Early Modern Era was to be found neither in Asia Minor nor in the Balkan peninsula, but in North Africa. It was forbidding terrain, bleak and sere, cruelly impoverished in its economic and social resources. Since the eighth-century Moslem conquest, the entire North African massif was fractured politically under rival dynasties loosely corresponding to present-day Algeria, Tunisia, and Morocco. Their governments, like their populations, were amalgams of Middle Eastern Arabs and indigenous Berbers.

Their Jews were also amalgams. Concentrated in the Atlas Mountain range of Morocco and Algeria, and in several oases, the little minority people belonged to clans that evidently had been Judaized in the early Middle Ages by traders or refugees from the Holy Land. Berber in race, language, and in many of their folk traditions, these *moghrebim* (from *Maghreb*, the Arabic term for the North African littoral) somehow remained Jewish in religion even following the Islamization of the surrounding majority population. No more impoverished Jews existed anywhere on earth. In the twelfth century, the fanatical Almohade dynasty in its missionary zeal consigned them to the lowest rung of dhimmi inferiority, and later rulers institutionalized that status. In their desperation, numerous moghrebim fled deeper into the desert interior, or, alternatively, into the fetid ghettos of the coastal towns. There, in ensuing centuries, these backwater Jews swooned into a long era of economic and spiritual atrophy.

In the fifteenth and sixteenth centuries, however, following the mass expulsion of Jews from the Iberian peninsula, as many as 50,000 refugee Sephardim made their way across the Strait of Gibraltar to North Africa. Their ordeal was a cruel one. Thousands were plundered and slain by local tribesmen. Others perished of starvation, disease, and exposure. Nevertheless, some two-thirds of them managed to survive, and gradually to make their way to the larger coastal cities, where local governors tolerated them for their commercial and professional skills. Consigned to the identical urban ghettos inhabited by the *berberiscos* (as the Sephardim contemptuously dubbed the native-born Jews), they also suffered the same legal restrictions of poll taxes, distinctive apparel, and limitations on synagogue construction. Yet there were occasional exemptions for important merchants, financial advisers, and physicians. Indeed, nearly every Moslem court had its Jewish physician. In Algeria, a later-arriving infusion of Italian Sephardim from Leghorn proved so rich in experienced merchants and commercial envoys that it won en bloc exemption from ghettoization.

Over the ensuing sixteenth and early seventeenth centuries, the larger part of the North African littoral came under Ottoman dominion. Only little Morocco, a kind of Iberian hinterland, fended off Turkish rule. But whether in Morocco or in Ottoman North Africa, lack of effective central government took its toll. Largely neglected by its Turkish overlords, the Maghreb gradually reverted to political and economic chaos. For the Jews, the ensuing centuries proved especially grim. Local Berber overlords confined them to the kinds of demeaning livelihoods that Moslems traditionally scorned, such as shoemaking, dying, weaving, petty shopkeeping, or peddling. In their isolation and debasement, North African Jewry became even more susceptible than the Jews of Europe to Kabbalism and to other varieties of mysticism and messianism. To some degree, their vulnerability reflected the mores of their Moslem neighbors, including the latter's predilection for amulets and incantations against demons and the ubiquitous evil eye (although a distinctly non-Moslem resort to alcoholism also became widespread among Moroccan Jewry). By the nineteenth century, as Moslem bands terrorized Jewish neighborhoods with growing frequency and destructiveness, emotional palliatives no longer sufficed. Assurance of physical security was needed.

Europe provided it. In 1830, France established a protectorate over Algeria, and later incorporated this largest of the Maghreb countries directly into the French national administration. Tunisia similarly came under French rule in 1883, as did Morocco in the years between 1904 and 1912. Here at last North African Jews were assured a certain elementary personal safety. Even in backward Morocco and Tunisia, they were released from their ghetto confinement and given access to French law courts and hospitals. Only their economic circumstances remained marginal. As craftsmen or small retailers, Jews in Morocco and Tunisia were hardly able to cope with the new flood of manufactured imports pouring in from France, or with the competition of growing numbers of European settlers. A poor community by any Western standards, they became poorer yet during the early years of the twentieth century. Living from hand to mouth, some two-thirds of their breadwinners subsisted as minor craftsmen or hole-in-the-wall retailers. In Casablanca, on the eve of World War I, almost a fourth of the Jewish community was unemployed, and some families were reduced to beggary.

It was in Algeria alone that a quantum improvement was registered in Jewish circumstances. For one thing, as an extension of metropolitan France, the nation enjoyed the advantage of massive French investment, both in private agriculture and industry and in governmental infrastructure. While all the native—Berber—inhabitants of Algeria profited from an impressive economic takeoff, the Jews as business people forged ahead almost as dramatically as did the European colonists. Moreover, in common with the growing numbers of European settlers, Jewish children were accepted almost immediately into the French school system. Soon almost every Jewish family became an *aspirant* to modernization, and specifically to French culture. Algerian rabbis delivered their sermons in French, and in the late nineteenth century the Torah crown in the main Algiers synagogue actually was fashioned in the shape of the Eiffel Tower. In 1870, impressed by Algerian Jewry's poignant Gallicization, and well apprised of the Jews' potential usefulness as clients of French imperialism, Emperor Louis Napoleon acceded to the appeal of the estimable Adolphe Crémieux. He bestowed full citizenship on the 60,000 Jews of Algeria.

The boon of the Crémieux Decree was not without its costs, however. It provoked deep resentment among Algeria's Moslem majority, themselves beyond the pale of the exalted French circle. In their frustration, local Berber mobs began tearing through Jewish neighborhoods, in Tlemcen in 1881; in Algiers in 1882, 1897, and 1898; in Oran and Sétif in 1883; in Mostaganem in 1897. Despite the best efforts of the French police, hardly a town of any size escaped the orgy of looting and synagogue-sacking, even occasional killing. Ironically, during these same late-nineteenth-century years, Jew-hatred also burgeoned up with comparable malevolence among Algeria's substantial enclave of European colonists. Insecure in their status as an expatriate minority, the *colons* discerned in their Jewish "fellow citizens"— numbering perhaps 90,000 by the turn of the century—a useful target for compensatory chauvinism. *Colon* xenophobia became particularly intense during France's Dreyfus Affair. In 1898, the wave of anti-Dreyfusardism brought to the French Chamber of Deputies such virulent antisemites as Max Regis, the mayor of Algiers, and Émile Morinaud, the deputy mayor of Constantine.

Indeed, it was from their experience in tension-ridden Algeria that French colonial officials decided not to risk the grant of equal citizenship to the Jews of Tunisia and Morocco, or even access to the French educational system. Thus, in fin-de-siècle Tunisia, with its 90,000 Jews, and in Morocco, with its nearly 200,000 Jews (by 1910), Jewish appeals for naturalization, for improved education, for special reward as enthusiastic *aspirants* to French culture—all were rejected. So it was, in the years before World War I, that Moroccan and Tunisian Jewry, representing more than two-thirds of the half-million Jews of French North Africa, remained among the most impoverished and culturally deprived Jewish communities in the world.

Aspirants of Westernization: Syria, Egypt, Iraq

Other Jewish enclaves that fell under the rule of the Ottoman Empire included communities tracing their lineage back even further than those of North Africa. Among the 7,000 to 8,000 Jews of Syria (by the latter 1800s) were families of *musta'arabin,* those whose tribal origins lay in the ancient Middle East. From the sixteenth century on, their numbers were augmented by small infusions of Sephardic refugees. Settling mainly in Aleppo, Damascus, and Beirut, Jews of both communities achieved the preeminent respectability of middle-class businessmen, functioning essentially as retailers and small-scale importers. Although continuing to live mainly in their own quarters, Syrian Jewry even managed to survive the trauma of the Damascus Affair. Following the withdrawal of the Mehemet Ali administration in 1840–41, Syria reverted to the torpid and essentially pluralistic toleration of Ottoman rule. The Jews then resumed the traditional rhythms of their mercantile and religiocommunal life. The principal modernizing influence among them, as among the Jews of the Ottoman Empire at large, was the Alliance educational network. By the late nineteenth century, the largest numbers of Jewish children in Damascus, Aleppo, and Beirut were enrolled in these Alliance Israélite Universelle schools. Well before World War I, and the subsequent establishment of the French mandate, French was becoming the principal commercial and social language of Levant Jewry—indeed, of the upper middle classes at large—and the marque of their instinctive orientation toward the West.

It was an orientation that became more palpable yet in the case of Egyptian Jewry. This was an irony. If North African and Syrian Jews in their origins harked back centuries, even millennia, all but 4,000 of Egypt's 35,000 Jews (in 1914) traced their native settlement back more than three decades. Most had been born in the Middle East, to be sure, but not in Egypt (except for a tiny Karaite enclave). Of these, many were émigrés from other Ottoman provinces, from Syria, Lebanon, and Palestine, from North Africa and Corfu. Since 1882, moreover, with the establishment of Britain's de facto rule in Egypt, Jews arrived in Alexandria and Cairo precisely to shed their Asian inheritance. Under British domain, Egypt offered immigrants special "status" under European consular protection. Jewish newcomers thus tended to regard themselves as "Europeans," members of that privileged economic and social class that eventually would include nearly a quarter-million British, French, Italians, Greeks, and Armenians.

They were almost exclusively a middle-class community. Beginning as petty merchants, the Jews soon flourished. In Cairo, together with the Greeks and Armenians, they established the most popular shops on Suleiman Basha and Ali Basha streets, and operated the largest textile firms in the city's Musky commercial quarter. Jewish financiers served as executives in Egypt's banking and insurance systems. Jewish brokers played leading roles in the currency, cotton, and stock exchanges. Other Jews prospered as doctors and lawyers. Among themselves, they spoke mainly French, the language of their Alliance schooling. As late as 1914, they tended also to live in their own somewhat pedestrian Harat al-Yahud quarters in Cairo and Alexandria; but in the postwar years, Jewish families began to purchase homes in Cairo's more attractive residential quarters of Heliopolis, Daher, and Zamalek, together with the nouveaux riches of other minority communities. Rarely did they encounter obstacles to advancement. If nationalist resentment festered beneath the surface of Egyptian public life, it was directed toward the British, rarely toward the other communities, and least of all toward the Jews.

Whatever their upward mobility, Egyptian Jewry also found time to maintain an unshakable ethnic cohesion and discipline. Their communal institutions included an elaborate network of Alliance schools, of Maccabi and HaKoah sports clubs, of B'nai B'rith lodges, mutual aid societies and hospitals, of youth, literary, and drama circles, and private associations of Sephardic, Ionian, and Italian Jews. As in other Middle Eastern lands, their abundant cluster of synagogues functioned under the juridical supervision of rabbinical councils. The government obliged the Jews to pay taxes to support these religious institutions, and they did so willingly. Affluent and Europeanized, somewhat less observant than the Jews of North Africa, possibly even than those of Turkey, Egyptian Jews nonetheless guarded their communal traditions proudly. Well into the twentieth century, ethnic cohesion functioned as tangible evidence of their status as quasi-Europeans.

During these same years of the late nineteenth and early twentieth centuries, Iraqi Jewry's economic and social circumstances achieved a superficial congruence with those of Egyptian Jewry. But, in fact, the background of the two communities could not have been more dissimilar. Tracing their ancestry to the oldest of Jewish diasporas, that of ancient Babylon, the Jews of Iraq comprised the most venerable Jewish community on earth. No Jewry in the Middle East was ever more thoroughly Arabized. Physically, too, Jews in Iraq were almost indistinguishable from their Arab neighbors, and spoke Arabic at home as in the street. By the early twentieth century, numbering approximately 115,000, they were dispersed mainly between Baghdad, Basra, and Mosul. Although they lived essentially within their own neighborhoods, and maintained the Ottoman tradition of administering their own affairs through their communal courts, they blended otherwise almost completely into the ethnographic landscape.

Following the Young Turk Revolution of 1908 (p. 408), the Jews of Iraq became Ottoman citizens in law and practical fact. Henceforth, they were spared the lingering status of dhinni and the psychological need to live exclusively in their own quarters. Indeed, they were authorized to send delegates to the 1908 Ottoman parliament in Constantinople, to serve in the nation's secular law courts and municipal councils. By then, too, Iraqi Jews had achieved a prosperity surpassed perhaps only by their kinsmen in Egypt. As far back as the nineteenth century, the opening of the Suez Canal had vastly augmented the importance of Baghdad and Basra in the developing British trade with the Orient. Sharing in that commerce, Iraq-Jewish businessmen participated actively in the country's role as an exchange center between Europe and the Far East. Several of them established trading outposts in Iran and India, in Hong Kong, Singapore, even in Australia. Among these merchant princes, the Sassoons, a family of renowned importer-exporters and bankers, emerged by the early twentieth century as among the wealthiest Jewish families in the world. Their prominence as members of the Governor's Council in the last year of Ottoman administration in Iraq prefigured the far more decisive, even dominant, role Jews subsequently would play in Britain's postwar Iraqi mandate.

It was a fin-de-siècle efflorescence that served no less as an epilogue to the long and often mottled odyssey of Jewish life under Turkish rule. From the fifteenth to the twentieth centuries, whether serving as haven for the fugitive Jews of Iberia, or as the conqueror of indigenous Jewish populations in the Middle East and North Africa, the Ottoman Empire kept its Jewish stepchildren alive and reasonably intact. This was no trivial achievement. The Ottoman epoch in Jewish history unquestionably produced its years of intimidation, even of brutality, as well as of toleration and solicitude. Yet it was significant that Turkish rule hardly ever was marred by the kind of widespread massacres once characteristic of Western and Central Europe, or by the systematic oppression that in Tsarist Russia produced the largest emigration of Jews in modern times, or by the industrialized West's exploitation of Jew-hatred for domestic political purposes. By the nineteenth century, the Empire of the Osmanlis unquestionably had become the "sick man of Europe." But whatever the Turks' cruelty to other peoples—to the Armenians and South Slavs, for example—their record in Jewish history over nearly half a millennium was essentially that of caretaker and protector. It was a role Jews elsewhere would not have scorned.

The Rise of Jewish Life in America

IN THE SOUTHERN HEMISPHERE

Notwithstanding Christopher Columbus's epic feat in discovering the New World, the great mariner's four voyages to the West achieved only a precarious territorial foothold for his royal patrons. Another half-century of exploration and conquest was required for others to secure Spain's vast new empire, and to structure the awesome magnitude of its terrain into the three viceroyalties of New Spain (Mexico, Central America, the Philippines), New Castile (Peru, all of South America except Brazil and the Guineas), and New Granada (encompassing the Central American region of Panama, Colombia, Venezuela, and Ecuador). For the Spanish government, colonization in the sixteenth and seventeenth centuries took precedence over trade. To foster that settlement, the Crown offered the inducements of extensive land grants for its soldiers and farmers, and substantial profits for the prospectors, engineers, and overseers of the southern continent's boundless silver mines. Ostensibly, the constraints of *limpieza de sangre* (untainted—that is, non-Jewish—blood) excluded "New Christians" from these ventures. Yet conversos aplenty found ways to immigrate to the Americas. Spain's notoriously venal bureaucracy was quite prepared to sell permits of exemption. Ship captains also could be bribed to disembark conversos at secret inlets.

The infiltration of these New Christians became something of an influx once the Spanish throne assumed its rule over Portugal in 1580. As on the Iberian peninsula itself, the transmigration of Portuguese New Christians to the Americas came to be known as the "penetración portuguesa." By the late sixteenth century, as many as 5,000 such Portuguese New Christians may have departed for the New World. They settled extensively in the major colonial cities, until by the 1630s virtually every town in Spanish America sheltered at least a scattering of converted Jews. A majority of these Sephardim gravitated toward commerce, but others became managers of silver mines, and were appointed to important colonial offices. In their midst, too, were to be found considerable numbers of marranos. Indeed, many of these putative Catholics hardly bothered to disguise their ancestral Jewish loyalties.

Yet if this was the Sephardim's best period in the New World, it was also a fleeting one. Before long, the Inquisition was introduced into Spain's overseas possessions, and its agents set about tracking marranos with ferocious single-mindedness, torturing and burning with a malevolence never exceeded, and rarely matched, in the homeland. By the early seventeenth century, as a result, the Inquisition wiped out any lingering pockets of Jews in New Spain, and the long, poignant struggle of vestigial Judaism flickered out in the empire. When it revived, two and a half centuries later, the flame no longer would be Sephardic (p. 668ff.).

BRAZIL

As in the Spanish possessions, virtually all Brazilian colonists in the 1500s and 1600s were on the qui vive for a swift payoff. Among them, none was more preoccupied with financial security than Portugal's beleaguered handful of *convertido* expatriates. One of these New Christians, Duarte Coelho, son of the Portuguese astronomer-navigator Gonçalo Coelho, became the first European to cultivate sugar in Brazil. Appointed governor of the province of Pernambuco, Coelho established the New World's earliest sugar mills on his own vast plantation, then brought over numerous relatives, also convertidos. Their origins actually were not secret. Intent on consolidating its holdings in Goa, Ceylon, and Angola, as well as in Brazil, the Portuguese Crown quietly allowed the enlistment of New Christians in the imperial cause. By the seventeenth century, therefore, in a multiracial frontier nation, New Christians fitted without difficulty into local European society. By 1620, Brazil's white population was estimated at 44,000. While possibly not more than 1,000 of these were convertidos, they represented at least 15 percent of all European settlers in the key frontier towns of Bahía, Olinda, Rio de Janeiro, and Recife. Moreover, as sugar emerged as Brazil's most lucrative export, the tiny sub-community of former Jews developed a significant proportion of planters and refiners. In the early seventeenth century, some 120 sugar mills were in operation, and as many as one-fifth of these were estimated to have been owned by convertidos. Who more efficiently could have shipped their products through the dense and sophisticated Sephardic trading network in Lisbon, Hamburg, and Amsterdam?

Most Brazilian Sephardim, to be sure, were wholesale and retail merchants, and were content simply to earn their modest livelihoods in peace and quiet. Virtually all New Christians had come for economic, not religious, purposes. Reared as Catholics, a majority of the convertidos in any case soon disappeared from the Jewish rolls. Nevertheless, a tiny marrano nucleus endured

somewhat longer among Portuguese New Christians than among their Spanish counterparts. In Brazil's raw frontier society, few of these secret Judaiz-
ers bothered to take elaborate precautions beyond occasional bribes to local
officials. Eventually, by the mid-1600s, inquisitional tribunals began arresting growing numbers of suspects and shipping them back to Portugal for
trial. Yet, even then, Brazil never quite matched the Spanish colonies as an
arena for doctrinal fervor. A nation with Portugal's modest demographic
resources was not yet prepared to jeopardize its single viable outpost in the
New World.

That outpost first came under threat as early as 1629. The Dutch West
India Company managed to capture the little Portuguese outpost of Bahía.
Moving on from Bahía, the company's armed mercenaries proceeded to invest
the much larger province of Pernambuco, a region comprising the heartland
of Brazil's sugar industry. The Dutch conquest in turn seemingly launched a
new era for the Jews. The marranos among them came out into the open. As
in the Netherlands itself, enjoying full liberty of religion, they were able to
establish synagogues and communal institutions for the first time in the history of the New World. Yet, as in New Spain, the respite proved a brief one.
The Dutch enclave was too limited in size and demographic depth to sustain
itself. In 1653, the Portuguese mobilized a sizable naval armada, recruited large
numbers of black former slaves for their army, and set out to recapture Bahía.
In January of the following year, their long siege finally starved out the
Dutch, who surrendered their last remaining garrison in Recife. The town's
six hundred remaining Jews now found themselves in desperate straits. On
the one hand, the Portuguese commander, General Francisco Barreto de
Menezes, was a large-spirited man who promised them complete safety
should they choose to leave. But if they stayed, Menezes announced regretfully, he could not protect them from the Inquisition.

And so they left. The majority returned to the Netherlands. Approximately
two hundred others decided to seek asylum elsewhere in the Americas. Some
departed for the French West Indies, where they found a haven. By decree of
France's King Louis XIII in 1615, Jews were not to be allowed henceforth on
French soil. But the law was hardly applied even in France, and in the colonies
no serious attempt ever was made to enforce it. The few dozen Jews who settled in these islands remained. With the tacit consent of England's government, Jews also found sanctuary and security in the British West Indies. In
the Dutch West Indies, of course, they were entirely safe. Establishing solid
communities in Surinam, in the Windward Islands and in the Leeward
Islands of St. Eustatius, Saba, St. Martin, and Aruba, they thrived as merchants, plantation owners, and slave traders.

The most substantial of the Dutch-Jewish settlements, however, was in
Curaçao. An island of 370 square miles off the coast of Venezuela, possessing

a superior natural harbor, Curaçao functioned as the Dutch West India Company's principal naval and commercial entrepôt in the Western Hemisphere. In 1649, five years before their flight from Recife, a dozen Jewish families had departed Brazil to settle there. Three years later, they were joined by fifty more families. Their presence was not a source of pleasure for Curaçao's governor, Pieter Stuyvesant, who sought initially to harass them by limiting their opportunities as wholesale and retail traders. But several additional score of Jews arrived with the fall of Recife, and that number was further augmented as kinsmen arrived directly from Holland. By the mid-eighteenth century, the Jews of Curaçao totaled not less than 1,500, fully half the island's European population. They thrived. Indeed, as owners of sugar and tobacco plantations, and as major players in the extensive Caribbean import-export trade, the Jews of Curaçao became the largest and wealthiest Jewish community in the New World. Their communal life was equally vibrant. Bringing over a rabbi from Amsterdam, and constructing a synagogue on the model of Amsterdam's renowned Esnoga, they developed a network of communal institutions, schools, kosher abattoirs, and ritual baths. As the Western Hemisphere's "mother Jewry," the Sephardim of Curaçao also played an indispensable role in nurturing other Jewish settlements in the Americas.

Nieuw Amsterdam

In February 1654, a month after the Portuguese reconquest, the Dutch schooner *Valk*, one of the two remaining vessels carrying Brazilian-Jewish refugees, sailed out of Recife. Bound for the French island of Martinique, the vessel was intercepted en route by a Spanish privateer and compelled to drop anchor in Jamaica, then under Spanish rule. Immediately, several baptized Sephardim among the passengers were incarcerated by the local Inquisition. The rest, twenty-three professing Jews, including four men, six women, and thirteen children, were allowed to depart. The little group's next anchorage was Cape St. Anthony, on the western tip of Cuba. Here they anticipated securing passage for Nieuw Amsterdam, the Dutch West India Company's outpost on mainland North America. Thus, at the cape, they negotiated an agreement with the captain of the French barque *Sainte Catherine*, who consented to transport them for the exorbitant fee of 2,500 guilders, 900 to be paid in advance.

But upon arriving at the ramshackle village of Nieuw Amsterdam, the Jews failed to produce the balance of their passage money. Immediately, the irate captain obtained a court order to attach their furniture. When a public auction still did not cover the debt, two of the Jews were clapped in the stockade. There they languished until October 1654, when kinsmen in Holland finally dispatched the needed payment. The situation of the other Jews remained desperate, however. They lacked funds for shelter or hot meals. It was the local Dutch Reformed Church that kept them alive, although its charity was sustained by the expectation that the Jews would soon be gone. Indeed, the newly appointed local governor, Pieter Stuyvesant, had had his fill of Jews during his previous assignment as governor of Curaçao. Describing them as notorious for "their usury and deceitful trading," he petitioned the West India Company for permission to expel them. Dominie Johannes Megapolensis, of the local Dutch Reformed Church, added his own warning to the church classis in Amsterdam:

> [A]s we have here Papists, Mennonites and Lutherans among the Dutch, also many Puritans and Independents, and many Atheists and various other servants of Baal among the English under this Government, who conceal themselves under the name of Christians, it would create still greater confusion if the obstinate and immovable Jews came to settle here.

But the "obstinate and immovable Jews" possessed their own contacts, among them Jewish stockholders in the West India Company, who reminded the company board that the original Recife fugitives had "risked their possessions and their blood in defense of the lost [Brazilian] Dutch colony," and that Jews had produced only economic benefit wherever in the Dutch Empire they had settled. The argument registered. In response, the board instructed Stuyvesant to allow the Jews to remain, "provided the poor among them shall not become a burden to the Deaconry or to the Company, but be supported by their own nation," and conduct their religious activities in private.

This the newcomers did. They earned their livelihoods as butchers, metal-workers, importers, and peddlers. Renting their own lodgings, they sustained their own burial ground, cared for their own indigent and orphaned. Evading Stuyvesant's persistent harassment, moreover, they gradually branched out into wider trade, purchased real estate, and soon were openly conducting religious services (albeit in a rented house). There was reason enough for Dutch forbearance. The Jews were white people, after all, subjects of the Dutch government in an outpost vulnerable to economic shortages, marauding Indians, and covetous British neighboring colonies.

And yet, within a few years, this tiny nucleus began to atrophy. Like many of their Dutch neighbors, the Jews sensed a precarious future in an outpost flanked north and south by much larger British colonies. Before long, most of them sailed off, either back to the Netherlands, or to Curaçao and other West Indian islands. By 1664, only one Jew remained of the pioneer band.

UNDER THE UNION JACK, AND AFTER

In Britain, meanwhile, the government had begun somewhat intermittently to follow the Netherlands' mercantilist example of allowing Jews to live openly, to worship and trade freely both in England proper and in its overseas empire (p. 96). Thus, over the seventeenth and eighteenth centuries, some 2,000 Jews settled in the British West Indies. They arrived initially as marrano refugees from Portuguese and Spanish America, and later as professing Jews directly from Holland and from Britain itself. By the early 1700s, as a result, Jews were to be found in every one of Britain's Caribbean possessions, including Barbados, Jamaica, Nevis, Tobago, St. Lucia, Antigua, and St. Kitts. Most of these Sephardim were small tradesmen. A few were coffee and sugar planters, as well as slave-traders. From their midst, too, emerged the Caribbean Basin's preeminent importer-exporters. By the eighteenth century, the largest share of the import-export trade between England and Jamaica was in Jewish hands. Living in full security, Jews were barred only from holding office and serving on juries.

It was in the mid- and latter 1600s, too, that small numbers of West Indian Jews spilled over to the North American mainland. Their initial port of call was New York, the former Nieuw Amsterdam (captured from the Dutch in 1667). Like their predecessors in the New World, most of the newcomers were Sephardim. By the mid-eighteenth century, however, their numbers were augmented by widening rivulets of Jews from German Europe. Most of the latter were *Dorfjuden,* village Jews who were fleeing burdensome limitations on their choice of livelihood and opportunities for marriage. Many of these young bachelors brought with them a modest quantity of savings as well as a considerable mercantile experience. Yet, even in the comparative freedom of North America, their life at the outset was far from easy. In the sternly Calvinist New England colonies, Jews often faced vexatious legal and economic obstacles. Many were denied lodgings, or barred from renting synagogue facilities, and virtually all of them at first were denied civic participation in juries or militias.

The situation varied, to be sure, in the mid-Atlantic and southern colonies. Some of the latter tended to be less restrictive. In any case, by the early eighteenth century, in a frontier society, Jews gradually won acceptance at least as fellow Europeans and as "non-Papists." They were helped when London set out to regularize the status of its overseas population. Under a new Uniform Naturalization Act of 1740, aliens were qualified for citizenship if born or long resident in a British colony, and if they swore loyalty to the Crown. On this basis, by the eve of the American Revolution, Jews throughout the British West Indies and most of the empire's mainland colonies acquired naturalization. With hardly an exception, too, they were exercising their de facto rights of domicile, trade, worship, and, increasingly, of jury and militia service. Unlike the restrictions on Roman Catholics, not a single law ever was enacted in British North America specifically to penalize Jews.

As elsewhere, the largest numbers of mainland Jews were traders. Continually supplemented by immigrant Dorfjuden, their population reached 2,000 by 1776. By then, New York had become the major focus of their settlement, although Newport, Philadelphia, Charles Town, and Savannah were close behind. Not a few Jews were beginning to prosper, as fur traders, land speculators, plantation owners, and merchant shippers. They could live where they pleased, engage in any trade, own homes anywhere, attend university, even vote in colonial and municipal elections. Altogether, by the late eighteenth century, the Jews of Colonial America were the freest Jews on earth.

In their political identification, too, they shared with their gentile neighbors the torn allegiances of the Revolution. Some Jews were British loyalists. A majority appeared to have favored the colonists. Approximately two hundred Jews performed military service for the Revolution. Several Jews became blockade-runners, among them the prominent merchant-fleet owners Isaac Moses and Aaron Lopez. The Polish-born Chaim Salomon emerged as a leading bill-broker, purchasing and selling at a discount the numerous currencies circulating along the Atlantic Seaboard. In Philadelphia during the Revolution, Salomon negotiated the sale of Continental bills of exchange for hard Dutch and French specie. Although the enterprise earned him little in short-term profit, in later years it paid off in goodwill for his business.

Once the Revolution began, the Declaration of Independence offered Jews and other minorities an umbrella of protection in its celebrated "all men are created equal" clause, for the clause was not limited to "all Protestants," or even to "all Christians." That protection later was reinforced in the Federal Constitution's guarantee that "no religious test shall ever be required as a qualification to any office or public trust under the United States." State constitutions were rather less progressive. It was not until 1868 that the final restriction was eliminated (in North Carolina) on the right of non-Christians to hold office. These lingering suspicions and prejudices notwithstanding, Jews by the early nineteenth century already were running for local and county office, even becoming prominent delegates in Democratic Party conventions. In New York, as elsewhere, Jews by the hundreds were achieving solid economic success in their mercantile and professional ventures. Moving out of their original Mill Street quasi-ghetto, constructing homes and synagogues farther north on Manhattan Island, they were becoming a respectable presence in the city.

But if the Jews no longer experienced significant economic or even political insecurities, they remained vulnerable in their demography. In their modest numbers, they still lacked critical mass. The sheer weight of the majority culture, as a result, began taking its toll. It was significant that the original, pioneering Sephardim among them already had intermarried so extensively with non-Jews that they had all but vanished from the Jewish rolls.

The Germanization of American Jewry

Between 1815 and the Civil War, however, a vast flood of German-speaking newcomers poured into the United States from Central Europe. As always, the impetus for migration of this scope was overwhelmingly economic. Agricultural enclosures and the inroads of the early Industrial Revolution impelled tens of thousands, and ultimately hundreds of thousands, of German villagers to seek a new future overseas. Their universal choice was the United States, a distant utopia that over the years had become romanticized and idealized in popular German literature. Nothing would stop the human tidal wave. German farmers and town-dwellers alike converged on their port cities by barge, horse and wagon, even by foot, and if they could not afford ocean passage, they signed on for their billets as indentured servants for American patrons.

Jews aplenty were among them. They, too, had suffered in the ruination left by the Napoleonic Wars, and by the disruption wrought by industrial change. In the post-1815 years of Metternichian reaction, moreover, they experienced the additional refinements of political and economic oppression (pp. 71–77). Thus, like their gentile neighbors, they seized eagerly upon the alternative of "golden America." Letters and guidebooks about the United States circulated extensively among them. Communal newspapers enthusiastically lauded the shining future awaiting Jews in the New World. "Why should not young Jews transfer their desires and powers to hospitable North America," editorialized Ludwig Philippson's *Allgemeine Zeitung des Judentums* in 1839, "where they can live freely alongside members of all confessions . . . [and] where they do not at least have to bear this?" The exhortation was superfluous. By then, emigration fever had grown so extensively among German Jews that, in their villages and in smaller towns, entire Jewish communities simply emptied out in the rush to Atlantic harbors.

Whether from Franconia or Bavaria, Prussia or Baden, the Jews who departed in the thousands still tended to be poorer, undereducated young males. Nevertheless, they did not anticipate a lengthy separation from their families. Once settled and solvent in the United States, they would waste little time before sending for parents, siblings, and fiancées. Thus, Joseph Seligmann, who years later in America would achieve eminence as an investment banker (p. 168), departed Bavaria in 1837 at age seventeen, and over a period of six years brought over his ten brothers and sisters and his widowed father. The pattern was typical. Jewish migration was a filial chain reaction. In 1820, some 3,400 Jews were settled in the United States; by 1840, 15,000; by 1850, 50,000.

Most of the newcomers gravitated to cities and larger towns. Thus, by 1858, the Jews of New York numbered 17,000 and comprised 30 percent of American Jewry. Philadelphia was home to 6,000 Jews; Baltimore, to 4,000. In the same antebellum decades, a new and vital Jewish nucleus was developing in the inland city of Cincinnati. It was a time when the paddle steamer functioned as the backbone of western commerce, and Cincinnati's location on a convenient bend in the Ohio River fostered the town's growth as a gateway to markets in the Midwest and South. By 1860, over 10,000 Jews lived there. They had accompanied the German migration inland, and as peripatetic merchants in the Old World, they continued to serve the retail needs of their fellow German-speakers in America. In fulfilling that role, they supplanted an earlier generation of Yankees as country peddlers by introducing the refinement of installment payments. By 1860, some 15,000 of these Jewish tradesmen roamed the American landscape.

As a rule, their lives were grudging and lonely. Typical was the experience of a twenty-three-year-old Bavarian Jew, Abraham Kohn, peddling in New England:

> On Saturday afternoon, May 20th [he wrote, working on the Jewish Sabbath], I saw a peddler pass by. "Hello, sir," I hailed him. "How are you?" It turned out to be Samuel Zirdorfer from Fürth. Alas, how the poor devil looked. Thus one man with eighty pounds on his back meets another with fifty pounds on his back some four thousand miles from their native towns. If I had known of this a year ago, how different things might be now!

Nevertheless, by hard work and thrift, the immigrant moved up to horse-and-cart "chapman," then to ownership of a tiny general store, even to wholesale distribution. Eventually, he might share in the actual manufacture of clothing. In this fashion, Cincinnati, Rochester, and Baltimore, as well as New York, became key Jewish manufacturing and distribution centers. It was not less common, during these antebellum years, for Jews to establish themselves as entrepreneurs of a range of secondary wholesale and retail establishments for clothing and other household items. In this fashion, whether on the Atlantic Seaboard or on the western frontier, German Jews in the United States were replicating their historic European stereotype as merchants.

It was not their only stereotype. Although less venomously than in Europe, the Jews in free America emerged as objects of derisive caricature, as cheap-jacks and sharpsters. In the hands of mass-market writers, the money-obsessed Jew became hardly less than a cliché in the literature of the early and mid-nineteenth century. More painful yet, Jewish businessmen tended to be disdained in Dun & Bradstreet ratings as "tricky" or "Israelite," and consequently often encountered painful obstacles in securing insurance policies or loans from banks. As always, then, they adapted, in this case organizing their own—Jewish—mutual-help networks of extended credit. Indeed, they improvised these mutual-help techniques virtually in the nick of time. By the mid-nineteenth century, a new and even larger influx of Central Europeans began to reach the United States. This time, the immigrants were reacting not simply to the convulsions of the European economy or to the failure of the 1848 political revolutions, but to significant improvements in European transportation. It was becoming a much less arduous, even a less expensive process to make one's way to the New World. Thus, between 1848 and 1860 alone, approximately 2.3 million immigrants reached the shores of the United States. Among them were some 100,000 Jews. Unmarried younger men still comprised a majority of these Jewish newcomers. But, increasingly, they were arriving as family groups, with wives and children. And for the first time, more of them came from the larger cities than from smaller towns and villages.

In still another break from their earlier immigration patterns, many of the arriving Jews joined the larger population movement inland. Although they augmented the older German communities of Cincinnati and St. Louis, new opportunities were also becoming available in the Deep South, and other locations west of the Appalachians. In the aftermath of the Mexican War, therefore, as the United States struggled to absorb the vast new expanse of western territories, Jewish young men accompanied other fortune-seekers in pushing beyond the Mississippi. Their success was extraordinary. By the time of the Civil War, and even more notably in the early postbellum years, Jews were winning security and status for themselves in the West as prospectors, businessmen, even as mayors.

The most common initial version of the frontier Jew was the familiar one of general storekeeper, innkeeper, or provisioner for army outposts. Friedrich (Fred) Salomon was all of these, establishing himself as an early Colorado tycoon, with holdings that included a general store, a brewery, a sugar-beet company, a real estate trust, and Denver's first piped-water company. Salomon also sat as a director of the First National Bank of Denver and as president of the city's Board of Trade, and eventually as the federally appointed treasurer of the Colorado Territory. The Goldwassers also were among the early merchants and prospectors of Arizona. Michael Goldwasser, the family patriarch, eldest of twenty-one children born to a Posen innkeeper (and himself the future grandfather of Senator Barry Goldwater), eventually nurtured his little general store into the principal supply center for a string of western army posts. With his earnings, Goldwasser braved the Indian wars to develop Arizona's largest department-store chain.

In California, sharing in the 1849 gold rush, a substantial minority of Jewish gold prospectors and frontier merchants became preeminent business leaders. Adolph Sutro pioneered the "Sutro Tunnel" that served the Comstock Lode, and subsequently became a successful San Francisco real estate developer. Wolff Haas laid the basis for the West Coast's largest produce company. Levi Strauss built the clothing empire that still bears his name. By the late nineteenth century, Jews of Central European origin had become senior figures in San Francisco's burgeoning economy.

THE AMERICANIZATION OF GERMAN JEWRY

In the manner of other German immigrants, the Jewish newcomers of mid-century sustained their native language for decades after their arrival. In home and shop, German was the medium of discourse. In synagogues, rabbis preached in German. Proud of their mastery of German culture, the immigrants became enthusiastic participants in German literary and musical activities. For many years, Rabbi Isaac Mayer Wise was president of the German Literary Association of Albany. Rabbi Max Lilienthal, resettled in Cincinnati after his inglorious withdrawal from the Russian Crown School project (pp. 68–69), was president of the national German-American Sangerfest, held in his city in 1870. Max Cohnheim founded New York's German-language theater, and for decades afterward Jews were among the theater's leading patrons.

It was less the immigrants' German than their Jewish identification that was equivocal. As late as 1860, numbering approximately 150,000 (triple their population of only a decade earlier), Jews still comprised only one-half of 1 percent of the American population. The majority still were bachelors. Scrabbling for a livelihood in the American hinterland, they married whomever they could. In the cities, at least half their spouses were non-Jewish, and in small towns the figure was higher yet. Although most of the immigrants still preferred to remain within their ancestral tradition, it was difficult for them to maintain the pieties of the Old World. Even Isaac Mayer Wise, a typhoon of sermonizing, publishing, and peripatetic synagogue visitation, who struggled heroically to keep the flame of Jewish identity alive (pp. 172–73), acknowledged the difficulty of the task in the New World. He recalled:

> [The] native Jews were . . . tinged with Christian thought. They read only Christian religious literature, because there was no Jewish literature. . . . They substituted God for Jesus, unity for trinity,

the future Messiah for the Messiah who had already appeared, etc. There were Episcopalian Jews in New York, Quaker Jews in Philadelphia, Huguenot Jews in Charleston, and so on, everywhere according to the prevailing sect.

In frontier America, synagogues tended to atrophy to their narrowest religious functions. Dispersed to all corners of the vast continent, Jews in their unrequited ethnic gregariousness preferred to engage in the Jewish secular and fraternal activities that spanned the limits of a single congregation, or even a single town. These were the associations that soon became central to their cultural and social life. New York's twenty-seven synagogues (in 1860) were less widely attended than the city's forty-four Jewish charitable and benevolent societies. In smaller towns, the focus of Jewish intermingling soon became that uniquely American innovation, the fraternal lodge. Thus, as far back as 1843, twelve young German-Jewish bachelors living in New York gathered in Sinzheimer's Saloon to organize their own Jewish fellowship, the B'nai B'rith (originally, the Bundes Brüder). Like its gentile prototypes, the Masons and the Odd Fellows, it proclaimed itself a mutual-aid society, but functioned more pragmatically as an instrument of conviviality and acculturation. One of its priorities was to teach Jews how to "behave" as Americans.

That "behavior" in turn could not avoid involvement in the major issues of American public life. By 1860, the most central of these manifestly was the burning question of slavery. Jewish reaction to the institution was largely shaped by the regions in which they lived. Southern Jews tended to be loyal states' righters. Some among them were slave-owners. Yet Southern Jews comprised a distinct minority of American Jewry, most of whom lived in the Northeast and Midwest. Even in these latter regions, Jews by and large were not fire-eating abolitionists. They had learned to fear populist emotions. Isaac M. Wise actually denounced the abolitionists as warmongers. But once the Civil War began, the slavery issue was immediately transcended by sectional loyalties. Some 8,600 Jews participated in military service, 6,000 of them in the Union army. In the Confederate forces, Lionel Levy served as judge advocate, Abraham Meyers as quartermaster-general, David Camden De Leon as surgeon-general. Eight Jewish generals served in the Union army. On both sides, Jewish young men enlisted in comparable proportions to non-Jews.

Notwithstanding this respectable military record, the Civil War, with its aroused nationalist passions, generated the first major upsurge of anti-Jewish prejudice in American history. The malice assumed official as well as popular expression. Congress turned down all requests to appoint Jewish chaplains to the Union army. It required President Lincoln's intervention, in 1863, to overcome congressional intransigence. As the economic pressures and frustrations of war mounted, government figures and newspapers in both the North and the South denounced Jewish businessmen as "extortionists," "counterfeiters," "blockade-runners," "gougers." In a particularly notorious episode of December 1862, General Ulysses Grant issued a directive, Order Number 11, for the expulsion of all Jews "as a class" from Tennessee, Mississippi, and Kentucky, a zone of Union military occupation. Northern carpetbaggers had descended upon this region, and in violation of government regulations were engaging in rampant cotton speculation. Jews among the speculators doubtless were identifiable by their German accents. In his exasperation, Grant indiscriminately singled out both Jewish carpetbaggers and other Jewish civilians living under military occupation. Men, women, and children alike, Jewish families were given forty-eight hours to clear out of their homes and depart the area.

Once news of Grant's Order Number 11 became known, American Jews reacted in shock and outrage, in both the North and the South. Cesar Kaskel, a Southern Jewish spokesman, urgently made his way upriver to Cincinnati to alert the renowned Isaac M. Wise. Wise in turn immediately mobilized his congressional friends in Washington, and these secured Kaskel an interview with President Lincoln. Upon learning of Grant's order, the president, much embarrassed, canceled it forthwith. But the damage was done. While numerous press editorials in North and South condemned Grant for bigotry, other Union newspapers directed their animus at the Jews themselves—for impugning the integrity of "brave General Grant." The episode left Jews in both the Union and the Confederacy much shaken. In 1868, therefore, when Grant became the Republican candidate for president, even Jewish Republicans anxiously raised the issue of Order Number 11. It could not deter Grant's election, to be sure. Yet the aftermath of the episode was ironic. On the one hand, cautioned by his political advisers, Grant as president emerged as a model of solicitude for Jewish concerns, both in the United States and abroad. On the other, the Jews had been profoundly chastened by the wartime evidence of their vulnerability. The malevolence of popular xenophobia would subside in the early postbellum era. Yet a more invidious, if more subtle, cultural and social discrimination eventually would take its place.

THE CONQUEST OF PROSPERITY

Initially, these dangers were occluded in the boom years of the Gilded Age. German Jews were forging ahead impressively in their quest for economic security. In 1889, the United States Bureau of the Census studied 18,000 Jewish families, of whom 80 percent were first- or second-generation Central Europeans. The data revealed that 50 percent of the men were merchants, 20 percent accountants, bookkeepers, or clerks, 2 percent bankers, brokers, or company officials, and 5 percent members of the liberal professions. Few peddlers remained among them. Rather, in the United States as in West-Central Europe, Jews had become solidly ensconced in the middle class. Indeed, several of them pioneered America's first department stores, and the testaments of their success were such household names as Garfinkel in Washington, Thalheimer in Little Rock, Goldsmith in Memphis, Sakowitz and Foley in Houston, Godchaux in New Orleans, Rich in Atlanta and Richmond, Cohen Brothers in Jacksonville, Kaufman in Pittsburgh, Filene in Boston, Gimbels and Saks Fifth Avenue in Philadelphia and in New York. In New York, virtually all the great retail emporia were Jewish, and included Abraham & Straus, Bloomingdale's, Lerner, and Lane Bryant. Macy's, founded by the Lazarus Straus family, became the largest department store in the world.

Whether as department-store magnates or modest retailers, however, Jews maintained their historic tradition of specializing in such nonperishable merchandise as household furnishings, tobacco, and, above all, dry goods. Again, as in Europe, the textile industry in the United States was Jewish. Clothing was Jewish. In New York, by 1880, fully 80 percent of all retail, and 90 percent of all wholesale, clothing companies were owned by Jews, a proportion largely replicated in smaller American cities and towns. It was in these postbellum years, too, that the Jews pioneered the manufacture of ready-made clothing for the retail market. The innovation was made possible by Isaac Singer's invention of the sewing machine in 1861, then by the vast mass-production requirements for uniforms in the Civil War. Thus it was that such major Jewish enterprises as Hart, Schaffner & Marx emerged, and similar firms up and down the East Coast, and as far west as Cincinnati. Between 1860 and 1880, the manufacture and distribution of ready-made clothing became a pillar of the German-Jewish immigrant economy.

The postwar boom decades accounted as well for other mighty Jewish business successes. As a newcomer in 1837, Joseph Seligman (né Seligmann) first earned his livelihood as a peddler, then as a proprietor of a general store in Lancaster, Pennsylvania. Upon accumulating a modest nest egg, he brought over his ten brothers and sisters and his widowed father (p. 162) and set about establishing branch stores throughout the West and Midwest. The enterprise flourished. But so, even more, did its credit and cash-loan services. Soon the family shifted over exclusively to investment banking. Transferring their office to New York, the Seligmans moved vigorously into the purchase and sale of Civil War bonds. Little time passed before bond-underwriting became the family specialty, and Seligman & Company became the principal bond-underwriting firm in the United States. Other Jewish investment bankers similarly were making their mark during the Civil War, among them Lehman Brothers, Goldman, Sachs & Company, Salomon Brothers, Kuhn, Loeb & Company, Jules Bach & Company, and Ladenburg, Thalmann & Company.

By the 1870s, these same companies turned increasingly from government to business underwriting, and specifically the bond issues of private American corporations. Indeed, Jewish firms in large measure provided the financing for the nation's greatest railroads. A preeminent figure in this enterprise was Jacob Schiff. German-born, Schiff as a young man was brought to the United States by a distant relative, Solomon Loeb, a partner of Kuhn, Loeb & Company. Starting in the firm as a junior executive, Schiff, upon marrying Loeb's singularly plain daughter Theresa, was duly anointed a full partner. He earned his keep. Under his astute leadership, Kuhn, Loeb & Company became the largest investment underwriter of railroads in American history. It was also the firm that underwrote Bethlehem Steel, United States Rubber, Westinghouse Electric, and AT&T. By the turn of the century, Kuhn, Loeb & Company had become Wall Street's largest Jewish investment house. And by the same token, Jacob Schiff, a classic *shtadlan*, emerged as the single most influential figure in American-Jewish communal life (p. 219).

The Gilded Age produced other mighty Jewish success stories. Adolf Lewisohn came to the United States in 1867 as the representative of his father's Hamburg-based brush company. In selling his copper-wire brushes to housewives for stove-cleaning, the young man soon grasped the manifold uses of copper wire in the developing American economy. Later young Lewisohn and his brothers purchased a small copper mine in Butte, Montana. The investment paid off spectacularly. In 1898, the Lewisohns merged their holdings with a number of Rockefeller interests to create the United Metals Selling Company, thereby controlling 55 percent of all copper produced in the United States. A comparable success was achieved by the Colorado Smelting & Refining Company, owned by M. Guggenheim & Sons. Meyer Guggenheim, son of a Swiss-Jewish tailor, arrived in the United States in 1848. Beginning as a peddler of stove polish, he earned enough to bring over his twelve brothers and sisters, then to risk a modest investment in two struggling Colorado lead and silver mines. The venture paid off, and Guggenheim and his siblings later acquired other, equally successful mines in the United States, Mexico, and Chile. At one point, the Guggenheims ranked as the third-wealthiest Jewish family in America, and one of the ten wealthiest families in the country altogether.

Joseph Pulitzer arrived from Hungary in 1864 as a seventeen-year-old. His first order of business was to enlist in the Union army, then to undergo a year of combat duty. Upon his discharge, the young man served as a reporter in St. Louis for Carl Schurz's German-language *Westliche Post*. Upon grasping the essentials of the journalistic trade, Pulitzer begged and borrowed enough money to acquire ownership of two foundering St. Louis newspapers, the *Post* and the *Dispatch*. He promptly merged the papers into the *Post-Dispatch*, expanded its news coverage and its focus on political exposés, and thereby spectacularly enlarged its circulation. With his growing fortune, Pulitzer in

1883 purchased (from Jay Gould) and rebuilt the *New York World.* Together with the *Post-Dispatch,* the *World* became renowned as a progressive, crusading journal, one of many that eventually would belong to the Pulitzer empire.

As these business tycoons thrived, they moved into palatial mansions, married off their children among one another, and in New York founded their own German-speaking Harmonie Gesellschaft, an uptown club for other German-Jewish eminences. They mingled as well with upper-class gentile society. Upon gaining a cautious acceptance into New York high society, they began to pull their weight in American culture. Young Berlin-born Oscar Hammerstein reached the United States in 1863. Employed as a cigar-maker in New York, he worked his way up to the editorship of the trade newspaper *Tobacco Journal.* Saving and investing wisely, Hammerstein then turned to his first love, opera. Without musical talent of his own, he became a brilliant impresario, pouring his savings and those of other investors into a series of theaters, most of them to become highly profitable. In 1906, Hammerstein achieved his life's ambition, the establishment of his own Manhattan Opera House, as a rival to the more staid Metropolitan Opera Company. Each enterprise then competed against the other, booking some of the great stars of the era. Indeed, the feud between the two houses, the Metropolitan, whose board chairman was the Jewish banker Otto Kahn, and the Manhattan, led by the flamboyant Hammerstein, made New York as opera-conscious as any city in the world.

Had the Jews in America "arrived," then? They were emerging not simply as financial dynasts but as social doyens and cultural icons. Some among them even became political figures. Isidore Straus, a senior member of the Macy's Department Store clan, served as a much-respected United States congressman, and was offered—but refused—the Democratic nomination for mayor of New York in 1901 (he and his wife went down on the *Titanic* in 1912). Another Straus brother, Oscar, a lawyer and expert reformer on numerous regulatory commissions, was appointed by President Grover Cleveland as minister to Constantinople in 1887 (a "safe" diplomatic billet for Jews; eventually four would hold this post). In 1905, Straus also would become the first Jew to sit in a White House cabinet, serving as Theodore Roosevelt's secretary of commerce.

But in 1877, the upward trajectory of Jewish private and public acceptance was shattered by a cause célèbre. The banker Joseph Seligman, a personal friend of former President Grant and the most prominent Jew in the United States, traveled with his wife and children to Saratoga Springs, New York, for their annual summer sojourn at the town's sumptuous Grand Union Hotel. To their disbelief, they were turned away by the hotel's management. The Grand Union was owned by the A. T. Stewart Company, a large mercantile conglomerate, and from 1876 was managed by Judge Henry Hilton. Hilton was a member of New York City's corrupt Tweed Gang, which lately had been exposed by the Committee of Seventy, a reformist civil body of which Seligman was a prominent member. Now Hilton secured his revenge by announcing that henceforth neither Seligman nor any other Jews would be accepted at the Grand Union. The episode rapidly aroused a storm of national condemnation and controversy between Jews and gentiles, liberals and conservatives.

The Grand Union Affair opened a Pandora's box. It revealed that, in the Gilded Age, a new image of the Jew was being superimposed upon the older, Civil War stereotype of economic predator. This was the image of the vulgar parvenu. Now at last gentile nouveaux riches, men of the genre of "Diamond Jim" Brady and Jim Fisk, could ascend the social scale on the backs of still another arriviste element. Moreover, the new Jewish image soon became all the vogue in the postbellum era, and not least in its popular literature. Indelicate Jewish types began peopling the novels of Beatrix Randolph and Francis Crawford, of Hall Caine and E. S. March. So did the vulgar stage caricature of the Jew, in grotesque makeup, plug hat, ungainly black coat, long beard, and large spectacles. More ominously, in the aftermath of the Grand Union Affair, there developed a vicious circle of gentile restrictionism and Jewish social ghettoization. As recently as the 1870s, Jews had believed that they were on the verge of full acceptance in the United States. Now the reality had to be faced, that a process of social congealment was under way, and that Jews were to be relegated to a palpably inferior social category. Indeed, the signs appearing outside one resort hotel after another—HEBREWS NEED NOT APPLY—testified to the fact. Town and country clubs similarly were closed off to Jews, as were chambers of commerce and athletic clubs.

For their part, the social rejectees would not fade away passively. Wealthy Jews now launched into the purchase or construction of their own vacation resorts and social clubs, often with facilities and amenities superior to those of their gentile counterparts. Still another response, however, was a vigorous new effort to develop their own alternative ethnic networks and outlets. A number of these were established, although it was B'nai B'rith that emerged as primus inter pares among them, reaching a membership of 30,000 by 1890 and developing a host of mutual benefit programs and communal and cultural activities. Young Men's Hebrew Associations also were organized, to train Jews in good citizenship and in the cultural amenities (p. 219).

THE AMERICANIZATION OF JUDAISM

It would have been useful, in these decades of challenge and transition, if the Jews had been offered authentic "spiritual" guidance for the crises of private and public life. Yet, well into the Civil War era, their synagogues encompassed a tangle of contentious ethnic liturgies, cantors, and lay "reverends." Almost imperceptibly, the patterns of Jewish worship tended to emulate those of their Protestant neighbors. A respected early preacher, Isaac Leeser of Philadelphia, worked closely with a dedicated lay volunteer, Rebecca Gratz, in adopting the Protestant model of Sunday school for Jewish children. What other choice was available? In a free and open country, second- and third-generation American Jews were rejecting Old World rites as obscurantist, or at least as irrelevant.

As far back as the 1820s, a group of acculturated Jewish professional men in Charleston, South Carolina, established a congregation, Beth Elohim, that incrementally modified the Orthodox liturgy. Although the sponsors failed to raise enough funds to keep their experiment solvent, it seemed plain that Reform was coming. The sheer amplitude of American society would tolerate change more rapidly than in Central Europe. Indeed, in 1835, Reform slipped in through the back door—again in Charleston. The city's Orthodox synagogue introduced an organ into its facilities and ritual, and no one said nay. Soon other changes included the excision of "redundant" prayers, of a separate gallery for women worshippers, of a predominantly Hebrew prayer book. Comparable modifications of both decorum and substance were adopted in other congregations, often borrowing from the Protestant model.

These innovations were given impetus by Isaac Mayer Wise, the first authentically protean figure to emerge in American-Jewish life. Born in Habsburg Bohemia in 1819, one of his schoolmaster father's heroic brood of thirteen children, young Wise attended a parochial *heder*, a series of *yeshivot*, but never managed to acquire a formal rabbinical degree before departing for the United States in 1846 with his wife and child. The family arrived in New York with two dollars to its name. Fortunately, Wise was an effective orator, and early on secured numerous itinerant preaching invitations. Mastering English with extraordinary rapidity, the "Reverend Dr. Wise" soon became a familiar presence before gentile and Jewish audiences alike. Upon being provided with his own congregation in Albany, he began systematically pioneering a number of liturgical reforms. In the process, however, it was significant that Wise no longer troubled to rely on surrounding Protestant models. By then, he was well seized of the doctrinal changes being introduced in Germany by Abraham Geiger and other reformers. These transformations struck him as even more appropriate for the United States than for the Old World. As Wise acknowledged later, "I began to Americanize with all my might and was as enthusiastic for this as I was for Reform."

Wise's reputation as a vigorous American patriot, courageous Jewish modernist, and charismatic preacher-pastor extended rapidly to other cities. In 1854, he was invited to B'nai Jeshurun, a new and well-funded pulpit in Cincinnati. "The Plum Street Temple" would continue as his base for the remaining forty-seven years of his life. From Cincinnati, Wise became a beloved fixture in American-Jewish communal affairs. He edited several widely popular German-language and English-language congregational newspapers, churned out an endless series of textbooks and religious tracts, and traveled extensively to dedicate new Reform congregations up and down the Midwest and South. A man of unflagging dynamism and tenacity, Wise also began to hurl himself into a project that would consume the rest of his adult life. It was to organize a federation of every synagogue in the United States. In that effort, Wise's vision was not specifically one of Reform, but of unity. As a minority people, he insisted, and still a vulnerable one, the Jews of America needed an "address," and a union of congregations presumably would offer that identification. It would soon become equally clear during the Civil War's upsurge of anti-Jewish xenophobia, that unity for Jews in America was hardly less than a matter of communal survival.

In 1873, therefore, with the help of his devoted midwestern followers, Wise became the impresario of a conference of lay and rabbinical leaders representing thirty-four separate congregations. It was this colloquium in turn that organized the Union of American Hebrew Congregations and also committed itself to the establishment of the New World's first rabbinical seminary. Prospects for the endeavor appeared favorable. The founding delegates had promised not to interfere in the doctrinal affairs of member congregations. Responding to this conciliatory approach, virtually all the major congregations in the East agreed to join. Indeed, by 1878, over one hundred synagogues had affiliated with the Union. Within these same five years, Wise also made impressive progress in organizing his cherished rabbinical seminary, the Hebrew Union College, in his home city of Cincinnati. In 1875, the school enrolled its first students, and in 1883 it prepared to graduate its first class. The celebration was a joyous one, graced by the presence of the mayor, local and state judges, clergymen, and other dignitaries.

Yet the euphoria of the graduation camouflaged the tensions between the remaining minority of traditionalists and the growing majority of reformers. The new breed of German immigrant rabbis were well trained, the recipients of university education. Some held doctorates. They were prepared to go much further in institutionalizing doctrinal Reform in America than Abraham Geiger had in Germany. But could this group coexist under a common Union umbrella with the traditionalists? Ironically, the answer was provided by the climactic banquet on the night of the graduation ceremony. The gentile caterer had not been alerted that a kosher meal was de rigueur for the event; his cuisine included shellfish and other distinctly nonkosher delicacies. In outrage, the traditionalist rabbis immediately left the banquet hall—and the Union of American Hebrew Congregations.

It is almost certain that the schism would have occurred with or without "the *trefe* [nonkosher] banquet." Indeed, Wise professed himself unfazed by the mass exodus of traditionalists. Now he could identify unambiguously with radical Reform, and with the nation's emergent Jewish majority. Thereafter, with his benevolent approval, the newer phalanx of secularly educated, modernist rabbis lost no time in preempting leadership of the Union of American Hebrew Congregations, and in ensuring that the organization, and the movement, came to be associated exclusively with Reform Judaism. Less than two generations after their arrival in a frontier society, the largest numbers of German Jews in the United States seemingly had redefined their collective identity far more forthrightly than had their kinsmen in the German *Vaterland* itself. That identity was one of unapologetic and triumphant acculturation.

X

False Dawn in the East: Alexander II and the Era of "Enlightenment"

LIFE IN THE PALE

Even during the grimmest years of tsarist oppression, the Jews of Eastern Europe managed to reproduce themselves at an extraordinary rate. At the opening of the nineteenth century, the Jewish population of Russia totaled approximately 1 million. Fifty years later, the number reached 3.2 million. By 1887, it approached 5.5 million. The principal area of Jewish concentration, the Pale of Settlement, comprising 362,000 square miles, encompassed 4 percent of the entire Tsarist Empire. According to the census of 1887, fully 600,000 Jews lived in former Congress Poland (p. 60), the rest were settled in Ukraine, southern Lithuania, Volhynia, and Belorussia. Nearly half of them were town- and city-dwellers, with the rest dispersed throughout the villages and hamlets of rural areas.

By mid-century, approximately 40 percent of the empire's Jews were engaged in commerce, with the rest divided between artisanry and personal service. The figure of 40 percent, however sizable by Russian standards, actually represented a much lower proportion of Jewish businessmen than in the West. But if not all Jews were merchants, nearly all merchants in the Pale were Jews. It was this vocational distention that induced tsarist governments, even the moderate government of the early Alexander II, to describe Jewish mercantile activity as "parasitism." The term was a misnomer. For most Jews of the Pale, the term "commerce" signified little more than shopkeeping and petty trade. It barely described the grocer whose store was a rickety stall by the side of a dirt road, the clothing salesman who peddled the used garments he carried on his back as he walked from door to door, the wagoner who slept in a stable with his horse, the carpenter who fed his wife and children less from the wages he earned than by the plot of soil he cultivated behind his shack, the glazier who patched up windows with wood planking and rags.

The Jews' life at mid-century remained as culturally insular as it was economically straitened. Jewish communal institutions displayed an astonishing imperviousness to change. In 1844, when Nicholas I officially abolished the kahals as organs of Jewish self-government, most of their public functions passed on, unofficially, to synagogue boards that preserved intact the full spectrum of kahal religious and philanthropic activities. As for the synagogue itself, its physical appearance gave little hint of its central role as a communal omnium-gatherum. A slate-gray wooden house, almost invariably dilapidated and often leaking, the typical *shul* was quite drab by any aesthetic standard. Within, virtually no ornamentation was evident beyond the Ark of the Torah and several flanking menorahs. In the Pale's larger communities, numerous such synagogues were maintained by separate vocational groups—butchers, tailors, carpenters, or even chimney sweeps. In the city of Vilna alone, by the end of the century, there were over one hundred such houses of worship, and these were exclusive of numerous Hasidic prayer rooms.

The diversity of synagogues was exceeded only by the bedlam of their devotional practices. The writer Isaac Baer Levinsohn (p. 180) described the chaos prevailing in a typical Volhynian shul:

> Each [synagogue] . . . abides by its own rules; there is no uniformity of service, only general disorder. This congregant demolishes what another has built; this one jumps while that one shouts; this one moans his loss while the other one complacently smokes; this man eats while that man drinks. One has just begun his prayer as another has finished it, one converses while the next one chants. . . . One aspires to the honor of being the sixth to come up to the Torah, another seeks the honor of taking the Torah out of the Ark and often they quarrel on that account. . . . Absence of decorum was the rule, and gossipers in the women's gallery above calmly ignored the strenuous entreaties of the beadle to quiet down.

Beyond its role as a house of worship and gathering place for benevolent and philanthropic societies, the synagogue was the community's principal conduit of information, as well as the social center for family and village celebrations.

Like synagogue attendance, education was universal. It was also implacably religious. At the age of four, the male child embarked upon his school career at the *heder,* the private, primary school, then continued with the *talmud torah,* the secondary school. For a talented few, the *yeshiva,* the religious seminary, was the educational capstone. The caliber of instruction in the Jewish educational system was primitive. Traditionally underpaid and irritable, the *melamed,* the primary-school instructor, demanded rote memorization rather than understanding from his students. Shmaryahu Levin, an eminent Jewish political figure of the late nineteenth and early twentieth centuries, recalled:

> Who knows how many genuine talents have been brutally done to
> death by the lash of the melamed, how many victims remained
> buried forever under the ruins of the heder? . . . I cannot stress too
> often the dominating, the exclusive role that the heder played in
> the life of the young Jewish boy. He saw his parents only for half
> an hour in the morning . . . and then for an hour in the evening . . .
> and the melamed became the lord and master of the Jewish
> child, and the heder, the narrow one-roomed school, lightless and
> unclean, laid its stamp on the Jewish child and brought ruin and
> misery on his tenderest years. . . . Only the very few chosen
> ones . . . escaped from those years of oppression more or less
> unharmed, with minds and bodies unruined.

No definite age limit marked the end of a pupil's schooling. If family circumstances permitted, a dedicated student might continue on to a yeshiva. But
even poor students attended these institutions, often supported by contributions from the general community.

Life in the Pale was not only parochial, it was insular. Until at least mid-
century, the political events and activities of official Russia were as remote to
the inhabitants of the *shtetl*, the Jewish small town, as the secrets of the Persian court. Contacts between Jews and gentiles were confined almost exclusively to intermittent business dealings. Russian life was a life of the earth, an
alien one to the Jews. "What are the [Jewish shtetl-inhabitants] shrinking
from?" asked Maurice Samuel, a renowned chronicler of Jewish life and literature. "Perhaps the loneliness and formlessness of space, perhaps the world
of the uncircumcised, perhaps the brutalizing influence of untamed nature.
They fear the bucolic. They fear, instinctively, the Man with the Hoe, not
because they live any better than he, but because his jaw hangs down." Apostasy exercised no gravitational influence whatever upon the Jews in Russia.
For them, Slavic culture appeared much too primitive to be worth the passport of conversion.

PREFIGURATIONS OF JEWISH ENLIGHTENMENT

Their evaluation of Russian intellectual potential was both harsh and premature. By the last years of the eighteenth century, a small minority of literate
and sentient Russians was being exposed to Western ideas. The contacts
widened after the Congress of Vienna, with a substantial increase of trade
between Russia and the West. Affluent merchants, government officials,
lawyers, physicians, and other Russian men of affairs were visiting Austria,
Germany, and France and returning with excited accounts of Western science, Western energy, Western political vitality. In the 1830s, the Russian

writers Alexander Pushkin, Vissarion Belinski, and Alexander Herzen braved censorship, even the threat of arrest, in their campaign for a selective acceptance of Western political and social institutions. "The destiny of Russia," wrote Belinski, "is to take into herself [only] the [best] elements of European and world civilization. . . . Of course the reception of those elements cannot be mechanical or eclectic, but must be organic and complete." Although none of these "Europeanizers" lived to share in the reconstruction of Russian society, they generated a more extensive awareness of the West, an undisguised admiration that in ensuing decades became the virtual obsession of Russian intellectual life.

It was an enthusiasm that was replicated in turn among a tightly limited minority of East European Jews. As in the case of Russia's incipient intelligentsia, the cultural horizons of these Jewish *maskilim* widened in tandem with the empire's commercial links to the West. The focus of the development actually was to be found on the borders of the Tsarist Pale, in Galicia, a Habsburg province straddling the crossroads of trade between Germany and Russia. The Galician cities of Lemberg (Lvov), Brody, and Tarnopol were heavily Jewish. By 1820, the 12,000 Jews of Brody comprised a near-totality of the local population and all but dominated its regional commerce. In common with the dense Jewish populations of Tarnopol and Lemberg, they acquired a functional acquaintance with the German, Polish, and Russian languages, and with the economic and legal vocabulary appropriate for cross-border trade. Within the Tsarist Empire, the Jews of Congress Poland (p. 60) added their own numbers to the disciples of Haskalah—of "enlightened humanism"—the maskilim who wished to place greater emphasis upon pragmatic, secular activity. So, even more extensively, did the Jews of Odessa. During the 1820s and 1830s, limited numbers of Jewish businessmen of the "first estate" were allowed to move to this dynamic Black Sea port, and thereby to share in Odessa's burgeoning economy and exposure to foreign visitors and ideas.

These were circumstances in which a vibrant nucleus of early-nineteenth-century Jewish enlightenment was to be found among Galician, Warsavian, or Odessan merchant families. Thus, Solomon Rapoport (p. 180), one of the earliest of the maskilim, was the son of an affluent tax assessor of Lvov, and was himself employed for many years as manager of an association of meat-tax "farmers"—officials who purchased from the government (at a discount) the right to collect taxes. Joseph Perl, another early maskil, was the son of a meat-tax farmer of Tarnopol. Nahman Krohmal was a distillery-tax farmer in Zolkiew. Altogether, the obsession with secular education that evolved into the very talisman of Haskalah first emerged from the requirements and circumstances of the merchant class. Businessmen with connections in Leipzig, Berlin, or Vienna, or even with government authorities in Galicia or Odessa, could not function without a mastery of German or Russian, and without at least a rudimentary understanding of geography and politics. It was this middle-class orientation that animated the social philosophy of the early maskilim. In exhorting their fellow Jews to "productivize" themselves, the emerging Jewish bourgeoisie grasped that the impoverished peddlers and hawkers of the Pale hindered the natural growth of an internal Jewish economy—and, by extension, of a productive interaction with the economies and societies of West-Central Europe.

Jewish Enlightenment: Scholarship, Prose, and Poetry

It was significant, however, that the beginnings of Haskalah in Habsburg Galicia, and among the affluent businessmen of Odessa, St. Petersburg, and later of Moscow, did not take the form of Russification. Here lay a crucial distinction between Jewish enlightenment in Eastern and in Western Europe. By Jewish estimation, Russian culture in the early nineteenth century appeared too embryonic to be worth emulating. If anything, the early maskilim tended to be admirers of Germany. Yet, here too their admiration was discriminating, and limited mainly to German dress, decorum, and technical efficiency. Like the Russian "Westernizers" (pp. 177–78), the Jewish maskilim of Eastern Europe never for a moment contemplated enlightening themselves "spiritually" or emotionally. In contrast to the emancipation-obsessed Jews of Germany, whose acculturationist agenda was heavily influenced by the political goal of full citizenship, the early Russian-Jewish maskilim sought to create the modern Jew, not simply the modern Jewish Russian. Respectful of Jewish tradition, they were uninterested in tampering with the ancestral religion, only with the Pale's obscurantist folk mores.

It was moreover their reverence for Jewish civilization that largely accounted for the choice of Hebrew as the initial language of the East European Haskalah. Largely, but not entirely, for reliance upon Hebrew was yet another way in which bourgeois modernists distinguished themselves from the Yiddish-speaking masses. Thus, Joseph Perl, a Galician Jew, devoted much of his Hebrew almanac, *The Wisdom of the Rabbis (T'vunat HaRabbanim)*, to the praise of enlightened monarchs, who were much to be preferred over "ignorant mobs." More fundamentally yet, Hebrew was the language of the Bible and Jewish history. Its revived use now as a contemporary medium signified that the humanists intended to remain within the mainstream of Jewish life. As the Lithuanian maskil Abraham Baer Levinsohn wrote in 1832: "[Hebrew] forms a bond of religion and national survival, and provides the global axis along which all Jews dispersed among peoples and languages are linked. . . . Ought not one be ashamed to call himself a maskil while remaining ignorant of the Hebrew tongue?"

Given this unwavering commitment to Jewish civilization, it was understandable that one of the earliest applications of secular, contemporary Hebrew should have been an East European version of *jüdische Wissenschaft,* the Science of Judaism (p. 132). The Galician-born Solomon Rapoport, who pioneered in the genre, not only earned a comfortable livelihood as manager of a tax-farming corporation, but married into still additional wealth, thereby enjoying the opportunity afterward to devote himself exclusively to scholarship. Like most early Jewish humanists, Rapoport remained an Orthodox religionist, and even underwent ordination as a rabbi. But the discipline of "objective" scholarship was as central to his research as it was to his Western Jewish counterparts. The first fruit of his labors, appearing in 1827, was an impressively "scientific" biography of Rashi, the renowned medieval Talmudic commentator, and it was followed by other historical monographs of comparable scholarly acumen.

In turn, Rapoport's effort to create an "eastern" Science of Judaism (p. 132) was enhanced by Nahman Krohmal, his contemporary and fellow Galician. Krohmal was not a prolific writer. Most of his scholarly career was spent in the preparation of a single magnum opus, *The Guide of the Perplexed of Our Time (Moreh Nevuhei HaZman).* Yet, upon its (posthumous) appearance in 1851, the work exerted a decisive impact on Jewish scholarship. In the manner of the German Idealists, Krochmal sought to interpret the defining "spirit" of Jewish civilization. With massive erudition, he identified that "spirit" with the Jewish people, rather than with the Jewish religion, and thereby helped lay the groundwork for the secular-nationalist interpretation of Jewish history that decades later would become the cultural impulsion for Zionism.

The yardstick of enlightenment was applied in its most pragmatic effect, however, less to scholarship than to polemics, and much earlier. Repeatedly, the Jews of Habsburg Galicia entreated their kinsmen in Tsarist Russia to expose themselves to European literature, to natural sciences, to vocational training. Outside the heder and market stall, they argued, the world in all its glories awaited the Jew, if only he would educate himself to appreciate it. The maskilim pressed their case most vigorously in tracts and essays. Like the philosophes of the eighteenth-century Enlightenment, Joseph Perl and his fellow Galician Isaac Erter frequently resorted to the contrivance of "dreams" or "visions" or "foreign visitors" to expose the Pale's shortcomings. Thus, in Erter's *Transmigration of the Soul (Gilgul HaNefesh),* parody was the technique by which a Talmudic scholar reappears as a helpless, wriggling mackerel; a cantor, endowed with every musical talent except a decent voice, assumes the shape of a hound, baying endlessly at the moon. Other East European caricatures were portrayed with comparable astringency.

It was thus by the 1820s and 1830s that Jewish enlightenment began to strike root in the Russian Pale itself. Isaac Baer Levinsohn (no relation to

Abraham), son of a wealthy mercantile family of Volhynia, was a polymath who had served as official translator (in Yiddish, Polish, and French) for the Russian army during the Napoleonic Wars. Settling in Galicia during the 1820s, Levinsohn joined Erter, Perl, and several other maskilim in the enlightenment campaign. His most influential work, published in 1823, *Testimony in Israel (T'udah b'Yisrael),* was unprecedented in the resonance it evoked throughout the length and breadth of the Russian Pale. In retrospect, the volume's astonishing popularity may have lain not only in the eloquence of its appeal for a wider and more eclectic learning, but in the prestige of its sponsorship. The tsarist government itself—the government of Nicholas I!—contributed 1,000 rubles for the book's publication, and Levinsohn accordingly projected the aura both of a Hebrew sage and of an imperial emissary. In a characteristic reaction, Matthias Strashun, a Jew of the Pale, wrote Levinsohn in 1834:

> From the day your book appeared, I read it from beginning to end, and could not put it down. I read it twice and thrice and could not have my fill; I wished that I were a dove, that I could fly to you, to be with you and embrace you, to be your dutiful servant forever. . . . Your book alone made me into a man.

Like Strashun, thousands of young Jews found a soul mate in Levinsohn.

Altogether, throughout the cities and towns of the Pale, aspiring young maskilim gathered in discussion groups to seek ways of generating a new cultural revolution. In Vilna, Abraham Baer Levinsohn defended the cause of enlightenment in an epic poem that joined scholarly exposition with penetrating satire. Entitled *Truth and Faith (Emet v'Emunah),* Levinsohn's work offered a Goethian-style allegory of the battle between knowledge and ignorance. The protagonists were listed variously as "Wisdom," "Truth," "Reason," and their counterparts "Ignorance," "Superstition," "Provincialism." In Berditchev, a Jewish physician named Rottenberg announced that he was forming a Society of Seekers After Enlightenment, which would unite all kindred souls in Russia in the cause of Haskalah.

In the 1840s and 1850s, moreover, polemics were fortified by pageantry, as Jewish humanism broadened its scope to portray the tactile grandeurs ostensibly awaiting beyond the Pale. The time was propitious for this new dimension. The reign of Nicholas I, for all its political ultraconservatism, also encompassed the zenith years of Russian literary romanticism. The language itself, which Pushkin and his admirers had substantially purged of its ancient Slavonic encumbrances, became in the hands of Lermontov and Gogol an instrument well attuned to the richness of nature, beauty, and emotion. The palette of aesthetic delights exerted its impact on mid-century Jewish literature. For the Jewish reading public, even more than for the Russian middle classes, romanticism offered escape from the sheer bleakness of life under the tsar. Thus, in 1848, when a Vilna maskil, Kalman Shulman, translated Eugene Sue's exotic *Mystères de Paris* into Hebrew, the book ran through nine printings. Shallow period piece though it was, the novel plainly answered the readers' yearning for an outgoing life of color and action.

Other Jewish humanists responded swiftly to this cultural nostalgia. Nature, beauty, love, action—all now were revisited by the translators, novelists, and poets of the Haskalah. Must Jewish life forever be identified with the squalid shtetl? these writers asked. Micah Joseph Levinsohn, the talented son of Abraham Baer, provided his own answer:

> *Once in a verdant tree, there was my home.*
> *Torn from a swaying branch, friendless I roam.*
> *Plucked from the joyous green that gave me birth,*
> *What is my life to me, and of what worth?*

For the Jews, there were historic glories to be revived, life "in a verdant tree," the robust agricultural life of ancient Israel, the exotic multicultural world of the Spanish Golden Age. These eras were now to be exhumed, reconstructed, and poignantly idealized in the poems and novels of Levinsohn and "Michaele" Shulman, and above all in the lush historical romances of Abraham Mapu.

Reared in the poverty of Slobodka, Lithuania, Mapu was educated in the region's characteristically Orthodox tradition. Possibly he would have become a rabbi if his first tutorial assignment, as a young man, had not brought him to the home of a Jewish farmer. Communion with nature was a revelation. "I was raised to live in the atmosphere of the dead," Mapu recalled, "and here I am cast among people who led a real life, in which I am unable to take part." Yet if Mapu was barred by physique and economic circumstances from life on the soil, he could re-create, even reinvent, that life and apotheosize it as literature. It was consequently in 1853 that he published a historical romance, *The Love of Zion (Ahavat Zion)*, a florid melodrama dealing with the wars and loves of King Ahab of ancient Israel. Although contrived and implausible, the book offered a thrilling release, particularly to younger Jewish readers, many of whom hid the novel inside the pages of their Talmud texts. It opened the world of action to them, of romance, even of violence. Later, as Abraham Baer Gottlober of Odessa wove the thread of this romanticism into an ongoing series of novels, poems, and histories, the reservoir of Haskalah-oriented readers increased even more decisively.

As it happened, the emphasis upon secular humanism gained its momentum in the very years that the tsarist government was instituting major political and economic changes throughout the empire. The transformations would not leave the culture of the Pale untouched.

THE ACCESSION OF THE "TSAR-LIBERATOR"

In 1855, in the midst of the Crimean War, Nicholas the Barracks Master died, and the prestige of his regime died with him. Through governmental ineptitude and corruption, Russia had suffered shattering defeats in the war. The tsar's very raison d'être, military efficiency, had been proved worthless. Among the literate upper middle class, revulsion against the sterile apparatus of oppression at last was voiced openly.

Nicholas's successor was listening. Ascending the imperial throne at the age of thirty-seven, Alexander II assured his people in an opening manifesto that he intended to initiate major domestic reforms. It was his intention, he declared, to provide "education, equal justice, tolerance, and humaneness" for every citizen of Russia. The very words—"equal justice, tolerance, humaneness"—had not been part of the tsarist vernacular for decades. Their use now seemed to betoken monumental improvements in the public welfare. The edicts, too, with which Alexander opened his reign appeared to validate their hopes. At his orders, the censorship was relaxed, together with restrictions on foreign travel. The inquisitorial Third Department of the Royal Chancery was stripped of much of its former power. Universities were opened to students drawn from all economic groups.

In 1861, Alexander turned his attention to Russia's 47 million serfs, whose fettered status represented the single most glaring anachronism of his realm. Humanitarian issues aside, the tsar recognized that personal bondage simply could not meet the empire's economic requirements. In the competition for international markets, the deficiencies of a labor source that functioned sluggishly and grudgingly, without hope of personal reward, had become painfully apparent. In March 1861, therefore, Alexander signed the emancipation manifesto. The measure doubtless was seriously flawed. It transformed the peasantry into hardly more than landless sharecroppers. Nevertheless, the imprimatur of their personal freedom became a landmark in Russian history. So, too, did other reforms. At Alexander's orders, a kind of town hall version of popular representation was introduced in the form of *zemstvos*, local assemblies. All Russian citizens were now proclaimed equal before the law, and the judiciary was transformed into an independent branch of government, with its court trials opened to the public. Finally, in 1874, Tsar Alexander reduced the obligation of military service from twenty-five to six years, and to an even shorter period for gymnasium and university students. If these innovations alone could not purge Russia of its economic backwardness and social inequities, at least they created far-reaching expectations.

No people sustained higher hopes for the future than did the 3.25 million Jews of the Pale. Sensing in the new tsar a modern-day Cyrus, they waited breathlessly for the chains of Babylon to be struck off. Their expectations were overdrawn. In 1855, when Minister of the Interior Sergei Lanskoi proposed that the Pale of Settlement be abolished as a first step toward "amalgamating" the Jews, the tsar demurred. He entirely shared the prevailing evaluation of Jews as monopolists of trade, and expected them to "earn" their civil rights through "moral improvement." Nevertheless, as early as 1858, Alexander allowed it to be known that his government welcomed a public debate "which may assist [it] to attain the goal of bringing the Jewish people closer to the other inhabitants of the Empire." In ensuing years, the Jewish question tended at last to become a more frequent subject for popular discussion—more than a century after the same issue had been addressed in the West. Government officials, university scholars, journalists, and private citizens of all backgrounds engaged in increasingly open discussions of Jewish economic and cultural behavior.

Altogether, public opinion in Russia was acquiring a new weight in the evaluation of major public issues. In the case of the Jews, liberal opinion similarly prefigured official reform. By mid-century, after all, the typical educated Russian now counted Western humanism as an integral feature of his own heritage, and an apparent consequence of this development was a more balanced image of the Jew. In 1858, an editorial in the *Russki Invalid* could proclaim:

> Let us be worthy of our age. Let us abandon the childish habit of presenting the Jews in our literary works as ludicrous and ignominious creatures. On the contrary, remembering the causes that brought them to such a state ... [let] us offer them a place among us, let us use their energy, readiness of wit, and skill as a new means for satisfying the growing needs of our people.

The provincial attorney of Belorussia, I. N. Kozakowski, begged the tsar to remove "the disabilities imposed on the Jews; to organize commercial and trade schools for them; and [the] ... people which currently is regarded as the scourge of the ... Western provinces will be transformed into arteries, carrying life-giving sap into all parts of the Empire."

Thus, whatever his distrust of the Jews, the tsar recognized that his inner circle favored some improvement in their status. While he remained unwilling to abolish the Pale altogether, as Sergei Lanskoi had proposed, he reacted favorably to a committee report of 1856, suggesting that a more "enlightened" approach was needed. In adopting that new flexibility, moreover, Alexander gave his initial attention to the single most notorious relic of his late father's Jewish policy. This was the "preliminary" six-year term of military cantonment decreed for Jewish conscripts. In 1856, the new tsar issued a ukase, abolishing the cantonment program. The reaction of Russian Jewry may be imagined. Throughout the Pale, thanksgiving services were conducted in synagogues packed to overflowing. Nor was the spigot of benedictions closed. In 1858, the frontiers of the Pale were readjusted, allowing Jews to live and work closer to the Austrian and Prussian frontier zones. Possibly most significantly of all, the tsar's national reforms no longer were tarnished by the hoary formula "Krome Evreiev"—"except the Jews." All Jews possessing the necessary agricultural or mercantile qualifications were granted "active" or "passive" suffrage within the new scheme of zemstvo self-government. New judicial regulations of 1864 similarly eliminated the traditional anti-Jewish discriminations; and, within a few years, a number of Jewish lawyers attained prominence as members of the Russian bar.

Nicholas I had penalized "useless" categories of Jews by heaping restrictions on them. But in his single most important "Jewish" innovation, Alexander II reversed the process by offering rewards to Jews in the more "useful" categories. A government decree permitted larger numbers of Jewish businessmen of the "first estate," together with skilled Jewish artisans, Jewish university graduates, and discharged Jewish veterans, to move into the Russian interior. It was the tsar's expectation that Jewish capitalists would be attracted to Russian industrial ventures; that Jewish artisans would provide useful services for Russia's backward rural population; that educated Jews might invigorate Russia's liberal professions.

In considerable measure, Alexander's expectations were fulfilled. During the 1860s and 1870s, new Jewish communities sprang up both within and beyond the Pale, consisting largely of wholesale merchants and incipient industrialists, of academicians and artisans. Several of their figures eventually made precisely the sort of contribution to the Russian economy that Alexander had envisaged. Thus, among a handful of important investment financiers was the Günzburg family, led first by Joseph Günzburg, who in 1859 founded a bank in St. Petersburg carrying his name; then by Joseph's son Horace, whom the archduke of Hesse-Darmstadt entitled a baron in 1871. As in Western Europe, it was the capital and initiative of Jewish financiers—the Poliakovs, Kronenbergs, Nathansons, Efroses, and Rafaloviches—that as late as the 1880s accounted for the construction of fully three-fourths of the (still rudimentary) Russian railroad system.

Few of these men could be compared to the Rothschilds, the Bleichröders, the Hirsches, the Pereiras, or other financial giants of West-Central Europe. Yet they shared a key similarity. They became their people's most committed advocates of pragmatic acculturation. Were they not themselves living examples of the blessings of modernization? Free to live wherever they wished, they spoke, wrote, and did business in Russian, sent their children almost exclusively to Russian schools, to Russian gymnasia and universities. As the new aristocrats of Russian-Jewish life, they regarded it appropriate that their fellow Jews should similarly "Russify" themselves, and in this fashion win commensurate privileges from the government. Many did. In 1872, when Moses Montefiore returned to St. Petersburg, he was astonished to discover in the capital a Jewish community that had evolved dramatically from the parochial shtetl population he remembered from his 1846 visit.

> I conversed [Montefiore noted in his diary] with Jewish merchants, literary men, editors of Russian periodicals, artisans and persons who had formerly served in the imperial army, all of whom alluded to their present position in the most satisfactory terms. All blessed the Tsar, and words seemed wanting in which adequately to praise his benevolent character. The Jews now dress like ordinary gentlemen in England, France, or Germany. Their schools are well attended, and they are foremost in every honourable enterprise destined to promote the prosperity of their community and the country at large.

In the 1860s, government figures appeared increasingly at celebrations in Jewish schools, at Jewish public banquets and weddings, even at occasional bar mitzvah ceremonies. For their part, Jews intermittently (although still rarely) were admitted into Russian social circles and Russian clubs. The ecstatic outburst with which a Jew of Kovno announced his election to the local "Nobility Club" might have been lifted directly from the memoirs of the Mendelssohnian Enlightenment: "What happened? . . . What miracles! . . . They elected me not in spite of my being a Jew but because of it, so that I might serve as an instrument for the expression of their highest ideals." "Soon, soon," rhapsodized Lev Levanda, a prominent maskil, "perhaps the door of our little hut will also open and we will rush forth to the great celebration of our good mother Russia." Sarin, the protagonist of Levanda's 1875 novel, *Fervent Days (Goryacheye Vremya)*, could declare: "My heart tells me that in time the Russians will come to us. We will make them love us. How? By our own love."

THE AGE OF REFORMS

So it was, in the vast template shift of Alexander II's reign, that Jews and Russians alike resonated to new opportunities. In the heady atmosphere of social and economic improvements, Russian writers abandoned their former predilection for romantic extravaganzas. *"Chto delat?"*—"What is to be done?"—asked Nicolas Chernyshevski. The question penetrated to the very roots of Russian society. The time for action had arrived. Chernyshevski and Dmitri Pisarev, who called themselves "positivists," after their hero Auguste Comte, exhorted their readers to devote themselves henceforth to immediate "practical" reforms, based on the calibrated methodology of the natural sciences. Useful, "positive" knowledge was the key, nothing else. "Mere" aesthetics was to be regarded as an unaffordable luxury.

By the same token, Jewish humanists also began to veer off on the new trend. Who knew how much longer the golden opportunity for practical improvement would continue? Was it not a wasteful luxury to labor away at some point of medieval history, or to reconstruct the glories of ancient Israel? Steps must be taken without delay for practical social and economic improvements. It was in this "positivist" climate of the 1850s and 1860s, therefore, that Jewish humanists set about producing a series of Hebrew-language journals, scientific essays, and pedagogical manuals devoted unreservedly to educational and vocational reform.

It was then, too, that the original Crown schools of Nicholas I's regime played a crucial, if belated, role. Sergei Uvarov's famed experiment had appeared in jeopardy following Max Lilienthal's precipitous departure for the United States in 1845. But requiems for the venture were premature. By 1855, seventy-one Crown schools were operating in the Pale, with an enrollment of some 3,500 students (pp. 69–70). Their curriculum adhered initially to the ministry of education's 1844 guidelines, by offering a balance of secular and Jewish subjects. From 1848 on, however, once Uvarov himself had been relieved of his ministerial portfolio (for reasons of his putative "liberalism"), the Crown schools' orientation became increasingly "practical" and secular. Training students for science and industry, their curriculum began to scale down Jewish subjects. Ironically, the shift evoked few objections from Jewish students or parents. The Crown program's inducements were not only educational, after all. By attending these institutions, young Jews avoided military conscription.

Then, within the first decade of his rule, Tsar Alexander II supplemented the Crown schools—and eventually doomed them—by opening the Russian state school system to Jewish students. Hereupon, responding with almost ferocious alacrity, young Jews clamored in their growing thousands for admission. For them, the inducements of a Russian education actually were more compelling than access to Crown schools. By a law of 1861, graduates of state schools, Jews and non-Jews alike, would be eligible for state employment, as well as for wider commercial and professional careers within the Russian interior. The law was hardly less than a revolution. Perhaps more than any single feature of the new tsarist legislation, it suggested the imminence of full and complete Jewish equality.

The hope seemed legitimate. The Jews were by no means an exclusively Yiddish-speaking community any longer. From the 1840s on, a growing minority among them spoke Russian as their daily vernacular; and by 1887, the official Russian census suggested that 50 percent of Jewish males read and spoke Russian as their principal language. Education both reflected and fueled this acculturation. In 1843, a mere 159 Jews were enrolled in Russian gymnasia. The number rose to 442 in 1863, then to 2,045 in 1870, then to 7,004 in 1880—12 percent of the entire secondary-school enrollment in Russia. In 1861, moreover, only 12 Jews were attending Russian institutions of higher learning. By 1876, their numbers had increased to 300, and eventually settled at about 2,000 by the 1880s, a figure that represented approximately 15 percent of the empire's entire university student population. In 1886, some 40 percent of the law and medical students at the University of Kharkov and at Odessa's New Russia University were Jews. Here, at last, was positivism in action. Here was the Haskalah vision of acculturation seemingly at the threshold of its climactic fulfillment.

An Apogee of Jewish Humanism

The preeminent spokesmen for this "positivist" phase of Jewish humanism were Judah Leib Gordon and Moses Leib Lilienblum. The Vilna-born Gordon was a classical product of the Crown school nucleus. Indeed, from 1857 to 1871 he earned his own livelihood as a Crown school teacher. They were not easy years. Beyond providing for his own wife and children, Gordon supported his mother and three younger siblings, and his remuneration as a teacher was barely enough to keep food on the table. In 1859, he was victimized in a case of mistaken identity and imprisoned for two years as a political conspirator. Nevertheless, transcending these vicissitudes, Gordon emerged as a paladin of Haskalah, and as an inexhaustible fount of Hebrew poetry and prose. In his earlier career, he had expressed himself essentially as a romantic, giving over his best literary efforts to biblical epics of the Mapu genre, to fables centered about the lives of King David and King Solomon, to lyric poetry on pastoral themes. But these initial efforts proved only intermittently successful. The Jewish reading public was becoming jaded by lush romances.

Gordon was duly chastened. From the 1860s on, his poetry and essays became exclusively "positivist" in their assault on the shortcomings of contemporary Jewish life. It was in the 1860s and 1870s, too, as he functioned simultaneously as Hebrew littérateur, Russian-Jewish journalist, and school-teacher in the service of the Crown schools and enlightenment, that Gordon's condemnation of Jewish insularity, his appeal for Jews to break free, to master

Russian and other European languages, approached a white heat of eloquence. His passion was best expressed in his "Awake, My People" ("Hakizah Ami"). Published in 1863, the ballad became the most widely celebrated positivist work of Hebrew literature ever produced in nineteenth-century Russia:

> *Awake, my people! How long will you slumber?*
> *The night has passed, the sunlight is dawning.*
> *Awake, cast your gaze near and far,*
> *Recognize your moment and your opportunity. . . .*
>
> *This paradise is now open to you,*
> *Its sons now call you "brothers."*
> *How long will you dwell among them as a stranger?*
> *Why do you spurn their friendship?*
>
> *So lift your head high, stand upright,*
> *Regard them now with love.*
> *Open your hearts to knowledge and reason.*
> *Become an enlightened people, speaking the [Russian] tongue.*
>
> *To the welfare of the state bring your own contribution,*
> *Bear your share of its wealth and opportunity.*
> *Be a man in the streets and a Jew at home,*
> *A brother to your countrymen and a servant to your ruler.*

"Be a man in the streets and a Jew at home"—no credo could have been more archetypical of the Haskalah at its apogee. Gordon's scorn for the caftaned Hasidim, the skull-capped pietists about him, was explicit and undisguised. It was intended, also, as an open challenge even to the earlier Haskalah vision of a specifically Jewish version of enlightenment; for it suggested, in the Western fashion, that his people's legitimate model was not the modern Russian Jew but the modern Jewish Russian.

Gordon's contemporary and fellow Lithuanian Moses Leib Lilienblum took an equally uncompromising position. As a child, Lilienblum had been apprenticed to an obscurantist and tyrannical melamed. Later, his parents married him off at the age of thirteen. Although desperate to escape the parochialist world that had ruined his youth, Lilienblum was obliged for years to earn his bread within its confines as an instructor of Talmud in the drab Lithuanian town of Wilkomir. The tensions of that near-schizophrenic existence gravely undermined his health. It also drove him to near-starvation, for his articles in the Haskalah journal *HaMelitz* went so far as to urge major reforms in Talmudic law. The response of Wilkomir's Jewish elders was to hound Lilienblum from the town. Ill and penniless, he moved on to Odessa in 1869, where he managed barely to support his family as a bookkeeper.

But it was also in Odessa, in the vortex of southern Haskalah, that Lilienblum finally could express himself as he wished. The opportunity was not neglected. During the 1860s and 1870s, he became a river of publishing creativity, appealing with unremitting passion for a social revolt against the "suffocation" of pietistic dogmatism.

> At a time [he wrote] when all thinking elements in Russia are aroused by the new ideas of Chernyshevski and Pisarev, which offer a solution to the great problem of universal happiness, our [Jewish] men of letters make a big noise about some comment on a biblical text, and pore over ancient times whose ideas are as dried up as withered leaves.

Lilienblum's commentary, if harsh, was solidly grounded in a vision of enlightenment that appeared on the threshold of cultural triumph.

Indeed, by then, the leaders of Jewish humanism no longer were voices in the wilderness. Tens of thousands of Russian Jews had become well acquainted with secular ideas and values. These were the halcyon days of Alexander II's quasi-emancipation, when a significant Jewish nucleus was beginning to make its way into Russian economic and even social life. Now, at last, the disciples of Haskalah were prepared to take seriously Gordon's injunction to "be a man in the streets and a Jew at home."

Peretz Smolenskin: The Pendulum Swings Back

The lucid, intelligible realism that became the crowning glory of modern literature awaited its pioneers in Russia until the mid- and late nineteenth century. But their appearance, if belated, was epochal. None in the West could surpass, and few could match, the capacity of giants like Tolstoy, Dostoevsky, Turgenev, or Chekhov to produce narratives and protagonists brimming with the authentic sap of life. It was during this cultural sunburst, moreover, that the literary course charted by others became a paradigm again for Jewish writers. While their numbers were hardly negligible, throughout the second half of the nineteenth century only one achieved a mastery of Hebrew prose that brooked no comparison among his fellow maskilim. It was the literary career of Peretz Smolenskin that represented both the apotheosis and the transfiguration of Jewish humanism.

He was born in Mogilev, Belorussia, in 1840, and his youth was the characteristic trauma of the Pale's sensitive spirits: a pietistic ghetto education, a brother dragged off to oblivion by army conscription agents, a wretched, poverty-stricken existence of Hebrew-teaching, and finally escape—in Smolenskin's case by freight car to Odessa, and from Odessa, in 1868, to Vienna. It was in Vienna, finally, that Smolenskin realized his long-cherished dream of founding a Hebrew-language literary monthly, *HaShahar.* For twelve years, he served as the journal's editor and principal contributor. In its columns appeared the installments of his six novels, works that in their cumulative impact during the late 1860s and 1870s laid the foundations of literary realism in the Hebrew language.

In the manner of his predecessors, Smolenskin in his novels ground the secularist ax of humanism. Although the books' plot structures often were uneven, their character portrayals were clinically accurate. Thus, under Smolenskin's pen, the maskilim among his protagonists are often revealed as opportunistic careerists; even as his pietists, far from emerging as one-dimensional fanatics, are portrayed with sensitivity, even compassion. Indeed, it was the author's deeply embedded reverence for the Jewish people in all their strengths and weaknesses that thrust him into the onrushing path of polemical enlightenment. In the manner of the Russian Slavophiles, disenchanted with the "false blandishments" of the West, Smolenskin was among the first to sense that Haskalah extremism might lead not simply to modernization, or even to Russification, but to the abandonment of Jewish loyalties altogether. He stated the warning plainspokenly in his most renowned essay, "Eternal People" ("Am Olam"):

> The willfully blind bid us to be like all other nations, and I repeat after them: let us be like all the other nations, pursuing and attaining knowledge, leaving off from wickedness and folly, and dwelling as loyal citizens in the lands whither we have been scattered. Yes, let us be like other nations, unashamed of the rock whence we have been hewn, like the rest holding dear our language and the glory of our people.

It is pointless to speculate whether Smolenskin alone could have blocked the momentum of a possibly indiscriminate Russification. In the 1870s, Tsar Alexander II, retreating from his earlier progressivist agenda, dampened hopes for an "amalgamation" of the Russian and Jewish peoples (pp. 184–85). Even as Smolenskin published his historic "Am Olam," in 1872, the Pale was giving closer heed to his trenchant defense of Jewish nationalism. The post-Mendelssohnian ideal of Judaism as a religious confession was bankrupt, Smolenskin insisted. So, too, was Judah Leib Gordon's conception of the duality of the Jew—"in the streets" and "in the home." Rather, the time had come to gird for the moral, even the political resurrection of the Jewish people as a national entity. In the last decade of his life, Smolenskin devoted several moving articles to this innovative theme, although he died before he could develop it.

Even before his passing, in 1885, others began to take up his cause. In 1880, Judah Leib Gordon, the preeminent exponent of cultural Russification, asked in one of his last poems, "For Whom Do I Toil?" ("L'Mi Ani Amel?"): "For whom have I toiled all my best years, denying myself contentment and peace?. . . . My fellow maskilim, possessed of 'true' knowledge, once loosely attached to the idiom of their people, now all but scorn the faithful old mother tongue." Isaac Erter (p. 180), also in the twilight of his life, joined Gordon in skewering the crude opportunism of self-proclaimed enlightened Jews, those who "cast off the folly of their own people in order to indulge in the folly of the gentiles." Yet if Haskalah had swung nearly full circle, from enlightened humanism to "amalgamation" and back to ethnic reaffirmation, one of its ideals proved enduring, and ultimately decisive, in Jewish history. This was the vision of economic and cultural activism, the categorical rejection of Pale fatalism and passivity. In the end, it was that vision above all others that would animate the political and migratory transformations shortly to sweep through the full breadth of the Russian-Jewish world.

*Russian Twilight: The Era of Pogroms
and May Laws*

The Realities of Jewish Life under Alexander II

Notwithstanding its imperfections and inequities, the "tsar-liberator's" emancipation of the serfs proved over the longer term to be a major stimulus to the empire's economy. Invigorated by improved labor productivity, Russian agricultural production expanded almost without interruption. With the help of foreign investments and state protection, a series of industrial enterprises in coal, steel, oil, and food-processing soon gained momentum. It was in the shorter term, however, that Tsar Alexander's liberation of the serfs, and their transformation into heavily indebted sharecroppers, produced cruel social displacements. The exodus to the cities of hundreds of thousands of these redundant peasants seriously exacerbated urban congestion, urban unemployment, and eventually social unrest.

The Jews, too, experienced the mixed consequences of accelerating economic change. Their population growth had been impressive over the decades, swelling from 3.2 million to 5.5 million between 1855 and 1887 (p. 175). But if their natural increase was impressive, and if enclaves of Jewish bourgeoisie increasingly were making their appearance in Russian cities and towns, the human circumstances for the Jewish majority by and large registered only modest improvements. In the best of times, Jews had functioned as small retailers, tavern-keepers, and artisans. Then, with the introduction of larger-scale industry and the influx into the cities of a huge, pauperized mass of former Russian farm workers, the traditional Jewish vocations of petty trade and cottage industry came under threat. As early as the 1860s, the impact of these changes on Jewish living conditions was becoming evident, particularly in the undernourished Lithuanian and Belorussian regions. In his survey of the province of Grodno, a government statistician recorded that "the bulk of the Jews there are poor. . . . [I]t is not uncommon for a three- or four-room dwelling to house as many as twelve families. . . . In most cases a pound of bread, a herring, and a few radishes comprise the fare of an entire family." Both in Grodno and in Belorussia, Jewish philanthropies were obliged to assume the tax indebtedness of nearly half the Jewish population.

Was this trauma an inevitable consequence of the economic transformations that affected the entirety of the Tsarist Empire? The evidence suggests that it was not, that the Jews' plight was the consequence specifically of their quarantined status in the Pale of Settlement. Wherever they were permitted to live outside the squalor and congestion of the Pale, they achieved a more widely diffused access to the Russian economy. Indeed, their contribution to that economy was significant. Some Jews of the "first estate"—possessing a comfortable income—became major financiers, railroad builders, industrialists, importer-exporters (pp. 185–86). Over the years, it was this affluent elite that persistently entreated the government to open the Russian interior still wider to the impoverished Jewish masses, to the Jews who were most urgently in need of breathing room. But even under the "tsar-liberator," the government's approach to the pressure cooker of the Pale remained cautious and incremental. As late as 1881, a mere 54,000 Jews had managed to secure official residential permits beyond the confinement of their geographical ghetto.

A more foreboding consequence of this economic distention, therefore, was an upsurge of antisemitism among tens of thousands of newly displaced Russian peasants. Ironically, it was the influx of these villagers into the cities that reduced local Jews to vocational marginality, and to an abrasive corelationship of shared impoverishment. Yet, from the perspective of Russian urban slum-dwellers, it appeared that Jewish competition alone was the source of their own displacement and misery. As their resentments deepened, the clamor grew more insistent for curtailment of the Jewish presence in the new urban economy. The mood of frustration was pungently summarized by the antisemitic *Novoe Vremie* in an editorial of March 23, 1880, entitled simply "The Yid Is Coming."

THE RISE OF SLAVOPHILISM

By the late nineteenth century, that brooding chagrin had evoked a uniquely Russian variant of the era's widely pervasive romantic nationalism. This was Slavophilism, an ideology given its most influential literary expression by Ivan Aksakov in the years following the humiliating defeat of the Crimean War, and summarized in Aksakov's famous credo, "Pera Domoi!"—"It is time to go home!" It was time, Aksakov contended, to stop aping the "decadent" West, with its materialism, its autocratic Roman Catholicism, its incipient mobocracy. Russia must be herself, and assert herself in the community of nations through her own authentic institutions, her peasant communes, her pacifism and "spirituality," her "true and glorious" Orthodox Church. In 1869, the renowned Pan-Slavist Nicholas Danilevski elaborated upon this doctrine in a celebrated volume, *Russia and Europe (Rossiya i Evropa)*. Laying his emphasis upon the "moral consciousness" of the Russian people, Danilevski warned that efforts to introduce the social or political institutions of Western Europe into Russia would almost certainly threaten the very foundations of the empire's Slavic civilization.

At first, there appeared little in Slavophilism, even in its later imperialist mutation of Pan-Slavism, that categorically endorsed political reaction. It was an ideology that venerated the *narod,* after all, the common folk. Yet in the vision of Fyodor Dostoevski, the "return home" took on distinctly illiberal characteristics. As the great novelist saw it, Russia's mission was to confront "the defiled humanity of the West" and transcend a Europe whose cultural legacy had been "eclipsed, lacerated, and brutalized" by rationalism and constitutionalism. "Whoever accepts a constitution according to the Western model," he wrote, "also has to bear the ultimate consequences of Western political life, social revolution with all its manifestations."

For all his early reforms, Tsar Alexander II was by no means immune to this Dostoevskian interpretation. In dealing with episodes of social unrest, he had never hesitated to employ the full machinery of governmental repression. Moreover, in his last years, the "tsar-liberator" confronted an ominous rise of populist terrorism. Initially, populism had not espoused violence of any kind. Based on the teachings of such respectable intellectuals as Alexander Herzen, Piotr Lavrov, and Nicholas Mikhailovski, the movement favored the cause of the "peasant masses," and urged simply a "moral" mobilization of the common people on behalf of social reform. But in the 1870s, as the moralistic approach proved ineffective in raising the peasantry's standard of living, a minuscule splinter group of some thirty men and women, the People's Will, set about achieving change through the more straightforward technique of assassination. Their prime target, moreover, was none less than Tsar Alexander himself, although in their "emperor hunt" they managed also to kill numerous other senior government officials. Early in 1880, the tsar narrowly escaped two attempts on his life, once by pistol, once by explosives planted under his train. On March 1, 1881, however, as Alexander's carriage turned onto a quay along the Neva River, a waiting terrorist hurled a bomb at him, and the ensuing explosion blew the tsar's legs off. He expired a day and a half later.

Alexander was succeeded by his thirty-six-year-old son, who assumed the throne as Alexander III. A powerfully built soldier, trained in a culture of military discipline, the new tsar was endowed with a grimly insular view of the world. He needed little persuasion that Russia's long-range interests, and his own, were best served by a policy of uncompromising Pan-Slavist insularity. Nor did he trouble to disguise his conviction that his father's murder was the end product of an ill-advised reformism. It was an approach not to be repeated. "We can have no other policy," Alexander III announced in April

1881, "except one that is purely Russian and national." Little time passed before his regime's orientation became clearer. Censorship of the press once again became rigorous, and soon reactionary newspapers had the field of public opinion to themselves. The imperial judiciary was returned to the government's executive branch, even as control of the zemstvos, one of the late Alexander II's key innovations, was largely reclaimed by the nobility.

Whatever imagination the new tsar lacked for implementing his policies was supplied for him by Konstantin Pobedonostsev, the arch-ideologue of administrative Pan-Slavism. A lawyer and former justice ministry official, fluent in several languages and broadly cultured, Pobedonostsev was immune to the blandishments of political liberalism, and had never disguised his reservations about Alexander II's "dangerous permissiveness." Nor, for his part, had the late tsar ever concealed his reservations about Pobedonostsev. In 1880, he removed Pobedonostsev from secular government by appointing him procurator of the Holy Synod, in effect, as lay administrator of the Russian Orthodox Church. Never had Alexander imagined that Pobedonostsev over the next quarter-century would transform the office into one of almost limitless political as well as "spiritual" power, disposing of 8 million rubles for an ecclesiastical superstructure that by 1898 encompassed 160,000 priests, nuns, and schoolteachers. For the procurator, the Church in effect served as the anointed guarantor of public behavior, of the Russian people's ongoing docility as "a colossal herd, obedient to the arbitrary will of one man."

In fulfillment of his vision of mass obedience, Pobedonostsev revealed himself as the bureaucrat par excellence, "a kind of wooden ruling machine in human shape," wrote a Russian journalist of the time, "to whom the living units of mankind are nothing, while the maintenance of bureaucratic 'order' is everything." Unlike the "pure" Slavophiles, Pobedonostsev had little faith in the common people. He once described Russia beyond the imperial palace as "an icy desert and an abode of the Bad Man." Fervent in his Great Russian nationalism, regarding parliamentarism as "the great lie of our age," he looked to the autocracy and clergy as the exclusive agents of public policy. The empire, Pobedonostsev frequently asserted, was best sustained by a combination of "Autocracy, Orthodoxy, and Nationalism," a phrase soon to be the epigraph of Alexander III's regime. Thus, to the new tsar, Pobedonostsev successfully argued for the dismissal of the Armenian-born Count Mikhail Loris-Melikov as minister of the interior. "Of an altogether oriental mentality and morality," the procurator wrote, such a man "does not understand Russia and the Russian people, whose aspirations evoke no echo in his heart." The non-Orthodox orientals of the Caucasus regions were of course even less welcome. Pobedonostsev fully endorsed a comment by the (Orthodox) Exarch of Georgia, that "Orthodox Russia may . . . tolerate Islam, Lamaism, etc., but it is not her business to safeguard the prosperity of these creeds."

Above all, the procurator was concerned about the crucial western provinces. Here the Orthodox clergy was obliged to compete with a highly articulate Catholic priesthood. Worse yet, the Vatican was to be regarded as a permanent ally of the Catholic Austrians and Poles, traditional enemies of the Russians.

For Pobedonostsev, racial animus initially was not a significant factor in his Jewish policy. His distrust was of a religious version. Indeed, he was quite prepared to make good use of such Jewish converts as J. F. Cyon, a former professor of physiology at St. Petersburg. Living in Paris during the 1890s, cultivating French intellectual and diplomatic circles, Cyon became as helpful as any professional diplomat in laying the groundwork for the Franco-Russian Alliance of 1894. Occasionally, the procurator also recommended to the tsar's attention distinguished artists of Jewish descent, like the composer-pianist Anton Rubinstein. When it suited Pobedonostsev's purpose, he maintained excellent relations even with such professing Jews as Samuel Poliakov, who had played a key role in developing the Russian railroad system. As elsewhere in Europe, however, by the late nineteenth century religious issues were becoming increasingly intermingled with ethnic resentments. Ivan Aksakov put the issue succinctly for the antisemites: "The Jewish religion is not so much a spiritual force as a racial and nationalist cult." Under Alexander III, the government's approach to Jews evinced a new and virulent amalgam of doctrinal and racial antipathy. "The passion for acquisition and money grubbing," a government commission report of 1888 observed, "is inherent in the Jew from almost the first page of biblical history." The observation was endorsed wholeheartedly by Pan-Slav chauvinists in the new tsarist era, not excluding Alexander III himself.

THE "EVENTS" OF 1881

Well before the assassination of Alexander II, there had been violence against Jews. Four major anti-Jewish pogroms had taken place in Odessa alone: in 1821, 1849, 1859, and 1871. Yet these riots evinced no specifically ideological agenda. The perpetrators tended to be Odessa's large minority of Greeks, reacting to growing Jewish economic competition in the city. It was the year 1881 that produced the first tremors of political change. An early catalyst was the suspected role played by a young Jewish woman, Hessia Helfman, in the assassination of Alexander II. In a collective trial of the conspirators, all the defendants were found guilty and sentenced to hang. But when the court was informed that Helfman was pregnant, it postponed her execution until forty days after she gave birth; and once her infant daughter was born, Helfman's sentence was commuted to life imprisonment. In any case, both mother and child died of mistreatment several months later.

Although no particular emphasis was placed on Helfman's Jewish background during the trial itself, in ensuing months it became yet another pretext for an antisemitic campaign that had been gaining momentum in the Slavophile press for several years. The Jews, it was charged, continued resistant to amalgamation, and stubbornly refused to abandon their baneful commercial habits. By the late 1870s and early 1880s, the economic upheavals of incipient Russian industrialization offered fertile ground for these accusations, and most notably in the empire's southern regions. It was the Ukraine that lately had become the magnet for job-hunters. Unemployed laborers from throughout Russia tended to gravitate there, seeking work in the new Ukrainian railroad and river navigation systems, in its sugar beet factories and coal mines. The restiveness and frustrations of this incipient proletariat became increasingly volatile during the spring thaw, when travel from the rural areas became easier, and growing numbers of migrants began converging on the cities in search of work.

In mid-March of 1881, the reactionary Odessa newspaper *Novorossiski Telegraf* began quoting rumors that attacks on Jews would be launched during the approaching Easter season. The reports soon reached nearby Elizavetgrad. Located on the Ingul River, a tributary of the Bug, Elizavetgrad was a major trading center of the Ukrainian steppe zone. By 1881, a third of its population were Jews, and much of the grain trade was in their hands. In their visibility and vulnerability, the Jews for their part were well aware of the festering hatred around them, and all the more during Easter season, with its intensified religious passions. Their fears were well grounded. The Russian Orthodox Easter was celebrated from Sunday, April 12, to Wednesday, April 15. During those four days, Elizavetgrad was teeming with idle visitors, both employed and unemployed. On April 15, a drunken worker began arguing with the Jewish owner of a tavern, then ran out, claiming that the Jew had struck him. Soon the cry was taken up: "The *zhidi* [yids] are beating Christians." Police attempted to disperse the growing crowd, but failed. Rioters then began looting and destroying Jewish shops. Eventually, troop reserves were called in to break up the mobs, but the rioters simply moved on to the outlying Jewish quarter, attacking Jewish homes and the local synagogue. By the following morning, peasants from nearby villages joined in the assaults, sharing in the pillage and destruction of Jewish property. The violence did not subside until April 17. Although over six hundred rioters eventually were arrested, it proved of little comfort to the Jews, who had suffered grave losses in homes, shops, and other property.

The events of Elizavetgrad were the merest overture to an escalation of pogroms. From April 16 to April 21, rioting spread to eighteen neighboring villages, then on to Jewish shtetls in the nearby Kherson province, to be followed by two weeks of further pogroms raging into other Ukrainian provinces. Indeed, on April 26, the assaults reached Kiev, and then continued on to the Ukrainian capital's surrounding villages, radiating out to the Kursk railroad line. By summer, much of southern Ukraine was consumed by pogroms, moving from shtetl to shtetl, not guttering out completely until August 16. In all, the violence of 1881 engulfed more than half the Pale's fifteen provinces. Its magnitude was not to be calculated only in the number of its Jewish casualties—40 persons killed, some 3,000 injured, together with approximately 200 women raped—but in its vast property destruction. Between 4,000 and 5,000 Jewish homes and businesses were ravaged. Even in the Pale's northwestern provinces, which initially had been spared violence, a series of mysterious fires destroyed large sections of Jewish neighborhoods in Minsk, Bobruisk, Vitebsk, and Pinsk, leaving at least 10,000 persons homeless and financially ruined. And then, on December 13, 1881, a pogrom of authentically massive dimensions exploded in Warsaw, leaving some 1,500 Jewish homes, shops, and synagogues sacked before troops could intervene. On March 29–30, 1882, in yet another grim aftermath, rioters destroyed nearly half the homes and shops in the largely Jewish town of Balta, in Podolia. Only then, almost a year after the initial outbreak in Elizavetgrad, did the violence come to an end.

For decades afterward, it was widely conjectured that the tsarist government itself had surreptitiously encouraged the chain reaction of pogroms. Archival research has since disproved this assumption. The turmoil was the consequence of frustration in an era of tumultuous economic change, of Pan-Slavist chauvinism, even of dramatic improvements in Russian communications, which allowed impoverished workers and peasants to converge rapidly on both outlying Jewish villages and urban Jewish neighborhoods. It was significant, too, that the new tsar's reaction to the pogroms was one of shock and dismay. On April 28, 1881, Alexander III suggested to his ministers that outside agitators must have incited the mobs against the Jews, and that reports of police and military laxity in quashing the pogroms were a "disgrace." He characterized as "inexcusable" the behavior of judges who were alleged to have treated rioters leniently. On May 11, receiving a Jewish delegation led by Baron Horace de Günzburg, the tsar assured his visitors that the government would not tolerate such "anarchist" and "socialist" outrages.

Yet, if the government did not precipitate the violence, its officials were egregiously negligent, even culpable, in their treatment of the pogrom activists. Relatively few persons were arrested, and those who were, were often released without being brought to trial. When sentences were handed down, they tended to be mild, usually running no longer than several months of imprisonment. Persons who returned stolen goods were not so much as prosecuted. The government's laxity reflected no particular calculated intent. As in its failure to suppress the original violence, its forbearing treatment of the perpetrators reflected essentially ineptitude and confusion. On the other hand, the Russian masses interpreted this sluggishness quite differently. For them, lethargy signified tacit official approval.

THE LAWS OF MAY 1882

This interpretation was lent credence by the government's longer-term reaction to the firestorm of pogroms. On August 22, 1881, at the recommendation of Minister of the Interior Nicholas Ignatiev, the tsar issued a memorandum. Dwelling on the "abnormal relations" between the Jews and the Russian people, Alexander ordered an investigation into "injurious" Jewish economic activities. He then appointed Ignatiev himself as chairman of the investigative commission. An undisguised Pan-Slavist chauvinist, the minister of the interior was a man grimly determined to extirpate "sedition" wherever he found it. Personally, he made no secret of his anti-Jewish feelings. "What can we do," he protested to the American chargé d'affaires in St. Petersburg, "if on the one hand there are five million Russian Jews, and on the other hand there are eighty-five million Russian subjects who insist that we expel . . . these five million Jews?" In December 1881, granting an interview to the editor of *Rastsvet*, the Russian-language Jewish newspaper, Ignatiev archly hinted at one solution to the Jewish question by noting that "[t]he western frontier is open to the Jews."

At the minister's direction, individual committees were established for each of the provinces that had undergone pogroms. Members of the local population were included in these bodies. Their conclusions, however, were prejudged by the guideline the tsar himself laid down for the Ignatiev Commission. "[R]ecognizing the detriment caused to the Christian population of the empire by the activity of the Jews," he declared, "their tribal exclusivity and religious fanaticism," he enjoined the commission to recommend ways to resolve "the exploitation [by the Jews] of the indigenous population." Responding to this genial mandate, the individual committees early on reached consensus that the Jewish role in Russian economic life should be severely restricted "for the sake of public order."

In October 1881, even before the Ignatiev Commission had completed its investigation, the tsar appointed still another committee to evaluate the "wider" Jewish question, this one under the chairmanship of Count Konstantin Pahlen, a veteran bureaucrat. The Pahlen Committee in turn would function under Ignatiev's general direction, but somewhat more independently. At first, its mandate did not appear to be quite as frontally antisemitic as Ignatiev's. The appearance was deceptive. In February 1882, the Pahlen Committee proposed a selective revision of the late Alexander II's legislation on the Jews (which had substantially eased Jewish restrictions). Until this revision could be drafted, however, the committee recommended that certain "temporary" measures be adopted to "calm" the Russian population. These measures were duly outlined, and the tsar, spared the need for making a final decision, accepted them three months later, in May. As matters developed, the "temporary" measures of May 1882—the notorious May Laws—proved to be far from temporary. Rather, they would continue in operation for the ensuing thirty-five years, until the Russian Revolution of March 1917.

Under the May Laws, no Jew was permitted to settle "anew" in any rural area in Russia, not even in the Pale. At one stroke, all exits from the crowded cities to the smaller towns and villages were sealed off to Jews. Although the May Laws did not bar all, only new, Jewish settlement in rural communities, in practical fact the legislation also was directed at Jews already living in the countryside, those who comprised approximately two-fifths of the Pale's Jewish population. Henceforth, gentile villagers had the right to expel "vicious" inhabitants by special "verdicts"—and provincial governors often encouraged local *muzhiki* to sign these documents. Jews who left their villages even for a few days were classified as "new visitors" and summarily barred from returning. Jews who rented their homes were denied new leases and thereby forced to depart. A Jew was not permitted to take in his widowed mother from another village, to inherit a father's home or business in another village, or to consult a doctor in another village, without facing expulsion. Additionally, provincial officials were authorized to reclassify many hundreds of small towns as villages; and, as "villages," these communities then were automatically closed to Jews. So it was, from the early 1880s on, that Jews by the hundreds of thousands poured steadily from the comparative amplitude of the countryside into the congestion of the cities. The process doubtless would have taken place in any case during the years of Russia's growing industrialization. But the May Laws ensured that the pace of Jewish urbanization was accelerated dramatically, prejudicially, and disastrously.

The May Laws signified yet another retrogression from Alexander II's vision of "amalgamation." This was a tightly limited numerus clausus for Jews in the Russian educational system. Beginning in 1887, as the laws underwent additional "refinements," Jews living within the Pale, where they often formed majorities of entire districts, were limited to 10 percent of all students enrolled in the empire's gymnasia and universities. For Jews living within the Russian interior, the quota was reduced to 4 percent; and in St. Petersburg and Moscow, to 3 percent. In 1889, the admission of Jews to the Russian bar was reduced initially from 22 to 9 percent; and six years later, no Jews at all could be admitted without special dispensation from the ministry of justice. The quota for Jewish physicians gradually was reduced to 5 percent. In ensuing years, young Jews by the thousands were obliged to find ways of traveling abroad for their higher education.

The May Laws were applied with officious and brutal inflexibility. Thus, large numbers of Jewish artisans were expelled from the Russian interior because their vocations had summarily been removed from the "artisan" classification. If a Jew used a machine in any phase of his craft, his status as artisan was canceled. A watchmaker who sold watch chains was stamped as a merchant of the "third estate" and his right to domicile was forfeited. Often, Jews were expelled on notice of only one or two days, with no opportunity to sell their homes or businesses. There were episodes of Jewish girls who arrived in St. Petersburg to attend university and found that, for the privilege of residence, they were obliged to register under the "yellow ticket" category, that is, as prostitutes. The May Laws achieved their apotheosis of refinement in the spring of 1891. It was then, at the instigation of Grand Duke Sergei, brother of the tsar and governor-general of Moscow, that Alexander issued a ukase ordering the removal of all Moscow Jews whose passports were "not in order."

The edict was published on March 29, the first day of Passover. Its consequences were described in an episode personally observed by Harold Frederick, Moscow correspondent of the London *Times:*

> Under [Cossack General] Bourkovski's personal supervision, the whole [Jewish] quarter was ransacked, apartments forced open, doors smashed, every bedroom without exception searched and every living soul—men, women, and children—were routed out for examination as to their passports. The indignities which the women, young and old alike, endured at the hands of the Cossacks may not be described. . . .
>
> Of these unhappy people, thus driven from their beds, and hauled off to prison in the wintry darkness, some were afterward marched away . . . chained together with criminals and forced along the roads by Cossacks. A few were allowed out of confinement; the rest were summarily shipped to the Pale . . . [whence] they were banished whether their passports were in order or not, and with them . . . into exile went their children and womenkind.

In this fashion, some 14,000 Jews were expelled, fully two-thirds of Moscow Jewry. The mass expulsion was repeated later that same year among the 8,000 Jews of Kharkov.

The Pale of the shtetl, the Jewish village, was fast approaching its end. So was the Pale of the merchant. Its place was soon to be taken by the Pale of the city and town, the Pale of the handicraftsman. The economic aftermath of the transformation may be discerned in the comments of a General Usarov, governor of one of the larger Bessarabian provinces:

The observer is struck by the number of Jewish signs in Bessarabian towns. The houses along second-rate and even back streets are occupied in unbroken succession by stores, big and small, shops of watchmakers, shoemakers, locksmiths, tinsmiths, tailors, carpenters, and so on. All these workers are huddled together in nooks and lanes amidst shocking poverty. They toil hard for a living so grudging that a rusty herring and a slice of onion are considered the tip-top of luxury and prosperity.

By the end of the nineteenth century, it was estimated that 40 percent of Russian Jewry were partially or completely dependent on charitable aid. There had never been oppression like this before, even under the grim rule of Nicholas I. But Alexander III's arch-ideologue Pobedonostsev evidently had anticipated its ramifications when he frankly acknowledged to a Jewish delegation in 1898: "One-third [of the Jews] will die out, one-third will leave the country, and one-third will be completely dissolved in the surrounding population."

During the 1881 pogroms, Judah Leib Gordon continued to editorialize away in the pages of *HaMelitz* in favor of Jewish reform—in business, in public behavior, in religious practice. But with the introduction of the May Laws, even Gordon was shaken into a fundamental reassessment. On the Ninth of Av, the Hebrew date commemorating the loss of the ancient Temple of Jerusalem, Gordon offered his readers a soul-stirring lament:

> What am I, what is my life after my goals were destroyed, my aspirations shattered, my ideals demolished without hope? . . . [L]ike the rainbow after a storm, my dreams faded with the passing of the years, until this disastrous year came and leached out the last tinges of color, blotted out the last rays of light to guide and inspire me.

RUMANIA: "LATIN OASIS"

Under Ottoman rule, the Danubian Principalities of Wallachia and Moldavia included among their Rumanian-speaking majority a small, comfortably ensconced Sephardic Jewish minority. Following the Crimean War, however, as the Rumanians gradually achieved de facto independence of Turkish rule, the number of Jews in their midst increased dramatically. These were Russian Jews, fleeing the squalor and poverty of the Pale of Settlement. By 1860, no fewer than 120,000 Jews had settled in Moldavia, and another 15,000 in Wallachia. In the 1870s and 1880s, as the Tsarist Empire underwent its economic disruptions, its pogroms, and then its May Laws, the Jewish immigration wave achieved even greater momentum. By the end of the century, 245,000 Jews were living in Rumania, amid a total population of approximately 6 million.

Although the proportion of Jews to Rumanians never exceeded 5 percent, they were a highly visible subcommunity, concentrated almost exclusively in the towns, where they formed almost the entirety of the nation's mercantile class. A few Jews prospered, and some actually became prominent bankers and newspaper owners, but most were wretchedly poor, functioning on the lowest margin of the "middle class" as owners of tiny shops or market stalls, or as itinerant peddlers in the countryside. Isolated in their Yiddish-speaking culture, the Rumanian-Jewish newcomers were universally detested by the native population as leeches, aliens, infidels. The Rumanian government barred them from citizenship, tightly restricted their "property" rights, and normally left them to the caprice of local officials, who extorted from them often to within an inch of their lives.

In these years of the latter nineteenth century, West European governments, prodded by such renowned shtadlanim as the Rothschilds and Moses Montefiore, interceded repeatedly with the Rumanian government to modify its harsh anti-Jewish policy. The responses from Bucharest were invariably conciliatory, offering a full plenum of ingratiating assurances of improved treatment. Nothing came of these promises. On Rumanian soil, the Jews remained pariahs, barely clinging to economic survival under bureaucratic and popular oppression. At last, in 1878, at the Congress of Berlin, Gerson von Bleichröder persuaded Bismarck and other Western diplomats to make Jewish equal citizenship the quid pro quo for diplomatic recognition of Rumanian sovereignty. Only then, it is recalled (p. 113), confronted by an apparently implacable European consensus, Rumanian Prime Minister Bratianu and Foreign Minister Kogalniceanu abandoned their resistance, agreeing to incorporate a provision in the Treaty of Berlin and in their own constitution, Article 44, assuring Rumanian Jewry of full and equal political rights, including the right of naturalization (p. 113). Bleichröder and the other Jewish financiers were exultant. For the Jews of Rumania, the long-delayed moment of emancipation was at hand at last.

It was a mirage, of course. The Rumanian leadership had not the faintest intention of bowing to the will of Europe. On the issue of their constitution, they evaded, dissembled, postponed, interpreting Article 44 as authorizing naturalization exclusively for the "veteran" Jewish minority that had long dwelled on Rumanian soil. Other Jews—the vast majority—would continue to be identified as foreigners, and thereby remain subject to special naturalization procedures requiring application on an individual basis. Confronted with this palpable violation of the Treaty of Berlin, would the Great Powers collectively withdraw their recognition of the Kingdom of Rumania? In fact, the

Western nations were tiring of the Rumanian issue. Although Bismarck himself, chivied by Bleichröder, held firm through the autumn of 1878, the governments of Italy, Austria, France, and Britain were eager to disentangle themselves from their earlier commitments to the Jews. It was the German chancellor himself who gave them their chance. In the autumn of 1878, Bucharest dispatched its finance minister, Dmitri Sturdaz, to Berlin. Meeting with Bismarck, the Rumanian emissary came up with several intriguing concessions. The Rumanian government would establish special "categories" of Jews, each to be naturalized en bloc, but seriatim. More fundamentally, Sturdz offered a financial payoff to German investors who had been mired in an ambitious but ill-conceived Rumanian railroad project. Accordingly, on October 3, 1878, over Bleichröder's anguished objections, Bismarck accepted the "compromise."

The formula divided Rumanian Jews into three categories: outright foreigners, Rumanian subjects, and Rumanian citizens. The first category included the bulk of Russian Jews who in recent years had been flooding into Moldavia. Jewish "subjects," comprising a smaller number of veteran Jews, would enjoy a limited number of basic rights, including those of land purchase and—qualified—medical and legal practice. But citizenship was another matter, both for new refugees and older settlers. Here applications had to be considered on an individual basis and be duly approved by special legislation. Only the tiniest minority of applications ever was approved. In February 1880, meanwhile, as Bucharest's nationalist politicians had anticipated, the governments of Britain, France, and Austria "expressed confidence" that Rumania's leadership would conform to the spirit of the Treaty of Berlin. A month later, they followed Bismarck's earlier example by announcing their de jure recognition of Rumania's sovereignty.

By the last decade of the nineteenth century, the bulk of Rumania's nearly quarter-million Jews remained impacted in the larger cities. Most continued to subsist as petty shopkeepers. In urban areas, all but a few Jewish "veterans" were barred from the export trade and from the liberal professions. In the countryside, Jewish physicians even of the "veteran" category were restricted in their practice to areas that were entirely lacking in "native" Rumanian medical care. Similarly, the number of Jewish patients admitted to hospitals was tightly limited. In 1891, the government of Prime Minister Ion Bratianu evicted the small number of Jewish children who had enrolled in Rumanian state schools, then blocked efforts by the Alliance Israélite Universelle to operate its own school system.

However painful these restrictions and humiliations, they were infinitely exacerbated by the Rumanian government's bland willingness to tolerate, even to encourage, pogroms. Each election season, Prime Minister Ion Bratianu artfully incited popular chauvinism by announcing a policy of "repression of the Germans and of the Jews who are everywhere their advance guard." Bands of thugs, fed and housed by Bratianu's acolytes, roamed Jewish neighborhoods, attacking local inhabitants, looting stores and homes. Over the turn of the century, tens of thousands of Rumanian Jews became dependent for their daily bread upon the charity of the Alliance and of other international Jewish welfare organizations. Nowhere in all of Europe, not even in Tsarist Russia under the May Laws, were the circumstances of a nation's entire Jewish population quite as dire.

In the late nineteenth century, as in the late eighteenth century, it is once again a sorely tried Jewry we encounter in Eastern Europe. The Pan-Slavist antisemitism of Tsarist Russia, the xenophobic malevolence of newborn Rumania, appeared for the first time to threaten the very continued survival of the single largest reservoir of Jews in Europe—in the entire world. In 1882, shortly after enactment of the May Laws, the prominent maskil Lev Levanda poured out his heart in the pages of the Russian-Jewish journal, *Rastsvet*. "When I think of what was done to us," he wrote, "how we were taught to love Russia and the Russian word, how we were lured into introducing the Russian language and everything Russian into our homes; how our children knew no other language [now] but Russian, and how we are now rejected and hounded . . . my heart is filled with corrosive despair from which there is no escape."

Yet there had to be some form of escape. Soon, in fact, the quest for a way out of the remorseless vise of East European oppression would precipitate a seismic transformation in Jewish life. In large measure, the years of Haskalah proselytization had already laid the groundwork for that upheaval. The revolution would be one of secular activism.

A Migration of East European Jewry: 1881–1914

A CONSTERNATION OF DEPARTURE

On August 11, 1881, a dozen of the wealthiest Jews in the Tsarist Empire filed into the palatial St. Petersburg home of Baron Horace de Günzburg, the renowned banker. Characteristically, these economic paladins functioned as the shtadlanim, the spokesmen-intercessors of Russian Jewry. This day they were in a state of grave anxiety. Their distress reflected not merely the ongoing pogroms, but the danger of mass Jewish flight. Such an exodus would be catastrophic, Günzburg and the others agreed, for it would convince the tsarist regime that the Jewish problem could be resolved simply by provocation and violence. Indeed, some four months later, in his interview with the editor of *Rastsvet,* Minister of the Interior Ignatiev all but acknowledged that the government had precisely that solution in mind (p. 200). At a second meeting in April 1882, therefore, Günzburg and his fellow notables issued a public statement abjuring any notion of organized emigration. A step of that magnitude would be "subversive of the Russian body politic," they insisted, "and of the historic rights of the Jews in their present fatherland." There was yet another reason for discretion on the emigration issue. The rabbinate was implacably against it. Where would Jews have fled, asked the Orthodox journal *HaTz'firah,* if not to the West? Was not the West a notorious breeding ground of secularism?

But the declamations of the intercessors and the rabbinate soon were revealed as irrelevant. The Jews of the Pale already had become well accustomed to movement. Decades even before pogroms and May Laws, the Europe-wide gravitation of village dwellers to towns and cities affected the Jews in common with other peoples. Within the Pale itself, they migrated by the tens of thousands from shtetl to town, from town to city, from undernourished Lithuania and Belorussia in the north to the more bountiful Ukraine in the south. In their growing urbanization, these peregrinating Jews were also in search of wider personal freedom beyond the scrutiny and intimidation of village rabbis. Soon, emigration beyond the Continent altogether would become a central fact of nineteenth-century life for Jews and gentiles alike. For Eastern and Southern European farm families, the termination of feudal landholding had proved as much a curse as a blessing. In their haste to bequeath their possessions to their children, peasants divided their tracts with such ill-judged alacrity that their descendants no longer could subsist on the soil. Agricultural enclosures merely compounded their landlessness. Movement to the cities unquestionably was one alternative. But if industry was unable to absorb them all, departure for the New World or Western Europe seemed a more logical choice. So it was that the westward migration of Serbs, Poles, Slovaks, and Italians swelled to over 2 million between 1880 and 1914. Even this vast outpouring was surpassed in the same period by a seismic efflux of 3 million men, women, and children from the Russian Empire.

Of the latter, fully two-thirds were Jews. Among them, too, immigration to the West had been growing well before the 1880s. In the two decades before the 1881 pogroms, approximately 65,000 Jews departed Russian and Habsburg Poland, and nearly 40,000 of these continued on to the United States. Unlike the majority of their gentile neighbors, East European Jews had earned their livelihood as middlemen between the countryside and the cities. Displaced now from that mercantile role, they discerned in factory labor a highly uncertain option. Gentile workmen threatened them. Religious and dietary constraints further limited their opportunities. Departure for the West thereupon began as early as the 1860s. Nevertheless, it was the pogroms of 1881–82 and the ensuing May Laws that decisively exacerbated the Jews' economic crisis and launched them on a mass flight unprecedented even in their own widely traveled history.

Emigration tended to follow several clearly defined routes. Jews from the western and northwestern Pale moved directly through East Prussia to the ports of Hamburg and Bremen. Jews leaving Rumania (pp. 211–12) passed through Vienna and Frankfurt en route to the harbors of Rotterdam and Amsterdam. The earliest, pacesetting group of émigrés, however, those fleeing the 1881–82 pogroms in Ukraine and Belorussia, made directly for the Habsburg Galician town of Brody, a railhead for trains continuing on to German or Dutch ports. The journey to this border community was memorable. Most of the fleeing Jews reached it only by traveling by train or carriage for at least sixty hours. Exhausted and hungry, they were obliged then to spend their last rubles on smugglers to help them negotiate the illegal frontier crossing. Once entering Brody, a town of some 15,000 souls, most of these also Jews, the fugitives encountered a spectacle of pandemonium, of soldiers and police and thousands of milling fellow refugees. For the newcomers, the experience was terrifying. They were not merely destitute. They were stranded. Lacking train tickets for the ports, or steamship tickets for the United States, they were denied transit across Austrian or German territory. Initially, some of them were taken in by local Jewish families. But others were obliged to crowd into synagogues, or even to sleep in the streets. Although local Jewish committees were rapidly established to provide food and shelter, the arrangements at best could only be temporary.

"Barbarians" at the Gate

Western Jews reacted swiftly and vigorously to the pogroms and the May Laws, with protest meetings and fund-raising campaigns. In June 1881, a German philanthropic committee, later to be known as the Hilfsverein der deutschen Juden, collaborated with Austria's Israelitische Allianz and Britain's Mansion House Fund (p. 216) to provide for the Brody refugees. The following month, France's mighty Alliance Israélite Universelle dispatched its field director, Charles Netter, to evaluate the situation at the border way station. Netter was stunned by the influx he encountered in Brody. From the horrifying account the newcomers related of their plight in Russia, it was immediately clear that they could not be repatriated. On the other hand, Netter's mandate was at all costs to keep these backward "Asians" out of Western Europe. Evidently the one and logical solution, then, was to arrange for their orderly transmigration to the United States, "to that vast, free, and rich country," Netter wrote back to Paris, "where all who wish to work can and will find a place. . . . Otherwise, we shall receive here all the beggars of the Russian Empire." Once the current wave of 12,000 Jews was dispatched, moreover, the migration would have to be stopped altogether.

In October 1881, an emergency conference of Jewish philanthropic leaders gathered at the Alliance headquarters in Paris. All the representatives shared Netter's conclusion that transshipment to America was the only feasible solution. To that end, they devised a rule-of-thumb allocation of responsibilities for the Brody refugees. France's Alliance would supply their food and shelter. The German Hilfsverein and the Austrian Israelitischen Allianz would provide transportation to the German and Dutch port cities. The Mansion House Fund and other British charities would cover food and lodging expenses in Southampton and Liverpool. From there, the Alliance again would underwrite transportation to the United States. Finally, in New York, the newly formed Hebrew Emigrant Aid Society—better known as the "New York Committee"—would receive the newcomers and arrange for their immediate needs. It was under this joint rubric, therefore, that the first selected contingent of nine hundred refugees was dispatched from Brody in November. Most were young men. Netter personally gave them their instructions, provided them with food rations for the journey to Hamburg, and supplied an additional stipend for meals and the purchase of bedding. As the men cheered him, the beaming Netter assured them that "the Americans will be delighted" with such "splendid human material."

In fact, the American-Jewish leadership was appalled. Even before 1881 they had reacted antiseptically to East European immigrants, branding them "unemployable" and "uncivilized." The very notion of a new, subsidized influx of *Ostjuden* was unthinkable to them. "Let those who do not possess a useful trade stay in Europe," pleaded Cincinnati's Isaac M. Wise, in his German-language newsletter, *Die Deborah*. Such people were divorced ("herausgerissen") "from all forms of modern civilization." Recoiling at the spectacle of Netter's selected nine hundred, Manuel Kurscheedt, a lawyer who served as voluntary secretary of the New York Committee, cabled the Alliance office in Paris, angrily branding the refugee contingent as *Luftmenschen,* in effect, as unemployable people. American Jews were themselves not secure enough to "afford to incur the ill-will of their compatriots," Kurscheedt insisted. His anguish was echoed in other American-Jewish communities. "If you send [us] any more Russians," insisted the New York Committee's distraught correspondent in Milwaukee, "they will be shipped back to you without permitting them to leave the depot." Indeed, in June 1882, when the New York Committee dispatched some four hundred of the newly arrived refugees to Boston, the latter's Jewish communal leaders promptly hustled them back to the rail depot for a return journey to New York. It was not the immigrants' destitution that concerned America's veteran Jews. It was their outlandish garb and Yiddish patois, at a time when American Jewry itself was confronting the shock of gentile social discrimination (pp. 167–71).

Faced with these protests and rejections, the European-Jewish philanthropies held a second emergency conference, this one in August 1882. Here, with much reluctance, the decision was taken to send back to Russia the 8,000 refugees still huddled in Brody. Whereupon, acting on this consensus, Charles Netter promptly dispatched announcements to leading rabbis and Jewish newspapers in the Pale, warning that additional fugitives would receive no further help. He then provided each of the remaining Brody Jews 200 rubles and train tickets for the return trip eastward. In the United States, in March 1883, the New York Committee was officially dissolved and local Jewish charities in New York and elsewhere assumed responsibility for the immigrants who had already arrived.

THE DIKES BREAK

But the effort to roll back the tide of fugitives was unavailing. In Russia, intermittent outbursts of anti-Jewish violence continued. Statements on Jewish issues by tsarist officials and press editorials were becoming more threatening, and the full import of the recently announced May Laws gradually was being absorbed. Less impulsively now, reacting in urgency if not in panic, Russian Jews in their tens of thousands began scraping together the minimum of funds needed for steamship tickets and the overland journey to Western ports. Daunting challenges still faced them. The logistics of rail travel were formidable. More intimidating yet was the bedlam at Atlantic ports, the need to find temporary lodgings, to purchase steamship passage at lowest cost. Sharpers and swindlers abounded, offering counterfeit tickets at "bargain" prices. And once the refugees managed finally to embark for the United States, their voyage was a cheerless ordeal. Dormitory accommodations in steerage were squalid, with kitchen and toilet facilities often dangerously unhygienic.

Arrival in the United States was hardly less terrifying than departure from Russia. For many years, the initial port of call was Castle Garden, functioning under the jurisdiction of the State of New York. Here many hundreds of immigrants passed daily under a great open rotunda, ushered from one "station" to the next to undergo a lengthy battery of personal and medical examinations. Even after approval for admission, few immigrants had family members or friends awaiting them. Initially, the New York Committee assigned agents to translate, to offer advice, to provide a meal and overnight lodgings. The service ended after 1883, however, when the committee dissolved itself. Afterward, the immigrants were left to their own resources.

These trials notwithstanding, the migration continued, and gained momentum. Between 1881 and 1883, some 19,000 East European Jews reached the United States. By the end of the decade, the number reached 161,000. Ironically, the post-pogrom influx actually evoked somewhat less panic in the West than in 1881. This time, the refugees were coming increasingly on their own, with fewer expectations of philanthropic help. The crisis of Russian Jewry also was briefly overshadowed by that of Galician Jewry, whose grinding poverty was exacerbated by the upheavals of early industrialization. The trauma of Rumanian Jewry was graver yet. By the late nineteenth century, Jews in this impoverished and xenophobic Balkan nation were undergoing the harshest ordeal of any Jewish population in the world, with each new administration in Bucharest vying with its predecessor in devising new torments for its despised Jewish minority. In 1899, moreover, to divert public attention from a grave economic depression, the Rumanian government began deporting large numbers of "socially unacceptable" Jewish peddlers across the Hungarian and Russian borders. By the turn of the century, tens of thousands of Rumanian Jews were streaming westward, moving by foot, train, and wagon to Vienna, and ultimately on to North Sea ports.

Responding to urgent appeals from Jewish leaders, the Western governments interceded repeatedly with Bucharest, citing Article 44 of the Treaty of

Berlin, with its guarantee of Jewish civic equality. But for the Rumanian government, these appeals and denunciations were an old story (pp. 204–6). Its spokesmen responded with their customary bland denials. Even a protest from American Secretary of State John Hay, in July 1902, was unavailing. The anguish of Rumanian Jewry continued, and with it a continuing upsurge of migration. Between 1881 and 1914, the number of Rumanian Jews who reached the United States alone came to 74,000—nearly 28 percent of the entire Rumanian-Jewish population of 270,000 (by the 1899 Rumanian census). It was a higher proportion of Jewish migration than from Habsburg Galicia or Tsarist Russia. From these three regions, in any case, some 2.4 million Jews departed for the West between 1881 and 1914. The figure represented one of every three Jews in Eastern Europe.

A Reality of American Acceptance

In May and October of 1891, representatives of the European-Jewish charities gathered in Berlin to reappraise the migration crisis. By then it was plain that Jewish circumstances in the East were collapsing irretrievably. Unstoppable, the tide of departures could only be channeled. The various Jewish philanthropies accordingly set about rationalizing and refining their efforts. They dispatched representatives to border posts, to railroad stations and ports of emigration. In the larger port cities, kosher food was provided, together with makeshift lodgings and emergency medical care. Explanatory literature in Yiddish also was available, with instructions and warnings against "shipping agents" offering "discount"—that is, counterfeit—tickets, and procurers lying in wait for unescorted girls (p. 220).

By the 1890s, moreover, America no longer was entirely terra incognita to these immigrants. A sizable avant-garde of kinsmen and former neighbors already had immigrated there. In growing numbers, the "veterans" awaited friends and family members at the dock, to provide them with temporary shelter and contacts for employment. Whereupon, responding to this incremental improvement, the new influx of immigrants included a much larger proportion of women and children—about 43 percent between 1899 and 1914. During these same years, recognizing that the immigration wave could not be reversed, America's Jewish "establishment" acknowledged that a new approach to the Easterners was needed. Thus, as early as 1882, a committee of the Union of American Hebrew Congregations suggested that efforts to foreclose immigration be superseded by a program of acculturation, for "[e]ducation, moral and religious, and instruction in manual labor will tend to elevate them." By the same token, a consensus was developing in favor of agricultural labor as the best means for "Americanizing," "productivizing," "civilizing" the newcomers.

It is of interest that not a few East European Jews shared this preference for agriculture. Like numerous Russian intelligentsia, the disciples of Haskalah had come to idealize the virtues of the *narod,* the common workers of the soil. By the late nineteenth century, a Zionist version of this pastoral romanticism was the BILU—a Hebrew acronym of "House of Jacob, Let Us Go"—contingent of young pioneers who departed for Palestine (pp. 261–62). Its counterpart among the immigrants to the United States was the Am Olam society, a name suggested by the Haskalah culture hero Peretz Smolenskin. Founded in 1881 by students at the University of Odessa, the Am Olam membership dispatched their initial vanguard of seventy men and women to the United States later that same year. Proclaiming their commitment to a "healthy" agricultural life in America, the youthful idealists were soon followed by other, smaller groups of Jewish *narodniki.* As they made their way to the Habsburg border, Jewish villagers along their route provided them with food and lodgings. Even Western Jewish philanthropists were prepared this time to provide railroad and steamship tickets. "Jewish agriculture will redound to the credit of Judaism," exulted Austrian Jewry's Israelitische Allianz.

That support was warmly reinforced by America's veteran Jewish leadership. In 1882, the renowned banker-philanthropist Jacob Schiff and a group of close associates shared in the purchase of a 2,400-acre tract on Sicily Island, Louisiana. Forty-eight young Am Olam immigrants made their way by train and wagon to Sicily Island and set to work clearing it. In less than a year, malaria and floods doomed the project. Nevertheless, in 1883 another forty-two aspiring immigrant farmers proceeded to a new tract, Cotopoxi, in Colorado; this one was provided by the still extant New York Committee. Once again, the venture quickly failed, as its colonists chose instead to earn guaranteed wages from a nearby mining company. Another endeavor, in South Dakota, underwritten by the Jews of St. Paul, Minnesota, expired after two years, as did still another effort on a Kansas tract, Beersheba, purchased by Isaac M. Wise's Hebrew Union Agricultural Society. In the end, only one of Am Olam's sixteen agricultural projects survived. This was in Vineland, New Jersey, where seventy-three families held on as chicken-farmers. Whatever their pastoral idealism, East European Jews evidently could not sustain the "heroic self-reliance" of the countryside in a new and strange land that offered them no Jewish historical associations.

But if the newcomers could not be dissuaded from congregating in the cities, perhaps a more acceptable alternative could be found to the congestion of New York's urban ghetto. To that end, Jacob Schiff and his fellow patriarchs in 1890 began discussing with B'nai B'rith leaders the notion of diverting immigrants to other, smaller communities, preferably west of the Allegheny Mountains. Here an additional source of financial support was available. It was Baron Moritz de Hirsch. The famed railroad tycoon thus far had concentrated his philanthropic efforts on the resettlement of Russian Jews in Argentina (pp. 673–74). Even so, his Israelite Colonization Association (ICA) had enough money left to fund worthy Jewish agricultural projects in Palestine and the United States. With his approval, then, a subsidiary Baron de Hirsch Fund of New York was set up, with Schiff and his colleagues named as its trustees. Some of the money went—vainly—to a few lingering Am Olam farm settlements, some to underwrite an agricultural school in Vineland, New Jersey, and the rest to support vocational and employment bureaus in New York and other cities. But the major effort was given to the establishment of the "Industrial Removal Office." Under IRO auspices, a network of agents set about negotiating employment and housing opportunities for Jews in midwestern and southern towns and cities. The undertaking in fact proved moderately successful. Between 1901 and 1914, the IRO dispatched approximately 60,000 male Jewish immigrants from the New York area to smaller inland communities.

Nevertheless, of the more than 2 million Jews reaching the United States since 1881, the proportion settling along the Atlantic Seaboard by the eve of World War I actually increased, from 40 to 71 percent. Elsewhere, too, whether in the East or in the Midwest, Jews manifestly preferred the larger cities. The trend was hardly unique to them, of course. America's demography altogether was shifting from country to city, and the pattern was replicated among the non-Jewish immigrants who flooded into the United States over the turn of the century. Yet, for the Jews, in all their perennial insecurity and ethnic cohesion, the instinct for urbanization remained more acutely developed than among virtually any other immigrant group.

A Permanence of Way Stations

The Jewish migration wave did not flow on exclusively to the United States. Shoals and eddies of Ostjuden soon developed in Western Europe. Initially, these were Jews whose resources were exhausted by the time they left Russian or Rumanian soil, and who could not afford steamship tickets to America. Thus, year by year, as Jews by the hundreds of thousands passed through Central Europe, significant numbers of them were obliged to accept temporary shelter and local charitable care in the slum neighborhoods of German and Austrian cities. Of these putative transients, at least 70,000 remained in the German Empire. Notwithstanding the formidable bureaucratic obstacles imposed by German officialdom, the dramatic growth of Berlin Jewry and of Munich Jewry was due almost entirely to this influx. As late as 1914, some 15 percent of all Germany's nearly half-million Jews were refugees or the children of refugees. In Austria, the proportion was far higher. No legal obstacles whatever were imposed on the movement of Galician Jews; after all, these people were Habsburg citizens. By 1914, therefore, of "integral" Austria's 240,000 Jews, approximately 100,000, or nearly 40 percent (most of these living in Vienna), were first- or second-generation East Europeans. Whether in Germany or Austria, the newcomers for many years tended to remain insular and Yiddish-speaking, maintaining their own Orthodox synagogues, their own immigrant clubs and associations. In both countries, too, their pungent ethnicity would help fuel a dramatic upsurge of antisemitism (p. 227).

The immigrant settlement pattern of Central Europe did not vary significantly west of the Rhine. By the early 1880s, France's 60,000 Jews had achieved an upward mobility not surpassed by their kinsmen in any other land. The majority were small-scale merchants or manufacturers, but a sizable minority were powerful financiers. Whatever their income or station, they all had long since acquired the fullest measure of economic opportunity and civil freedom, and important numbers of them were on the verge of a wider social acceptance. Then, from 1881 to 1914, as the great East European migration moved westward, some 80,000 Russian and Rumanian Jews arrived in France (by 1939, their numbers would double), laying down their roots mainly in Paris. As elsewhere, the newcomers settled in poorer neighborhoods, earning their livelihoods essentially in their traditional garment trades. These were the circumstances in which the Marais, comprising essentially Paris's third and fourth arrondissements, became the capital's most densely congested Jewish quarter. The immigrants were Yiddish-speaking and intensely ethnocentric. They shunned consistorial synagogues in favor of their own makeshift little shuls, their own Orthodox dietary commissions and religious schools, and, increasingly, their own left-wing Bundist societies.

France's veteran Jews, soon to become a minority of their nation's Jewry, regarded the newcomers with distinct unease. Social insecurities played their usual role, of course. Yet, in the case of France, a political factor significantly exacerbated these concerns. In 1881, when news first arrived of the Russian pogroms, the leadership of the Consistoire Central refrained from organizing the kind of public protest meetings then taking place in England and the United States. Not a single French-Jewish leader bestirred himself to seek official French intercession with Tsarist Russia. The reason was not arcane. During the 1880s, France and Russia were drawing closer in their shared suspicion of the Central Powers, and French Jews no less than the French government accepted the importance of diplomatic restraint. Indeed, once the Franco-Russian Alliance was formalized in 1894, Jewish circumspection approached the threshold of obsequiousness. It was also the year when Alexander III died. As the Russian tsar lay on his deathbed, prayers were offered up on his behalf in all the consistorial synagogues of France. The tsar had greatly persecuted Jews, acknowledged Grand Rabbi Zadoc Kahn, "nonetheless, he was an honest man and a believer. . . . [A]bove all, we must remember that he was a friend of France and that in the interest of our Fatherland his life is precious."

Otherwise, in their demographic growth, if not in their diplomatic stance, the parallelisms between French Jewry and Anglo-Jewry were striking. In the last years before 1881, England's Jewish population roughly approximated that of their coreligionists across the Channel. Of the nation's 56,000 Jews, all but 10,000 lived in London. A majority of them, too, had reached the middle-income level, and a significant minority was quite well-to-do. Unlike French Jewry, however, the Jews of England had achieved their emancipation gradually, painlessly, almost offhandedly. In ensuing years, they experienced no psychological compulsion to prove their patriotic bona fides or their cultural Anglicization. Thus, in the spring and summer of 1881, when news of the Russian pogroms reached England, the Board of Deputies of British Jews unhesitatingly set about recruiting the nation's most eminent public figures to denounce the anti-Jewish violence. Among those who signed a petition to condemn the "unprecedented atrocities" were Foreign Minister Shaftesbury, the Archbishop of Canterbury, and scores of members of Parliament of all factions. On February 1, 1882, in a public protest meeting held at the Mansion House, London's mayoral residence, Prime Minister William Gladstone was the keynote speaker.

But if the Anglo-Jewish establishment was not timorous in protesting the East European outrages, neither was it eager for a wave of Russian Jews to descend upon England's shores. On the one hand, a philanthropic enterprise, the Mansion House Fund, was launched on behalf of the refugees. Yet the money raised was disbursed with the clear understanding that newcomers in transit at British ports would either return home or continue on their journey to the United States. Some of the refugees actually did return to Russia, for the Board of Deputies and the Jewish Board of Guardians alluded repeatedly to the "hardships awaiting refugees in England." In 1884, Chief Rabbi Nathan Adler warned his rabbinical colleagues in Russia and Rumania: "Many [immigrants] are lost without livelihoods. . . . [A]t times they contravene the will of their Maker on account of poverty and overwork, and violate the Sabbath and Festivals." Thus, as Anglo-Jewry continued to provide migrating Jews with food, shelter, legal advice, and transportation, it was with the plain-spoken intention of keeping the refugees moving, pressing them to continue on from British ports until they reached the Western Hemisphere.

As many as 50,000 refugees did in fact sail on to North America. Nevertheless, despite all admonitions, the numbers of those remaining in England grew steadily. By 1900, London's Jewish population had grown by 100,000 souls, and by 200,000 by 1914. Of the 250,000 Jews living in Britain on the eve of World War I, at least two-thirds were East European immigrants.

Of these, in turn, the great majority were living and working in London, most of them concentrated in the Borough of Stepney, which included areas of Whitechapel and Mile End, near the docks or rail terminals where they had disembarked. Congested industrial quasi-slum though it was, the East End at least provided cheap housing, and was close to the apparel factories and workshops where immigrants in large numbers earned their livelihoods.

Meanwhile, without abandoning its efforts to move the refugees on to the United States, Britain's veteran Jewish leadership was obliged increasingly to emphasize the need for Anglicization and "social control." As Nathan Joseph, a communal leader, warned in 1893, the immigrants "will drag down, subvert and disgrace our community if we leave them in their present state of neglect." At the turn of the century, therefore, new branches of the Jews' Free School, of youth clubs and Boy Scout groups, were established throughout London and in other cities, all with the forthright purpose of weaning immigrant youngsters away from Yiddish and training them in "British values." It was a familiar acculturationist program by then, and one well launched in the much larger English-speaking milieu across the Atlantic.

SURVIVAL IN THE IMMIGRANT CITY

As early as 1890, immigration swelled the Jewish population of New York to nearly 165,000; of Philadelphia, to 26,000; of Boston, Baltimore, Cleveland, and Chicago, to approximately 20,000 each. Thirty years later, these figures had quintupled from city to city. In whichever community, the newcomers lived in their own densely populated immigrant neighborhoods. New York was their paradigm. With the best harbor in the Western Hemisphere, Manhattan alone between 1865 and 1914 functioned as the principal gateway to the United States, and thereby became a city comprised overwhelmingly of immigrants.

By the turn of the century, approximately 330,000 East European Jews had settled into Manhattan's Lower East Side. Within walking distance of their original port of disembarkation, this two-mile, forty-block enclave—essentially the Tenth Ward—was hardly less than a Jewish Hong Kong. Most of its population was packed into some 2,000 tenements. In 1908, a sanitary inspector reported of these multistory dwellings: "The rooms were damp, foul, and dark; the air was unbearable, the filth impossible, the crowded conditions terrible. . . . The life of the children was endangered because of the prevailing contagious diseases, and children died like flies." The sheer rankness of the Tenth Ward actually was more reminiscent of a medieval European town than of a modern American city.

The squalor notwithstanding, Manhattan's East European Jews were more favorably situated than were the Italians, Slovaks, or Poles, their fellow immigrants. The Jews had not been peasants in the Old World. As travelers and traders, they had learned to deal with corrupt bureaucracies. They had tasted the fierce competition of the marketplace. To be sure, as many as a quarter of New York's immigrant Jewish "merchants," still without capital, barely subsisted as hole-in-the-wall retailers, as sidewalk tradesmen and pushcart peddlers. Others, the majority, survived initially as blue-collar workers. Among this latter group, a significant number labored as bakers, carpenters, painters, glaziers, shoemakers, or cigar-makers. Most, however, earned their livelihoods in the "needle trades." In the United States, no less than in Europe, the production of ready-made clothing remained the Jewish industry par excellence.

The invention of the sewing machine in the 1850s was a key factor in this growth, together with the military clothing requirements of the Civil War (p. 168). The subsequent appearance of the rotary cutting machine in the 1870s fostered an even wider mass production of men's apparel. In the 1880s, moreover, the invention of the steam pressing iron launched the mass production of women's clothing. As a further stimulus to the industry, the sources of raw textiles were close at hand, in the mills of New York State, New Jersey, and New England. In New York, moreover, the garment industry was owned almost entirely by German Jews. Here the immigrants faced no antisemitism, no ethnic anomie. And, above all else, the women's garment industry was labor-intensive, and in the explosion of Jewish immigration the factory owners found their ideal workforce. More than any other immigrant group, Jews had acquired an earlier familiarity with the needle trades. In the Pale, closed out of Russia's mills and factories by gentile hostility or by their undersized physiques, they had needed only a sewing machine to operate in their own homes as tailors and milliners. Their proficiency in the genre was unmatched.

These were the circumstances in which the needle trades became New York's largest single industry. By 1910, of 23,000 factories in Manhattan, 47 percent were devoted to clothing production. They employed 215,000 people, 46 percent of the city's industrial labor force, and the overwhelming majority of these were immigrant Jews. The garment workers' lot was by no means easy. In the industry's early decades, its defining feature was the "subcontracting" system. Manufacturers found it cheaper to subcontract the "finishing" labor on raw garments, the trimming and stitching of collars, cuffs, and buttonholes. Bidding competitively for these finishing rights, subcontractors—immigrant Jews themselves—initially waited at the docks to round up their labor among arriving kinsmen and former neighbors from the Old Country. Hustling the newcomers to tenement flats that had been converted into workshops, the subcontractors set the newcomers to work on awaiting sewing machines. Paid by the subcontractors on a piecework basis, the immigrants endured a form of wage slavery in these "sweatshops." But at least they were among their own, working in a Yiddish-speaking milieu, observing their own religious holidays and diet. And they avoided the abject mendicancy of the Russian shtetl or the Rumanian market stall.

Noblesse Oblige

Well before the turn of the century, America's veteran German Jews, accepting the irreversibility of the East European immigration, set about organizing a network of more solidly funded relief societies. Their task henceforth was to find housing and employment for the newcomers, to provide them with clinics, orphan asylums, old-age homes, and vocational training courses (see below). By 1910, New York's United Hebrew Charities alone was spending $10 million annually on these social programs. The biggest givers, led by Jacob Schiff, Isidore Straus, Meyer Lehman, and other German-Jewish patriarchs, monitored these dispensations. By then, Schiff had emerged as the premier patron-spokesman of American Jewry, and no detail of the immigrants' absorption was too trivial for his attention or flinty solicitude.

As in Western Europe, the patriarchs were determined that the newcomers be "civilized" as quickly as possible. Characteristically, Detroit's *Jewish American* editorialized in 1891: "The minority is always judged by its lowest representatives. Our great duty, therefore, is to raise our race. . . . It has become a question of self-defense." So it was, in their own version of America's turn-of-the-century Progressivist movement, that the Jewish leadership organized educational programs to teach the immigrants English, civics, and American history. A favored instrument of this acculturation campaign was the Young Men's Hebrew Association, initially established during the German-Jewish immigration (p. 171). Modeled on the Young Men's Christian Association, the YMHA developed a curriculum of evening classes in English, civics, and "self-improvement." As always, Schiff was the major benefactor, purchasing the Y's spacious new building on East Ninety-second Street and funding its program. Similar Y's were established in other major cities.

Their activities were paralleled by the settlement houses. Founded in England as an outgrowth of the late-nineteenth-century Christian Socialist movement, the settlement-house program became even more widespread in the United States around the turn of the century. Once adapted for Jewish (and other) immigrant neighborhoods, these institutions augmented basic welfare services with a wide diversity of courses in English and civics, in manual trades and home economics. Led by New York's famed (Jewish) Educational Alliance, the settlement houses in larger American cities developed programs of classes and public lectures that by 1901 were drawing the participation of tens of thousands of newcomers. Ultimately, over seventy-five such

Jewish settlement houses functioned as indispensable social-service agencies and as instruments of functional Americanization.

In this same era of massive East European immigration, Jewish society matrons began to find a new creative role for themselves. Their "Sisterhoods of Personal Service" became integral components of every major Jewish community, and in 1893 were organized nationally as the National Council of Jewish Women. Although the council's agenda included the education of social workers and the establishment of juvenile courts, its principal efforts were devoted to the care of immigrant Jewish girls. Inspired by Bertha Pappenheim's Bund der jüdische Frauen in Germany, the council focused on a malignancy threatening the moral health of the Jewish people. This was the cancer of prostitution, and its origins lay in the collapse of East European Jewish life. With fathers departing for America, many of their teenage daughters later followed on their own. Alone and vulnerable, they often became the victims of predators, most of these Jewish, as well, who offered them false promises of shelter and security, even of marriage. Too late, the luckless young females discovered the true import of the promises.

It was the fate of these girls, in turn, that impelled the National Council of Jewish Women to seek them out as they arrived at the ports, and to offer them care and protection until lodgings and employment could be found for them. In New York, an even more aggressive antiprostitution campaign was launched by the Committee of Fifteen, a group of Uptown Jewish patriarchs and Lower East Side Jewish social workers. Working with federal, state, and local law-enforcement bodies, the committee helped ferret out Jewish traffickers in women. Some of these predators were tried and convicted for violating the Mann Act (a law barring the transportation of female minors over state borders for immoral purposes). Most simply were harassed into departure. By the late 1920s, the distinctive connection between Jews and prostitution finally was broken.

Nevertheless, at its height in the years before World War I, Jewish prostitution drew its sustenance from an even wider substratum of corruption. From the 1890s on, reflecting the circumstances of immigrant poverty and disorientation, a substantial Jewish criminal underworld emerged in New York and other major cities. In 1906, New York State government statistics revealed that 30 percent of youngsters confined in city and state correctional facilities were Jewish. Some graduated to violent crime. As far back as the 1880s, Isaac Zucker operated New York's largest ring of arsonists. In ensuing years, Edward Osterman and a gang of fellow Jews strong-armed votes for "Big Tim" O'Sullivan, the local Tammany boss. Over the turn of the century, Jacob Zelig operated New York's most notorious extortion racket. Gambling became a favored Jewish avocation. Protected by "Big Tim," the Lower East Side's presiding dukes of illegal gambling were Jews. Among them, the best known was Arnold Rothstein, who soon went on to such cognate fields as loan sharking, debt "collection," prostitution, and extortion. In the last years before World War I, as prosecutors dredged up one Jewish name after another, the stereotype of Jewish criminality became widely disseminated. In their mortification, American Jewry's veteran leadership acknowledged that urgent corrective measures had to be taken.

It was a Reform rabbi, Dr. Judah Magnes, occupying the pulpit of New York's august Temple Emanu-El, who took the lead in this countercampaign. In 1912, he persuaded Schiff and other patriarchs to organize and fund a "Bureau of Social Morals" to combat Jewish corruption. Beneath the cosmetic title, the bureau would function in effect as a Jewish secret service, to cooperate with the New York district attorney's office in identifying and apprehending Jewish criminals. Private Jewish citizens then enthusiastically offered their help in the venture, supplying law-enforcement agencies with a wealth of data on Jewish malfeasance. The bureau operated for five years, and its accumulated data helped to indict some two hundred Jewish criminals, and to convict more than half of them. Yet, as lawlessness began to recede as a major factor in the Jewish immigrant community by the early postwar period, it was above all prosperity that turned the tide. In the hundreds of thousands, Jews were moving out of the Lower East Side to middle-class neighborhoods, where they no longer remained either perpetrators or easy marks of organized crime.

Still another danger remained for the immigrant community, however, one that proved more difficult to overcome. As waves of Jews poured from the Old World to the New, many of the best and brightest among them turned their backs not only on Eastern Europe but on a traditional religious value system. The newcomers' struggle for a foothold in the United States eventually would transcend the barriers of economic privation and gentile prejudice. But their most bedeviling challenge, in a society far more open in its tantalizing alternatives than the ones they left behind, would remain the struggle for psychological and moral anchorage.

XIII

The Onset of Modern Antisemitism

THE LEGACY OF FOLKLORISTIC JUDEOPHOBIA: CENTRAL EUROPE

Of the plurality of obstacles European Jews confronted in their struggle for political emancipation, the most formidable was their lingering image as aliens—in religion, culture, and vocation. As late as the nineteenth century, even the medieval fear of Jews as "ritual murderers," as fiends who supped on Christian blood for their Passover ceremony, had not yet been exorcised. Thus, in the eastern, predominantly agricultural regions of the Habsburg Empire, twelve ritual-murder indictments against Jews took place between 1867 and 1914. Several of these indictments resulted in trials, and at least two of them were exploited for political purposes. The atmosphere was conducive to religioethnic xenophobia. During its last decades, the empire seethed with irredentism, with nationality conflicts between Germans and Czechs, Poles and Ukrainians, Magyars and Serbs. Many of these fears and hatreds were exacerbated by the economic upheavals of rural displacement. Thus, in 1882, Gysl Istoczy, a country lawyer, won election to the Hungarian legislature on a program committed to "national defense" against the mounting influx of Polish and Jewish immigrants. Istoczy's demagoguery both exploited and fueled the hatred aroused by a particularly notorious blood-libel trial.

The episode began in a small Hungarian village, Tisza-Eszlar. The local inhabitants were Catholics, Calvinists, and Jews. On April 1, 1882, a week and a half before Easter, a fourteen-year-old Catholic housemaid, Esther Solymossy, left her employer's home to buy paint. She did not return. Her employer and her widowed mother looked for the girl until evening but found no trace of her. When Esther was not back after a week, Tisza-Eszlar's sheriff organized an extensive search of the entire district, but in vain. Rumors then began circulating. It happened that the district to which Tisza-Eszlar belonged was represented in the Hungarian parliament by Deputy Onody, a virulent antisemite and protégé of Gysl Istoczy. When both Istoczy and Onody launched into accusations of ritual murder, the sheriff and the district examining magistrate felt obliged to investigate further.

On May 19, the two men arrived in Tisza-Eszlar with an entourage of mounted policemen and immediately directed their attention to the family of Joszef Sharf, custodian of the local synagogue. In early April, Sharf had sought to reassure Mrs. Solymossy that Esther would turn up, and this expression of sympathy the magistrate found suspicious. Yet he shrewdly began his interrogation by questioning not Sharf but Sharf's five-year-old son, Samuel. Mixing gifts of candy with "suggestions," the magistrate obtained a statement from the youngster. "Papa called Esther into the house," said the boy, "washed her, and took her to the synagogue. The [kosher] butcher slaughtered her. My brother Moritz and I saw the blood being caught in a plate." The magistrate then turned to Moritz, a fourteen-year-old. Using threats instead of bribery, he extracted a similar "confession." It stated:

> My father, the synagogue officer Joszef Sharf, called Esther Soly-
> mossy into our house from the street. . . . [H]e led her into the
> synagogue, laid her on the floor there, and undressed her down to
> her shift. In addition to my father . . . the others present were the
> [town's three kosher butchers and several others]. . . . The [others]
> held Esther fast while the butcher Schwarz cut her throat with a
> knife. The blood was caught and poured into a pot.

With these statements, the sheriff promptly set about rounding up the eleven men whom Moritz had named. When all indignantly declared their innocence, they were forced to drink ice water by the quart until, in their agony, they "confessed." Preparations were made then to arraign the jailed defendants.

On June 18, however, the gamekeeper of Tisza-Eszlar's woodland recovered the body of a girl from the neighboring Nyiregyhaza River. The dead girl's left hand clutched a cloth saturated in zinc crystals, a key ingredient in paint. No trace of a wound appeared on her throat. The magistrate immediately summoned Esther's mother to identify the corpse. Mrs. Solymossy adamantly insisted that the body could not be that of her missing daughter. She gave no reason for her opinion, and the magistrate did not ask for any. The next morning, he summoned two local physicians to determine if the girl had been approximately fourteen years old, and whether she could have been lying in the river since April 1, the day of Esther's disappearance.

After their examination, the physicians stated that the dead girl had been "at least eighteen and probably twenty years of age," that she could not have lain under the water for more than ten days, and that her white and tender skin suggested that she belonged to the upper class. Plainly, none of these observations applied to Esther Solymossy. Yet the magistrate was not content. His distrust of Jews led him to suspect a link between the discovery of this body and the Jews of Tisza-Eszlar. Was it not likely that friends of the arrested Jews had dressed another corpse to create the impression that Esther had drowned, and that the prisoners consequently were innocent? Then, on a "tip" from a local gentile, the magistrate ordered the arrest of three other local Jews. These, too, were given the ice-water treatment until they similarly "confessed." Jailed, they awaited their trial, together with the alleged murderers of Esther Solymossy.

By July of 1882, newspaper accounts of the Tisza-Eszlar affair had aroused extraordinary interest and passions throughout the Habsburg Empire. In several of Hungary's smaller towns, local Jews were beaten and Jewish homes were pillaged. Christian servants left their Jewish employers. In Tisza-Eszlar, the examining magistrate received letters with alleged Jewish recipes for "the best way to prepare a meal with the blood of Christian virgins." Yet, at the same time, a number of Hungary's most prominent attorneys offered to represent the Jewish prisoners. One of these was a noted liberal parliamentary deputy, Karl von Eotvos. From the reports he had heard, Eotvos, an experienced criminal lawyer, instantly discerned the superficiality of the country doctors' autopsy report. In December 1882, he asked the state prosecutor's office for permission to have the corpse exhumed and examined by several respected pathologists in Budapest. The request was granted. Two weeks later, the pathologists completed their report. The dead girl assuredly was not older than fourteen or fifteen, it stated. Her body could easily have lain in the river for up to three months without decomposing. Her "upper-class" skin was tender and white because blood slowly had leaked through it.

With this information in hand, Eotvos laid out his defense in the trial that began in mid-June 1883, in the district courthouse of Nyiregyhaza. The proceedings by then had attracted journalists and lawyers from throughout Europe, all of them fascinated by the struggle being played out between rationality and superstition. For two months, they watched in disbelief as the prosecution elaborated upon its charges of ritual murder, citing medieval sources, among them twisted paraphrases of the Talmud. Yet even a jury of local rustics could not ignore Defense Attorney Eotvos's scientific data. On August 3, it acquitted the defendants. Immediately, anti-Jewish demonstrations erupted in Budapest. Jews were assaulted in the streets, in the parks, in trams. Jewish shops were smashed and looted. More than a week passed before order could be restored, when army units were brought in to reinforce the Budapest police.

A half-year earlier, in the spring of 1882, the antisemitic politician Gysl Istoczy launched *Tizenket Ropirat,* a periodical of unprecedented xenophobic scurrility. Its articles were so brazen in their demand for a mass eviction of the Jews "[as] a foreign race, with corrupt morals, baleful character, filthy self-interest," that the Hungarian lower house of parliament voted to bring a libel suit against Istoczy. The trial took place in Budapest in June and July 1883, almost simultaneously with the proceedings of Tisza-Eszlar. It was a time of severe economic disruption. In his florid trial defense, therefore, Istoczy shrewdly raised the specter of the Rothschilds and Jewish international banking, of the Hungarian nation "writhing in the octopus tentacles of the Jewish money kings" and the "all-powerful" Alliance Israélite Universelle. The jury required less than thirty minutes to issue a verdict of acquittal. Flushed with victory, Istoczy then proceeded to establish the National Antisemitic Party, with the professed goal of eliminating Jews from the nation's political and economic life. In the ensuing national election, seventeen of the party's candidates won parliamentary seats.

Elsewhere in the Habsburg Empire's backward and ethnically mixed provinces, the Jews remained as exposed and vulnerable a minority as in the Hungarian countryside. Here, too, in the 1880s and 1890s, the blood libel was periodically revived. The most notorious of these episodes occurred in March 1899, when a nineteen-year-old seamstress, Agnes Hruza, disappeared in the Brzina Forest near Polan, a middle-sized Bohemian town. Agnes's body was discovered on April 1, the day before Easter Sunday. An autopsy determined that she had been stabbed and strangled (although not sexually molested). Once again the rumor circulated that the Jews had found a victim for their forthcoming Passover Seder. Within the week, a Jewish suspect was taken into custody. This was Leopold Hilsner, an unemployed shoemaker. Hilsner had known Agnes Hruza and had followed her home several times before, and a search of his lodgings revealed clothes that appeared to be covered with foliage and dried blood. The evidence was sufficient to arraign Hilsner and put him on trial in the circuit court of Kutenberg. Yet the prosecuting attorney, Dr. Schneider-Svoboda, embellished his case by invoking the ritual-murder charge, citing various Jewish sources, including the Talmud, as "proof" of this practice. On September 16, 1899, the jury convicted Hilsner of murder. The judge sentenced him to be hanged.

Once again, newspapers throughout the empire gave wide coverage to a ritual-murder case. Without taking an editorial position, all devoted extensive space to scholarly and ecclesiastical views and counterviews on the Passover-blood charge. It was in the aftermath of the trial, too, that a professor of philosophy at Prague's Karl-Ferdinand University produced an assessment of unique critical weight. The author was Tomas Masaryk, a prolific scholar of the Czech Reformation and a renowned cultural icon among his people. Indeed, not long before, his admiring countrymen had elected him as one of their delegates to the Habsburg Reichsrat, where he became an eloquent champion of the Czech national cause. Above all else, Masaryk was an enlightened humanist. Thus, in 1899, reacting to the ritual-murder accusation against Hilsner, he provided Vienna's *Neue Freie Presse,* the empire's most widely read newspaper, with a concise historical overview of the blood libel. His indignation barely suppressed, the professor concluded in apocalyptic language that "[i]t is blasphemy for a Christian to state that ritual murder comes from the spirit of the Jewish religion." Although Masaryk's reputation alone could not have reversed the Hilsner verdict, it assured close judicial attention upon appeal. In late summer of 1900, the court of claims in Vienna ordered a new trial. This time, the issue of ritual murder no longer was invoked. Hilsner simply was found guilty of acting as an "accomplice" to murder, and sentenced to life imprisonment.

Yet Masaryk paid dearly for having adopted an unpopular public position. When he appeared for class on November 10, 1900, in the week following Hilsner's retrial, he was greeted by placards urging students to boycott the lectures of a professor "who had taken up the cause of a Jew." Ruefully, Masaryk acknowledged later that "not only the student body but the whole [of Karl-Ferdinand University] was infected with the uncultivated virus of street antisemitism. . . . I have taken part in many struggles, but the battle against antisemitism cost me the most in both time and pain."

THE LEGACY OF CLERICAL JUDEOPHOBIA: HABSBURG AUSTRIA

It is worth recalling that the ritual-murder accusation, originating as far back as the twelfth century, was the product not only of folk superstition but of clerical endorsement. Well into the High Middle Ages, the friars of the Franciscan and Dominican orders were particularly vigorous in circulating the charge. Although the blood libel survived principally in backward Eastern Europe, the accusation underwent a certain unanticipated revival even in the West, and even as late as the nineteenth century. Once again, the initial sponsorship was clerical. In 1870, following the Italian *Risorgimento*, the Vatican was stripped of its rule over the city of Rome. Accordingly, in its vindictive counterassault on secular liberalism, papal spokesmen left no doubt that Jews and Freemasons were the driving force behind this sinister new movement. In 1871, moreover, Pope Pius IX uttered not a word of criticism or caution when August Rohling, a Catholic priest and professor of theology at Karl-Ferdinand University, published *Der Talmudjude*, a volume that made much of the Jews' alleged propensity for ritual murder. Indeed, Rohling published and lectured so widely on this issue that he was called as a prosecution witness for the Tisza-Eszlar trial. Throughout the 1880s, the papal press quoted extensively from his writings.

Leo XIII, who acceded to the pontifical throne in 1878, following the death of Pius IX, fully shared his predecessor's enmities. At Leo's initiative, some 130 Catholic newspapers and periodicals were launched in Italy alone, all of them committed to the war against secular liberalism, and against the Jews as the movement's putative sponsors. Possibly the single most influential of these publications was the Jesuit biweekly *La Civiltà cattolica*. In 1880, with Vatican approval, the newspaper embarked on a series of thirty-six articles unsurpassed in the malignity of their attacks on Jews. The Jews were atheists and freethinkers, editorialized the *Civiltà cattolica*, the "nucleus of the secret sects that . . . threaten the ruin and the extermination of Christian society." The accusation was paralleled in *L'Osservatore romano*, the Vatican's semiofficial daily newspaper. In May 1882, warning that the Jews constituted a "rapacious tyranny," *L'Osservatore romano* allowed it to be known that "[t]he Holy Father [Leo XIII], while condemning violent means, upholds the antisemitic movement as long as it is carried out in a legal fashion, as in Germany, for example."

It was also in the latter nineteenth century, with clerical hostility linked increasingly to modern nationalism and to lower-middle-class insecurity, that a new dimension was added to the Jews' unique and anomalous status in Christian thinking. Who were the Jews? The question remained both spoken and unspoken in European consciousness. Where did these mysterious and potent wizards come from? They bore, as Leo Pinsker suggested in his little volume *Self-Emancipation* (p. 259), all the attributes of nationality, but possessed no country of their own. Like faceless Gypsies, they skulked through the backstreets of Europe's cities. While pledging loyalty to the lands of their domicile, they remained a people of international ties, and they expressed their unshakable cohesion in a multitude of religious, ethnic, and financial ways.

In Catholic Europe, the culture shock of a Jewish presence loomed largest in Vienna. The presence was a comparatively recent one. In the nineteenth century, responding to the erratic trajectory of emancipation, Jews from the Habsburg Empire's outlying provinces, from Galicia, Bukovina, Moravia, and Slovakia, began moving into its larger cities, into Prague, Budapest, and above all into Vienna. By 1910, Viennese Jewry numbered some 175,000, fully 9 percent of the city's population. Quite impoverished, most of the newcomers congregated initially in the drab, quasi-ghetto Leopoldstadt quarter. Yet, whatever their humble origins, under their beloved Emperor Franz Josef the immigrants perceived only hope for themselves in this magnificent capital, with its unsurpassed economic and cultural opportunities. In their optimism and sheer bulldog tenacity, they forged ahead, year by year. By 1914, with few exceptions, the city's Jews had achieved middle-class status.

Indeed, a significant minority among them, veterans and newcomers alike, rose to economic and professional eminence. In Austria as in Hungary, Jews were the principal builders of the nation's steel mills and railroads, of its textile, sugar-refining, and meatpacking industries, of more than half its larger banks, and virtually all of Vienna's fashionable retail shops. Almost one in five of the empire's military reserve officers were Jews (albeit principally in the medical and technical-service branches). By 1918, no fewer than 450 Jews had been ennobled in Austria, and 346 in Hungary. Their record of upward mobility extended to the liberal professions. Here, given the Jews' passion for education, their record of overachievement should have been even less surprising. Jews, after all, comprised one of every three students in Vienna's gymnasia, one in four at the University of Vienna, one in three in the university's schools of law and medicine.

It was not a phenomenon the Church regarded congenially, not in this largest Roman Catholic nation in all of Europe. Moreover, in his campaign of anti-Jewish "enlightenment," Pope Leo XIII discerned both a moral imperative and a political weapon formidable enough to exploit against other non-Catholic and secularist elements. It was also in this clerically inspired effort that attention was shrewdly drawn to the Rothschilds. The prominence of the great banking family was by no means singled out by the Church alone. Neither was it targeted only in Austria. In France and Germany, numerous articles and several books were devoted to the "octopus-like power" of the renowned "sixth dynasty of Europe" (pp. 102–16). Yet, as a political weapon, anti-Jewish rhetoric focused on the Rothschilds more effectively in Austria than in Germany or even in Catholic France; for in Austria the economic power of the Rothschilds survived more extensively than in any other country. It was in Vienna, too, that Jews in business and the professions loomed larger in public visibility than in any other European city. Thus, theologians like August Rohling (p. 226) and Josef Decken, a noted political polemicist, vigorously denounced the "Judaization" ("Verjudung") of Austrian culture.

In the years after 1873, moreover, the crash of the Vienna stock exchange, and the ensuing economic depression, induced Karl Lueger to develop a political campaign directed largely against "Jewish" financial power. A man of proletarian background who had worked his way through university, Lueger was first elected to Vienna's municipal council in 1875, and ten years later was elected to the imperial Reichstag. Eloquent and charismatic, the young politician soon found his métier in stigmatizing Jewish bankers as the manipulators of the recent economic collapse and as the authentic source of Vienna's endemic underemployment. Throughout the 1880s, Lueger pressed for nationalization of the Rothschild-owned Kaiser-Ferdinand Railroad. In 1891 he went much further, establishing a Christian Socialist Party as his vehicle to the mayoralty of Vienna. In his campaign program, Lueger outlined his scheme for creating job opportunities on behalf of "deserving Catholics." It included the imaginative device of extensive public works projects, the dismissal of all Jewish municipal employees, and the transfer of municipal contracts from Jewish to Christian providers. Lueger's closest aide, Ernst

Schneider, genially fortified the platform by suggesting that the Austrian government should offer a prize to any good Christian who killed a Jew.

While the monarchy and members of the aristocracy adopted a cool reserve toward Lueger's demagoguery, the Austrian clergy from the outset were unflagging in their support. On Lueger's fiftieth birthday, in 1894, he was presented with a greeting by five hundred Austrian priests. Pope Leo XIII gave the "Christian Socials" an approbation that was all but explicit, not disguising his pleasure at their emphasis upon antisemitism. In August 1899, Cardinal Emilio Taliano, the papal nuncio in Vienna, took "great pleasure" in informing Cardinal Mariano Rampolla, the Vatican secretary of state, ". . . that the Christian Socials are steadily enlarging their base of operations and spreading not only into the countryside . . . but also into the most important towns, where liberalism and Judaism, united together, still control local governments and oppose the people." In reply, Rampolla conveyed the pope's "delight."

These were the circumstances, by the late nineteenth century, in which Lueger, widely perceived as the unofficial candidate of the Church, emerged as a formidable candidate for Vienna's mayoralty. Indeed, he actually was elected to the office three times, but on the first two occasions he was vetoed by Emperor Franz Josef, who feared the blatancy of his populism and antisemitism. In 1897, however, after eliciting Lueger's assurance of nondiscrimination, the emperor finally authorized him to take office. By then, Lueger's party assumed control not only of the mayoralty but of the provincial Diet of Lower Austria. Throughout the subsequent fourteen years of his mayoral incumbency, Lueger actually proved to be an innovative and effective executive. The range of his government's municipal services was unprecedented in Vienna's history. He managed as well to keep his promise to the emperor, muting his antisemitism. "Wer ein Jude ist, bestimme ich," he joked with confidants. "I decide who is [and is not] a Jew." Nevertheless, Lueger's earlier years of anti-Jewish campaigning had inflicted their damage. White-collar antisemitism, always socially acceptable, had now been institutionalized as politically functional.

THE JOINDER OF CLERICAL AND NATIONALIST XENOPHOBIA: FRANCE

Superficially, the Jews of France appeared rather less exposed than those in Austria. They were a much less visible community, numbering between 80,000 and 90,000 at the end of the nineteenth century. Moreover, their acceptance into the nation's body politic seemed more complete than in any other major continental nation. Here Jews enjoyed unlimited access both to

France's economy and to its public offices (p. 110). In 1891, commemorating the centennial of Jewish emancipation, Chief Rabbi Zadoc Kahn struck a popular chord among French Jewry in apotheosizing the date as "our exodus from Egypt. . . . It is our modern Passover."

Nevertheless, undercurrents of both religious and political reaction were not lacking in these same years. The aristocracy found it difficult to make its peace with France's liberal new government, and the clergy remained even more discomfited. Although Pope Leo XIII had resignedly authorized French Catholics to accept the newly established Third French Republic, and to defend the cause of the Church within the framework of republican politics, the pontiff's injunction was not accepted literally. Rather, during the 1880s, the Jesuits, who had been barred from France since the Revolution, managed quietly to return to the country and establish close connections with the tight-knit royalist nucleus. Shrewdly, the Jesuits played on the country's nationalism, urging all true patriots to repudiate a republic that was the "captive" of Protestants, Freemasons, and Jews. The appeal evoked particular resonance among followers of the Boulangist movement. General Georges Boulanger, minister of war in 1886–87, had envisaged himself as a leader capable of governing the nation with true "military efficiency" and ultimately of winning a war of revenge against Germany. In the 1889 parliamentary election, the general won a substantial plurality vote and appeared on the verge of a coup d'état. At the last moment, however, he lost his nerve and decamped to Belgium, never to return.

Boulanger's followers were not to be that easily dispersed. Dubbing themselves nationalists, they attracted numerous reactionary elements from the royalist, clerical, and even urban petit bourgeois camps. Under the nationalist flag, antisemitism became their favored rallying point. The most prestigious spokesmen among them were Henri de Rochefort, François Lauer, Maurice Barrès, and the Marquis de Morès, all of whom discerned in antisemitism an exemplary technique for stigmatizing the republic itself as a front for Jewish predators. Thus, in February 1890, a great Boulangist-nationalist rally in the Paris suburb of Neuilly marked the "official" birth of political antisemitism in France, for the event's sponsor was the newly established Ligue Antisémitique. While Morès, Lauer, Rochefort, and Barrès were among the league's charter members, its presiding eminence was a man who already had achieved national recognition as France's "pope of antisemitism." This was Édouard Drumont.

Born in Paris in 1844, Drumont was the son of a municipal clerk. As a young man, fascinated by journalism, he dropped out of lycée to work for a succession of fringe newspapers, most of them of the scandal-sheet variety. At the same time, Drumont was strongly influenced by the militant reactionism of the Catholic press, and in 1867 managed to publish his first anti-Jewish article, in the *Revue du monde catholique,* accusing the Jews of economic parasitism. The contribution evoked much praise and encouragement among both priests and Catholic laymen. Over the ensuing two decades, therefore, Drumont published almost exclusively for the Catholic press. Although clerical antisemitism was hardly a newer phenomenon in France than in Italy or Austria, Drumont's uniqueness lay in his ability to merge and magnify Catholic, nationalist, and populist antipathy to the Jews in a single vision. For him, France's defeat in the Franco-Prussian War was the end product of a "Freemasonry of Treachery" that was manipulated principally by Jews. Indeed, the specter of Jews as German spies within the gates would remain one of Drumont's choice battle cries. And so would the well-familiar diabolization of the Rothschilds.

It was in 1876 that the stocky, heavily bearded Drumont began work on his volume *La France juive (Jewish France).* Ten years later, with the help and advice of his close friend the writer Alphonse Daudet, the book eventually was published. In the racy, sensationalist prose that had become the vogue in French journalism, *La France juive* developed a stereotyped image of the Jewish role in history, of a people incarnating a composite of social and political deviances that included alcoholism, socialism, capitalism, warmongering, espionage, and child sacrifice. Even the Jews' physical characteristics had to be described in racist, scatological terms, with detailed attention given their "trailing odor of excrement." The volume proceeded then to focus on the Jews' role specifically in modern France. By its account, the new, liberal, republican regime was nothing less than the Jews' creation and their cash cow. The suppression of the monarchy, that historic protector of Catholic values and virtues, was and remained the work of the Jews, and principally of the Jewish bankers—the Rothschilds, Bleichröders, Hirsches, and other financial vampires. *La France juive* reached its climax with an appeal for all "true" Frenchmen to drive Jews from the country, even, if necessary, by resorting to full-scale massacre.

Notwithstanding its tone of hysteria, even of palpable derangement, *La France juive* almost immediately won vast and indiscriminate praise from right-wing, clerical newspapers and journals. Indeed, the volume went through twenty-eight printings in its first year, and soon established the basis of a comfortable estate for Drumont. It also launched Drumont as France's "pope" of antisemitism. In 1892, he was able to capitalize upon that reputation. A wealthy businessman set him up as editor of his own newspaper and lavishly funded its expenses. From then on, Drumont's staff was drawn almost exclusively from the Ligue Antisémitique. Others who were continually in and out of the newspaper's office were Morès, Barrès, Lauer, Rochefort, Daudet, right-wing priests, members of the effete Jockey Club, and other ideological soul mates. In his newspaper, as in his volume, Drumont continued to hammer away almost exclusively at the Jewish menace. Letters of praise and gratitude inundated his editorial office. The circulation of *La Libre Parole* grew steadily in its first months, eventually reaching 70,000. Possibly, it would have remained at that impressive, if unspectacular plateau, if Drumont had not scored yet another populist coup, this time by exposing the "Panama Canal Scandal."

Thirteen years earlier, in 1879, Ferdinand de Lesseps, builder of the Suez Canal, launched a comparable engineering venture for the Isthmus of Panama. Leaving the engineering details to his son, Charles, Lesseps concentrated on the business of raising share capital for his project. In that effort, he had recourse to a banker, Marcel Lévy-Crémieux, who formed an underwriting syndicate. Bribes were placed strategically to win press support (a common practice in France), and to secure political influence in the parliament. Ultimately, more than 60,000 Frenchmen purchased shares in the company. It was money down the drain. An uninspired engineer, Charles de Lesseps badly miscalculated the different sea levels of the Atlantic and Pacific oceans, and heavy cost overruns ultimately became prohibitive. In February 1890 the Panama Canal Company was placed in bankruptcy. Thousands of life savings were destroyed. Shock waves swept through France.

Covering these developments, *La Libre Parole* launched immediately into sensational accusations of a "Jewish publicity campaign to deceive Frenchmen," a "Jewish conspiracy to destroy the French economy." Even without evidence, Drumont had stumbled on the incontrovertible fact that a number of Jews, men such as Cornelius Herz, Baron Jacques de Reinach, and Léopold Arton, had served as "intermediaries," that is, bribe dispensers, between the company and parliament. Before *La Libre Parole* could so much as publish the information, moreover, Reinach suddenly panicked, rushed to Drumont, and promised to reveal details of influence peddling if his own name was not mentioned. Drumont agreed, revealed the information—and included Reinach in his accusations. Soon afterward, Reinach committed suicide. Herz fled to England. As for Ferdinand and Charles de Lesseps, in 1893 they were jointly put on trial for fraud. Convicted, both father and son were given five-year sentences (although, upon appeal, they avoided prison on a technicality). All these revelations and developments meanwhile did wonders for *La Libre Parole*'s readership. In 1893, the paper's circulation exceeded 200,000 and its editor had become the toast of Paris.

L'Affaire

For Drumont, that popularity was to be exploited first and foremost in his ongoing campaign against the Jews. In the pages of *La Libre Parole*, it was the Jews alone who were to be identified with the vast and tragic multiplicity of

France's social ills. As he flailed away against the "people of vampires and traitors," Drumont harshly assailed War Minister Auguste Mercier for allowing Jews, a people notorious in their "propensity for treason," to serve as military officers. In the eyes of Drumont and much of the nation at large, the officers' corps was the very distillation of the "true" France. As products of France's "best" families and of its finest Catholic secondary schools, these men were the guardians of the ancient Gallic virtues of obedience and discipline, and thereby the repository of France's anguished dreams of revenge against Germany. What were Jews doing among them? What was the future of a nation that permitted several hundred Jews to hold military commissions?

One of the beneficiaries of this republican egalitarianism was Alfred Dreyfus. Born in 1859, Dreyfus was the youngest of thirteen children of a prosperous Alsatian-Jewish textile manufacturer who had moved his family to France in the aftermath of the Franco-Prussian War. After attending the Collège Saint-Barbe, Dreyfus was admitted to the École Polytechnique, one of several training schools for military officers, and was graduated as a sublieutenant. In 1889, he was promoted to captain of artillery, and a year later to the École de Guerre. In 1893, upon completing his studies, Dreyfus was assigned to the General Staff. It was an exemplary record. Married, with two children, the young captain seemed on the threshold of a brilliant career, one that apparently was impregnable to the thinly veiled distaste of his Catholic fellow officers. Yet those anti-Jewish resentments suddenly became entangled in an apparent new threat to the nation's security.

France had been "out-intelligenced" in the Franco-Prussian War. As a corrective, the army put much effort afterward into the improvement of its own intelligence services. One of the Bureau of Intelligence's key departments was that of counterespionage, the so-called Section of Statistics, under the command of Colonel Jean Sandherr, and of Sandherr's deputy, Major Hubert Henry. Among Henry's responsibilities were guarded dealings with shady informants. One of these agents was a cleaning woman in the German embassy who had succeeded lately in dredging up material from the office of the German military attaché, Lieutenant Colonel Maximilian von Schwartzkoppen. The recoveries suggested that Schwartzkoppen was actively seeking out information on France's military dispositions. In April 1894, the cleaning woman–informant ferreted from Schwartzkoppen's wastebasket the copy of a recent letter suggesting that a certain "D" on the French General Staff was providing the German attaché with this intelligence. The copy was immediately rushed to Major Henry at the Section of Statistics. Duly alerted, Henry and his staff investigated diligently but could find no clue to the traitor's identity. Yet the critical "D" would remain acutely in the consciousness of French intelligence.

The guilty party in fact was Major Ferdinand Walsin Esterhazy, battalion chief of the Seventy-fourth Infantry Regiment. A gambler and wencher, chronically in debt, Esterhazy had approached Schwartzkoppen on his own and brazenly offered to sell information to the German attaché. Upon consulting with Berlin, Schwartzkoppen received permission to deal with the renegade Esterhazy. Further communication between the two men soon produced new deliveries—and new interceptions for the French Section of Statistics. In September 1894, War Minister Mercier was informed that still another intriguing document had been retrieved from Schwartzkoppen's wastebasket. It was a *bordereau* (a letter bordered in blue), promising to deliver to the German attaché key information on a new French artillery manual. The discovery touched off a flurry of meetings within the senior French military command, including the Bureau of Intelligence and its counterintelligence subdivision, the Section of Statistics. Again, the evidence pointed to a staff officer, presumably an artillery specialist. The handwriting was studied and restudied. Soon a consensus was reached that the traitor might well be Captain Alfred Dreyfus, the one staff officer bearing the initial "D."

On October 13, 1894, Dreyfus was called in to "take dictation" from Commandant du Paty de Clam, an assistant to Army Chief of Staff General Raoul de Boisdeffre. Suddenly, Paty de Clam snatched the notepad from Dreyfus's hands, studied it, then bellowed: "In the name of the Republic, I arrest you. You are accused of the crime of high treason." A pistol was left on the table for Dreyfus to do "the honorable thing." Shocked and outraged, Dreyfus demanded to know his crime. Instead, he was arrested and marched off to prison, still protesting wildly. For five days, he would be left alone in his cell, half-mad with horror and rage. Meanwhile, the army's top officers remained in continual meeting, conferring with graphologists. Comparing the *bordereau* with samples of Dreyfus's own handwriting, the handwriting experts failed to agree that Dreyfus was the author of the mysterious letter. At this point, uncertain of their ground, Generals Mercier and Boisdeffre considered dropping the accusation against the imprisoned captain. Suddenly, their hands were forced.

On October 29, Drumont's *La Libre Parole* appeared on the streets with a strident headline: "Arrest of the Jewish Officer A. Dreyfus." In ensuing days, the newspaper released a sequence of lurid accounts, describing the alleged crime and the "confirmed evidence" against the "Jewish traitor." It later developed that, from beginning to end, Major Henry was the source who alerted his friend Drumont, and who continued to feed him information on Dreyfus. With the sensational press release of October 29, the army command hesitated no longer. On November 1, it announced that it would proceed with a formal court-martial. The process then duly began on December 19. Over the next three days, before a panel of six army officers, testimony was offered by Colonel du Paty de Clam, who declared, mendaciously, that Dreyfus had a long history of suspicious behavior, that graphologists had "conclusively" identified the handwriting on the *bordereau* as his. But when the testimony began to appear suspiciously fragile, it was Major Henry who decided the issue, asserting that the Dreyfus file contained other incriminating details that could not be revealed "for reasons of state security." On this putative evidence, the court-martial proclaimed Dreyfus's guilt, on December 22, 1894, and sentenced him to life imprisonment.

All the while, other right-wing newspapers followed the lead of *La Libre Parole*, sharing in the antisemitic vilification. Thus, *La Croix*, organ of the Assumptionist Order, proclaimed that "Jewry . . . has rotted out everything. . . . It is a horrible cancer," and then joined *La Libre Parole* in demanding the collective banishment of French Jewry. Other clerical press accounts asserted that Dreyfus was under the protection of the Rothschilds and of a "league" of Jewish bankers. Altogether, the moment was one of supreme vindication for the Church and its clerical Orders, one to be exploited to the limit. In earlier years, Prime Minister Léon Gambetta, "father" of the Third Republic and an ardent secularist, had embarked on a program to create a dominant public school system. His success was impressive. By 1894, fully 86,000 public schools were functioning in the country. Nevertheless, 15,000 private, Catholic schools continued to operate, and it was in these that children of the "best" families received their education, including graduates who went on to the military officers' corps. These were the elements of Church and army that had only awaited an opportunity to reassert their influence in the despised republic. It appeared now that they had found it.

On January 3, 1895, as Dreyfus was drummed out of the army in the courtyard of the École Militaire, huge crowds outside shouted "Death to the Jews!" On February 21, removed from his prison and transferred to an icy cell in a naval cruiser, Dreyfus was carried across the Atlantic to Central America, to imprisonment on Devil's Island, off the coast of French Guiana.

THE RESURGENCE OF REPUBLICAN IDEALISM

Dreyfus's family would not abandon him. His brother Mathieu, who directed the family textile business, was determined to secure a reversal of the court-martial verdict on grounds of insufficient evidence. Yet, as he sought political support in his effort, he made little progress. Even among the nation's moderate and leftist parties, no one could be found to take up the cause of the convicted Jewish officer. Writing in *La Justice* on December 25, 1895, the Radical Socialist Georges Clemenceau observed that "[Dreyfus] has . . . no love of anything, no human or even animal ties, nothing but an obscene soul and abject heart." The Socialist leader Jean Jaurès declared forcefully that Dreyfus should have been sentenced to death. Even the Jews of France, shamed and mortified, remained convinced of Dreyfus's guilt. Others knew better. One was Colonel Schwartzkoppen in the German embassy. In 1895, he disentangled himself from Esterhazy, turning down the latter's repeated offers to sell information. Esterhazy, in turn, endemically short of funds, now sought "loans" from Jewish fellow officers, those for whom he had occasionally hired himself out as a "second" in duels. His entreaties were rejected. So was his appeal to a former lycée classmate, Baron Edmond de Rothschild.

Toward the end of the year, Colonel Jean Sandherr retired as chief of the army's Statistical Section. His place was taken by the Alsatian-born Lieutenant Colonel Georges Picquart. With Major Henry remaining on as his deputy, Picquart was quite prepared to accept the latter's assurance that no need existed to revisit the Dreyfus case, except for a perfunctory review of the convicted prisoner's file. But in March 1896, a new development unexpectedly shook this assumption. It was then that the cleaning woman–informant in Schwartzkoppen's office recovered a small blue piece of stationery from the German attaché's wastebasket. "Le petit bleu" spoke vaguely of payments still due. The return address on the envelope was Major Walsin Esterhazy's. Picquart immediately ordered an undercover investigation of the officer. Letters were secretly "borrowed" from Esterhazy's apartment and photographed. They alluded to the major's private contempt for his fellow officers, his wish that he could lead a company of German uhlans in putting them to the sword. As Picquart read through these copies, his memory was jogged. He studied the Dreyfus file again, and noted that the handwriting on *le petit bleu* and on the original *bordereau* were identical. It followed that the *bordereau* must also have been written by Esterhazy, not by Dreyfus. With this astonishing information, Picquart over the summer and autumn of 1896 repeatedly dispatched memoranda to the army command, explaining the significance of his discovery. The replies were succinct: the Dreyfus case was closed. Picquart persisted. On September 15, 1896, he secured an interview with General Charles-Arthur Gonse, the deputy chief of staff. Gonse heard Picquart out, but remained unshakable. "What does it matter to you that the Jew is on Devil's Island?" he asked finally.

"But since he's innocent—" protested Picquart.

"It doesn't matter," interjected Gonse. "These are not issues which ought to enter into consideration."

"What you are saying is abominable, *mon général*," exploded Picquart. ". . . . I will not take this secret to the grave with me."

Yet it appeared at first as if Picquart would have to. On October 27, after refusing all subsequent warnings to desist from his "obsession," he was reassigned to a nondescript garrison in eastern France. At the same time, Major Henry, in his alarm that the Dreyfus case might be reopened, began "thickening" the Dreyfus file with forged documents suggesting that the imprisoned officer had engaged in an even wider-spread conspiracy. But Picquart was not through. He provided Mathieu Dreyfus with copies both of Esterhazy's handwriting and of the *petit bleu*. These in turn were circulated to newspapers, many of which reproduced the copies in their pages. Bank officials needed little time in confirming that the handwriting was Esterhazy's. He had long been notorious among them for circulating bad checks.

Here at last, in the spring of 1897, the effort to win support for a retrial began to gain important support. Prominent intellectuals such as Anatole France, Charles Péguy, and Émile Zola now joined the "Dreyfusard" cause. So, belatedly, did Georges Clemenceau, Jean Jaurès, Senate Vice President Auguste Scheurer-Kestner, and other liberal and socialist political figures. Not least of all, among the formerly timorous Jewish community, champions of the Dreyfusard cause began to emerge, among them such literary figures as Marcel Proust and Léon Blum (although the chief rabbinate, the Rothschilds, and other members of the Jewish "establishment" continued to remain discreetly silent). Among the "progressive" newspapers, editorial pressure mounted for President Félix Faure to order a revision of Dreyfus's conviction (Faure would not respond). Only Alfred Dreyfus himself remained unaware of these developments. His life was one of complete isolation on Devil's Island, with a stockade fence erected around his hut. At night, he was chained to his cot. In October 1897, he appeared so close to death from hopelessness and exhaustion that the prison commander ordered him measured for a coffin.

In November, however, the army leadership felt impelled to conduct a brief, superficial investigation of the unsavory Esterhazy. It then developed that the evidence against him simply was too compelling to ignore. Accordingly, a court-martial was scheduled for January 11, 1898. On that day, Picquart was called as a witness—and was virtually crucified by the panel of military judges. The following day, Esterhazy was acquitted, to be carried out of the courtroom on the shoulders of an exultant crowd. The army command then wasted little time in stripping Picquart of his commission and pension for "traducing" his commanders. All hope appeared gone for a revision of the Dreyfus verdict.

It was at this point that an elemental force intervened. This was the renowned novelist Émile Zola. On January 13, 1898, one day after the Esterhazy court-martial ended, Zola published an open letter to President Faure. Appearing on the front page of the Radical Socialist newspaper *L'Aurore*, the letter was the renowned "J'accuse," charging both the army's senior commanders and President Faure himself of having knowingly collaborated in the conviction and life imprisonment of an innocent man. Indeed, beyond his indictment of the president and the army command, Zola was assaulting the "virtues" of traditional France, its religious passions and prejudices, its military chauvinism and social rigidities. The letter was a bombshell. Within hours of its appearance, over 300,000 copies of *L'Aurore* were sold. "Dreyfusardism," recalled Léon Blum, "was reinvigorated...."

For its part, the army command saw no alternative but to bring action against Zola for criminal libel. This it did on February 4. Plainly, Zola could not prove his accusation of "knowing collaboration" (nor had he cared to), and it was not a difficult matter for the prosecution to win a conviction. Zola was sentenced to a year's imprisonment but then was discreetly allowed to "escape" to England. He had accomplished his purpose. By the late winter and early spring of 1898, the *Affaire* had effectively split France politically and socially. All the forces of liberalism, secularism, and republicanism now at last were fully mobilized against the entrenched interests of conservatism, clericalism, and royalism.

It was among these latter elements that popular antisemitism reached a new pitch of ferocity. Throughout January and February 1898, in Nantes, Rennes, Tours, Poitiers, Toulouse, Angers, Marseilles, Rouen, and Châlons, mobs attacked and pillaged Jewish homes and shops. In Paris during the Zola trial, Jules Guérin, chairman of the Ligue Antisémitique, led his "troops" menacingly around the courthouse and the Palais de Justice, many of them carrying placards demanding "À MORT LES JUIFS!" In Algeria, the European *colons* discerned in the Dreyfus Affair an opportunity to isolate the 80,000 Jews who presumed to share their citizenship. Hardly a day passed in 1898 without attacks against Algerian-Jewish homes and businesses. In the parliamentary elections of May 1898, Max Régis, a fiery spokesman for Algeria's Europeans, led the victorious four-member bloc of deputies that would be known as the "antisemitic caucus" in the French Chamber of Deputies.

Perhaps most ominously, in these two years of 1897–98, clerical antisemitism set the tone for much of French daily life, whether in churches, Catholic schools, or private homes. At religious services, a substantial minority of priests invited the faithful to continue the sacred battle against the "deicidal people," an "accursed race who sold Our Lord," who sought to "enslave all the nations on which they sweep down like so many vultures." The Augustinian publishing house, La Maison de la Bonne Presse, issued *La Croix* and *Le Pèlerin*, newspapers that matched *La Libre Parole* in the frontal malevolence of their Jew-hatred. For the Augustinians, arguably the most flagrantly antisemitic of the Catholic religious orders, the terms "parasites," "Jews," and "Freemasons" were interchangeable with "Judas," "the Rothschilds," and "Dreyfus." Their crusade of vilification in turn evoked resonance not only among aristocrats, army officers, the petite bourgeoisie, and much of the peasantry, but among numerous members of the liberal professions and other intellectuals. Nor was it the Catholic press alone that sustained the campaign of anti-Jewish denunciation. The Christian Democratic Party, unofficially linked to the nation's Catholic hierarchy, included in its official platform the commitment to ongoing struggle against Jews and Freemasons. At the party's national convention in November 1896, the keynote speaker was Édouard Drumont.

The *Affaire* Liquidated

In May 1898, General Auguste Mercier retired as war minister. He was succeeded by General Godefroy Cavaignac, a nonpolitical career soldier. The following month, Cavaignac received an unexpected visitor. It was Chrétien Esterhazy, youthful nephew of Major Walsin Esterhazy. As Chrétien recounted to the war minister, Major Esterhazy the previous year had inveigled 40,000 francs from his widowed sister-in-law—Chrétien's mother— explaining that he could profitably invest the money for her with "his friend," Baron de Rothschild. When ugly accusations began surfacing against Esterhazy, the major assured his sister-in-law that his "contacts" in the Intelligence Bureau were protecting him by "thickening" the Dreyfus file. In the intervening months, Chrétien explained bitterly, Esterhazy had ignored all appeals to return the "invested" money. Would the general then be interested to know about the "thickened" dossier? asked Chrétien.

Cavaignac was indeed interested. He directed Major Henry to bring him the file. Little time was needed for the war minister and his staff to discover that, of the additional "secret" Dreyfus correspondence, lines and even entire pages of the handwriting attributed to the Jewish captain in fact were pasted, mismatched, even forged. From beginning to end, Henry's "secret information" on Dreyfus was a clumsy frame-up. On August 30, 1898, Cavaignac ordered Henry's arrest. General de Boisdeffre, the army chief of staff, who was present at the cross-examination, immediately submitted his own resignation. That same night, in jail, Henry wrote a letter to his wife, insisting that "what I have done . . . was for the good of the country and the army." He then slit his throat with his razor. The next morning Dr. Léon Levy, a young Jewish physician doing his military service at army headquarters, found Henry's body and pronounced him dead.

Henry's suicide, and his evident complicity in Dreyfus's imprisonment, shook the nation to its depths. Frantically attempting to regroup, the rightist press began describing the late Henry as "a martyr for a just cause," the author of "a patriotic forgery." Jules Guérin's Ligue Antisémitique organized mass demonstrations outside the Chamber of Deputies. Nor did the Assumptionists, Augustinians, and Jesuits abandon their anti-Jewish campaign. Yet the Dreyfusards now sensed that the battle was shifting their way. The haute bourgeoisie and working classes by and large were supportive. So was the new, moderate government of René Waldeck-Rousseau. The prime minister and his cabinet interposed no objections, on October 27, 1898, when the Court of Appeal approved a retrial for Dreyfus.

Only then was military censorship lifted on correspondence to Alfred Dreyfus. On November 16, for the first time, a letter from his brother Mathieu arrived explaining the events—political, legal, and journalistic—that had swirled around the *Affaire* during the past four years. It was then, too, that guards removed the stockade around Dreyfus's hut, permitting him his first view of the ocean. Slowly, the prisoner began to return to life and hope. Yet the army was not prepared to relent. In ensuing months, the high command filed petition after petition to the High Court to overrule the Court of Appeal. When the High Court refused, the army command appealed directly to President Faure, a right-winger, to hold fast against revision. But on February 16, 1899, Faure died of a stroke in the arms of his mistress. He was succeeded by Émile Loubet, a moderate, who acknowledged that he favored revision. So at last, on June 9, 1899, the cruiser *Sfax* arrived at Devil's Island to bring Dreyfus home. He had been imprisoned for four years and three months. Arriving in France a week later, he was carried off to the military garrison town of Rennes, the venue of the impending court-martial, and put in a comfortable hotel "detention." The next morning his wife arrived to greet him. Her face was ravaged. Dreyfus's was unrecognizable. His hair and many of his teeth were gone. His limbs had atrophied to brittle sticks. He was thirty-nine years old.

The court-martial began on August 7, 1899. The courtroom was packed with journalists from throughout Europe and the United States. For over a year, in fact, the *Affaire* had been followed in other countries almost as avidly as in France. Once again, testifying for the army, Mercier, Boisdeffre, Sandherr, and Paty de Clam leveled all the old accusations against Dreyfus. But this time the hard evidence of massive forgeries and conspiracies was incontrovertible. The trial ended on September 7. Subsequently, the officer-judges required only two and a half hours to reach their verdict. It was an ingeniously political one, and doubtless formulated well in advance to save the judges' own military careers and the army's reputation. The panel found Dreyfus guilty of betraying France. Yet the judges agreed that there were "extenuating circumstances," and Dreyfus's original life sentence therefore would be reduced to ten years. It became clear only afterward that the court was leaving open the possibility—almost certainly the likelihood—that the president would pardon Dreyfus. And so it happened. On September 20, at the recommendation of Prime Minister Waldeck-Rousseau, the pardon was forthcoming from President Loubet.

Ironically, Dreyfus's lawyer, Fernand-Gustave Labori, would have preferred to battle the verdict to a full and complete exoneration. It was Mathieu Dreyfus who persuaded his brother to accept the pardon. Exoneration would come later, he argued. It did. In November 1903, the Dreyfus defense team prevailed upon the High Court to review the extensive record of the case. In July 1905 the judgment was handed down. The original December 22, 1894, verdict was set aside. Dreyfus was proclaimed innocent. Even earlier, in July 1903, the Chamber of Deputies restored both Dreyfus and Colonel Picquart to the army, with full back pay. Picquart was promoted to brigadier general, Dreyfus to major. Both were inaugurated into the Legion of Honor. In 1908, Picquart served briefly as minister of war. In January 1914, after suffering a fatal horseback fall, he received a state funeral. When the World War began, Dreyfus was given command of an artillery column. In September 1918, he was promoted to lieutenant colonel, and in July 1919 he was appointed a "chevalier" of the Legion of Honor. He lived privately afterward, dying in 1935.

In the aftermath of the *Affaire,* the political right, shamed and chastened, was thrown onto an apparently permanent defensive. Conversely, Radical Socialists and other liberals intensified their demands for decisive state control over the Church hierarchy and the various clerical orders in France. Supporting their cause, all the parties of the left won an impressive electoral victory in May 1902, returning 339 out of 590 seats, and uniting again behind the Radical-Socialist government of Waldeck-Rousseau. The victory was widely interpreted as one of republicanism over the last feckless remnants of the ancien régime.

During the next two years, a strenuous political debate raged over the future of the Church in France. On June 27, 1903, the government ordered closure of 120 religious schools. A law of July 7, 1904, banned the religious orders from teaching in France altogether. When Pope Pius X strenuously protested this legislation, the French government riposted by severing diplomatic relations with the Vatican. In July 1905, by parliamentary vote, Church and State were formally separated. Henceforth, the functionaries of all religions in France—Roman Catholic, Protestant, and Jewish—ceased to receive state funding or to conduct their affairs under state supervision. France in effect was reproclaiming itself a secular nation, evincing neither favoritism nor even interest in matters religious. More fundamentally, its ensuing *belle époque* became one not merely of prosperity and tranquillity, but of revived and reinvigorated egalitarianism. The fate of a single Jewish officer had resolved that commitment apparently for good and always.

Others drew the opposite conclusion. One of these was the Paris correspondent of Vienna's renowned *Neue Freie Presse.* On January 3, 1895, Theodor Herzl had witnessed the ceremony of Dreyfus's degradation in the courtyard of the École Militaire, and had heard the shout of the crowds outside: "À mort les juifs." The experience would resonate in his memory ever afterward.

The Mutation of Racism

Antisemitism and the *Machtstaat*

In 1871, within weeks of Prussia's shattering victory over France, a united German Empire emerged from a heterogeneity of independent sovereignties to cast its shadow over much of West-Central Europe. The accomplishment, largely Otto von Bismarck's, was all the more remarkable inasmuch as the "Iron Chancellor" had forged his vast new realm without invoking the Continent's fashionable ideology of liberalism. To be sure, several key features of representative government were adopted, among them a two-house parliament and universal male suffrage. Yet in other respects German constitutionalism remained notably attenuated. The kaiser alone was authorized to appoint and dismiss key officials of government, and Bismarck ensured that old Wilhelm I chose these personnel almost exclusively from the Prussian Junker class. Over the course of his ensuing two decades as chancellor, Bismarck was able to administer his national agenda through a powerful coalition of his fellow aristocrats and of the equally conservative members of the Center Party. Even the middle-class industrialists, with their ideological commitment to individual freedom, were lured into cooperation with the kaiserian regime. Bismarck softened their reservations by offering them the glittering new prospect of imperial nationalism, together with a selective basket of civil rights—of which the most important evidently was the right to make money in the empire's huge, unrestricted new trading market.

Few arguments are as powerful as those rooted in success. The sheer magnitude of Bismarck's political miracle accounted for a concomitant upsurge of triumphalist literature. Had not military autocracy worked? Had it not created the empire? Prosperity? National self-respect? For sixty years before the emergence of the new Germany, such revered cultural icons as Kant, Herder, and Fichte had argued that the needs of a Christian-German state deserved precedence over those of the individual German citizen. Leopold von Ranke and Johann Droysen had probed deep into German history to support this contention. And now, in one massive coup de main, Bismarck validated all the theorizing that had gone before. If conservative nationalism had been a respectable ideology in pre-Bismarckian days, it appeared irrefutable after 1871.

Among the supporters of the new *Machtstaat* was the philosopher Friedrich Nietzsche. Profoundly impressed by the growth of the new imperial administration, Nietzsche was unsparing in his contempt for the "outworn" values of the old order—"philistine slave morality," democracy, middle-class "self-satisfaction." None of these putative ornaments of Western civilization had contributed to Germany's ascendancy, after all. Two of Nietzsche's more celebrated works, *The Will to Power (Der Wille zur Macht)* and *Thus Spoke Zarathustra (Also sprach Zarathustra)*, provided Germany's intelligentsia with morbidly attractive slogans: "might makes right," "blond beast," "superman." However distorted by his more impressionable readers—Nietzsche actually had little use for militarism—these were the maxims that eventually became the ideological tools of the empire's aggressive nationalism. Nietzsche's admirers were joined in their contempt for "nineteenth-century morality" by Heinrich von Treitschke. A professor of history at Heidelberg, then at Berlin, Treitschke envisaged the state as the authentic embodiment of the German spirit, as an all-embracing, self-determined entity, unbound by rules of individual behavior or morality, or by any limitation beyond its own carnivorous power to grow. The state was the "divine will" as it "exists on earth." Popularized versions of Nietzsche's and Treitschke's writings became scripture for tens of thousands of educated young Germans who were eager to buttress the triumph of conservative nationalism. Only a few additional weapons were needed to render the Leviathan State impregnable. One of these was antisemitism.

From the early 1860s, the few lingering restrictions on Jewish emancipation crumbled rapidly (p. 95). By 1871, once the *länder* of southern Germany joined the newborn empire, the Emancipation Act adopted by the North German Confederation two years earlier was applied to Germany in its entirety. Bismarck resisted all subsequent efforts to abolish or weaken the measure. Nevertheless, hostility to Jewish civil equality did not expire. As far back as 1850, Paul de Lagarde, a brilliant if rancorous philologist, argued that the future of the German people would remain uncertain without a dynamic "spiritual" revival. The Protestant Church no longer could accomplish this rejuvenation, Lagarde argued. Rather, a new, "cleansed" version of Christianity offered a better solution, one that would find a place for the historical Jesus, yet dissociate itself from all connection with Judaism. In Jewry, Lagarde discerned a sinister cabal intent on ruling Germany's press, academia, law, medicine, and theater, no less than its economy. Near the end of his life, execrating the Jews as "vermin," "bacilli," as "the cancer of our entire existence," Lagarde recommended their speedy eradication.

Enjoying far wider intellectual recognition than Lagarde, Treitschke was among the first of Germany's conservative nationalists to identify Jews with the twin dangers of liberalism and internationalism. What stake could Jews possibly have in the future of the German nation? Treitschke asked. Were not Jews everywhere revolutionaries and atheists? In a series of widely read articles in *Das Preussische Jahrbuch* of 1879, Treitschke called attention to the growing power of "Jewish solidarity," to the emergence of a separate and elitist German-Jewish caste. Germany must be transformed into a Lutheran *Kulturstaat,* he warned his fellow citizens, and purged of all "cosmopolitan" influences, for "[t]his element of Jewry is hostile to everything that is authentically German." Treitschke's monumental *History of Germany in the Nineteenth Century* was equally replete with harsh invective against the Jews.

As it happened, the 1870s were critical years for Central Europe's lower middle class, particularly after the crash of the Austrian and German stock markets in 1873. Throughout the ensuing half-decade, shopkeepers, schoolteachers, civil servants, and others of modest means and savings appeared perilously close to losing their coveted white-collar status. It was during this interregnum of economic malaise that Adolf Stöcker came to prominence. A Lutheran minister, the son of a jail warden, Stöcker by dint of a keen intelligence and a charismatic sermonic ability worked his way up from pastor of a working-class church to appointment as Kaiser Wilhelm I's court chaplain. Sharing the prejudices of his imperial parishioners, Stöcker made no secret of his distrust of modern industrial capitalism. Like Karl Lueger in Vienna, he empathized with members of the struggling lower *Mittelstand,* and the pride that inhibited these "respectable" elements from gravitating to Marxist socialism, cheek by jowl with blue-collar workers. Stöcker in ensuing years made it his life's work to provide the lower middle class with a version of non-proletarian socialism that would bring it into alliance with the propertied conservatives.

To that end, in 1877, the court chaplain launched his own Christian Social Workers' Party, and undergirded it with an ambitious agenda for social reform, one that envisaged trade corporations, government-controlled insurance, and a number of related social-welfare concepts that managed to avoid the tenets of classical Marxism. It was only in later years, as he stumped through white-collar and working-class neighborhoods alike, that Stöcker honed an innovative technique for enhancing his program's appeal to a wider cross section of the empire's harassed underclasses. "I have emphasized," he said, "that the social revolution has to be overcome by healthy social reform, built on a Christian foundation. . . . I do not want culture that is not Germanic and not Christian. That is why I am fighting against Jewish supremacy." In 1881, as an opening broadside in his fight, Stöcker organized and presented to Bismarck an antisemitic petition, bearing a quarter-million signatures, demanding a ban on Jewish access to all governmental offices.

Although the Christian Socials made little substantial progress in that year's national elections, Stöcker had managed by then to transform social antisemitism into an increasingly formidable political issue in Germany, and this barely a decade after Jewish emancipation had been completed in the empire. More than any other figure, it was the charismatic court chaplain who lured a major proportion of the lower middle class, and of selected proletarian elements, away from the political left and into the camp of the Prussian squirearchy. Stöcker was too cautious a man, perhaps even too sincere a Christian, to espouse the doctrine of racism. By twentieth-century standards, his antisemitic strictures bore little relation to the wild nihilism of his successors; for he demanded merely "reasonable" limitations on Jewish participation in German public and economic life. Yet, like Karl Lueger in Vienna, he managed to sensitize Imperial Germany's modest white-collar elements to "Jewish power." More than Lagarde or Treitschke, it was Stöcker who awakened right-wing German politicians to the functional utility of antisemitism as a party issue.

In the 1880s and early 1890s, moreover, a number of respected Conservative newspapers ventured to stigmatize ideological liberalism by drawing attention to the prominent role of Jews, men such as Eduard Lasker and Ludwig Bamberger, in the leadership of the National Liberal Party. As titular leader of the still dominant Conservative Party, Bismarck himself was unwilling at first to ride the hobbyhorse of political antisemitism. He had espoused Jewish emancipation in Germany, after all, and once had observed that the breeding of a "German stallion" and a "Jewish mare" would provide the country with valuable offspring. The chancellor's intimate association with Gerson von Bleichröder similarly precluded a departure from the political high ground. Yet the exigencies of party strife, and specifically attacks on Bismarck by Junkers and other archreactionaries who resented his dalliance with business interests, eventually forced him into greater dependence upon *völkisch* (ethnic-chauvinist) elements.

In some measure, the shift also was influenced by far-rightist accusations that Bismarck himself was the "captive" of Bleichröder and of other Jewish financiers, those who ostensibly had caused the financial crash of 1873. Among the first to propagate the charge was Otto Glagau. A journalist for the mass-circulation family journal *Gartenlaube*, Glagau in December 1874 launched a series of articles on corruption in high capitalist circles, most of which he attributed to Jews. The series concluded with the warning:

No longer should false tolerance and sentimentality prevent us Christians from moving against the excesses, excrescences, and presumptions of Jewry. No longer can we suffer to see the Jews push themselves everywhere to the front and to the top, to see them everywhere searching for leadership and domination over public opinion. They are always pushing us Christians aside, to put us up against the wall, they take our air and our breath away. . . . God be merciful to us poor Christians.

Glagau was followed in 1875 by a right-wing politician, Franz Perot, whose series of articles in the *Kreuzzeitung*, a conservative Protestant journal, produced a sensation by denouncing Bismarck's economic policies as "Judenpolitik," and Bleichröder as the chancellor's "éminence grise."

At a time of German economic frustration, therefore, the Jewish question manifestly was gaining a new political dimension, one that even Bismarck no longer could ignore. In the Reichstag, increasing numbers of Centrist and Conservative delegates had begun to identify themselves with the antisemitic ideology. For that matter, accusations of Jewish financial malfeasance were emanating even from Social Democratic circles. Accordingly, in the spring of 1881, persuaded that antisemitism was indispensable in wooing lower-middle-class support, Bismarck finally ventured the cautious observation: "I should like to see a state which for the most part consists of Christians, and penetrated to some extent by the principles of the religion which it professes." With this widely publicized remark, the chancellor provided antisemitism with a new dimension of political respectability. In 1888, at their party convention in Tivoli, a German resort town, the Conservatives followed Bismarck's lead in adopting a mildly antisemitic plank, deprecating "Jewish influence" in the economic life of the empire. Ironically, the new political "respectability" of antisemitism came too late for Adolf Stöcker. Within a month of the Tivoli convention, he was dismissed as court chaplain by the new kaiser, Wilhelm II, for "irresponsible extremism." It was the extremism of socialism, not of antisemitism. Once antisemitism had been endorsed by the party of the great Bismarck, it would endure henceforth as a legitimate tactical weapon of the German political right.

THE BIRTH OF RACISM

In these same late-nineteenth-century years, Central Europe's conservative nationalists began to experiment with the volatile new doctrine of racism. The concept offered multiple appeals. It supplied Germany's iron state machine with a biological rationale, ostensibly proving German "ethnic" superiority over neighboring peoples. More prosaically, for domestic politics, rightists and populists of the Stöcker genre had found antisemitism useful in making inroads among the country's *Kleinburgertum,* and they were prepared now to fortify the appeal by infusing it with a new, racial ideology.

In its initial incarnation, German racism evolved out of the Aryan myth, a theory that found its "scientific" beginnings as far back as the late eighteenth and early nineteenth centuries. It was then that the Semitic languages were first identified and classified. In 1833, the German philologist Franz Bopp traced the Romance, Germanic, and Slavic tongues to a common "Aryan"—Indo-European—source. But here science ended and pseudoscience began, inasmuch as philologists erroneously assumed that a common linguistic origin signified a common racial origin. August Pott and Theodor Pösch reconstructed a mythological people, blond and blue-eyed, that reputedly had migrated to Europe from Central Asia. In 1855, Count Arthur de Gobineau, a French diplomat, published a widely influential two-volume book, *Essai sur l'inégalité des races humaines.* A great synthesizer, Gobineau drew upon anthropology, linguistics, and history to reconstruct an elaborately upholstered intellectual edifice in which race explained everything. Like his predecessors, citing linguistic "proof," he favored the notion of Aryan "racial" superiority, and contended that "Aryanism" incarnated the virtues of love, freedom, honor, and spirituality. To Gobineau's professed dismay, the Aryan peoples appeared to be facing the threat of "degeneration." The source of the peril, as he saw it, was miscegenation with other, "inferior" races.

By the late nineteenth century, the Aryan archetype gradually came to be associated with Germans, and Aryan virtues thereby were identified with German virtues. By the same token, the legend of Aryan superiority was taken over principally by German historians and anthropologists. These were also the cultural eminences who drew invidious comparisons not only between the German race and races beyond the German-speaking world, but specifically with a race that lived within the very midst of that world. Here it was, too, that the antithesis first was charted between the limitless superhumanity of the German people and the debilitating subhumanity of the Jews. Thus, the "Aryanist" Otto Wigand could write in 1858:

> How can the race difference between a German and a Slav, of a German and a Dane, be compared to the race antagonism between the children of Jacob, who are of Asiatic descent, and the descendants of Teut and Hermann, who have inhabited Europe from time immemorial, between the proud and tall blond Aryan and the short, black-haired, dark-eyed Jew! Races which differ in such degree oppose each other instinctively....

The argument was accepted and given its widest "respectability" by Germany's most venerated culture icon, Richard Wagner. Ironically, it was not a stance that would have been predicted of him as late as 1848, for the great composer then was an ardent liberal, a friend of Heinrich Heine and of several other Jewish members of the Jung Deutschland circle. But not long afterward Wagner set about developing his notion of a revolutionary new Christianity, a "social-revolutionary" Christianity that somehow would cast off the shackles imposed by the Jews, who had rejected Jesus's message of "love" for one of "law." It did not take Wagner long to begin linking his social-revolutionary antisemitism with the emergent new doctrine of race. Indeed, racial-cultural elements first appeared in his Nibelungen cycle of operas. In the program notes to *Die Götterdämmerung*, Wagner stated explicitly that the Nibelungs represented the Jews. Alberich is "swarthy, swampy, and sulfurous," while Mime is "gruesome, grizzled, and gray, cramped and crooked, with hanging ears stretching, bleary eyes staring." The Nibelung manner of speech, Wagner explained, should be in "the Jewish manner . . . shrill, hissing, buzzing, a wholly foreign and arbitrary distortion of our national idiom."

It was in the September 1850 issue of the *Neue Zeitschrift für Musik,* under the pseudonym of "K. Freigedank," that Wagner published his celebrated essay "Judaism in Music" ("Das Judentum in der Musik"). This time the message was straightforward. Living outside the German *Volk,* the Jew was a foreigner, and thereby was incapable of producing an authentically German culture, whether of speech or music. "The tragedy of [Felix] Mendelssohn," wrote Wagner, "is that, despite his natural gifts, his racial origins make it impossible for him to achieve any profound, meaningful utterance." Some thirty years later, in yet another essay, "Heroism and Christendom" ("Der Helden und die Christenheit"), Wagner cautioned that if a Jew intermarried with a German, the Jew's "impure" qualities would only contaminate the purity of the German partner. And in 1882, in a letter to his patron, King Ludwig II of Bavaria, the composer added:

> I hold the Jewish race to be the born enemy of pure humanity and everything noble in it. It is certain that [the Jews] are running us Germans into the ground, and I am perhaps the last German who knows how to hold himself upright in the face of Jewry, which already rules everything.

By 1890, Wagner's cultural reputation in Germany far transcended his musical achievements. Some three hundred branches of the Wagner Society were functioning throughout the empire, and his home in Bayreuth had become a kind of national shrine where the flame of the German "spirit" was jealously preserved.

It was also in the latter nineteenth century that Wagner's message was given resonance by a steadily widening diversity of interpreters. Thus, in 1879, a sensation-mongering journalist, Wilhelm Marr, the son of a Jewish actor and a gentile mother, published a pamphlet, *The Victory of Judaism over Germanism (Der Sieg des Judentums über das Germanentum)*. In this tract, which first launched the term "antisemitism," Marr warned that the Jews were perpetually at war with the German race, and actually winning that war through their materialism, liberalism, and racial "infestation." Marr himself was a person of little consequence, but many of his followers and successors were figures who evoked attention and respect. It happened that in the 1880s and 1890s the pseudoscience of Aryanism was undergoing a merger of sorts with still another field of research, one that appeared distinctly more respectable in its scientific bona fides. This was the study of "eugenics."

The new inquiry focused principally on the hereditary characteristics of individuals and ethnic groups alike, and on the possibility of "socially engineering" their traits for improvement of the "national well-being." The notion drew its intellectual premises from the pioneering discoveries of Charles Darwin, specifically in the popularized doctrine of selective breeding. During the mid- and latter nineteenth century, Darwin's nephew by marriage, Francis Galton, became a widely admired figure on his own account in British scientific circles for his research in genetics. In his London office, Galton developed a statistical method for tabulating, classifying, grading, and assessing physical types. Eventually, he extended his research beyond physiology, developing an imaginative battery of "anthrometric" tests and statistical analyses that categorized "degrees" of human intelligence. In 1869, Galton summarized his findings in a pathfinding volume, *Hereditary Genius*. The title also summarized its content, namely, that exceptional abilities were strictly a matter of inheritance. On the basis of his data, Galton suggested that it was possible to anticipate which parents would produce children of greater or lesser "civic worth." Once this information was evaluated, he insisted, it would be legitimate, even obligatory, for the British government to encourage the propagation of individuals of "good stock" and discourage unions among those who manifestly were "unfit." Over the ensuing years, Galton published the fruits of his substantial research in a series of articles and books that won him an extensive following among many of Britain's most eminent public figures.

Yet it was Galton's disciple, Karl Pearson, who most vigorously extended the range of eugenics research into the study of "fit" and "unfit" races. By the early twentieth century, Pearson devised categorizations of "inferior" stock that included Africans and various strains of Asian and even South Mediterranean peoples. They included East European Jews, as well. Focusing on Jewish immigrant children from Tsarist Russia, Pearson drew attention to physical indicators suggesting the "potential pathology" of Jews as a "racial" element. In his old age, Pearson became an admirer of Nazism. Even so, "scientific" racism never gained quite the momentum in England that it achieved on the Continent, or even in the United States (pp. 380–83). Rather, it was in Germany that the *Archiv für Rassen-und Gesellschaftsbiologie*, founded in 1904, was devoted undisguisedly to the proposition that the very survival of the German race was linked to racial "hygiene," that is, to the protection of its "uncorrupted integrity." As a founder of the eugenics movement in Germany, Alfred Plötz similarly argued in *The Fitness of Our Race and the Protection of the Weak (Die Tüchtigkeit unserer Rasse und der Schutz der Schwachen)* that the "tall and blond" German race was the preeminent culture-bearing race in the world—and more than any other, therefore, the German race deserved protection against miscegenation with inferior breeds.

Among the "inferior" breeds, it was the Jews whom German eugenicists singled out as a distinct and unique threat to the national "stock," for the Jews alone were extensively intermingled among the German people. In a succession of widely quoted articles on the ethnology of the Jews, Carl Stratz ventured the generalization that "European Jews have a greater percentage of physically handicapped individuals than the peoples among whom they live." "In addition to knock knees, flat feet, hunched backs, concave chests," argued Stratz, Jews suffered from a variety of "inherited constitutional illnesses," with "neurasthenia" preeminent among these ailments. By the early twentieth century, German ethnographic studies in growing numbers suggested links between the Jews' physiology and their sociology. Jews, it was asserted, were innately incapable of performing physical labor, and consequently were ill-suited to perform the duties of citizen-soldiers. The notion of sexual "degeneracy" was also extensively identified with Jews, an affliction attributed to their historic inbreeding. Indeed, the medical literature of early-twentieth-century Germany drew extensive parallelisms between inbreeding and sexual as well as other "Jewish" degenerative diseases. Similarly, Ernst Dühring, Otto Ammon, and Ludwig Wilser, university professors all, provided quasi-anthropological "evidence" that the German blood mixture was endangered by sexual contact with Jews. So, too, did such respected historians as Johann Droysen (p. 242), Constantine Frantz, and Heinrich von Sybel.

It was not entirely ironic, given the origins of the eugenics movement, that the most influential exponent of racism in fin-de-siècle Germany was an Englishman. Houston Stewart Chamberlain was born in Southsea in 1855, the son of a British admiral and a German mother. Traveling to Germany in his early manhood, he became a disciple of Richard Wagner's Aryanism, and eventually settled in Germany, where he later married Wagner's daughter.

At the same time, immersing himself in the writings of Galton, combining Galton's theories with the pseudoscience of German Aryanism, Chamberlain in 1899 produced a book that became the magnum opus of German racism, *The Foundations of the Nineteenth Century (Die Grundlagen des Neunzehnten Jahrhunderts)*. In this formidable two-volume publication, packed with impressive, if specious, documentation, Chamberlain traced the saga of the putative Aryan race. It was his thesis that the most enduring achievements of virtually every civilization were the products of German Aryanism. Thus, in the *Grundlagen*, even Jesus was transformed into an Aryan. The Jews, by contrast, were a race of cheapjacks, who had produced nothing of value in their entire history, not even the Bible. Although it was not central to the book's thesis, Chamberlain also felt obliged to give warning about the Jews. Their principal mission on earth, he argued, was to contaminate the German racial stream, and to "produce a herd of pseudo-Hebraic *meztizos,* a people beyond all doubt degenerate physically, mentally, and morally." In the same measure, therefore, the German people were obliged to fight back, not merely to survive but to conquer; for they alone were destined to be a nation of masters, to govern in the "chaotic jungle of peoples. . . ."

Chamberlain's portentous scenario much impressed Kaiser Wilhelm II. On the one hand, the German ruler was prepared to maintain courteous relations with a select number of Jews—"Kaiserjuden," they would later be dubbed—among them such major figures in the developing imperial economy as Max Warburg, the Hamburg banker; Albert Ballin, president of the Hamburg-Lloyd Packetboat Line; Walther Rathenau, chairman of the huge AEG electric conglomerate; and James Simon, a renowned art connoisseur and collector. Nevertheless, the kaiser evinced only distaste for the Jews as a class, and privately characterized them as "a fungus upon the German oak." Chamberlain's *Grundlagen*, therefore, so enthralled Wilhelm that he invited the author to be his personal weekend guest, and assured him later that it "was God who sent your book to the German people, and you personally to me." Avoiding in his text any vulgar antisemitic invective, or appeals to violence, Chamberlain had devoted the bulk of his mighty opus to Aryan splendor and superiority, a theme that was music to the kaiser's ears.

The Institutionalization of Racism

By the late nineteenth century, the notion of German racial superiority in its most general terms was well embraced by a significant number of conservative nationalists, including the "All-Highest" in the royal palace. Yet antisemitism of the racist variety was treated more cautiously. By and large, it was avoided by tradition-bound Junkers and by other "respectable" antisemites of the Conservative Party, even by Adolf Stöcker, whose antisemitism in any case functioned as only one ingredient of a wider populist agenda. For these political figures, racist antisemitism, or simply antisemitism in its literal meaning, seemed to possess uncontrollable, nihilistic potentialities. Rather, the authentically racist Jew-baiters tended to be peripheral figures, those unwilling to accept the civilized restraints of law and order either in the domestic or in the international community.

The notion of a political faction based exclusively on radical, racial antisemitism was first mooted by Moritz Busch, an obscure press attaché in the German foreign ministry; and by the half-Jewish journalist Wilhelm Marr (p. 249). Marr, who actually founded a threadbare "League of Antisemites," gained little personal following. Instead, it was Otto Böckel, elected to the Reichstag in 1887, who became the first antisemitic deputy to remain independent of official Conservative Party sponsorship and to be elected exclusively on his racist agenda. In any case, like Marr, he failed to generate a significant political ideology or party. It was a somewhat more noisome racist, Hermann Ahlwardt, who attracted wider attention, although essentially through blatant decibel power. Originally the principal of an elementary school, Ahlwardt was dismissed in 1890 for embezzling from the school treasury. Afterward, he launched his antisemitic "career" by producing a series of furiously racist essays that were the ultimate in vituperation, incendiarism, and sheer madness. Ahlwardt achieved little political power in his own time, for he was uninterested in public office. But the sizable crowds that attended his lectures at the turn of the century prefigured an ominous transition in German political thinking. They suggested that the older "ideological" Judeophobia was likely soon to be overshadowed by the newer, pseudoscientific concept of racism.

Georg von Schönerer, the preeminent European visionary of political racism, was a citizen not of the German but of the Austrian Empire. The son of a wealthy Viennese railroad engineer, Schönerer managed only a haphazard education and an even less certain livelihood in the Habsburg civil service before turning full-time to politics. In 1873, he got himself elected to the Reichstag as a left-wing Liberal. Over the ensuing decade, however, Schönerer underwent a sea change of ideology, possibly even of temperament. Denouncing Jews, Slavs, and others of the empire's non-German races and nations, in 1885 he organized the Pan-German Union, whose program favored a total dismemberment of the Habsburg patchwork quilt, to be replaced by a union of its core "Aryan" population with that of Wilhelminian Germany. In articulating his new vision, moreover, Schönerer proved to be a master of public relations. It was he who pioneered many of the propaganda techniques later to be used by the Nazis, including the use of anthems, postcards, matchbooks, and signboards; and within three years, he managed to cobble together a substantial aggregation of followers, many of them from

Austria's urban *Kleinburgertum.* Schönerer was less successful, however, in winning encouragement from Bismarck. The German chancellor evinced no interest whatever in transforming Austria into an appendage of the German Empire.

Nevertheless, in promoting his agenda, Schönerer was the first demagogue who understood the potential of antisemitism in eradicating not simply Jewish equality of civil status, but the structure of an entire nation. In that effort, he exploited numerous "conventional" weapons in the antisemitic arsenal. Among these was the well-worn specter of the Jewish banker, whom Schönerer identified with the Austrian government itself, and whom he singled out as the éminence grise behind every imperial institution in the Habsburg realm. Indeed, for Schönerer, who fastened upon the emergent new doctrine of racism, no Jew was exempt from the damning identification, for Jewishness no longer was a matter of religious loyalty, but of racial inheritance. On that premise, he urged the government to enact "authentically" anti-Jewish legislation that would denaturalize even baptized Jews. Such draconian measures of course would hardly have been possible within the legal and economic structure of the multinational Habsburg realm. In recognition of the fact, Schönerer nurtured an audacious strategy. It was to provoke the empire's core German population into a mass uprising against Franz Josef's "obstructionist" government. Once this goal was achieved, the reunion of German Austria with Imperial Germany presumably would follow in due course.

Yet at the very moment that Schönerer's propaganda campaign appeared to be gaining credibility, it was ruined by a spectacular blunder. In 1888, a liberal newspaper prematurely announced the death of Germany's ailing Kaiser Wilhelm I. Acting on the erroneous information, Schönerer organized a raid on the newspaper's Vienna office in order to declare his personal loyalty to Germany's Hohenzollern dynasty. Presumably, he anticipated that the German crown prince, the future (and short-lived) Kaiser Friedrich I, would respond by annexing Austria. Instead, it was the Austrian government, its patience exhausted by Schönerer's near-treason, that seized upon this latest indiscretion to disenfranchise him, to disbar him from the Habsburg Reichstag, and to strip him of his patent of nobility. His power broken, Schönerer eventually dissolved his Pan-German Union and abandoned his struggle for a union of the Germans of both empires.

He gave up too soon. In Germany itself, over the turn of the century, the vision of a gradualistic, "respectable" Pan-Germanism was gaining its own momentum. Reflecting the sentiments of Kaiser Wilhelm II, and of an influential group of army officers and industrialists, the Pan-German League evolved into a uniquely German adaptation to the new age of imperialism. During the years in which Britain, France, and other maritime powers were swallowing up Africa and large tracts of Asia, a land power such as Germany was obliged to think primarily in terms of imperial expansion within Europe itself. The potential for this expansion lay in the necklace of *Volksdeutsche* (ethnic German) communities extending along the eastern perimeter of the Continent—in Hungary, Bohemia, Poland, the Balkans, in the Russian Baltic and Black Sea regions. Ardently, the Pan-Germans set out on their mission of nurturing German "cultural and national values" among these fellow German-speakers, and establishing "closer ties among all peoples of the Germanic race."

While antisemitism did not initially figure in the Pan-German program, the movement was shot through with racist ideology. By no coincidence, its shining light and revered intellectual guru was Houston Stewart Chamberlain. In 1906, moreover, the unofficial became official when the Pan-German League barred Jews from membership. By then, of all the race-based political and neopolitical ideologies and movements, the Pan-German League may well have emerged as the most accurate weathervane of the German future. Embracing the dream of Aryanism and "racial hygiene," the league also discerned in the Jews the classic symbol of a bankrupt internationalism. In their imperialist agenda, the Pan-Germans were the first of the empire's *Vereinen* to express open impatience with the chimera of the Concert of Europe, or with the European balance of power altogether. It awaited only an Adolf Hitler to grasp the manner in which a "superior Aryan *Volk*" might disrupt that balance, by striking at the most international of Europe's peoples, and thereby purging an entire continent of Jewish "racial degeneracy."

XV

The Rise of Zionism

The Birth of Jewish Nationalism

As late as the nineteenth century, a cherished feature of the East European Jewish cultural heritage was the memory of the ancestral homeland, the lost and lamented Zion that was enshrined in the folklore and religious liturgy of virtually every observant Jew. Throughout the centuries of Jewish dispersion until modern times, rabbis, poets, philosophers, and mystics in Spain, North Africa, the Middle East, and Europe expressed a universal nostalgia for the ravished cradle of their peoplehood. For Russian Jews, distraught and quarantined under the tsars, clinging fast to their accumulated sacred literature, the recollection of Zion was a visceral wound. On the ninth day of the Hebrew month of Av, commemorating the destruction of the ancient Temple of Jerusalem, they fasted and mourned as if they personally had been witnesses to that catastrophe. In the manner of other ethnic-religious eastern communities—of Greeks, Armenians, or Georgians, for example—they continued tenaciously to nourish the dream of a future miracle, the restoration of the vanished national hearth.

Jews in the Russian Pale doubtless resisted all attempts to "force the end." Their vision of a mass return to the Holy Land was of a rather abstract halcyon era that alone would betoken a final collective redemption in Zion. Nevertheless, infused as it was with religious overtones, Jewish nationalism perhaps inevitably achieved its earliest modern expression at the hands of rabbis. One of these was Judah Alkalai, an obscure Sephardic preacher from Semlin, near Belgrade. In 1839, Rabbi Alkalai published a slim Ladino-Hebrew booklet, *Pleasant Paths (Darhei Noam)*, proclaiming that the redemption of Zion depended initially upon vigorous secular action, and specifically upon the establishment of Jewish colonies in the Holy Land. A year later, Alkalai cited the role of Adolphe Crémieux and Moses Montefiore in winning release of the imprisoned Damascus Jews. This kind of pragmatic initiative, he argued, offered a precedent for future stages of liberation, in Palestine.

Alkalai's views were paralleled by those of his contemporary Rabbi Zvi Hirsch Kalischer, who occupied a pulpit in the Polish-speaking town of Thorn, in East Prussia. In 1843, Kalischer's two-volume work, *An Honest Faith (Emunah Yesharah)*, similarly described the progressive triumph of Western Jewish emancipation as an augury of redemption in Palestine. Why, then, should the Jewish people not achieve salvation in Zion through the identical, "natural," political means? The advent of the Messiah was hardly required, only the formation of a society of wealthy Jews to underwrite the colonization of the Holy Land. Kalischer himself was a man of action. Through his persistent intercession, the Alliance Israélite Universelle in 1870 agreed to underwrite a small Jewish agricultural school, Mikveh Yisrael, near the port of Jaffa.

But Alkalai and Kalischer were issuing their appeals in the heyday of Western Jewish emancipation. Their exhortations for the redemption of the Holy Land evoked little practical interest. By the 1850s and 1860s, moreover, a messianic age of sorts appeared to have opened even in the Russia of Alexander II. With opportunities widening for Jewish enterprise, the Jewish bourgeoisie of the Pale were asking now if the time had not come for all Jews in the Tsarist Empire to "modernize," to "productivize" themselves on the soil of Russia itself. Indeed, the rise of Haskalah encouraged growing numbers of Jews to wrest themselves from the insularities of the shtetl and to seek normal discourse and interaction with the surrounding gentile population (pp. 180–81). Yet, if Jewish secular humanism seemingly deemphasized the traditional messianic yearning for Zion, it also generated ideas that eventually would be absorbed into Zionist ideology. In its demand for vocational "productivization," for example, Haskalah extolled the merits of physical labor in field and factory, a concept later to become the very bedrock of Labor Zionism. It also idealized a new secular Jew who appraised the world about him clear-mindedly, and with a determination to resolve the Jewish problem logically and dynamically, rather than by a fatalistic immersion in traditional pietism.

Not least important, Haskalah revitalized the Hebrew language, wresting it from synagogue and religious school and transforming it into a vehicle for contemporary expression. The secular, literary use of this classical tongue in turn evoked a rich skein of historical associations. Thus, in Hebrew, it was natural to invoke innumerable biblical allusions, to contrast the circumstances of the Russian-Jewish shtetl with the legendary (and idealized) glories of ancient Zion. In the ornately tapestried romances of Kalman Shulman and Abraham Mapu (p. 182), the Land of Israel was projected as a terrain of historic glory, inhabited by robust farmers and soldiers, by epic heroes. During the 1870s, the Pale's Hebrew-language journals enlarged upon this biblical ideal in a kind of preadumbrated Zionism.

EUROPEAN NATIONALISM AND PALESTINIAN REFUGE

If incipient Zionism was latent both in religious messianism and in secular humanism, it was stimulated as well by the emergence of other nineteenth-century nationalist and irredentist movements. "Let us take to heart the examples of the Italians, Poles, and Hungarians," wrote Rabbi Kalischer in his later, 1862 volume, *In Search of Zion (Drishat Zion)*. "All the other peoples have striven only for the sake of their national honor. How much more should we exert ourselves, for our duty is to labor ... for the glory of God Who chose Zion!" The romantic-nationalist Jung Deutschland movement of the mid-nineteenth century (pp. 124–25) much impressed Micah Joseph Levinsohn, who lived in Berlin from 1861 to 1864. Eliezer Perlman (later Ben-Yehuda), a witness to the Pan-Slavism sweeping through the Balkans during the Russo-Turkish War of 1877–78, asked: "Why should we be any less worthy than any other people? What about our nation, our language, our land?"

The earliest and possibly most imaginative response to the upsurge of European nationalism was that of Moses Hess. Born in 1812 to an Orthodox family of Bonn, Hess as a young man disdained his family's business opportunities to move into the intellectual ferment of pre-1848 German radicalism. He ceased to be a practicing Jew. Wandering across Germany, he fitfully tried his hand at teaching and writing. For a while, he attended the University of Bonn. A "tall, scrawny man, with benevolent eyes and a cock-like curve to his neck," as he was described later by his fellow student Karl Marx, Hess preached mildly of love and justice for the poor. Later, in Paris, where he joined Marx in coediting a socialist journal, he went so far as to marry a prostitute out of socialist compassion.

In 1837, responding to the Hegelian interest in history then current in Germany, Hess published his first book, *The Holy History of Mankind (Die heilige Geschichte der Menschheit)*. It sank without a trace. So, in 1841, did a second volume, *The European Triarchy (Die europäische Triarchie)*. It was in this latter book, moreover, that Hess made clear his opposition to the separate existence of a Jewish people. Their special role as a "ferment" among the nations was exhausted, he insisted. Nevertheless, exposure to periodic outburts of anti-semitism could not have left him unaffected. In 1857, living in Belgium, where he perused the writings of the Italian nationalist Giuseppe Mazzini, Hess came across the works of Rabbi Kalischer. Fascinated, he then belatedly took up the study of Jewish history. Indeed, in 1862, he quite astonished his fellow socialists by producing his extraordinary volume, *Rome and Jerusalem: The Last National Question (Rom und Jerusalem, die letzte Nationalitätsfrage)*.

"Here I stand again in the midst of my people," Hess acknowledged at the outset of *Rome and Jerusalem*, "after having been estranged from them for twenty years." His encounters with European nationalism, he continued, his studies in ethnicity, had persuaded him that his original cosmopolitan vision of a single homogeneity of nations was outdated. Each people, he wrote, nurtured its own individual traits, its own unique ambition and specific "mission." Indeed, developments even then taking place in Italy confirmed that view, for "on the ruins of Christian Rome a regenerated Italian people is rising." It then followed, Hess argued, that "the orphaned children of Jerusalem must also be permitted to share in the great renaissance of the nations," for the Jews represented the last great national problem in Europe. "Only a national renaissance can endow the religious genius of the Jews . . . with new strength," he concluded, "and raise their soul once again to the level of prophetic inspiration." *Rome and Jerusalem* was unique in its prefigurations of later and better-known Zionist doctrines. It anticipated the writings of the Labor Zionists in projecting the Land of Israel as ideal terrain for the Jews to return to the soil, to shed their stereotype as parasites in the lands of other peoples. Moreover, only on barren and largely uninhabited soil would Jewish labor find it possible to organize on "correct socialist" principles. With these and other insights, Hess's book was a dazzling tour de force of ideological prophecy. Even so, *Rome and Jerusalem* evoked no response in the Jewish world of the 1860s. It was not published as a book in Hebrew until 1899.

The relevance of Hess's vision evidently was confirmed only a few years after his death in 1875. The explosion of Russian xenophobia, the pogroms and May Laws, shook East European Jewry's lingering illusions of opportunity on Russian territory. Shaken, too, was their faith even in the pragmatic value of humanistic enlightenment within the Tsarist Empire itself, for numerous Russian intellectuals had joined in the new anti-Jewish campaign. "I intended to devote my strength and energy to serving the interests of my country," wrote Chaim Hissin, a Jewish medical student, "and honestly to fulfill the obligations of a good citizen. . . . And now suddenly we are shown the door. It is too much for a sensitive Jew." Where did the door lead? The likeliest destination was America. Yet Peretz Smolenskin, the most renowned of Haskalah figures, envisaged another solution. Abandoning his earlier conception of the Jews as a uniquely "spiritual" nation, Smolenskin appealed instead for mass emigration to Palestine. "Now is the time to circulate this idea," he wrote in 1881, "and to raise funds to help settle those who will go to the Land of Israel." Smolenskin was joined in his reorientation by Moses Leib Lilienblum, another classic maskil (pp. 189–90). During the pogroms of 1881, Lilienblum had been reduced to huddling for safety in a basement. The experience enraged him emotionally and reoriented him intellectually. Afterward, in a series of articles entitled "The Way of the Return" ("Dereh HeHazarah"), Lilienblum acknowledged that the solution to the Jewish problem no longer was to be found in integration but in the creation of Jewish national self-awareness, "for aliens we are and aliens we shall remain even if we become filled to the brim with [Russian] culture."

Neither Smolenskin nor Lilienblum, however, no more than Alkalai or Kalischer before them, offered evidence that the tide of gentile prejudice might not eventually crest, perhaps even be dissipated by political change within Russia itself. Hundreds of thousands of Jewish liberals and socialists continued to nurture that dream, after all, and in Western Europe they were witnessing its apparent realization. Under these circumstances, what rationale was there for immigration to the wilderness of Zion? In fact, one such rationale existed, and it took the form of a rigorous, "scientific" analysis of the Jewish condition. Yehuda Leib (Leo) Pinsker was the son of a cultivated maskil family of Odessa. After earning a medical degree at the University of Moscow, he won high esteem as an army surgeon during the Crimean War. Like many of his generation, Pinsker had shared in the optimism of the era of Alexander II, and he was a frequent contributor to *Rastsvet,* where he expressed the prevailing hope for a pluralistic Russia. Then came the shock of the pogroms and the May Laws. Upon reflection, Pinsker concluded that neither ignorance nor bigotry alone was the source of the Jewish tragedy. The crisis lay, rather, in the very structure of contemporary society.

In late 1881, Pinsker departed for the temporary quietude of Berlin to write, and in 1882 to publish, a small book. Entitled *Self-Emancipation (Selbst-emanzipation),* the volume asserted plainspokenly that the Jews were the one people on earth who could never be treated with national respect. The reason was not arcane. They lacked the indispensable prerequisite of national identity. "The Jewish people has no fatherland of its own," Pinsker observed, "no center of gravity, no government of its own, no official representation." Rather, they were perceived as a kind of "phantom people," displaying many of the salient characteristics of nationhood, but lacking the final, indispensable attribute of a land. As a phantom people, therefore, the Jews inspired fear among their gentile neighbors; and that which people feared, they hated. The solution to the Jewish condition accordingly lay not in reliance upon the will-o'-the-wisp of emancipation, but in a concerted effort by Jews to restore a national home of their own. "Let 'now or never' be our watchword," Pinsker declaimed. "Woe to our descendants ... if we let this moment pass by!" It was illustrative of Pinsker's "scientific objectivity," however, that he attached no particular sentimental importance to Palestine. The tract of land might be anywhere, so long as it produced a recognized sovereign nationhood.

In the clarity and dispassion of its analysis, *Self-Emancipation* much impressed the Russian-Jewish intelligentsia. Indeed, soon after the book's appearance, they prevailed upon Pinsker to assume the leadership of a loose collection of Zionist cultural groups, the Hovevei Zion, the Lovers of Zion. Little branches of these Hovevei Zion already were developing as early as the 1870s. But in 1884, Pinsker, with his newly won prestige, took the initiative in summoning a national conference of senior Hovevei Zion leaders, with the aim of developing a pragmatic agenda. To evade tsarist restrictions on minority nationalism, the thirty-four delegates gathered in Kattowitz, in Germany. Here they reached unanimous agreement that the Holy Land alone must be their goal, and that practical steps consequently should be taken to encourage immigration there. Pinsker acquiesced. Moreover, he proved to be as able a propagandist and administrator as an analyst of the Jewish condition. By the time of his death, in 1891, the physician-sociologist had provided the Hovevei Zion with a clear organizational structure and had nurtured its growth to approximately one hundred branches, with a membership of 14,000. If the movement was never large, its constituency included some of Russian Jewry's most respected cultural figures, including many of its university-trained professionals. Among the latter, significantly, were to be found most of the Russian Jews studying in Western European universities. It was this constituency that ultimately would provide Theodor Herzl with some 90 percent of his delegates at the First Zionist Congress in 1897 (p. 268).

The Beginning of the Return

As late as three hundred years after the destruction of the Jewish Commonwealth of antiquity, a vestigial Jewish presence of perhaps 2,000 souls continued barely to subsist in the Holy Land. The remnant began to revive only after the Arab conquest in the seventh century, and much more substantially under the rule of the Seljuk Turks a century and a half later. By the year 1000, the Jewish population of the Holy Land may have revived to as much as a quarter-million. But the interlude of renewal ended abruptly, and quite gruesomely, with the arrival of the Crusaders. The butchery of Jews was so extensive under Christian rule that, in 1168, when the Spanish-Jewish traveler Benjamin of Tudela visited Palestine, he found barely a thousand Jewish families alive. The number would not rise appreciably for nearly half a millennium.

It was the mass expulsion from Spain in 1492 that propelled a wave of Jewish refugees into the newly established Ottoman Empire. Some 15,000 of these fugitives made their way to Ottoman Palestine. Over the years, the tiny enclave was augmented by additional rivulets of Jews, essentially pietists from Central and Eastern Europe who arrived to live out their days in the four "holy" cities of Tiberias, Hebron, Safed, and Jerusalem. Yet even this modest settlement was intermittently depleted by plagues, and once, in 1837, by a massive earthquake in the Galilee. By the early nineteenth century, not more than 6,000 Jews remained in the Holy Land. Taxed and tyrannized by Turks and Arabs alike, they regarded their presence in Zion essentially as a testament of repentance.

If there were auguries of hope for this vestigial Jewry, they were to be found in the emergence of Palestine itself from its legendary mists, and into the realm of international attention. Napoleon's invasion of Egypt in 1789, Mehemet Ali's conquest of Syria in 1833, the Crimean War at mid-century, and Britain's occupation of Cyprus and Egypt in the 1870s and 1880s—all opened up the Ottoman Empire as a critical new arena of world politics. Moreover, as the price for guarding that empire against the expansionist designs of Tsarist Russia, European governments extracted a major concession from the Turks. This took the form of "capitulations," a kind of legal extraterritoriality bestowed on Europeans traveling or living in Ottoman lands. Additionally, by an understanding of 1846, secured through the good offices of the British consul in Jerusalem, the same "capitulatory" protection was extended to Jewish residents of the Holy Land. With this inducement, a modest immigration of East European Jews began to resume by mid-century. Most of the newcomers settled in Jerusalem, where their initial circumstances were quite marginal. As pietists, they were content to subsist on little more than charitable remittances dispatched from Jewish communities in Europe. But in the early 1870s, these same communities organized "building societies" to help fund small Jewish colonies outside Jerusalem's medieval walls. At the same time, Europe's growing network of institutions in the Middle East—of archaeological societies, religious missions, churches, hospices, as well as trading companies—encouraged the Ottoman government to improve road transportation and security measures within Palestine. Responding to these measures, the Jewish population in the Holy Land inched upward, to approximately 32,000 by 1881.

Then, between 1881 and 1903, 24,000 additional Jews entered Palestine. Most were refugees from tsarist oppression. Among these, too, religionists still comprised the majority. Yet, for the first time, a substantial minority were also Zionists, most of them arriving under the auspices of the Hovevei Zion. At first, the newcomers tended to settle in Jerusalem or Jaffa, where they resumed their former vocations as modest shopkeepers and artisans. But early in 1882, the immigrants also included some two dozen former students at the University of Kharkov, who made known their determination to revive Jewish life in the Holy Land "productively," by working on the soil. Calling themselves BILU, the vanguard of young idealists laid out a plan for creating a new, autonomous society, imbued with the "highest principles of duty and national generation." In that effort, they sought their first employment as agricultural laborers at the Alliance Israélite Universelle's training tract of Mikveh Yisrael (p. 256). The experience proved unsuccessful, even grim. Under the harsh supervision of professional French agronomists, they were driven to exhaustion—and despair. Most of the "BILUists" eventually departed Mikveh Yisrael to settle in the towns, and half of them eventually returned to Russia.

Notwithstanding these initial discouragements, the numbers of aspiring farmers continued to grow. In May 1882, a contingent of some two hundred young Rumanian men, women, and children disembarked in Jaffa with sufficient funds to purchase a small coastal tract. Although lacking previous experience on the land, they managed to clear the soil and establish an agricultural village, eventually to be known as Zichron Ya'akov. At the same time, the Hovevei Zion organization accumulated enough funds to purchase several additional tracts for other groups of young Zionist idealists. Most of these early ventures barely remained viable. To discourage Europeans from land ownership, the Ottoman government confronted them with an endless maze of regulations and restrictions. Although the settlers managed to circumvent many of these difficulties through bribery, the expenditure left hardly any money for agricultural equipment, or even for the basic necessities of food and medicine. Fortunately, a patron came to the rescue in the form of Baron Edmond de Rothschild. The great Parisian banker was by no means a Zionist, but he approved the notion of restoring Jews to productive, agricultural labor. Ultimately, Rothschild's Palestine Jewish Colonization Association—PICA—would provide over 20 million francs to ensure the survival of these fledgling Zionist farm colonies.

Such were the mixed circumstances of the *Yishuv,* the Jewish settlement in Palestine, at the end of the nineteenth century. By then, approximately 57,000 Jews were living in the country. Yet the largest majority still was ensconced in Jerusalem, and half of these were at least partially dependent upon charity. The Jewish rural population had grown to some 5,000 individuals, living in twenty villages (nearly that many villages had been abandoned), but fifteen of the settlements were subsidized by Rothschild's PICA. Even with this help, the Jewish farm economy remained heavily dependent on cheap Arab labor. Neither did the Zionists' Hebrew-cultural aspirations seem likely to be realized. Their initial handful of schools was underwritten either by PICA or by the Alliance, and thus French served as the language of instruction. For that matter, the prospect of any meaningful Jewish demographic growth seemed equally remote, as Turkish officials continued to raise innumerable bureaucratic obstacles to their settlement. If the Jews had achieved a Yishuv on the soil of their ancient homeland, it remained the most fragile and precarious of enclaves.

THEODOR HERZL AND THE RISE OF POLITICAL ZIONISM

On June 2, 1895, the railroad tycoon Baron Moritz de Hirsch received a visitor in his Paris mansion. Hirsch was a legendary figure, not only of capitalist enterprise but of philanthropic generosity. Earlier in the decade, Hirsch had poured tens of millions of francs into the effort of transporting Russian Jewry en masse to the agricultural plains of Argentina. That scheme had failed, as it happened. Fewer than 3,000 Jews had availed themselves of Hirsch's largesse (pp. 673–74). Nevertheless, the baron had persisted in expending vast sums on refugees in Europe and the Americas, and his munificence evoked the highest respect of Jews and non-Jews alike. Then, on May 24, 1895, a request for an interview arrived in the mail from Theodor Herzl, an author and journalist of Europe-wide reputation; and the letter, reflecting this dignity, contrasted markedly with the fawning solicitations that ordinarily reached the baron's desk. "Until now you have been only a philanthropist," Herzl had written. "... I want to show you the way to become something more." Intrigued, Hirsch had consented to the meeting.

The visitor was a striking figure, with dark, soulful eyes, chiseled features, and a rich "Assyrian" beard. His demeanor was consciously aristocratic. Indeed, his explanation for Hirsch's Argentine debacle approached conde-scension. "You breed beggars," Herzl calmly informed his host. "As long as Jews are passive recipients of charitable funds, they will remain weaklings and cowards." Rather than philanthropy, Herzl continued, the Jews were in need of political education for self-support, and ultimately for self-government, in a land of their own. When Herzl began elaborating on this theme, Hirsch interrupted with vigorous objections. These were not trivial. Although the Holy Land did not figure specifically in Herzl's presentation, the baron assumed that Palestine was its ultimate objective; and on the basis of Hirsch's long and unpleasant railroad dealings with the Turkish government, he doubted that any Ottoman province would bring the Jews security. As he had written to the board of the German-Jewish Hilfsverein four years earlier: "I point out the danger . . . in sending [Jewish refugees] into Asia and Turkey. I know that land better than anybody . . . and am in a position to judge the mis-ery and deceptions that await any [Jews] that may be sent there haphazardly." In any case, Hirsch was convinced that much of the Ottoman Empire, including Palestine, was destined to fall into the hands of Russia, "the arch-enemy of the Jewish people." When Herzl in turn sought to respond to these objections, the baron cut the interview short. Yet the import of the conversa-tion lingered, both annoying and intriguing Hirsch. What manner of man was this Herzl, he asked later of Zadoc Kahn, the Grand Rabbi of Paris, to utter thoughts so shockingly at variance with the affirmation of Europeanism, the Napoleonic Sanhedrin's dominating tradition in Western Jewish life?

In truth, the thirty-five-year-old Herzl was the very quintessence of acculturated Europeanism. Son of an affluent Jewish banking family of Budapest, he was raised to cherish the painfully achieved opportunities of Habsburg citizenship. In his case, those opportunities included education at the University of Vienna, where in 1884 he received a law degree (with its grandiloquent Central European title, "doctorate of jurisprudence"). The diploma actually became an irrelevance in Herzl's career. He preferred to devote his spare moments to writing literary and political essays, and within a year he abandoned the practice of law entirely for journalism. The decision was a useful one. In journalism, Herzl achieved almost instant success as a columnist on a wide range of political and social issues. In 1891, he was appointed Paris correspondent for the *Neue Freie Presse,* Vienna's most respected newspaper. Presumably, the young man should have relished his professional success. But emotional satisfaction was lacking. His wife was high-strung and unstable. Separations were frequent, and after the birth of their third child the couple lived together only intermittently.

By the last decade of the century, too, Herzl was increasingly preoccupied with the poisonous new upsurge of West European antisemitism. Indeed, in 1894 he dashed off a short play, *The New Ghetto (Das neue Ghetto),* that addressed the issue of Jewish vulnerability with a pessimism evident in its title (the protagonist was a high-minded Jewish lawyer who was driven to suicide by the bigotry of vindictive business associates). Herzl's despairing obsession with the Jewish question was intensified by the degradation of Captain Alfred Dreyfus on January 3, 1895, in the courtyard of the École Militaire, which Herzl had witnessed personally (p. 235). It was a critical moment of recognition. At some point in the spring of 1895, the Zionist idea evidently took form in Herzl's mind, and inspired his interview with Moritz de Hirsch in June of that year.

Although a disappointment, the meeting with the baron merely impelled Herzl into an urgent formulation of his new Zionist idea. Within days, he began transcribing his thoughts in his diary. The opening pages describe a vision that possessed him "walking, standing, lying down, in the street, at the table, at nighttime. . . . I believe that for me life has ceased and world history has begun. . . . The Jewish State is a world necessity." With Hirsch unavailable to him, Herzl decided to turn next to the Rothschilds. Indeed, an early "chapter" of the diary was titled "An Address to the Rothschilds," for Herzl intended to read it to the great banking family assembled in council. First, however, he read it to a friend, Max Nordau. Eleven years older than Herzl, the son of a Budapest rabbi, Nordau had been trained as a physician, but subsequently had achieved a far wider reputation as the author of numerous volumes exposing the neuroses and debilities of contemporary society. For most of his adult life, Nordau had considered himself a cosmopolitan. Changing his original name from Sudfeld to the more Germanic Nordau, he had left Judaism behind as a "mere memory." But the Dreyfus Affair also had dispelled the chimera of assimilation for him. Accordingly, when Herzl read the "Address," Nordau reacted with intense enthusiasm. Promising his friend the fullest measure of personal support, Nordau from then on would remain Herzl's most intimate collaborator. With this encouragement, Herzl duly set about reworking his "Address to the Rothschilds." Within two months, it was completed as a sixty-five-page booklet, and entitled *Der Judenstaat*.

The title has been translated most frequently as *The Jewish State*. In fact, it is *The Jew State*, a term Herzl flung into the teeth of antisemites and of acculturated Western Jews who preferred such euphemisms as "Israelite" or Germans or Frenchmen of the "Mosaic persuasion." Published in Vienna in February 1896, the pamphlet was immediately republished in French and English, and not long afterward in Russian and Yiddish. The subject of its subtitle, "An Attempt at a Modern Solution to the Jewish Question," was developed straightforwardly in Herzl's first chapter. Jew-hatred was an ineradicable fact of life, he argued. Neither a social nor a religious question, "[antisemitism] is a national question, and in order to solve it we must . . . transform it into a political world question, to be answered within the councils of civilized peoples." Herzl then elaborated upon his central thesis. Having failed to win acceptance within their host nations, the Jews were left with only one alternative, and this was a mass exodus to a land of their own. "Political principle will provide the basis," he argued, "technology the means, and the driving force will be the Jewish tragedy." It was Herzl's contention, too, that Europe itself would cooperate in the Jewish departure, for an "inner" migration of gentiles then could fill positions abandoned by the Jews. "The [Jewish emigration] will be gradual . . . [but] its very inception means the end of antisemitism."

The greater part of the essay was given over to the actual "mechanics" of transplantation. Above all, insisted Herzl, it should avoid the failed method of "gradual infiltration," as was currently taking place in Palestine. The right of collective Jewish settlement demanded international recognition, whether directed toward Argentina or Palestine—although Palestine, "our unforgettable historic homeland," logically would be the first choice. Two instruments would be created, a "Society of the Jews," to function as legal representative of the national idea, and a "Jewish Company," a joint-stock corporation to finance both Jewish emigration and the physical construction of the Jewish state. Once established in a country of their own, the Jews would organize their society on the latest scientific principles. Herzl was less specific on cultural matters. He hardly made reference to a national language except to speculate that the state might emerge as a linguistic federation, as in Switzerland. But such details were less important than the sheer compulsion to immigrate and build a Jewish nation. And to that end, mass propaganda was needed:

> The idea must radiate out until it reaches the last wretched nests of our people. They will awaken out of their dull brooding. Then a new meaning will come into the lives of all of us. . . . We shall finally live as free men on our own soil and die peacefully in our own homeland.

As one assesses the phenomenon of a thoroughly Europeanized Jew producing a work of this startling nature, it is worth recalling that Herzl was a citizen of a multinational, multilingual empire. Both as a Jew and as a Habsburg citizen, he was in no sense the outsider that Lilienblum or Pinsker were in Tsarist Russia. Habsburg society was entirely pluralistic, and well accustomed to the spectacle of ethnic and national minorities contending for influence within the larger framework of empire. Many of the lawyers who pleaded the cause of their kindred Czechs, Croats, Serbs, or Slovenes were themselves entirely Germanized in language and culture. There was thus nothing particularly atypical in a German-speaking, agnostic Jew like Herzl propounding Jewish separateness, without being steeped himself in the Jews' own language and culture. But if there were precedents for this sort of advocacy within the Habsburg experience, there was none within the Jewish experience. Earlier formulations of Jewish nationalism—Smolenskin's, even Pinsker's—had issued from a solid grounding in Jewish religion and folklore. Herzl, conversely, writing in ignorance of these Zionist predecessors, was uninhibited by their emphasis on Jewish culture as a major objective of revived Jewish nationhood. His nationalism emerged more characteristically from Western concepts of political sovereignty, rather than from a devout, but insular, Russian-Jewish traditionalism.

Yet Herzl's very intellectual eclecticism may actually have helped him in his one-track endeavor. More cautious and less superficial thinkers would have feared to tread where he did. None, in any case, possessed his credentials for dealing in international affairs. Herzl's version of Zionism was the first to be articulated by a man of the world, by a distinguished political observer and a broadly traveled journalist. *Der Judenstaat*, in short, introduced Zionism to European readers, to editors, university men, politicians, diplomats, and other molders of public opinion precisely in the kind of language they were accustomed to reading.

The Zionist Organization

Nevertheless, the initial reception of *Der Judenstaat* was inauspicious. The European press ridiculed Herzl as the "Jewish Jules Verne." The renowned literary figure Stefan Zweig recalled:

> I can still remember the general astonishment and annoyance of the middle-class Jewish elements of Vienna. . . . Why should we go to Palestine? Our language is German and not Hebrew, and beautiful Austria is our homeland. Are we not well off under the good Emperor Franz Josef? . . . Why does [Herzl] . . . place arguments in the hands of our worst enemies and attempt to separate us, when every day brings us more closely and intimately into the German world?

But derision and exasperation were not the only reactions, even in the West. *Der Judenstaat* was received warmly by Kadima, the Zionist student society of Vienna. Many Russian-Jewish students attending universities in Austria, Germany, and Switzerland were thrilled by the book. These, in turn, were the first to apprise Herzl of the writings of Smolenskin, Lilienblum, and Pinsker, and of the emerging Zionist cultural renaissance in Eastern Europe.

At the same time, along his own chosen route of personal diplomacy, Herzl was making useful contacts. One was the Grand Duke of Baden, uncle of the German kaiser. Kindly disposed to Jews, the grand duke reacted well to Herzl's vision of a Jewish state and promised to discuss the matter with his royal nephew. In the meanwhile, he put Herzl in touch with a debt-ridden Polish aristocrat, Count Philip de Nevlinski, who maintained important friendships among the demimonde of European royalty. Intrigued by the offer of Herzl's private subsidies, Nevlinski in June 1896 actually secured an interview for Herzl in Constantinople with the Turkish prime minister and foreign minister. In their meeting, Herzl ventured a striking proposal. It was for "influential Jewish financiers" to assume responsibility for the Ottoman Public Debt in return for a charter of collective Jewish settlement in Palestine. The reaction of the two ministers was one of polite noncommittal.

Undaunted, Herzl traveled on to London, the financial capital he envisaged as the headquarters of his "Jewish Company." Attempting to sell his idea to a group of Anglo-Jewish businessmen, he was rebuffed once again, equally politely. In July 1896, finally, he secured an interview in Paris with Baron Edmond de Rothschild, whose ongoing largesse to the Palestinian colonies seemingly augured well for Herzl's project. Yet the baron curtly shot the notion down, describing a Jewish state as likely to bring 100,000 "schnorrers" (beggars) to Palestine. "You were the keystone of the entire combination," Herzl observed sadly. ". . . . I shall [now] have to do it in a different way. I shall launch a great agitation which will make the masses still more difficult to keep in order."

It was no idle bluster. By then, Herzl's name and legend were growing in the Russian Pale. In the recollection of Chaim Weizmann, an early Zionist who years later would become the movement's preeminent statesman: "Here was daring, clarity, and energy. The very fact that [Herzl] came to us unencumbered by our own preconceptions had its appeal. We were right in our instinctive appreciation that what had emerged from *Der Judenstaat* was less a concept than a historic personality." Telegrams and letters of thanks poured in to Herzl from Hovevei Zion societies throughout Eastern Europe, all calling upon the "new Moses" to accept leadership of the movement. During his otherwise unsuccessful visit to London, Herzl was cheered by a tumultuous crowd of Russian-Jewish immigrants in the East End. "About me, a faint mist is rising," he admitted in his diary, not without pleasure. Finally, on July 21, 1896, three days after his abortive meeting with Rothschild, Herzl made the decision to organize a Zionist congress. Together with Nordau and other close associates, he eventually settled on Basel, Switzerland, as its site. By then Herzl, the austere Viennese journalist, was rapidly being transformed into a dynamic man of political action. In advance of the congress, he ensured that his proposed agenda was distributed among Zionist leaders throughout Europe, requested the election only of the most "eminent" representatives, and outlined the congress's procedural rules and regulations.

Herzl's energetic preparations were well repaid. On August 29, 1897, 204 delegates arrived in Basel from twelve European countries, as well as from the United States, Algeria, and Palestine. They convened in the Stadt Casino, a local concert hall, where a newly designed Zionist flag was hanging at the auditorium entrance. Dignity was the key. All the delegates wore frock coats and white ties. The galleries were packed with visitors, including correspondents from Europe's leading newspapers. And when Herzl rose to speak, the delegates leaped to their feet in a thrilled fifteen-minute ovation. The opening words of Herzl's address were as unequivocal as those of *Der Judenstaat*. "We are here to lay the foundation stone of the house which is to shelter the Jewish nation." Then, after genuflecting to the East Europeans' concern for "spiritual revival," he proceeded to reemphasize his diplomatic agenda, insisting that the older method of piecemeal colonization in Palestine no longer was adequate. A new, permanent homeland, "öffentlich, rechtlich" ("openly recognized, legally secure"), was the only solution; and to that end, a new, permanent, "official" body was required.

Herzl had learned much of parliamentary techniques during his years covering the French Chamber of Deputies. Skillfully now, he presided over the

Zionist sessions. During the ensuing three days of the congress, the various delegations presented reports on the circumstances of the Jews in their respective countries. The accounts were bleak, for the most part, particularly those from Eastern Europe and Palestine. The congress then followed Herzl's guidelines by establishing as its instrument a permanent, popularly elected Zionist Organization (the "Jewish Society" of his *Judenstaat*), with its Central Executive to be comprised of the leadership residing in Vienna (essentially Herzl and Nordau, and their closest associates). As its final act, the congress unanimously elected Herzl president of the Zionist Organization, and concluded with the singing of a Hebrew anthem, "Hatikvah," composed for the event. When the delegates rose, weeping and embracing, they carried Herzl through the hall on their shoulders. "If I were to sum up the Basel Congress in a single phrase," Herzl wrote later, ". . . I would say: in Basel I created the Jewish state."

The remark was not hyperbole. Even more than Herzl had anticipated, the congress gave powerful impetus to Zionist propaganda throughout the Jewish world. Zionism soon became the leading Jewish issue of the day, infusing a new vitality into Jewish communities everywhere. A second, then a third Zionist Congress in the ensuing two years would bring additional delegates from the hundreds of new Zionist societies that were springing up to augment, and eventually to supersede, the old Russian Hovevei Zion groups. All expressed a renewed commitment to the Yishuv, the Palestine Jewish settlement, by both immigration and fund-raising, and all simultaneously endorsed the goal of a charter for collective Jewish settlement in the Holy Land.

Indeed, for Herzl, acquisition of a charter remained his idée fixe. As a keen student of international affairs, aware that the Ottoman Empire was gravitating into the German economic and diplomatic orbit, he sensed that the route to Constantinople passed through Berlin. To exploit that route, Herzl offered a shrewd inducement for German political support. As he explained to Count Philip zu Eulenberg, Germany's ambassador to Vienna, a Zionist enclave in Palestine might serve as the cultural outpost of German influence in the Middle East, inasmuch as the entirety of Zionism's executive leadership were German and Austrian nationals. The argument registered. Eventually, in the autumn of 1898, it secured Herzl an audience with the kaiser himself.

Significantly, the meeting took place in Constantinople, on October 18, during the course of Wilhelm II's state visit to the Ottoman Empire. Arriving at the Yildiz Kiosk, where the German royal entourage was lodged, Herzl maintained his own "regal" poise and eloquence, as befitting a "leader" of the Jews. The kaiser received him correctly. Nevertheless, during the hour-long interview, Wilhelm implied that his interest in Zionism was at least obliquely antisemitic. "There are among your people," he observed, "certain elements whom it would be a good thing to move to Palestine." Herzl remained unruffled. Outlining his plan for a charter of Jewish settlement in the Holy Land, he laid emphasis on the imperial advantages for both Germany and Turkey of a German protectorate over a Jewish enclave in the Middle East. The kaiser reacted well to this approach and intimated that he would discuss the matter with Sultan Abd al-Hamid II. Two and a half weeks later, as Wilhelm visited Palestine, Herzl followed in his wake, and was given a second audience, this one outside Jerusalem. This time the meeting was a disappointment. The German emperor was noncommittal. Herzl soon grasped that his envisaged route through Berlin was foreclosed.

The aftermath of the unproductive German negotiations represented a bleak period for the Zionist leader. Thus far, all his diplomacy with statesmen apparently had been in vain. For the ensuing two years, therefore, he found himself engaged essentially in pedestrian Zionist propaganda and fund-raising efforts. Yet, even then, Herzl did not abandon his diplomatic objective. Only his tactics changed. He decided once again to direct his major effort to the Ottoman government. To that end, moreover, in 1900, he added yet another intermediary to his private payroll. This was a Hungarian Jew, Arminius Vambery, a former professor of oriental languages at the University of Pest, and subsequently private tutor to Princess Fatima, Sultan Abd al-Hamid II's younger sister. Eventually, in May 1901, through the discriminating use of his patron's baksheesh funds, Vambery actually managed to secure an interview for Herzl with the sultan.

It was a dinner meeting at the royal palace. Abd al-Hamid went to great lengths to be amiable, emphasizing his own friendship for the Jews, even presenting Herzl with the Order of Medjije (second-class). Herzl responded by quoting the fable of Androcles and the lion. "His Majesty is the lion, perhaps I am Androcles, and perhaps there is a thorn—the Ottoman Public Debt—which I could withdraw." He went on to intimate that his Jewish associates might supply the needed funds in return for "the proclamation of a measure particularly favorable to the Jews." The sultan appeared to be impressed, and asked for a written memorandum. Herzl was ready. The next day, he submitted his prospectus for a chartered company to the prime minister. With the finance minister, he discussed his plans for refunding the Ottoman Debt. The proposal envisaged a syndicate of Jews buying up the debt's bonds over a period of three years, beginning with a down payment of 1.5 million pounds sterling; while the sultan in turn would grant the Zionist Organization a charter for a land settlement company in Palestine. Leaving the Turkish officials to chew over this offer, Herzl then returned to Vienna.

Convinced that his years of effort were approaching fruition, Herzl anticipated that at long last he had achieved the leverage necessary to raise a down payment of 1.5 million pounds for the charter. But again he was doomed to disappointment. None of the Rothschilds expressed interest. Neither did the

Montefiores in London. Fighting for time, Herzl subsequently entered into a lengthy series of written exchanges with the Ottoman prime minister, suggesting that the sultan should take the initiative by offering the Jews their charter. But the prime minister, an experienced bargainer, insisted first on seeing the color of the Jews' money. Finally, in mid-July 1902, desperate to buy additional time from the Ottoman government, Herzl set out again for Constantinople. And there he encountered a shock. The Turks had been using the Zionist connection simply as a bargaining pawn with a visiting consortium of French bankers. The diplomatic route to Palestine evidently was closed.

AN IDEOLOGICAL SCHISM

By the summer of 1902, Herzl faced yet another series of crises. These were related not to the diplomatic world, however, but to the Jewish world. The Jewish establishment in Western Europe and the United States remained implacable in their hostility to political Zionism. For these acculturated veterans, Zionism was akin to blatant treason, and a provocation to antisemitism. Within the Zionist movement, on the other hand, Herzl confronted mounting impatience at his fixation with diplomacy, his apparent indifference to the unspectacular but steady growth of Zionist membership both in Europe and in other continents. It was in a mood of growing desperation, therefore, in July 1902, that Herzl visited England upon his return from Turkey. Friends had arranged for him to testify as a "Jewish expert" before a parliamentary commission that was then studying the threat posed to British workers by cheap immigrant labor in London's East End (p. 217). The immigrants were principally Russian Jews. Appearing before the commission, Herzl in his broken English attempted to describe the wretched conditions in the Pale that had impelled the refugees' flight and expressed the hope that Britain would keep its doors open. At the end of his testimony, however, he made the point of adding: "But if you find that they are not wanted here, then some place must be found to which they can emigrate without raising the problems that [you are investigating]. The problems will not arise if a home can be found for them which will be legally recognized as Jewish."

By chance, the Zionist allusion picqued the interest of Britain's colonial secretary, Joseph Chamberlain. An ardent imperialist, Chamberlain was known to favor the use of client peoples as instruments of British rule. Conceivably, the Jews might fulfill this purpose. He invited Herzl to a meeting and listened with interest as the Zionist leader intimated that he was receptive to possible alternatives to the Holy Land. One was al-Arish, an extension of the Sinai Desert that evoked historical memories of the Hebrew exodus from Egypt. Chamberlain responded favorably, and authorized Herzl to appoint a Zionist commission to explore al-Arish's potentialities for Jewish settlement.

Yet, in ensuing discussions over March and April of 1903, the Egyptian government blocked the plan, citing "inadequate irrigation." Herzl fell into black despair. "It's simply done for," he wrote in his diary on May 11.

At this point, Herzl conceivably was prepared to abandon Palestine, and its extended hinterlands, as his intended state. The torment of Russian and Rumanian Jewry affected him deeply. Unless he could present his followers with a diplomatic coup in the early future, he suspected that the entire Zionist enterprise might collapse. For that matter, Herzl did not know how many years of leadership he could offer. His personal estate had been gravely depleted by heavy expenditures in travel and subsidies. One gains insight into his concerns through a slim, polemical novel, *Altneuland (Old-New Land)*, that Herzl dashed off in his recent months of ebbing morale. The book envisages a futuristic Zionist Palestine, Altneuland, a community thriving with prosperous agriculture and flourishing cities, sustaining a cooperative social and economic order in which all citizens live together in amity—worker and employer, Arab and Jew. Is it all a dream, a mere vision? asks Herzl's protagonist. The novel closes with the epilogue: "But if you will it, it is no fable."

While *Altneuland* was assured a respectable audience within the Zionist movement, it was among these readers that the book's lacunae were noted most acutely. The description of the country's emergent culture placed no emphasis whatever upon Hebrew, whether in the school system, literature, press, or theater. For Herzl, evidently, *Judenstaat*—Altneuland—served as a functional answer to Jewish oppression, nothing more. By then, too, his fixation with diplomacy, his apparent indifference to Jewish "spiritual" values, was evoking growing concern, notably among the East Europeans. The principal intellectual spokesman for that dissidence was a Russian-Jewish writer, Asher Ginzberg, who published under the pen name of Ahad Ha'Am ("One of the People"). Born in Kiev in 1856 to a Hasidic family, Ginzberg endured the prototypical Jewish childhood of a sensitive mind imprisoned in the obscurantism of the Pale. He was married off at the age of seventeen to a girl he had not set eyes on until the day of the wedding. Afterward, he was locked into a modest family business for which he exhibited little enthusiasm or aptitude. Ginzberg's escape from material circumstances was almost entirely cerebral. Like other, often forgotten geniuses of the Haskalah era, he became an omnivorous reader in virtually all the major European languages. His horizons were additionally broadened when he took up residence in Odessa, in the years of that port city's emergence as a major Jewish intellectual center, and afterward in London, where he was employed as an auditor in the English branch of the Wissotzky Tea Company.

From his earliest writing career, this spare little man, goateed and pincenezed, devoted his phenomenal erudition and mastery of the Hebrew language to a single and exclusive issue: "The Solution of the Jewish Problem" (the title of one of his essays). As an active member of the Hovevei Zion, Ginzberg was obsessed with his people's need for spiritual and cultural awakening, and far less with the establishment of a Jewish political presence in the Land of Israel. Expressing that concern in an austere lucidity of style rarely equaled in modern Hebrew, he soon developed a substantial following even among the most relentless "practical" Zionists, those committed to nation-building in Palestine. One of these, Chaim Weizmann, recalled of Ginzberg: "He had the profoundest effect on the Russian-Jewish students in Europe. . . . [T]he appearance of one of [his] articles was always an event of prime importance. He was read and discussed endlessly."

Indeed, by the turn of the century, Ginzberg had emerged as a revered intellectual mentor for the tens of thousands of East European Jews who were flocking to the Zionist cause. Detecting and mercilessly exposing the lack of Hebraic content in Herzl's original *Judenstaat,* he chose to attend the First Zionist Congress as a visitor rather than as a delegate, "like a mourner at a wedding feast," he wrote afterward. In ensuing years, Ginzberg waged an unrelenting campaign against "mere political Zionism" and against Herzl's diplomatist leadership. For Ginzberg and his followers, among them Weizmann and a nucleus of younger Russian-Jewish delegates, Herzl's preoccupation with a diplomatic coup, with a charter of territorial settlement, with a polyglot, Europeanized society in the Land of Israel—all gravely trivialized the more enduring role of Zion as the wellspring of a Jewish cultural and moral renaissance.

For Herzl, by contrast, issues of "cultural" or "moral" revival were luxuries. They could not be allowed to overshadow the urgency of the Jewish plight in Europe, particularly in Eastern Europe. In May 1903, the Kishinev pogrom had shaken the entire Jewish world (p. 289). Herzl himself visited Russia the following August in a—largely successful—effort to win legal status for Zionism in the Tsarist Empire. At the same time, during his interviews with government officials, he grasped the bottomless depth of their antisemitism. In Minister of the Interior Vyacheslav von Plehve, a key instigator of the pogroms, Herzl discerned "a cold panther, ready to spring," and in the Pale he sensed a doomed Jewry. Thus, upon returning to Vienna, he decided to give serious attention to a proposal that had merely been hinted at by Britain's Colonial Secretary Chamberlain the previous April, when it appeared that the al-Arish project was foundering.

Chamberlain had visited South Africa late in 1902, in an effort to explore a reconciliation with the Afrikaner population following the Boer War. Stopping off briefly in Kenya, the colonial secretary gave special attention to the newly completed East African Railroad, extending from Mombasa on the coast up to Nairobi in the hill country. Chamberlain envisaged the rail line as an ideal projection of British imperialism in the Dark Continent. He would have cherished an even wider European settlement in these areas, particularly in the highlands. Then he remembered his earlier conversation with Herzl. "On my travels," said Chamberlain in his subsequent, April 1903 meeting with the Zionist leader, "I saw a country for you: Uganda." The reference to "Uganda" actually was erroneous. The territory fell within the frontiers of Kenya. "On the coast it is hot," Chamberlain noted, "but in the interior the climate is excellent for Europeans. You can plant cotton and sugar. I thought to myself: that's just the country for Dr. Herzl. But *he* must have Palestine. . . ." "Yes, I must," Herzl responded. "The base must be in or near Palestine."

By late summer of 1903, however, following his visit to Russia, Herzl was prepared to consider alternate sanctuaries. "We must give an answer to Kishinev," he explained to Max Nordau, "and [Chamberlain's proposal] is the only one. . . ." By reacting favorably to the colonial secretary's offer, he added, "we [will at least], in our relationship with [England] . . . acquire recognition as a state-building power." The rationale was impressive, and Nordau was persuaded. Chamberlain, in turn, informed of Herzl's reassessment, suggested that the Zionists once again appoint a commission, as they had for the earlier al-Arish proposal, to investigate the East Africa terrain. Herzl then began the preliminaries. Yet, at the same time, preparations had to be made for the impending Sixth Zionist Congress, this one scheduled again in Basel, in late August. So it was, on August 22, 1903, as the delegates entered the Stadt Casino, that they suddenly recognized the extent to which the issue of physical Jewish rescue now had shifted Herzl's focus and that of his colleagues on the Zionist Executive.

It had been a tradition in earlier congresses for a map of the Holy Land to be draped on the wall behind the dais. This now had been replaced by a map of East Africa. Herzl himself confirmed the new approach when he informed the delegates of Chamberlain's offer. East Africa, he acknowledged, was to be regarded exclusively as an emergency measure. Nordau characterized it as a "Nachtasyl," an asylum for the night. Both men stressed the thrilling new connection with the British government, and its potential for the future. The congress delegates then reacted with a burst of rousing applause. But after several minutes, a muffled disquiet became evident in the auditorium. Numerous delegates still had not overcome their resentment at Herzl's recent meeting in Russia with Minister of the Interior Plehve, the "architect of Kishinev." This latest, East African, proposal was a source of even graver consternation. The dismay was given its first expression on the rostrum by Yehiel Tchlenow, an East European Zionist leader. "There fills us all an inexpressible joy," Tchlenow acknowledged, diplomatically, "that a great European Power . . . has recognized with this offer the national demands of the

Jewish people. But to this is linked the great sorrow that we must refuse the offer, because our needs can only be satisfied by Palestine." Other speakers were less restrained. The debate became impassioned. Warnings and accusations—"Suicide!" "Criminal!" "Treachery!"—began flying from all sides.

Eventually, when a vote was taken on the seemingly innocuous resolution to dispatch an investigative commission to East Africa, it passed by an unimpressive tally, 295 to 177, with 100 members abstaining. Even this "victory" became a Pyrrhic one for Herzl. The congress was polarized, and a gathering of "purists" went so far as to meet in a rump caucus to condemn Herzl and to reassert their commitment exclusively to the Land of Israel. In a white heat of indignation, Asher Ginzberg (Ahad HaAm) published an article, "HaBohim" ("Those Who Weep"), proclaiming the final bankruptcy of "political Zionism." Within weeks, the crisis between the "politicals" and the "practical-culturals" ignited a major upheaval in the Zionist movement. Transcending countries of origin, the cleavage was profound. Family bonds and lifelong friendships were shattered on the issue.

As it happened, the debate over East Africa was becoming academic. The small nucleus of British colonists inhabiting the Kenyan highlands strenuously opposed any notion of a mass influx of Russian Jews. Somewhat embarrassedly, Colonial Secretary Chamberlain then felt obliged to withdraw the offer. Herzl in turn was almost relieved that the issue had resolved itself, and with it the threat of a conceivably permanent disruption of the Zionist movement. For him, the relationship with England was all that mattered. "You will see," he told his colleague Max Bodenheimer, "the time is coming when England will do everything in her power to have Palestine ceded to us for the Jewish state."

Yet the bitter internecine struggle had taken its toll. A friend was startled by the change in Herzl. "The imposing figure now was stooped," he wrote later, "the face was sallow, the eyes . . . darkened, the mouth drawn in pain and marked by passion." In the late spring of 1904, Herzl suffered a mild heart attack, and in June left for Edlach in the Semmering Mountains to recuperate. But on July 3, he suffered another attack and died. He was forty-four. In the Zionist world, all factional recriminations immediately ended. The "great eagle" was gone. In Vienna, 6,000 people walked behind his funeral cortege. Stefan Zweig recalled "a sort of elemental ecstatic mourning such as I have never seen before or since at a funeral. And it was this gigantic outpouring of grief . . . that caused me to realize for the first time how much passion and hope this lone and lonesome man had borne into the world through the great power of a single idea." It became clear only later that, for all his shortcomings, Herzl's redeeming greatness was his ability to elevate a domestic misery, one that traditionally had been addressed through stopgap measures, into a challenging international issue. He removed the Jewish problem from the waiting rooms of philanthropy and introduced it into the chancellories of European diplomacy.

It was no less significant that Herzl bequeathed to future Zionist leaders—Chaim Weizmann and Nahum Sokolow, among others—far more than precept and example. In his own career, he actually developed the contacts they later would exploit. Arthur James Balfour was prime minister in 1903, when Herzl secured the British offer of territory in East Africa. Years later, as foreign secretary, Balfour would recall Herzl's vision of a Jewish homeland. So would David Lloyd George, whose law office, at Herzl's request, drew up the initial draft charter for a Jewish settlement in East Africa. Sir Edward Grey, vital to Weizmann in 1916, had been politically attracted to Zionism by Herzl in the course of the al-Arish and East Africa negotiations. Much that Herzl had anticipated, from high diplomacy to the patient cultivation of influential public figures and solicitation of funds, he himself put into action. "Everything directed from one center with purposeful and farsighted vision," he had written Baron Moritz de Hirsch after the abortive meeting of 1895. "Finally, I would have had to tell you what flag I would unfurl, and how. And then you would have asked in mockery, 'A flag, what is that? A stick with a cloth rag?' No, a flag, monsieur le baron, is more than that. With a flag you can lead men where you will—even into the promised land."

AN IDEOLOGICAL IMPULSION FOR THE LAND OF ISRAEL

Under Herzl's successor, David Wolfssohn, a Lithuanian-born lumber merchant based in Cologne, the Zionist Organization in ensuing years focused less on diplomacy than on the movement's pragmatic growth. By then, Zionism was "officially" committed to the development of the Yishuv in Palestine. Nevertheless, the movement's initial momentum was palpably slowed. Herzl's death was not the decisive factor. Reacting to the sheer desperation of their circumstances in Eastern Europe, most Jews in the prewar years concentrated either on immigration to the West or on political revolution in the Tsarist Empire itself. Meanwhile, the Ottoman government continued to oppose the immigration of Europeans into Palestine, or the purchase of land for cultivation or home construction. Even with the extensive use of baksheesh, the restrictions could be evaded only torturously and minimally.

Reacting to these difficulties, Wolfssohn and his colleagues could do little more than adopt a compromise approach between "cultural" and "practical" Zionism—that is, between fund-raising and cultural activities in the Diaspora on the one hand, and support for infiltrationist settlement in Palestine on the other. While the approach ignited no fires of popular enthusiasm, it achieved a number of solid, if unspectacular, successes. By 1914, fully 127,000 Jews throughout the world had become dues-paying members of the Zionist Organization. Hebrew-language schools were being organized in Eastern and Western Europe alike. The little blue-and-white Jewish National Fund box, devoted to land purchase in Palestine, could be found in tens of thousands of Jewish homes. So it was that *Gegenswartsarbeit*—pragmatic, functional spadework—became the leitmotif of prewar Zionism.

The approach was not without its dangers. By recommitting itself to nationalist political activity on Russian soil, Zionism revived the tsarist government's suspicion, and in June 1909 the movement was finally and decisively outlawed. From 1910 on, arrests and prison sentences of Zionist activists multiplied, and in 1913 some 160 trials of Zionists took place on charges of illicit fund-raising. Yet the movement was tenacious enough even in these prewar years of harassment and intimidation to foster a diversity of intramural ideologies. In elections to its annual international congresses, candidates were fielded not only by "General" Zionists, but by thousands of Orthodox Jews. Recruited into the movement by Rabbis Shmuel Mohilever and Isaac Reines, they joined a *Mizrahi* faction, religionists who envisaged a redeemed Land of Israel as the arena for a "Torah-true Judaism." Even hard-core Bundists, members of Russian socialism's Jewish "faction," became potential recruits to the Zionist cause. Admittedly, this formidable left-wing constituency posed a tougher challenge to the movement than did the Orthodox. Obsessed with the achievement of economic and political emancipation within the Tsarist Empire (p. 292), the Bundists regarded Zionism as a kind of bourgeois utopianism, a movement that ignored the political and economic aspirations of millions of Jews on Russian soil, that depended upon the goodwill of the reactionary Turkish government and the largesse of Jewish capitalists.

But if the competition between Zionism and socialism was conducted in an atmosphere of unrestrained ferocity, with each group often shouting down and even physically breaking up meetings of the other, tentative efforts to achieve reconciliation were launched as early as 1898. In that year, a young doctoral student in Berlin, Nahman Syrkin, published an essay, "The Jewish Question and the Socialist Jew-State" ("Der Judenfrage und der sozialistischen Judenstaat"), arguing that socialism would solve the Jewish problem only in the remote future and that the immediate and urgent need was for a Jewish state. "The *form* of the Jewish state," Syrkin insisted, "is the only debatable issue involved in Zionism. Zionism must be responsive to the needs of the Jewish masses. . . . [I]t must of necessity fuse with socialism." Most Bundists rejected Syrkin's argument, regarding it as absurd that the struggle for social justice should be transplanted to an arena outside mighty Russia, the domicile of over 5 million Jews. Under the mounting hammer blows of tsarist oppression, however, both Zionists and socialists evinced a growing willingness to seek an accommodation.

It was in the city of Poltava, in 1905, that Ber Borochov, a twenty-four-year-old university student and former Bundist, formulated a unique theory of Marxist Zionism. In his Yiddish-language essay "The National Question and the Class Struggle" ("Der natzional Frage und dos klassishe Anstrengung"), he read off before a Zionist study group his synthesis of both ideologies. As a Marxist, Borochov did not seek to justify the choice of Palestine along romantic-nationalist lines. He chose a different approach. In other countries, he explained, the absorptive capacity for immigration, and surely for Jewish immigration, was quite limited. The Jews required a land in which their labor force could freely enter all branches of the economy. The land would have to be semiagricultural and thinly populated. Such a country was Palestine, for Palestine alone was lacking in a national tradition, in attraction for other European immigrants, or in existing cultural or political institutions. Only in Palestine, therefore, "parallel with the growth of [Jewish] economic development, will come the growth of [Jewish] political independence." From the contemporary vantage point, Borochov's formulation may appear riddled with inconsistencies and misapprehensions. But for the déclassé and radicalized Jews of early-twentieth-century Russia, his rationale appeared to make Zionism ideologically more respectable.

It was not yet a rationale that impelled them to abandon the Russian battlefields for the sandy wastes of Ottoman Palestine. As late as the turn of the century, fewer than 60,000 Jews were living in the Holy Land, and of these barely 5,000 were to be found in the Yishuv's twenty rural colonies. A new, major influx was touched off only after the Kishinev pogrom in 1903 and, even more, after the failure of the 1905 Russian Revolution. Continuing until the outbreak of the World War, this Second *Aliyah*—Second Wave— of immigrants eventually added 30,000 newcomers to the Jewish population. Most of them were refugees plain and simple from tsarist persecution, and in Palestine's bleak and fearsome wilderness most would take their employment wherever they could find it. Yet they included in their midst a significant minority of Labor Zionists, and ultimately it would be this dedicated core group that would emerge as the political leadership of Palestine Jewry.

Like the BILU idealists of the 1880s (p. 261), the youthful visionaries of the Second Aliyah evinced a genuine sense of guilt for having been alienated from the soil. Their obsession with the land reflected more than a *narodnik,* or even a Tolstoyan idealization of agricultural labor. It also evinced unconscious resentment at the creeping Industrial Revolution in Eastern Europe, a social transformation that dislodged Jews socially and confronted them with the new and more vicious antisemitism of the urban lower middle class. Agriculture alone, then, would make the Jews independent. As Labor Zionists, the newcomers appreciated that socialist thinkers from Marx to Lenin had cited the absence of a Jewish peasant class as evidence that the Jews were not a nation, but rather a peculiar social or functional entity. It was this assertion that now had to be disproved.

Sadly, the prospect awaiting the Labor idealists appeared hardly less forbidding than it had for the BILUite predecessors. Whichever farm colony they approached, they encountered the identical circumstances of unemployment, exhaustion, and dispiritedness. In Petah Tikvah, largest of the Jewish rural villages, the attitude of the established capitalist planters was hostile. Israel Shohat, a young immigrant, recalled that the main task of the Petah Tikvah farmers "was to ensure that the Arab [employees] worked properly. . . . Before dawn, hundreds of Arab laborers daily tramped into Petah Tikvah to look for work, and mostly they found it. . . . Jews were considered virtually unemployable." The farmers' distrust of the tatterdemalion newcomers was influenced not only by the immigrants' lack of experience but by their new socialist theories. The orange growers' journal, later entitled *Bustani,* warned that the arriving young Jews "want power, economic and social dictatorship over the agricultural domain and those who own it." Faced with this antagonism, the immigrants wandered from settlement to settlement, often in rags and suffering from malnutrition. David Ben-Gurion (then David Gryn), a nineteen-year-old former university student, succumbed to malaria and nearly perished. A doctor urged him to return quickly to Russia. "Half the immigrants who came to Palestine in those early days took one look," Ben-Gurion wrote later, "and caught the same ship home again." Indeed, more than half. Possibly 80 percent of the Second Aliyah returned to Europe or continued on to the United States within weeks of their arrival.

CONQUERING AND GUARDING THE LAND

Well apprised of these forbidding prospects, the Zionist Organization grasped early on that it would have to provide the Yishuv with more active and direct encouragement. Accordingly, in the immediate aftermath of the Young Turk Revolution in 1908 (pp. 408–9), the promise of a liberalized Ottoman administration encouraged the Zionist Executive in Vienna to open a permanent office in Palestine. Its first director was a thirty-two-year-old German Jew, Dr. Arthur Ruppin. A graduate of the Universities of Berlin and Halle, trained in sociology, Ruppin had earned wide respect as director of the Bureau of Jewish Statistics in Berlin. Indeed, upon taking up his new Palestine assignment, Ruppin characteristically embarked on a detailed investigation of settlement possibilities. Five months later, he presented his recommendation to the Zionist Executive in Vienna. It was for the Jewish

National Fund (JNF) to purchase some 2 million dunams (approximately 5 million acres) of land in Judea and Galilee. Later, the tracts would be sold or rented on easy terms to Jewish immigrants. The proposal was daunting in its fund-raising requirements, yet the Zionist Executive accepted the challenge immediately and unanimously.

As JNF funds began to arrive, Ruppin then set about locating and purchasing a series of tracts both on the coastal plain and in the interior. The land subsequently was divided into modest plots suitable for cultivation. In this fashion, nine additional agricultural villages sprang up within six years. Immigrants who were prepared to work the land were given temporary lodgings and agricultural training before being settled on the new plots. Occasionally, Ruppin was obliged to take liberties with JNF and other Zionist funds, paying Arab landowners their often inflated asking price rather than engaging in protracted negotiations, and providing decent housing and ample farm equipment for new settlers. In justifying these expenditures, he emphasized that "our farms must, for the time being, serve other and larger goals than the production of a profit. . . . Instead of dividends [the farms] will provide us with something more necessary: men."

This was also the vision that Ruppin applied in nurturing one of the Yishuv's most noteworthy innovations, the kibbutz. As early as 1907, entirely as an independent venture, a group of eighteen young Labor Zionists who had secured work at Sejera, one of the PICA—Rothschild—farms, succeeded in persuading its French overseer to let them operate an untilled portion of the tract on their own responsibility. Indeed, this time the PICA acted with uncharacteristic generosity. Its management lent the group livestock, seed, and equipment. The fourteen men and four women then launched their venture on a purely collectivist basis. Disdaining recourse to hired Arab labor, they arranged their own division of work, shared all hardships in common, and within two years harvested a modest crop and repaid their loan. Witnessing the success of this experiment, Ruppin in 1911 decided to turn over a somewhat larger tract to thirty-six other young aspiring collective farmers. This settlement, to be known as Degania, proved even more successful. Soon other young socialist immigrants moved onto JNF land to establish fourteen additional collectives. All the villages survived. None had recourse to cut-rate Arab labor. Although their profits were meager by any Western standard, the settlers regarded themselves as pioneers of social justice. Perhaps they were not wrong. The kibbutz was destined to become early Zionism's most innovative experiment in human relations. Without it, the Jewish "return to the soil" probably would have remained an unrealized dream.

In the early years of the Second Aliyah, that dream would be fortified by yet another one, "the religion of labor." It was an ideology whose prophet and practitioner, Aaron David Gordon, was one of the authentically epic figures of Zionist history. Russian-born, educated in Orthodox Jewish schools, Gordon later had followed the classical Haskalah path, teaching himself Western languages and history. In adulthood, he was taken on as financial manager of the rural estate of Baron Horace de Günzburg. It was a comfortable position, and Gordon held it for twenty-three years. During his leisure hours, immersing himself in the writings of Nietzsche and Tolstoy, he began to develop his own unique philosophy of Zionism as an act of personal redemption. When the Günzburg estate was sold in 1903, leaving him without employment at the age of forty-seven, Gordon made a soul-searching decision that was not unlike Tolstoy's flight to Yasnaya Polyana. He departed for Palestine. Here he was offered an office job at Petah Tikvah, but shunned it in favor of manual labor in the orange groves. Afterward, he worked in various other farm settlements. A contemporary recalled of Gordon: "There were many in the Second Aliyah who exceeded him in labor energy and skill. But in their labor one felt [that] their efforts [were] . . . to prove that the Jews, and not only the Arabs, knew how to work. The work of Gordon was of another sort entirely. It was a kind of worship, a pure prayer."

As Gordon saw it, the vital element in nationhood was creativity, and physical labor was the bedrock of creativity. Without physical labor, the Jews would remain an island in an Arab sea. "A living people," he would write, "always possesses a great majority to whom labor is its second nature. Not so among us. We despise labor. . . . There is only one path that can lead to our renaissance—the path of manual labor. . . . Our people can be rejuvenated only if each one of us re-creates himself through labor and a life close to nature." Gordon's exhortation far transcended the written word. Until the last days of his life, he dwelt among the immigrant workers, sharing a room and tilling the soil with them, participating in their communal life. A beloved figure, with his great Tolstoyan beard and Russian peasant blouse, he was an unquenchable source of encouragement to younger men who faltered. Gordon's wife, who came to share his life in Palestine, died of malaria, and his only surviving son died in Russia. Gordon himself was afflicted with cancer, at the age of sixty-six. Through all his vicissitudes, he rejected pity, insisting almost to his last breath on preaching his faith in the redemptive significance of labor. That faith came to be shared by younger newcomers in Palestine, whatever their economic and political ideologies. It was well expressed in a common folk song of the prewar period: "Anu banu Artza, liv'not u'l'hibanot ba"—"We've come to the Land of Israel to build, and to be rebuilt, here."

There were numerous forms of "rebuilding." As early as September 1907, ten young Jewish farm workers gathered in a Jaffa rooming house to discuss a method of linking Jewish "conquest of the soil" with its natural corollary, the "conquest of defense." If it was unthinkable for Jews to depend indefinitely upon hired Arabs to work Jewish farms, then it was equally unacceptable to continue hiring Arab or Circassian guards to protect Jewish property. On this premise, the group organized itself into a secret society of exclusively Jewish guards, eventually to be known as HaShomer (the Watchman), and set about training themselves in the use of firearms and in horseback-riding. Once satisfied with their progress, they offered their services to the Jewish farm colonies.

Sejera was the first to take a chance on the young watchmen. The experiment succeeded. It had been a frequent occurrence for bedouin to infiltrate Jewish fields and corrals and abscond with crops and livestock. But in their first encounter with "rustlers," the Jewish guards beat the intruders off. Soon another colony, Mescha, dismissed its Moroccan watchmen and engaged the Shomer guards instead. Although the experiment again succeeded, it was not without risks. In the years after the Young Turk Revolution, Ottoman authority was loosened in Palestine, and Arab bandits roamed the countryside at will, often substituting force for stealth in making off with Jewish farm property. HaShomer trained its recruits well, however, and succeeded in placing them in one agricultural colony after another. Mounted, armed, wiry, and increasingly confident in bearing, they soon evoked respect among the Arabs, whose incursions or occasional armed attacks slackened. By 1914, the watchman's guild had placed over one hundred men throughout the Jewish-inhabited areas of Palestine's countryside, and gradually attuned the Zionist community to the legitimacy and indispensability of self-defense.

THE CONQUEST OF LANGUAGE

In the earliest years of the Zionist redemptive effort, Hebrew-language educational facilities were nonexistent in the Holy Land. The rudimentary networks of elementary and vocational schools, sponsored by France's Alliance, and later by Germany's Hilfsverein, employed their respective European languages for instruction. The small numbers of locally established Jewish schools were Orthodox in sponsorship, and conducted their instruction in Yiddish on antiquated parochial lines. The Hebrew that was read and occasionally written by small numbers of Zionist idealists was the Haskalah's ornately tapestried and over-"literalized" version. It awaited the achievements of a frail little philologist, Eliezer Ben-Yehuda, to transform Hebrew into a language capable of secular, vernacular use as a spoken tongue.

Born Eliezer Perlman in tsarist Lithuania in 1857, Ben-Yehuda (as he later Hebraized his name) joined other thousands of his generation in turning from pietism to Haskalah secularism, then to Zionism. It was as a medical student at the Sorbonne in the late 1870s that he came to appreciate the role of literature in the development of modern French nationalism. Soon he abandoned his medical studies for an intensive immersion in philology. "I have decided," he wrote his fiancée in 1880, "that in order to have our own [Jewish] land and political life, it is also necessary that we have a language to hold us together . . . a [modern] Hebrew language in which we can conduct the business of life." The following year, the two were married and departed for Palestine. From the moment they boarded ship in Odessa, they vowed never again to speak any other language but Hebrew.

The couple's next years in Palestine were as grimly impoverished as any endured by the early Zionist farmers. In Jerusalem, Ben-Yehuda earned a pittance teaching Hebrew for an Alliance school. At times, he and his wife were barely able to feed their growing family. Yet their every free moment was devoted to editing a succession of Hebrew-language newspapers, then to writing Hebrew-language textbooks for the growing chain of Zionist farm villages. Very slowly, the Hebraization campaign began to bear fruit. In 1905, modestly underwritten by grants from Rothschild's PICA and from the Zionist Organization, Ben-Yehuda was able to turn his major effort to the preparation of a modern Hebrew dictionary. The project ultimately would run to six volumes (and after Ben-Yehuda's death, to seventeen), and become the authoritative source work for Hebrew speech and literature. In the last years before the war, moreover, when both the Alliance and Hilfsverein chains of schools adopted Hebrew as their principal medium of instruction, it was evident that Hebrew was emerging as primus inter pares among the immigrants' heterogeneity of languages. In 1916, a Zionist census indicated 40 percent of the Yishuv's population (except for Jerusalem's tightly knit Orthodox community) spoke Hebrew as its principal vernacular.

How far, then, had the return of Zion materialized by the eve of the First World War? Some 85,000 Jews were domiciled in Palestine. If no longer a fragile settlement, the Yishuv was still an uneven one. The total farm-based Jewish population did not exceed 12,000. Town-dwellers comprised the rest, and of these, more than half were pietists who subsisted essentially on philanthropy. Yet there were auguries of creativity in the urban sector, as well. A widening collection of Jewish workshops and small industries offered the promise of accelerated economic growth. Jewish hospitals and clinics were going up, together with a teachers' training college, an academy of arts and crafts, a modest "national" library, a polytechnical institute, a school of agriculture. Tel Aviv was developing on the outskirts of Jaffa as an exclusively Jewish suburb. In the countryside, the necklace of groves and farms, some capitalist, others collective or cooperative, was sustained predominantly by Jewish labor and protected by Jewish watchmen. It was essentially between the years 1904 and 1914 that the foundations of the Jewish national home were laid, and its ideological configuration charted. "Above all," recalled the Zionist statesman Chaim Weizmann, "we got the feel of things, so that we did not approach our task after the Balfour Declaration like complete strangers."

XVI

The Evolution of Jewish Radicalism: Tsarist Russia

STIRRINGS OF REVOLUTIONARY CHANGE IN RUSSIA

In 1894, Tsar Alexander III died. His successor, Nicholas II, was as malleable and irresolute as his father had been forceful and obdurate. Indeed, his inner circle in St. Petersburg had difficulty taking seriously a man who at the age of twenty-six was still playing hide-and-seek with his companions, and filling his diary with enthusiastic accounts of picnics and hunting parties. It was an open secret, too, that Nicholas was inordinately susceptible to personal influences at court. Dominant among these were the éminence grise Konstantin Pobedonostsev, whom he inherited as "ideological" adviser; the notorious roué and blackmailer Prince V. P. Meshcherski, editor of the Slavophile newspaper *Grazhdanin;* and above all the tsar's own wife, the former Princess Alix of Hesse-Darmstadt, a woman consumed by superstition and mystical fantasies. When Nicholas affirmed to a gathering of zemstvo representatives in January 1895 that "I shall preserve the principle of autocracy as undeviatingly as my father did," he was reflecting emotional vulnerability no less than ideological commitment.

Whatever Nicholas's frailties, it remained by his sufferance alone that senior government officials exercised their powers, that "untrustworthy persons" could be exiled from towns or entire provinces, that newspapers and factories could be shut down, and public or private gatherings banned simply on hearsay information. By the turn of the century, the empire's collection of police forces was invested with virtually unlimited powers of arrest and incarceration, and nowhere in Europe were the police as omnipresent as in Russia. There were political police, railroad police, even factory police. In reserve, the army was available to cope with large-scale public disorders or unrest of any kind.

Evidence of that restiveness was developing widely over the turn of the century. Its sources were first and foremost economic. As recently as 1853, Russia's urban population was estimated at not more than 4 million. By 1897 that figure had climbed to 16 million as a consequence of the liberation of the serfs and an emerging surfeit of agricultural labor. A significant minority of these displaced former peasants was absorbed by the empire's incipient Industrial Revolution: in its expanding railroad network, its newly opened metallurgical complexes, its textile factories and sugar refineries. By the early twentieth century, the empire had produced a small but strategically placed urban proletariat. Yet, for most of this element, the social trauma of change, in submarginal labor conditions, rampant woman and child labor, and sheer slum misery, exceeded the grimmest working and living environment even of Dickensian England. These were the circumstances that rendered the empire's working classes susceptible to a new breed of social activists.

In the 1880s and afterward, the most influential of the radicals tended to be living not in Russia but in exile in Switzerland. Many were former narodnik intellectuals, men and women who had learned through bitter experience that their original vision of a peasant revolution was obsolescent. Rather, the future of political and economic change lay with the "scientific" socialism of Karl Marx. It was in 1872 that Marx's *Das Kapital* was translated into Russian, and eleven years later that the first Russian Marxist group came into existence, in Zurich. Its founding father was Georgi Plekhanov. The product of a landowning family, Plekhanov was the first member of his class to defect to the narodniki. Yet, by the same token, he was also the first narodnik to defect from the populist-agriculturist ranks. In 1883, Plekhanov founded a Marxist organization known as the Group for the Liberation of Labor, a faction that placed its emphasis henceforth on the education of the industrial proletariat in the class struggle. Under his leadership, during the 1880s and 1890s, these Marxist study groups began to make their initial headway among Russian university students, both in Switzerland and in Russia.

Jews would figure prominently in early Russian radicalism. By the time Alexander II's government turned reactionary, in the 1870s, the number of Russian-Jewish university students had grown significantly, both within the Tsarist Empire and elsewhere in Europe. It was most notably among these young men (and several women), with their developing ties to the Russian intelligentsia, that the incidence of revolutionary activity mounted. Several young Jewish radicals initially envisaged themselves as putative narodniki. Their participation in the violence-prone Narodnaya Volya (People's Will) faction was extensive, possibly comprising 20 percent of its active membership. One of them, Hessia Helfman, was implicated in the assassination of Alexander II, and died in prison (p. 197). Nevertheless, Jews by and large proved ineffectual in the populist and later in the Socialist Revolutionary movements. They were distrusted as outsiders. In the pogroms of 1881–82, moreover, following the assassination of the tsar, large numbers of peasants, and not a few narodniki, shared in the anti-Jewish violence. As a result, most of the Jewish participants soon left the populist cause. Yet, even then, they did not drop out of the revolutionary movement. They simply cast about for a more effective, and doubtless less anti-Jewish, version of reform. It would also have to be a version that more effectively confronted the transformation of their own economic circumstances.

In part, the transformation reflected the Industrial Revolution beginning to make its inroads in Russia at large. To a far greater degree, however, it was the consequence of the May Laws, and the enforced urbanization of the Pale's vast Jewish population. Thus, the Russian census of 1897 revealed that fully half that population of nearly 5 million had become town- and city-dwellers. The congestion of Jews in such industrial centers as Lodz, Bialystok, Vilna, and Brest-Litovsk revolutionized their economic circumstances far more dramatically than that of non-Jews. Although a majority of the Jewish urban population sought to remain in commerce, most of these "merchants" barely subsisted at the level of petty trade, and many sank to the quasi-mendicancy of peddlery. By the last decade of the nineteenth century, some half-million Jews had turned to urban manual labor. This per capita proportion was far larger than among the gentile majority.

Yet, if urbanization and industrialization accounted for the Jews' vocational displacement, it similarly excluded them from the emerging factory economy. There were reasons for this anomaly. Russian factory laborers often brutalized the few Jews who worked beside them. Instances of maiming and killing were not unknown. Aware of this danger, factory-owners tended not to hire Jews. Even such Jewish-owned industries as textiles, sugar-refining, food-processing, or tobacco-rolling preferred to avail themselves of cheap, unskilled former villagers. By the 1890s, of the half-million Jewish manual workers throughout the Pale, only about 40,000 were employed in factories. The rest found themselves confined largely to cottage industry, in effect, to artisanry. In their economic marginality, too, they gravitated to livelihoods that required little investment, for example, shoe-repairing, carpentry, or locksmithing. Above all, Jews subsisted as garment finishers, laboring over their sewing machines at home, often together with their wives and daughters. Here, too, the competition was cutthroat. Indeed, it was largely "intramural," confined to the Jewish economy itself, as Jewish factory subcontractors played off one tiny Jewish workshop enterprise against another. The practice would soon be replicated among Jewish immigrants in the United States (p. 218).

It was specifically among this urbanized, quasi-industrialized Jewish underclass that socialist activists found their likeliest following. Marxism offered literate Jews a number of compelling inducements. In its adaptation of the Hegelian "dialectic," its intellectual sophistication appealed to Jews. Its platform rejected the People's Will approach of political assassinations. Even its Marxian emphasis on proletarian revolution was appealingly "gradualistic," with its blueprint of a two-phase process en route to a classless society. Above all, socialism as an internationalist ideology transcended ethnic rivalries. Spurning the reactionary proto-Slavophilism of Narodnik and other Russian populist movements, it similarly rejected all forms of chauvinism and nationalist xenophobia. In short, it rejected antisemitism. With this formidably progressive amalgam of inducements, Marxian socialism soon came to exert a near-mesmeric appeal to idealistic young Jews.

It was all but predictable that Jews should have produced some of the earliest intellectual leaders of the Russian Social Democratic movement. In Zurich, the movement's initial forcing ground, expatriate Jewish students in disproportionate numbers were available and eager to participate in the Marxist effort. Among them, Pavel Akselrod and Lev Deitch ranked almost as coequals with Georgi Plekhanov as founder-theorists of the original Liberation of Labor cell. Indeed, Akselrod was one of the two or three outstanding figures altogether in the early history of Marxian socialism. With the Germans Karl Kautsky and Eduard Bernstein, he would become one of the founders in 1889 of the Second International, the confederation of socialist parties and movements worldwide, and for almost sixty years he functioned as mentor and guide of two generations of Russian and European socialists. (Uri Martov and Leon Trotsky were among the scores of prominent figures in modern Marxism who came under the spell of Akselrod's almost hypnotic intellect.) Other Jewish Marxists of this "university" period also functioned as intermediaries between Eastern and Western socialism. Gera Dobrodzanu became famous as a pioneer of Marxism in Rumania. Anna Kuleshov helped organize the Italian Socialist Party and for thirty-five years edited *Critica sociale,* the party's organ.

Not least of all, Social Democratic cells began springing up in the Pale itself in the late 1890s. Soon almost every substantial Jewish community produced at least one Marxist "study group." There was nothing specifically Jewish in the groups' tone or content. In all instances, their language was Russian. Indeed, their "preceptors" usually were younger men and women who came from acculturated, middle-class families. Maxim Litvinov's father was a prosperous, well-traveled produce merchant in Bialystok; Adolf Joffe came from a wealthy merchant family in the Crimea; Angelica Balabanov's family were wealthy landowners in Chernigov; Leon Trotsky's parents were middle-class farmers in the Ukraine (p. 327); Uri Martov's father was active in the intellectual life of Odessa's Jewish upper middle class. As in other revolutionary movements, these were the individuals who had enjoyed a certain access to travel, who were familiar with the non-Jewish world, with foreign languages, and with the writings of non-Jewish thinkers.

An Awakening Volcano

Beyond this sophisticated Jewish leadership, however, even beyond the unique circumstances of Russian Jewry in an era of urbanization and tsarist persecution, still other factors ensured a ground-level Jewish shift to radicalism. By the 1890s, the Jews no longer were alone in their resistance to oppression. Initially, during the shock of the May Laws, Russian Jewry had felt isolated as much by populist revolutionaries as by rightist reactionaries, and assuredly by a majority of the Russian population. But in ensuing years, with the intensifying social misery of industrialization, opposition to tsarist autocracy gained a new momentum among the Russian people at large. Socialist Revolutionary propaganda in the countryside, Marxist propaganda among the urban proletariat, and an upsurge of terrorism sponsored by the People's Will Party accounted for the assassination of some 3,000 members of the tsarist bureaucracy. In 1903, a major work stoppage by miners in the Urals was met by mass shootings. The episode in turn touched off a wave of strikes, reaching the empire's major cities by 1904. By then, revolutionary unrest had become fulminant and all but uncontrollable.

It was in 1903–4, too, that the tsarist government in its beleaguerment set about intensifying the late Alexander III's thirteen-year war against the Jews. The campaign possibly could be justified as punishment for Jewish radicalism. By 1900, after all, some 30 percent of the political arrests in the Russian Empire were of Jews (and would climb to 37 percent by 1905). In 1903, upon visiting Russia, Theodor Herzl was assured by the—comparatively moderate—Russian statesman Count Sergei Witte that at least half of all Russian revolutionaries were Jews. The assessment was not far off the mark. Yet, more than punishment, the renewed anti-Jewish campaign would emerge as a political diversion for public unrest. Nicholas II required no encouragement in this effort. For him, the Jews had long evoked only distrust and revulsion. He used the word "zhidi" (yids) as a pejorative for all his pet hates, including the British and the Japanese. Now the moment had arrived to translate that enmity into practical action, by systematically debasing the Jews in Russian eyes as the underlying source of the empire's poverty and weakness. In 1902, the tsar had given the portfolio of minister of the interior to Vyacheslav von Plehve. A Baltic German, a former imperial police chief in the Duchy of Finland, and the gravedigger of Finland's struggle for wider autonomy, Plehve needed little encouragement to deal harshly with any of the non-Russian minorities. Personally, he entertained few anti-Jewish opinions. But if the tsar so desired, the minister would make a good job of Jew-baiting. In that effort, violence would play a critical role.

Dramatic evidence of the new policy surfaced in April 1903, in the city of

Kishinev, administrative capital of the province of Bessarabia. A multiethnic community, Kishinev consisted of approximately 50,000 Rumanians, 50,000 Jews, 8,000 Russians, with the rest a mixture of Balkan peoples. For years, the Jews had lived there in comparative tranquillity. Lately, however, Pavlochi Krushevan, editor of the province's single newspaper, *Bessarabets,* had transformed the organ into an antisemitic screed. In the process, Krushevan received important government help. Minister von Plehve recently had turned over a substantial slush fund to him and simultaneously had denied publication licenses to other newspapers in Kishinev. During the late winter and spring of 1903, moreover, Krushevan was presented with a unique opportunity to ingratiate himself with his patron. On February 13 of that year, the body of a twelve-year-old boy, Mikhail Rybachenko, was found in a neighboring village. The official postmortem revealed twenty-four stab wounds on the corpse. Almost immediately, *Bessarabets* began printing rumors of Jewish "ritual murder." Alarmed at the potential for incitement, a delegation of Kishinev Jews then appealed to Bessarabia's Vice Governor Sergei Ostrogov to censor the newspaper. Ostrogov refused. In ensuing weeks, *Bessarabets* repeated and expanded upon the accusations.

On April 18, one day before Easter, a group of interior ministry officials arrived in Kishinev from St. Petersburg to engage in secret conversations with Krushevan and with local functionaries. Several hours afterward, handbills, printed on the *Bessarabets* press, were scattered about the city, urging townsmen to inflict a "bloody punishment" upon the Jews. And so it was, the next morning, Easter Sunday, that violence erupted. Bands of teenage boys, followed by throngs of laborers, rampaged through Jewish business and residential neighborhoods, vandalizing and looting. Overwhelming small groups of Jewish defenders, the rioters soon began killing, mutilating, raping. The mayhem continued for two days. Among the Jewish victims were 42 dead and 424 wounded, including scores of women violated. Over 700 homes and shops were burned down. Neither the police nor the army moved in until the evening of the second day. There is no conclusive proof that Plehve himself encouraged the violence. In the trials afterward, however, it was significant that fewer than two dozen of the perpetrators were sentenced, and most of these to one-year terms; while 181 Jews were given identical one-year sentences for "sharing" in the unrest. When a Jewish delegation from Odessa visited Plehve several months later, the interior minister responded with threats: "In the western provinces some ninety percent of the revolutionaries are Jews," he warned, "and in Russia, at least forty percent. . . . [I]f you do not deter your youth from the revolutionary movement, we shall make your position untenable to such an extent that you will have to leave Russia, to the last man!"

Outrage was not limited to the Jews of Russia, or even to numerous prominent Russian cultural figures, including Leo Tolstoy and Maxim Gorky.

Beyond the Tsarist Empire, mass protest meetings were organized under both Jewish and Christian auspices. The German kaiser discreetly expressed his concern to the tsar, as did the Austrian emperor. From Washington, President Theodore Roosevelt dispatched a personal note of "grave reservation" to St. Petersburg and joint resolutions of outrage were issued by Congress. The protests were unavailing. Indeed, Kishinev turned out to be the merest beginning of a chain reaction of pogroms. In September 1903, violence raged in the Belorussian city of Homel, where some 20,000 Jews formed half the population. In 1904, even as the Russo-Japanese War raged, forty-three pogroms of greater or lesser magnitude churned through the Pale, in tandem with a newspaper campaign denouncing the Jews for treasonable collaboration with the Japanese (at a time when 30,000 Jewish troops were serving on the battlefront in Manchuria). Finally, in late summer of 1904, the government ordered a halt to the violence, concerned that it might disrupt the war effort.

In these same months, still another reaction to the pogroms ultimately would play a decisive role both in the collective psyche and in the political stance of Russian Jewry. It was given literary expression by Chaim Nahman Bialik. Thirty years old, Bialik already had won recognition as the greatest Hebrew poet of his time. After the events of Kishinev, the Jewish Historical Society of Odessa dispatched him to the scene of the horror to conduct a thorough, firsthand inquiry into its causes and effects. This Bialik did. His report to the committee was thorough and detailed. But he chose to express his personal reaction in an epic poem, "In the City of Slaughter" ("B'Ir HaHaregah"). In a work of 268 rhymed couplets, execrating the Bessarabian hooligans who committed the massacre, Bialik nevertheless directed his rage principally to the Jewish men of Kishinev, those who had allowed the massacre to unfold, who had permitted their wives and daughters to be defiled while

> They lay, in their shame and watched—neither moving nor flinching,
> Neither gouging out their eyes nor going mad,
> And perhaps only praying, each man in the privacy of his soul. . . .
> The agony of it all was profound; so was the disgrace.
> Which then was the greater? . . .

The poem became a sensation among Russian Jewry. It was all but canonized by the entirety of their political leadership. Bialik had precisely captured the visceral change in mood that now swept through the Pale.

That shift was translated into action during the Homel pogrom of September 1903. By then the city's local Jewish population already had developed powerful Zionist and Bundist (socialist) organizations. In the aftermath of Kishinev, these were the groups that began training and arming self-defense squads. On September 11, 1903, when the first crowds of peasants and workers began assaulting Jewish neighborhoods, the squads rushed into action, and continued their resistance for three days until vigorous police and military intervention finally ended the rioting. Although four Jews were killed, eight Russians also were slain, and dozens on both sides were seriously wounded. News of the resistance did much to strengthen Jewish morale throughout the Pale. The Russian Social Democratic Party in Kharkov sent its Jewish colleagues in Homel a congratulatory message. The Homel resistance in fact marked a watershed for Russian Jewry. Enraged by the bankruptcy of their earlier submissiveness, they moved now toward a new dynamism of mind and action.

The Rise of the Jewish Bund

A principal source of this transition lay in the Russian Social Democratic movement, and specifically in the role of its Jewish "Bundist" component. The origins of the Bund actually harked back to the well-established tradition of Jewish self-help in the Pale, as manifested in such cooperative institutions as the *hevra*, a benevolent society that provided charitable and other emergency aid to needy families; and the *kassa*, a credit society to provide loans for Jewish small businessmen. As early as the 1880s, numerous of these agencies, springing up in the factories and workshops of Vilna, Bialystok, Minsk, and other industrial cities, also took on the characteristics of trade unions. Marxist intellectuals soon began preempting their leadership, and set about threatening employers with strikes to extract wage-and-hour concessions. The pace for this militantly leftist orientation was set in Vilna, whose population encompassed the most densely concentrated Jewish working-class population in the empire. Here, in the early 1890s, a group of young Jews began preaching the new Marxist dogma to the city's impoverished Jewish workers. Exclusively Russian in language and content, however, the propaganda at first was only minimally effective. Jewish workers in any case were interested less in Marxist dialectic than in resolving the discrimination they endured both as workers and as Jews.

In 1894, therefore, the socialist agitators agreed to concentrate exclusively on the issue of discrimination, and to conduct their discussions in Yiddish. As the prominent Social Democrat Uri Martov explained to a gathering of fellow socialists in Vilna, Jewish workers had problems unique to their status as Jews. It was entirely appropriate for them to be organized along both class and ethnic lines, and in a separate, Yiddish-language federation within the larger Russian Social Democratic Party. His argument was gratefully endorsed by Vilna's predominantly Jewish labor unions. From then on, the unionist-socialist movement, both in Vilna and in the Pale at large, assumed more of a Jewish folk quality, and in 1897 even adopted its own proprietary title, the General Jewish Workers' Union (Bund) of Poland and Russia.

The individual who orchestrated the transition was Arkadi Kremer. A stolid, pragmatic man, an engineer by training, Kremer had been drawn to the Social Democratic movement while a student at the Riga Polytechnikum. He personally had little appreciation for the "outworn" values of Jewish culture. Yet it was his very "scientific objectivity" that persuaded him, as it had Martov, of the unshakable ethnocentrism of the Jewish people. Meeting with the Bund leadership in Vilna in 1897, Kremer transcended Martov's "linguistic" socialism by defining the Bund's multiple objectives as

> the special task of defending the specific interests of the Jewish workers, carrying on the struggle for the civic rights of the Jewish workers and above all carrying on the struggle against discriminatory anti-Jewish laws.

The Jewish working class responded enthusiastically to Kremer's formula, and accepted it from then on as the virtual credo of the Bund. By the turn of the century, the movement's ranks had grown to some 20,000 dues-paying members.

Yet by then, too, the Bundists had enlarged their field of vision well beyond the achievement of full economic and civil rights. They were encouraged increasingly to embrace the goal of full "national" rights within the framework of the Tsarist Empire. Here they drew inspiration from several of Russian Jewry's most respected intellectuals. One of these was Dr. Chaim Zhitlowski, a widely published journalist-philosopher, who argued that "cosmopolitanism," whether Marxist or tsarist, was merely a cloak for the Russification of the empire's minority peoples. No self-respecting Jew could accept it. The argument was fortified by an even more venerated cultural figure. This was Simon Dubnow, an internationally renowned historian of Russian Jewry and the authentic "father of Diaspora nationalism." The Jews were not merely a separate nation, argued Dubnow, but the "highest" form of nation, a "cultural-spiritual" nation, one that did not require territorial definition for its fulfillment, whether in Russia, in Palestine, or in any other land. Instead, the Jews' national autonomy could be achieved in Tsarist Russia itself through their own separate and powerful communal organization, their own autonomous Jewish school system, offering instruction in their own, legally recognized languages—whether Yiddish, Hebrew, German, or Russian.

The notion of Jewish cultural autonomy soon was embraced as a Bundist principle. It did not spring full-blown from the brow of Zhitlowski or of Dubnow alone. Rather, it was sold to Jewish workers by a charismatic new personality, Vladimir Medem, who soon took over from Arkadi Kremer the mantle of leadership in the Bund. In his espousal of "Diaspora nationalism," Medem climaxed a unique spiritual journey. He was born in 1879 to a completely assimilated Russian-Jewish family of Libau. His father, one of the first Jews to graduate from the St. Petersburg Military Medical Academy, served for many years as an army doctor. Eventually, both Medem's father and mother converted to Russian Orthodoxy and had their children baptized. But as the son grew up, he became increasingly uncomfortable with his parents' apostasy, and by his second year in gymnasium in Minsk he took up the study of Yiddish and began attending synagogue. In 1899, while studying law at the University of Kiev, Medem also was drawn to socialism and soon became active in a student Marxist group. For his efforts, he was expelled from the university. At this point, he made the decision to commit himself exclusively to the Bund. From his branch office in Minsk, he also took the initiative in the Bund's struggle for an autonomous "federative" membership within the Social Democratic Party. Moreover, in the brilliance and vigor of his campaign, the twenty-one-year-old Medem soon took over leadership of the Bund altogether.

It was accordingly at the Bund's fourth convention, in 1901, that the party's delegates unanimously adopted Medem's resolution in support of a Social Democratic movement based upon a federation of nationalities, allowing full administrative autonomy for each national group, including the Jews. Once news of the resolution became known, however, it was furiously denounced by leaders of the Russian Social Democratic Party. In harsh language, these veteran Marxists—Akselrod, Trotsky, even Martov—warned the Bundists to fuse with the Russian proletariat and forthwith end their retrograde "deviationism." Vladimir Lenin, by then emerging to prominence in the party, was sufficiently incensed to write a scathing article in the Russian Social Democratic newspaper, *Iskra,* warning the Bund that it faced expulsion from the party's ranks. But Medem and the Bundist leadership would not back down. Eventually, the issue came to a head at the Russian Social Democrats' Second Congress, meeting in Brussels in July 1903. Lenin, Martov, and Trotsky were among the "purists" leading the assault against a federationist party structure. Medem in turn forcefully reminded Lenin and the other Social Democratic veterans that the Bund's membership was three times larger than that of the entire Social Democratic Party, and that its record of physical resistance to tsarist oppression already had become legend (pp. 290–91). But Lenin and his colleagues were not having it. They spurned all appeals for "reactionary" autonomism. Hereupon, announcing that the Bund would function independently of the Social Democrats, Medem led his colleagues out of the congress hall.

The unflinching display of independence actually strengthened the Bund's hold among the Jewish masses and it opened the way for an intensive new burst of nationalist activism. Thus, in the following years, it was supremely the Bund that stood at the Jewish forefront in launching demonstrations and strikes against the government's antisemitic legislation. It was the Bund that organized, armed, and trained the paramilitary units that led the defense against pogroms. Indeed, Bundist resistance during the Homel pogrom stood in dramatic contrast to the terrified passivity of Jews during the earlier Kishinev massacre. So did its resolute defense of other Jewish communities in the upsurge of pogroms during and after the 1905 Revolution.

The Revolution of 1905

As the twentieth century opened, an escalation of strikes, student disturbances, and protest marches swept through the Russian Empire. The largest numbers of these were organized by the Social Democrats. The year 1904 was a particularly threatening one for the tsarist regime. The war against Japan was going badly, consuming thousands of lives, revealing a military command structure that was as inept as the government's civil administration. Moreover, with the army 6,000 miles away in Manchuria, unrest at home became increasingly unrestrained. Terrorist plots now were focused against the highest officials in government. In July 1904, an anarchist threw a bomb into Minister of the Interior von Plehve's carriage, killing him instantly. In January 1905, the largest mills and factories in European Russia were virtually paralyzed by work stoppages, and the nation appeared on the threshold of civil war. On Sunday, January 22, tens of thousands of workers embarked on a march to St. Peterburg's Winter Palace, seeking to present a list of reformist demands to Tsar Nicholas II himself. A police guard then raked the crowd with gunfire, killing 130 demonstrators and wounding at least twice that many. At this point, the events of "Bloody Sunday" touched off a series of popular outbursts throughout the empire, including a succession of terrorist acts that culminated in the murder of Grand Duke Sergei, uncle of the tsar.

Meanwhile, the Russo-Japanese War produced still additional military defeats. These were climaxed on May 27–29, 1905, with the sinking of the Russian fleet in Tsushima Strait. In ensuing months, strikes and demonstrations closed down the nation's railroad, telegraph, gas, and electric services. Soon Russia's major cities all but ceased to function, and red flags were raised in one part of the empire to another. Tsar Nicholas now recognized that the dynasty itself was hanging in the balance. Panic-stricken, he appointed a former minister of finance, Count Sergei Witte, a respected moderate, as his principal cabinet adviser, and on October 30 he accepted Witte's counsel to issue a conciliatory official manifesto. The document represented a historic break with imperial precedent. By its provisions, the Russian people for the first time were guaranteed a wide array of civil liberties, including a Duma—

a parliament—with the right to initiate, accept, or reject all proposed laws, and a promise further to liberalize the nation's social order. In short, the October Manifesto seemingly betokened the transformation of the tsarist autocracy into a constitutional monarchy.

From the very onset of the political upheaval, the Jews faced the issue of deciding their own role in the looming new changes. The Bund, it appeared, was best prepared of all Jewish political factions to share in a revolutionary experiment. By 1905, it had become a well-organized party, endowed with a coherent ideology, a relatively efficient staff, and numerous clandestine printing presses for publication of newspapers and proclamations. As an underground movement that had sacrificed several thousand of its members to prison, exile, and death, it inspired awe in the Jewish world far beyond the working classes themselves. As early as June 1903, Chaim Weizmann noted in a memo to Theodor Herzl that "almost all [Jewish] students belong to the revolutionary camp. Hardly any of them escape its ultimate fate. . . . It is a fearful spectacle . . . to observe the major part of our youth . . . offering themselves for sacrifice as though seized by a fever."

Weizmann could not yet have known the extent of those sacrifices. In the aftermath of Nicholas II's October Manifesto, the government launched over six hundred pogroms, striking out not only against the Pale but at communities of acculturated Jews living in the Russian interior. In Odessa, 300 Jews were killed that month and 4,000 were seriously injured, while the value of destroyed Jewish property was estimated at 3.75 million rubles. It was a four-day horror that all but pauperized the city's Jewish working-class majority. In Minsk, 100 Jews were killed, 400 wounded. During the ensuing months, pogroms and their attendant heavy casualties were reported from Kiev, Kherson, Ekaterinoslav, Simferopol, and again from Kishinev. From October to the end of 1905, the total of Jewish dead in the Pale alone was estimated at 990, with thousands of other Jews injured and at least 200,000 ruined economically. The violence continued into 1906. "Since the days of [the seventeenth-century Ukrainian insurrectionist] Bohdan Chmielnicki," wrote one correspondent, "the Jews have not suffered through such bloody days." In the aftermath of violence in the city of Lodz, the correspondent of *Iskra,* Lenin's Social Democratic newspaper, reported on June 11:

> I cannot but emphasize the great respect in which—over the past year, and especially in recent months—Christian Lodz holds the Jews. The heroic conduct of the Jews in the clash with the police and the army units arouses admiration everywhere. . . . Legends are circulated about yesterday's battle between the Jews and the Cossacks on the Waschodnaja [boulevard], legends that describe the Jewish workers as virtual Samsons.

Was the cause worth the sacrifice? Nicholas II's manifesto represented a new era for Jews and non-Jews alike. Yet, unrecognized in the events of October 1905 was an emergent fissure within the revolutionary movement. Russia's liberals and moderates, most of them identified with the Constitutional Democratic ("Cadet") Party, were prepared to accept the guidelines of the October Manifesto. It was assumed that these might eventually produce a full constitutional convention. The illusion was not shared by the Social Democrats, however. For them, the Manifesto was a fraud. They would not participate in a "fake" election. With the opposition thus split, the government achieved a certain room for maneuver, and gradually began to eviscerate its initial concessions.

A Duma election in fact did take place in April 1906, based ostensibly on full manhood suffrage. The Cadets actually emerged as the largest party in the Duma, and were further augmented by other groups of the left. But on April 23, 1906, virtually on the eve of the Duma's first session, the government "reinterpreted" its October Manifesto to ensure the tsar's ongoing control of the executive, the police, and the armed forces. More fundamentally, Nicholas retained veto power over all legislation. When the Duma was not in session, the tsar could issue ukases with the full power of the law (although the Duma was obliged to ratify such legislation post factum). Not less than 40 percent of the budget also remained outside the Duma's purview. Moreover, under altered new property qualifications, substantial elements among the proletariat were disenfranchised.

It was this last revision that affected the Jews' role in the forthcoming election. For the first time in Russian history, Jews were granted the vote. Yet the amended property qualifications persuaded the Bundists to join with their fellow Social Democrats in boycotting the election. For this reason, all the Duma's twelve elected Jewish delegates shared an essentially middle-class background. Nine of the delegates belonged to the Cadets, and three to the Trudovik (labor) group, a newly created quasi-populist faction. Nevertheless, all twelve shared a common and urgent commitment to full Jewish emancipation, and all of them willingly and immediately joined ranks to advance that agenda in the new Duma.

Initiative in the effort was taken by Maxim Vinaver. History may well rank Vinaver as the preeminent Jewish statesman of the late tsarist era. Born in Warsaw in 1860, he completed his legal studies at the University of Warsaw, then settled in St. Petersburg under the "liberal profession" estate, where he became a distinguished advocate in the field of civil law. At the same time, Vinaver's devotion to the welfare of Russian Jewry was unsurpassed. During the court trials that followed the Homel pogrom in 1904, he won immense respect for his successful defense of the alleged Jewish "provocateurs." Moreover, as a founder and first vice chairman of the Cadet Party, Vinaver in 1906

became one of that party's first delegates in the new Duma. With this prestige, he was also the logical figure to recruit the other Jewish delegates into the
Union for the Attainment of Full Equality for the Jewish People in Russia—
in effect, a Jewish caucus.

As chairman of that caucus, Vinaver displayed his diplomatic skills in persuading the other caucus members to refrain from demanding Jewish rights
on a narrow, "parochial" basis, but to adopt a wider platform on behalf of all
races and religions in the empire. "We Jews," he declaimed before the full
Duma, meeting in the Tauride Palace, "representatives of one of the most tormented nationalities in the land, have never uttered a word about ourselves."
All his people asked, he insisted, was a law to normalize the status of *every*
inhabitant of the empire. In that shrewdly modulated appeal, Vinaver won
the unanimous support of his own Cadet Party. Thus, on May 16, 1906, the
Cadets introduced a bill to establish a "basic law" on civic equality. The measure was sent to committee and appeared certain of approval for final passage.
In cities and towns throughout the Pale, Jews gathered in their synagogues to
conduct prayer meetings for the success of the legislation.

By early July, before the final vote could be taken, the largest part of the
Russian army had returned from Manchuria. On the ninth of the month,
seventy-three days into the Duma session, a detachment of troops surrounded the Tauride Palace and posted the government's announcement that
the First Duma was being dissolved for its "grave misstep" in dealing with
matters "outside its legitimate jurisdiction"—but actually for its lèse-majesté
in openly criticizing the tsarist government's refusal to allow the Duma full
legislative authority. In the case of the Jews, the opportunity for any practical
legislative emancipation was apparently blocked. Yet, even then, their hopes
did not fade. Elections for a Second Duma were scheduled for February 1907,
and before the new delegates convened in March, presumably there would
be renewed leeway to achieve full civil equality in a liberalized Russia. Their
optimism would prove misplaced.

The previous July, following dissolution of the First Duma, some two
hundred Cadet delegates had gathered in an emergency colloquium in the
Finnish town of Viborg. Here they signed a manifesto of their own, this one
denouncing the government and calling upon citizens to refrain from paying
taxes or accepting a military draft until convocation of a new Duma. It was a
rash step. The Russian population, intimidated by the return of tens of thousands of imperial troops from Manchuria, hesitated to respond to the Viborg
appeal. Worse yet, by order of the ministry of justice, the Viborg participants
lost the right to stand for election to the Second Duma. Thus, when the new
legislature convened in March 1907, the composition of its leftist and rightist
membership shifted further to the wings, leaving a shrunken and dysfunctional center. As for the Jews, most of their previous Duma members had

been Cadets and accordingly, were now "disbarred" for their participation in the Viborg conference. Only four Jews sat in the Second Duma (and two in the Dumas that followed). Their best opportunity for a bill of civil equality had also passed. In later parliaments, it would never again so much as be tabled for discussion.

A YIDDISH CULTURAL RESPECTABILITY

During 1906 and 1907, even as the tsarist government regained the political initiative and moved ominously toward counterrevolution, the Bundist movement appeared to be moving toward an offensive of its own. Under the impression that its membership no longer risked quite the existential dangers of the previous fifteen years, its leadership opened new offices and embarked upon vigorous new recruitment campaigns. Workers' educational clubs and newspapers proliferated. In the window of opportunity when free speech still was permitted, public meetings and lectures became almost daily occurrences. After some hesitation, the Bundist congress of August 1906 belatedly approved participation in the ensuing parliamentary elections, and two of the party's members actually were seated in the Third and Fourth Dumas. Nevertheless, at the very apogee of its prestige, the Bund soon found itself caught up in a furious ideological struggle with competitive parties and movements. These were Jewish parties and movements.

Preeminent among them were the Zionists, whose faction only then was beginning to emerge as a serious political force in the Pale. The bitter rivalry between Bundists and Zionists was seemingly implacable (p. 277) and appeared to deepen with each passing year. In 1908, Vladimir Medem, his sense of "Diaspora patriotism" outraged by Zionist propaganda, denounced a Zionist congress in Kharkov:

> Journey preparations, travel-fever! Pack your belongings! Turn your back on our life, on our struggle, on our joys and sorrow. You have decided to desert the Diaspora. Well, leave it in peace. Don't interfere in our affairs, don't show your generosity by throwing alms . . . [to us] . . . from the windows of your rail carriage—and please, don't talk about defending our rights here.

There were occasional ideological compromises between the two groups, as in the Labor Zionist movement; but, otherwise, Zionists and Bundists remained at each other's throats. It appeared, too, that the revolution had tipped the balance decisively against the Zionists. Oriented as it was toward the Holy Land, the Zionist program had ill prepared its adherents to take an active part in Russian politics, and in 1905, the movement could offer nothing comparable to the dynamic relevance of the Bund. Zionism supported the revolution, to be sure, in common with all Russian Jews. Five of the Jewish Cadets in the First Duma were pro-Zionist, and they participated actively in Maxim Vinaver's Jewish caucus. Nevertheless, the Zionist leadership could only speak vaguely in favor of political and ethnic-nationalist equality. Everyone knew that their territorial focus lay elsewhere.

Still another factor allowed the Bund to sustain its constituency for years even after the October Revolution failed. This one was linguistic. Yiddish, the transplanted medieval German-Jewish demotic, was the vernacular of the uneducated Jewish masses, and the Zionists as a matter of nationalist principle refrained from public activities in that language. The Bund, on the other hand, embraced Yiddish as a matter of proletarian principle. It was the language of their program and propaganda, and of a future Jewish cultural autonomy on Russian soil. Indeed, the sheer effervescence with which Yiddish now was mobilized on issues of far-reaching political and economic importance infused the language with a new dignity. It also enhanced the usage of Yiddish for the first time in belles lettres. This was a unique development. Well into the eighteenth century, Yiddish writing tended to be limited to *Spielmann* romances, religious fables, and folk songs. As literature, Yiddish in these earlier stages functioned essentially as a recreational, or a "woman's," language. Even the surging eighteenth-century Hasidic movement employed written Yiddish almost exclusively for religiopietistic themes.

The yeasty old vernacular emerged as a "modern," secular literature only in the mid-nineteenth century, when the full force of Haskalah realism began to shape the basic lineaments of Jewish prose-writing, in Hebrew and Yiddish alike. The transition was initiated by Sholem Abramovich, "grandfather" of modern Yiddish literature, who was best known by his pen name of Mendele Mocher S'forim—Mendele the Bookseller. Mendele, born in Kapuli, Belorussia, in 1835, considered himself a humanist, but for many years he was obliged to earn his bread as director of a parochial talmud torah in Odessa. He found time nevertheless to translate German scientific texts into both Yiddish and Hebrew, and to produce occasional literary essays before turning full-time from Hebrew to Yiddish fiction. It was an audacious venture. "[I]f I started writing in this 'unworthy' language," he wrote later, "my honor would be besmirched. . . . But my concern for utility conquered my vanity and I decided . . . that I would take pity on Yiddish, that rejected daughter, for it was time to do something for our people."

From the late 1860s on, Mendele was the fighting satirist, directing his mockery at the squalor and uncouthness of Jewish life in the Pale. In this vein, his best-known shorter works were *Die Klyatsche (The Nag)*, *Dos kleine Menschele* (most frequently translated as *The Parasite*), *Die Takse (The Tax)*, and *Fishke der Krumer (Fishke the Lame)*. Yet his most highly regarded novel was

Masot Benyamin HaShlishi (The Travels of Benjamin the Third), a picaresque work featuring a timid and vacillating Jewish Don Quixote who wanders aimlessly through the Pale, encountering everywhere insularity, backwardness, and superstition. While the book's tempo remains as slow and clubfooted as the tempo of the Pale itself, it was in this climactic effort that Mendele's literary style achieved a precision and refinement unique for a pungent but otherwise inelegant vernacular.

In attuning Yiddish to literary requirements, Mendele laid the groundwork for his even more widely admired successors. Few writers so decisively captured the imagination of their readers as did Sholem Aleichem, the culture hero of East European Jewry. Born in Pereyaslav, Ukraine, in 1859, he later moved to Voronkova, a small town that would become the model for his imaginative literary shtetl Kasrilevka. His actual name was Sholem Rabinovich, but he, too, chose to write under an easily recognized nom de plume, best translated as "Hello to All." Sholem Aleichem's literary productivity was vast. From his first Yiddish story in 1883 until his death in 1916, he produced forty volumes of stories, novels, and plays, and found time as well to establish a distinguished literary journal, *Die Yiddishe Folks Bibliotek*.

Again, like Mendele, Sholem Aleichem concentrated on developing a literature purely of delight. It was thus as a gentle, discursive, somewhat Chekhovian humorist that he became the most beloved Jewish writer of modern times. Sholem Aleichem chose the short story as his principal métier, and the plain folk of the typical shtetl as his subject matter. Under his pen, they emerged as a memorable gallimaufry that included Tevye the milkman, the poverty-stricken, wryly optimistic philosopher-manqué; Menahem Mendel, the harebrained, dauntly incorrigible promoter; Hapke, the pockmarked maid. The retinue included Rabchik, the Jewish dog; Methuselah, the Jewish horse; and untold numbers of Jewish goats, cats, and chickens. Sholem Aleichem's characters were walking medical exhibits, suffering from every typical affliction of the Pale: scurvy, cataracts, tuberculosis, asthma. Yet the typology was never a mere promenade of caricatures. They stepped off the page. Beyond comparison, Sholem Aleichem was the folk writer of his people, more widely beloved and "internalized" than any of his literary contemporaries.

With Yehuda Leib Peretz, on the other hand, Yiddish literature achieved the zenith of its "classical" development. Peretz was very much the student of European thought and literature. Born in a small Polish town in 1873, he experienced an early manhood scarred by an unhappy arranged marriage, and by disbarment from the practice of law due to a brief flirtation with the revolutionary movement. Ultimately, Peretz was reduced to earning his bread as a bookkeeper at Warsaw's Jewish Community House. By then, fortunately, he had discovered his solace in writing. In embarking on that avocation, he followed in the footsteps of his predecessors, first undergoing a "patrician" phase, writing in Russian, Polish, or Hebrew. It was not until he was forty that he arrived at Yiddish, his "last stop." Unlike Mendele's picaresque moralizing, or Sholem Aleichem's affectionate portraits of shtetl life, Peretz's work was "sophisticated," attuned to the electric nervousness of Jewish Warsaw. More than his predecessors, it was Peretz who elevated Yiddish literature to the level of European realism, endowing it with crisp dialogue and clinically accurate descriptions that matched the best products of Gerhart Hauptmann and Charles Péguy (the writer to whom he was most often compared). At the same time, his compassion for the piety of simple people led him to a reevaluation of Hasidism. In that growing attraction, Peretz evidently was influenced by the Europe-wide reappraisal of mysticism, which was pioneered during his lifetime by such men as Baudelaire, Mallarmé, Verlaine, and Maeterlinck.

Other gifted Yiddish writers followed the classical triad of Mendele, Sholem Aleichem, and Peretz into the twentieth century. Among these were Sholem Asch and I. J. Singer (brother of Isaac Bashevis Singer), authors of epic *Bildungsromane* of East European Jewish life. Their contemporaries Joseph Opatoshu, Zalman Schneuer, and David Pinski devised styles that frequently were naturalistic, vivid, even erotic. In Jassy, Rumania, a vibrant Yiddish theater produced translations of European playwrights, together with experimental dramas crafted by Jews themselves. In effect, the "literazation" of an essentially plebeian vernacular addressed the cultural needs of Eastern Europe's impoverished and still inchoate Jewry, those whom the Hebraic elitists of Haskalah had largely ignored.

STOLYPIN'S NECKTIES

It was in April 1906 that Nicholas II issued his Declaration of Fundamental Laws, sharply attenuating the provisions of the manifesto he had issued only the previous October. Simultaneously, the tsar dismissed Count Witte, his moderate and conciliatory prime minister, replacing him with the obsequious I. L. Goremykin. Yet the authentic power in the cabinet would devolve into the hands of the minister of the interior, Pyotr Stolypin, who was appointed prime minister in 1906. An experienced and energetic former provincial governor, it was Stolypin henceforth who would set the legislative agenda for the empire. Although lacking breadth of intellect, he was renowned as both a hard-driving administrator and a forceful speaker. Nor was Stolypin by any means a blind reactionary. He understood the importance of primary education and of land reform. At every opportunity, he encouraged these projects, sensing that they would win over the peasantry and help defuse pressures for more extensive political reform.

By the same token, Stolypin genuinely hoped to work with the new Duma, to seek cooperation at least with that body's more centrist elements. Once it became evident, however, that the Cadets insisted upon full legislative authority for the Duma, Stolypin lost patience with the parliamentary process altogether and resorted to more draconian "emergency" legislation and to a wider-ranging campaign of arrests throughout the empire. Indeed, repression became progressively harsher in tandem with a mounting wave of terrorism that included a bomb thrown at Stolypin's summer dacha in August 1906, killing twenty-seven people and seriously wounding the minister's two young children. Within weeks, the empire was operating under martial law. By the thousands, political activists suspected of terrorism were arrested and imprisoned. Not a few were executed without trial, often hanged on gibbets that soon came to be dubbed "Stolypin's neckties."

Meanwhile, a new election was authorized for a Second Duma, in February 1907. Although it took place on schedule, it resulted in a wider political polarization. This time the far-left Socialist Revolutionaries and Social Democrats had decided to participate, and their delegates filled the vacuum left by numerous banned Cadets. Thus, when the Duma convened in March, a legislative deadlock ensued, with right and left refusing all cooperation or compromise. Stolypin had seen enough. For him, the decisive issue was the Duma's refusal to follow his orders in stripping parliamentary immunity from a group of Social Democratic "traitors." On June 16, he persuaded the tsar once again to dissolve the Duma. Afterward, the government wasted little time in narrowing property qualifications for the franchise even more drastically. Accordingly, elections were held for a Third Duma, which convened in September 1907, and which this time brought in a solid right-wing majority consisting mainly of landowners. Now at last, politically housebroken and functioning under a "peace of exhaustion," the Third Duma would be allowed to serve out its full term, until 1912.

For the tsarist government, the time had come to throttle the residual pockets of political liberalism sine die. In that effort, too, it was confident that it possessed an effective tactic. This was to focus public frustration on the Jews. The decision was not Stolypin's. As far back as February 1907, on the eve of the election for the Second Duma, the prime minister actually had suggested a partial amelioration of Jewish circumstances, arguing that it might defuse Jewish participation in revolutionary unrest. But the aristocracy, and the tsar himself, forcefully rejected the proposal. "An inner voice more and more resolute," explained Nicholas II, "tells me not to take this decision upon myself." And after the dissolution of the Second Duma in June 1907, as he confronted ongoing violence, the tsar became even more implacable. In a conversation with General Drachevski, the recently appointed police chief of

Rostov-on-Don, Nicholas remarked: "You have a lot of zhidi there in Rostov and in Nakhichevan." The general sought to reassure the tsar, explaining that many Jews had perished during the revolutionary disturbances and pogroms. "No, not enough," Nicholas retorted. "I had expected that more would die." While normally disapproving of violence, the ruler by then was quite prepared to have the revolution stigmatized and throttled as a "Jewish plot."

In that effort, Nicholas relied upon the support of a cunning ally. This was the Union of the Russian People, a cabal that had been organized in October 1906. The Union's initial membership of prominent landowners was broadened gradually to include substantial numbers of Russia's incipient white-collar class, including small businessmen, clerks, and minor government functionaries, specifically the elements that regarded themselves threatened by the emergence of modern and progressive industrial capitalism. With the blessing of the tsar, who wore the Union's badge proudly on his breast, the Union directed its animus not merely at the Jews as an "unassimilable" people (the classic refrain of earlier tsarist regimes), but first and foremost as revolutionary harbingers of Russia's emergent liberal middle class. In the fashion of West European antisemitism, it was this dynamic and forceful bourgeoisie that was now to be stigmatized in public consciousness as tools of "Jewish parasitism." During the winter and spring of 1907, therefore, the Union's agents set about distributing handbills in town squares, warning the Russian people that the Jews were their true oppressors, that the Jews were in league with the German factory-owners, the Japanese, the Poles, and the British.

Stolypin was prepared to tolerate the Union's propaganda. Indeed, it was under his aegis now that the wholesale expulsion of Jews from the Russian interior assumed the character of an epidemic. The numerus clausus for Jews in the liberal professions became a virtual ban. Jewish cultural and religious institutions were forced increasingly to close down. The right-wing press was encouraged to brand Jews as "werewolves," "a criminal race," "bloodsuckers," "traitors." In his diary, the former prime minister, Sergei Witte, lamented: "Never before has the Jewish question been treated with such unspeakable cruelty." Witte was premature. In February 1911, the ultra-rightist United Nobility Party issued a warning that the government's measures were insufficient, that it would be more appropriate "not to abolish the Pale of Settlement . . . but to cleanse Russia of the zhidi [altogether]. . . . The government must recognize that the Jews are dangerous to the life of mankind in the same measure as wolves, scorpions, reptiles, poisonous spiders, and similar creatures." To buttress its case, the United Nobility commissioned a Ukrainian former Catholic priest, Justin Pranaitis, to formulate a report "documenting" the Jewish practice of ritual murder. The tactic proved eerily prophetic.

THE CASE OF MENDEL BEILIS

On March 20, 1911, the body of a thirteen-year-old boy, Andrei Yustschinski, was discovered near a brick factory on the outskirts of the Ukrainian capital of Kiev. An autopsy discovered numerous knife wounds on his corpse, inflicted evidently by "random slashing." In earlier years, the murder normally would not have aroused much public interest, but lately there had been an upsurge of serious crime in Kiev. It developed later that a well-organized band of thieves had been operating in the city, grouped around one Vera Cheberiak, wife of a post-office clerk. A tough harridan, Vera currently was making plans to rob priceless icons from the great Kiev Cathedral of Santa Sofia. By chance, her son Zhenya was a friend of one of the students at the cathedral school, Andrei Yustschinski. The two youngsters often met at the Cheberiak apartment, with its accumulation of stolen goods and intermittent conclaves of plotting thieves. On March 12, the boys happened to quarrel, and Andrei petulantly threatened to inform the police about the Cheberiak activities. Zhenya mentioned the remark to his parents. That very night, Vera Cheberiak arranged for Andrei to be killed.

Eight days later, when the body was discovered and the report of its numerous knife wounds was issued, rightist organizations sensed a unique opportunity. Within the week, pamphlet accusations, printed by the Union of the Russian People, were in extensive circulation. A typical document stated:

> ORTHODOX CHRISTIANS! The zhidi have tortured Andryusha Yustschinski to death. Every year, before their Passover, they torture to death several dozens of Christian children in order to get their blood to mix with the *matzoti*. They do this in commemoration of our Savior, whom they tortured to death on the Cross. . . . Russians, it is time for the Christian world to understand where the enemy is and with whom it has to fight. . . . When the guilt of the Jews in the murder of Andrei Yustschinski has been established, there will be no doubt that the abolition of the Pale of Settlement, which the zhidi so hopefully expected, will not be approved by the Imperial Duma, and that the very consideration of the question of equality for the zhidi will be postponed indefinitely.

In Kiev and other major cities, rumors of pogroms began to circulate. Minister of Justice Ivan Shcheglovitov on April 16 telegraphed Kiev District Procurator Chaplinski to investigate the case personally. Chaplinski complied, ordering a second autopsy, this one by two Kiev University medical professors. The latter's report, issued on April 25, stated that the victim had been almost completely drained of blood, and that, "[i]nasmuch as the most severe hemorrhaging was in the left temple region . . . we must assume that it would have been more convenient to collect blood from Yustschinski's body from these wounds. . . ." The intimation was plain that a ritual murder had been committed. Years later, it would be learned that the ministry of justice had slipped the two doctors a 4,000 ruble bribe.

Meanwhile, Chaplinski's next priority was to find a likely suspect. He was given his "clue" by a man named Golubev, a member of the local Kiev branch of the Union of the Russian People, who noted that the cave where Andrei Yustschinski was discovered was near a brick factory owned by "the zhid Zaitzev. The manager of the . . . factory is the zhid Mendel [Beilis]. . . . My personal opinion is that the murder was . . . committed [by Beilis] either here or in the Jewish clinic. Naturally, I cannot present evidence of this." With or without evidence, the district attorney sought to follow this lead.

At the same time, the local Kiev police followed up on their own investigation, under the direction of Chief Detective Mitshiuk. In June, Mitshiuk unearthed sufficient evidence to warrant the arrest of Vera Cheberiak, together with three other suspected murderers in her gang, all ex-convicts. But when the detective brought Vera in for questioning, Chaplinski angrily ordered the woman to be released. Hereupon, the district attorney sensed that he would have to act without delay to propitiate the ministry of justice. Accordingly, in July, his staff produced a "witness" for him. It was a local lamplighter, who testified that he had seen a member of the Cheberiak gang carrying Andrei Yustschinski's body into a cave. Upon being "interrogated," however, the lamplighter changed his mind, and agreed that the person he had seen was Mendel Beilis. For Chaplinski, this was evidence enough. At his orders, on the night of July 21, a small expeditionary force of gendarmes forced its way into Beilis's home and arrested him. An ex-soldier, the thirty-seven-year-old Beilis was the father of five children. He had worked as dispatcher at the Zaitzev brickworks for fifteen years and was universally liked by his non-Jewish neighbors, including the parish priest. Nevertheless, citing the blood ritual, Chaplinski formally arraigned Beilis. At an initial hearing, at which the lamplighter again testified, a nine-member grand jury agreed to indict Beilis for murder.

Six weeks later, in the first week of September 1911, Nicholas II visited Kiev to unveil a statue of his grandfather, Alexander II. Shortly after his arrival, the tsar ordered Chaplinski to meet with him personally to submit a progress report on the Beilis case. Plainly, the entire enterprise had evoked his interest and approval. It was also during the tsar's visit, attending a gala performance of the Kiev Opera on September 6, that Nicholas was targeted by a young Jewish terrorist, Dmitri Bogrov. Bogrov's pistol shot missed Nicholas, but struck and killed Stolypin, who was sitting in the royal box. On September 10, four days after Bogrov was summarily hanged, Minister of Justice Shcheglovitov rushed from St. Petersburg to Kiev to ensure that the case against Beilis was pressed with renewed vigor. There was reason for urgency. With antisemitism now poisoning the nation's atmosphere as never before, and elections for the Fourth Duma scheduled early the next year, the government was intent on driving the final nail into the revolutionary cause.

Nevertheless, the case against Beilis was far from airtight. Detective Mitshiuk and the Kiev police stolidly continued to accumulate incriminating new information on the Cheberiak gang. In his exasperation, District Procurator Chaplinski promptly ordered the evidence filed away unseen, then arranged for a convicted felon, one Ivan Kozachenko, to be confined in Beilis's cell, with the promise of a quick release if he would function as a police informer. Gratefully, Kozachenko soon came up with a report that Beilis had offered to pay him, Kozachenko, to poison the lamplighter, "but naturally I would not do such things because I do not want a zhid to drink Russian blood." At Chaplinski's orders, this "evidence" was added to the Beilis file. The Cheberiak material was not included.

THE PENDULUM SWINGS

In the late spring and summer of 1912, Mitshiuk and several of his fellow detectives began leaking their information about Vera Cheberiak to a friendly journalist, Boris Brazhul-Brushkovski, a columnist for the Kiev newspaper *Kievskaya mysl*. A committed liberal, and married to a Jewish woman, Brazhul-Brushkovski needed little encouragement to embark on his own investigation. Thus, once apprised of the Cheberiak gang's likely involvement in the murder, he managed to win the trust of Vera's half-brother, Andrei Singayevski; and Singayevski, after being plied with vodka, boasted that he and two accomplices had done the actual stabbing. He added that Vera had inadvertently killed her own small daughter by sedating the child in advance of a police interrogation. All this information appeared in Brazhul-Brushkovski's newspaper articles, and was widely reproduced by other journals, both in Russia and in the West.

By early autumn of 1912, in the wake of the Brazhul-Brushkovski revelations, only Russia's most unregenerately right-wing elements, led by the United Nobility and the Union of the Russian People, were prepared to give their unqualified support to the tsarist autocracy. Conferring then with other government officials, Minister of Justice Shcheglovitov acknowledged that the case against Beilis was so shaky, and the political atmosphere in Russia so uncertain, that it would be safer to postpone the trial until after the election for the Fourth Duma, scheduled for late November. This was done. But once the election took place, and the Cadets and other reformist parties found themselves counterbalanced by a "safe," if still narrow, majority of rightist delegates, the government decided to move ahead with the Beilis prosecution. Ironically, even with these advantages, Chaplinski was unable to organize the prosecution to his satisfaction until September of 1913. By then Beilis had languished behind bars for nearly two and a half years, and his case had burgeoned into an international cause célèbre. Indeed, once the trial finally began, on September 15, it was covered by hundreds of journalists from Russia, Europe, and the United States, all fascinated by the unfolding spectacle of a "Russian Dreyfus Affair."

The government picked the judge, Fyodor Doldreiev, a committed reactionary, who ensured that the jury was selected principally from the semi-literate peasantry of the surrounding Kiev countryside. As prosecutor, the ministry of justice brought down from St. Petersburg its premier trial attorney, Chief Procurator Yevgeni Vipper. It was Vipper who presented the court his full panoply of government witnesses. The first of these was none other than Vera Cheberiak, queen bee of the entire criminal plot. Vera in turn "quoted" her son Zhenya, asserting that he personally had seen Beilis kidnap his friend Andrei. The lamplighter and his wife repeated the testimony Chaplinski had extracted from them in 1911. As for Singayevski's role in the killing (as reported in Brazhul-Brushkovski's newspaper account), Vipper blandly assured the jury that "[none] of [Singayevski and his friends] is guilty. . . . The government would have indicted them if they were guilty."

The defense then presented its case, and its choice of counsel proved an unpleasant surprise for the prosecution. Leading the team was Basil Makhlakov, president of the Liberal Party, and widely regarded as the most distinguished trial attorney in all of Russia. He had volunteered his services. So had his principal associate, Oscar Gruzenberg, the leading Jewish criminal lawyer of his generation. Makhlakov and Gruzenberg needed barely three days to expose the government's witnesses as felons and bribe-takers. Called to the witness stand, Brazhul-Brushkovski gave ample testimony of his discoveries about the Cheberiak gang. So did Dmitri Makhalin, a former member of the Kiev police force, who cited District Attorney Chaplinski's role in suppressing evidence on Vera Cheberiak. The jury was visibly shocked.

More shocking yet, however, was the government's counter-riposte to the defense. In the third week of the trial, Prosecutor Vipper summoned to the witness stand the redoubtable Justin Pranaitis. The former Catholic priest would testify as an "international authority on Jewish ritual murder." Indeed, upon being sworn in, Pranaitis lost no time in launching into a description of the Jews as "ghouls," "vampires," and "fiends." He went on to declare:

> A curse was laid upon the Jewish people by Moses, who said: "God will smite you with the curse of Egypt." We see clearly that this

curse has been fulfilled, since all European Jews have eczema of the posterior, all Asiatic Jews have mange upon their heads, all African Jews have boils on their legs, and American Jews have a disease of the eyes, as a result of which they are disfigured and stupid. The wicked rabbis have found a medical cure that consists of smearing their afflicted parts with Christian blood.

When Pranaitis finished, Vipper assured the jury that it had heard "definitive, unimpeachable" evidence of the Jews' historic usage of the blood ritual.

By then, cascades of protests against the "Russian Dreyfus Affair" had inundated the tsarist government. They included messages of outrage from such Western eminences as Gerhart Hauptmann, Thomas Mann, Tomas Masaryk, the archbishops of Canterbury and York, H. G. Wells, John Masefield, Georges Clemenceau, Charles Péguy. Protest petitions from the United States contained the signatures of senators, congressmen, mayors, and presidential candidates. Discreetly, the French and British governments expressed concern that the trial was imperiling their special diplomatic relationship with St. Petersburg. In Russia itself, not least of all, public revulsion was widespread. Writers, lawyers, doctors, professors, students, even workers and peasants, held protest meetings and called strikes. Tram workers in Kiev took up a collection for Mendel Beilis's family. For its part, the tsarist government in its acute beleaguerment engaged in a frenzy of censorship, confiscating entire editions of newspapers and arresting their editors. When the St. Petersburg Bar Association wired its support for the editors, the government prosecuted twenty-five of the association's members, among them Alexander Kerensky. Except for the empire's most unregenerate nucleus of political and clerical reactionaries, the trial had become an embarrassment of monumental proportions. As far back as 1817, Alexander I had publicly condemned the blood libel as "a superstitious belief . . . unworthy of discussion." Now, almost a century later, another tsar and his government had made the blood libel a pillar of imperial policy.

On October 28, 1913, the case went to the jury. The jurors required less than a day to return a unanimous verdict of not guilty. When Mendel Beilis was escorted out of the courtroom, he was mobbed by thousands of cheering spectators. Both he and his defense team were flooded with telegrams of congratulation from throughout Russia and the West. By contrast, the government in its chagrin chose to interpret the verdict as its "moral" victory for having "alerted" the Russian people. Tsar Nicholas personally conferred medals and cash awards on the numerous officials who shared in the prosecution. District Procurator Chaplinski was appointed to Russia's Supreme Court.

It is of interest that most of these tsarist favorites received a different kind of reward several years later at the hands of the Bolsheviks. In 1918, Shcheg-lovitov, the former minister of justice, was shot. Chief Procurator Vipper was discovered in hiding in 1919. Summarily convicted, he later died in prison. The ex-priest, Pranaitis, was shot in 1917. Vera Cheberiak and her half-brother Singayevski also were shot in 1918. Brazhul-Brushkovski, a hero to the nation's liberals, was arrested during the Stalinist purges of 1937 and never seen again. Mendel Beilis, meanwhile, all but broken in health, departed Russia in 1914. He immigrated first to Palestine, but was unable to support his family there. In 1922, he moved on to the United States, where again he failed to earn a living. Eventually, he became a charitable ward of New York Jewry, and died in 1934.

As for the great mass of Russian Jewry in this blackest night of counter-revolution, even the Bundists, the most activist of the Jewish political factions, no longer discerned a meaningful future for their people under tsarist rule. The sunburst of 1905–6 had come and gone. By 1913, the acquittal of Mendel Beilis had occurred too late to persuade even the most optimistic among them that Nicholas II's corrupt and dysfunctional regime would ever be liberalized. Only a force majeure would effect their salvation, and few Jews, or Russians, could have anticipated a transformation of that magnitude.

XVII

Socialist "Internationalism" in Western Europe: The Trauma of World War I

WEST EUROPEAN SOCIALISM IN THE PREWAR ERA

In 1847, attending a congress of the League of the Just, an assemblage of radical reformers in London, the twenty-nine-year-old Karl Marx, stocky and heavy-bearded, read off a new guideline for social transformation. It was published in February 1848 under the title *The Communist Manifesto (Manifest der Kommunistischen Partei)*. The essay's premise was unequivocal. The Industrial Revolution had transformed the worker from an artisan who owned his own tools into a propertyless, destitute factory hand, dependent for his livelihood on the capitalist who owned the means of production. With the capitalist's profits deriving from the surplus value of the worker's product, the exploiter was becoming richer, and the exploited was becoming poorer. The process, according to Marx, could end only with the violent overthrow of the existing order. The working poor, trained in class consciousness and prepared for this event, would launch the inevitable revolution to usher in the new order of a classless society.

No sooner had Marx published his German-language declamation, however, than he was branded a dangerous radical and denied residency rights in his native Rhineland, or anywhere else in Germany. Accordingly, he remained in London—indeed, for the next thirty-five years, until his death in 1883. Although employed intermittently as a stringer for the *New York Herald*, Marx and his family in these years received their principal financial support from Friedrich Engels. A fellow Rhinelander, son of a wealthy industrialist, it was Engels as a conscience-stricken idealist who gave Marx the leisure to pursue his years of research at the British Museum. The fruit of that effort was Marx's magnum opus, *Capital (Das Kapital)*, whose third and final volume (edited by Engels) appeared posthumously in 1885. In rich detail, the work provided historical context for the thesis Marx earlier had outlined in his *Communist Manifesto*.

Even as he labored on this epic work, Marx in 1864 set about organizing the First International Workingman's Association. Although the "First International" never quite gained practical momentum in Marx's own lifetime, six years later a Second International Workingman's Association was organized by the Frenchman Édouard-Marie Vaillant and the German Wilhelm Liebknecht. This one resonated far more dramatically than had its predecessor. By 1889, the very term "socialism" betokened a new era of elementary human justice for all the downtrodden of the earth, for worker and peasant, man and woman, gentile and Jew. Within a quarter-century of its establishment, the Second International had grown prodigiously in strength, encompassing Socialist, or Social Democratic, parties throughout the world.

In fact, that growth reflected a subtle if unofficial revision in the original Marxist commitment to a violent class revolution. The modification was the achievement of another German Jew, Eduard Bernstein. Born in 1850, one of fifteen children of a lower-middle-class Berlin family, Bernstein secured his earliest employment as a clerk in the local branch of the S. & L. Rothschild Bank. In 1872, like many Jews of his background, he was attracted to Germany's recently founded Social Democratic Party. Six years later, when Bismarck persuaded the Reichstag to outlaw the Social Democrats, Bernstein chose to immigrate, first to Switzerland, and eventually to England. Spending eleven years in England, the "workshop of the world," Bernstein underwent a crisis of intellectual conscience. In 1894, in a series of articles written for *Die Neue Zeit*, he introduced a shocking proposal to his fellow socialists. It was to reject the key Marxist tenet that capitalist society was on the verge of collapse. Bernstein's experience in England had convinced him that the circumstances of the laboring class were not deteriorating under the weight of modern capitalism. Rather, they were improving, however erratically and unevenly.

If that was the case, argued Bernstein, far better to abandon the classical socialist goal of revolution in favor of bread-and-butter improvements in working-class conditions. As he saw it, those improvements also logically encompassed a democratization of the property-based suffrage; of military conscription, from which the wealthy and privileged could be exempted; and of the bias of the law, which favored the rich. In truth, without admitting the fact, most socialists in Europe already were directing their efforts less to the chimera of revolution than to Bernstein's pragmatic goals of improved working and living conditions, and of a more democratic and humane society. By the turn of the century, only one of Marx's original premises appeared to remain intact, the one to which even "revisionist" socialism apparently remained committed. This was the goal of internationalism, of world peace, a peace in which working people everywhere would never again become cannon fodder for chauvinist, capitalist-ruled governments.

JEWS AND WEST EUROPEAN SOCIALISM

During these same fin-de-siècle years, a growing minority of West European Jews proved to be almost unique among members of the middle class in their growing political affinity for socialism. In Germany, Jewish partisans of the burgeoning Social Democratic Party included not only desperate East European fugitives from tsarist oppression, firebrands like Rosa Luxemburg (p. 492) and Leo Jogiches, but a vibrant minority of "respectable" native-born families. Indeed, most of these young men and women were products of *Mittelstand* homes, and in earlier years they had gravitated almost instinctively to the National Liberal Party. But now they were reevaluating their political loyalties.

Several factors accounted for the shift. One, surely, was the "treason" of German political liberalism. Anchored in a vast and open trading arena, the resplendent new Reich was generating unprecedented material prosperity. As businessmen, the National Liberals found themselves increasingly tempted to give their support to the authoritarian imperial regime, and expediently to ignore the growing cartelization of the national economy, the alliance of industrial magnates with landowning Junker reactionaries. Not so the Jews. Their political allegiance historically had been linked to "authentic" liberalism, the movement that had produced their emancipation. Neither could educated young German Jews turn a blind eye to the passivity with which the National Liberals accepted the triumphalist new militarism that was becoming all the vogue in the empire. More ominously, the National Liberals appeared to be equivocating on the issue of antisemitism. Although the party leadership had never formally embraced the reactionary ideology, neither had they unequivocally rejected it. In their disillusionment with the putative "Liberals," therefore, Jews of all backgrounds tended to give new attention to the SPD (Sozialdemokratische Partei Deutschland), the Social Democratic Party, as their alternate haven. More than any other faction, the SPD espoused "authentic" democracy and a humane social agenda. Not least of all, the Social Democrats unambiguously condemned antisemitism.

These were the circumstances under which substantial numbers of Jews began transferring their loyalties to the Social Democrats, some of them appearing among the party's candidates to the Reichstag. Indeed, eight Jewish Social Democrats were elected in 1898, and thirteen in 1903, a figure that comprised approximately 10 percent of the entire SPD Reichstag delegation. They were lawyers, journalists, or economists, by and large, and it was their superior education and grasp of world affairs that propelled them to visibility and leadership. Few of them were radicals. Like their non-Jewish colleagues, they gravitated almost instinctively to the party's moderate-revisionist center.

Eminent among this group were Hugo Haase and Ludwig Frank. Haase, a Baden lawyer who for years contributed his services pro bono to workers, was elected deputy party chairman in 1911, and cochairman (with Friedrich Ebert) in 1913. But smaller numbers of Jewish Social Democrats also attached themselves to the party's revolutionary, "purist" faction. These included Laura Lafargue, Marx's daughter and keeper of his literary legacy, and the renowned party attorneys and Reichstag members Paul Levi and Kurt Rosenfeld. All were native-born. Rosa Luxemburg, however, a Polish-Jewish immigrant, was the most visible figure in this group, and antisemites subsequently tended to dub her entire faction as "Russian buffalo-Jews." But whether of the party's center or left wing, the Jewish minority within the SPD became a convenient bête noire for a vindictive German right.

In the Habsburg Empire, during these same years, the Jewish role in the labor and socialist movements possibly was no less striking than in Germany. The Social Democratic Party's two outstanding intellectuals were Victor Adler and Otto Bauer. Adler, a physician who had been reared in Vienna's heavily Jewish Leopoldstadt quarter, contributed much of his early medical practice to working-class families. In the process, he was shaken by the poverty and squalor he encountered beneath the capital's glittering surface. The experience drew him to Marxism. So, too, did the poisonous bigotry he had encountered since his university years, and which even an expedient conversion to Protestantism did not spare him. By his mid-thirties, Adler had abandoned his medical practice to devote himself exclusively to Social Democracy. In that effort, he formulated a compromise program that blended orthodox Marxism and moderate revisionism. By the early 1900s, it was an agenda that had become particularly attractive to Jewish professionals, most of whom spurned the notion of violent revolution in favor of humanism and peaceful internationalism, ideals that Liberal Party members in Austria were abandoning as rapidly as their counterparts in Germany.

One of those Liberal defectors was Otto Bauer. Son of a prosperous Jewish textile manufacturer, trained as a lawyer, Bauer in 1907 published a volume of pathbreaking originality. Entitled *The Nationalities Issue and Social Democracy (Die Nationalitätenfrage und die Sozialdemokratie),* the work projected an enlightened, federal-autonomist approach to the empire's contentious non-Austrian peoples. Widely acclaimed for intellectual acuity, Bauer soon rose to the position of secretary of the SPD faction in the Austrian Reichstag, and became a founding editor of *Der Kampf,* the principal theoretical organ of Austrian Social Democracy. At the same time, together with Adler and Bauer, an entire galaxy of febrile Jews was ascending to eminence in the party, most commonly as newspaper editors, political theoreticians, economists, and publicists.

THE WAR AND EUROPEAN JEWRY

It was also in these early-twentieth-century years that socialists of all gradations found themselves grappling with urgent new issues of nationalism and
military preparedness. As war clouds gathered, the party's rank and file in one
country after another tended increasingly to adopt the stance of militant
patriotism. Even the French socialist leader Jean Jaurès, widely esteemed as
the "conscience" of European pacifism, found himself marginalized by his
party's nationalist majority. And when hostilities broke out, in July 1914, it was
Germany's mighty SPD, the putative vanguard of European socialism, that
led all its European counterparts in voting to support the government's war
policy. Among the tiny handful within the SPD leadership that opposed the
majority decision, one was Karl Liebknecht (son of the revered Wilhelm
Liebknecht, a founder of the party). The other was Rosa Luxemburg. Both
were jailed for their passionate antimilitaristic "incitement." In her prison correspondence, Luxemburg continued her relentless denunciation of the
SPD—"shamed, dishonored, wading in blood and dripping with filth"—for
its betrayal of peace. But to no avail. A small dissident faction, the "Independent" Socialists, led by Karl Kautsky and two Jews, Hugo Haase and the
famed revisionist Eduard Bernstein, was equally unwilling to disgorge Germany's recent military gains.

Elsewhere throughout the Continent, Jewish socialists and nonsocialists,
businessmen and professionals, virtually competed with their fellow citizens
in a feverish effusion of patriotism. In France, even the unsavory prospect of
Tsarist Russia as an Entente partner failed to shake the loyalty of the nation's
veteran Jewish population. Thus, in 1915–16, French Jewry dismissed as German propaganda reports of a mass forced relocation of Russian Jewry. In
Austria, the socialist theorist Otto Bauer set a personal guideline for his colleagues when he volunteered for the army, then served on the Eastern front.
The renowned littérateur Stefan Zweig, writing to a colleague, acknowledged
that "in spite of all my hatred and aversion for war, [m]y great ambition . . . is
to be an officer with you in the . . . army, to conquer in France." To his intense
joy, Zweig was accepted for military service, and spent the first half of the war
in an artillery regiment. Sigmund Freud, although overage for army duty, was
among these Jewish loyalists. "All my libido is given to Austria," he acknowledged to a friend. Two of Freud's sons served in the army. The elder, a lieutenant, won the Military Cross.

In Germany, too, once hostilities began, the nation's various Jewish
Gemeinden appealed to their members to "devote your resources to the Fatherland above and beyond the call of duty! . . . All of you—men and women—

must place yourselves in the service of the Fatherland through personal help of every kind and through donations of money and property." "I foresee a great victory for Germany and Germanism," exulted Jakob Wassermann in a diary entry of August 12, 1914. "Germany is becoming a world power." For the renowned Judaic philosopher Rabbi Dr. Hermann Cohen, Jews bore an obligation "piously to respect Germany, their spiritual home." In August 1914, the German-Jewish poet Ernst Lissauer whipped off a doggerel, "Hymn of Hate Against England" ("Hassgesang gegen England"). Set to music, its stanzas immediately were on everyone's lips, and the kaiser personally bestowed a medal on Lissauer.

Years later, German Jewry's national Cultusverein published statistics on the Jewish war record. These revealed that some 100,000 Jews (in a total Jewish population of 500,000) had served in Germany's armed forces, and 12,000 had died in combat. Civilian contributions were not less impressive. In numbers unimaginable before 1914, Jews were recruited for key public positions. Albert Ballin, chairman of the great Hamburg-Lloyd (Hapag-Lloyd) Packetboat Company, was charged with the establishment of a central acquisitions agency, Reichsinskauf, for the purchase of supplies vital to the civilian economy. Walther Rathenau, chairman of AEG, the nation's largest electricity conglomerate, organized the government's raw materials department to husband resources indispensable for military purposes. The immunologist August von Wassermann produced his tetanus vaccine essentially as a treatment for war wounds. Fritz Haber, a renowned chemist (and later Nobel laureate), mobilized some 150 leading scientists and aggressively coordinated their efforts to meet Germany's military and civilian needs.

At a time of inflamed chauvinism, however, the record of Jewish patriotism availed little. By the winter of 1915–16, with the war locked in stalemate, nationalist frustrations coalesced increasingly around the Jews. The military leadership soon was inundated with denunciations of Jewish treachery and malfeasance, with charges that Ballin, Rathenau, and other Jews in public service were "taking over" German national institutions. From the onset of hostilities, the Reichshammerbund (Imperial Brotherhood of the Hammer), a xenophobic cabal led by Theodor Fritsch—later to become a prominent Nazi official—pressed for a *Judenzählung,* a census to determine if Jews were making their "fair share" of sacrifices. Fritsch enjoyed support in high places. In December 1915, a conference of other ultra-rightists, including the future Nazis Count Klaus Reventlow and Adolf Bartels, similarly approved a research survey, to be titled *The Jews in the Army (Die Juden im Reichswehr).* Under these pressures, the government then tacitly permitted the army to conduct its own inquiry. Jewish soldiers were obliged to fill out a questionnaire that pressed for details of where, how, and when they were fulfilling their military service. A number of senior officers began transferring Jews under their command to frontline duty simply to avoid accusations of pro-Jewish favoritism.

The results of the survey were not made public until after the war, when it was revealed that the proportion of Jewish casualties and medal recipients actually exceeded the proportion of Jews in the nation at large. But, in the meanwhile, the effect on Jewish morale of the *Judenzählung* and the deluge of antisemitic accusations was devastating. Hermann Cohen spoke of a "stab in the heart." "We have become marked men," agonized Hugo Haase, the former Social Democratic Reichstag deputy, now serving as an army lieutenant, "second-class soldiers." In shock, Ernst Simon, who had enlisted in 1914, noted two years later that the *Judenzählung* evidently "reflected genuine popular attitudes." It did. The old prewar suspicions had been fanned into intensified racism. At the moment of German Jewry's ultimate commitment to the Fatherland, the Wilhelminian Empire had offered them nothing in return but contempt and suspicion. In their disillusionment, it was perhaps inevitable that most of them would extend a cautious welcome to the popular revolution of autumn 1918.

RUSSIA AT WAR

During the earliest weeks of hostilities, as the German Reichswehr launched its preemptive Schlieffen Plan offensive against France, the tsarist government moved swiftly to fulfill its treaty obligations to its embattled Western ally. In that effort, the Russian armed forces embarked on a two-pronged offensive of their own. One was directed at Galicia (Habsburg Poland), and proved dramatically successful. In its early months, tsarist divisions overran the Galician provincial capital of Lemberg (Lvov) and tens of thousands of square miles of surrounding hinterland. Here lived between 200,000 and 250,000 Jews. Terrified of falling under Russian domination, some two-fifths of this dense Jewish population fled westward, into other provinces of the Habsburg Empire. Indeed, fully 75,000 Galician Jews moved directly to Vienna. Here they survived on a dole provided by Austrian-Jewish philanthropy.

For Russian Jewry, however, the war brought not simply hardship but overwhelming tragedy. In their effort to relieve German pressure on France, the Russians had launched the second prong of their military offensive at East Prussia. Here it met disaster. A German rearguard force, led by General Erich Ludendorff, outflanked and all but annihilated an entire Russian army near the city of Tannenberg. Afterward, to exploit this spectacular victory, the Germans promptly launched a counteroffensive of their own on the Eastern Front. It began in the spring of 1915, and within a period of two months succeeded in driving tsarist forces almost completely from Habsburg Galicia. In Russian Poland, the German steamroller pushed on directly into Warsaw, then Kovno, then Brest-Litovsk, then Vilna. Thus it was, by August 1915, that the largest areas of northwest Poland, Lithuania, and Ukraine had fallen under the occupation of German and Austrian armies. Within this vast terrain lived approximately 1.75 million Jews. Initially, it had appeared that their fate might actually take a turn for the better. Intent on winning over Jewish loyalties, General Ludendorff, the Eastern Front commander, went so far as to dedicate synagogues and publish proclamations of friendship (An Meinen Liben Yiden in Poilen) in choicest Yiddish. The occupied areas were largely devastated. Although administered by the famously "efficient" Central Powers, they could offer their inhabitants little economic security. But whether under German or Austrian rule, the Jews in these occupied areas fared infinitely better than those—the largest numbers—who remained under direct tsarist rule.

The circumstances of Russia's captive Jewish population in some measure reflected a wider and more generalized tragedy. In the aftermath of the Tannenberg disaster, and the tsarist army's ensuing military retreat, Grand Duke Nicholas, Russia's military commander in chief, proclaimed a scorched-earth policy for the abandoned territory. Homes, chattels, and crops all were to be put to the torch, and the area's inhabitants were to be moved inland, beyond the range of the advancing German armies. The Great Retreat was a horror for all its victims, Jews and non-Jews alike. Perhaps as many as 2 million refugees were propelled into flight eastward, most of them eventually to be dispersed in or near the larger cities of the Russian interior. Although local charities worked frantically with government committees to provide a bare subsistence amid the chaos, tens of thousands of inhabitants perished of hunger and exposure.

It was among the Jews, however, that the tsarist evacuation ultimately inflicted its most lethal consequences. From the moment the war began, regarding the Jews as endemically untrustworthy, the government maintained intact the entire apparatus of Jewish repression. Some 450,000 Jews were serving in the Russian army, yet none was allowed to receive officer's ranking, except in the medical corps. Indeed, military and civil authorities vied with each other in treating the Jews essentially as an enemy population. Yiddish was declared an alien language, and its public use was banned. Rumors were circulated of Jews extending aid and comfort to the enemy, of Jews dispatching nocturnal messages to German couriers. When the vast transplantation began, therefore, it was inflicted on the Jews not as refugees but as suspected traitors. As Minister of the Interior N. B. Shcherbatov privately acknowledged to the cabinet: "[O]ne does not like to admit this, but . . . the army wished . . . [to impute to] the local Jews imaginary actions of sabotage against the Russian forces . . . to represent them as . . . responsible for [the army's] own failures and defeat at the front."

In December 1914, even before the mass retreat, the army on its own began to deport Jews. By January 1915, approximately 60,000 Jewish refugees from smaller Polish towns were crowded into Warsaw. Jews from western Ukraine were driven into Kiev. And with the great omnibus evacuation of the spring and summer of 1915, Jews were driven from the entirety of the western Pale area, including major sectors of Belorussia, Lithuania, and Ukraine. Their displacement was conducted with a unique and gratuitous brutality. A non-Jewish deputy in the Duma, one Dzhubinski, wrote later:

> As a representative of our Fifth Siberian Division, I was myself on the scene and can testify with what incredible cruelty the expulsion of the Jews from the province of Radom took place. The entire population was driven out within a few hours during the night. . . . Old men, invalids, and paralytics had to be carried on people's arms because there were no vehicles. The police . . . treated the Jewish refugees precisely like criminals. At one station, for instance, the Jewish Commission [kehillah] of Homel was not even allowed to approach the trains to render aid to the refugees or to give them food and water. In one case, a train which was conveying the victims was completely sealed and when finally opened most of the inmates were found half-dead, sixteen down with scarlet fever and one with typhus.

By June 15, 1915, approximately 600,000 Jews had been uprooted from the Pale, by far the largest proportionate transplantation among the various populations of the empire's western provinces. With most of the able-bodied Jewish men serving in the army at the front, those affected by the expulsions were essentially women, children, sick or elderly men, and crippled Jewish war veterans. Families often were separated, their members sent off to different areas of the interior. When transportation was provided, the deportees were loaded into freight cars and dispatched to inland towns and villages on a waybill. Elsewhere, thousands of Jews were compelled for weeks to sleep in wagons, boxcars, or in open fields. Estimates of the numbers who perished of starvation and exposure during the great expulsion of 1915 ranged between 60,000 and 80,000.

THE UKRAINIAN TRAUMA

The Jews' climactic agony occurred within the single densest area of their settlement in the Tsarist Empire. This was the southwestern, Ukrainian quadrant of the Pale. It was a region with a blood-drenched history. Here the Ukrainian people had waged a gallant three centuries' struggle for national independence. In the seventeenth century, that effort took the form of the explosive Chmielnicki uprising against the ruling Polish Commonwealth (pp. 11–13). In later years, following the partitions of Poland, the Ukrainians continued to stage periodic revolts against both the Tsarist Empire and the Polish landowning aristocracy. By 1914, their numbers approached some 23 million, a peasant and largely illiterate population, and still an unquenchably nationalistic one. Their latest and best opportunity to wrest free of alien rule appeared to revive with the Russian Revolution of March 1917. Organizing their own government and army, the Ukrainians began functioning as an autonomous nation. From their capital in Kiev, their parliament appointed Mikhail Hrushevsky as the nation's first president and Simon Petliura as its minister of defense.

As the months passed, however, and as the Communists seized power in Russia in November 1917, the Bolshevik leader Vladimir Lenin became alarmed at the prospect of losing the Ukraine's rich agricultural resources, its naval ports and army bases, and he insisted on a more limited version of Ukrainian autonomy. He was rebuffed. Instead, in January 1918, the Hrushevsky government proclaimed full Ukrainian independence. It was a challenge Lenin could not ignore. Two weeks later, he dispatched a 60,000-man Red Army force, which swiftly overcame Ukrainian resistance and occupied Kiev. The occupation in fact proved to be short-lived. In February, General Max Hoffman, Germany's plenipotentiary at the still ongoing Brest-Litovsk peace negotiations, concluded a treaty of "recognition and peace" with the Ukrainian separatists. Hereupon, the Reichswehr sent the Red Army to flight and restored a Ukrainian council in Kiev. It was a sham "restoration," of course. The occupying German forces determined national policy. Indeed, under the terms of the March 1918 Brest-Litovsk Treaty, the puppet Ukrainian council was obliged to deliver vast quantities of grain and livestock to the Central Powers.

For the Jews, meanwhile, the Ukrainian nationalist struggle became an ordeal of unsurpassed horror. Under the tsarist census of 1897, Jews in the Ukrainian regions numbered 1.927 million almost 10 percent of the area's total population, and the largest concentration of Jews in the Tsarist Empire altogether. As a consequence of the May Laws, most of these people had become town-dwellers. "Infidel," alien, urban, and commercial, they also remained a perennial target of Ukrainian xenophobia. On the one hand, in July 1917 the recently established Ukrainian legislature made a point of assuring full civil rights and even communal autonomy to all ethnic minorities under its jurisdiction—Russians, Poles, Belorussians, and Jews alike. These peoples were to be represented in the Ukrainian government by their own "undersecretaries"; and in November 1917, Jews were guaranteed no fewer than fifty delegates in the Ukrainian parliament. But if a "honeymoon" seemingly was under way between the Ukrainians and the Jews, it did not endure. In February 1918, as the terms of the Brest-Litovsk Treaty still were under negotiation, the Germans imposed their puppet regime in Kiev. Although the Jews played little role in this administration, they believed themselves at least physically safe under the rule of "civilized" Germany. Doubtless they were; but the issue soon became moot. In the autumn of 1918, as the German presence in Eastern Europe deteriorated, Ukrainian nationalist forces moved once again to reclaim their territory. Hereupon their reinstated Ukrainian parliament appointed a new executive directorate, this one under the presidency of Simon Petliura.

A veteran Ukrainian nationalist, Petliura as minister of defense in the initial Ukrainian government of March 1917 had set about mobilizing a Ukrainian brigade to defend his nation's newly proclaimed autonomy. The effort was premature, of course. The Germans soon were in effective occupation of Ukraine, and ensured that Petliura remained under house arrest in East Prussia. But with the German collapse in the autumn of 1918, Petliura was released, and in November the reinstated Ukrainian government selected him as the nation's *ataman,* its president. A man of progressive, even socialist ideals, Petliura doubtless would have preferred to revive the democratic regime of the previous year, but he was not granted that luxury. In February 1919, a Soviet Red Army invaded Ukrainian territory from the north, while General Anton Denikin's White, counterrevolutionary, army drove into Ukraine from the south. Compressed into a shrinking territorial enclave, Petliura's troops fell back to the west. By the spring of 1919, they were reduced to a tatterdemalion force of barely 20,000. So it was, throughout the year, in the march and countermarch of rival armies, that the Ukrainian Republic collapsed in pandemonium, and then in pillage and anarchy.

These were also the circumstances in which Ukrainian army units, demoralized and enraged by their defeat at the hands of both the Red and White legions, redressed their losses by turning on unarmed local Jews. Throughout 1919–20, not a single Jewish city, town, or neighborhood escaped pogroms and mass pillage. At least half a million Jews were reduced to destitution in this period, while tens of thousands of others were murdered outright, mutilated, and often raped by Ukrainian military and guerrilla forces. Thus, in March 1919, Ukrainian Cossack units marched into the largely Jewish-populated town of Proskurov. As one Ukrainian observer testified later, the troops

> swarmed out into the ... streets that were inhabited exclusively by Jews. . . . [Entering the] houses, [they] drew their swords and began to cut down the inhabitants without regard to sex or age.

They murdered old men, women, and infants at their mothers' breasts. They were not content with killing, but thrust their victims' bodies through with bayonets.... The Jews were dragged out of the cellars and lofts and murdered. Hand grenades were thrown into the cellars, and [in this manner] entire families were put to death.

The massacres continued from town to town. Between March 1919 and March 1920, at least 30,000 Jews perished.

Yet the slaughter committed by Ukrainian irregulars actually was superseded by the mayhem inflicted by General Anton Denikin's White army. A former tsarist military commander, Denikin managed to escape from his Bolshevik imprisonment and, in April 1918, to emerge as generalissimo of all White forces in southern Russia. Under his experienced and vigorous leadership, the counterrevolutionary troops soon were able to invest most of the Caucasus and, in May 1918, to launch a wider-scale invasion directly into Ukraine. By the summer of 1919, Denikin's army had cleared the region both of Petliura's shattered rear guard and of isolated Russian Bolshevik units. Unlike Petliura, who still hoped to enlist Western support, Denikin felt no need to maintain a pretense of liberal moderation. Thus, in August 1919, periodic White assaults on Jews, the well-familiar scapegoats of the former Tsarist Empire, burgeoned into mass pogroms that far transcended any atrocities committed even under the rule of Nicholas II. Eventually, by late autumn of 1919, the Red Army's larger manpower reserves began to press Denikin's forces back to the southwest. But the turn in the tide of battle produced no respite for the Jews. In their frustration, the Whites descended with vindictive ferocity upon the surviving belts of Jewish towns and villages. Anathematizing the Jews as Bolsheviks and Antichrists, Denikin's troops often burned or buried their victims alive. Estimates of casualties varied, but none assessed the numbers slain by Denikin's army at less than 80,000.

A final chapter remained to be written in the Ukrainian tragedy. In late 1918, a Polish army under the command of Jozef Pilsudski launched its own invasion of Ukraine. For nearly two years, battles raged back and forth between the Poles and the Soviet Red Army. Finally, exhausted, both sides expressed interest in negotiating a peace. In April 1921, a formal treaty was signed in Riga. Under its terms, the newborn Polish government accepted Soviet Russian domination over the largest part of Ukraine. In turn, Polish sovereignty was recognized over the territory of Galicia—essentially western Ukraine. As for the Ukrainian nationalists, after four years of struggle, they were left with nothing. Their casualties, military and civilian, may have reached 750,000. But the Jews had endured a proportionately far greater trauma of terror and loss. Beyond the death of between 60,000 and 80,000 of their people in the original, forced Russian exodus of 1915, the Petliura-Denikin massacres of 1918–1920 annihilated possibly 120,000 additional Jewish lives and orphaned at least twice that many children. Until the era of Adolf Hitler, the East European horror of World War I represented the profoundest catastrophe in modern Jewish history.

The unprecedented scope of this tragedy was not lost on Western Jewry. Indeed, as early as 1915, the American-Jewish leadership moved urgently to provide relief for the hundreds of thousands of East European Jews trapped in the zone of conflict between Russia and the Central Powers. By 1916, they succeeded in establishing the American Jewish Joint Distribution Committee, to be known ever after simply as the "Joint." Raising $15 million by the time the war ended, and an additional $7 million in the immediate postwar, the Joint eventually would maintain a network of some five hundred soup kitchens and clinics throughout the Polish-Ukrainian-Russian battle areas. At the same time, functioning in the vortex of the storm, it was the Joint's personnel who were the first to witness and assess the sheer magnitude of Jewish vulnerability and desperation. They wasted no time in transmitting this information to Jewish communities in America and Western Europe.

For their part, Western Jewish leaders reached an early consensus that all diplomatic efforts in behalf of their kinsmen in the East should be focused on the impending Paris Peace Conference. Here, in the French capital, the assembled Allied statesmen would determine the fate not only of the defeated Central Powers but also of a host of successor states—the Baltic countries, Czechoslovakia, Poland, Serbia, and "successor" Rumania. Beyond the inaccessible, Bolshevik-ruled Eurasian landmass of Soviet Russia, these were the nations, old and new, that encompassed the largest reservoir of European Jewry. All of them presumably would be compelled to accept the guidelines imposed by the Allies at the peace conference. It was in Paris, therefore, that Jewish spokesmen from the Western democracies anticipated a historic diplomatic opportunity at long last to safeguard their tormented people's future on the European Continent.

XVIII

The Triumph of Bolshevism

THE FALL OF TSARDOM

In the course of the Great War, the Russian army mobilized 15.5 million troops, and suffered 1.65 million killed, 3.85 million wounded, and 2.41 million prisoners. The deaths of civilians trapped in the war zones approached another 1.4 million. These losses might have been endured by a traditionally fatalistic Slavic population, but no longer when naked graft and venality compounded sloth and gross incompetence at the command level. More tragically yet, Tsar Nicholas II remained delusional in his visions of leadership omniscience. In the autumn of 1915, he departed for the army's advance headquarters at Mohilev to assume personal direction of his nation's military effort. In effect, the government was left in the hands of his wife, Tsaritsa Alexandra, and her closest "adviser," the louche Siberian faith healer Grigori Rasputin. At Rasputin's suggestion, the empress in February 1916 persuaded her husband to appoint a new prime minister, Baron Boris von Stürmer, a thoroughly incompetent Baltic German of suspect loyalties. The calamitous sequence of administrative decisions became the turning point in the fate of the monarchy.

In January 1917, rumors began circulating that Nicholas was preparing once again to dissolve the Duma. The prospect of yet another dissolution, the third within the space of eleven years, was too much even for conservative legislators. In February, a splinter group of rightist delegates joined with the centrist Cadets to formulate a demand for the tsar's abdication. The issue was forced less than a month later, when a series of workers' strikes and protest demonstrations erupted in Petrograd. This time the turmoil was exacerbated by the royal garrison, which mutinied. On March 12, sensing the collapse of government authority, the Duma took the initiative in electing its own "provisional committee," in effect, a new government executive. The committee was a liberal body. The chairman it selected for its new Council of Ministers was a leading Cadet, Prince Georgi Lvov; its new foreign minister, Pavel Miliukov, was chairman of the Cadet Party; while Alexander Kerensky, a Socialist Revolutionary, would function as minister of justice, and soon afterward as minister of war. Three days later, abandoned by all political factions, even of the right, Nicholas finally relinquished the throne. Hereupon, the Council of Ministers unilaterally declared the monarchy at an end and proclaimed itself the "Provisional Government."

If the March Revolution (or the "February Revolution" as it is commonly titled, under Russia's Julian calendar) evoked rejoicing among tens of millions of citizens, none were more thrilled than the former empire's minority peoples. On April 4, 1917, the Provisional Government decreed an end to all restrictions based on class, religion, and nationality. For the Jews, above all, the decree signified an end to their historic collective afflictions, to the Pale of Settlement, the May Laws, the foreclosure of educational and professional opportunities. Within weeks, they also embraced as never before the opportunity of free and open expression, of public meetings and public organizations. Schools, musical and dramatic societies, a proliferation of religious and political activities—all at last began to emerge from a shadowy underground existence. With them appeared an unprecedented diversity of publications in Hebrew, Yiddish, and Russian.

Much of this avalanche of print reflected the appearance of a multitude of specifically Jewish parties: Zionist, Bundist, Labor Zionist, Populist, Democratic, Religious Orthodox. Indeed, with all bans lifted on ethnic aspirations, and with separatist movements burgeoning as well among Poles, Ukrainians, Finns, Armenians, Georgians, and other minority peoples, virtually every Jewish party declared in favor of communal and cultural autonomy. Whatever their ideological coloration, these autonomist factions seemingly vindicated the formula of the historian Simon Dubnow (p. 292), who as far back as the First Duma in 1906 had strenuously pressed the case for Diaspora nationalism. Now even the Zionists agreed that the Jews' initial priority must be to assert that national identity, on Russian soil. It would be expressed not only through political activism but in a virtual renaissance of communal and cultural creativity.

THE BOLSHEVIK REVOLUTION

Meanwhile, on March 12, 1917, the very day the Provisional Government came into existence, it faced a serious rival. This was Petrograd's Soviet (Council) of Workers' and Soldiers' Deputies, a group of populist militants that now set about producing its own legislative agenda in the Tauride Palace, across from the main hall where the "official" Duma continued to hold its sessions. The uneasy cooperation between the Duma and the Soviet produced a curious, bicephalous arrangement that soon became dysfunctional. Indeed, all the more so as Prince Lvov and his newly formed cabinet offered no blueprint for extricating Russia from a widely detested war. On the battlefields, the hemorrhage of lives continued. Responding to the national passion for peace, the Soviet in the late summer and early autumn began to assert its political muscularity as the more authoritative body at the Tauride Palace. Within the Soviet, moreover, the Bolsheviks were asserting themselves as the dominant faction.

The modern Bolshevik Party had emerged from the early-twentieth-century schism within the Russian Social Democratic Party. The largest number of Social Democrats had remained committed to Marx's initial vision of a two-stage revolution, and favored admitting into their ranks all those who accepted that formula. Vladimir Lenin, however, editor of the party journal, *Iskra,* advocated a small, tightly knit group of disciplined revolutionaries who would launch the revolution the moment the tsarist regime appeared to be faltering. In 1903, at the SD congress in Brussels, Lenin won in the first test on that issue, yet by so narrow a margin (and only after a walkout of the Jewish Bund) that it left the party all but sundered. Nevertheless, tenaciously continuing his struggle, Lenin gave his faction the name of Bolshevik (majority), and labeled the opposition group Menshevik (minority). The two wings would fight, reunite, fight again, until Lenin ultimately decided to lead his Bolshevik hard core out of the Social Democratic Party altogether.

In March 1917, Lenin was still living in exile, in Zurich, when the tsar unexpectedly was overthrown. His reaction was instantaneous. Through Swiss intermediaries, he managed to establish contact with representatives of the German government and to request their help in securing his return to Russia. Once back in Petrograd, he explained, he would organize a more decisive upheaval that would extricate Russia from the war. In Berlin, the German War Council mulled over the proposal for several weeks, then decided to gamble on it. In early April, Lenin and his political entourage were allowed to journey by train through German lines to the Finnish border. Once in Finland, Lenin continued by Russian railroad directly to Petrograd, where he was awaited by his local Bolshevik followers. Hereupon, Lenin wasted little time in proclaiming that the "bourgeois" phase of the revolution had taken place. The Russian peasantry must now set about taking over the land, he insisted, and Russian troops must wrest control of the army from their officers. The appeal evoked wide enthusiasm at a time when the Provisional Government's link with the Russian masses was growing tenuous. In July 1917, however, when Lenin sought to force the issue by organizing a coup against the Provisional Government, his timing was premature. The minister of war, Alexander Kerensky, managed to rally the capital's military garrison, and Lenin was compelled to beat a tactical retreat to Finland.

The Bolshevik leader's setback was brief. In ensuing weeks, Kerensky, whom the cabinet now appointed prime minister, found his government increasingly dependent upon the army, and the army was becoming steadily Bolshevized. By late October, the political atmosphere in the capital was volatile enough to allow Lenin to return. During his absence, under the tactical leadership of Leon Trotsky, the Bolsheviks had achieved a majority in the Petrograd Soviet. The moment appeared ripe at last for a "true" revolution. But speed was crucial. Kerensky had announced his intention to attend a forthcoming Inter-Allied conference in Paris, where he would seek approval for withdrawing Russia from the war. It would be fatal for the Bolshevik cause if peace were achieved under other, non-Bolshevik auspices. Moreover, a second All-Russian Congress of Soviets was meeting then in Petrograd. Lenin was convinced that this body commanded enough popular support to launch a complete governmental takeover. On November 7, therefore, at his order, Bolshevik soldiers and sailors stormed the Tauride Palace and arrested leading members of the Provisional Government. Two days later, a Bolshevik-controlled cabal, the Council of People's Commissars, duly proclaimed itself the new government of Russia.

Yet, even then, Bolshevik authority was less than certain. Six weeks earlier, Kerensky and the Provisional Government had set in motion plans to conduct a national election for a Constituent Assembly, and preparations were too far advanced to be canceled. Instead, the election took place as scheduled, on November 25. By the time the results were tabulated, on January 5, 1918, it became clear that, of 707 elected delegates, only 170 were Bolsheviks. The others—the majority—came exclusively from such progressivist, but nondictatorial factions as the Cadets and Socialist Revolutionaries. Alarmed by this repudiation, Lenin and his colleagues agreed that their only remaining alternative was to move preemptively. On January 18, when the Constituent Assembly's delegates finally gathered at the Tauride Palace, Bolshevik soldiers and sailors packed the galleries. Under Lenin's direction, they blocked all further proceedings. The next day, the assembly hall was given over to the Bolshevik-dominated Council of People's Commissars. Lenin's revolution was now complete.

JEWS IN THE BOLSHEVIK UPHEAVAL

The largest numbers of Russian Jews had never adopted a Bolshevik political agenda. As late as 1917, most of their breadwinners earned their marginal and precarious livelihoods essentially as petite bourgeoisie, a category that in their case included even manual workers, most of whom were cottage artisans. The Bolshevik economic program was distinctly unattractive to this minority population, as was Lenin's rejection of nationalist autonomism. Indeed, before the war, Jewish socialists by and large had opted for the Bund, or at least for the more gradualistic Menshevik branch of the Russian Social

Democratic Party. Following the original, March 1917 revolution, Simon Dubnow, the historian and Diaspora nationalist, observed in a diary entry of May 1 that "[t]he dictatorship of the proletariat is spreading like a contagious disease; following the plan of Lenin and his followers, it can only lead to violent expropriations." The evidence is compelling that Dubnow spoke for the Jewish majority.

As in Western Europe, however, the prominence of literate, urban Jews among the leadership of "communism" (the term that would increasingly be applied to the Leninist, totalitarian version of socialism) was far more evident than among the movement's rank-and-file membership. Thus, by December 1917, five of the twenty-one members of the Communist Central Committee were Jews, including the commissar for foreign affairs, the president of the Supreme Soviet, the deputy chairman of the Council of People's Commissars, the president of the Petrograd Soviet, and the deputy director of the Cheka, the political police. Never before had so many Jews served in any European cabinet. Their names, mentioned in either awe or hatred, included Leon Trotsky, Grigori Zinoviev, Mikhail Uritzki, and Grigori Sokolnikov. If Lenin himself did not "qualify" as a Jew, inasmuch as only his maternal grandfather was Jewish (a fact not known at the time), the half-Jew Lev Kamenev traditionally was added to that number.

By common recognition, Trotsky was the "star" among them, the one member who was equal in stature to Lenin himself. Born Lev Bronstein in 1879, in the Kherson province of Ukraine, he was the son of a Jewish farmer and the grandson of one of the 40,000 Jews whom Tsar Alexander I had lured to the thinly populated southern provinces by offering free land. Leon Trotsky (as we shall call him) had a difficult childhood, quarreling often with his brutal and illiterate father. As a teenager, sent off to study at an Odessa gymnasium, he was swept up almost immediately in the revolutionary fervor of his late-nineteenth-century student generation, and upon graduation he severed all ties with his family. For a while Trotsky became a narodnik, living and working among the peasants in a neighboring commune. Later, after a brief stint at the University of Odessa, he veered off into an even more progressivist group, this one somewhat closer to the Socialist Revolutionary Party. For his activities, he was arrested, tried, and given a four-year sentence in Siberia. The young man would not be broken. Upon acquiring Marxist literature from several fellow prisoners, and devouring the material by candlelight at night, he found his ideological home at last in Social Democracy.

In 1902, two years into his Siberian exile, Trotsky evaded his guards by hiding in a peasant hay cart. Upon reaching a junction of the Trans-Siberian Railroad, he succeeded in making his way to western Russia, protected by fellow Marxists from town to town. Soon afterward, in October of the same year, Trotsky turned up unannounced at the London apartment of Vladimir

Lenin. Lenin received him warmly—the young man's reputation had preceded him—and immediately appointed him to the editorial board of the Social Democratic newspaper, *Iskra*. From then on, Trotsky became an intimate of some of the leading figures of Russian Social Democracy. He also became a spellbinding orator. At the party's 1903 Brussels congress (p. 293), one of the participants described the twenty-four-year-old expatriate as "a lean, tallish man, with large fierce eyes and a large, sensual, irregular mouth, perched on the platform like a bird of prey."

It was in Brussels that the split occurred between Bolshevik "extremists" and Menshevik "gradualists." Although Trotsky refused to make a definitive commitment to either faction, he was careful not to break off his respectful relationship with Lenin. For their part, Lenin and the Bolsheviks remained continually impressed by Trotsky's socialist dedication and extraordinary personal courage. Typical was the young man's reaction to the 1905 Revolution. Although still listed as an escaped convict, he returned secretly to Russia, where he harangued the working classes to reject the tsar's October Manifesto (p. 295), and to move forthwith into an authentically social revolution. With this kind of commitment, he achieved a reputation that elevated him above factional divisions.

Indeed, Trotsky's career soon began to achieve a drama that fiction could hardly match. In November 1906, he was rearrested in Petrograd and sentenced to life imprisonment in Siberia. With other convicts, his horse-drawn prison wagon carried him off to the penal colony of Obdorsk, lying on the rim of the Polar Circle. En route, Trotsky sensed that his choice was escape or certain death. Shortly before reaching Obdorsk, therefore, he managed to bribe a local peasant with several hundred rubles he had brought with him in a secret pouch. The peasant in turn secured a native guide for Trotsky, together with a sleigh and a team of reindeer. With this equipage, the two men traveled night and day for three weeks. Freezing and starving, changing reindeer at villages en route, they finally reached the Ural Mountains. Soon afterward, an "underground railroad" of Marxists smuggled Trotsky to autonomous Finland, where he was awaited by Uri Martov and Lenin. To all who followed his career, it was plain by then that Trotsky was no ordinary man. During the ensuing years of tsarist counterrevolution, living in exile in Vienna, where he earned a modest salary editing the SD journal *Pravda*, Trotsky became an awe-inspiring figure among socialist leaders in Central and Western Europe. His speeches (in Russian, German, and French) were widely attended, and his essays were reprinted in the major European socialist journals.

Trotsky was in Vienna with his wife, son, and daughter when the war began. To avoid internment as a Russian national, he and his family immediately decamped to neutral Zurich. It was an astute choice. The heartland of revolutionary exiles, Zurich also was the temporary home of Lenin, Karl Radek, and Nicholas Bukharin. It was thus in Zurich that Trotsky took a leading role in denouncing the "treason" of European socialist parties for supporting their countries' war efforts. In 1915, he helped organize an international conference of socialist purists in the village of Zimmerwald, where the celebrated Zimmerwald Manifesto of denunciation was formulated. But a year later, venturing a return visit to Paris in the hope of winning support for his antiwar agitation, Trotsky was arrested for incitement and hustled with his wife and two children across the frontier to Spain. In January 1917, the Spanish authorities, for their part, put the family on a ship bound for the United States. At last, in New York, the four expatriates seemingly reached a secure haven. They were greeted enthusiastically by the local colony of Russian socialist émigrés, which settled them in a Bronx tenement and appointed Trotsky editor of their journal, *Novy mir.*

Ironically, Trotsky's sojourn in the United States lasted a mere two months. When news arrived of the March 1917 revolution, he was no less desperate than Lenin in Switzerland to return home to guide events. Again, his fellow expatriates came to the rescue, purchasing steamship tickets for him and his family, and sending them off to Europe. Following three additional weeks of internment in Nova Scotia, Trotsky eventually continued on, arriving in Russia in mid-May. In Petrograd, a large crowd waited at the Finland Station to hoist him on its shoulders. Within days, he and Lenin reached agreement to collaborate in the effort to overthrow the Provisional Government. Thus, in July, when Lenin went into tactical hiding in Finland after his failed coup attempt, it was Trotsky who remained behind as caretaker of the Bolshevik cause. Although he himself suffered yet another imprisonment, he was released in September. By then, Prime Minister Kerensky needed the Petrograd Soviet's help in quelling a threatened right-wing coup, led by General Lavr Kornilov. Trotsky ensured that support. Indeed, it was his courage and dynamism alone that shifted the balance against the Kornilov danger. By October, when Lenin felt safe enough to return from his Finnish sanctuary, the ground was well laid for the ensuing Bolshevik takeover.

By then, too, leadership of the emerging Soviet regime had devolved into a de facto partnership between Lenin and Trotsky. In April 1918, soon after the Brest-Litovsk Treaty had disengaged the nation from the European conflict, the Communist Central Committee appointed Trotsky commissar for war and president of the Supreme War Council. No role could have been more vital, not even Lenin's as chairman of the Central Committee. Russia was convulsed by a widening civil conflict between the Communists and their political enemies, and a new Red Army had to be created without delay. To meet that challenge, Trotsky, a transplanted Jewish civilian, moved with a ruthless vigor more characteristic of an experienced military officer. Rejecting all notions of Communist egalitarianism, he insisted at the outset upon a conventional command structure and conventional military discipline, and did not hesitate even to recruit some 30,000 experienced former tsarist officers—although he appointed political "commissars" to monitor their loyalty.

Possibly the most effective of Trotsky's weapons, however, was his own well-tested personal charisma. He made a point of appearing at one military front after another, often standing on an armored car in the midst of battle, exhorting, challenging, rallying his troops. In March 1920, as the tide of war shifted in favor of the Communists, the Central Committee proclaimed Trotsky "Father of Victory" and awarded him its first Order of the Red Banner. By then, he and Lenin were functioning as alter egos, each often making key policy decisions in the absence of the other.

It was also in this period of civil war that other Jews in large numbers gravitated to the Communist regime, particularly during the widespread Petliurist and Denikin massacres, when sheer physical survival obliged them to depend upon the protection of the Red Army. The record of that army was itself not unblemished. In 1920, the Jewish writer Isaac Babel described occasional anti-Jewish atrocities carried out by Red Cossack units. Yet these episodes were not typical, for Lenin had issued strict orders for the Red Army to protect Jews from counterrevolutionary terror. In their gratitude, moreover, young Jews in large numbers then volunteered for military service. They also began to appear at all echelons of the Soviet bureaucracy. Indeed, beyond their eminence in the Communist Central Committee, Jews during the early 1920s comprised between 15 and 20 percent of the delegates elected to party congresses. Among the 246 figures who occupied the first and secondary tiers of Communist leadership during the early years of the Soviet regime, 41 were Jews. In the Communist bureaucracy, Jews were represented even more extensively as technocrats—as mid-level administrators, publicists, researchers, translators, and clerks. It was a presence in the Soviet apparatus that eventually would produce dire consequences for this minority people, both in Russia itself and in the West.

THE TRAUMA OF COMMUNIZATION

By the spring of 1921, as the civil wars and the Russo-Polish War (p. 412) guttered out, the Soviet nation lay in a state of economic prostration. Vast quantities of its agricultural and industrial infrastructure had been carved away or demolished. Diplomatic isolation, the loss of Western markets and resources, compounded the fragility of the new Communist utopia. So did the process of economic collectivization. Even before the government took title to private landholdings, peasants had set about a rule-of-thumb distribution among themselves. If the process reflected a certain elementary justice, it did little in the first years to restore the prewar efficiency of Russian agriculture. Neither did Lenin's decision to nationalize the country's industry and commerce. Any enterprise with more than ten workers was confiscated by the state. All banks were nationalized and private savings were sequestered.

The impact of these decrees all but ensured Russia's economic collapse. The nation's industrial output in 1921 was one-sixth that of 1913. Fuel was virtually exhausted. With the urban population starving, the government in its desperation ordered farmers to turn over their agricultural "surpluses" to official collection stations. Far from complying, the peasantry burned their crops and slaughtered their livestock. Soon primitive barter took the place of monetary exchange. In 1920–21 alone, some 3 million people died of famine or hunger-induced diseases. By late 1921, Trotsky, for one, was enough of a realist to understand that a compromise was in order, and he gradually won Lenin over to his view. At their initiative, the Central Committee then scrapped the program of "War Communism" and in its place announced a "New Economic Policy" that would reinstate private trading, modest individual farm holdings, and a measure of private property and individual enterprise in the urban economy. A limited salary-and-income differential also was revived to encourage productivity in factories and commercial enterprises. Very slowly, then, in response to these emerging rectifications, the worst of the human ordeal began to ease.

During these grim early postwar years of Communist rule, the circumstances of the Jews were fully as parlous as those of the nation at large. Under the decrees of War Communism, it was specifically the bourgeoisie, the "speculators," who were stripped of their possessions. Even the smallest shops were nationalized. As a result, between 1918 and 1921, approximately 80 percent of the Jewish population of the former Pale was left hovering at the edge of starvation. Had it not been for Lenin's strategic retreat to the NEP—the New Economic Policy—the largest majority of these people almost certainly would have perished. As it was, the Jews themselves often were stigmatized as "NEP-men" and profiteers, and thus became renewed targets of antisemitism. Their economic breathing space in any case was short-lived. The proliferation of industrial cooperatives virtually doomed any possibility for the revival of small businesses. By 1923, the government census listed some 250,000 Jews as out of work. A rescue program for these "half-beggars" was urgently needed.

Since 1915, the Joint—the American Jewish Joint Distribution Committee—had been operating a chain of soup kitchens and clinics in the traumatized Pale of Settlement regions. Initially, the relief program was directed almost exclusively to war victims. But after the war, the Joint was obliged to widen its efforts to include the hundreds of thousands of Jews whom communism had rendered economically "redundant." By late 1921, moreover, it was becoming evident that charity alone could not sustain this population, and that a longer-term solution was needed. In fact, one such alternative was proposed by the Joint itself. It was the inspiration of Dr. Joseph Rosen, a Russian-born agronomist who had returned from the United States after the war to help direct Joint activities throughout Eastern Europe. In discussions with Soviet officials, Rosen noted that 7 million acres in the southern Ukraine and the Crimean peninsula had recently been confiscated from their aristocratic and clerical owners. Would this land not be ideal for the transplantation of large numbers of economically ruined Jewish small businessmen? If Moscow agreed, Rosen suggested, the Joint might help fund the project.

The Soviet leadership was interested, although less for reasons of humanitarianism than for access to hard currency. The scheme was especially appealing to Mikhail Kalinin, the Soviet president. Possessing numerous Jewish friends, and sentient to the importance of Jewish public opinion abroad, Kalinin in 1923 helped establish the Society to Settle Working Jews on Land in the USSR, to be known by its Russian acronym, OZET. Now much would depend on the extent of American-Jewish support. In fact, with Rosen serving as liaison between the Russians and the Americans, prominent board members of the Joint reacted well to the proposal. Among them, Louis Marshall, Otto Warburg, Herbert Lehman, and other Jewish patriarchs discerned social and "moral" value in the agricultural resettlement of déclassé Russian Jews, as they had, years earlier, in supporting the Am Olam project (p. 213). Additionally, if Rosen's project worked, it would provide a non-Zionist alternative to Jewish marginality, an objective the American-Jewish establishment shared with the Soviet government.

After extended negotiations, therefore, Moscow in 1924 agreed finally to set aside some 1 million acres in the Crimea and in Ukraine's Kherson and Dniepropetrovsk districts. In each of these regions, as many as thirty-six farm colonies could be established. For its part, the Joint would underwrite the venture financially, through a subsidiary organization to be known as Agro-Joint. Agro-Joint's fund-raising target was set at $10 million over ten years. Remarkably, over the ensuing decade, the goal was met, even exceeded. By 1934, some $14 million had been subscribed, and 217 Agro-Joint colonies were supporting fully 175,000 Jewish colonists, a number that exceeded the entire Jewish agricultural population of Palestine. It was the project's high point.

And then, in ensuing years, the Jews' demographic on the soil fell off sharply—to 110,000 by 1938, and the numbers of Jewish farmers would continue to decline. Indeed, in 1938, Agro-Joint officially ceased its operations in the Soviet Union. Several factors accounted for the implosion of this once promising experiment. One was the government's massive program of agricultural collectivization, which reversed its original policy of allowing private or even cooperative land ownership. Still another influence was the endemic antisemitism of the surrounding Ukrainian peasantry, who continued to find ways of harassing and intimidating the Jewish "islands" in their own agricultural hinterland. More important yet was Joseph Stalin's sequence of five-year industrialization programs (p. 337), and the accompanying inducements these offered for city life. Perennial town-dwellers, the Jews were unable to resist these attractions. Additionally, as far back as the late 1920s, even as it encouraged the Agro-Joint project, the government was simultaneously beginning to explore a parallel role for Jewish farmers. This one, however, was rather more strategic than economic.

Soviet officials were concerned by the infiltration of Chinese and Japanese into a distant, Far Eastern region lying at the confluence of the Biro and Bidzhan rivers. Extending across some 14,000 square miles, the territory was meagerly inhabited by less than 200,000 Koreans, Kazakhs, and a few primitive Tungus tribesmen. From Moscow's viewpoint, it would have been strategically useful if this region could be transformed into a buffer enclave, in the event of a future clash with the Japanese. Yet the territory's climate was exceptionally harsh, and few Russians were interested in settling there. Here it was that the government conceived the notion of encouraging a mass immigration of Jews to Biro-Bidzhan by offering them full communal autonomy and the promise of eventual nationality status. Thus, in May 1934, Soviet President Mikhail Kalinin proclaimed Biro-Bidzhan an *oblast,* an autonomous (Jewish) region, and promised that, "as soon as Biro-Bidzhan encompasses one hundred thousand Jews, it will be transformed into a full-fledged Soviet Jewish Republic, on an equal basis with the Soviet Union's other national republics."

Initially, the scheme evoked its widest interest among Jews abroad. For Jewish leftists in the West, exposed to harsh Depression-era antisemitism, the Biro-Bidzhan project seemed an intriguing opportunity to achieve an authentically "national" life on Diaspora territory. But among Soviet Jews themselves, the project failed to evoke enthusiasm. In 1928, the first group of Jewish volunteers did not exceed 654 immigrants. Over the next five years, their numbers in Biro-Bidzhan were augmented by a mere 6,000 to 8,000 annually. At its apogee, in 1934, the Jewish population did not exceed 36,000. The settlers enjoyed significant communal and cultural freedom, to be sure. They established their own Yiddish-language schools, newspapers, and other autonomous institutions. The streets in Biro-Bidzhan were named after Mendele Mocher S'forim, Sholem Aleichem, Peretz Smolenskin, and other Jewish folk icons. But cultural-communal autonomy was meager consolation for grim physical circumstances. Settlers were obliged to build their own homes, usually from materials in the surrounding forests. They were not provided with adequate construction machinery. Agricultural machinery also was lacking, and horses and cattle had to be transported from the west—only to die by the hundreds of local diseases. Deluged by heavy rains, the region also swarmed with insects. By 1939, barely 15,000 Jews remained on. Biro-Bidzhan's role in Jewish history survives essentially as a poignant footnote.

The Joys of Communist Utopianism

In 1917, the great majority of Russian Jews had reacted to the Bolshevik Revolution with grave reserve, even dismay. Alexander Kerensky recalled:

> [It is true that] many of the Bolshevik chiefs are Jews, unfortunately so for the Jewish people. But, on the other hand, ninety-nine percent of the Russian Jews are against the Bolsheviks, and during the whole of the [revolutionary period] the Jewish intellectuals and the Jewish masses . . . were . . . faithful to the [democratic] revolution.

None more so than the Bundists. Once the Bolsheviks cemented their grip on the Russian state, the Bund split, with its smaller, more radical wing gradually blending into the Communist Party, but its larger constituency still maintaining a "parochialist" loyalty to the Jewish people. Acutely aware of this fact, the Soviet government for its part appeared willing at first to reach a certain accommodation with Jewish and other ethnic "progressives." One of its first public documents was the Declaration of Rights of the Nations of Russia, signed by Lenin and by Commissar for Nationalities Joseph Stalin. Two of the declaration's key paragraphs stated that the government would assure "freedom of development" for all national minorities and ethnic groups. To that end, Stalin in January 1918 established the Commissariat for Jewish National Affairs, with the task of "bridging the gap" between the government and the Jewish "masses" (i.e., the Bund). The Commissariat in turn established the Yevsektsya, a special Jewish department, to fulfill this essentially propagandistic role.

The idea was the brainchild of the Jewish Commissariat's first director, Semyon Dimanshtein. Originally an ordained rabbi, Dimanshtein had been drawn into Social Democratic circles while still a comparatively young man. Arrested in 1906, he escaped, was rearrested, and eventually served five years in Siberian exile before the Revolution of March 1917 set him free. Throughout his ensuing career, as director of the Commissariat, Dimanshtein won respect among the Jewish leadership as a patient and reasonable man. Yet no one doubted that his central purpose was to employ the Yevsektsya as an instrument for dissolving all political competitors among Russian Jewry. Communism would not tolerate pluralism. Indeed, the largest numbers of the

Yevsektsya's personnel were themselves former Bundists, and they hurled themselves into a proselytization campaign with all the fanaticism of the recently converted.

Thus, it was they who orchestrated the early Jewish relocation program in the Ukrainian and Crimean farm colonies, who liquidated the Jewish kehillot, closed down all Zionist offices, all Hebrew schools and Hebrew publications. The Habimah, recently established in Moscow as an avant-garde Hebrew-language theater, managed to stage its brilliant productions through the early 1920s, but in 1926 its funds were cut off, forcing its staff to decamp to Palestine. Between sixty-five and seventy synagogues and seminaries were closed, and their rabbis were denied permission even to conduct private services. Indeed, Jewish rituals of any kind were banned, including the traditional rite of circumcision and kosher slaughter. It was only among the venerable "Mountain Jews" of the distant Caucasus communities that a limited resistance was maintained against this escalating anti-Judaism, anti-Hebrew campaign. Otherwise, by the end of the 1920s, the Communists had succeeded in eliminating all Jewish political parties and cultural movements, in suppressing Zionism and the Hebrew language, in driving Jewish worship underground, and thereby in gaining a monopoly of political and communal power on the "Jewish street."

Yet the question remained: Could destruction of the traditional Jewish community be followed by "amalgamation" of the Jews into the Russian population at large? The tsars had engaged in this effort for a century and a half, and had not succeeded. Or should a separate Jewish subculture at long last be acknowledged and tolerated, on condition that it base itself on secularism and Communist internationalism? The answer seemed to be the latter. The Declaration of Rights of the Nations of Russia had promised "freedom of development" for all national minorities and ethnic groups. In prerevolutionary years, to be sure, Lenin had ridiculed the concept of the Jews as a nationality (p. 279), and had warned that "Jewish national culture" was the slogan of the rabbis and the bourgeoisie, of "our enemies." But after the revolution, he and other Soviet leaders appeared increasingly willing to experiment with an alternate method of winning over Soviet Russia's diversity of peoples. This was to allow "the flowering of the nationality cultures." The technique was to invest in the nationalities' native-language schools, theaters, newspapers, and other ethnic institutions, so long as these remained under Communist direction and guidance. In 1920, Stalin even offered a famous new definition of proletarian culture as "national in form, socialist in content."

By no coincidence, the genuflection to cultural autonomy was almost a mirror image of the provisions recently incorporated into the Paris Peace Conference's Minorities Treaties (pp. 400–401). It reflected Moscow's effort to maintain the goodwill of "progressive" elements abroad, no less than in the

Soviet Union itself. But the experiment would remain tightly controlled. In the case of the Jews, its linguistic application would apply exclusively to Yiddish, "the language of Jewish proletarians," and would be used exclusively for the development of a new, secular, Communist society. Thus, wherever Jews lived in compact communities, they would be allowed to employ Yiddish in all public and commercial documents, in their own cultural and communal activities, including most specifically their own school systems. Throughout the 1920s, Moscow actually provided generous subsidies to Yiddish cultural endeavors. By 1927, it was underwriting publication of some 300 Yiddish books annually, and no fewer than 50 Yiddish newspapers. The number increased to 431 by 1930. In 1924, the government subsidized 21 Yiddish newspapers, and by 1927 at least 50. The number of secular Yiddish schools also grew dramatically in the 1920s, from 366 in 1923–24 to 1,100 in 1929–30. In that same period, student enrollment in Yiddish-language schools climbed from 54,000 to 130,000—representing almost half the school-age Jewish children still living in the former Pale.

With government subsidies, numerous eminent Yiddish literary figures flourished in this period, as well, among them David Bergelson, Peretz Markish, and Dov Nister, members of the so-called Kiev Group. Although the Jewish Commissariat ensured that these authors expressed themselves within general Communist guidelines, ideological control at first was not oppressive, and leeway existed for some quite distinguished prose, poetry, and literary criticism. The star of the brief history of Soviet Yiddish culture was the Moscow Yiddish Theater, which won wide renown for producing numerous Yiddish classics, among them works adapted from the writings of Sholem Aleichem, Yehuda Leib Peretz, and Mendele Mocher S'forim. Marc Chagall designed a number of the theater's sets and several dazzling murals. The government lavished considerable support on this remarkable institution, nurturing it into one of the preeminent theaters in the world, with its own school of dramatic art, and over twenty "satellite" theaters performing throughout the Soviet Union.

By the early 1930s, however, the much-touted Yiddish cultural revival began to fade. The atrophy reflected a wider phenomenon that was transforming the country at large. In 1927, the Communist leadership reached a consensus that the nation's economy was trapped in a series of vicious circles. Still enmeshed in the NEP version of quasi-capitalism, the Soviet Union fully a decade after the revolution was hardly closer to socialism than before 1917. Apparently a firm, coherent policy was needed to feed the cities, raise industrial output, and build a widely based proletarian class that would guarantee the new society. To achieve these multiple purposes, the new Communist leader, Joseph Stalin, who succeeded Lenin upon the latter's death in 1924 (p. 340), launched the Soviet regime on a massive program of forced industrialization and agricultural collectivization. Over a period of more than a decade, Stalin whipped and drove his people into the single most protracted economic transformation ever endured by a single nation in the history of modern Europe. The human costs were notoriously grim. In agriculture, as early as 1930, some 8 million independent peasants and their families had been forcibly hounded into kolkhozes, giant collective farms, an ordeal that took perhaps 5 million lives.

For several years, in its reluctance to forfeit Agro-Joint money, the Yevsekt-sya leadership managed to protect the Jewish colonies from the collectiv-ization program. But Stalin was not the man to tolerate exemptions. The government's control over the Agro-Joint program soon became tighter, with the imposition of heavy taxes, accelerated delivery schedules, confiscation of farm equipment, and interdiction of "bourgeois ideology" in the colo-nies' schools. Year by year, too, Joint personnel were forced out of the Agro-Joint administration. By the late 1930s, the great experiment of Soviet-Jewish land settlement was approaching its end. As late as 1939, some 95,000 Jews remained on the land, but most of these had been absorbed into the kolkhozes.

At the same time, Stalin pushed ahead with his relentless program of forced industrialization. Under the First Five-Year Plan, scheduled to run from 1928 to 1933, it was his objective to massively increase Soviet heavy industry and the nation's electrification and transportation infrastructure. To a remarkable degree, he succeeded. By 1933, despite innumerable bottlenecks and shortages, and incredible human suffering, Soviet heavy industry had increased by possibly 300 percent. And with the completion of the Second Five-Year Plan in 1938, Russia by some estimates had replaced Britain in third place as a major industrial power, and ranked only behind the United States and Germany in overall industrial production. It was an achievement, in turn, that had required unprecedented exertions of labor reeducation. To that end, Russians by the millions, driven off the soil by agricultural collec-tivization, streamed into urban centers to be trained as workers in factories, on hydroelectric dams and construction projects, and as transportation personnel.

In this great migration to the cities, Jews shared in even greater proportions than non-Jews. The process of their urbanization had been given its initial, enforced momentum as far back as the May Laws of the 1880s. Now, ironi-cally, a half-century later, the direction of the migration was reversed, and channeled from the former Pale of Settlement areas specifically to the Soviet interior. In 1920, barely one-quarter of the state's remaining Jewish popula-tion of 2.75 million lived in urban areas. By 1939, with their numbers approaching 3 million, approximately 40 percent of Soviet Jewry had left the Soviet provinces of the former Pale of Settlement area altogether and resettled in the cities of the Russian and Belorussian republics. At first, to be sure, there was little in the disintegration of their former geographical ghetto to set the Jews to dancing in the streets. The immediate impact of "crash" industrialization was even more traumatic for them than for non-Jews, in view of the government's determination to liquidate déclassé, "non-productive" categories. Displaced, vocationally redundant, tens of thousands of transplanted Pale migrants suffered intensely as planning commissions grappled with the challenge of retraining and reassigning them.

Within a comparatively short period, however, the largest numbers of these Jewish former merchants and handicraftsmen were integrated into the immense industrialization program. In the factories of Dniepopetrovsk alone, 10,000 young Jews labored to construct fabricated sections for the giant hydroelectric dam. The industrial cities of Magnitogorsk and Kukznetskstroi were built under the supervision of Jewish engineers and technicians, while other thousands of Jewish workers could be found in the plants and on the girders. By 1930, only two years after the launching of the First Five-Year Plan, more Jews were employed in the metal industries than in the traditional Jewish needle and leather trades. For the first time, too, a majority of Jewish manual workers had become authentic proletarians, working with machines in factories and mines. Altogether, between 1926 and 1938, the number of Jewish wage-earners in the Soviet Union nearly tripled, rising to over 1.1 million.

Yet within the same years, approximately one-third of this vocationally transformed group, some 364,000, had become white-collar employees. Jewish literacy and familiarity with urban living played a key role. But so, even more, did a near-total emancipation from the anti-Jewish restrictions of the tsarist era. From the early 1920s, Jews in unprecedented numbers rushed to enter the Soviet Union's proliferating network of gymnasia, universities, and polytechnical institutions. Thus, by 1934, Jews comprised 18 percent of all students in Soviet higher education. With their new degrees, they were free to move into research institutes, hospital staffs, editorial boards, university faculties, and the officer ranks of the Soviet military corps.

The bonanza of upward mobility accelerated still another trend within the Jewish population. It was immersion in Russian culture. In 1926, only a quarter of the nation's Jews listed Russian as their native language. By the eve of World War II, more than half did so. As late as 1927, approximately 160,000 Jewish children still were receiving their instruction in Yiddish-language schools. By 1940, the figure was 80,000—barely one-fifth of the Jewish student population. Neither students nor parents complained. For them, the Russian language was the passport to vocational upward mobility, and none of Russia's minorities was more ardent to master it than the Jews. Thus, by the mid-1930s, official repression of Jewish political, religious, and communal institutions was becoming gratuitous. Geographic, vocational, and linguistic integration was "amalgamating" Jews far more effectively than any of the tsars could have anticipated (or than Jewish grandparents would have wished). By 1937, in the Soviet Union's Russian, Belorussian, and Ukrainian federal republics, nearly a third of all Jewish marriages were with non-Jews, an unimaginable phenomenon in earlier decades.

Equally unimaginable were the Jewish-born literary giants who found spiritual inspiration in Russian history and culture. Osip Mandelshtam and Boris Pasternak (both of them converts to Orthodox Christianity) achieved national renown as the Soviet Union's most respected literary figures. Beyond the shrinking Yiddish cultural firmament, one of the few Jewish writers in the Russian language who fearlessly addressed the impact of revolutionary upheaval on Jewish life was Isaac Babel (p. 342). Odessa-born, the product of a Yiddish-speaking home, Babel served as a volunteer in General Semyon Budennyi's Red cavalry during the wars of 1918–20. His terse, surgically accurate description of his experiences, in his *Red Cavalry* stories (p. 342), remains among the underappreciated jewels of twentieth-century Russian literature. And so, no less, do his accounts of Russian-Jewish daily life in Soviet Russia. His portrayal of the Jews' criminal underworld are as authentic as his depiction of Soviet triumphs and failures, Soviet idealism and corruption. Well into the early 1930s, a number of Babel's most unsparingly "objective" short stories managed to achieve publication both within and outside the Soviet Union.

STALINISM AND THE FATE OF "NATIONAL IN FORM"

In the aftermath of the civil war, once the Communists established control over the full breadth of their nation, it was anticipated that antisemitism as a relic of the tsarist era would disappear. It did, as official policy. But it survived in popular sentiment and expression. The sheer visibility of Jews in the early Soviet regime helped keep the animus alive. During the years of the New Economic Policy, the peasantry charged that communism had made them dependent on "the Jewish NEP men." Throughout the grim, sacrificial ordeal of the First Five-Year Plan, the competition of Jews in the new industrial economy often led to serious harassment of Jews in factories, in schools, even in universities. In the 1920s and early 1930s, the government gave serious attention to this painful anomaly. Thus, in a 1931 interview with a reporter for the Jewish Telegraphic Agency, Stalin forthrightly condemned antisemitism as a "survival of the barbarous practices of the [tsarist] . . . period. . . . [It is] profoundly hostile to the Soviet way of life." As late as 1936, this statement was reprinted in *Pravda*.

Over the years, Stalin maintained close relations with Jews, both politically and personally. His daughter-in-law, the wife of his oldest son, Yakov, was a Jew. His daughter Svetlana was briefly married to a Jew, and consequently their children—Stalin's grandchildren—were half-Jews. Yet Svetlana recalled that her father "never liked Jews." Throughout the first decade and a half of the Soviet regime, Stalin refrained from expressing that animus. Nevertheless, the severe restrictions imposed on Jewish culture, as well as on individual Jews during the 1930s, suggested that the party chairman nurtured a private anti-semitic paranoia even within his broader-ranging terror campaign against his political rivals.

That campaign began while Lenin was still alive. In the immediate aftermath of the civil war, in 1921, Leon Trotsky was at the apogee of his power and prestige. Doubtless he was less than fully occupied, inasmuch as the commissariat of war no longer functioned as the hub of government. Nevertheless, he still managed to throw himself into the new economic and social problems of the state, and to lead numerous commissions dealing with these issues. He also continued to be ranked with Lenin himself as Soviet Russia's principal intellectual guide and authority on Marxism. Yet, by the same token, it was also Trotsky's unique stature that was beginning to evoke jealousy. As the Central Committee's general secretary, Joseph Stalin made no secret of his personal resentment. In turn, well aware of this festering envy and political ruthlessness, Lenin sought to warn his colleagues against Stalin. But Lenin was felled by a stroke in 1922 and left incapacitated. In January 1923, unable to speak, he dispatched a brief memo to the committee members, urging them to "remove Stalin" from his office. He was too late. Over the ensuing year, Lenin suffered three additional strokes, and these left him completely paralyzed.

Trotsky, meanwhile, had maintained close relations with a number of other powerful members of the Central Committee, among them Grigori Zinoviev and Lev Kamenev, both of whom ostensibly shared Trotsky's militant socialist idealism. With these two men, Trotsky sought belatedly to rebuild his strength against Stalin's relentless bureaucratic entrenchment. In January 1924, however, the Thirteenth Congress of the Communist Party gathered in Moscow, and at this conclave it became evident that Kamenev and Zinoviev had been induced to turn against Trotsky. Together with Nicholai Bukharin, another prominent member of the Central Committee, the new "triumvirate of expediency" denounced Trotsky for "petit bourgeois deviation from Leninism." The party congress immediately endorsed the scathing condemnation. By then Lenin had died, and Trotsky's key protector was gone. For the while, he was allowed to remain in the Council of People's Commissars, but soon his position became untenable. Later in 1924, he saw the War Commissariat slip from his hands, and when the Council of Commissars formally demanded his resignation, he acquiesced without formal protest.

Although in ensuing months Trotsky continued to serve as chairman of several technical commissions, his power clearly was gone. Stalin had little difficulty in besmirching his reputation, playing upon the slogan "socialism in one country," as if there were important ideological issues between the two men. Moreover, in this final purgation of his rival, Stalin shrewdly exploited Russia's venerable wellspring of antisemitism as he set about courting right-ist-nationalist elements within the party. Few of communism's senior Jewish figures, whether Trotsky, Sokolnikov, Radek, or even Kamenev or Zinoviev until their recent, expedient defection, had been allied with the Stalin camp. Rather, those Jewish Communists who hung on tended to be older, Trotsky-style internationalists—and Stalin exploited the fact. In November 1926, packing the Fifteenth Party Congress with his own people, the general secretary venomously denounced Trotsky as a "traitor to Leninism." As Trotsky sought to defend himself, he was shouted down as "a deviationist," "a traitor," "a Jew." The congress then expelled Trotsky from the party on the grounds of "counterrevolutionary insurrectionism." Hundreds of other Jewish veterans of the revolution also were expelled (one of these, Adolf Joffe, committed suicide). In January 1927, Trotsky, his wife, son, and daughter were deported to Alma-Ata, in Soviet Asia, near the Chinese frontier. At first, they were decently housed in a local inn, permitted their own library, even granted a modest income. In late 1928, however, Trotsky's mail suddenly was cut off. The following January, he and his family were transported to Odessa. There Trotsky was escorted onto a ship bound for Istanbul, while his wife and son for the while remained behind (his daughter had since died).

Even then, Stalin had not revealed the full extent of his vindictiveness. His expulsion of "counterrevolutionaries" was merely a prelude to a wider and more brutal series of public purges. In December 1934, the assassination of Sergei Kirov, one of Stalin's closest associates, became the pretext for the arrest of some one hundred alleged "traitors" of the leftist opposition. The men were tried, convicted, and shot. Stalin's campaign against his suspected political opponents, active or potential, would continue for three and a half additional years, vastly widening in scope into an epic trauma of mass arrests, imprisonments, and executions. Among the victims were perhaps 80 percent of all the original Bolshevik stalwarts who had come to power with Lenin and Trotsky. By mid-1938, finally, Stalin was satisfied that his control of the party and government was unchallengeable.

Yet, for Soviet Jewry, the gravest shock of the terror campaign was less its sinister byzantinism than its undertone of Great Russian chauvinism and antisemitism. No one could miss the implications when Stalin's show trials achieved an apotheosis of virulence in their prosecution of Jewish defendants, among them Zinoviev, Kamenev, Radek, as well as the exiled Trotsky. It was general knowledge that the proportion of Jews among the Bolshevik Old Guard, those now slated for eradication, was much larger than in the party as a whole. On occasion, Stalin himself casually reminded the country's news media that Zinoviev's and Kamenev's original names were Radomyslski and Rozenfeld. Treason, espionage, and other heinous crimes were repeatedly and publicly identified with these veteran Jewish Bolsheviks. Following their convictions, the nation was artfully reassured that the Soviet Union had been cleansed, almost in the nick of time, of the poison of "cosmopolitanism."

It was in this same period of Stalinist repression that the texture of Jewish "ethnic" life was shattered irrevocably. Within the All-Union Association of Proletarian Writers, Yiddish-language sessions were subjected to harsh new controls and censorship. In 1934, the concept of "socialist realism" became official doctrine when Andrei Zhdanov emerged as the party's new authority on cultural affairs (after World War II he would lead the campaign against "rootless cosmopolitanism"). Several authors ventured to express their reservations about the new trend, among them the Yiddish writers David Bergelson, David Hofshtein, and Peretz Markish, and even converts like Boris Pasternak and Osip Mandelshtam. Courageously denouncing Stalin as the "peasant-slayer from the Caucasus," with "fingers fat as worms" and a "cockroach mustache," Mandelshtam was arrested in May 1934 and in 1938 was exiled beyond the Urals. He failed in a suicide attempt but died later in the Gulag Archipelago. Isaac Babel also would fall victim to the "counterrevolutionary" purge. His fate probably was sealed by the unflattering references in his *Red Cavalry* stories to Generals Budennyi, Timoshenko, and Voroshilov—all of them old cronies of Stalin. Babel was arrested in 1939 and a year later sentenced to life imprisonment. He died in an unknown place in 1941.

These men were joined by other, more forthrightly Jewish figures. By 1938, either executed or left to die in prison, were Semyon Dimanshtein, the former guiding spirit of the Yevsektsya, together with other dutiful Soviet *apparatchiki* who had interacted extensively with the Jewish world. In the remaining Yiddish-language schools, the teaching curriculum was drained of any hint of Jewish content. All institutions relating to Jewish culture were closed down, including the world-renowned *Yevreiskaya starina (Jewish Antiquities)*, the journal of the Jewish Historical Society, founded by Simon Dubnow. Deprived of spokesmen, of semiautonomous agencies, newspapers, publications, or schools, and with almost two-fifths of the nation's Jews dispersed outside the former Pale, Jewish group cohesion in the Soviet Union was becoming more fragile with every passing year.

It was at the beginning of the third decade of Soviet rule, moreover, in

August 1939, that Jewish group morale was given a particularly cruel blow by the Nazi-Soviet Pact. Portents of that treaty appeared as early as the previous April, when *Izvestiia* suddenly discontinued publishing the Paris dispatches of its most renowned political reporter, Ilya Ehrenberg, and when Foreign Minister Maxim Litvinov, also a Jew, was replaced in office by Vyacheslav Molotov, a "pure" Russian. These steps manifestly were taken to clear the atmosphere for an understanding with Hitler, whose power Stalin greatly feared. When the understanding reached its Nazi-Soviet Treaty stage on August 23, 1939, its most ominous feature was not the two nations' mutual commitment to "non-aggression," but the "secret" codicil by which they agreed to divide Poland between them, and to assure Russia its former "primacy of interest" in the Baltic republics. From then on, until Hitler's actual invasion of the Soviet Union on June 21, 1941, the Kremlin found it expedient to ban the publication of any further articles on the persecution of Jews in the Third Reich.

For Stalin, in any case, the Nazi totalitarianism of Adolf Hitler was hardly more to be feared than the kind of Marxist-Leninist idealism represented by Leon Trotsky. No one grasped the fact better than Trotsky himself. On December 28, 1938, preparing to depart Norway, one of several countries that had briefly extended and then withdrawn sanctuary, Trotsky was seized by a premonitory vision. "[Stalin] wishes to strike not at the ideas of his opponent," he noted in his diary, "but at his skull, at his very life force." On August 20, 1940, that fate was confirmed at Trotsky's latest refuge, in Coyoacán, Mexico, when a Stalinist agent who had managed to work his way into his confidence suddenly plunged an ax into Trotsky's brain. In later years, the Jews of the Soviet Union, whom Trotsky had abandoned long before departing the land of his birth, would experience the wider consequences of Joseph Stalin's unrequited paranoia and malevolence.

The Balfour Declaration and
the Jewish National Home

PALESTINE JEWRY AND THE GREAT WAR

For all its impressive economic progress, the Yishuv, the Jewish settlement in the Holy Land, comprising some 85,000 souls, remained the most vulnerable component in the Zionist movement after the outbreak of World War I. Since the nineteenth century, Palestine Jewry had learned to rely principally upon the European consuls to ensure their physical security. But with the Ottoman Empire's entrance into the war in November 1914, that assurance was gone. The following month, Beha-a-Din, the aged and irascible Turkish governor of Jaffa, ordered the immediate expulsion of the 6,000 Russian Jews living in his port city. Within forty-eight hours, the police rounded up their first 700 deportees, loaded them onto an Italian steamer, and shipped them off to Alexandria. Aghast at this development, Jews elsewhere in Palestine hurriedly began packing for departure. Within a single month, 7,000 of them had fled the country. The rest—the majority—unable to pull up stakes at short notice, decided to apply for Ottoman citizenship as their only alternative to disaster. By the end of 1914, approximately 12,000 did. The number doubled in the ensuing year. Gradually, the threat of large-scale expulsion declined.

Other dangers remained. Before the war, it had been the tradition for Christians and Jews to buy exemption from Ottoman military service by paying special taxes. That option was canceled now. The best non-Moslems could hope for, as members of an educated elite, was privileged "labor." By the winter of 1915, however, labor service had become all but penal. Young men and old were drafted, consigned to verminous barracks, put on near-starvation rations, and set to work paving roads or quarrying stone. Remarkably, even treatment this punitive failed to discourage the Zionist leadership from asserting their loyalty. David Ben-Gurion, a future prime minister of Israel, was among those who petitioned Turkish authorities for a Jewish militia to share in the defense of the country. General Ahmed Djemal Pasha, commander of the Ottoman Fourth Army and military governor of Palestine, favored the idea. He was dissuaded from accepting it only at the last moment by Beha-a-Din. The Jaffa governor was irredeemably hostile to the Zionists. Nevertheless, other young Jews volunteered for regular army service. A few were accepted, among them Moshe Shertok and Dov Hoz, both later to become prominent figures in Palestine Jewry.

The ambivalence of Ottoman policy toward the Zionists was soon resolved. In February 1915, Djemal Pasha returned from a failed military expedition against the Suez Canal. In a black mood, determined to reduce Palestine's non-Turkish communities to a state of terrorized submission, the general ordered the closure of Zionist newspapers, schools, banks, and political offices. All Zionist public activities were banned. When Ben-Gurion ventured to protest these measures, he and other Zionist leaders were summarily exiled. The circumstances of the Jewish labor battalions soon became increasingly precarious. Many hundreds of young men were marched off to prisons in Damascus, while others were sentenced to a living death in the granite pits of Tarsus.

It was not Djemal's hostility alone that threatened the survival of the Yishuv. The "normal" hardships of war were painful enough. The British naval blockade choked off food imports and philanthropic remittances from abroad. The citrus crop withered and died on the trees. Crushing war taxes were levied on Jewish and Arab farms. Livestock and foodstuffs were confiscated. During the first two years of war, some 35,000 inhabitants of Syria-Palestine perished of starvation or disease. Between 6,000 and 7,000 of them were Jews. It was only the intercession of influential Western Jews that helped keep the others alive. One of these intercessors was Arthur Ruppin, director of the Zionist Organization's Palestine Office. As a German citizen who was known to enjoy the esteem of Foreign Minister Arthur von Zimmermann, he was allowed to distribute German-Jewish charitable funds. Equally vital was the solicitude of the United States ambassador in Constantinople, Henry Morgenthau. A Jew himself, Morgenthau at first circumspectly avoided showing favoritism toward Palestine Jewry. Yet the ambassador was a humanitarian, and in the spring of 1915 he could no longer avoid interceding on behalf of Jews and other minorities under Ottoman rule. At his request, the Turks allowed American naval vessels to bring occasional relief shipments and money to the Holy Land. Until April 1917, when diplomatic relations between Washington and Constantinople were severed, it was this uncertain trickle of overseas supplies and funds that enabled the largest numbers of Palestine Jewry to survive.

Meanwhile, Ottoman brutality was not forgotten by the Jews who had been forcibly exiled. By March 1915, some 10,000 of their number had found asylum in Egypt, where half of them were interned in refugee camps and sustained by Jewish communal funds. It was specifically among these embittered expatriates that the first efforts were launched to recruit a Jewish military legion for battle service against the Turks. The proposal was initiated by Vladimir Jabotinsky, a Russian-Jewish journalist and Zionist activist (pp. 354–55), and by Joseph Trumpeldor, himself one of the internees. Trumpeldor in his native Russia had been trained as a dentist. Serving as a volunteer medical officer in the Russian army, he had lost an arm and had been decorated for heroism in the Russo-Japanese War. Upon being discharged from military service, Trumpeldor had immigrated to Palestine to work as a farmer-pioneer on a kibbutz in the Galilee. But when the Ottoman Empire entered the World War, Trumpeldor was among those whom the Turks deported to Egypt. It was also in his Alexandria internment camp that he met Jabotinsky, and the two promptly collaborated in the effort to recruit a Jewish fighting force to share in the liberation of Palestine. The British authorities were cautiously receptive. In principle, they agreed to organize a Jewish military unit, but they preferred that it serve on an alternate war front, which they did not identify. Despite Jabotinsky's initial misgivings, Trumpeldor persuaded his fellow internees to accept the arrangement. As long as the enemy was the Turk, he insisted, "any front leads to Zion." Thus, in the spring of 1915, some five hundred Jews were enrolled in a special transportation unit, the Zion Mule Corps, and allowed to wear their own shoulder patches bearing the Shield of David.

Their assignment was the Gallipoli campaign in the Dardanelles. A British army colonel was placed in charge of the force, although its animating spirit was Trumpeldor, now commissioned a captain. Upon disembarkation at the beaches of Gallipoli, the Zion muleteers led their supply animals to the front trenches through heavy fire, suffering casualties in common with other Allied troops. With the subsequent evacuation of Gallipoli, in the late winter of 1915, the Jewish corps also was withdrawn, and the British disbanded it. Nevertheless, unrecognized at the time, the episode of the Zion Mule Corps represented an initial step in a developing Anglo-Zionist collaboration.

THE MIDDLE EAST AND BRITISH WAR POLICY

Following the outbreak of war, England based its Middle Eastern military strategy on a central and immutable criterion, the security of the Suez Canal. This indispensable passageway for British commerce, the artery of transport for the military manpower reserves of the overseas empire, was threatened twice in the course of hostilities by Ottoman invasion expeditions of January 1915 and August 1916. Although repelled each time, the Turkish offensives fixated British attention on the vulnerability of the canal to assaults from neighboring Palestine. To cope with the threat, military headquarters set about devising a new political approach. This was to mobilize the Ottoman Empire's restive subject peoples in a joint military effort against the Turks.

The idea in fact had been mooted initially by a distinguished Arab figure, the Emir Abdullah al-Hashimi, eldest son of Hussein, the Hashemite *sherif* (guardian) of the Holy Cities of Mecca and Medina. Shortly before the war, Abdullah had visited General Horatio Kitchener, Britain's high commissioner in Egypt, to request British help in protecting his father's dynasty against its suspicious Ottoman overlords. Negotiations were resumed later in the year, and continued after the war began, this time in direct correspondence between Sherif Hussein and Sir Henry McMahon, who had succeeded Kitchener as high commissioner in Egypt. In the course of their written exchange, the two men reached an understanding. The crucial letter, from the high commissioner to Hussein on October 24, 1915, stated that the British government was prepared "to recognize and support the independence of the Arabs within the limits demanded by the Sherif [namely, the entire Arab rectangle, including Syria, Arabia, and Iraq]," with the exception of those "portions of Syria lying to the west of the districts of Damascus, Homs, Hama and Aleppo. . . ." In return for British support in fostering their independence, so the understanding went, the Hashemite Arabs would join the Allied war effort against Turkey, and accept British "advice" in developing their postwar government. On this basis, the Arab Revolt began in June 1916, under the leadership of Hussein's second son, the Emir Feisal, and later with the help of such British liaison officers as T. E. Lawrence. During the ensuing year and a half, the participation of up to 20,000 Arab guerrillas fulfilled a useful supplementary role in the British military campaign against Turkish forces in Arabia and eastern Palestine.

Yet, if the British made a commitment to the Hashemites, they scrupulously protected not only their own postwar interests but those of their Entente partners. The Ottoman Empire, after all, was more than a source of danger to the Suez Canal. With its untutored Moslem populations, it also offered a far likelier arena than Europe for Allied imperial aggrandizement. In recognition of this territorial opportunity, the British dutifully apprised the French and Russian governments of their impending compact with Sherif Hussein. And at the same time, even as High Commissioner McMahon was preempting for Britain the key "advisory" role over a future Arab government, he also made clear to Hussein in the letter of October 24, 1915, that western Syria was being reserved for a possible French relationship. Indeed, during the winter of 1915–16 this relationship was confirmed in a series of negotiations among the Entente governments themselves. It was in January 1916 that Sir Mark Sykes, the British representative, and Charles François Georges-Picot, the French emissary, affixed their signatures to a treaty allocating postwar spheres of influence in the Arab world. Under this document, Britain would be invested with supervision over Arab territories encompassing the largest part of Iraq, as well as most of the terrain east of the Jordan River. France would exercise ascendancy over southern Turkey, Syria, and upper Iraq. By later agreement with Russian Foreign Minister Sergei Sazonov, Russia too would be recompensed, essentially in the Armenian sectors of the Ottoman Empire.

What was the fate of Palestine under the Sykes-Picot arrangement? From London's perspective, terrain of this strategic proximity to the Suez Canal could not be allowed to fall into the grasp of another nation, even of an Entente nation. Yet Foreign Secretary Sir Edward Grey was unprepared to offend the French or the Russians by demanding unilateral control for Britain. Instead, each of the Allies would be awarded specific spheres of influence in the Holy Land. Thus, skirting Palestine's central zone, Britain would control the Haifa Bay area, southern Palestine, and the country's eastern, trans-Jordanian highlands, thereby assuring that Palestine would be encompassed on three sides by British-controlled territory. To the French sphere of influence would be allocated the totality of northwestern Palestine, including the upper Galilee region. Finally, the venerated Jerusalem-Bethlehem area would be transformed into a "condominium," an enclave whose governance would be shared by all the signatory powers—including Italy, which in April 1917 muscled its way into the anticipated Middle East partition.

From the summer of 1916 onward, however, Sinai and Palestine came to function increasingly as Britain's chosen battlefield against the Turks. Early British expeditions in the Middle East, at the Dardanelles and in Iraq, had been sanguinary failures. The Sinai peninsula offered a possibly more direct and efficient invasion route toward the Ottoman Levant. In June 1916, therefore, British military headquarters in Cairo set about organizing a 150,000-man Egyptian Expeditionary Force in anticipation of a straight-line thrust into Palestine. In December of that year, the ponderous army ventured out toward Palestine. Al-Arish and Rafa were overrun en route. At last, in March 1917, the expeditionary force moved against Gaza, the historic "gateway" to Palestine. But here it was twice repelled by a formidable Turkish defense. In late spring of 1917, the British commander, Archibald Murray, was replaced. His successor, General Sir Edmund Allenby, reorganized his forces and made plans for a climactic breakthrough toward the north of Palestine's Negev Desert.

But even as Allenby's troops were preparing for their offensive into the Holy Land, the British War Cabinet began to experience misgivings about the prize its diplomacy seemingly had forfeited. The compromise of quasi-internationalization might have been unavoidable at a time when the British were on the defensive in the Middle East, licking their wounds after the Gallipoli disaster. As the months passed, however, the prospect of a French military enclave in Palestine, even linked to an Allied condominium, became increasingly unpalatable to London, and all the more so, in the spring of 1917, when Allenby was marshaling tens of thousands of imperial troops for the offensive into the Holy Land. In late April, therefore, Prime Minister Lloyd George informed his ambassador in Paris that "the French will have to accept our protectorate over Palestine," for an international regime in the Holy Land "would be quite intolerable to ourselves. . . . Palestine is really the strategic buffer of Egypt." Even so, a more "idealistic," "moralistic" rationale for British rule would have been preferred at a time when Mark Sykes's signature was hardly dry on the 1916 agreement with Georges-Picot. Initially, the prime minister failed to grasp that such a rationale already existed. It had been provided by an unlikely source, the Jews.

The Origins of the Anglo-Zionist Alliance

At the outbreak of the war, the Zionist Organization would have appeared the unlikeliest of diplomatic partners for any major power. In no country had Zionism yet won decisive support even among its Jewish population. In Russia, the Bund still vigorously contested for the loyalty of the Jewish working classes; while Orthodox Jewry tended to remain suspicious of Zionism. In the Western nations, the acculturated Jewish "establishment" rejected the very notion of an official Jewish homeland. The war itself, finally, ruptured the precarious unity of the Zionist movement. In the hope of preserving at least a functional contact between its members throughout Europe, the Zionist Organization in 1914 established a special Bureau for Zionist Affairs in neutral Copenhagen. The device was notably ineffective. The principal Zionist leaders remained in their native countries and barely dealt with the Copenhagen office. More significantly, they shared the general patriotic enthusiasm of their fellow countrymen. In Austria, the Zionist Federation announced that it expected all its young members to register for military service. In Germany, the official Zionist weekly "recognize[d] that our [Jewish] interest is exclusively on the side of Germany."

Indeed, throughout Europe, efforts were mounted not simply to identify all Jews with the various national causes, but to persuade their respective governments to embrace the Zionist movement as a potential diplomatic asset. It was wasted effort, however. Unprepared to alienate its Turkish ally, Berlin rejected Zionist overtures. Other foreign ministries shared a widespread suspicion of Zionism. The government of France, recalling that Herzl, Nordau, Wolfssohn, and other early Zionist leaders were Central European Jews by training and culture, tended to regard Jewish nationalism as "the advance guard of German influence." In Petrograd, the tsarist government hardly was inclined to express sympathy for Jewish nationalism at a time when it was driving 600,000 Jews like cattle into the Russian interior (pp. 317–18). Even in Britain, where East European immigrants had become the majority among that nation's quarter-million Jews, most of these newcomers were too poor or harassed to exert meaningful influence in Jewish public or communal affairs, let alone in national affairs. Meanwhile, the British government remained essentially indifferent to the Zionist renaissance.

In the eyes of at least some British politicians and statesmen, however, Zionism was no longer either an unknown or a suspect movement. Beyond Herzl's negotiations with Joseph Chamberlain, the Fourth Zionist Congress was held in London in August 1902, and its sessions had been given considerable publicity. Afterward, the al-Arish and East Africa schemes had been raised and debated in a House of Commons that included Lloyd George and Balfour. In ensuing years, the governmental connection was maintained and cultivated by a vibrant group of Zionist activists who lived in England. By 1914, their acknowledged, if still unofficial, spokesman was Chaim Weizmann, a forty-year-old chemistry instructor at the University of Manchester. Russian-born, educated in Germany and Switzerland, Weizmann proved to be as compelling an advocate in England as in his youthful leadership of the Ahad HaAmist–"cultural" faction during the early Zionist congresses (p. 273). He soon won a loyal following for Zionism among a number of eminent figures in the Anglo-Jewish community. Among these was Harry Sacher, a lawyer and journalist who had served on the editorial board of the Manchester *Guardian*.

More influential yet was Herbert Samuel, president of the Local Government Board, and afterward home secretary in the Asquith cabinet. In fact, Samuel had taken a mild interest in Zionism even before meeting Weizmann, and by the time the war broke out with Turkey, he was already contemplating the possible diplomatic advantage of a British protectorate over a Palestine Jewish homeland. Upon meeting Weizmann in December 1914, through the auspices of Charles P. Scott, editor of the *Guardian*, Samuel and Harry Sacher moved energetically to introduce Weizmann to several key public figures. One of these was Charles Wickham Steed, editor of the London *Times*, whose earlier interest in Zionism was now rekindled. Through Scott and Steed, in turn, Weizmann made the acquaintance of the nation's political leaders, including Lloyd George, Winston Churchill, and Lord Robert Cecil. His relationship with these men was further strengthened by a vital service he performed for the Admiralty. In March of 1916, Weizmann was summoned to London to help solve the shortage of acetone, an ingredient vital for the cordite used in naval explosives. After some ten months of laboratory research, he accomplished the task by devising an innovative fermenting process.

During this war service, too, the contacts Weizmann had made earlier were cemented at the highest level. Years later, Sir Ronald Storrs, secretary of the British government administration in Palestine, described Weizmann as

> a brilliant talker with an unrivaled gift for lucid exposition. . . . As a speaker almost frighteningly convincing, even in English . . . in Hebrew, and even more in Russian, overwhelming, with all that dynamic persuasiveness which Slavs usually devote to love and Jews to business, nourished, trained and concentrated upon the accomplishment of Zion.

Weizmann's eloquence and charisma were enhanced by other factors. Pre-eminent among them was his uncompromising devotion to Britain, his repeated insistence that the fate of Zionism was inexorably linked to that of the Allies. Thus, a letter written by Weizmann in 1916, in which he terminated his relations with the "neutralist" Zionist Bureau in Copenhagen, was kept by Scotland Yard—Weizmann was a foreign national—and further disposed the authorities in his favor.

British statesmen did not formulate national policy on the basis of emo-tion or philanthropy, of course. In the last weeks of 1916, Lloyd George, a Liberal, became prime minister, and Balfour, a Conservative, became foreign secretary in a coalition government. For Lloyd George, who had favored an aggressive Middle East policy since the beginning of the war, British rule over a Jewish Palestine would have represented a logical and climactic tour de force of imperial diplomacy. He personally had played no part in negotiating the Sykes-Picot Agreement, and subsequently he made no secret of his con-tempt for it as a "fatuous document" based on erroneous calculations. The Zionists, he believed, might well open new possibilities of revision. The view was heartily shared now by Lord Milner, the colonial secretary and Lloyd George's closest friend in the cabinet; by Lord Robert Cecil, the new perma-nent undersecretary of the Foreign Office; by Philip Kerr, the prime minis-ter's adviser on foreign policy; and most important, by the War Cabinet's three young undersecretaries for Middle Eastern Affairs: Mark Sykes, Leo-pold Amery, and William Ormbsy-Gore.

A CRUCIAL INTERMEDIARY

Sykes was the most influential of this group, the official who served as "mar-riage broker" in the developing relationship between the government and the

Zionist leadership. Although initially hesitant to disrupt the 1916 agreement with France, Sykes in ensuing months came to share his colleagues' interest in a revised approach to a Middle Eastern settlement. Thus, the chain of liberated national groups—Armenians, Arabs, Greeks—whom Sykes envisaged as Britain's logical Middle Eastern clients against the Turks would, necessarily, include the Zionist Jews. By the time Sykes met Weizmann on February 7, 1917, it already had become his diplomatic raison d'être to wed Zionist and British interests. "From the purely British point of view," he told Amery, "a prosperous Jewish population in Palestine, owing its inception and its opportunity of development to British policy, might be an invaluable asset as a defense of the Suez Canal against attack from the north and as a station on the future air routes to the East."

There was little time to waste before embarking on the diplomatic volte-face. By the opening weeks of 1917, the British military offensive in Palestine already was under way. In his February meeting with Weizmann, therefore, Sykes hinted to the Zionist leader that the government might be prepared to favor a Jewish national entity in the Holy Land. He could not yet reveal the existence of the agreement he himself had signed with Georges-Picot and the restrictions this treaty placed on the War Cabinet's freedom of action. Rather, Sykes observed simply that the Zionists themselves would have to take the initiative in persuading the Allied governments to endorse the notion of a Jewish national home in Palestine. Once this thesis was accepted, the corollary of a British protectorate would be easier to negotiate. Weizmann and his colleagues required no further inducement. They set about immediately presenting their case in Paris and Rome.

Yet it was Sykes, in the background, who stage-managed the negotiations. Nahum Sokolow, Weizmann's most intimate collaborator in these Allied discussions, wrote later:

> As I was crossing the Quai d'Orsay [in Paris] on my return from the Foreign Ministry I came across Sykes. He had not had the patience to wait. We walked on together, and I gave him an outline of the proceedings.... [In Rome, in April 1917] I went to the British Embassy; letters and instructions from Sykes were waiting for me there. I went to the Italian Government Offices; Sykes had been there, too; then to the Vatican, where Sykes again prepared my way.

These efforts made important progress. Although the French Foreign Ministry was resistant to any changes in the Sykes-Picot Agreement, it was prepared to express a friendly interest in Zionism. Apparently, it had little choice, for rumors of an impending pro-Zionist statement by Berlin (which turned out to be false) convinced French officials that in Jewish nationalism it was "up against a big thing." Thus, on June 4, 1917, the Foreign Ministry dispatched a letter to Sokolow assuring him that "the French Government . . . can only feel sympathy to your cause, the triumph of which is bound up with that of the Allies." In Rome, Pope Benedict XV evinced a similar vague cordiality. In the pontiff's case, a gesture of friendship to the Jews was as tactical as it was atypical. A British-sponsored Jewish enclave in Palestine at least would forestall a Russian Orthodox presence.

By the spring of 1917, none of the Allies was left in doubt of Britain's purpose in fostering Zionism. As early as April 6, Sykes frankly informed Georges-Picot that Britain's military efforts in Palestine would have to be "taken into account" at the peace conference. "[Picot] is convinced," France's President Raymond Poincaré ruefully noted in his diary on April 17, "that in London our agreements are now considered null and void." Neither were the Zionists ignorant of their function as an extension of British policy. They welcomed the role; for the support and friendship of this mighty imperial power—Herzl's cherished hope during his 1902–3 negotiations with Joseph Chamberlain (p. 271)—at long last appeared to be reaching fruition.

Yet, by the same token, Weizmann and his colleagues, impatient for a public declaration of support from the War Cabinet, were mystified that an open commitment was not yet forthcoming. They knew nothing of the prior understanding with France. "It was not from [Sykes] that we learned of the existence of the agreement," Weizmann recalled, "and months passed before we understood what it was that blocked our progress." Scott of the Manchester *Guardian* was the first to uncover the details of the Sykes-Picot Agreement. Inadvertently, he let the information slip to Weizmann. The Zionist leader was appalled. When he confronted Lord Robert Cecil with the information, the undersecretary neither confirmed nor denied it. Cecil intimated, however, that possibly even more could be done in persuading the government to declare an identity of British and Zionist goals. It would be helpful, he observed, if Jews not simply in England but in other lands should express themselves in favor of a British protectorate in the Holy Land, and, indeed, in favor of the Entente cause altogether.

The Quid Pro Quo of Jewish Friendship

The hoary legend of international Jewish wealth and influence could be traced back as far as the late seventeenth and early eighteenth centuries, when Jewish court bankers functioned as reliable supporters of European dynasties. It was taken with even greater seriousness in the nineteenth century, the heyday of the Rothschilds and of other great European-Jewish merchant bankers. Thus, in 1840, reacting to Mehemet Ali's threatened attack on Constantinople, British Foreign Secretary Lord Palmerston discreetly importuned the Ottoman government to allow large-scale Jewish settlement in Palestine "because the wealth [the Jews] would bring with them would increase the resources of the Sultan's dominions. . . ." Nor was Jewish influence regarded with less deference in the twentieth century. In February 1917, Sykes reminded Georges-Picot: "If the great force of Judaism feels that its aspirations are . . . in a fair way to realization, then there is hope for an ordered and developed Arabia and Middle East." Nearly all the major belligerent governments shared this awe for the alleged power of world Jewry. It was significant that both Germany and France included Jewish "advisers" among their wartime missions to the United States, in the hope of mobilizing the support—still uncertain—of American Jewry for their respective causes.

Lloyd George, too, shared the widespread presumption of Jewish influence in other lands. If the notion was spurious, this was less important than the prime minister's belief, and Lloyd George's belief in 1917 was conditioned by the worst crisis of the war: Russia virtually hors de combat; France exhausted, its troops mutinying after the bloodbath of Verdun; Italy demoralized after the rout at Caporetto; German submarines taking a lethal toll of Allied shipping; not a single American division yet in the trenches. The need to keep Russia in the war and to exploit America's resources was overpowering. "In the solution of these two problems," Lloyd George acknowledged years later, "public opinion in Russia and America played a great part, and we [believed] . . . that in both countries the friendliness or hostility of the Jewish race might make a considerable difference." The prime minister's belief was erroneous. The potential animus or goodwill of American Jewry was a negligible factor once the United States entered the war, while the Russian Zionist attitude toward the Entente was hopelessly poisoned by hatred of the tsarist regime. That animus became evident in June 1917 when Menahem Ussishkin and other Russian Zionist leaders sent word to Weizmann and to Louis Brandeis (p. 396) that they were unprepared to identify the cause of Zionism with one or another of the combatant powers.

Vladimir Jabotinsky discovered this opposition the hard way. A Russian-Jewish writer, orator, and linguist of remarkable virtuosity, thirty-four years old when the war began, he served as correspondent on the Western Front for the liberal Russian newspaper *Russkiye vyedomosti*. The moment the Ottoman Empire joined the Central Powers, Jabotinsky sensed the unique opportunity that would accrue to Zionism if the Turks could be driven from Palestine. To that end, he hurled himself into the endeavor to organize a Jewish legion. But the first fruit of that endeavor, the Zion Mule Corps, was sent to Gallipoli and afterward disbanded (p. 346). Early in 1916, when Jabotinsky paid a return visit to Russia, he found himself ostracized by the Zionists, who regarded any military effort on behalf of the Entente as simply another attempt to succor the despised tsarist government. In his hometown of Odessa, Jabotinsky was branded a traitor from the synagogue pulpit. His mother was accosted in the street by the Zionist activist Menahem Ussishkin, who declared that "your son should be hanged."

From then on, Jabotinsky concentrated his recruiting efforts in London. There, too, he nearly met disaster. Addressing crowds of Russian-Jewish immigrants in the ghetto of the East End, he was furiously hooted off the platform. It was evident that in England, as in Russia, the Jews wanted no part of a legion dedicated to combat against the enemies of the tsar. Even the leaders of Anglo-Zionism, except for Weizmann, Sacher, and Sokolow, were cool to Jabotinsky's scheme, although for a different reason. They recognized that the Yishuv was an Ottoman hostage. If it became known that Jews abroad were mobilizing specifically to liberate the Holy Land, Palestine Jewry conceivably might suffer the fate of the Armenians, whom the Turks recently had all but annihilated as potential traitors.

This analogy was by no means far-fetched. In 1917, the same tragic results were almost provoked by a small group of Palestinian Jews engaged in transmitting military data to the British. The driving force behind the clandestine operation was Aaron Aaronsohn. The son of a pioneer Zionist farmer, Aaronsohn was an agronomist of recognized genius. In 1906, he won international acclaim for discovering a weather-resistant primeval wheat. Four years later, encouraged by the United States Department of Agriculture and funded by Julius Rosenwald, a wealthy American Jew (who later would help subsidize the Agro-Joint program in Soviet Russia), Aaronsohn set up an experimental station in Atlit, a coastal village outside Haifa. There, in ensuing years, he carried out intensive research in dry-farming techniques. Yet even as he explored methods of reviving Palestine's soil, Aaronsohn sensed that the Yishuv had no future under the corrupt and brutal Ottoman regime. The outbreak of the war, the expulsions and sequestrations carried out against Jews and Arabs alike, the horror visited upon the Armenians, whose pathetic refugees straggled in dying bands through the countryside, appeared to confirm this premonition. The Jews' best hope, Aaronsohn believed, was to wrest Palestine away for themselves. His view was shared by a small group of associates, including his father, brother, and sister, and by several other young Jews who worked with him in the research station.

Aaronsohn and his companions had anticipated a British invasion once the war began. When the landing took place instead at Gallipoli, the Atlit group decided on its own to establish contact with the British and to offer them systematic information on Ottoman military dispositions in Palestine. Aaronsohn's brother Alexander and another member of the group managed to pass successfully through the Turkish lines, to reach Egypt, and eventually to meet with British officials in Cairo. To no avail. The latter expressed meager interest in a relationship with an unprepossessing band of Palestinian Jews. In August of 1916, however, Aaron Aaronsohn in Atlit received ominous information that the Turks were concentrating large numbers of troops for a second campaign against the Suez Canal. Somehow the British had to be warned. It was vital, too, that they appreciate another danger. Unless Palestine was swiftly liberated, its inhabitants might not survive the famine that was penetrating every corner of the land. Aaronsohn's problem was to find a way of reaching England and speaking directly with the appropriate officials.

An invasion of another kind, of locusts, gave him his opportunity. In a meeting with Djemal Pasha, describing the need to develop alternate food supplies, Aaronsohn asked the military governor to let him depart for Germany in order to carry out "research on a variety of sesame rich in oil." The permission was granted. But once in Germany, Aaronsohn traveled on to neutral Copenhagen, and through the Zionist Bureau there devised a plan to reach England without appearing to defect. In October 1916, he embarked from the German port of Bremen for the United States. En route, by pre-arrangement, a British destroyer intercepted his ship, "arrested" Aaronsohn as an Ottoman national, and carried him back to England. Literally within hours of his arrival in London, the Palestinian agronomist was pouring out his information to Sir Basil Thomson, chief of Scotland Yard, and offering substantial evidence of Turkish vulnerability to an invasion through Palestine. Thomson was impressed, and in late November sent Aaronsohn to Egypt for discussions with military commanders there. Equally impressed, the officers this time promised their active collaboration with the Jewish spy ring.

While Aaronsohn remained in Cairo as liaison between the British and the Atlit group, his family and friends worked for the next eight months under the very noses of the Turks. Aaronsohn's sister Sarah, and an associate, Yosef Lishanski, directed the effort, collecting information on Ottoman troop movements and transmitting it to a British frigate that anchored off the Atlit coast every two weeks at nightfall. The intelligence proved of critical importance to the British. When General Allenby assumed command of the Egyptian Expeditionary Force in the spring of 1917, he asked the Jewish spies for information on Turkish defenses around Beersheba, the contemplated site of his forthcoming offensive. Sarah Aaronsohn and her associates secured it. Their dispatches included vital data on the location of water sources for cavalry horses, on the condition of every known route to Jerusalem from the Negev Desert. "It was largely the daring work of the young [Jewish] spies," wrote Captain Raymond Savage, Allenby's deputy military secretary, ". . . which enabled the Field Marshal to accomplish his undertaking so effectively."

The espionage came to an end in September 1917, when one of the spy network's carrier pigeons fell into the hands of the Turks. Eventually, the Atlit group was discovered and arrested, including nearly all of Aaronsohn's family. They were tortured for information, then executed (Sarah Aaronsohn committed suicide rather than implicate other members). Aaron Aaronsohn himself, operating out of Cairo, managed to survive the war. In May 1919, however, the airplane carrying him from London to the Paris Peace Conference crashed in the English Channel.

A Declaration Is Issued

The fate of the Jewish spies might have inhibited Weizmann and his colleagues in their attempt to extract a pro-Zionist commitment from the British government. But their discovery of the Sykes-Picot Agreement convinced them that any risk of Turkish retaliation was worth taking to avoid the dismemberment of Palestine, and its Jewish settlement, into isolated zones of conflicting foreign sovereignties. With Allenby's military offensive imminent, the War Cabinet for its part sensed the compelling need for a public statement that would imply future unilateral British control over the Holy Land. On June 17, 1917, therefore, Foreign Secretary Balfour called Weizmann to his office and suggested delicately that it would be useful if the Zionists themselves now formulated the draft for an appropriate declaration. If the draft were acceptable, Balfour would submit it to the War Cabinet for endorsement. Immediately, then, Weizmann and his closest associates, Sacher and Sokolow, embarked on the preparation of a suitable text, in consultation with Sykes and Ormsby-Gore, the War Cabinet's Middle East expert. The draft was submitted to Balfour on July 18. It did not lack for forthrightness. "His Majesty's Government," it stated, "accepts the principle that Palestine should be reconstituted as the National Home of the Jewish People. His Majesty's Government will use its best endeavours to secure achievement of this object and will discuss the necessary methods and means with the Zionist Organization."

When the document was formally discussed in a cabinet conference of September 3, it elicited the ministers' near-unanimous approval. Ironically, the most forceful opposition came from the one Jew in the Lloyd George government. This was Edwin Montagu, secretary of state for India, and a cousin of Herbert Samuel. Although reared in affluence (his father was the banker Lord Swaythling), Montagu had fought an uphill battle to escape his Orthodox origins and to win acceptance in the privileged circles of government. In this case, a "national home" for the Jews seemed to raise embarrassing questions of dual loyalty. "If you make a statement about Palestine as the national home for the Jews," he had warned Lloyd George earlier in a private memorandum, "every anti-Semitic organization and newspaper will ask what right a Jewish Englishman, with the status at best of a naturalized foreigner, has to take a foremost part in the Government of the British Empire." And now, on September 3, 1917, Montagu further insisted that a pro-Zionist statement would alarm the Moslems of India. The vehemence of his opposition to Zionism as "a mischievous political creed" persuaded the cabinet to leave the issue temporarily unresolved.

Neither the Zionists nor their supporters in the government accepted the setback as more than temporary. Lloyd George confidently put the matter of the declaration on the agenda for the next cabinet session. But when the meeting took place on October 4, Montagu opposed the statement with even more intensity than before. His opposition, and that of his supporters—Lord Curzon, a Conservative member of the War Cabinet, and Gertrude Bell, an Arabist adviser to the Foreign Office—had the effect of persuading Lloyd George, Balfour, and other pro-Zionists that a milder text was needed simply to dispose of the question. Accordingly, Leopold Amery and Lord Milner took it upon themselves to devise a compromise formula. It was the one that became the final draft of the Balfour Declaration. The earlier phrase, "that Palestine should be reconstituted as the National Home of the Jewish People," was dropped in favor of a more equivocal statement (pp. 359–60). Although the Zionists were chagrined by the alteration, they were fearful of tampering with it.

Lloyd George was prepared at last to force the issue through the cabinet. Before taking the final step, however, he was determined to win a commitment of diplomatic support for Zionist aspirations, assurance that a declaration, with its implied corollary of a British protectorate, would not face international opposition at the peace conference later. Ultimately, it was the prestige and influence of the American government that would prove vital. Although Washington had not declared war on the Ottoman Empire, it was understood that the United States would exert a major impact on all phases of the peace settlement, including the future of the Holy Land. Would President Woodrow Wilson endorse a declaration linked to a postwar British protectorate in Palestine?

Wilson could not have been ignorant by then of the growing shift of American-Jewish sentiment toward Zionism (p. 361). Indeed, as they adopted this orientation, the Jews of the United States were influenced by their new role as host to the Zionist movement's de facto headquarters "in exile." When the war began in August 1914, a member of the Zionist Executive, Shmaryahu Levin, was en route from New York back to Europe. His ship turned back immediately and Levin remained in New York to establish a "Provisional" Zionist Executive Committee for General Zionist Affairs. It was this committee's vigilant liaison that ultimately helped save the Yishuv. Its intercession with the State Department fortified Ambassador Morgenthau's humanitarian efforts on behalf of Palestine Jewry. Additionally, the committee's chairman,

Louis D. Brandeis, was a man of national prominence. In 1916, he became the first Jewish appointee to the United States Supreme Court. It was thus at Weizmann's suggestion, and with Balfour's full concurrence, that Brandeis was asked to use his influence with the president on behalf of London's impending pro-Zionist statement. The effort succeeded. Wilson's approval was forthcoming on October 16, and Lloyd George had the endorsement he needed. The War Cabinet voted for the declaration on October 31, over the last forlorn objections of Lord Curzon (Montagu by then was on the high seas en route to India and did not participate in the final vote).

Significantly, the declaration's principal rationale by then was no longer the need to avert participation by the other Allies in a Palestine "condominium." Allenby's army was on the verge of conquering the Holy Land, and the issue plainly would be decided by the substantial presence in Palestine of the Egyptian Expeditionary Force. Rather, the War Cabinet's decision was influenced by the obsessive desire to win the friendship of "world Jewry." Lloyd George was counting on that support. "The Zionist leaders," he wrote later, "gave us a definite promise that, if the Allies committed themselves to . . . a National Home for the Jews in Palestine, they would do their best to rally to the Allied cause . . . Jewish sentiment and support throughout the world. They kept their word in letter and spirit. . . ." Other factors possibly helped set the atmosphere for the cabinet's vote. One was the genuine religious affinity of Balfour (and Jan Christian Smuts and Lloyd George) for the Holy Land, and their appreciation for the historic role of the Jewish people in the rise of Christianity. "Near the end of his life," wrote Lady Blanche Dugdale, Balfour's niece, "he said to me that on the whole he felt that what he had been able to do for the Jews had been the thing he looked back upon as the most worth doing." Others in the cabinet may have been at least marginally influenced by even more complex motives, for example, Protestant millenarianism, an uneasy conscience about Jewish suffering, conceivably the need to endorse a humane and productive act in the midst of the havoc of war.

The declaration itself seemed curiously bland, however, and devoid of religious or mystical overtones of any kind. It took the form of a letter on November 2 to Lord Lionel Walter Rothschild, titular president of the British Zionist Federation, and stated:

> Dear Lord Rothschild, I have much pleasure in conveying to you, on behalf of His Majesty's Government, the following declaration of sympathy with Jewish Zionist aspirations which has been submitted to, and approved by, the Cabinet:
> "His Majesty's Government views with favour the establishment in Palestine of a national home for the Jewish people, and will use their best endeavours to facilitate the achievement of this

object, it being clearly understood that nothing shall be done which may prejudice the civil and religious rights of existing non-Jewish communities in Palestine, or the rights and political status enjoyed by Jews in any other country."

I should be grateful if you would bring this declaration to the knowledge of the Zionist Federation.

The original Zionist text of the declaration had called for the reconstitution "of Palestine *as* [italics added] the National Home of the Jewish People." The phrase "national home," employed in both versions, actually was unknown in international usage. The Zionists had coined the expression at their initial, 1897 congress to avoid the term "Jewish state," which the Turks might have found provocative, and the Zionist draft followed this circumspect approach. The Balfour version in fact proved even more discreet, for in endorsing "the establishment *in* Palestine of *a* [italics added] national home," it precluded the need to define the boundaries of a Jewish settlement in Palestine. The "national home" might be no more than a small enclave within the country. Only five years later, the broad trans-Jordanian uplands would be sheared away, and fifteen years after that a further amputation would be proposed by a British royal commission—all without violating the letter of the declaration. Moreover, the need to protect "the civil and religious rights of existing non-Jewish communities in Palestine" ultimately would serve as the pretext for limiting Jewish immigration in order to placate Arab hostility.

Yet the eventual fate of the declaration was not necessarily consonant with the original intention of its authors. "My personal hope," Balfour told a friend in 1918, "is that the Jews will make good in Palestine and eventually found a Jewish State." In 1920 Winston Churchill, who had served as minister of munitions when the declaration was issued, spoke of "a Jewish State by the banks of the Jordan . . . which might comprise three or four million Jews." Lloyd George was quite explicit in his description of the cabinet's proposal: If the Jews became a majority in the Holy Land, Palestine would

> thus become a Jewish Commonwealth. The notion that Jewish immigration would have to be artificially restricted in order to ensure that the Jews should be a permanent minority . . . would have been regarded as unjust and as a fraud on the people to whom we were appealing.

It is worth assessing the effectiveness of the appeal to "world Jewry." The Jews of England were thrilled, as their public meetings and resolutions of thanks made evident. Heartened by this response, and intent upon duplicating it in other countries, the government established a special Jewish section within the department of information, staffing it primarily with Zionists. Under the latter's direction, copies of the Balfour Declaration were distributed by the tens of thousands in Jewish communities throughout the world, including leaflets dropped by the Royal Flying Corps over German and Austrian towns. When news of the declaration arrived in Russia, huge, cheering crowds of Jews gathered outside British consulates in the larger cities. Cables of congratulation flooded in on Balfour from Jewish communities as far removed as Alexandria, Shanghai, and Cape Town. Indeed, so fearful were Britain's enemies of the propaganda value to be reaped by the declaration that belated efforts were launched to match it. In Constantinople, Mehmet Talaat Pasha, Turkey's minister of the interior, announced his intention of canceling restrictions on Jewish immigration to Palestine; and in January 1918, Talaat went so far as to approve establishment of a chartered company to foster an autonomous Jewish settlement in Palestine. In Berlin, two days later, Undersecretary of State Joachim von dem Busschi-Haddenhousen formally endorsed the Turkish proposal.

Yet, in practical fact, the Balfour Declaration did not significantly affect the loyalties of Jews in other belligerent nations. Although Weizmann and Brandeis cabled friends in Russia, entreating them to intercede with the new Communist government on behalf of the Entente cause, the effort was wasted. Not one of the Jews in the Communist Central Committee evinced the faintest interest in Jewish nationalism. Meanwhile, Jews in the German and Habsburg empires remained steadfastly loyal to their countries. French Jewry responded to news of the declaration with a certain mild enthusiasm. Henri Bergson, Edmond Fleg, Léon Blum, and other eminent French-Jewish figures expressed their satisfaction. But the official Consistoire Israélite maintained an ambivalent posture on the issue of Jewish nationalism. There was nothing equivocal about the reaction of American Jews, to be sure. Among them, public demonstrations were mounted, including large parades in New York, Philadelphia, Chicago, and other major cities. But the United States was already at war. The hated Russian tsar had fallen. Nothing remained to inhibit the enthusiastic participation of American Jews in their war effort, and nothing further, even a Balfour Declaration, was required to inspire it.

THE LIBERATION OF THE YISHUV

Perhaps the one tangible military result of the declaration was Vladimir Jabotinsky's belated success in organizing a Jewish Legion. Following the March Revolution of 1917, Russian-Jewish opposition to the plan began to weaken. Moreover, in late spring, the imminence of a British offensive in

Palestine largely dispelled fears of Turkish reprisals. In the interval, Jabotinsky had persuaded Lord Edward Derby, the war secretary, that Zionist and British interests would be equally served by a Jewish military unit entrenched in Palestine; and in August, Prime Minister Lloyd George officially approved the establishment of a special Jewish infantry regiment that would be assigned for combat exclusively on the Palestine front. Hereupon, the task of organizing the regiment's first unit, the Thirty-eighth Battalion of Royal Fusiliers, was given to Colonel John Patterson, former commander of the Zion Mule Corps. Predictably, the colonel's first recruits were some 120 veterans of that original transport unit. This time, too, with the active proselytizing efforts of Jabotinsky, who served now as Patterson's aide-de-camp, the unit's members were supplemented from the immigrant Jewry of London's East End.

Nor was the recruitment effort limited to England. In November 1917, the department of information's "Jewish" section ensured that recruitment circulars were distributed among Jewish communities in North and South America. The Balfour Declaration had just been issued, and in the United States and Canada volunteers soon began registering at British consular offices. Among the first of the 6,500 to enlist was David Ben-Gurion, whom Djemal Pasha had exiled from Palestine in 1915, and who had traveled halfway around the world to New York. The recruits then were sent on to basic training camp in Nova Scotia, and by August 1918 were on their way across the Atlantic as members of the Thirty-ninth and Fortieth battalions of the Royal Fusiliers. After further training in England, the troops were loaded onto transports and carried across the Mediterranean. Meanwhile, the Legion's initial, Thirty-eighth Battalion had disembarked at Alexandria as early as March 1918.

Their arrival was hardly premature. During 1917, the circumstances of the Yishuv in Palestine had become dire. In late March of that year, anticipating a British offensive, Djemal Pasha ordered the evacuation of all remaining Jews in Jaffa and its suburban quarter of Tel Aviv. Even Jews who had applied for Ottoman citizenship long before were suspect now as potential traitors. Driven out of their lodgings, they clambered onto wagons or donkeys and fled toward the settlements in the highlands of Judea for temporary shelter. Other refugees moved northward, farther yet from a potential battle zone, to the Jewish farm colonies of Galilee. Employment and food were in desperately short supply well before this influx from the coast. Soon the refugees faced starvation. Many of them were obliged to forage for roots. Several hundred Jewish girls remained alive by selling themselves to Turkish and German soldiers who were quartered in the Galilee. Then, in October 1917, Allenby launched his invasion of Palestine. The initial phase of the campaign was successful beyond the general's highest expectations. Augmented by tens of thousands of Australians and New Zealanders, the Egyptian Expeditionary Force struck quickly into the country's interior, overrunning Beersheba, capturing Jaffa on November 16 and Jerusalem three weeks later. On December 11, 1917, Allenby himself marched into the historic capital to address a gathering of Moslem, Christian, and Jewish notables that had been convened on the steps of the Tower of David, and to promise "a new era of brotherhood and peace in the Holy Land."

Jewish rejoicing was ill timed. With the winter rains, Allenby's campaign stalled, and Jews in the north remained hostages under Ottoman military rule. Their last remnants of security were gone by then, for Turkish soldiers began indiscriminately confiscating Jewish food reserves, and army deserters by the thousands ran amok, terrorizing Jewish settlements, looting property, even killing. It was during this final trauma of Ottoman occupation in Palestine that the Yishuv endured its worst torment. By the time the British resumed their offensive in the spring of 1918, and ultimately set the last of the enemy's forces to rout in September, the Jewish population had been reduced from its prewar figure of 85,000 to approximately 55,000. Some 20,000 had departed or had been expelled from the country, but no fewer than 8,000 had perished of hunger, illness, or exposure.

The Jewish Legion shared in the 1918 campaign. In the spring, its Thirty-eighth Battalion was assigned to patrol the Jordan Valley against a threatened Turkish counterattack. In later months, after repeated appeals from Colonel Patterson, the—now augmented—Legion was permitted to join Allenby's climactic autumn offensive. At this point, its ranks numbered 5,000, one-sixth of the British army of occupation. If modest in size, it was distinctly more than a symbolic force, and its participation in the last stage of the Palestine conquest eventually signified as much as the ordeal of the early Zionist pioneers, and hardly less than the Balfour Declaration itself, in reinforcing the Jews' claim to a national home. Once achieved under British patronage, that armed and self-proclaimed Jewish bridgehead would not easily be foreclosed.

ESTABLISHING THE PALESTINE MANDATE

On April 25, 1920, the Paris Peace Conference formally confirmed the allocation of the Middle East's Arab rectangle to Britain and France. Yet the Allies' final boundaries for their respective mandates in Palestine and Syria did not produce the viable frontiers the Zionists had anticipated for their National Home. To the north and northeast, Palestine was deprived of its most important potential water resources, including the Litani River, a key fount of the Jordan, as well as the greater length of the Yarmuk River. The boundaries similarly ignored the historic entity "from Dan to Beersheba" envisaged in the original negotiations leading to the Balfour Declaration. By failing to approximate any natural geographic demarcations, moreover, the borders left the country perennially exposed to neighboring armies. It was a heritage of economic and military vulnerability that would haunt the Palestine mandate, and later the State of Israel, for decades to come.

Notwithstanding these territorial disappointments, the Zionists had grounds for optimism. In designating Palestine as a British mandate, the Allied Powers at Paris ensured that the full text of the Balfour Declaration was incorporated in the award. In the course of its military occupation, too, the British gave priority to the revival of Palestine's desolated economy and the sustenance of its shrunken population of 55,000 Jews (and ten times that many Arabs). To achieve these goals, General Allenby established a taut, efficient military administration. British officers and civil servants held its senior posts, while Palestinian Arabs and Jews were encouraged to apply for positions in its lower echelons. The system worked effectively enough to set the pattern for most of the ensuing years of the mandatory government. Steps were taken to improve the health and sanitation of Palestine, as cisterns and sewage lines were dug and hospitals and clinics opened. With the purchasing power of a large British garrison coursing through its towns and villages, the country's economic circumstances improved markedly. In June 1920, the growth potential of the Jewish National Home would become even more hopeful, when the Lloyd George government appointed as Palestine's first civilian high commissioner none other than Sir Herbert Samuel, himself a Jew of known Zionist sympathies (p. 521).

Moreover, during the earliest months following General Allenby's capture of Palestine, the Arabs' Hashemite leadership did not appear to react adversely to the Jewish National Home. In January 1918, shortly after issuance of the Balfour Declaration, Commander D. H. Hogarth, research director of the Arab Bureau in Cairo, was dispatched to Jidda, Arabia, to reassure Sherif Hussein that the Zionist program for Palestine represented no threat to the emerging Hashemite realm. In turn, sensing the potential advantages of Arab-Jewish cooperation, the sherif issued the Jews several warmly phrased invitations to return to their "sacred and beloved homeland." This evident cordiality was further reaffirmed by the Emir Feisal, Hussein's second son and leader of the wartime Arab Revolt. In meetings with Weizmann at the Red Sea port of Aqaba in the summer of 1918, and in London in the winter of 1918–19, Feisal gave his fullest assurance of Arab friendship. The exchanges of courtesies were formalized on January 4, 1919, in a "pact" signed by Weizmann and Feisal, anticipating "the closest possible collaboration [between Arabs and Jews] in the development of the Arab State and Palestine. . . ."

By the late spring of 1919, however, as the Zionists moved vigorously to ensure wider opportunities for immigration and land purchase, Palestinian Arab restiveness began to surface. In February 1920, a party of Arab raiders attacked several Jewish agricultural colonies along Palestine's northern border, in a twilight area between the British and French zones of occupation. Among those who were killed defending the outposts was Joseph Trumpeldor, the Jews' wartime leader of the Zion Mule Corps. In April of that year, Arab riots outside Jerusalem led to the deaths of some two dozen Jews and Arabs. Thirteen months later, in May 1921, an upsurge of Arab violence extended more widely throughout Palestine. Before British army units managed to suppress the unrest, forty-seven Jews and forty-eight Arabs had been killed and several hundred others of both peoples wounded. A British commission of inquiry subsequently revealed an extensive array of Arab grievances, ranging from distaste for Jewish "socialist" equality between the sexes to fear of rising Jewish immigration and land purchases.

By coincidence, in that same spring of 1921, Colonial Secretary Winston Churchill had summoned a gathering of senior military and imperial officials to Cairo to formulate a new approach to Britain's unsettled Iraq mandate. Churchill's visit now also provided a logical occasion to discuss the exploding tensions in Palestine. The solution Churchill and his advisers devised, in late May, was to transfer Palestine's high plateau land east of the Jordan River to the rule of Emir Abdullah, eldest son of the Sherif Hussein. Henceforth, the Jewish National Home would be restricted to the narrow corridor of Palestine west of the Jordan River. In July 1922, further to dispel Arab misgivings, the Colonial Office issued the Churchill White Paper, a document that specifically rejected any notion of a future Jewish state in Palestine. It cautioned, too, that Jewish immigration henceforth would be limited to the "economic absorptive capacity of the country."

The Zionists had suffered a reverse, but hardly a fatal one. The Churchill White Paper had reaffirmed that the Jewish National Home existed as of right, not as of Arab sufferance. On September 29, 1922, the League of Nations, like the Paris Peace Conference two years earlier, incorporated the Balfour Declaration verbatim in its award of the Palestine mandate to Britain, and imposed on Britain the obligation not simply to permit but to "secure" the Jewish National Home, to "use their best endeavours to facilitate Jewish immigration and settlement on the land." Nor did there appear any doubt that Britain intended to stand behind its commitments to the Jews. The Bonar Law government, which succeeded the Lloyd George coalition in October 1922, firmly rejected every Arab effort to alter Britain's support of the Jewish National Home.

By mid-decade, the future of that Zionist vision appeared increasingly hopeful. When Britain assumed responsibility for the Holy Land, it took over an economic cripple, a territory that was impoverished well beyond the destruction of the recent war. Underpopulated, possessing little industry or trade and few known natural resources, Palestine was further debilitated by famine and administrative chaos. The newly arrived British military and civilian staffers were obliged to devote their first efforts simply to the restoration of a minimal degree of public order. The task was fulfilled, despite occasional outbreaks of rioting. Perhaps the mandatory's single most impressive administrative achievement was the establishment of an honest and efficient judiciary. Its operation was based on successive tiers of courts that included Arab and Jewish as well as British judges. The system worked well. At the same time, both the content and the administration of the law were decisively transformed. Virtually the entire Ottoman criminal and commercial code (except for land matters) was replaced by the English Common Law. Only issues of "personal status"—marriage, divorce, testamentary wills—remained within the jurisdiction of Moslem, Jewish, and Christian religious courts. It was essentially in this form that the legal system of Palestine would be adopted in 1948–49 by the State of Israel.

The British mandatory government similarly expended much effort and talent on the development of agriculture, a sector of the economy the Turks had ruinously neglected. Research stations were constructed for the improvement of cultivation and livestock. Modern, efficient procedures were instituted for land registration, and customs taxes were raised to protect citrus and other agricultural crops. Wide-ranging improvements in communication were achieved by enlarging the rail network, building roads and bridges, and further modernizing and augmenting postal, telegraph, and telephone services. Air links were established with Europe and other Middle Eastern nations. An international airport was constructed at Lod. Plans were under way to enlarge the port of Haifa. By the mid-1920s, these improvements, both physical and governmental, were substantially reflected in the growth of the Jewish population, from 55,000 in 1919 to 108,000 in 1925. Much of the progress unquestionably was the fruit of Zionist enterprise (p. 369). Yet it reflected no less Britain's contribution in providing a quality of security and order, justice and administrative integrity, far superior to any the Holy Land had ever known.

BUILDING THE JEWISH NATIONAL HOME

The establishment of the Palestine mandate offered the Jewish National Home considerably more than a diplomatic imprimatur. Within the guidelines laid down by the Peace Conference, and later by the League of Nations, the Jews were authorized to provide their own "agency" to work as an active partner with Britain in developing the Palestine Jewish economy. Provisionally, the Executive of the Zionist Organization in effect anointed itself as this Jewish Agency. Functioning henceforth as a kind of quasi-government for the Jewish National Home, the Agency in turn organized its own departments of political affairs, immigration, labor, colonization, education, and health. Chaim Weizmann, president of the Zionist Organization (an acclamation bestowed upon him for his monumental achievement in negotiating the Balfour Declaration), launched into a worldwide fund-raising effort to broaden Palestine Jewry's economic and social infrastructure.

The urgency of this fund-raising effort hardly could have been exaggerated. In the postwar period, Jewish immigrants were arriving in Palestine in unprecedented numbers—over 50,000 between 1919 and 1925 alone. A significant minority within this postwar influx had received a kind of makeshift exposure to agriculture in Eastern Europe, on Zionist training farms organized by the *HeHalutz* (Pioneer) movement. Although nominally apolitical, HeHalutz in practical fact was overwhelmingly influenced by the doctrines of Labor Zionism. Most of the trainees also were committed to A. D. Gordon's ideal of physical labor and self-resurrection on the soil (pp. 280–81). To achieve that goal, the fund-raising campaign of the Jewish National Fund moved into its highest gear. The small denominations gathered up from hundreds of thousands of blue-and-white contribution boxes became the sustaining currency of Zionist land purchases in Palestine. Upon this public soil, in turn, elaborating upon the techniques innovated before the war, the newcomers set about establishing new belts of collective and cooperative farms.

Yet a majority of the postwar settlers did not opt for agriculture. In contrast to the socialist idealists of the prewar Second Aliyah (p. 278), the immigrants of the 1920s were refugees pure and simple. With few exceptions, they were in flight from the successor-state xenophobia of newly independent Poland. By 1928, some 70,000 of these economically "redundant" immigrants, supplemented by approximately 8,000 Jews from the Caucasus and the Middle East, raised the Jewish population of Palestine to 154,000. On the other hand, if few of the newcomers were animated by Labor Zionist or even Gordonian ideals, they laid the basis at least for the Yishuv's expanding urban economy. Within five years, they doubled the Jewish population of Jerusalem and Haifa. It was their immigration, moreover, that transformed Tel Aviv into an authentic city. By 1928, the population of this former Jaffa suburb had grown to 46,000, and the city's growth produced its own self-sustaining momentum. By 1939, Tel Aviv encompassed 160,000 inhabitants, all Jews. Much of this urban growth was based upon an emergent substructure of Jewish industry that included electric power stations, saltworks, flour mills, and cement, brick, textile, olive oil, and soap factories, together with a proliferation of light industrial workshops. Above all, home construction dominated early Jewish urban growth. Whatever the strain the inflow of East European newcomers imposed, it also sustained and propelled a construction industry that played the central role in the National Home's economic growth.

Monitoring this development closely, the leadership of the dominant

Labor Zionist movement was persuaded that in the cities, as on the soil, their task was to "conquer" the Palestine Jewish economy and shape it in the socialist image. Rudimentary workers' organizations actually had appeared in the Jewish agricultural colonies as early as the turn of the century, but the effort to create labor unity gained momentum only in the last years before the war, when several Labor Zionist factions joined together to found the *Histadrut*, the rather portentously titled Federation of Jewish Labor. At first, the Histadrut's few hundred members tended to belong to the agricultural settlements, and this accordingly became the sector where the labor federation placed its heaviest emphasis to secure employment for new immigrants. Not all its techniques were conciliatory. Neither were they limited to strikes against employers. To ensure that employment priority was given to Jews, picketers occasionally used strong-arm tactics against Arab migrant labor. The Arab economy was self-contained, they argued, but employment for Jewish immigrants was literally a matter of life or death. By the late 1920s, the employment issue was essentially resolved in favor of Jewish labor, but by methods that did nothing to improve Arab-Jewish relations.

Meanwhile, with the bulk of postwar Jewish immigration pouring into towns and cities, the Histadrut also began organizing urban labor exchanges and urban workers' unions. It similarly approached the problem of employment with considerable imagination by organizing its own economic projects and welfare services. These included its own construction corporations, its own medical insurance fund, its own banks, cooperative purchasing and marketing outlets for communal farms, even its own network of—ideologically socialist—primary and secondary schools. Over the years, too, in its political dimension, the Histadrut forged the basis for Palestine Jewry's single largest party, Mapai, the acronym for the Land of Israel Workers' Party. More than any other element, therefore, it would be this Labor Zionist coalition of workers and farmers that would shape the ideology and institutions of Palestine Jewry, and later of the early State of Israel.

By the end of the Jewish National Home's first decade, its tangible accomplishments, although numerically modest, were qualitatively impressive. Some 162,000 Jews lived in Palestine by 1930, comprising 17 percent of the country's inhabitants. Of these, 37,000 lived on the soil, in 111 agricultural settlements and 13 Zionist agricultural schools and experiment stations. Citrus crops were growing in size and profitability. Some 1,500 Jewish-owned workshops and factories were in operation. The quality of life was slowly improving. By 1930, the broad Histadrut health network, together with such overseas philanthropic organizations as Hadassah-WIZO, had established four hospitals in Palestine, a nurses' training school, fifty clinics and laboratories, and a wide-ranging maternity and child-hygiene service. Within the Jewish sector, at least, the historic scourges of the Holy Land—malaria, trachoma, and typhoid—were being systematically reduced, and the Jewish mortality rate fell from 12.6 per thousand in 1924 to 9.6 per thousand in 1930 (Jewish infant mortality dropped from 105 per thousand to 69 per thousand in the same period).

Here, in sum, was the measure of the Yishuv's growth. Comprised largely of recent transplants from Eastern Europe, Palestine Jewry had developed its own quasi-government, its own largely autonomous agricultural and industrial economy, its own public and social welfare institutions. Its schools were providing some 28,000 children with a basic education and a Jewish "national" self-assurance unprecedented even in the most pluralistic communities of the Diaspora. More than the expansion of landholdings, of financial resources, or of world Jewish support, it was this dimension of self-assurance that ultimately would prove decisive in girding the Jewish National Home against the future challenges of British diplomatic equivocation and Arab hostility.

XX

The Legacy of Progressivism:
Immigrant Jewry in the United States

THE STRUGGLE FOR A LABOR FOOTHOLD

By 1914, America's 3.5 million Jews had become the largest Jewish population in the world. New York's 1.5 million Jews outnumbered by five to one those of Warsaw, the world's second-largest Jewish community. Yet demographic increase signified only the most visible feature of American Jewry's transformation. The East European newcomers of the twentieth century were a far less insular element than the shtetl Jews who had preceded them a generation earlier. Over the decades, they had read the works of Russian and German writers, had shared in parallel Yiddish literary developments in Warsaw, Vilna, Bucharest, and Jassy, and had begun to work loose from the constraints of religiocultural insularity. Earning their livelihoods in industry or in small workshops, they had shared in the new revolutionary movements sweeping through Europe, and tens of thousands of them had been members of the Bund.

These were the militant immigrant Jews of the early twentieth century. Infused with the ideals of socialism and labor activism, they gravitated to Bundist-style organizations in New York and other large cities. Some were lured into anarcho-syndicalism by the fiery German radical Johann Most. In far larger numbers, however, they gave their support to socialism, and to the American Socialist Party's much respected leader, Eugene Debs. Beyond repudiating violence, Debs evinced a gratifying willingness to allow "ethnics"—Czechs, Hungarians, Poles, Serbs, Finns, Jews, and others—to register in the party on an autonomous basis, in their own foreign-language constituencies. The Bundists of course had fought for this dispensation in Russia. They grasped, too, that the Socialist Party in the United States was solidly rooted in the American tradition of agrarian populism. By 1911, a Socialist, Victor Berger, was serving in the United States House of Representatives, and seventy-six Socialist mayors held office. For even the most doctrinaire former Bundists, the evident grassroots respectability of American-style socialism was an advantage to be taken seriously.

Few Jews entertained illusions of a Socialist victory in a presidential election. Rather, they had tended to cast their votes for Republican candidates. The Republicans were the party of Lincoln, after all. More important, Theodore Roosevelt's or William H. Taft's signature was on the Jews' immigration certificates. But on the local level, in New York's Lower East Side, the Socialist Party developed a substantial following among voters seeking an alternative to the Democrats' corrupt Tammany machine. Indeed, immigrant Jews themselves produced two Socialist folk heroes, Morris Hillquit and Meyer London. Hillquit, a lawyer, was five times a candidate for the House of Representatives from the Ninth Congressional District. In each election, however, Tammany Hall worked in cynical association with the Republicans to assure his defeat.

But if Tammany stopped Hillquit, it could not always overwhelm Meyer London. Ukrainian-born, London had come to the United States in 1886, at the age of sixteen, and worked his way through New York University Law School. Never hesitating to donate his services to his fellow immigrants, he began running for Congress in 1910, and eventually, in 1914, with multiparty Jewish support, he won. It was a moment of rejoicing for the Lower East Side. Indeed, the victory of New York's first Socialist representative was hardly less than a political sensation. Much of the press, and many of the "uptown" Jews, did not hide their concern that London might prove to be a wild-eyed radical in Washington. Their anxiety was unwarranted. A model of tact and graciousness, London evoked only respect among his fellow congressmen for his personal integrity and open-mindedness. Once the United States entered the World War, he felt obliged to adopt his party's stance of pacifism, and he lost his second bid for reelection. Nevertheless, both London and Hillquit remained the East Side's beloved elder statesmen. Both captured its ambience of militant utopianism. Whether in the immigrant ghettos of New York, Chicago, Philadelphia, or other major cities, Jews magnified every incident and event in the struggle for workers' progress and minority rights in the archetypical Bundist spirit of righteous protest.

Initially, the East Europeans' leftist militance availed them little. They had reached the United States, after all, at the very apogee of unrestrained American capitalism. Early working-class efforts to unionize, to strike, invariably failed. Among immigrant Jews, these early unionizing ventures were additionally frustrated by the very structure of their immigrant economy. It was centered in the garment industry, where most Jews worked in sweatshops, in tenement quarters too small and dispersed to foster opportunities for collective organization. In the late nineteenth century, their strike efforts were comparatively few, and as a rule flickered out unproductively. In 1888, Morris Hillquit led the effort to establish an umbrella organization for Jewish workers, to be called the United Hebrew Trades. Its purpose was one essentially of

"consciousness-raising," or fostering unionization within the garment industry and other "Jewish" vocations. But the effort was unsuccessful. Upon resolving a specific grievance, the early garment workers often allowed their
union dues to lapse.

Over the turn of the century, however, the United Hebrew Trades gradually was subsumed into a rather larger working-class organization. Its leader,
Samuel Gompers, would emerge as one of the major figures of American
social history. He was also one of the unlikeliest. Born of Dutch Sephardic
parents in the ghetto of London, Gompers had come to the United States as
an adolescent, in the midst of the Civil War. He secured his first employment as a cigar-roller on New York's Lower East Side. Helping to organize
the cigar-makers' union, Gompers steadily worked his way up through the
German-language Central Labor Council. In 1886, it was he who personally
led the negotiations that produced the American Federation of Labor and
who then became the AFL's first president. A phlegmatic, rather colorless
man, a pragmatist through and through, Gompers evinced no interest whatever in political ideologies, and in socialism least of all. Appraising the
nation's booming economy in the post–Spanish-American War era, he concluded early on that free enterprise was a fact of life, and labor's rights would
have to be secured within that system. To that end, Gompers shrewdly and
patiently negotiated a series of bread-and-butter wage and hour improvements that validated his cautious moderationism to employers and employees
alike. In 1900 alone, some 45,000 new workers flocked to the AFL. Jewish
workers, too, then agreed to forgo ideology. Encouraged by Hillquit, London, and eventually even by the Socialist Party leader Eugene Debs, they
accepted the AFL's pragmatic guidelines. In the long run, the decision proved
a sound one.

In the short run, however, it was a series of "intramural" developments
that gave Jewish unionism an unexpected new vitality. One was the early-
twentieth-century wave of immigrating Bundists. Well accustomed to confrontation with employers and tsarist police, these hard-edged activists
brought a new tenacity and discipline to the Jewish labor movement in
America. Another factor was the growth of the garment industry itself. Over
the first decade of the new century, women's clothing manufacture—mainly
Jewish-owned—became the third-largest consumer-goods industry in the
United States. In 1900, the number of its factories totaled 1,224; in 1910, the
figure grew to 21,701. During the same period, the numbers of its workers rose
from 31,000 to 84,000. With this growth, and the introduction of more efficient machinery, the older sweatshops gradually disappeared in favor of integrated factories. It was a transformation, in time, that provided a more effective
basis for unionization. No longer dispersed among tenement flats or isolated
from one another, employees who labored in a common workplace were posi-

tioned to share their grievances and to collaborate for group action. Thus, in 1900, responding to the exhortation of Gompers and the AFL leadership, the various individual unions within the women's garment industry agreed to collaborate in an umbrella organization, the ILGWU—International Ladies' Garment Workers' Union.

By 1909, the ILGWU had grown to sixty-three local branches encompassing nearly 20,000 workers. Although its membership would increase exponentially in future years, the period of its early gestation was also its most intensely idealistic. Much of that idealism was generated not only by the union's own Bundist core but by the working conditions of the clothing industry itself. Employees labored sixty-five hours a week, and often longer at the height of the fashion season. Frequently, they had to provide their own needles, threads, irons, even sewing machines. Within the factory, a sinister "internal" subcontracting procedure reduced employees to working for their foreman on a piecework basis. The ordeal was more arduous yet for women, who comprised the majority of the workforce, for they were paid much less than men for equivalent work. It was in the largest of the women's garment factories, the Triangle Shirtwaist Company, in September 1909, that the ILGWU local called for a strike. All 1,000 of Triangle's women employees responded. It was the first women's strike in American history, and its participants paid for their initiative. Marching on the picket line, they were taunted, threatened, jostled by hired toughs, even arrested on charges of "malingering" and "vagrancy." But when the entirety of the ILGWU membership voted to support the walkout, over 20,000 other shirtwaist workers—virtually all of them Jewish women—now joined the Triangle strikers.

Stunned by the outpouring, the employers then mobilized the police and local judges against the strikers. But not all New York's "respectable" elements were hostile. The press was generally sympathetic. So were many Protestant and Catholic clergymen, as well as the totality of the Reform rabbinate, who sermonized on behalf of the strikers. Many upper-class New Yorkers were moved by the spectacle of impoverished immigrant girls defying police and company goons. Wealthy matrons provided bail money, even joined the strikers on the picket line. By early 1910, management understood that it had lost the war of public opinion. It came to terms, agreeing to reduce the workweek to fifty-two hours and to provide four legal holidays with pay. Employees no longer were obliged to supply their own tools, or to pay off foremen on a piecework basis.

The strike established a precedent for collective action in the men's cloak and suit industry. Here the employees were largely immigrant Jewish men, many of them former Bundists, and their factory working conditions were as harsh as any in the United States. In July 1910, with AFL support, 65,000 of the employees voted to go on strike. Again, the workers had to undergo the intimidation of police and company strong-arm men, of exhausted savings and family privation. Indeed, the economic impact of the huge walkout soon ramified through the economy of the entire Lower East Side. Hundreds of small businesses closed. Finally, in late summer, a group of influential "uptown" Jewish spokesmen, led by Jacob Schiff, pressed management and strikers to utilize the good offices of Louis Brandeis, a progressive Boston lawyer with much experience in labor relations cases. Both sides agreed. In September, Brandeis's negotiating skills produced results. An agreement was hammered out that established the principle of a fifty-hour workweek, paid legal holidays, overtime compensation, the abolition of "inside" contracting, and a joint labor-management committee to monitor physical conditions in the factory. The workers were jubilant. The day after signing, they celebrated wildly, with parades and brass bands. The so-called Protocol of Peace was the first in American labor history. The rights achieved in the men's garment industry, whose workers united under the AFL umbrella as the Amalgamated Clothing Workers of America—the Amalgamated—soon would be achieved by other heavily Jewish New York unions: of cigar-makers, bakers, butchers, painters, and glaziers.

Yet it required a final catalyst to transform immigrant Jews into a major presence on the American industrial scene. On Saturday, March 25, 1911, some eight hundred young women and a few dozen young men were at their sewing and cutting machines on the top three floors of the ten-story Triangle Shirt-waist Company building. Notwithstanding the agreement of the previous year, sanitary conditions remained marginal, with piles of oil-soaked scraps lying on the floor. These suddenly caught fire, and flames leaped through the workroom, then from floor to floor, transforming the overcrowded plant into an inferno. The owners fled the building without unlocking the heavy steel exit doors. Many of the terrified girls suffocated, others fought their way to windows. There, screaming, they jumped with their clothing ablaze. The fire was not brought under control until darkness. By then the toll was 147 women and 21 men killed. Several days later, in a mass funeral, over 100,000 workers and their families marched in a silent cortege through streets whose store-fronts were draped in black. Lower East Side businesses were closed for the day. In a sobbing funeral eulogy, Rose Schneiderman, a leader both of New York's Women's Suffrage Party and of the Women's Trade Union League, reminded her listeners that "it is up to the working people to save them-selves. The only way they can save themselves is by a strong working class movement."

That movement henceforth was irreversible. Despite the Protocol of Peace and its arbitration provisions, between 1913 and 1916 both the ILGWU and the Amalgamated felt obliged to resort to a series of swift, sharp strikes to resolve their grievances. In each instance, the employers retreated, fearing to lose the "season." By the end of World War I, the combined membership of the women's and men's garment unions would exceed a quarter-million, and employees felt secure enough to begin turning their efforts to welfare union-ism (p. 376). Yet it was not improved labor conditions alone that tempered the workers' flaming Bundist zealotry. They well understood that the United States was not the Pale of Settlement, that their "enemies," management, were not Russian gentiles or tsarist police officials, but usually Jews like them-selves, often the same people whose solicitude had built the protective canopy of Jewish philanthropies and social services. Each group could talk to the other, each shared a minority people's commitment to security in the New World.

THE EMERGENCE OF IMMIGRANT COMMUNITY

For the East European newcomers, the quest for religious, cultural, or even psychological stability often was more complex than the struggle for eco-nomic dignity. The Orthodox rabbinate, denied its authoritative Old World function as arbiters of Jewish personal and communal behavior, failed to sus-tain its historic influence or prestige in the New World. In truth, the shift to a more activist and secular way of life had been prefigured even before the great migration from Europe. In the free and open United States, the trend simply gained momentum. Over the years, Jewish communal leadership was pre-empted by such nonreligious institutions as the Socialist Party, labor unions, fraternal lodges, and the Yiddish press and theater. Like their German-Jewish predecessors, the East Europeans almost from the moment of their arrival set about establishing philanthropic and benevolent associations. Their models tended to be the *hevrot* of the Old World. As in the Pale of Settlement, these mutual benefit associations included burial societies, orphanages, old-folks' homes, even modest clinics and hospitals. In New York alone, over a thousand of these bodies were in operation, and most of them functioned independ-ently of the synagogues.

A particularly vibrant example was the *landsmanshaft*, a kind of informal club of Jews who shared a common town or village of origin, and who regrouped in the United States for self-help or welfare-insurance purposes. Pioneered by the Bialystok Mutual Aid Society in 1886, these *landsmanshaftn* eventually represented nearly every city, town, and village that sent its kins-men to America. A few, like the Pruskurower Society, blossomed into umbrella organizations of several thousand members. The United Brisker Relief Society developed branches extending from New York to Los Angeles. Some landsmanshaftn maintained their own cafés and meeting halls. By 1924, at the end of the Great Migration, over a million Jews had been enrolled at one time or another in a landsmanschaft. Whatever its nomenclature or diversity of purpose, this "brotherhood of memory" served as an indispensable bridge of adaptation to the United States.

At the same time, for affiliated and unaffiliated Jews alike, it was Yiddish, the transplanted language of the Pale, that functioned as the common denominator of ethnicity in America. Indeed, the pungent old vernacular achieved its plateau of literary refinement not in Europe but in the United States. The reasons were entirely functional. For newcomers, a common language obviously served as a refuge from anomie. But not less important was a fractionally improved margin for leisure in the wealthy United States, even during the earliest and most harassed years of immigrant settlement. Accordingly, it was in New York, Philadelphia, and Chicago, not in Vilna, Warsaw, or even Odessa, that renowned Yiddish émigré intellectuals achieved their widest audiences. Lectures became a particularly important medium, whether sponsored by landsmanshaftn or by such larger organizations as the socialist Workmen's Circle (Arbeiter Ring) or National Workers Alliance (Farband). As a Yiddish newspaper observed in 1905:

> Friday, Saturday, Sunday there are lectures. Hundreds of listeners . . . fill the hall. During the winter there are several hundred lectures. Big societies have series of lectures; the tiny ones have single, irregular ones. Some big clubs attract several hundred people. Statistics show that there are thousands and thousands of Jews coming to be enlightened by lectures. . . . [Even the most uneducated masses are being reached.]

Others read and watched. In New York alone, before 1914, over 150 weekly, monthly, quarterly, and festival journals and yearbooks were published in Yiddish. Even as that literature opened the doors of world affairs and American life to hundreds of thousands of immigrants, its preeminent conduit at all times was the Yiddish press. By 1910, almost every immigrant Jew in America read a New York–published Yiddish newspaper. With few exceptions, these publications tended to reflect the major political and ideological trends within the Jewish community. Thus, two pioneering newspapers included the *Tog*, politically centrist and self-described as "the newspaper of the Yiddish intelligentsia," and the *Morgn Djurnal*, much prized by the Jewish middle class and boasting columns by some of the most respected Jewish thinkers of the day. In the proletarian ghettos, on the other hand, it was the socialist press that captured the widest readership, and specifically in the years when the incipient Jewish trade-union movement was struggling for a voice. One of these journals, the *Forverts*, became the largest Yiddish newspaper in the world.

From the outset of its publication in 1897, the *Forverts* was cautiously social-democratic. The approach reflected the multicultural experience of its editor, Abraham Cahan. In the Pale of his birth, Cahan had attended a Crown secondary school, where he was exposed to secular subjects and became fluent in Russian. In 1882, at the age of twenty-two, after a conspiratorial eighteen months evading the police in the socialist underground, he fled to the United States. Enrolling in a Lower East Side primary school with twelve-year-olds, Cahan acquired functional English in six months, even as he earned his bread at night as a finisher in a sweatshop, then as a tobacco-stripper. Within two years, he found his métier as a freelance journalist.

Soon Cahan was contributing articles in Russian to Russian newspapers, in Yiddish to the Yiddish press, in English to American newspapers. In 1897, taken on as a reporter for the *New York Commercial Advertiser,* he spent the ensuing four years covering assignments that ranged from murders and fires to interviews with "Boss" Croker, Buffalo Bill, and President William McKinley. Thus, by 1901, upon accepting the editorship of the *Forverts,* he brought with him both well-honed skills as a journalist and a more realistic understanding of American life. Almost single-handedly, afterward, Cahan transformed the *Forverts* from an obscure sectarian newspaper, with a modest readership of 6,000, into the great voice of Yiddish journalism. By 1912, the paper's circulation had reached 140,000; by 1917, not less than 200,000, a figure rarely matched even by English-language newspapers.

Cahan never abandoned his working-class constituency. His columns expressed their socialist and unionist aspirations. It was largely the *Forverts* that orchestrated Meyer London's congressional election campaign, that served as unofficial headquarters for the garment workers' unions and for numerous other labor-oriented organizations. Yet Cahan would not allow his newspaper to engage in tendentious socialist polemics. All articles were to be informative, clearly written, and infused with the spice of human interest. Cahan regarded himself above all else as an educator of immigrants to the realities of America. Thus, in his columns he offered fatherly homilies. He urged mothers to provide their children with fresh vegetables and clean handkerchiefs, to permit them to engage in sports and other forms of exercise. It was also to educate the immigrant masses that Cahan introduced the *Forverts*'s single most widely read feature, "Bint'l Brief" (literally, "Collection of Letters"), a kind of Yiddish prefiguration of Dear Abby–style advice columns. Whether printed or not, each letter was answered personally by the department editor. An entire generation of immigrants understood its debt to Cahan. When he died in 1955, at the age of ninety-one, some 10,000 mourners waited outside the memorial hall to pay tribute to the "Lower East Side's First Citizen."

ON THE THRESHOLD OF AMERICANIZATION

In the last decade before World War I, an additional half-million Jews arrived in the United States. The expanding American economy absorbed them all—and more. The garment workers' "Great Revolt" reflected that new stability, for theirs was a revolution of rising expectations. In 1908, the United States Immigration Commission reported that 37 percent of New York's immigrant Jews already were employed in white-collar jobs. In growing numbers, former garment workers were opening their own small workshops. Other Jewish "proletarians" were investing their modest savings in real estate, particularly in New York's outlying boroughs. In 1908, the first subway to Brooklyn went into operation, and soon real estate agents were touting Brownsville, the subway's first stop in Brooklyn, as a "pastoral village" where "Jews could live as in the Old Country, without any rush or pressure." By 1914, approximately 230,000 Jews had settled there, and Brownsville was a "pastoral village" no more. In contrast to the Lower East Side's tenements, dwellings in Brownsville were solid three-story brownstones. Similar areas of Jewish "second settlement" were emerging in the Bronx. Learning the lay of the land, mastering functional English, the first generation of East European Jews was taking root. Although prosperity still eluded most of them, the immigrants no longer were quite the penniless, terror-stricken novices who once had traveled alone and friendless from East European border stations to the looming pandemonium of industrial America.

It was the crisis of World War I, ironically, that solidified their still undefined identity with their new country. When hostilities in Europe began in the summer of 1914, the emotional loyalties of thousands of America's German-Jewish families at first remained as closely bound to Germany as those of German-Americans at large. Even the banking patriarch Jacob Schiff refused to allow his firm, Kuhn, Loeb & Company, to subscribe the Anglo-French loans in 1916 so long as "one cent of the proceeds of the loan would be given to Russia." Hatred of the tsarist regime was even more visceral a fact of life among the East European immigrants. New York's eight Yiddish newspapers were implacable in condemning the very notion of support for the Russian war effort. "All civilized people sympathize with Germany," the *Forverts* editorialized in the spring of 1915. "Every victorious battle against Russia is a source of joy."

Then, suddenly, all was changed by the Russian Revolution of March 1917 and the ensuing political emancipation of Russian Jewry. Almost immediately, Jacob Schiff underwrote a $10 million loan to Russia. Louis Marshall, president of the American Jewish Committee, a collection of German-American patriarchs, exulted: "We are seeing a paean of victory. We are rejoicing at the answer to our prayers." As for the immigrant community, its reaction to the fall of the tsar was ecstatic. "It means freedom," declared Abraham Cahan in the *Forverts*. "We are facing a miracle," proclaimed the *Yiddishe Volk*. "And one claims that the times of miracles are over!" rhapsodized the *Fraynd*. On March 20, 1917, in a rally organized jointly by the *Forverts*, the Bund, the United Hebrew Trades, the Socialist and Russian Social Democratic parties, and the Workmen's Circle (Arbeiter Ring), some 15,000 Jews gathered to celebrate in Madison Square Garden, and thousands of others milled about outside.

For American Jewry, one of the revolution's most decisive consequences was the support it ensured for entrance of the United States into the war, on April 6. The two events were separated by less than a month. Now even the German-Jewish leadership was prepared to give full-hearted commitment to the American military effort. "I am German by birth," declared Schiff at a meeting of the American League of Jewish Patriots, an ad hoc group he himself had helped organize, "and I love the German people. But I do not love the German government as it exists today." The *Bulletin* of the Solomon Seligmann Society, another ad hoc German-Jewish group, declared: "We must win the war. We must forever banish the imperialistic principles of the Kaiser and his cohorts." Among East European Jews, the shift was less dramatic than the volte-face of the older, nativized group. Numerous principled Socialists, Morris Hillquit and Meyer London among them, hewed to the party line of opposing participation in a "capitalist" war. Indeed, all the party's ethnic federations—Slavic, Finnish, Italian, German, as well as Jewish—subscribed to that position.

Yet the visibility of Jewish (and other immigrant) pacifists obscured the routine and artless wartime commitment of the Jewish immigrant masses. Within three months of America's entrance into the war, even the leftist unions underwent a substantial deradicalization. The ILGWU purchased $100,000 in Liberty Bonds. The Amalgamated Clothing Workers and Workmen's Circle adopted resolutions supporting the war effort, and the United Hebrew Trades and the Furriers' Circle raised $12 million in bond drives conducted on the Lower East Side. In common with a majority of immigrant communities, hundreds of thousands of other Jews were swept up in the mood of the war and intensified American patriotism. In 1918, Jews comprised 3.3 percent of the nation's population. They provided 5.7 percent of the armed services. Of 250,000 Jewish soldiers and sailors, 51,000 were enlistees.

THE JEWISH PRESENCE UNDER REAPPRAISAL

Whether in the years before or after this record of wartime commitment, the attitude of "Old Americans" to the Jewish immigrant presence was one of distaste and alarm. The parochial insecurities of rural and small-town Americans, the misgivings that had flared up in the populist movements of the late nineteenth century, appeared to intensify in the twentieth. The rise of industry and the city, the influx of millions of Eastern and Southern Europeans, the growth of political radicalism and urban crime—all persuaded inhabitants of the "heartland" that they were losing control of the society their forebears had painstakingly established. As far back as the 1890s, in books and articles, Frederick Jackson Turner, a historian of the American frontier, praised the "Old Immigration" from Northwest Europe and warned that the "New Immigration" from Eastern and Southern Europe was a "loss to the social organism of the United States." Turner's views were heartily shared by Edward A. Ross of Stanford University, a renowned progressivist economist, and by William Graham Sumner, a pioneering Yale sociologist. Once again, the invidious comparison between "old" and "new" immigrants was applied with particular intensity to the Jews. In *The Old World and the New* (1914), Ross echoed Turner's argument that the new immigrants, and particularly the Jews, were "beaten men from beaten breeds . . . moral cripples, their souls warped and dwarfed by iron circumstances. . . ."

The invidious distinction between the two waves of immigration was expressed with frontal straightforwardness by Prescott F. Hall, a Boston Brahmin and founder in 1894 of the Immigration Restriction League.

> Our institutions were established by a relatively homogeneous community [wrote Hall], consisting of the best elements of a population selected by the circumstances under which they came to the New World. Today, much of our immigration is an artificial selection . . . of the worst elements of European and Asiatic peoples.

For Hall and other Old Americans, it was the immigrant Russian Jew whose ghetto-based mores and sheer exotic "alienism" evoked the most visceral revulsion and fear. In truth, eminent intellectuals were no more immune to this culture shock and nativism than were farmers or small-townsmen. Returning from England to the United States in 1904, Henry James toured New York City for the first time in twenty years. In *The American Scene* (1907), James described

> [a] great swarming that had begun to thicken, infinitely, as soon as we had crossed to the East Side. . . . There is no swarming like that of Israel when once Israel has got a start, and the scene here bristled, at every stop, with the signs and sounds, inimitable, unmistakable, of a Jewry that had burst all bounds.

Even as they confronted the spectacle of the alien tidal wave, American sociologists, biologists, and anthropologists tended to be influenced by the pseudoscience of Aryanism, the new racist ideology then sweeping through Western Europe. The evident triumph of white imperialism in Africa and Asia, and the victory of American armed forces over the "decadent" Latin Spaniards, tended further to popularize the notion of "Aryan," Nordic superiority. The theory was given further credence by Francis Galton and Karl Pearson's extensive research in eugenics. Once adapted to the American scene by Charles Davenport, the eugenicist notion that selective breeding might protect a nation's "good" racial traits, and prevent their corruption by "bad" ones, was seized upon by Old Americans and applied to the New Immigration, and specifically to the Jews.

Thus, William Z. Ripley's widely popular *The Races of Europe* (1899) expressed a rather more extreme reaction than Henry James's culture shock. He laid his emphasis on the Jews' "physical degeneracy." "The great [Polish-Jewish] swamp of miserable human beings," warned Ripley, "threatens to drain itself off into this country, as well, unless we restrict its ingress." For Charles Davenport, the offspring of mixed Jewish and non-Jewish couples were "half-breeds"; while medical specialists attributed the Jews' "psychopathic" behavior to "racial incest." It was above all the image of congenital enfeeblement that appeared with growing frequency in numerous turn-of-the-century literary descriptions of the Jew. In this fashion, a more broadly defined Jewish stereotype emerged in the United States, one that transcended earlier versions of economic shrewdness or dishonesty. It was of a race somehow unwholesome, a threat not only to the nation's cultural homogeneity but to its very physical and moral vitality.

Whether rooted in culture shock or in eugenics-based racism, popular opposition to the New Immigration encouraged the federal government to begin reappraising the traditional American policy of unrestricted immigration. In 1891, when President Benjamin Harrison asked Congress to tighten the legislative ban against "paupers," Congress acted with dispatch and the president signed the bill that same year. In 1892, New York State Commissioner of Immigration John B. Weber led a committee of investigation into Jewish persecution in the Tsarist Empire. Traveling to Russia, the group expressed its concern at the treatment of the Jews. Some of that anxiety doubtless was humanitarian, but it reflected more fundamentally the impact of mass Jewish departure on America's social economy. The consequence of these visitations, reports, and the widening stream of eugenist publications eventually induced Congress to pass two bills in 1907, one imposing a literacy test on immigrants, and the other adding a "means" test.

It was in 1907, too, that Senator William Dillingham, Republican of Vermont, an avowed nativist, chaired a commission to evaluate the impact of the recent immigration on the nation's economy and society. The Jews by then knew what to expect, and their fears were confirmed a year later when the Dillingham Commission entertained lengthy testimony from the Immigration Restriction League, from the Patriotic Order of the Sons of America, the Daughters of the American Revolution, and other anti-immigration groups. Published in 1908, the Dillingham Report comprised forty-seven volumes and was packed with statistics, testimony, scientific and pseudoscientific horror stories of urban slums, urban crime, reduced literacy, and debased moral and physical standards. One entire volume, *A Dictionary of Races,* provided a detailed eugenicist categorization of nationalities and ethnic groups. Armed with the Dillingham Report, congressional restrictionists then moved to the offensive in their campaign for even tighter literacy and means tests. In February 1913, their draft legislation passed both houses of Congress. But five days later, responding to the anguished appeals of Jews and other immigrant groups, President William Howard Taft, in one of the last acts of his expiring presidency, vetoed the bill. So did President Woodrow Wilson in January 1914 when a new draft of the legislation reached his desk. The outbreak of the World War that summer then temporarily blocked further immigration. Yet the temper of Congress, and of much of the American people, was quite apparent.

It was the Bolshevik Revolution that provided restrictionists with still another weapon. This was Jewish "radicalism." Like the kinsmen they had left behind, America's immigrant Jews had greeted news of the Bolshevik triumph with grave trepidation. But in the ensuing Russian civil war, the horror inflicted on the Pale by White armies lent the Soviet regime growing prestige as the defender of Jewish lives. Thus, in the United States, when 70,000 far-left members of the American Socialist Party reestablished themselves in 1922 as the American Communist Party, Jews comprised some 15 percent of the Communist membership, and not less than 45 percent of its leadership. Conversely, the triumph of bolshevism in Russia evoked a militant counter-response from "respectable" Americans of all backgrounds. In June 1918, Congress drastically amended the wartime Espionage Statute to include such nonmilitary offenses as "profane, scurrilous, and abusive" language against the government and Constitution of the United States. Ultimately, some 2,000 individuals would be prosecuted under this vaguely worded law. Indeed, within a year, the United States slid naturally from wartime anti-German chauvinism to anti-Red hysteria. In 1919–20, A. Mitchell Palmer, President Wilson's attorney general, launched a wide-ranging series of raids against suspected radicals in New York and elsewhere. Over 4,000 suspect aliens were rounded up and held in special detention pending deportation. A majority were Jews.

Most of these deportees, like the fiery Emma Goldman, were committed radicals, and if they represented only a small minority of the Jewish immigrant population, they were linked increasingly in American public consciousness with the Bolshevik regime in Russia. The theme was endlessly embellished by the right-wing press. "The aims of the Jewish-radical party," explained the *Chicago Tribune,* "[have] nothing behind them beyond the liberation of their own race." "The Russian Jews . . . have no real national feeling," echoed *Life* magazine. "They are loyal to socialism, to internationalism . . . but are not bound by more than the loosest ties to any country or form of government." The American Defense Society, the American Protective League, and other self-defined patriotic organizations mounted campaigns against "unclean" foreign influences, particularly the "Bolshevik Jew." By late 1920, the acutest phase of the Red Scare had passed in the United States. Nevertheless, the image of the immigrant Jew as active or incipient Bolshevik was not easily to be dissipated. More even than the populist stereotype of financial Shylock or the eugenicist stigma of racial degenerate, that radicalist image would cling like the mark of Cain to a second and even a third Jewish generation.

It was exacerbated, too, by an antisemitic booklet, *The Protocols of the Elders of Zion,* a clumsy forgery that attributed the rise of bolshevism to a sinister Jewish plot for world domination (p. 471). Circulated throughout Europe by a group of embittered White Russian émigrés, the *Protocols* was republished in the United States by the renowned automobile manufacturer Henry Ford. Indeed, for several years Ford's private newspaper, the *Dearborn Independent,* and then his privately published book, *The International Jew,* quoted extensively from the *Protocols,* and issued repeated warnings against the putative Jewish menace to world order. It was not until 1927, facing a libel suit initiated by a group of American Jews, that Ford grudgingly repudiated his endorsement of the *Protocols* and issued a public apology. But the damage had long since been done. With his vast prestige as America's industrialist-statesman, Ford had delivered a blow to the Jews' self-confidence as grave as any inflicted by their mounting phalanx of enemies in the United States.

A FORECLOSURE OF JEWISH INGRESS

Meanwhile, Jewish immigration, choked off by the war, had fallen to 26,000 in 1915, to 15,000 in 1916, and then had stopped altogether during the years of American belligerency. As the restrictionists had feared, however, the demand for admission to the United States burst all bounds once the war ended. For hundreds of thousands of Ukrainian, Polish, and Rumanian Jews, overseas sanctuary was a matter quite literally of survival (pp. 413–14). Thus, in 1922, the Jewish influx reached its pre-1914 level of 190,000, nearly 15 percent of all immigrants to the United States that year; and some 300,000 more were known to be preparing for departure. While South Slavs and Italians also were swelling the immigrant tide, antisemitism manifestly had become the most pervasive feature of the restrictionist mood. Ranging from eugenicist tracts to Red-baiting journalistic polemics, the barrage of anti-Jewish litera-ture mounted steadily. In the House of Representatives throughout 1920, committee hearings on immigration did nothing to mitigate the fear of a Jewish inundation. Reports from the United States consul in Warsaw argued that "[i]t is impossible to overestimate the peril of the class of emigrants com-ing from this part of the world. . . ." Another Foreign Service officer, Wilbur J. Carr, insisted that

> [most of the emigrants] are Polish Jews of the usual ghetto type. . . . They are filthy, un-American and often dangerous in their habits. . . . [They are] socially undesirable. . . . Ninety percent lack any conception of patriotic or national spirit, and the majority of this percentage is mentally incapable of acquiring it.

These and other warnings made their impact. Immigration legislation accordingly was fashioned by Congressman Albert Johnson, Republican of Washington, and co-sponsored in the Senate by the formidable William Dillingham. Approved by Congress in the spring of 1921, and signed by Presi-dent Warren Harding, the Johnson Act established an annual ceiling of 350,000 immigrants. Under that restriction, newcomers would be limited to 3 percent of the number of foreign-born of each nationality present in the United States in 1910. The bias of the legislation was undisguised. It favored immigrants from the traditional "heartland" of Northwest Europe, those who still comprised the great majority of foreign-born in 1910, even as it disfavored—that is, virtually barred—newcomers from Southern and Eastern Europe. In 1924, the Johnson Act was tightened even further, shifting the base year for determining quotas from 1910 to 1890, while the maximum propor-tion of immigrants altogether was reduced from 3 percent to 2 percent. Under these constraints, Jewish immigration to the United States dropped from 190,000 in 1920 to 43,000 in 1921, to 7,000 in 1926, and the numbers would continue to decline. In effect, the door was closed specifically on the vast, tor-mented reservoir of Polish, Lithuanian, Ukrainian, and Rumanian Jews who were undergoing pogroms and economic strangulation. Yet, even as late as the mid-1920s, no one could have anticipated that the closure prefigured a fate much graver than ongoing discrimination and impoverishment.

In the United States itself, meanwhile, Jews over the turn of the century were confronted with a parallel closure of "inner" doors. Indeed, gentile reac-tion to Jewish upward mobility became evident as early as the 1880s, in the

Gilded Age of nouveau-riche American status-seeking. It was then that discrimination first manifested itself in summer resorts and in city and country clubs. By the eve of World War I, virtually all resort hotels in the Midwest and Far West were limited to gentile clientele. B'nai B'rith could not find a single Minnesota hotel willing to accommodate the organization's summer convention. Masonic lodges blackballed Jews. Soon bias transcended the social and extended to the more functional sectors of American life. In New York, in the last years before the war, immigrant Jews moving from ghetto neighborhoods into areas of "second settlement" found themselves blocked from renting apartments in the more desirable areas of Upper Manhattan. Realtors in Long Island and Westchester County adopted the device of "restrictive covenants" to close off entire residential communities to Jews. In the early 1920s, the pattern rapidly extended throughout the Atlantic Seaboard and into the Midwest.

More painfully yet, restrictions began to affect higher education. The children of Jewish immigrants reached college age in the last years before World War I. It was then, for the first time, that Ivy League and other prestigious institutions began introducing a severe Jewish numerus clausus. During the early postwar years, the barrier was raised not only against the children of immigrants but against the more acculturated, "refined" progeny of older nativized German-Jewish families. Thus, in 1926, the proportion of Jews admitted to Harvard's freshman class was limited to 14 percent; two years later, to 10 percent. At Yale, the Jewish quota dropped from 13 percent in the early 1920s to 8 percent by the early 1930s. Other prestigious eastern colleges similarly reduced their Jewish quotas. Soon the pattern of discrimination extended westward. By the 1930s, it was universal in the nation's private schools.

The restrictions may have been humiliating, but they were never an insurmountable obstacle to a college education. If Jews were barred increasingly from elite institutions, they could and would go elsewhere, to public universities in their own cities and states. As in Europe, however, the tightening quotas also affected opportunities for professional training and employment. In medical schools, by the late 1920s and early 1930s, the quota for Jewish students had atrophied to a negligible 6.7 percent. For Jews who were accepted for medical school, hospital residency appointments after graduation were minuscule. During the 1920s, in New York and other large cities, Jews similarly began facing restricted access to law schools. Dominating the legal profession, the larger gentile law firms viewed with horror the prospect of admitting persons of "immigrant stock" into their austere bailiwick.

In the business world, dominated by Old American capital, the pattern of discrimination became no less institutionalized throughout the 1920s. Firms large and small limited their hiring and directed advertising exclusively to "Christian" office help. Hardly a white-collar area was unaffected, from junior management down to secretarial and clerical positions. The scars of the 1920s and 1930s would be felt for years afterward. Of the 180,000 directors of corporations listed in the 1934 edition of *Standard & Poor's Register,* less than 5 percent were Jews. In 1936, a *Fortune* magazine survey listed only three Jews in the (lower) executive ranks of the automobile industry. None could be found in coal, rubber, chemicals, transportation, utilities, engineering, or construction. Of 93,000 commercial bankers in the United States, less than 1 percent were Jews (again, almost exclusively German Jews). As late as the 1950s, Jews remained dramatically underrepresented at executive levels of industry, banking, transportation, and insurance. In the interval, their best hope lay in alternate white-collar employment in "safe" Jewish firms, or in precarious business or professional ventures they themselves would launch.

THE GHETTO WALLS FALL

Under this cloud of suspicion and distaste, the economic status of East European Jews in the United States underwent no instant revolution during the boom era of World War I and the 1920s. As late as 1933, Jews comprised three-fourths of all factory workers in New York's garment district. Thousands of other Jews continued to earn their livelihoods as carpenters, painters, plumbers, glaziers, and locksmiths. It was in smaller or middle-sized towns that immigrant Jews were more likely to achieve white-collar status, usually as small retailers, but even these were hardly storming the ramparts of the middle class. Jews in America, as in Western Europe between the wars, at best remained a petit bourgeois community.

Nevertheless, there were several important areas in which even East Europeans managed to leave their mark. Preeminent among these, of course, was the garment industry, still the bedrock of Manhattan's social economy. Nationwide, the needle trades by 1939 employed 700,000 men and women, a majority of these still foreign-born Jews. It was a sector, moreover, that lent itself to diffusion into small units. A "shop" with 100 workers could operate as efficiently as a factory with 1,000 workers. The decentralization was ideally suited to those former employees who had accumulated modest nest eggs. Thus, in the postwar years, the management of garment manufacture in the United States shifted gradually from German to East European hands. Other areas of the economy soon acquired an East European coloration. In the United States, as in Europe, scrap was the marginal vocation of a marginal people. Immigrant Jews made a good thing of it in the prewar and early postwar years. Virtually the entire market in waste products, including iron, steel, nonferrous metals, rubber, paper and cotton residue, was founded by Jews and remained within the Jewish economy. The manufacture of cigars and cigarettes also drew substantially from the early Jewish immigrant vocation of cigar-rolling. Three of America's largest cigar manufacturers, including Fred Hirschorn's General Cigar Company, were established by Jews, as were the P. Lorillard and Philip Morris cigarette companies.

Transplanted to the United States, the European-Jewish tradition of distilling and tavern-keeping also produced several of America's greatest liquor companies. In 1899, the American Distilling Company—the ill-starred "Whiskey Trust"—was organized by a group of immigrant Jews, who managed briefly to control production through much of the Midwest and South. In 1916, Samuel Bronfman of Montreal, one of eleven children of Russian-Jewish immigrants, opened a local retail liquor outlet, then went on to purchase the old Canadian distillery of Seagram & Company. Soon Bronfman developed a thriving market for his products. That market was less profitable in Canada, however, than in the United States, and specifically during the Prohibition years, when Bronfman developed vast expertise in sending clandestine shipments of whiskey across Lake Erie to awaiting American bootleggers. So many of these bootleggers also were Jews that Lake Erie came to be known as the "Jewish Lake." The traffic laid the basis for Seagram's formidable post-Prohibition eminence in the United States, where the family eventually shifted its headquarters. In the same fashion, Lewis Rosenstiel, a Cincinnati distiller, built his Schenley Corporation by smuggling in contraband liquor from Canada and Scotland. Bronfman's and Rosenstiel's epic rivalry produced raids on each other's personnel, even the reputed "disappearance" of key shippers. It was a ruthless game.

Real estate, too, was becoming an important vocation for immigrant entrepreneurs (p. 378). After the war, Jewish contractors responded with vigor and imagination to an acute urban housing shortage by erecting medium-sized apartment buildings in the areas they knew best, the Jewish secondary-settlement neighborhoods in Brooklyn and the Bronx. Elsewhere throughout the United States, Jewish builders similarly were among the earliest to lay the basis for a substantial postwar construction of apartments and row houses. Among the thousands of middle-sized immigrant builders and developers, occasional grand visionaries began to surface, particularly in New York. Louis Horowitz covered Manhattan with some of its mightiest skyscrapers, including the Woolworth and Chrysler buildings, and the Waldorf-Astoria Hotel. A. E. Lefcourt and his partners were simultaneously erecting skyscrapers on Fifth, Madison, Lexington, and Seventh avenues.

Other fortunes were built in cosmetics. First-generation East Europeans established three of the nation's largest beauty firms—Revlon, Max Factor, and Helena Rubinstein. John Keeshin of Chicago, the son of immigrants, built his Transcontinental Freight Lines into the largest trucking company in the United States. Samuel Zemurray, born in Kishinev in 1877, arrived in America as a youngster to work in an uncle's country store in Selma, Alabama. Afterward, toiling as a dock laborer in the port of Mobile, young Zemurray sensed an opportunity to buy up discarded, "pre-ripened" fruit for a pittance, then to deliver it at cut-rate prices to regional grocery stores. Within seven years, he became a bulk importer of Central American bananas. By the eve of World War II, Zemurray owned banana plantations in Honduras, Guatemala, and Costa Rica, and his United Fruit Company became the single largest privately owned agricultural domain on earth.

Entrepreneuring a Popular Culture

As an immigrant people, the Jews for the most part had acquired their initial economic foothold in "safe" vocations, where Jewish predecessors were well ensconced. The garment, tobacco, and liquor industries were early examples. So was entertainment. Peripheral to the central economy, indifferent to pedigree, the field had been open to raw talent from its nineteenth-century beginnings. Indeed, popular-music publishing had become extensively Jewish even before the East European influx. The nation's largest music-publishing firm, M. Witmark & Sons, was founded in 1886 by three young German-Jewish brothers. But the great majority of Jewish music publishers who followed were Russian immigrants. By 1910, most of these companies had set up shop in "Tin Pan Alley" (a sobriquet evoked by the sounds of hundreds of clinking piano keys), on West Twenty-eighth Street, adjoining the theater district.

Tin Pan Alley thrived by providing the endless quantities of songs needed for the many hundreds of new theater and vaudeville houses rising in the nation's cities. Oscar Hammerstein's huge Olympia Music Hall, a combination theater and cabaret, opened in 1894 at the site of the present Times Square and became the virtual capital of New York show business. More than any other individual, it was the Berlin-born Hammerstein (p. 170) who subsequently launched New York on its frenzy of theater construction. Beginning at Thirteenth Street and extending along Broadway as far north as Forty-fifth Street, thirty-three theaters launched over seventy productions in the 1900–1901 season alone, and new theaters were continually opening. So they would in other major cities, for it was the national market that determined a play's financial success or failure. By 1914, between two hundred and three hundred road companies were touring the country, and large circuits of theater-booking companies were organized to exploit them. Most of these chains were owned by Jewish impresarios, and specifically by a monopolistic "Syndicate" of seven Jewish theatrical promoters, all of German background, led by Abraham Lincoln Erlanger.

Even before the war, however, another family rose to challenge the Syndicate. These were Samuel, Jacob, and Lee Shubert, sons of impoverished East European immigrants in Syracuse, New York. Working as an usher in a local theater, Sam Shubert gradually worked his way up to manager. His brothers joined him. With borrowed funds, they began producing their own plays. The Syndicate monopoly then demanded a substantial share of the Shuberts' revenue. Instead, defying Erlanger and his partners, the brothers Shubert resorted to importing plays from England, then set about purchasing, renovating, renting, or building their own theaters for road-company productions. By 1910, the brothers had sixty productions running throughout the United States, and by 1929 they had broken the back of the Syndicate. By then, too, over 75 percent of Broadway productions were Shubert-financed and -managed, and Shubert Alley had become synonymous with New York theater. So, even earlier, had the impresarial talents of Florenz Ziegfeld, an Austrian-born half-Jew whose Ziegfeld Follies were the diadem of Broadway musicals in the prewar and early postwar decades, and the launching pad for a host of Broadway talents.

Even as Jews guided Broadway to its central role in American legitimate theater, motion pictures would represent their breakthrough to far larger audiences. Jews did not invent motion pictures, but in the early twentieth century they were among the first to grasp the potential of these primitive "flickers." By the eve of the war, some 3,000 "nickelodeons" were operating in the United States, and by no coincidence they thrived most vigorously in immigrant neighborhoods. Besides their cheap admission price, the photoplays required only a minimal understanding of the English language. Moreover, the field was a new one. With only a modest investment in equipment, bright young Jews grasped that they could get in at the start without having to trip over established gentiles. Thus, by 1914, some of these newcomers already had become owners of small chains of nickelodeons.

With accumulated earnings, graduating to theater ownership, eight or ten venturesome immigrants began organizing rickety little production companies to provide two-reelers. Among these pioneers, Carl Laemmle, the German-born son of a Württemberg Jewish merchant, put together the Universal Film Company. Still other immigrant entrepreneurs, Adolf Zukor and Marcus Loew, who began their American careers as furriers in North Dakota, eventually moved in the prewar period from nickelodeons to theater ownership to production companies, then established a partnership with another theater owner, Jesse Lasky, to form the Paramount Pictures Corporation. Lazar Mayer, disembarking in New Brunswick, Canada, in 1892 with his Russian-Jewish parents, peddled junk in St. John, Nova Scotia. Moving to Boston while still a teenager, venturing briefly into the junk business on his own, Mayer soon purchased a nickelodeon, then two film theaters, then a film distribution office. In 1923, "Louis B." Mayer joined forces with a group of other immigrant Jews to launch a production company, the Metro-Goldwyn-Mayer Corporation.

California was becoming a favored locale among these aspiring producers. Clement weather for outdoor filming was one advantage. A more important one was the proximity of the Mexican border, which served as a convenient escape route for evading process servers dispatched by the patent monopolists of early film technology. Within a few years, however, the "interlopers" generated sufficient financial resources to defy the film trusts, and either to win their cases in court or to negotiate settlements. Several of the newcomers even began to devise important technological breakthroughs of their own. Jack, Harry, Sam, and Albert Warner, sons of an immigrant junk-dealer in Ohio, started out as nickelodeon operators in New Castle, Pennsylvania, in 1913. By the mid-1920s, Warner Bros. was a profitable studio, but hardly in the front ranks. That status changed almost overnight as a result of a courageous gamble. Purchasing the shaky Vitagraph Company in 1925, the Warners subsequently acquired the rights to a sound-recording process devised by an engineer at Western Electric. They bet their shirts on developing it through their new Vitagraph subsidiary. The result was a revolution in motion pictures that set a new standard for all production companies, compelling them to develop rival sound systems of their own.

Throughout its critical gestation years, the film industry remained a fellowship essentially of outsiders. Even its bank financing was not provided by Old American firms, with their tradition of genteel antisemitism. Rather, it was largely Jewish investment companies that underwrote their earliest undertakings, together with an immigrant Italian banker, Amadeo Giannini, chairman of the Bank of America. The investments paid off spectacularly. In 1919, with 15,000 theaters serving as their outlets, film-producing companies registered a gross income of $750 million. Only seven years later, with $1.5 billion invested in their operations, motion pictures had become the fifth-largest industry in the United States.

THE CULTURE OF AMERICANIZATION

Old World legacies died hard. In the early postwar period, some twenty Yiddish theater companies in New York continued to attract sizable audiences. In that same period, the Yiddish press achieved the meridian of its readership, when some twelve major newspapers generated a combined circulation of nearly 400,000. By the latter 1920s, however, Yiddish theaters began to close, newspaper circulation began to fall off, and Yiddish trade papers ceased publication altogether. A vibrant linguistic heritage was fading.

So, apparently, was a religious heritage. With the immigrant community still well exposed to socialist secularism, and acculturation the tantalizing vision of young, second-generation Jews, conventional piety no longer had a chance, even within the shrinking urban ghettos. Orthodox rabbis were ill equipped to challenge this trend. From their tiny makeshift *shuls*, often carved out of former stores or warehouses, they frowned on any compromise with Americanization. Their obdurateness proved spectacularly ineffectual. At the other end of American Jewry's religious spectrum, the Reform movement remained committed to its vigorous rejection of Talmudism, dietary laws, and the separate and inferior status of women. Its uncompromising emphasis on modernism was reaffirmed in 1903 when Kaufmann Kohler assumed the presidency of the Hebrew Union College. A domineering administrator, Kohler forbade skullcaps and prayer shawls at his seminary and rejected numerous traditional prayers and commandments.

Yet it was also during Kohler's tenure, ironically, and that of his successor, Julian Morgenstern, that the Hebrew Union College over the next three decades attracted growing numbers of students from East European immigrant homes—indeed, fully 75 percent of the student body by 1937. The "demographic" shift in turn reflected the multiple inducements of Reform. The movement was well funded and solidly structured. Its "nativist" origins permitted an oblique identification with the Jewish "aristocracy." Above all, Reform was humanistic and modernistic. It appealed to both the cultural sensibilities and the social aspirations of educated, second-generation Jews; and, in its social activism, it was "relevant." Uninterruptedly, then, the Reform movement maintained its trajectory of growth. From 136 congregations in 1900, its Union of American Hebrew Congregations expanded to 411 by 1939.

Still another of the factors that assured Reform's intellectual and social eminence in the interwar years was the leadership of a fascinating group of charismatic rabbis. In their ardent commitment to social reform, they evoked a unique resonance among immigrant families with Bundist roots in the Old World. The best known of these preachers was Stephen S. Wise. Born in Budapest in 1874, himself the son of a non-Orthodox but traditionalist (Neologue) rabbi, Wise was brought to the United States as a child when his father accepted a New York pulpit. Attending public school, then City College, the younger Wise earned a doctorate in Semitics at Columbia University. His rabbinical ordination was achieved in Europe under Adolf Jellinek, the renowned "enlightened" rabbi of Vienna. In 1899, against the advice of family and friends, Wise accepted a call from a Reform congregation in Portland, Oregon. If Oregon was frontier country in those days, this was specifically its appeal to a vigorous, self-assured young man like Wise. It offered him scope to formulate his own dynamic conception of the rabbinate. Exploiting the opportunity to the hilt, Wise hurled himself into Oregon's public issues, sermonized against municipal and state corruption and liquor and gambling interests, and campaigned for liberal political causes and candidates.

With his reputation as a social activist and powerful orator, Wise in 1905 was invited to be interviewed for the pulpit of New York's august Temple Emanuel, the prestige plum of the Reform rabbinate. But when the board resisted Wise's demand for freedom of expression on public issues of social and political policy, Wise declined further negotiations. Instead, remaining in New York, and with the financial backing of his growing circle of admirers, he organized a "Free Synagogue." Besides offering freedom of the pulpit, Wise emphasized, the new congregation could be committed to "abolition of distinction between rich and poor as to pews and membership privileges." In short, there would be no "establishment" here. Wise incorporated his mission into the very organizational structure of the congregation. A "social service division" maintained an employment office, conducted welfare activities for the Jewish indigent, and operated a child-adoption center. By 1913, nearly half the congregational budget was devoted to social service.

At all times, too, Wise sustained his well-developed role as a public activist. He sermonized endlessly on behalf of workers' right to unionize and strike against "intolerable working conditions." In New York, as earlier in Portland, Wise took dead aim at corruption in municipal and civil affairs. "For me," he insisted repeatedly, "the supreme declaration of our Hebrew Bible was and remains: 'Justice, Justice shalt thou pursue.' " In 1907, Wise's sermons against the notorious former Tammany boss "King Richard" Croker played a substantial role in blocking Croker's return to power after an expedient self-exile in Ireland. In 1912, again under Wise's pressure, Mayor William Gaynor appointed a blue-ribbon civic committee to investigate police corruption. In the 1920s and early 1930s, Wise's dramatic philippics against the city's venal mayor, James J. Walker, helped launched the reformist campaign that drove the mayor from office.

Neither did Wise and numerous of his fellow Reform rabbis hesitate to trim Jewish ceremonials and rituals to accommodate the practical realities of life and work in the United States. Yet, by the same token, it was specifically this flexible approach to Jewish tradition that evoked growing misgivings among Reform's "moderates." Borrowing from the precedent of Zacharias Frankel in Germany (p. 136), a small group of American Reform rabbis and laymen sought to devise a workable compromise between Orthodoxy and Reform. As early as the 1880s, these self-styled "Conservatives" sought to organize their own "Jewish Theological Seminary," whose faculty and rabbinical graduates presumably would lay the intellectual foundations for compromise. The project foundered, and for some years the effort to produce a new Conservative version of Judaism appeared moribund. It was revived, ironically, by the crisis of East European immigration. Although unshakably Reform themselves, the German patriarchs grasped that a seminary producing "moderate," traditionalist rabbis would help ease the newcomers' adjustment to America. To that end, in 1901, Schiff, Warburg, the Lewisohns, the Guggenheims, and other establishment stalwarts contributed $500,000 for the Jewish Theological Seminary endowment fund.

To direct the new enterprise, the sponsoring group turned to Solomon Schechter, one of Europe's most renowned Jewish scholars. The product of a Rumanian Hasidic family, Schechter had been drawn to a broader intellectual outlook while still in his teens. In 1865, he had traveled to Vienna to enroll at the Israelitische Theologische Lehranstalt, the enlightened "Jellinek Yeshiva" (which Stephen Wise also attended), and was ordained there at age nineteen. His intellect barely whetted, young Schechter then pursued advanced research in oriental studies at the universities of Berlin and Oxford. In 1890, already a prolific author, he was appointed Cambridge University's first lecturer in Judaic Literature. It was during his Cambridge incumbency, moreover, that Schechter won much renown for his discovery in Cairo of the Hebrew original of the Ben-Sira, a long-lost volume of near-canonical quality, resembling the Book of Proverbs. It was one of the great literary finds of history. Afterward, Schechter continued to pour out a felicitous series of essays on Jewish historical and religious issues that further augmented his scholarly reputation. Who in the Jewish world could challenge the credentials of so prodigious an intellect? It was in 1901, therefore, at the age of fifty-four, that Schechter was offered and accepted the invitation to direct a revived Jewish Theological Seminary.

He did not disappoint his constituency. Within two years, he assembled a distinguished faculty, and in 1910 ordained his first dozen rabbis. At the same time, Schechter's approach to Judaism evoked respect from wide sectors of American-Jewish life. He described it as "K'lal Yisrael"—"catholic Israel." More tolerant than the Orthodox fundamentalists, less pliant than the Reformers, Schechter insisted that there was room in the Jewish tradition for a wide variety of rituals and ceremonials. The formulation prefigured a decisive trend in American Judaism. Building on Schechter's conception of an all-embracing "catholic Israel," the Conservative movement by and large avoided confronting ideological problems. So long as congregants accepted the central role of the "peoplehood" of Israel, they were free to compromise on issues of religious ritual. With this flexibility, it became possible for second-generation Jewish humanists to rationalize their identification with the synagogue, to claim that they were observing tradition for the sake of "Jewish peoplehood." Additionally, to give organizational structure to his movement, Schechter in 1913 set about identifying the growing network of Conservative-oriented congregations as the United Synagogue of America.

Two years later, Schechter died suddenly of a heart attack. Afterward, under leadership less dynamic than his own, the Conservative movement began to languish, and "catholic Israel" soon reduced itself essentially to the line of least resistance, a comfortable but rather bland compromise position in American-Jewish life. Nevertheless, the ideological and structural basis for the movement had been laid. In the post–World War II era, with the birth of Israel and the resurgence of emotional and ideological "peoplehood," Conservatism would enter into a new era of vitality as American Jewry's most widely accepted "middle school."

THE ERA OF THE GREAT DEPRESSION

In 1929, the onset of the Great Depression inflicted a series of shattering blows on America's Jews, immigrant and second-generation alike. For industrial workers, the painfully achieved collective bargaining guarantees of the prewar Great Revolt era vanished almost immediately. In a reversion to the old sweatshop days, entire families began slaving away again at piecework. As for white-collar Jews, these remained concentrated in small mercantile or handicraft operations, and thereby were precisely the marginal entrepreneurs hardest hit by the economic collapse. In 1931 alone, a nationwide review of thirty Jewish welfare agencies disclosed a 42 percent increase in relief recipients during the first nine months of the year. In Baltimore, the increase was 77 percent; in Minneapolis, 100 percent! Yet the most debilitating wound of all for Jewish middle-class families was an upsurge of vocational discrimination. More even than in the 1920s, employment in the corporate sector was barred to Jews. In 1938, an American Jewish Congress report noted that anti-Jewish restrictions in want-ads had reached their highest level in the nation's history.

The old Bundist ideals now resurfaced. Indeed, the Depression accelerated a process of radicalization that had begun in the immediate aftermath of Russia's Bolshevik Revolution. In those early postrevolutionary years, a left wing sprang up within the American Socialist Party. Attaching itself to the Comintern—the Moscow-sponsored Third International—the faction eventually would reincarnate itself as the American Communist Party (p. 382). It was among this hard-edged minority, in turn, that Jews once again played as visible a role as in the Communist parties of Europe. Yet it was significant that the militant Jewish nucleus evoked little following among Jewish blue-collar workers. In the garment industry, Jews had learned through bitter experience that Communists and fellow travelers were ideological doctrinaires who evinced little practical concern for workers' laboring and living conditions. Although unions of predominantly Jewish membership would remain ardently leftist well into the early 1930s, it was not from them that the Communists would draw their most impressionable Jewish sympathizers during the Great Depression.

Instead, the response came from the children of immigrants, those in their early and mid-twenties who had just arrived at the threshold of economic security. Most were recent college graduates. Many had lately entered the white-collar ranks as teachers, city and state government clerical employees, and social workers. Now their hopes of career advancement and "respectability" lay blasted, apparently by an irredeemably ruthless economic system. Nor did it escape these embittered young people, blocked in mid-passage by depression and discrimination, that the Soviet Union had resolved the problem of unemployment for its own citizens, and also had taken the lead in mobilizing resistance to fascism and antisemitism in their own country and elsewhere in Europe. In the United States, too, the Communist Party appeared to be positioning itself in the forefront of every campaign for racial and economic justice.

These were the circumstances, during the early years of communism's revival, in which the Jewish component surfaced even more notably than it had a decade earlier, in the aftermath of the Bolshevik Revolution. During the 1930s, the State of New York accounted for one-fifth of the Communist Party's membership, and that one-fifth was predominantly Jewish. All the senior editors of the *Daily Worker* were Jews. If the party failed to make headway in the bread-and-butter-oriented garment unions, it managed successfully to infiltrate white-collar unions, with their extensive Jewish membership. More significantly, tens of thousands of Jews throughout the country were drawn to Communist-front organizations, most of which disguised themselves as "anti-fascist" groups. Impressionable and idealistic, Jewish students were uniquely susceptible to these leagues and alliances, both in New York's "subway circuit" of public colleges and in numerous other public universities throughout the East and Midwest.

It was in the Depression era, too, that Jewish belletrists, critics, and essayists wielded the literary sword for the fellow-traveling left. The novelists Michael Gold and Meyer Levin, the playwrights Clifford Odets, Irwin Shaw, Marc Blitzstein, and Sidney Kingsley, the screenwriters Samuel Ornitz, John Howard Lawson, and Albert Maltz, produced social dramas with aggressively leftist themes. They captured the anguish of an entire generation of afflicted and distraught young Jews. Even the many tens of thousands among that generation—still the majority—who had managed to resist the appeals of communism, tended to thrash out despairingly for an effective route to social justice.

In 1933, they began to find it. Entering the White House in January of that year, Franklin Roosevelt promptly set in motion a vigorous program for resolving America's massive unemployment. At the president's initiative, Congress approved an unprecedented series of federal works projects to cope with a "national emergency . . . as grave as that as if the nation were at war" (Roosevelt's words). Social security, labor, and securities-and-exchange legislation followed in rapid order. The unconventionality and dynamism of the program evoked a groundswell of hope among tens of millions of citizens of all backgrounds. For the Jews, however, that hope was lent even greater credence by the people Roosevelt co-opted to serve under him. If the president had little time for conventional domestic restraints, neither did he for conventional domestic bigotries. To launch his vast New Deal enterprise, he would forfeit no person of talent. Here Louis D. Brandeis and Felix Frankfurter played key roles as intellectual mentors of his program. Over the turn of the century, Brandeis, the son of Czech-Jewish immigrants, became a renowned crusading lawyer in Massachusetts, where he drafted much of the state's pioneering reformist economic and social legislation, and subsequently negotiated the Protocol of Peace for New York's garment industry (p. 374). As an avowed enemy of corporate giantism, Brandeis swiftly won the admiration of Woodrow Wilson. Indeed, in 1916, Wilson defied the right-wing legal establishment by appointing Brandeis to the Supreme Court, thereby making him the first Jew to hold that honor.

Austere and intellectually rigorous, Brandeis proved himself the ablest juridical draftsman the high tribunal had ever known. No man of his generation so fully grasped the inner workings of the nation's economic system, or the relationship of jurisprudence to the needs of economic public policy. Nevertheless, for almost two decades, Brandeis's was a minority voice on the court. After Wilson's departure, three successive Republican administrations had cut him off from access to the White House. Only in 1933, following the Roosevelt electoral landslide, was the opportunity revived for personal influence. The new president held Brandeis in high esteem, and consulted with him periodically on major social welfare legislation. More decisive yet was the impact Brandeis exerted indirectly through key technocrats. Indeed, not a few of these young lawyers and economists owed their appointments or promotions to the justice's intercession. That intercession was never direct, however. For Brandeis, there was a better conduit.

Felix Frankfurter, one of six children of a Viennese-Jewish immigrant family, arrived in the United States in 1894, at the age of twelve. The family settled initially in New York's Lower East Side. After attending City College, Frankfurter went on to Harvard Law School, where he compiled a brilliant academic record. With these credentials, he seemed likely to overcome even the "Jewish barrier," and to enjoy a lucrative private practice. Yet, as an irrepressible activist, Frankfurter was drawn instead to public service: as assistant United States attorney for New York; as campaign manager for Henry Stimson's (unsuccessful) campaign for governor of New York; then as assistant to Stimson during the latter's tenure as secretary of war in the Taft administration. It was in Washington that Frankfurter came to know Brandeis, and to become the great man's disciple and alter ego. Upon returning to Cambridge afterward as a professor at the Harvard Law School, Frankfurter also befriended Roosevelt, who by then had become governor of New York. On numerous occasions, Frankfurter advised Roosevelt in Albany on the state court system, on public utilities and staff appointments. Following Roosevelt's election to the presidency, Brandeis prepared a detailed blueprint for much of the New Deal program, and discussed it at length with Frankfurter. It was Frankfurter who then set about identifying talented young lawyers and economists to help activate Roosevelt's New Deal.

A significant minority of these technocrats were Jews. Sons of immigrants, recently trained in the conventionally "Jewish" professions of law, economics, and social work, few of them had ever so much as seen the inside of a corporate law office or a major corporation. Now theirs was the opportunity to draft regulatory legislation against the very interests represented by these august Wall Street firms. It was Roosevelt himself who encouraged these young people to come to Washington. Rising to political maturity in New York State politics, he had developed a genuine admiration for the numerous Jewish progressives who flocked to his program. By the time he became New York's governor, and even more when he became president, Roosevelt had come to depend on the commitment of these people to his social objectives. Despite the contumely he endured for employing Jewish advisers and technocrats, nothing would inhibit him from mobilizing them for his administration. The most influential among them may have been Benjamin V. Cohen, general counsel of the Treasury Department, and a master drafter of New Deal legislation. Others included David Lilienthal, who served as first chairman of the Tennessee Valley Authority; Mordecai Ezekial, general counsel of the Agriculture Department; Charles Wyszanski, general counsel of the Labor Department; Robert Nathan, director of the national-income division of the Commerce Department; Isador Lubin, director of the Bureau of Labor Statistics. Approximately 4,000 Jews operated at various middle-level and senior echelons of government during the 1930s, an unprecedented number for any Western government.

Grateful as they were for Roosevelt's rejection of a numerus clausus of any kind, American Jews were even more impressed by the president's willingness to grapple forthrightly with the deepest structural problems of American society. Admittedly, he did not accept a socialist blueprint for these problems, but neither any longer did the largest numbers of Jews. Except for an implacable Communist and fellow-traveling minority, the message resonated through every sector of Jewish life: political liberalism, rather than communism, or even socialism, now offered a likelier avenue to their welfare and security. By the time the president launched his reelection campaign, in 1936, he had become a kind of secular Jewish messiah. That year, he garnered

86 percent of the Jewish vote. In the same presidential campaign, Norman Thomas, the Socialist candidate, won a meager 188,000 votes, only one-fifth of his 1932 showing. The evidence was compelling that Jews were his principal defectors. It was under Roosevelt's leadership that they decisively abandoned the immigrant legacy of radical utopianism, to venture at long last into the mainstream of American liberalism. If the shift of political stance was belated, it appeared in future years to be all but irreversible.

XXI

Successor States and Minority Guarantees: 1919–1939

A MINORITY "BILL OF RIGHTS"

In 1914–15, the Jews of the United States moved urgently to provide relief for the more than 1 million of their kinsmen trapped in the zone of conflict between Russia and the Central Powers. Within months, they succeeded in establishing the American Jewish Joint Distribution Committee (p. 322). No philanthropic instrument ever proved more effective than the "Joint" in raising funds and dispensing supplies to victims in these war areas. Tens of thousands of Jews survived as a result of Joint emergency food and medical help. Far from ending with the surrender of the Central Powers, moreover, the Joint program was broadened during the savage "intramural" military campaigns in Ukraine. By 1920, the great philanthropy maintained a network of over five hundred soup kitchens and clinics throughout the battle areas. At the same time, witnessing the magnitude of Jewish vulnerability and suffering in the East, Joint personnel were the first to share their information with Jewish leaders in the United States.

Those leaders still tended to be the more affluent and acculturated veterans of German-Jewish background. From their midst came the board members of the American Jewish Committee, a small, self-appointed elite group of between fifteen and twenty prominent business and professional men who traditionally functioned as philanthropic patrons and intercessors on behalf of East European Jewry. Although the committee's financial Maecenas remained the banker Jacob Schiff, the organization's president was Louis Marshall. A highly successful New York corporation attorney, Marshall proved as able a strategist in Jewish communal life as in his legal practice. Within the committee, his clarity of analysis and powers of persuasion established him almost instantly as first among equals. In 1911, when the tsarist government refused to grant visas to American Jews, it was Marshall who organized the political campaign that torpedoed renewal of the Russian-American Commercial Treaty. In 1914–15, responding to the brutal mass evacuation of hundreds of thousands of Jews in the Pale's border regions,

Marshall took the initiative in organizing public demonstrations and congressional resolutions of protest against the tsarist regime.

And in the last months of the war, shifting his attention to the victims of Ukrainian and Polish atrocities, Marshall worked assiduously to formulate an American-Jewish strategy for the anticipated Peace Conference. On November 7, 1918, he dispatched the first in a long series of memoranda to Woodrow Wilson. Calling the president's attention to pogroms and economic boycotts against Polish Jews, Marshall urged that the Polish government, in exchange for international recognition, be compelled to accept a treaty of guarantees for its minority peoples. It was in this correspondence, too, that Marshall laid his finger on one of the most intractable issues to be confronted by the Allied statesmen. Struggling with the task of establishing a chain of successor nations out of the debris of the former Russian, Austrian, German, and Turkish empires, the Western leaders soon grasped that the emergent new states could not be territorially sculpted to assure ethnographically homogeneous populations. Ultimately, some 30 million minority members would find themselves living as unwilling minorities within successor-state borders, a figure that represented nearly one-fourth of the populations of East-Central Europe altogether. It was specifically this archipelago of minority races and nations that demanded the rights both of civil-political freedom and of national-communal "self-determination"—that is, the freedom to maintain their own linguistic and communal autonomy.

The Jews of liberated Eastern Europe, most notably in Poland and the Baltic republics of Latvia, Lithuania, and Estonia, shared in that appeal. Whether Zionist or non-Zionist, socialist or religionist, they all pressed vigorously not only for guarantees of civil and political equality, but for the opportunity to maintain the widest ambit of cultural and administrative "self-government." In that campaign, they enjoyed the enthusiastic support of their kinsmen, the East European immigrant Jews of the United States. It was specifically this ethnocentric immigrant majority that pressed Louis Marshall and other board members of the American Jewish Committee to endorse their program. At first, the committee patriarchs did not react congenially to the East Europeans' political agenda, and still less to their demand for participation in a future Jewish "diplomatic" mission to the Paris Peace Conference. After extended and often acrimonious negotiations, however, Marshall and his colleagues accepted the new arrangements, with the understanding that Marshall himself continue as American Jewry's senior spokesman.

Indeed, in Paris, Marshall emerged as the preeminent negotiator both for American Jewry and for other Jewish national delegations—from Britain, France, Italy, as well as from the East European nations themselves. It was Marshall's eloquent advocacy that won over Woodrow Wilson and the other Allied statesmen to the concept of minority guarantees. Shrewdly, Marshall based his case on the archetypal American precedent of a "bill of rights," a proposition he then fortified by applying it to all the minorities in Europe's emerging successor states, not merely to the Jews. Once President Wilson and his advisers accepted this formula, it was not difficult for Marshall to sell it to an inter-Allied committee.

The fruits of this diplomacy first appeared in the Minorities Treaty imposed on the Polish delegation. On June 24, 1919, the document was signed by Polish Prime Minister Ignacy Paderewski, in Versailles's Hall of Mirrors. Although the treaty consisted of only twelve articles, its guarantees were precise and unequivocal. The first of these awarded full civil, religious, and political rights to all citizens of the new Poland, with the term "citizen" applied broadly to all persons either born or "habitually" resident on Polish territory. The provision was not original, of course. It had been prefigured in the "Jewish" clauses imposed on Rumania at the Congress of Berlin of 1878 (p. 204). It was rather in its "cultural-autonomous" articles that the treaty charted new terrain. Here for the first time appeared ironclad linguistic rights, guaranteeing Poland's minorities "free use" of their language in commerce, in the law courts, and, most crucially, in primary schools in whichever region minority peoples formed sizable compact groups. The Polish government was obliged to incorporate this "bill of rights" into its very constitution and to accept the emergent League of Nations as its guarantor.

The treaty set a historic precedent. Virtually identical documents would be signed in ensuing weeks by Czechoslovakia, Serbia, Rumania, Greece, and Armenia. Special minority provisions also would be integrated into the peace treaties subsequently imposed upon defeated Austria, Bulgaria, Hungary, and Turkey. Louis Marshall's diplomatic achievement was an extraordinary one. Returning to the United States, the lawyer-statesman addressed an overflow crowd of Jews at Carnegie Hall on July 19, 1919. To his thrilled listeners, he offered assurance:

> You, my friends, are celebrating an event which the Almighty in His wisdom willed.... For the first time, the nations of the world have recognized that, in common with all other peoples, we are entitled to equality in law.... It has now become an established principle that any violation of the rights of a minority is an offense not only against the individuals but against the law which controls all of the civilized nations of the earth.

A PROFESSOR OF CONSCIENCE

Marshall's enthusiasm was by no means shared by the successor-state governments. They regarded the minorities treaties as a gratuitous infringement upon their painfully achieved national sovereignties. On May 31, 1919, led by Ignacy Paderewski, the delegations of Rumania, Hungary, Serbia, and Greece actually ventured a "Revolt of the Small Powers," protesting that alleged infringement; and Austria, Bulgaria, and Turkey similarly made known their opposition. In the end, however, confronting a stone wall among the senior Allied statesmen, each of the protesting delegations signed its respective treaty.

It is of interest that only one successor-state leader required no pressure of any kind to accept the minorities guarantee. This was Tomas Masaryk, president of Czechoslovakia. No statesman ever represented his people with greater moral leverage. In the prewar years, as an ardent and eloquent Czech nationalist, Masaryk was elected by his admiring countrymen as one of their delegates to the Habsburg parliament. In that capacity, he emerged as the preeminent champion of the entire Slav opposition bloc in the Reichsrat, defending the cause of Serbs and Croats in common with those of Czechs and Slovaks. The stance was not without its risks. When war broke out, Masaryk was obliged to flee the country. As a fugitive, then, making his way to Western Europe, he set about importuning and eventually winning the support of the Allied governments for his people's freedom. Most critically, in his wartime visits to the United States in 1916 and 1918, Masaryk held several warm interviews with President Wilson, and the two men developed a mutually admiring relationship. By June 1918, Wilson joined Britain's Foreign Secretary Balfour in recognizing Czechoslovakia as a sovereign ally. With the collapse of the Central Powers in November, Masaryk returned in triumph to Prague, where the Czech National Council promptly elected the sixty-eight-year-old statesman-scholar as president of their newly proclaimed Republic of Czechoslovakia.

Masaryk held office in a nation of approximately 8 million Czechs, 3 million Slovaks, 2.8 million Germans, 700,000 Hungarians, and 300,000 Poles. Additionally, some 360,000 Jews were represented in the new successor state. Of these, 90,000 lived in Bohemia, 38,000 in Moravia, 136,000 in Slovakia, 7,000 in Silesia, and 93,000 in Ruthenia. The mosaic represented the sixth-largest Jewish population on the Continent outside of Soviet Russia. It was also a disparate population. The Jews of Slovakia were small-townsmen, either merchants or artisans. Their culture was ethnocentric and Yiddish-speaking. The Jews of Bohemia-Moravia tended to live in cities and large towns, and were a quintessentially middle-class, German-speaking community (pp. 403–4). In the last months of the war, as it happened, Habsburg Jews of all backgrounds, whether parochial or Western-oriented, had watched in alarm as their empire began to implode, and its various nationalities began preparing for independence. Protection had to be sought from the anticipated excesses of newly emergent Slavic nationalities. To that end, on October 14,

1918, an "intercommunal" Jewish congress was organized in Vienna. Arriving from the principal Habsburg cities, the delegates elected a Jewish National Council and issued a policy statement that was intended as a message to the Allied Powers. Whatever the empire's fate, they declared, the Jews expected to be awarded the identical civil and collective recognition, and thus the identical protection, extended to any other nationality. Two weeks later, when the Republic of Czechoslovakia was formally proclaimed, Max Brod, chairman of the new country's parallel (Czech) Jewish National Council, was received by Masaryk. In his explanation to the new president, Brod observed that the Jews' acculturation had been to an essentially German empire, and not to a Slavic majority whose behavior toward the Jewish minority was less than reassuring. And Masaryk, with his unique personal experience of antisemitism (pp. 225–26), had every reason to understand the Jews' chronic insecurity.

Imperial Bohemia and Jewish Memory

The Jews' presence in Bohemia-Moravia was a venerable one, traceable to the twelfth century. Their population grew slowly, decade by decade, as rivulets of kinsmen arrived from the Balkans and Poland, from German Franconia and Bavaria. Even as late as the sixteenth century, their enclave in Prague did not exceed 1,000 souls. Nevertheless, within their Josefstadt ghetto, they were free to worship and to conduct their affairs as a community unto themselves. The trajectory of their growth did not go uninterrupted. In 1745, Empress Maria Theresa, fervid in her Catholic pieties, ordered a full-scale expulsion of the empire's Jews. Yet the ban would not endure, not in an Age of Enlightenment. The empress's son and successor, Joseph II, issued his celebrated Toleranzpatent in 1792, marginally easing residential and vocational restrictions on Jews. In 1867, moreover, under Emperor Franz Josef, a general political emancipation was extended to Jews throughout the entire Habsburg realm (p. 94).

It was this climactic benediction that opened the floodgates for an influx of village and small-town Jews into the larger imperial cities. They came from Galicia, Bukovina, Slovakia, Moravia, as well as from Bohemia itself. By the mid-nineteenth century, some 20,000 Jews were living in Prague. By 1910, the figure rose to 34,000 among Prague's total population of 443,000. The figure was deceptively modest. Those 34,000 Jews comprised not less than half the city's German-speaking minority. Moreover, from the beginning of their settlement to the very end of the Habsburg Empire, Prague Jewry identified wholeheartedly with the realm's enlightened German civil administration and reigning German culture. Thus, Franz Kafka's father, a rural Jew who spoke Czech in his native Bohemian village of Wossek, promptly cast his lot with the city's German-speaking community from the day he settled in Prague, in 1873. If there were few social contacts between the two peoples, the German enclave at least accepted the Jews as pragmatic allies against the Czech majority. In turn, Prague's Jewish intellectuals largely set the tone of the city's German "higher culture." With the single exception of Rainer Maria Rilke, the most renowned German writers and poets of early-twentieth-century Prague were Jews: among them, Franz Werfel, Max Brod, Egon Kisch, and Franz Kafka. Czech Jewry's passion for the German connection signified above all a commitment to the Habsburg throne. They owed everything to the empire, after all, their civil rights, their economic and social mobility, and not least their physical protection against the rising tide of modern Czech nationalism.

During the 1880s, a period of economic depression, antisemitic riots in Prague culminated in assaults on Jewish shops and individual Jews. The sensational trial of Leopold Hilsner in 1899 (p. 225) was only one of a series of ritual murder accusations that periodically erupted among the Czech rural population. For that reason, Masaryk's role in denouncing the blood libel registered powerfully on the Jews. They never forgot his courage and integrity. During Masaryk's 1916 wartime visit to the United States, Supreme Court Justice Louis Brandeis, whose own parents had emigrated from Bohemia in the nineteenth century, secured the professor his first interview with Woodrow Wilson. "I was more than compensated . . . for any part [I played] in the Hilsner affair," Masaryk acknowledged later.

And in 1919, as president, Masaryk was keenly sentient to of the ongoing dangers of xenophobia, and of possible future Hilsner trials in his newborn Czechoslovak Republic. In full understanding of the Jews' need for reassurance, he promised Max Brod that he, the president, favored "recognition of the legitimate position of the Jewish nationality in the Czechoslovakian state." In fact, the Jews' priority was less one of communal self-expression than of collective self-protection. In November 1918, units of the Czech Legion, a volunteer force that had participated in the nation's uprising against Habsburg rule, engaged in a widespread pillage of Jewish shops and homes in Slovakia (the violence would recur a year later in the aftermath of a brief Hungarian incursion into Slovakia). It was hardly paranoia, therefore, that impelled Max Brod and his colleagues to request still additional commitment from Eduard Benes, Czechoslovakia's newly appointed foreign minister. Benes, educated in Paris, thoroughly steeped in the Western liberal tradition, warmly endorsed his president's "Jewish" guidelines. The Jews would be given "equal rights of citizenship and all other minority rights," he assured the delegation.

The promise was honored on September 10, 1919, when Benes signed Czechoslovakia's own version of the Minorities Treaty, and Masaryk then ensured that the document was promptly incorporated into the republic's constitution. Henceforth, in common with others of Czechoslovakia's ethnic communities, Jews were entitled to a full panoply of linguistic, communal, and educational rights. Those guarantees were fulfilled in letter and spirit. Thus, in Slovakia and Ruthenia, virtually all Jews opted for registration as a minority nationality and for their own separate, Yiddish-language school system. The government funded these schools in their entirety. In Bohemia-Moravia, a majority of Jews still preferred to send their children to the public schools, where Czech now was the language of instruction. Yet, in whichever province, all Jewish communal institutions, all Jewish holidays, enjoyed full juridical recognition and protection. It was an impressive achievement, and a near-unique one. In contrast to the reaction of other successor-state governments, the award of Jewish communal rights in Czechoslovakia had been swift, forthcoming, and condign. If ever an individual set the tone for this achievement, it was the scholar-statesman in Hradcany Castle, Prague's presidential residence.

The nation's economic prosperity shared in that fulfillment. Before 1914, the natural resources and burgeoning industry of Bohemia-Moravia and the Sudetenland had functioned as the locomotive that drove the Habsburg imperial economy. In the postwar period, functioning on its own, the Czechoslovakian Republic emerged as one of the rare economic success stories of East-Central Europe. Boasting a substantial middle class, the nation joined Finland as one of the even rarer stable democracies to emerge from the wreckage of the prewar empires. The Jews, in turn, as an urbanized, middle-class element, operated comfortably in the new *Stimmung* of independence and democracy. They owned and managed several of the nation's largest factories. In postwar journalism, literature, and academia, their intellectuals, led by the novelists Franz Kafka and Frantisek Langer, and by the renowned literary critic Otokar Fischer, swiftly approached the eminence they had enjoyed in prewar Bohemia as the doyens of German culture. None other of the republic's minority peoples ever made the transition from German to Czech, from one culture to another, with greater speed or acuity. Here, at least, in this single region of East-Central Europe, the Jews' future appeared secure.

A Precarious Sephardic Oasis in the Balkans

In 1918, Serbs, Croats, Slovenes, Dalmatians, Bosnians, Montenegrins, Turks, Greeks, Bulgars, Jews, Gypsies—all were incorporated into a jerry-built nation of 17 million, eventually to be known as the Kingdom of Yugoslavia. Within that dense heterogeneity of peoples, the Jews alone transcended regional, cultural, and linguistic divergences to sustain a common religiocultural loyalty. The 13,000 Jews of Bosnia-Herzegovina and the 8,000 Jews of Serbia clung tenaciously to their Sephardic identity (pp. 147–48). Yet they participated jointly in national and regional Jewish organizations, together with the 25,000 Romaniot (Greek-speaking) Jews of the Vojvodina and Macedonia, and the 24,000 Ashkenazic Jews of Croatia and Slovenia.

Whatever their cultural background, they had sustained their tradition of communal self-government over the centuries of Ottoman rule. Would Yugoslavia's ruling Serb dynasty and its associated politicians respect that tradition? After all, the Serb delegation to the Paris Peace Conference was among those that had participated in the Revolt of the Small Powers. Yet the Serbs' "revolt" was directed essentially at Yugoslavia's residual communities of Turks and other Moslems, and in later years at the Croats and Bulgars. The Jews were not the targets. Indeed, for many decades even before the war, Jews living in the independent Kingdom of Serbia had enjoyed the fullest measure of political and economic security. During the Balkan Wars of 1912–13, and then in the World War, 1,600 Jews, virtually all the community's able-bodied, younger males, volunteered for the Serbian army, and 400 were killed in battle. In the postwar Yugoslav government, the Serbs for their part ensured that the Jews' equality of juridical status and communal self-expression remained intact. The royal household set the tone of that cordiality. King Alexander I granted frequent audiences to Jewish delegations and bestowed numerous honors upon prominent Jews. Under its minorities-treaty obligations, the government provided subsidies for the nation's extensive network of religious, educational, and social service institutions. Like priests and cadis, rabbis were paid by the government. During Jewish religious holidays, Jewish children were excused from schools, Jewish civil servants from work, and Jewish soldiers from military duty.

As in other successor states, however, Jews often were the first to experience shifting political circumstances. At the end of the war, over three-fifths of Yugoslav Jewry were German- or Hungarian-speaking. Most of them had settled in Croatia, Slovenia, and the Vojvodina, where they functioned under Hungarian administration. As a somewhat better-educated and more affluent group than their Sephardic coreligionists in Serbia and Bosnia, Jews in these former Habsburg provinces now found themselves caught up in the widening postwar rivalries between Croats and Serbs. By the 1930s, in the region's classic tradition of interethnic strife, the Croatian Peasant Party and the Slovenian People's Party began exploiting antisemitism as an integral feature of their anti-Serbianism, and stigmatized the Jews as mere appendages of Serbian hegemony.

The technique was adopted even more frontally by the Ustasha, a league of Croatian fascists. Operating mainly in exile, in Italy, the Ustasha was subsidized by Mussolini, who coveted Yugoslav territory in the Adriatic. It was the Ustasha, in 1934, that hired and trained the Macedonian gunman who assassinated Yugoslavia's King Alexander I. In turn, genuflecting toward Hitler as a "protector" against Mussolini, Yugoslav Prime Minister Milan Stojadinovic felt obliged to support the German revisionist program in Europe, even to introduce a program of domestic antisemitism. In September 1939, following the German invasion of Poland, the Yugoslav government set about expelling Jewish children from state secondary schools and establishing a tight numerus clausus for Jews in the nation's business and professional life.

In some measure, the circumstances of Yugoslav Jewry were replicated in other, formerly Ottoman-governed regions of the Balkans. One of these regions was the Macedonian port city of Salonika, with its historic community of some 90,000 Sephardim (p. 145). In the early years of the twentieth century, on the verge of reclaiming its once vaunted reputation as the "Jerusalem of the Balkans," Salonikan Jewry suddenly was caught up in an international crisis. It was the first of the two Balkan Wars, in 1912, that drove the Turks from Macedonia and established Greek rule over the region's queen city of Salonika. Immediately, then, Greek Prime Minister Eleutherios Venizelos, determined to shift economic advantage in Salonika to the local Greeks, imposed a series of punitive taxes upon such traditional Jewish vocations as textile manufacture and retailing. The process of "Hellenization" was further accelerated following the World War. In 1922, the Turkish nationalist commander Mustafa Kemal drove the occupying Greek army out of Asia Minor. In the process, Turkish forces simultaneously uprooted over a million Smyrniot Greeks—citizens of Izmir and its hinterland—and sent them fleeing into the Kingdom of Greece (p. 409). Ultimately, more than 100,000 of the fugitives were resettled in Salonika.

The arrival of this Smyrniot tidal wave all but doomed the Jews' historic commercial role in the city. Offered every financial and tax benefit, the Greek-speaking newcomers soon achieved decisive control over Salonika's trade and industry. In 1923, moreover, Prime Minister Venizelos, who had participated in the Paris Peace Conference's Revolt of the Small Powers, now set about openly flouting his nation's obligations under its Minorities Treaty. A new law banned all commercial activity in Greece on Sunday. As a result, Jews who observed their own Saturday Sabbath were obliged to close their businesses for an extra day. A series of education laws required the network of Alliance Israélite Universelle schools in Salonika to drop French, even Ladino, as the language of instruction.

More ominously, throughout the 1920s the Venizelist press engaged in a thinly veiled campaign of antisemitism, editorializing against "those interlopers who suck the blood of our people, who are in the forefront of communism." It was true that Jews constituted an influential minority in Salonika's vigorous and vocal Communist Party, but much of that radicalism expressed frustration at Prime Minister Venizelos's economic and cultural discrimination. Worse yet, throughout Macedonia, chauvinist political and paramilitary groups became rampant in the postwar period. In 1930, when a congress of Balkan Jewish sports organizations gathered in Sofia, a Bulgarian Jew thoughtlessly parroted Bulgarian nationalist claims in Macedonia. Greek newspapers immediately seized upon the comment, and rightist hooligans then attacked Salonikan Jewish neighborhoods, razing some three hundred homes while the police stood by. It was accordingly in the 1930s that the earlier, fin-de-siècle trickle of Jewish emigration grew into an uninterrupted stream. Seventeen thousand Salonikan Jews sailed off to Palestine, and nearly that many departed for France and North and South America. By 1939, the Jewish population of Salonika had shrunk from its 1912 apogee of some 90,000 to an estimated 65,000.

AN OASIS BLIGHTED AT THE SOURCE

Yet it was Turkey itself, encompassing approximately 125,000 Jews by the early twentieth century—the world's largest Sephardic population—that bore principal responsibility for the atrophy of this once legendary Jewish civilization. As late as 1908, it was not a fate that would have been predicted, for the brutal and ineffectual government of Sultan Abd al-Hamid II that year had been overthrown by the Committee of Union and Progress. A select coalition of junior military officers, lawyers, doctors, academics, and businessmen, these "Young Turks" were committed to a fundamental political and economic liberalization of the Ottoman Empire. With hardly an exception, Turkey's Jews ardently welcomed the coup. A small number of them even played important roles in the Young Turk government. Alluding to that participation, Britain's Ambassador Sir Lewis Mallet suspiciously attributed the Young Turk Revolution to a "Jewish conspiracy." The charge was specious. Ethnic Turks thoroughly dominated the Committee of Union and Progress and the government.

Indeed, the new regime would soon become fulminantly xenophobic. No sooner were the Young Turks in office than they confronted a renewed onslaught of European imperialism that stripped the empire of Bosnia-Herzegovina (1908), Bulgarian Rumelia (1908–9), Crete (1911), Tripolitania (1911), and Macedonia (1912). In its rage and helplessness, the government increasingly vented its frustrations upon the empire's non-Turkish peoples. Upon Turkey's entry into World War I, moreover, the Jews were among the first to experience the backlash. This was an irony, for Ottoman Jews were among the earliest and most enthusiastic supporters of war against the hated tsarist enemy. But their commitment would avail them little, for in Palestine the perversion of Young Turk "liberalism" became tragically apparent. Here the forced expulsions, the expropriations of food and livestock, the grim labor battalions, the death marches to the Taurus granite pits, all shocked and shattered a Yishuv that until then had been almost obsequiously loyal to its Ottoman overlords.

The wartime ordeal of Ottoman Jewry was not limited to Palestine, nor did it end with Turkey's military surrender in October 1918. Five months later, the Allied Powers authorized the Kingdom of Greece to "administer" southwestern Asia Minor, a sector extensively inhabited by Ottoman Greeks. At first, in common with their Turkish neighbors, Jews living in the city of Smyrna (Izmir) suffered the pillage of their homes and shops by occupying Greek military units. Then, in the late summer of 1922, a revived Turkish army counterattacked the Greek invaders, driving them from Asia Minor and eventually forcing the Greek government to negotiate a humiliating peace treaty. Nor did the eviction of the Greeks bring relief to either the Smyrniot or the Salonikan Jews. Under terms of the 1923 Treaty of Lausanne, the 1.2 million Smyrniot Greeks of Asia Minor, and the 460,000 Macedonian Turks living within the Kingdom of Greece, were to be permanently resettled among their kinsmen in each's respective "motherland." The shock was severe for both peoples. Although few Jews shared in the population exchange, large numbers of them lived in the zones of Greek-Turkish repatriation and disruption, and thus shared in its economic consequences.

Well before 1923, indeed, since the turn of the century, Jews had been seeking respite from the despotism of Sultan Abd al-Hamid, then from the upheaval of the 1912–13 Balkan Wars, then from the World War, and eventually from the Greco-Turkish War of 1920–22. Thus, in addition to the prewar expatriates of Salonika, some 12,000 Sephardim from integral Turkey also departed for France and the Western Hemisphere in these years. In Latin America, they were known as *turcos,* and virtually all of them started out as peddlers, accommodating their Ladino vernacular to the local Spanish- and Portuguese-speaking populations. Even larger numbers of Ottoman Sephardim made their way to the United States. By 1930, their population in American cities approached 30,000. Nevertheless, the bulk of Turkish Jewry, numbering between 115,000 and 120,000, chose not to join the postwar exodus. It was in Turkey itself, therefore, that they were exposed to the thunderous new personality and ideology of Mustafa Kemal, the "gray wolf" of modern Turkish nationalism.

Kemal was forty-one years old in 1922, a professional officer with fifteen years of hard military service. Notwithstanding the ravages of drinking and wenching, the man's dynamism and charisma were unprecedented perhaps since the days of the original Mehmet the Conqueror. In 1915, it was Kemal, as Turkish area commander, who shattered the British expedition at Gallipoli. In 1921–22, it was this same elemental force who reconstituted a ragtag militia, survivors of the defeated wartime army, to block the Greek invaders at the very gates of Ankara, then to launch his soldiery on the furious counteroffensive that drove the enemy out of Turkey altogether, together with over a million Smyrniot Greeks in their wake. The achievement, brutal as it was, represented merely the first act of the nation's resurrection. The following year, 1923, Kemal personally inaugurated the Grand National Assembly that abolished the sultanate and declared Turkey a constitutional republic, and that subsequently elected him as its first president.

The mantle of constitutionalism was largely a façade. Kemal functioned as virtual dictator of his nation, and he gave his people no rest. Soon after taking office, he enlarged the former imperial program of economic autarchy by establishment of étatism—of government monopolies—in such basic industries as tobacco, salt, matches, and munitions. The policy reflected ethnic nationalism as much as economic pragmatism. Until the World War, Turkish industry and commerce depended heavily upon networks of Greek and Armenian businessmen, and upon an even smaller minority of Jewish financiers and importers. Most of the Greeks and Armenians were gone by then, but some 125,000 Jews remained. Could they function, or even survive, under leadership committed to a policy of implacable ethnic Turkification?

It was an issue the Jews confronted in 1923. The Treaty of Lausanne included the identical minority guarantees that had been imposed on other postwar successor states. Non-Turkish citizens thus enjoyed the prerogative of maintaining distinctive communal, social, and linguistic institutions, including their own school systems. Yet the treaty had hardly been signed before the Kemalist government suggested that the Jews "reconsider" whether they wished to be regarded as a "national" minority, and thereby the object of possible foreign interference in domestic Turkish affairs. The intimation was all but explicit that the Jews were risking exposure to the fate of the Greeks and Armenians. At this point, Chief Rabbi Haim Bejerano endorsed the suggestion of Turkish Jewry's most prominent laymen, that his people forgo the "protected" status of a national minority. In 1923, the Jews also relinquished their *millet* (religious community) status, with its quota of guaranteed seats in the Grand National Assembly.

The subservience went unrewarded. The government moved relentlessly to preempt commerce from Jews and Christians. Moslem Turks were now given preference in import-export licenses. In 1934, with Turkey languishing in the world Depression and with unemployment rampant, Moslem crowds stormed Jewish homes in Thrace and the Chanak peninsula, looted Jewish property, and sent 3,000 of the region's 13,000 Jews fleeing to Istanbul. The Jews of Edirne faced a comparable upsurge in violence. Two of their synagogues were razed. When pressure mounted on the Jews of Gallipoli to depart, their spokesmen ventured a complaint to President Mustafa Kemal himself. He brushed them off. There is little evidence that Kemal personally entertained strong feelings on Jews one way or another. Yet his regime's militant nationalism would not spare any minority. Although Jews now were recruited in the army, together with other Turkish citizens, few even of the best educated of them were accepted for officers' ranking. By the late 1920s, virtually no Jews remained in the civil service.

Meanwhile, in the same postwar years, determined to root out the last vestiges of clerical influence in Turkey, Kemal and the Grand National Assembly set about abolishing the caliphate (a theocratic title traditionally held by the former sultans), dethroning Islam as the state religion and stripping the Moslem religious hierarchy of its lingering jurisdiction over civil litigation and public education. As an integral feature of this anticlerical program, the government simultaneously banned religious instruction in schools operated by the non-Moslem communities—Jewish, Greek, Bulgarian, Armenian. Turkish now was mandated as the principal language of instruction, and French and Ladino thus ceased to be teaching languages in Jewish primary schools (although they remained in secondary schools). The impact of the decrees soon became apparent. As late as the 1927 census, 80 percent of Turkish Jews had registered Yahudice (Ladino) as their mother tongue. Eight years later, the percentage had dropped to 54 percent. At the same time, Jews were barred from affiliation with international Jewish organizations. None could participate in the World Jewish Congress, the World Zionist Congress, or even in Orthodox religious federations. It was an unaccustomed vulnerability for a people that, as late as the nineteenth century, had functioned under the corrupt but essentially pluralistic toleration of their Ottoman overlords.

POLAND'S STRUGGLE FOR CONGLOMERATE IDENTITY

Like Mustafa Kemal in Turkey, Jozef Pilsudski, president of the newborn Republic of Poland, evoked almost universal admiration as the champion of his people's recent liberation. Born in 1867 to an aristocratic Polish-Lithuanian family, a citizen of the Tsarist Empire, Pilsudski as a university student joined the socialist branch of the underground Polish freedom movement, where he rose swiftly to a position of leadership. In the last years before the war, moving to Lvov (Lemberg), in Habsburg Galicia, he set about organizing an émigré Polish Legion. Once hostilities began in 1914, Pilsudski led his modest, 5,000-man force into tsarist territory and pressed the Central Powers to support his people's claim for postwar independence. Instead, the Germans placed him under house arrest in East Prussia, where he remained until the end of the war. Only with Germany's surrender in November 1918 was Pilsudski, by then a national hero, released and escorted by his admirers to Warsaw, there to assume office as his nation's chief of state.

Although the Paris Peace Conference awarded Poland the former

German- and Austrian-ruled territories of pre-partition Poland, Pilsudski was determined also to assert his nation's historic claim to its former Ukrainian dependency. Thus began the brutal two-and-a-half-year Russo-Polish War. The conflict did not end until the spring of 1921, in the Treaty of Riga, when both sides agreed to partition Ukraine between them (p. 321). In consequence of these territorial accessions, the Republic of Poland had grown from a nation of some 20 million, at the end of the World War, into a nation of 29 million, by far the largest of the East-Central European successor states, and the sixth-largest state on the Continent altogether. But the price of these acquisitions was heavy. The march and countermarch of armies had left Poles, Ukrainians, Russians, Belorussians, Lithuanians, Jews, and other minorities in economic and communal ruin. In the case of the Jews, Ukrainian irredentism had inflicted the grimmest toll of all. But the Poles, too, in their burgeoning imperialism, did not hesitate to ravage the former Pale of Settlement regions, killing hundreds of Jews, and wreaking havoc on their homes and shops. It is certain that Pilsudski himself did not countenance this brutality. Indeed, in November 1918, as one of his first acts as chief of state, he assured a delegation of Jewish leaders of his full-hearted commitment to their people's security.

Yet Pilsudski, the lifelong Social Democrat, with his pluralistic vision of Poland as a federation of nationalities, was by no means speaking for his people. The average Pole viewed with horror the very notion of living on a basis of political and communal equality with non-Polish minorities, elements that made up fully 33 percent of the state's population. Amid this vast conglomeration, Ukrainians comprised 12 percent; Belorussians, 4 percent; Lithuanians, 4 percent; Germans, 3 percent; and Jews, 9.6 percent. It was the argument of Roman Dmowski, leader of the powerful Endek (National Democrat) bloc, that Poland simply did not possess the resources to spare for "non-nationals." The sacrifices of almost uninterrupted conflict had destroyed much of the nation's economy. Flanked by powerful revisionist enemies, Germany and Russia, the country was obliged to devote a third of its meager budget to national defense. These costs, and the still heavier ones of reconstruction, were complicated by the integration of Poland's enlarged territories, with their 9 million new inhabitants and their patchwork of inherited laws, administrations, civil services, and currencies.

Moreover, political dysfunctionalism compounded economic infirmity. Poland's electoral system was based on proportional representation rather than majority rule. Dmowski's Endeks and Pilsudski's Social Democrats were obliged to negotiate deals with a host of smaller parties, and government soon was reduced to precarious coalitions that were endlessly collapsing under the blackmail of marginal political factions. Even the Social Democrats found themselves beholden to the most chauvinist of these factions.

Over the years, as a result, Poland's Minorities Treaty was eroded to virtual meaninglessness. In defiance of its cultural guarantee, the government refused funding for the school systems of Ukrainians, Lithuanians, Belorussians, Germans, or Jews. Non-Polish farmers were denied access to state land sales, to state subsidies for agricultural cooperatives, to government employment. Discrimination conceivably would have been even more onerous had it not been for the threats and protests of neighboring "brother states"—Soviet Russia in the case of Poland's Slavic minorities; Germany, in the case of Poland's German minority. Lacking this "brother-state" intercession, however, it was the nation's second-largest minority, its 9.6 million Jews, that would soon become the most vulnerable of reborn Poland's heterogeneity of peoples.

A Jewish Bill of Rights in Polish Action

In the renewed anti-Jewish onslaught of the postwar years, Roman Dmowski's Endeks continued to set the nationalist tone. They would consent to the ingestion of Ukrainians and Belorussians, so long as these people of "lower civilization" accepted cultural Polonization. But the Jews could never be assimilated—nor should they be. As far back as 1903, Dmowski in his *Political Testament* had insisted that "[i]n the character of this race, so many different values, alien to our moral constitution and harmful to our life, have accumulated that assimilation with a large number of [Jews] would destroy us." Publicly or otherwise, other parties shared this abhorrence of the huge Jewish minority. By the early 1920s, sensing the depth of his nation's xenophobia, even Pilsudski muted his traditional pluralism.

These were the circumstances under which antisemitism in Poland remained a central feature both of popular ideology and of public policy. The issue of citizenship was an early harbinger. The Minorities Treaty had committed Poland's government to accept as citizens all individuals "habitually resident" in the newly acquired territories. But of all the peoples in these regions, Jews possessed the least official proof of "habitual" residence. They had been driven from pillar to post by the incursions of rival armies and would be kept on the move until the border wars ended in 1921. Afterward, as some half-million bedraggled fugitives sought to return to their homes, they came without funds, chattels, or papers of any kind. Polish officials needed little pretext to confine these refugees to a juridical no-man's-land, denying them legal protection for either residence or business ownership. It was only after repeated Western appeals that the government agreed to resolve the issue, but strictly on a case-by-case basis. The process consumed nearly a decade, and remained a bureaucratic nightmare for tens of thousands of Jews, particularly in the annexed border regions. Similarly, the Minorities Treaty's elaborately crafted provision for government funding of Jewish schools was exposed to immediate attack. As in the case of other non-Polish communities, the expenditure was declared an "unaffordable luxury." Yet the ministry of education might have countenanced private Jewish sponsorship, as in the case of the German school system. It did not. Under various pretexts, the government systematically harassed, obstructed, even closed down privately financed Yiddish- and Hebrew-language schools.

In the 1920s, too, the government also found ways to restrict Jewish economic activity. The rationale was Jewish overcrowding in commerce and the professions. Here, in fact, statistics bore out the charge. By 1922, Jews comprised 52 percent of Poland's tradesmen and owned 48 percent of the nation's retail shops (although most of these were diminutive market stalls). A majority of attorneys in larger cities were Jews, and in medicine the Jewish presence ranked second only to the German. Intent upon preempting these business and professional sectors for Poles, the government adopted a heavy hand. By 1929, its taxes on commercial ventures were raised so sharply that Jews were paying 40 percent of all direct taxes in Poland. The new republic's program of étatism—state capitalism—also fell heaviest on the Jews. To jump-start the ravaged economy, the government in the 1920s set about establishing new industries under its own direction, or nationalizing private businesses already in existence. These sectors included public transportation and power utilities, sales-brokerage offices, as well as the salt, tobacco, liquor, paper, and match industries—all enterprises and services that historically had been pioneered, managed, and largely staffed by Jews. The policy was by no means animated exclusively by antisemitism, but the manner of its application was. Jews employed in these fields were immediately dismissed and their positions were given over to Poles. In the former Habsburg Galician areas, Jews had been extensively represented in the civil service. Here, too, they were replaced by Poles.

Meanwhile, in the United States, witnessing the collapse of their months of intensive Peace Conference diplomacy, Louis Marshall and his American Jewish Committee colleagues entreated the State Department to intercede with Warsaw. To no avail. Under the Harding and Coolidge administrations, the United States had opted out of European affairs. For the British and French governments, the issue of Jewish rights was even less a diplomatic priority. Lacking a "brother state" to press their cause, therefore, either directly or through the League of Nations (p. 425), the Jews alone of Europe's ethnic minorities found themselves bereft of diplomatic leverage. Was political leverage available? At first, it appeared not. In January 1919, the first elections were held for the Sejm, the Polish parliament. Comprising nearly 10 percent of the country's population, the Jews had anticipated a substantial share of legislative representation. Instead, they gained only 13 out of the Sejm's total of 444 seats. Worse yet, the rightist parties (most of them Endeks) held an intimidating plurality in parliament. Their deputies often engaged in derisive heckling whenever Jews rose to speak.

In ensuing years, however, Jewish political leaders formulated several imaginative strategies for achieving a more substantial legislative presence. One was devised by Yitzhak Gruenbaum, chairman of the General Zionist Party, the largest Jewish faction in the Sejm. A successful Warsaw lawyer and an adroit political operative, Gruenbaum in 1921 proposed fashioning a "Bloc of National Minorities," a united electoral list of all non-Polish peoples, with each ethnic group accorded its own appropriate proportion of Sejm seats. Thus, in 1922, Gruenbaum negotiated an alliance with most of the other minorities. In the new Sejm elections of that year, the Bloc returned eighty-one deputies, and of these, thirty-five were Jews. The marriage of convenience appeared to be a major breakthrough. In fact, the Bloc endured less than two years. Implacably antisemitic, the Ukrainians refused to join. Among the Jewish parties, the Bundists at the last moment chose to ally with the Polish Social Democrats rather than with the parties of Jewish "capitalists" and "pietists." During its brief existence, the Bloc failed to alleviate a single one of the government's anti-Jewish measures.

In 1924, the General Zionists came up with an alternate strategy. This was to negotiate a *ugoda* (a pact) directly with the government in an effort to achieve Jewish-Polish cooperation on issues specific to the two peoples. Prime Minister Wladyslaw Grabski was receptive. He was no friend of the Jews. Indeed, he personally had devised the punitive tax measures on Jewish businessmen. Yet Grabski was in active search of investment capital abroad, and he sensed the potential usefulness of American-Jewish financiers. Thus, as a quid pro quo for Jewish restraint on the issue of Poland's "hegemonic" treatment of its border populations—essentially the Ukrainians and Belorussians—the prime minister agreed to permit Jewish businessmen access to the state credit bank, to bid on state contracts, even to enjoy a five-year moratorium on étatist measures of nationalization. Hereupon, pocketing an apparently clean bill of health on the Jewish question, Foreign Minister Aleksander Skrzynski sailed off to the United States to meet with Jewish bankers and communal spokesmen. The meetings were equable. They were also unproductive. Well-informed American-Jewish leaders noted that Grabski already was dragging his feet on the *ugoda*. In the end, his government's single, cosmetic gesture to the Jews was to include Yiddish as an official language in the Polish postal-telegraph system.

A Shift to Political Reaction

Effective legislative government altogether was becoming problematic in Poland. By 1926, the nation had undergone 118 changes in cabinet personnel and had swooned into an administrative catatonia reminiscent of the eighteenth-century era of the liberum veto. In May of that year, therefore, Jozef Pilsudski had seen enough. The soldier-statesman had withdrawn from political life three years earlier, retaining only command of the army. But with the country in political disarray, the old marshal turned to the veteran senior officers of his wartime Polish Legion to unseat the current government. Their coup was bloodless and efficient. Afterward, exercising power behind the scene, Pilsudski installed loyal technocrats as his handpicked protégés; while the Sejm, thoroughly intimidated, supinely allowed rigged elections to "endorse" Pilsudski's personal choices. Presumably, a firm, non-political regime would find ways to cope with Poland's chronic economic stagnation.

It did not. The Depression transformed stagnation into mendicancy. In 1929, the national per capita income of France (by the measurement of Polish zlotys) had fallen to 2,000; of Germany, to 2,400; of Britain, to 4,200. In Poland, it had fallen to a starvation-level 600. In the Polish countryside, destitution became so acute that parents were selling their children for adoption. The economic misery of Jews in Poland matched that of their gentile neighbors. As always, their ordeal was exacerbated by public policy. Étatism remained one of its most painful features. In 1932, Minister of Finance Stefan Strzynski co-opted still wider areas for nationalization, and specifically in the commercial and banking sectors, with their extensive Jewish component. The tens of thousands of Jews who became "redundant" encountered a bureaucratic stone wall. Public-works jobs, credit banks, and other forms of government relief undisguisedly favored Poles.

Indeed, under the impact of this emerging "cold pogrom," nearly a third of Poland's Jews of working age were unemployed by 1932. Two years later, a fourth of Polish Jewry had become partially or completely dependent on philanthropy. By 1936, the proportion reached two-thirds, and some 300,000 Jewish schoolchildren were estimated to be suffering from malnutrition. Once again, the Joint Distribution Committee was obliged to function as the principal source of communal relief, organizing scores of clinics, X-ray stations, infant-care dispensaries, and small-credit funds for businesses and workshops. Yet these measures were the barest palliatives in a catastrophe so dire that it appeared incapable of becoming worse.

Politically, however, it did worsen. Pilsudski's initial military coup of May 1926, although authoritarian, was based on no particular chauvinist agenda. But once the Depression struck, the "liberals" in Pilsudski's entourage lost their influence, and the cabal gradually shifted its coercion to such "leftist" institutions as rural cooperatives and trade unions. In 1934, Pilsudski became ill and incapacitated (he would die in May 1935). Far-rightists then began to take over the government. Their strongman, Colonel Edward Rydz-Smigly, dictated policy to a sequence of compliant prime ministers. None of his measures succeeded in reversing the economic emergency. Finally, in its turmoil and confusion, the colonels' regime moved toward fascist populism. An initial step on this route was Rydz-Smigly's decision to genuflect to the Endeks, still the nation's most intimidating political faction. In September 1934, the government formally renounced Poland's adherence to the 1919 Minorities Treaty. For the Jews, the implications of that renunciation would swiftly become explicit. So they would, elsewhere, in the largest part of successor-state Europe.

XXII

The Triumph of East European Fascism

THE POLITICS OF REDUNDANCY

From September 1934 on, following Warsaw's cancellation of the Minorities Treaty, the status of Polish Jewry emerged as the single most ulcerated issue in the nation's domestic agenda. It was not political opportunism alone, or even "spontaneous" xenophobia, that focused public animus on the Jews. The Polish Church had long played a central role in shaping government policy and public opinion. Throughout the 1920s and 1930s, in parochial schools, religious periodicals, and pastoral sermons alike, clerical denunciations of Jews and Judaism achieved an unprecedented intensity. In earlier years, the Church had stigmatized Jews essentially as deicides. But as the Depression became increasingly acute, and with it the threat of social radicalism, the Jews were depicted more frequently as Bolsheviks, as purveyors of moral corruption, as carriers of disease, to be ranked with "the louse, the bedbug, the locust, the typhus bacillus, and the cholera and plague bacillus." In a pastoral letter of May 1939, Cardinal August Hlond, the Primate of Poland, laid down an ecclesiastical guideline on the Jews:

> It is a fact that Jews oppose the Catholic Church, are steeped in free-thinking and represent the avant-garde of the atheistic movement, the Bolshevik movement, and subversive action. . . . It is true that Jews commit fraud, usury, and are involved in [prostitution]. . . . [Consequently] one does well to prefer his own kind in commercial dealings and to avoid Jewish stores and . . . stalls in the market, although it is not permissible to demolish Jewish businesses.

In the anti-Jewish assault, Poland's white-collar class also emerged for the first time as a major influence, and specifically its "intelligentsia," its doctors, lawyers, engineers, professors, and mid-level government bureaucrats. In a joint statement of April 1934, the Union of Polish Catholic Lawyers, the Union of Catholic Writers, the Coordinating Committee of Academic Corporations, and the Union of Technicians and Engineers straightforwardly entreated "all Christians not to sell to Jews any land or houses, not to buy from Jewish stores, not to employ Jewish lawyers, physicians, engineers, architects, artists, or any other professional men." In June 1935, Endek partisans in Grodno launched a series of anti-Jewish attacks, destroying and looting shops in the main Jewish business quarter. Other assaults soon followed: in Bialystok, Brest-Litovsk, Minsk-Mazowiecki, Pryzytyk, Resc, Bugiem, and Czestochowa. In Czestochowa, the pogrom continued for three days, producing four deaths and some three hundred injured.

Yet special-interest groups alone, or even the Church hierarchy, could not have orchestrated a campaign of this range and intensity. It was endorsed by a widening spectrum of political parties. Beyond the Endeks, these included several "respectable" factions, among them the socially prestigious Conservative Party. Funded mainly by landowning magnates, the Conservatives at their annual convention in December 1937 approved the formula "We accept the injunctions issued by . . . Cardinal Hlond, which . . . regard it permissible to fight against Jewish influence in the economic and moral spheres." Even the nation's first prime minister, the pianist-statesman Ignacy Paderewski, who in 1919–20 had been a key liaison between Poland and American-Jewish leaders, now endorsed an anti-Jewish stance for his new Camp of Labor Party. At its founding convention in January 1938, the party advocated "the complete elimination of Jews from industry, trade, and business. . . . The party regards as the best solution of the Jewish problem a mass emigration of the Jews."

The Diplomacy of Redundancy

As the furor against the Jews gained momentum throughout the Depression, the colonels' regime began to accept the pragmatic usefulness of embracing antisemitism openly and officially. Thus, in the spring of 1936, in a seemingly innocuous bill introduced in the Sejm, the government proposed imposing restrictions on *shehita*, the slaughter of animals in Jewish abattoirs under Jewish dietary laws. Terming shehita "a cruel practice," Rydz-Smigly and his colleagues in practical fact hoped to inflict a crippling blow to Jewish religiocultural identity. It was revealing that the Sejm prolonged the debate on the shehita issue through fully half its sessions between 1936 and 1939. In March 1939, finally, its legislation banned shehita altogether—although the ban was not scheduled to take effect until 1942. Other measures cut no less deeply. Whatever their political and economic insecurities, Jewish families in the postwar period still nurtured the dream of a higher education for their children, and with it a future of economic self-sufficiency. The illusion was one of the first to be punctured. Almost simultaneously with Polish independence, a Jewish numerus clausus was introduced in Polish universities. In 1921–22, of the nation's 34,266 university and polytechnical students, 8,426 were Jews. By 1938–39, of Poland's 49,968 university students, 4,613 were Jews.

For the shrinking Jewish student minority, university life became an acutely humiliating ordeal. As early as 1922, gentile classmates harassed Jews out of school dormitories and obliged them to find separate housing. By the 1930s, right-wing student groups went rather further, agitating for the classroom segregation of Jews. In the effort, they mounted campus demonstrations, then physical attacks on Jewish students. In April 1937, Minister of Education Jozef Ujejski felt impelled to broadcast an appeal for the nationalist groups to avoid using life-threatening weapons. In return, he promised, the government would "reconsider" the question of segregation. And five months later, "for the maintenance of peace," Ujejski's successor, Wojciech Swietoslawski, authorized the rector of the University of Warsaw to allocate the left side of classrooms for Jews, where special benches would be provided for them. In galled response to these "ghetto benches," Jewish political parties in October 1937 organized a mass meeting and a six-hour work stoppage in Warsaw's Jewish quarter. The demonstrators were joined by a small but dedicated minority of Poles, academicians and others, who wrote letters of protest to newspapers and to the government. But the majority of professors and other university officials did not protest. Nor did a single member of Poland's Church hierarchy.

By then, too, the government had begun orienting its "Jewish" policy toward a more draconian solution. This was mass Jewish departure. There was little dissimulation or ambiguity in that objective. In January 1938, the colonels' regime publicly endorsed the concept. "The solution to the Jewish problem in Poland," party spokesmen declared flatly, "can be achieved above all by the most considerable reduction of Jews in the Polish state." In January 1939, responding to a petition from the Sejm's 116 Endek deputies as well as those of other rightist factions, Prime Minister Slawoj-Skladkowski affirmed that his administration "would do all in its power to obtain outlets for [Jewish] emigration by international action."

"International action" in fact had been under government exploration for many years. As early as 1927, the foreign ministry's consular bureau began formulating a detailed program for "encouraging" Jewish departure. Under this scheme, all remaining Jewish employees would be dismissed from state-subsidized cultural institutions—from music, theater, and the allied arts. The numerus clausus in the professions would be tightened to the point of closure. More fundamentally, entire categories of Jews would be disenfranchised, specifically those who had been absorbed into Poland with the annexed territories.

Reacting to these pressures, some 430,000 Jews actually managed to immigrate between the wars, to North and South America, to Western Europe and Palestine. The numbers plainly would have been much larger but for immigration restrictions abroad. In 1921, once the United States began closing its doors to East Europeans, other nations somewhat erratically followed this course. The onset of the Depression in 1929 produced an even more remorseless tightening of immigration quotas. At the same time, in response to Arab unrest, Britain's Colonial Office during the 1930s severely limited the number of Jews it would admit into Palestine (pp. 518–25). For the Polish government, therefore, the priority no longer was to devise techniques for hounding Jews to mass departure, but to seek out alternative destinations for them.

Thus, in early 1937, visiting Paris for conferences with Prime Minister Léon Blum, Poland's Foreign Minister Jozef Beck raised the possibility of French Madagascar as a haven for "surplus" Polish Jews. Blum voiced no objection, provided Poland itself or other nations funded the resettlement. Wasting little time, the Polish government then dispatched a commission of Polish and Jewish experts to Madagascar, led by Major Mieczyslaw Lepecki, president of his nation's International Colonization Society. Evidently the prospects in Madagascar were unenticing. If the commission report was ever completed, it was not published. The Polish government forged on, however, establishing three new emigration bodies in 1939 to explore other possibilities, in Africa and Australia. Yet the committees scarcely had begun their discussions before World War II began. The Warsaw government in any case always had taken less interest in Africa or Australia than in Palestine, a site offering the advantage of its "official" designation as the Jewish National Home. In the 1920s and 1930s, Jozef Pilsudski expressed an expedient sympathy for Zionism. Other Polish leaders often had cooperated with the Zionist leadership. In 1933, the right-wing Zionist activist Vladimir Jabotinsky (p. 354), who discounted the very notion of a meaningful Jewish future in Poland, actually was invited to broadcast his Zionist appeals on Polish state radio.

Like Jabotinsky, at least one other prominent Zionist had concluded that his people's future no longer could be salvaged in Poland. In 1933, Yitzhak Gruenbaum, leader of the Sejm's "Jewish caucus" and architect of the short-lived Minorities Bloc, already had made his own commitment to Palestine. Emigrating that year, he accepted a position on the Executive of the Jewish Agency, the Jewish National Home's quasi-government. A decade and a half later, when the State of Israel was established, Gruenbaum would become its first minister of the interior. His mandate was immigration. His clients by then would be the meagerest remnant of the first internationally "guaranteed" Diaspora community in the history of the Jewish people.

HOSTAGES OF "LATIN" CIVILIZATION

The Kingdom of Rumania, a comparative newcomer among the family of nations, a product of the 1878 Congress of Berlin, continued over the turn of the century to nurture irredentist claims upon the millions of ethnic Rumanians who remained under Russian and Hungarian rule. With its modest population of fewer than 7 million, the nation even as late as 1914 could not realistically hope to liberate these kinsmen on its own. A mutual defense agreement with the Central Powers appeared at first to offer a more promising strategy for "unification." Yet, once the World War began, Rumanian Prime Minister Ionel Bratianu, son of Ion Bratianu, Rumania's prime minister in 1878, chose to emulate his father's diplomatic strategy by playing each set of belligerents against the other "like a peddler in an oriental bazaar," contemptuously observed French Foreign Minister Paul Cambon. In 1916, negotiating a better deal from the Entente Powers, Bratianu led his country into war against his former German and Austrian treaty partners. The move was ill-advised. In the autumn of that year, the German Reichswehr effectively destroyed the hapless Rumanian army, and forced Bratianu's government to accept a satellite status under German and Austrian hegemony. Then, in the summer of 1918, as the Western democracies seemed poised at last to turn the military tide, the Rumanians once again smoothly repudiated their peace treaty with the Central Powers and reentered the war at the side of the Allies.

No sooner had the war ended, moreover, than Bratianu set about pressing his nation's territorial demands as if it had been a key partner in the Allied victory. The sheer brazenness of his tactics outraged the Allied leaders. Nevertheless, conceding the usefulness of an anti-Bolshevik cordon sanitaire in East-Central Europe, the Western leaders in the end grudgingly acquiesced in the full spectrum of Rumanian territorial claims. On December 19, 1919, as Bratianu affixed his signature to the Austrian and Hungarian peace treaties, his Rumanian "Old Kingdom" added to its domain the neighboring territories of Russian Bessarabia, together with Hungarian Transylvania, Bukovina, Dobrudja, and Temesvar. A prewar nation of 80,000 square miles and a population of 7.2 million now encompassed 176,000 square miles and a population of 16.6 million. The demographic revolution was also an ethnic one. At least 92 percent of the Old Kingdom's inhabitants had been Rumanian, with a shared language that could be traced back to the territory's status as Dacia, a colony of the ancient Roman Empire. The annexed provinces of 1919 now added 4.5 million new inhabitants, many of whom were distinctly non-Latin in their origins. Of these, 1.9 million were Hungarians. Other annexed populations included 1.1 million Ukrainians, 340,000

Germans, 290,000 Bulgars, 200,000 Turks, Russians, and Gypsies—and no fewer than 556,000 Jews.

In Rumania as elsewhere in Eastern Europe, the Great War had generated a renewed frenzy of xenophobia. A military staff order had decreed that "[a]ll Jews must be placed in the front line at the beginning of an attack." Another warned that "Jews cannot be tolerated in the hospitals for wounded and sick." Jews were exposed to random pogroms, to widespread governmental confiscation of food and possessions, to bouts of forced labor. Their single hope of meaningful emancipation would lie with the Western Allies, at the impending peace conference. Others of Rumania's new diversity of annexed minorities similarly awaited protection, among them Transylvania's sizable enclave of Hungarians. But the Jews, their numbers swollen from 240,000 before the war to 796,000 afterward, well understood the historic uniqueness of their vulnerability. Although 70,000 of these had left for the United States between 1912 and 1914, they still comprised 5 percent of the entire Rumanian population now. Their engorged presence was certain to become a bone in the Rumanian throat. Accordingly, they counted on the statesmen at Paris to impose conditions on the Rumanians far more ironclad than those negotiated in Berlin in 1878 (p. 113). The Allied leaders needed little persuasion. Once committed to the principle of minorities treaties, they were prepared to force the issue with the detested Rumanians even more unrelentingly than with the Poles. Prime Minister Bratianu, as guileful on minority issues as on territorial ones, sought to dilute the treaty through "interpretive" ruses. But Clemenceau, Lloyd George, and Wilson would not budge.

In December 1919, therefore, the Rumanians signed the treaty. Although the communal-autonomist features of the Polish treaty also appeared in the Rumanian version, its "Jewish" reference, Article 7, went much further. Ostensibly, its language plugged the lacunae of the 1878 Treaty of Berlin by affirming that "Rumania undertakes to recognize as Rumanian nationals ipso facto, and without the requirement of any formality, Jews inhabiting any Rumanian territory who do not possess another nationality." Moreover, upon ratifying the treaty, the Rumanian parliament duly incorporated its principal articles into its constitution. But the commitment would prove as fraudulent in 1919 as in 1878. Once again, the Rumanians would sabotage their obligations in both letter and spirit.

THE "NEW" RUMANIA

The enlarged kingdom was all but awash in natural resources, in rich topsoil and a luxuriance of forests, in a subterranean cornucopia of oil, iron, coal, copper, and aluminum. Yet, for all its amplitude, the inheritance would continue to devolve into the hands of the nation's privileged boyars, with the peasantry left to eke out a precarious subsistence as tenant farmers. In the immediate postwar period, moreover, each of the nation's political parties chose to ignore these structural inequities, preferring instead to accuse "foreign elements" of dominating the country's economic life. There was some truth in the charge, although it bore little relevance to land ownership. It also related essentially to the annexed provinces. Here, Germans and Hungarians maintained their preeminence in the banking and oil sectors. By the same token, they became choice targets for political retaliation. Thus, in defiance of its minorities-treaty obligations, Bucharest withheld funds to German- and Hungarian-language schools, imposed punitive taxes on German and Hungarian businesses, and relentlessly squeezed non-Rumanians out of the civil service.

But none of the ethnic minorities was dealt with as brutally as were the Jews, or demonized as the principal source of the nation's economic ills. None other, after all, was as uniquely "infidel," urban, or mercantile a presence among an overwhelmingly rural population. Jew-hatred plainly had been endemic to the Old Kingdom long before the war. After 1918, however, Rumanian xenophobia focused with a revived and unsurpassed malevolence on the dense Jewish populations in the annexed territories. Any Western illusions that the Minorities Treaty would be honored toward the Jews, of all nationalities, were instantly dispelled. As Foreign Minister Alexandru Voievod murmured to an aide upon signing the treaty in December 1919: "The Allies have written the treaties, but we Rumanians will know how to interpret them."

Thus, with the identical deviousness they exhibited in "interpreting" the 1878 treaty, Rumania's statesmen applied the 1919 document's "citizenship" clauses exclusively to the "veteran" inhabitants of the Regat, the Old Kingdom regions. The far larger Jewish populations of the new territories would have to achieve their naturalization through special legislation. Eventually, by the late 1920s, some 35,000 Jewish families achieved a belated citizenship, but the process was so dilatory and byzantine that scores of thousands of others remained without passports. Living in a juridical limbo, these noncitizens were barred from registering their children in public schools, from entering into business contracts, even from owning land in their own names. Subject to eviction at any moment, they paid off local Rumanian police officials simply to remain where they were, as squatters.

As for the cultural-autonomist provisions of the Minorities Treaty, these were simply ignored. Yiddish-language schools were denied accreditation, let alone funding. Economic discrimination also was an integral feature of government policy. Income taxes were assessed on a graduated basis, the lowest rate to be paid by ethnic Rumanians, the highest by annexed non-Rumanians.

The measures did not significantly distinguish between Jews and other minorities, but the Sunday closing laws did. So did Rumania's characteristic successor-state program of étatism. Once the government set about nationalizing match, tobacco, salt, and liquor production, the Jews who formerly predominated in these fields were dismissed sine die.

Throughout the 1920s, Louis Marshall of the American Jewish Committee, and Lucien Wolf, executive secretary of the Anglo-Jewish "Conjoint" (the Board of Deputies of British Jews and the Anglo-Jewish Association, working in tandem), appealed repeatedly to the Rumanian government to honor its treaty obligations, and above all to put an end to the physical and economic intimidation of Jews. Bucharest's responses invariably were bland disclaimers. Appeals to the League of Nations proved equally unavailing. As early as October 1920, the League Council had devised a cumbersome, multistage procedure for dealing with minority grievances. The first stage established the minority's right of petition to the League secretary-general. Upon receiving the bill of complaints, the secretary-general was obliged to notify the offending state, giving it opportunity to respond. Once that response was in hand, the secretary-general might then forward the original petition (and the ensuing correspondence) to the full League Council. Yet even this initial process might consume months. Afterward, in still another "filtering" stage, the petition would require a Council member's sponsorship for additional investigation. Only then could the secretary-general appoint a "committee of investigation," consisting of three other members of the Council. In turn, the committee's first objective was to resolve the dispute through "mediation." But this process, too, could devour still additional months, and in any event might produce no result. By the mid-1920s, with most of the successor states fighting the minorities treaties tooth and nail, the Jews of East-Central Europe had all but given up on the League of Nations.

THE FOUNDATIONS OF POLITICAL RACISM

It was in the early years of the twentieth century, as romantic nationalism achieved a growing intensity in the Balkans, that several Rumanian intellectuals began to develop the mythos of a common "Latin" ancestry for their people. In the process, it became fashionable to characterize minorities such as Greeks, Jews, and assorted varieties of Slavs as threats to the nation's cultural integrity, and ultimately to its political independence. In the case of the Jews, moreover, that threat was seen as profoundly compounded by the vast prewar influx of refugees from the Russian Pale of Settlement, and after 1918 by the far larger numbers of Jews incorporated together with the annexed provinces. Even in the last years before the war, the history professors Nicolae Iorga and Alexandru Cuza were concentrating their animus on the Jews as aliens whose presence represented a particularly lethal threat to the Rumanian people. After the war, projecting himself as the high priest of Rumanian "intellectual" antisemitism, Cuza determined that "the only feasible solution of the Jewish question . . . is the elimination of the *yids,* which implies immediate action, in all fields. . . ." The call for action resonated widely throughout the country. Cuza, like Iorga, was no "mere" professor. In 1922, both men joined the poet Octavian Goga in becoming charter members of LANC, the racist Christian National Defense League, and Cuza served as LANC's first parliamentary deputy.

Yet Cuza's most enduring achievement was the inspiration he provided for a younger protégé, Corneliu Zelea Codreanu. In 1919, the twenty-year-old Codreanu enrolled at the University of Jassy Law School. It was in this Moldavian district capital, inundated by thousands of "new" Jews from recently annexed Bessarabia, that the young man was swept up in a particularly virulent new wave of antisemitism and simultaneously exposed to the "ideological" Jew-hatred of the renowned Professor Cuza. Codreanu even earlier had given serious thought to the threat of bolshevism and to the likelihood of rescuing his impoverished nation through an alternate variety of "Christian" populism. To this redemptionist vision, he could now link Cuza's favored strategy, of saving Rumania's "soul" by purging the country of its vast new Jewish population.

Codreanu seemed all but predestined for the role of populist messiah. Tall, handsome, eloquent, he swiftly mastered the knack of cultivating his fellow students' blood lust, exhorting them to intimidate their Jewish classmates, to hound them out of the lecture rooms by threatened or actual violence. Within the year, he won thousands of followers to his cause (still nominally the LANC cause) by defining the Jewish issue as one of atheistic communism against racial purity, of Semitic alienism in a nation struggling for cultural homogeneity. Yet Codreanu was no mere rabble-rouser. He activated his ideology by personal example. In 1923, when police broke up one of his noisome campus rallies, he filed suit against the local police prefect for brutality. A court hearing exonerated the prefect. Enraged, Codreanu then exacted his own justice by shooting the prefect dead. The episode became a turning point in Codreanu's political career. The government put him on trial, shifting the venue from inflamed Jassy to Turnu Severin, at the far western edge of the country. The trial itself was wasted effort. So intense was public fervor on behalf of the young demagogue that the jury needed less than an hour to exonerate him. Codreanu's trip back to Jassy thereupon burgeoned into a triumphal procession of some 30,000 jubilant LANC partisans—who did not hesitate to attack Jewish neighborhoods and businesses en route.

Prime Minister Bratianu regarded the orgy of violence with mounting concern. If the mayhem continued, Rumania's already tarnished credit rating would be further damaged. At his initiative, therefore, Corneliu Codreanu was "encouraged" to leave the country for an extended period of study abroad. But three years later, in 1925, exploiting the government's preoccupation with other political issues, Codreanu made his way home without incident and immediately reclaimed control over his antisemitic crusade. This time, however, his agenda far transcended mere violence, or even racist incitement. The twenty-nine-year-old repatriate announced that he was acting on a "vision." The Archangel Michael had appeared to him and enjoined him to guide the Rumanian people to moral resurrection. To achieve that goal, Codreanu now set about organizing the League of the Archangel Michael, a fellowship of patriots who would combat Rumania's corruption and decay by engaging collectively in national reconstruction. "We want to build, from the smallest to the greatest," he proclaimed, ". . . even villages, even cities, even a new Rumanian state."

The response was instantaneous. Thousands of unemployed young men flocked to Codreanu's banner, eager to join a program that combined such unobjectionable public projects as road-building and hospital construction with the dynamic of the leadership principle, with military-style drills and public parades and raucous demonstrations against the "Jewish menace." Codreanu envisaged his uniformed lumpenproletariat—soon to be known as the Iron Guard—as the nucleus of a revived political movement, All-for-the-Fatherland-Front. Indeed, during the 1928 national elections, Codreanu led his followers to an impressive 15 percent of the popular vote. Both as a party and as a paramilitary force, Codreanu's crusade plainly was emerging as a serious alternative to Rumania's established political alignments. By then, it had burgeoned into a fascist-style tidal wave.

Hostages of Civil Struggle

In that same year, 1928, unable to cope with Rumania's stagnant economy, Ionel Bratianu, Rumania's "hero" of the Peace Conference, resigned as prime minister. His National Liberal Party was succeeded by the faintly more progressive National Peasant Party, under the premiership of Iuliu Maniu. A rarity in his nation's politics, Maniu was an honest man. Upon taking office, he launched into a conscientious attempt to democratize the government, even to address minority grievances. His effort was unsuccessful. The obstacle lay not only in Rumania's suppurating racism, or even in the chronic venality of its civil service. It related to the anomalous status of the Rumanian monarchy.

Crown Prince Carol, well educated and hardworking, might have developed into a productive national talisman. But the royal heir was encumbered by a half-Jewish mistress, Elena Wolff, more commonly known as Magda

Lupescu. In 1923, hopelessly smitten by the divine "Magda," Carol divorced his wife, Princess Helen of Greece, to settle in with his femme fatale. Hereupon, under Church and government pressure, Carol was obliged to renounce his succession to the throne and live in Paris. In 1928, however, several months after the death of King Ferdinand I, the new Maniu government decided to bring Carol home as a symbol of domestic stability. Accordingly, in 1930, following two years of political negotiations, the royal exile was ushered back to Rumania, duly to be proclaimed King Carol II.

A problem soon developed. The restored monarch had assured Maniu that he would not bring his mistress with him. Yet no sooner had Carol returned than Magda Lupescu also mysteriously reappeared, taking up residence in a Bucharest villa near the royal palace. The public's reaction to this development was not congenial. Nor did Prime Minister Maniu seem the man to resolve it. He had been in office for two years and manifestly was failing to resolve the far graver crisis of the Depression. He proved equally incapable now of dealing with King Carol, who soon revealed his intention not simply to reign but to rule in the manner of the much admired Mussolini government in Italy. Before 1930 was out, therefore, the premier was maneuvered into resignation. Over the next three years, Carol similarly forced the resignation of Maniu's three rather nondescript successors, and manipulated into office his own handpicked "Government" Party. By 1933, it was the populist racists, Codreanu's Iron Guard, who remained Carol's most formidable political enemies. Indeed, from then on, Rumanian political life devolved into an escalating civil war between the Iron Guard and the king. Mass Iron Guardist demonstrations against the government, coupled with hooliganism against Jews, set the political atmosphere of the mid-1930s.

More than ever before, it was in this malaise of economic depression and chauvinist frustration that Jews became the target of choice for the nation's rightist political and professional organizations. At its convention in June 1936, one of those factions, the National Soldiers Front, ordered a "spiritual mobilization . . . against the vast Jewish plot [to cripple] Rumania's economy." In May 1937, the Federation of Rumanian Free Professional Associations requested its constituent groups to purge their membership of all remaining Jews. The Rumanian Cultural League, whose president was the veteran xenopobe Professor Nicolae Iorga (p. 425), appealed for an economic boycott of Jews. To this crescendo of anti-Jewish imprecations and accusations, the Rumanian Orthodox Church lent its spiritual endorsement. In June 1935, Ion Motta, the Orthodox archdeacon, called for drastic measures against the Jews along the lines of "the great master, Adolf Hitler." Motta's proposal was echoed by Grand Patriarch Dr. Miron Cristea. "Why should the Jews enjoy the privilege of living like parasites upon our backs?" Cristea declaimed.

"Why should we not get rid of these parasites who suck Rumanian and Christian blood? It is logical and holy to react against them."

It was in any case expedient. In 1937, Carol's Government Party polled only 37 percent of the vote. The Goga-Cuza LANC dropped to 9 percent. By contrast, Codreanu's All-for-the-Fatherland Front achieved a stunning 21 percent of the vote, thereby emerging as the third-largest party in Rumania. The king now found himself in a painful dilemma. The notion of bringing Codreanu and the Iron Guard into a coalition cabinet was unthinkable. Their raging populism, the blatant incendiarism of their Jew-hatred, their pornographic diatribes against Magda Lupescu, all persuaded Carol to devise a stopgap solution. He would turn to the Goga-Cuza coalition. By appointing to the prime ministry a man like Octavian Goga—poet, verbose ideologue, co-leader of a tiny electoral minority—the king might still exercise a certain control over public policy.

The decision shocked the nation's dwindling residue of liberals. Rumania was now to be led by a crypto-Nazi, essentially a fatter and duller version of Codreanu. In any case, the new government proved entirely inept, enduring barely seven weeks, until February 1938, when its sheer incompetence brought Rumania to the brink of economic collapse. During his abbreviated tenure, however, Goga managed to keep a single promise, the one that had recommended him to the king as a firebreak against the Iron Guard. He would propitiate the antisemites. The very day he entered office, the poet-premier announced that he would seek a parliamentary bill to "review," in effect, reverse, all postwar naturalizations, thereby abrogating the painfully negotiated citizenship of those tens of thousands of Jewish families that had come under Rumanian sovereignty in the aftermath of the Peace Conference.

Once more, international Jewish organizations registered their protest. From Washington, President Franklin Roosevelt let it be known that the American people were "anxiously watching developments." The Soviet government, monitoring Rumania's shift toward the fascist powers (p. 431), used the episode as a pretext to recall its ambassador from Bucharest. This time, the adverse publicity gave pause to King Carol's rubber-stamp cabinet. Goga agreed to postpone his bill for several months. Yet the prime minister required no formal legislation to put much of his agenda into effect; for, by act of parliament, the government was empowered to annul any certificate of naturalization if the document had been obtained by "misrepresentation." Under this pretext, some 14,000 Jews in the winter of 1938 had their citizenship reversed. The nation itself, however, paid an unanticipated price for these punitive measures. Thousands of Rumanian Jews, even those with unchallenged credentials, resorted to a campaign of passive resistance. Closing their businesses and offices, they left behind a vacuum of crucial managerial experience. Soon the shock of these Jewish closures began jeopardizing Rumania's already precarious credit reputation.

The king had seen enough. In February 1938, he dismissed Goga, appointing in his place a technocratic Government of National Consensus under the leadership of Dr. Miron Cristea, the Orthodox patriarch. At Carol's "suggestion," the patriarch assured Rumania's Chief Rabbi Jacob Niemerower that the revisionist naturalization program would be "postponed." Yet, all but predictably, the assurance turned out to be mendacious. The rescissions of citizenship quietly proceeded, under administrative subterfuges. Thus, in June 1938, it was announced that some 28,000 Jews in the annexed territories had failed to prove their claim to citizenship, and were thereby denaturalized. Facing the imminent loss of their livelihoods and homes, these newly stateless Jews were reduced once more to paying off Rumania's officialdom. By then, however, even bribery offered no certainty of protection. In that same June of 1938, all denaturalized "residents" of Czernowitz, the capital of Bukovina district, with its extensive, middle-class Jewish population, were ordered to liquidate their businesses within a fortnight.

HOSTAGES OF *Realpolitik*

Throughout the late 1930s, as Rumania's economy continued its free fall under the impact of world Depression and governmental chaos, public support for the Iron Guardists widened from month to month. Yet even as Codreanu sought to identify the national crisis first and foremost with the monarch (and Magda Lupescu), Carol's patience was approaching its end. In the spring of 1938, he decided to move forcefully against his nemesis. At his orders, Codreanu was arrested on a charge of criminal libel. Tried in an "administrative" court, he was sentenced to ten years' imprisonment. During the summer and autumn, the police managed to round up some 3,000 additional Iron Guard activists and place them under "administrative" detention. Finally, on November 30, Carol's personal bodyguard garrison hauled the Iron Guard's senior officers from their concentration camps, trucked them to a deserted road, and shot them. One of the executed prisoners was Codreanu himself. After eight years of political maneuvering, the king apparently had established himself as the nation's uncontested dictator. Requiring no further political firebreaks, no tactical marriages of convenience with chauvinist elements, he would govern Rumania henceforth with order, authority—and venality.

Was there time for the nation's Jews to breathe more easily? The opposite was the case. By 1939, Rumania's political future was rapidly being transformed by the shifting balance of European power. Throughout the 1920s, the nation had been an enthusiastic member of the Little Entente, the French-sponsored alliance of East European successor states, all of them sharing a vested interest in the postwar territorial status quo. By the mid- to late 1930s, however, France no longer appeared to be a reliable guarantor of the postwar map. It had remained passive as Nazi Germany successfully repudiated the constraints of the Versailles Treaty, reoccupying the Rhineland in 1936, and swallowing Austria and the Czech Sudetenland in 1938. Thus, as the inheritor of the former Habsburg Empire's extensive trading arena in Danubian Europe, the Third Reich by late 1938 was in a position to draw the region's chronically impoverished successor nations into its widening economic orbit. At the same time, the strident dynamism of Nazi antisemitism was proving irresistible to the fascist movements of these xenophobic, multiethnic states.

In November 1938, as Germany augmented its frontiers and economic leverage in East-Central Europe, even King Carol felt obliged to visit Hitler in Berchtesgaden and to profess his friendship. Afterward, Carol periodically dispatched reminders to Berlin that the struggle to maintain his royal prerogatives was entirely unrelated to issues of foreign policy, or even of racist ideology. For the while, the führer stayed his hand. But in the summer of 1940, with France's surrender in World War II, Rumania was obliged to make its own payoff to Germany's entourage of allies and dependencies. At Hitler's orders, the Bucharest government was "directed" to return Bessarabia to Soviet Russia (Germany's ally since the Nazi-Soviet Pact of August 1939), as well as northern Transylvania to Hungary, and the southern Dobrudja to Bulgaria. The amputations sheared away one-third of Greater Rumania, and one-fifth of the country's population.

At Berlin's "recommendation," too, a pro-German government was installed in Bucharest under the leadership of General Ion Antonescu. Hereupon, fatally compromised as "guardian" of Rumania's independence, the hapless Carol was forced to abdicate. On September 6, 1940, he fled the country with his mistress. For years, he had functioned at best as an indifferent and imperfect shield of the third-largest Jewish population in Europe outside the Soviet Union. His fate henceforth was the harbinger of their own.

HUNGARY AND THE LEGACY OF UTOPIANISM

On March 21, 1919, a senior Hungarian government official arrived at Budapest's aging Marko Street jail for a meeting with one of its prisoners. The visitor, Zsigmond Kunfi, was minister of education in Hungary's Social Democratic government. The prisoner, Bela Kun, was chairman of Hungary's Communist Party. The improbable interview reflected Hungary's chaotic military and political circumstances. During the recent World War, the country had suffered over a million casualties in dead, wounded, and prisoners. In the city streets, starving workers were rioting. Count Istvan Tisza, the wartime premier, who had ordered troops to fire on peace demonstrators, had himself been assassinated. Accordingly, on November 3, 1918, Count Mihaly Karolyi, the new prime minister, won cabinet approval to seek an armistice, then to dissociate the nation from the "imperial warmongers" of Vienna by proclaiming Hungary's independence. At the same time, Karolyi attempted desperately to restore some degree of social order before confronting the Allies at the Peace Conference. To that end, he restructured his cabinet to include both moderate Liberals and Social Democrats.

But in his efforts, Karolyi was ill served by the Allied governments. During the last weeks before the armistice, Hungary's subject peoples—Serbs, Croats, Slovaks, Transylvanian and Bukovinian Rumanians—were proclaiming their independence or their union with neighboring successor states. By early January 1919, Hungary already had lost more than half its prewar population, and the Rumanian army was pushing across the Tisza River, deep onto Hungarian soil. Two months later, on March 20, 1919, the Allies demanded an extensive Hungarian troop pullback from the nation's eastern borders. Horrified by a directive that manifestly anticipated even more extensive territorial amputations, Karolyi resigned that same day. Yet the prime minister's decision was impelled by more than simple outrage. He sensed the possibility of a last-minute military alliance with Bolshevik Russia. The chances for that alliance plainly would be enhanced if Hungarian Communists entered the national cabinet. These were the circumstances, on March 21, in which the minister of education visited the Communist chairman in his prison cell to determine if he would assume responsibility with the Social Democrats in forming a new government. The proposal approached surrealism. The emissary, Zsigmond Kunfi (Kohn), and the prisoner, Bela Kun, were Jews.

The Hungarian-Jewish world that produced both men was a comparatively recent one. As late as 1789, 85,000 Jews lived in the country, most of these from the neighboring Habsburg province of Galicia. Over the years, they had settled principally in northeastern Hungary, functioning as estate agents and tax collectors for the local boyars. An early turning point in their demography, in both Hungary and Austria, came in 1782, when Emperor Joseph II issued his Toleranzpatent, allowing a select number of Jews to rent dwellings and workplaces throughout the realm's cities and towns. Exploiting this opportunity, Jews in far greater numbers began migrating to (Greater) Hungary from neighboring Poland. By 1840, they numbered 240,000. They also stood at the threshold of a decisive emancipation. The political turning point for Hungarians and Jews alike was the Ausgleich, the constitutional "reconfiguration" of 1867 that transformed the empire into the Dual Monarchy of Austria-Hungary (p. 94). Enjoying full internal self-rule under a common Habsburg dynasty, exposed to the winds of Europe's ascending liberalism, Hungary soon emulated its western, Austrian partner in extending political and civil equality to all its minorities.

From Russia's Pale of Settlement, therefore, as well as from impoverished Habsburg Galicia, the westward migration of Polish Jews became a flood. By 1910, Jews living under Hungarian rule had reached a critical mass of 910,000 within the nation's conglomerate population of 21 million. To be sure, more than two-thirds of these Jews lived in Hungary's Slovakian, Transylvanian, Bukovinian, and Serbo-Croatian provinces. But even within "integral" Hungary, a population of 270,000 Jews represented a substantial presence. In Budapest alone, numbering 205,000, they made up over a fifth of the capital's 1 million residents (cynics dubbed the city "Judapest"). By 1910, too, Jews comprised Hungary's preeminent mercantile and professional community. More than half of Budapest's commercial firms were owned by Jews, as were 85 percent of all Hungarian banks. Indeed, Jewish-owned banks played the decisive role in funding Hungary's industrial expansion, much of which also was pioneered by Jews. In the professions, by 1910, the Jews represented 46 percent of Hungary's journalists, 51 percent of Hungary's lawyers, 62 percent of Hungary's private physicians.

A significant minority of Jews even became politically prominent, although most of these tended to be Christian converts, or the children of converts. Between 1900 and 1918, twenty-six deputies of Jewish ancestry sat in the parliament, and at least twelve served as cabinet ministers. Given the magnitude of their acculturation and upward mobility, therefore, it was little wonder that Hungarian Jews engaged in a virtual competition of nationalist devotion. With the outbreak of war in 1914, no ethnic community in the empire greeted the conflict with a more fervent effusion of loyalty. Some 214,000 Jews from Greater Hungary served in the armed forces, and at least 10,000 perished in combat.

Nevertheless, as in other nations, they also became scapegoats for the war's hardships and sacrifices. Antisemitism had not originated during the conflict, of course. For several decades before 1914, the animus had been simmering among the nation's déclassé minor nobility and lower middle classes. By early 1918, however, as the tide of battle shifted decisively against the Central Powers, and as the threat of starvation mounted, charges of Jewish economic exploitation burgeoned ominously. These resentments were further exacerbated by culture shock, as tens of thousands of insular Galician Jewish refugees, many of them caftan-wearing Hasidim, flooded in from the Eastern battle zone. In 1918, the right-wing Christian Socialist Party based its political campaign largely on the need to "crush Jewish rule." Almost overnight, so it appeared, Hungary's most thoroughly acculturated minority race found itself widely execrated as the principal source of the nation's misfortunes.

A HUNGARIAN LENIN

Although Jews in prewar Hungary for the most part were archetypes of middle-class respectability, their political haven by the latter war years had become the Social Democratic Party. As elsewhere on the Continent, they appeared in disproportionate numbers among the party's leadership cadres. Urbanized and literate, often members of the liberal professions, they gravitated instinctively to a movement that preached and practiced egalitarian ideals at a time when the upper strata of Hungarian society jealously preserved conservative and Catholic values. By the early twentieth century, Social Democracy's coterie of intellectuals, the so-called Galilei Circle, was largely Jewish. Its chairman was the Jewish-born Erwin Szabo.

Like their counterparts in Europe's other major powers, Hungary's Social Democrats initially supported the decision to enter the war. By 1916, however, the military stalemate and purposeless carnage affected socialists everywhere. In Hungary, as in Germany and Austria, a significant minority within the Social Democratic Party fell under the influence of radicals, particularly in the aftermath of Russia's Bolshevik Revolution. Thus, in the nation's factories, workers' "soviets" began springing up as the preferred instrument of social deliverance. In January 1918, Erwin Szabo, who recently had become chairman of the party's left wing, and another Jew, Sandor Osztereicher, chairman of the "inter-factory soviet," were arrested for sedition. At that point, Otto Korvin-Klein and Jeno Landler, both former moderate-revisionists (and former Jews), assumed leadership of the radicals, and both men vigorously set about organizing mass protest meetings and wildcat strikes.

By autumn of 1918, with the war essentially lost, the—mainline—Social Democrats had become too powerful to be barred from Prime Minister Karolyi's coalition government. The agenda they brought with them included universal suffrage, the secret ballot, full civil liberties, and the progressive income tax. Yet virtually none of this program could be translated into practical action. In the chaos of the early postwar months, Karolyi was uninterested in projecting an image of Hungary as a hotbed of "bolshevism"—not at a moment when the Allies were sharpening their knives in anticipation of the Peace Conference. In turn, throughout January 1919, the Communists and the SD left wing intensified their demonstrations and strikes. Still, Karolyi dug in his heels. On February 21, the prime minister ordered the arrest of over one hundred prominent Communists. Among them was Bela Kun.

Born in 1886 in a small Transylvanian town, Kun was the son of a Jewish notary. Like most of the local Jewish population, his family was culturally Magyarized, and he himself attended a Calvinist school. After a brief, indifferent stint in law school, Kun found his métier as a political journalist. Mingling with workers, attending trade-union meetings, he himself became a committed Social Democrat. When the war began, however, Kun shared the patriotism of most of his fellow socialists and promptly enlisted in the army. As a university graduate, he was selected for officers' training school, and as a young lieutenant he saw intermittent battle action on the Eastern Front. Then, in late spring of 1916, overwhelmed by a massive Russian offensive, Kun and his entire company were taken prisoner and carried off for internment in Siberia. Although Kun was entitled to a special officers' billet, he found the privilege meager comfort. His fellow officers endlessly harassed him as a Jew. He chose instead to join with other political soul mates in organizing a Marxist discussion group.

Throughout the great network of Austrian-Hungarian POW compounds in Siberia, these "camp revolutionaries" by and large had been prewar socialists, and a large proportion of them were Hungarian Jews. Literate and multilingual, they also succeeded early on in establishing contacts with radical elements among the surrounding population. Thus, following the outbreak of the Bolshevik Revolution, several of these Marxist POW groups actually found themselves transformed into local Red Guard auxiliaries; and Kun, as leader of the single largest POW Bolshevik unit, was selected by Lenin to direct the entire POW Bolshevik organization in Russia. By the end of the war, most of the POW revolutionaries made their way back to their native countries, often to become active in their respective leftist political parties. Yet none quite achieved the eminence of Bela Kun. Upon reaching Budapest, the young activist actually flaunted a personal letter from Lenin, authorizing him to assume leadership of Hungary's Social Democratic left wing and transform this faction into the Hungarian Communist Party. It was a mission Kun accomplished within a single week. Organizing a party office, he wasted no time in launching an explosive campaign of demonstrations and strikes on behalf of "full and total socialization." In that effort, six of the eight members of Kun's newly structured Communist Central Committee also were Jews, all of them, typically, the products of higher education and doubtless of social discrimination.

In late February 1919, as demobilized soldiers and unemployed workers grappled with the police in clashes of increasing violence, the provocation became too much for Prime Minister Karolyi. He ordered Kun arrested and Communist Party offices closed. Yet the stern measures did nothing to ease Hungary's ordeal. The ongoing Allied economic blockade and diplomatic pressure merely compounded internal chaos. These were the circumstances, on March 20, that impelled Karolyi to resign, thereby allowing his emissary, Zsigmond Kunfi, to invite Bela Kun to assume a decisive role in forming a new government. Upon receiving assurance that his Communists would dominate that government, Kun accepted the offer.

REVOLUTION ...

Kun's new cabinet included thirty-three "commissars," with virtually all the key positions held by Communists. The public's initial response to this political transformation was surprisingly favorable. Even the middle classes secretly hoped that the Kun experiment might bring relief to their mutilated country and foil the Allied statesmen at Paris. But the mood would soon change. Kun revealed himself to be a Bolshevik-style doctrinaire, lacking even the faintest ability to administer a planned economy. His government clumsily set about confiscating not only the nation's privately owned factories, banks, and larger businesses, but its private homes and possessions, even its private art and stamp collections. His cabinet increased pensions for veterans and the unemployed, then simultaneously cut taxes on the urban working classes. Little time passed before the treasury ran out of funds to support the enlarged public-welfare program. In the agricultural sector, the Communists decreed nationalization of the larger estates but made no provision for dividing the land among impoverished small farmers.

By summer of 1919, a particularly ugly feature of the Kun government revealed itself. Communist enforcement squads rounded up suspected "counterrevolutionaries." Under the command of Jozsef Czeny and Tibor Szamuely, both former POWs in Russia, these vigilante-hoodlums fostered a reign of terror, breaking into private homes, requisitioning "illegal" foodstuffs and chattels, dragging the hapless owners off to local jails, where they often had to face the summary justice of revolutionary courts. Although the "Red Terror" executed possibly less than two hundred victims, its psychological impact was severe, and not least in its post factum consequences for Hungarian Jewry. It was this little people's gravest misfortune that their fellow Jews figured prominently in the nation's Communist regime. Tibor Szamuely was commander of all paramilitary activities. Otto Korvin-Klein, now acting as commissar of the interior, became Szamuely's counterpart as chief political prosecutor. Other Jews served in high-visibility positions not only as cabinet members but as revolutionary judges, propagandists, and as leaders of Communist cultural and youth groups. Bitter charges of a "Jewish conspiracy" fell on receptive soil.

Possibly even more fatal to the Kun government than its Jewish associations was its eventual abandonment by Bolshevik Russia. As Lenin's chosen protégé in Hungary, Kun had made it one of his priorities to secure a military alliance with Moscow. Yet, in the midst of its own civil war, the Soviet regime could spare no troops to protect Hungary against ongoing Rumanian incursion. On July 29, 1919, as the Rumanian invaders resumed their drive toward Budapest, the Allies issued an ultimatum to the Hungarian government. Kun must be removed from office, they insisted, and his Red cabinet dismantled in favor of a moderate, middle-class coalition. Only then would the Western Powers ensure a Rumanian military withdrawal and terminate their economic blockade. The terms were acceptable to Kun's Social Democratic partners. On August 1, 1919, they demanded Kun's resignation and that of his fellow Communists.

The next day, helpless to resist, Kun and eight of his closest associates and their families departed Budapest by train. Under diplomatic immunity, they were allowed to cross the frontier into Austria, where the entire group was interned. Less fortunate were the Communist ex-officials who tarried behind in Hungary. Tibor Szamuely was denied entrance into Austria. Before he could be turned over to the Hungarian "White" authorities, he shot himself. Nine others of Kun's commissars similarly were turned back from the Austrian frontier. All were arrested, most were imprisoned, and three, including Otto Korvin-Klein, were executed by the counterrevolutionary government.

. . . AND COUNTERREVOLUTION

By the time Kun and his retinue left Hungary, the Allies possibly would have honored their commitment to expel the Rumanians and lift their economic blockade. But Rumania's Prime Minister Bratianu clung to his own agenda. In a secret deal with a reactionary Hungarian boyar, Istvan Friedrich, Bratianu sent his regiments into the defenseless Hungarian capital and installed Friedrich as puppet premier. Hereupon the Rumanians launched into a nightmare of pillage. For the next sixteen weeks, their troops systematically looted Budapest and other occupied cities, not departing until mid-November, and then only under dire warnings of Allied military intervention. Afterward, to restore order in the nation until a final peace treaty could be formulated in Paris, the Western Powers authorized still another military force to fill the vacuum of the departed Rumanians. This one, however, was native Hungarian, and its leadership was fully as authoritarian as that of the late Kun regime.

Under the direction of Vice Admiral Miklos Horthy, the wartime commander of the Habsburg navy, the "caretakers" were structured around a loose confederation of minor boyars and former mid-level imperial officials, all of them militantly right-wing. In November 1919, the Allies were impressed enough by the Horthy group's anti-Communist bona fides to promise their support to his government, but on strict condition that it avoid "counterrevolutionary excesses." With this assurance, the resplendently bemedaled Horthy led his troops into Budapest. From the inception of his "regency," however (the façade of a caretaker royalist government would be preserved), Horthy's pose of moderation was a sham. His government's key personnel were ultraconservatives. Indeed, it was this constituency that lent its financial and moral support to the Society of the Awakening Magyars, a collection of lumpenproletariat vigilantes. Commanded by a wartime officer, Captain Gyula Gombos, the paramilitaries set about their "cleansing operation" by rounding up suspected "Bolsheviks" and "national traitors." By late autumn of 1919, the counterrevolution developed into a full-fledged "White Terror." In addition to suspected Communists and Communist-sympathizers, its victims included the staffs of liberal newspapers, trade unions, and Social Democratic Party leaders.

And once again, as in Ukraine, Poland, Rumania, and Bavaria (pp. 495–96), the White Terror in Hungary concentrated with particular ferocity on the Jews. Although the Jews had always been the most exposed of Hungary's ethnic minorities, it was specifically the role played by Kun and his Jewish colleagues in the late Communist regime that would not be forgiven. In the first three months of Horthy's rule, approximately 3,000 suspected former Kun partisans were killed, and a majority of these were Jews. Throughout 1920, others would be hunted down and slain. They were particularly vulnerable in provincial towns and villages. Here Gombos's Awakening Magyars seized Jews at random and shot them in scores. From January to June 1920, an estimated 10,000 terrified Jews rushed to convert to Christianity, and thereby to achieve a precarious measure of clerical protection. The White Terror did not begin to ebb until spring 1921, when the government finally turned its attention to the task of stabilizing a drastically attenuated nation. By then, however, some 6,000 "detainees" had been executed, a majority of them Jews.

The "Stability" of Authoritarianism

Of all Paris's basket of peace settlements, the Treaty of Trianon was the most punitive. Signed in June 1920, the pact amputated fully 65 percent of Hungary's territory, 60 percent of its population, and major portions of its natural and industrial resources—all in favor principally of Yugoslavia, Czechoslovakia, and Rumania. Afterward, the nation's resulting strategic and economic vulnerability all but determined its foreign and domestic policies. Regent Horthy sensed now the importance of cultivating a "moderate" image on the world scene, of avoiding any provocation that might incur a reimposition of the Allied economic blockade. To that end, in April 1921 he asked Count Istvan Bethlen, leader of the conservative Unity Party, to assume the prime ministry. Bethlen, a Calvinist Transylvanian nobleman, shared Horthy's commitment to a restored social "equilibrium." Accordingly, by allowing the opposition parties to resume a certain limited political activity, he was able to direct his principal attention to the restoration of Hungary's shattered economy. By late 1922, his efforts began to produce results, even to win a generous League of Nations loan.

The legal protection of Hungarian Jews similarly began to improve during the nearly ten years of the "Bethlen era." Yet their exposure was of a different nature. The Jews were diminished in numbers, to be sure. Under the 1910 census, their population was listed as 910,000 in a nation of 21 million (p. 433). But once Hungary itself was reduced to a population of 8 million, large segments of the prewar Jewish minority also were sheared away: 182,000 going to Rumania; 231,000 to Czechoslavakia; 43,000 to Yugoslavia. Even with these excisions, however, the remaining critical mass of 473,000 Jews actually signified a proportionate increase, from 4.64 percent of prewar Hungary's population to 5.92 percent after the war, and to emerge as the truncated nation's single largest ethnic minority. Over half of them lived in Greater Budapest, where they comprised 23 percent of the capital's population.

Yet it was not visibility alone that became the marque of the Jews' vulnerability. Their newly accentuated distinctiveness was economic as well as ethnic. In the postwar years, scores of thousands of white-collar Hungarians who had functioned as civil servants or office employees in the former territories now suddenly became unemployed refugees in a rump Hungary. Their numbers were further swollen by new waves of university graduates. With the Jews traditionally "overrepresented" in the professions and commerce, the reaction of the newly déclassé Hungarians took the form of an even more virulent antisemitism. Their professional societies, whether of engineers, lawyers, or physicians, blackballed Jewish members and pressed relentlessly for tough quotas on Jews both in the professions and in the universities that trained them.

As elsewhere in postwar Europe, it was academia that conducted the most aggressive anti-Jewish campaign. By 1920, Jews accounted for at least 25 percent of Hungary's university students. For gentile classmates and faculty members alike, the ratio was intolerable. Indeed, it was specifically in response to their demands that Hungary's parliament in September 1920 passed an education bill that admitted students to universities on the basis of the "proportion of [students'] race or nationality in the country." Under this guideline, the quotient of Jews would be reduced to 6 percent of the student body. The law plainly represented a frontal violation of Hungary's 1919 Minorities Treaty. Hereupon, on behalf of Hungarian Jewry, England's Anglo-Jewish Conjoint Committee and France's Alliance Israélite Universelle appealed to the League of Nations for redress. But their protest had to wend its way through a hesitant and dilatory League Council, and did not achieve "resolution" until December 1927. It was only then that the Bethlen government agreed to replace the "race and nationality" quota (a feature Hungarian Jews found particularly threatening) with "geographic" quotas that in effect favored the provinces over Budapest. It was a shrewd countermaneuver. With more than 70 percent of the nation's Jews living in Budapest, the practical consequences of the new classification were essentially identical with the original 1920 law, and the Jews' access to Hungary's universities remained severely curtailed.

THE TRIUMPH OF POLITICAL FASCISM

Except for the numerus clausus issue, however, Count Bethlen during his ten-year premiership offered the Jews a certain breathing space. With their physical security assured, they shared extensively in Hungary's wider economic recovery. Most Jews remained small businessmen, but the elite among them continued, as in the prewar, to forge well ahead of other Hungarians. Thus, Jews maintained proprietorship of at least 70 percent of Hungary's largest industrial enterprises. As late as 1937, an extraordinary 83 percent of Hungary's millionaires were Jews, and the average Jewish per capita income was four times higher than that of non-Jews, most of whom were either farmers or urban workers. Notwithstanding discrimination at universities and in professional societies, Jews still comprised one-fourth of all doctors in Budapest, and nearly one-third of the capital's lawyers. Theater and film in Hungary were almost entirely in Jewish hands, while journalism was overwhelmingly a Jewish vocation, with the four principal Budapest newspapers Jewish-owned and largely Jewish-staffed. During the 1920s, Jews even began venturing back into politics, mainly through the Social Democratic Party. Seven Jews sat in the 1928 parliament. Although counterrevolutionary antisemitism still festered, the animus no longer appeared capable of wreaking its initial, postwar havoc.

The reprieve ended with the onset of the Great Depression of 1929. Over the next two years, as the economic crisis in Hungary became acute, destitution among both the agrarian and urban populations often approached the threshold of starvation. The collapse overwhelmed Prime Minister Bethlen. In August 1931, he resigned. But his immediate successor also proved ill equipped to cope with the nation's escalating social unrest. It was in September 1932, therefore, that Admiral Horthy, fearing a national revolution, reluctantly turned to Gyula Gombos, the former commander of the White Terror's Awakening Magyars.

Throughout the 1920s, Gombos's right-wing proclivities remained undiminished, and seemingly uncontrollable. Indeed, it was for this reason that Prime Minister Bethlen in 1928 had sought to placate the army's chauvinist younger officers by appointing Gombos as his minister of defense. But Gombos had always regarded the position as merely a stepping-stone. Vain and aggressive, he fancied himself another Mussolini, and consciously mimicked the Italian Duce in uniform and demeanor. In contrast to Mussolini, on the other hand, antisemitism had always been a central feature of Gombos's agenda. In 1926, he and his political ally Tibor Eckhardt had even gone so far as to convene a rather seedy World Antisemitic Congress in Budapest. For the time being, however, Gombos was capable of adjusting his strategy to political opportunism. Thus, in 1932, on the threshold of the premiership, he consented to Horthy's demand to mute his Jew-baiting. "To Jewry," Gombos declared, ". . . I openly and sincerely emphasize that I have revised my position. Whichever part of Jewry that throws in its lot with the Hungarian nation I wish to regard as brothers, as I do my Hungarian brothers."

The display of goodwill was fraudulent. By 1934, as his fiscal program proved ineffective against the Depression, Gombos reverted to type. He countenanced a wider array of antisemitic movements and political parties, including one that openly dubbed itself the Hungarian Nazi Party. When student riots against Jews began flaring up, the government declined to intervene. Rather, Gombos suggested that it would be useful for Jewish businessmen to give preference to non-Jewish employees. To encourage the process, he directed his minister of industry, Geza Bornemisza, to circulate questionnaires among the nation's principal industrial enterprises, to ascertain the "religious identification" of their employees.

In October 1938, Gombos succumbed to cancer. Immediately, Horthy seized upon the opportunity to install a new prime minister, Kalman Daranyi. Like the regent himself, Daranyi was an ultraconservative who nevertheless detested the vulgar race-baiting of the fascist populists. Yet by then he and Horthy alike failed to grasp the burgeoning strength of far-rightist extremism. Its most politicized faction, soon to be known as the Arrow Cross, had gestated during the months of Gombos's protracted illness into the largest of the nation's agglomeration of reactionary parties; and its leader, Ferenc Szalasi, a former army major, was intent on replicating Gombos's chauvinist agenda. Although sincere in his populism, Szalasi was even more committed to the restoration of Hungary's amputated provinces. Shrewdly, then, he linked his social compassion to a fiery, rather mystical pan-Magyarism. And on the all-devouring Jewish question, Szalasi was implacable. He wanted all Jews out of the country.

By the latter 1930s, thousands of "Gombos orphans" were flocking to Szalasi's banner. For most of them, the Arrow Cross program offered a tantalizing alternative both to failed capitalism and to "vapid" liberalism. It was known, too, that Szalasi was on excellent terms with senior German officials; and following Hitler's Anschluss with Austria in March 1938, a relationship with Germany seemingly offered Hungary its best chance to revise the Treaty of Trianon. Moreover, as Szalasi saw it, the surest route to German goodwill was a "congenial" domestic political agenda, that is, a total exclusion of Jews from all sectors of Hungarian economic and cultural life.

The flagrant brutality of this Nazi-style program alarmed Horthy and Daranyi. Intent on blocking it, the regent and prime minister then devised a political firebreak. They would produce their own agenda of "prophylactic" antisemitic legislation, a program based on the Bournemisza "industrial" survey that had been authorized by the late Gombos. In March 1938, Daranyi informed the parliament that the Bournemisza data confirmed the "overweening role" played by Jews in the nation's life. To reduce that influence, the prime minister appointed Dr. Bela Imredy, president of the Hungarian National Bank, to come up with appropriate legislation. Whereupon, turning to his task with alacrity, Imredy within three weeks produced his own version of a "Jewish Bill." It was a shocker. For the first time, Jewish employment quotas were established in such "chambers" as the press, theater, medicine, law, commerce, white-collar office work—in all vocations where "Jews can be admitted in numbers . . . only in such proportion . . . that does not exceed 20 percent of the total chambers." Moreover, salaries paid to Jewish white-collar employees were limited to 20 percent of the salaries paid "Hungarian" white-collar employees. With hardly a demurrer, the bill sailed through the parliament in May 1938. As a reward to Imredy, Admiral Horthy then dropped the somewhat hesitant Daranyi as prime minister and replaced him with Imredy himself.

Ironically, the fascists did not react well to this new law. They regarded it as too mild. Nor could their anger be ignored. In the period of a single year, the membership of Szalasi's Arrow Cross movement had risen from 20,000 to over 100,000, and their marches, demonstrations, and oratory mounted in scope and decibel level. Hungary's equable relationship with Nazi Germany had to be preserved, as well. In September 1938, Hitler blackmailed his way into the Czech Sudetenland. Two months later, in return for Budapest's "loyalty and understanding" on the Sudeten issue, the führer issued his first Vienna Award, returning to Hungary a 6,500-square-mile enclave of land along the Slovakian border, together with its nearly 1 million, predominantly Hungarian, inhabitants. As it happened, 78,000 of those newly incorporated inhabitants were Jews.

Whatever his gratification at the territorial accession, Imredy regarded the unexpected new influx of Jews with unalloyed horror. For him, this was not the moment to exacerbate Hungary's Jewish problem. Hereupon the prime minister decided to achieve multiple objectives in a single maneuver. He would cordon off the nation's Jews, Slovakian and Hungarian Jews alike, from the national economy and in the process ingratiate his government even further with Nazi Germany. Thus, in December 1938, Imredy introduced into the parliament a "Second Jewish Bill." This "Christmas present for the Jews," as the prime minister jocularly described it, went much further than its recent predecessor. For one thing, the new measure was as overtly racist as Hitler's Nuremberg Laws (pp. 508–9). It defined a Jew simply as anyone with at least one Jewish parent or two Jewish grandparents. And while the first law restricted the proportion of Jews in commerce to 20 percent, this new one reduced the quotient to 12 percent in commerce and to 6 percent in the professions. At the same time, Jewish householders were barred from purchasing or renting residential plots larger than (the equivalent of) nine hundred square feet. Finally, those Jews who had acquired Hungarian citizenship after the outbreak of the World War would now be denaturalized.

The bill achieved a solid legislative majority. With considerable reluctance, Horthy decided to let it pass, and signed it on May 4, 1939. The consequences for Hungarian Jewry proved almost immediately ruinous. Although some Jews managed to operate their business or professional activities through gentile "fronts," at least half the nation's Jewish breadwinners were stripped of any practical means of earning a livelihood. In the provinces, where a Jewish identity could not be disguised behind a "front" of any kind, entire Jewish communities soon began departing for the larger cities, abandoning homes, businesses, synagogues, and cemeteries. A proud and distinguished minority people now faced destitution.

The scope of the tragedy was compounded by Hungarian Jewry's lack of psychological defense. Unlike the Jews of Poland and Rumania, the Jews of Hungary had committed themselves to acculturation with a passion not exceeded by their nation's gentile majority. Did they deserve such abasement, they queried rhetorically now in their letters to the press and in petitions to the government—they, a people whose only desire had been to be Hungarian and Hungarian only? A people who had fought Hungary's enemies on so many battlefields and contributed so extensively to the nation's economic and intellectual achievements? The lamentation was an old one, and in Hungary, as elsewhere on the Continent, it would evoke the same practical resonance.

XXIII

A Final Symbiosis of Jewish and Western Culture

THE PHENOMENON OF JEWISH INTELLECTUALISM

In 1925, Hugo Bettauer, an Austrian-Jewish convert to Protestantism, published an intriguing little roman à clef, *The City Without Jews (Die Stadt ohne Juden)*. The book was a cold-eyed portrait of contemporary Austria, of its turgid xenophobia and confused, dysfunctional Jewish minority. As Bettauer's narrative unfolds, Austria's popular chancellor, Karl Schwartzfegel (transparently based on Vienna's renowned fin-de-siècle mayor, Karl Lueger), appears before parliament to offer a solution for the nation's widespread unemployment. It is to expel the Jewish population. As Schwartzfegel explains:

> [T]he trouble is simply that we Austrian Aryans are not a match for the Jews. . . . With their uncannily keen intelligence, their worldliness and freedom of tradition, their catlike versatility and their lightning comprehension . . . they overpowered us, became our masters, and gained the upper hand in all our economic, spiritual and cultural life. . . . Either we, who make up nine-tenths of the population, must perish, or the Jew must go.

Cheering, the parliamentary deputies then overwhelmingly approve the chancellor's bill of eviction. The public, too, reacts in a delirium of joy at the prospect of gaining access to Jewish businesses and homes.

The response of the Jews of course is one of terror and chaos. Within the legislation's "merciful" six-month grace period, they rush frantically to liquidate their properties and estates. Except for a perfunctory love story, Bettauer treats these people less than sympathetically. But his sharpest barbs are reserved for the chancellor and the latter's constituents in parliament, who become increasingly frustrated as their blueprint for economic resurrection flounders. Jewish holdings devolve into the hands not of Austrian gentiles but of foreign banks. The sheer bureaucratic expense of administering the expulsion depletes public resources. Worse yet, bereft of Jewish patronage, the opera has closed, together with the theaters, the museums, the publishing houses and libraries. Without Jewish doctors and lawyers, the hospitals and law courts become hopelessly congested with patients and litigants. Ultimately, public frustration with the entire enterprise leads to the fall of the government, and elections afterward produce a new parliament, which immediately reverses the law of expulsion. The nation's Jews thereupon return en masse to Austria, much to public relief and jubilation.

Bettauer's mordant satire offers a revealing insight into the European world of his time. Well before 1914, Jewish participation in the Continent's intellectual life had assumed unprecedented dimensions. Virtually no field of cultural activity lacked a vibrant Jewish quotient, often a Jewish nucleus. In the realm of music and theater, Jews ranked among the most numerous and esteemed of Europe's concert performers, symphonic conductors, theatrical producers and directors. As scientists, Jews in disproportionate numbers achieved recognition as chemists and biologists, physicists and mathematicians. The "per capita" ratio of Jews in medicine and law, in "higher" criticism and journalism, as "lay" professionals or as research scholars in universities, was virtually exponential. Nor did any other ethnic element match them as patrons of the arts, letters, and music. As Thomas Mann acknowledged that contribution:

> Jews "discovered" me, Jews published and propagated my reputation, they performed my impossible plays. . . . And when I go out into the world, and visit its cities, it is almost always Jews, and not only in Vienna and Berlin, who welcome, shelter, dine and pamper me. . . . It is a fact that simply cannot be denied that, in Germany, whatever is enjoyed only by "genuine Teutons" and aboriginal *Ur*-Germans, but scorned or rejected by the Jews, will never really amount to anything, culturally.

The evaluation was prescient. Well beyond the fondest hopes of Moses Mendelssohn and his coterie of eighteenth-century "enlighteners," Jews by the end of the twentieth century had achieved recognition as respected practitioners of European culture. Indeed, they were flourishing as the virtual arbiters of that culture.

The efflorescence of Jews in the modern intellectual firmament was rooted as much in the European social structure as in their own. By the early post-Napoleonic era, the commonwealth of intellect no longer remained the closed preserve of aristocracy and Church. In their control of the civil service and army, the nobility remained preoccupied with the defense of their political and economic seniority. Few craved identification with the arts and sciences, preferring to leave such "esoteric" vocations as literature, art, and science to the bourgeoisie. In turn, among all the members of the middle class, Jews were the element most prepared to venture into the "emancipated" professions. Their objective, first and foremost, was self-employment, and thereby insulation from economic discrimination. Here the "classic" professions were law and medicine. It was symptomatic, by 1910, in the German section of Prague's Karl-Ferdinand University, that four of every ten students in the law and medical faculties were Jews; at the University of Vienna, one of three. As early as 1890, a majority of Vienna's attorneys were Jews; and by 1900, half of Vienna's physicians. In 1924, of the nearly 30,000 physicians in Prussia (Imperial Germany's largest state), 4,500 were Jews—15 percent. In Berlin, in 1928, more than half the practicing lawyers were Jews.

Yet vocational pragmatism alone could not explain the growing numbers of Jews who moved beyond law and medicine into the study of literature, philosophy, and history, and in such proportions that the terms "intelligentsia" and "Jews" became virtually interchangeable. Thus, in Budapest, Berlin, Vienna, and Prague before 1914, the largest numbers of mass-circulation newspapers were either Jewish-owned or extensively staffed by Jews. Of the twenty-three best-known authors within the Jung-Wien circle that virtually defined Austrian literature until 1938, sixteen were Jews. In Germany, during the first three decades of the twentieth century, beyond the five Jews awarded Nobel Prizes (out of the nine awarded to German scientists altogether), Jews in the humanities and social sciences produced such heavyweights as the philosophers Ernst Cassirer and Edmund Husserl, the historians Ernst Kantorowicz, Gustav Mayer, and Erwin Panofsky, the sociologists Karl Mannheim and Franz Oppenheimer. In 1913, the critic Moritz Goldstein noted with some concern that "German cultural life seems to be passing increasingly into Jewish hands. . . . We Jews are administering the spiritual property of a nation which denies us our right and our ability to do so."

That "right" and "ability," however, stemmed as much from religious tradition as from vocational opportunism. Historically, the Jews "practiced" intellect as an integral feature of their religious sociology. A this-worldly construct of rules and rituals, Judaism had consecrated a literature that was densely legalistic, requiring the discipline of intellectual mastery. With the exception of the Hasidic movement in Eastern Europe, piety and scholarship were entwined in an identical regimen. Even in emancipated Western Europe, well after "traditional" religiosity began to fade, veneration of scholarship endured, although translated increasingly into secular expression. It was a rather poignant fact of Jewish life that the most coveted spouse for the daughter of a wealthy Jewish family was the professional man—a doctor, lawyer, scholar, or, less frequently now, a rabbi. The ongoing genuflection to intellect similarly was evident in those families whose quest for wealth had been exhausted within the space of two or three generations. The Rothschild who became an ornithologist, the Warburg who became an art historian, the Sassoon who became a poet, even the Rathenau who became a social philosopher manqué, were characteristic of the affluent businessmen's sons who were anxious to emancipate themselves from cold money-making, to flee the clamorous marketplace for the idealized retreat of intellect.

Perhaps most decisively, talented Jews soon discovered that if mere wealth did not guarantee social equality, fame almost invariably did. It might have been possible to exclude a parvenu Jewish millionaire from upper-middle-class society, Marcel Proust described the phenomenon with piercing acuity, but it was unthinkable to reject a distinguished artist or scientist. The European haut monde, bored with its own wealth, tended increasingly to resonate to the far less common spectacle of genius; and the "radiant power of fame," in Stefan Zweig's characterization, was the leverage by which social outcasts established a foothold on gentile terrain. "They came," recalled Jakob Wassermann of his fellow Jewish intellectuals, "imbued with a fierce resolution to hold their own. They came as conquerors. . . ." And as "conquerors" they moved resolutely to circumvent the still formidable social barriers of Christian Europe.

ASPECTS OF JEWISH INTELLECTUALISM
Innovation

The ancestral traditions and contemporary insecurities that impelled Jews to achievement produced a sequence of impressive intellectual triumphs. Manifestly, only a small number of Jews who ventured into the liberal professions were giants of creativity, of new discoveries, innovations, or formulations. But if pioneers and revolutionaries among them were a minority, they were a strikingly protean minority. The evidence registered in the widest diversity of intellectual expression. Gustav Mahler, the legendary conductor of the Vienna State Opera from 1897 to 1907, dared as a composer to approach the symphony much as Wagner had approached opera. For Mahler, the symphony was a vehicle not only for aesthetic pleasure but for a vast panorama of expression and emotion, for the nostalgically recollected innocence of childhood, spectral gaiety, martial bombast, power, despair, exaltation, even frenzy. Altogether, Mahler's innovations allowed the symphony to incorporate a range of expression never attempted or so much as imagined earlier.

It was form rather than content that defined the innovations of Arnold Schönberg. Born in 1874, a product of Vienna's Leopoldstadt ghetto, Schönberg was obliged to enter the workforce at the age of sixteen, to earn his pittance as a junior bank clerk. In his every spare moment, the youngster managed to teach himself the fundamentals of piano and violin, and the essentials of orchestration. Eventually, with Mahler's help, several of Schön-berg's compositions were performed by local and provincial symphony orchestras. By 1914, as one of Vienna's best-remunerated musical instructors, Schönberg was comfortably ensconced in the Austrian musical establishment. Yet, in the privation of the war and early postwar, even a modest teaching bil-let in Berlin's Academy of Music offered him a wider professional opportu-nity and the intellectual latitude to develop a project that in recent years had consumed his most intensive creative efforts.

This was a new approach to tonality, an extension of the harmonic scale from eight to twelve tones, a range that then could be manipulated, inverted, or reversed to produce a dramatically wider palette for composition. The new harmonic system was exceptionally complex and at first evoked resistance from conductors and critics alike. Nevertheless, in Weimar Germany's vigor-ously experimental atmosphere, Schönberg's fascinating innovation gradually won acceptance. By 1933, when the Nazis dismissed him from his faculty posi-tion, his twelve-tone system had become irreversibly incorporated into the modern musical vocabulary. In different ways, both Mahler and Schönberg had added new dimensions to music. Mahler's contribution was perhaps richer in content and orchestration, and exerted an enduring impact on com-posers of the caliber of Alban Berg, Dmitri Shostakovich, Benjamin Britten, Aaron Copland, and Leonard Bernstein. Yet Schönberg's twelve-tone system found its way not only into orchestral and chamber music but into opera and modern musical comedy. The time would come when even a bitterly critical Igor Stravinsky paid him the compliment of adopting his technique.

In the world of theater, it was Otto Brahm (né Abrahamsohn) who intro-duced Ibsenite realism to fin-de-siècle German audiences. Indeed, as producer-director of Berlin's prestigious Deutsches Theater, Brahm all but single-handedly ensured the genre's conquest of the German stage. Possibly of even greater theatrical importance, however, was Brahm's discovery and initial sponsorship of the young actor-director Max Reinhardt (né Gold-mann), whose name remains synonymous with the most vibrant period of Central European drama. During the prewar and early postwar years, it was Reinhardt who transcended an increasingly formulaic realism with a more versatile style, mobilizing the services of such allied arts as dance, music, pan-tomime, painting, and architecture. In addition to his imaginative use of light and space, and the perfection of nuance he evoked from his actors, Reinhardt developed a mastery of crowd scenes that transformed his productions into breathtaking aesthetic spectacles. Over the turn of the century, Reinhardt's revolution in drama swept Brahm from directorship of the Deutsches The-ater, and the position was given to Reinhardt himself.

In ensuing decades, under Reinhardt's tutelage, drama "mattered" as never before. The great man soon brought his spectacles to Soviet Russia, to

England, to the United States—all to rapturous public and critical acclaim. Eventually, Reinhardt's influence extended well beyond the theaters in which he himself produced and directed, to those where his protégés were employed. One disciple, Leopold Jessner, directed the Berlin Staatstheater; another, Victor Barnowsky, staged productions in three separate Berlin theaters; another, Sandor Revai, director of Budapest's National Theater, was acclaimed as the "Max Reinhardt of Hungary." In this fashion, well into the twentieth century, Jewish producers and directors became as synonymous with the European stage as did their Jewish counterparts with Broadway in the United States.

No less than in the realm of "artistic" culture, the groundwork for Western Europe's most decisive scientific achievements was laid in the last years before World War I. By no coincidence, it was also in the late Wilhelminian Empire that the "special calling" of science obliged German universities to make room for Jewish overachievers. In contrast to the humanities, science made no claims as an "Aryan" monopoly. Indeed, the field was almost unique in its willingness to allow Jews to share in the empire's rise to scientific eminence. A pioneer in this breakthrough was Fritz Haber, whose success in fixating ammonia and nitrogen won him directorship of the mighty Kaiser Wilhelm Institute of Physical Chemistry and Electrochemistry (and in 1918, the Nobel Prize). During the war, beyond his personal role in devising the formula for poison gas, Haber bore principal responsibility for mobilizing the resources of German science to serve the armed forces.

It is of interest, too, that in 1914 Haber personally recruited Albert Einstein to the Kaiser Wilhelm Institute. Born in 1879 to middle-class Jewish parents in Ulm, Swabia, Einstein as a young man evaded the still formidable Jewish numerus clausus in German universities by taking his doctoral degree, in theoretical physics, at Zurich's Polytechnical Institute. It was in Zurich, under the influence of a famed Jewish mathematician, Hermann Minkowski, that Einstein was drawn to the study of electromagnetism and its relationship to space, an issue that lately was shaking the traditional Newtonian-mechanical theory of the universe. Although Einstein secured his first employment after graduation as a technical expert for the Swiss Federal Patent Office, he continued to immerse himself in this promising new field of electromagnetism. Subsequently, in 1905, at the age of twenty-six, Einstein published a series of four concise scientific papers, any one of which would have established his reputation. It was the third of these, however, "On the Electrodynamics of Moving Bodies," that introduced the theory of relativity to the world. At the age of twenty-six, Einstein had come up with the shattering notion of a cosmos in which stars and entire galaxies moved in relation not to space but exclusively to one another. In 1908, two articles by Minkowski gave mathematical endorsement to Einstein's dazzling but purely physical theory of relativity; and a year later, in 1909, the German physicists Max Planck and Max Born published their own research papers, further buttressing Einstein's theories.

Only then did the young genius's career begin to flourish: initially as an associate professor at Prague's Karl-Ferdinand University; then, in 1914, at the Kaiser Wilhelm Institute, where Fritz Haber appointed him the first director of the institute's department of physics. Yet, when the war began, Einstein did not allow his gratitude to Haber or the government to occlude his shocked awareness of German chauvinism, as displayed by his academic colleagues, or by the military command in the brutality of its U-boat campaign. He denounced them both. To his credit, Haber protected his young protégé from retribution and freed him for his research. With this leeway, Einstein in 1916 expanded his initial theory of relativity into a longer, fifty-three-page article for the *Annalen der Physik*. Entitled "The Foundation of the General Theory of Relativity," the thesis explored in greater detail the concept of "space curvature," the renewed claim that light did not move in straight lines, and that the universe could be viewed from the earth only through the distorting, that is, relativistic, spectacles of gravity. In November 1919, astronomers studying an eclipse off the coast of Africa confirmed the theory, discerning that light from the stars was deflected when passing through the gravitational field of the sun. Einstein then became the single most famous scientist in the world, and in 1921 the recipient of the Nobel Prize in Physics.

In that eminence, Einstein also became one of Weimar Germany's most important assets. His frequent visits abroad throughout the 1920s helped reduce anti-German hostility by directing attention to the achievements of German culture and science. Repeatedly, he signed petitions imploring the Western Powers to save the famished German people from starvation, and in this way to encourage the new and democratic Weimar Republic. If Einstein's views on German chauvanism were increasingly troubled, the one constant in his attitude was his internationalism, his touchingly naïve advocacy of a universal world government. But here the great scientist was courting disaster. Within the German academic community, memories of Einstein's pacifism were long. Some colleagues even attacked his scientific credibility. In 1920, his effort to defend his theory of relativity at a meeting of the German Association of Science evoked an uproar of protests. Apparently Einstein and too many other Jewish "radicals" were playing fast and loose with the very foundations of German science.

Among these "radicals" were Hermann Minkowski, who first devised the concept of a four-dimensional time continuum; Tullio Levi-Cività, who developed the absolute differential calculus, the instrument with which Einstein developed his theories; Albert Abraham Michelson, who first disproved the existence of ether as the medium for the transmission of light rays; and

Max Born in Germany and Leon Silberstein in the United States, who were the first to interpret the significance of Einstein's discoveries. Little wonder that German ultranationalists contemptuously dismissed this pioneering role as "Judenphysik." Their reaction was not unlike the outrage provoked by Schönberg's music. Both innovations, Schönberg's and Einstein's, evidently robbed the Germans of the categorical absolute vital to their *Volkswesen*, their national essence. In the seismic transformations of the postwar years, Germans needed above all to cling to "das Altewährte," their "old home truths." For them, Jewish intellectuals altogether were inveterate troublemakers and *Querulanten* (provocative question-askers) of a nonstable society.

The genius for innovation that animated Mahler, Schönberg, Reinhardt, Einstein, and hundreds of other Jewish intellectuals hardly could be explained on a religious basis, as the economic historian Werner Sombart once had sought to explain the Jewish role in the rise of capitalism. Similarly, a neo-Darwinian interpretation for Jewish intellectual vitality, the notion that persecution somehow enabled the best and brightest to survive, was disproved by the virtual collapse of productive Jewish intellectualism under calamitous circumstances, for example, in the fifteenth-century era of exodus from Spain, or the seventeenth-century Chmielnicki massacres in Ukraine—horrors that produced the disorientation of Cabbalistic mysticism and its ensuing gravitation to a sequence of false messiahs. Conceivably, the most plausible explanation for Jewish innovationism was offered by Sigmund Freud in his letter of thanks to the B'nai B'rith Lodge of Vienna, which in 1926 celebrated his seventieth birthday. "Only to my Jewish nature," wrote Freud, "did I owe the two qualities that had been indispensable to me on my hard road. Because I was a Jew I found myself free from many prejudices that limited others in the use of their intellect; and, being a Jew, I was prepared to enter opposition and to renounce agreement with the 'compact majority.' "

It was an intriguing suggestion. The very minority status that had barred the Jews from the protection of feudal and clerical hierarchies, that had force-fed their talents as mobile and resourceful businessmen, almost certainly was the desperation-rooted initiative that liberated them from the intellectual dogmas and prejudices of the "compact majority." In tandem with a widening access to secular education in Western Europe, it may well have been their very marginalism that impelled a crucial minority of Jewish scientists, artists, and humanists to view the world about them, to probe the universe, minds, bodies, literatures, and folk mores of their neighbors, with a sense of urgency neither characteristic nor required of the surrounding majority population.

A Sanctification of Life

Noteworthy, in the modern era, was the large number of Jews who gravitated to the profession of medicine. In common with the practice of law, medicine undoubtedly offered an opportunity for self-employment and financial security. Yet pragmatic considerations alone would not have accounted for the extraordinary "overproportion" of Jews in medical research. In the 1920s, Jews in Germany and Austria represented not less than 25 percent of the physicians who had abandoned the remunerative opportunities of private practice to devote themselves exclusively to salaried research. The names of many of these scholar-scientists read like a roll call of medical history. Ferdinand Cohn was the founder of bacteriology. Moritz Schiff laid the basic groundwork for the study of endocrinology. Adam Politzer and Robert Barany established the field of otology. Paul Ehrlich has widely been regarded as the greatest biochemist of modern times. Waldemar Haffkine devised the method of inoculation against cholera. Bernard Zondek co-developed the Zondek-Ascheim test for pregnancy. Albert Frankel isolated the micrococci of pneumonia. Casimir Funk discovered vitamins. Countless diagnostic and surgical techniques similarly were pioneered by Jewish medical figures.

Among the factors possibly accountable for the gravitation to medicine was the dignity with which Jewish tradition endowed the profession. That distinction, in turn, may not be fully interpreted without reference to the distinguishing essence of Judaism itself. This was the "sanctification" of life. The historic uniqueness of Judaism was its rejection of paganism's indifference to life, on the one hand, and Christianity's emphasis on life in a world to come, on the other. Reverence for life on earth eventually became so integral to Jewish religious sociology that it was all but institutionalized in the countless blessings, regulations, and injunctions that governed the most prosaic as well as the most austere activities of daily existence. Whether in the pro forma inclusion of medicine in the curriculum of medieval rabbinical training, or in the triviality of a toast, "l'Haim" ("to Life"), with which Jews shared their drinks, the sanctification of life maintained its focal centrality in Jewish tradition. By no means were Jewish doctors of the modern era responding to an ancient religious sanction. Indeed, it was not unlikely that the largest numbers of them were secularly inclined. But the veneration of life had endured long enough in Jewish sociology to endow with unique prestige the man who could save life. A dignified calling in the gentile world, medicine among Jews was a profession that was hardly less than exalted; and it was primarily among Jews that Jewish doctors would be living.

One branch of medicine, psychoanalysis, for many years was essentially a Jewish monopoly. The field did not exist before Sigmund Freud created it. As a young man, Freud possibly was influenced by Jewish factors in his decision to specialize in neurology. Throughout the nineteenth and early twentieth centuries, hysteria and "neurasthenia" were classified as degenerative diseases, and ascribed principally to heredity. Neurologists often linked these illnesses to specific ethnic groups, and most commonly to Jews (p. 250). The view was shared even by a number of Jewish scientists, including Max Nordau, a Viennese physician (and close Zionist associate of Theodor Herzl), whose 1892 book, *Degeneration (Entärtung)*, stressed the biological-hereditary nature of the disease. In France, too, the notion that the Jews were a race uniquely susceptible to "degeneracy" was taken seriously in medical circles, not least by Professor Jean-Martin Charcot, at whose famous Salpêtrière Hospital for Degenerative Diseases Freud spent eighteen months on a research fellowship. It was an argument that racists such as Édouard Drumont and Georg von Schönerer seized upon with ferocious alacrity. During his fellowship at the Salpêtrière, Freud could not have avoided the political implications of these studies in "ethnic" hysteria.

Freud's own epochal discoveries are now integrated into the cultural no less than in the purely medical vernacular of the contemporary world: his exploration of the hidden ocean of the unconscious; his compartmentalization of the unconscious into the id, ego, and superego; his use of "free association" to probe the dreams and traumas of childhood; his guidance of a patient's recollected memories to eventual relief of psychic disturbances. Much of the immense biographical literature on Freud has sought to identify a hidden Jewish agenda in his work. Freud personally rejected these speculations, insisting that his discoveries should be regarded as universalistic. Yet the social circumstances of his life as a Jew in modern Austria were entirely relevant to his choice of a medical career. Doubtless he was influenced at least in part by a characteristic Jewish need to be self-employed. But prejudice almost certainly played a concomitant role in Freud's decision to specialize in psychiatry.

Notwithstanding the young physician's brilliant early record as a neurologist, the University of Vienna denied him a professorship and instead consigned him to the traditional "Jewish" rank of *Dozent*, in effect, adjunct. Indeed, a key factor in drawing large numbers of other Jews to psychiatry in its early decades was the field's sheer marginality. Often described as the "forensic specialization of deviate behavior," psychiatry was regarded as the basement of Viennese medicine, and thus it remained one of the few specialties open to Jewish physicians. Characteristically, Freud's most intimate personal and professional relationships in his early career were the neurologists Josef Breuer and Wilhelm Fliess, both Jews. With only two exceptions, his colleagues in the famous Psychological Wednesday Evening Circle, which met at his apartment at Berggasse 19, were Jews.

By the same token, the gravitation of Jews to psychoanalysis may have reflected their own unconscious desire, functioning on the vocational and social periphery, to unmask the emotional dysfunctionalism of an antisemitic gentile world. Even Jews who were not psychoanalysts took pleasure in the "new thinking" and its potential for social retaliation. In 1910, Freud joined the B'nai B'rith Lodge of Vienna. Serving as an alternative to the professional societies that blackballed him, the international Jewish organization provided Freud with a guaranteed audience. It was an appreciative audience, delighting in Freud's theories at a time when the city's medical authorities were denouncing him as a charlatan. In the end, however, the most decisive compulsion drawing Jews to psychoanalysis almost certainly was the empathy shared by members of a minority people, themselves afflicted by a dense mantle of personal and social insecurities, for the neuroses and frustrations of others. Few Jewish psychoanalysts escaped these Jewish-rooted complexities. Even Freud, for all his tough-mindedness, was inhibited for decades from visiting Rome, a city that he identified (by his own later acknowledgment) as the very fount of his people's historic mistreatment. Exacerbated by vulnerability, the Jew's sensitivity to psychic no less than physical suffering may have been yet another defining feature of his identification with the healing arts.

ALIENATION

During these same fin-de-siècle years, Jewish humanists achieved their climactic mastery of European literature, and a concomitant European acceptance of Jewish belletrists, essayists, literary and drama critics as preeminent interpreters of contemporary culture. In that achievement, they fulfilled the classic role of Jews as "outsiders," marginal figures who found themselves in a position to evaluate the circumstances of their host societies with a unique detachment and objectivity. Modern Europeans actually expected this role of their Jews. It precluded the need to invent "Persian" or "Chinese" visitors, as in the era of the eighteenth-century philosophes.

The largest numbers of modern Jewish litterateurs hardly sought that function for themselves. Instead, the role sought them out, even in the heyday of their acculturation. At first blush, there appeared no more archetypically English playwrights than Arthur Wing Pinero or Henry Arthur Jones; no more characteristically Parisian literary sophisticates than Adolphe Philippe d'Ennery or Henri Bernstein; no Germans more militantly Prussian than Ernst Lissauer, whose "Hassgesang gegen England" became the Reichswehr's unofficial marching anthem during the World War; or Walther Rathenau, industrialist, political philosopher, and eventual foreign minister (p. 499), whose lyrical devotion to Germany—"Blood and steel-blue corn and air / Blessed lakes the eyes of heaven / . . . Country, my country, thou, my love"— was shrewdly discerned by his friend Count Harry Kessler as afflicted by a "lack of self-confidence . . . deepened by . . . the fact that he was a Jew. . . ."

Sharing in that transparent passion for acceptance were the children of Jewish millionaires, who crowded the arts and belles lettres, patronized museums and art galleries, sought appearances in rotogravures as fashion plates, but scrupulously avoided a frontal identification with Jewish communal life. A French Christian, Jacques de Lacretelle, depicted this insecurity in his literary portrait of a Jewish schoolboy, "Silbermann":

> "Oh, I'm not going to deny my origin," [Silbermann] said emphatically, with the little quiver of the nostrils which with him indicated a feeling of pride. "On the contrary, to be a Jew and a Frenchman seems to me the most favorable condition possible for accomplishing great things." He raised a finger prophetically. "Only I want to form the genius of my race according to the character of this country. I want to unite my resources with yours. If I write, I want to make it impossible to be reproached with the least sign of a foreign characteristic. I do not want to hear, of anything I produce, the judgment: 'It is thoroughly Jewish.'"

In his 1921 autobiography, *My Career as German and Jew (Mein Weg als Deutscher und Jude)*, Jakob Wassermann, the most widely read of postwar German novelists, was among the first to dispense with Silbermann's, and Rathenau's, feckless quest for a seamless acculturation. With refreshing candor, Wassermann affirmed his unique angle of vision, the duality of his culture. "I am a German and a Jew," he wrote. "I am completely imbued with elements from both spheres, the oriental and the occidental." Although he penetrated with rare insight into the soul of the German people, Wassermann acknowledged that his work was the expression of a Jewish mind and heart. His duality was shared by other giants of postwar German literature—Max Brod, Ernst Toller, Arnold Zweig, Lion Feuchtwanger—who forthrightly acknowledged the distance between themselves and non-Jews, even the non-Jewish intellectuals among whom they interacted.

Estrangement was distinctly more than the mood of Franz Kafka's writings. It was the message. In the twelve years between 1912 and 1924, this slim, introspective Prague Jew produced some of the most fearsome commentaries on the human condition ever to appear in modern Europe. In their detachment from time and place, his tales were stark, even surrealistic. Immemorial dreams appear in them, primeval shapes emerge from mistlike surroundings. Arrests, executions, transformations into vermin are recounted in casual, even pedestrian terms. Beyond all else, the theme of alienation reveals itself in everything Kafka wrote. If man is alienated from his fellow human beings—it is the central motif of Kafka's novel *The Trial (Der Prozess)*—he seems also to be distanced from God. The entirety of *The Castle (Das Schloss)* revolves about a surveyor's fruitless effort to secure an interview with the Lord of the Manor. When at last "K," the surveyor-protagonist, attempts to telephone the Lord, the castle's chatelain observes sardonically:

You haven't once until now come into real contact with our authorities. All those contacts of yours have been illusory, but owing to your ignorance of the circumstances you take them to be real. . . . There's no fixed connection with the Castle, no central exchange that transmits our calls further. . . . For who would take the responsibility of interrupting in the middle of the night the extremely important work up there . . . with a message about his own little private troubles?

Kafka's preoccupation with the dilemma of estrangement may have stemmed partly from the barrier that separated him from his father, an overbearing philistine. It surely reflected his inability to savor the physical pleasures of life, notably in his last and most productive years, when his creativity struggled with the laryngeal tuberculosis that eventually killed him. Yet, in the end, Kafka's defining insecurity was that of a Jew, and a Jew of Prague at that, a member of a minority within the German minority. The word "Jew" does not appear in *The Castle,* but the Jew's isolation is there. K is lost in a strange village. Exhausted, he asks an old peasant, "May I come in for a while?" The peasant mumbles something indistinctly. Later K asks an unfriendly schoolmaster whether he may visit him sometime. The schoolmaster responds, "I live at Swan Street, at the butcher's." Everywhere K is politely but firmly rejected. The issue of collective fragility appears as well in his tale "Josephine the Songstress, or the Mice Nation" ("Josephine die Sängerin, oder das Volk der Mäuse"). Critics traditionally have interpreted the "Mice Nation" as a euphemism for the Jews.

The absence of "fixed abode" almost certainly enhanced the importance that a vibrant nucleus of Jewish intellectuals attached to the ideal of international community. In the world of "higher intellect," it was not coincidental that the literary, art, and drama critics who were the earliest to introduce foreign talent to local audiences were Jews. In Denmark, Georg Brandes (né Morris Cohen) was the recognized "father" of modern European criticism and the first of his profession to interpret Polish and Russian literature for Western Europe. Alfred Kerr, "dean" of Berlin's drama critics in the Weimar era, achieved his reputation largely for his prescience in identifying talented contemporary playwrights in other countries. Jewish patrons and impresarios almost invariably were the first to organize exhibitions for promising foreign painters, to sponsor concerts by foreign musicians and soirées for foreign writers. "Whoever wished to put something through in Vienna," recalled Stefan Zweig (confirming Thomas Mann's evaluation), "or came to Vienna as a guest from abroad and sought appreciation as well as an audience, was dependent on the Jewish bourgeoisie."

Surely not all Jewish intellectuals were political internationalists. Their passion for acculturation produced more than a few Ernst Lissauers and Walther Rathenaus. But in proportions distinctly larger than among non-Jewish intellectuals, they turned earliest in revulsion from the meaningless carnage of war. Like Franz Werfel, Albert Einstein, Marcel Proust, or Karl Kraus, they tended to become socialists less for economic than for pacifist reasons. Still uncertain of acceptance in their native lands, and with their initial wartime patriotism unrequited (pp. 315–16), they exorcised in short order local prejudices against neighboring peoples and neighboring cultures. However superficial their identification with Judaism, or even with the Jewish people, a few even identified their "antichauvinism" specifically with their Jewishness. Thus, Bernard Berenson, the renowned art historian (American-educated but living his adult life in Italy), expressed a frequently shared view when he observed:

> The Jew still has a mission. . . . In the future he should cultivate the qualities that anti-Dreyfusards and other anti-Semites have reproached him with. He should not identify himself with the rest of the nation in its chauvinism, in its overweening self-satisfaction, self-adulation, and self-worship. He should be in every land the element that maintains a standard of human value and cultivates a feeling of proportion and relations. He should be as supranational as the Roman Church claims to be.

Stefan Zweig evinced the qualities of internationalist humanism as passionately as any individual of his generation. The quintessential man of letters, Zweig was the definitive arbiter of literary taste, the paradigm of sophisticated European culture in its last postwar efflorescence. Thirty-three years old in 1914, Zweig had been the youngest member of the original Jung-Wien group (p. 446). Although he had taken his university degree in law, it was literature that almost immediately became his exclusive vocation. Publishing a string of well-received short stories, novellas, and plays, Zweig in ensuing years achieved his greatest eminence as biographer and interpreter of historic literary figures, from Shakespeare to Goethe, from Tolstoy to Proust. By the late 1920s, as polymath, historian, and critic, Zweig towered over every literary figure on the Continent. With the possible exception of Thomas Mann, no one in German-speaking Europe, and few literary personages in any culture, could match him in sheer range of erudition and fecundity of publication.

With his works translated into every European language, Zweig became an international cult personality and was in continual demand before lecture audiences throughout the Continent. His substantial foreign royalties also enabled him to purchase an elegant home on the Capuchin Hill overlooking

Salzburg. There he reigned like a philosopher-king, hosting an endless stream of visitors from many countries. And there, too, as the consummate humanist, Zweig presided as Europe's major intellectual figure in the world peace movement. During the war, he had taken the initiative, together with Leonhard Frank, Franz Werfel, Georg Brandes, as well as numerous eminent non-Jews, in establishing an "international community of intellectuals." In that cause, after 1918, Zweig was tireless in producing a deluge of articles, lectures, and personal correspondence with the network of cultural celebrities who shared his devoted internationalism.

The governments of Europe meanwhile were not laggard in sensing that Jews, whether as intellectuals or businessmen, might fulfill a unique role as diplomatic intermediaries. Almost to the eve of World War I, the British and German governments encouraged the joint mediation of their two eminent Jews, the London banker Sir Ernst Cassel and the Hamburg maritime tycoon Alfred Ballin, in the hope that these "blood brothers" somehow would produce a formula to keep the peace. During the war, the German government made its first overtures to the Allies through the intermediary of the German Zionist Federation. Notwithstanding the failure of both sets of negotiations, they achieved a perverse significance in antisemitic propaganda, both in England (pp. 469–70) and, supremely, in postwar Germany. Whenever the Nazis execrated the "international Jew," for that matter, their bête noire was the Jewish intellectual, "the debaser of European culture," no less than the Jewish banker.

An Ongoing Cultural Defection

As late as the twentieth century, the quest for a "passport to European culture," the hoary issue that had bedeviled West European Jews during the pre-emancipation era, had not yet been entirely resolved. There still remained more than a few Jewish intellectuals who departed Judaism for Christianity essentially for careerist reasons. In the fin-de-siècle era, Austria's young nephew-royal, Franz-Ferdinand, was the spokesman for a new, ascetic, reformist Catholicism that attracted to his circle numerous writers, artists, and musicians. In light of Franz-Ferdinand's personal antisemitism, it was an irony that a number of gifted young Jews were drawn (or professed to be drawn) to his ideology, among them Hugo von Hofmannsthal, Adolf Loos, Karl Kraus, and Gustav Mahler. As a Jew, Mahler had been excluded from directorship of the Vienna State Opera. By tradition, if not by law, positions of this eminence were denied to professing Jews. Once proclaiming his interest in "reformist Catholicism," however, and accepting baptism, Mahler encountered no further obstacle to this crown jewel in the Habsburg musical establishment. A similar blend of careerism and aestheticism may have accounted for Bernard Berenson's apostasy. Living in a richly illuminated world of Venetian and Florentine painting, immersed in the splendor of Renaissance and Baroque artistry, Berenson, like Heine, accepted baptism ostensibly to transcend the cultural limitations of a small "tribal" people.

There were still Jews to be found, however, whose flight from Jewish identification was impelled less by careerism, or even by cultural aestheticism, than by shame. Arnold Zweig described the "so-called Jewish 'self-hatred' as a specific Austrian form of ego denial, [as a] Jewish *Weltschmerz*, Jewish doubt, the passionate drive to deny one's own being." In 1903, Otto Weininger, twenty-three years old, a precocious Viennese Jew and aspiring philosopher, published *Sex and Character (Geschlecht und Charakter)*, a savage tirade against women and Jews. Regarding Jews as afflicted with both feminist and materialist "decadence," Weininger interpreted the struggle between Aryan Christianity and Semitic Judaism as a battle between masculinity and femininity, in effect, between good and evil. The volume became an instant bestseller, going through twenty-eight printings. Yet its success proved inadequate to rescue its mentally unstable author. He committed suicide only a few months after the book's appearance.

Weininger's former gymnasium classmate Arthur Trebitsch, a tall, fair-haired young Jew, surpassed even his late friend in developing Aryan racial theories comparable to the most virulent ideologies then sweeping through Central Europe. Like Weininger, Trebitsch became deranged, although he was institutionalized before he could do away with himself. Less fortunate were his contemporaries the chemist Max Steiner, the philosopher Paul Rée, and the poet Walter Calé, all of whom became delusional in their Jewish insecurities and committed suicide. Others survived their own variations of malaise and self-abasement to offer commentary on the Jewish people's debilities and transgressions.

Prominent among these critics was Karl Kraus, Western Europe's notorious journalistic Cassandra, and an early convert to Catholicism. If moral hypocrisy, chauvinism, philistinism, arrivism, and sheer vulgarity were Kraus's bêtes noires, for him no people embodied those vices more quintessentially than the Jews; and on no subject did he wax more acidulous. In 1897, Kraus's first published essay, "The Ruined Literature" ("Die demolierte Literatur"), evinced the author's contempt for the largely Jewish clique that congregated at the "literary" Café Griensteidl. During all the thirty-seven years in which issues appeared of Kraus's monthly journal, *Die Fackel*, hardly any lacked a snide allusion to one or another variety of Jewish miscreants. Whether the "effete" Jewish publishers of Vienna's "morally corrupt" newspapers, or the climbers who were the first to "wrap themselves in the flag of Habsburg patriotism once war began," or the "uncouth" *Ostjuden*, pouring into Vienna form Galicia and Bukovina, Kraus reacted to them indiscriminately as if they were his private gall and wormwood.

Whatever the insecurities of the prewar era, these were infinitely exacerbated under the much graver tensions and frustrations of the 1920s and 1930s. Arthur Schnitzler had shrewdly anticipated that exposure as far back as his 1907 novella, *The Road to the Open (Der Weg ins Freie)*. In a famous passage, the gentile protagonist reflects: "Wherever he went, he met only Jews who were ashamed of being Jews, or others who were proud of it and feared people who might think that they were ashamed." The theme appears years later in *Auto-da-Fé* (the "English" title used for *Die Blendung*), a 1935 novel by Elias Canetti, a Bulgarian-born Viennese Jew, and subsequent literary Nobel laureate. When the Jewish protagonist, Siegfried Fisherl, first meets a non-Jew, he is preternaturally anxious to determine whether the gentile is an antisemite. How could one tell? The world was swarming with antisemites. But those "antisemites" were not lacking among the Jews themselves. Canetti's Fischerl, a dwarfed, hunchbacked, hook-nosed swindler, could not have emerged a more grotesque caricature even from the pen of a Nazi.

The malaise fled with Central European Jews across the Atlantic. Thus, in 1930, the Austrian immunologist Karl Landsteiner, a Jewish-born Nobel laureate, filed an injunction to restrain the publisher of *Who's Who in American Jewry* from including his biography in a new edition. "It will be detrimental to me," argued Landsteiner in his legal petition, "to emphasize publicly the religion of my ancestors; first, as a matter of convenience; and, secondly, I want nothing that may in the slightest degree cause any mental anguish, pain or suffering to any members of my family. . . ." The *Selbsthass* was expressed more forcibly yet by the French-Jewish philosopher and critic Simone Weil. Not content merely to reject identification with the Jews, Weil ventured to equate the spirit of Nazism with that of Judaism, and insisted that Hitler was seeking only to revive under another name and for his own benefit the God of Israel, "earthly, cruel, and exclusive."

A PRAGMATIC IDENTIFICATION

Notwithstanding the circumstances of Jewishness that influenced their careers, few Jewish intellectuals were interested in overtly repudiating their ancestry or religion. Most simply remained within the Jewish group, accepting the fact of their Jewish birth and their Jewish social status, even as they ceased almost entirely to be practicing Jews. Sigmund Freud exemplified this qualified "ethnic" identification. From his earliest manhood, he evinced little patience with traditional ritual. Following his betrothal to Marthe Bernays, he sought to wean her from her "religious prejudices" and "foolish superstitions." Freud had consented to a Jewish wedding, but afterward permitted no Jewish prayers or holiday observances in his family home. Nevertheless, throughout his life, Freud's professional and personal associations remained overwhelmingly Jewish. "I was born on May 6, 1856, at Freiberg, Moravia," he declared forthrightly at the opening of a brief autobiographical essay. ". . . My parents were Jews, and I have remained a Jew myself." His enduring admiration for the Jews as a people at the least was a mirror image of his personal self-respect, and was reflected as well in the gallantry with which he confronted antisemitism head-on.

Almost certainly it was this pride that explained Freud's disdain for Jews who opportunistically apostatized, a careerism that he regarded as hardly less than a pathology. In 1926, discussing with Professor Sandor Ehrmann the recent conversion of an eminent Polish-Jewish intellectual, Freud rejected Ehrmann's suggestion that baptism was an entirely personal matter. Such an act also "endangered the common interest," he insisted. Yet more even than self-respect influenced Freud's rejection of apostasy. At the turn of the century, as Karl Lueger's Christian Socialist antisemitism became a public issue (pp. 228–29), Dr. Max Graf, a colleague of Freud's, wrestled with the notion of expediently arranging his son's conversion. Graf sought Freud's advice. Sternly, Freud counseled against the step. "If you do not let your son grow up as a Jew," he warned, "you will deprive him of those sources of energy which cannot be replaced by anything else." Freud would make the same point to numerous colleagues and friends over the years. His letters to Karl Abraham asserted repeatedly that Jews found it much easier than gentiles to accept "subversive" ideas, for Jews after all were possessed of "our ancient Jewish toughness."

Some Jewish intellectuals preserved more than ethnic "toughness." In an age of secularism, a few actively explored ways of sustaining a meaningful relationship with the ancestral tradition. Franz Kafka was one of these. In Prague, in 1910, he took a lively interest in a visiting group of Yiddish actors from Eastern Europe. Spending hours analyzing their idioms and mannerisms, he discussed Hasidism with one of them, and systematically jotted down his observations in his "Jewish" journal. Kafka began then to take up the study of Jewish history and literature, and later discussed these subjects perceptively in his essay "The Literature of Small Peoples" ("Die Literatur von kleinen Leuten"). In the last years of his life, during his love affair with Dora Dymant, a Jewish girl from Poland, Kafka went so far as to attend classes in Hebrew and Talmud at the Freies jüdische Lehrhaus in Berlin (p. 468), then to make plans with Dora to immigrate to Palestine, where they would live a "simple," "authentically Jewish" life.

If Kafka's "spiritual" quest rose from solid anchorage in Jewish peoplehood, Albert Einstein's approach came from the opposite direction. Originally, the great scientist's tenuous attachment to Judaism was sustained by his intellectualized conception of God. For him, the Almighty was not a tribal god of the Jewish people, but the austere, rather arid deity of Maimonides and Spinoza, a force that reflected simply Einstein's oft-stated belief that a rational truth lay concealed behind the phenomena of nature. The son of assimilated parents, he had received only a perfunctory introduction to Jewish ethics and ceremonial during the "religious" hour mandated by the Swabian educational system. As a young man in Milan, Einstein renounced both his German citizenship and his membership in the Jewish Cultusgemeinde. It was only later, as a visiting professor in Prague's Karl-Ferdinand University, that Einstein found himself exposed to an "authentic" version of Jewish group life. In Prague, during the last prewar years, the Jewish community was undergoing a tentative intellectual renaissance, led by Martin Buber, Hugo Bergmann, and Max Brod. Although Einstein himself did not participate in communal activities, or attend a single lecture at Buber's Bar-Kokhba Society, he came to know several of the Bar-Kohba members and listened attentively to their ideas.

Afterward, during the war and in the 1920s, when Einstein lived in Berlin at a time of renewed and virulent German antisemitism, his Jewish and Zionist interests acquired sharper definition. He helped Chaim Weizmann raise funds for the Hebrew University during an American tour shared by the two men in 1921. In 1923, Einstein visited Palestine and described the experience as the "greatest event in my life." Although remaining an entirely nonobservant Jew, in January 1930 he appeared in a Berlin synagogue, wearing a skullcap and playing his violin to help raise contributions for a new Jewish community center. Einstein had long since identified the source of his ultimate loyalties, and confirmed to his friend Kurt Blumenthal that "the best in man can only flourish when he loses himself in a community."

An Intellectual Reformulation of Judaism

If the apostasy of Mahler and Berenson, the self-hatred of Landsteiner and Weil, were not typical of the majority of Jewish intellectuals, neither was the belated spiritual-communal Jewish identification of Kafka and Einstein. Far more characteristic was the matter-of-fact ethnic Jewishness of Sigmund Freud. The fin-de-siècle in any case saw widening opportunities in Western Europe for a purely "secularist" identification. Thus, in Germany, the CV, the Cultusverein deutscher Staatsbürger jüdischen Glaubens, the central administrative organ of the affiliated Jewish community, operated essentially as a secular body, and functioned both as an anti-defamation league and as an umbrella organization for the development of Jewish senior citizens' homes, employment agencies, loan offices, orphanages, adult education, and other programs for Jewish culture. In its nondoctrinal eclecticism, the CV increasingly drew into its ambit lawyers, politicians, educators, and lay administrators; for its field of action was less the synagogue than the courtroom, individual *Land* (province) diets, the imperial Reichstag, and the national press. Together with other European-Jewish communal organizations—the Board of Deputies of British Jews, Austria's Cultusverein, even France's Consistoire Central—the CV represented a decisive transformation in a formerly religion-based communal framework.

Altogether, throughout Western Europe during the early twentieth century, a network of societies and organizations functioned within the secular arena of Jewish civilization, among them unions of associations for Jewish history and literature, Jewish libraries, central archives for Jewish public records, the *Germania Judaica* journal, and its sister *Archives juives* in France. There were Jewish sporting clubs and student fraternities, B'nai B'rith lodges, Zionist federations, associations promoting the collection of statistics and folkloristic data among German and Austrian Jews, the German Jewish Women's League (jüdischen Frauenbund)—and all these in addition to innumerable philanthropic organizations, extending from the German Hilsverein and the Austrian Israelitische Allianz to France's venerable Alliance Israélite Universelle and Britain's Mansion House Fund and Jewish Board of Guardians. The emergence of an authentic Jewish renaissance plainly made room for all varieties of Jewish "civilization" well beyond those of traditional religiosity. In 1904, addressing a German-Jewish women's group, Rosalie Perles, widow of the rabbi of Königsberg, offered a sentient observation:

> Let us imagine that our grandfathers, especially those who had . . . feared a gradual assimilation within the non-Jewish surroundings, would return to life and step in front of us. . . . How they would be astonished that the assimilation [of which they had warned] did not occur, that instead exactly the opposite happened! . . . The [Jews of] today proudly display their Judaism. . . . Jewish artists, painters, and sculptors tend to depict Jewish topics. . . . There are long concert evenings with Jewish melodies, Jewish folk songs and liturgical music, which are performed by our best singers. There are recitals of Jewish poems and legends. . . . Some revive our old prophets on the stage, while others describe the life of the *Ostjuden* or of the Palestinian settlements. . . . Our grandfathers would not have had to worry so much, had they seen this future while they were still alive.

Frau Perles did not mention that the grandfathers would have been even more gratified had the new renaissance been a religious one rather than a movement essentially from "confession to culture." If modern science, Darwinism, biblical criticism, even psychiatry, were making serious inroads on the religious loyalties of Jewish and Christian intellectuals, they exerted their belated impact on nonintellectuals, as well. Thus, a significant minority of West Europeans was beginning to modify profoundly its traditional religious beliefs and practices. Others, perhaps a majority, remained nominally within their churches and synagogues, but sought to reconcile their inherited faiths with the spirit of science. Even within this latter element, however, the struggle to salvage the "essence" of religiosity appeared to be failing. Indeed, it was to meet the challenge of modernity that a group of Christian philosophers addressed the task of reconciling science with traditional Christian doctrine. To that end, the Italian thinker Benedetto Croce fashioned a "philosophy of the spirit" whose purpose was to interpret the content of world history in terms less of its factual data than of its guiding "spirits." The most creative of those spirits, argued Croce, was the religious. The French theologian Jacques Maritain formulated a kind of twentieth-century neo-Scholasticism that proved unexpectedly successful in reconciling the traditionally formidable differences between science and Catholicism.

Within the framework of Judaism, the détente between religion and science was attempted by Hermann Cohen, arguably the profoundest Jewish thinker of the early twentieth century. German-born, the son of a small-town synagogue cantor, Cohen dutifully respected his family's wishes by undergoing ordination at Breslau's theological seminary. Afterward, however, he went on to earn a doctorate in philosophy at the University of Halle, then moved immediately into the world of academia. In 1897, after laboring for more than a decade as a *Dozent,* he was appointed professor of philosophy at the University of Marburg, a rare achievement for a Jew in Wilhelminian Germany. In ensuing years, rejecting his earlier, rather antiseptic "objectivity" toward his ancestral religion, Cohen came gradually to recognize the "Eigenart," the specific character of Judaism. He described that Eigenart in 1912, in his monumental volume *The Religion of Reason from the Sources of Judaism (Die Religion der Vernunft aus den Quellen des Judentums),* one of the authentically seminal contributions to the modern philosophy of religion.

Like Cohen's earlier articles, the volume was straightforwardly Kantian in its orientation, for it stressed the importance of the "categorical imperative," or, in religious terminology, the idea of right and wrong. Ethics, law, moral behavior—these were central to Cohen's thinking, as in Kant's—and religion to him was valid and purposeful only insofar as it encouraged rigid adherence to ethical law. In the Kantian tradition, too, Cohen envisaged religion not as a separate discipline but as a complement to rational ethics. Once allied in a "religion of reason," the two approaches produced a guideline capable of directing mankind to a society of moral perfection. Yet it was ironic, even as he presented his case in sound, airtight, rationalistic terms, that Cohen employed the terminology of high pathos, prophetic rather than academic, and it was possibly his language even more than his message that lent his "religion of reason" the fervor that moved and inspired his readers. If not always successful in grasping the depth of Cohen's argument, the typical Jewish layman was vaguely aware, and gratified, that this effervescent little rabbi-professor had managed to identify the Jewish "spirit" with the ideas of Germany's most venerated philosophic figure.

A Mobilization of the Spirit

It was possibly for this reason of status satisfaction that Cohen's "neo-Kantianism" appealed rather more to the Jewish man in the street than to the Jewish intellectual, who normally would have chosen to relax from a diet of philosophical theology, even to find a more inspirational route to the "living presence" of God. By the early twentieth century, as it happened, Europe witnessed a general revival of interest in negotiating specifically that route—through myth and mysticism. Thus, the poet Stefan George and his "circle" employed Germanic myths and Eastern spiritualism as sources for their literary creativity; and the publisher Eugen Diederichs translated and produced a highly popular collation of classical mystical texts. In 1906, Gustav Landauer (p. 495) published the first modern translation of the great German mystic Meister Eckhart. After the war, distraught and impoverished Germany would become even more susceptible to mystic and neo-mystic ideologies and movements, from naturism to "Blut-und-Boden."

For European Jewry, the interest in myth and personal communion was addressed initially by Martin Buber. Vienna-born in 1878, Buber was reared by his grandparents in Lemberg (Lvov), Galicia, where he attended both Jewish parochial and German-language secular schools; and in 1904 he acquired his doctorate in religion and philosophy at the University of Berlin. Over the ensuing decade, Buber earned his livelihood as a part-time instructor in philosophy at the University of Frankfurt, as the editor of a rather impecunious German-Jewish philosophical journal, *Der Jude,* and as a frequent lecturer before Jewish student and academic circles. It was accordingly in Frankfurt, in 1911, with the publication of his *Lectures on Judaism (Reden über das Judentum),* that Buber moved into the forefront of the "New Romanticism," the European literary effort to recover the lost traditions of myth and mysticism.

An unplumbed reservoir of those traditions lay in the world of Hasidism. In 1898, a full decade before Buber set about publishing his Hasidic tales, an informal circle of German-Jewish intellectuals, led by the Hamburg rabbi Max Grünwald, founded a Jewish folklore association. The group's journal, *Mitteilungen zur jüdischen Volkskunde,* was replete with articles about Hasidic "wonder rabbis," about *tzaddiks, dybbuks,* and other dramatis personae of Hasidic mysticism. Soon other, more traditional scholarly Jewish organizations, like the venerable Verein für jüdischen Wissenschaft (p. 132), had to take into account the revived interest in Jewish "folklore." Yet it was above all the mass wartime influx of Galician- and Bukovinian-Jewish refugees that acquainted Central and West European Jews with the deep-rooted folk traditions of the *ostjüdische* world. By then, Buber had emerged as the master interpreter of those traditions.

As he explained to his readers and listeners, the Hasidim had discerned a central truth, that the wellspring of spirituality lay in the subterranean world of rich and vibrant folkloristic tradition, not in the deracinated Judaism, the "synagogue Judaism," of the bourgeois establishment. From this premise, Buber projected two central concepts: first, that the individual Jew must learn to embrace in his heart the spirit, or collective, subterranean soul, of his entire people; and second, that it was possible, as the Hasidim had learned, for an individual to confront God as a person, to enter into "dialogue" with God. In ensuing years, Buber went on to elaborate upon this theory of "dialogue," particularly in his slim but highly influential volume *Ich und Du (I and Thou),* published in 1923. By maintaining the "tension" of a conversational attitude to God, Buber argued, man could sense the actual personality of the Supreme Being; and by encountering that personality as an equal, man exalted himself to the full extent of his own potential divinity.

Buber's neo-Hasidism exerted much interest among his fellow intellectuals. Yet, in his writings and lectures, as in his sponsorship of student organizations like Prague's Bar-Kohba Society, Buber fostered an even wider interest in his uniquely "mystical" conception of Zionism. The nineteenth-century "confessionalization" of Judaism had atomized West European Jews, Buber insisted, and uprooted them from the deepest springs of their existence, their "community of blood." They were living in a void, and only the healing power of the Land of Israel offered a creative potency for the Jewish soul. It was an interesting notion, although hardly an original one. In truth, Buber's Zionism drew less from neo-mysticism than from the upsurge of frustrated romanticism that was sweeping through the German world in the early postwar years, and that inspired such crypto-fascist *Vereinen* as the student *Wandervogel* hiking and nature associations, with their blend of nationalism and the *Führerprinzip,* their adulation of strong, dynamic leadership. When the antisemitism in these youth movements became increasingly flagrant, Jewish students were obliged to form their own societies, principally the Zionist Blau-Weiss hiking group—an alternative warmly embraced by Buber as a legitimate expression of the Jews' own "community of blood."

For all the interest evoked by Buber's "spiritual," "mythical" Judaism, Central Europe's Jewish renaissance of the postwar period continued to develop essentially along secular lines. Indeed, during the 1920s, it was another figure, Franz Rosenzweig, who emerged as the "programmatic" catalyst of that renaissance. Born into an acculturated family of Cassel in 1886, Rosenzweig studied history and classics at the University of Freiberg. In Berlin, later, he earned a doctorate, and then embarked on a career as a minor literary editor. In 1913, following the lead of a much-respected distant cousin who had become a Protestant theologian, Rosenzweig prepared to convert to the Lutheran faith. Opportunism was not a factor in his decision. Yearning for a religion of "personal" belonging, Rosenzweig was convinced that he would not find it in a "legalistic" Judaism of moral rules and regulations.

Yet, determined to enter Christianity as did its founders, as a Jew, not a pagan, Rosenzweig attended synagogue services in the period immediately preceding his intended baptism. It happened to be the eve of Yom Kippur, and the religious ceremonies in the small Berlin congregation were particularly awe-inspiring. Rosenzweig was shaken. By the time he left the temple, he had discarded all notions of conversion and resolved instead to work out his theology within the framework of his ancestral religion. In that effort, and with the encouragement and friendship of Hermann Cohen and Martin Buber, Rosenzweig embarked on a program of Jewish studies. Yet, before he could seriously begin, the war broke out and he promptly enlisted in the kaiser's army.

It was during his military service on the Eastern Front that Rosenzweig made his initial contact with Polish Jewry. The experience had important consequences for his thinking, for the image of the "integral" *Ostjude* remained with him, as with Buber (and Franz Kafka), as a kind of yardstick for measuring the "fragmentary" existence of the Western Jew. Assigned to the Macedonian front in August 1918, Rosenzweig then began formulating his magnum opus, *The Star of Redemption (Der Stern der Erlösung)*. The book was written between maneuvers, battles, hospitals, and after the collapse of the front line, on the road with the retreating German army. Rosenzweig would jot down his writings hurriedly on postcards and scraps of paper, then send them on to his mother for transcription. When the volume finally was published, in 1922, it became the core of a religious philosophy that Rosenzweig would refine in a succession of later essays. A religion of fulfillment, he insisted, depended upon more than a legal system, or even upon "ethical behavior." Like Buber, Rosenzweig was persuaded that the "life of faith" was the only true religious experience, and consequently should be lived on a plateau where God and man were linked by a bond of personal dialogue.

If that vision drew extensively from Buber, Rosenzweig proved much more adept in translating their shared goal of a Jewish renaissance into a practical agenda. Upon completing *The Star of Redemption,* he projected as his life's work the task of reintroducing educated Jews to the classics of Jewish literature and history. Thus far, he noted, Jewish education had been devoted almost exclusively to children, and, at that, was confined principally to a shrinking network of Orthodox institutions. Now the time had come to reach out to adult Jewish circles, to offer them a program of Jewish courses that would complement their mature intelligence. Buber and Hermann Cohen enthusiastically shared this ambition. Indeed, at their request, the Jewish *Gemeinde* of Frankfurt invited Rosenzweig to organize a program of Jewish studies in their community. It would be known as the Freies jüdisches Lehrhaus—the Free Jewish Study Institute.

The course of weekly evening studies was launched in 1922, and its faculty consisted of the elite of German-Jewish scholarship, such eminences as Simon Rawidowicz, Norbert (Nahum) Goatzer, Ernst Simon, Leo Strauss, Gershon Scholem, Bertha Pappenheim, as well as Buber, Cohen, and Rosenzweig. The lay people who attended their classes rarely exceeded fifty in number, but their interest and appreciation were keen. Soon other adult education courses were established in a half-dozen other large communities, including Berlin and Breslau. It was also during the early 1920s that Rosenzweig and Buber collaborated in the effort to publish a new and modern translation of the Bible, the first since the eighteenth-century Torah version produced by Moses Mendelssohn and Naphtali Herz Wessely. Yet, even as Rosenzweig pressed on in these multiple projects, he was stricken by lateral sclerosis, which in 1923 began wasting his body. For the ensuing six years of his life he conducted his activities strapped in a chair, his neck supported by a pulley, using a specially constructed typewriter to communicate with family members and colleagues. In 1929 he died, at the age of forty-three.

The Jewish cultural renaissance that Rosenzweig, Buber, Cohen, and others fostered during the Weimar years produced impressive results. Beyond adult education programs, and the new translation of the Bible, a monumental *Encyclopaedia Judaica* was published in 1928 by the newly founded Eshkol House, as was a compact five-volume *Jüdisches Lexicon*. In the 1920s, too, the Soncino Society was established for the publication of an even wider range of books of more general Jewish interest. Magisterial works of Jewish scholarship flowed from the pens of Ismar Elbogen, Simon Rawidowicz, and the mighty Simon Dubnow, then living in Berlin as an expatriate from Communist Russia. Several scores of handsome new synagogues and temples, Jewish hospitals, and senior-citizens' homes were erected, a number of them designed by the renowned architect Erich Mendelssohn. For the Jewish population of West-Central Europe, it was a bittersweet irony that the dying years of German humanism should have produced a sunburst of Jewish culture, one that was unsurpassed, and rarely equaled, in any earlier era of European history.

XXIV

A Climactic Onslaught of Postwar Antisemitism

AN OSCILLATION OF BRITISH SUSPICION

In the last prewar years, the influx of East European immigrants into Britain, and their congestion in London's East End, evoked growing tremolos of public concern. It was then that Major W. Evans-Gordon, M.P., founded the anti-immigrationist British Brothers League and led the restrictionist clamor that ultimately produced the Aliens Act of 1905. Rather moderate in its constraints, the new legislation over the ensuing nine years did not substantially inhibit Jewish immigration. Nevertheless, by 1914 the British public had become distinctly "Jew-conscious." Indeed, the war crisis transformed consciousness into active suspicion. Rumors almost immediately gained momentum of a secret German-Jewish conspiracy, a plot that accounted for every lurking danger, from pacifist propaganda to wartime food shortages to the subversion of the British pound on international currency exchanges.

In some measure, these suspicions drew from the confusion with which Anglo-Jewry itself reacted to the approach of war. The Jewish financiers and industrialists Sir Ernst Cassel, Edgar Speyer, and Sir Alfred Mond were of German origin and were involved in various German economic enterprises. Widely known on both sides of the English Channel was the last-minute effort mounted by Cassel and Albert Ballin, the Jewish director of Germany's Hamburg-America Packetboat Company (Hapag-Lloyd), to stave off war between their two countries. In late July 1914, the British Rothschilds similarly interceded with Chancellor of the Exchequer Lloyd George and with Lord Northcliffe, publisher of the London *Times,* in an effort to maintain British neutrality. Only a week before the outbreak of war, London's *Jewish Chronicle* added its editorial voice to the peace effort, condemning as "an outrage and a crime" the very notion of a military alliance with Tsarist Russia.

Once hostilities began and Germany invaded neutral Belgium, the *Jewish Chronicle* immediately changed its position, as did the entirety of the Jewish "establishment." During the course of the war, 41,000 Jews served in the British armed forces. Yet the volte-face came too late to erase popular suspicions. The *National Review* was unrelenting in its accusations of Jewish pro-Germanism, charges that were repeated intermittently by the *Times* and the *Morning Post*. In May 1915, the *Times* asserted that Jewish circles in both Germany and Britain applauded the U-boat sinking of the *Lusitania*. Anti-German riots during the war occasionally spilled over against the Jews as "German agents," and a two-day riot in Leeds was directed against Jewish homes and shops, inflicting much property damage and numerous personal injuries.

A rather more legitimate source of public resentment was the ambivalent response of immigrant Jews to military service. When Parliament introduced conscription, in May 1916, some 45,000 male Russian Jews in England had not been naturalized, and thus technically were exempt from the draft. Of these, 31,000 chose to register for service. Yet 14,000 did not, in spite of repeated appeals by the Anglo-Jewish communal leadership. Even the March 1917 Revolution in Russia, and the overthrow of the tsar, could not bestir this hard core of draft-evaders. Finally, in response to outraged public opinion, Parliament in May 1917 enacted an Aliens Conscription Act that obliged resident nationals of "friendly" countries to perform military service or face deportation home. Hereupon, some 4,000 immigrant draft-evaders finally accepted conscription; but 2,000 others accepted passage back to Russia, and the rest somehow escaped British military service altogether. The episode was an unsavory one, and it rankled in Anglo-Jewish history.

More painful yet was the impact of the Bolshevik Revolution, in November 1917. It was the near-unanimous view of the British press that Jews were the central players in the Bolshevik upheaval. Victor Marsden, the *Morning Press*'s correspondent in Petrograd, voiced the prevailing opinion that Jews headed "the entire Bolshevik terror apparatus." "The Bolsheviks are not Russians," insisted the *London Globe*. "[T]hey are international Jews of the vilest sort, whose aim is to destroy all Christian civilization and culture. . . ." With minor variations, the charge was endorsed by a number of senior government figures. In April 1920, Lord George Curzon, the foreign secretary, intimated to a Conservative Party audience that the Ukrainian and White Russian pogroms against Jews did not lack justification. "These [White] prejudices have been strengthened by the belief," Curzon asserted, ". . . that the Bolshevik movement has been led and exploited by Jews for their own ends." "Nor is the action of Jewish revolutionaries confined to Russia," added Foreign Undersecretary Lord Robert Cecil, the following month. ". . . [T]here is scarcely a dangerous revolutionary movement in any part of Europe which has not at the back of it a Jew, driven into enmity of the whole existing order of things by the injustice . . . which he or his relatives have suffered from the hands of the old Governments." In a May 1920 article for the *Illustrated Sunday Herald*, entitled "Zionism versus Bolshevism: A Struggle for the Soul of the Jewish People," Minister of Munitions Winston Churchill argued that the conflict between good and evil "nowhere reaches such an intensity as in the Jewish race." The Jews were responsible for the benefits of Christianity, acknowledged Churchill, but now they could well be responsible for "producing another system of morals and philosophy, as malevolent as Christianity was benevolent."

Even as these articles evoked wide attention and distrust, a new and far more sinister publication would fuel the simmering brushfire of anti-Jewish suspicion and denunciation.

The Protocols of the Elders of Zion

In its English translation, the little volume began circulating early in 1920, initially among British military personnel in the Middle East, then among Western delegates at the Paris Peace Conference. Numbering approximately one hundred pages, and entitled *The Protocols of the Elders of Zion,* the booklet described a secret meeting of twelve Jewish "wise men," who gathered (at an unspecified time) in a Prague cemetery to devise a scheme for world domination. In a turgid and melodramatic style, the senior figure of the cabal specifies twenty-four "protocols"—that is, methods—by which the Jews might achieve this world rule. Their tactics will range from the dissemination of liberalism and socialism through Freemasonry and other "godless" secret societies, to the manipulation of gold prices for the purpose of creating an international financial crisis. Eventually, the senior wise man explains, "there should be in all states of the world, besides ourselves, only the masses of the proletariat, a few millionaires devoted to our interests, and our own police and soldiers." Once this vast undertaking is completed, mankind will be united in the single religion of Judaism, "under a Jewish sovereign."

No author was listed for the bizarre tract, but the *Protocols* was lent a specious authenticity by the cachet of its publisher, Eyre & Spotteswoode, "His Majesty's Printing Office." The English version eventually would go through six printings. Its credibility was further enhanced when the *Times* queried rhetorically on May 8, 1920: "What are these 'Protocols'? Are they authentic? If so, what malevolent assembly concocted these plans, and gloated over their exposition? . . . Have we, by straining every fibre of our national body, escaped a 'Pax Germanica' only to fall into a 'Pax Judaica'?" All elements of the English press gave comparable attention to *Protocols*. The *Morning Post* published a series of articles under the general title "Cause of the World Unrest," interpreting the entire course of history in the light of the *Protocols*. By 1921, the *Protocols* was appearing in book form throughout the world. There were two German, three French, and two Polish versions, as well as translations in Swedish, Italian, Danish, Arabic, Spanish, and Finnish. In the United States, the *Protocols* was published in a newspaper owned by Henry Ford, as part of a larger and wider-ranging series entitled "The International Jew." In its subsequent book version, Ford distributed 200,000 copies of *The International Jew* (p. 383).

Suddenly, in August 1921, the London *Times* produced an astonishing revelation. Philip Graves, the *Times* correspondent in Constantinople, had lately met with a Russian monarchist émigré, Mikhail Raslovlev, who was then working for the American Red Cross in the Turkish capital. Raslovlev presented Graves with a copy of a small novel, published in Brussels in 1864, by an émigré French lawyer, Maurice Joly. The book had been intended as a parody on the regime of France's Emperor Napoleon III. Inasmuch as direct criticism of the emperor had been forbidden then in France, Joly had cast his satire in the form of a *Dialogue aux Enfers entre Montesquieu et Machiavel.* Montesquieu presented the case for liberalism, and Machiavelli the case for despotism. At least one-third of this "dialogue" subsequently was reproduced in the *Protocols.* It did not appear in "pure" form, however. As Graves subsequently learned, it was taken from a later plagiarism of Joly's work by a German writer, one Hermann Gödschke, who in 1868 published a melodramatic novel, *Biarritz.* One of the novel's chapters was entitled "In the Jewish Cemetery in Prague," and it further "modified" Joly's text into a kind of slapdash Jewish prophecy for the future.

Indeed, it developed that the Joly novel had undergone still further reincarnations. In 1892 (as Philip Graves later confirmed), the chief of the tsarist secret police, Piotr Rahkovski, engaged one Sergei Nilus, a right-wing publicist, to reformulate the *Biarritz* chapter as a book-length "documentary" entitled *The Great Within the Small,* which in turn incorporated Gödschke's plagiarism of the Joly satire. The adaptation was intended simply to entertain the tsar's family. Following the Bolshevik Revolution, however, and the ensuing Russian civil war, the *Protocols,* distilled and adapted from the Nilus version, was exploited to a fare-thee-well by Russian reactionaries attached to the White armies. Updated, the new version attributed bolshevism to the Jews. The authors' intention manifestly was to persuade Western governments to intensify their military intervention in Russia. Did not the *Protocols* reveal that the conflict in Russia was no mere civil war, but a logical extension of an "international Jewish plot" to subject all respectable governments to Jewish rule?

This was the sequence of forgeries that Philip Graves revealed in his three lengthy articles for the *Times* in August 1921. Presumably, the exposé would have buried the *Protocols* for good and always. But the myth of a worldwide Jewish conspiracy was not easily to be laid to rest. Although the *Times,* which first had given credence and publicity to the *Protocols,* was also the first to expose and discredit the work, the archconservative *Morning Post* continued to play up the immense influence of "international Jewry" not only in Soviet Russia, but equally in the British Labour Party. Indeed, that alleged influence was apparent in the episode of the "Zinoviev Letter." The letter ostensibly had been dispatched from Moscow on December 2, 1924, virtually on the eve of Britain's general elections, by Grigori Zinoviev, the (Jewish) chairman of the Comintern, and was directed to Communists in England, urging them to give full support to Labour candidates. This "letter," too, was soon revealed to be a rightist forgery; but, like the *Protocols,* it kept the myth of a Jewish plot alive and caused the electoral defeat of the Labour government before its fraudulence could be revealed. Campaigning against the "plot" at an election rally in Leicester, George Curzon warned his audience again that the Russian government was composed of "a small group . . . few of them Russian by birth, and most of them Jews in origin," who were "preying like vultures on the bodies of that unhappy people."

Fortunately for British Jewry, the more paranoid varieties of antisemitism began to ease by the mid-1920s, as the nation's postwar economic circumstances improved. At the political fringe, Henry Beamish, a veterinarian, founded England's first avowedly antisemitic organization, the Britons. It made little impact. Neither did the British Fascisti, the first English movement openly to espouse the ideology of fascism. Less than a thousand individuals joined the group, although one of its early members was William Joyce, a part-time tutor in English literature at London University, who during the Second World War became widely known as the Nazi broadcaster "Lord Haw-Haw."

It was the Depression-era 1930s that produced a more substantial fascist-style conglomeration. In 1929, Ramsay MacDonald and a Labour government returned to office, and one of its younger junior ministers was Oswald Mosley. The son of a Lancaster baronet, Mosley boasted a good war record, important social connections, and in 1918 was first elected to Parliament as a conventional Liberal Unionist. In 1920, he married Cynthia Curzon, daughter of Foreign Secretary Lord Curzon, in a wedding attended by King George V and Queen Mary. Later, shifting his allegiance to Labour, Mosley advanced rapidly through the party ranks as an expert on economic issues. An effective speaker, he might eventually have achieved a senior cabinet position. Yet Mosley had little patience with the Labour government's equivocation at a moment of national economic crisis. He himself favored the more populist approach, of creating millions of new jobs through public works and deficit spending. To that end, in 1930, he resigned from Labour and in 1931 founded the New Party. It went nowhere. In his frustration, Mosley then visited Mussolini. Impressed by Il Duce's vigor and dynamism, he promptly set about transforming his New Party into the British Union of Fascists. Here Mosley began adding distinctly authoritarian features to his populist agenda, even dressing his followers in black shirts. By 1934, in the abyss of the Depression, the Union had grown to 40,000 dues-paying members.

Initially, antisemitism did not figure in Mosley's program. But the mounting anguish of Depression-era unemployment, and the fear of embroilment in a new war, led Mosley in his public addresses to begin harping about the threat of "aliens," the power of "international Jewish finance," and an alleged Jewish effort to maneuver Britain into a new confrontation with Germany. To fortify this emerging racism, the Union began conducting its meetings in London's East End, in the very midst of the still extensive immigrant Jewish population. Inevitably, there were pitched battles, requiring police reinforcements. In 1937, the government banned the wearing of uniforms. Yet, black-shirted or not, the Mosleyites continued to mount their parades, marching through the heart of the East End, chanting their new refrain: "The Yids, the Yids, We've Come to Beat the Yids!" In 1939, Mosley's newly renamed Union of Fascists and National Socialists was fielding candidates for Parliament on its own ticket. Although failing to win a single constituency, the Union in its strident antisemitism managed to keep the Jewish issue alive among the British public at large.

The more existential anti-Jewish threat actually lay not in a single party or faction, but in the faceless hostility of the government bureaucracy. The animus was directed less at British than at European Jews. In the pre-1914 period, one of the more avowed xenophobes in the House of Commons was William Joynson-Hicks. During the 1901–5 debates on the Alien Restriction bill, it was Joynson-Hicks who led much of the public clamor against the "alien threat." In 1905, the bill enacted by Parliament may have been anodyne. But the wartime, 1916 version of the Aliens Act was not. As further amended in 1919 and 1920, the legislation imposed far more rigorous "means" and "national security" tests. The bias of these measures was scarcely disguised. Between 1921 and 1929, Joynson-Hicks served as home secretary in a series of Conservative governments, and East European Jews found him an implacable enemy. Throughout the 1920s, he ensured that their immigration was steadily throttled, and did not exceed 30,000 during the entire decade. Well before the exodus of Jews from Nazi-dominated Europe, it was becoming clear that Britain's tradition of open-ended hospitality to political or religious fugitives no longer applied, and least of all to East European Jews.

A REBIRTH OF FRENCH XENOPHOBIA

In these same early years of the twentieth century, the Jews of France remained a middle-sized community. As late as 1914, their numbers did not exceed 130,000. Of these, two-thirds lived in Paris. Most had reached the comfortable middle ranks of the bourgeoisie. Their political status appeared equally secure. Following the liquidation of the Dreyfus Affair, royalist and clerical reaction seemingly had shot its bolt. The Third French Republic had broadened its anchorage in secular egalitarianism. Between 1899 and 1914, in the belle époque of economic and cultural efflorescence, Jewish upward mobility continued unimpeded. Some Jews, then and earlier, had become titled aristocrats, and counted among their numbers such fabled dynasties as the Rothschilds, Camondos, Cahan d'Anvers, Pereiras, Königswärters, Menasches, Hirsches, and d'Almeidas. There were Jewish deputies in parliament, Jewish army officers (including the redeemed and promoted Dreyfus), Jews in university faculties, in literature and the arts. They included theatrical figures like Henri Bernstein and Sarah Bernhardt, composers like Jacques Offenbach and Jacques Fromental Halévy, artists like Camille Pissarro, Amadeo Modigliani, and Marc Chagall, the sociologist Émile Durkheim, the anthropologist Claude Lévi-Strauss, the political journalist Bernard Lazare, the poet André Spire, the philosopher Henri Bergson. In these golden prewar years, the nation appeared reconfirmed in the exuberant liberalism it had displayed in the earliest decades of the Third Republic.

Little wonder that France's Jews responded to the outbreak of war in an orgy of patriotism. In October 1915, the Consistoire Central and the Alliance Israélite published a joint appeal to the Jews of neutral countries, reminding them of all they owed France, "the initiator of the emancipation of Israelites throughout the world." Admittedly, the military alliance with Russia created a problem. In 1915, the tsarist government was conducting its mass evacuation of the Pale's borderland Jews. To cope with this embarrassing tragedy, a joint Consistoire-Alliance committee issued a public statement claiming that "reassuring signs have already appeared [that] the victory of the great liberal powers of the West, united with Russia for the defense of justice, cannot fail to achieve the emancipation of our brethren in Russia." The committee then organized and dispatched a delegation of eminent French Jews to the United States, to conduct propaganda there on behalf of the Allies.

Even in the last prewar decade, however, antisemitism was far from moribund in France. Édouard Drumont may have been politically crippled long before his death in 1917, but others picked up the torch of chauvinist bigotry. Coining the phrase "integral nationalism," Maurice Barrès emphasized the "spiritual" character of France's blood and soil. Jacques de Bainville evoked the mystic grandeur of the nation's royalist past. Yet it was Charles Maurras who almost single-handedly transformed ideological reaction into an inflammatory xenophobia. Charles-Marie Photius Maurras, son of a provincial tax collector, was registered by his parents in a Catholic lycée in Paris in 1885. It was the youth's first exposure to a cosmopolitan city, and to its intermingled population of Jews and other "non-Gallic" types. In 1894, as a twenty-six-year-old fledgling literary critic for the right-wing *Cocarde*, Maurras described these elements as *"métèques,"* that is, aliens, a term he borrowed from the ancient Athenians and which he later enlarged to include Protestants and Freemasons. By the turn of the century, retrieving the mantle of the discredited Drumont, Maurras and several colleagues organized themselves into a league, the Action Française, and formulated a program to resuscitate a monarchical France, a nation purged of Jews and other *métèques*.

In ensuing years, under Maurras' dynamic guidance, branches of the Action Française were organized among a wide diffusion of lingering anti-Dreyfusard and other antisemitic elements. In 1908, the league established a newspaper, also *L'Action française*. A nucleus of wealthy contributors, including Léon Daudet, who doubled as circulation editor, ensured the paper's economic base. It was from the densely packed, garishly headlined pages of *L'Action française* that a torrent of xenophobic abuse poured out. "The *métèques* are our foreign guests," Maurras editorialized, "domiciled or recently naturalized. . . . The Jews are foreigners." Jews were not only masters of high finance and incipient traitors (the old anti-Dreyfusard accusation), they were aliens, with an alien disdain for national traditions or ideals. In the last prewar years, exploiting that putative alien threat, the Action Française league corraled widening support from disgruntled military, aristocratic, and petit bourgeois elements. Its youth organization, the "Camelots du Roi" (literally, the "King's Vendors"), disseminated anti-Jewish wall posters and hooted performances by Jewish musicians and theatrical artists.

In this campaign, acting out the gospel of "integral nationalism" more frontally than had Barrès or even Drumont, the Action Française and other similar leagues emerged as the cutting edge of an ominous right-wing revival. During the war, even Maurras was obliged to acknowledge that "many Israélites, settled among us for generations . . . are natural members of the national body." But following the armistice, chauvinist passions would not be limited to the former German enemy. Rather, in 1923–24, they were further inflamed when an ill-judged and costly military occupation of the German Ruhr produced a collapse of the French franc, and a virtual liquidation of French lower-middle-class savings. Henceforth, the nation's petite bourgeoisie (like its counterpart in Germany) would become the marching infantry of the nation's political right wing.

Even in the worst of the economic crisis, ironically, at the height of France's irascible chauvinism in the 1920s, some 3 million foreigners were allowed to immigrate, mainly from Eastern and Southern Europe. It was the largest postwar immigration accepted by any Western nation. Yet the open-door policy was inspired not by humanitarianism but by strategic and economic logic; France was obliged to compensate demographically for its catastrophic battlefield losses. Among the newcomers, some 185,000 were

Jews, most of them from Eastern Europe. By 1939, they would comprise more than half of the French-Jewish population of 300,000—to be supplemented by approximately 50,000 refugees from the Nazi Reich (p. 483). The largest numbers of them settled in Paris's Marais district, encompassing the third and fourth arrondissements, bordering the aged rue de Rivoli and Métro St.-Paul, where they formed the nucleus of the capital's apparel industry. An ethnocentric community, they maintained their own institutions, their own Yiddish press, their own synagogues, and (more frequently) their own Bundist societies.

French gentiles were repelled by the newcomers' strident leftism. For them, it was a mirror image of Jewish prominence in the Bolshevik Revolution, the disaster that had threatened France's military survival and repudiated the massive bond debt to French investors. Now ultra-rightists had more grist for their political agenda. For Maurras and Léon Daudet, the mood of postwar chauvinism could be further exploited under the guise of resistance to a "Judéo-Bolshevik" conspiracy. In his nationalist demagoguery, Maurras even managed ingeniously to identify Germany, Jews, and bolshevism in the same camp. Thus, after 1918, he stigmatized Germany as the "stem and root" of Russian bolshevism, inasmuch as German Jews were "the masters in Moscow." Even "respectable" conservatives in the Chamber of Deputies shared in the denunciation, together with such prestigious Church journals as *La Documentation catholique* and *La Revue internationale des sociétés*. In July 1920, the Consistoire Israélite reported that antisemitism in senior military circles approached the level of the Dreyfus Affair, forcing many Jewish officers to apply for early retirement.

An Incipient Fascism

Following evacuation from the Ruhr and the resumption of—modified—German reparations payments in 1925, the French economy appeared briefly to stabilize. But France's political structure, with its multitude of splinter parties, remained fragile, and chronically vulnerable to the nation's socioeconomic inequities. It was the Great Depression that profoundly exacerbated those underlying tensions. In June 1932, a new election produced a certain rickety, arm's-length parliamentary cooperation between the Radical Socialist Party (neither radical nor socialist) and the Socialist Party (blandly social-welfarist). Yet the policy alignment lasted barely six months and effected no meaningful reforms in the nation's regressive tax structure or submarginal industrial working conditions. The coalition's principal "achievement" was to frighten the political right. Indeed, from 1933 onward, fearful that even the centrist Radicals might open the floodgates of leftist extremism, France's conservative parties moved incrementally closer to fascist ideology. They were in congenial company. By then, much of the Continent had gone that route, from Italy and Germany to a majority of France's Little Entente allies in Eastern Europe.

Exploiting this political and social polarization, Maurras and his Action Française associates Léon Daudet and Jacques de Bainville moved vigorously to organize lectures and demonstrations throughout the country, invoking the familiar perils both of a resurgent Germany and of a Bolshevik, "non-Gallic" France. With its formidable membership of some 100,000, the Action Française by the early 1930s had been joined by numerous other fascist or crypto-fascist imitators, most of them sharing a common impatience with "effete" parliamentarism and an instinctive preference for strong leaders. The most intimidating of these were Pierre Taittinger's Jeunesses Patriotes, and Count Casimir de la Rocque's Croix de Feu. With a combined membership of nearly a quarter-million, all three leagues conducted their marches and demonstrations in full military accouterment, with uniforms and torchlights, mobilizing lumpenproletariat and petit bourgeois followers alike under a common umbrella of "national vigilance" against leftist, alien influences.

The moment for these and other reactionary leagues to flex their muscles came in the winter of 1933–34. Mired in the Depression, the nation witnessed only governmental ineptitude in dealing with the economic crisis. Since the 1932 elections, the Radicals and Socialists had dominated the Chamber of Deputies. After their brief six-month partnership, however, each party afterward had blocked the other's program. The results were five governments between April 1932 and December 1933 alone, and public outrage approaching the threshold of conflagration. The spark was provided by the Stavisky Affair. The son of an immigrant Russian-Jewish dentist, Serge Stavisky was a high-living confidence man who specialized in buying up semipublic corporations with watered bonds, "guaranteeing" repayments with the anticipated payoffs of his other corporations. The Ponzi-style operation finally was exposed in December 1933, with the revelation that thousands of Stavisky's investors had been bilked. The police immediately launched a search for the mysteriously absconded Stavisky and tracked him down to a border village in the French Alps. Before he could be arrested, he shot himself. This was the official version.

But few people in France believed the official version. It was the popular consensus that the police had murdered Stavisky to prevent the revelation of his many connections among public figures. Those contacts were not trivial. They extended up to the brother-in-law of Camille Chautemps, prime minister of the incumbent Radical Socialist government. The political right smelled blood. By mid-January 1934, the *Action française* harangued its readers to descend on the Chamber of Deputies in massive waves and "Drive the Thieves Out" (in the words of the newspaper's headline). Indeed, all the rightist leagues now sensed that the moment was ripe for a decisive blow against the "corrupt," "effete" parliamentary regime. Over the ensuing weeks, rightist demonstrations outside the Chamber of Deputies mounted in scope and violence.

By January 28, 1934, Prime Minister Chautemps had had enough. He submitted his government's resignation. Yet the appetite of the leagues had only been whetted. Their riots picked up momentum. An attempt to patch together a new government under a Radical prime minister, Édouard Daladier, proved unavailing. The mobs wanted no more "leftists" (Daladier hardly was that) in office. On the night of February 6, an unprecedented wave of some 10,000 demonstrators threatened to break into the Chamber of Deputies. Only a massive police effort drove them back. By then, however, fifteen rioters and policemen had been killed and over three hundred seriously injured. At this point, the thoroughly intimidated Daladier submitted his resignation. For the second time in ten days, a legally elected government had fallen victim to right-wing intimidation. Over the ensuing week, still another government was cobbled together. Ostensibly based upon Radical Socialist leadership, most of its key cabinet ministers in fact came from the political right, even the far right. Plainly, the forces of reaction were entrenching themselves in France.

An Unlikely Republican Champion

As the violence raged on the evening of February 6, 1934, and as league paramilitaries battered at the doors of the Chamber of Deputies, Premier-designate Daladier found his one source of political support among the Socialists, and particularly the Socialist Party chairman, Léon Blum, who promised to stand with him against the mob. Who was this thin, bespectacled figure, with his elegant pince-nez and foppish lapel flower, who courageously held his ground at a moment of grave political and personal danger? Born in 1872, one of five sons of a prosperous Alsatian-Jewish silk-ribbon manufacturer who had resettled his family in Paris after the Franco-Prussian War, Léon Blum early on was drawn to the world of intellect. A precocious student of classical literature, he contributed highly polished essays to French literary magazines. Although Blum studied law, upon receiving his degree in 1894 he chose to become a public attorney in France's chancery court, principally to ensure himself enough time for his cultural and communal interests. It was the era of the Dreyfus Affair, and those interests inevitably turned to public causes.

They also turned to socialism, for in 1898 Blum came to know Jean Jaurès, the charismatic parliamentary leader of France's Socialist Party. Becoming the great man's protégé and devoted friend, Blum in 1904 was appointed deputy editor of the party newspaper, *L'Humanité*. When a demented super-patriot assassinated Jaurès on the eve of the war, Blum acceded to the party's leadership. In that capacity, he maintained the late Jaurès's commitment to democratic, nonrevolutionary socialism—and thus found himself in the minority, in 1920, when the party split into Communist and "moderate" factions. Over the ensuing years, revealing formidable political skills, Blum worked tenaciously to rebuild the original, mainstream Socialist Party to its former strength. In the process, as a member of the Chamber of Deputies, Blum also established a legendary personal reputation for intellectual and moral integrity.

Those qualities never appeared to better advantage than during the Stavisky crisis of February 1934. As rightist mobs threatened to storm the parliament, Blum offered to mobilize his Socialist Party in support of Édouard Daladier, the newly appointed premier-designate, and to cooperate in a coalition government. But Daladier's nerve was gone, and he resigned. In turn, witnessing the new cabinet devolving into the hands of political rightists, Blum made his decision to seek an alternate coalition with the Communist Party. In previous years, the Communists would not have agreed to the proposal. But more recently, the Soviet leadership in Moscow, alarmed at the growing triumph of fascism in one European nation after another, decided that expediency dictated a modus vivendi with the Socialists. Thus, in the spring of 1935, after months of negotiations, the two parties reached agreement for a Popular Front. To defeat the forces of reaction, they would cooperate in the impending April 1936 parliamentary elections. Those candidates of either party who scored highest in the first round of voting would receive joint support in the second, decisive round. Belatedly, too, Daladier of the Radicals persuaded his colleagues to enter the Popular Front coalition.

It was well understood that, if the Popular Front were victorious, Blum, as chairman of the largest party in the triad, would become prime minister. But in France's envenomed political climate of the 1930s, was the prospect of a Jewish prime minister realistic? The full impact of Depression-era xenophobia had refocused on the Jews, and with growing ferocity on Blum himself. Over the years, the Socialist chairman had become well acquainted with antisemitic venom. As early as December 1920, Léon Daudet had warned readers of the *Action française* that "a simian little *youtre* [yid] like Blum is utterly indifferent and even hostile to French interests." In Blum's initial parliamentary years, he endured continual ad hominem taunting even during his most cogent addresses to the Chamber. Maurras would write of him in 1928: "There is a man who should be shot, but in the back." A January 1934 issue of *Solidarité*, journal of the Jeunesses Patriotes, carried a full-page photograph of Blum, with the caption: "Public Enemy Number One."

And now, in early 1936, as the election campaign gained momentum, so did the cascade of vitriol against Blum. On February 13, as he was being driven home from his office, a group of Action Française militants dragged him from his automobile and savagely beat him, leaving him bleeding on the street with a severed neck artery. Rushed to the hospital, Blum underwent surgery and survived, although he would be obliged to convalesce throughout the remaining spring election contest. Ironically, the episode evoked widespread public sympathy for Blum. For a brief moment, like Dreyfus at the end of the nineteenth century, he emerged as a symbol of the Republic itself.

A Lightning Rod for Reactionaries

The national elections, taking place in two rounds of April 26 and May 6, 1936, produced a solid triumph for the Popular Front. As the single largest party in the Chamber, the Socialists at long last would assume decisive leadership in the new government, and Léon Blum thereby would become the first authentically Socialist prime minister in French history. Yet his election plainly represented a more stunning innovation yet. Antisemitism even in the polarized atmosphere of the 1930s had not become quite as inflammatory an issue in French public life as at the height of the Dreyfus Affair. But the lesson learned during the years of the *Affaire,* that Jew-hatred could be exploited as the cutting edge of an assault on political democracy itself, was put to far more systematic use in the postwar period. It was supremely the Depression era that fused antisemitism with paramilitary fascism.

Blum's Jewish ancestry now provoked a frenzy of rightist diabolization. Georges Suarez, editor of a racist screed, *Gringoire,* popularized the phrase "That man is not from here." "Here is a man to shoot down," editorialized Maurras. "Human detritus should be treated as such." On June 7, 1936, the day Blum presented his list of ministerial appointments to the Chamber of Deputies, Xavier Vallat, a stalwart of the far right (and future official in the wartime Vichy government), solemnly warned Blum: "M. Le Premier . . . [f]or the first time this ancient Gallo-Roman land is to be ruled by a Jew. . . . To govern this peasant nation of France, it would be better to have someone whose origins, however modest, lie deep in our soil, rather than a subtle talmudist." (The Chamber then erupted in a bedlam of taunts and countertaunts.) Blum personally remained unintimidated by the vilification. Yet France's veteran Jewish leadership failed to match his stoic dignity. The overwhelming majority of French Jews may have cast their votes for the Popular Front. In the immediate aftermath of his electoral victory, however, *L'Univers israélite,* a publication of the Consistoire, and *La Tribune juive Strasbourg-Paris,* organ of the venerable Alsatian-Jewish community, exhorted their readers to display restraint, to mute all displays of enthusiasm for Blum's election. Grand Rabbi Jacob Kaplan, in a private letter, even gently suggested that Blum forgo the premiership altogether (there was no response).

Upon assuming office, Blum honored the Popular Front legislative program in letter and spirit. The agenda he submitted to the Chamber in the summer of 1936 bore an acknowledged resemblance to Franklin Roosevelt's New Deal. It called for a forty-hour workweek, paid vacations, collective bargaining, reform of the tax system in favor of the laboring classes, introduction of unemployment insurance, and enlargement of free, compulsory schooling. And like Roosevelt's program, Blum's New Social Charter won massive parliamentary approval. Nevertheless, France's political opposition was far from chastened. The Chamber of Commerce and the nation's professional associations declared war on the Charter. The army command publicly opposed the government's "naïve" commitment to the League of Nations. The Church hierarchy reacted with alarm to Communist participation in the new government. As for the rightist leagues, their rage was foreordained by the new cabinet's decree, in June 1936, to close down all paramilitary organizations.

These crypto-fascist consociations did not go quietly into the night. Upon being terminated as a uniformed league, the Croix de Feu ingeniously reconstituted itself as a political party, the Parti Social Français. By 1938, the PSF's membership was estimated at 600,000, and its rolls included 3,000 mayors, over 1,000 municipal councilmen, and a dozen parliamentary deputies. Another former paramilitary league, the Parti Populaire Français, touting Mussolini and Hitler as models for France, accumulated 170,000 members by 1938, and surpassed even Maurras' reincarnated Parti de l'Action Française. Other former leagues now reinvented themselves under various façades. In their anticommunism, antiparliamentarism, and incendiary Jew-hatred, they fanned the nation's internecine hatreds at a moment of growing international tensions.

The Demise of Republican Democracy

It was in fact a European crisis that torpedoed the Popular Front government. With the outbreak of the Spanish Civil War in July 1936, Blum's instinctive reaction, and that of his fellow Socialists, was to provide military aid to the embattled Spanish Loyalists. Getting wind of his intention, Britain's Conservative government immediately warned Blum to stay clear of the Spanish maelstrom. So did the French right, of course, wanting no part of the "Communist butchers" of Madrid. And so, too, even more critically, did Blum's Popular Front ally, the Radical Socialists. Blum then was helpless to provide the Spanish Republicans with meaningful aid. In turn, outraged by his "betrayal" of the Spanish left, Blum's Communist partners turned against him. A series of clashes with Communist-dominated unions in Paris's industrial suburbs further splintered the Popular Front. In June 1937, abandoned both by the Communists and by substantial elements among the Radical Socialists, Blum submitted his resignation.

The second and "reconstituted" Popular Front government now functioned under the Radical Socialists, and in ensuing months the party's chairman, the redoubtable Édouard Daladier, set about burying the achievements of Blum's New Social Charter. Dismantling the forty-hour workweek, the government eviscerated the remaining public-works programs and crushed workers' strikes in mines and railroads. Daladier's management of foreign affairs proved even more tragic. He collaborated obsequiously in Britain's sacrifice of Czechoslovakia to Nazi Germany in September 1938 and March 1939. Unrecognized at the time, moreover, Daladier's foreign and domestic policies were intimately linked. International crises gave the premier the pretext for both reversing social reforms and for restricting civil liberties. Thus, in September 1939, exploiting public outrage at the Nazi-Soviet Non-Aggression Pact, which had been signed only the month before, Daladier outlawed the Communist Party and jailed forty-four Communist deputies. As the prime minister saw it, a harsh stance toward the political left also would help placate Hitler. So would a harsh stance toward "nonnationals." Almost predictably, the Jews became the principal "nonnationals" to bear the brunt of the government's sharp swing rightward.

France's economic doldrums alone would have compounded Jewish vulnerability. In the Depression-ridden 1930s, some 50,000 new Jewish refugees poured into France, most of them as fugitives from the Nazi Reich. By their "invasion," the newcomers represented more than a threat to Gallic culture. They were competition in the labor market. Worse yet, the Jews ostensibly threatened to embroil France in complications with Nazi Germany. Even in the latter 1930s, the nation's mood was one of peace at almost any price. Thus, immediately following Daladier's sellout of Czechoslovakia in September 1938, the rightist former league commanders—Colonel de la Rocque, Charles Maurras, Jacques Doriot, and others—issued public testimonials in praise of the government for "keeping the peace." Afterward, as Nazi Germany's threat to Danzig and the Polish Corridor burgeoned during the spring and summer of 1939, France's right-wing journals engaged in a frenzied campaign of alarmism against the Jews as the ultimate source of anti-German warmongering. In his editorial "Attention les Juifs!" Maurras warned that the Jews would pay dearly for their provocation.

Over the years, France's governmental bureaucracy had been giving heed to the mounting confluence of anti-Jewish suspicions and hostilities. In 1933, it began imposing tight limitations on the number of foreigners allowed to practice medicine and pharmacy, a measure transparently directed at Jewish professionals fleeing Nazi Germany. Restrictions abated somewhat during

Blum's Popular Front administration. But in 1938, with Daladier as prime minister, the anti-immigrant policy regained its momentum. "[We have] reached the saturation point," explained Henri Béranger, France's delegate to an international conference on refugees at Évian-les-Bains in July 1938 (p. 516). ". . . [It] does not permit [us to receive] any more refugees without tipping the social balance." Béranger doubtless expressed a national consensus.

By then, the Daladier cabinet was considering an alternate solution to the problem of Jewish immigration. This was the resettlement of refugees in French Madagascar. Ironically, it was an alternative that the Polish government in recent years had been seeking for its "redundant" Jewish population (p. 421). Now, suddenly, Madagascar emerged as a possible dumping ground for France's own "redundant" Jews. During a visit to Washington in October 1938, Foreign Minister Georges Bonnet raised the proposal in talks with Undersecretary of State Sumner Welles. Could the United States help underwrite such a transmigration of refugees? The United States could not. The following month, the Daladier government issued a pronouncement of authentically sinister implications. It warned that French nationality might be stripped even from those foreign-born persons who already had been officially naturalized, should they be judged "unworthy of the title of French citizenship." Jews were not specifically mentioned in the warning. They did not have to be.

A PAPAL BENEDICTION

If much of postwar Europe found itself afflicted by a revived new strain of Jew-hatred, the role of the Catholic Church also had to be taken into account. The Church's stance on *The Protocols of the Elders of Zion* offered a useful litmus test. In both Italy and France, the principal disseminators of the forgery were Catholic prelates. Since the turn of the century, Monsignor Umberto Benigni, a former senior official in the Vatican secretariat of state, had been publishing denunciations of Jews as ritual murderers who worked in tandem with Protestants, Freemasons, and others of the Church's "heterodox" enemies. In 1920, however, Benigni directed his animus exclusively at the Jews, and in his *Bollettino antisemita* that year he set about publishing chapters of the *Protocols*. As the forged description of the Jewish world conspiracy began circulating in Western Europe, the official Vatican daily, *L'Osservatore romano*, similarly turned to the Jewish question, calling attention to Jewish "hostility toward Christianity, driven by racial hatred and by the thirst for domination."

In France, Monsignor Ernest Jouin devoted much of his writing career to an exposé of the Jewish danger. In his translations of the *Protocols* in 1920,

Jouin signed his foreword: "E. Jouin, Prelate of his Holiness," a reminder that Benedict XV had honored him with this title for his distinguished publishing role on behalf of the Church. The vocation had begun in 1912 when Jouin launched his *Revue internationale des sociétés secrètes,* a journal that focused unremittingly on the Jewish-Masonic conspiracy. Soon after Cardinal Achille Ratti became Pius XI, in 1922, he honored Jouin with a private audience. "Continue your *Revue,*" declared the pope, ". . . for you are combating our mortal enemy." To foster Jouin's work, Pius XI then appointed him "Apostolic Prothonotary." In 1926, a group of Dutch priests, alarmed by the Vatican's quasi-official endorsement of antisemitism, founded a new association, the Friends of Israel, with the purpose of countering anti-Jewish libels. Two years later, the Holy Office ordered the association dissolved for its "erroneous initiatives." As the virulence of antisemitism mounted in Europe throughout the 1920s, it evoked not a word of condemnation from the Vatican.

Thus, in Austria, virtually every Catholic organization in the interwar years was openly and avowedly antisemitic, their publications overflowing with denunciations of Jews. At a meeting of the Catholic Men's Association, the so-called Piusverein, the group's director, Father Victor Kolb, alerted its members that "wherever you look, you always see Judaism's work . . . backed by unlimited means, always aimed at supremacy, in every form." For Kolb, the task of the Verein was to ensure "protection of the German people . . . from Jewish penetration, from the destructive work of the Jews." Even Bishop Joachannes Geföllner of Linz, one of a handful of "liberal" Austrian prelates, who cautioned against the dangers of Nazi-style racism, felt obliged to qualify this warning with another: "It is beyond any doubt that many Jews . . . exercise an extremely pernicious influence in almost all sectors of modern civilization. . . . Not only is it legitimate to combat and to end [that] influence, it is in fact the firm and solemn obligation of every informed Christian."

In Germany, meanwhile, the sheer pagan brutality of Nazi racism became a source of growing concern to the papacy. Nevertheless, in 1933, Pius XI saw no alternative but to seek a politically expedient understanding with Hitler. To that end, a German-Vatican Concordat was negotiated by the pontiff's secretary of state, Eugenio Pacelli, ostensibly to protect the autonomy of Catholic institutions on German soil. No sooner had the agreement been signed, however, than the Nazis began to violate it, muzzling clerical sermons, censoring Catholic publications, subsuming the Catholic Youth Organization into the Hitlerjugend. Eventually, in March 1937, Pius XI felt impelled to issue an encyclical, *Mit brennender Sorge (With Burning Anxiety),* reproving Berlin for violating the terms of the Concordat. The document then went on to warn against the deification of race and state and called for the free exercise of religion. Yet, even then, no explicit mention was made of the persecution of Jews. During the first half of 1937, a semiofficial Vatican newspaper, the widely read *Civiltà cattolica,* had circumspectly recommended that Catholics desist from overt acts of antisemitism lest these prove inimical to conversionary efforts. But in autumn 1938, on the very eve of Kristallnacht in Germany (p. 513), *Civiltà cattolica* resumed its traditional condemnation of Jewish "penetration."

Two months earlier, in September 1938, during the last year of Pius XI's papal incumbency, Mussolini announced the first of Italy's series of anti-Jewish laws (p. 542). As justification, Il Duce cited among other reasons the Church's own long record of warnings against the Jews. Once these new laws were put into effect, neither Pius XI nor his successor, Pius XII, who assumed the papal throne in 1939, nor any other Church authority, opposed the Italian government's measures to throw Jewish children out of school and to dismiss large numbers of adult Jews from their employment. Altogether, in the post–World War I decades, the Vatican's stance on the Jewish issue lent the mantle of "spiritual" approbation to the Jewish policies of Europe's fascist movements and governments.

JEWISH "RADICALISM" IN AUSTRIA

Nowhere in postwar Europe was the ideological dichotomy between Catholic "traditionalism" and Jewish "radicalism" given wider political attention than in Austria, a nation that in its earlier imperial incarnation had been the largest Catholic state in Europe.

It was on November 11 of 1918, in horrified recognition of their impending isolation as a remnant nation, that Austria's deputies in the Habsburg imperial Reichstag "accepted" the abdication of Emperor Karl, and declared "German Austria" a "democratic" republic. A veteran Social Democrat, Karl Renner, then assumed office as provisional chancellor. The following month, the new republic held its first official elections. Although the Social Democrats won the largest plurality, they failed to win a majority, and thus were obliged to enter a coalition government with a group of nationalist factions. It was a marriage of political convenience that soon would prove unworkable.

At the Peace Conference, the Allied statesmen turned their attention to Austria only after dealing with Germany. But in September 1919, they obliged the Renner government to accept a document, the Treaty of Saint-Germain, that stripped Austria not only of its prewar imperial domains but also of two-fifths of the German-speaking homeland. From a mighty conglomeration of 52 million inhabitants, Austria now was transformed into a hunchback republic of barely 7 million; and the city of Vienna alone encompassed a third of this remaining population. Worse yet, the nation was surrounded by its former Habsburg subject peoples, a majority still hostile, and all intent on maintaining stiff tariff barriers against Austria's modest exports. The country was left threadbare and hungry, "too small to live, too large to die," as political commentators described it. This was the grim legacy with which the Social Democrat–dominated coalition now had to grapple.

It was Otto Bauer, returning from Russia in a prisoner exchange in September 1918, who played a central role in coping with the new state of affairs. The product of an acculturated Viennese-Jewish family, trained as a lawyer, Bauer shared in the liberal-humanist Jewish milieu that provided much of the socialist leadership in the last decades of the empire. In 1907, at the age of twenty-six, he produced the monumental volume *The Nationalities Issue and Social Democracy (Die Nationalitätenfrage und die Sozialdemokratie)* that laid out the guidelines of an enlightened, pluralistic approach to the subject peoples. It also won Bauer an immediate appointment to the Social Democratic Party's delegation in the Austrian Reichstag, as well as editorship of *Der Kampf*, the chief theoretical organ of Austrian Social Democracy.

With the establishment of the republic, it was Bauer and the Jewish intellectuals who emerged even more decisively than before the war as the Social Democrats' most vibrant nucleus. Although the non-Jewish Karl Renner became chancellor of the postwar coalition government, Bauer became foreign minister, taking over from the redoubtable Victor Adler, who died one day after the provisional republic was established. Indeed, Bauer soon transcended his portfolio, orchestrating a major part of the cabinet's domestic agenda. It was at his initiative that the ensuing two years of Social Democratic governance produced the most far-reaching working-class legislation in Austria's history. The program included an eight-hour workday, paid holidays, prohibition of child labor and night work for women, and a quantum increase in unemployment and health insurance. Vienna, under the perennial control of the Social Democrats, developed the single most enlightened municipal administration in the world.

It was in the early 1920s, too, that Austrian Jews essentially completed the prewar shift in their political loyalties from the Liberals to the Social Democrats (p. 313). Internationalism remained the party's key inducement. More than any other faction, Social Democracy had purged itself of its residual chauvinism and antisemitism. By contrast, the party's main rival, the Christian Socialist Party—the "Christian Socials"—had been founded by Karl Lueger on a program of ideological antisemitism, and maintained a close if unofficial relationship with the Catholic hierarchy. Soon the Jews' en bloc reorientation to the left became evident in their preeminence at the upper echelons of the Social Democratic leadership. By the end of the war, of the 137 "senior" figures in Austrian socialism, no fewer than 88 were Jews or part-Jews.

Perhaps inevitably, then, the parliamentary elections of December 1918 witnessed the Christian Socials reverting to type, structuring their political campaign almost exclusively around the "Jewish danger." On this occasion, the effort did not produce an electoral victory, although it secured the party a slot in the Social Democratic coalition cabinet. But in December 1920, the impact of the peace-treaty amputations and the raging inflation forced yet another national election. Exploiting antisemitism to the hilt once again, the Christian Socials this time won leadership of a restructured coalition. Indeed, Ignaz Seipel, who replaced Karl Renner as chancellor, was a monsignor of the Catholic Church. Aloof and sophisticated, Seipel personally disdained rabble-rousing of any kind. His "Jewish" objective was simply to limit Jewish cultural and political influence in Austrian life. Otherwise, the new chancellor was preoccupied with the effort to dampen the nation's raging inflation. This he achieved, but only through the painful surgery of terminating numerous public projects and laying off thousands of civil servants. If Seipel's measures achieved a certain economic stability, it was the salaried, white-collar class that paid most heavily. Their bitterness henceforth would remain a permanent feature in Austrian public affairs.

As in the prewar period, therefore, Christian Socialist politicians in the 1920s directed their most creative efforts to diverting lower-middle-class frustrations. In that effort, it was a simple matter to identify Jews with the political radicalism then sweeping through Russia, Hungary, Germany, and Austria itself. As far back as October 1916, Friedrich Adler, a physicist and the frail, intellectual son of Victor Adler, shot and killed the Austrian prime minister, Count Karl von Stürgkh. At his trial, the younger Adler defended his act as a protest against the regime that was destroying the Austrian people (he was sentenced to death, but in 1917 the imperial court, unwilling to risk worker unrest, commuted the sentence to eighteen years). In the immediate postwar years, moreover, as funds and propaganda literature flooded into Vienna from Bolshevik Russia, local radicals embarked on *putsch* efforts of their own. Again, Jews played a central role. One of the best known was the Prague-born journalist Egon Kisch. In November 1918, Kisch and several of his fellow Red Guards launched an armed raid on the offices of the *Neue Freie Presse,* Austria's leading newspaper. A bastion of moderate liberalism, the paper was a particular bête noire for the Communists. Although the assault was repelled without loss of life, the image of Jewish radicalism was not easily to be erased. It was to the Jews, not least of all, that the Christian Socials attributed the punitive taxes and social egalitarianism of "Red Vienna," and the widespread economic misery of the nation's déclassé white-collar elements.

Never before had Jews loomed so prominently in Vienna's life. In 1910, they numbered some 175,000 in a metropolitan population of 2.3 million. By 1923, although war losses and economic privation had reduced Vienna's population to 1.865 million, the Jewish population actually had grown to about 200,000, owing to the wartime influx of Galician and Bukovinian refugees. Moreover, despite the rigors of the war and of the early postwar years, Viennese Jewry remained an overwhelmingly middle-class community. As late as 1934, in the professions, they comprised 62 percent of the city's lawyers and 47 percent of its physicians and dentists. In business, at least 70 percent of the city's wholesale and retail trade was concentrated in Jewish hands. Most of these businesses actually were quite small, even marginal, but the typical Austrian gentile knew only what he saw; and wherever he turned, Jewish names appeared on offices and storefronts. Before 1914, in a comparatively prosperous empire, a seemingly elitist Jewish presence could be accepted or ignored. But not in the misery of the postwar, and even less when that presence was equated with the political radicalism of Red Vienna, with its latest infusion of culturally objectionable East European refugees.

Thus it was, in the late teens and early 1920s, that antisemitism acquired dimensions unprecedented in recent Austrian history. In 1919 a series of thuggish rampages tore through Vienna's largely Jewish Leopoldstadt quarter, ending only after Jewish war veterans hastily organized a defense force. In the autumn of 1920, when Albert Einstein accepted an invitation to lecture at the University of Vienna, police had to be summoned to cordon off the campus against threatened anti-Jewish violence. Rallies and demonstrations against Jews became almost weekly occurrences. For two and a half years the wave of xenophobia continued, not subsiding until the spring of 1923, when Chancellor Seipel insisted that the Christian Socials adopt a more subdued middle-class orientation, if only to ensure the nation's credit rating.

The Rise of Austrian Fascism

The ominous political divergence between Social Democrats and Christian Socials continued well into the late 1920s, with each side going so far as to organize its own paramilitary "defense" force. Ultimately, the pressure of governing amid this polarization became too much for Chancellor Seipel. In June 1929, the monsignor resigned. His successors faced a new and even more debilitating series of crises. Over the ensuing two years, the Great Depression ramified throughout the entirety of Europe. In May 1931, Austria's renowned Kreditanstalt chain of banks collapsed, and within a year the country's rate of industrial production (in 1928) dropped by two-thirds, while its unemployment rate doubled. In a desperate effort to cope with the metastasizing economic crisis, one Christian Socialist chancellor followed another. No other party would enter a government coalition. Otto Bauer, ideological leader of the Social Democrats, refused to share in "administering the affairs of a doomed capitalism."

In the parliamentary elections of 1932, the Austrian people decided to place their trust in yet another Christian Socialist government, this time under a charismatic new chancellor, Engelbert Dollfuss. A much decorated war veteran with a rural, archconservative background, Dollfuss was first and foremost an unregenerate Austrian patriot. Ideologically wedded to the Church, he and his fellow Christian Socials would not allow their little Catholic nation to be swallowed up by Germany, a largely Protestant *Machtstaat*. Thus, by committing himself to strict observance of the 1919 Treaty of Saint-Germain, and its injunction against an Anschluss with Germany, Dollfuss won important trade concessions from Benito Mussolini, who needed an independent Austria as the northern "buffer" for Italy. It was a shrewd diplomatic stance, but a difficult one. The chancellor faced stiff competition from the Austrian Nazi Party, whose members dutifully parroted Hitler's demand for an Anschluss. In June 1933, then, Dollfuss outlawed the Nazi Party.

Yet, at the same time, to protect his rightist base after banning the Nazis, Dollfuss felt obliged to deal even more harshly with the Social Democratic opposition. He found his pretext in February 1934, when the SDs launched a general strike in Vienna to protest Dollfuss's emergent authoritarianism. Soon both sides hurled their respective paramilitary forces against each other. In the ensuing two days of furious internecine battle, over 600 workers were killed and some 2,000 wounded before the their leadership surrendered. Immediately afterward, the chancellor had eleven of those leaders executed for "treason" and dissolved their Social Democratic Party altogether. Otto Bauer and numerous of his surviving comrades fled for their lives to neighboring Czechoslovakia. Henceforth, Austria would function under an undisguised fascist-style dictatorship.

As the nation veered steadily rightward, its Jews needed little reminder that their most implacable enemy was the Austrian Nazi Party. Indeed, before being outlawed, local Nazis had declared open season on Jewish shops in the Leopoldstadt quarter, breaking windows, painting antisemitic epithets on doorways, driving Jewish bystanders off sidewalks and out of parks. Attacks on Jewish university students in Austria were an old story, of course, well predating the Republic. Yet they achieved a special intensity in the Depression years. At the medical school, Jewish students were obliged to seek the protection of HaKoah, the Zionist sports organization, which ushered them in "convoys" to and from their classes.

Although the Christian Socials were hardly less antisemitic than the Nazis, Chancellor Dollfuss himself offered little evidence of personal bigotry. Before assuming office in 1932, he fraternized with a number of Jews, and upon becoming chancellor he followed Mussolini's lead in rejecting Hitler's racial theories. But once Dollfuss outlawed the Nazi Party, he had become a marked man. Directed from Berlin, local Nazi violence against his government included bomb attacks on Austrian government facilities and murder attempts against public officials. The campaign of mayhem was climaxed on July 25, 1934, when a band of Austrian Nazis, seeking to wrest control of the chancellery building, shot and killed Dollfuss.

The attempted putsch failed. Austria's president, Wilhelm Miklas, named Minister of Justice Kurt von Schuschnigg as chancellor; and Schuschnigg immediately made plain that the rule of law, if not democracy, would prevail in Austria. Yet Schuschnigg well appreciated that Austria's survival ultimately depended on the protection of Fascist Italy. Endlessly genuflecting toward Mussolini, the new chancellor structured his government even more closely than his predecessor's on the Italian "corporate" model. In the end, however, the tight-wire gamble proved ineffective. By 1935, Mussolini, newly isolated in the West as a consequence of his recent invasion of Ethiopia, saw no alternative but to draw closer to Nazi Germany. Schuschnigg, in turn, felt obliged to reach a protective "understanding" of his own with Hitler. Thus, by terms of an agreement reached between the two men in July 1936, Schuschnigg promised to legalize the Austrian Nazi Party and appoint selected Nazis to key positions in his cabinet. From then on, a German sword of Damocles would dangle over the Austrian Republic—and assuredly over Austria's Jews.

Until these last years of Austrian political reaction, Jews had managed to retain their cultural preeminence in Vienna. The city's Jewish physicians still attracted patients from throughout the world, and Jewish attorneys continued to be regarded as the doyens of the legal profession. Of the four Austrians who became Nobel laureates in the 1920s and 1930s, three were Jews. Playwrights and theater directors, symphony orchestra conductors and concert performers, journalists and newspaper critics, remained substantially Jewish. Nor was Chancellor Schuschnigg personally a rabid antisemite. For reasons of political expediency, however, his government began adopting its own thinly veiled methods of isolating Jews: countenancing regulations that in practical effect denied Jewish businessmen the required licenses for commercial enterprises; virtually barring Jewish students from medical and law schools, and Jewish physicians access to hospital internships.

As late as 1937, a majority of Austrian Jews appeared to nurture the illusion that they would find time to exploit their well-honed ability to adapt, or at least to negotiate a cautious, selective, and painless emigration. In that illusion, they remained a mirror image of their kinsmen elsewhere in Central Europe—even those living in the vortex of the Continent's nascent racist tornado.

XXV

The Triumph of Nazism

GERMANY: THE WAGES OF RADICALISM

On May 31, 1919, a partly decomposed corpse was spotted in one of the locks of Berlin's Landwehr Canal. The body was retrieved and taken to the city morgue, where it was promptly identified as that of Rosa Luxemburg. Two weeks later, on the day of her interment, mourners in seemingly endless thousands filed by to pay their respects to a woman who had emerged as a legend of socialist idealism.

Rosalia Luksemburg was born in 1871, in Zamocz, within the Polish-inhabited Lublin district of the tsarist Pale of Settlement. Her father, a prosperous merchant, was an acculturated Jew who later moved with his wife, sons, and daughter to Warsaw, where they could be exposed to Western influences. The daughter fully exploited that opportunity. An intellectual overachiever, she was invariably first in her class each year of her—secular—schooling. It was as a gymnasium student, too, that she was caught up in the revolutionary socialism of her generation, and as a nineteen-year-old escaped arrest only when her family smuggled her over the border to Austria. Soon afterward, like numerous other young Jewish expatriates, Rosa Luxemburg moved on to Switzerland, where she enrolled at the University of Zurich, eventually to earn a doctorate of social sciences in 1897.

It was during these Zurich years that Luxemburg maintained her ardent socialist commitments and soon became a delegate and much-admired speaker at international socialist congresses. In 1898, she settled in Germany in order to participate in that country's powerful Social Democratic Party. Characteristically, Luxemburg needed little time to rise to the party's inner circle, where she became an influential voice of "orthodox," nonrevisionist socialism. Yet, for all the respect she evoked, in the war crisis of July 1914, Luxemburg and Karl Liebknecht were the only senior party members to oppose Germany's entrance into war. So vigorous was their opposition that both were sentenced to prison terms for "incitement." It was in prison, therefore, that Luxemburg wrote her celebrated *Junius* pamphlet, mercilessly exposing the war as an imperialist "swindle." Once the document was smuggled out to her followers, it was secretly published and soon became the inspiration for a tightly knit group of fellow "Spartacists," those who embraced her cause of "authentic," "revolutionary," "internationalist" socialism.

On November 9, 1918, an exhausted German nation erupted in mass uprisings against the war. Hereupon, the Social Democrats belatedly came into their own as champions of peace. Facing no opposition, Friedrich Ebert, the SPD chairman, assumed the chancellorship, sent the kaiser into exile, negotiated an armistice, and organized a Soviet of People's Commissars based on a cabinet of three Social Democrats and three Independent Socialists. It was in this same ten-day explosion of activity, moreover, that Ebert announced his intention to organize elections for a constitutional assembly. The announcement quite horrified Rosa Luxemburg. Upon their release from prison on November 9, she and Karl Liebknecht had anticipated a government based on an authentic "proletarian" revolution, not on a middle-class electoral process. Immediately, then, the two purists mobilized their Spartacist followers, exhorting them to organize a Red Guard, to replace Ebert's "fraudulent" soviet with a true "people's" soviet.

It was significant, however, that Luxemburg rejected the very notion of a Leninist-style dictatorship. Her vision was of a working-class constituency that carefully and painstakingly would be nurtured to political maturity, with all governing authority to emerge logically and peacefully from their own midst. Assuredly, she opposed any precipitous move to overthrow the Ebert cabinet by violence. But events soon got out of hand. Liebknecht and other Spartacists were recruiting several thousand workers and demobilized soldiers, taking over army weapons depots in preparation for establishing an "authentic" socialist government. Under the circumstances, Luxemburg saw no alternative but to exhort all "true socialists" to join the Spartacist uprising. Yet neither could Friedrich Ebert, a moderate-revisionist Social Democrat, tolerate a revolutionary challenge. Fully supported by the army command and the Freikorps, a paramilitary force comprised of some quarter-million right-wing army veterans, the chancellor moved vigorously against the "bolshies." In January 1919, over the course of a four-day running battle through the streets of Berlin, the government crushed the Spartacist uprising, inflicting over 3,000 casualties.

Luxemburg and Liebknecht fled, a price on their heads. Wall placards denounced "Red Rosa" as a fanatic, a Bolshevik, a Jew. In May 1919, the army tracked the two fugitives to a secret hideaway in Berlin's drab Wilmersdorf district. They were seized, beaten senseless, dragged away, and shot. Aware of Luxemburg's great personal popularity, the government felt it safer then to announce that she had been abducted by a mob, that her whereabouts were unknown. But her true fate was revealed on May 31, the day her body was recovered in the Landwehr Canal. In the ensuing months, Luxemburg's legacy of idealistic socialist radicalism came to be incorporated into the program and folklore of Germany's Communist (formerly Spartacist) Party. The chairmanship of that party subsequently devolved into the hands of another Jew, Paul Levi. Although fully as committed a Marxist as the late Luxemburg, Levi proclaimed an end for the while to revolutionary conspiracy, and placed his emphasis henceforth on political activity within the framework of the new republic. Yet, by then the "Jewish" image of violent radicalism was well established in public consciousness.

The Legacy of Jewish Radicalism

In southern Germany, too, the initial postwar surge toward socialist radicalism generated its highly visible Jewish component. Although Catholic Bavaria traditionally had been the single most conservative state in the German Empire, its acute wartime suffering turned its population as sharply leftward as that of any other of Germany's *Länder*. On November 4, 1918, Bavaria actually was the first of these states to become a socialist "republic." The process was guided by an unlikely figure, Kurt Eisner, a man of distinctly moderate, non-Bolshevik temperament. He was also a Jew.

Son of a Berlin shopkeeper, Eisner had served a journalistic apprenticeship for the Social Democratic newspaper *Die Forwärts* before rising to the paper's editorship early in the century. Ironically, he was fired in 1905 for being too hesitant in his editorial support of Russia's 1905 Revolution. Afterward, still uncertain of his ideological stance, and in and out of favor with the party, Eisner moved to Bavaria to subsist as a freelance journalist. It was in Munich, in 1917, that he became a founding member of the Bavarian branch of the Independent Socialist Party and in the process adopted a position somewhat to the left of the mainline Social Democrats. During the last year of the war, upon being imprisoned for his pacifist views, Eisner unexpectedly became something of a hero to Bavaria's younger socialists. Thus, upon being set free in late October 1918, in the midst of Munich's revolutionary chaos, he exploited his inflated reputation to organize a network of "soviets," and on November 8 to lead his followers in a peaceful takeover of the Bavarian Diet, then to proclaim a Bavarian Socialist Republic. Functioning as a coalition of Independent Socialists and Social Democrats, Eisner's regime was virtually a mirror image of the Ebert government then being established in Berlin. Indeed, this moderate social-welfarist regime followed the Berlin model by promising free, democratic elections.

Whatever Eisner's good intentions, his cabinet was equivocal and unimaginative in its diplomatic and economic policies. Seeking exemption from the Allied blockade against Germany, Eisner proclaimed Bavaria's "autonomy."

The strategy did not impress the Allies, who tolerated no exemptions from the blockade. As in Germany at large, food shortages and unemployment mounted. Taxes could not be collected, pensions could not be paid. Inevitably, the public soon identified the crisis with Eisner himself and with other prominent Jews in his government. In the state election of January 1919, his party candidates were soundly repudiated. On February 21, therefore, Eisner dutifully set out for the Diet to submit his cabinet's resignation. As the chancellor neared the building's entrance, a young man approached from behind and shot him fatally. The assassin, Count Anton von Arco-Valley, was the son of a respected Bavarian aristocrat. Yet he was also the son of Emma von Oppenheim, a Jewish woman, a blemish that had barred him from membership in the Thule Gesellschaft, a racist society. Infuriated, young Arco-Valley by his act of murder evidently intended to prove his "Germanic" bona fides.

In March 1919, a month following Eisner's assassination, a new, equally moderate Social Democratic government was organized in Bavaria. But it proved as helpless as its predecessor in coping with Bavaria's economic crisis. At this point, a group of exasperated far-leftists agreed that the time had come to establish an "authentic" soviet. The moment seemed ripe, for Spartacist uprisings were still periodically flaring up in the Ruhr, and the Bela Kun regime lately had taken over in Hungary. Thus, in April 1919, the "new" radicals seized control of the chancellery and the Landtag, proclaimed a Soviet Republic of Bavaria, and broke off all remaining connections with Berlin. The guiding spirits of the new regime were Gustav Landauer, Erich Mühsam, and Ernst Toller. None was a Bavarian or even a Christian. All three were Jewish intellectuals from other parts of Germany, and so politically inept that their "republic" lasted barely a week and a half. Thoroughly intimidated by Bavaria's ongoing chaos and widening starvation, the three-man junta gave way without protest to an even more militantly Communist trio. This time, the three newcomers, Tovia Axelrod, Max Levien, and Eugen Leviné, were not even Germans. All were Russian citizens. All were Jews. Dispatched by Lenin to implant an unqualifiedly Bolshevik regime in Bavaria, the three promptly launched into the organization of a Red Army and a program of forced collectivization.

This latest, even more draconian and clumsy, version of political musical chairs was too much for Germany's national government. In Berlin, Chancellor Ebert and his colleagues decided to "liberate" Bavaria once and for all. At their orders, in late April 1919, Defense Minister Gustav Noske dispatched a substantial Freikorp detachment southward, backed by regular army troops equipped with tanks, flamethrowers, even airplanes. In less than ten days of "White Terror," partisans of all of Bavaria's current and former leftist regimes, Communists and moderate socialists alike, were hunted down indiscriminately. Landauer and Leviné were captured and executed. Mühsam was given a lengthy prison sentence and eventually shot by the Nazis in 1934. Toller, a renowned dramatist, was dealt with somewhat more gingerly. Given a four-year sentence, he survived imprisonment to become a traveling activist for antifascist causes worldwide. In 1934, a fugitive from the Nazis, penniless and despondent in New York, he hanged himself in a local hotel.

The events in Bavaria, as in Germany at large, during these early postwar years allowed political reactionaries to direct their animus almost exclusively to the Jews. The entire revolutionary movement, they argued, could be attributed to this dangerous people. No distinction was made between the hard-edged bolshevism of Levien and Leviné, the vigorous but nonviolent messianism of Luxemburg and Paul Levi, the progressive leftism of Kurt Eisner, or even the bland social welfarism of Hugo Haase and Otto Haase, who sat in Chancellor Ebert's coalition cabinet. All of them sooner or later would perish at the hands of their political enemies. In German public consciousness, too, all of them—indeed, the Jews at large—were a people to be linked irredeemably with the terrifying peril of alien radicalism.

The Wages of Jewish Respectability

On January 19, 1919, the week following suppression of the Spartacist uprising in Berlin, the German people went to the voting booths and produced a solid triumph for Friedrich Ebert and the Social Democrat moderates. Moving to Weimar (to avoid intermittent political violence in the capital), the National Assembly drafted and approved a new constitution, then reconvened in Berlin in April as a normally functioning Reichstag. There, too, the government waited to learn Germany's fate at the hands of the Paris Peace Conference. That fate was decreed on June 28, 1919, when German representatives were ordered to affix their signatures to the Versailles Treaty.

Besides stripping Germany of its overseas empire and the provinces of Alsace and Lorraine, the document established a "Polish Corridor" across eastern Germany, internationalized the city of Danzig, demilitarized the Rhineland, and imposed heavy reparations obligations on the German government. Whether or not the treaty was unavoidable, the Social Democrats would not survive their identification with it. In the ensuing Reichstag elections of June 1920, their party lost sixty seats, as did their smaller allies, the Centrists and Democrats. By contrast, the two main conservative parties doubled their strength. Socially polarized, Germany had created a political monster, a Reichstag that henceforth would live on without a pro-democratic majority. The Weimar Republic would not overcome the crippling legacy of its birth.

Neither would the nation's Jews. Still a middle-class community, their social values had remained substantially *Mittelstand*, and even more substantially patriotic, well into the postwar era. In the early Weimar years, a majority of Jews continued to vote for the liberal Democratic Party. A prominent Jewish member of the party, Dr. Hugo Preuss, professor of jurisprudence at the Berlin College of Commerce, was the principal author of the Weimar Constitution. But the Jews were rapidly gaining visibility among the leadership of the leftist parties, including the Communists. Paul Levi would remain the party's chairman until well into the 1930s, and a substantial number of its Reichstag delegates also were Jews. Nevertheless, a far larger number of Jews were continuing their prewar gravitation to the Social Democrats (p. 312), and for the identical reasons of SPD commitment to egalitarianism and internationalism. Indeed, by 1925, Jews comprised 10 percent of the delegates to the Social Democratic congress. Of the sixty Jews who served intermittently in the Reichstag from 1919 to 1932, thirty-five were Social Democrats, while the rest were either Democrats or Communists.

In these same Weimar years, however, the leftward repositioning of Jewish political loyalties was accompanied by another, related development. This was the diminution of Jewish political influence altogether. After Kurt Joël, a nonparty appointee, held the justice portfolio in 1931–32, no Jew ever again served as a government minister, and the number of Jews in *Land* governments also steadily shrank. Fourteen Jews had sat in the first Reichstag, in 1920. In 1932, there was one. The ground-level shift of Jews to the political left, and the atrophy of Jewish political influence at the upper levels of government, were linked phenomena. Both reflected a dramatic upsurge of political and popular antisemitism.

The Politicization of Antisemitism

The chaos of the postwar period fostered Jew-hatred of a virulence unprecedented in modern German history. The animus drew from multiple sources. The most obvious, even the most simplistic, was the role of Jews in the left-wing extremism of the late teens and early 1920s. Another was the historic anti-Jewish bias of Germany's religious denominations, Protestant and Catholic alike. Racism played its insidious role, of course (pp. 250–51). So did the Pan-Germanist view of Jews as "internationalists" and "treasonous pacifists." Prewar conservatives had stigmatized liberalism as Jewish. Now, in the postwar, far-rightists devised the strategy of characterizing the entire Weimar experiment as nothing less than a "Jew Republic."

The antisemitic onslaught was orchestrated with authentic German efficiency. In February 1919, gathering in Hamburg as an antirevolutionary convention, a wide spectrum of far-rightist societies, leagues, and miniparties laid the groundwork for a German People's League for Protection and Defiance (Deutsch-völkisch Schutz- und Trotzbund). In ensuing months, the league itself served as the nucleus for a Community of German People's Unions (Gemeinschaft deutschvölkischer Bunden). By 1922, the "community" had grown to 250,000 members in 250 branches. All focused on the Jews: as war malingerers, profiteers, economic parasites, political subversives, internationalists, racial degenerates, and, above all, as the éminences grises behind the Weimar Republic.

It was in the 1920s that Jew-hatred acquired its highly politicized virulence, especially among the Kleinbürgertum, the members of the lower middle class, who had become déclassé as a consequence of the postwar inflation, and thus far more inclined than in earlier years to take compensatory solace in their "superior" racial pedigree. Prefigurations of this white-collar vindictiveness were particularly rampant among university students. Fear of Jewish professional competition was one factor, and another was a *völkisch* and increasingly racist version of romanticism. Under Weimar law, a numerus clausus was illegal in public universities. As a result, discrimination took the "social" form of excluding Jews from student societies and hazing them out of dormitories. Jewish professors also were harassed, even the mighty Einstein. Evincing a distaste for Jewish "modernism," "leftism," and racial "levantinism," large numbers of academicians began gravitating to the political right. Meanwhile, outside the universities, episodes of physical assaults were gaining momentum. On November 5, 1923, following the collapse of the German mark, several thousand impoverished Germans, blue- and white-collar alike, descended upon Berlin's Scheunenviertel district, inhabited principally by *Ostjuden,* and for two days beat hundreds of Jews and ransacked nearly a thousand Jewish shops before police managed to put an end to the violence.

Most ominous of all, amid the revolutionary and counterrevolutionary hatreds of the early postwar, was the mounting frequency of political assassinations—at least 375 between 1918 and 1922 alone—nearly all of them committed by rightist elements. Although one of the victims was Matthias Erzberger, the Catholic statesman who had signed the armistice document, the majority of these "executions" were committed against Jews. Most of the victims were political leftists, including Luxemburg, Eisner, Landauer, Mühsam, even Hugo Haase, the Independent Socialist who cochaired the Ebert cabinet. But the single most shocking assassination was that of a nonsocialist Jew.

Walther Rathenau, the austere, highly cultured director of AEG, a huge electrical conglomerate that was often described as "the General Electric of Germany," had volunteered his services to his government during the war. As the nation's industrial "tsar," Rathenau managed to allocate vital raw materials between civilian and military needs so effectively that the army gained possibly an extra year of fighting capacity. After the war, returning to his business empire, Rathenau in his early fifties was too restless and *engagé* a man to withdraw entirely from national affairs. Rather, he produced a sequence of books and articles offering imaginative social programs for the mutual benefit of capital and labor. One of Rathenau's ardent admirers was Josef Wirth, leader of the Catholic Center Party, who assumed the nation's chancellorship in May 1921. Soon after taking office, Wirth prevailed upon Rathenau to accept the portfolio of foreign minister. It was a shrewd move. The Treaty of Versailles had saddled Germany with an immense reparations burden. A man of Rathenau's economic experience was precisely the individual to grapple with this problem.

For his part, Rathenau understood that the best hope for alleviating reparations was to win the trust of the Allies through *Erfüllungspolitik,* a sincere effort to meet Germany's treaty obligations, and thereby persuade the Allies gradually to moderate their demands. But the effort proved unavailing. Finally, at an international monetary conference, meeting in Genoa in April 1922, Rathenau came up with a shrewd alternate strategy. One of the statesmen at the conference was the Soviet foreign commissar, Georgi Chicherin. Like Rathenau, Chicherin represented a nation that Europe had consigned to diplomatic pariahdom and commercial isolation. Thus, when Chicherin proposed a secret meeting with Rathenau at the nearby town of Rapallo, the German foreign minister agreed immediately. Within hours, the two men reached agreement. Their ensuing Treaty of Rapallo established diplomatic and trade relations between Germany and Soviet Russia. In a single brilliant coup de main, Rathenau and Chicherin breached the Allies' diplomatic-economic quarantine against their two nations.

Within Germany, however, Rathenau's achievement evoked sharply mixed reactions. It was praised by socialists and centrist-moderates. But right-wingers, long outraged at the very notion of *Erfüllungspolitik,* now seized upon the Rapallo Treaty to denounce Rathenau not only as a Jew but as a Bolshevik traitor. The foreign minister became a marked man. On the morning of June 24, 1922, as his chauffeured automobile pulled away from his home in a Berlin suburb, a group of young men, armed with pistols and grenades, lay in wait for him. They were members of the ultranationalist League of the Upright (Bund der Aufrechten), loosely associated with the Freikorps' sinister assassination unit, the Organization Consul. It was the latter's refrain that was widely invoked among Germany's ramifying network of political reactionaries:

> *Knallt ab den Walther Rathenau*
> *Die gottverdammte Judensau*
> *(Liquidate that Walther Rathenau*
> *The goddamned Jew-pig)*

And now, on the morning of June 24, 1922, the exhortation was carried out. Rathenau was cut down by a fusillade of bullets.

THE WELLSPRINGS OF ADOLF HITLER

In January 1923, after Weimar Germany failed to meet its treaty-mandated schedule of reparations payments, the French government responded with a simple but draconian solution. It dispatched an army of occupation to the German Ruhr to operate the great industrial zone's mills and mines under military direction, and physically to carry off the required coal and steel shipments to France. Hereupon, the fragile German economy imploded. In the most ruinous inflation of contemporary history, money lost all value. Life insurance policies, mortgages, annuities and other pensions, accumulated savings in cash and securities—all were transformed into worthless paper. With their disappearance, Germany's lower middle class, traditionally a bulwark of political conservatism, was left in ruin and desperation.

Not all wounds could be attributed to Allied vindictiveness. Some were self-inflicted. In the immediate postwar period, Friedrich Ebert's Social Democratic cabinet had moved vigorously to quash a series of Communist uprisings. Yet it was also the Ebert government that failed to move with comparable decisiveness against the German right. Almost predictably, then, the forces of reaction waited with ill-concealed impatience for their opportunity to return to power. The defenders of the former imperial regime, among them the judges and other mid-level bureaucrats, the senior Reichswehr officers, and the Prussian Junkers, were men of prestige, often of veneration. Presumably, they had to be treated with deference and circumspection. Even in the grimmest period of the inflation, therefore, the Social Democratic government never quite generated the courage to curtail the interlocking estates and industries that drew on the accumulated wealth of centuries of privileged aristocrats, or to dismiss those military and civilian officials who made no secret of their ideological commitment to the defunct empire.

With hardly an exception, moreover, the ingredients of gestating National Socialism—Nazism—traced back not to Allied retribution, nor even to Social Democratic political timorousness, but to the *Weltanschauung* of imperial Germany. These included the idealized Teutomania of mid-nineteenth-century romanticism (p. 248), Bismarck's autocratic-militaristic wizardry in building a *Machtstaat* that gloried in the benediction of a generation of intellectual yea-sayers, from Hegel to Nietzsche to Treitschke. In the same fin-de-siècle period, the Pan-Germans, committed to an expansion of the glittering new empire as far as the driving power of its industry and armed forces would permit, drew extensively from the Aryan mythology of Dühring, Chamberlain, Ahlwardt, Wagner, and other ideological racists.

Neither were there lacking quasi-scientific currents to feed into the cauldron of German racism. The eugenics movement, born in England (p. 249), was developing a unique orientation of its own in postwar Germany. Alfred Plötz, founder-editor of his country's principal eugenics journal, the *Archiv für Rassen-und Gesellschaftsbiologie,* argued that each generation could be assured its proper quotient of genetically healthy individuals by restricting fertilization to the "best" of the nation's pool of germ cells. If the proposal was of questionable morality or even practical feasibility, its attractiveness in Weimar Germany bespoke a gradual transformation of Galton's ideal of eugenics into the vision of *Rassenhygiene,* a term Plötz himself adopted. Led by Fritz Lenz, Erwin Bauer, and Eugen Fischer, other eugenicists of the postwar era accepted the notion that mighty Germany's recent military defeat was the consequence of biological degeneration, a phenomenon that in turn was the predictable consequence of racial impurity. "The Nordic race marches in the van of mankind," argued Lenz, depicting other races as lacking the indispensable Nordic capacity for genius, truth, honor, "civilization." Above all, Lenz warned against any mixture with Jews, a "mental race" that gained control of other peoples through cunning and economic parasitism. During the 1920s, such was the prestige of Lenz, Bauer, and Fischer's version of "racial science" that it came to be adopted wholesale by the Nazi movement.

Whatever the different interpretations of his biographers, there is a consensus that Adolf Hitler's life was decisively shaped by that racist ideology. The essential facts of his career are well known. Born in 1888 in Braunau, Austria, he was the son of a Habsburg customs official, a white-collar factotum who managed by and large to provide adequately for his family. As a student in gymnasium, Hitler displayed a genuine talent for art. Yet, arriving in Vienna in 1907, he failed to gain admission to the Academy of Fine Arts, and for the ensuing six years subsisted on the modest pension bequeathed by his late parents, and on the proceeds from watercolors he occasionally sold to art dealers. Although Hitler was living in Vienna when the war began in August 1914, he chose to enlist in the German Reichswehr, an alternative permitted by the Habsburg and German governments. Spending the ensuing four years on the Western Front, he fought bravely, and on the recommendation of his company commander, Lieutenant Gutmann, a Jew, he was awarded the Iron Cross.

It was shortly before the end of the war that Hitler was gassed and thus confined to a military hospital at the time of the armistice. Remaining in uniform after his recuperation, Hitler subsequently earned a few marks working for the Reichswehr intelligence service, which was intent on infiltrating suspect leftist movements. In the unit to which he was assigned, his company commander, seeking to test the thirty-year-old corporal's ideological bona fides, asked him to write his personal explanation for Germany's defeat in the war. Here it was, on September 16, 1919, in this lengthy memorandum, that Hitler's attitude toward the Jews first becomes evident. The Jews, he insisted, were exploiters who specialized in undermining their host nations by infecting them with a kind of racial tuberculosis. The solution to this danger was for Germany to adopt an "antisemitism of reason," a series of legal measures to eliminate Jews from all levels of the nation's economic and cultural life.

Beyond his lower-middle-class frustrations, and his exposure to the antisemitic ideologies of prewar Vienna (pp. 227–28), were there clues in Hitler's personal life for this sudden eruption of Jew-hatred? His mother's physician, Dr. Eduard Bloch, was a Jew, and was held in much esteem by the family. In Vienna, Jews were the only art dealers who purchased Hitler's paintings, and who treated him generously. It is more likely that his racism was sexual in origin. "For hours," he wrote in *Mein Kampf*, "the black-haired Jew-boy, diabolic joy in his face, waits in ambush for the unsuspecting girl whom he defiles with his blood. . . ." Elsewhere he wrote of the "nightmare vision of the seduction of hundreds of thousands of girls by repulsive, crook-legged Jew-bastards." Later in *Mein Kampf*, he referred to Jews as "the seducers of our people," and described the phenomenon as *Rassenschande*, racial shame.

Plainly, the fixation with "blood poisoning," with "racial pollution," or, more directly, with incest, occupied a central position in Hitler's thoughts. Relations in his family were so convoluted as to border on incest. It was uncertain whether Hitler's mother, Klara, was her husband's second cousin or niece. The relationship in any case was intimate enough to require an episcopal dispensation for marriage. There may also have existed a troubled relationship between Adolf Hitler and his own niece, Geli Raubal, the daughter of his half-sister Angela. Apparently, a love affair developed between them in Munich, where Hitler had settled in the late 1920s. Geli subsequently died of a bullet wound. Whether her death was suicide or murder, Hitler afterward sank into a profound depression. Both before and after this event, the fear of incest, of "blood poisoning," seemed to have obsessed him.

But "sociological" factors also shaped Hitler's views on the Jewish question, as he acknowledged in *Mein Kampf*. Living in Vienna before the war, he became familiar with the Jewish theories of Mayor Karl Lueger and of the Pan-Germanist Georg von Schönerer. He had already been repelled by Vienna's racial diversity, and specifically by the Galician-Jewish newcomers. It enraged him that the senseless constitutionalism of the Habsburg Empire permitted such "alien" types to be classed as citizens. From then on, by his own account, he regarded Jews as worthless middlemen, economic parasites, pornographers who contaminated German culture. Morally and physically repugnant, they defiled German women with their blood. "Gradually I began to hate them. . . . I was transformed from a weakly world citizen to a fanatic antisemite."

It was after the war, earning pocket money as an informer for the army, that Hitler happened across a small political faction that aroused his interest. It called itself the German Labor Party, and its leader, Gottfried Feder, a former lumberman, had come up with a populist, non-Marxist version of socialism that apparently borrowed some of its ideas from Karl Lueger's Christian Socialism. Hitler was struck, too, by Feder's distinction between *raffendes* (predatory) capitalism, which was Jewish, and *schaffendes* (creative, useful) capitalism, which was "German and Christian." Intrigued, Hitler joined the group as the seventh member of its executive committee. Brimming with enthusiasm and imagination, he soon managed to co-opt the leadership position from Feder. It was he personally who changed the group's name to the National Socialist German Workers' Party, who laid renewed emphasis upon revision of the hated *Diktat* of Versailles, and selected the "Aryan" swastika as the party's logo.

In February 1920, Hitler also reworked the Nazi program to ensure that six of its twenty-five points were explicitly or implicitly devoted to Jews. Thus, Article 4 denied the Jew, no matter how venerable his ancestry in Germany, the right to full citizenship. Article 5 applied the lowly status of aliens to noncitizens (most of whom were Polish Jews), who would live in Germany on sufferance alone, and under special laws. Article 7 demanded the expulsion of all aliens in periods of economic distress. Article 8 called for the expulsion of those non-Germans who had entered Germany since the war. Aricle 23 sought to ensure the "purity" of the German press by eliminating non-Germans from journalistic positions. Finally, Article 24 called on all Germans to preserve Christianity by maintaining a ceaseless struggle against "the Jewish materialistic spirit." In later years, still other "Jewish" articles and amendments would be added to the program.

From the very outset of his political career, Hitler exhibited a shrewd insight into the German mentality. He swiftly came up with the notion of giving his followers uniforms, and dubbing them storm troopers (Sturm Abteilung), an innovation that appealed to the nation's lumpenproletariat possibly more even than Nazism's rather turgid platform of chauvinism and antisemitism. By 1923, the party's membership had grown to 11,000. In November of that year, determined to exploit the fragility of Bavaria's relationship with Prussian-dominated northern Germany, Hitler and his group launched an attempted putsch in Munich. Impetuous as it was, the uprising enjoyed the participation of several prestigious figures, among them Field Marshal Erich Ludendorff, the air force ace Hermann Göring, and other admired former military figures. But the putsch failed. The Bavarian police easily dispersed Hitler's followers, and most of them fled ignominiously into side streets, and eventually into self-imposed exile.

Hitler was one of the few plotters who was arrested. His trial, in February 1924, gave him a platform and a national audience for Nazi propaganda. Reviewing the sorry state of affairs in Germany, the thirty-five-year-old fire-brand denounced the policies of the Weimar Republic and boldly predicted that he would come to power despite his judges. In fact, his judges, veterans of the imperial civil service, were sympathetic. They sentenced Hitler to a paltry thirty months of imprisonment, and he was paroled after only nine months. Moreover, Hitler used those months to political advantage. It was then that he dictated his political autobiography, *Mein Kampf,* to his cellmate Rudolf Hess. Besides its surfeit of nationalist and racist antisemitism, the book also included a feature that had come to Hitler's attention only recently. This was *The Protocols of the Elders of Zion.* He acknowledged now that the machinations of the Elders of Zion represented the supreme expression of the Jewish race. This was a world conspiracy, the product of the ineradicable will to evil inborn in every Jew. A colleague of Hitler's in the early Nazi Party, the journalist Dietrich Eckhart, later would argue that it was Hitler's genius to combine the *Protocols* with *völkisch*-racist ideas to formulate the entirety of his philosophy of history.

THE TRIUMPH OF NAZISM

Upon his release from prison on Christmas Eve, 1924, Hitler settled in a modest Berlin apartment. He lived comfortably by then, drawing a respectable salary from the party. But his political future remained uncertain. Although the Nazis' membership had climbed dramatically to 108,000 by 1928, it had returned a mere 12 delegates to the Reichstag. The national economy, profiting from a relaxation of reparations obligations and by substantial American investments, enjoyed a modest recovery. For the while, Nazis and Communists alike were consigned to the political margins. The world Depression changed all that, of course. In Germany, as elsewhere, political extremists suddenly achieved a new credibility. The lower middle class, struggling to recover from the postwar inflation, now fell back again into despair. They were joined by millions of fellow citizens of all backgrounds, as unemployment in Germany reached 6 million by 1930 and 9 million by 1932.

Under the circumstances, Nazi strength revived spectacularly, climbing to 107 Reichstag delegates in 1930. Once again, it was Hitler who personally orchestrated the party parades and pageantry, replete with torchlights, armed storm troopers, and military bands. With his commitment to *schaffendes* capitalism, and his execration of "Asian bolshevism," he was also winning important financial support from the billionaire cartelists Fritz Thyssen, Emile Kordorf, and Alfred Hugenberg. It was this amplitude of financing that helped make possible the Nazis' extraordinary return to political credibility in

1930, giving them their 107 seats in the Reichstag and transforming them almost overnight into Germany's third-largest political party. It was a growth that was further underscored by the government's sheer ineptitude in coping with the nation's mounting unemployment. Thus, in 1932 alone, three more elections followed—two for president, one for a new Reichstag. In the first election, Hitler himself had the temerity to campaign against the incumbent president, the revered General Paul von Hindenburg, and polled an astonishing 11 million votes in March and over 13 million in the runoff in April. In the Reichstag election in August, the Nazis won 12.7 million votes and 230 seats, the largest number won by any party in the brief history of the republic.

Yet, even in the spring of 1932, Hitler was not called upon to form a government. The little cabal of National Party leaders that dominated the senile old president exhausted their ingenuity to avoid bringing Hitler into office. Moreover, Hindenburg regarded the Nazis with grave trepidation. Their nihilistic racism shocked and alarmed him. In August 1932, shortly after the Nazis won their massive 230-seat return, he responded to Jewish appeals by letting it be known that he opposed any attempt to restrict the constitutional rights of "our Jewish citizens, who have contributed to Germany's cause so gallantly on the battlefields of the recent war." But Hindenburg, and the Jews, underestimated their mutual vulnerability.

The 1925 census listed the number of Jews in Germany at 568,000. In 1933, as a consequence of immigration to the Americas and elsewhere, their population may have dipped slightly to perhaps 530,000. The figure in any case represented barely 1 percent of the German population, and even this proportion would have been smaller had it not been for the earlier influx of 50,000 to 60,000 wartime refugees from Poland. Yet the Jews' modest demography was belied by their unparalleled visibility. Here was a people that had become almost entirely urbanized. By 1925, over 70 percent of German Jews lived in cities of 100,000 or more. Their vocational profile was overwhelmingly middle class. Approximately 60 percent of Jewish breadwinners were engaged in commerce, with another 22 percent listed in the professions. Moreover, it was their middle-class status that drew attention to the seeming disproportion of Jews in the postwar German economy. As late as 1930, Jews owned almost half of Germany's textile companies, a quarter of its wholesale food companies, two-thirds of the nation's larger department and chain stores. Although no longer preserving their former dominance in banking, renowned financial families such as the Mendelssohns, Bleichröders, Schlesingers, and Warburgs owned half the country's private banks. Jews dominated the publishing sector. Germany's two largest publishing houses, Ullstein and Mosse, were Jewish-owned, and Jewish journalists remained overwhelmingly prominent in the liberal and left-wing press. Elsewhere in the professions, Jews by 1930 represented 11 percent of Germany's doctors, 16 percent of its lawyers and notaries, and more than 50 percent of the lawyers in Berlin (p. 446).

Yet statistics alone did not give an accurate picture of Jewish economic vulnerability. The great majority of Jewish businessmen operated small-scale enterprises. The typical Jewish merchant was a modest shopkeeper, who was as exposed to the vicissitudes of the economy as any other German. During the postwar inflation, Jews suffered in the identical proportions as non-Jews. In 1923, Berlin's Jewish Cultusverein had to maintain nineteen soup kitchens and seven homeless shelters. A decade later, the Depression would leave 60,000 German Jews unemployed. As elsewhere in Europe, however, non-Jews knew only what they saw; and in good times and bad, they saw Jewish names on shops, and on commercial and professional offices. In the Depression, economic vindictiveness alone would have fueled German antisemitism. Widely infused with racism, the animus now achieved an unsurpassed political dynamism.

Even then, Hitler's political success could by no means be attributed exclusively to the manipulation of antisemitism. Jew-hatred, after all, was only one of many planks in the Nazi platform. Nor were its other planks, chauvinism and populism, unique to the Nazi political program. Rather, it was Hitler's genius to link all the party's inducements—chauvinism, populism, white-collar vindictiveness—to a single enemy. Antisemitism could not by itself have won over so wide a conglomeration of voters of all backgrounds. It was antisemitism that reinforced all the other features of the Nazi agenda: the *Jewish* Bolshevik, the *Jewish* capitalist, the *Jewish* department-store owners, the *Jewish* "November criminal," the *Jewish* blood polluter of an Aryan nation. As the historian Karl Schleunes has brilliantly shown, antisemitism permitted Hitler to obfuscate the fact that Nazism was all things to all people. These were the circumstances, both of antisemitism and of political sleight of hand, that Hitler exploited in his final drive to the chancellorship.

On January 30, 1933, the little governmental cabal of Franz von Papen, Kurt von Schleicher, and their industrial bankrollers "inveigled" Hitler—so they believed—into accepting the provisional leadership of a coalition government that they fully intended to control. With a Reichstag election scheduled for March 5, Hitler's sponsors confidently anticipated that the balance of power would shift to the Nationalists or to other rightist factions. On the evening of the Nazi triumph, therefore, as thousands of torchbearers, swastikas on their armbands, marched exultantly along the Wilhelmstrasse, and the new chancellor bowed for hours from his balcony window, the politicians who had engineered his incumbency remained unfazed. They were confident that they had brought a puppet to office.

HITLER'S JEWISH POLICY IN ADMINISTRATIVE ACTION

Within one month of his appointment to office, the new chancellor revealed himself as far more adroit and ruthless a political tactician than his National-ist patrons had ever imagined. In organizing his campaign for the scheduled Reichstag elections, he well understood that he was running the risk of still another political standoff. It was not a gamble he was prepared to take. He had appointed his close associate Hermann Göring as minister of the inte-rior, and with that portfolio, Göring moved swiftly to take full personal con-trol of the Prussian police force. At his decree, the "auxiliary" police (actually, the Sturm Abteilung) set about breaking up meetings of opposition parties. On February 27, moreover, less than a week before the elections, there came a "sign from heaven." The Reichstag building was mysteriously set ablaze. Although it still remains uncertain that the arson was executed by the Nazis themselves, the event ideally served their purpose. That same day, broad-casting to a terror-stricken nation, Hitler charged the Communists with the crime, ostensibly as part of their attempt to take over the country. At his request, President Hindenburg agreed to a series of emergency decrees restricting freedom of speech, press, and assembly. Most of the Communist leaders then were arrested.

Remarkably, the Communists still managed to win eighty-one mandates in the ensuing elections. But inasmuch as they were never permitted to take their seats in the Reichstag, the Nazis, with 44 percent of the seats, obtained a working legislative majority. Afterward, Hitler bought off the Catholic Cen-trists by negotiating a Concordat with the papacy (p. 485), thereby, on March 23, achieving the larger, two-thirds majority he needed to win passage of an all-important Enabling Act. Emulating the precedent initially adopted by Mussolini in Italy, Hitler exploited the Enabling Act to secure legislation by decree, and the Reichstag accordingly was reduced to a meaningless political appendix. In August 1934, moreover, following the death of President Hindenburg, Hitler combined the offices of president and chancellor, assum-ing the title of führer. The Nazi dictatorship was now in place.

German Jewry lived through these early months of the Nazi regime in an agony of uncertainty. Would the ax fall on them? Not immediately, it seemed. Hitler's initial priorities were to consolidate his power. Uninterested in clut-tering up his program with an anti-Jewish purge, he spoke only vaguely of depriving Jews of their "privileges" through "administrative, legal means." Yet Hitler also knew that he had to propitiate the SA, the storm-troop element that had played a key role in his ascent to power. These uniformed thugs were brimming with explosive anti-Jewish enthusiasm, and mere administrative measures scarcely could assuage an organization schooled in terror. Indeed, during the first two weeks of March, the SA on its own embarked on a spontaneous anti-Jewish rampage. Local storm trooper units, eager for blood and pillage, often simply kidnapped individual Jews and demanded ransom from the families, or dragged Jewish lawyers and doctors into the street and disrobed them in public; or invaded Jewish-owned department stores, creating havoc by intimidating customers.

Hitler did not approve of these tactics. He was concerned that they might sabotage the "legitimacy" of his regime. For the moment, however, he could not quite afford a showdown with Ernst Röhm, the SA commander and a close ally. But perhaps he could buy time by steering the storm troopers' passion into less destructive channels. Thus, on March 26, he acquiesced in a nationwide boycott of Jewish businessmen and professionals. Under the direction of Julius Streicher, editor of the SA weekly *Der Stürmer* (and arguably Germany's most rabid antisemite), "Boycott Day" was launched on April 1. The original intention was for the boycott to continue indefinitely, until Jews had been eliminated from the German economy altogether. But when rumors of the plan leaked on March 28, prices on the Berlin stock exchange dropped, and Foreign Minister Konstantin von Neurath urged Hitler to modify his approach. Hitler agreed. He limited the boycott to a single day. It was a day that began with SA men taking up positions in front of every Jewish store and office, with the purpose simply of "dissuading" citizens from entering. Yet discipline soon was abandoned. Windows were broken, graffiti were painted on stores, and acts of physical abuse became rampant. When the German public reacted coldly to the hooliganism, the boycott was canceled before the day was out. From then on, all anti-Jewish measures would follow bureaucratic, "legal" procedures.

Within the next months, therefore, a series of laws dismissed "non-Aryans" from the civil service, including all teaching professions and government medical and juridical programs. A minuscule Jewish numerus clausus, 1.5 percent of the student body, was established in public and private educational institutions. Other administrative anti-Jewish measures followed in the next year. By autumn 1934, the entire process of categorization, separation, and exclusion was completed with "legal" precision. Ironically, it was that very façade of legality that convinced most Jews that their future in Germany was not yet foreclosed. In the private sector, it appeared that Jewish business and professional activity might still continue without interference, that the worst of Nazi antisemitic "legislation" was over. In spite of a sharp initial spike in emigration, most Jews were prepared to remain on in Germany.

Little time passed before the ground shifted under their feet. No determination had yet been made on the racial factors that constituted a Jew. But in September 1935, addressing the annual Nazi Party rally in Nuremberg, Hitler informed his audience that a new "clarification" had been reached on the Jewish issue. It took the form of a "Law for the Protection of German Blood and Honor" (Gesetz zum Schutz des deutschen Blutes und der deutschen Ehre), actually an ongoing series of four racial laws and thirteen supplemental decrees that extended into 1936. A key feature laid down that "non-Aryans" henceforth were to be divided into two categories: Jews and *Mischlinge* (individuals of mixed blood). Jews were defined as those who descended from at least three "racially" Jewish grandparents, or from two "racially" Jewish grandparents whose Aryan spouses had become members of the organized Jewish religious community. "Half-Jews" were those who descended from three racially Jewish grandparents, or from two racial and professing Jews who did not belong to the Jewish religion. Such half-Jews were to be categorized as *Mischlinge* of the "first degree." One-quarter Jews became *Mischlinge* of the "second degree."

Under these definitions, the Nuremberg Laws deprived racially identified Jews of their German citizenship. From then on, as mere "nationals," they were stripped of all residual political rights, including pension rights. Other social and economic deprivations prohibited marriage and extramarital relations between Jews and non-Jews, banned Jews from the practice of medicine, except for a limited number of doctors who ministered exclusively to Jewish patients. Subsequent regulations and "clarifications" excluded Jews from places of public entertainment, from public swimming pools and parks. Jewish Cultusgemeinden, official Jewish communal organizations, were divested of taxation authority, and thus of their ability to fund their programs and institutions. For identification purposes, Jewish males were to bear the name "Israel," and Jewish females, the name "Sarah."

The year 1936 witnessed a brief lull in the regime's Jewish legislation, to avoid a public relations crisis in the period before the Berlin Olympics. But in 1937 and 1938, seeking to drive Jews into the larger urban centers, the government ordered the dissolution of all Jewish businesses and the sale of all Jewish homes outside the cities. Even within the cities, new decrees required Jewish owners of such larger-scale enterprises as department stores and banks to place their holdings "in trust" with Aryan administrators. Jews were forced out of their last remaining professional activities, even among Jewish patients and clients—out of medicine, dentistry, law, and accounting. By 1939, as a consequence of this sequence of economic hammer blows, approximately one-third of all Jews living in Germany were reduced to destitution and dependence upon communal assistance.

At first, Jewish reaction was confused and ambivalent. Before 1933, German Jewry possessed no central institution in the manner of French Jewry's Consistoire Israélite or Anglo-Jewry's Board of Deputies. Their communal structure, like that of the German government, was highly federalized. In September 1933, Jewish leaders managed to patch together an emergency organization, the Reich Representative Council of German Jews (Reichsvertretung der deutschen Juden), to deal with the government. But the Reichsvertretung had no constitution or fixed rules. Even one of its logical responsibilities, the management of immigration to Palestine, continued to be handled exclusively by the German Zionist Organization, and immigration elsewhere remained under the direction of the venerable Hilfsverein. In 1938, moreover, the government narrowed the Reichsvertretung's function essentially to the publication and clarification of official rules and regulations on the Jews.

A somewhat more effective Jewish response was the proliferation of mutual support groups. In a newly shared sense of Jewish identity, rich and poor alike tended now to come together more naturally and frequently. In one community after another, synagogues and Jewish *Lehrhäuser*—adult education institutes—reported an upsurge of seminars in Jewish history, culture, and Zionism. Jewish artists devoted their talents increasingly to Jewish themes. Under Zionist auspices, Jewish sports organizations multiplied. Entirely spontaneously, without funds or certainty of immigration opportunities, Jews in growing numbers made plain their determination not to go quietly into the German night.

GERMAN JEWRY IN FINAL TRANSITION

As late as 1934, some 505,000 identified Jews remained in Germany, although others, nonidentified or half-Jewish, may have raised the figure by another 30,000 or 40,000. By 1939, approximately 230,000 of these people had emigrated. The pace of their emigration was erratic, however. The explanation lay not only in the difficulty of securing asylum. On the one hand, the government encouraged Jewish departure. On the other, it gave pause to all but the most affluent by imposing heavy "emigration taxes" on them, and partial or even total confiscation of property. Thus, in 1933, some 37,000 Jews departed, then 23,000 in 1934, and 21,000 in 1935. Even after 1935, when the impact of the Nuremberg Laws began to be felt, the rate of departures was uneven: 25,000 in 1936, and 23,000 in 1937. Until 1938, moreover, the Nazi regime was content simply to wear the Jews down through economic desperation, rather than to expel them at the point of a gun. Even the tactic of ruining Jews economically was cautious until Economics Minister Hjalmar Schacht was dismissed in September 1937. Between 1933 and early 1938, therefore, as more than 150,000 Jews departed Germany, a majority of the Jewish population remained in place.

It was the winter of 1937–38 that became the dividing line in the Nazis' Jewish policy. By then, Hitler had successfully defied the Versailles Powers by introducing military conscription and sending his troops into the Rhineland.

Exultant at his success, the führer saw no further need for moderation in either domestic or foreign policy. Thus, in preparation for additional expansion into Austria and Czechoslovakia, he set about purging all the "moderates" from office, among them, Schacht, Generals Blomberg and Fritsch, and Foreign Minister von Neurath. The hard-core Nazi "radicals" soon were in full control of the government, and this change also produced a radicalization in the government's approach to the Jews. Beginning in 1938, Reichsmarshal Hermann Göring became Hitler's chief policy-maker on Jewish issues. Although he held no official designation in fulfilling this role, it was Göring who lent the anti-Jewish program a new intensity. In some measure, he was responding to the demographic consequences of Germany's recent diplomatic triumphs. The Anschluss with Austria in March 1938 undercut the work of over five years of Jewish emigration from Germany, for it brought 240,000 new Jews into the Nazi empire, and soon even this number would more than double with the ingestion of Czechoslovakia. It was time to become even more remorseless with the Jews, to find ways of driving them from the Greater Reich by every resource of economic compulsion and physical brutality.

Thus, on March 27, 1938, two weeks after the Anschluss, Göring informed his associates that the entirety of Austria's 240,000 Jews should be removed without further delay. Their expulsion must be swift and total. Hereupon, the Nazis launched into a campaign of Jewish delegitimization that they had not yet displayed in Germany proper. With a renewed and single-minded efficiency, they began closing down Jewish businesses and professional offices and seizing Jewish property outright. An SS major, Adolf Eichmann, who worked for the Reich Main Security Office (RSHA)—an umbrella organization for the SS, the Gestapo, and for other police or quasi-police agencies— was put in charge of the Central Office for Jewish Emigration in Vienna. Eichmann's mandate was unequivocal. It was to remove the Jews from Austria by any and all means.

To that end, setting himself up in a former Rothschild mansion, Eichmann operated with an eerie, assembly-line efficiency in administering the mass expulsions. Thousands of Jews were simply rounded up in buses and trains and dumped across Austria's borders. Other thousands were given the choice of leaving the country immediately or suffering concentration-camp imprisonment. Within six months, Eichmann managed by these means to expel at least 50,000 Jews from Austria, most of them in a state of destitution. By November 1939, when emigration was largely choked off by the war, no fewer than 118,000 Jews had been driven out or had fled. By the same token, following Hitler's occupation of Czechoslovakia in March 1939, that nation's 360,000 Jews confronted an identical fate. Czech-Jewish business offices and homes were subjected to a frenzy of confiscations that made no pretense, as in

Germany, of Aryan "trusteeships." If nearly 200,000 Jews still remained in Czechoslovakia as late as autumn 1939, the reason lay only in the shorter time span before World War II began.

The model of frontal ruination and expulsion adopted in Austria, and later in Czechoslovakia, soon was applied to Germany itself. Gradualism, incrementalism, Aryan "trusteeships"—all now would go by the board. Henceforth, Jews were obliged to register all their property holdings valued at over 5,000 marks, in effect, virtually anything and everything. With these lists of Jewish assets, the government set about an immediate process of confiscation. Pauperization, then abject destitution, soon became an irresistible inducement for mass and immediate departure. There were also other inducements. Until 1938, physical brutality had not yet played a decisive role in German-Jewish emigration. But in August of that year, Göring made plain his intention to launch a "fundamental cleanup" *(grundlegende Vereinigung)* of the Jewish question. The catalyst was provided in November.

Months earlier, in March 1938, at the time of the Anschluss, Hitler had incorporated into the Greater Reich not only the Jews of Austria but approximately 20,000 Polish Jews, expatriates who for years had been living in Vienna. At this point, the Polish government, determined not to allow these former citizens to flee Hitler and return home, gave them a deadline of October 30, 1938, to revalidate their Polish passports. Warsaw knew full well that most Jews would not have time to complete the deliberately complex bureaucratic procedures, and that most of them in any case would take the chance of remaining in Austria. Yet the German government, determined not to allow them that chance, ordered that they be immediately rounded up and deported back to Poland. Thus, on the night of October 28–29, a series of widespread police raids corralled some 18,000 Polish Jews, many dressed only in their bedclothes. They were hustled into sealed trains and carried off immediately to the Polish frontier. Here many of them were literally pushed across the border at the point of a gun. At most frontier crossings, however, Polish police managed to keep them out. Eventually, these doubly unwanted families were shunted into makeshift frontier holding pens, where they faced exposure and starvation.

A seventeen-year-old Polish Jew, Herschel Grynszpan, studying in France, learned that his parents and sister were among these interned Jewish victims. On November 7, crazed with grief, he walked into the German embassy in Paris and asked to see the ambassador. Instead, he was directed to the office of a minor official, Ernst vom Rath. The youth then pulled a revolver from his briefcase and shot Rath fatally. Upon learning of the episode, Hitler decided to exploit it by authorizing the SA to "have a fling." The "fling" was an unprecedented paroxysm of destruction on November 9–10, 1938. During those night hours, the storm troopers conducted a nationwide pogrom, smashing the windows of Jewish businesses and of many Jewish homes, burning and gutting most of Germany's five hundred remaining synagogues, as well as dozens of other Jewish communal institutions. The littered shards of broken glass, glittering like crystal, gave the night its sobriquet, Kristallnacht. Over 30,000 Jews were jailed in concentration camps, half of them never to return. Göring then compounded the horror by imposing a 1 billion mark "fine" on the Jews for "cleanup" expenses—this in addition to the expenses Jews incurred for repairing the damage to their homes or businesses. Some quarter-billion marks in personal insurance claims also were forfeited to the state.

Ironically, soon after Kristallnacht, Hitler criticized the "haphazard" approach to Jewish policy and demanded that "the Jewish question . . . once and for all be coordinated or solved in one way or another." To that end, Göring now formally and officially assumed responsibility for "solving" the Jewish question and focused all his attention exclusively on emigration. It was then, too, impressed by Adolf Eichmann's success in Vienna, that Göring ordered Reinhard Heydrich, chief of the Reich Main Security Office, to have Eichmann relocate his Central Office for Jewish Emigration to Berlin. Thus, by March 1939, operating out of the German capital, Heydrich and Eichmann pressed ahead with their customary brutality and efficiency. Under their direction, Gestapo teams adopted the "Austrian approach" of dumping Jews across frontiers at gunpoint, hustling them into chartered German and Italian tramp steamers to be carried off—usually without foreign visas of any kind—to Western ports for transshipment abroad. At all costs, and by any means, the Reich was to be cleansed of the last of its Jews before the führer launched upon the reconfiguration of Europe altogether.

XXVI

The Quest for Sanctuary: 1933–1939

A Failure of European Refuge

In the brief period between Kristallnacht and the outbreak of war, approximately 80,000 Jews left Germany, raising to 230,000 the number who emigrated in the years 1933–39. Refugees from Austria and Czechoslovakia brought the total figure to roughly 350,000 in this same period. Yet, as late as October 1941, an estimated 263,000 Jews remained in Germany, between 190,000 and 200,000 in Czechoslovakia, and 80,000 in Austria. Most of these people would not survive. Neither would the largest numbers of Jews who were driven to neighboring countries in the period between Kristallnacht and September 1, 1939. When the German Wehrmacht later overran these nations, refugee Jews would be their first civilian victims.

During the 1920s and early 1930s, France had remained Western Europe's most dependable haven for political and religious refugees. Its hospitality manifestly represented less compassion than demographic self-interest (p. 476). Nevertheless, from the mid-1930s on, even France gradually succumbed to right-wing pressures, and with the fall of the Léon Blum government in 1937, restrictions against fugitive Jews tightened to the point of closure. Altogether, not more than 30,000 Jews from the Greater Reich were given legal admission to France after 1933, although possibly another 20,000 to 25,000 managed to reach the country illegally and to remain on clandestinely (again, to become early victims of the ensuing German conquest).

Unlike France, Britain after World War I no longer was inclined to accept religious or political refugees. The country's immigration restrictions were gradually tightened. In the 1930s, with the economy mired in the Depression, there appeared no serious likelihood of a change in government policy. Seeking to modify that implacable stance, Anglo-Jewry's Board of Deputies in 1933 promised the Home Office that all expenses of accommodating Jewish refugees would be borne by the Jewish community itself. The offer was politely declined. The number of Jews admitted into the country did not exceed 5,000 in each of the next five years. Only in late 1938, following the

Kristallnacht crisis, did the Home Office agree to a partial relaxation of its stringent quotas. It admitted 10,000 Jewish children, together with 6,000 adult Jews. Yet the move was not altogether one of compassion. It was also taken essentially in recompense for the Chamberlain government's recent decision to close off Palestine to Jewish immigration (p. 525). By the time World War II began, a thin dispersion of some 110,000 Jewish refugees was strung out across Europe. Overseas, Argentina and Brazil each accepted approximately 10,000 Jews; South Africa, 5,000; and Canada and Australia, about 2,000.

One of the more significant areas of refuge, ironically, turned out to be the unlikeliest. This was China, and specifically Shanghai, whose 4 million inhabitants by 1933 already included approximately 100,000 foreigners. Impoverished, squalid, crime-ridden, Shanghai nonetheless possessed a unique advantage for Jews and other refugees. It was an "open" city, virtually the only place in the world requiring no visas or other documentation for entry. Even before 1933, some 4,000 Jewish refugees from the Russian civil war were living there. In 1936, the Japanese army occupied the city. Its presence at first had little effect on the Jews, most of whom resided in the International Settlement area that was controlled in effect by representatives of the major powers. It was in this period, however, that Jewish refugees from Central Europe began entering Shanghai in large numbers, particularly after the Anschluss and Kristallnacht. Thus, by 1939, approximately 17,000 new Jewish fugitives had arrived, to vegetate in a state of abject poverty. In 1940, through Red Cross auspices, the Joint Distribution Committee negotiated a fascinating contract with the Japanese. By its terms, the Japanese agreed to extend credit to Jewish relief organizations in Shanghai in sums equivalent to $25,000 a month— the so-called Shanghai dollars—until hostilities ended in Asia. Afterward, the Joint would repay the Japanese. Both sides honored the agreement. The Jews of Shanghai survived the war. The postwar Japanese government was reimbursed.

During the 1930s, meanwhile, even as some 130,000 Jews negotiated sanctuary in European, Latin American, and Asian havens, there remained hundreds of thousands of others from the Greater Reich who lingered in a twilight world between life and death. With the nations of the free world struggling to recover from the Depression and confronting their own varieties of embittered chauvinism, refugee Jews were the last encumbrance they wanted. Significant was the fate of the autonomous Office of High Commissioner for Refugees from Germany. Established in 1933, this was a curious, hybrid institution. Although it invoked the moral authority of the postwar League of Nations Refugee (Nansen) Commission, the new entity was not an official component of the League. Rather, it was funded by several charitable foundations, most of these underwritten by Jewish groups, and allowed a dotted-line accreditation to work "in cooperation" with the League. Its high commissioner, James McDonald, a former Columbia University professor, was charged with the task of coordinating the efforts of the various private refugee organizations, of negotiating passports, visas, laissez-passers, work permits, and temporary residence certificates. In fact, McDonald achieved a few modest successes, winning sanctuary for several thousand—mostly Jewish—refugees in Australia, South Africa, and Latin America. But in 1935 an upsurge of Rumanian and Hungarian antisemitism intensified emigrationist pressures. The situation became unmanageable, with all doors closing even tighter. In November, a frustrated McDonald stepped down as high commissioner.

Three years later, in March 1938, eleven days after the German-Austrian Anschluss, President Franklin Roosevelt in Washington endorsed a new approach to the refugee issue. Suggested to him by Undersecretary of State Sumner Welles, it was to call an international conference on refugees. Conceivably, such a gathering might yet produce alternate sanctuaries. In ensuing weeks, invitations went out to some fifty governments, including Germany's. Thirty of these agreed to participate (Germany's not among them). The meeting would take place in early July, in the French resort town of Évian-les-Bains. Yet virtually all the participating governments, including the American, were adamant that their own countries would not become refugee havens. London added a warning that the question of immigration to Palestine must not be raised.

Inhibited by these limitations, the Évian Conference was further afflicted by a bias that was scarcely disguised. The Australian delegate stated plain-spokenly that "as we have no real racial problem in Australia, we are not desirous of importing one." The Canadian delegate repeated the observation of Frederick Blair, his nation's commissioner of immigration, that the Jews themselves were responsible for their suffering (Prime Minister Mackenzie King earlier had asserted that the Jews were a people who were bound to pollute Canada's "bloodstream"). The conference's single accomplishment was to establish the Intergovernmental Committee on Refugees, with headquarters in London, and to endow this body with a mandate to seek out employment opportunities for refugees in countries that already had accepted them. The committee's subsequent discussions concentrated almost exclusively on the need to persuade Berlin to "alter" its Jewish policy.

AN EQUIVOCAL AMERICAN SANCTUARY

In the aftermath of the Évian failure, Franklin Roosevelt responded to Jewish and liberal appeals by directing Sumner Welles to explore alternate sites for Jewish colonization "in any part of the world." The president also consulted his immigration expert, Professor Isaiah Bowman of Johns Hopkins University, on the possibility of havens in Central America, in Tanganyika, even in Italian-ruled Ethiopia (Mussolini coldly ignored a letter from the White House on this proposal). At all times, Roosevelt's overriding objective was to avoid raising immigration issues in the United States. In no sense was the president indifferent to the plight of European Jews. Yet, in assiduously seeking out alternate sanctuaries for them, he was equally sensitive to the realities of American politics and public opinion. Even as late as 1938, the United States had not managed to free itself from the crippling Depression. Millions of its citizens, still unemployed, did not react congenially to the prospect of immigrant competition in the labor market.

Additionally, the resentments of an economically unrecovered nation provided fertile ground for nativist and antisemitic elements. In the latter 1930s, one of these was a charismatic Catholic priest, Charles Coughlin, an economic populist and spellbinding orator. Coughlin broadcast weekly on a radio network he himself had put together, execrating Roosevelt's monetary policies by identifying them with Jewish bankers and the New Deal's highly visible minority of Jewish technocrats. Coughlin's oratory appealed widely to low-income Irish Catholics, whose ethnic distaste for Jews was further inflamed by abhorrence of Jewish political leftism. It was in any case galling for this city people, who once had flourished as the dominant political force among America's urban immigrants, to have to share municipal patronage with Jews. By 1939, led by activists in Coughlin's neofascist Christian Front organization, some fifty rallies were taking place weekly in New York alone, arousing an ominous upsurge of threats and even physical violence against Jews.

While Coughlin's Christian Front was the largest and best organized of the anti-Jewish factions, smaller xenophobic organizations were not lacking, among them such populist and conspiratorialist leagues as Gerald Winrod's Defenders of the Christian Faith, Billy James Hargis's Christian Crusade, William Dudley Pelley's Silver Shirt Legion, and George Deatherage's Patriotic Defenders. In the years before 1932, only five or six antisemitic factions of any size had existed in the United States. Between 1933 and 1940 the number exceeded 1,000. None of them was quite politically potent enough to win a congressional election. But if the United States generated no sustained right-wing movement, its hate cabals in the bleak Depression years poisoned the national atmosphere against Jews even more extensively than in the early 1920s, when Henry Ford was publishing and widely distributing *The Protocols of the Elders of Zion.*

Far more than in any earlier era, too, populist antisemitism had its spokesmen in Congress, particularly from the more insular and agrarian southern and far western states. Franklin Roosevelt depended upon these economically straitened regions to help put through his New Deal domestic legislation. None, he knew, would tolerate a relaxation of immigration quotas for Jews. Even Judge Samuel Rosenman, a presidential adviser and speechwriter, and himself a prominent member of the veteran German-Jewish establishment, warned the president that any effort to tamper with immigration quotas could be politically dangerous.

In the original restrictionist legislation of 1917, 1921, and 1924, those quotas had been aimed specifically against immigrants from Eastern and Southern Europe (p. 384). The quotas from "Nordic" Western Europe initially were less stringent. But in 1932, as the Depression worsened, the Hoover administration issued a directive that reinterpreted a key provision in the three immigration acts. That provision initially had authorized the government to reject any immigrant who posed the "likelihood" of becoming a public charge. The Hoover Directive now substituted the word "possibility" for "likelihood." It was this "public charge" clause that soon became the nemesis of German-Jewish refugees. As a consequence of its alteration, the numbers of German-Jewish immigrants rose only modestly, from 1,372 in 1933 to 4,137 in 1934 and to 4,837 in 1935—numbers far lower than those actually permitted under the Western European quota. Nor would that quota ever be filled. Congress would not permit Roosevelt to alter the Hoover Directive.

Still another factor sabotaged the president's efforts to introduce flexibility into the immigration quotas. It was the obdurateness of State Department bureaucrats. Largely of Old American stock, these officials evinced a thinly veiled distaste for Jews, and ensured that the Hoover Directive was followed to the letter and applied with the fullest rigor. It was not until the Nazi Kristallnacht, in November 1938, that a horrified Roosevelt reacted decisively in behalf of the refugees. Ignoring any political consequences, and sternly forbidding any bureaucratic obstructionism, the president ordered the State Department to combine the German and Austrian immigration quotas, and to give every possible "humanitarian" consideration to refugee applications. As a consequence of this modification, the number of German- and Austrian-Jewish immigrants climbed sharply, to 33,000 by the end of 1939.

Between April 1933 and June 1941, some 104,000 Jews from the Greater Reich entered the United States. The number was hardly negligible. Yet, had all the existing Central European quotas conscientiously been filled, even under the constraints of the Hoover Directive, the total number of refugees from the Greater Reich would have reached at least 212,000.

A Problematic Zionist Sanctuary

Presumably another alternative was available. This was the Jewish National Home in Palestine, which had been established as an internationally recognized haven for the beleaguered Jews of the world. In Germany, before 1933, the Zionist movement had attracted only small numbers of the adult Jewish population; and, of these, none had anticipated a catastrophic mass departure for Palestine. But once disaster struck, Germany's Zionist leadership responded swiftly. The Palästina-Amt, the Zionist office in Berlin, emerged as the single Jewish organization in Germany capable of providing centrally organized guidance for immigration.

Indeed, it was the Palästina-Amt that engaged the Nazi regime in a unique version of pragmatic "diplomacy." It alone had been authorized by the British administration in Palestine to distribute the coveted immigration certificates for German Jews. The British issued these certificates according to specific categories: for manual workers, for "capitalists" (those with assets equivalent to not less than 1,000 English pounds), and for students whose support in Palestine could be guaranteed. In a period of world Depression, the British plainly were issuing many fewer certificates than in earlier years. Even so, the chances remained better for individuals in the "capitalist" category, those who could bring a certain minimum of funds with them. Here the Palästina-Amt in Berlin sensed a possible room for maneuver with the German government. The Nazis might be willing to enter into a mutually useful arrangement to encourage the emigration of Jewish "capitalists."

The notion of transferring capitalists actually was preceded by a plan for transferring Jewish capital. In March 1933, it was Heinrich Wolff, the German consul in Jerusalem, who first brought the idea to the attention of the German foreign ministry. Married to a Jewish woman (and two years later dismissed for that reason), Wolff had maintained equable relations with Jewish businessmen in Palestine. Accordingly, he was sought out by Sam Cohen, owner of a middle-sized Palestinian citrus company. Cohen was interested in utilizing German-Jewish funds to enlarge investments in his firm, as well as in other Palestinian agricultural and industrial ventures. Could an agreement be worked out to facilitate such a transfer? Reacting affirmatively, Wolff wrote Berlin in March, endorsing Cohen's idea.

The scheme of a capital transfer was also favored by the Jewish Agency, particularly by the director of its political department, Chaim Arlozorov, who discerned in the proposal even wider possibilities than did Cohen or Wolff. Arlozorov knew Germany well, and had been a friend of Magda Quandt, the woman who became the wife of Joseph Goebbels, the Nazi minister of propaganda. Thus, with Arlozorov's approval, Cohen departed for Berlin to conduct personal discussions with German government officials. The negotiations went well. Indeed, they transcended even the original proposal Cohen had brought to Wolff in February. In August 1933, an agreement was signed by representatives of the Jewish Agency and the Reich Ministry of Economic Affairs. The agreement, henceforth to be known by its Hebrew title of

Ha'avarah (Transfer), allowed German Jews with capital to purchase German industrial goods that were needed in Palestine, mainly irrigation pipes, cement mixers, and other production equipment, and to pay for these supplies in German marks. In turn, the Jewish Agency in Palestine, through its financial arm, the Anglo-Palestine Bank, would find local buyers who would deposit the equivalent sums in British pounds to pay for the goods, which would then be shipped to Palestine. When the German Jews who made the original mark payments subsequently arrived in Palestine, they would receive their money back from the Anglo-Palestine Bank in pounds sterling.

For the Nazi government, too, the Ha'avarah agreement offered clear advantages, even though it provided Germany with no hard currency. At the least, it augmented the government's supply of marks, which it acquired at bargain rates from the departing Jews. From May 1934 on, moreover, Berlin levied a heavy "capital flight" tax on all sums exceeding 50,000 marks, a source of revenue that compounded the transfer agreement's usefulness for Germany, and those taxes continued to rise in future years. Well beyond these financial considerations, however, the Ha'avarah agreement facilitated and encouraged the emigration of Jews. It was this decisive inducement that won over the foreign ministry and the economics ministry.

Thus it was, during the 1930s, that some 20,000 middle-class Jews, approximately 37 percent of all German-Jewish immigrants to Palestine, managed to depart Germany. Upon arrival, retrieving their funds in pounds sterling, many were in a position to make still further capital investments. It was this evident advantage that overcame lingering Zionist opposition to the agreement. Admittedly, the immigrating Jewish "capitalists" did not reach Palestine with quite the funds that they or the Jewish Agency had anticipated. They lost 25 percent of their capital in "departure taxes," and even more after 1937, together with another 30 percent through Nazi manipulation of the exchange rates. Nevertheless, over the six years of its duration, the Ha'avarah program transferred to Palestine the equivalent of 140 million German marks. In the same period, the departure of upper-middle-class German Jews encouraged the emigration of 30,000 other German Jews who otherwise would have been reluctant to exploit the meager immigration quota still available to them.

It was well that they overcame their reluctance. In January 1939, the Nazi government terminated the Ha'avarah program, and with it permission for Jews to immigrate to Palestine altogether. The cancellation was determined not by economic but by diplomatic factors. In the latter 1930s, the Nazi regime, and its Italian Fascist partner, sensed greater long-range advantages in cultivating Arab goodwill than in exploiting and evicting to Palestine a shrinking number of Jewish "capitalists."

An Upheaval of Arab Palestine

Between 1932 and 1936, the Jewish population of Palestine doubled, from 185,000 to 375,000. Most of the newcomers were fugitives from successor-state oppression in Eastern Europe. But a significant minority were Central European Jews, among them many who possessed business and professional skills as well as capital resources. With their help, even in the midst of the Depression, the economy of the Jewish National Home achieved impressive growth. In 1938, the Jewish agricultural sector, with its 105,000 settlers, was registering its first substantial profits. Although most of Palestine Jewry's industrial firms were still quite small, they too had grown impressively in number, from 6,000 in 1930 to 14,000 in 1937. Electricity usage in these same years increased seven times over.

Neither was the Palestine Arab community standing still. Indeed, its growth was almost precisely the consequence of the growing Jewish market for Arab agricultural products. In 1920, approximately 600,000 Arabs lived in Palestine. By 1931, the figure had climbed to 840,000, and represented 81 percent of the country's inhabitants. Most were farmers, and of these a majority dwelt in the hilly northern and central regions of the country. With access to the burgeoning Jewish economy, they generated a standard of living measurably higher than that of Moslem Arabs elsewhere. In the earliest years of Britain's Palestine mandate, both peoples, Arabs and Jews, lived together in a state of cautious forbearance (p. 364). As in other countries, however, it was the emergence of a native middle class that fostered the nationalism of Palestine Arabs. More critically yet, Palestine Arab restiveness was exacerbated by the displacement of Arab political hopes elsewhere in the Middle East.

The heartland of the Arab nationalist movement lay in Syria, and was structured around Emir Feisal, charismatic leader of the wartime Arab uprising, and putative ruler of an "independent" Syrian Arab state. But in 1920, leading a popular uprising against the French mandatory government, Feisal was dethroned and exiled. A year later, the British offered him a surrogate throne under their own "tutelage," in Iraq, but on condition that he refrain from nationalist provocation. It was then that Arab nationalist restiveness shifted to Palestine, to focus specifically on the country's Jewish-inhabited enclave. Here the Zionist settlement appeared to be more vulnerable to Arab political and military pressure than were the French in Syria or the British in Iraq. Leadership of the Arab nationalist movement in Palestine then tended to devolve around the Husseini family, the wealthiest landowning clan in the region. In 1921, the British high commissioner, Sir Herbert Samuel, augmented this family's prestige by appointing one of its senior members, Haj Muhammad Amin al-Husseini, to the vacant post of Grand Mufti, the

Islamic high judge of appeal. With that prestige, Husseini eventually assumed the chairmanship of a wider colloquium of secular and religious leaders, to be known as the Arab Higher Committee.

Over the ensuing years, the Grand Mufti set about organizing a campaign of resistance to the Jewish presence in the Holy Land. In August 1929, responding to his series of inflammatory sermons in Jerusalem's venerated al-Aqsa Mosque, Arab riots flared against Jewish settlements throughout Palestine. The violence left several hundred Jews and Arabs dead. For the British, the shock resonated back to London. A new Labour government recently had come to power under Prime Minister Ramsay MacDonald. Hereupon, the government's colonial secretary, Lord Passfield (formerly Sidney Webb, the renowned social reformer), dispatched a Parliamentary Royal Commission to Palestine. Under the chairmanship of Sir Walter Shaw, a veteran civil servant, the commission engaged in five weeks of hearings, then issued its report in March 1930. Although apportioning blame for the unrest on both sides, the Shaw Report drew particular attention to Arab bitterness at the steady rise of Jewish immigration into Palestine. It noted, too, that the increase of Jewish land purchases from absentee Arab landlords often resulted in the divestiture of tenant farmers from their plots. In view of these tensions, the Shaw Commission and a follow-up, the Hope-Simpson Commission, recommended tighter restrictions on Jewish land purchases and immigration into Palestine. In London, Lord Passfield wasted little time in registering his own reaction. He issued a White Paper that transcended the commission's recommendations by suspending Jewish immigration and land purchases altogether.

Stunned and outraged, the Zionist leadership loosed a hue and cry that ramified through much of the Labour and Liberal political establishments in Britain, where Jewish participation was extensive. In turn, taken aback by the depth of this pro-Zionist reaction, Prime Minister MacDonald announced in February 1931 that he was "reinterpreting" the Passfield White Paper—in effect, canceling it. But the Jews took only momentary comfort in the "reinterpretation." They were shaken at the unanticipated fragility of their National Home in Palestine, barely a decade after the Paris Peace Conference had confirmed the Balfour Declaration.

Graver perils lay ahead. By the mid-1930s, German and Italian consular and press officers throughout the Arab world, as well as German and Italian overseas broadcasting transmissions, steadily intensified their propaganda campaign to encourage Arab violence against Britain's presence in the Middle East. The strategy was shrewd. Britain's diplomatic position as a mandatory ruler of Arab peoples was awkward enough. But as "guarantor" of a Jewish minority in Palestine, Britain was more vulnerable yet to Arab resentment. This was an irony, of course, inasmuch as Nazi Germany, in the brutality of its antisemitic program, was itself the main instigator of Jewish immigration to Palestine. Nevertheless, the Arab leadership was impressed by Berlin's sympathetic assurances of a shared Jew-hatred. To exploit that sympathy and implied support, the Grand Mufti in the spring of 1936 concluded that the moment was ripe to strike back at Britain's protected Zionist enclave.

Britain Repudiates the Jewish National Home

Arab attacks against Jewish farm villages resumed in April 1936. By midsummer, the scale of fighting escalated sharply, as Arab guerrillas infiltrated into Palestine from neighboring Syria and Iraq. By August, the violence had produced approximately 1,300 casualties, most of these Arabs, but also some 200 Jews, as well as a score of British military and civilian personnel. In response, following urgent consultations with the Palestine mandatory government, the Colonial Office warned the Arab Higher Committee of stern repression, but linked the warning to a parallel commitment. If hostilities ended, the British government would embark on a thorough investigation of Arab grievances. The Mufti and his colleagues accepted the offer. Fighting stopped.

London in turn honored its promise by dispatching still another Royal Commission to Palestine, in November 1937. This one was chaired by Lord Robert Peel, a former secretary of state for India. Peel was an able public official, and the other members of his commission included experienced diplomats and jurists, as well as an Oxford professor of colonial history. The group conducted six weeks of detailed hearings. By January 1937, it was becoming plain that Arabs and Jews were at an impasse. The Arabs insisted upon an immediate end to all Jewish immigration and full Arab self-rule in the totality of Palestine. The Jews remained adamant on their right of free immigration within an autonomous Jewish National Home. It was then that the commission's academic member, Professor Reginald Coupland, offered an innovative proposal. It was for the Holy Land to be partitioned into separate Jewish and Arab states, with each nation to enjoy sovereignty within its own territory. Impressed, Coupland's colleagues then accepted his solution as the least objectionable of alternate solutions, and endorsed it in their commission report.

The reaction of the Zionists to the Peel Report was distinctly mixed. Vladimir Jabotinsky, the inspirational force behind the wartime Jewish Legion, harshly opposed any further attenuation of the Jewish National Home. He and his followers had not forgotten that, only fifteen years earlier, the original Balfour Declaration award to the Jews had been "redefined," and Palestine's largest hinterland had been reconstituted as the (Arab) Emirate of Transjordan. Now, apparently, even the rump area left to the Jews was to be further resected and its largest portion transferred to the Arabs. The proposal was unthinkable for Jabotinsky and his associates. In their territorial maximalism, these "Revisionists" henceforth would become an increasingly formidable component within the Zionist world. But if the Revisionists were enraged at the notion even of discussing the Peel Report, a majority of the Zionist Organization's membership was cautiously prepared to explore the proposal. David Ben-Gurion, chairman of the Jewish Agency Executive, sent word to his Arab contacts that he was ready to discuss with them a modified version of the Peel Report, even to offer financial help to the envisaged Arab state. His overture was rejected with contempt, both by the Arab Higher Committee and by the surrounding Arab governments. If Britain should attempt to put the partition scheme into effect, warned Arab spokesmen, they, the Arabs, would not hesitate to turn "elsewhere" for help. The allusion to Italy and Germany was all but explicit.

In September 1937, with encouragement from Mussolini and Hitler, the Arabs renewed their uprising. This time they launched their attacks equally at the British and the Jews. The revolt soon assumed major dimensions, inflicting heavy casualties on British troops and serious damage on British installations. Eventually, fighting among Arabs, Jews, and British would claim over 4,000 lives and inflict tens of millions of pounds in property damage. In the summer of 1938, the British government was compelled to ship in two new infantry battalions and two additional RAF squadrons. Meanwhile, in April 1938, London dispatched still another Royal Commission to Palestine. Led by Sir John Woodhead, a veteran of the Anglo-Indian administration, this one conducted its hearings over the ensuing two months with a sense of mounting urgency. There was reason for alarm. At a moment of acute international crisis in Europe, the financial and diplomatic costs of protecting the Jewish National Home threatened to outweigh the Palestine mandate's strategic advantages for Britain.

A CLOSURE OF SANCTUARIES

The Woodhead hearings took place at a particularly dire moment in Jewish history. By the spring of 1938, the Nazis were embarked on a climactic eradication of the Jewish presence in the German Reich. For the Jews, the issue of free immigration to Palestine manifestly was becoming one of life or death. The gravity of Jewish circumstances was further heightened in July 1938 by the debacle of the Évian Conference on refugees. And on November 8, when the Woodhead Report was submitted to Parliament, it confirmed the Jews' worst fears. The Peel Commission partition plan was unfeasible, the report declared, inasmuch as the prospective Jewish state would encompass a huge Arab minority, and the remaining land area would be insufficient to accommodate further infusions of Jews. Neither would the prospective Arab state be large enough to function viably. The Woodhead

Report suggested, then, that a better solution would be an enforced economic union between two states, each of them to be deprived of jurisdiction over all issues affecting economic policy, including the issue of immigration. Such matters would remain under British control. The report enraged the Jews. The Arabs expressed cautious satisfaction.

So did the British cabinet. In late December 1938, Prime Minister Neville Chamberlain announced that he was summoning Zionist and Arab leaders to a Round Table Conference in London, scheduled for February 1939. In London, presumably, some version of the Woodhead Report would be negotiated. Yet, when the conference began at St. James's Palace, the Arab delegations (including those from the various Arab governments) refused even to sit in the same room with the Jews, and the British were obliged to confer with each delegation separately. The discussions thus continued unproductively over the ensuing weeks, producing no agreement large or small. The Arabs demanded an end to the mandate and full independence for an Arab-dominated Palestine. The Jews insisted that free immigration for their people was nonnegotiable. In mid-March, with neither side budging, the British government in its exasperation suspended the conference.

The Chamberlain cabinet at this point discerned no alternative but to impose its own solution on the volatile Holy Land mandate. On May 17, 1939, that solution took the form of an official White Paper on Palestine. In its preface, the document asserted Britain's intention to organize a fully independent Palestinian state within the period of ten years; and in the first half of that time span, Jewish immigration would be limited to an annual quota of 10,000 persons, with a climactic ceiling of 25,000 in the fifth and final year. After this period, no further Jewish immigration would be permitted without Arab acquiescence. The sale of land to the Jews would be prohibited immediately. In effect, Britain was foreclosing on the Jewish National Home.

At the Twenty-first Zionist Congress, convening in Geneva in mid-August 1939, the prevailing reaction of the delegates was one of shock and defiance. All of them regarded the White Paper as a likely death warrant for their hopes in Palestine, and conceivably for their people in Europe. From Palestine, David Ben-Gurion led a Jewish Agency group that urged a campaign of militant resistance. But Chaim Weizmann, Zionism's elder statesman, reminded the congress that Britain was facing the likelihood of war with Germany. In that confrontation, the British and other Western democracies had to be assured of the widest measure of international support. "It is my duty in this solemn hour to tell England," declared Weizmann, ". . . [that we] have grievances. . . . But above our regret and bitterness are higher interests. What the democracies are fighting for is the minimum . . . necessary for Jewish life. Their anxiety is our anxiety. Their war is our war." Then he added:

"If . . . we are spared in life and our work continues . . . perhaps a new light will shine upon us from the thick, black gloom. . . . There are some things which cannot fail to pass, things without which the world cannot be imagined." Deep emotion gripped the congress. Tearfully, Weizmann embraced his colleagues on the platform. Few of the European delegates would survive the war.

XXVII

The Holocaust of European Jewry

THE THEORY AND PRACTICE
OF THE FINAL SOLUTION

In the summer of 1941, Europe was at war. During the previous year, the Nazi Reich had overrun western Poland, the Low Countries, Norway, and France, driven the British army from the Continent, and swallowed much of the Balkans. On June 22, 1941, intent upon fulfilling his vision of ruling Slavic Europe, Adolf Hitler tore up the Nazi-Soviet Non-Aggression Pact of August 1939 and launched into Operation Barbarossa, his long-planned invasion of the Soviet Union. Once again, the Wehrmacht's blitzkrieg tactics proved devastatingly effective. By mid-August 1942, German armored columns penetrated to the outskirts of Stalingrad, at the southern outlet of the Volga River. The Nazi empire was at its apogee, extending over more of Europe than any other domain since Julius Caesar's.

Now, too, Hitler was presented with unprecedented scope to translate his concept of Aryan blood purity into demographic practice. His scheme for "breaking the resistance of the settled populations" envisaged the physical extermination of many millions of Slavs, and the enforced transplantation of peoples of all races by hunger and forced labor. Accordingly, under the guise of antipartisan warfare, the Germans slaughtered between 25 million and 40 million Russians (statistics are continually being updated from newly opened Soviet archives), 2.5 million Poles, 2 million Greeks and Serbs, 200,000 Gypsies, while some 12 million others of all races perished of hunger and disease.

The Jews, too, were among the peoples who fell victim to Nazi "biologists." As late as September 1, 1939, there remained 185,000 Jews in "integral" Germany, together with 70,000 in Austria and 190,000 in Czechoslovakia. Of these, even after the war began, approximately 90,000 fled or were driven from the Greater Reich, and nearly that many—temporarily—escaped from Nazi-occupied France, from the Low Countries, and the Balkans. Most of the rest frantically sought visas to free countries, with the United States their favored port of call. But in June 1940, Congress passed the Alien Registration Act, closing off all further immigration from Europe. Seventeen months later, the issue of refuge became moot. On October 23, 1941, Berlin announced that Jews no longer would be permitted to depart from German-controlled Europe. The sheer magnitude of Hitler's conquests in the East had dictated a shift in Nazi racial policy. It was a transition from mass departure to mass murder.

The process developed in stages. Following Germany's initial, September 1939 occupation of western Poland (a region henceforth to be known as the General Government of Poland), the Nazis found themselves with nearly 1.6 million Jews on their hands. Accordingly, the notion was floated of driving this vast Jewry to the very frontier of eastern Poland, the territory allocated to the Soviet Union under the Nazi-Soviet Pact, in the hope that large numbers of Jews would find their own way into the Soviet zone. But in ensuing months, the congestion of hundreds of thousands of these debilitated and panic-stricken Jews along the demarcation line all but overwhelmed German administrative and logistical resources. Hans Frank, gauleiter (regent) of the General Government, pleaded with Berlin to find another solution. In late March 1940, therefore, attention was directed to Madagascar, the huge French-owned island off the East African coast. Here as many as 3 million Jews conceivably might be settled. The idea seemed feasible, inasmuch as France by then appeared ready to collapse, and Britain presumably would come to terms with Germany soon afterward. But the British did not capitulate. The Royal Navy maintained its control of the seas, and thereby blocked German access to Madagascar.

Meanwhile, as early as the winter of 1940–41, Hitler was increasingly preoccupied with his impending invasion of the Soviet Union. He confided to his associates that he expected to find as many as 5 million Jews in this vast Communist empire (in fact, there were about 3.4 million). The West obviously did not want these people. By implication, there remained only one resolution of the Jewish Question. And with the launching of Operation Barbarossa on June 22, 1941, the implication became all but explicit. On July 31, from his vantage point on the Russian front, Hermann Göring dispatched a telegram to Reinhard Heydrich, the SS officer who was director of the RSHA, the Reich Main Security Office in Berlin. It instructed Heydrich to begin making "all necessary organizational, functional, and material preparations for a total solution [Gesamtlösung] of the Jewish question in the German sphere of influence in Europe." The transition from emigration to extermination had moved a step closer.

Even before the war began, Göring had delegated the Jewish question to the Nazi regime's specialists in terror, the Schutzstaffel, the political police. The SS was the most powerful institution in Hitler's realm. Under the direction of SS Reichsführer Heinrich Himmler, its tentacles extended into all corners of German life, even into the army. Yet for all Himmler's brutality and organizational talent, he lacked the imagination to handle the Jewish question with the scope and finality that Hitler would soon demand. Rather, he preferred to turn the matter over to Reinhard Heydrich. Unlike his superior, the thirty-eight-year-old Heydrich was brilliant, polished, and flashy, an accomplished violinist, an airplane pilot, skier, and fencer. He was also an unashamed sadist, prepared and eager to cope with the Jewish question "decisively." To that end, in March 1939, Heydrich opened a special "Jewish" office within the RSHA's Security-Police Bureau (Sicherheitsdienst), and placed it under the leadership of Adolf Eichmann, who had proved his bona fides as the highly efficient director of the Jewish Emigration Office, first in Vienna, then in Berlin. It was Eichmann's suite of rooms in the main RSHA building on Berlin's 116 Kurfürstendammstrasse that would become the nerve center of Jewish extermination.

Following Göring's telegram of July 31, 1941, and another half-year of careful preparations at Heydrich's and Eichmann's headquarters, the final strategy for dealing with the Jews was formulated. It was revealed at a conference of January 20, 1942, held at Grossen Wannsee No. 42–48, a lakeside villa outside Berlin. The meeting was convened by Heydrich, and present were fifteen of the Reich's senior SS officials. Here it was that the RSHA chief informed the group that plans had been laid for a Final Solution (Endlösung) of the Jewish question.

> In the course of the Final Solution [Heydrich explained], the Jews now should be brought under appropriate direction . . . to the East for labor utilization. Separated by sex, those Jews capable of work will be led into these areas in large labor columns to build roads, where doubtless large numbers of them will fall away through natural reduction. The inevitable final remainder . . . will have to be dealt with appropriately, since they represent a natural selection . . . which . . . is to be regarded as the germ cell of a new Jewish development.

No mention was made of extermination, but the euphemism "appropriately" was clear to all those present.

"ANTIPARTISAN" WARFARE IN THE SOVIET UNION

Even earlier, in Poland, and then in the Soviet Union, the Jews were being dealt with "appropriately." The Final Solution in practical fact proceeded from east to west, with the Grossen Wansee Conference representing an "administrative" watershed dividing military from civilian extermination. By the summer of 1940, the Nazis already were launched on the process of starving and debilitating the 1.6 million Jews living in the General Government of western

Poland. But eastern Poland, as well as Latvia, Lithuania, Estonia, Bessarabia, and other territories the Soviets had annexed under the terms of the 1939 Nazi-Soviet Pact, remained beyond Hitler's grasp. Here lived approximately 1.7 million Jews.

A full year before the German invasion, the Kremlin had deported to Soviet Central Asia and Siberia as many as 250,000 to 300,000 of these "annexed" Jews, most of whom were suspect as socialists or Zionists. Ironically, that deportation saved their lives. Once Operation Barbarossa began, too, the Soviet government ordered an immense general civilian evacuation inland, well beyond the Urals, to western Siberia, Uzbekistan, Tajikistan, and the distant Caucasus republics. Between 12 million and 15 million Russians, Ukrainians, and Belorussians shared in this transplantation, both from the territories annexed under the Nazi-Soviet Pact and from the "integral" Soviet Union. With them migrated approximately 900,000 Jews, including 600,000 to 700,000 from the annexed regions. Although the circumstances of this epic transmigration were grim, most of the Jewish evacuees survived the war. Among other Jews who did not fall helplessly into German hands were the approximately 500,000 who served in the Soviet armed forces. Of these half-million, some 200,000 perished in battle, in common with other Soviet military personnel. Yet, even with these "exemptions," fully 1.4 million Jewish civilians remained behind in the areas of Wehrmacht advance, in both annexed and integral Soviet territory.

At first, Hitler's plans for the Jews in this vast eastern terrain were as tentative as for those elsewhere in Europe. As late as March 1941, when Operation Barbarossa was under preparation, the führer had not yet committed himself to ethnic annihilation. It was in that month, however, that he issued a directive relating to the treatment of civilians in the Soviet territories. He wanted the "Jewish-Bolshevik" intelligentsia to be eliminated. Did the term mean all Soviet Jews? The guidelines were not clear. Nevertheless, once the invasion began in June 1941, the Nazis launched a campaign of widespread extermination of Jewish men—with or without "Bolshevik" identification. It soon became clear, too, that dead Jewish men were leaving behind women and children who could not fend for themselves. Executions then also came to include these helpless dependents. By August, the systematic and indiscriminate shootings of all Jews became routine.

The executioners were the special shock units of the SS, the so-called Einsatzgruppen, who dogged the heels of the invading Wehrmacht. Heydrich assigned four units of Einsatzgruppen, one for each military front, to follow in the wake of the army, each unit functioning under the command of an SS general. Each was invested with supreme authority over all civilian affairs behind the front lines. No military officer was permitted to interfere with the Einsatzgruppen's activities. But inasmuch as none of the SS units ever comprised more than nine hundred men, local Polish, Ukrainian, and Lithuanian militias were usually co-opted to help in the dirty work of rounding up and executing Jews. Thus, in Lvov, on July 25, 1941, immediately after the Germans occupied the city, Ukrainian militia commanders proclaimed "Petliura Day" (in memory of the Ukranian nationalist hero who in 1926 was assassinated in his Paris exile by a Jewish avenger), and embarked on a three-day pogrom that massacred 6,000 Jews. Moving into Soviet towns, they sought out the local Jewish council and obtained a list of all Jewish inhabitants. If the list had been destroyed, Ukrainian and other "supplemental" forces usually managed to locate the missing victims. The Jews then were transported to nearby woods or steppes where they were machine-gunned to death.

It was not a complicated matter to dispose of the hundreds of thousands of Jews who were concentrated in the larger towns of Belorussia and Ukraine. In Minsk alone, 76,000 Jews fell into German hands and were systematically liquidated. In Kiev, 33,000 Jews were murdered within two days on September 29–30, 1941, in the single most concentrated massacre of the war. They were shot and buried in the huge Babi Yar ravine where, a few days later, their gas-bloated bodies literally caused the earth to heave. In October 1941, the 30,000 Jews of Dniepropetrovsk were machine-gunned and buried in the antitank ditches outside the city, and additional mass executions followed until March 1942. Another 20,000 Jews were slaughtered at Poltava, 20,000 at Kharkov (many of them buried alive in their huts), 35,000 in Odessa, 10,000 in Simferopol. In Latvia, some 170,000 Jews perished, and in Lithuania fully 250,000. As the blitzkrieg moved deeper into Soviet territory, the killings increased in speed and efficiency.

By the end of 1942, the SS and its accomplices had largely completed their assignment in occupied Soviet terrain. Over 1.4 million Jews had been executed by then—approximately 600,000 from the annexed territories and 800,000 from the "integral" Soviet Union. Yet even the mass annihilation of Soviet Jews was transcended by the efficiency and scope of the Final Solution in the General Government of Poland.

THE LAST DAYS OF POLISH JEWRY

In this western sector of the Republic of Poland lived some 1.6 million Jews. It was to determine their fate that Reinhard Heydrich conferred with his subordinates on September 21, 1939, immediately following the Nazi conquest of this territory. After much discussion, the decision was reached to use the General Government as the principal dumping ground for Polish Jewry. Soon afterward, however, at the request of Gauleiter Hans Frank, the notion of concentrating this vast population along the east-west frontier was aban-

doned (p. 528). On December 14, 1939, Heydrich then issued a modified directive. Henceforth, all rural and small-town Jews in the General Government
were to be transported to the larger Polish cities. There they would be quarantined from the rest of the Polish population and kept under tight SS surveillance. Frank launched into action the very next day. By the tens of thousands,
Jews were systematically rounded up and transported or force-marched into
specially designated urban ghettos. By late winter of 1940, this mass movement of people into the slums of Warsaw, Lublin, Cracow, and Kovno was
largely accomplished. In Warsaw alone, 450,000 Jews eventually were compressed into an area, the city's traditional Jewish districts, that had accommodated 145,000 persons before the war. In each of these ghettos, brick walls
were erected to prevent contact with the non-Jewish population.

It was Frank's objective to reduce large numbers of these Jews to starvation, leaving a more "manageable" population to be disposed of in the future.
The scheme proved quite effective. The daily food-ration limit for Jews was
set at eight hundred calories, and rations consisted mainly of potatoes and
synthetic fat. Although smugglers were punished by immediate execution,
children occasionally made their way through tunnels under the ghetto walls
to beg or steal grain from the Polish sections of the city. But the amount of
food that illegally reached the Jews was negligible. People were reduced to
walking cadavers. By spring 1941, the death rate by starvation and typhus had
reached 30 percent of the ghetto populations.

Even as the Nazis systematically reduced their Jewish problem to "manageable" size, they were obliged to devise techniques for ensuring that these captive urban populations remained passive and obedient. For that purpose, they
authorized a Judenrat (Jewish Council) to operate in each of the important
ghettos. Each Judenrat operated under an appointed president, through
whom the SS issued their decrees and from whom they obtained their "relocation" quotas, in effect, their victims. The efficiency of the system varied from
city to city. Some of the Judenrat presidents were obsequiously cooperative,
and possibly corrupt. An example was Dr. Chaim Rumkowski, the seventy-
two-year-old president of the Lodz Judenrat. Invested with extraordinary
power by the SS, Rumkowski was permitted to raise taxes, to print currency,
even to engrave postage stamps with his likeness. Aware of the death camps
(p. 533), Rumkowski sought to keep the information from his "subjects" and to
discourage every hint of Jewish resistance. In the end, he gained little by his
cooperation, either for his fellow Jews or for himself. When the SS evacuated
the Lodz ghetto in August 1944, Rumkowski was hurled into one of the last
departing freight cars for Auschwitz. For the most part, however, the Judenrat
presidents, conceivably even Rumkowski, genuinely hoped to alleviate Jewish
suffering through personal intercession. Dr. Adam Czerniakov of the Warsaw

Judenrat and Dr. Lukasz Rotfeld of the Lvov Judenrat eventually committed suicide rather than collaborate with the Final Solution.

Notwithstanding starvation and disease, by March 1942 approximately 800,000 Jews were still alive in Poland's General Government. Himmler and Heydrich agreed then that more "systematic" extermination measures were required. To that end, they delegated the project of eradicating the remaining Jewish population to a veteran Austrian Nazi, Odilo Globocnik, who was then serving as SS police chief for Lublin province. "Globus" Globocnik, a hard-drinking fanatic with a moral record unsavory even by Nazi standards, enthusiastically launched into the task of organizing concentration centers for extermination. In fact, three such facilities already existed: in Belzec, Chelmno, and Treblinka. Others—Lublin, Sobibor, Auschwitz, and later Majdanek—would be added; but Globocnik was the man who put them all into operational order.

Thus, in April 1942, under SS orders, the Judenrat police began rounding up tens of thousands of Polish ghetto inhabitants and dispatching them to the extermination camps in sealed cattle trains. Here a unique fate awaited them. As early as autumn 1941, the SS had begun experimenting with large-scale gassings of Red Army prisoners of war. The instruments of execution were simple vans, large boxes mounted over the exhaust pipes of captured Russian tank engines. In December 1941, van gassings were applied to Jewish prisoners in Auschwitz. But the method of asphyxiation by carbon monoxide fumes, even experimentally by crude cyanide fumes, was imperfect. The torment and screams of the victims often proved unnerving even to the SS executioners. Accordingly, in May 1942, Lieutenant-General Heinz Kammler, the Wehrmacht engineer who later would design Germany's rocket bases on the French coast, was sent to Poland to devise a more efficient method of death-camp extermination. One of Kammler's innovations was to employ a particularly swift and toxic cyanide gas, Zyklon B. At the same time, he supervised the construction of an ingenious system of gas bunkers. To conceal their purpose from their intended victims, he installed furnaces on their upper tiers, beyond eye level. The lower levels, where the actual gassings took place, were disguised as shower rooms.

Each day, trainloads of Jews arrived at Auschwitz, Belzec, Sobibor, or at other death centers. The prisoners were ordered to strip, to surrender all valuables at "checkrooms." Afterward, separated by sex, they were marched into huge "shower rooms." Unsuspecting, they waited for the water to pour. Instead, Zyklon B crystals were dropped into awaiting buckets of water, and gas escaped from the perforations in the sheet-metal columns. When the prisoners caught sight of the emerging gas vapor, they stampeded toward the locked steel door. Here they piled up in pyramids, clawing and mauling one another before expiring. A half-hour later, electric exhaust pumps removed the poisoned air, the door slid open, and Jewish work detachments entered, wearing gas masks. Hosing off blood and wastes, they pulled the victims apart with hooks to search for gold teeth. The booty usually was stacked in separate boxes. Soon rail wagons arrived to transport the bodies up the concrete levels to the furnaces. Once the corpses were burned, a mill ground the human remains to fine ash, and trucks later arrived to scatter the ash into neighboring streams. In some death camps, melted body fat was preserved for the manufacture of soap.

By early 1943 the Jewish population in the General Government of Poland had been reduced to approximately 350,000. Each day, between 6,000 and 10,000 men, women, and children were loaded onto the trains that ran continually from the ghettos to the death camps. Throughout the rest of that year, the remaining ghettos were thinned out. In August 1944, the last Jews in the work camps of Lodz were dispatched to Auschwitz for gassing.

THE FATE OF JEWS IN WEST-CENTRAL EUROPE: THE ALTREICH

West of the Soviet Union and Poland the eradication of Jews fell essentially within the purview of Adolf Eichmann. The man was by no means a senior eminence. Born in Solingen, Germany, in 1906, he initially had moved with his family to Austria, where he was employed briefly by an oil company. Upon losing his job, he drifted into the Austrian Nazi movement. In 1933, after participating in an unsuccessful putsch effort against the Austrian government, Eichmann fled to Germany. There he began his career in Heydrich's incipient security apparatus, serving as a minor functionary in charge of the card file on Freemasons. Later, when he was given responsibility for organizing a police museum on Jewish ritual objects, Eichmann began making a systematic study of Jewish history and folklore, even of Hebrew and Yiddish grammar books. Impressed by the Zionist movement, which he recognized as a potential vehicle for Jewish emigration, Eichmann in 1937 actually flew to Palestine to study the Jewish National Home (upon being recognized by British Intelligence agents, he was hustled back onto an airplane the next day). A year later, following the Anschluss, he was appointed director of the Central Office for Jewish Emigration, with the task of directing the exodus of Austrian Jewry (p. 511). Upon fulfilling his task with brutal efficiency, Eichmann was brought back to Berlin, promoted to major, and placed in charge of the RSHA's department "IV-A, 4b," the inconspicuous office responsible for administering Jewish emigration from the entirety of the Third Reich.

By 1941, as that responsibility gradually was transformed from emigration to extermination, Eichmann was given wider rein to administer the Final

Solution through the entirety of German-ruled Europe, "independent of geographic frontiers." Yet he tended to leave the liquidation of Soviet Jewry to the Einsatzgruppen, and of Polish Jewry to Globocnik. He chose to devote his principal attention to the 1.3 million Jews west of Poland. Here Eichmann moved cautiously, waiting until the destruction of Soviet and Polish Jewry was well under way. At the outbreak of the war, in the Altreich, the "homeland empire" of prewar Europe, there were still as many as 185,000 identified Jews in Germany itself, approximately 80,000 in Austria, as well as 190,000 in the Czech areas of Bohemia and Moravia.

The condition of these "homeland" Jews was grim. Allowed only minimal food and clothing rations, they were barred from public facilities and public transportation, forced into congested ghetto lodgings, and obliged to wear the yellow star. Yet at first they did not appear to be in danger of their lives. Early in 1942, however, following the Grossen Wannsee Conference, all "homeland Jews" also began to be loaded onto trains and dispatched eastward. At one time or another, some 135,000 of these veterans of German culture were temporarily confined to the "privileged" concentration camp of Theresienstadt, in Czechoslovakia. These included families of Jewish military veterans who had been decorated in World War I, or who had achieved eminence in German economic or intellectual life. But eventually most of these "privileged" figures also were shipped on to Poland's gas chambers. The largest majority of the Altreich's remaining Jews shared that fate.

Eichmann's plans for Jews living beyond the Altreich were far less equivocal. He was dealing with militarily conquered territory, after all, where there was less need for discretion. Within the scope of the Nazi genocide, it was the fate of the venerable Balkan Jewish communities that possibly was unmatched for sheer prolonged brutality. Requiring a clear Balkan "shoulder" for his anticipated invasion of the Soviet Union, Hitler in April 1941 launched his Wehrmacht on Yugoslavia. Italian, Hungarian, and Bulgarian units then joined the invasion. They also shared in the spoils. When Yugoslavia's royalist government surrendered two weeks later, the Germans occupied Serbia, northern Slovenia, and the Banat. Hungary was allocated a portion of the Vojvodina, a territory it had lost to the Serbs after World War I. Bulgaria in turn assumed control over Yugoslav Macedonia (lost in the Balkan War of 1913). Italy's reward was Dalmatia, an area it had coveted but had been denied at the Paris Peace Conference. The remainder of Yugoslavia, encompassing Croatia, Bosnia, and Herzegovina, was reconstituted as the independent state of Croatia, and ruled by Ante Pavelic, the self-appointed prime minister of a puppet Ustasha (fascist-nationalist) regime.

Under German rule, the fate of Serbia's 14,000, largely Sephardic, Jews was predictable. At the outset, they were ghettoized. In the following months,

Serbia's scores of venerable synagogues and libraries were pillaged and destroyed. Then, in the summer of 1942, the SS rounded up 4,000 Jewish males in Serbia and transported them to penal compounds. In October, those who survived exposure and starvation were shot. Soon afterward, 6,000 women and children in Belgrade were similarly gathered together and transported to a makeshift local concentration camp, where they were asphyxiated in gas vans. Another 3,000 Jews, hiding in the countryside, perished of debilitation. In this fashion, Serbia and northen Slovenia were left *judenrein*—purged of Jews.

Meanwhile, the Germans had allocated Bosnia and Herzegovina to the Independent State of Croatia. At Dictator Pavelic's orders, Ustasha irregulars promptly launched into a widespread butchery of tens of thousands of the country's Serbs. In the process, they had time and energy to spare for Jews. Before the war, some 29,000 Jews (most of them Ashkenazim) lived in Croatia, and 13,000 (mostly Sephardim) in Bosnia and Herzegovina. During the autumn of 1941, captive Bosnian Jews were herded into concentration camps, where they were subjected to torture, mutilation, and eventual death, often by decapitation. All but 2,000 of Bosnia's Jews were liquidated. In Croatia itself, the Ustasha began rounding up Jews in the capital Zagreb in January 1943, and by spring 8,000 Jewish males were done to death in the infamous torture camp at Jasenovac. Yet the largest number of Croatia's Jews—some 13,000 men, women, and children—were delivered to the Germans, who in turn sent them on to Auschwitz for gassing. Some 3,000 Jews from Slovenia, and another 4,000 from the Vojvodina and western Macedonia, also perished of exposure and spot executions. By the end of the war, approximately 54,000 of Yugoslavia's prewar Jewish population of 71,000 had perished. It was a mortality rate of over 70 percent.

That fate, and that proportion, were shared by the 70,000 Jews of Greece. Nearly four-fifths of this veteran, predominately Sephardic, minority were concentrated in Salonika, long the commercial and cultural center of Balkan Jewry (p. 145). The German invasion of April 1941 doomed them. At first, during the initial months of Nazi occupation, the 55,000 remaining Jews of Salonika experienced a false sense of security. Although subjected to acute privation, they were not uprooted. But in the summer of 1942, most of their population, like the Jews of Athens and smaller Greek towns, were evicted from their homes and penned in ghettos. Those who managed to flee to the Italian zones of occupation were protected (p. 542). In September 1943, however, all of Greece came under German military rule. Thousands of Jews already had died of ill treatment in forced-labor battalions, but now systematic roundups of Jews were conducted throughout the country, even on the islands of Corfu, Crete, and Rhodes. By the spring of 1944, approximately 58,000 Jews had been annihilated, most of them at Auschwitz. Salonikan

Jewry, which lost 52,000 of that total, suffered the largest proportional geno-cide of any Jewish community in the world.

The eradication of Dutch Jewry, if no less uncompromising, was achieved at least far more rapidly. At the time of the German occupation, in March 1940, approximately 140,000 Jews lived in the Netherlands, including 34,000 refugees from the Altreich. In February 1941, once it became known that the SS was preparing to segregate the Jews, possibly for deportation, the Dutch underground was successful in helping approximately 16,000 of them to escape. But in ensuing weeks, fewer likely hiding places remained in the Netherlands' flat terrain. Throughout 1941–42, some 110,000 Jews were rounded up and deported to Auschwitz and Sobibor. On October 9, 1942, Anne Frank, hidden with her family in an Amsterdam warehouse, wrote in her diary: "The British radio speaks of their being gassed." By then, most of these people knew the fate that awaited them.

The survival rate of Belgian Jewry was somewhat higher. Of a population numbering 57,000 in 1940, and divided almost equally between Antwerp and Brussels, 29,000 Jews remained alive at the end of the war. They had received important support from the Belgian underground, and from the Catholic prelates Cardinal van Rooey of Antwerp and Bishop Kerkhofs of Liège, who exhorted their clergy to share in the rescue effort. With this help, and that of the socialist and Communist underground, several thousand Jewish children were successfully hidden among private families. King Leopold III, and the king's mother, Queen Elizabeth, worked vigorously to raise funds and locate sanctuary for Jewish fugitives. These efforts doubtless would have been even more successful but for the pro-Nazi collaboration of many Belgian Flem-ings, who traditionally resented the nation's French-speaking economic-cultural elite and evinced an emotional kinship with the Germans. Of the 28,000 Jews whom the SS rounded up for deportation, most were captured in Antwerp and its Flemish environs.

It is ironic that the highest proportional Jewish survival rate in Nazi-occupied Europe was also numerically the smallest. In 1940, the Jews of Den-mark, nearly all of them living in Copenhagen, numbered approximately 7,500 in a Danish population of 4.2 million. Of these, 1,300 were the offspring of mixed marriages, and another 1,500 were fugitives from the Altreich. It was this minicommunity that was trapped in April 1940, when Germany occupied its little Scandinavian neighbor. In fact, during the first two and a half years of German rule, Jews and non-Jews were treated alike. Ostensibly sharing a common "Aryan" heritage with Germany, Denmark was declared a Musterprotektorat, a "model" protectorate. It was the Nazis' calculation that decent treatment of all Danish citizens conceivably would send a message of reconciliation to the "Aryan" British. Yet the interlude of forbearance ended in the autumn of 1943. By then, the emergence of a Danish resistance movement had forfeited the country's privileged status. Accordingly, the German administration scheduled its long-postponed roundup of Jews. The date was set for September 30.

One member of the German administration, Georg Duckwitz, had been living in Copenhagen since 1928, as the representative of a German coffee firm. "Infected" by the venerable Danish tradition of democratic pluralism, Duckwitz immediately alerted the nation's senior political figures. The latter rushed to warn Denmark's Chief Rabbi Marcus Melchior and other Jewish communal leaders. Hereupon, Jews and gentiles alike set about informing every Jew in Copenhagen and arranging hiding places for them among the gentile population. By September 30, when contingents of SS troops arrived and set about raiding Jewish homes, they were able to seize only 202 persons, most of these ill and elderly people. Although the search continued for several more days, only 270 additional Jews were captured. By then, the largest numbers of the Jewish population were being loaded onto Danish fishing schooners for transport across the three-mile Malmö Sound to Sweden. Several days before the scheduled roundup, on a secret visit to Stockholm, the indefatigable Duckwitz had won assurance from Prime Minister Per Albin Hansson that his government would offer sanctuary to any Jews who reached Sweden.

Hansson's reaction signified an interesting volte-face in Swedish cabinet policy. Although Sweden's 7,000 Jews enjoyed full and equal rights, the country's government until then had been highly circumspect in its dealings with Germany. In the spring of 1940, intimidated by threats from Berlin, it had allowed a Wehrmacht army corps to pass through Swedish territory en route to a land invasion of Norway. Nor did the Swedes hesitate to sell Germany steel and other vital industrial commodities. By the autumn of 1943, however, the tide of the war had shifted. Seeking to project a different face to the Allies, Hansson offered the Jews his country's asylum. It was with that assurance that the Danish underground managed to bring over 6,500 Jews from their hiding places in the countryside, to load them onto a flotilla of fishing vessels, and within the space of a week to bring virtually all of them safely to Sweden. In Sweden, local Jewish charities cared for the internees until the end of the war. As for the Danes, if their effort in the rescue endeavor was less opportunistic than Sweden's, it also reflected the high rate of Jewish-Christian intermarriage. In many instances, the Danes simply were helping their relatives. Moreover, the middle-aged German occupation troops by and large were not fanatical Nazis. Uninterested in helping the SS, most simply turned a blind eye to Jewish escape.

Elsewhere, the genocide of West-Central European Jews was carried out on "schedule." It also was carried out as far distant from Germany as logistics permitted. Whether from France, the Low Countries, the Balkans, or the

Altreich itself, the largest numbers of victims were dispatched in cattle cars to the General Government of Poland, and divided there among the six major Polish gassing centers of Treblinka, Majdanek, Sobibor, Belzec, Chelmno, and Auschwitz. (In Germany, such "nongassing" centers as Dachau, Buchenwald, Ravensbrück, and Bergen-Belsen functioned as "traditional," if homicidal, concentration camps, intended for political and Jewish prisoners alike.) Then, in August 1942, SS Reichsführer Heinrich Himmler selected Auschwitz as the principal extermination center for Western Jewry. Auschwitz was camouflaged; it had been planned initially as the site for a huge synthetic oil and rubber industry. It was also well supplied with housing. During World War I, Auschwitz had served as a Habsburg cavalry barracks; and early in World War II it also had functioned briefly as a concentration camp for Polish POWs. Located at the marsh-ridden juncture of the Vistula and Sola rivers in the southern sector of the General Government of Poland, Auschwitz overflowed into some twenty-five square miles of northern Moravia. At its full capacity, the vast reticulation could accommodate up to 140,000 prisoners. Eventually, its five crematoria were capable of burning 10,000 bodies a day.

The largest number of Auschwitz's gassings took place in spring and summer. Winter cold would decimate the prisoners and preclude the need for extermination actions. Thus, the work of bricklaying performed by the inmates was meaningless, its routine only occasionally broken by homicidal roll calls and by human experiments conducted at the hands of German medical men. The typical inmate stayed on his feet bricklaying from twelve to fourteen hours a day, living on a watery turnip soup until he became a Muselmann, a living corpse, wrapped in a scrap of blanket and waiting his turn to die. In these conditions, more prisoners expired of starvation, exhaustion, and disease in Auschwitz than in the gas chambers. Whether its victims died by gassing or debilitation, however, Auschwitz was the single largest extermination center in Nazi Europe. Within its confines approximately 1 million Jews perished.

The Wages of Collaboration: Western Europe

Beyond the Altreich, in an area encompassing some 2 million Jews, a key role in the Final Solution was taken by non-German governments and peoples. Among them, Slovakia and Croatia were satellite states that had been established by Germany. Italy, Bulgaria, Rumania, and Hungary were active allies of Germany. France, however, a defeated former enemy, was a special case, owing to the rather unique surrender formula that established "Occupied" and "Unoccupied" (Vichy) sectors. At the outbreak of the war, approximately 350,000 Jews lived in France. Some 50,000 to 55,000 of these were refugees from the Greater Reich. The rest, French citizens, were fairly evenly divided between veteran, acculturated Jews and more recent immigrants, largely from Eastern Europe (pp. 476–77).

Once the French government surrendered, in June 1940, native and foreign-born Jews alike immediately began fleeing southward to the Vichy zone, until by the end of the year some 195,000 of them were concentrated in Unoccupied France. Yet approximately 150,000 Jews remained in the Occupied Zone. It was accordingly in Occupied France, in the autumn of 1940, that the German administration ordered a census of all Jews and the registration of all Jewish businesses for purposes of "Aryanization." Subsequently, in April 1941, Jews were banned from a wide variety of professional occupations, from access to public transportation and public facilities, and ordered to wear the yellow star. Then, in May and August 1941, the first roundups of foreign-born Jews began in Occupied France. A year later, in May 1942, Adolf Eichmann arrived in Paris with a mandate to "resettle" all Jews, regardless of place of birth. The victims' initial destination was an internment camp in Drancy, a Paris suburb. From Drancy, they were packed into cattle cars at a local rail siding and sent off to Auschwitz.

In Unoccupied France, meanwhile, Marshal Henri-Philippe Pétain, who assumed the office of "head of state" in July 1940, was hesitant at first to adopt flagrantly anti-Jewish measures. It was his vice premier, Pierre Laval, who displayed less squeamishness. At Laval's initiative, and under the direction of the Commissariat des Affaires Juives, French citizenship was stripped from all recently naturalized Jews. Other regulations barred Jews from practicing medicine or law. Then, in October 1940, a new Statut des Juifs defined Jews on racial lines and excluded them, native and foreign-born alike, from employment in public service. In ensuing months, large numbers of Jewish enterprises and properties were "Aryanized." At the same time, an edict of October 7, 1940, swept away the Crémieux Decree of 1870, a law that granted French citizenship to the Jews of Algeria (p. 150).

It was the internment camps, however, that prefigured the darkest chapter of the Vichy period. From early 1941 on, some 10,000 "stateless" Jews were packed into these barracks under inhuman conditions, and 3,000 ultimately died there. In the summer of 1942, 23,000 other stateless Jews were deported from the Vichy Zone to the Occupied Zone, ostensibly to serve the Germans as "industrial labor," but in fact to be dispatched to Auschwitz. Then, in November 1942, following the American invasion of French Algeria, German troops swept across the demarcation line between France's two zones to extend their occupation to the entire country. The SS, by then well launched on the Final Solution in the Occupied area, immediately set about extending its "resettlement" to all parts of France. By the same token, roundups and deportations no longer differentiated between native and foreign-born Jews.

During 1943–44, another 33,500 Jews from all parts of the country were shipped on to Drancy, and thence to Auschwitz. Before France was liberated, in the summer of 1944, an estimated 74,000 French Jews had been deported to the Polish morgue. Another 16,000 to 18,000 died as a result of detention-camp brutality or spot executions. For many years after the war, much of France's political and cultural leadership made the case that they had lived under occupation, and consequently had been helpless victims of German rule. The collaborative role of much of that leadership in the deracination of French Jewry was glossed over.

Ironically, it was a role that contrasted sharply with that of Mussolini's Italy, Germany's wartime partner. The Jews there were as thoroughly acculturated as those in any nation in Europe, more so even than in Germany or France. Comparatively few East Europeans were to be found among them. As far back as 1891, Luigi Luzzatti was appointed minister of finance, and in 1910 he was elected prime minister. Another Jewish cabinet member, Salvatore Barzilai, was a member of the Italian delegation to the Paris Peace Conference. Baron Sidney Sonnino, the Protestant son of a Jewish father and a Catholic mother, served as finance minister, as foreign minister, and twice as prime minister. Giuseppe Ottolenghi became minister of war in 1902. Among the 7,000 Jews who fought in World War I, fifty-one were generals.

Benito Mussolini's rise to power in 1922 produced little discernible alteration in the Jews' status. Indeed, some 5,000 of them, sharing the widespread public fear of mounting syndicalist and anarchist violence, were themselves drawn early to the Fascist Party. Aldo Finzi, a wartime fighter pilot, became a member of the Fascist Grand Council. Dante Almansi served as vice chief of the national police; Guido Jung, as minister of finance; Ludovico Mortara, as president of Italy's supreme court. The Jewish-born Margherita Sarfatti was one of Il Duce's early mistresses and an influential adviser. In Italy as elsewhere, to be sure, the largest numbers of Jews actively or passively supported the nation's anti-Fascist parties and movements. Nevertheless, Mussolini was willing for many years to overlook the Jews traditional propensity for liberalism. He displayed no more interest in antisemitism than did the average Italian. In 1928, the government established a rabbinical seminary in Rhodes (under Italian rule since 1912) and endowed a chair in Italian literature at the Hebrew University of Jerusalem. These gestures plainly were intended to augment Italian influence among Sephardic Jews throughout the Mediterranean world, and to some extent they succeeded.

By the latter 1930s, however, the shared territorial revisionism of Fascist Italy and Nazi Germany drew the two nations closer together. In the spring of 1937, reflecting this congruence, Rome launched a farrago of press attacks on "Jewish bolshevism" and "Jewish dual loyalties." The following year, genuflecting even more obsequiously to Hitler, Mussolini shifted to a flagrant

Nazi-style racism. In July, his party newspaper, *Il Popolo d'Italia,* published a Manifesto of Racial Scientists, signed by ten academicians (none a scholar of reputation). Invoking the jargon of racial pseudoscience, the document asserted that the Italians, like the Germans, were of pure Aryan origin, and the Jews did not belong to "our Italian race." The declaration in turn was followed by establishment of a new government Office of Demography and Race. In November 1938, it was this bureau that formulated a list of anti-Jewish rules and regulations. Virtually overnight, Jews suddenly found themselves banned from the ownership or management of any company employing over 150 workers, from their positions in the party and government, in the arts, sciences, universities, and eventually in the armed services. In later months, Jewish children were barred from public schools and Jewish doctors from employment in hospitals. Marriages between Jews and gentiles were prohibited. Some 8,000 refugees from the Third Reich were given a six-month deadline to leave the country.

From its outset, however, Mussolini's antisemitic program was ambivalent. Jews continued to receive their government pensions, and at least partial compensation for their sequestered industrial or commercial properties. Jewish doctors and lawyers were allowed to function within the Jewish economy. Decorated war veterans usually managed to negotiate "exceptions" for themselves and their families, as did Jews whose public accomplishments defined them as persons of "special merit." Bureaucratic venality played its characteristic Mediterranean role. But so did humanitarianism. With the help of numerous Church officials, the issuance of baptismal certificates over the next three years enabled 6,000 Jews to undergo an expedient conversion and exemption from antisemitic legislation. At no time did racism achieve a solid popular base among the Italian people.

In 1938, the Italian census recorded a Jewish population of 47,000 (including 7,000 refugees). With Mussolini's declaration of war in June 1940, the status of these people immediately deteriorated. The government froze all Jewish bank accounts and drastically tightened Jewish vocational restrictions. By year's end, fully a third of the nation's Jews were subsisting on charity provided by the Joint. The circumstances of foreign Jewish refugees became far more precarious. Nearly half were arrested and confined in internment camps. Yet, even then, the restrictions were porous. Eventually, most of the internees were allowed to reside in neighboring towns and villages under surveillance and curfew, and Jewish communal representatives were permitted to assist them. Nor would Mussolini's government give even the remotest consideration to deporting Jews back to German-occupied Europe.

Nevertheless, in midsummer 1943 the threat of deportations suddenly intensified. The war was going badly for the Axis. Allied troops were fighting their way up the Italian peninsula from the south. On July 24, in a conspiracy of disgruntled former Fascist Party members, Marshal Pietro Badoglio led a group of senior officers in overthrowing the government. Placing Mussolini in custody, the insurgents prepared to extricate Italy from the war. For the Jews, the coup promised a decisive liberation. As the nation's racial laws almost immediately became inoperative, refugees began to emerge from hiding, and local Jews slowly returned to their homes and businesses. Like other Italians, they gave hardly any attention to a powerful German army remaining on the peninsula in the north. On September 12, however, German glider troops suddenly swooped down to rescue Mussolini from his confinement outside Rome. Carried back to the German-occupied north, he was proclaimed dictator of the "Italian Social Republic." In that same late summer, SS units were embarked on a silent hunt for Jews in the northern region. The operation was small-scale and never publicly reported. The much larger Jewish population of Rome was unaware of it. But two weeks after the rescue of Mussolini, SS detachments appeared outside Rome and prepared to launch a *Judenrazzia* (Jew roundup) of the capital's 12,000 Jews.

On September 25, 1943, Commandant Herbert Kappler, the SS attaché at the German embassy, summoned to his office Ugo Foà, president of the Rome Jewish Community. The fate of the Jews was sealed, Kappler informed Foà bluntly. Nevertheless, they might yet spare themselves deportation if they could pay fifty kilograms of gold or its equivalent within the next thirty-six hours. Kappler then dismissed Foà with the observation that "the clock is ticking." Foà and his terrified colleagues immediately set about organizing a "contribution" center in Rome's largest synagogue and alerting as many of their fellow Jews as they could reach. In his desperation, Foà on September 27 also approached his Vatican contacts in the hope of securing a papal loan. The hope was vindicated. Almost immediately Pius XII sent back word that he was prepared to lend the Jews any amount of gold they might need (p. 564). In fact, none was required. As local Jews deluged the synagogue with their contributions of jewelry and silverplate, the collection campaign reached its goal. By the morning of September 28, the treasure was delivered in cartons to Kappler's office.

The ransom effort was wasted; Kappler's offer had been fraudulent. From Berlin, Adolf Eichmann dispatched his personal aide, SS Captain Theodor Dannecker, to supervise a decisive *Judenrazzia* in Rome. Two and a half weeks later, on the night of October 16, the roundup began. SS troops surrounded the eight-block Lungotevere—former ghetto—area, where some 4,000 of the city's 12,000 Jews still lived. Of these, the SS now collected over 1,000 men, women, and children and carried them off for rail shipment to Poland. The following month, the roundup of Jews picked up momentum elsewhere in Italy, in Milan, Siena, Florence, and Bologna. By December 1943, nine deportation trains already had left Italian soil, carrying 5,000 Jews to Auschwitz.

Although not a few Italian police and other government personnel collaborated in the Final Solution, the wider public reaction was far more humane. In rural areas, Jews were offered hiding places in rooming houses, resort hotels, even private farms. In cities, Jews moved in with gentile friends, or rented private rooms in distant neighborhoods. Everywhere, in the countryside and cities alike, simple farmers, maids, janitors, and other private citizens hid Jews in attics or cellars, or saved their possessions, or took in and saved their children. Altogether, the survival of nearly 38,000 Jews out of a population of 45,000 (in 1943) was almost unique for Nazi-occupied Europe.

THE WAGES OF COLLABORATION: EAST-CENTRAL EUROPE

East and south of the Altreich of German-speaking Europe, there were also gradations of participation in the Nazi genocide. Bulgaria was a case in point. Following that nation's defeat in World War I, and its extensive territorial losses, the public mood was embittered and xenophobic. During the postwar years, a collection of right-wing parties sprang up, obsessed with Bulgaria's irredentist grievances in Macedonia, and the perceived failure of democratic government. By the late 1930s, Nazi political ideology similarly gained a wider acceptance, and in 1939 Hitler succeeded in wooing the Sofia government into his Anti-Comintern Pact of fascist solidarity. In turn, bending with the political winds, King Boris III in February 1940 appointed a rabid Germanophile, Bogdan Filov, as his prime minister. The following year, Filov won legislative approval to allow Wehrmacht troops access to Bulgarian territory; and in April 1941, Bulgaria became a launching base for Germany's devastating invasion of Greece and Yugoslavia.

As a payoff for this help, Hitler awarded Bulgaria extensive areas of conquered Greek and Yugoslav Macedonia, and portions of Greek Thrace. These were the circumstances in which 13,000 Macedonian and Thracian Jews fell under Bulgarian rule. Almost immediately, Bulgarian fascist paramilitaries launched into the pillage of Jewish communal offices, synagogues, and private homes and businesses. Yet the chauvinist rampage was insufficient to satisfy Berlin. In Sofia, Germany's special representative on Jewish affairs, the peripatetic Theodor Dannecker (p. 543), dunned the Bulgarian government relentlessly for decisive measures against Bulgaria's "integral" population of 50,000 Jews. Prime Minister Filov did not object. Even earlier, in December 1940, his cabinet had stripped citizenship from several hundred naturalized Jews and dispatched them on three aged vessels in the general direction of

Palestine. Only one of the leaking hulks, the *Salvador*, got as far as the Sea of Marmara. Caught in a storm there, it sank less than a mile from the Turkish coast. Of the 204 passengers who drowned, 66 were children. During the ensuing months, the Filov cabinet adopted a comparably punitive approach to Bulgaria's native-born Jewish population, slashing their food rations, banning their ownership of telephones or radios, denying their children admission to public schools.

In June 1942, approximately 6,000 Jewish males of military age were shipped off to road-building camps and to subhuman living and working conditions. Their fate, and that of other Jews, was linked to the even more dire circumstances of the Jews in occupied Macedonia and Thrace. By then, Dannecker, the German SS representative, was pressing for a mass deportation of the entire Bulgarian-Jewish population. Again Prime Minister Filov was prepared to cooperate. Yet he sensed that King Boris and much of the Bulgarian parliament would not. For them, the veteran Jewish population, almost exclusively Sephardic, had long fitted comfortably into Bulgaria's heterogeneous ethnic landscape. As Germany's Ambassador Adolf Beckerle noted ruefully in his dispatch to Berlin in January 1943: "Raised partly among Greeks, Armenians, Gypsies, and Jews, the average Bulgarian does not fathom the significance of the fight against the Jews, especially since he is not too concerned with racial issues." Sentient to that lingering pluralism, Filov moved to appease the Germans with a partial payment. In March 1943, he turned over to them the 13,000—non-Bulgarian—Jews of occupied Macedonia and Thrace. The captives were duly loaded into convoys of trucks and railcars, and sent off toward Poland. En route, thousands of them perished of suffocation. Those who survived were delivered to the death camp of Treblinka, where they were annihilated to the last soul.

Dannecker remained unappeased. He intensified his demand for the mass deportation of Bulgaria's "integral" Jewry, nothing less. At this point, Filov decided on a significantly wider concession to the Germans. In the same month that the Macedonian and Thracian Jews were dispatched to Treblinka, the prime minister ordered a roundup in Sofia of 8,000 Jewish "undesirables," essentially business and cultural leaders and their families. Then, at the last moment, even as rolling stock was assembled for their deportation, several Jewish communal leaders managed to secure an interview with Orthodox Archbishop Kiril, and to inform him of the impending tragedy. Shaken to his depths, Kiril demanded an immediate audience with the king. The meeting took place in the royal palace on March 17, 1943, and the archbishop minced no words in warning Boris that if he permitted this atrocity, he would jeopardize his immortal soul. At the same time, forty-two Bulgarian parliamentary members dispatched an urgent letter to the king, reminding him that the

Allies were threatening retribution against officials implicated in mass murder (p. 567). The warnings registered. Boris stiffened and vetoed the deportations. Filov in turn sought to reassure Dannecker that he, the prime minister, would find a way secretly to ship off some 25,000 Jews living or working in the provinces. But in May, the plan leaked, and the king blocked it again. No further Jews were deported.

King Boris would pay, however. On August 24, 1943, he was summoned to Berlin, where Hitler personally subjected him to a harsh browbeating on the Jewish issue. Obsequiously, but vaguely, the king promised his cooperation. He returned home on August 26. Two days later, he died. There were rumors that the Nazis had exacted their revenge by poisoning him, or by causing his weak heart to fail by engaging in aerial maneuvers upon flying him back to Sofia. Whatever the explanation, the Jews of "integral" Bulgaria had been spared the fate of their kinsmen elsewhere in the Balkans. Although 4,000 of them perished of work-camp brutality, the great majority of the nation's 50,000 Jews survived the war.

That stroke of "good fortune" was not to be shared by the other Jewish populations of East-Central Europe, whose fate almost mathematically reflected the vicissitudes of postwar diplomacy. Thus, the Kingdom of Rumania, the single most engorged of the post–World War I successor states, unexpectedly became the victim of a secret deal negotiated between Nazi Germany and the Soviet Union. Only months after signing the Nazi-Soviet Pact in August 1939, the Soviets "preempted" Bessarabia and northern Bukovina from Rumania. With the same German support, Hungary and Bulgaria "reclaimed" Rumania's Peace Conference awards of northern Transylvania and southern Dobrudja. In turn, blaming King Carol for supinely accepting the nation's dismemberment, Rumania's fascist leagues compelled the monarch to abdicate, then assumed power themselves (p. 431). Under the ensuing dictatorship of General Ion Antonescu, the military chief of staff, the regime wasted no time launching into a policy of "national unification." Its purpose manifestly was to recover its lost territories, a goal that seemed achievable after June 1941, with Hitler's invasion of the Soviet Union. Yet, to fulfill that objective, Antonescu was obliged to commit Rumania's armed forces to active combat on the Soviet front. The price would be a heavy one for the Rumanian people.

It would be heavier yet for the Jews. Even as it collaborated in Germany's military campaign, the Antonescu government coordinated its Jewish policy with Berlin's. The pattern was established in the first week of the war. Following a Soviet air raid on Jassy, the Rumanian army and native fascists organized their own "retaliation" against the city's Jews. Approximately 8,000 Jewish men and boys were shipped off in cattle cars to dead-end sidings, where nearly all perished of suffocation. Another 3,000 Jews were shot or hacked to pieces in the street. It was the merest overture to Rumania's exercise in "ethnic cleansing." Moving along the flanks of the Wehrmacht, the Rumanian army reoccupied Bessarabia, seized Bukovina, then pushed on across the Dniester River, eventually sharing in the capture of the port of Odessa. The territory seized by the Rumanians on the eastern bank of the Dniester was substantial. They dubbed it Transnistria. With Berlin's permission, Transnistria would remain under Rumanian jurisdiction (although under joint military occupation) to serve as Rumania's principal Jewish killing ground.

Thus, before the Nazi invasion, some 300,000 Jews lived in Bessarabia and Bukovina. Once the war in the Soviet Union began, the Rumanians and Germans found it simpler to herd much of this vast population across the Dniester into Transnistria. Here two-thirds of them were liquidated in August 1941. Most of the executions were carried out by the German SS; but in the autumn, when a Rumanian general and his staff were killed in an explosion at their Odessa headquarters, Antonescu ordered a "reprisal" against the Jews at a ratio of 100 to 1. Hereupon, the Rumanian army itself assumed responsibility for slaughtering at least 185,000 additional Jews, including 90,000 in Odessa. In the process, they shocked even the Germans in their fondness for mutilating corpses.

At the same time, the 406,000 Jews of the Regat—"integral," pre-1938 Rumania—fared somewhat better than those in the occupied territories. On the one hand, Bucharest tightened its already grim constraints on these civilians, ghettoizing them, reducing them to subsistence rations and exposure to widespread confiscation of property, forcing large numbers of their men and boys to serve in penal labor brigades. Nevertheless, there appeared no thought of deportation. But in the summer of 1942, Adolf Eichmann's personal representative, SS Major Gustav Richter, negotiated an understanding with the Antonescu regime. It was to deport this entire "integral" Jewish population to Transnistria, where the Germans would "take care of them."

Here, too, however, mass deportation was not to be easily accomplished. It awaited the accumulation of substantial quantities of rolling stock. The logistical delay extended into late autumn, and on into the winter. Then the German defeat at Stalingrad in February 1943, together with the decimation of four Rumanian divisions, convinced Antonescu that the war was shifting against the Axis, and that the threat of Allied retribution no longer was remote. In that same February, therefore, Antonescu began sending out peace signals to the Allies (p. 568), and simultaneously resisting all further German demands for Jewish deportation. Debilitated and demoralized though they were, most of the Jewish "core" population survived. Their solace was bittersweet. Once the Rumanian government surrendered to the Red Army in

August 1944, the wider impact of its anti-Jewish collaboration with the Germans could be assessed. Fully 380,000 Rumanian Jews had perished, most of them in the German-occupied territories.

The scope of that mass slaughter actually was exceeded in neighboring Hungary. It was an asymmetry that could not have been anticipated before the war. In contrast with Rumania's tradition of antisemitic thuggishness, the circumstances of Hungary's 454,000 Jews remained at least physically tolerable well into the mid-1930s. It was only following Germany's Anschluss with Austria, in March 1938, that Hungary's government began genuflecting to the Nazi führer by enacting a succession of harshly discriminatory "Jewish laws" (pp. 442–43). A generation earlier, the nation's veteran Jewish families had regarded themselves as among Hungary's economic and cultural aristocracy. Now, humiliated and broken, they possessed less moral defense in depth than did their fellow Jews in Poland and Rumania. Their single consolation lay in their apparent physical security.

Yet the fate of Hungary's newly annexed Jews became an ominous augury. In November 1938, barely one month after Germany's occupation of the Czech Sudetenland, Hitler returned to Hungary extensive tracts of its pre-1919 Slovakian territories. In these regions lived 87,000 Jews. In March 1939, after swallowing the rest of Czechoslovakia, Hitler threw Hungary another territorial bone, this one containing 72,000 Jews. In the summer of 1941, moreover, as a payoff for collaborating with Germany in the invasion of the Soviet Union, Hitler's "Second Vienna Award" authorized the Hungarians to occupy still additional terrain at the expense of both the Rumanians and the Russians. Whatever its logistical advantages, the territorial increment also brought with it 156,000 additional Jews, thereby raising Hungary's Jewish population to nearly 800,000.

For the Budapest government, a Jewish engorgement of this magnitude was unacceptable. With the tacit approbation of Prime Minister Miklos Kallay, therefore, the Hungarian army gave over some 40,000 Jews in the occupied regions to the German SS, which promptly massacred them. Yet, even as late as 1942, Kallay resisted all Nazi demands for the deportation of Hungary's "integral" Jews, and adopted instead the well-perfected diversion of an intensified program of domestic antisemitism. Thus, in the summer of 1942, Kallay steered a bill through parliament depriving Jews of their final rights to own real estate. At the same time, he agreed to supply 50,000 Jews for labor battalions on the Russian front, where all but 7,000 of them were literally worked to death.

In the winter of 1942–43, as the German army suffered its shattering defeat at Stalingrad, some 80,000 Hungarian troops froze to death in the Don campaign near Voronezh. At this point, Regent Horthy and Prime Minister Kallay sensed that the tide of the war was shifting. Secretly, then, they began dispatching peace overtures to the Allies—and simultaneously easing a number of the government's harshest anti-Jewish pressures. Even at that late date, 744,000 Jews remained alive in Greater Hungary, 450,000 of them in "integral," prewar Hungary. When Berlin protested the "laxity" of Hungary's Jewish policy and demanded additional deportations, Kallay held firm. Moreover, as the German Wehrmacht suffered wider-ranging defeats, additional voices were raised to dissociate Hungary from the Axis and specifically from Hitler's Jewish policy.

Yet the führer himself would have something to say about this volte-face. On March 18, 1944, he launched Operation Margarete, the dispatch of four Wehrmacht divisions into Hungary. Admiral Horthy was in Berlin at the time, having responded to Hitler's personal invitation. When the news of Operation Margarete was sprung on him, it was accompanied by a warning that the Hungarian government would find it useful to accede to Germany's demands, including an appropriate "common position" on the Jewish question. Shaken, the regent then promised his full cooperation. Upon returning to Budapest, he appointed a new prime minister, Dome Sztojay, a militant fascist. Almost immediately, Sztojay's cabinet set about issuing a series of decrees that stripped Jews of their last remnants of dignity. They were obliged to wear the yellow star, to surrender their telephones and radios, to refrain from using public transportation. These measures soon were followed by a registration of Jewish assets, a freezing of Jewish bank accounts, and finally a selective expropriation of Jewish properties. By April 1944, Hungarian Jewry was reduced to destitution.

A still grimmer fate awaited. That month Adolf Eichmann arrived in Budapest and wasted little time in personally formulating plans for a decisive Jewish "resettlement." As early as April 13, 1944, the Jews of the annexed territories were being rounded up and concentrated in urban ghettos. Now, however, on May 15, with the full cooperation of the Hungarian police, Eichmann launched into the deportations of Jews from the entirety of Greater Hungary. Over the ensuing eight weeks, 437,000 Jews were shipped off to the Polish death camps. Only the 325,000 Jews packed into Budapest and its immediate surroundings remained to be disposed of. But at the same time, news of this climactic liquidation reached the Allied governments. In turn, their warnings to Horthy were plainspoken. He would be held personally responsible for war crimes (p. 558). Changing course yet again, the regent on July 2, 1944, ordered a halt to all further deportations, and Eichmann was "advised" to return to Germany. Seven weeks later, Horthy dismissed the pro-German Kallay government, then dispatched a secret mission to Moscow to begin armistice negotiations. Finally, on October 15, in a broadcast to the nation, Horthy confirmed that he had signed an armistice with the Soviet Union, and under its terms his government now was declaring war on Germany.

Four days later, the Germans struck back. Wehrmacht reinforcements poured into Hungary, and an SS unit abducted Horthy's son and "interned" him in Germany as a hostage. At the same time, Hungary's pro-Nazi Arrow Cross Party forced the regent's abdication, and the party's leader, Ferenc Szalasi (p. 441), assumed office as prime minister. Within days, Adolf Eichmann returned to Budapest to assume personal direction of a definitive Jewish liquidation. In ensuing weeks, as the Red Army battered its way closer to Hungary's borders, SS troops and Arrow Cross police joined forces to "thin out" the vast concentration of Jews in the capital area. Whereupon, some 5,000 Jews were shot or drowned, nearly 100,000 others were herded into trucks and railcars or force-marched by foot, to perish either en route to Auschwitz or within the confines of the death camp itself.

By the time the Red Army reached Budapest, approximately 119,000 Jews remained alive, most of them in the Budapest area. In August, an additional 72,000 returned from detention camps, together with 11,000 from penal work gangs, and isolated groups of some 15,000 others from the provinces. Of the 800,000 Jews of "Greater Hungary" (at its 1941 apogee), it later was estimated that approximately 575,000 had perished. Of these, slightly over 400,000 had been nationals of "integral" Hungary. By either calculation, the death toll represented the single widest-ranging genocide of Jews in all of "collaborationist" Europe.

XXVIII

The Final Solution *and the Struggle for Jewish Survival*

JEWISH RESISTANCE

In his monumental three-volume *Destruction of the European Jews,* Raul Hilberg, dean of holocaust historians, is unsparing in his criticism of European Jewry's "almost complete lack of [wartime] resistance." By his evaluation, the Jews "avoided 'provocations' and complied instantly with [Nazi] decrees and orders." Hilberg attributes this passivity both to the Jewish leadership and to the Jewish masses. Their entire culture, he explains, was one of obedience to authority, and in the end that tradition proved their downfall.

Hilberg's judgment on Jewish passivity, although once shared by most historians, has been challenged in recent decades. In the era of the Third Reich, entire nations under the Nazi heel failed to generate effective uprisings against the German military machine. The Jews, locked in the central killing ground of Poland, lacked weapons, and faced the certainty of brutal collective retaliation. More fundamentally, they were surrounded not merely by thousands of armed German soldiers, by Polish and Ukrainian guards under German command, but by Polish and Ukrainian populations the intensity of whose antisemitism was a grimly authenticated fact of modern history. General Tadeusz Bor-Komorowski, commander of the Polish Home Army, who later would lead the August 1944 Warsaw underground revolt, issued a directive in September 1943, accusing Jewish anti-Nazi partisan groups in the Polish forests of "bolshevism" and "banditry," and ordered their extermination. In Soviet Lithuania and Ukraine, antisemitism was possibly more virulent than in Poland. Even Jews serving in the Red Army faced the danger of being shot in the back if their officers were Ukrainian. In all these East European nations, the very notion of Jewish resistance efforts might have appeared surrealistic.

Yet resistance efforts did take place. Some of these originated with members of the Polish Zionist parties, those who had been inspired by the activist tradition of kinsmen in Palestine. Thus, in Warsaw, during the summer of 1942, a youthful Warsaw Zionist, Mordecai Anielewicz, won over Jews of other political backgrounds to the cause of resistance. Immediately, a core group of seven hundred younger men and women set about digging bunkers and underground shelters. Money was scraped together to purchase modest quantities of small arms from Polish Communist intermediaries. By the end of the year, at a time when barely 40,000 Jews remained alive, the Jewish guerrilla nucleus had emerged as a dominant force among Warsaw's ghetto population.

In January 1943, Heinrich Himmler personally visited Warsaw and issued the order for a final deportation of the city's remnant Jewry. Weeks passed before sufficient rolling stock could be accumulated, but on April 13, SS Major-General Jürgen Stroop arrived from the Balkans to execute Himmler's order. He had under his command some 2,000 men, half of them Poles and Lithuanians, the rest a mixed collection of SS and regular army troops. Stroop anticipated that the roundup would be completed within three days. On April 19, at dawn, he sent his men into the ghetto. No sooner had the detachments moved into position, however, than they were greeted by a fusillade of bullets and Molotov cocktails from tenement roofs and windows. In response, Stroop ordered up artillery and flamethrowers. When put into action, these weapons effectively destroyed the Jews' firing positions in surrounding buildings. Even then, the defenders descended into bunkers and sewers, and continued their resistance. The SS brought up mechanical drills, dynamite, and gas shells. Sewers were flooded. Police dogs were unleashed. Fighting still continued.

Although the Polish underground immediately learned of the uprising—the sounds of battle carried well beyond the ghetto wall—it was powerless to intervene. At most, it succeeded in transmitting news of the unfolding struggle to the Polish government-in-exile in London. The Allied governments then were informed. None could offer help. In London, on May 11, 1943, Szmuel Zygelboim, an expatriate former official of the Polish-Jewish Bund, whose own wife and daughter already had perished in Warsaw, flung himself from his upper-story hotel window. He left behind a suicide note, declaring: "I wish to make my final protest against the passivity with which the world is looking on and permitting the extermination of the Jewish people." Five days after Zygelboim's suicide, General Stroop's action in the ghetto was completed, three and a half weeks after it had begun. German casualties did not exceed 150 men. In all, some 40,000 Jews perished—7,000 by military action, 20,000 by deportation to Treblinka, and the rest simply buried and burned under the debris. Only a few dozen Jews managed to escape through the sewers, eventually to join partisan groups.

There were other, less publicized episodes of resistance among the approximately four hundred ghettos in the General Government of Poland. In Bialystok, organized fighting erupted in August 1943, and guerrilla resistance continued intermittently for weeks afterward. In that same month, uprisings were attempted (equally futilely) in Treblinka and Auschwitz. Except for the Warsaw ghetto uprising, the single other marginally effective episode occurred in Sobibor, in October 1943. Here one of the prisoners, Alexander Pecherski, a Soviet-Jewish officer, carefully organized and personally led a mass breakout of 600 Jews. Of these, some 400 managed to overpower their Ukrainian guards and escape to the surrounding woods. Most of them eventually were caught and immediately shot. But sixty-two men and women, Pecherski among them, survived and eventually joined partisan units. Other Jewish escapees were less fortunate. Ukrainian and Polish guerrillas either drove them off or killed them. Elsewhere, throughout Poland and Ukraine, some 15,000 Jews eventually reached partisan units attached to the Red Army, and these were allowed to fight on. In other countries, Jews tended to organize their own underground units. In Yugoslavia, these fought in intimate collaboration with Tito's partisans. In France, the Éclaireurs Juifs (Jewish Scouts) similarly fought in their own units.

In Palestine, meanwhile, during the winter of 1942–43, the Jewish Agency leadership intensified their appeals to the British authorities for permission to assist the mortally beleaguered Jews of Europe. As David Ben-Gurion reminded the British, Jews in Rumania, Hungary, Slovakia, and Bulgaria were still "reachable." With proper leadership, they could still be organized for resistance or escape. The trained Zionist fighters of Palestine were the logical source of that leadership, Ben-Gurion insisted, for many of them had come from these enemy nations, spoke the languages, had families and friends there to serve as contacts. Yet the British Colonial Office rejected the proposal. It feared complications with the Arabs.

In early spring of 1944, however, a more favorable response was forthcoming, and from Prime Minister Winston Churchill himself. The prime minister's son, Randolph, a military officer serving in the Middle East, was rather taken with the notion of arming the Jews, and he won over his father. Winston Churchill then authorized the training of up to five hundred Palestinian parachutists for the specific purpose of rescuing their kinsmen in Europe. Even then, the Colonial Office and the mandatory government in Palestine interposed numerous bureaucratic obstacles, and eventually whittled down the number of selected volunteers to thirty-two. Finally, in late summer 1944, RAF bombers airlifted the Palestinians to the selected targets. Nine of the parachutists were dropped into Rumania, three into Hungary, two into Bulgaria, three into Italy, six into Slovakia, nine into Yugoslavia. Of these volunteers, all but one were caught and executed. Two of the parachutists were women. One of them, Haviva Reik, managed to organize a Jewish underground unit in Slovakia, even established a transit camp for escaping Russian prisoners of war, before she was captured and shot. The second woman, Hannah Szenes, a twenty-three-year-old Hungarian Jew, was caught by Arrow

Cross police while secretly visiting her mother in Budapest and subsequently was turned over to an SS firing squad.

The parachutist episode accounted for the escape of between 2,000 and 3,000 Jews, who were alerted in time to seek out hiding places. Yet, notwithstanding its moral or symbolic usefulness for collective self-esteem, Jewish resistance could achieve few practical results in collective survival. In the end, rescue probably would have to depend upon a far older Jewish strategy, one that had been well tested over the centuries. Ironically, it was the Germans themselves now who suggested its adoption.

RANSOM DIPLOMACY: NAZI-STYLE

During the course of the Final Solution in Italy, a new dimension of Nazi policy emerged. This was financial blackmail. In September 1943, SS Commandant Herbert Kappler achieved a monetary payoff from the Jews of Rome (p. 543). Did the episode represent merely the peculation of a single, avaricious German officer? The collective exactions demanded in Slovakia, in 1941, and in Hungary, in 1944, suggested otherwise. In Slovakia, the collaborationist government was ruled by the Slovak People's Party, an anti-Czech, antisemitic regime of undisguised fascist orientation. In March 1939, the party's leader, Jozef Tiso, a Catholic monsignor, had cooperated with Hitler in the spoliation of Czechoslovakia by declaring the "independence" of Slovakia under his own presidency. In this "independent" Slovakia lived 89,000 Jews. Almost immediately, the new Slovak government set about issuing a series of anti-Jewish laws, culminating in the mass expropriation of Jewish property in September 1941.

Since August 1940, Germany's "adviser on Jewish affairs" in the Slovakian capital of Bratislava was SS Captain Dieter Wisliceny. A former theology student, Wisliceny had tried his hand in business before joining the Nazi Party in 1931 and the SS in 1934. He brought a businessman's instincts to his assignment in Slovakia. In the summer of 1941, when the Tiso government refused the German labor ministry's request for 20,000 Slovak workers and offered Jews instead, Wisliceny came up with the brainstorm of sending the Jews' families with them—at the Slovakian government's expense. In February 1942, one month after the Grossen Wansee Conference (p. 529), as Heydrich and Eichmann pressed vigorously for a swift and total implementation of the Final Solution in Slovakia, Wisliceny devised an equally imaginative approach. It was for the Tiso government to reimburse Germany for the Jews' transport to Poland, at the rate of 500 marks per head. On that basis, the mass deportations duly began on March 26, 1942, with an initial transport of girls, ages eight and up.

One day later, through intermediaries, Slovakia's Chief Rabbi Michael

Weissmandel and the Slovakian Zionist leader, Gisi Fleischmann, dispatched a frantic message to Wisliceny. It was a plainspoken offer of a bribe (ostensibly from "world Jewish sources") to stop the shipments. On March 29, Wisliceny sent back an equally plainspoken reply. He wanted $50,000 in cash. With much difficulty, the money was raised, most of it from the Joint Distribution Committee. The funds were transmitted through a go-between in Switzerland, Saly Mayer, a retired Jewish businessman and former president of the Union of Swiss Jewish Communities. Yet the deportations did not stop. Rather, by late July, 52,000 Jews already had been dispatched to Poland. Only 29,000 still remained, most of these children. Throughout the summer and early autumn, therefore, Mayer frantically sought to arrange a new ransom of $100,000. But in the meantime Wisliceny sent word that he was raising the ante, to $200,000. Although appalled at this new extortion, Mayer nevertheless struggled on grimly to secure the additional funding. Wisliceny for his part then twice postponed his deportation deadlines. By late summer of 1943, the rest of the $200,000 was accumulated. It reached Bratislava via Istanbul. But the effort ultimately proved fruitless. On September 18, 1943, at the personal order of Adolf Eichmann, the deportations were resumed from Slovakia. The country's remaining Jews were doomed.

Yet it developed that Wisliceny was not the only German official behind the Slovakian negotiations. Himmler and Eichmann had been informed and had approved the blackmail. For Himmler, the inducement almost certainly was not the paltry sums involved. More likely it reflected his awareness that Jewish contacts might be useful in protecting Germany's range of diplomatic options in the event the war continued to go badly. Indeed, those contacts soon were extended to collaborationist Hungary, with its far larger Jewish population of three-quarters of a million. Throughout 1942 and 1943, the circumstances of Hungarian Jewry, while grim, had not yet approached the scale of mass annihilation, not even in Hungary's recently annexed territories (p. 548). Then, on March 18, 1944, Hitler ordered German troops into Hungary in an effort to forestall Admiral Horthy's separate armistice with the Soviet Union. At the same time, Horthy was ordered to participate unequivocally in the Final Solution. Thoroughly intimidated, the Hungarian regent acquiesced. In April and May the movement of "resettlement" trains to Auschwitz resumed its momentum. Again, the first regions to feel the deportations were the annexed Vienna Award territories. Altogether, between May 18 and July 7, 1944, approximately 437,000 Jews were deported to Auschwitz. Those who remained were some 350,000 Jews in Greater Budapest, the majority of them jammed into the capital's Erzsebetvaros (Jewish) district.

It was in the midst of this spring-summer nightmare that a new phase of Nazi-Jewish relations developed. Arriving with the German army in March 1944 was an SS unit led personally by Adolf Eichmann. Attached to Eichmann's staff was the avaricious Dieter Wisliceny, who had been brought from Slovakia specifically to investigate a possible financial deal with the Jews. Wisliceny had been informed by his Bratislava contact, Rabbi Weissmandel, that a useful negotiating contact in Budapest was Reszoe (Rudolf) Kasztner (evidently it was not yet clear that Slovakian Jewry was altogether doomed). In 1943, Kasztner, a former Transylvanian journalist, and more recently a prominent spokesman in Budapest's still modest Zionist movement, had helped organize an Aid and Rescue Committee, known loosely as the Va'adah. One of Kasztner's closest Va'adah associates was Joel Brand. Also born in Transylvania, Brand had been a Communist agent in Germany until 1934, when he fled back to Transylvania, and later yet to Budapest, where he was employed in his wife's small glove factory. In 1942, Brand joined Kasztner in the Va'adah's effort to save refugees. Now, in the spring of 1944, they were identified by Wisliceny as the likeliest interlocutors for a ransom agreement.

A month after arriving in Budapest, Wisliceny was replaced as negotiator by Eichmann himself. On April 25, therefore, it was Eichmann who summoned Joel Brand to SS headquarters on Budapest's Schwabenberg. As Brand later recalled, Eichmann's greeting was terse:

> You know who I am. I am the man who liquidated the Jews of Poland, Slovakia, and Austria, and now I have been appointed head of the liquidation commando in Hungary. I am willing to do business with you: human lives for merchandise. What do you want? Women who can bear children? Men who can make them? Children? Whatever is left of your people's biological potential?

While Brand remained speechless, Eichmann elaborated upon the German demands, and it soon became clear that he was also speaking in the name of Himmler. Initially, Eichmann's offer was to release 100,000 Jews. In ensuing discussions, however, he successively raised the offer to 1 million Jews, both from Hungary and from other European countries. He was prepared to let them go in installments, he explained, to Spain or anywhere else, except to Palestine, for the führer had promised his friend Grand Mufti Amin al-Husseini not to permit that. In exchange, Eichmann demanded from the Western Allies no fewer than 10,000 trucks, together with 1,000 tons of coffee or tea, and 1,000 tons of soap. The trucks would be used exclusively against the Russians, he assured Brand, on the Eastern Front.

Brand could only guess at the SS's purpose in authorizing these negotiations. Almost certainly it was not to allow 1 million Jews to go free. Was the objective a separate peace with the Western Allies? Although it seemed unlikely, the very process of negotiations might itself save lives. Brand was convinced that it had to be pursued. But when he conveyed the offer to Kasztner and the other Va'adah members, the latter were skeptical and reluctant to proceed. In fact, it was Eichmann himself who made the decision. He sent word that Brand was to depart immediately for Turkey, where he would present the offer to "world Jewish representatives" on neutral soil. Kasztner and his associates then had no choice but to acquiesce.

On May 17, 1944, Brand was flown in a German courier airplane from Budapest to Istanbul. Awaiting him there were two representatives of the Jewish Agency for Palestine, Wenja Pomeranz and Menahem Bader, who had been alerted to his visit. After hearing Brand's astounding account, and questioning him intensively, the two men returned to Palestine to confer urgently with David Ben-Gurion, the Jewish Agency chairman. Ben-Gurion and his colleagues took the offer seriously. Yet, upon informing the British authorities, they evoked only suspicion. Sir Harold MacMichael, Britain's high commissioner for Palestine, suspected a Nazi ruse to split the Allied front. In any case, it was unthinkable even to consider the delivery of war matériel to Germany. Ben-Gurion did not disagree. He argued, however, that negotiations at least should be undertaken, and if possible strung out, for Himmler and Eichmann might then be willing to postpone Jewish deportations. But when the proposal was relayed to the Allied governments, Britain's Foreign Secretary Anthony Eden immediately shot it down, as did United States Secretary of State Cordell Hull. Both men agreed that if Moscow got wind of Allied negotiations with the Nazis, it would suspect Western treachery. Indeed, to ensure that the scheme got no further, the British transported Joel Brand from Turkey to Syria and kept him there in "temporary internment."

Even as these discussions were taking place, Kasztner and his Va'adah associates in Budapest frantically awaited Brand's return. The shipment of Jews to Auschwitz was gaining momentum each day. On his own initiative, then, Kasztner himself met with Eichmann in June to propose that selected groups of Jews be allowed to depart Hungary forthwith as a token of German "good faith." Eichmann needed barely forty-eight hours to consult with Berlin, and to secure agreement in principle—provided a substantial sum of money was paid over. Within ten days, the money was forthcoming, although the actual amount (possibly $1 million) and its source have never been determined. Immediately, Kasztner returned to his hometown of Cluj. There, on June 10, he selected 388 members of his own extended family, as well as groups of family friends. Numbering 1,684 in all, the exempted Jews were carried away by train on June 15, 1944, and brought safely to Switzerland. At the "request" of the German embassy, the Swiss government this time admitted them without asking questions. Eichmann's and Himmler's motives in agreeing to the rescue train, and for an apparently paltry sum, still remain unclear. Possibly they assumed that a token selection of Jews might serve as bait for later arrangements with "world Jewry."

Kasztner, meanwhile, conducting his negotiations throughout the summer without the absent Brand, pressed Eichmann for a wider number of exemptions. There had been a brief glimmer of hope in early July when Admiral Horthy, shaken by grave Allied warnings of retribution, took it upon himself to halt the Jewish deportations. Yet the interruption was very brief. On August 14, under mounting Nazi pressure, Horthy allowed the deportations to resume. In his desperation, Kasztner then sought out another member of Eichmann's staff. This was Kurt Becher. Serving earlier with the SS in Poland, Becher had personally shared in the plunder of the Warsaw ghetto. Aware of this record, Kasztner suspected that Becher might be "reachable." He was. The two men then arranged a private meeting with Saly Mayer, the Swiss-Jewish intermediary. Eventually, four meetings between the three men took place in late August and early September 1944, on the Rhine River's Sankt Margareten Bridge between Switzerland and Germany.

Although Becher at first held firm on Eichmann's original demand, that is, for 10,000 trucks and other supplies, eventually he intimated that 20 million Swiss francs might be an acceptable "down payment" to postpone further deportations. Mayer then urgently discussed the matter with representatives of the Joint, and with Roswell McClelland, operating in Switzerland as a representative of the United States War Refugee Board (p. 568). Nothing came of the proposal. Washington vetoed it. Even then, Mayer and Becher continued their meetings throughout the autumn and into December 1944. But the contacts became increasingly meaningless. By the end of 1944, two-thirds of Hungarian Jewry had been immolated, and in any case the Reich itself was crumbling. Ultimately, it was the collapse and the chaos of Wehrmacht withdrawal from Hungary, not the feckless ransom negotiations with SS officials, that accounted for the survival of some 215,000 Hungarian Jews.

AN EQUIVOCATION OF NEUTRALISM

Turkey, an initial site for those ransom contacts, might itself have appeared a logical haven for many tens of thousands of Jewish refugees. In earlier centuries, no other nation had functioned as a more generous sanctuary for waves of Jewish fugitives (p. 139). Even during the 1930s, the Turkish government had granted permanent residence status to some 4,000 Jews from the Nazi Reich, specifically to those who could be useful to the national economy. But once the war began, the Turks adopted a stance of diplomatic circumspection. Intimidated by the sheer magnitude of Germany's military victories and by the looming proximity of the Wehrmacht in the Balkans and in southern Russia, Turkey's President Ismet Inonu and his cabinet set out to placate Berlin in every fashion short of entering the war at Germany's side. Authorizing the sale to Germany of vital supplies of manganese and mercury, the Turkish leadership also turned a blind eye as German embassy and consular offices in Ankara and Istanbul became hotbeds of Middle Eastern espionage.

For the same reason, the Turkish government no longer was prepared to offer even temporary asylum to Jewish refugees. Fearful of angering either the Germans or the British, Inonu and his colleagues required all refugees to possess official entry papers for Palestine, and Syrian transit documents, before being admitted. Few Jews did. In December 1941, the *Struma,* a rickety, Bulgarian-owned schooner, dropped anchor in Istanbul harbor. Several weeks earlier, the vessel had departed the Rumanian port of Constanta, bound for Palestine. Carrying 767 Jews, the overloaded boat had limped along the Black Sea coast. Now, with its engine malfunctioning and its hull leaking, the *Struma* was obliged to dock in Istanbul. Here representatives of the Joint implored the Turkish government to grant the refugees a temporary haven. The appeal was repeatedly turned down. In February 1942, declaring their patience exhausted, the Turks ordered the *Struma* to weigh anchor. Five miles out at sea, the vessel, still carrying the flag of Bulgaria, a nation at war with Russia, was torpedoed by a Soviet submarine. It sank with the loss of all passengers, including seventy children.

Nor did Turkey's own Jewish population of 120,000 escape the effects of minority vulnerability. By 1942, the war had largely closed off civilian shipping in the eastern Mediterranean, a blockade that imposed grave economic hardships on the Turks. To help resolve its budgetary shortfall, the government contrived an ingenious solution. In December 1942, it moved to impose a capital tax on those "mercantile elements" who had engaged in "profiteering"—a code phrase for the nation's minority communities of Greeks, Armenians, and Jews. Known as the Varlik Vergisi, the impost was savagely vindictive. In some instances, it exceeded the entirety of individuals' capital assets, and the government then ensured "reimbursement" by confiscating and auctioning off the delinquents' businesses, homes, and possessions. Those whose property failed to cover the bill were sentenced to punitive labor.

Ultimately, some 10,000 "defaulters" were carried off to road-building camps. More than half the victims were Jews. Work conditions were brutal, food was in short supply, illness was common, and there were numerous deaths. Although the Allied governments condemned these measures, the Turks held firm. Eventually, by 1943, as the tide of the war turned, the Turkish government expediently allowed the Joint and the United States War Refugee Board to conduct their relief and rescue operations openly in Istanbul. Yet it was not until March 1944 that Turkey's Grand National Assembly abolished the Varlik Vergisi, and another seven months after that before the last of the prisoners were released. The tax had raised 315 million Turkish liras. In the process, it also had pauperized a third of Turkish Jewry. Few of them ever recovered.

It was of interest that Spain, whose historic fifteenth-century expulsion decree was the principal source of Turkey's once extensive Jewish population, was beginning to countenance a limited Jewish revival half a millennium later on its own soil. During the 1920s and 1930s, some 2,000 Jews were living and working in the country, most of them Sephardic refugees from the Balkan Wars of 1912–13. Notwithstanding Spain's lingering medievalism, its reactionary Church hierarchy and quasi-feudal social structure, the prognosis for Jewish communal revival seemed encouraging, particularly between 1923 and 1930, under the "benign" dictatorship of Prime Minister Miguel Primo de Rivera. Moreover, in 1931, once the Bourbon dynasty was overthrown in favor of a republic, local Jews were extended full and equal status as Spanish citizens. Later, the country's doors were opened to Jewish refugees from Nazism. By 1936, approximately 6,000 Jews were living in the country.

The idyll of toleration ended that year with the outbreak of the Spanish Civil War. Beyond the nearly 2,000 foreign Jewish volunteers who died as members of the Loyalist International Brigade, several hundred resident Jews suffered execution or imprisonment at the hands of the fascists. A majority of Spain's Jews simply fled the country. For those who remained—less than 1,000—all earlier guarantees of religious liberty were abrogated, the synagogues of Madrid and Barcelona were shuttered, and Jewish religious worship was forced underground. Once World War II began, Spain's dictator, Francisco Franco, adopted an undisguised stance of pro-German collaboration. The nation's tiny Jewish enclave accordingly was reduced to a tremulous vigilance, uncertain when the sword of Damocles might fall.

In fact, no government measures were directed specifically against Jews. Even foreign Jewish refugees were not barred altogether. In 1940, with the surrender of France, thousands of French Jews accompanied other fugitives in applying for Spanish visas, at least for transit purposes to the United States or other Western nations. Madrid's policy was stringent. Applicants were required to possess official Vichy exit permits and documents certifying that permanent refuge was available elsewhere. Nevertheless, over the ensuing two years, and despite these unforgiving entrance qualifications, some 30,000 Jews were among the much larger avalanche of refugees who gained admission into Spain, to continue on to Lisbon, and eventually to other temporary havens.

In September 1942, however, the period of legal rescue through Spain ended. Under German intimidation, Vichy canceled all exit permits for Jews, and Madrid in turn denied the necessary transit documents. Two months later, the German Wehrmacht flooded across the demarcation zone between

Occupied and Vichy France, and the hunt for Jews attained new scope and momentum. In their terror, the fugitives resorted to illegal crossings into Spain. Most were caught. Although most were sent back to France, many were consigned to Spanish internment camps. By early 1943, approximately 7,000 Jews were incarcerated in these bleak compounds, together with an even larger number of non-Jews. There, they subsisted for the next two years under near-starvation conditions, exposed to the often brutal antisemitism of their fellow internees. It was not until 1945, with Allied victory in sight, that Madrid circumspectly permitted the Joint to assume responsibility for the Jews' food and lodgings.

During the Nazi epoch, it was ironic that Switzerland, a nation of unchallengeably democratic credentials, should have proved as grudging a haven as contemporary Turkey and Spain. In 1933, some 18,000 Jews lived in Switzerland, sharing comfortably in that democratic nation's public and private life. With the flight of refugees from the Third Reich, however, Swiss immigration legislation became harsh, even discriminatory. Indeed, in 1938, Dr. Heinrich Rothmund, commander of the Swiss Federal Police, insisted that Jews carrying German passports be specifically identified as Jews. No other democratic nation required such identification, but Rothmund argued that Jews were less likely than other "temporary visitors" to return home. Under this guideline, fewer than 7,000 Jewish fugitives were admitted to Switzerland before the outbreak of war. Once war began, the doors closed even more tightly. Between the summer of 1939 and the summer of 1942, only about 1,000 Jews were admitted. Inhibited by fear of provoking Germany, the Swiss rationalized their exclusionist policy with the slogan "The lifeboat is full." Eventually, the Swiss admitted a total of 22,000 Jews, but nearly all of these after 1944, once it became clear that the tide had shifted decisively against Germany. With the end of the war, moreover, the Swiss government moved vigorously to repatriate most of the refugees, even to prosecute those of its own citizens who had violated the law by helping Jews enter the country, and caring for them.

Other legacies of the brief Jewish presence endured in Switzerland for decades after Germany's surrender. These were tens of millions of dollars in Jewish bank accounts. In a frantic attempt to save their estates, European Jews had transferred these funds to Switzerland before the war. The deposits remained frozen upon the deaths of their owners. In the postwar period, invoking its traditional law of bank secrecy, the Swiss government would neither identify nor release these accounts to relatives of the deceased. Nor would the Swiss provide information on Jewish assets seized and liquidated in German-occupied Europe, then deposited by the Nazis in Swiss banks during the last months of the war. Throughout the 1980s and 1990s, a protracted Jewish legal and diplomatic campaign eventually persuaded Swiss banks to release these funds—although not until the weight of the United States government was brought to bear.

The role of Sweden, like that of Switzerland, shifted with Germany's fortunes in the war. The country's most widely publicized rescue effort was the en bloc asylum its government provided Danish Jewry (p. 538). But other significant developments followed. In July 1944, as the Final Solution approached its crescendo in Hungary, Stockholm dispatched Raoul Wallenberg to Budapest as one of its embassy attachés, with a mandate to help rescue Hungarian Jews. In that effort, Wallenberg set about distributing thousands of official Swedish "certificates of protection" for Jews. Through this imaginative tactic, he eventually achieved a stay of deportation for nearly 30,000 individuals. But the respite was brief. By October 1944, thousands of other Budapest Jews were hounded from their ghetto congestion and force-marched toward German territory. Wallenberg's effort to provide the deportation convoys with food and clothing ultimately availed little. Indeed, it possibly assured Wallenberg's own doom. In the early spring of 1945, he was arrested by the occupying Soviet authorities on charges of espionage, and his subsequent fate remains unknown.

In April of 1945, however, as preparations were made to transfer the last remaining thousands of prisoners into the shrinking pockets of the Reich, Heinrich Himmler sought urgently to transform his image among the Allies. In that effort, he entered into negotiations with Count Folke Bernadotte, president of the Swedish Red Cross, to devise a formula for a "mercy gesture." The discussions consumed nearly three weeks, but arrangements finally were made to ship as many as 21,000 concentration-camp prisoners to Sweden. Of these, approximately 3,500 were Jews, most of them from Hungary.

A CLERICAL EQUIVOCATION

It is uncertain that the full magnitude of the Final Solution was widely known among the German people in the first years of the war. Yet the mass slaughter of Jews on the Soviet front was no secret to large numbers of Wehrmacht troops, many of whom informed their families and friends during home leave. From 1942 on, moreover, the sheer scope of Jewish deportations to Poland from Central and Western Europe could not have gone unnoticed by the various civilian populations—including members of the clergy. In Germany, to be sure, the pastorate of the Lutheran churches remained as silent as in the prewar years. But in other countries, the record of the Protestant churches was mixed. In Denmark, during the abortive SS roundup of Jews in September–October 1943, Lutheran pastors throughout the nation conducted prayer services on behalf of "our Jewish brothers and sisters." In the Netherlands, by contrast, the German administration offered

Protestant and Catholic clergy an enticing concession. If they would refrain from engaging in public protest against the deportation of Jews, the SS would not deport Jewish converts. The Dutch Reformed Church then accepted the offer, breaking ranks with local Catholic prelates.

Nevertheless, among the leadership of the major Western religions, it was the Vatican that bore heaviest responsibility for moral failure. Before the war, as long as antisemitic legislation was not brutal, violent, or openly based on "neopagan" doctrines of blood and soil, it evoked little reaction from the Holy See. Even Pope Pius XI, who reigned in the years of Hitler's investiture of Germany, and who privately expressed deep reservations about Nazism (p. 485), was uninterested in bestirring himself on behalf of the Jews. Rather, as late as 1932, the pontiff expressed concern for "the spiritual dangers to which contacts with Jews can blind souls." In 1938, shortly before his death, protesting Hitler's violation of the July 1933 Concordat (p. 485), Pius XI alluded obliquely to Nazi racial persecution, but avoided any mention of Jews. In 1939, Pius XI was succeeded by Cardinal Eugenio Pacelli. In early decades, whether as papal nuncio to Berlin or as Vatican secretary of state, Pacelli displayed a thinly veiled antipathy to Jews. It was his Concordat agreement with Hitler that thwarted any possibility of organized German Catholic opposition to the Nazi antisemitic program. Thus, while publicly repudiating racist theories throughout the mid- and late 1930s, Pacelli, like Pius XI, was unwilling to sanction an open or official protest by Germany's Catholic episcopate.

Once the war began, Pacelli, now enthroned as Pius XII, similarly opposed any pontifical appeal on behalf of the Jews at the level of international politics. When the Germans overran Yugoslavia and established a puppet Ustasha fascist state in Croatia, the Ustasha dictator, Ante Pavelic, loosed a campaign of extermination against 2 million Orthodox Serbs and the smaller numbers of Jews and Gypsies under his rule. The acts of murder and torture were so heinous that they shocked even hardened German troops. Croatia was largely a Catholic region and presumably susceptible to ecclesiastical influence. Indeed, in August 1941, the papal nuncio in Zagreb interceded with Pavelic to halt the wanton slaughter. The effort was unavailing. Neither was it repeated. Five weeks later, granting an audience to the Croatian ambassador, Pius XII expressed pleasure at the letter he had received from "our Pavelic," and alluded only to the "one, real, and principal enemy of Europe . . . bolshevism."

In the spring of 1942, when the pope began receiving authenticated information on the Final Solution from the World Jewish Congress and other Jewish organizations, he made no public reaction. As the deportations of Jews continued, from country to country, and accounts mounted from shocked Catholic clergy scattered throughout German-occupied Europe, Pius XII continued to remain silent. Even when France's Vichy government participated in these roundups, the pontiff, receiving Cardinal Emmanuel Suhard of Paris in January 1943, "warmly praised the work of the Marshal [Pétain]," according to an eyewitness, and "took a keen interest in government actions that are a sign of the fortunate renewal of religious life in France." Three weeks earlier, on December 18, 1942, Lord Osborne, Britain's representative to the Holy See, had provided the Vatican with detailed information on the mass killings of Jews, and pleaded for a clear denunciation of this horror in the pope's Christmas Eve broadcast to the world. It was here at last, in his lengthy radio address, that Pius mentioned the "hundreds of thousands, who without any fault of their own, sometimes only by reason of their nationality or race, are marked for death or gradual extinction."

Soon the Nazi Final Solution would strike closer to home. It was in late September 1943 that the Jews of Rome were presented with SS Major Kappler's ransom demand (p. 543). When the Jewish community president, Ugo Foà, appealed to the Vatican for a loan to meet Kappler's deadline, the pope himself sent back word that the money would be forthcoming. As is recalled, the papal loan was not required; the Jews raised the necessary ransom themselves. The payoff was unavailing in any case. On October 16, a procession of German army trucks arrived outside the Lungotevere ghetto, in preparation for a mass roundup. Alerted to this development, the pontiff seemed prepared again to react forthrightly. Word was sent to Ernst von Weiszäcker, Germany's ambassador to the Vatican, that the pope might find it necessary to speak out against the impending deportation. Weiszäcker then alerted Berlin. Nevertheless, the roundup of Jews proceeded, and, at the last moment, Pius chose silence. As he explained on October 18 to Harold Tittman, the United States representative to the Vatican, a "demonstrative censure" might provoke a clash with the SS "that could benefit only the Communists." Five days after the deportation train left Rome, its 1,060 Jewish passengers were gassed at Auschwitz and Birkenau.

Ultimately, the pope's decision to refrain from a "demonstrative censure" on behalf of Rome Jewry produced still farther-reaching consequences. In November, additional thousands of Jews were rounded up in Florence, Genoa, Venice, and elsewhere in northern Italy. Had they been alerted to the impending danger in preceding weeks, it was all but certain that they would have taken measures to save themselves. Moreover, if the Vatican had issued a threat of excommunication against soldiers or civilians participating in the deportations, numerous German Catholics in Italy and in other nations might have refused their cooperation in the Holocaust.

Pius XII's timorousness offered a stark contrast to the compassion and courage of innumerable Catholic clerics. Several French bishops outspokenly condemned the first SS roundups of Jews in the summer of 1942. In Italy and Belgium, as well as France, many hundreds of individual priests and nuns hid Jews in their monasteries, convents, and hospices, always at the risk and often at the cost of their own lives. By contrast, Pius XII adopted a tradition-bound interpretation of the papal role. Intent upon proving his "impartiality" between secular belligerents, he made no secret of his hope that Berlin sooner or later would call on his services as a "trustworthy peacemaker." Beyond even his distrust of Jews, it was this antiseptic commitment to "neutrality," linked with an abiding fear and hatred of communism, that proved decisive in Eugenio Pacelli's epic moral failure.

The Role of the Western Democracies

Meanwhile, Britain's austere approach to the crisis of Jewish refugees from the Third Reich did not end with the outbreak of war. Once hostilities began, even those 40,000 Jews who had been admitted onto British soil confronted a new crisis. Most of them found themselves suddenly designated as "enemy aliens." In 1940, during the fifth-column hysteria that fixated the nation following the surrender of France, some 30,000 foreign nationals, most of them Jewish refugees, were confined in grim internment centers and nearly 8,000 were deported to Canada and Australia, where additional space was available for confinement. Altogether, in the first years of the war, London was in the forefront of the effort to bar Jewish escape routes to England from the Continent, and banned food and medical shipments to the ghettos and concentration camps of Europe. "The Jews have done nothing but add to our difficulties by propaganda and deeds since the war began," complained J. S. Bennett of the Colonial Office. The view was echoed in September 1944 by A. R. Dew of the Foreign Office, who argued that "a disproportionate amount of the time of this office is wasted in dealing with these wailing Jews."

The government's chill reaction was paralleled by concern lest Jews flood into Palestine. From 1937 onward, in its effort to assuage Arab unrest in the Middle East, Britain's Colonial Office imposed increasingly stringent limits on Jewish immigration into Palestine and in May 1939 issued its climactic White Paper (p. 525). Henceforth, Britain would terminate its post–World War I experiment as patron of a Jewish National Home by the straightforward method of phasing out Jewish immigration altogether. The foreclosure effort was not entirely seamless, however. In the last fifteen months before the outbreak of World War II, an ongoing flotilla of refugee ships brought some 11,000 Jewish "illegals" to the shores of Palestine. Although the Royal Navy intercepted most of these vessels and carried off their passengers to internment centers in Mauritius and South Africa, the clandestine traffic continued well after the war began. A few of the unseaworthy little steamers were purchased by Jabotinsky's revisionists (pp. 523–24), but most were owned by Greek or Bulgarian gangsters and were paid for by the desperate refugees themselves.

Initially, the Nazis encouraged this smuggling effort. In 1940, the Gestapo actually put a Jewish businessman, Berthold Storfer, in charge of the refugee shipping program. Within the year, Storfer's organization succeeded in dispatching three medium-sized passenger vessels to Palestine with 3,600 immigrants. In November 1940, the British intercepted two of them, escorted them to Haifa, and transferred the refugees to a dormitory ship, the *Patria*, which was assigned to carry them to Mauritius for internment. But on November 25, members of the Jewish underground detonated a mine under the *Patria*, intending to cripple it and prevent it from sailing. Instead, the vessel capsized, taking 240 victims with it (the British afterward permitted the survivors to remain). Then, nine months later, on August 23, 1941, Heinrich Himmler in Berlin gave the first public intimation that his government was adopting a new approach to the Jewish question. Henceforth, all departures of Jews from German-occupied Europe were banned. It was in that same month, ironically, as news of widespread Nazi massacres began to leak, that the British partly relented and allowed individual refugees who reached Turkey to proceed on to Palestine under the White Paper's minimalist immigration quota of 10,000 a year. Nevertheless, by war's end, the total number of European Jews who had reached Palestine since May 1939 did not exceed 58,000, well below the White Paper's cutoff figure of 75,000.

For all the gruesome accounts of Nazi atrocities that reached the West, none quite seemed to reveal a master plan for Jewish extermination. In July 1942, however, a bombshell suddenly dropped in the lap of Gerhart Riegner, the World Jewish Congress representative in Geneva. It came in the form of information conveyed by a German industrialist, Dr. Eduard Schulte, director of the Giesche Mining Company. Schulte's business activities gave him access to important government officials. From them, he had learned of a plan under discussion in Hitler's inner councils. It envisaged destruction of the entirety of Europe's Jewish population. A staunch anti-Nazi, the horrified Schulte managed to transmit his intelligence to contacts in Switzerland, and the latter shared it with Riegner.

Riegner moved urgently, arranging for the information to be cabled to the World Jewish Congress's New York office. Upon receiving it, Rabbi Stephen Wise, the congress's founder and senior figure, rushed to Washington to hand the report personally to Undersecretary of State Sumner Welles. Welles was incredulous. He asked Wise for time to confirm the story through the department's own contacts in neutral European governments. Within three weeks, the report was corroborated. Until then, the Allied governments had largely remained silent on the Jewish tragedy, concerned that atrocity reports might divert attention from the war itself. But the Riegner dispatch could not be ignored. Welles then promised Rabbi Wise that it would reach President Roosevelt's desk. It did. After further discussions between London and Washington, several measures were taken. On December 1, 1942, Roosevelt and Churchill issued a joint public statement revealing the dire facts of the Nazi extermination program, and issuing a solemn warning that individuals engaged in it ultimately would be tried as war criminals (p. 546).

At the same time, genuflecting to liberal pressures, the United States and British governments agreed to convene a joint conference for the purpose of exploring a possible resettlement of refugees. To that end, representatives of the two Allied Powers gathered in Bermuda in April 1943. Britain's delegation consisted exclusively of Foreign Office personnel. Most of the American representatives also were State Department professionals, except for the cosmetic choice of their chairman, Harold Dodds, president of Princeton University. No Jewish spokesmen were represented. From April 12 to April 24, the assorted diplomats lived and worked at the Horizons, Bermuda's most luxurious seaside resort. Throughout their leisurely discussions, it became clear that neither the British nor the Americans would relax their immigration restrictions. Palestine was foreclosed from the agenda. So was the notion of secret deals with the Axis. The one token gesture agreed upon was the establishment of a "model" camp in North Africa as shelter for 3,000 refugees currently subsisting in their oppressive internment compounds in Spain and North Africa itself. The results of the twelve days of discussions were so negligible that they evoked virtually no press coverage. Nor, subsequently, were any refugees transshipped from Spain to North Africa.

Nevertheless, by the summer of 1943, with the improvement of the Allied war situation, Franklin Roosevelt felt impelled to devote closer attention to the Jewish tragedy. In July of that year, he received Jan Ciechanowski, ambassador of the Polish government-in-exile, based in London, and Jan Karski, a Polish underground courier. Both men confirmed the unfolding genocide of European Jewry. Although the president was moved, he discerned no possibility of rescue action. A more decisive influence, however, was Secretary of the Treasury Henry Morgenthau, Jr., an old political ally of Roosevelt's, and the single Jew in the president's cabinet. For some months, a group of young (non-Jewish) technocrats working at the Treasury directly under Morgenthau—among them John W. Pehle, Josiah E. DuBois, Jr., and Randolph Paul—had become increasingly alarmed at the thinly veiled bigotry they had encountered in their dealings with State Department visa officials. Quietly, they assembled a dossier on the State Department's "Jewish" record, and in December 1943 presented their eighteen-page memorandum to Morgenthau. Entitled "Report to the Secretary in the Acquiescence of This Government in the Murder of the Jews," the indictment cited chapter and verse of State Department's "procrastination and willful failure to act . . . even of willful attempts to prevent action from being taken to rescue Jews from Hitler." In the report's conclusion, Randolph Paul, the Treasury's legal counsel, warned: "Unless remedial steps . . . are taken immediately . . . this government will have to share for all time responsibility for this [Jewish] extermination." Paul then urged that refugee policy be removed from State Department jurisdiction.

Morgenthau took the report to the president on January 16, 1944, and summarized it for him. This time, Roosevelt was visibly shaken. On the spot, he accepted the document's proposal, and within the week, by executive order, he transferred refugee policy from the State Department to a newly established War Refugee Board. The WRB would be composed of representatives from the Treasury, War, and State departments, but with the State Department's participation entirely nominal. Indeed, Morgenthau's young protégé, John Pehle, was appointed the board's director. It was Pehle who assigned his WRB field staffers to the frontiers of Axis Europe—to Switzerland, Turkey, Sweden, Portugal, and North Africa. Invested with diplomatic status, exempt from currency regulations, authorized to coordinate the expenditures of such private organizations as the Joint and other Jewish philanthropies, the agents were free at last to negotiate, to threaten—to bribe. Their likeliest interlocutors were collaborationist regimes, and specifically those known to be using their captive Jews for bargaining purposes, both financial and diplomatic.

Several of the WRB initiatives proved almost immediately effective. Thus, in May 1944, responding to John Pehle's urgent appeal, Cardinal Angelo Roncalli (later Pope John XXIII) forwarded thousands of baptismal certificates to Papal Nuncio Angelo Rotta in Hungary. In this fashion, approximately 3,000 Jewish children were saved. It was the WRB's stringer in Sweden, Stig Olsen, who secured Swedish diplomatic endorsement for Raoul Wallenberg's rescue effort in Hungary. With Joint subventions, too, WRB emissaries helped eke out food rations for the thousands of French-Jewish refugees confined to Spanish internment camps. In Switzerland, Roswell McClelland, the board's representative, distributed Joint funds for relief operations in Hungary and Bulgaria, for the distribution of bribes and the preparation of false documents. It was McClelland, together with Saly Mayer, who conducted negotiations with Kurt Becher in the clandestine (and eventually unsuccessful) effort to strike a ransom deal for Hungarian Jewry.

In the late winter and spring of 1945, moreover, Rumania's dictator Ion Antonescu actually took the initiative in seeking out an "arrangement" with the WRB. It was known that thousands of Jews remained interned under appalling conditions in Transnistria. These could yet be saved, Antonescu intimated, in the event the Allies were prepared to be "forbearing" in their treatment of Rumanian government leaders. The discussions were conducted between the Rumanian ambassador in Ankara and Ira Hirschmann, the WRB representative in the Turkish capital. Hirschmann could make no diplomatic commitments. As he strung negotiations along, however, the Antonescu government dispatched nearly 40,000 Jews from Transnistria back into integral Rumania. At least half their number survived the grim penal treatment reserved for them. Altogether, by war's end the War Refugee Board saved the lives of an estimated 90,000 Jews. Yet the number, while not altogether negligible, plainly was tragically inadequate when measured against the many additional hundreds of thousands who might have been rescued had the Allied governments been prepared earlier to accept these victims as immigrants, or at least as temporary internees.

A Final Tabulation

During World War II, between 55 million and 60 million people died in all theaters of conflict and conquest. Of these, at least a third were civilians, and among the civilians approximately 5.9 million were Jews, a proportion that far exceeded the death rate of any other people. Unlike other massacres before or since, every single one of Europe's Jews was marked for extermination. The Nazis very nearly achieved their goal. In 1939, the world Jewish population was calculated at slightly over 16.5 million. Of this figure, the Jews of Europe (including the Soviet Union) comprised 9.5 million. After Germany's surrender, the number of Jews in Europe was closer to 3.5 million. For months even after the war, thousands of the 230,000 liberated Jewish death-camp inmates continued to expire of debilitation and disease. Before the war, 57 percent of the world's Jews lived in Europe. After the war, the figure was 32 percent, the majority of them in the Soviet Union.

The Nazi Party, and its instrument, the SS, manifestly were the prime movers of this genocide. But there were others in the Third Reich who could not be absolved. The Wehrmacht high command was an undeniable accomplice. It may have regarded the SS as ungovernable brutes, but senior officers at the front interposed no obstacles to the liquidation of Jews. By the same token, despite numerous moving episodes of German civilian appeals and protests on behalf of Jewish neighbors, the evidence was more extensive of public indifference to the Jewish tragedy. Well into the twenty-first century, new information continues to be unearthed of the "Aryanization" of Jewish property throughout the Reich, ranging from the crucial participation of such large German financial institutions as the Dresdner Bank and the Deutsche Bank, to the hundreds of thousands of "deserving" German and Austrian *Volksgenossen* who eagerly shared in the distribution of Jewish businesses, homes, furniture, objets d'art, and other personal possessions. As for the collaborative role in the Final Solution of the Polish, Ukrainian, Hungarian, Baltic, and Rumanian peoples, there is even less historical disagreement than on the role of the German and Austrian peoples.

Inasmuch as the ultimate and essential guilt lay with the Nazi leadership, however, the question remains: why did they do it? The exploitation of anti-semitism as one of a number of useful tactics to achieve political victory was one matter. But a program of mass annihilation long after the consolidation of political power was another. Why was the immolation of the totality of European Jewry so indispensable to Hitler and his collaborators that they were prepared to disrupt Germany's military transportation, even at the most crucial phase of the war, by placing all available rolling stock at the disposal of the SS? Thus, on March 15, 1943, in the aftermath of the Stalingrad disaster, Hitler informed his propaganda minister, Joseph Goebbels, that the liquida-tion program should not "cease or pause until no Jew is left anywhere in the Reich." In the spring of 1944, when Germany was being pounded incessantly, and invasion from the West was imminent, SS units found time to hunt down every Jew they could lay their hands on, even a tiny community of 260 Jews on the island of Crete.

One purely mechanistic explanation for this obsession was provided by Goebbels himself in a diary entry of March 2, 1943: "We are so entangled in the Jewish question," he wrote, "that henceforth it is impossible to retreat. All the better. A movement and a people that have burned their bridges behind them fight with a great deal more energy . . . than those who are still able to retreat." When one considers Hitler's determination, toward the end of the war, to pull everything and everyone down with him in a last Götterdämmerung (a decision aborted by Armaments Minister Albert Speer at the peril of his life), this explanation gains plausibility. But assuredly there were more fundamental impulses yet for the Final Solution. From begin-ning to end, the führer and his closest associates were transfixed, mesmerized in their racist phobia. All survivors and scholars of the Nazi epoch agree that Hitler personally believed with every fiber of his being that the Jews were the one international force that seriously threatened his master plan for dominat-ing the Continent. Worse than cosmopolitans, the Jews represented a diaboli-cal racial threat to Aryan Europe's very survival. The war against the Jews accordingly was no mere political tactic for Hitler and his followers. It was a biological necessity. "The Jews are no people like any other people," wrote Goebbels, "but a pseudo-people welded together by hereditary criminality. . . . The annihilation of Jewry is no loss to humanity, but just as useful as capital punishment or protective custody against other criminals."

On April 30, 1945, Adolf Hitler ended his life. On the previous afternoon his secretary, Frau Traudl Junge, had typed out the concluding words of his political testament. It was the führer's climactic valedictory to the European civilization that had spawned him. "Above all," he declared, "I bind the leadership and its subordinates to the painful observance of the racial laws and to merciless resistance against the world-poisoner of all nations, international Jewry." Hitler's directive was gratuitous. A century and a quarter after their forebears had tendered their National Affirmation to France's Napoleon Bonaparte and to Prussia's Friedrich Wilhelm IV, those few hundred thousand of Europe's "world-poisoners" who survived the Final Solution and made their way to the quasi-freedom of Western displaced-persons camps had internalized a new reality. Their destiny no longer was to be fulfilled among "all nations."

XXIX

The Birth of Israel

AN EXASPERATION OF ZIONIST PATIENCE

David Ben-Gurion, chairman of the Executive of the Jewish Agency, the Zionist "quasi-government" in Palestine, shared his people's shock at Britain's White Paper of May 1939, a policy statement whose manifest purpose was to scale down and eventually terminate future Jewish immigration to the Holy Land. In his initial reaction, Ben-Gurion angrily and impetuously proposed that the Jewish Agency adopt a policy of civil unrest against the British. Before the notion could gain serious consideration, however, World War II began. "Let us fight against Hitler as if there were no White Paper," Ben-Gurion conceded then, "and let us continue our political struggle against the White Paper as if there were no war against Hitler." The formula accurately reflected Palestine Jewry's collective instinct. Their campaign against the White Paper for the time being would have to remain essentially diplomatic. But in the war against Germany they would mobilize the totality of their economic and military resources.

Thus, within the Jewish National Home, some four hundred new factories were constructed exclusively for the purpose of supplying Britain's Middle Eastern forces. In June 1941, approximately two hundred members of the Haganah, the locally trained Jewish militia, were allowed to participate in a British–Free French invasion of Vichy Syria and Lebanon. More substantially, 11,000 Palestinian-Jewish volunteers were serving in North Africa, in their own company-sized units under British Eighth Army command. In the late summer of 1944, acceding to repeated Zionist appeals, Prime Minister Winston Churchill authorized the Eighth Army to incorporate a full brigade of Palestinian Jews into its ranks. It was this "Jewish Brigade," comprising 3,400 volunteers and flying its own blue-and-white flag, that was organized, trained, and shipped off for combat duty in Italy. In their gratification and pride, the Zionist leadership discerned in the Brigade a symbolic British commitment to political dispensations after the war.

Nevertheless, at a time when their families were being exterminated in

Europe, growing numbers of Palestinian Jews were unprepared to await the end of the war to force Britain's hand on immigration. One of their militant factions, the Lech'i (a Hebrew acronym for "Fighters for the Freedom of Israel"), launched an underground campaign against British immigration policy. Avraham Stern, the group's founder, had briefly studied in Italy during the 1930s, where he became an admirer of Mussolini's brand of fascist "direct action." In 1940, he led his several hundred Lech'i followers in occasional guerrilla attacks on British offices and military installations. In 1942, Stern was cornered and fatally shot in a Tel Aviv apartment. Yet the Lech'i remained a cohesive band under successor leaders, and intermittently engaged in gun battles with the British police. In November 1944, two Lech'i members actually traveled to Cairo and assassinated Britain's resident minister for Middle Eastern affairs, Lord Moyne. Shamed and horror-stricken, Ben-Gurion and his Jewish Agency colleagues fiercely execrated the assassination as criminally irresponsible. As the ban on immigration remained in effect, however, Zionist patience with the British mandatory government was visibly expiring.

It was in May 1945, once hostilities in Europe ended, that the full magnitude of the Nazi catastrophe was revealed. Its consequences were most poignantly evident in the residue of uprooted humanity left in the wake of the Third Reich. In West-Central Europe alone, this legacy of German mass transplantation and slave labor included 7 million "displaced persons," among them 1.6 million Poles, 465,000 Russians and Ukrainians, 340,000 Czechs, 300,000 Dutchmen, 300,000 Belgians, and 200,000 Frenchmen. Most of the refugees eventually made their way home on their own. But at least 3 million other displaced persons, bereft of transportation, food, shelter, or certainty of destination, found themselves adrift. It was to cope with this human overflow that Allied military occupation forces in Germany and Austria rushed to organize a network of temporary encampments, where the DPs could be provided with elementary lodgings, meals, and basic medical care.

The emergency effort soon all but overwhelmed American and British resources. In late 1945, therefore, General Dwight D. Eisenhower, the Supreme Allied Commander, ordered that the vast army of refugees now be returned immediately to their nations of origin. All civilian and military transportation and other logistical facilities would be made available for that purpose. The massive repatriation effort was put into effect without delay, and by mid-1946 was largely completed. The largest numbers of European DPs were returned to their homelands. But the Jewish survivors presented a unique and complex challenge. At the time Eisenhower issued his repatriation directive, approximately 100,000 Jews, many of them from Central and Western Europe, either had emerged from hiding or had been liberated from the concentration camps of Mauthausen, Dachau, Bergen-Belsen, Buchenwald, Ravensbrück, and other Nazi detention centers within the former

Altreich. Packed into the barracks of these former encampments, living on army rations or, later, United Nations relief funds (see below), the survivors categorically rejected the very notion of returning to their former homes and living among their former neighbors.

The Jewish DPs unquestionably were a difficult group. Few of them appeared susceptible to Allied "management." Malcolm Proudfoot, who served in the displaced-persons branch of the American military command, found the Jews to be "in an unbalanced emotional condition." However understandable their behavior, wrote Proudfoot later, "their mental state was frequently so abnormal and offensive that it required a real effort for even the most friendly non-Jews to keep from being goaded into discriminatory action." Before long, serious political trouble began to grow out of this tragic standoff. UNRRA. The United Nations Relief and Rehabilitation Administration initially had been given responsibility for operating the network of DP camps. But UNRRA functioned under Allied military command, and the military's personnel were not social workers. Little time passed before they became altogether exasperated by this psychologically traumatized agglomeration of refugees. General George Patton, whose American Third Army governed the largest part of occupied Germany, suggested that the Jews should be treated like prisoners and kept behind barbed wire. If not, he warned, "they would . . . spread all over the country like locusts."

Then, in the summer of 1945, responding to the appeals of American-Jewish spokesmen, President Harry Truman appointed Earl Harrison, dean of the University of Pennsylvania Law School, to make a survey of refugee conditions in the American zones of occupation. Completing his investigation in August of that year, Harrison dispatched to the president an extended and harshly critical report on the military's treatment of the Jewish DPs. These survivors should be turned over exclusively to UNRRA jurisdiction, Harrison suggested, independent of army control. They were. At Harrison's recommendation, too, the UNRRA was provided with new and vigorous direction under the leadership of Fiorello La Guardia, the dynamic former New York City mayor. Within a few months, La Guardia oversaw a dramatic reversal of policy. Henceforth, Jewish DPs were quartered separately from other prisoners, many of whom were antisemitic East Europeans. Their physical facilities were improved, as were their food and clothing allotments, much of which now was supplied privately by the Joint.

Yet it was at best an interim solution. The Jewish survivors had not dug in their heels against repatriation simply to vegetate indefinitely as wards of the United Nations, or even of Western Jewish philanthropy. Their idée fixe was permanent departure from Europe, nothing less. That obsession soon was reinforced by emissaries from Palestine. Operating under Jewish Agency directives, the Palestinians set out to organize the survivors into an "army" capable of surmounting Britain's White Paper immigration barrier. The most authoritative of those emissaries was David Ben-Gurion himself. Addressing a gathering of Jewish DPs in Landsberg, Germany, in the autumn of 1945, the Jewish Agency chairman assured his listeners that they were not simply refugees. They were a political force. "Do not be afraid if you hear of new laws against us tomorrow or the day after," he declaimed. "A Jewish power has arisen which will fight together with you for a proud, independent Palestine."

The Jewish National Home Repudiates the Mandate

Ben-Gurion's new militance was impelled by a seismic political reorientation not only in Palestine but in the United Kingdom. In July 1945, national elections in Britain had overthrown the Conservative government of Winston Churchill and replaced it with a Labour cabinet under Clement Attlee. The astonishing Labour victory was a source of vast gratification to the Zionist movement worldwide. Notwithstanding Churchill's personal support of the Zionist cause, and his gravitas as the most admired statesman of the free world, it was, after all, his Conservative Party that had issued the 1939 White Paper and that had maintained the wartime ban on Jewish immigration. Anthony Eden, Churchill's foreign secretary, a veteran Arabophile, was also suspect as a closet antisemite. With few exceptions (p. 522), the Labourites traditionally had expressed a warm friendship for Zionism, and Labour's campaign platform included a vigorous condemnation of the White Paper and a commitment to open Jewish immigration to Palestine.

Witnessing this extraordinary political upheaval, Ben-Gurion and his colleagues immediately interpreted it as a decisive crossroads in Anglo-Zionist relations. As they saw it, the Jewish National Home no longer should be regarded as a tiny and vulnerable supplicant of British protection. Its population had grown to 560,000. Its economy had been dramatically stimulated by the war. Its troops had given an impressive accounting of themselves on the battlefield. These achievements surely deserved acknowledgment and reward. Thus, eager and impatient to test the intentions of Britain's new government, Ben-Gurion personally led a Jewish Agency deputation to London within weeks of the Labour takeover. Upon meeting with George Hall, the new colonial secretary, he laid out a full list of Zionist demands. These did not err on the side of understatement. They included cancellation of the White Paper and the immediate admission into Palestine of the 100,000 Jews currently languishing in Europe's displaced-persons camps. Beyond this reversal of British immigration policy, the Jewish Agency also sought control over Jewish land purchase in Palestine, and full internal political autonomy for the Jewish National Home. The magnitude of Ben-Gurion's claims, no less than the aggressiveness with which he presented them, astonished and offended the colonial secretary. Hall's response, then, was equally blunt and uncompromising. The White Paper ban on Jewish immigration would remain in effect "for the time being."

Whatever the shock it inflicted on the Zionist world, Labour's unanticipated obduracy reflected the hard facts of Britain's postwar economic and strategic vulnerability. The new Attlee government was intent upon carrying out an unprecedented program of social welfare. Yet the nation was virtually bankrupt, its population hungry and threadbare. Under these austere circumstances, ongoing access to the vast oil resources and pipelines of the Middle East was indispensable, both to fuel Britain's industry and to sustain its foreign-currency income. Nothing should be done to provoke Arab unrest in a region so vital for the British people's economic survival. By the same token, the Middle East represented a potential access route for Soviet penetration; and by war's end, the Russians were beginning to exert heavy diplomatic and military pressure on Turkey, Greece, and Iran. In view of this threat, Britain's traditional bases in the Arab world functioned as a critical defensive shield against the Soviet threat. They dared not be jeopardized by provoking Arab ill will.

Ernest Bevin, foreign secretary in the new Labour government, had been a reliable friend of the Zionists during the prewar. In 1930, he had interceded with the Ramsay MacDonald government to reverse the Passfield White Paper, an early plan to limit Jewish immigration to Palestine (p. 522). Subsequently, as chairman of Britain's Trade Union Council, he had championed the Zionist cause at international labor conventions. Ben-Gurion personally had developed equable relations with Bevin at these and other socialist conclaves. But now, in 1945, bearing responsibility for the wider spectrum of Britain's foreign-policy interests, Bevin was rapidly seized of his nation's acute economic and strategic vulnerability. On Middle Eastern affairs, his principal advisers were the Foreign Office's veteran specialists on the Middle East. For Bevin, the "crash course" offered by these pro-Arab experts was sobering. His former support of Zionism would have to be reappraised. As for Prime Minister Attlee, no reappraisal was needed. He had long regarded the entire Balfour Declaration undertaking as a historic mistake. Both men agreed that there could be no modification of the 1939 White Paper until a "new" approach to Palestine could be formulated.

In the interim, Ernest Bevin was convinced that the plight of tens of thousands of Jewish displaced persons could best be resolved not through Palestine but through the United States. His hope was to persuade Washington to share responsibility for these survivors by opening America's doors to them. He suspected, in any case, that the American government was as disinclined as his own to favor a Zionist solution. It was a well-founded suspicion.

Although Franklin Roosevelt had publicly expressed friendship for the Zionist cause, privately he had intimated his reservations about a self-governing Jewish commonwealth in Palestine. As for the State Department professionals, these were as unambiguously anti-Zionist as were their counterparts in London.

On the other hand, the new American president, Harry Truman, adopted a more equivocal approach. He had come to the White House at a moment when the trauma of the displaced persons first became acute, as it had not in Roosevelt's lifetime. Without Roosevelt's prestige or experience in international affairs, the untutored former Missouri senator was more vulnerable to ethnic political pressures. Thus, as Jewish appeals on behalf of the refugees mounted, Truman expressed a cautious willingness to intercede on the Palestine issue. At the Potsdam Conference of July 1945, he expressed his hope to Churchill that Britain might consider easing its White Paper restrictions on immigration. Before Churchill could react, he was voted out of office. It was soon afterward that Truman dispatched Earl Harrison to study the conditions of the Jewish DPs, and subsequently acted on Harrison's recommendations.

As it happened, one of those recommendations was for 100,000 Jews to be admitted into Palestine forthwith. Hereupon, disregarding State Department advice, Truman promptly endorsed Harrison's proposal and sent it on to Clement Attlee on August 31, 1945. The president's intervention, in turn, so discountenanced the new prime minister that he and Bevin required two and a half weeks to prepare a response. Issued on September 16, Attlee's reply signified a distinct hardening of the Labour government's stance on Palestine. Rejecting the notion that Jewish DPs had suffered more than any other victims of Nazism, his letter stated:

> In the case of Palestine, we have the Arabs to consider as well as the Jews, and there have been solemn undertakings . . . given by [the late Franklin Roosevelt], yourself, and by Mr. Churchill, that before we come to a final decision . . . there would be consultation with the Arabs. It would be very unwise to break these solemn pledges and so set aflame the whole Middle East.

The British response may have been a serious tactical error. Had Attlee and Bevin agreed to accept 100,000 Jewish DPs, they might have avoided an ugly confrontation with Washington. More important, a good deal of the stridency might have been leached from the Zionist demands. It would have been useful, too, if Bevin, still as rough-edged as in his trade union days, had exercised verbal discretion, rather than respond to parliamentary questioning, on November 2, 1945, with the observation that "if the Jews, with all their suffering, want to get too much at the head of the queue, you have the danger of another antisemitic reaction through it all." The remark elicited a day of mourning in Palestine.

Throughout the years of the British mandate, Ben-Gurion consistently had rejected the doctrinaire view of Jewish extremists, who had condemned the very notion of cooperation between the Zionist leadership and "imperialist" Britain. For the Jewish Agency chairman, relations with Britain always were pragmatic, not ideological. It was he, after all, who in 1939 had called upon Palestine Jewry to support Britain in the common struggle against Hitler (p. 572). But now, confronted with Bevin's inflexibility on the refugee question, and with mounting evidence that the foreign secretary might himself have succumbed to "the danger of another antisemitic reaction through it all," Ben-Gurion decided that the time had come to adopt harsher measures against Britain's presence in Palestine.

In November 1945, at the Jewish Agency's initiative, the commanders of the Haganah, the "official" Zionist militia that had been organized as far back as the 1920s to confront Arab violence, and of the Lech'i and the Etzel, the two "unofficial," militantly right-wing Jewish underground elements, reached a temporary agreement to join forces under Haganah direction. For the next eight months, with weaponry smuggled back from the wartime battlefields of North Africa, the three groups mounted a series of coordinated attacks against British military installations in Palestine. In October 1945, they stormed the gates of a British detention camp, liberating several hundred interned Jewish DPs who had been intercepted en route to Palestine. That same month, another underground operation dynamited the rail network at two hundred different sites in the country, seriously limiting British troop movements. Other acts of sabotage were conducted against British naval installations, airfields, radar stations, and coastal lighthouses.

Ultimately, the British were compelled to send in military reinforcements, including a full army division and a light naval squadron. But the raids continued, and with a savage efficiency that quite shocked the British, who until then had regarded violence in the Holy Land as an exclusively Arab reaction. General Sir Evelyn Barker, Britain's military commander in Palestine, had to admit later that "the Jews knew all government secrets and military plans within a day of our making a decision. Their intelligence system is uncanny." No less relentless, however, was the British government's determination to solve the refugee issue in its own way.

Fully two months had passed since its negative response to Truman's appeal for 100,000 Jews to be admitted into Palestine. When the president expressed his disappointment, Attlee on November 13, 1945, responded with a new, compromise proposal. Refusing to accept "the view that the Jews should be driven out of Europe," the prime minister now suggested that a joint

Anglo-American committee investigate the problem of refugees and devise a solution to it. The proposal was a shrewd one. It was manifestly based on the assumption that Washington would cooperate not only in devising a solution, but in putting that solution into effect. And, for his part, Harry Truman promptly accepted the challenge.

THE UNITED STATES ENTERS THE PALESTINE IMBROGLIO

Organized in early December, the Anglo-American Committee included six British and six American members. Among the British participants, the most influential were the chairman, Sir John Singleton, a high court judge; Herbert Morrison, a senior Labour politician; and a young Labour M.P., Richard Crossman. The American chairman was also a judge, Joseph Hutchison, a seventy-year-old ultraconservative from Texas. Other leading members included James McDonald, the former League of Nations high commissioner for refugees, and Bartley Crum, a prominent San Francisco lawyer and pro-Zionist. The joint body heard their first Jewish and Arab witnesses in New York, each side uncompromising in its demands: the Arabs demanding Palestine for themselves, the Zionists demanding control of immigration to the Jewish National Home.

Proceeding then to London in January 1946, the committee members encountered the full force of British governmental anti-Zionism. Experts from the Colonial and Foreign offices direly predicted a bloodbath in Palestine if thousands of additional Jews were allowed in. But it was in the Holy Land itself that the full force of Arab nationalism was ventilated by successive local Arab eminences (although the Mufti, Amin al-Husseini, a wartime pro-Axis collaborator, remained in exile in Syria). Their fear of Jewish immigration, their bitterness at being denied statehood in Palestine, were transparently genuine and evoked the sympathy of American and British committee members alike.

The basis of the Jewish case was made even before the committee reached Jerusalem. Shortly after departing London, in February 1946, the group visited the European DP camps. "The abstract arguments about Zionism and the Jewish State seemed curiously remote after this experience of human degradation," Richard Crossman wrote afterward. "We had been cut off from what had previously been reality." At the instigation of Ben-Gurion, the refugees themselves early in 1946 had organized a Congress of Jewish Displaced Persons in Munich, and demanded the right of large-scale immigration to Palestine. Supervised by Palestinian emissaries, an extensive program of Zionist activities was in operation, including classes in Hebrew, Jewish history, calisthenics, and agriculture. The Anglo-American Committee witnessed this phenomenon as it toured the DP centers. Its members also understood Jewish desperation somewhat better after encountering the poisonous antisemitism lingering in Central Europe, even at the highest governmental level. "[My colleagues] found themselves increasingly regarding Palestine as the Jews of Europe regarded it," wrote Crossman, "as a solution rather than as a problem."

Subsequently, in Jerusalem, when Ben-Gurion and Chaim Weizmann testified before the committee, they astonished its members by disdaining the Truman proposal for the admission of 100,000 refugees. Their demand now was for full Jewish statehood in Palestine. To make their case, the Jewish Agency leaders presented graphs and statistics rebutting Arab claims of Jewish economic exploitation. Surveys conducted by teams of economists and hydrologists were cited as evidence of Palestine's capacity to absorb up to a million immigrants over the next decade. The visitors were impressed. "I had to admit," wrote Crossman, "that no Western colonists in any other country had done so little harm, or disturbed so little, the life of the indigenous people [as had the Jews]."

At the end of March 1946, the committee carried its mass of data to Lausanne, Switzerland. There the material was boiled down into a unanimous report of some one hundred pages, and was published in May. The document recounted the unbearable physical and psychological conditions of the European-Jewish survivors and the improbability of their repatriation to their former homes. "We know of no country to which the great majority can go in the immediate future other than Palestine," the report continued. Although the committee did not propose Jewish statehood, it recommended the immediate admission of 100,000 Jews into Palestine, and the continuation of Jewish immigration so long as it "does not threaten to create a Jewish majority for the entirety of the Holy Land"—an unlikely scenario, given the high Arab birthrate.

Whatever the report's limitations, none of the members anticipated that it would be rejected, for it appeared to fulfill the principal desiderata that Bevin had outlined to the Anglo-American Committee during its visit to London. It was unanimous. It favored a unitary Palestinian state under an ongoing British mandate. It enjoyed American moral and (presumably) financial support. Nevertheless, much to the committee's dismay, the Labour government's response was frigid. Britain was unprepared, explained Bevin, to open Palestine to an additional 100,000 Jews. Such a move almost certainly would antagonize the Arab world, and perhaps the larger Moslem world, at a critical juncture of British diplomacy in Egypt, Iraq, Iran, Turkey, and India.

Yet if the committee members had never anticipated outright rejection of the fruits of their efforts, Bevin in turn had not imagined that their recommendations would receive official support from Washington, at least without prior consultation. The moment the report was published in the United

States, however, on May 1, 1946, Truman astounded the British Foreign Office, and his own State Department advisers, by publicly endorsing its recommendations for admitting 100,000 Jews into Palestine. Stunned and enraged, Bevin immediately cabled his protest to Washington. The foreign secretary then compounded his irascible reaction by declaring publicly that the Americans favored the admission of 100,000 Jews into Palestine because "they did not want too many of them in New York." At this point, in their despair, the Zionist leadership concluded that additional negotiations with London would be futile. Henceforth, their diplomacy would be directed first and foremost toward Washington. Their dealings with the British would take other, distinctly nondiplomatic forms.

A ZIONIST COUNTEROFFENSIVE

By the time London rejected the Anglo-American Committee Report, the circumstances of Europe's Jewish refugees had taken a sharp turn for the worse. Some 300,000 Polish Jews who had shared in the mass wartime civilian evacuation to the Soviet Urals were slowly making their way westward, anticipating a return to their original homes. But the reception that awaited them was one of overwhelming hostility, even violence. Reporting from Warsaw as early as December 1945, British Ambassador Victor Cavendish-Bentinck reported that "the Poles appear to me to be as antisemitic as they were twenty-five years ago." The assessment was accurate. In the summer of 1946, when several hundred Jews sought to regain their homes in the city of Kielce, a mob attacked and killed forty of them, and wounded many more. Over the course of 1946 and 1947, as many as 1,500 returning Polish Jews were murdered.

Tens of thousands of these East European refugees consequently saw no alternative but to move on westward, toward the "safety" of the American zones of Germany and Austria. For its part, the Polish government encouraged their departure, granting them passports that were valid exclusively for exit purposes. Over the course of 1946, therefore, an additional 150,000 Polish-Jewish survivors flooded into the DP camps, raising their numbers of Jews to approximately a quarter-million. It was this vast new influx, occurring in tandem with London's refusal to open the gates of Palestine, that impelled Ben-Gurion and his colleagues to intensify their pressure on the British administration in Jerusalem. The Zionist campaign assumed two forms. On the night of June 17, 1946, Haganah units launched the most daring attack of their underground campaign thus far, blowing up ten of the eleven bridges connecting Palestine with surrounding nations. In response, on June 29, the British army embarked upon a cordon and search that continued for two weeks. Tel Aviv and other cities were combed block by block, houses and buildings were searched from basement to attic for weapons caches. Many hundreds of civilians were arrested on suspicion of sabotage operations.

In authorizing this underground resistance, Ben-Gurion and the Jewish Agency had issued firm instructions to avoid, at all costs, inflicting harm on British military and civilian personnel. But the two smaller, non-Haganah, paramilitary organizations were uninterested in following this directive. Even before its wartime assassination of Lord Moyne (p. 573), the Lech'i had discarded any notions of moderation, and engaged freely in acts of anti-British sabotage and murder. The somewhat larger underground group, the Etzel (the Hebrew acronym for "National Military Organization") was no less remorseless in its choice of targets. Functioning as the paramilitary wing of the late Jabotinsky's revisionist Zionists, the Etzel was led by Menahem Begin, and its most draconian measure was perpetrated on July 22, 1946, when it blew up an entire wing of Jerusalem's King David Hotel, specifically the wing that had been appropriated by the British administration for its Criminal Investigation Division. In the blast, ninety-one Britons, Arabs, and Jews were killed, and forty-five were seriously injured. The action infuriated Ben-Gurion and his colleagues. Such acts of "indiscriminate mayhem," they warned, "can only imperil the moral legitimacy of the Zionist cause."

By then, in any case, the Jewish Agency had perfected a distinctly more compelling weapon against the British immigration blockade. This was a full-scale "underground" migration of Jewish DPs from Europe to Palestine. Far from a clandestine smuggling effort of a few thousand refugees, the Zionist leadership had in mind a traffic of tens of thousands of Jews. The homelessness of these victims of Nazism was to be exploited fully, even ruthlessly, to dramatize the callousness of British immigration policy in Palestine. The exodus, in short, was intended as fulfillment of Ben-Gurion's earlier promise to the displaced persons at Landsberg (p. 575): "You are not only needy persons, you are also a political force." To exploit that force, Palestinian-Jewish emissaries, many of them veterans of the wartime Jewish Brigade, were dispatched to the various DP camps throughout the German and Austrian zones of American occupation. With funds supplied by the Joint and other Western Jewish philanthropies, the Palestinians from late 1945 onward arranged frontier crossings, established transit stations, secured lodgings, food, and clothing, and purchased ships and repair facilities at French Mediterranean ports.

It is of interest that none of these activities would have been feasible without the tacit approval of the French government, many of whose senior officials shared a deep-seated resentment at Britain's preeminence in the Middle East. With their help, by autumn of 1946, the number of "illegals" exceeded 1,000 a month. With the Palestinians directing their migration from one transit point to the next, the DPs eventually reached French coastal inlets, where their ships were waiting. Hardly one of these aged and undersized vessels was fit for a Mediterranean crossing. Nevertheless, each of them was crammed from lower to upper decks with hundreds of the refugees, and sent off to sea.

The illegal immigration had its counterpart in Palestine itself. Although the British naval blockade was airtight, and not less than 80,000 British troops were patrolling the country by mid-1946, Jewish underground agents often secured copies of British interception plans and monitored radio messages between the police and the government's intelligence headquarters. Ruses were employed to decoy British personnel while the refugees landed. Thus, in the first two months of 1946, half a dozen ships slipped through the British coastal watch, unloading 4,000 refugees. The Royal Navy then extended its surveillance to the French and Italian Mediterranean coasts. Here its quarantine became more effective. Identifying the refugee ships early on, British destroyers trailed them to Palestine territorial waters, where they "escorted" the vessels to Haifa. Upon being offloaded under military guard, the refugees were reloaded—often forcibly, over bitter resistance—onto British transports and carried off to nearby Cyprus, where they were confined in internment camps. Photographs of these interceptions appeared in many of the leading newspapers of Europe and the United States, and profoundly stirred Western sympathies. As the Jewish Agency had intended, the impact of the refugee migration on world opinion turned out to be possibly the Zionists' most effective weapon.

Britain's Deteriorating Foothold in Palestine

By the late spring of 1946, the confluence of Jewish refugee flotillas and Jewish underground violence in Palestine made its impact on British foreign policy, too. However belatedly, the Labour government was beginning to grasp that the crisis of Jewish refugees could not be resolved except in relation to Palestine, that neither the Jews nor the United States government would accept an alternative approach. Evidently, the Palestine mandate itself would have to be fundamentally restructured. And once this new flexibility was communicated to Washington, President Truman for his part indicated a willingness to share the task of altering Palestine's status. Thus, in May, a second Anglo-American committee, this one of governmental technocrats functioning under the joint chairmanship of Henry Grady, an assistant secretary of state, and Herbert Morrison, a British Labour politico, spent two months devising a new, "compromise" formula for Palestine.

When published on July 31, however, the Morrison-Grady Plan turned out almost immediately to be a nonstarter. Under its provisions, a British-dominated trusteeship would supervise the operation of separate Arab and Jewish "provinces." The Jewish "province," to be limited to 17 percent of Palestine, represented the most drastically attenuated territorial blueprint ever envisaged for the Jewish National Home. Moreover, the province's autonomy, like that of the Arab province, would be essentially fraudulent. The British high commissioner would maintain authority over all key areas of public life, including a veto power over all legislation for a five-year period. To be sure, 100,000 Jews would be admitted during the first year, but afterward the high commissioner would determine immigration on the basis of the Jewish province's economic absorptive capacity. In effect, the plan reflected the interests essentially of the British Colonial Office, which had inspired it. "It is a beautiful scheme," one British official later summarized the plan. ". . . [I]t gives nothing to either party, while it leaves us a free run over the whole of Palestine." And for that reason, both Arabs and Jews contemptuously rejected the proposal.

So did Harry Truman. Together with Undersecretary of State Dean Acheson, he accepted the Zionist evaluation of the plan as a ghetto, a betrayal of the Jews. To Prime Minister Attlee, the president cabled on August 12, 1946: "The opposition in this country to the plan has become so intense that . . . it would be impossible [for] . . . this Government to give it effective support." Seven weeks later, on October 4, the eve of Yom Kippur, Truman issued the customary presidential statement of greeting to American Jewry, but then went on to urge that "substantial" refugee immigration into Palestine commence immediately, for the plight of the DPs "cannot await a solution to the . . . [Palestine] problem." In London, upon being informed of Truman's statement, Bevin publicly and furiously accused the president of making a blatant play for the Jewish vote at a time when congressional elections were only one month off. "In international affairs," protested the foreign secretary, "I cannot settle things if my problem is made the subject of local elections."

Despite their exasperation, Attlee and Bevin by the winter of 1946–47 were prepared grudgingly to accept the reality of the Zionist-American alliance. Thus, in January 1947, in a more conciliatory gesture, they invited Ben-Gurion and his foreign-policy adviser, Moshe Shertok, to visit them in London. Upon their arrival, the two Jewish Agency leaders went into immediate conference with Bevin. Exhausted and dispirited, the foreign secretary informed his visitors that his government had decided to terminate Britain's mandatory administration in Palestine. The burden it imposed on the nation's taxpayers and on its relations with the Arab world had become intolerable. Ben-Gurion, in turn, acknowledging Britain's strategic dilemma in the Middle East, responded with a bluntness matching the foreign secretary's. "Tell me frankly what you need in Palestine. Military bases? Harbors? Perhaps we

Jews would be willing to help. Perhaps our interests coincide." This was language Bevin understood. Reacting cautiously, he then mentioned the importance of air force bases in the Negev Desert, and naval access to Haifa.

But the moment of possible Anglo-Zionist accommodation soon faded. In February 1947, Bevin retreated to a straightforwardly pro-Arab stance. The formula he came up with that month actually was less palatable to the Zionists than the Morrison-Grady scheme. It was for a provisional British trusteeship over a series of Arab and Jewish cantons in a unitary state, with the Arabs to be assured a voice in determining immigration policy. The Jewish Agency this time refused even to discuss the proposal. The deadlock was complete. On February 14, therefore, a despairing Bevin announced that he was referring the entire Palestine imbroglio to the United Nations.

The foreign secretary's decision was taken not simply out of weariness and frustration on Palestine. Britain's economic resources by then were strained to the limit. Only six days later, Prime Minister Attlee appeared before the House of Commons to announce that his cabinet intended to transfer the government of India to the Indians not later than June 1948. One day after this declaration, the Foreign Office revealed that it was terminating its military and financial commitments to Greece and Turkey. Thus, in the course of a single week, London had foreshadowed the divestiture of a historic sphere of British imperial influence. It was not yet certain that Attlee and Bevin had entirely abandoned the notion of maintaining a British presence in Palestine. But events in the Holy Land gradually doomed any expectation of resolving the Arab-Jewish impasse.

In these same winter months of 1947, the Etzel and Lech'i guerrilla organizations intensified their coercive efforts, blowing up officers' clubs, raiding arms depots, killing and maiming British military and civilian personnel with brutal impartiality. Altogether, the most significant development in Palestine throughout 1946 and 1947 was the collapse of security in the Holy Land. By then, in addition to the 80,000 troops Britain had dispatched to this tiny country, a full regiment of the Transjordanian Arab Legion was stationed there, together with 16,000 British and local police. This was a combined military-police establishment four times larger than the one of 1938, at the height of the prewar Arab uprising (pp. 523–24). To pay for this security apparatus, British taxpayers had spent over 50 million pounds during Labour's year and a half in office. The burden of Jewish desperation, and Arab intransigence, was too heavy for a near-bankrupt nation.

PALESTINE BEFORE THE INTERNATIONAL COMMUNITY

As the British government turned to the United Nations, it selected the General Assembly as its organ of choice to deal with Palestine, rather than the

smaller and more efficient Security Council. In this decision, Bevin even at
the last moment revealed his lingering hope that the United Nations, failing
to provide a solution, might turn the matter back to London, presumably with
a wider latitude in dealing with Zionist obstructionism. Harold Beeley, the
Foreign Office's Palestine expert, said as much to David Horowitz, a Jewish
Agency representative:

> In order to obtain a favorable decision, you will need two-thirds of
> the votes of the countries [in the General Assembly], and you will
> be able to obtain it only if the Soviet bloc and the United States
> unite and support . . . the same formulation. Nothing like that ever
> happened, it cannot possibly happen, and will never happen.

Nevertheless, on May 13, 1947, when the Assembly established the United
Nations Special Committee on Palestine—UNSCOP—the new eleven-
member body proved to be reasonably balanced between Eastern and
Western Bloc nations and politically "neutral" countries. Indeed, when Arab
UN delegations sought repeatedly to divorce the Jewish refugee problem from
the Palestine issue, a majority of the UNSCOP members rejected the
attempt. Hereupon, the Arab Higher Committee, the political arm of Arab
Palestine (p. 522), announced that it would boycott the UNSCOP hearings.
The decision was a tactical blunder. It forfeited an opportunity to counter
the Jewish Agency's elaborately documented testimony. More fundamentally, the atmosphere in Palestine itself had changed for the worse. Etzel
and Lech'i violence reached its apogee in the midsummer of 1947. The
UNSCOP members were shocked and dismayed by the killings, and the evidence they saw everywhere around them of elaborate British military precautions, of barbed wire, armored-car patrols, searchlight beams at night. Yet
they sensed, too, that they were witnessing in the mandate a doomed political
entity.

If the UNSCOP visitors needed additional proof of Jewish desperation,
they found it in a dramatic episode that occurred while they were in Palestine
in mid-July. Earlier in the month, a battered little American coastal ferry,
packed with 4,500 DPs, departed from a port in southern France. Waiting
offshore were seven British destroyers. These naval vessels immediately
"escorted" the refugee ship, appropriately renamed *Exodus 1947*, across the
Mediterranean. Twelve miles off the Palestine coast, the British armada
closed on the *Exodus* for boarding. The Jews resisted. In a furious hand-to-
hand struggle, three of them were killed and over one hundred others
wounded. The crew surrendered only when the warships began ramming the
vessel. Listing badly, the *Exodus* then was towed into Haifa harbor. Under
ordinary circumstances, the British would have transshipped the boat's pas-

sengers to Cyprus. But this time, Foreign Secretary Bevin personally decided to "make an example" of the illegals. He ordered them carried back to the French port of Marseilles, and from there to DP camps in Germany, where they were interned again.

The *Exodus* affair, prolonged over three months, was given extensive international news coverage. The UNSCOP members could not have remained unaffected. Upon leaving the Middle East for Geneva in late July, they voted to dispatch a subcommittee to the refugee centers in Germany and Austria. And there, in the DP camps, they witnessed precisely the spectacle that Earl Harrison, President Truman's emissary, and Richard Crossman, of the Anglo-American Committee, had encountered a year and a half earlier: a community of refugee Jews, nearly 250,000 by this time, who measured their very existence against the hour of departure for Palestine.

Spending most of August weighing alternatives, the UNSCOP finished its report at the end of the month. The document contained eleven guiding principles, but the most important stated that the British mandate should be ended and independence granted Palestine as early as possible, that the economic unity of Palestine should be maintained, and the security of the Holy Places assured. Not least of all, the UN General Assembly should immediately arrange to solve the urgent problem of a quarter-million Jewish refugees in Europe. Applying these principles, the UNSCOP then divided into a majority favoring the partition of Palestine into separate Arab and Jewish states, and a minority recommending a Palestinian federation. In supporting partition, the majority scheme envisaged an Arab area encompassing western Galilee, the hill country of central Palestine (except for the Jerusalem-Bethlehem enclave, which would be placed under UN trusteeship), and the southern coastal plain. The Jewish area would encompass the coastal plain, eastern Galilee, and the northern Negev Desert. During a two-year interim period, Britain would administer Palestine under UN supervision, while Jewish immigration would continue at the rate of 6,250 persons monthly.

The Arab leadership, in and out of the United Nations, furiously denounced the majority report, with its recommendation of partition, and warned that they would never accept it. There was little in its proposals, for that matter, to set the Zionists to dancing in the streets. Territorially, its provisions would have awarded both peoples asymmetrical segments that appeared strategically complex and dangerous. Nevertheless, the majority report offered the Jews at least two indispensable prerequisites. These were sovereignty, and an uninterrupted flow of immigration into the foreseeable future. The Jewish Agency consequently expressed cautious satisfaction. At this point, with no room for negotiations between Arabs and Jews, the future status of the Holy Land was turned over to the UN General Assembly.

The Struggle for Partition

In the alignment of blocs within the United Nations, the influence of the Soviet Union would prove of decisive importance among the nine "socialist" delegations at the General Assembly. Here the Jews initially discerned little reason for optimism. Zionism had long been outlawed within Soviet territory as a subversive movement (p. 335), and Moscow in its opposition to British imperialism traditionally had supported Arab nationalism in the Middle East. Yet the Jews were about to receive a stunning surprise. In May 1947, the Soviet ambassador to the United Nations, Andrei Gromyko, lent his government's support to the partition plan. The shift in Soviet stance in fact evinced the logic of Realpolitik. Moscow had concluded by then that the establishment of a vigorous and progressive Jewish state in Palestine was more likely to undermine British influence in the Holy Land, and possibly elsewhere in the Middle East, than would a backward Palestine Arab regime, heavily dependent on Britain for money, weapons, and advisers. Whatever Moscow's ulterior purpose, this reversal of its diplomatic position assured the Jews the votes of the second-largest bloc in the General Assembly.

For Arabs and Jews alike, however, the most critical diplomatic factor remained the attitude of the United States, by then widely recognized as the most powerful nation in the world. The American attitude in turn was mightily influenced by several contending influences within its own government. One was the growth of American economic and strategic interests in the Middle East since World War II. By far the most vital of those interests were American oil holdings in Saudi Arabia. With much urgency, State and Defense Department officials reminded the White House that these wells and pipelines could be threatened by Washington's support for Zionism. Indeed, as late as September 22, 1947, General George Marshall, recently appointed as secretary of state, instructed the American delegation at the United Nations to refrain from supporting the UNSCOP majority report, with its recommendation of partition.

But other factors exerted a decisive pro-Zionist influence on the White House and Congress. Chief among these was the importance political leaders placed on the Jewish vote in states with large urban Jewish populations. This influence in turn would hardly have been effective if American Jewry itself had not been won over to Zionism through decades of cultivation. Indeed, by the end of the war, the revelations of the death camps and the plight of the Jewish displaced persons effectively transformed Zionism into the single most urgent force within the American-Jewish community. By 1947, fundraising drives on behalf of European survivors and the Palestine sanctuary were raising $100 million a year, far surpassing the philanthropic efforts of any other American charity or any other American ethnic group. Mobilized by such eloquent Zionist leaders as Stephen Wise, Abba Hillel Silver, and Arthur Lelyveld, American Jewry deluged the White House and Congress with letters and telegrams, activated the support of labor leaders, the press, and sympathetic Christian clergymen, and organized rallies, conferences, and letter-writing campaigns.

When Harry Truman assumed the presidency in April 1945, he was subjected instantly to the full force of that Zionist appeal. Although frequently exasperated by it, he could not ignore it, or the advice of several pro-Zionist liberals whose judgment he trusted, including Eleanor Roosevelt, widow of the late president; Herbert Lehman, former governor of New York; and his own White House legal counsel, Clark Clifford. It was the influence of these and other pro-Zionist advisers that evoked Truman's early pressure on Britain to admit 100,000 DPs into Palestine and subsequently to reject the Morrison-Grady scheme (pp. 583–84). Moreover, on October 9, 1947, the president learned that the Arab League Executive had requested its member nations to dispatch troops to the Palestine border, in anticipation of invasion. Truman's back was up. He then instructed Secretary of State Marshall to support the partition plan.

On October 21, therefore, when the UNSCOP majority report was sent on to the United Nations General Assembly, its signatories included the United States and the Soviet Union. It was a formidable combination. Yet the State Department had managed to impose one constraint upon the Truman directive. No American pressure was to be applied to other governments. If the Zionists hoped to win over the remaining UN delegations, they understood that they would have to do so on their own. Hereupon, responding to that challenge, the American-Jewish leadership set about vigorously exploiting their business and diplomatic connections among a group of six smaller nations that had tended initially to reject the partition report. Ultimately, most of these "waverers" agreed to support partition. Except for minor territorial modifications, the blueprint now to be submitted to final General Assembly consideration provided for an Arab state encompassing 4,500 square miles, 804,000 Arabs, and 10,000 Jews. The Jewish state would encompass 5,500 square miles, 438,000 Jews, and 397,000 Arabs. The two states would be linked in an economic union, share a joint currency and joint transportation facilities, as well as all postal and telecommunications services. Each year the Jewish state would pay the Arab state a 4 million pound subsidy, reflecting the former's anticipated superior economic development.

On November 29, the partition resolution was submitted to the General Assembly for a final vote. It passed by a margin of 33 to 19, thereby giving it the necessary two-thirds majority. The political maneuvering of Jews and Arabs had continued to the last moment. The Americans and the Soviet Bloc of states were committed to partition. So were France, Norway, Canada, and the group of former "waverers"—among them Haiti, Ethiopia, Liberia, and the Philippines—whom the Zionists had won over. Yet the sizable number of Moslem delegations, together with India, Yugoslavia, and Greece, continued unshakable against the majority report. As matters developed, the pivotal bloc of votes in favor of partition was cast by the Latin American delegations. Ironically, political pressures exerted virtually no influence on them, for none of their governments possessed any interests either way in the Middle East. Rather, the evidence is compelling that simple compassion for the Jewish refugees was the decisive influence in their votes.

Altogether, Jewish and Arab pressure tactics appeared to have influenced the United Nations vote only marginally. Far more important was the rare and impressive phenomenon of Soviet-American agreement on an international issue. In any case, there appeared little valid alternative to the partition plan. Both Arabs and Jews had insisted that they would not accept the minority report's blueprint for a federalized Palestine. Partition, on the other hand, claimed the support of at least one of the parties to the dispute. The Arab scholar Albert Hourani later offered possibly the most incisive insight into the partition decision. The Jews belonged mainly to the West, he observed. They were far better known than the wholly alien Arabs. Their plight, registering directly and intimately on the conscience of Western nations, was magnified by the latter's sense of guilt for the Holocaust. They could exorcise that afflicted conscience now principally by supporting the establishment of a Jewish state.

Jewish Statehood in the Balance

The United Nations partition formula anticipated a reasonable degree of British cooperation on a number of crucial issues. These included use of a port adequate for substantial Jewish immigration, and a willingness to share the administration of Palestine with an appointed UN commission during a transitional period of British departure. But the British flatly refused any cooperation, rejecting the UN-specified departure schedule of February 1, 1948, in favor of their own, August 1 (although several weeks later the British advanced the timetable to May 15). Neither would there be a gradual transfer of British authority. When Ben-Gurion, premier-designate of a future Jewish state, visited British High Commissioner Sir Alan Cunningham at Government House in Jerusalem to seek information on the reserves of food and fuel in the country, and permission to organize a militia, he was coldly rebuffed.

Instead, determined to maintain Arab goodwill at any cost, the British government removed Palestine from the sterling economic bloc and froze

Jewish Agency currency accounts in London—measures that threatened to bankrupt the embryonic Jewish state. At the same time, even as they maintained their embargo on Jewish immigration and Jewish weapons acquisition, the British continued to sell weapons to Iraq and Transjordan under its treaty relations with those states. General Sir Gordon MacMillan, Britain's army commander in Palestine, received instructions to deliver over to the Arabs the largest British army camp and others of the country's strategically placed fortresses. The Arabs made good use of these facilities. Within days of the UN partition vote, the Arab Higher Committee began recruiting volunteers, and these guerrillas soon began launching hit-and-run attacks on Jewish farm settlements and on the Jewish quarters of Jerusalem, Haifa, and Jaffa.

On December 12, 1947, moreover, the Arab League voted to provide funds, weapons, and volunteers for an impending Palestine war. Hereupon, under the command of an Iraqi staff officer, Ismail Safwat Pasha, an "Arab Liberation Army" established its headquarters outside Damascus and gave over field command to Fawzi al-Qawukji, a veteran guerrilla leader of the Palestine civil war of the 1930s. By January 1948, Fawzi began moving larger detachments of men into northern Palestine, until 7,000 of them were conducting organized assaults on the Jews' Galilee communities. Soon, Fawzi was able to establish a central command, which he subsequently delegated to Abd al-Qadir al-Husseini, a nephew of the Mufti. By winter and spring of 1948, these forces succeeded in intensifying their attacks on the Jewish "New City" of Jerusalem and in isolating all roads between Tel Aviv and Jerusalem, and between Haifa and the Galilee. The Jews' military situation, particularly in Jerusalem, became very grave. As late as the spring of 1948, the reserves available to the Jewish Agency numbered 21,000 men and women, and most of them were only partially trained and were inadequately equipped. To circumvent British restrictions, weapons had to be purchased and smuggled in from Europe in isolated odd lots, and these frequently could not be openly used. Altogether, in the spring months of 1948, Palestine Jewry faced the grimmest period of its struggle for independence.

Washington, meanwhile, in endorsing partition, had counted on a swift, surgical division of Palestine into its two component states. But with the escalation of hostilities, this gamble seemingly had failed. The State Department then began hedging its bets. Beginning in December 1947, it turned down repeated Jewish Agency appeals for arms-purchasing licenses and for financial loans. Moreover, on February 21, 1948, when the Arab League voted to deny American oil companies pipeline rights in the Middle East until Washington altered its Palestine policy, Secretary Marshall and his departmental officials pressed the White House to rethink its support of partition. And on March 19, Warren Austin, the American ambassador to the United

Nations Security Council, stunned the General Assembly by suggesting that it consider postponing partition in favor of a "temporary" trusteeship over Palestine "without prejudice . . . to the character of the eventual settlement."

Shaken by this sequence of retrenchments, the Zionists deluged the White House with telegrams and petitions, buttonholed congressmen and senators, organized large and politically suggestive parades of American-Jewish war veterans. On March 23, Ben-Gurion cabled the State Department a warning of his own: he and his colleagues would oppose with all their strength any postponement of Jewish independence. And so, too, apparently, would most of the UN delegations, who made plain that "postponement" would represent a serious blow to the authority of the world body. Eventually, as international opposition to the American plan mounted, the White House dropped all further reference to it. In any case, by April 1948, both Arabs and Jews were well embarked on the establishment of their own realities in the Holy Land.

BEN-GURION FORCES THE ISSUE

In late March 1948, Palestine Jewry's military position was crumbling under the weight of the Arab guerrilla offensive. It was then that their army commanders proposed a strategy of desperation to supply the beleaguered Jewish communities in Jerusalem and the Galilee. They would abandon their defensive posture and instead concentrate all their resources on an offensive campaign to seize control of Palestine's key heights and road networks. The gamble was a dangerous one, for manpower and weapons were still in short supply, and an offensive campaign would not only leave key settlements unprotected, but even risk the danger of a pitched battle with the British. Yet Ben-Gurion discerned no alternative to a single, hammer-blow offensive. On April 1, therefore, in an urgent meeting with his senior Jewish Agency colleagues, he forced the issue through.

Until that moment, no decision Ben-Gurion ever took was fraught with profounder risks. His willingness to accept the challenge revealed the true dimensions of the man's tenacity and boldness. Only then, in fact, did the Jewish Agency chairman become a household name outside Palestine itself. Yet no Jew alive had ever been more fully identified with the Yishuv than Ben-Gurion, since the moment in 1906 of his arrival in Jaffa harbor from Poland as a nineteen-year-old youth named David Gryn. From then on, every facet of his career reflected a stage in the history of the Zionist redemptive effort. In the years before 1914, he labored as a farmhand in the citrus groves. During World War I, he served in the Jewish Legion. After the war, he became a leader of the Jewish labor movement, then a secretary-general of the Histadrut (p. 368). In 1935, he was elected chairman of the Palestine

Executive of the Jewish Agency and found himself thrown willy-nilly into the world of statecraft.

Ben-Gurion was no suave diplomat in the Weizmann manner. At heart, he remained the tough union leader, as forceful and outspoken as Bevin, yet no less stubborn. He looked the militant role he was to play: short, stocky, his hands still callused, his face hard and weather-beaten, with a granitic chin thrusting belligerently forward. Ben-Gurion's colleagues remembered a single-minded devotion to the cause of the Jewish National Home that approached fanaticism, a total disregard for material comforts, and a lack of personal vanity that was not to be confused with indifference to authority. Certain in his mind where the fate of the Yishuv lay, Ben-Gurion was determined to ensure his nation's security against any opposition and any odds. It was with this approach that he browbeat the members of the Jewish shadow government into approving the plan to clear the Palestine interior.

Fortunately for the impending operation, weapons purchased abroad by Zionist emissaries were beginning to arrive from France and Czechoslovakia, both of whose governments discreetly favored the Jewish cause. Much of this equipment was unpacked almost literally on the eve of battle. Thus, from early April on, the Jews threw everything they had into a furious offensive effort to break open their supply lines. The fighting continued for a month, often at heavy cost in casualties both to Jewish troops and to Palestine-Arab villagers and householders, who fled or were driven from Jewish-controlled territory. After a month of fighting, however, the ragtag Jewish militiamen eventually managed to secure the interior lines of their projected state. Henceforth, they were able to concentrate upon the anticipated invasion of the surrounding Arab armies.

It was also in the second week of May, on the eve of the termination of the British mandate, that the Jews were beginning to fill the administrative vacuum left by Britain's departing government personnel. An interparty committee approved a provisional Council of State, under Ben-Gurion's chairmanship. The body's embryonic cabinet then agreed that all taxes in the Jewish sector would be collected on the same basis as before, that Jewish Agency officials would remain at their posts with their former, quasi-official functions now transformed into governmental responsibilities. A national loan was authorized. Almost at the last minute, a printer's shop in Tel Aviv managed to run off a design for postage stamps and paper currency. Yet these measures were slapdash at best. By all odds, the most critical decision faced by the emergent Zionist government was the choice between postponing the declaration of statehood or confronting the certainty of full-scale invasion by neighboring Arab armies. It was in acute recognition of that danger, on May 12, that Secretary of State George Marshall appealed to Ben-Gurion to hold off a decision for independence. Courteously, but firmly, the appeal was refused.

Two days later, on the morning of May 14, the British lowered the Union Jack over the High Commission's office in Jerusalem. At 4 p.m., senior members of the Zionists' Provisional Government gathered at makeshift facilities in the Tel Aviv Museum. It was there, speaking by radio to the nation, that Ben-Gurion, prime minister–designate, read off the declaration of independence of the State of Israel. Completed in its final draft only the night before, the declaration informed the world that the Land of Israel was the historic birthplace of the Jewish people, that the Zionist movement was testimony to the role the Holy Land had fulfilled in Jewish history and religion, that the Balfour Declaration, the United Nations Partition Resolution, the sacrifices of the Zionist pioneers, and the torment suffered by Jews in their Diaspora—all had laid the moral and legal foundations for the new state. Israel, it was announced, would be open to all Jews everywhere in the world, and would extend full equality to all its citizens without distinctions of religion, race, or gender. The broadcast ended with a final plea: "We extend our hand in peace and neighborliness to all the neighboring states and their peoples, and invite them to cooperate with the independent Jewish nation for the common good of all."

The appeal was poignant, but evidently unrequited. The newborn state was confronting an invasion launched by the organized armies of five Arab nations. It seemed almost a genetic ordination of the Jewish odyssey through history. In the 1930s, by the time the Jews had belatedly discerned in Palestine their one and final sanctuary, the British had closed its doors and European Jewry was doomed. In the early postwar period, even those Jews who had survived the Final Solution and managed to undertake the clandestine postwar journey to Palestine were hardly more than human derelicts, apparently incapable of functioning except as permanent dependents of philanthropic benevolence. At best, the UN Partition Resolution seemed an uncharacteristic, and possibly cosmetic, expression of the Western conscience. Gentile pity (or guilt), after all, did not translate into guarantees of protection for Palestine Jewry, no more than it had for European Jewry. While the Arab nations presumably could be depended upon to take care of their own, the Jews faced the distinct and imminent possibility of another genocide. Nothing in their Diaspora experience would have prepared them for a better fate. As it developed, the Jews of independent Israel were not a fatalistic community.

XXX

Eastern Jewry in the Postwar: A Failed Convalescence

A CRIPPLED SOVIET BLOC DIASPORA

The demography alone offered eloquent testimony. By the end of 1940, following its annexations of eastern Poland, Bessarabia, Bukovina, and the three Baltic republics of Latvia, Lithuania, and Estonia, the "greater" Soviet Union had encompassed a Jewish population of 3.02 million. By the end of World War II, that population was reduced by almost a third. As late as the first postwar Soviet census of 1959, the entirety of the Jewish population was calculated at 2.269 million. It was an ethnic hemorrhage undergone by no other Soviet nationality. Of this cruelly mutilated Jewry, moreover, only 221,000 remained in the annexed territories, where the Nazi Final Solution had inflicted its most grievous losses. The largest numbers of Soviet Jews who survived the war, by and large, were those living in eastern Ukraine, the Russian Republic, and the Transcaucasus and Central Asian republics—where some 350,000 Jews had been relocated following the German invasion.

During the war years, the Jews' military contribution of a half-million officers and men was highly valued. So were their potential international connections. Intent on mobilizing goodwill among Jews in the Allied nations, and through them, of their governments, the Kremlin in 1942 had authorized the establishment of a "Jewish Antifascist Committee." Under the chairmanship of Solomon Mikhoels, director of the prestigious Jewish State Theater, the committee included some of the nation's most respected Jewish authors and artists. None doubted the role they were expected to fulfill. Dispatched to England and the United States to lecture before Jewish audiences, Mikhoels and his colleagues invoked the unity of the Jewish people and described the genocide of Soviet Jews then unfolding under the Nazi invaders. Once the war ended, the committee, still intact, also began to function as a kind of center for Jewish cultural activities in the Soviet Union, and its Yiddish-language newspaper, *Eynigkeit,* became the forum for all genres of Jewish literary expression. Throughout the country, Jews discerned in this cultural revival the augury of an improved future under Stalin.

Hope similarly was kindled by an unanticipated shift in the government's foreign policy. Before the war, Zionism was as illegal a movement among Soviet Jewry as political nationalism among others of the USSR's heterogeneity of races and peoples. But from March 1947 on, the Kremlin intimated its support for the notion of partitioning the Holy Land into independent Arab and Jewish states, and on November 29, 1947, Soviet Bloc delegations actually joined in the decisive UN General Assembly vote in favor of partition (pp. 589–90). Indeed, after extending diplomatic recognition to the newborn State of Israel in May 1948, Moscow countenanced a wide-ranging program of military aid to the Jewish republic, most of it funneled through its Czechoslovakian dependency.

As for Soviet Jewry, news of Israel's birth evoked a near-euphoria of pride and gratification. Many thousands of Jews of all backgrounds attended synagogue services of thanksgiving. In September 1948, when Israel's newly appointed minister to the USSR, Golda Meyerson (later Meir), appeared at Moscow's Great Choral Synagogue on the eve of the Jewish New Year, she was overwhelmed by the reception tendered her. As she wrote later:

> Instead of the 2,000-odd Jews who usually came to synagogue, a crowd of close to 50,000 people was waiting. . . . Within seconds, they had surrounded me, almost lifting me bodily . . . surging around me, stretching out their hands and saying . . . "Shalom, shalom," and crying.

But if Israeli independence was a thrilling development for Soviet Jewry, it was also a remote one. Most of the Jewish younger generation still entertained high hopes for their future on Soviet soil. Enjoying equal access to the mighty cultural resources of the Soviet state, they found it difficult to sustain a vision of life in an exclusively Jewish nation.

An Uncertain Residue: Bulgaria, Yugoslavia, Czechoslovakia

Was their reaction characteristic of Jews elsewhere in Eastern Europe? However decimated, enclaves of Jews were still to be found among these Communist satellite republics, and a number of them were quite substantial. The 45,000 Jews who remained alive in Bulgaria comprised the largest proportion of Eastern Bloc Jews to survive the Nazi Holocaust. The challenge awaiting them in the postwar years unquestionably was grave. Many of their homes had been destroyed or damaged, or were occupied by squatters. Under orders of the new Communist regime, priority in housing was given over to veteran party members. Few Jews belonged to this category, and months passed before homes and shops were returned to them, often in uninhabitable condition. Afterward, their hopes of reviving their mercantile careers were destroyed by Communist nationalization decrees. Nearly destitute, subsisting largely on Joint philanthropic subventions, Bulgaria's Jews discerned no alternative but emigration. In the prewar period, they had achieved a reputation as the most ardent Zionist community in the European diaspora (p. 147). Now they required no further incentive to apply for permission to depart for Palestine.

Their decision was taken in the period when Moscow was undergoing its reversal of position on the Jewish National Home and lending its diplomatic support to partition. Thus, adapting to the twists of Soviet diplomacy, the Bulgarian government in late 1947 agreed to a limited immigration to Palestine of 7,000 younger Jews as "fighters against British imperialism." In 1948, Sofia negotiated a secret and wider-ranging deal with the Jewish Agency. Jews of all categories would be free to leave for Israel, provided they relinquished all claims to their Bulgarian property. Under this formula, the departure of Jews swiftly picked up momentum. By 1950, no more than 5,000 of them remained in Bulgaria. They were free to pray in their own synagogues, to maintain several Hebrew schools and two decrepit communal centers in Sofia and Plovdiv. But with each passing year, fewer of these survivors bothered to maintain the ghost of their once fecund Sephardic tradition.

In neighboring Yugoslavia, approximately 53,000 Jews had been wiped out (pp. 535–36), while 18,000 others saved their lives by taking refuge in the Italian-controlled zone in Dalmatia, or by joining the Titoist resistance in the partisans' mountain retreats. After the war, approximately a third of these survivors chose to depart for refugee camps in Austria and Germany, and from there to Palestine. Marshal Tito's Communist government did not stop them. Nor did it stop others, once Israel was born. Over the next two decades, another 7,500 Jews emigrated. Of the remaining 4,500, the "ethnic" ratio continued essentially as in the prewar: two-thirds Ashkenazim, one-third Sephardim. In common with their non-Jewish neighbors, they experienced a gradual improvement in their material circumstances following Tito's break with the Kremlin in 1948, when the Communist economy was decentralized and small traders and commercial managers were permitted to function again. Other Jews earned their livelihoods as mid-level civil servants or as doctors and lawyers. Although in Sarajevo, Belgrade, and Zagreb a few—restored—synagogues and communal centers continued to operate, Yugoslavia's shrinking Jewish enclaves, with their high intermarriage rate, offered little evidence of future cultural vitality.

Of all the minorities to fall within the postwar Soviet sphere, it was Czechoslovak Jewry that had undergone the most radical proportionate deracination. Barely 70,000 of their numbers survived the Nazi genocide, of a prewar Jewish population of 360,000. Yet, however shrunken their demography, the prospects for their revival were not altogether bleak. Czechoslovakia had been spared the physical devastation of battle. Its economic infrastructure remained in place. So, apparently, did its newly restored democratic institutions, for Moscow had decided for the while to allow Czechoslovakia to function as a kind of showpiece of Soviet forbearance. The nation's president, Edvard Benes, and its foreign minister, Jan Masaryk (son of Tomas Masaryk), responded generously to Jewish needs. As in the pre-1938 years, Jews and other ethnic minorities were assured complete civil equality and cultural autonomy. Between 1945 and 1947, the Prague government unhesitatingly opened the nation's frontiers to Polish-Jewish survivors in transit to the American zones of Germany and Austria, and cooperated with the Joint in providing them food and lodgings en route. Additionally, following Moscow's lead, Czechoslovakia in 1948 became a principal source of weapons for Israel during the Jewish state's military struggle for independence. By late summer of 1948, when the supply effort was phased out, Czechoslovakia had supplied Israel with 60,000 rifles, 22 artillery pieces, 84 fighter airplanes, and 22 tanks, together with large quantities of ammunition.

This record of Czech solicitude notwithstanding, Jewish survivors even in the first postwar years discovered that their restitution claims often were denied, on the pretext that Jews belonged to the despised "German" or "Hungarian" minorities. In backward Slovakia, with its more deeply rooted anti-semitism, Jewish efforts to reclaim their prewar homes and shops frequently erupted in violence. And in February 1948, once Moscow abandoned its policy of restraint and officially transformed Czechoslovakia into a "Socialist People's Republic," there could be no question of returning commercial property to anyone, Jew or non-Jew. Such enterprises were nationalized altogether. Jewish communal institutions similarly were taken over by Communist apparatchiki, contacts with Jewish organizations abroad were terminated, and the Joint was ordered to close down its operations in Czechoslovakia. It was this sequence of reverses that produced a wave of departures. By 1952, approximately 53,000 Jews had left the country. Of the 17,000 who remained, most were highly assimilated, and many were Communist sympathizers.

POLAND, HUNGARY, RUMANIA

In 1946, the more than 300,000 Polish Jews who had escaped during the war to the Soviet interior began returning to Polish soil. There they encountered Europe's quintessential graveyard. Barely 85,000 of their people remained alive on Polish soil. Moreover, the treatment meted out to both groups of survivors, "locals" and repatriates, proved more brutal than anywhere else in Communist Europe. Claims for restitution of homes and shops were greeted with open hostility, even with pogroms. By late 1946, as a result, the tide of Jewish migration to the displaced-persons camps in Germany regained its initial postwar momentum (p. 581). It did not ebb until the summer of 1949 when the Polish government, essentially to preserve a reservoir of skilled manpower, decided to seal the exit routes. By then, not more than 90,000 Jews stayed on in Poland.

The majority of them fell into the repatriate category—those who had survived in the Soviet Union during the war. Many had been won over to communism during those years, and some 5,000 others were veterans of the Polish Communist Party, where they had comprised fully 26 percent of the party's pre-1939 membership. Upon their return, it was specifically the latter whom the Soviets pegged for a leadership role in postwar Poland. Among them, three became leading members of Poland's Communist Politburo, and three others were deputy members. Many of the directors-general of government ministries were Jews. So were numerous police chiefs and army officers. The visibility of these Jewish eminences was deeply repugnant to the Polish population, who regarded them as a despised alien elite administering an equally despised social system on behalf of a traditional Russian oppressor.

If Jewish Communists were sentient to the hatred around them, it was not Marxist idealism alone that persuaded them to remain. Postwar Poland had shifted westward to the Oder-Niesse Line, acquiring the highly industrialized former German territory of Silesia and East Prussia. Once the inhabitants of these regions were forcibly repatriated to Germany, a vacuum existed for skilled, educated personnel to take their place, and a sizable nucleus among the Jewish survivors possessed the necessary background. Accordingly, they were offered comfortable (formerly German) apartments and decent salaries to remain on. Many accepted, to become technocrats in the government, in public corporations and nationalized industry, or to establish successful practices as doctors, dentists, lawyers, and accountants. They appeared secure. In marked contrast to the successor-state Polish government of the 1920s, moreover, the post–World War II Polish regime was prepared to fund Jewish communal centers and Jewish schools, while the Joint underwrote Jewish newspapers, literary journals, libraries, theatrical and musical activities. Was a spark of life flickering amid the ashes of the Nazi inferno, amid the gray aridity of the Communist "People's Republic"?

Hungary, too, lay in ruins when the war ended, its economy shattered, its citizens threadbare and often starving. The Jews among them plainly faced the grimmest ordeal of all. During the war, 405,000 of their numbers had perished—more than half their critical mass in the Greater Hungary of 1941, and at least two-thirds of their population in "integral," pre-1938 Hungary. At war's end, some 155,000 Jews survived in Budapest, and approximately 60,000 in the provinces. Throughout the spring and summer of 1945, in their ongoing debilitation, they continued to die off at the rate of seven hundred a week. Their crisis eased only late in the year, with the opening of a network of Joint canteens and clinics.

As in the aftermath of World War I, Hungary's new Communist leadership included substantial numbers of Jews. A few of them were veteran commissars from the Bela Kun era who had managed over the years to survive in Soviet exile. In 1945 they returned in the wake of the Red Army. Their leader was Matyas Rakosi. The illegitimate son of a Jewish miller's daughter and a gentile coachman, Rakosi before World War I had studied at Vienna's elite school for diplomats before joining the Communist Party. In 1919, captured after participating in the short-lived Bela Kun regime, he was spared execution but spent a decade and a half in and out of Hungarian prisons. Upon Rakosi's final release in 1940, he departed for Moscow. Eventually, at war's end, he returned as party first secretary (and later prime minister) at the head of a quintet of fellow Jews that included Erno Gero, the Communist government's economic overlord; Mihaly Farkas, its military and defense chieftain; Jozsef Revai, its cultural "pope"; and Gabor Peter, chief of the dreaded Communist security police. Of the twenty-five members of the first Communist Central Committee in postwar Hungary, nine were Jews, and at the lower echelons, Jews also were extensively distributed at key positions.

It was specifically this Jewish leadership that now tolerated a resurgent wave of popular antisemitism, believing that time was needed to recruit a larger party base. In 1946, when Jewish efforts to secure the return of homes and businesses touched off riots in several provincial towns, the government refrained from intervening. Three years passed before the Communists consolidated their grip on the country. Not until 1949 did they move decisively to stamp out anti-Jewish violence. Yet by then the government's nationalization program had all but liquidated the Jews' traditional status as a middle class. As late as 1949, half the nation's remaining Jewish population was dependent on Joint philanthropic help. In 1951, moreover, the Rakosi government began deporting expropriated "capitalists" from Budapest and other cities to distant villages, where they were confined in penal conditions. Thus it was, in a grim throwback to the Bela Kun episode of 1919, that Rakosi and his detested regime, widely identified as Jewish, dealt with the Jews more brutally than with any other element in Hungary.

It was more ironic yet, in these same postwar years, that the government authorized a limited reactivation of Jewish (and non-Jewish) religious, cultural, and educational institutions. Under a cabinet decree of 1945, the property of the decimated prewar Jewish communities was taken over by the Central Board of Hungarian Jews. Two dozen of prewar Hungary's 142 Jewish schools were reopened, a Jewish museum was reestablished, an institute of Jewish music, even a "Free Jewish University" (more impressive in title than in facilities or curriculum). If this was the government's strategy to divert Jewish interest in immigration to Palestine, the effort would have seemed vain at a time when Zionism for the first time became virtually the raison d'être of the Jewish school network, even of the Central Board of Hungarian Jews with its veteran, traditionally acculturated leadership. Nevertheless, the statistics of departure revealed a still fragile Zionist popular base. The numbers of immigrants to Palestine from Hungary remained proportionately smaller than those from Poland or Rumania. Of the approximately 70,000 Hungarian Jews who departed for the DP camps of Germany, only half chose to continue on to Palestine. The rest settled in Western Europe or eventually found their way to the United States. In any case, fully 145,000 Jews remained behind, still as convinced as in the prewar era that they were Hungarian by right and tradition, that they might yet live out their remaining years in the land of their birth.

It was not a prospect coveted by their kinsmen across the frontier in Rumania. By 1948, the "Latin Island" had been systematically transformed into a Socialist People's Republic, an apparently dependable satellite of the USSR. Here lived 360,000 Jews, the largest surviving Jewish community in Eastern Europe except for the Soviet Union. On the edge of starvation at war's end, they were kept alive during 1945–46 almost exclusively by the Joint's massive program of emergency relief. The most urgent of their needs were not only food and medical services, but restored housing and business property. Yet in Rumania, as in most of the other People's Republics, government leaders were unwilling to press the issue of restitutions lest they appear to be favoring their own. For here, too, Jews were prominent within the tiny Communist nucleus, and had been since the 1920s and early 1930s, when nearly half the party's Central Committee members were Jews.

At the end of the war, the architects of the Communist takeover were the "Muscovites," those who had returned from exile in the Soviet Union under the protection of the Red Army. Their leader was Anna Pauker, daughter of a *shohet*, a Jewish ritual butcher. A formidably plain woman of harsh dynamism, it was she, not the party's chairman, Gheorghe Gheorghiu-Dej, who made the key policy decisions in her triple capacity as deputy premier, foreign minister, and deputy secretary of the Communist Central Committee. At Pauker's direction, the nationalization of private business enterprises simply completed the Jews' economic ruin. By 1960, fully 140,000 Jews were deprived of any source of regular income. Together with other, non-Jewish "parasitic elements," some 20,000 Jewish businessmen were mobilized as forced labor on public works projects. Under these desperate circumstances, the guarantee of full and equal citizenship in an authoritarian state, even the legalization of Jewish communal institutions, provided meager consolation.

In their desperation, therefore, from the early postwar years on, Rumanian Jewry discerned in mass emigration their one viable hope for the future. Long before the war, their political ideology had become overwhelmingly Zionist, and by the summer of 1947, their revived Zionist Organization maintained no fewer than ninety-five branches and twelve youth training farms. Some 150,000 Jews had registered for emigration visas. Initially, too, the applicants encountered little government opposition. The Communist leadership discerned only advantage in reducing the economically redundant Jewish population to "manageable" size—and, if possible, in ridding the nation of this historically despised alien race altogether. To achieve that goal, in the first two and a half years after the war, 35,000 Jews were quietly allowed to depart, either via the port of Constanta, or overland, to the American occupation zones of Central Europe.

It was in February 1948, following Moscow's break with Yugoslavia's Marshal Tito, that Zionism in the Eastern Bloc suddenly came under renewed suspicion as a "deviationist" movement. The Zionist Organization was outlawed, Zionist funds sequestered, Zionist training farms liquidated. Nevertheless, in the case of Rumania, Jewish emigration was not entirely foreclosed. In private negotiations conducted in early 1949, Anna Pauker reached an "understanding" with Reuven Rubin, Israel's minister to Bucharest. Jews would be allowed to depart at the rate of 4,000 a month. The deal was characteristically Rumanian, for it was produced by a handsome Jewish Agency subvention to the Rumanian government in hard currency, at the rate of $3,000 per emigrant. By December 1951, approximately 160,000 Jews had departed for Israel, where they became a major component of that little nation's postwar population.

The Stalinist "Black Years"

During the Great Patriotic War, even as Joseph Stalin tolerated a limited Jewish cultural revival, he simultaneously appealed to Great Russian nationalism, and the seeds of antisemitism were never lacking in this ideology. Nor were they, under German occupation, when tens of millions of citizens in the western Soviet regions were exposed to Nazi racist ideology. As these areas were progressively liberated between 1943 and 1945, Jews returning from beyond the Urals confronted a blast of antisemitism fully as intense as in the prewar years. In Kiev, the popular mood suggested the imminence of a pogrom. It was an atmosphere that also reflected the barely disguised suspicions of Stalin himself.

From the Soviet dictator's viewpoint, the kinds of Jews who remained alive in such recently annexed areas as the Baltic states, eastern Poland, and Moldavia represented a danger to his empire. These were ethnocentric, "authentic" Jews, with memories of a vigorous prewar Jewish communal life. Moreover, of all the races and nations in Eastern Europe, the Jews alone possessed their largest ethnic hinterland among the Western democracies. Those newcomers who were attached now to the Soviet Union, as fellow citizens of the more thoroughly sovietized Jews of Russia and the "inland" Soviet republics, were a potential conduit for such alien Western influences as Zionism, "Trotskyite" socialism, possibly even democracy. For Stalin, all the old suspicions of the Jews as carriers of these Western "viruses" flared up again—and all the more in 1948, with the defection from the Soviet Bloc of Yugoslavia's Marshal Tito. The threat of heterodoxy would have to be eradicated, possibly by invoking Great Russian chauvinism.

It was thus in 1948 that the campaign against "Titoist deviationism" and "anti-Soviet treason," first launched under the aegis of Stalin's deputy Andrei Zhdanov, shifted its focus to the Jews. The most frequently employed pejoratives now were "homeless," "rootless," "tribeless vagabonds," and "cosmopolitans." Although the individuals singled out as bearers of these anti-Soviet qualities were not specifically identified as Jews, their original Jewish names usually were printed in newspaper accounts. "They are persons devoid of any sense of duty toward the people, the state, or the party," warned *Pravda*. "It is our pressing task . . . to smoke them out of their lairs." The campaign was waged also against Jewish institutions. Central among these was the Jewish Antifascist Committee.

The government actually had been taking aim at the committee ever since its leadership began moving beyond its specific wartime mandate. From 1944 on, Solomon Mikhoels and other committee members devoted their efforts increasingly to the revival of Jewish cultural and communal life. Then, in February 1948—by no coincidence the month of the Soviet break with Tito— Mikhoels was killed. According to the official version, he had perished in an "automobile accident." Almost simultaneously, twenty-five other prominent figures of the committee were arrested. Kept in incommunicado imprisonment for four years, they finally were put on trial in July 1952. Only then was the charge against them revealed. Allegedly, the defendants had plotted the "amputation" of the Crimea from the USSR, and the transformation of the peninsula into a "Zionist bourgeois republic," a base for American imperialism. The instrument of this putative conspiracy was the Joint, acting on behalf of the United States Central Intelligence Agency. However surrealistic the accusations, the court routinely accepted them. It found the hapless Jewish prisoners guilty. In August 1952, twenty-four of them were executed. Lina Shtern, the one woman in the group, was sentenced to life imprisonment. Also sentenced to lengthy prison terms were hundreds of other Jewish intellectuals.

Throughout 1952 and 1953, the arrests or mysterious disappearances of many hundreds of prominent Jews continued, in tandem with venomous press attacks on "cosmopolitans" and Zionism and dozens of secret trials of Jews for alleged treason. Thus, in 1952, eight Jewish communal leaders in Biro-Bidzhan, several of them famed war heroes, were arrested, imprisoned, and eventually charged with "artificially trying to establish a Jewish state in the Far East with the help of the spying Jewish Antifascist Committee." Pronounced guilty, two of the prisoners were sentenced to death, the rest to varying terms of hard labor in the Gulag Archipelago. In that same year, some two dozen Jews were tried before the military court of Kiev for embezzling state property. Found guilty, three of the defendants were sentenced to death, the others to long prison terms. The Kiev trial in turn inaugurated a flood of Soviet press accounts dealing with the alleged widespread Jewish embezzlement of food, clothing, building and industrial supplies, or private vehicles. Many of the accused were described as possessors of Zionist connections. The charges usefully diverted attention from the regime's economic failures. Yet for Stalin, in his paranoid fixation with Titoism and pro-Westernism, they served the even further-reaching purpose of linking deviationist threats to a Zionist-American plot against the Soviet people.

These were terrifying years for Soviet Jewry. Beyond exposure to possible arrest and punishment, to public and private hostility and social ostracism, Jews faced vocational demotions and dismissals. Between 1948 and 1953, over three hundred senior Jewish military officers were "retired," until not a single Jew remained in the upper echelons of the Soviet armed forces. As late as 1939, nine Jews sat in the Central Committee of the Communist Party. By 1952, only one remained, the veteran Lazar Kaganovich. Nor were Jews to be found any longer in other key sectors of their former prominence, in the secretariat of the Central Committee, or among party first secretaries in the various Soviet republics. Jews lost their jobs in trade unions, information agencies, and university faculties and research institutes. The role of Jews in Soviet history was rewritten and minimized. In the 1953 edition of the *Great Soviet Encyclopedia,* the article on the Jews was abbreviated from its former 108 columns to 4 columns. All but a handful of Jewish communal offices, newspapers, and journals were closed down.

The anti-Jewish onslaught reached its climax in January 1953. In that month, *Pravda* shocked the nation with its front-page "revelation" of a sinister conspiracy of "physician-saboteurs," most of them bearing Jewish names, who in recent years allegedly had murdered a number of high Soviet officials. These "monsters in human form" were identified as hirelings of the "international bourgeois-nationalist organization," the American Jewish Joint Distribution Committee. Many of the Soviet officials had been "murdered" years before, among them Andrei Zhdanov in 1948, but the world evidently had to wait until 1953 for the "true facts" of their deaths to emerge. A leading figure of the Politburo, long regarded as Stalin's heir apparent, Zhdanov had been the very symbol of Soviet anti-Westernism and leader of the original campaign against "cosmopolitanism." The murder perpetrated by the Jewish doctors consequently was described as an act of reprisal by a vengeful people. "The black hatred of our great country," declared the journal *Krokodil*, "has united in one camp American and British bankers, colonialists, kings of arms, Hitler's defeated vengeful generals, representatives of the Vatican, and loyal adherents of the Zionist kahal." In ensuing weeks, Soviet diatribes against Jews, Israel, and Zionism became almost psychotically vindictive. In February and early March of 1953, warnings were issued throughout the Eastern Bloc for "revolutionary vigilance" against "Zionist nests."

As Stalin's anti-Zionist and anti-Jewish offensive gained momentum, waves of accusations followed against other Jewish doctors for negligent and abusive treatment of patients. Hundreds of these physicians were dismissed from their hospital positions. Indeed, the government hardly needed to orchestrate a panic that drew from folkloristic wellsprings of Jew-hatred extending back to the Mendel Beilis case, and beyond (pp. 304–9). In the wake of retribution against Jewish doctors, thousands of other Jews were dropped from state enterprises. Jewish children were harassed in school. The ex-foreign minister Vyacheslav Molotov was obliged to remain silent as his wife, a Jew, was exiled from Moscow. On the eve of his death, Stalin was rumored to have formulated a plan for repeating the epic wartime mass evacuation of Jews from the USSR's western regions, this one allegedly to the remotest eastern and Siberian reaches of the country. The years between 1948 and 1953 were the darkest of the Jewish experience under Soviet rule.

The Antisemitic Campaign in the Satellites
Czechoslovakia

In the Eastern Bloc states, even more than in his own country, Stalin was fearful that the Communist leadership might yet follow Tito's example in breaking free of Soviet control. It was thus from February 1948 on that party officials in the various satellite nations became instantly suspect as former colleagues and friends of the Yugoslav dictator. To cauterize any possibility of "infection," Stalin launched into a chain reaction of purges from one end of the Iron Curtain to the other, culminating in the trial, execution, or imprisonment of hundreds of senior party and government figures.

Among all the states of the Eastern Bloc, the most extensive "cleansing action" occurred in Czechoslovakia. Here, since the end of the war, the Soviets had maintained a calculated restraint, allowing the Prague government, much beloved of the West, to function autonomously as a socialist-oriented ally but not as a fully ruled satellite nation. But with the defection of Yugo-slavia's Marshal Tito in February 1948, Stalin no longer could afford this permissive relationship. That very month, he personally supervised the trans-formation of Czechoslovakia into a subservient Communist police state, then launched a thoroughgoing purge of party and government officials. Between 1948 and 1951, no fewer than 25,000 of these personnel were arrested.

At the same time, Czechoslovakia's new puppet regime in 1951 followed Moscow's initiative in linking the putative threat of Titoism and bourgeois nationalism to Zionism, with the very term "Zionism" functioning as a code word for Jewry. Early that year, a sensational "conspiracy" was uncovered, this one in the Central Secretariat of the Communist Party itself, and implicating fourteen senior party and government officials. The master conspirator was alleged to be the party's secretary-general, Rudolf Slansky. The other thirteen were identified as Slansky's intimate collaborators. Eleven of the fourteen were Jews, including Slansky himself, and after the name of each defendant the indictment added the words "of Jewish origin." When the trial finally began, in the autumn of 1952, the government prosecutor announced that the prisoners' crime, "Zionist conspiracy," was an integral feature of a more widely based plot, devised by Jewish leaders in the United States and Israel, to under-mine the socialist order and to give away billions in Czech currency reserves to foreign capitalists. Here, too, the Joint was identified as the conduit of Zionist penetration, its techniques ranging from espionage and sabotage to black-marketeering and smuggling. Even the charge of medical assassination was raised in the Prague trial (two months before announcement of the Doc-tors' Plot in Moscow), with the Joint accused of helping Slansky arrange an attempted poisoning of the nation's president, Klement Gottwald.

The defendants, who had been held incommunicado for more than a year and a half before the trial began, and who presumably had been subject to "persuasion," now vied with one another in confessing their role in the "Zion-ist plot." In November 1952, the court handed down the sentence of death for Slansky and ten of the other defendants, with three receiving life terms. The executions were carried out on December 3. A second trial, in May 1953, con-victed Richard Slansky, brother of Rudolf, and two other senior party offi-cials. All were Jews. All received extended prison sentences. At the same time, from the outset of the first trial down to the final convictions, the media sus-tained their barrage against the Zionist conspiracy. Jews in every echelon of national life were expelled from their positions in government, party, or industry. Even Stalin's death in March 1953, and the ensuing "thaw" within the Soviet Union itself (p. 712), did not initially ease the Jewish ordeal. A full decade would pass before the imprisoned survivors were released and legally rehabilitated, and the pall of suspicion gradually lifted from the nation's shrunken minority of 17,000 Jews.

Poland

As late as 1948, among Poland's far larger remnant population of 90,000 Jews, there appeared at least an even chance for a modest cultural-communal revival. The hopes were soon punctured. In that year, as Stalin launched his anti-Tito witch hunt, Poland's Socialist People's Republic was transformed into a classically totalitarian dictatorship. Jewish revival was stopped in its tracks. Over the ensuing half-decade, as antisemitism emerged as a key feature of the Stalinist "anti-deviationism" campaign, the Joint and other international Jewish philanthropies were closed down. Jewish schools were nationalized, followed by Jewish credit cooperatives and welfare institutions, senior citizen and orphan homes, Jewish newspapers, theaters, and youth organizations. It was in this period of cultural strangulation, during the early 1950s, that rivulets of illegal immigration to Israel further shrank the Jewish population, to approximately 60,000 by 1956.

Ironically, the death of Stalin in 1953, which loosed a far-reaching "thaw" throughout the Soviet empire, produced only mixed results for Polish Jews. As elsewhere in Eastern Europe, the relaxation of Communist totalitarianism in Poland opened a major schism within the party leadership. Since late 1944, control of the party had been in the hands of the Muscovites, those Polish émigrés who had lived in the Soviet Union during the war, and who had returned to assume power in Warsaw directly under Soviet sponsorship. By contrast, the Partisans, Communists who had survived as members of the Polish wartime underground, had largely been dismissed from positions of leadership. But now, in the post-Stalin years, much of the Polish people's hatred of Communist domination was focused on the Muscovites, and specifically on the prominent Jews among them.

The opposition became all but uncontrollable following the death in March 1956 of Boleslaw Bierut, the (non-Jewish) party chairman, and a veteran Stalinist. In June, a series of popular demonstrations culminated in a workers' riot in Poznan. At this point, the Muscovites in the Politburo deemed it expedient to invite a number of Partisans to share responsibility with them. One of these was Wladyslaw Gomulka, a wartime underground veteran who in recent years had been kept under house arrest. Yet it was too late to appease the Partisans. In July of the same year, under Gomulka's leadership, they seized control of the Central Committee and, over the ensuing months, fended off all Soviet threats to restore the Muscovites.

At last, on October 20, a deeply alarmed Soviet delegation, led personally by Party Secretary Nikita Khrushchev, flew into Warsaw. Over the next three days, in a tough bargaining session, the Soviet leadership finally agreed to enlarge Polish autonomy in domestic matters, on condition that Gomulka—now functioning as party first secretary—and his colleagues remained aligned with Moscow on foreign policy and military issues. Then and later, Gomulka kept his part of the bargain. But at the same time, he embarked on a series of vigorous internal reforms: decentralizing the economy, easing restrictions on press and assembly, reintroducing Catholic religious instruction in the public schools. These were measures that gave the new regime a certain measure of popularity and staying power.

So did a shift in the government's approach to the Jews. On the one hand, Jewish communal institutions were allowed a limited revival. Several Jewish schools were reopened, and a Jewish newspaper was authorized to publish news about Israel and Jews in other lands. The Joint was permitted to resume its philanthropic activities in Poland. But the other face of "liberalization" proved much less congenial. It unleashed an upsurge of popular antisemitism. Jewish graves were desecrated. Antisemitic placards appeared on synagogue walls. Jewish children were harassed in schools and playgrounds. Gomulka personally was not an antisemite. Indeed, he was married to a Jewish woman. Yet the first secretary knew his own people. As restraints on their traditional xenophobia were loosened now, he feared even graver consequences, possibly even violence. For this reason, Gomulka intimated that those Jews who wished to leave for Israel could do so. Many accepted the offer. Between 1956 and 1958, an estimated 33,000 Jews departed Poland and journeyed directly to Israel. Although the 27,000 who remained included principally the aged, who feared losing their pension benefits, they also included an important nucleus of technocrats, unwilling to abandon well-paying employment, who were convinced that the antisemitic revival would burn itself out.

It did not. Throughout the 1960s, the Gomulka regime proved incapable of solving Poland's economic problems. As the nation's temper became increasingly restive, General Miczlyslaw Moczar, minister of the interior, discerned an opportunity to gain political advantage over Gomulka. In the spring of 1968, students at the University of Warsaw launched into public demonstrations, demanding wider political liberalization. Several of the more prominent student activists were Jews. Exploiting that visibility, Moczar now denounced Gomulka's policies as "lacking in Polish nationalism." It was surely no accident, the minister suggested, that the country's public institutions were riddled with "non-Poles." At this point, sensing the way the wind was blowing, Gomulka himself belatedly joined in the condemnation of "anti-patriotic elements."

Afterward, a succession of party conclaves demanded a purge of Jews at all echelons of Polish life. Gomulka did not militate the demand, but he complied with alacrity. Between March and June 1968, some 8,000 Jews at all levels of government, party, and cultural life were dismissed from their positions. Their cultural and communal institutions were closed down. In 1969 and 1970, responding to a burgeoning wave of antisemitism in the private sector, another 17,000 Jews abandoned their apartments, pensions, and savings, and departed Poland. A thoroughly acculturated element, most of them bypassed Israel for Western Europe. Barely 10,000 remained behind, a testament to the improbability of life after death.

Hungary

In Hungary, too, as an integral function of Stalin's "anti-Tito" campaign of the late 1940s and early 1950s, the Communists tightened their grip on the government and on other public institutions. The nation's remaining 125,000 Jews were among the first to experience the darkening atmosphere of anti-pluralism. In these years, their newspapers and journals were gradually discontinued, and their communal schools were systematically nationalized. One of the most lamented casualties of the Stalinization campaign was the Joint's extensive network of canteens, clinics, and credit banks. Between 1945 and 1952, the Joint had poured $52 million of relief and welfare assistance into Hungary, the great philanthropy's single largest European welfare program outside Germany's DP camps. In 1953, it was all closed down. And so were the Zionist offices. As early as 1949, the government began selectively arresting members of the Zionist leadership and banning emigration.

Neither was the Communist Party's Jewish elite to be spared. As he grasped the implications of Stalin's antisemitic frenzy, Prime Minister Matyas Rakosi hastened to save his own skin. He ordered the arrest of several of his closest allies, including Gabor Peter and senior Jewish officials of the security police, together with numerous other prominent Communists who happened to be Jews. The lists of those dismissed from their positions extended from the president of the Hungarian state radio to scores of Jewish executives at all levels of the bureaucracy. But in the end, Rakosi himself could not escape the purge. In February 1953, the order came down from Moscow that he should leave his office as prime minister, although he was allowed to remain on as the party first secretary. Two other members of the "Rakosi quintet," Mihaly Farkas and Jozsef Revai, also lost their posts. Later, at Moscow's directive, the Hungarian Communist Politburo appointed a colorless party apparatchik, Imre Nagy, as the new prime minister and warned him to cleanse the party of any remaining Jewish influence. Nagy obsequiously complied.

It was the death of Stalin in March 1953 that gradually eased several of the heavier-handed features of Communist repression in Hungary. In June of that year, even Nagy felt safe in abandoning measures of dictatorial collectivization. Opening the doors of the forced-labor camps, he released the "economic parasites" who had been exiled from Budapest. These measures evoked relief among Jews and Hungarian liberals alike. As party first secretary, to be sure, Rakosi ventured a last shot. Exploiting the power struggle within the Soviet Union, he dismissed Imre Nagy as prime minister in February 1955 and expelled him from the party. But Rakosi had made his move too late.

It was in October 1956 that the political upheaval in neighboring Poland (pp. 607–8) became the catalyst for a parallel uprising in Hungary. Workers and intellectuals alike launched into public demonstrations, demanding the reinstatement of Nagy and the evacuation of Soviet troops based in Hungary. Rakosi, in turn, intimidated by this new display of mass belligerency, promptly reinstalled Nagy as prime minister. Presumably, he anticipated remaining the power behind the scenes. It was a miscalculation. Yet Nagy, in turn, committed an even graver one. He was prepared now to accommodate the rebels, even going so far as to promise free elections and closer relations with the West. For Moscow, Nagy's provocation was too flagrant. Hungary had been an Axis partner in the recent war, after all, and Nagy evidently was prepared to renew contacts with the (West German) Bundesrepublik. On November 4, 1956, Soviet army units unleashed a massive attack on Budapest, instantly and brutally suppressing the popular revolt. Even as Nagy and his colleagues took refuge in the Yugoslav embassy, the Soviets installed a more "reliable" Communist functionary, Janos Kadar, as the new Hungarian prime minister (weeks later, Nagy was carried back to the USSR, where he was subsequently executed).

Jewish students had been prominent participants in the uprising. Once it failed, they were certain that a revived Stalinist-style reaction would follow. Thus, of the 170,000 refugees who fled across the Austrian border, between 35,000 and 40,000 were Jews. Some 90,000 other Jews remained behind, essentially older people who were unwilling to be uprooted yet again. For them, ironically, as for other Hungarians, the Kadar government developed into a rather unlikely surprise. In return for "stability," the new prime minister was willing to offer his people major concessions. These included a much wider freedom of expression in Hungary's cultural life, in journalism, drama, literature, and in university classrooms. In the 1960s, a "New Economic Model" was introduced, allowing more extensive profit opportunities for Hungarians in all vocations, including the professions and industrial and commercial enterprises. Moscow was prepared to allow Kadar this leeway. On the foreign-policy issues that mattered most to the Kremlin leadership, he remained scrupulously loyal to the Soviet Bloc.

No element of the Hungarian population welcomed the new "relaxation" more gratefully than did the Jews. They shared fully in its economic blessings. Indeed, from the 1960s on, they were to be found prominently again among the nation's reviving business community. They served as editors and columnists in newspapers. Once again, as in the prewar years, theater and cinema in Hungary became overwhelmingly Jewish. More than half of Budapest's newspaper editors and columnists, its physicians, lawyers, and university professors, were Jews. Moreover, within a single decade since the 1956 uprising, Jews found political appointments increasingly open to them. Those serving in the Kadar government included the deputy prime minister, the ministers of the treasury, foreign trade, transport, and post, the deputy ministers of defense, foreign affairs, and internal commerce, in addition to the president of the national bank, and several score directors-general of government bureaus. In the 1970s, three Jews sat in the thirteen-member Communist politburo, eight Jews in the party presidium, thirty-seven Jews in parliament. Altogether, the tiny Jewish minority remained far more visible in the country's public and intellectual life than in any other "socialist" nation. With the government's benign approbation, too, Jewish communal life was allowed to revive. By the 1980s, some thirty synagogues were functioning in Budapest and the provinces, as well as eleven Jewish old-age homes, a major hospital, a religious high school, even a resurrected (if quite feeble) rabbinical seminary. Not least of all, after years of isolation, Hungary's Jews were permitted to resume extensive contacts with international Jewish organizations, and with Israel.

In view of these quiet transformations, the collapse of the Soviet Bloc in 1989–90 effected no spectacular alteration in the status of either Jews or Hungarians at large. The transition from quasi-freedom and a neo–market economy to full democracy and modern capitalism proved comparatively seamless. The shrinkage of Hungary's Jewish population by steady, modest departures to Israel was hardly to be distinguished from the ongoing attrition of intermarriage and a low birthrate. By the opening of the twenty-first century, the Jewish population was estimated at 51,000. Even then, Hungarian Jewry remained the largest community of Jews in Eastern Europe, except for those in the territories of the former Soviet Union.

COMMUNIST "ACCOMMODATIONISM," RUMANIAN-STYLE

As late as 1952, it appeared that Rumanian Jewry's "critical mass" would remain the largest among the Communist satellite states. In that year, the burgeoning immigration wave to Israel had been stopped in its tracks as a consequence of Stalin's "anti-Zionist" terror campaign throughout the Eastern Bloc. Anna Pauker was removed from office, and the Moscow-trained party apparatchik Gheorghe Gheorghiu-Dej assumed decisive control of Rumania's state machinery. Under Gheorghiu-Dej's rule, the anti-Zionist campaign sustained its ferocity. Even after Stalin's death, scores of Rumania's Zionist activists were sentenced to long prison terms. It was not until the mid-1950s that the "thaw" extending throughout the Soviet Bloc eventually had its effect in Rumania. Pressure on the Jews gradually eased.

Indeed, the post-Stalinist years of Communist "moderation" gave

Gheorghiu-Dej and his associates the opportunity for a more flexible stance in international affairs. So, also, did the emergent Sino-Soviet confrontation, and the temporary immunity from Soviet retaliation that schism afforded the Rumanians. Thus, in July 1958, Gheorghiu-Dej negotiated the departure of Soviet troops from Rumanian soil. Four years later, seizing upon Soviet Prime Minister Nikita Khrushchev's recent humiliation in the Cuban Missile Crisis, the Rumanian government announced that henceforth it would adopt an "independent Socialist policy." Nor did Gheorghiu-Dej's death in 1965 reverse this new approach. Nicolae Ceauşescu, the newly appointed party first secretary, was determined to maintain his government's independence of action in domestic and international affairs.

Fortunately for the country's nearly quarter-million Jews, the daring shift in Rumanian policy was not accompanied, as in Poland, by an upsurge of antisemitism. This was not an accident. In its divergence from Moscow, the Bucharest regime was intent upon reinforcing its freedom of maneuver by establishing new links with the West. To that end, Gheorghiu-Dej and his associates early on had begun to examine the potential usefulness of the Jews as intermediaries. Here it was that Rumania's Chief Rabbi Moses Rosen played a key role. In 1961, Rosen, a suave and by no means self-effacing politician, was allowed to travel to the United States on a lecture tour of Jewish communities. In his visits, the chief rabbi described the "vitality" of Jewish life in Rumania, emphasizing the "fairness" with which Bucharest was treating its Jews. Rosen was embellishing the facts. Nevertheless, his statements were accepted at face value as evidence of Rumania's growing independence from Moscow, and they helped soften the American government's reservations toward the Gheorghiu-Dej regime. Soon afterward (although plainly not as a consequence of Rosen's visit alone), relations between Washington and Bucharest eased, and the Rumanian ambassador became an increasingly welcome visitor at the State Department. As for Rosen, when he flew back home from his first visit to America, Gheorghiu-Dej received him as a hero, praising his "marvelous diplomatic accomplishment."

The new atmosphere of trust, not to mention the reduced Jewish demographic presence in Rumania, made it possible for the government to countenance a modestly enhanced opportunity for Jews in public life—although never again in the dominating role of the Anna Pauker era. Gheorghe Gaston-Marin and Leonte Rautu served as deputy prime ministers. At different periods, Simeon Bughichi served as foreign minister or deputy foreign minister. Several of the nation's leading intellectual positions also were held by Jews, who emerged as professors, editors, physicians, and theater directors. By the same token, Rabbi Rosen now exploited his leverage to secure tangible concessions for his people. With government approval, a network of Jewish day schools was revived throughout the late 1960s and 1970s. In that same period, over one hundred synagogues were repaired, and the government itself contributed substantially to the project. Funding also was provided for the maintenance of Jewish cemeteries and memorials. A Jewish museum was established. The country's once-renowned Yiddish theater was revived and enlarged. In 1969, the government authorized resumption of contacts between the Rumanian-Jewish federation and international Jewish organizations. By far the most important of those international agencies was the Joint. Thus, in 1969, for the first time in twenty years, the great American philanthropy was permitted to resume its activities in Rumania, where it immediately began underwriting a wide array of social welfare institutions—and thereby disbursed millions of dollars in hard American currency.

Yet Nicolae Ceaușescu, who succeeded Gheorghiu-Dej as first secretary (and later as president) following the latter's death in 1965, sought an even more meaningful American dispensation than hard currency. This was nothing less than most-favored-nation trading privileges with the United States. Here again, Rosen was among those selected for an intermediary role. The wily chief rabbi was eager to cooperate. To help secure American goodwill, he knew, the Ceaușescu government was willing to pay in coin of even more decisive significance to the Jews. The compensation this time would be a relaxation of the ban on immigration to Israel. It had not escaped Rosen that, as far back as the early 1950s, as the Bucharest regime explored a new leeway for itself in international affairs, it seemed intent on developing a more flexible Middle East policy. It began to abstain in the United Nations on various Soviet-sponsored resolutions against Israel. Ultimately, Rumania's most significant departure from the Kremlin line was its refusal to sever diplomatic relations with Israel following the 1967 Six-Day War. By then, Ceaușescu had come to envision himself as an "honest broker" between Israel and its Arab enemies. In 1972, he tendered an elaborate state banquet to Israel's Prime Minister Golda Meir; and five years later yet, he conducted extensive private discussions in Bucharest with Menahem Begin and (afterward) with Egypt's President Anwar al-Sadat. These meetings in turn helped pave the way for Sadat's historic 1977 visit to Jerusalem.

Once the specter of Israel was exorcised from Rumanian foreign policy, it was an easier matter for the government to contemplate Jewish emigration there. As late as 1958, some 230,000 Jews lived in Rumania, still the largest Jewish enclave in Eastern Europe except for the Soviet Union. In that year, following the precedent of numerous other, prewar Rumanian politicians, Gheorghiu-Dej studied the possible advantage of thinning out this dense minority population. Jewish emigration would provide jobs and apartments for the emerging Rumanian middle class; and if the departure of Jews could produce additional dividends in American goodwill, so much the better. In September 1958, therefore, the government authorized a limited number of

Jewish exit visas for Israel. The response was a tidal wave of applications. On this occasion, only 33,000 Jews managed to leave before Gheorghiu-Dej shut the door again, in response to Arab protests. But in 1961, the Bucharest government decided to ignore Arab reaction and to open the door wide.

From 1961 on, there would be no reversal of policy. Diplomatic relations between Bucharest and Washington were steadily warming. Indeed, in 1974, the United States government formally extended Rumania the long-coveted desideratum of most-favored-nation trade relations, on a par even with the democratic countries of the West. Between 1961 and 1975, therefore, fully 160,000 additional Jews left the country. Most of them settled in Israel, where they soon comprised that nation's second-largest bloc of European immigrants, after Polish Jews. In ensuing years, Rumania's remaining minority of 37,000 Jews would continue to diminish. So would the rate of departure, for the Jewish population comprised a proportionately higher number of the aged and ill. Nevertheless, by the turn of the century, a decade after the final implosion of the Communist empire, Rumania's once massive and historically tormented Jewish enclave had been reduced to fewer than 10,000 souls—this in a nation that only two generations earlier had encompassed the third-largest Jewish population in Europe, and the fourth-largest in the world.

A Residual Middle Eastern Diaspora: Turkey and Iran

By 1939, the numbers of Jews living in the Middle East reached 1.7 million. At a time when Jews of European origin totaled some 15 million, this figure represented barely 11 percent of the world Jewish population. Yet, within a period of five years, the Nazi slaughter of European Jews had the unexpected effect of nearly doubling the proportion of non-Europeans among world Jewry.

Did the 120,000 Jews of Turkey, overwhelmingly of Sephardic origin, belong in the European or the non-European category? Perhaps, like Turkey itself, they might have been defined as a kind of nexus between their people's European and oriental worlds. Although spared extermination at the hands of the Nazis, they remained a sorely afflicted community. The Varlik Vergisi was a decisive factor (p. 559). Together with other, impoverished kinsmen, it was principally those Jews whose estate had been devoured by this crippling wartime impost who sailed off for Israel in the first years after 1948. They numbered 52,000. The Turkish government made no effort to block their departure.

In 1956, moreover, an outburst of Turkish violence was ignited by the perennial Cyprus crisis. Rumors circulated that Greeks had destroyed Mustafa Kemal's birthplace in Salonika. Soon mobs raged through the Greek quarter of Istanbul, wreaking damage on shops and dwellings. The rioting then spilled over to the Armenian quarter, and finally to Jewish commercial and residential neighborhoods. Business establishments with non-Turkish names were pillaged and burned. The Pera district, where virtually all the shops were Jewish, was gutted. Deeply shaken, another 15,000 Jews pulled up stakes and departed for Israel. In Turkey's other, internal, political crises of the 1960s and early 1970s, possibly 10,000 more Jews left the country. By 1973, as a result, a national census revealed that barely 42,000 Jews remained in Turkey, and their numbers continued to decline—to an estimated 18,000 thirty years later. Most of them lived in Istanbul.

Virtually all the working members of this shrunken population earned their livelihoods in business and the professions. While few were wealthy, most lived comfortably, often in the apartments and villas of Istanbul's northern suburbs. By the opening of the twenty-first century, whatever the uncertain fortunes of democracy in Turkey, Jews no longer were singled out for discrimination. The rise of Israel had produced no adverse effect on them, except "residually," when Arab terrorists launched two spectacular and bloody attacks on Istanbul's venerable Neveh Shalom Synagogue (p. 739). Although nearly all Turks were Sunni Moslems, they harbored little affection for the Arabs, their former subjects, and their admiration for Israel as a warrior state and unofficial ally against Islamic terrorism spilled over in some measure toward their own Jews.

It was not Turkish Jewry's security, but its cultural vitality, that appeared slowly to be waning. By the turn of the century, religious observance had become as perfunctory among the Jews of Turkey as among most of their kinsmen in Europe. The great majority of Jewish children attended state schools or, whenever economic circumstances permitted, a small number of elite foreign-language schools. Among the younger generation, Jewishness was an identification almost entirely of ethnicity and was sustained by a score of Jewish cultural, sports, and social clubs. If Turkish Jews in no sense were a moribund population, neither were they the vibrant nucleus that, as recently as World War I, ranked them among the most distinguished Sephardic communities in the Diaspora.

Much of that historic pluralism reflected the comparatively forbearing tradition of Sunni Islam. But in the easternmost region of the Middle East, in Iran, Jewish circumstances were profoundly different. Until the twelfth century, this vast and mountainous land encompassed a substantial Jewish population estimated variously at between a quarter-million and a half-million. By the Early Modern Era, however, large numbers of Iranian Jews had dispersed to other parts of the Middle East, and by 1914, those who remained did not exceed 110,000. Plain and simple official brutality accounted for their flight and dispersion. For more than seven centuries, government policy in this militantly Shi'ite realm was uncompromising in its theocratic fundamentalism. The nation's Jews accordingly were subjected to painful extortions and humiliations. Tightly ghettoized, branded by the Shi'ite mullahs as "ritual polluters," they were forbidden to walk in the rain lest water touching them come into contact with Moslems. Jewish men experienced harassment, beatings, even occasional murders. Their women intermittently suffered abduction and rape. Over time, driven from craft and mercantile guilds, Jews were confined to the demeaning vocations of itinerant peddlery, money-lending, amulet-making, and cesspool-cleaning.

It was not until an army coup established the Pahlavi dynasty in 1925 that Iranian Jews experienced a modest improvement in their circumstances. The new shah, Reza Pahlavi, was determined to crush the power of the Moslem hierarchy and embark on a Mustafa Kemal–style program of secular modernization. At his direction, the juridical authority of the mullahs was limited to the narrowest ambit of personal status. All commercial activities henceforth came under the protection of the secular courts. In 1941, with the accession to the throne of Pahlavi's son, Mohammed Reza Pahlavi, whose wartime reign coincided with the Allied occupation of his country, the conditions of Jewish life were further liberalized. A few Jews actually were given civil service employment, and Jewish children for the first time were accepted into state schools.

During Iran's oil boom of the 1950s and 1960s, moreover, as the country's population shifted from smaller towns to the larger cities, Jews shared in the migration. They also gained wider security in middle-class urban vocations. The businessmen among them were quite aware of the rampant bribery that infested every echelon of the economy, including the payoff received by the shah's family on public contracts. But like non-Jewish other businessmen, they adjusted, paying baksheesh for every major deal that came their way, but sharing in the ample remaining profits. Under the protection of the young shah (who in turn remained sentient to American goodwill), Jews now also were routinely enrolling in universities and achieving upward mobility as doctors, lawyers, journalists, and professors. Indeed, in no other Middle Eastern nation did Jewish circumstances improve as dramatically and within as short a period.

It was of note that Shah Mohammed Reza Pahlavi also reacted equably to Israeli statehood. In 1950, his government extended de facto recognition to Israel, and de jure recognition in 1960 (although without establishing formal diplomatic relations). Following Israel's victory in the 1967 Six-Day War, the two countries extended their economic and commercial ties. Israel purchased most of its oil from Iran. El Al, Israel's national airline, operated a regular schedule between Tel Aviv and Tehran. Many Israeli technical experts worked in Iran as advisers, particularly in the military industry, to strengthen Iran's defenses against their common enemy, Iraq. Not least of all, Iranian Jews were free to immigrate to Israel. As in other Jewish exoduses from Islamic lands, those who first availed themselves of the opportunity tended to be poorer or more devout Jews, many from outlying, smaller towns. Their numbers were substantial. Indeed, by 1966, they comprised a majority of the 40,000 Jews who departed for the Jewish State. By contrast, the 70,000 who remained behind generally belonged to the more prosperous business or professional classes. Comfortable in their middle-class status, they saw no reason to pick up stakes.

By the latter 1970s, however, as the government squandered vast quantities of hard currency on elaborate state armaments and public building programs, inflation raged through Iran, and the nation soon was convulsed by social upheaval. The mullahs and ayatollahs, bitter at the shah's appropriation of religious foundation lands, encouraged strikes and demonstrations. Watching these developments with growing anxiety, the Jews kept a low profile. Those who still lived in outlying towns began moving to the cities. Others, more affluent, established bank accounts overseas. The precautions were not gratuitous. Followers of the Ayatollah Khomeini, the most prestigious of Iran's religious leaders, already were extending their assaults on government buildings to Jewish-owned shops and offices. Two firebomb attacks were launched against the El Al office in Tehran. By 1978, leading ayatollahs publicly warned Iranian Jews to cease acting as defenders of "Zionist aggression." Thus, in February 1979, the last month before the fall of the shah, no fewer than 30,000 Jews cleared out of the country.

Ironically, in Paris during this same period, where he had been living as an émigré, Ayatollah Khomeini reassured Western journalists that Iranian Jews would be unmolested. But in March 1979, once the Islamic Republic was proclaimed, the assurance rang increasingly hollow. The Israeli embassy was ordered closed, and its premises were turned over to Yasser Arafat's Palestine Liberation Organization. At the universities, Islamist students intimidated Jewish professors into "voluntary" retirement. Once again, as in the pre-Pahlavi era, storekeepers would not allow Jews to touch food on the shelves, and surrogate buyers had to be found. Then, in May 1979, Habib Elghanian, president of the Council of Federations of Iranian Jewish Communities, was arrested, convicted for "Zionist spying," and summarily executed. In ensuing months, nine other Jewish businessmen were arrested. Convicted on the identical charge of "aiding Zionism," they were shot by firing squad. In terror, another 10,000 Jews then rushed to leave the country.

Their timing was fortuitous. In September 1980, fearing a hemorrhage of capital and talent, the Islamic government announced that henceforth no Iranian, whether Moslem or Jew, would be allowed an exit visa. Iran's remaining 30,000 Jews now appeared trapped inside the country. Nevertheless, over the next few years, through extensive baksheesh payments, another 5,000 Jews succeeded in making their way across the borders of Pakistan or Turkey, eventually to reach the United States or other Western countries. The circumstances of the shrinking Iranian-Jewish minority became increasingly delicate. Synagogues were allowed to remain open, but communal institutions and schools were monitored by the government and substantially de-Judaized in curriculum and enrollment. With the ebbing of the initial passions of the Islamic revolution, the Jews' physical safety no longer appeared to be in serious jeopardy. Nevertheless, over the years, their numbers were depleted by still another 15,000, as homes and savings were forfeited to negotiate secret passage to the West. With intermittent arrests and imprisonments of suspected "Zionist spies" continuing even into the twenty-first century, Iran's remaining 11,000 Jews lingered in a state of psychological limbo, endlessly sensitive to future changes in the barometer of public toleration.

THE ARAB MIDDLE EAST

In other Moslem nations, the Jews' fate after the birth of Israel tended to be resolved more swiftly and decisively. An example was the Imamate of Yemen, an obscure little realm in the southwestern corner of the Arabian peninsula. Here a Jewish presence traced back nearly two millennia, to the destruction of the Jewish Commonwealth of antiquity. As Jewish exiles from Palestine were scattered throughout the Middle East, a number of them settled in Yemen. There, in the sixth century, they even managed briefly to Judaize the royal household of King Yusuf As'ar Dhu Nuwas. The Yemeni ruler in turn secured the conversion to Judaism of thousands of his subjects. These, it is assumed, became the ancestors of the Yemenite Jews.

The era of large-scale proselytization was fleeting, however. Once subjected to Moslem rule in the seventh century, the Jews of Yemen were transformed into a dhimmi people. Afterward, as infidels, and banned from the practice of agriculture, they were confined to isolated ghetto quarters in Tsan'a, the Yemeni capital, and obliged to pay special taxes, to perform the despised chore of collecting animal carcasses, even to give right-of-way to Moslems in the streets. Living in a society later governed by Shi'ism, the less tolerant of the two main branches of Islam, they remained virtual untouchables. It was not until the nineteenth century, under Ottoman rule, that their material circumstances eased somewhat and they were allowed to rebuild their homes and synagogues. Yet, even then, confined exclusively to handicrafts, underfed and small of stature, the Yemenites remained as marginalized and impoverished as Jews anywhere else on earth.

In their tenacious piety, too, the Yemenites nurtured the messianic conviction that sooner or later they would return to Zion. The dream acquired an apocalyptic reality in 1880, when accounts reached them that Jews elsewhere were beginning the process of return. All but overcome by the news, some one hundred Yemenite families immediately disposed of their homes and set out for the Holy Land. Sailing up the Red Sea in tiny dhows, they continued afterward by land to Alexandria, then by steamer to Jaffa, and again by donkey cart or by foot to Jerusalem. Less than half their number survived the voyage. Nevertheless, each year afterward, the Yemenites were joined by several hundred more of their kinsmen. In Jerusalem and its surroundings, they subsisted as they had in Yemen, as artisans or as menial laborers in the Jewish economy. By 1948, their population in Palestine had grown to 40,000.

For the nearly 50,000 Yemenites who remained behind in the Imamate, the birth of Israel offered divine confirmation that the moment of redemption had indeed arrived. By then, too, life in Yemen had become insupportable. Enraged by Arab defeat in the Palestine War, mobs attacked and pillaged Tsan'a's Jewish quarter. At this point, through the mediation of the local British consul, the ruler of Yemen, Imam Yohya, reached agreement with the Jewish elders. He would allow their people to depart en masse, provided they left their homes, workshops, and chattels to his government. At the same time, and under a parallel arrangement, the Jewish Agency paid off the various Arab sheikhs through whose territories the Yemenites would have to pass to reach the British Crown Colony of Aden. Subsequently, across this bleak terrain, Yemen's remaining Jews made their way by foot down the Red Sea coast, eventually reaching the Jewish Agency transit camp in Hashed, adjoining Aden. Here, more dead than alive, they were taken in hand by Jewish Agency personnel and provided with rest and recuperation. Once restored to health, the Yemenites were loaded onto the Agency's chartered transport planes and flown off to Israel. So it was, in the course of Operation Magic Carpet, between January 1949 and June 1951, that 48,000 Yemenites became the one Jewish community in the world that was transported down to its last soul to the Holy Land.

Although the transplantation of Iraqi Jewry essentially matched that of the Yemenites in scope, no two communities could have been more dissimilar in sociology. Following the Young Turk Revolution of 1908, the 120,000 Jews of Iraq, descendants of the most venerable of Middle Eastern Jewries, became full and equal Ottoman citizens. Like their Moslem neighbors, they were permitted now to send delegates to the imperial parliament in Constantinople, to serve in law courts and municipal councils. Even earlier, they had begun to share in Iraq's widening prosperity as a major crossroads of Ottoman international trade (p. 153). After 1920, upon establishment of the British mandate, Iraqi Jewry flourished more handsomely yet as major contractors for British military installations, as owners of the nation's principal import-export houses, as leading executives in local branches of British companies, as upper-level civil servants in the British mandatory administration and as prominent attorneys and physicians. By 1939, numbering approximately 140,000, the Jews in Iraq had achieved an economic and educational distinction unsurpassed in the Arab world.

These favored circumstances were unexpectedly threatened following the outbreak of World War II. In April 1941, with British forces on the defensive in the Middle East, a pro-German military cabal briefly assumed control of the Iraqi government, and for several weeks Jews were subjected to a reign of terror. Before a British relief column arrived the following month, some two hundred Jews were killed, and nearly a thousand injured. Even later, the restoration of normalcy proved to be only temporary. Three years after the end of the war, in the spring of 1948, Britain began withdrawing its garrisons under a new treaty arrangement with the Iraqi government. Immediately, demonstrations against the Jews revived. This time, however, they were fueled by the outbreak of the Arab-Israeli war. With Zionism now a capital offense, hundreds of Jews were arrested on this charge and tried, fined, or imprisoned. One Jew was hanged. By September 1949, the worst of the hysteria abated. Yet the economic impact on Jews was only beginning. Their import licenses as wholesalers were revoked, together with the licenses of their larger-scale retail firms. Even the most respected Jewish businessmen, those with the heaviest commercial and residential investments, now merely awaited an expedient moment to depart.

That moment apparently came in March 1950. The government announced then that Jews wishing to immigrate to "occupied Palestine" would be permitted to do so, on condition of renouncing their Iraqi citizenship. In fact, the entire Ezra and Nehemia Operation had been carefully organized by the Jewish Agency. Over weeks of negotiation through local Jewish intermediaries, the Agency had won permission to use the Baghdad airport to fly the emigrants to Israel. Thus, some 14,000 Jewish householders lined up at makeshift registration offices to secure emigration permits for themselves and their families. They were joined by an additional 14,000 Jews from the mountainous Kurdish territories, who poured into the larger cities, camping in synagogue courtyards as they also awaited their opportunity to register. For the Iraqi government, the official dispensation was shrewdly calculated. The departure of the middle-class Jewish population would open their positions to local Arabs. In ensuing weeks, therefore, after selling their homes and businesses at distress prices, the Iraqi Jews departed with only the smallest residue of their savings. Their economic loss in fact was so egregious that it induced the 55,000 remaining Jews to hold on a while longer, in expectation that selling conditions would improve.

In February 1951, however, with thinly disguised government concurrence, anti-Jewish violence broke out again. Attacks on Jewish homes and businesses were accompanied now by synagogue bombings. At this point, the remaining Jews were prepared to sell out for whatever they could get. But they had waited too long. In March, the government announced a three-month deadline for Jewish emigration. In the interim, it froze all Jewish assets and announced that emigrating Jews henceforth were allowed to take with them a maximum of 40 Iraqi pounds—and a single suitcase. So it was, in June 1951, as the emigration deadline expired, that the second wave of Jews left the country, this time departing as paupers. In all, between March 1950 and June 1951, the bulk of the Iraqi-Jewish population, 110,000 men, women, and children, relinquished their citizenship and were flown off to Israel. Barely 6,000 remained, and in future years, as most of this remnant bought or smuggled its way out of the country, finis was written to the single oldest Jewish community in the world.

In Egypt, meanwhile, as early as 1946, seeking an end to the British presence on their soil, nationalists in the government covertly encouraged anti-British and antiforeign unrest. Initially, the nation's 65,000 Jews were not prime targets of this militance. But soon the festering Palestine issue began to undermine their security. Anti-Jewish demonstrations became more frequent, including the pillage of Jewish shops, even the torching of a synagogue. In 1947, as the Palestine partition issue approached its climax in the United Nations, the Egyptian government enacted a Companies Law requiring that at least 75 percent of all private-business employees hold Egyptian citizenship. The measure was a crippling blow for family-staffed Jewish enterprises. Worse yet, with the declaration of Israel's independence in May 1948, and the outbreak of the Palestine War, hundreds of Egyptian Jews were arrested on suspicion of Zionist activities. Bombs were set off in Jewish neighborhoods, killing and wounding 252 individuals. Jews were "persuaded" to contribute hundreds of thousands of pounds to the Egyptian war effort. Jewish schools were ordered closed. By government decree, ninety-four large Jewish companies were sequestered outright, and permission to operate as cotton brokers, to practice medicine and law, was restricted exclusively to Egyptian citizens.

With the end of the Palestine War, the wave of public and private chauvinism appeared to subside, and Jewish circumstances slowly began to improve. The government released most of the confiscated Jewish assets. Jewish schools were reopened. More significantly, "non-Moslems" were allowed to leave the country, even to take their assets with them. Thus, between 1949 and 1951, approximately 30,000 Jews disposed of their homes and businesses, transferred their liquid assets to Western banks, and summarily departed for Europe, where approximately a third of them continued on to Israel. Yet fully three-fifths of Egypt's Jews remained in Egypt, optimistic that national stability had been restored.

That assumption endured barely three years. In 1952, a revolution of senior army officers overthrew the corrupt monarch, Farouk I, and established a putative republic, one that functioned under military rule. Within the space of two years, a dynamic young colonel, Gamal Abd al-Nasser, emerged as leader of the officers' junta. Hereupon, fanning the flames of anti-British and anti-Israel resentment, Nasser focused public rancor on "foreign domination" of Egyptian economic life. Soon his government barred the major European companies from the stock and cotton exchanges and from other key sectors of the economy. It was the Jews, however, who were singled out with particular vindictiveness, ostensibly as an Israeli fifth column. The government foreclosed their import and foreign-currency licenses. Their money transfers abroad were blocked, even as the market for Jewish properties collapsed. Egypt's 35,000 remaining Jews were reduced to economic marginality.

Then came the Suez-Sinai War of 1956. In the wake of the Anglo-French assault on the Suez Canal, and Egypt's humiliating battlefield defeat at the hands of the Israelis, President Nasser reacted in a vindictive spasm against the entirety of the nation's remaining European population. Tens of thousands of these foreign nationals were stripped of their business and work licenses and thereby compelled to depart the country. Once again, however, retribution was harshest against the Jews, some 20,000 of whom were expelled from the country forthwith. Stripped of the entirety of their remaining estates, they were permitted to take with them a maximum of 30 Egyptian pounds for each family unit. By the end of 1959, another 15,000 Jews managed to negotiate their departure, again under conditions of financial destitution. The émigrés settled variously in Israel, France, Italy, and Brazil. By June 1967, on the eve of the Six-Day War, not more than 4,000 Jews remained in Egypt. Under tight police scrutiny, they were reduced to earning their livelihoods afterward as small retailers. Eventually, by special dispensation negotiated with other governments, groups of these families intermittently secured exit visas. By 1979, the year of the Egyptian-Israeli peace treaty, barely 200 Jews remained.

The ordeal of their Syrian kinsmen was somewhat more prolonged. At the end of World War I, Syrian Jews numbered approximately 30,000 and were settled almost evenly between Damascus, Aleppo, and Beirut. Under French mandatory rule, they shared in the Levant's dramatic post–World War I economic upsurge. In Lebanon—detached administratively from Syria in 1925—the tiny Beiruti enclave of 5,000 Jews did best of all. Living at the very gateway of Mediterranean commerce, they flourished under French benevolence. Even the emergence of Lebanon to independence in 1946 did not undermine their security. Dominated by Maronite Christians, the Lebanese government remained largely detached from Moslem nationalist passions. Thus, following the establishment of Israel in 1948, as Jews from Syria and other Arab countries relocated themselves in Lebanon, this sophisticated trading nation became the single Arab state in which Jewish numbers actually increased, from 6,000 in 1944 to 9,000 in 1949. As late as 1962, several dozen Jews held important positions in the Lebanese civil service, even in the Lebanese delegation to the United Nations. Nevertheless, by 1980, immigration to Israel and to other nations all but emptied this population.

The circumstances of Syrian Jewry were far more dire. Numbering approximately 20,000 in the early postwar period, they began to experience the full force of Moslem hostility following the passage of the UN Partition Resolution in November 1947. Attacks on Jewish neighborhoods were frequent. The Syrian government imposed discriminatory restrictions on Jewish businesses and prohibited Jewish emigration in fear of augmenting Israel's military manpower reserves. In ensuing years, therefore, Syrian Jewry's devouring obsession was escape. Nothing would inhibit their efforts. People took extraordinary risks, paid exorbitant fees, to be smuggled across the frontier to Lebanon, or directly to Israel. If caught, they faced imprisonment and torture, as well as retaliation against their families. Nevertheless, they exploited every opportunity to flee. By 1967, no more than 8,000 Jews remained in the country.

It was in that year, however, that Syria experienced the crowning humiliation of defeat in the Six-Day War. In its rage, the government barred Jews from traveling more than three miles from their homes, and intermittently imposed nighttime curfews on them. And still the escape efforts continued. By 1970, barely 5,000 Jews remained, most of these in Damascus, and all living in a state of acute insecurity. It was in the ensuing decade, however, that they experienced an unanticipated redemption. The Ba'athist government of Hafez al-Assad, eager for American support against Israel's ongoing presence on the captured Golan Heights, was persuaded by visiting American congressmen gradually to lift the ban on Jewish departure. As a result, Syria's Jewish population over the turn of the century fell to a tremulous residue of fewer than 1,000.

NORTH AFRICA

As late as World War II, the single largest remaining hinterland of non-European Jews, totaling some half-million, was to be found in the Maghreb, the vast, French-ruled North African littoral. Approximately 265,000 lived in Morocco, with Algeria accounting for another 135,000, and Tunisia for an estimated 105,000 (pp. 148–51). Among this dense Jewry, it was the Moroccans who remained the most deprived, both economically and culturally. The establishment of the French protectorate in 1912 had assured them a reasonable physical security, even a measure of economic improvement (p. 149). But as late as 1939, fully two-thirds of Morocco's Jewish working population earned their modest livelihoods as artisans and small shopkeepers.

Concentrated mainly in Casablanca, Marrakesh, and Fez, they lived for the most part in their own quite shabby *mellahs*. Perhaps the principal benefaction of the French presence was the admittance it provided Jewish children to a network of Alliance schools and other Alliance social services. As always, the beacon of French culture shone tantalizingly before Jewish eyes.

The interregnum of Vichy rule signified a painful retrogression for Moroccan Jewry. Even the small numbers of affluent and acculturated families among them were barred from European urban neighborhoods, from access to tightly rationed supplies or opportunities to secure new business licenses. The period of active Vichy harassment fortunately was brief, ending with the Allied invasion of North Africa in the autumn of 1942. Yet economic hardships continued until the end of the war, and even into the postwar. As late as 1950, the Joint was obliged to provide relief for tens of thousands of Moroccan Jews. Soon, too, a new threat developed to North African Jewry. This one reflected the political changes of the postwar period. In 1948–49, the establishment of Israel and the Palestine War unleashed a series of Berber pogroms. The worst of the violence was felt in neighboring Libya (formerly under Italian rule), where a chain reaction of mob attacks in 1948–49 eventually caused the flight of the entire Jewish population of 32,000 to Israel and to Italy. But in Morocco, too, Berber mobs invaded the Jewish section of Oujda in June 1948, killing forty men, women, and children and wounding at least a hundred others. The assault touched off a wave of departures to Israel.

As elsewhere, the émigrés were comprised initially of Moroccan Jewry's poorest and least Gallicized elements. By 1952, approximately 70,000 of these had fled the country and its volatile Berber mobs. Meanwhile, a development even more traumatic than random native violence was the emergence of the Moroccan independence movement. By the early 1950s, a series of riots and demonstrations against the French Protectorate brought the little country to the verge of revolution. In 1954, to be sure, France's Prime Minister Pierre Mendès-France managed to quell the unrest by committing his government to the establishment of Moroccan—and Tunisian—independence within the next two years. But the prospect of Berber rule deeply unsettled Morocco's remaining Jewish population.

It is of interest that their fear no longer related to physical violence, or even to political discrimination. Indeed, the Moroccan nationalist leadership had promised full and complete equality for all inhabitants, and upon achieving independence in 1956, that promise was honored in letter and spirit. Jewish neighborhoods were protected. A senior nationalist eminence, Hassan Muhammad ibn Yusuf (who in 1961 formally assumed his country's throne, as Hassan II), ordered the arrest of anyone engaged in anti-Jewish violence or even of anti-Jewish propaganda. A Jew was appointed to the first Moroccan cabinet. But these assurances notwithstanding, it was the likelihood of economic failure that most alarmed Moroccan Jewry. With the imminent loss of French investment and institutions, the nation was swooning into near-bankruptcy. As a result, an additional 35,000 Jews left the country in the two years before the end of the French Protectorate, a majority of them settling in Israel; and in 1956, during the first ten months of Moroccan independence, another 33,000 departed. Further emigration continued intermittently during the ensuing decades. By the end of the century, Morocco's once vast Jewish population of 265,000 had dwindled to 7,000. Approximately two-thirds of the émigrés settled in Israel.

Meanwhile, for Tunisia's 105,000 Jews, World War II was an even more fearful experience than for their kinsmen in Morocco. In addition to the legal and economic harassments of Vichy rule, in 1942 Tunisia fell directly under the occupation of General Erwin Rommel's Afrika Korps. It would take the American army six months to clean the Germans out, and until then Tunisian Jewry remained at their mercy. Fortunately, the SS had little time to launch a *Judenrazzia* beyond imprisoning a number of Jewish communal leaders. Moreover, the Italians, who exercised political "supervision" over Vichy-ruled Tunisia, once again held firm against any racist cleansing. The Germans did not press the issue. Yet even after liberation and the end of the war—indeed, well into the 1950s—Tunisian Jews in their painful economic recovery remained heavily dependent upon the Joint's extensive program of philanthropic relief.

In was in these same postwar years that approximately 18,000 of their number departed for Israel. Initially, as in Morocco, the emigrants tended to be poor and pietistic families from the *bled*, the Berber interior. Few urban Jews at first were interested in joining them at a time when kinsmen in Israel were writing of the hardships and dangers of life in the struggling new Zionist state. In 1956, moreover, when Tunisia achieved its formal independence from France, President Habib Bourguiba assured the Jews full civil and political rights in their new republic. He kept his word. Several Jews were offered prominent positions in the Tunisian cabinet and public administration, and others became influential journalists.

Nevertheless, concerns about the new republic's economic stability were not dissipated. On the eve of Tunisian independence, in 1955, the nation's Jewish population totaled approximately 90,000. By 1962, it had fallen to 60,000, with two-thirds of the émigrés choosing to settle in France. Even then, a majority of Tunisian Jewry remained at home. But their lingering ambivalence was abruptly resolved by the events of 1962. Early that year, responding to nationalist pressures, President Bourguiba decided to reclaim the port of Bizerte, a facility that had been reserved to France by earlier treaty arrangement. Yet when Bourguiba ordered his troops into the protected area, they were annihilated by the French garrison. An orgy of strikes followed, and the nation's economy soon was all but paralyzed. For the Jews, caught up in this nationalist upheaval, it was not the time to risk further delay. Within the following year, as they decamped in wholesale numbers for France, their remaining population declined by half. Afterward, a steady, if slower, exodus continued. Adopting a policy of economic étatism, the Tunisian cabinet declared a state monopoly in sugar, coffee, tea, fruits, grain, hides, and cattle. Thousands of Jewish businessmen subsequently witnessed the elimination of their occupations. By 1965, fewer than 8,000 Jews remained in Tunisia; and, by the end of the century, only a few hundred.

It was a fate to be replicated among the even larger Jewish population of Algeria. For this community, France had been not simply their protector, but their *patrie*. By 1939, the Jews in Algeria numbered 135,000. If their population was only half that of Moroccan Jewry, it represented nearly 14 percent of the country's 950,000 European *colons*. Since 1870, too, Algeria's Jews had shared all the latter's rights and privileges of French citizenship (p. 150). Living for the most part in Algiers, Oran, and Constantine, they were a mercantile constituency, although economically and culturally somewhat more advanced than their kinsmen in Tunisia and Morocco. Several thousand Algerian Jews were members of the civil service. It was specifically that juridical and political equality that galled the colons. In classic irredentist tradition, the xenophobia of this overseas European minority, surrounded by an ocean of Berbers, was more acutely inflamed than the nationalism of their fellow citizens in France itself. During the period of the Dreyfus Affair, their antisemitism had been more vocal and violent than that of the anti-Dreyfusards on the mainland (p. 238). Years later, during the 1930s, their hatred of Léon Blum's Popular Front government erupted in riots, in the vandalization of synagogues and Jewish shops in Algiers, and the murder of a score of Jews in Constantine.

In Algeria, therefore, as in metropolitan France, the establishment of the Vichyite regime was a moment of vindication for these Europeans. If it was not possible to ship Jews to the mainland, and into German hands, the local Vichyite administration nevertheless swiftly introduced its own program of antisemitic restrictions and penalties. It stripped Jews of their French citizenship, purged Jewish employees from the civil administration, expelled Jewish children from French schools. Business and professional licenses were summarily canceled for Jews, as well as access to vital commercial and residential supplies. The ordeal lasted for two and a half years, until November 1942, when American troops invaded North Africa. It was significant of the colons' political orientation that Jews, not they, comprised 316 of the 377 activists who took part in the underground preparation for the American landings. Yet, even after the Americans and Free French were well ensconced in Algeria, none of these scores of young Jews were brought into the country's leadership. Instead, the Free French liaison officer, General Henri Giraud, persuaded the Americans not to reverse the Vichyite anti-Jewish decrees, for fear of "inciting" the European population. The legislation was canceled only in the spring of 1943.

For Algerian Jewry, the period of belated normalcy and security endured only a decade. By the mid-1950s, Moslem resentment of French rule exploded into a full-scale nationalist insurrection, and soon into a prolonged slaughter and counterslaughter that devoured tens of thousands of lives, French and Berber alike. The Jewish reaction to the Algerian revolt was confused. Members of their younger generation, most of them socialists, empathized with the Berber struggle for self-rule. Not a single major act of Moslem terrorism had been committed against Jews, after all. Indeed, like their counterparts in Morocco and Tunisia, the FLN—Berber nationalist—leadership repeatedly promised the Jews the fullest measure of security and equality in an independent Algeria. On the other hand, it was known that much of the FLN's military equipment was coming from Egypt's President Nasser, and the Jews were unsettled by the prospect of an Algerian regime beholden to one of Israel's most implacable enemies. As a result, Algerian Jews, like those of Tunisia and Morocco, tended to avoid committing themselves politically. Remaining publicly neutral, they still hoped privately that Algerian self-government could be achieved under French supervision and military protection.

The hope was not to be realized. Once Charles de Gaulle consolidated his political base as president of France's new Fifth Republic, in 1959, he did not disguise his intention of phasing out the last of the colons' privileges in Algeria. It was during the ensuing three years of political transition, moreover, that Berber xenophobia unexpectedly erupted against the Jews. In December 1960, widespread anti-Jewish riots culminated in the pillage of the Great Synagogue of Algiers. Although the violence was immediately repudiated by the FLN leadership, the Jewish population was gravely alarmed. It was even more thoroughly unnerved by de Gaulle's decision, in July 1962, to accord full sovereignty to Algeria and to evacuate the French army. Indeed, it was then that the totality of the European settlement, 950,000 strong, embarked on a vast collective exodus to France. Their homes, farms, businesses, and public institutions, the legacy of a century and a quarter of French rule—all now were left behind. Algeria's 135,000 Jews shared in the departure.

Until this moment, the Israeli government had been confident that Algerian Jewry would follow the example of tens of thousands of other Maghreb Jews, particularly those of Morocco, and immigrate to Israel. The expectation was naïve. The long process of Gallicization had done its work. Of French nationality and culture, the Jews of Algeria were intent upon claiming all the rights extended to the colons. Paris had guaranteed them loans, housing, employment, and social-welfare benefits once they reached France. Straitened little Israel could not yet match these inducements. Ultimately, not more than 5,000 Jews chose to go to Israel. Of the rest, nearly 130,000 returned "home."

Upon the establishment of national independence, the Israeli government as its first priority set about emptying the DP camps in Germany, Austria, and Italy. To that end, between September 1948 and August 1949, fifty-two refugee centers were closed in Europe and their inhabitants shipped to Israel, while 35,000 internees similarly were removed from the three Cyprus detention camps. At almost the same time, a full-scale transfer of Bulgaria's Jews was set in motion, paralleled by the migration of Yugoslav and Turkish Jews. It was in 1949–50, too, that the Communist regimes of Poland, Rumania, and Hungary opened their gates for the emigration of tens of thousands of Jewish survivors and Soviet returnees. The East Europeans' numbers, in turn, would be dramatically augmented by the influx of Jews from the Middle East, and later by the tidal wave from the vast Jewish reservoir of North Africa.

So it was, in the first eighteen months after Israel's Declaration of Independence, that 340,000 Jews arrived in the newborn Zionist republic. They came by passenger liner, by rickety dormitory steamer, by airplane, and in some instances by clandestine land routes. Even as war still raged and the little state faced possible destruction or bankruptcy, the newcomers continued to flood in. During the British mandate, the rate of immigration had averaged 18,000 a year. During the first three years of Israeli statehood, the average reached 18,000 a month. Between May 15, 1948, and June 30, 1953, the Jewish population of the country doubled, from 640,000 to 1.3 million By June 30, 1956, it tripled, to 2.1 million. No influx like it had been witnessed in modern times. It was a deluge into an entryway that older, larger, and vastly wealthier countries would long since have closed. But none other had been established to fulfill the internationally mandated role of a homeland for a nation of perennial stepchildren and stateless refugees. Whatever the future vicissitudes of Israel's citizens, the entryway would remain open. It was the Zionist republic's ongoing raison d'être.

XXXI

A Precarious Revival in Western Europe

A RETURN TO THE EYE OF THE HURRICANE

In the first years after the war, as the numbers of Jewish displaced persons approached a quarter-million, the American Jewish Joint Distribution Committee and other Western philanthropies assumed principal responsibility for their medical and other social services. Yet, by 1949, the task of rebuilding the survivors' lives, whether in Israel or Western Europe, proved too onerous to be borne exclusively by Jewish welfare funds. For a growing number of Jewish leaders, it appeared more appropriate that Germany, the nation most responsible for the mutilation of the Jewish people, should bear at least part of the cost of their rehabilitation. It was a view, in fact, that was shared by the German government.

At war's end, the notion of seeking help from Germany would have been inconceivable. The former Reich was a shattered land, after all, its own population hungry and freezing. Yet, within four years, a combination of Marshall Plan aid and the sheer hardworking diligence of the German people themselves produced a significant economic improvement. It was this resurgence, in 1949, combined with a pragmatic need to invoke Western goodwill, that persuaded Konrad Adenauer, chancellor of the (West) German Bundesrepublik, to favor an atonement gesture to the Jews. Accordingly, over the ensuing months, in private German conversations with Jewish and Israeli leaders, agreement was reached in principle that the gesture should take the form of financial compensation. In Israel itself, to be sure, where national pride ran high, there existed much popular and political resistance to the proposal. The very act of sitting down with the Germans, so the argument went, would imply forgiveness for Germany's sins. But Prime Minister Ben-Gurion understood well that his beleaguered little republic could not afford the luxury of self-righteousness. The nation's economy, strained to the limit by the massive influx of refugees, teetered on the verge of collapse. The issue of a financial infusion was one not of morality, Ben-Gurion argued, but of survival.

Eventually, after another year of intense discussions among Israeli and Diaspora Jewish representatives, the prime minister's viewpoint prevailed.

In March 1952, the Israeli government, together with a consortium of
twenty-two international Jewish organizations (the Jewish Claims Conference), entered into formal negotiations with representatives of the Bundesrepublik. Notwithstanding the preliminary discussions of earlier months, the
talks consumed another half-year of—often acrimonious—bargaining and
counterbargaining. Periodically, they approached the verge of breakdown.
But at last, in September 1952, agreement was reached, and formally and ceremonially signed, in the City Hall of Luxembourg City. Under its terms, Germany would provide Israel with $822 million in "reparations" over a span of
between twelve and fourteen years. Payments would take the form of goods,
including such heavy capital equipment as rolling stock, merchant vessels,
harbor supplies, agricultural and industrial machinery, and telecommunications. It was the combination of these German reparations, as well as supplementary loans from the United States government and the World Bank, that
literally saved Israel from bankruptcy. Indeed, it launched the Jewish state on
its period of economic "takeoff."

Yet reparations were only one component of the Treaty of Luxembourg.
The West German government had also agreed to provide funds for the rehabilitation of Jewish victims living outside as well as inside Israel's frontiers.
The payments would assume two forms. The first would be en bloc grants to
Jewish communal institutions in their various lands of survival. The second,
and farther-reaching, indemnification would be paid to hundreds of thousands of individual survivors of the Nazi era for their property and income
losses, and for their personal suffering. Here, too, as in the case of the reparations payments to Israel, the Germans met their obligations punctiliously. By
the end of the century, the Bundesrepublik had transferred the equivalent of
$31 billion in "atonement" funds to Israel, to Jewish communal organizations,
and to individual Jewish survivors. Money alone obviously would never compensate for the trauma of the Hitler epoch. Even so, Germany's outpouring
was substantial, and it played a major role in the rehabilitation of hundreds of
thousands of Jewish survivors worldwide, and not least in Western Europe.

Of the various West European Jewish communities, the largest in the prewar era had been that of Germany itself. At its apogee in 1933, German Jewry
numbered at least 510,000 individuals. During the first six years of Nazi rule,
295,000 Jews fled the country, leaving some 215,000 by 1939. Of these latter,
180,000 perished. At war's end, possibly 35,000 remained alive in the shattered Reich and elsewhere in Europe. Between 1945 and 1952, at least a third
of this surviving remnant departed for Israel or for other countries. Of the
20,000 to 25,000 who remained in Germany, approximately half were pensioners, too old or ill to move on again, and most of the rest were half-Jews or

married to non-Jews. Few appeared likely material for a communal revival. But after 1952, a sudden influx of 20,000 additional Jews arrived in West Germany. Perhaps a fourth of these came from East Germany (the Deutsche Demokratische Republik), whose Communist regime even then was sharing in the Stalinist "antideviationist" purge campaign. Although many of the newcomers joined the ranks of Jewish pensioners, others developed useful careers in West German business, public media, the professions, as well as in the federal and state governments.

But refugees from the DDR were not typical of the Jewish influx into West Germany. Most of the newcomers were "authentic" East Europeans—Jews from Poland, Hungary, or Rumania, who had congregated in the early postwar as displaced persons in the American-occupied zone of Germany. Earning a small stake as petty traders, these former DPs remained on to take up livelihoods in the reviving West German economy. They were not an easy group. Many had been twisted by their wartime ordeal and often were less than scrupulous in their business activities. Yet their numbers continued to grow, and were augmented over the years by small groups of repatriates from Israel. In the 1980s and 1990s, their ranks were swollen by an unanticipated and much larger influx of 120,000 Jews from the imploding Soviet Union. Thus, by the turn of the century, Germany's Jewish population had grown to an estimated 200,000, and thereby into the third-largest Jewish community in Europe, outside Russia.

Concentrated for the most part in Berlin, Munich, Hamburg, and Frankfurt, "veteran" Jews and Eastern European newcomers alike were treated with infinite consideration by German state and local authorities, which funded their Cultusgemeinden, synagogues, old-age homes, schools, libraries, and other communal institutions. This support was in no sense a mere public relations gesture. By any objective standard, the German people had undergone a profound metamorphosis since 1945, when the post-Hitler generation confronted the shame and horror of the Nazi epoch. Rooted in prosperity, the nation's democratic institutions had gained solid anchorage, and all the more following the reunion of East and West Germany in October 1990. In turn, the revived Jewish population reacted to these developments with growing confidence. Jewish young people shared in a host of Jewish functions, belonged to B'nai B'rith lodges, visited and contributed generously to Israel. Unlike their parents and grandparents in the immediate postwar period, the second and third generations of Jews no longer were "sitting on their suitcases." They had long since internalized the words of David Ben-Gurion, uttered in 1951: "The Germany of Adolf Hitler is no more."

In contrast to Germany's postwar record on the Jews, that of Austria was equivocal, even duplicitous. It was a nation, after all, whose pre-Anschluss population of 7 million produced 537,000 registered members of the Nazi

Party, a higher quotient of the voting rolls than in pre-Hitler Germany. During the war, approximately one-third of the functionaries working for the SS extermination program were Austrian or former citizens of the Habsburg Empire. This unsavory record notwithstanding, the Allies as early as the Moscow Conference of 1943 proclaimed Austria "the first free nation to fall victim to Hitlerite aggression"—thus confirming the Austrians' sense of blamelessness for their tainted past. Later, under Allied occupation, the Austrian parliament felt it expedient to enact a war-criminals law and to conduct a few perfunctory trials. But the moment the nation regained its sovereignty in 1955, a series of presidential decrees granted amnesty to the largest numbers of convicted prisoners. Austrian Nazis who were tried and convicted in other lands enjoyed full civil rights upon completing their sentences and returning home.

The nation's attitude of self-forgiveness was particularly evident in the treatment of Jewish financial claims. As late as 1935, Vienna's Jewish community was Europe's third-largest, numbering approximately 200,000, nearly 3 percent of Austria's total population. Although the majority succeeded in fleeing soon after the 1938 Anschluss (p. 511), at least 60,000 were trapped, and all but 9,000 of these eventually were liquidated. Together with those who had fled earlier, the survivors had been cruelly despoiled by the Nazi regime. In 1956, to be sure, the Austrian government committed itself to a full restitution of prewar Jewish property. Yet it soon became evident that "full restitution" would apply exclusively to properties currently "identifiable" in Austria. Sadly, little remained to be identified. Between the wars, most Viennese Jews were renters; only a small minority had owned their homes. Their possessions also had long since disappeared, through confiscation and multiple sales, and all remaining "heirless" Jewish property had reverted to the state. The single initial concession extracted by the Jewish Claims Conference was a relief fund for Austrian Jews who had been imprisoned in concentration camps, and this only after the German Bundesrepublik agreed to provide half the capital. Otherwise, for nearly a half-century afterward, the survivors of one of Europe's largest and most distinguished Jewish communities remained disfranchised from meaningful restitution or indemnification.

Vienna's initial importance in postwar Jewish life was essentially strategic, as a transit point for Jews from Eastern Europe. Indeed, most of the 44,000 Jews impacted in the DP camps of Austria were originally from Poland, Rumania, and Hungary. As in Germany, a small minority, 3,000 or 4,000, decided to remain in Europe. They tended to be hardened survivors, who accommodated well to the thriving Austrian black market. The 1,400 Viennese-Jewish "veterans" would not touch them, least of all the Hasidim who arrived from Hungary after 1956, to become small merchants. But Eastern European newcomers in any case soon overwhelmed the older Jewish nucleus. By 1960, they comprised some four-fifths of Vienna's 9,000 Jews. Although most remained small shopkeepers, a few became prosperous businessmen, particularly in furs, jewels, and other luxury items. And astonishingly, one Jew—albeit a native-born Viennese—rose to his nation's political leadership.

Bruno Kreisky was a paradox for modern Austria. A veteran Social Democrat, he returned to Vienna in 1945 from his wartime exile in Sweden to work his way up to the party's chairmanship. In 1970, when parliamentary elections gave the SDs a majority, it was Kreisky who assumed the chancellorship. Was he an "authentic" Jew? On the one hand, he never denied his origins. On the other, he no longer meaningfully identified with the Jewish people, and made a point of adopting a detached attitude toward Israel. That "detachment" became particularly evident in September 1973. For some years, the Jewish Agency had maintained a transit camp outside Vienna to accommodate arriving Soviet Jews, before flying them on to Israel. But now, suddenly, as a train carrying Soviet Jews crossed the frontier in Austria, three Arab terrorists seized five Jewish passengers as hostages and demanded air transportation to an Arab capital. The abductors in fact got more than their flight east. Fearful lest his country become a venue for the Arab-Israeli vendetta, Kreisky ordered the Jewish Agency to close its transit camp altogether. When Israel's Prime Minister Golda Meir rushed to Vienna in a last-minute effort to change Kreisky's mind, she failed.

The chancellor's antiseptic attitude toward Jews and Israel availed him little. Most Austrian political writers, acutely conscious of Kreisky's background, tended to describe him as "tricky." It was a characteristic reaction. A public opinion poll in 1973 revealed that 70 percent of adult Austrians nurtured antisemitic feelings. Right-wing deputies in parliament openly boasted of their "subconscious antisemitism." In 1986, the "subconscious" feeling became overtly "conscious." Elections that year were scheduled for the presidency of Austria. One of the candidates was Kurt Waldheim, the former United Nations secretary-general. By then, Waldheim's wartime role as a Wehrmacht lieutenant in the Balkans, functioning as a liaison with SS units engaged in the hunt for Jews, had been revealed and extensively publicized by the World Jewish Congress. In voting Waldheim into office, therefore, the Austrian electorate appeared to be deliberately flouting Jewish outrage and expressing their own resentment at the Jews for having raised the issue of Waldheim's past. Israel's ambassador to Vienna was immediately summoned home for "consultations" and did not return through the ensuing six years of Waldheim's presidential term. A comparable episode occurred only a decade later, when Joerg Haider, governor of Carinthia province and chairman of Austria's far-right Freedom Party, praised Hitler's "decent employment policies" and described SS troops as "men of character." In February 2000,

Haider's party won sufficient votes to become a coalition partner in the Austrian government. The shock was far-reaching enough to provoke a European moratorium on dealings with Vienna. Once again, Israel withdrew its ambassador.

Meanwhile, in the late 1990s, with the active support of the Clinton administration in the United States, the World Jewish Congress finally persuaded several of Europe's "delinquents" to meet their obligations to Holocaust victims. The Swiss government was one of these, agreeing belatedly to release hundreds of millions of dollars of unclaimed Jewish bank accounts in Swiss banks, and to make payments to the Jewish Claims Conference for having "sheltered" Nazi money extracted from Jewish victims (pp. 561–62). Austria was another retrograde case. In January 2001, following two years of negotiations with representatives of the World Jewish Congress and the United States Treasury Department, the Austrian government finally confirmed its "moral responsibility" and acknowledged that it was "facing up to the light and dark sides of the past deeds of all Austrians, good and evil."

MIXED SIGNALS FROM ROME

The record of the Italian people, whose government had collaborated with Nazi Germany during the war, proved distinctly more benevolent toward the Jews than that of "the first free nation to fall victim to Hitlerite aggression." It was the Italians' fundamental humanity, after all, that accounted for the survival of 28,000 Jews (4,000 of them refugees from other countries), not to mention thousands of other Jews in other lands who fell within Italian zones of occupation. The survival was a precarious one, to be sure, even into the early postwar period. Italian Jews managed to resume their lives within a far more limited ambit, essentially in Milan and Rome. Most of their smaller communities had long since atrophied through conversion, internal migration, and a low birthrate. Even this residual population sustained its communal vitality in large measure through an influx of Jews from Libya, following that nation's emergence to independence from Italian rule in 1951. Indeed, over the course of the 1950s, Italian Jewry acquired a new demographic profile. One-third were Ashkenazim, one-third indigenous Sephardim, and the last third essentially newcomers from Libya.

The political role of Italian Jewry remained limited in a nation whose first postwar years were dominated by the Christian Democratic Party, a faction closely allied with the papacy. Yet antisemitism remained as negligible a factor in Italian public life as before 1938. Compassion for Jewish victims and survivors of the Holocaust was deeply felt. Numerous streets and squares were named for Jews or for those who had helped Jews, and Jewish organizations and leaders were frequent recipients of public awards. The crisis of Italian Jewry in the latter twentieth century was not of political security but of cultural vitality. If the Jews' communal life had been quite feeble before the war, it was virtually moribund after 1945. Most of their religious and cultural institutions remained heavily dependent on Joint and Claims Conference subventions.

Even before Mussolini's anti-Jewish laws, for that matter, a significant minority of Italian-Jewish families had joined the Catholic Church. Indeed, between 1910 and 1931, government data suggested that as many as 10 percent of the Jewish population underwent conversion. After the Holocaust, demoralized and exhausted, far larger numbers of Jews were anxious to "pass," simply to avoid any future complications in their lives. Thus, in the late 1940s and 1950s, the conversion rate approached 20 to 25 percent. The intermarriage rate climbed to nearly 50 percent. In later decades, when the communal journal *Shalom* announced "Jewish marriages," it referred increasingly to marriages between Libyan Jews. Otherwise, among the Europeans, it was the combination of intermarriages, conversions, and a low birthrate that reduced the Jewish population to fewer than 30,000 by the turn of the century. As elsewhere in Western Europe, devotion to Israel became the principal talisman of an uneven ethnic identity.

The erratic and tremulous revival of Italian Jewry occurred in tandem with a painful and cautious reappraisal of Jewish-Vatican relations. In the early postwar years, local and international Jewish organizations devoted their initial efforts to the retrieval of Jewish children who had found wartime refuge among Catholic families. To that end, Gerhart Riegner of the World Jewish Congress met repeatedly at the Vatican with Monsignor Giovanni Montini, the Vatican's acting secretary of state (and the future Pope Paul VI). Montini procrastinated. "I cannot give orders for the return of those children unless I have their exact addresses," he insisted. Nearly three years passed before the Vatican softened its position, calling in general terms for the return of Jewish children. Even after this rather vague appeal, or perhaps because of it, individual prelates in Western Europe were hesitant to cooperate. At the same time, Pope Pius XII (the redoubtable Eugenio Pacelli) fended off Jewish appeals for an encyclical that would decisively repudiate the theological basis of antisemitism.

Then, in 1958, Pius XII died and was succeeded by Angelo Roncalli, who assumed the pontifical throne as John XXIII. Renowned for his broad humanity, the new pope set out immediately to demonstrate his friendship for the Jews. In 1959, he invested Israel's ambassador to Italy with the Grand Cross of the Order of Sylvester, a gesture of significance in view of the papal Curia's earlier refusal to engage in communication of any kind with the Israeli

government. In that same year, the Vatican announced the pontiff's intention
to convene a Second Vatican Council (an earlier gathering had been planned
shortly before the war). Vatican II was scheduled to meet in 1962 and to continue until 1965. Sensing a historic opportunity, Jewish representatives wasted
little time in securing an interview with John XXIII, to ask that the issue of
antisemitism be placed on the agenda of the forthcoming council. The pope
was sympathetic. He turned the matter over to Cardinal Augustin Bea, president of the Secretariat for the Promotion of Christian Unity.

Seventy-eight years old, a German-born Jesuit and former confessor of
Pius XII, Bea was a leader of the progressive element in the Vatican. He had
witnessed the SS *Judenrazzia* in Rome in 1943, and the memory of that horror
never left him. In recent years, he had supported Jewish pleas for an encyclical
on the Jewish question, although without result. But now at last, in the
enveloping compassion of John XXIII, he found his man. Accordingly, Bea
consulted with Gerhart Riegner and with representatives of other Jewish
organizations, who promised to draft a proposed statement for the anticipated conclave. Negotiations among the Jews themselves were not easy; and
even when their compromise draft finally was submitted, in April 1960, it
encountered further delays among the Vatican's conservative elements. Ironically, renewed momentum was provided by Israel's capture of Adolf Eichmann, the Nazi master administrator of the Final Solution. The 1961 trial
sessions of Eichmann in Jerusalem raised painful questions of Christian
complicity in the Holocaust. Moreover, in December 1961, the (Protestant)
World Council of Churches issued a forceful condemnation of antisemitism.
Cardinal Bea exploited these embarrassments as he pressed his colleagues for
action.

Nevertheless, opposition remained. Several members of the Curia were
thinly disguised antisemites. Others were susceptible to Arab pressures. In
1963, John XXIII died, and his successor, Giovanni Montini, was enthroned as
Paul VI. The new pontiff's traditional suspicion of Jews was compounded by
his support of Roman Catholic claims on Jerusalem, and by his fear of possible Moslem retaliation against Latin Christians in the Middle East. During
his visit to Christian Holy Places in Jerusalem a year later, Paul's single allusion to Israel was to "the authorities in Tel Aviv." In the end, however, it was
not only Bea's persistence but strong political pressure from liberal Catholic
elements in the United States (among them, President John Kennedy) that
eventually forced a draft declaration through the Lateran Council. In 1965, in
the fourth and final session of Vatican II, Bea and his supporters at last prevailed. The bishops voted a *Schema* on the Jews.

The *Schema* was perhaps less than a dithyramb of friendship. Suggesting
that all mankind, not simply part of it, was guilty of the Crucifixion, the
document went on to state:

Although the Jewish authorities and those who followed their lead pressed for the death of Christ, nevertheless, what happened to Christ in his Passion cannot be attributed to all Jews without distinction to those then alive, or to the Jews of today. Although the Church is the new People of God, the Jews should not be represented as rejected by God or accused as if this followed from Holy Scriptures.

Finally, the declaration observed that the Church "deplore[d] on religious grounds any display of anti-Jewish hatred or persecution."

Later that year, on the basis of the *Schema*, Paul VI belatedly authorized the establishment of an International Catholic-Jewish Liaison Committee to discuss Catholic-Jewish relations. He himself would appoint the Catholic members, while the various Jewish organizations would select a delegation from among themselves. These negotiations also bore fruit—nine years later. At last, in the spring of 1974, the Vatican published a series of "Guidelines and Suggestions for Relations with Judaism." The "guidelines" actually transcended the *Schema*. They rejected the widespread notion that Judaism was a religion of fear and inflexible law. Rather, the history of Judaism was declared to be an ongoing one, "creating new and rich religious values." The publication concluded with instructions for Catholics everywhere to embark on a serious dialogue with Jews at all levels and actively to fight antisemitism. The Vatican then gave practical effect to the "guidelines" by dropping its insistence on a Catholic upbringing for the children of mixed Jewish-Catholic marriages. The implications for thousands of such youngsters and their parents were far-reaching.

Paul VI died in August 1978. Following an incumbency of only a few weeks, the next pope, John Paul I, died unexpectedly. It was the latter's successor, Karol Wojtyla, a Pole, who assumed the papal throne as John Paul II, thereby becoming the first non-Italian pontiff in centuries. He was also the first papal incumbent to possess extensive knowledge of Jews, and specifically of East European Jews. During the Nazi occupation of his country, Wojtyla had served in the Polish underground, where he had sought to save Jewish lives. For many years afterward, he had been associated with Zanak, a Cracow-based group of Catholic intellectuals. In reaction to Poland's notorious antisemitism, Zanak had always been unreservedly pro-Jewish. It had also been pro-Zionist, understanding well that Zionism would be a useful antidote to communism among Polish Jewry.

Now, as Pope John Paul II, Wojtyla remained available to his Jewish friends, visiting their synagogues, repeatedly affirming the depth of his respect for Judaism and the Jewish people. During the millennial year 2000, upon visiting the Christian shrines in the Holy Land, John Paul held cordial talks with Israeli political and religious leaders. It was in the aftermath of that visit, too, in an epochal departure from precedent, that the pope issued a statement of contrition for the Church's centuries-long role in fostering anti-semitism, and enjoined Roman Catholics everywhere to accept the Jewish people as their brothers. The pronouncement manifestly fell short of an encyclical dispensation. But as an ecclesiastical guideline for the vast pastoral and educational apparatus of Latin Christendom, its potential was highly significant. From Pius XII to John Paul II, the Church had come far in the space of forty years.

A Demographic Transposition: The Low Countries

In May 1940, at the time of the Nazi invasion, 140,000 Jews were living in the Netherlands, 34,000 of them as refugees from the Third Reich. Within the next two and a half years, 110,000 Jews were transported to the death camps. About 6,000 survived. Added to this number were approximately 24,000 Jews who had fled the country and returned in the postwar.

Concentrated in Amsterdam, they swiftly resumed their former vocations in commerce and the professions. The goodwill of the Netherlands government was exemplary. Homes and shops were returned to their Jewish owners almost immediately. Special restitution courts were established only months after the war, and in 1953 the parliament allocated the equivalent of $7 million to help recompense Jews for their untraceable chattels and securities. Two years later, when the German Bundesrepublik negotiated an agreement with twelve European nations for a lump-sum reparations payment equivalent to $280 million, the Dutch used their share to deal even more generously with Jewish survivors and Jewish communal institutions. Nowhere else in Europe were representatives of the government, often of the royal family, as likely to attend Jewish memorial commemorations and other communal affairs. The Anne Frank House was declared a national museum. Jewish religious and historical issues were given extensive coverage by the nation's press. In the 1970s and 1980s, three mayors of Amsterdam were Jews. Other Jews served in the government cabinet. Friendship for Israel in the Jewish state's early, beleaguered decades was profound. During the Six-Day War of 1967, thousands of Dutch young people conducted a sympathy march for Israel in Amsterdam.

Political and economic security, however, could not be translated into demographic revival. Dutch Jewry was an aging community, with a lower birthrate, a higher death rate, than the population at large. The Holocaust had sharply reduced the number of prospective spouses, and by the turn of the century, intermarriage reached the 50 percent level. Indeed, by then, the Jewish population of 28,000 (among 15.5 million Dutch fellow citizens) had fallen below its early postwar level. Only a small minority of its young people received more than a perfunctory Jewish education. As elsewhere in Western Europe, commitment to Israel emerged as the common denominator of ethnic identification.

If there was a qualitative difference between the Jews of the Netherlands and those of Belgium, it was to be found in the latter's powerful Orthodox subculture. On the eve of the German invasion, in March 1940, some 57,000 Jews remained in Belgium (at least 20,000 others had already fled), where they comprised slightly less than 1 percent of this small country's 9.3 million inhabitants. A majority of them were post–World War I immigrants, predominantly from Eastern Europe, together with some 14,000 more recent fugitives from Hitler's Reich. Divided between Antwerp and Brussels, they tended to be self-employed, particularly in Antwerp's diamond trade, which was largely in their hands. Portable assets for an insecure people, diamonds remained a historic Jewish vocation. Indeed, well before World War II, or even before World War I, Antwerp had become an international gem center. Its cutters and dealers were the first to exploit the newly discovered stones of the Belgian Congo, and the city rapidly attracted other Jewish gemologists, who similarly maintained close links with their—largely Jewish—retail clients throughout the world. For its part, the Belgian government valued this unique Jewish contribution to the nation's economy and was intent on restoring it.

Thus, at the end of the war, when approximately 21,000 Jews remained alive in the country, the government set about repatriating some 26,000 Jews who had fled to other lands, most of these to Britain and to the United States. The effort was well intentioned but only modestly successful. By the end of the twentieth century, Belgian Jewry achieved a plateau of 32,000 (in a Belgian population of 10.2 million): 20,000 in Brussels, the rest in Antwerp. Most Jews still were of non-Belgian origin, and scarcely more than half of these were naturalized. Even so, they enjoyed the identical civil rights possessed by other Belgians. The government, endlessly responsive to their needs, subsidized the nation's half-dozen Jewish day schools, in common with other religious-school systems. In Brussels, the Jews were an upper-middle-class mercantile and professional community, almost entirely acculturated and French-speaking. Not so in Antwerp, where Orthodoxy remained the dominating motif among the 3,000 or 4,000 diamond-dealers and their families. Dressed in Hasidic garb, with their numbers swollen by as many as 4,000 émigré Israelis, the Antwerp Jewish community made an elaborate display of its right-wing pietism, a stance (here as elsewhere) intended as a kind of guarantee of business probity. While the Jews of Brussels maintained an antiseptic distance from the Antwerp shtetl, each community in its own way shared in the Israeli renaissance, and commitment to the Jewish state became as decisive an integument of Jewish vitality in Belgium as elsewhere in Europe.

A FLICKERING SEPHARDIC LEGACY

In proportion to demographic mass, the fate of Greek Jewry was arguably more tragic that of any other Jewish community during the Holocaust. Not more than 12,000 of Greece's 70,000 Jews survived. Their economic condition was more desperate even than that of the Greek population at large. Each day after liberation, scores of survivors—starving, half-naked, lacking roofs over their heads—expired of disease and debilitation. Little public assistance was available, and the widening civil war between the royalists and the Communist EOKA rebels blocked access to Joint assistance until late 1946. At the same time, the postwar Athens government, unwilling to dispossess thousands of Greek squatters, was notorious for its procrastination in restoring confiscated Jewish property.

The government's attitude almost certainly evinced its awareness that most of the Jewish survivors belonged to the leftist camp, whose underground forces earlier had helped them during the German occupation. Indeed, as the internecine fighting reached its climax in 1948–49, the royalist press once again chose to label Marxism a "world Jewish intrigue." Jews were accused of fostering heresy, of seeking to weaken the Orthodox Church as a barrier to communism. Impoverished Jewish families often were denied help from government welfare centers on the grounds that Jewish charities were available. In Salonika and Athens, taxes on the few remaining Jewish shopkeepers were assessed at a much higher level than on Greek businessmen. It was accordingly in these years of postwar discrimination that more than half the Jewish survivors immigrated to Israel.

In later decades, the 4,000 Jews who remained in the country underwent no significant communal revival. With Salonikan Jewry all but eradicated, so was the ambience of an integral Sephardic culture. In 1955, helped by a $1 million Claims Conference grant, Greece's Central Jewish Council opened a primary day school in an Athens suburb. It sustained its modest enrollment only intermittently. Mixed marriages over the years exceeded 50 percent. In the last years of the twentieth century, Greek Jewry, whose principal enclave, Salonika, once had functioned as the cultural and economic center of the modern Sephardic world, was fast approaching the threshold of exotica.

By contrast, Jewish life was reviving in an even more historic Sephardic context. This was Spain itself. During the early postwar years, the Franco government's approach to the Jews remained as ambivalent as in the prewar. Well into the 1950s, the nation's press and pulpit continued to disseminate anti-Jewish propaganda. Yet, from 1945 on, the Falangist dictatorship grasped the importance of cultivating goodwill in liberal circles abroad, particularly in the United States. Here as always, the Jews appeared a logical intermediary.

Thus, in 1946, Madrid enacted a series of laws guaranteeing non-Catholics the right to practice their religion, although not in public buildings. In the early 1950s, Spain offered transit facilities to the Jewish Agency during the mass immigration of Moroccan Jews to Israel and France (p. 625). In the 1956 and 1967 Arab-Israeli wars, Spain extended its diplomatic protection to some 3,000 Sephardic Jews in Egypt, enabling them to leave the country.

Responding to these hopeful auguries, Jewish settlement in Spain began to revive, particularly during the country's economic boom of the 1950s and early 1960s. Although a majority of the newcomers were Moroccan Jews, and most settled in Barcelona, a significant minority of Europeans also began taking up residence in both Madrid and Barcelona. By 1967, approximately 8,000 Jews were living in Spain. Most of them held permanent-resident status and enjoyed perfect freedom to conduct their business and personal activities. Their security was further enhanced that year as the Franco government, seeking membership in the UN and NATO, took additional steps to ingratiate itself with the Western democracies. A new law guaranteed non-Catholics full religious liberty, including the right of public worship. It was a major concession for Franco's Spain. In 1968, the government symbolically embellished it by revoking Ferdinand and Isabella's 1492 expulsion decree. And in 1978, three years after Franco's death and the restoration of the Bourbon monarchy, the Spanish people voted their approval of a new, democratic constitution. One of the document's key provisions affirmed "freedom of ideology, religion and worship for individuals."

In the 1970s and 1980s, Jewish immigration to Spain gained further momentum. This time most of the newcomers arrived from Argentina and Chile, where political and economic conditions were worsening (p. 678). By the turn of the century, augmented by an influx of émigré Israelis, Spain's Jewish population reached 12,000. If the figure was modest (all the more in a Spanish population of 64 million), it nevertheless exceeded the Jewish enclave of Austria or of any Scandinavian country. Still divided essentially between Barcelona and Madrid, virtually all the Jews were businessmen. Their religious and communal activities were vigorous. Both cities possessed synagogues, Jewish community centers, and day schools. Chairs and institutes in Semitic and Sephardic studies were established at Spanish universities.

In the last decades of the twentieth century, endlessly on the qui vive for American goodwill, the Spanish government issued postage stamps to mark the rededication of Toledo's El Tránsito Synagogue, a jewel of Sephardic Jewry's medieval golden age, and organized an extensive series of "Sephardic" tourist programs. In 1992, to commemorate the quincentennial of Ferdinand and Isabella's expulsion decree, King Juan Carlos and Queen Sofia paid a ceremonial visit to the Madrid synagogue, and in ensuing years the royal couple extended other gestures of cordiality and respect on Jewish religious occasions. In 1996, ignoring Arab diplomatic protests, the Spanish government formally exchanged ambassadors with Israel.

FRANCE: A BELLE ÉPOQUE REVIVED

The Holocaust reduced France's prewar Jewish population from 340,000 to 250,000. In 1944, following the liberation, and intent on exorcising the shame of wartime French collaboration, the government of France immediately canceled all anti-Jewish laws and set about reinstalling Jewish survivors in their former homes and business premises, and in their former civil service positions. An additional feature of the national catharsis was the virtual open door extended to Jewish immigrants. Some 50,000 Jewish displaced persons availed themselves of the opportunity, raising the postwar Jewish population to approximately 300,000 by 1951. The task of caring for these immigrants still fell largely on the Joint. But in 1954, the government of France received its share of German reparations, a treaty payoff of 1 billion marks ($300 million), and afterward disbursed the equivalent of $30 million to Jewish victims of Nazi oppression. Jewish Claims Conference funds similarly were applied to French-Jewish welfare and cultural needs. Perhaps most important, the nation's economic health was reviving, and the Jewish population shared in that recovery.

Indeed, Jews were achieving distinction as well as security at all echelons of French life. Active in many sectors of the economy, from the textile industry to heavy steel and machinery (the automobile manufacturer André-Gustav Citroën was a Jew, as was Marcel Dassault, chairman of France's leading military aircraft company), Jews also played their traditional role in high finance. The Rothschilds continued to rank as the largest of the nation's private bankers, their investments extending from the Peugeot automobile company to Club Méditerranée. Among widely respected figures of the early postwar decades were the political commentator Raymond Aron, the sociologist Georges Friedmann, the novelist Joseph Kessel (member of the French Academy), and four postwar winners of the Prix Goncourt—Anna Langfus, Roger Ikor, Romain Gary, and André Schwarz-Bart. As elsewhere in Europe, Jews were prominent in theater and cinema. And to a degree unprecedented in the prewar era, they were also assuming a vibrant role in politics. René Mayer served briefly as premier of a socialist-dominated coalition government in 1953, even as Daniel Mayer (no relation) succeeded Guy Mollet as secretary-general of the Socialist Party. Jules Moch served as minister of the interior in a number of socialist governments. Michel Debré, the baptized son of Jewish parents, held the office of prime minister under de Gaulle's presidency in 1958.

By far the most important of these political figures, however, was Pierre

Mendès-France. Descended from a Sephardic family that had lived in France since the seventeenth century, the son and grandson of decorated war heroes, Mendès-France as a young lawyer and committed socialist was elected to the Chamber of Deputies in 1932, and served until the outbreak of war. Enlisting then as an air force officer, he escaped German capture in 1940 and eventually made his way to England, where he joined the Free French air force and participated in bombing raids over Europe. Following liberation, Mendès-France served briefly as minister of national economy in the provisional government, then resumed his former seat in the Chamber of Deputies. In those years, he rose swiftly to leadership in the Socialist Party's "progressive" left wing, and in that capacity he was chosen premier in 1954.

A trim, square-jawed man of forty-seven, at the height of his intellectual powers, Mendès-France acted swiftly to introduce a disciplined program of Keynesian reforms that substantially energized his nation's economic growth. In foreign policy, the premier's skill in devising a formula for awarding independence to Morocco and Tunisia in 1954–55 was exceeded only by his success in negotiating an end to the Indochina War, a conflict that had raged for eight years and taken a heavy toll of France's manpower and wealth. By these achievements, Mendès-France won the respect of every major political group in the nation. Indeed, a virtual Mendèsist cult developed in France. After seven months in power, the Socialist Party split again into factions, and Mendès-France left the premiership. Yet he remained perhaps his nation's most beloved political figure, a symbol of all that was idealistic in the French socialist tradition.

If France's acceptance of Jews approached philo-Semitism in the latter 1950s, part of the reason could be ascribed to widespread admiration for Israel, whose growing military prowess served France's interests in facing a common enemy, Egypt's President Gamal Abd al-Nasser. Nasser had launched a campaign of subversion both against the French presence in Algeria and against Israel's very existence in the Middle East. The emerging Franco-Israeli alliance was cemented in October 1956 when the two nations collaborated in the Sinai-Suez War. For nearly a decade after that partnership, Israel and France remained linked in a tight, mutually supportive friendship. Within France, an influential pro-Israel bloc developed in the parliament, while the Alliance France-Israël included some of the nation's most respected political and cultural leaders. Much of this friendship for "our gallant little ally" in turn subliminally influenced the popular attitude toward Jews. Even French rightists (among the strongest advocates of the partnership) found it often confusing to distinguish between "Israéliens" and "Israélites," between the Jews of Israel and those of France. If the era between the end of the Dreyfus Affair and the outbreak of World War I was the belle époque of French Jewry, the decade of the mid-1950s to the mid-1960s might have been termed a second golden age, a period when approbation for Jews became virtually a weathervane of France's reconfirmed liberalism.

A Demographic Transfusion

These same years, however, were rather less than a belle époque for French Jewry's religious and cultural vitality. As late as the mid-1950s, a mere twenty-one rabbis were to be found in all of France. The Séminaire Rabbinique, established in the previous century, was attended by fewer than a dozen students. The Consistoire Israélite, the Jews' religious "establishment," at first displayed little initiative or imagination in attracting North African Jewish immigrants or in providing for their specialized religious traditions. In the first postwar decades, the totality of Jewish students attending afternoon religious schools in Paris did not exceed 2,400, in a local Jewish school population of 34,000. During the late 1940s and early 1950s, the lingering wartime trauma could also be discerned in an upsurge of conversions to Catholicism and the widespread exchange of Jewish family names for "native" French names. Even before 1939, French Jews had been famously uninterested in seeking creative expression for their Jewish identity. But in the early postwar years, they appeared to have regressed into a minority so palpably lacking in Judaic élan as to hover on the threshold of communal atrophy.

Then, beginning in the mid-1950s, a much larger influx of newcomers from North Africa and the Middle East launched French Jewry on a sudden and dramatic religiocultural transformation. For one thing, the tidal wave of Maghreb-Jewish immigration, totaling at least 300,000 by the mid-1960s, almost doubled France's Jewish population. Within the space of a single generation, the number of identified French Jews achieved a critical mass of between 560,000 and 580,000, thereby becoming the second-largest Jewish community in Europe and the fourth-largest in the world. The resettlement of these newcomers unquestionably presented a significant challenge. Even with financial help from the Joint and the Jewish Claims Conference, France's Jewish social services were obliged to work overtime to establish absorption centers for the many tens of thousands of immigrants, to find housing and employment for them.

Nevertheless, the North Africans managed the ordeal of resettlement better than their East European predecessors in the interwar years. They arrived in a period when the national economy was expanding. They spoke French. Virtually all of them were literate (unlike many of their kinsmen who immigrated to Israel). Even the undereducated Moroccans and Tunisians were able to fill the quasi-proletarian role that once had been performed by the East Europeans. Settling in Paris's drab Belleville quarter, the Moroccans and Tunisians worked in leatherware ateliers and in modest textile and clothing manufactories. Others found employment as plumbers, mechanics, or electricians. If few of them achieved acceptance into the nation's social structure, by the late 1950s they succeeded at least in winning an economic foothold for themselves.

The Algerians did even better. At the time of their resettlement during the 1960s, under the Gaullist repatriation program (pp. 627–28), they had access to a full spectrum of French government assistance. The ethnic barriers that had limited their advancement under colonial rule in Algeria were more easily surmounted in France. Having barely achieved petit bourgeois status in the Maghreb, Algerian Jews now earned their livelihoods as middle-level retailers, as proprietors of workshops, as government employees, teachers, pharmacists, notaries, and increasingly as physicians and lawyers. Dispersed somewhat more extensively around the country than their European forebears had been, reviving moribund Jewish settlements in Marseilles, Nancy, Toulouse, Nice, and other, smaller cities, the Algerians managed a swift and comparatively painless integration into the French social economy.

A Communal Revolution

Beyond their impact on France's Jewish demography, the Maghreb newcomers profoundly transformed the sociology of French-Jewish communal life. However much they regarded themselves as *aspirants* to French civilization, they sustained a vigorous Jewish ethnocentrism that contrasted sharply with the pale "cultism" of France's veteran Jews. To their credit, the leaders of the Consistoire were prepared to help rebuild the North Africans' institutions according to the latter's taste and experience. Thus, for the first time in sixty years, and with the help of substantial Jewish Claims Conference funds, a major program of synagogue construction was launched throughout France. A Sephardic seminary was established for the training of rabbis, cantors, teachers, and youth leaders. Day-school facilities were enlarged, new afternoon religious schools were opened in Paris and the provinces, together with a network of Jewish community centers. These latter were an American innovation. With their attractive facilities and broad-ranging social and cultural programs, the centers became magnets for younger North African Jews. Increasingly, too, the Maghreb immigrants began to make their own mark in Jewish communal life. Early on, they achieved a monopoly of the chief rabbinate. In ensuing decades, the newcomers and their children served enthusiastically on the various Jewish public committees, and by the turn of the century they occupied more than half the seats on the National Jewish Community Council and the United Jewish Welfare Fund.

The "integral" Jewishness of the North Africans eventually proved infectious even among veteran French Jews. The phenomenon was evident less in

formal religiosity—a tradition that had been fading even in the Maghreb—
than in renewed ethnic pride and self-assurance. Beginning in the 1960s, a
spate of new books was published dealing with French-Jewish issues. By the
1970s, conferences of Jewish intellectuals met on an annual basis. Courses in
Jewish studies were offered and well attended in leading French universities.
Above all, commitment to the security and welfare of Israel assumed a vigorous, even militant new dimension among French Jews of all backgrounds. As
in other Jewish communities, the process became notably evident during the
Six-Day War crisis of 1967. Large pro-Israel demonstrations were mounted,
blood donated, financial contributions dramatically enlarged. From then on,
even French Jewry's most acculturated representatives identified themselves
unreservedly with Israel's fate. Among them, Guy de Rothschild served as
chairman of a special emergency fund-raising appeal. Pierre Mendès-France
mobilized his political colleagues. Raymond Aron, dean of French political
writers, recruited the support of his fellow intellectuals.

Yet it was uniquely the North Africans who supplied the critical mass in
this Jewish, and Zionist, renaissance. Their new muscularity was first tested in
response to President Charles de Gaulle's 1967 diplomatic shift in favor of the
Arabs, a policy maintained by de Gaulle's presidential successors Georges
Pompidou and Valéry Giscard d'Estaing. Reacting to that anti-Israel stance,
the new Jewish activist leadership organized a series of pro-Israel demonstrations that drew crowds of over 100,000 and served warning that French Jewry
now should be regarded as a militant ethnic political bloc. However anathema
to the older Jewish establishment, with its lingering tradition of discreetly
Gallicized political identification, that bloc was powerful enough in the 1981
national election to tip the political balance in favor of François Mitterrand
and the Socialists in some forty parliamentary districts. Upon his inaugura-
tion, Mitterrand knew how to reciprocate. He became the first president of
France to pay a state visit to Israel.

Not all of Mitterrand's successors in office adopted as pro-Israel a position.
In May 1995, Jacques Chirac acceded to the presidency of France, thereby
ending fourteen years of Socialist ascendancy. Although a veteran Gaullist,
Chirac was too experienced a politician to emulate de Gaulle's austere chill
toward the Jewish state. Indeed, a year after his election, he also paid a state
visit to Israel. But he issued repeated warnings that Europe could not indefinitely tolerate Israel's settlements' policy in Arab Palestine; for the Middle
East conflict, he insisted, threatened sooner or later to embroil Europe. On
the other hand, Chirac balanced these warnings with a gesture of goodwill
toward French Jewry that had not been prefigured by any earlier French
political leader, not even by François Mitterrand.

The gesture was needed. In these same years of the 1990s and early twenty-
first century, Jean-Marie Le Pen's National Front Party coarsely exploited

public alarm at the mounting influx of hundreds of thousands of non-European immigrants. In his frontal racism, Le Pen directed his heaviest attacks at Moslems and black Africans. Yet he and his supporters barely troubled to disguise their antipathy to Jews. Chirac would not have it. In July 1995, only two months after assuming office, the new president courageously, even greatheartedly, acknowledged France's shared wartime responsibility for Jewish deportations. "Yes, the criminal folly of the [Nazi] occupier was assisted by the French people, by the French state," he declared publicly at a ceremony commemorating the notorious French police roundup of Paris's Jews in 1942. "These dark hours tarnish our history forever." Chirac's Jewish audience was profoundly moved by the gesture of contrition and empathy. Even so, they had undergone too much in their history to accept it as a sure and certain guarantee of future solicitude.

XXXII

The Jews of British Commonwealth

GREAT BRITAIN: AN ENSCONCEMENT OF POSTWAR SECURITY

As late as 1914, fully three-quarters of Britain's Jewish population of approximately 265,000 remained concentrated in London. Of these, at least four-fifths continued to live in the capital's squalid East End. It was only after World War I that the pattern began to shift, and by 1930 less than a third of London Jewry still made their homes in or near the eastern Stepney and Bethnal Green areas of immigrant settlement. The migration was accelerated by World War II. Large areas of Stepney were flattened by Luftwaffe bombardment, and many families were moved elsewhere. At the same time, rent controls placed housing in London's more desirable northern and northwestern boroughs within the means of numerous East End dwellers. Throughout much of the postwar era, homes in these quarters remained comfortably middle-class, and comfortably Jewish. Not until the latter twentieth century did the Jews of London, by then comprising fully two-thirds of Anglo-Jewry's population of some 285,000 (down somewhat from its early postwar plateau of nearly 300,000), embark on a belated migration to the suburbs.

The shift reflected the climactic embourgeoisement of a predominantly East European community. By World War II, the immigrant population had begun to pull its weight economically, and as early as mid-century some 60–70 percent had achieved entrepreneurial status. While most were small businessmen, a growing minority did substantially better. Arnold Weinstock, son of an immigrant Polish tailor, joined his father-in-law's electrical and radio business, then went on after a series of dazzling takeovers to become chairman of a mammoth company embracing three of the proudest names in British engineering: General Electric, English Electric, and Associated Engineering Industries. Other Jewish businessmen imaginatively developed the concept of mass merchandising. Thus, Montague Burton climbed out of the East End to build a network of six hundred shops retailing tailor-made suits. By the eve of World War II, he dominated the mass tailoring business. John

Cohen, son of a Whitechapel tailor, served in the Royal Flying Corps in World War I, then returned to trade in surplus military foodstuffs. After a half-century of aggressive expansion, his company, Tesco, became the largest chain of food stores in post–World War II England. Other Jews displayed the same shrewd instinct for the mass market: among them, the Glueckstein brothers and Barnett Salmon, who built Lyons Teashops into a chain that by 1970 achieved a turnover of 129 million pounds, sold nearly 40 percent of all the ice cream eaten in Britain, owned a quarter of the frozen-food market, and operated a string of hotels.

The paragons of entrepreneurial merchandising in Britain may have been Isaac Wolfson and Michael Marks. One of eleven children of an immigrant furniture-maker who lived in the slums of Glasgow, Wolfson moved to London in 1920 and began selling clocks, mirrors, and upholstery covers. His main chance came in the Depression, when he was hired as chief buyer for Great Universal Stores, a Jewish-owned mail-order company. Sensing the firm's potential, Wolfson purchased its controlling shares with borrowed money, then set about buying up small retail businesses and continued these purchases through World War II. By the 1970s, Great Universal Stores had become Western Europe's largest mail-order chain.

Even better known than the vast Wolfson conglomerate was the chain of Marks & Spencer stores. Arriving as a youth from Bialystok in 1882, Michael Marks began as a stall operator in Leeds, then eventually graduated to a "penny bazaar." He worked on a low profit margin, but his volume soon enabled him to open additional penny bazaars in different northern English towns. By the time Marks died in 1908, he had left behind a prosperous company. In ensuing years, under the direction of his son, Simon, and son-in-law, Israel Sieff, the firm began marketing a wider range of quality goods. During the 1930s, the brothers-in-law concentrated on building "superstores," until, by mid-century, Marks & Spencer had become England's largest chain of all-purpose department stores, the nearest equivalent of Sears in the United States.

Other vocations besides mass merchandising were pioneered and largely preempted by East European Jews and their children. Thus, two out of three major motion picture chains, Odeon and Granada, were built by Jewish entrepreneurs. By the late twentieth century, a sizable proportion of the entertainment business, stretching from Associated Television to London's Palladium, was in the hands of the three Grade brothers, sons of Polish-Jewish immigrants who had started life as tap dancers in the music halls of the East End. During Britain's post–World War II real estate boom, at least one hundred Jews made their fortunes in imaginative property development. In 1969, Harold Samuel acquired the huge (but ailing) City of London Real Property

Company, thus becoming the single largest property owner in the world. By 1990, of the five hundred leading companies listed in the *Times* index, seventy-four were Jewish-owned.

In recompense for their efforts, some of Anglo-Jewry's tycoons achieved the official recognition that counted most in Britain. They were inducted into the knighthood, and more than occasionally into the peerage. Isaac Wolfson became Sir Isaac Wolfson. Both Simon Marks and Israel Sieff moved from baronetcy to barony, as did Sieff's son, Marcus. The registry of knighthood included the widest spectrum of Jewish entrepreneurs, from Sir Arnold Weinstock to Sir John Cohen to Sir Lew Grade. The Salmons and Glueck-steins of Lyons Tearooms boasted among them two privy councillors, seven knights, six commanders of the British Empire, three members of the House of Commons, a chairman of the Greater London Council, a high court judge, and a cabinet minister.

As in the United States, the Jewish drive for entrepreneurial success had stabilized by the late twentieth century. Increasingly, the children and grand-children of immigrants enjoyed the leisure to seek new outlets in the liberal professions. By the mid-1980s, statistics began to reveal the profile of a community not only secure and acculturated, but increasingly elitist. Comprising a mere one-half of 1 percent of the British population, Anglo-Jewry already was producing 3 percent of all university students, 5 percent of the nation's doctors, and 9 percent of its lawyers. Their role as academicians was beginning to approach that of American Jews, and at every level. Even before World War II, Arthur Goodhart, an American-born Jew, was appointed master of Oxford's University College. David Daiches, son of a Scottish rabbi, was dean of the School of English and American Studies at Sussex University. Max Beloff, Gladstone Professor of Government, resigned his chair at Oxford in 1972 to accept appointment as president of University College of Buckingham (and later yet, upon retirement, appointment to the House of Lords).

Isaiah Berlin, professor of social and political theory at Oxford, emerged as a near-legendary figure in Britain's academic constellation. In 1966, he was appointed first president of Wolfson College and afterward was showered with honors, including a baronetcy, the Order of Merit, membership in the British Academy, and later the academy's presidency. A useful index to Jewish prominence in the learned professions in the first three post–World War II decades was the rising number of Jews elected as fellows of the Royal Society: from twelve to forty-nine; and as fellows of the British Academy, from four to twenty-two in the same period. Then and later the reservoir of Jewish professionals came to include hundreds of Jewish musicians, composers, directors, producers, writers, and playwrights. By the opening of the twenty-first century, it was no longer possible to find any significant area of British life from which Jews were excluded.

To a significant degree, that upward mobility also came to include public life. In the post–World War II decades of intermittent Labour rule, the historic snobberies and inequities of the prewar years were substantially dissipated, and the British people settled into a comfortable acceptance of their new role as a second-rate power but an increasingly first-rate democracy. Within that new ambience, Jews moved much more freely into the top echelons of public life. From their midst came a chairman of the Commonwealth Telecommunications Board, a permanent undersecretary of the ministry of development, a permanent representative to the European Economic Community, a chief scientific adviser to the ministry of defense.

Soon, too, public service came to embrace political as well as civil service. From the 1970s on, solidly ensconced in the middle and upper-middle income brackets, British Jews might have been expected to vote Conservative. There was even precedent for that affiliation. A century earlier, wealthy Jews exerted a certain influence within the Tory Party, and as late as 1900, of twelve Jewish MPs, eight were Tories. Throughout the first third of the twentieth century, however, most Jews, even affluent Jews, gravitated increasingly to the Liberals. The party was conservative enough not to put off Jewish millionaires, yet was trusted by Jews of all income levels for its traditional championship of religious liberty and equal political rights (pp. 96–97). As a result, when the Liberals faded as a major force after World War I, Jewish representation in politics similarly declined for many years.

Socialism, too, apparently had lost its brief, early appeal for East European immigrants. During the interwar years, the Labour Party tended to pick its MPs from among the gentile working classes. It was only after World War II that Jews began turning in increasing numbers to Labour. The change was largely a reaction to the Conservatives' record of genteel antisemitism and anti-Zionism (Winston Churchill notwithstanding). In the early postwar period, almost all Jewish MPs were Labourites, and no fewer than forty-two during the 1970s, at the apogee of this relationship. Yet the influence of Jews within the party rarely was substantial. Most of them were left-wingers, and in the first decades after the war Labour was dominated by centrists such as Clement Attlee, Hugh Gaitskell, and Harold Wilson. Harold Laski, once a major Labour theorist, saw his influence swiftly erode during the Attlee government.

Whatever their political affiliation, throughout the entirety of the twentieth century it was almost unthinkable for Jews to regard themselves as a separate ethnic voting bloc. Even occasional surveys of Jewish voting patterns tended to embarrass the Jewish Board of Deputies, which was swift to reject any notion of a "Jewish vote" in the pattern of the United States (or, increasingly, of France). For British Jews, political "objectivity" was proof of their acculturation. The British voting public accepted that evaluation. In the 1980s and early 1990s, as Jewish progressives tended increasingly to emulate their non-Jewish neighbors in voting their pocketbooks and social status, there was a resurgence of Jews elected to the House of Commons on the Conservative ticket. Several occupied key positions in Margaret Thatcher's government. Sir Isaac Wolfson's nephew David was Thatcher's chief of staff. Sir Keith Joseph, one of three Jewish cabinet members, was her closest domestic adviser. Thatcher's successor as prime minister, John Major, upon winning election on his own account in 1992, appointed Malcolm Rifkind as Britain's first Jewish foreign secretary.

The apotheosis of Jewish political respectability, however, occurred in 2003, when the Conservative Party elected Michael Howard as its chairman, and thus as its designated candidate for prime minister. Born in Llanelli, Wales, in 1941, Howard was the son of a Rumanian-Jewish shopkeeper. The family name of Hecht was anglicized to Howard. After attending Cambridge, where he was president of the Cambridge Union, Howard achieved a brilliant career as a barrister. In 1983, he won election to Parliament as a Conservative member for Folkestone and Hythe. Rising almost immediately in party councils, he held various cabinet ministries under Margaret Thatcher, and in 1993 under John Major was given the important portfolio of home secretary, where he became known as a man uncompromisingly tough on crime. With the fall of the Major government, Howard retained his seat in the House of Commons during the ensuing incumbency of Tony Blair's Labour administration. His aggressiveness in debate and his shrewd political skills much impressed his colleagues. When the Conservative leader, Iain Duncan Smith, proved ineffectual in stemming Labour's landslide 2003 election, his party replaced him as chairman in favor of Howard. A dues-paying member of a Liberal synagogue, Howard thereby became the first professing Jew in British history to lead one of the nation's major political factions.

A COMMUNAL TRANSFORMATION

Anglo-Jewry's instinct for respectability was no less evident in its "ecclesiastical" affiliations. By the opening of the twenty-first century, some five hundred synagogues were functioning in Britain. Approximately half of these belonged to the United Synagogue, founded in the nineteenth century as the Jewish "establishment's" nearest equivalent to the Church of England. With an income approaching 3 million pounds a year, this largest of Jewish religious organizations still wielded enough influence to nominate the "chief rabbi," whose authority extended to Ashkenazic congregations not only in

Britain but throughout the entire Commonwealth, except for Canada. The United Synagogue also supported Jews' College, a seminary for the training of Orthodox rabbis, and supplied religious instruction for Jewish students in state schools. Over the years, this record of institutional service was all that the United Synagogue's members asked of it. Orthodox in their affiliation out of respect for their parents and grandparents, most second- or third-generation Jews were content that their religious representation, like that of the wider British community, remain bland, tolerant, gentle, avoiding the strictures of "legalism." The typical British rabbi continued to embody a certain pallid blending of English and Jewish cultures—rather like a Jewish version of an Anglican parson, down to the canonical collar.

Meanwhile, the Federation of Synagogues, established in 1887 by a more rigorously Orthodox group of East European immigrants, continued to hold its own. By the twenty-first century, the federation's nearly 200 constituent congregations embraced some 18,000 families. Even further to the right, an ultra-Orthodox conventicle of Hasidim, comprised almost exclusively of Holocaust survivors and their families, burgeoned in the decades after World War II. Known as the Adat, and numbering between 3,000 and 4,000 families, the Hasidim moved aggressively toward the self-segregation of their American counterparts, and in the latter twentieth century their members tended to congregate in Stamford Hill, London's counterpart to Brooklyn's Crown Heights. Other alternatives to the United Synagogue establishment were more likely to be found on the left. Thus, by the late 1900s, Reform Judaism encompassed some 10,000 families and supported twenty-eight congregations. A somewhat more modernist version of Reform, Liberal Judaism, resembling the American model, drew approximately the same number of congregants, and as early as 1956 managed to open its own theological seminary, later called Leo Baeck College. Eventually, the seminary was underwritten by both groups, even as both established the joint Council of Liberal and Reform Congregations. As late as the turn of the century, however, the two movements together attracted barely 10 percent of the United Synagogue's membership.

But if British Jews, through habit and sheer inertia, tolerated the United Synagogue's authority, they were not prepared to allow their children to vegetate in quite the same torpor. Until well after World War II, a majority of Jewish pupils received their religious education in late afternoon synagogue classes. Upon undergoing a perfunctory bar or bat mitzvah, few youngsters afterward continued to study. Then, in the 1960s and 1970s, a network of Jewish day schools began to emerge. The inspiration for this development, sociological possibly as much as ideological, was the growing influx of African and Moslem children into neighborhood schools. Confronting the phenomenon, British Jews responded with a belated discovery of the values of private Jewish education. By the late twentieth century, Jewish day schools were attended by one out of every seven Jewish youngsters in Great Britain, and the ratio appeared likely to grow.

It is probable that the older Jewish establishment, the affluent families who once dominated Anglo-Jewry's communal institutions, would have found alternative ways of coming to terms with the circumstances of British society. But that establishment had long since given way to the East European immigrant community. The process had been powerfully enhanced in the 1920s and 1930s not merely by the East Europeans' numerical preponderance, but by the rise of Zionism. The old guard, including most of the Rothschild family, initially had scorned the very notion of political Zionism. The East Europeans had embraced it early on, but somewhat ineffectually during their years of settlement and impoverishment.

It was only when Chaim Weizmann and Harry Sacher, both of Russian-Jewish background, had succeeded in extracting the Balfour Declaration from the War Cabinet in November 1917, that the older families began to be outflanked. Until then, whenever a Jew wished to approach authority, he did so through the acculturated mandarins of the Board of Deputies. Weizmann now opened out a direct contact with the government. As London became the fulcrum of international Zionism between the wars, the movement accordingly gained in prestige among Anglo-Jewry itself. During the 1920s and 1930s, the Jewish veterans still ensured that the Board of Deputies maintained a discreetly "non-Zionist" position. But the board's rank-and-file membership increasingly reflected the preponderance of the East Europeans. In 1939, when Selig Brodetsky, born in the tsarist Pale and reared in London's East End, assumed the board's presidency, Zionism ever after remained a central feature of its agenda. The organization's fund-raising and public affairs efforts on behalf of Zionism, and later of the State of Israel, remained as intensely tenacious and generous as those of American Jewry.

By the twenty-first century, the status of Anglo-Jewry could hardly be described as one of efflorescence. Numbering between 280,000 and 290,000, the community's demographic resources could not generate the vibrance and effervescence of its counterpart in North America. Yet its economic and political security was as solid as any Jewish community's in the Western world. If its "Jewish" intellectual achievements still reflected the limitations of its modest population, the seriousness of its efforts to interpret, enrich, and disseminate higher Jewish culture deserved respect. In tandem with the United States and France, philanthropic endowments underwrote courses in Jewish studies in a wide range of universities, from Oxford and Cambridge to the major regional and municipal universities. As recently as the 1980s, the profile of Anglo-Jewish communal life struck some observers as bland and unimaginative. By the twenty-first century, that evaluation would be less reserved. Well anchored in economic and political security, the Jews of England appeared at last to have found their voice in a self-assured and pluralistic creativity.

The Legacy of Empire: Canada

In their late-nineteenth-century flight from tsarist persecution and economic redundancy, tens of thousands of East European Jews flocked to Britain's European-inhabited dominions: to Canada, Australia, New Zealand, and South Africa. Aside from Britain itself, it was Canada that eventually became the single largest haven for this swelling tide of emigration. More than twice the size of the continental United States, rich in soil and minerals, the country lacked neither for space nor resources. Self-governing, democratic in political structure, Canada had attracted immigrants from all sectors of Europe during the entire course of the nineteenth century, including a small number of Jews from Central Europe. Indeed, well before the East European influx, German Jews were to be found in the far western reaches of British Columbia and Saskatchewan. One of them, Lumby Franklin, was elected mayor of Victoria, and another, David Oppenheimer, was four times elected mayor of Vancouver. By the late 1870s, a dozen synagogues were functioning in Canada, serving a Jewish population of approximately 3,000.

Yet their numbers did not grow dramatically, even in the immediate aftermath of the May Laws. For Russian Jews, the great northern dominion was still an unknown entity. Those who arrived in the late nineteenth century did so essentially by accident, when British ships, offering cheap passage to the United States, made Canada their first port of call. The odyssey of these early East Europeans in some measure replicated that of nineteenth-century German Jews in the United States. Among them were hundreds of storekeepers who settled in the tiny railroad villages throughout the Canadian West. Only recently arrived from the belt of mixed populations of southeast Europe, the typical Russian-Jewish trader of this type was able to make himself understood among the Germans, Ukrainians, Poles, and Serbs who settled in the interior. Living in the windblown "bush" with these tough, hard-drinking workmen and farmers, housing his family in a converted railroad car or in the back of his little store, the Jewish merchant served as provisioner, banker, translator, letter-writer, and adviser for a growing and heterogeneous population.

The Jewish immigration rate accelerated only in the twentieth century. The process was familiar. As in the United States, the small groups of Russian Jews who had initially disembarked and earned a modest security in Canada mailed remittances, and eventually steamship tickets, to relatives in the Pale. The more fundamental incentive for "temporary" residence in the north, however, was the United States' harshly restrictive Johnson Act in 1921. Altogether, from 1900 to 1939, some 125,000 Jews settled in Canada. While the figure represented barely 2 percent of the country's total immigration in those years, by the eve of World War II Jews comprised the nation's seventh-largest ethnic group. Most of them were settled in Canada's three largest cities—43 percent in Montreal, 23 percent in Toronto, 8 percent in Winnipeg.

As in the United States, the majority of them found their initial employment in the needle trades. The story was a familiar one. Over time, the immigrants moved from sweatshops into ownership of a textile and clothing industry that became the earliest Jewish contribution to Canada's economic life. Yet there were other Jewish success stories in commerce and industry. Samuel Bronfman, starting out as a small retail liquor dealer in Montreal, prospered sufficiently to purchase the old Canadian distilling firm of Seagram's. In the 1920s, selling his whiskey both in Canada and (illicitly) in the United States during the years of Prohibition, Bronfman laid the basis for the largest distilling empire in North America (p. 307). By the 1950s, the Reichman brothers already were emerging as the largest commercial land-developers in North America (and, briefly, in England). Altogether, by mid-century, the immigrants had achieved their characteristic middle-class profile.

They had never questioned their basic security, not in a vigorous parliamentary democracy such as Canada's. Nevertheless, a dominion structured on a complex legacy of federal quasi-autonomy posed obstacles to Jewish integration. The most serious of these arose in Lower Canada, in the largely French-speaking province of Quebec. Here lived nearly half of Canada's Jews, most of them in Montreal. The province maintained a unique educational system. In the absence of secular public schools, each of the two major religiocultural groups, the French-Catholic and the Anglo-Protestant, supported its own network of parochial schools and funded them out of provincially authorized property taxes. The method worked reasonably well as long as the province's children came exclusively from Catholic or Protestant homes. But as Montreal's Jewish immigrants developed into a homogeneous minority, they confronted the problem of finding a hospitable school system for their own children.

At first, Jewish students attended the Protestant schools. By an agreement reached in 1903, and subsequently legalized by the provincial legislature, these youngsters shared the full rights and privileges of the Protestants. In return, the Jews paid their school tax into the Protestant "panel." It was an unsatisfactory compromise. Jewish children found themselves segregated in separate classrooms and denied official permission to be absent during Jewish holidays. After years of fruitless Jewish litigation in the courts, the Protestant representatives in 1931 finally agreed to terminate segregated classes and to excuse Jewish youngsters on Jewish holidays and from compulsory study of the New

Testament. Even then, the agreement did not work well. Jewish children still tended to be ghettoized in their own classes. Nor would the Quebec legislature, controlled by the Francophone majority, provide sufficient funds for schools with large numbers of Jewish students. It was essentially this tax dispute that obliged Jewish families to turn increasingly to private Jewish day schools. By mid-century, 18 percent of Montreal's Jewish schoolchildren already were receiving all their education in these parochial Jewish institutions, and the proportion would grow steadily with the decades. Because the arrangement was an involuntary and expensive one, Jews could only regard it with mixed emotions.

Through the 1920s and early 1930s, moreover, the school controversy opened a vein of flagrant antisemitism. As the legal battle continued, many of the French-Canadian newspapers alluded to Jews in libelous terms. Even after the settlement of 1931, anti-Jewish feeling suppurated throughout French-speaking Quebec. Altogether, the episode underscored the lingering backwardness and insularity of the Québécois population. For years, its Catholic Church hierarchy was among the most obscurantist in the world. In the Depression era, parish priests actively extolled the virtues of such Catholic-authoritarian regimes as Fascist Italy's and (later) Franco's Spain. In 1935, too, the campaign of reaction was given official sanction when Quebec's premier, Maurice Duplessis, publicly encouraged a boycott of Jewish businesses. The antisemitic upsurge was more spectacular than effective, however. Most of Quebec's industrial and commercial interests—shipping, railroads, lumber, insurance—were in the hands of the "Anglos." The latter condemned the French-Catholic boycott campaign, which soon foundered.

Yet, even then, the dominion's venerable tradition of ethnic suspicion appeared to survive intact. Assuredly, it was powerful enough in the 1930s to bar the door to Jewish refugees (p. 516). Even as late as the 1950s, few Jews were to be found in the upper echelons of government. No Jewish attorney sat as a judge until Harry Batshaw was appointed to the superior court in 1950. The election of Nathan Phillips as mayor of Toronto in 1954 created as much astonishment as delight among Canadian Jewry. For many years after World War II, Jewish lawyers in search of gentile clients remained limited to damage suits and other small tort cases. If they represented small businesses, these were almost invariably Jewish-owned. Only a small minority of Jewish physicians succeeded in obtaining appropriate hospital staff appointments, and their patients tended to be predominantly Jews. No Jew held a seat on the Montreal stock exchange. By tacit agreement, no Jew was ever a partner in an insurance company or a bank. Masonic lodges, the Royal Canadian Legion, the Press Club, and other veterans' and professional associations admitted only occasional token Jews. Very rarely were Christian and Jewish families on visiting terms.

The country's implacable separatism was not the product exclusively of antisemitism. It was the consequence as well of Canada's historic kulturkampf between the Anglos and the French, a parochialism that endured in Canada with only slightly less tenacity among the Italians, Poles, Ukrainians, and other ethnic groups. In any case, without a significant German-Jewish "establishment" to encourage and guide their acculturation, the Jews accepted the fact of intracommunal clannishness as further inducement to maintain their East European traditions and institutions. With few exceptions, synagogues in Canada were Orthodox or Conservative. Well into the mid-twentieth century, the Yiddish language remained in wide use. *Landsmanschaftn*, associations of Jews who had been neighbors in the Pale (p. 375), survived and thrived. It was an ethnocentrism that was manifest as well in the passionate devotion of Canadian Jews to Zionism, and in an extravaganza of programs and activities sustained by the Canadian Jewish Congress.

Even into the late twentieth century, the Jews of Canada, numbering barely one-fifteenth the population of United States Jewry, remained heavily dependent upon the cultural and organizational resources of their kinsmen to the south. It was from the United States that they imported nearly all their rabbis, the executive directors of their synagogues and Jewish centers, the administrative apparatus of their B'nai B'rith, Zionist, and United Jewish Appeal organizations, and of innumerable other Canadian-Jewish religious, cultural, and philanthropic associations. For many years, accepting the reality of that dependance, Canadian Jewry did not question that it would continue into the indefinite future.

Toward Communal Identity

Yet, in some measure, the prognosis of dependency was belied by the impressive late-twentieth-century expansion of the Canadian economy, and by a concomitant growth of the nation's Jewish population. From the late 1970s on, exploiting the growing liberalization of the nation's immigration laws, successive infusions of Jews arrived from North Africa, Israel, and the Soviet Union. Almost imperceptibly, Canada's Jewish demography went "critical." Indeed, after five decades of quiet postwar growth, the nation's Jewish population nearly tripled, from its 1939 plateau of 125,000 to almost 360,000. By the year 2000, Canada's Jewry had become larger than Britain's, and in a Canadian population—27 million—less than half as large as the mother country's. It had become a "re-migrated" community, as well, shifting from Montreal to Toronto, and even to Vancouver, on the Pacific coast. Demographic surveys in 2002 calculated that the Jewish population of metropolitan Toronto had grown to 175,000; while Montreal Jewry, numbering 95,000, had lost both its numerical and proportional "seniority."

The altered balance could be attributed in some measure to the distinctive pattern of late-twentieth-century Jewish immigration. Its sources were over-whelmingly the Soviet Union and Israel. The newcomers chose Toronto both as Canada's business center and as a city in which they could use their second language, English. But no less decisive a factor was the resurgence of French-Canadian ethnicity. Unlike its earlier incarnation before World War II, this new version reflected the self-assurance of an increasingly prosperous and vigorous Francophone middle class. Politically, the development was reflected in the triumph of the Parti Québécois in the 1976 provincial elections. René Lévesque, the party's fiery leader and newly elected provincial prime minister, defined a maximalist goal for his followers. It was nothing less than secession from federal Canada and the establishment of an independent Québécois republic. Fortunately for the Anglophones—a group that emphatically included the Jews—Lévesque's secessionist dream foundered early on, in a national referendum. Nevertheless, during its nine years of political rule, the Parti Québécois was able to inflict a serious trauma on the province's English-speaking minority.

Thus, shortly after assuming office, the Lévesque government passed a new language bill requiring all newcomers in Quebec to send their children to schools in which the first language of instruction was French. If the measure was a shocker for the Anglos, it proved even more so for the Jews. Indeed, it all but precluded any further Jewish immigration to Montreal. More funda-mentally, the Québécois government required non-French schools substan-tially to increase the hours of instruction given in the French language. By 1976, fully 60 percent of Jewish children in Montreal were attending their own Jewish primary day schools, and the remaining third attended Jewish secondary day schools. With Hebrew traditionally the second language of instruction in these institutions, the new linguistic requirement sharply lim-ited the time available for Hebrew and other Jewish studies.

Beyond the school crisis, moreover, all Jews in Canada were intent on maintaining their principal economic and cultural links with the English-speaking world, both in the United States and in the British Commonwealth. It was unthinkable for Jews as a minority community to be further encysted as a minority within a minority. And so they began to leave. As in South Africa (p. 667), the professionals and others with exportable skills were the first to depart. Nonprofessionals were obliged to proceed more cautiously in liquidat-ing or transferring businesses; but once the Québécois government tightened the screws by mandating the use of French in mercantile displays and other advertisements, businessmen similarly began to transfer their operations to Toronto or points farther west.

If Jews moved to the English-speaking provinces, however, they rarely found it necessary to leave Canada altogether. Indeed, opportunities were now theirs that had never been dreamt of in the prewar period or even in the early postwar years. As elsewhere in the British Commonwealth, the last third of the twentieth century witnessed a relaxation of the unspoken barriers to Jewish advancement. A rapidly growing Canadian economy, the influx into the country of numerous additional ethnic groups from Eastern Europe and the Far East, educational improvements within Canada at large, tended gradually to replace exclusionism with a new and more tolerant cultural pluralism. Now at last Jewish businessmen in far greater numbers emerged as major players in the nation's economic takeoff, as movers and shakers in discount merchandising, property development, the theatrical and film industry, and in the professions. Indeed, in the professions, Jews had long since achieved a characteristic distinction, serving as medical professors, as university department chairmen and deans, as presidents of Toronto's York University and of Montreal's McGill University. Government service in all branches, both on the federal and provincial levels, became increasingly familiar to upwardly mobile Jews, who served as local mayors and municipal board chairmen, as parliament and cabinet members, as supreme court justices, commission chairmen, and as ambassadors to foreign nations (including the United States).

It was inevitable that the new affluence and visibility should also have generated a more vibrant Jewish cultural self-assurance. Thus, by the latter twentieth century, it was a rare Canadian university that did not offer at least one course in Jewish studies. At the University of Toronto and at McGill University, large and solidly funded departments of Judaic studies matched in quantity and quality comparable programs at several of the most eminent American institutions. Perhaps the best evidence of this coruscating vitality, equally as Jews and as Canadians, was the acerbic glee with which a Montreal novelist like Mordecai Richler could transmit the flavor of arriviste Jewish society, and the undisguised delight with which Canadian reading audiences of all ethnic backgrounds could claim him as their own.

Australia: The Comforts of Multiculturalism

In January 1788, the first of England's flotilla of convict transports dropped anchor at Sydney harbor, New South Wales. Among its nearly eight hundred prisoners were eight Jews. These included sixteen-year-old Esther Abrahams of London, sentenced to an Australian penal farm for stealing a piece of lace. Possibly as many as a thousand Jewish prisoners, most of them convicted for petty thievery or fencing, reached the Australian colonies before the practice of shipping felons was terminated, in 1844. Afterward, as "emancipees," they were joined by other—free—immigrants, both from England and from Central Europe. By 1881, Australia's Jewish population reached 9,000. Approximately half of them settled in Sydney, the rest in Melbourne, the capital of the state of Victoria. From the beginning, emancipees and immigrants alike enjoyed full civil and political rights. Jewish numbers doubled again by 1914, with the largest influx of Jews arriving from Eastern Europe. Often starting out as itinerant peddlers, the newcomers won their foothold in a thriving frontier economy. After World War I, they moved from peddling to small shopkeeping. A minority of Jews even began to win success as bankers, financiers, brewers, clothing manufacturers, and, increasingly, as professionals.

Early on, too, several Australian Jews achieved a distinction unimaginable to their kin in Britain. John Monash, the son of Galician immigrants, was trained as a civil engineer and patent attorney. Active in the military reserves while still a university student, Monash climbed steadily in the reservist ranks until, in 1918, he was appointed commander of the Australian Expeditionary Force in France. On the Western Front, his military-administrative skills achieved several brilliant successes, particularly in the final breakthrough of the Hindenburg Line. Lloyd George called him "the most resourceful general in the whole of the British Army." Decorated many times, knighted, the recipient of almost every honor the governments of Britain and Australia could bestow, Monash at the time of his death in 1931 was the single most respected Australian of his generation.

Isaac Isaacs, born in Melbourne of Polish immigrant parents, became a successful lawyer before entering political life. After occupying a number of ministerial and judicial positions in Victoria, he was appointed chief justice of Australia in 1930. The following year, Prime Minister James Scullin nominated Isaacs as the country's first native-born governor-general. Initially, King George V was hesitant to appoint a Jew, until he was apprised that social snobbery was far less common in Australia than in England. In virtually all the day-to-day opportunities that mattered, Jews continued to find the great frontier nation open and fair-minded. Although immigration barriers were tightened in the Depression years of the 1930s, and racism played its role in the government's unwillingness to accept refugees (p. 516), no significant economic or professional opportunities were closed to the country's long-resident Jews.

After World War II, moreover, even the obstacles to immigration were lowered. Before 1939, regarding their nation essentially as an outpost of Anglo-Saxon civilization, Australians fully supported the preference given British immigrants. But from the latter 1950s on, with the recent danger of Japanese invasion still fresh in their minds, they began to grasp the military-security value of an augmented population. Both the nation's Liberal and Labour parties agreed, too, that racial diversity was an unavoidable corollary of enlarged immigration quotas. Between 1946 and 2000, at least 6.6 million newcomers were admitted to Australia, contributing to the nation's population growth in those years from 7.2 million to 19.1 million. Less than 40 percent of the immigrants were British. Indeed, less than half came from Europe altogether. The largest influx this time was from Vietnam, Thailand, and other Southeast Asian nations.

The Jews shared in the nation's demographic growth. Between 1946 and 2000, their numbers in Australia more than doubled, approaching 100,000. Virtually all were East European refugees, although between 25,000 and 30,000 of them arrived via an initial immigration to Israel. Intensely ethnocentric, a majority of the newcomers tended to bypass Sydney, with its older Jewish enclave, in favor of Melbourne, a more polyglot city. By the turn of the century, Melbourne's Jewish population had reached 49,000; Sydney's, 38,000, with smaller communities taking root in Adelaide, Brisbane, and Canberra. Wherever they settled, the Jews comprised an overwhelmingly white-collar element, concentrating in business and the professions.

Their political loyalties reflected that middle-class status. Voting their pocketbooks, Jews from the 1970s on abandoned their traditional allegiance to the aggressively left-wing Labour Party in favor of the more centrist Liberals. The latter, once regarded as the citadel of "Anglo" snobbery, had long since become as pro-immigration (and as pro-Israel) as the Labourites. Representing both major parties, Jews themselves served as lord mayors of Sydney and Melbourne, and as members of the federal and state parliaments. And once again, in 1978, a Jew, Sir Zalman Cowen, was appointed governor-general of Australia.

With more than half the nation's adult population foreign-born, meanwhile, Australia was prepared, even obliged, to accept "multiculturalism" as the norm. The new context plainly was as congenial to Jews as to other ethnic groups. Now one among many immigrant communities, they experienced only minimal social pressures to conform. Their own institutions and organizations flourished. These included the Executive Council of Australian Jewry, welfare agencies, Zionist societies, Jewish cultural movements of all trends, even a Yiddish theater in Melbourne with a semiprofessional repertory company. Far more than Britain, or even Canada, day-school education became a major fact of Jewish life. By the end of the twentieth century, Sydney's three day schools educated a third of the city's Jewish children. In Melbourne, eight day schools were educating 90 percent of the city's Jewish children of primary-school age, and 40 percent of children in the secondary-school age group. One of these institutions, Mount Scopus College, was the largest Jewish private school in the world. If much of the community's ethnocentrism veered toward cultural parochialism, it was also as enviably relaxed a form of Jewish identification as could be found anywhere in the Diaspora.

SOUTH AFRICA: FLAWED EL DORADO

In 1795, during the Napoleonic Wars, officers of the British navy planted the Union Jack on the southern tip of Africa, thereby preempting the harbor of Simonstown from possible French occupation. Moving up the coast to establish their rule in Cape Town, British marines encountered a small agricultural community of Dutch and Huguenot settlers. They also encountered a handful of Sephardic Jews. Like their Protestant neighbors, the Sephardim over the previous century had fled Spanish and French Catholic persecution to establish new lives in an open and unclaimed frontier.

Beyond establishing their own military rule, the British would not interfere in the lives or institutions of the Cape Province's local settlers. Thus, in ensuing decades, the tiny Jewish emplacement would be joined by additional numbers of British and German Jews. Most were peddlers. But from the 1830s on, growing numbers of Afrikaner (Dutch and French Huguenot) farmers moved into the interior to avoid the British presence, and several hundred Jews followed in their wake. Traveling from the Cape by ox or mule wagons, the peddlers dragged themselves up mountain passes toward the inland *veld* to seek out their traditional customers in isolated farm villages. Several enterprising Jewish merchants opened modest stores, and a few became local councilmen and magistrates.

None of them anticipated that they were emplacing themselves in terrain of unimaginable natural potential. But in the 1850s, veins of diamonds were unearthed in the northeastern corner of Cape Province; and in the 1870s, goldfields were discovered in the interior, in the Witwatersrand reef of the Afrikaner-ruled Transvaal Republic. Some 2,000 additional Jews then joined the cascade of fortune-hunters that poured into South Africa. Of German or British origin, the newcomers initially followed the tradition of their predecessors as peddlers or storekeepers. But several became important diamond buyers, and a few became wealthy in the diamond trade. Barney Barnato and Lionel Phillips eventually achieved vast fortunes as company directors in several Transvaal gold mines. Ranging further afield, Samuel Marks, a Lithuanian immigrant, used his profits in gold and diamonds to develop a large industrial complex in coal and iron mines, in brick and glass factories, in breweries and distilleries.

In the 1880s, moreover, in the aftermath of the Russian pogroms and May Laws, a larger influx of some 10,000 Jews arrived from Eastern Europe, a majority of them also from Lithuania. Close enough to the Baltic for a window on the world, and inspired by the legendary success of their compatriot Samuel Marks, the Litvaks came in family groups. At first, most of them established themselves in the Cape Province. But soon afterward, they moved extensively into the mineral-rich Transvaal Republic, and into the Transvaal's small Afrikaner satellite, the Orange Free State. In the pattern of their Jewish predecessors, the East Europeans also began as peddlers and storekeepers. Most eventually settled in Johannesburg, the Transvaal's burgeoning frontier capital. By the turn of the century, some 12,000 of the 15,000 Jews in South Africa made their homes there.

Even as they lived and thrived under Afrikaner administration, however, the Lithuanian newcomers continued to place their greatest value on the British connection, with its link to the great and liberal democracy of England. Thus, in 1899, with the onset of the Boer War, a majority of Jews in the Afrikaner republics joined in the exodus of Anglos to the British coastal provinces. But in 1902, when the conflict ended, virtually all of them returned. Indeed, in ensuing years, Jews broadened their base in South Africa. Increasing numbers of them played a role in its public life. In 1909, Harry Graumann became the first Jewish mayor of Johannesburg. Other Jews were elected to the Transvaal and Cape Province legislative councils. In 1910, when the country was reconstituted as the Union of South Africa, its new federal parliament included seven Jews. Each year, too, ongoing infusions of Litvaks reflected their widely shared conviction that an unlimited future was opening for them in this African El Dorado. By 1933, numbering approximately 70,000, Jews comprised nearly 5 percent of the country's white population.

But the mood of ethnic accommodation was changing. In 1924, the Afrikaner-dominated National Party swept into office. Committed to an insular policy of "South Africa for the South Africans," the Nationalists in the ensuing six years packed the civil service exclusively with kinsmen. In 1933, when the Depression brought a more moderate Afrikaner leader, Jan Christiaan Smuts, to leadership in a "United" coalition government, the right-wingers set about organizing a new, "purified" National Party, this one even more unregenerately xenophobic than its predecessor. Embittered by widespread unemployment, the Nationalists were convinced that the solution to their problems lay in eliminating all further influence by "foreigners," that is, the British and the Jews, who dominated the industrial and commercial sectors of the economy. For the while, the United coalition managed to preserve the British connection. In 1939, under Smuts's premiership, the government even brought South Africa into World War II on the side of the Allies. But the coalition majority was always a precarious one.

Yet, the Smuts era represented the last gasp of political moderation in South Africa. During their years in opposition, the Nationalists continued to fan the flames of Afrikaner rancor. Finally, with their electoral triumph of May 1948, and with the accession of their party chairman, Daniel Malan, to the prime ministry, the Nationalists' moment of vindication had arrived. By the same token, Malan's accession was a thunderbolt for the Jews of South

Africa. Haunted by fear of an impending Nazi-style regime, the South African Jewish Board of Deputies found itself at a loss. Should Jews immigrate en masse to Britain? To Israel? Or should they stand fast to resist an impending program of militant Afrikanerdom? The moment was a terrifying one.

In fact, the Nationalist leadership had reevaluated its priorities by then, and central among them was a harsh new program of apartheid, of enforced segregation and "regulation" of the nonwhite races. As Prime Minister Malan embarked on this agenda, he no longer discerned a need gratuitously to alienate the Jews, a powerful middle-class element that constituted 15 percent of white Johannesburg. Thus, in discussions with the Jewish Board of Deputies, Malan emphasized that he was uninterested in any further talk about the "so-called Jewish question." Whereupon, immensely relieved, the Board of Deputies in turn was prepared to meet the government more than halfway. Even as the Nationalists muted antisemitism as an issue in public life, Jewish spokesmen learned to remain silent on the government's emerging program of discrimination against nonwhite races.

As individuals, to be sure, Jews were more visible than any other white element in their opposition to apartheid. Throughout the 1950s and early 1960s, they figured prominently at virtually every level of the struggle, among reformist liberals and Communists, in the courts (whether as defendants or as counsels for black defendants), in the lists of "bannings" (political quarantine), and among those who fled the country to evade arrest. Although Jews represented a mere 3 percent of South Africa's 4.2 million whites by 1960, they comprised 60 percent of the nation's white political defendants. In 1959, a Jewish member of Parliament, Helen Suzman, wife of a Johannesburg physician, broke from the United Party for reasons of the latter's "cowardice" on apartheid, to found the Progressive Party and to lead it in a lonely and courageous struggle for racial justice. But gallantry was not the "official" Jewish position. The Jewish Board of Deputies remained thunderously silent on the issue of apartheid. Not even the government's 1960 Sharpeville Massacre of black protesters induced the board, the Jewish press, or the rabbinate, to break their silence. Rather, during the years of apartheid, Jewry's official spokesmen vied with one another in praising Prime Minister Malan and his Nationalist successors in office for their "statesmanship."

If one explanation for the Jews' communal obsequiousness was their minority insecurity, another was the intensity of their Zionism. Nowhere in the Diaspora was Zionism so integral a feature of Jewishness itself. A mosaic of racial and cultural traditions, South African society encouraged this kind of ethnic identity. Here, alone in the Jewish world, the Zionist Federation was the senior communal organization, founded in 1898 and antedating the Jewish Board of Deputies by more than a decade. The government, partially as an expression of Calvinist devotion to the Holy Land, but even more transparently as a tactic of encouraging Jewish emigration there, was unremitting in its support of Zionism. Thus, as a member of the British War Cabinet in 1917, Jan Christiaan Smuts was one of the authors of the Balfour Declaration. During all the ensuing years of his prime ministry, even as he discreetly closed South Africa's doors to Jewish immigration, Smuts insisted that the answer to the Jewish question was "free immigration to the Jewish National Home in Palestine." In May 1948, Smuts was one of the first government leaders to extend recognition to the State of Israel.

In 1953, Prime Minister Malan actually trumped Smuts's gesture by becoming the first head of government to visit Israel. More significantly, Malan and his successors relaxed South Africa's stringent currency-export laws. As a result, South African Jews year in and year out were able to raise a cornucopia of (non–tax-deductible) funds and transmit them to Israel. For the Nationalists, approbation of Zionism was a cheap price to pay for Jewish silence on apartheid. In turn, these governmental benedictions permitted the Jewish leadership a comfortable rationale, namely, that if Judaism imposed a moral imperative to oppose racial discrimination, there was a national Jewish imperative, too, to strengthen the State of Israel—and Malan's government was helping in that process.

Keeping their peace on apartheid, then, the Jews of South Africa continued to thrive mightily. Success was hardly difficult for them, of course, or for any white community, in a land so bountifully endowed with agricultural, mineral, and industrial wealth, including a vast pool of cheap black labor. With these considerable advantages, the Jews pioneered South Africa's discount-chain stores and such light industries as clothing, leather goods, furniture, tobacco-processing, and candy-making. In the 1960s and 1970s, turning to the service sectors, Jews built more than half of South Africa's hotels, including the Sun International Group, the nation's largest conglomerate, and put together the country's principal theater and cinema chains. By 1990, replicating their vocational pattern elsewhere, 22 percent of the Jewish working population had moved to the professions, where they comprised 12 percent of South Africa's doctors and dentists, 11 percent of its accountants, 15 percent of its academicians, and 10 percent of its lawyers.

For all its economic success, however, this remained a community that lived its social life almost exclusively among its own. Its organizational activities were overwhelmingly Jewish, encompassing the Zionist Federation, the Board of Deputies, and innumerable other Jewish committees and associations. Not less than 60 percent of Jewish school-age children attended Jewish day schools, most of these Zionist-sponsored. The Jews' synagogue federations and other religious institutions were almost entirely in the hands of Orthodox rabbis (most of them quite right-wing). Yet, despite the considerable funds and energy poured into this intricately structured communal edifice, the investment ultimately proved incapable of salvaging South African Jewry's anchorage in their South African Elysium. The failure could not be attributed to "assimilation"—not in a golden Jewish cocoon where the endogamous marriage ratio exceeded 90 percent. Neither was the explanation to be found any longer in government hostility or Afrikaner antisemitism. It was the black ocean this time.

Until 1974, white rule in South Africa had been protected by comparable European regimes in nearby Rhodesia and in the neighboring Portuguese colonies of Angola and Mozambique. Then, unexpectedly, Portugal abandoned its African possessions. Five years later, Rhodesia acquired its own majority black government and transformed itself into Zimbabwe. Meanwhile, in June 1976, a serious eruption of violence occurred in Johannesburg's black Soweto ghetto, and in later years outbreaks among the nation's disaffected African population grew in frequency and bitterness. If South Africa's white minority felt itself beleaguered, the Jews experienced a double vulnerability. Approximately 6,000 Jews, most of them younger people, departed almost in the immediate aftermath of the Soweto uprising. In ensuing years, South African Jewry sustained additional shocks to its comfortable status quo. In 1985, an international boycott was imposed against the nation's apartheidist government. Ultimately, the pressure became economically unbearable. Even the Nationalists recognized that there existed no alternative to a fundamental liberalization of the country's political structure.

That change began in 1990 when Prime Minister F. W. de Klerk ordered the release of Nelson Mandela, a charismatic black activist who had been imprisoned since 1962 for political incitement. A year later, Mandela was ushered into office as South Africa's first native African prime minister, and in 1995 he was formally elected to the presidency in the nation's first all-racial election. However peaceful, the revolution all but traumatized South Africa's white population—Afrikaners, Anglos, and Jews alike. In the ensuing momentum of emigration, Jews tended to be in the vanguard. Uncommitted to the soil, keeping their assets comparatively liquid, often possessing "transferable" professional skills, they departed in growing numbers for England, Canada, the United States, and Israel. In 1948, the Jewish population of South Africa was estimated at 118,000. By the year 2004, the figure was estimated at 60,000. Only the Jews of the former Soviet Union had undergone a comparable demographic shrinkage (pp. 734–35). In 1984, even before South Africa's climactic political transformation, the Anglo-Jewish writer Chaim Bermant recalled his visit to a Jewish day school in Johannesburg: "My wife and I spoke to the sixth form . . . and asked how many of the students proposed to go to Israel when they left school. About a quarter of the hands went up. [But] when we asked how many proposed to make their home [permanently] in South Africa, not a *single* hand went up."

XXXIII

A Latin Israel in the Southern Hemisphere

A Revival of Jewish Security: Central America and Uruguay

It was the haunting fear of a Spanish or Portuguese reconquest that inhibited Jews from resettling in Latin America until quite late in the nineteenth century, long after most of the native populations had won their independence. When the connection finally was risked, Mexico was the initial port of call. Ladino-speaking Sephardim characteristically were the first to venture a return after fleeing the New World's Inquisition. Arriving from Turkey and the Balkans in the latter nineteenth century, several hundred of these *turcos* (as the locals called them) began as peddlers of household and farm goods. Their presence in Mexico was augmented in the early years of the twentieth century by a modest infusion of West European Jews, among them José Yves Limantour, who became the financial genius of the Porfirio Díaz regime. Several hundred other West European Jews participated in Mexican mining and railroads. It was only in the 1920s, however, when the United States closed its doors to immigration, that large numbers of Polish and Rumanian Jews altered their route southward. Some 20,000 of them settled in Mexico before World War II.

Like their Sephardic predecessors, most of these East Europeans began as door-to-door peddlers or as proprietors of tiny market stalls. They were joined by perhaps 5,000 to 6,000 West European fugitives from Hitler. The war boom of the 1940s fortified their economic security. In the postwar years, Jews branched out into wider-scale commercial and light-industrial ventures. By the late twentieth century, their children and grandchildren were among Mexico's most prominent engineers and doctors. Numbering approximately 40,000 in a population of 95 million, and comprising the fourth-largest Jewish community in Latin America, virtually all of them lived in Mexico City. Here their network of synagogues, day schools (embracing 85 percent of all school-age Jewish children), journals, and newspapers, their palatial community center—all emerged less from classical Jewish political beleaguerment than from cultural ethnocentrism. Since Mexico's early-twentieth-century revolutionary period, the country's politics had been liberal and anticlerical. At no time were Jews confronted here with overt, Church-generated anti-semitism. As a result, they remained an inbred minority throughout the years, self-satisfied and materialistic both in their private lives and in their communal activities. Within their luxurious suburban enclaves, their homes, perhaps even their consciences, appeared firmly insulated against the Indian and mestizo majority population.

By contrast, Uruguay, the "Switzerland of Latin America," was an oasis of Europe in a non-European continent. Perhaps two-thirds of its 3.1 million citizens (in the early twenty-first century) were descendants of Spaniards, French, and Italians. Inhabiting a beautiful little country, with a temperate climate and rich soil, the Uruguayans were renowned in the Southern Hemisphere for the breadth of their middle class. The nation's political ambience was as mild as its climate. Uncharacteristically for Latin America, Uruguay functioned as a viable democracy for more than a century and a half. Even a brief civil conflict in the 1970s was hardly more than a political frisson by the standards of neighboring countries. It was an attractive sanctuary for Jews. With little significant marrano prehistory, their settlement here was almost entirely a twentieth-century phenomenon.

Initially, in 1907–8, it was a limited immigration of a few hundred Sephardim from Izmir and fifty or sixty Jews from Eastern Europe. The first sizable influx, 18,000 Polish Jews, occurred in the 1920s. It was followed a decade later by a wave of German-Jewish refugees, and after World War II by a smaller group of East European displaced persons. By the late twentieth century, Uruguayan Jewry numbered approximately 50,000. Settled in Montevideo, they comprised the third-largest Jewish community in Latin America. No obstacles barred their way as they rose swiftly to upper-middle-class status. From the 1950s on, there were Jewish senators, ministers and deputy ministers, a director of the central bank, and a rector of the national university. Uruguay was the first Latin American government to recognize Israel. Indeed, for many years the two states found much in common as small, democratic, progressive nations. A Jewish program in Spanish, *Kol Yisrael en Uruguay,* was transmitted on the state radio station two hours each day during the choice afternoon listening time, a privilege unmatched in any other Diaspora community except New York's. Although a lavish sports-communal center, Maccabi, was the focus of Jewish social life, it was Zionism, here as elsewhere in Latin America, that remained the common denominator of Jewish organizational and emotional life.

Unlike Mexico or even Uruguay, Venezuela provided a cherished sanctuary for Jews in both the worst and best of times. The first marrano refugees from the Portuguese Inquisition arrived here from Brazil in the seventeenth century. Their descendants intermarried and eventually were interspersed among

Venezuela's most aristocratic European families. Early in the nineteenth century, in the aftermath of its recently won freedom from Spain, Venezuela began to attract professing Jews, including a contingent of some four hundred Sephardim who arrived from neighboring Curaçao. By the opening of the twentieth century, a functioning Sephardic community was in place, with its own synagogue and network of social services. In the ensuing decade, modestly augmented by newcomers from Morocco and the Middle East, the Jewish enclave totaled a modest 3,000.

Typically, Jewish life in Venezuela achieved its most impressive growth immediately before and after World War I, when East Europeans began arriving in substantial family groups. In the classical immigrants' profile, they were followed by German-Jewish refugees in the 1930s and 1940s, then by smaller quantities of displaced persons after 1945. By the opening of the twenty-first century, Venezuela's Jewry numbered 18,000 (in a national population of 14 million), virtually all of them living in Caracas. Almost to the last soul, they were middle class. While a majority of the businessmen among them were importers, several hundred Jews owned factories producing textiles, clothing, and furniture. Their children tended to be professionals, not a few of them holding faculty positions at the National University. Relations with the government and the Catholic clergy were quite equable.

Two large synagogues functioned in Caracas, one Ashkenazic, one Sephardic, along with a dozen smaller congregations. With hardly an exception, Jewish children attended their own day schools. One of these, the Herzl-Bialik School, was regarded as the best private school in Venezuela and was attended by the children of high-ranking government officials. Both the Sephardic and Ashkenazic communities functioned under a confederative roof organization, and cooperated in a joint fund-raising drive for Israel. Here, too, Zionism was primus inter pares among their communal endeavors. As late as 2002, more than 1,000 Venezuelan Jews had settled in Israel. Even those who remained behind tended to regard Israel as a safety net. In recent decades, Venezuela's economic and political future had become uncertain. Despite ambitious government programs in social welfare, the nation's widespread poverty, underemployment, and illiteracy remained seemingly ineradicable. Caracas's gleaming skyscrapers overlooked a nightmare of slums. Perched on this kind of social volcano, no middle-class community, least of all the Jews, could regard the future with equanimity.

THE JEWS OF POLITICAL INSECURITY

It was a lesson already well learned by other once proud Jewish communities in Latin America. Chile was a case in point. Its population of 15 million (in 2002) was stratified quite sharply between a European elite, 30 percent of the nation, and an impoverished mestizo majority. Marranos had figured prominently here among the early conversos of the sixteenth century, and the Inquisition, implacably hunting them down, remained in place in Chile for nearly three centuries afterward. Indeed, religious freedom was not explicitly recognized in Chile until 1925, when the country adopted its new constitution. The first significant influx of professing Jews accordingly was quite recent, arriving from Eastern Europe in the years immediately following World War I. Yet it was a not unwelcome infusion. By then, the *criollo* "aristocracy" regarded immigration as essential to the nation's economy and racial composition. In the Depression years, to be sure, the quotas for immigrants would be tightened. Yet, even in the 1930s, no fewer than 18,000 German Jews managed to find their way into Chile, soon to comprise its single largest Jewish community. After World War II, 8,000 displaced persons and some 2,000 fugitives from North Africa and the Middle East augmented the earlier settlement. By 1970, approximately 30,000 Jews were living in Chile, two-thirds of them Central Europeans. Settling for the most part in Santiago, they rapidly achieved their traditional eminence in commerce and played a major role in the establishment of Chilean light industry. Here as elsewhere in the Southern Hemisphere, their children and grandchildren gravitated almost reflexively to law, medicine, or academia.

Although each Jewish community—German, East European, Sephardic—characteristically maintained its own network of synagogues and social services, Chile's was one of the more acculturated Jewries in Latin America. Attracted to the European ambience of Chilean culture, Jews of all backgrounds tended quite early to conduct their public and private activities in Spanish. Barely 20 percent of Jewish schoolchildren attended day schools. Yet, even among the Central Europeans, however, Zionism soon emerged as the binding integument of their communal identity, and all the more so in the crisis and euphoria of the Six-Day War. Indeed, only three years afterward, commitment to Israel was revealed as a farsighted personal investment. In 1970, an avowed Marxist, Salvador Allende, was elected president of Chile and immediately set about nationalizing the country's banks and larger industries. The development was as alarming to the Jews as to the rest of the nation's middle classes. At least 6,000 of them departed for Israel or the United States. The leftist era was a brief one, as it happened. In 1973, the Allende government was overthrown by an American-sponsored coup, led by General Augusto Pinochet, Chile's military chief of staff.

Under the ensuing right-wing Pinochet cabal, a reign of terror was inflicted on suspected "leftists," some of them Communists but most of them liberal moderates. Over a three-year period, at least 100,000 Chileans were arrested, and (by some estimates) as many as 30,000 of these were tortured and killed. At the same time, the Pinochet regime entirely reversed its predecessor's nationalization program. It was the evidence of economic "stability" rather than of political autocracy that most reassured the émigrés of the Allende period, Jews and gentiles alike. The majority of them returned, although the number of Jews in Chile did not reach 30,000 again, and possibly not 25,000. Their security in any case appeared ensured under the Pinochet autocracy. Several hundred held positions in the administration. In common with the rest of the nation's middle class, they anticipated order and prosperity.

For a while, they got both. But in late 1981 the economic revival abruptly ended. Chile suffered a catastrophic drop in exports and production, and the unemployment rate climbed to a quarter of the nation's workforce. Until this setback, most Chileans had been prepared to overlook Pinochet's repressive government. But as the economy continued its free fall, protests against the regime became increasingly vocal and evoked increasingly harsh countermeasures. Each year brought widening chaos, repression, and economic havoc. Finally, in 1989, under intense pressure from Washington, Pinochet consented to a plebiscite. The vote massively repudiated his government. The following year, free elections installed the democratic administration of Patricio Alwyn, and Pinochet departed Chile for self-imposed exile in England. But nearly twenty years of uncertainty and trauma had left the fragile Chilean economy and political system profoundly shaken. During the 1980s, the avalanche of émigrés had included 8,000 Jews. Settling in Israel and the United States, only a small number of them returned. By the end of the century, Chile's Jewish population had shrunk to 21,000, a reduction of one-third in the space of a generation. In a region of the world all but synonymous with economic and political instability, an immigrant people was reminded again that sanctuary at best was a relative term.

They learned this lesson in Colombia, where chronic unemployment, runaway inflation, staggering population growth, and drug-based terrorism reduced a once vigorous and distinguished bourgeois Jewish community from 12,000 in 1980 to barely 4,000 at the end of the century. They learned it in Cuba, too, where the Castro revolution in 1959 eventually impelled all but a few hundred of the nation's 12,000 Jews to join the middle-class exodus to the United States. However belatedly, the lesson was learned in still other tyrant-plagued Caribbean nations, in the Dominican Republic, Nicaragua, El Salvador, each of whose minuscule Jewish communities departed almost to the last soul. Even the 2,000 Jews of Panama (one of whose feckless presidents, Dr. Eric del Valle, was himself a Jew) displayed characteristic symptoms of alarm under the corrupt rule of General Manuel Noriega, until the latter's deposition and imprisonment in 1989 at the hands of the United States Army.

Yet, in the end, it was even more ironic that the fragility of refuge was a lesson Jews learned earliest of all in Argentina, the single most European and culturally advanced nation in the entirety of Latin America.

Argentina: "Whitener" of the Southern Hemisphere

In 1897, Julio Roca, president of Argentina, dispatched immigration agents to Europe to seek out cheap agricultural labor. The vast plains of his country's interior were underpopulated except for the backward, half-Indian gauchos. Europeans were needed. Apprised of Jewish suffering in Tsarist Russia, the president's emissaries visited the Pale of Settlement. In their meetings with Jewish leaders, they promised ample homesteads and excellent credit terms for immigrants prepared to settle in Argentina's Entre Ríos province. Hereupon, intrigued by the offer, and supplied with travel fare by the Alliance Israélite, nearly one hundred families ventured the lengthy voyage from Odessa to Trieste to Buenos Aires, and then inland. As promised, they found the tracts—but nothing else. Neither credit nor agricultural equipment was forthcoming. Soon the hapless pioneers were reduced to destitution. A dozen of them starved. Two years later, getting wind of their plight, the renowned financier-philanthropist Baron Moritz de Hirsch came up with an inspiration. It was to solve the problem of Russian-Jewish suffering in one fell swoop by purchasing vast stretches of the Argentina pampas and transplanting several million Jews there. In pursuit of that vision, Hirsch established a foundation, the Israelite Colonization Association (ICA), funded it with $40 million of his private fortune, bought up 1.4 million acres of Argentine (and some Brazilian) soil, and hired a battalion of economists and agronomists to administer the project.

East European Jews did not stampede to avail themselves of Hirsch's generosity. For them, the "golden land" was the United States. In 1891, the first year of the ICA experiment, only 1,348 Jews settled on its Argentine tracts. Neither did the flow of immigrants widen significantly in any future year. By 1927, the Jewish farm population in Argentina reached its highest figure of 33,000, barely 1 percent of the transplantation Hirsch had envisaged. The vocational patterns of the Diaspora evidently could not be transformed within the span of a single generation, or withstand the momentum of Argentina's demographic shift from countryside to city. Yet the experiment was far from an unqualified failure. As late as 1922, nearly a quarter of Argentina's Jews were settled in agricultural communities, a higher proportion than in Palestine, and they proved to be capable farmers. "[They] have nothing of the ghetto bend about them," marveled a visiting observer, Elkan Adler, in 1903. "Fearless and high-spirited, the boys and girls ride the horses bare backed, and they at least are really attached to the land." Indeed, these transplanted narodniki pioneered a series of agricultural cooperatives that became models both for the Argentine countryside at large and for the Jewish banks that were founded later in the cities. As in Israel, the farmers and their descendants over the years became an aristocracy of sorts among the Jews of Argentina. Nevertheless, their most enduring significance was the plain and simple foothold they established for a future Jewish community that soon would rank as the largest in South America.

Other Europeans were becoming aware of Argentina's attractions. The land offered seemingly inexhaustible supplies of grain and cattle. It was endowed with a superb ocean seaport and inland maritime communications, and with a relatively literate white population that produced the largest middle class and one of the longest records of political stability in Latin America. It was hardly surprising that in Spain and Italy, in the Balkans and southern Russia, Europeans soon responded to the inducements of Argentine immigration agents. Between 1890 and 1914, over 4 million new settlers arrived. The largest numbers were Italians, followed closely by Spaniards. Although hundreds of thousands of these newcomers resumed their former livelihoods as agricultural or industrial laborers, by 1914 one in four was living in Buenos Aires, until almost half of Buenos Aires's 1.5 million inhabitants were foreign-born or the children of foreign-born.

Jews were the third-largest immigrant group. Of the 150,000 Jews in Latin America by World War I, 113,000 were to be found in Argentina, and 90,000 of these already were living in Buenos Aires. Even after the war, when immigration restrictions gradually were introduced, additional thousands of East European Jews, blocked from entrance to the United States, managed to enter Argentina. Ultimately, between 1890 and 1939, the country absorbed no fewer than 210,000 Jews, a figure representing 5 percent of the total European-Jewish migration overseas, and by far the lion's share in Latin America. Their numbers also included 45,000 Central European Jews who arrived during the Hitler era. After World War II, they would be augmented by 10,000 East European displaced persons.

Approximately 190,000 of the Jewish population would make their homes in Buenos Aires. Here, much to the discomfiture of the criollo elite, the hard-working immigrants, Jews and gentiles alike, included an urban proletariat that had been widely exposed to Europe's Marxist and syndicalist ideas. Many of the Jews were veteran Bundists. Sheer distance from the Old World's religious influences possibly was a factor in exacerbating their radicalism. Few rabbis had accompanied them. In Argentina, the void in Jewish spiritual leadership was filled increasingly by social activists. Indeed, more than in any other Diaspora community, more even than in New York, the Jews of Buenos Aires would foster a highly secularized and politicized culture.

On May Day 1909, during a workers' demonstration in Buenos Aires, a

Jewish anarchist murdered a local police chief. Retaliation was savage, as rioters attacked and sacked Once, the city's predominantly Jewish small-retail business quarter. Even this violence was overshadowed a decade later, in January 1919. Alarmed by labor unrest, conservative elements published warnings against the "Jewish Bolshevik conspiracy." Again, police and right-wing agitators descended upon the Once ghetto, this time killing sixty Jews, injuring hundreds more, and burning a square mile of Jewish stores and workshops. In Argentine folklore, the episode is recalled as La Semana Trágica (the Week of Tragedy).

For the Jews and other southeast European immigrants, the Argentine government's reaction to La Semana Trágica was to tighten entry restrictions and to crack down forcefully on leftist political activity. Temporarily inhibited, Argentine Jews over the ensuing two decades tended to channel their political energies into cultural and communal life. These were the circumstances under which Argentina, with the United States, emerged during the interwar years as one of the two great centers of Yiddish language and publication outside Europe. By 1939, the Jewish community supported thirty-four Yiddish newspapers and periodicals, four Yiddish repertory theater companies, and a host of Yiddish-language libraries and lecture groups. Whatever the medium, themes of social protest continued to dominate. The socialist ethos was equally apparent in Argentine Jewry's densely organized welfare network, in its cooperative banks and wide variety of philanthropic, mutual insurance, and educational programs.

During the 1920s, too, the Asociación Mutual Israelita Argentina (AMIA), the federation of Jewish communal associations, engaged much of its social energy in unremitting battle against a Polish-Jewish "guild" of white slavers. Until the arrival of this element, prostitution in Argentina had largely been monopolized by French procurers. The Jews proved to be superior businessmen. By the eve of World War I, they had taken control of more than half of Buenos Aires's licensed brothels, and hapless Jewish immigrant girls were their likeliest captives. Outraged by this cancer in their midst, the AMIA in ensuing years organized groups of Jewish vigilantes to raid the procurers' bases of operations. Yet it was not until the early 1930s that the increased stringency of Argentina's immigration laws effectively closed off the brothels' principal source of "raw material." By 1934, the "guild" was out of business.

There were not lacking other public crises for Argentine Jewry during the era of the Depression and World War II. Since 1930, the government had been in the hands of a right-wing military junta led by General José Uriburu. Ideologically sympathetic to Mussolini and Hitler, the army command began choking off liberal expression in press and public debate. Within the officer corps, too, a number of younger men, led by Colonel Juan Perón, maneuvered themselves into political power by offering the nation a populist agenda of grandiose wage and unemployment benefits. Formally assuming the presidency in 1946, Perón banned freedom of the press altogether, and jailed political opponents. At the same time, the young colonel-president transformed Argentina into the world's principal sanctuary for Nazi war criminals (including Adolf Eichmann), and authorized the appointment of several ex-Nazis to important posts in the Argentine police and army. Inevitably, Jew-baiting emerged as a popular tactic in Peronist mass rallies, and periodic defacements of synagogues and Jewish communal institutions occurred with little police interference.

It was a deeply unsettling period for Argentine Jewry, but, so it appeared, a comparatively brief one. By 1947, obsessed with the vision of "national economic self-sufficiency," the Peronist regime embarked on a large-scale program of forced industrialization. However visionary, the effort was fatally undermined by a simultaneous effulgence of social benefits (many of them dispensed through Perón's flamboyant wife, Eva) and an exhaustion of foreign-currency reserves. The inevitable consequence of this governmental schizophrenia was rampant inflation. Hereupon, desperate in his need for United States goodwill (and spare parts), Perón impetuously shifted his approach 180 degrees. Purging the fascists from his administration, he adopted the opportunistic and well-honed tactic exploited by other rulers in other times, of proclaiming his friendship for Jews and (after 1948) for the State of Israel.

Even during its earlier "fascist" incarnation, ironically, the Perón era had offered the Jews a certain unintended advantage. They had shared in the Argentine war boom. Their proletariat had largely disappeared, and they had become a middle-class community. Although they suffered with other businessmen from Perón's bloated social-welfare program, they could hardly disapprove the president's enforced industrialization and tariff protection. Many Jews began to thrive in the closed Argentine market. Their textile mills and clothing factories were emerging among the nation's largest. Jews were also among the most successful pioneers in food products, in lumber and steel, in printing and publishing. Others were achieving eminence as bankers, builders, and developers, as engineers, doctors, and lawyers. By the early 1950s, even as their numbers in Argentina approached 240,000, a significant minority of Jews was taking up residence in Buenos Aires's fashionable Belgrano and Palermo districts.

A Renewed Vulnerability in the "Europe" of the South

In 1955, thoroughly exasperated by the government's ineptitude and Perón's unsavory personal extravagances, a rival military junta overthrew the president and sent him into exile. Over the ensuing decade, closely monitored by the Argentine army, a succession of civilian governments struggled to reconcile fiscal stability with social reform. But in 1963, when President Arturo Illia, a hack politician, appeared likely to capitulate to Argentina's strident, pro-Peronist union leadership, the army command stepped in once more, this time to organize a military administration of its own under General Juan Ongania. So it was, for the ensuing eighteen years, that the 23 million inhabitants of Latin America's most sophisticated "European" nation again found themselves governed by the kind of regime associated with the lowliest Caribbean banana republic. By the same token, these years of alternating turmoil and autocracy soon developed into the grimmest in Argentine-Jewish history.

Several thousand Jewish small businesses were bankrupted. So were at least a dozen Jewish banks and credit cooperatives, whose failure in turn crippled numerous Jewish communal and educational institutions. More ominous yet, the post-Perón years developed into the acutest period of Jewish political vulnerability since the onset of their settlement in Argentina. Intent on diverting worker unrest, the government tacitly countenanced underground hate groups that swelled in numbers and boldness after the fall of Perón. The most notorious of these was the Tacuara, founded and led by a Jesuit priest, Julio Meinville. Its members were youths from the upper strata of Argentine society, classically fascist in their views. Although their animus was directed principally at democratic institutions and the political left, the Jews as always served as a convenient target, particularly after Israeli commandos abducted Adolf Eichmann from Argentina in 1960.

The unfolding pattern of 1960s violence was reminiscent of the successor-state hooliganism of Eastern Europe. Synagogues were intermittently fire-bombed, homes and businesses defaced, adults and schoolchildren beaten and terrorized. More alarming even than the brutality against Jewish individuals and property was the government's indifference to the violence. During his first months in office, General Ongania decreed the removal of all Jews from civil service positions. In 1966, on government orders, the police in Buenos Aires launched a series of raids in the predominantly Jewish business districts of Once and Calle Libertad, arresting eight senior officials of Jewish credit cooperatives for alleged peculation. Although the prisoners had to be released for lack of evidence, Police Chief Enrique Green, Ongania's son-in-law, afterward launched a "morality campaign" against "liberal atheism"—essentially a series of interrogations and beatings of Jewish professors and students at the University of Buenos Aires. In the late 1960s, under pressure from Washington (which itself was responding to Jewish appeals), the Ongania government agreed to a respite in the antisemitic onslaught. But in 1971 and 1972, economic paralysis again suggested a diversionary campaign against the Jews, and the military regime tolerated a renewal of antisemitic abuse.

As they confronted this reign of intimidation, Argentine Jewry discerned in the State of Israel more than an object of romantic nationalism. For years, they had identified wholeheartedly with the Israeli republic, and had contributed their funds and energy on its behalf. During Israel's 1967 and 1973 wars, Argentine-Jewish rallies and military volunteering were extensive and enthusiastic. The Israeli ambassador was a perennial guest of honor at every major Jewish function. As early as 1956, the Israeli party-list system was incorporated directly into elections for the AMIA, the Jewish community federation. However eccentric the transplantation of Israeli politics to a Diaspora electorate, the phenomenon in Argentina was far more pragmatic than ideological. From the Perón era onward, Argentine Jews, like South Africa's Jews, had come to regard Israel as their ultimate guarantee of sanctuary. Between 1948 and 1972, approximately 20,000 of them immigrated there.

The events of the 1960s and 1970s and after merely exacerbated this insecurity. By then, Argentina had reached a political crossroads. For nearly two decades, an oscillation of civilian and military governments had proved either inept or lawless. Perón's faction had been banned during that time, but Peronism as a populist movement remained a vital force among the working population. No other figure could match the ex-president's charisma. In the election of 1973, with Argentina in economic and political turmoil, the army no longer dared risk a civil war by denying Peronists the right to campaign. The latter then triumphed decisively. Soon afterward, the aging Juan Perón himself returned from his Madrid exile to be acclaimed president once more. The most dedicated of his followers were young leftists in the Montonero guerrilla movement, who were convinced that their hero would now set the government on a revolutionary Castro-style course. But others among the president's supporters were right-wingers who expected him to restore some degree of order and fiscal stability to the nation.

In July 1974, before Perón could reconcile these conflicting forces, he died at the age of seventy-eight. He was succeeded by his widow, a former cabaret dancer (whom he married after the death of his earlier wife, the unforgettable Evita), who thereupon became the puppet of her minister for social welfare, José López Rega. A committed reactionary, López Rega immediately set about purging suspected leftists from the government and party. His opponents fought back with equal violence. Soon Argentine political life devolved into a nightmare of kidnappings, assassinations, dynamiting, and counter-dynamiting between the right and left wings of the Peronist movement. In 1975, following still another military coup, the violence escalated into a civil war between the army and the far-left Montoneros. Throughout the remainder of the decade, guerrilla attacks and the army's campaign against both Montoneros and honest liberals reduced the nation virtually to a state of siege.

Like other Argentinians, Jewish businessmen were facing ruin. On the one hand, the intimidation and violence of the Montonero guerrillas had become a curse to them, destroying their livelihoods and security. But the danger from the right was more sinister yet. Although the military junta's repression of leftists and liberals was by no means aimed specifically at Jews, its antisemitic undertones were unmistakable. Over nine hundred Jews were on the lists of "disappeared" prisoners, and those who survived continued to be singled out for particularly harsh interrogation. When a series of ugly financial scandals in the 1970s implicated several Jewish financiers, among them the banker David Graiver, the embezzlement of whose bank shares ruined many thousands of Argentine investors, government propaganda made the most of an alleged "Jewish conspiracy" to funnel money secretly to the Montonero guerrillas. One of those arrested for alleged involvement in the scheme was Jacobo Timerman, publisher of the liberal newspaper *La Opinión*. Timerman was imprisoned and brutalized for nearly two years until vigorous pressure from the Carter administration in the United States secured his release in 1979. It was thus in the latter 1970s and early 1980s that an additional 8,000 Jews departed Argentina, raising their expatriate population in Israel to nearly 30,000.

Well into the twenty-first century, Argentine Jewry still comprised the seventh-largest Jewish community in the world. Notwithstanding the abuse and contumely they had endured in recent decades, their role in Argentine-Jewish economic and cultural life remained vibrant. Their sociologists insisted that the gravest threat to Argentine-Jewish survival ultimately was less political than demographic. It was the old story: of a low birthrate, an aging population, rising intermarriage, of widening "assimilation." Compared with these purely "internal" developments, so the argument went, political dangers were entirely secondary, possibly even overrated.

Moreover, in 1983, Argentina's military regime collapsed in disgrace, one year after its failed war in the Malvinas (Falkland) Islands. Afterward, a new, democratically elected civilian government embarked on a root-and-branch liberalization of political life. Did this change not betoken a hopeful new era for all Argentinians, including the nation's remaining 210,000 Jews? Not likely. The overspill of Arab-Israeli violence would take its toll on Jewish institutions and lives (p. 739). Of possibly longer-term significance, a series of financial crises early in the twenty-first century thrust the country once again to the verge of bankruptcy and sent an additional 11,000 ruined Jewish businessmen off to Israel and the United States. Democracy in this perversely volatile land, the "Europe of Latin America," remained a sure and certain hostage to the vicissitudes of the national economy; and for the Argentine people, the fragility of the economy was the oldest story of them all.

BRAZIL: THE JEWS OF COMPLACENCE

Following Portugal's seventeenth-century reconquest of its Brazilian colonies from the Dutch West India Company, and the reintroduction of the Inquisition, the Jews of this Amazonian behemoth fled en masse to other lands, certain that they would never return (p. 157). But they did return. The connection was resumed in 1824, two years after Brazil achieved its independence from Portugal. It was then that the country's first constitution proclaimed toleration for all non-Catholics, and a marrano group in northern Pará province immediately declared its Judaism openly and established a synagogue in Manáus, the nation's rubber capital.

In the late nineteenth century, new Sephardic immigrants arrived, many settling in the northeastern rubber provinces. Their ports of origin were the traditional non-Ashkenazic hinterlands of Morocco, the Balkans, and Syria. In the twentieth century, they were joined by additional infusions of Sephardim, most of whom were post–World War II refugees from Egypt and the Levant. Reestablishing themselves in São Paulo and Rio de Janeiro, the newcomers, many of them Ladino-speaking, managed early on to win a stable economic foothold, essentially as merchants and small manufacturers of clothing and costume jewelry, and as functionaries in the nation's banks, insurance companies, and import-export houses. Steadfast in their Jewish loyalties, they maintained their own elaborate federation of social services and enrolled nearly half of their children in Jewish day schools, a much higher ratio than among the Ashkenazic Jews. Observance of Jewish tradition remained a central feature of their existence. By the late twentieth century, the Sephardim numbered approximately 30,000. Although by then they comprised less than one-third of Brazilian Jewry, they did not hesitate to proclaim themselves the "conscience" of their European kinsmen.

The Ashkenazim in turn were rather slower in grasping Brazil's immense economic potential. During the larger part of the nineteenth century, only a few hundred of them arrived, principally as technicians, mining engineers, and businessmen from Germany. In the 1890s, however, attracted at last by Brazil's evidently limitless supplies of rubber, diamonds, and timber, immigrants of all European backgrounds began arriving at the rate of approximately 100,000 a year. Among them were some 2,000 Russian Jews, who had been brought over by the ICA foundation, which transplanted them in farm colonies the late Baron de Hirsch had purchased in the southern Brazilian state of Rio Grande do Sul. These agricultural experiments proved even less enduring than their Argentine counterparts. The settlers gradually drifted off to the cities. As late as 1914, the Jewish population of Brazil did not exceed 7,000, still almost equally divided between Ashkenazim and Sephardim and other Middle Eastern Jews.

A far more significant influx took place after World War I, as the United States closed its doors to immigration. By 1933, Brazil's Jewish population had climbed to 42,000. Unlike their predecessors, most of these later arrivals were East Europeans, and a majority of them gravitated to São Paulo. The economic locomotive pulling Brazil, São Paulo between the wars accounted for half the nation's industrial output and was on the threshold of even more impressive growth. As the Jewish newcomers rented cheap flats and settled in the city's Bom Retiro quasi-ghetto, they found an open terrain for their talents as spinners and weavers, tailors and modest shopkeepers. Working from dawn to dusk in their tiny stores or workshops, many eventually accumulated enough capital to open larger retail establishments or small factories. By 1929, Jews owned several of the nation's medium-sized textile mills and paper factories, as well as many of the largest wholesale clothing and food distributorships and department stores.

The Depression struck Brazil hard. The international market for coffee sharply declined. In 1930, exploiting the crisis, Getúlio Vargas, a wealthy landowner and president of the state of Rio Grande do Sul, seized control of the nation's presidency. In ensuing years, Vargas silenced opposition through censorship, arbitrary arrests, and assassination. Although not personally anti-semitic, the president tolerated Jew-baiting to placate his right-wing landowner and lumpenproletariat constituency. Many of the latter gave their support to the Integralista Party, a collection of green-shirted toughs who drew their inspiration from Italian and Portuguese fascism. With the tacit support of important Church leaders, the Integralistas devoted an entire branch of their secret service organization to the surveillance of Brazilian Jewry. It was an ominous moment.

Fortunately, Vargas soon began to have second thoughts about foreign-inspired propaganda on Brazilian territory, and in 1935 he suppressed the Integralistas. Nevertheless, to cope with the ongoing problem of unemployment, the Vargas regime in 1937 introduced severe restrictions on immigration—at the very moment that refugees from Hitler were turning to Brazil for sanctuary. Eventually, 14,000 Central European Jews managed to enter the country before the outbreak of the war, although perhaps 4,000 others afterward made their way in from neighboring Latin American countries. Modest as it was, the latest immigration was not altogether negligible. In time, German Jews and their descendants would comprise a fourth of São Paulo's Jewish population. But their early years were hard. Most of the newcomers gained admission only through the bribery of officials, and many were obliged to pay extortion money for years. Nor could they be employed without permanent residency permits. The multiple harassments drove a number of the refugees to suicide, among them the Austrian writer Stefan Zweig and his wife.

In 1945, President Vargas was deposed and constitutional government was restored. Immigration restrictions soon were eased. In the ensuing two decades, approximately 20 million newcomers from Europe and Asia were admitted into the country. These included several thousand Jews, most of them from Hungary, Syria, Egypt, Turkey, and Israel. By 1970, the number of Jews in Brazil had climbed to 85,000, and by the end of the century to approximately 100,000, in a total Brazilian population of 170 million. They were dispersed widely around the country: 42,000 in São Paulo, 38,000 in Rio de Janeiro, 12,000 in Pôrto Alegre, 3,000 in Recife, and perhaps 1,000 each in Manaus, Bahia, Belo Horizonte, and Curitiba, with several hundreds in various other, smaller communities.

With rare exceptions, the Jews had achieved solid economic anchorage as early as the 1950s. Literate and well versed in business affairs, they were in the forefront of Brazil's spectacular postwar takeoff. It was ironic that a military coup in 1964 actually sped this process. The army regime was technocratic and procapitalist. It encouraged Brazil's transformation from an agrarian to an industrial economy. Indeed, the rate of growth in annual GNP in the 1960s and 1970s was hardly less than spectacular, as the government orchestrated a massive construction of roads, dams, power plants, and other infrastructure. Sharing in this action, Jewish businessmen by then had begun shifting the scale of their operations from the immigrant vocations of garment-making and merchandising to larger-scale manufacturing. The range of their products soon extended to plastics, electronics, automobile parts, chemicals, pharmaceuticals, and paper. One company, Leon Feffer & Cia., operated the largest integrated pulp-and-paper combine in Latin America, with nearly 15,000 employees.

By the late twentieth century, too, the barriers to Jewish political and social integration were as minimal as in the economic sphere. The nation's industrial takeoff was one factor. A certain public esteem for Israel may have been another. Throughout most of this period, relations between the two countries remained cordial, and scientific and cultural exchanges between them for many years were extensive. More fundamentally, Brazil's military regime, covetous of United States goodwill, was uninterested in arousing antisemitism or in exploiting group frictions of any kind. Jews served in the national cabinet, in state and municipal cabinets, as mayors of Curitiba and Rio de Janeiro—where squares and streets were named for Theodor Herzl, David Ben-Gurion, Anne Frank, Selman Waksman, and other Jews. The nation's cultural life was as widely influenced by Jews as that in any Western land, from the conductors of symphony orchestra and directors of state academies and institutes to deans of universities. Interfaith activities were common, with Church leaders benignly participating. Friendly descriptions of Jewish holidays and interviews with Jewish leaders appeared periodically in the popular press.

Over the years, too, the cohesion of Jewish organizational life survived intact. The country abounded in synagogues for almost every ethnic trend, and these generally were well attended. In São Paulo, approximately 20 percent of Jewish students attended the community's day schools; in Rio de Janeiro, with its larger quotient of Sephardim, the proportion was 50 percent. The extensive network of Jewish federations and Zionist societies sponsored lectures, art festivals, occasional theatrical performances. In Rio and São Paulo, several publishing houses periodically brought out translations of Jewish scholarly works. In Brazil, as elsewhere in Latin America, Zionism could be depended upon as a unifying talisman. Israeli music and dance ensembles performed before large and enthusiastic audiences. The country's local Jewish federation elections, like Argentina's, were contested by Israel-style party lists. Annual giving for Israel (under various euphemisms, owing to restrictions on currency export) invariably were generous.

Yet it was significant that the principal focus of São Paulo's Jewish activity was a luxurious country club–community center, Hebraica. Lavishly equipped with a golf course, tennis courts, swimming pools, restaurants, and a theater, as well as ample picnic and playground areas, Hebraica set the tone of São Paulo's Jewish life. A comparable facility in Rio performed an identical function. In earlier years, during the crest of the Brazilian economic boom, the effulgence of Jewish communal life tended to blend with a more widely diffused prosperity. There was little evidence that social achievement here projected a sense of *Judenschmerz* or ethical commitment. With the exception, typically, of university students and a handful of progressives in the state and national legislatures, few Jews were prepared to take a stand on the nation's horrifying social inequities. Living in comparative affluence, accepted by the elite strata of Brazilian society, they appeared content by and large with a military regime that was benign by Latin American standards. In Brazil, as in Chile and Argentina, most Jews remained suspicious of populist democracy and skeptical of majority rule.

In 1979, the military junta authorized a gradual return to parliamentary democracy, and in 1989 the nation held its first popular election in twenty-nine years. Yet, even as Brazilians prepared to accommodate to authentically democratic government, it was questionable whether they could adjust to their nation's economic realities. Over the turn of the new century, uncontrollable inflation was rapidly outstripping earnings. Soaring energy costs were driving the national economy to the threshold of insolvency. At least half the Brazilian population was believed to be afflicted with a near-medieval array of diseases, many of them malnutrition-induced, from tuberculosis to parasitic infections. Almost surrealistically in debt, chronically on the verge of defaulting on tens of billions of dollars in American and World Bank loans, the government apparently no longer could give even passing attention to measures of public improvement. Although the treasury's hard-currency reserves unexpectedly spiked between 2003 and 2005, the long-term political prognosis of a notoriously volatile economy was not encouraging to the nation's middle class. For the Jews, in their classic minority exposure, it was all the less so.

XXXIV

The Efflorescence of American-Jewish Community

THE ERA OF THE GREAT FEAR

In the course of World War II, 550,000 Jews served in the American armed forces, approximately 11 percent of the total Jewish population in the United States. If the proportion was slightly higher than the national average, it reflected the Jews' overwhelming preponderance as city-dwellers, and the tendency of their men to marry and raise families later in life than small-town Americans, leaving fewer of them eligible for deferment. Some 29 percent of all Jews in the army served in the air force, with one in five of these a pilot. Otherwise, there were no divergences from the wider pattern of American military participation. Jews suffered 35,000 casualties, including 10,000 deaths, and won 36,000 decorations. In contrast with World War I, when large numbers of Jewish servicemen were immigrants, most Jews of military age in World War II were native-born. At the highest echelons, these included nineteen generals and three admirals.

Notwithstanding this respectable record of patriotism, the stigma of alienism that had clung to American Jews in the 1930s and early 1940s, that had imposed quotas on their employment and educational opportunities and choked off the rescue of their European kinsmen, was not immediately to be dissipated in the postwar years. Rather, in the next two decades, a threat that initially had flared up in the immediate aftermath of World War I revived with all its former virulence. This was political intimidation under the guise of anticommunism. The initiative in the new campaign was taken by Congressman John Rankin, a Mississippi Democrat and rabid antisemite whose bigotry was grounded in the fertile xenophobia of the Deep South. In 1945, Rankin warned his colleagues that communism was an instrument devised by world Jewry to extirpate Christianity, that the gravest issue facing America was "Yiddish communism versus Christian civilization." Rankin then set about resuscitating the House Un-American Activities Committee, a body that had functioned briefly in earlier years ostensibly to root out subversive organizations.

The committee then embarked on a year and a half of intermittent and somewhat scattershot investigations of the American Communist Party. But in the winter of 1946–47, Rankin and his committee colleagues turned their attention to the film industry. In their renewed zeal, they exploited the recent congressional elections of November 1946, which produced the single most right-wing legislative majority the nation had known since 1920. It was the Congress that brought Richard Nixon to the House and Joseph McCarthy to the Senate. Almost immediately, the House Un-American Activities Committee began inviting spokesmen of the American League of Patriots, the Watchmen's Society, the American Vigilance Union, and other reactionary leagues, each of whom denounced Hollywood as a nest of Communist traitors. Within a year, the hearings took on all the features of a Hollywood premiere, with batteries of floodlights, a promised cast of the film industry's most right-wing directors, studio executives, and actors, who provided dire accounts of Communist or fellow-traveling conspiracies within the Screenwriters and Screen Actors guilds.

Of the figures named as Communist or pro-Communist, most were Jews. Many of them had indeed been active in fund-raising efforts on behalf of Communist-front organizations, although few had managed to translate their ideas into film. Several dozen of the accused were duly subpoenaed to appear before the committee. When ten among them refused to answer their congressional interrogators, they were promptly indicted, convicted, and imprisoned for contempt. Eventually, in a desperate tactic of self-protection, fifty of the nation's top film executives (all but two of them Jews) decided to preempt further congressional action by dismissing all leftist elements in their employ, whether cited, acquitted, or simply "exposed." So began the notorious Hollywood blacklist. It was destined to torment the film industry, and eventually the entire entertainment industry, for nearly a decade. Fearful of attack not only by Congress but by right-wing interest groups, the major film, stage, radio, and television studios denied employment to any actor, writer, or director under even the remotest shadow of hearsay suspicion. Employees at all levels lost jobs, careers, homes, and marriages, and in several instances their lives, through illness or suicide.

The House Un-American Activities investigations revealed no evidence of espionage, exposed very little effective Communist propaganda before, during, or since the war, and provided little meaningful information beyond the marginal sociology of a distraught generation of Depression-era Jews. It was a purgation of undesirables, virtually none of them hard-core Communists, only a few of them relapsed party members, but most of them simply naïve petition-signers on behalf of leftist front organizations. The campaign's single and exclusive achievement was to revive the disreputable image of Jewish radicalism.

The Rosenberg Trial and Its Aftermath

During these same postwar years, the tragedy of Depression-era communism reached a cruel denouement. In New York, a decade and a half earlier, Julius Rosenberg, his wife Ethel, and Ethel's brother David Greenglass—all products of impoverished immigrant Jewish families—had become committed Marxists and had participated in Communist Party meetings during the late 1930s and early 1940s. During the war, they sought ways to provide help for America's embattled Soviet ally. In that effort, Rosenberg, a civilian engineer working for the Army Signal Corps, found opportunity to copy and turn over to a Soviet consular official several items of classified military information. These included blueprints of radio tubes, proximity fuses, and a bombsight component. An even better opportunity developed for clandestine help when Greenglass, a skilled machine-tool maker then serving in the army, was assigned to the atomic bomb project in Los Alamos, New Mexico. At Rosenberg's request, Greenglass managed to acquire vital information on the bomb's fabrication, including specifications for the manufacture of "implosion lenses." Making sketches of these processes, Greenglass turned his drawings over to a special courier whom the Soviets had dispatched to New Mexico.

The courier was Harry Gold, also the son of Russian-Jewish immigrants, who had earned a modest livelihood as a chemist in a New Jersey soap factory. Lonely and embittered by the Depression and by his frequent encounters with antisemitism, Gold also had been drawn into Communist-front activities, and during the 1930s had delivered over to Soviet agents various patented formulas for industrial solvents. Gold took no money. He was doing something positive to fight injustice, he believed. Subsequently, in 1943, while exempted from military service due to chronic asthma, he embarked on espionage of a new and more ominous nature. His contacts included a man who had recently come to the United States from England, Klaus Fuchs, a German-born scientist. The contacts were limited and not especially productive, but Gold's single mission as a courier to New Mexico vindicated all his more pedestrian earlier efforts. Meeting Greenglass in Albuquerque, he took the sketches of the implosion lenses, returned with them to New York, and delivered them to Soviet agents. The war ended not long afterward. Gold left his New Jersey company to work in a Philadelphia hospital laboratory. Rosenberg and Greenglass opened a small machine shop together in New York. None engaged any longer in Communist activity, but the memory of their wartime contribution to "social justice" presumably would warm their hearts forever.

Four years later, in 1949, while deciphering a Soviet codebook, the FBI determined that Klaus Fuchs, the German-born scientist and secret Communist, had taken part in wartime espionage on behalf of the Soviet Union. Upon being grilled, Fuchs broke down and acknowledged his earlier activities, including his transmission of classified atomic information that had been provided to him by the courier, Harry Gold. In May 1950, the FBI visited and interrogated Gold. The latter similarly broke under interrogation and confessed his role in delivering Greenglass's "implosion" sketches to the Soviets. Soon afterward, the FBI swooped down on Greenglass. Apprised of Fuchs's and Gold's confessions, Greenglass also crumpled, revealing the entire story of his wartime collaboration with his sister and brother-in-law, Ethel and Julius Rosenberg. With this information, the FBI in June 1950 arrested the Rosenbergs. Six months later, the two were indicted, together with Greenglass and Morton Sobell, the latter a Rosenberg friend who allegedly had shared in the conspiracy plot, and Anatoli Yakovlev, the Soviet vice-consul in New York who had served as Gold's "control," but who no longer was in the United States. Harry Gold by then had been convicted and imprisoned and was serving mainly as a prosecution witness.

In March 1951, by the time the four defendants were placed on trial in the federal district court in Manhattan, the American public had been regaled for months with press accounts of a vast, sinister Communist, and apparently Jewish, conspiracy on behalf of the Soviet Union. The trial's Jewish atmosphere was further enhanced by its dramatis personae. Beyond the defendants themselves, the government prosecutor, Irving Saypol, and Saypol's assistant, Roy Cohn, as well as the trial judge, Irving Kaufman, were Jews, as was the Rosenbergs' defense attorney, Emanuel Bloch. Very possibly it was Jewish insecurity that accounted for Saypol and Cohn's furious tenacity of prosecution, demanding capital punishment for all the defendants, even for Ethel Rosenberg, whose guilt at worse was passive knowledge of the conspiracy; and Sobell, against whom evidence of conspiracy was thin. Apparently Judge Kaufman also felt obliged to overcompensate in his patriotism. When the jury returned guilty verdicts against all the defendants, Kaufman sentenced Sobell to thirty years' imprisonment, Greenglass (a cooperative witness) to fifteen years, and both Julius and Ethel Rosenberg to death. After numerous appeals and postponements, the Rosenbergs were executed in June 1953, leaving two young children behind.

Antisemitism played little role in the arrests and convictions. Yet public reaction to the highly visible Jewish component in both the earlier congressional inquiries and the later espionage prosecutions was a different matter. The frequency with which Jewish employees in government were purged as "security risks" could hardly be missed. In 1950, a consortium of rightist vigilante groups nearly succeeded in blocking the appointment of a distinguished public servant, Anna Rosenberg (no relation to the executed couple), as assistant secretary of defense. In 1953, Jews comprised a majority of the employees who were suspended as alleged security risks from the army radar laboratories in Fort Monmouth, New Jersey—and for reasons so flagrantly antisemitic that the Department of Defense felt compelled to rescind the suspensions. Also in the 1950s, right-wingers attacked the loyalty and significantly crippled the effectiveness of David Lilienthal, a Jew, chairman of the Atomic Energy Commission and former chairman of Franklin Roosevelt's Tennessee Valley Authority. By 1955, some five hundred Atomic Energy Commission scientists, more than half of them Jews, had been either dismissed on security grounds or denied clearance for promotion. Among the latter was J. Robert Oppenheimer, scientific director of the wartime Manhattan Project that had produced the atomic bomb.

In these same postwar decades, the miasma of suspicion extended beyond the government to nearly every sector of American life. University faculties came under attack, and some professors were hounded off campuses by accusations of communism or fellow-traveling. In the assaults, a prominent role was played by overt or thinly veiled antisemitic groups. Jewish defense agencies worked assiduously to expose these accusers but could do little in New York City, where charges for dismissal were brought against several hundred teachers for current or past membership in "listed" organizations. Most of the accused were Jews, children of immigrants who had been scarred in the Depression and whose "progressive" affiliations were largely toothless. Most of them were dismissed from their jobs.

In its pragmatic impact on American Jews, however, even this era of the "Great Fear" could not quite be equated with the eugenicist antisemitism of the teens and early 1920s, and assuredly not with the neofascist antisemitism of the Depression era. The bigotry of a Rankin and of other congressional nativists failed to evoke the resonance once achieved by a Henry Ford or a Father Coughlin (p. 517). The late 1940s and 1950s, after all, were years of unprecedented affluence for the United States. Even fear of communism sooner or later had to give way to the widening mood of American optimism. Moreover, the Jews themselves, in their emerging third-generation acculturation to American mores and ideals, no longer appeared as formidably alien as in earlier decades, or as reflexively susceptible to radical ideologies. What need had they any longer of leftist utopianism? In the 1930s and 1940s, Jews and their children had undergone the transition from proletarian to a precarious white-collar status. During the economic boom of the war, and even more dramatically by the mid- and late 1950s, they had all but completed their transition to the middle and even the upper middle class. It was inevitable that the political orientation of American Jews in their—increasingly moderate—liberalism would reflect that new social profile.

THE EAST EUROPEANS' PLACE IN THE SUN

It was a profile of upward mobility far surpassing that of other twentieth-century immigrant groups. Moving vigorously into business and professional life, the Jews were exceeded in earning power only by Episcopalian and Presbyterian Old Americans. By 1974, a *Fortune* magazine survey determined that the average Jewish family income was one-third higher than the national average. Despite all lingering constraints and prejudices, in a free and wealthy land this little minority had vaulted to first place among the nation's economic success stories.

The process was uneven. The same *Fortune* survey found that Jews still were extensively identified with the vocations they had made their own, that is, the garment and liquor industries, entertainment, "secondary material" products, and above all mass discount merchandising. Over the previous two decades, pioneering Jewish discount chains included such giants as E. J. Korvette, Best & Co., Interstate Stores, and Levitz Brothers Furniture Corporation, all of whose slashed prices generated profits matching or surpassing those of "conventional" department stores. The Jewish emphasis on consumer goods was evident as well in such fast-growing areas as automotive parts, electronic supplies, and most dramatically in cosmetics. In 1946, Joseph Lauder, the son of immigrant parents, formed a partnership with his wife, Esther, to market preparations developed by her chemist uncle, John Schatz. The enterprise subsequently grew into the Estée Lauder line of products, with sales worldwide eventually surpassing those of the older Jewish cosmetics empires of Helena Rubinstein, Max Factor, Revlon, Clairol, and Fabergé. Similarly, the toy industry, a $4 billion annual business by 2000, was dominated by the Jewish-founded companies Toys "R" Us, Mattel, Mego, Hasbro, and FAO Schwarz.

But if East European entrepreneurialism increasingly surpassed the great German-Jewish fortunes, it was real estate that provided the most spectacular margin of difference. After World War II, a new generation of Jewish developers became pacesetters in the nation's residential and commercial building boom. In New York, from the 1950s onward, the great majority of landlords were Jews. Among those emerging to national prominence was Harris Uris, a Russian immigrant. With his son Harold, Uris put up 13 percent of all the office buildings erected in Manhattan between 1945 and 1965. Julius Tishman and his son Louis developed much of the upper-crust elegance of Park Avenue, as well as a vast conglomerate of hotels and office buildings. William Zeckendorff, Benjamin Swig, Charles E. Smith, Joseph and Harvey Meyerhoff developed some of the great commercial areas in other cities, from Washington to San Francisco.

Yet it was William Levitt, more than any of his peers, who transformed the social landscape of American home ownership. During the acute housing shortage of the immediate postwar years, Levitt borrowed funds to purchase 4,000 acres of potato-farm land on Long Island. There, during the late 1940s and early 1950s, he used cut-rate, mass-production techniques to build 17,000 single-family homes, which he proceeded to sell—to military veterans only— at prices young families could afford. On this same tract, Levitt simultaneously laid out six "village greens," twenty-four playing fields, and nine community swimming pools, as well as ample sites for schools and houses of worship. Ultimately, "Levittown" became a clean and pleasant community of 82,000 persons. This and other Levitt development projects in other parts of the country became models for comparable developments that eventually put affordable housing within the range of lower-middle-income Americans.

Meanwhile, if the Jews' role in mass entertainment continued preeminent on Broadway and in Hollywood, it soon acquired a new and potentially wider dimension in radio and television. The great networks were largely their handiwork. Samuel Paley climbed out of Chicago's Maxwell Street ghetto to become a multimillionaire cigar manufacturer. His son William became advertising director of the family company. In 1928, William Paley invested $50 a week to sponsor a half-hour program on an early Philadelphia radio station. The expenditure was well placed. Cigar sales climbed impressively. Paley gave closer attention to the potential of radio. That same year, purchasing a struggling network of sixteen radio stations for a half-million dollars, he became the youthful president of the Columbia Broadcasting System. In ensuing years, Paley attracted affiliates by offering them an initial series of free programs. The gamble paid off, and by 1937 CBS member stations had climbed to 114, and annual earnings to $279 million. After World War II, the CBS television network continued to grow and by the end of the century included 500 stations and generated some $1 billion in annual profits. From the 1950s on, the fledgling American Broadcasting Company under the chairmanship of its founder, Leonard Goldenson, similarly developed into one of the great media empires (and eventually would be merged with the Disney Corporation, under the direction of another Jewish dynamo, Michael Eisner).

Yet the decisive role of broadcasting in American life, and later of television, ultimately owed most to David Sarnoff. Sarnoff's career was a classic immigrant success story. He was brought to America in 1900 as a child. Reared in Lower East Side poverty, the youngster dropped out of school before the ninth grade. After a stint as a newsboy, he was taken on as a messenger for the Commercial Cable Company. Between delivering messages, young Sarnoff took courses in telegraphy at the Jewish Educational Alliance (p. 219), and at age fifteen became an operator for the American branch of the Marconi

Wireless Telegraph Company. Assigned to the remote Marconi station on Nantucket Island, he employed his spare time devouring manuals on mathematics, science, and telecommunications. Three years later, at age eighteen, Sarnoff was appointed chief wireless operator of the Marconi organization. It was in 1912 that his station on the roof of New York's Wanamaker Department Store picked up the faint signals of the sinking *Titanic*. The episode vastly increased interest in radio.

By then, the young Sarnoff was refining an inspiration. Why not advance radio from an audience of one receiver to an audience of thousands? The technology might even transmit music. From the outset, Sarnoff also discerned the revenue to be earned from the sale of "radio music boxes," as well as from advertising for sponsors of broadcasts. By 1917, as director now of Marconi's commercial department, Sarnoff devoted all his energies to the transformation of radio into a mass medium. A year later, Marconi and General Electric collaborated to establish an independent American company, the Radio Corporation of America. With Sarnoff as its chairman, RCA during the 1920s acquired some 2,000 patents, covering all the basic elements of an integrated radio-transmission system. Thus, in 1926, dominating the early broadcasting field, RCA launched its own broadcasting network, the National Broadcasting Company. At the same time, it embarked on the manufacture of its own "radio music boxes." Soon output reached 75,000 units a month. No product in American history, not even the automobile, achieved sales velocity so quickly.

Sarnoff's imagination never rested. By 1933, upon moving his entire operation into the RCA Building in Rockefeller Center, he was already thinking ahead to television. As early as 1929, he had hired Vladimir Zworykin, an immigrant Jewish scientist who developed the cathode-ray tube for the television receiver. Throughout the Depression, Sarnoff unstintingly bankrolled Zworykin's research, never doubting that someday television would become RCA's lifeblood. By 1939, the basic technology was available. But soon afterward, war intervened, and RCA was converted almost exclusively to military production. Indeed, in 1944, Sarnoff, at the age of fifty-four, volunteered his services to the military. Commissioned a brigadier general and appointed Eisenhower's chief of communications, he rapidly organized all radio communications for the Western Front.

Finally, in the postwar era, Sarnoff was free to pour his company's resources into television. Together with the technology, the stations were also in place. The existing network had only to convert from radio to television transmission. Moreover, in 1945, the first RCA television sets began rolling off the company's production lines. A year later, 250,000 sets were marketed, and sales tripled and quadrupled throughout the 1950s and 1960s. By the 1960s, Sarnoff was possibly the most admired man in American industry, the recipient of innumerable awards and honorary degrees. As much as Henry Ford, Thomas Edison, Carl Laemmle, or Louis B. Mayer, he had revolutionized the quality of American life.

THE GATES OF HIGHER CULTURE

Would the children and grandchildren of East European immigrants have opportunity to make their mark beyond the American business world? With an academic provenance not yet comparable to that of the distinguished Central European refugees of the 1930s, it was uncertain that their role could extend beyond the realm of popular culture, beyond Tin Pan Alley, Broadway, and Hollywood. But the outlook for their educational and professional opportunities was improving. By the late 1940s, in the aftermath of the crusade against Nazism, President Harry Truman's commissions on higher education, civil rights, and employment practices, and his initiative in deseg-regating the armed forces, responded to a general postwar restiveness at the lingering inequities in American society.

It was perhaps inevitable that change would also extend to higher educa-tion. Prodded by the American Jewish Congress and the Anti-Defamation League, the New York City Council in 1948 voted to deny municipal funds and tax-exempt status to local colleges and universities that discriminated. New York's state legislature passed an identical bill, then New Jersey's, then state legislatures in other parts of the country. Economic factors also played a key role in this upsurge of public conscience. With the G.I. Bill—the federal subsidy of college tuition for military veterans—encouraging a vast new influx of students into the nation's universities, the demand for instructors opened up new teaching slots for Jews. So did the exploration of space in competition with the Soviet Union. And so did the Jews' own predominantly middle-class status, with their ability to pay the price for the best education America had to offer. In 1947, 62 percent of college-age Jews were enrolled in college. For non-Jews, the figure was 27 percent. By 1973, the respective pro-portions were 80 to 40.

Almost imperceptibly, restrictions began easing at the more eminent pri-vate institutions, at Ivy League universities and Seven Sisters colleges. At the same time, no longer harassed for economic survival, young Jews often exploited their quality education to bypass their fathers' businesses for more intellectually stimulating professional careers. In the 1960s and 1970s, they moved in vastly disproportionate numbers to graduate training. By 1973, a B'nai B'rith survey found that 58 percent of Jewish graduate students were enrolled in the nation's ten most respected graduate schools, precisely double the ratio for non-Jewish graduate students. By then, too, a significant propor-tion of American professors also were Jews. The same B'nai B'rith survey revealed that Jews comprised one-tenth of the faculty members in university graduate schools, and one-sixth of the faculties at major research-oriented institutions. As in their student days, they continued to be overachievers. In 1985, the quarterly *Public Interest* cited thirty-two Jews among its list of the nation's seventy most eminent intellectuals. Their accumulation of publications, scholarly innovations, and scientific discoveries, and the acknowledgment of their achievements with titles, honorary degrees, and prizes (among these, 38 of the 118 Nobel Prizes awarded to Americans by 1989) already surpassed the record of their Central European predecessors.

In law and medicine, as in academia, the changing social climate similarly began to make its impact. As late as 1946, the "Jewish quota" at law schools averaged 11 percent. But in ensuing years, these restrictions rapidly eased and then all but disappeared. By 1960, an analysis of four law schools (two Ivy League, one Catholic, and one New York metropolitan) revealed an average Jewish ratio of 47 percent. Employment opportunities matched this growth. In the postwar period, substantial numbers of Jewish former New Deal and other Washington attorneys were carving out new careers as lawyers for corporations with major interests before the government. By the 1960s, it was a rare big-city firm that did not include at least one Jewish senior partner. In 1966, the American Bar Association elected its first Jewish president. That year, too, Jews were deans of twelve law schools and sat at all echelons of state and federal judiciaries, including the supreme courts of eleven states. By the end of the century, thirty-four law school deans and two United States Supreme Court justices were Jews.

Acceptance in the medical profession became an even more telling litmus test of Jewish vocational advancement. Well into the 1940s, the minuscule quotient of Jews who secured admission to medical schools found even more limited hospital opportunities upon receiving their degrees. It was the shortage of hospital appointments in turn that accounted for the proliferation of Jewish-sponsored hospitals. By 1972, seventy-three of these Jewish hospitals were functioning in thirty cities (the number would increase to eighty-one by the end of the century). Yet, by then, too, medical schools, like law schools, were relaxing their Jewish quotas. The ratio of Jewish students moved slowly upward, from 18 percent in 1956, to 25 percent in 1978, to 39 percent in 1986—a figure that oscillated only slightly in ensuing years. The increase was matched almost precisely in appointments to leading hospitals and to medical school faculties. The impact of this progress was notable in other ways. By 1997, of sixty-one Americans who had been awarded Nobel Prizes in the medical sciences, twenty-two were Jews.

These were proportions that did not deviate significantly from the emerging norm of Jewish professionalism altogether. Entries in the 1988 edition of *Who's Who in America* suggested that Jews were "overrepresented" by 308 percent in the medical sciences (one of every five American doctors), 299 percent in dentistry, 231 in nonmedical sciences, and 263 in law. Like their Central European predecessors in the early decades of the twentieth century, the third and fourth generations of American Jews craved a soul-satisfying blend of economic security and intellectual creativity. By the turn of the century, they had achieved it.

THE SOCIOLOGY OF ARRIVISM

The demographic patterns of American Jews kept pace with their upward mobility. The post–World War II era altogether was one of movement, particularly from city to suburb. Living in or near the nation's ten largest cities, Jews fully shared in that migration. The development was not without its obstacles, however. In prewar New York, Jews were barred from access to at least a third of Manhattan's most desirable new cooperatives and condominiums (p. 385). In the postwar suburbs of New York and other large cities, barriers were even more ironclad. Normally, these took the form of restrictive covenants, that is, commitments by landowners and realtors to sell or lease their property exclusively to white Christians.

Most of the new Jewish suburbanites were not thinking of prestige value. They were simply young marrieds, often war veterans, seeking access to decent homes for themselves and their children. In the effort to eradicate these restrictions, the American Jewish Congress and the Anti-Defamation League counted on public and government support. It was a realistic expectation. Since the war, discrimination in housing came to be regarded as unacceptable a social anachronism as discrimination in employment and education. As far back as 1939, New York State included in its public-housing law a prohibition against discrimination. Now, in 1947, New York City moved further, barring discrimination in private housing. Pittsburgh followed with a similar law in 1958. Colorado passed a statewide fair-housing law in 1959; other states followed, until the last barriers for home purchase eventually were breached. In this fashion, the gates were opened for a stream of Jewish movement out of second-settlement neighborhoods into the suburbs of the nation's major cities, with all their environmental amenities.

Yet, as Jews became more widely dispersed from their parents' immigrant neighborhoods, they sensed that it was no longer possible to maintain their religious and cultural identification on the basis simply of ethnic cohesion. A more active effort was required. Like their gentile neighbors, who rushed to join community churches, the new Jewish suburbanites wasted little time in registering for local synagogues. Their reasons were less pietistic than sociological. Whatever the degree of their own religious commitment, Jewish parents wanted their children to marry "among their own," and only a sense of

Jewish identity would assure that time-honored endogamy. Although synagogue schools were available for the youngsters, the parents themselves would first have to belong to synagogues. By no coincidence, then, the postwar boom decades were also the great era of synagogue-building. Nearly a thousand new synagogues and temples were erected between 1945 and the end of the century, each vying with the next in size and all-purpose functionalism, each serving as a talisman of "respectable" American religiosity.

In the decades before World War II, it was Reform Judaism that had emerged as the aesthetic and ideological paradigm of that respectability (p. 391). For essentially the same reasons, Reform maintained its steady growth well into the postwar era. Thus, by 1971, the number of Reform congregations had reached 698, encompassing over 1 million dues-paying members (the figures would reach 900 congregations, and 1.5 million members by the end of the century). By the latter 1900s, too, the great majority of these members were of East European background. Intent upon preserving at least the spirit of their parents' traditionalism, most of the second- and third-generation Reformers now ensured that increased emphasis was placed on afternoon religious-school classes for their children, on Hebrew both in the school and in the liturgy, together with extensive references to the State of Israel. But even with these genuflections to "ethnic" Judaism, Reform's constituency remained the most acculturated, socially fashionable, and modernized stratum within American Jewry. Its Union of American Hebrew Congregations developed efficient, well-staffed departments for religious education, men's clubs, sisterhoods, and youth work. As always, the Union took a vigorous stand on American economic and social issues.

In these same postwar years, however, Reform gradually was matched and briefly surpassed in its membership growth by the Conservative movement. In 1948, a mere 210 Conservative congregations existed in the United States. In 1971, the number had burgeoned to 832. Indeed, a national survey that year estimated that 40 percent of American Jews regarded themselves Conservative; 30 percent, Reform; 10 percent, Orthodox. For suburban Jews in the process of abandoning old Orthodox ties, Conservatism evidently provided a more convenient framework for sustaining a mildly observant, sentimental ethnicity. Although Reform innovations such as mixed seating and organ music were accepted now in Conservative synagogues, these were balanced by a more conscientious preservation of older traditions, including skullcaps, prayer shawls, and a predominantly Hebrew liturgy. Much earlier than the Reformers, too, Conservative rabbis sensed that the synagogue would function as it had in Eastern Europe, as a kind of "ethnic church," an omnium-gatherum for a wide variety of Jewish communal activities—religious, educational, social. There was little pretense to prophetic universalism among the Conservatives, or, for that matter, to the liberal causes dear to Reform

Judaism. From beginning to end, the Conservatives' emphasis was upon Jewish peoplehood in all its manifestations.

By contrast, Orthodoxy, a way of life that once claimed the allegiance of the largest numbers of immigrants, appeared to be eroding rapidly in its financial and numerical strength. Over the years, second- and third-generation Jews almost instinctively departed their parents' rather decrepit little *shuls* for Conservative or Reform congregations. Even where they managed to survive, Orthodox synagogues possessed few of the ancillary groups, the men's clubs and sisterhoods, the social service and educational programs, of their more affluent counterparts. Even the establishment of a theological seminary in 1897, the Isaac Elhanan Spector Yeshiva, together with a dozen, smaller Orthodox rabbinical yeshivot, did little to dissipate the stereotype of Orthodoxy as out of date. A century later, not more than six hundred of Elhanan Spector's approximately one thousand graduates held permanent pulpits.

Nevertheless, a kind of "underground" version of Orthodoxy was developing in the post–World War II years that almost imperceptibly began to develop a powerful gravitational field of its own. Between 1948 and 1952, some 100,000 European-Jewish survivors immigrated to the United States, a majority of them under the provisions of the Displaced Persons acts of 1948 and 1950. Thousands more would arrive in the 1960s, following the Kennedy administration's further liberalization of immigration quotas. Virtually all the newcomers were East European, and nearly half of these were members of Hasidic sects. Well into the twentieth century, Hasidism's leadership had scorned the United States as a spiritual wasteland and had adjured their followers not to go there. But Hitler would have something to say about Jewish migration patterns. In the initial decades following the Holocaust, a demographic basis for Hasidic revival apparently no longer existed in Europe. Neither, in the late 1940s and 1950s, did Israel appear to be a solution. Dominated in its early decades by secular socialists, the Zionist republic was known to impose on its citizens the obligation of hard work and military service. The principal remaining destination, therefore, was the United States.

Among the sudden influx of Hasidic immigrants, the most influential was Joseph Isaac Schneerson, the "Lubavitcher *rebbe*." Scion of a Ukrainian dynasty that as late as 1939 "governed" some 150,000 adherents worldwide, Rabbi Schneerson was stranded in Poland at the time of the Nazi invasion. Fleeing to the Soviet sector in 1941, he was brought to the United States after the war under the privileged "clergyman" category. Upon setting up headquarters in the Crown Heights section of Brooklyn, the rebbe organized a yeshiva and dispatched missionaries throughout the world to win Jews back to the "true" faith. Upon his death in 1951, he was succeeded by his rabbinical son-in-law, Menahem Mendel, who followed Hasidic tradition by adopting the dynastic name Schneerson. The new rebbe proved to be even more dynamic than the old. Without delay, he launched into the organization of an international "Habad" movement, a network of Lubavitcher yeshivot, schools, and youth activities, even a college organization—all dedicated to the precepts of Hasidic ultra-Orthodoxy. Above all, the rebbe addressed himself to those elements of the intellectual elite whose emotional exhaustion or disillusionment, he sensed, rendered them fair game for fundamentalism. By the opening of the twenty-first century, the Lubavitcher movement in the United States may have encompassed as many as 80,000 adherents.

Additional Hasidic sects developed enclaves of their own throughout Brooklyn and Sullivan County (the Catskill region), among them conventicles from Satmar, Belz, Tzelem, Stelin, Papa—all deriving their names and identifying their dynastic rebbes from their Hungarian, Ukrainian, or Polish towns of origin. Ultimately, by immigration and unrestrained reproduction, the Hasidic subcommunities comprised between 100,000 and 125,000 members. To ensure that their children continued on the true path, the sects placed overwhelming emphasis upon their own version of parochial education. They maintained fifty or sixty little yeshivot to train their own rabbis and teachers, then channeled the rest—the bulk—of their resources into primary and secondary schools. Most of these latter were academically marginal. In perhaps two-thirds of them, the principal language of instruction was Yiddish, and nearly half their curriculum was devoted to Bible, Talmud, Hebrew, and other Jewish studies. General studies, conducted in English to meet state educational regulations, were taught by Hasidic teachers of often suspect pedagogic qualifications.

Nevertheless, it was the Hasidic immigration that propelled the day-school movement into the forefront of postwar Jewish education. Once the Hasidim achieved the major breakthrough for the movement in Brooklyn and other large communities, Orthodox groups of more established vintage moved swiftly to exploit the new possibilities. By the end of the century, over 90 percent of Jewish day schools throughout Greater New York were Orthodox-sponsored. In no sense were these institutions to be equated with the intensely parochial Hasidic schools. Together with a solid nucleus of Jewish studies, they offered secular courses that met state-approved standards. In growing numbers, even non-Orthodox families then began enrolling their children. To compete with this Orthodox growth, the Conservative movement then set about establishing its own network of Solomon Schechter day schools, institutions that provided a quality of instruction often surpassing that of the best public schools.

By the late twentieth century, it appeared likely that at least a substantial minority of families registering their children in Jewish day schools were of non-Orthodox background, or possibly even of non-Conservative background. Their choice was dictated less by Jewish theology than by American sociology. Day schools offered a cosmetic method of evading racial integration in the public school system.

A REINVIGORATION OF ETHNICITY

For the Jewish population at large, ethnicity far more than religiosity had long since established itself as the benchmark of communal identity. The entire socialist-Yiddishist culture of the Lower East Side had emerged out of that fact of life, after all, and so had modern Zionism. The great majority of American Jews lived by that identity. Unconsciously, perhaps, they found themselves sharing in the "reconstruction" of Judaism as pioneered by an eminent Jewish philosopher, Mordecai Kaplan. During the early post–World War II years, Kaplan, a Conservative rabbi, had refined a theory of "Reconstructionism," arguing that Judaism was less a theology or even a legal system than a "civilization." Within the ambit of that civilization, every variety of Jewish creativity was to be regarded as a legitimate expression of the Jewish spirit. Without acknowledging the fact, second- and third-generation American Jews evidently had been "Reconstructionists" most of their lives.

Never as much so as in the latter twentieth century, when a virtual explosion of Jewish institutional growth was matched by an effulgence of Jewish-studies courses in every major American university. The preeminent source of that renewed vitality was the birth of Israel. In its sheer emotional impact, the Jewish state profoundly energized American-Jewish communal life. Indeed, a prefiguration of that new vitality was the appearance of a coruscating new group of second-generation Jewish intellectuals. In the tradition of Franz Rosenzweig's Lehrhaus students in Weimar Germany (p. 468), prominent figures among the New York Jewish intellectual elite—among them Irving Howe, Alfred Kazin, Nathan Glazer, Milton Himmelfarb—felt impelled to explore the richness of Jewish literature and tradition and to write extensively on those themes.

Several interesting postwar enterprises helped structure this revived "community of memory." One was a renowned Jewish publishing house, the Schocken Verlag. Established originally in Weimar Germany by Zalman Schocken, the firm produced exquisitely printed volumes in Hebrew and German, among them works by S. Y. Agnon, Martin Buber, Franz Rosenzweig, Franz Kafka, and Max Brod. In 1946, Schocken's son Theodor opened Schocken Books in New York to provide translations of German-Jewish authors for American readers. It was through the Schocken company that Kafka's works first reached the United States (and Hannah Arendt received her first employment in New York as a Schocken editor).

An influential magazine similarly helped revive and focus the "community of memory." In 1945, the American Jewish Committee sponsored publication of *Commentary*, a monthly journal of Jewish life, and appointed Elliott Cohen its editor. Cohen had a clear vision of his editorial role. It was to prove that Jewish identity could be intellectually respectable enough to win over not only educated Jews, but Jewish intellectuals who already had won distinction in the American cultural scene at large. A number of these figures—most notable among them Irving Howe, Alfred Kazin, and Lionel Trilling—were induced to contribute articles on both Jewish and general issues. With these vibrant resources in hand, Cohen was able within three years to develop an important cultural vehicle, dealing with sociological discussions, political analysis, literary criticism, even fiction that touched directly or indirectly on all issues affecting American Jews. During the ensuing decades, *Commentary* functioned as a vital halfway house in which a former "lost generation" of talented Jews could negotiate their return to Jewish identity and creativity.

Possibly more dramatic evidence yet of the Jews' emergence as a pluralistic force on the cultural scene was their success in founding a nonsectarian university. The venture drew from respectable American precedents. Of the approximately two hundred colleges and universities established in the United States before Horace Mann began his nineteenth-century crusade for public education, all but twenty-five were denominationally sponsored, although nonsectarian in curriculum and student body. Yet, among the nation's major religious communities, the Jews alone had failed to produce a nonsectarian college (Yeshiva University, a later addendum to the Elhanan Spector seminary, was established under Orthodox auspices originally for Orthodox students). There was a certain irony in the lacuna. Since World War I, Jews had attended universities in far greater proportion to their numbers than had any other denomination. Nor were they ungrateful for the education they and their children had received. Their philanthropists had contributed generously, even munificently, to existing institutions. Nevertheless, throughout the first half of the twentieth century, American Jews had been inundated by other emergency pressures, from mass East European immigration, to the rescue of Jews from Nazi-dominated Europe, to the rescue of Holocaust survivors and the establishment of the State of Israel.

In 1948, however, a group of Boston and New York Jewish businessmen decided to wait no longer in embarking on a university venture. The president of a defunct medical school in Waltham, Massachusetts, had offered them his ninety-acre campus and its few aging buildings, if they could maintain a viable educational program. Taking over the campus, they promptly named the incipient institution Brandeis University, in honor of Louis Brandeis, American Jewry's most revered icon, and offered the school's presidency to Abram L. Sachar. A historian and educator, a former national director of the Hillel Foundation, the forty-nine-year-old Sachar hurled himself into the

Brandeis challenge with characteristic second-generation energy. To achieve instant parity with older, established universities, he set about accumulating the nucleus of a distinguished faculty within the school's first year of operation. Brandeis's endowment was still modest. Yet, on faith and borrowed funds, the trustees offered blue-chip salaries for scholars of national reputation. The gamble paid off. Brandeis won full academic accreditation in 1954, and that same year began opening its graduate schools.

In 1954, too, American Jews celebrated their people's three-century presence in the New World. The tercentenary commemoration offered a logical moment for reappraisal and self-congratulation. Only 5.5 million in number, comprising less than 3 percent of the American population, Jews could be found in every state in the Union. Even that early, they had achieved an average income significantly above the national median. Their role in the nation's cultural life, as in its economic and philanthropic life, already was beginning to loom far out of proportion to their modest demographic base. More notably, the largest numbers of American Jews had clung fast to their ancestral heritage. Their federations had taken care of their own. Voluntarily uprooted from neighborhoods of first and second settlement, they were embarked upon the establishment of a formidable new series of collective ventures, of community centers, seminaries, religious and cultural societies, and now universities. The largest and most powerful community in Jewish history, American Jews in the aftermath of World War II no longer were engrossed in crises of economic security or political toleration. Rather, their preoccupation from mid-century on was the encouragement and apparently limitless enhancement of group creativity.

XXXV

The Jewish State and World Jewry

ISRAELI INDEPENDENCE AND DIASPORA PRIDE

On the evening of May 14, 1948, the Jews of New York reacted to Israel's declaration of independence with a jubilation approaching euphoria. When the Israeli flag was unfurled outside the Jewish Agency building, throngs of Jewish youngsters danced the hora outside, and traffic on East Sixty-eighth Street came to a halt. The next day, the American office of Magen David Adom (the Israeli equivalent of the Red Cross) opened a blood bank for Israel on West Thirty-ninth Street that was soon packed with donors. The "official" celebration, sponsored by the American Zionist Emergency Council, took place at Madison Square Garden on May 16. An estimated 75,000 people had to be turned away. Similar rallies were held in other cities, including one that packed 25,000 people into the Hollywood Bowl. Altogether, throughout the Western Diaspora, the birth of Israel produced an explosion of relief, pride, and joy unprecedented in modern Jewish history. It had been prefigured by similar demonstrations in November 1917, when the Balfour Declaration was issued. But the intensity of the Jewish reaction in 1948 struck gentile observers as something unreal, surreal, inhuman. No people had waited longer, or had suffered more, for this ultimate dignity. It was the apotheosis of the Jewish experience.

American Jews put their money where their hearts were. Even before Israel was born, $8 million was discreetly raised for the secret purchase of arms-manufacturing machinery, much of the equipment to be dismantled and its parts shipped to Palestine Jewry as "irrigation components." Jewish veterans of the United States Air Force ferried some fifty surplus military airplanes to Israel via secret Caribbean bases. Altogether, 1,750 American Jews participated in Israel's war of independence as members of the Mahal, an international brigade of volunteers from Jewish communities throughout the West. The American record doubtless was less impressive when measured against the 700 volunteers provided by the tiny Jewish community of South Africa, the 450 provided by Canada, including the Mahal army commander, General

Ben Dunkelman, the 500 each provided by Britain and France. Yet the role of the Americans proved decisive in Israel's fledgling air force, to which they dispatched some 300 pilots. The Mahal's best-known volunteer, moreover, was Colonel David Marcus, a West Point graduate and war veteran who arrived in Palestine to assume a key planning role in the Israeli general staff (and later to be killed in the battle for the Jerusalem Road).

Yet, in the end, the most dependable of American Jewry's contributions was the well-tested one of financial support. The Holocaust had laid the emotional basis for the unprecedented United Jewish Appeal campaigns of the postwar era. During the climactic struggle for Israel in 1947–48, the campaign raised $205 million, four times more than the Red Cross collected that year from the entirety of the American population. The figure was supplemented by $11 million raised by Hadassah and other Zionist welfare and educational funds. The fund-raising effort charted a new course in American-Jewish sociology. For the Jews of the United States, together with those of other Western Jewish communities, the success of their Israeli kinsmen in achieving and defending their homeland generated an upsurge of self-esteem too profound to be described as vicarious. Each passing year, commitment to Israel's growth and welfare emerged as the uncontested emotional and ideological focus of Jewish communal life.

The renaissance of Diaspora pride was manifested even in the most broadly acculturated of Western Jewish communities. Zionism had grown only slowly in France, whose Jewish leadership traditionally had placed heavy emphasis on "Gallic" values, and the Fédération Sioniste had not become entirely respectable among the nation's 300,000 Jews (in 1948) until the actual birth of Israel. But in England, Zionism had been a much admired movement ever since Chaim Weizmann and his colleagues negotiated the Balfour Declaration in 1917. Twelve years later, in 1929, the Board of Deputies of British Jewry officially affiliated itself with the newly formed Jewish Agency for Palestine. In future years, in addition to military volunteers in Israel's war of independence, Anglo-Jewry provided migrants to the Jewish state. Within a decade after 1948, the immigration of British Jews raised Israel's Anglo-Jewish population to 10,000, and they were joined by an additional 3,000 kinsmen after the Six-Day War of 1967. Indeed, British Jews established three of Israel's most respected kibbutzim, and eleven other agricultural settlements become predominantly "Anglo-Saxon" in membership. Altogether, British Jews played a distinguished role in Israel's business and professional life, in its public service, government, and Jewish Agency offices.

Their commitment was matched and even eclipsed by the 118,000 Jews of South Africa. No Diaspora community anywhere was quite as intensely Israel-oriented as this demographically modest population (p. 667). In the years before 1948, South African Jewry's contributions to Zionist funds were second only to American Jewry's, and proportionately three times larger. By 1967, nearly 4,000 South Africans had settled in Israel, and ten years after that the number had grown to 6,000—again, the highest proportion of immigrants from the Western Diaspora. Approximately 1,000 settled on the land, while another thousand resumed their medical and dental practices in Israel, or served in the nation's diplomatic and military services. Two South Africans were members of the cabinet, another was a member of the Knesset, two were mayors. Most South Africans were businessmen, however, and a number of Israel's important commercial and industrial enterprises owed their growth to South African capital and executive leadership, among them El Al, the national airline. Perhaps the most visually impressive South African contribution was the Mediterranean port city of Ashkelon, founded in 1953 by private South African investors in partnership with the South African Zionist Federation and the Israeli government. Within ten years, the results of this joint enterprise were visible in a handsome garden city of 15,000, one of the showpieces of Israel (it has since tripled in size).

Yet it was the settlement of American and Canadian Jews in Palestine that dated back farthest of any Western Jewry. As early as 1900, approximately 1,000 North Americans had arrived in Palestine. With few exceptions, these newcomers were European-born, many of them Orthodox pietists, others fugitives from tsarist persecution who regarded America essentially as a way station to Zion. During World War I, some 2,000 Americans and Canadians served in the Jewish Legion, and a third of these remained in Palestine during the British mandate to become citrus farmers, pioneers of the cooperative movement, as well as founders of the towns of Ra'anana and Herzlia. Approximately 3,000 American small businessmen also joined their numbers during the mid-1920s, and nearly a thousand others in the years before World War II. In the course of the illegal refugee immigration between 1945 and 1948, American and Canadian Jews manned ten refugee vessels and helped transport some 40 percent of the displaced persons to Palestine—well before the contribution of North American Jews to Israel's 1948 war of independence.

Yet, the principal growth of American and Canadian immigration awaited the "normalcy" of statehood. Afterward, between 1948 and 1967, the population of North Americans in Israel grew to 14,000. Among them were founding members of sixteen kibbutz settlements, while hundreds of others joined existing collective and cooperative agricultural communities. As in the case of other "Anglo-Saxons," however, the majority of Americans and Canadians resumed their former middle-class vocations, in business and the professions. Nearly a thousand others found employment in public institutions, in the Jewish Agency, the Jewish National Fund, the United Jewish Appeal and Israel Bonds offices, as well as in the government. One was elected mayor of

Jerusalem, two were appointed justices of the supreme court, and two became prime ministers.

ISRAEL REFORMULATES ZIONISM

It was the view of David Ben-Gurion and many of his colleagues that these settlers in Israel were the only Jews who had the right henceforth to call themselves Zionists. Shortly after the establishment of statehood, the issue of Zionism's role erupted into prolonged debate between the Israeli government and the American Zionist leadership. One source of the quarrel lay in a characteristic Israeli attitude toward the Diaspora. It seemed to Ben-Gurion, as to many who had fought in his nation's war of independence, that the overseas community was inhabited by an inferior breed of half-Jews, who preferred the comforts of life abroad to the challenges and dangers of life in Israel. For the prime minister, the very term "Zionist," unattached to actual settlement in the Jewish state, evinced a kind of officious, outdated windiness. In his eyes, Jewish life overseas was bankrupt. Moreover, in his rejection of the notion that Zionism could be limited simply to ideology, Ben-Gurion revealed another, more practical and political consideration. "There is a fundamental difference between Israeli Jewry and Diaspora Jewry," he insisted. "We are also an independent factor in international life. We appear like any other free people at the United Nations. We meet with representatives of large and small states on an equal footing. We don't need shtadlanim any more."

The prime minister's trepidation lest Zionist leaders overseas presume to speak for Israel was by no means paranoia. To be sure, there was mutual recognition that world Jewry would continue to bear a heavy financial burden for the ingathering of Jews from throughout the world. It was actually at Ben-Gurion's insistence that the Zionist Organization, in August 1948, agreed that the Jewish Agency should be maintained as a body independent of the government and continue its historic mission of transporting and settling refugees; for this was a humanitarian task legitimately to be borne by Diaspora Jewry no less than by the beleaguered citizenry of Israel. Indeed, further to strengthen that mission, Ben-Gurion in 1952 went so far as to approve Knesset legislation, entitled "Law on the Status of the Zionist Organization–Jewish Agency," which specifically invested both these organizations with the task of rescue and relief.

But the notion of allocating wider-ranging public, quasi-governmental, or quasi-diplomatic responsibilities to the Jewish Agency, and thereby to its parent body, the Zionist Organization, with the latter's heavily weighted American membership, was a very different issue. Well after 1948, the Zionist Organization continued to function on the basis of its traditional international party structure. In doing so, it prolonged the anachronism of biennial congresses, their delegates elected by parties—Labor Zionist, General Zionist, Zionist Religious, and others—most of whose constituents lived in the United States, Britain, South Africa, and elsewhere. In 1949, Nahum Goldmann, Abba Hillel Silver, Emanuel Neumann, and other veteran leaders of American Zionism warned that separation of the Jewish Agency from Israel's public-policy issues threatened the very survival of Zionism in the Diaspora. The Agency must have some role in determining Israeli public policy. Ben-Gurion was not having it. With the support of his numerous American-Jewish admirers, he forced the resignation of Silver and the latter's colleagues on the Jewish Agency Executive. The prime minister, who had labored all his life to achieve a sovereign Jewish state, was implacable in his unwillingness to share governmental functions even with the most devoted veteran Zionists living abroad.

A RELATIONSHIP BECOMES A PARTNERSHIP

Yet even as Ben-Gurion sternly reformulated Israel's relationship to world Jewry, the Jews of the Diaspora, particularly those of the United States, found it necessary to redefine their own attitude to Israel. In fact, a small number of American-Jewish communal and intellectual spokesmen were prepared to accept Ben-Gurion's dire prognosis of a threatened Jewish future outside Israel, and to affirm that the one and single hope for creative Jewish survival lay in immigration to the Jewish state. At the other end of the ideological spectrum, an even smaller minority of American Jews rejected not merely the obligation of departure for Israel but the legitimacy of Jewish statehood altogether. This anti-Zionist faction was identified essentially with the American Council for Judaism. A numerically modest group comprised essentially of ultra-Reform Jews, the council since the early 1940s had tenaciously rejected the nationalist component in Jewish history and religion. Several decades later, in the 1960s and 1970s, their numbers were augmented by an articulate group of Jewish university students, members of the "New Left," a movement that in its doctrinaire anti-imperialism regarded Israel's very existence as an affront to the "Third World."

Nevertheless, anti-Zionists and New Leftists hardly were typical of those who expressed the most penetrating criticism of Diaspora Jewry's overwhelming Zionist bias. Rather, there were others, sensitive Jewish intellectuals, themselves fully committed to Israel's well-being, who questioned whether a political state could appropriately fulfill its emergent role as the touchstone of Western Jewish communal life. Among these critics, the American rabbis Jakob Petuchowski and Jacob Agus, both eminent scholars of Judaism, rejected the proposition that Western Jews were living in a featureless limbo of exile. They even found suspect the classical Zionist argument that a Jewish state would somehow normalize Jewish life in the Diaspora. In the United States, they argued, Israel's existence actually disrupted Jewish life. It forced American Jews to be nationalists about Israel, when Jews traditionally distrusted nationalism or flag-waving of any kind. It raised troubling public concerns about Jewish dual loyalties by mobilizing Jewish political lobbying on behalf of Israel. Anyway, these critics asked, was Israel performing a "mission" for Diaspora Jewry? Was it fulfilling the prophetic role of social justice in its own country? How did the Israelis treat their own minorities, most specifically their own residual Arab population? To what extent did ethics and morality influence Israel's political and business life? Its religious establishment? The answers were not always encouraging.

But if the rise of Israel produced troubling reservations among important segments of Western Jewish life, particularly in the affluent and pluralistic United States, these appeared to be dissipated in the apocalypse of the Six-Day War. From mid-May 1967, during the period when Egypt's President Nasser forged a tightening cordon of Arab armies around Israel, American and other Western Jews watched in anguish as their Israeli kinsmen seemingly faced another Holocaust. In near-continual session, American-Jewish communal organizations formulated a stream of pro-Israel position papers, importuned the White House and Congress for diplomatic and military help to Israel, and bombarded the press with full-page newspaper advertisements in Israel's behalf. On May 28, 1967, more than 150,000 New Yorkers marched along Riverside Drive to express solidarity with Israel. Similar demonstrations were mounted in London, Paris, São Paulo, and Buenos Aires.

And when news arrived of the outbreak of war on June 5, tens of thousands of American and other Western Jews rushed to their synagogues to pray, to commune together, to await further information. On campuses, special lectures and "teach-ins" were held for Jewish students and faculty. Some 10,000 young American Jews lined up at Israeli consulates to volunteer their services to Israel. Neighborhood committees were formed to solicit food, blood, and medical supplies for Israel. Above all, American Jews responded with an effusion of funds unmatched in the history of Western philanthropy. The cascade of financial pledges was of such magnitude that United Jewish Appeal staffers, and their equivalents in other countries, were hard-pressed to cope with the deluge. In community after community, synagogues froze their building campaigns, and businessmen often applied for bank loans and turned the proceeds over to the UJA, while others turned over the cash surrender value of their insurance policies. Ultimately, American Jews raised $430 million for Israel in 1967, and Jews of other Western countries raised an additional $207 million (as well as thousands of volunteers for military service).

The unprecedented financial response signified but the tip of an iceberg of

Jewish support. In April 1968, exploiting Diaspora rapture at Israel's military victory, Prime Minister Levi Eshkol convened an International Economic Conference in Jerusalem, bringing together five hundred prominent Jewish businessmen from throughout the world. Its aim was to devise joint projects for promoting Israel's economic development. The meeting was followed by another, the Conference on Human Needs, sponsored by the Jewish Agency. This time, two hundred American UJA and Jewish Federation delegates, and their counterparts from other lands, gathered in Jerusalem to devise long-range programs to meet Israel's urgent social-welfare requirements. Finally, in the post-1967 years, American Jewry generated a migration to Israel of some 25,000 individuals, far exceeding the numbers of earlier decades (although this figure subsequently was more than doubled by a wave of American Jews, most of them Orthodox pietists, who were intent on settling not in integral Israel but in the Palestinian West Bank). And even this infusion was transcended by that of other Western Jews, 64,000 by 2002, particularly from Latin American countries and South Africa (pp. 672, 678, 703).

A Partnership Is Re-evaluated

Could the warmth of this mutual embrace be sustained? From the latter 1970s on, and specifically during the prime ministry of Menahem Begin and the latter's right-wing successors, Diaspora Jewry witnessed the convulsions in Israel's domestic and diplomatic programs with growing misgivings. An important source of discomfiture to third- and fourth-generation American Jews was the implacability of Israel's Orthodox rabbinate, which blocked every effort by Western Reform and Conservative Jews to achieve equality of juridical status for their congregants and programs in Israel. In earlier years, in the United States and elsewhere, Jews of all backgrounds tended to mute their criticism of Israel's perceived shortcomings rather than tarnish the Jewish state's public image. But from the 1980s on, these reservations could no longer be disguised. By then, too, they tended to focus on Israel's widening occupation of the Palestinian West Bank, and on the aggressiveness and tenacity of Israeli settlement groups.

Diaspora unease at Israeli policy initiatives was largely, but not exclusively, directed at Jerusalem's right-wing governments. Indeed, American-Jewish distress burst into the open in 1985, at a moment when Shimon Peres's Labor cabinet was in office. Nor was the catalyst this time Israel's creeping annexationism in the "territories." In November of that year, the FBI arrested Jonathan Pollard, a thirty-one-year-old Jewish civilian employee of United States Naval Intelligence. It developed that Israeli agents had lured Pollard into providing classified American satellite data on Middle Eastern weapons systems, including the location of Syrian antiaircraft batteries and of Iraqi nuclear test sites. Pollard's data also included classified information on Israel's "outer ring" of enemies—Saudi Arabia, Libya, and Tunisia. Washington doubtless could have released much of this information to Israel, so long as parts of it were censored to protect its sources. Failing to block out any of these documents, however, Pollard unintentionally compromised a number of key United States intelligence services and agents.

News of the arrest burgeoned into a national sensation. The Reagan administration already had been embarrassed by earlier disclosures of widespread espionage. Among these was the treason committed by the John Walker family, which through the years had turned over to the Soviet Union the navy's most closely guarded secrets. The disclosure now of Pollard's activities proved almost unbearably mortifying. In jail, Pollard was grilled intensively. He proved cooperative, exposing the full extent of Israeli involvement. In March 1987, Pollard was sentenced to life imprisonment and was ever after kept in solitary confinement "to protect his life from other inmates."

Was the damage inflicted on Israeli-American relations irretrievable? An Anti-Defamation League survey found little evidence to that effect. But the ADL's conclusion was not reassuring to most American Jews. With few exceptions, a poll revealed, they were acutely chagrined. In their view, the Pollard case gravely threatened the goodwill for Israel that they, loyal American citizens, had been cultivating assiduously for some forty years. Indeed, the danger seemed palpable in the immediate aftermath of Pollard's arrest. Suspecting a broader Israeli espionage network in the United States, Justice Department officials repeatedly interrogated Pollard to name his alleged accessories among various American-Jewish organizations. In turn, the leadership of these organizations reacted in panic, demanding assurance from the Israeli government that it never again would expose them to this mortification. How would their neighbors in the future ever accept at face value the painfully achieved record of Jewish patriotism?

AN INDISPENSABLE SANCTUARY

Notwithstanding these and other oscillations in Diaspora-Israel relations, it did not escape Western Jewry that Israel continued at least to fulfill the minimal purpose anticipated by the early Zionist ideologues. It still functioned as an indispensable sanctuary for beleaguered Jewish populations in other lands. In the latter twentieth century, that role was dramatized in two critical venues, one Ethiopia, the other Eastern Europe. Encompassing much of the Horn of Africa, Ethiopia since the mid-twentieth century had proved of considerable strategic value for Israel. With its extended Red Sea coastline, the vast, 437,000-square-mile behemoth served as Israel's maritime gateway to the Dark Continent, even as it offered buffer protection against Egypt along

Israel's sea route to Asia. Israel reciprocated the courtesy. During the 1950s and 1960s, it offered Ethiopia's Emperor Haile Selassie economic and military cooperation against Nasserist subversion.

In 1973, however, during the upheaval of the Yom Kippur War, as Israeli troops countercrossed the Suez Canal to threaten "integral," African Egypt, Haile Selassie reluctantly succumbed to pressure from his Moslem neighbors and severed diplomatic relations with the Jewish state. Ironically, soon afterward, the emperor himself was deposed by a Marxist-oriented military junta. Yet even Haile Selassie's successor, President Mengistu Hale Mariam, was unable to relinquish the Israeli connection altogether. In 1976, facing an insurrection of Eritrean rebels along his nation's northeastern coast, Mengistu and his fellow officers secretly enlisted the help of Israeli military advisers. And following Israel's 1982 invasion of Lebanon, Israel negotiated a substantial shipment of captured Soviet arms to Ethiopia.

The clandestine relationship between the two countries in fact transcended purely strategic considerations. Some 28,000 black-skinned Jews also lived in Ethiopia, most of these congregated in the highlands of Gondar province. Known to their neighbors as Falashas (strangers), the members of this tiny group preferred to call themselves Beta Israel. Their origins were uncertain, but it seemed that they were ethnic Ethiopians, descendants of as many as a quarter-million Africans who had converted to Judaism in the Early Middle Ages. In the sixteenth century, a Christian emperor, Sarsa Dengael, launched a systematic extermination of "infidels," and these included two-thirds of the Falasha population. Of the less than 100,000 survivors, most were persecuted in ensuing centuries, many were sold into slavery, and the rest were barred from owning more than the tiniest strip of cultivable land. Soon this remnant Jewish population devolved into an impoverished pariah community of sharecroppers and handicraftsmen. By the nineteenth century, their numbers had been reduced to less than 30,000.

Yet it was also in the nineteenth century that Ethiopian Jewry was rediscovered by the Scottish explorer James Bruce, and subsequently by a French-Jewish philologist, Joseph Halévy. Both men confirmed that the Falashas' rites had become a poignant amalgam of crypto-Jewish, Christian, and animist traditions. In 1903, Professor Jacques Faitlovitch, a former student of Halévy's, visited the impoverished little community in its mountain retreat and made it his mission henceforth to reintroduce the Falashas into the Jewish mainstream. Subsidized by Baron Edmond de Rothschild, Faitlovitch over the years established a skeletal school system for these lost sheep of Israel. By 1948, the Falashas were well apprised of the outer Jewish world, and specifically of the birth of the Jewish state. Indeed, from then on, departure to the land of their "ancestors" became their compelling obsession.

The immigration of Ethiopian Falashas was less than a priority for the government of Israel. During the 1950s and 1960s, the Jewish nation was overwhelmed by a tidal wave of refugees from Europe, North Africa, and the Middle East. The fate of a black, primitive community, whose bona fides as Jews in any case were not accepted by the nation's chief rabbinate, hardly seemed a burning issue. But with the overthrow of Haile Selassie in 1974, and the ensuing Ethiopian conflict with Eritrea, the Falashas' very physical survival suddenly hung in the balance. At last, in March 1979, with the help of the Carter administration in the United States, the Israeli government arranged a discreet transfer of funds to the private Swiss bank account of Sudan's President Ja'afar al-Numeiri. Numeiri in turn agreed to grant Ethiopian Jews temporary asylum in Sudan, with the understanding that they would be quietly transported afterward from Sudan to Israel. Yet even after this agreement, the initial migration southward of over 9,000 Falashas proved a terrifying ordeal. They moved entirely by foot. En route, they endured disease, starvation, robbery, rape, until eventually they reached their way station at the Israeli-operated refugee compound at Um Raquba. From Um Raquba, in the spring of 1981, Israeli agents transported the Falashas down the Red Sea coast by truck, where some 4,000 of them were loaded into awaiting freighters, which then carried them to Israel. It was anticipated that at least three times that many would follow by the end of the year.

But in the autumn of 1981, Sudan's President Numeiri canceled his arrangement. He had been unnerved by the recent assassination of Anwar al-Sadat in Egypt. Approximately 24,000 Falashas remained behind, 5,000 in their Sudan encampment, the rest in Ethiopia. Israel would not give up on them. Rather, in 1983, the Mossad, Israel's overseas intelligence agency, devised a new scheme, Operation Moses. The plan was to use a swift, surgical airlift to evacuate those Falashas who still were vegetating in Um Raquba, to be followed by others who would be brought down from Ethiopia. Would Numeiri agree? Once again, the role of the United States was decisive. Through the intermediary effort of Vice President George Bush, Washington deposited another $100 million of Jewish Agency funds in Numeiri's Swiss account. To avoid compromising the Sudanese president before the Arab world, the Israelis would fly the refugees initially to Europe, and only afterward to Israel. Operation Moses duly began then in November 1984. Under cover of darkness, the Falashas were trucked from Um Raquba to the Khartoum airport. The air carrier, a private Belgian charter line, flew the Ethiopians from Khartoum to Brussels, and afterward from Brussels to Israel.

Virtually all the 5,000 Um Raquba "transits" were brought out before the secret leaked. The Arab governments protested, and Numeiri closed the Sudanese route—this time permanently. Although as many as 18,000 Falashas remained behind in Ethiopia proper, a second Operation Moses did not appear realistic, for Ethiopia's Mengistu regime was uninterested in provoking Arab ire. Neither did Ethiopia's mountainous terrain lend itself to secret evacuation by air. But seven years later, in May 1991, an insurrectionist faction of anti-Mengistu rebels began converging rapidly on Addis Ababa. Acutely at risk, the Falasha community would have to be flown out without delay. Over the preceding six months, in fact, sentient to the threat of Ethiopia's civil war, Jewish Agency representatives had been transporting thousands of Falashas by truck and bus from outlying villages to Addis Ababa, where makeshift hostels awaited them. At the same time, the Israeli government had transferred some $40 million to the Swiss bank accounts of key Ethiopian ministers. Yet, as in 1984, it was the intercession of the United States government that ultimately proved decisive. Responding to a personal appeal from Prime Minister Yitzhak Shamir, President George Bush exhorted the Ethiopians not to block the Falasha evacuation.

Even with that passive cooperation, the sheer logistical challenge to a mass airlift—this one code-named "Operation Solomon"—was daunting. By the night of May 23, rebel artillery could be heard outside the capital, and Israeli officials sensed that only days remained to complete their mission. Thus, in relays, their fleets of chartered buses rushed the Falashas to the Addis Ababa airport. Awaiting them were thirty-three Israeli military and civilian aircraft, from air force transports to El Al 747s, all parked wingtip to wingtip. Within less than two days, flying in daylight and darkness, Operation Solomon whisked more than 14,000 Ethiopian Jews out of Addis Ababa and brought them to Israel. Although some 4,000 remained behind in their Gondar highland, these too, in ensuing years, were quietly (if less dramatically) brought out in small groups to Israel. Their integration into Israeli life would remain a formidable task. But they were safe.

An Uncertain Soviet Thaw

On March 5, 1953, Joseph Stalin died. Within months, a process of liberalization was inaugurated at almost every level of Soviet life. During the next year and a half, emerging as leader of his party and nation, Nikita Khrushchev called a halt to the worst excesses of Stalinist terrorism. Hundreds of thousands of prisoners of all nationalities were released from labor camps, and the reputations of thousands of Stalin's former victims, living or dead, were rehabilitated and their families were emancipated from pariah status.

Initially, the Jews, too, were among the beneficiaries of the new thaw. Only weeks after Stalin's death, an official government statement denounced the recent Doctors' Plot (p. 606) as a criminal fraud. The surviving physicians (one had died in captivity) were released almost immediately from their imprisonment. The alleged instigator of the ghoulish affair, Mikhail Ryumin, then deputy minister of security, was himself denounced, tried secretly, and shot in July 1954. Among other prisoners to be released were the small numbers of Jewish poets and writers who had survived the nightmare of arrests and convictions following the liquidation of the Jewish Antifascist Committee. Throughout 1955–56, these people were slowly returned from the Gulag Archipelago, most of them broken in health and incapable of further productive work. The Sovietski Pisatel publishing house meanwhile was authorized to bring out selected works of the Jewish poets who had been executed. In this fashion, a limited financial and moral compensation was provided to the writers' families, and the world was informed obliquely that Jews in the USSR were respectable again.

It was apparently to court Western goodwill, too, that the Soviet government in 1958 tolerated a modest publication of works in Yiddish, mainly by such classical, nonpolitical writers as Sholem Aleichem, Y. L. Peretz, and other pre-Soviet figures. A Yiddish-language journal, *Sovietish Heymland,* was inaugurated, the first of its kind since the demise of *Eynigkeit* in 1948 (its topics were predictably anodyne). The Kremlin even displayed a new forbearance toward the Jewish religion. Jewish leaders from abroad were welcomed to the USSR and encouraged to attend the nation's few remaining synagogues. In 1957, the government authorized the publication of 10,000 prayer books, the baking of matzot for Passover, and the establishment of a small rabbinical seminary (which soon expired for lack of students).

This cautiously permissive approach during the first post-Stalin decade evinced the government's ambivalence not only toward the Jews, but toward the USSR's entire mosaic of nations and races. Under Stalin, priority had been given to the support of Russian culture, and the Russian language was promoted as the lingua franca of the non-Russian republics. But several years after Stalin's death, Nikita Khrushchev authorized a tentative "cultural" relaxation. However belatedly, the non-Russian peoples were to be allowed to resume their ancestral traditions, to teach their own national histories, to rehabilitate their national heroes. Even as Khrushchev appeared to be genuflecting to a policy of cultural federalism, in practice he shrewdly revived and even intensified the earlier Soviet program of political integration under the rule of Moscow. This seeming ambivalence of policies in fact reflected the government's awareness that the non-Slavic peoples demographically would soon outnumber the Slavic "heartland" populations. Accordingly, all meaningful state power, whether in the Politburo, the Council of Ministers, or state committees, would have to remain overwhelmingly in Russian hands. Cultural relaxation, in turn, might serve as camouflage for political consolidation.

Yet it was precisely the encouragement of cultural and administrative self-expression among the non-Russian peoples, on the one hand, and the reinforcement of Russian political hegemony, on the other, that in the end produced a whipsaw effect on the Jews. For one thing, notwithstanding their fearful losses in World War II, the Jews remained an exceptionally visible group. Numbering 2.15 million in 1970 (a drop of 5 percent from the 1959 census), they were dispersed through all fifteen of the USSR's republics. They were also heavily concentrated in urban areas. The 1970 census listed the Jewish population in Moscow at 252,000 (although it may have been much higher), 133,000 in Leningrad, 143,000 in Kiev, 47,000 in Minsk, 50,000 in Kishinev, 31,000 in Riga, 20,000 in Tbilisi, and 16,000 in Vilnius (Vilna). It was specifically this urbanization, accompanied by the cultural Russification of Soviet Jewry, that accelerated the familiar Jewish trend toward economic elitism. Even the "black years" of Stalinism had not quite succeeded in reversing this process. As late as 1959, some 395,000 Jews had achieved the honored status of party members, fully 17 percent of the Soviet-Jewish population. No other national group matched this ratio. No fewer than 190 Jews served as deputies to the Supreme Soviet. Despite the expulsion of all Jews from the Communist Central Committee by 1947, other Jews remained active within the party at lower levels, and Benyamin Dymshits continued as a kind of showcase Jew, in the position of deputy chairman of the Council of Ministers.

Moreover, even if Jews in the late 1940s were substantially purged from the Foreign Ministry and the military senior command, they continued to be well represented on the secondary and tertiary levels of government administrative positions and in state enterprises. Their representation in education and the professions was all but overwhelming. Notwithstanding restrictions on their access to the better universities, Jews continued to produce three times their proportion of university graduates. Among their graduates, too, the ratio of Jewish professionals was similarly distended, relative to those of other nationalities. As late as 1963, Jews comprised 13 percent of all Soviet doctors, 10 percent of all lawyers (perhaps half the lawyers in Leningrad and Kharkov, and 40 percent of those in Moscow), 8 percent of all writers and journalists, 7 percent of all musicians and artists. Jewish membership in the prestigious Academy of Sciences was 10 percent.

It was precisely this inordinate visibility in many of the higher echelons of Soviet life that became the measure of Jewish vulnerability in Khrushchev's "federalism." The brutal and physically threatening antisemitism of the Stalin years may have ended. But something nearly as ominous was afoot. The hale and hearty Khrushchev, with his Jewish grandson, was the first Soviet leader to speak openly about a need for adjustment in the "ethnic balance" to sustain the political loyalties of the USSR's welter of nationalities. In authorizing these "adjustments," the Kremlin consciously permitted, even encouraged, the various national administrations to give preferential treatment to their own peoples as they staffed their local bureaucracies. Ukrainians henceforth tended to favor their own, as did Belorussians, Uzbeks, Kazakhs, and, of course, the Russians themselves. Throughout the Soviet Union, by the late

1950s and early 1960s, the Jews found themselves expendable, or at least reducible, to less important positions in the party, the government, and the economy.

Nowhere did this revived numerus clausus exert a profounder impact than in higher education. Traditionally the nation's educational elite, whether as students or faculty members, Jews now were shunted flagrantly into second-rate institutions. The implications were devastating for a people that had regarded educational discrimination as the single most painful feature of their life under the tsarist May Laws. Indeed, the end of those restrictions after 1917 had evoked such gratitude among Soviet Jews that they were prepared in the 1920s and 1930s to accept all the inequities and shortcomings of Communist rule. The sons and daughters of tailors, peddlers, and Talmudists had become the intellectual aristocracy of a mighty nation. Now Khrushchev and his successors were threatening to attenuate that coveted access to higher education and its opportunities. The shock to the Jewish intelligentsia was profound.

Hardly less so was another development of the early 1960s. Palpably failing to improve the nation's standard of living, the Soviet government once again sought to dissemble—and divert. As in Stalin's time, it embarked on a new series of show trials against "parasitism" and "economic crimes." During 1962–63, over two hundred persons were reported to have been executed for these offenses. Nearly two-thirds of them were Jews. Surely not all of them were innocent. Neither could all of them have been guilty. It was significant that the publicity given the defendants in lurid newspaper accounts emphasized Jewish names and featured antisemitic caricatures. Nor was the assault directed exclusively against the Jews' alleged financial peculation. It focused, as well, on their intellectual "domination" and their "web" of international connections. Judaism itself again became a target. Although the antireligious campaign similarly impugned Roman Catholicism and Islam, in the case of the Jews the denunciations were grotesquely vindictive. Propaganda depicted elderly pious Jews as cunning profiteers, and characterized rabbis as "loathsome and filthy ticks." In 1963, the Ukrainian Academy of Sciences published Trofim Kichko's *Judaism Without Embellishment,* an account that equated Judaism with "money-worship," "thievery," "bribery," and "the exploitation of non-Jews." The book's jacket displayed a hooked-nose rabbinical figure, standing at his pulpit with a sack of overflowing gold coins in his clawlike hands.

If these strictures were intended as diversion from the Kremlin's failures, why were the victims still predominantly Jews? And why so long after Stalin's death? Plainly, the Jews remained an exposed target for the accumulated generations of Slavic folk suspicion. But from the government's perspective, the Jews above all represented a current and pragmatic danger as the appendage

of an international people most of whose kin lived in the West. Not less critically, Jews served as the demographic hinterland of the State of Israel, the
putative "outpost of Western imperialism" in the Mediterranean, the silent
partner of NATO air forces and navies whose missiles were directed against
the USSR's exposed southern republics. Not long before, in 1956, the Israelis
had collaborated with these Western nations in a military offensive against
Moscow's client, Egypt. Manifestly, the Jews were not like the rest of the
Soviet peoples. None other was regarded as a potentially more traitorous subject nationality. Nor was any other quite as vulnerable to a far-reaching campaign of political diabolization.

XXXVI

Israel, the United States, and the Struggle for Soviet Jewry

ISRAEL'S SILENT COUNTEROFFENSIVE

In September 1948, when Golda Meir arrived in Moscow as Israel's first minister to the USSR, she and her colleagues were eager to assess the extent of surviving Jewish identity in the Soviet Union. The ecstatic reception she received at Moscow's Great Choral Synagogue provided the clue (p. 596). It was apparent that Soviet Jewry remained far from moribund in their ethnic loyalties. Yet, in these initial years of Soviet diplomatic and military support, Israel's government leaders were hesitant to risk the Kremlin leadership by cultivating the Zionist potential of Soviet Jews. It was only in the early 1950s, when Moscow adopted an increasingly pro-Arab orientation, that the Israeli government took the decision to embark on a more vigorous effort to link Soviet Jewry to the newborn Jewish state.

The vision sprang largely from the brow of David Ben-Gurion. The Israeli prime minister had repeatedly emphasized his determination to forge a network of contacts between the Soviet-Jewish hinterland and the Israeli republic. Accordingly, in 1953 Israel's Mossad intelligence organization dispatched an agent to the Soviet Union. This was the Estonian-born Nehemia Levanon, a veteran emissary who had achieved much success in developing Zionist youth groups in Western Europe. Levanon took up his duties at Israel's embassy in Moscow, with the title of "agricultural attaché." The cover was a useful one, for it allowed him and his staff to tour much of the Soviet Union ostensibly to study Soviet agricultural methods. In the course of these visits, however, Levanon arranged numerous discreet meetings among local Jews and distributed literature about Israel among them. The Soviet KGB assuredly knew of Levanon's clandestine activities, yet it rarely intervened. No pretext should be offered for reprisals against Soviet diplomatic personnel in Israel. Moreover, the KGB was satisfied that Levanon and his associates were uninterested in intelligence. The Israelis scrupulously restricted themselves to the distribution of Jewish and Zionist information, nothing more. Thus, for five years, Levanon was able to move relatively freely and to develop a small but committed network of Zionist "study groups."

In 1958, his tour of duty over, Levanon returned to Israel to establish and direct the Mossad's "Liaison Office" in Tel Aviv. The office in fact would become the planning center for the campaign of "reaching" Soviet Jewry. In turn, Levanon picked as his replacement in the Soviet Union a resourceful and experienced agent, Arieh Eliav. Russian-born, "Lova" Eliav had been brought to Palestine as a child and had fought in the Jewish Brigade during the war. Subsequently he had proved a brilliant and dynamic organizer in the illegal-immigration movement of Jewish displaced persons. His ensuing role in building settlement communities in the northern Negev similarly had honed his negotiating skills among immigrants of numerous backgrounds. Once in Moscow, therefore, functioning under the title of "first secretary," Eliav set about widening the contacts Levanon had pioneered. He had much to work with. By the late 1950s, it was becoming plain that Soviet Jewry remained quite sentient to its collective identity. Golda Meir had verified the fact. So had Levanon. So did various Israeli delegations to international conferences and conclaves sponsored by Soviet cultural and scientific organizations.

Building on this hard evidence of Jewish cohesiveness, Eliav and his staff of eight moved with vigor and growing expertise to seek out Jewish contacts, to distribute Israeli "mementos" that ranged from condensed Russian-Hebrew dictionaries and prayer books to plastic diskettes of Israeli music and miniature bottles of Israeli wine. Every trip through the Moscow metro, every tour outside the capital, was carefully arranged to draw attention to the visiting Israelis. Carrying El Al bags, wearing Stars of David on their briefcases and their collars, the emissaries could "sense" Jews watching them. Increasingly, persons began to approach them. There were quick, furtive conversations, and the Israelis swiftly distributed their material. The work was prosaic, but indispensable.

Indeed, within months of his arrival in the Soviet Union, Eliav was sought out by Jewish activist groups, all of them eager to receive and pass on information about Israel. At the outset, the most promising center of this activity was Riga. This Latvian-Jewish community had been fearfully depleted by the Holocaust, but 31,000 Jews survived there. As in the prewar years of Latvian independence, the vestigial Riga nucleus sustained its identity, even a militant version of right-wing Zionism. Throughout the 1950s, its members conducted discreet Zionist meetings. In *samizdat* (underground) literature, they spread the word of Israel's growth and international recognition to other Zionist groups in the Soviet Union. Eliav's staff kept their various underground "cells" informed of one another's activities, carried messages between them, and offered advice for transcribing underground literature. Their efforts were fortified by Kol Yisrael, the Israeli state radio. Beginning in the late 1950s, Jerusalem transmitted its first Russian-language broadcasts to the USSR. Carefully refraining from criticism of the Soviet Union, or from expressing opinions on East-West issues, the program was left unjammed, and thereby reached growing thousands of Soviet-Jewish listeners.

In 1958, meanwhile, as the Khrushchev "cold pogrom" became increasingly flagrant, Nehemia Levanon, now directing the Mossad's Liaison Office in Tel Aviv, persuaded his government to move to the offensive, to focus world attention on the plight of Russia's huge and historic Diaspora population. Ben-Gurion agreed. Henceforth, Levanon's mandate would be to awaken the West to the cultural strangulation of Soviet Jewry and then gradually to seek out methods of easing their plight. To avoid further compromising Israel's delicate relationship with Moscow, however, the project was organized in the form of local Jewish institutions within Western cities. Thus, in London, it functioned under the euphemism of a "Contemporary Jewish Library." Similar "libraries" were established in Paris and Rome, in Buenos Aires and São Paulo. Their task initially was to enlist the support of overseas Jewish communities, then to recruit non-Jewish diplomats and public figures.

To that end, in 1961, Levanon organized an International Congress of Intellectuals, devoted to the cause of Soviet Jewry. Most of the delegates who attended the gathering in Paris were Jews, among them such eminences as Martin Buber, Nahum Goldmann, and René Mayer, a former French prime minister; but a few leading non-Jewish figures also attended, including Lord Bertrand Russell, the renowned British philosopher. The participants appealed for an end, essentially, to the cultural persecution of Soviet Jewry. Press coverage of the gathering was extensive. Similar protest meetings were conducted throughout Latin America.

In the United States, the task of recruiting Jewish leaders took somewhat longer. Since the war, American Jews had devoted themselves almost exclusively to the establishment and sustenance of Israel. Levanon and his staff required several years of patient education to redirect American-Jewish attention to the plight of the Soviet-Jewish hinterland. Slowly, however, the effort began to make headway. By the mid-1960s, a worldwide organization of Jewish leadership was in place, as well as an impressive roster of non-Jewish public figures willing to speak out for Soviet Jews. By then, too, the United States government was prepared to intercede on behalf of Soviet Jews, albeit for political rather more than for ideological reasons. In a 1964 "summit" meeting at Glassboro, New Jersey, President Lyndon Johnson raised the issue of Soviet Jewry with Khrushchev's successor, Soviet Prime Minister Alexei Kosygin (p. 721). Kosygin reacted coolly. In recent months, he had been angered by the series of pubic meetings Levanon had organized in the West, by the "vigils" of American and European Jews outside Soviet embassies, and by the protest demonstrations outside theaters and concert halls whenever visiting Soviet artists performed.

Although Israel's Liaison Office had needed six years of hard work to effect this coordination, its structural fulfillment in the United States achieved "official" form in 1964 with the establishment of the National Conference on Soviet Jewry. The new body included twenty-five American-Jewish organizations and was coordinated by an office in New York, although in fact its wider strategy was formulated by Israel's Liaison Office. Under the aegis of the National Conference, a mammoth protest rally on behalf of Soviet Jewry was held at Madison Square Garden. It was also the National Conference that obtained a congressional resolution calling on Moscow to grant Soviet Jews the "rights to which they are entitled by [Soviet] law." Groups of jurists, scholars, clergymen, and labor leaders were enlisted to endorse the resolution. It was significant, however, that these appeals were concerned only with Jewish legal "rights" within the Soviet Union. They said nothing yet about the "right" of emigration.

THE JEWS OF PROTEST

Others did. As early as 1962, the Riga activists had been pressing Israeli diplomats to speak out in behalf of Jewish emigration. Yet here they encountered reservations. Yosef Tekoah, Israel's ambassador to Moscow between 1962 and 1965, understood well that a campaign for Jewish equal rights as a Soviet nationality conceivably was viable. Soviet leaders had a certain respect for legality, provided their government's interests were not threatened. Mass emigration, however, was a very different matter. No Soviet nationality possessed that right, not in a closed society that was susceptible to "infection" by Western ideas. In any case, the USSR had lost as many as 40 million of its citizens in World War II. Laboring to achieve economic parity with Western nations, it could ill afford now to lose its Jewish scientists, engineers, and other skilled personnel. Most critically of all, the grant of en bloc permits to one people would establish a precedent for other nationalities, and particularly for the USSR's Moslem peoples, whose kin lived directly over the southern and eastern frontiers, in Turkey, Iran, and Afghanistan. Israel's embassy officials thus felt obliged to move circumspectly on the emigration issue. Time was needed, both for a general softening of Soviet policy vis-à-vis all its subject peoples, perhaps in response to better relations with the West, and for Israel's campaign of Jewish "consciousness-raising" within the Soviet Union to take wider effect.

In fact, the opportunity for Israel to move to the offensive developed even sooner than anticipated. By 1964, Nikita Khrushchev's failures had come home to roost. He had blundered in the Cuban Missile Crisis, exacerbated the diplomatic rift with China, and seriously aggravated the shortfall of agricultural production. An embarrassment to the Communist Central Committee, he was replaced. His successors as premier and party first secretary, Alexei Kosygin and Leonid Brezhnev, were "safe" party veterans. They were expected to keep liberalization within narrow bounds, and in some measure they did. Ideological and intellectual controls were tightened. Nevertheless, the post-Khrushchev regime was unable to stem the nationalist restiveness of the USSR's non-Russian peoples, most notably in Ukraine, or in the reannexed Baltic republics, or in the Moslem East. In Lithuania, dissent approached the threshold of a mass movement, with large-scale demonstrations and occasional riots. In Ukraine, unrest became sufficiently impassioned in 1965 to provoke the arrest and imprisonment of scores of prominent activists. The Baltic Germans, a diffuse group of nearly 2 million that had been driven far into the interior during the war, also launched clamorous protest marches. So did the Crimean Tatars, the Armenians, and the Georgians. It was this groundswell of unrest in turn that created both precedent and inspiration for the Jews.

To an even greater degree, so did the emergence of a vibrant human rights movement among Soviet intellectuals. Its initial catalyst was the arrest in February 1966 of Andrei Sinyavski and Yuli Daniel, whose novels and essays, published abroad, had trespassed an unspoken boundary in their criticism of the Soviet system and its literature. Alarmed, many Soviet intellectuals detected in the government's repression of the two writers an augury of revived Stalinism. Their determination to challenge this threat was stiffened by other arrests and trials of prominent critics. By 1968, the human rights turmoil had developed into a formidable movement. For the first time in years, people dared to organize in groups on behalf of persecuted individuals, to stage demonstrations, to engage in *samizdat* publications that detailed government abuses, and to transmit this material to foreign tourists, journalists, and diplomats.

From the outset, possibly as many as half the leaders of the human rights movement were Jews. Yuli Daniel, whose arrest triggered the dissident protest, was a son of the Yiddish writer Meir Meierovich. Convicted for "anti-Soviet slander," Daniel was sentenced to forced labor together with Andrei Sinyavski, who, although non-Jewish, wrote under the name of Abram Tertz, an anonymous Jewish underground figure. Daniel's wife, Larissa, also the child of a Jewish writer, became a leading force in the movement and ultimately was exiled to Siberia. The movement's star, the physicist and Nobel laureate Andrei Sakharov, was not Jewish, but his wife, Yelena Bonner, was half-Jewish. Dozens of other Jews were prominent in the human rights campaign, among them Pavel Litvinov (son of the diplomat Maxim

Litvinov), Yevgenyi and Aleksandr Ginzberg, Benyamin Kovesin, Osip Brodski, and Piotr Yakir.

The impact of these dissidents on the Zionist emigrationist movement was crucial. From them, the Zionists learned the technique of invoking the Soviet constitution as legal justification for their demands, of reaching Western readers by exploiting the presence of Western diplomats and newsmen. Years later, one of the USSR's prominent Zionists, Mikhail Zand, paid tribute to the dissidents:

> Our national [Jewish] movement could not . . . have existed without the democratic movement. . . . They created the climate that made dissent possible. . . . Without their bravery and assistance, it would have been difficult to give vent to our views, because we had little experience in such things. . . . To turn our backs on them would be impossible to us as Jews.

But eventually the Jews did turn away from the dissident movement. There was little choice after June 1967. It was the Six-Day War that marked them again as targets of Soviet frustration and vindictiveness. The Arab debacle was at once an economic, diplomatic, and political defeat for the Soviet Union itself. Fully $2 billion in Soviet military equipment was destroyed or captured by the Israeli armed forces. More painful yet was the Soviet government's loss of prestige among its own satellites. Although most of these Communist regimes followed the Kremlin's lead in severing diplomatic relations with Israel, it was evident that popular sentiment among the East Europeans markedly favored the victors. In their eyes, Israel was a symbol of effective resistance to Soviet might, and they drew the appropriate parallels.

Rarely in history did the Kremlin react to a foreign-policy setback with a more explosive outburst of vilification. In late July 1967, Moscow launched an unprecedented propaganda campaign against Zionism as a "world threat." Defeat was attributed not to tiny Israel alone, but to an "all-powerful international force." As in the Stalin era, that "international force" was equated now with Jewish communities everywhere, and not least with expressions of national feeling among Jews in the Soviet Union. The term "Zionist" once again became interchangeable with "Zionist Jew," or with the "rich Jewish bourgeoisie." In its flagrant vulgarity, the new propaganda assault soon achieved Nazi-era characteristics. The Soviet public was saturated with racist canards. Extracts from Trofim Kichko's notorious 1963 volume, *Judaism Without Embellishment*, were extensively republished in the Soviet media. Yuri Ivanov's *Beware Zionism*, a book that essentially replicated *The Protocols of the Elders of Zion*, was given nationwide coverage. Two antisemitic novels, *In the Name of the Father and the Son* and *Love and Hatred*, were published under the imprimatur of the ministry of defense. Never before in Soviet literature had such a rogues' gallery of Jews been portrayed, most of them as sinister power brokers who were funded surreptitiously by the unlimited wealth of world Jewry. Western observers, even members of Communist parties in Western lands, were stunned by the Nazi-like onslaught.

It exerted its effect on Soviet Jewry, as well. The Six-Day War had all but electrified them. For years, even before the fighting began, the Kremlin's Middle Eastern policy had kept the Israel issue alive in the press, and thus in the consciousness of Soviet Jews everywhere. Avid readers, they were made aware that Israel and the Jewish Diaspora evidently were a powerful force on the international scene. In the aftermath of the war, the Kremlin inadvertently reinforced this dynamic image by further exaggerating the "power of world Jewry." It was in the non-Russian territories, particularly the Baltic and Caucasus republics, with their "authentic" Jewish populations, that the impact of the Six-Day War was most far-reaching. The Zionist underground that had begun stirring more than a decade earlier as a nucleus for cultural nationalism swelled now into a militant, widely organized Jewish struggle for mass departure.

THE EMIGRATIONIST CAMPAIGN

On February 15, 1968, a group of twenty-six Jewish lawyers, doctors, and scientists in Vilnius (Vilna) addressed a letter to the Central Committee of Lithuania's Communist Party. Alluding to widespread governmental discrimination against Jews, and to the suppression of Jewish culture, the letter appealed in straightforward language for the "right" of repatriation to Israel, the "ancestral Jewish homeland." Through Western tourists, a copy of this document made its way to the United States, where it was published in *The Washington Post.* Other appeals followed, and these, too, were reproduced in Western newspapers. The emphasis upon the "right" to emigrate was not merely rhetorical. Much attention was paid to the innovative approach of Dr. Boris Zuckerman, a young Moscow physicist. Stung by an editorial in *Literaturnaya Gazeta* that had branded as a traitor anyone seeking to forsake "Mother Russia," Zuckerman wrote the editor to argue that neither the constitution nor Soviet legislation denied a citizen the right to leave the country. Rather, Soviet law specifically countenanced "family reunions" in one's former homeland. Eventually, Zuckerman received his reply, and although it was vague, acknowledging only the "principle" of family reunions "in special circumstances," he had forced the authorities at least to take notice. Hereupon, satisfied that the law could be a weapon in the struggle to emigrate, Zuckerman alerted the extensive samizdat readership.

Several thousand Jews, again predominantly in the Baltic regions, then began applying for *vyzovs* (exit visas). In October 1968, the unimaginable suddenly came to pass. The ministry of the interior began issuing vyzovs to several hundred applicants. The moment the astonishing news broke, thousands of Jews began lining up each day at ministry offices in Riga and other Baltic cities. Their bureaucratic ordeal proved to be formidably complex. An applicant was required to cable relatives in Israel, who would authenticate his bona fides as a Jew seeking "family reunion" in his "native homeland." Even with these papers in hand, the applicant was obliged to secure a *kharakteristika* (character reference) from his employer or school principal, then to resign his job or position in school, trade union, or army reserves. Finally, if the vyzov were approved, the applicant was charged 900 rubles ($1,000) for himself and for each family member. The sum represented approximately six months' wages for the average Soviet professional. Nevertheless, the applicants resolutely fulfilled their bureaucratic requirements. Their tenacity achieved results. The number of Jews receiving the coveted vyzovs rose from 213 in 1968 to a modest but hardly insignificant 3,033 in 1969.

The Soviet government's reasons for authorizing this limited increase were not quixotic. Foremost among them was the hope for détente with the West. A cautious loosening of emigration restrictions apparently would serve as proof of the Kremlin's good intentions. In any case, the Jews were not demanding political reform, but simply the opportunity for "family reunions." Boris Zuckerman had reached the mark. There were precedents for this concession even in recent Soviet history. In the 1950s, approximately 200,000 (non-Jewish) Poles, living in the Soviet interior since 1939, had been repatriated to Poland. Additional thousands of Volga Germans, Mongolians, and Koreans similarly had been "reunited" with their families. Moreover, if some Jews, particularly those in the annexed Baltic provinces, were agitating to leave for Israel, perhaps it would be wiser simply to allow them to depart and thereby limit the danger of "infection" spreading to the Jews of the "heartland" Slavic republics. If these were the Soviet leadership's assumptions, they soon proved to be radically in error.

Once the government's relaxed emigration policy was verified, the number of Jewish applicants for departure quadrupled, from 7,000 in 1968 to 27,000 in 1969. The scope of the response quite shocked the Kremlin. At this point, fearful that it would burgeon altogether out of control, the government's hard-liners asserted themselves decisively. From late 1969 on, they ensured that the issuance of vyzovs was all but terminated. The policy reversal was a particularly cruel one for Jews who already had submitted their applications. Having burned their bridges, thousands of them now found themselves suspect in the eyes of their superiors. Many were dismissed from their jobs or demoted, and their children were harassed in school. With little to lose, therefore, they decided to fight openly for their right to emigrate. Henceforth, employing techniques they had learned from the dissident movement, they set about dispatching thousands of letters and petitions to the Soviet government and to influential figures and institutions in the West.

As late as 1969, Nehemia Levanon, from his vantage point as director of Israel's Liaison Office, remained convinced that Soviet Jews were more likely to be extricated through clandestine operations, the method Israel had used in rescuing displaced persons in the prestate period of 1945–47 and in achieving the Jewish exodus from Rumania, Bulgaria, and Poland during the 1950s. Golda Meir, now serving as prime minister, accepted Levanon's argument that Israel's role behind the emigration movement should not be publicly acknowledged (although Moscow was entirely aware of it). Otherwise, if provoked, the Soviet leadership might exploit the relationship to extract concessions from Israel in the Middle East. It was vital for Israel to keep the two issues separate.

But the Soviet-Jewish activists themselves tended to discount this logic. Those who had managed to reach Israel argued that it was specifically the glare of publicity, not Israel's quiet diplomacy, that had originally induced the Kremlin to relax its emigration policy. In any case, the damage was done. "Tens of thousands of our brethren continue to face the risk of arrest and imprisonment," the activists protested, "and mainly because of the inspiration provided by our courageous Israeli kinsmen." Although the protest was somewhat overblown (by the late 1960s, loss of job security was a more common fate than imprisonment), both sides may have been right. Whatever the risks, Mrs. Meir decided to acquiesce in the emigrants' appeal. In November 1969, she announced that the government of Israel in the future would openly champion the cause of Soviet-Jewish emigration. A Knesset resolution then solidly endorsed this policy. Thus, for Soviet Jews, a "second front" had been opened. It proved to be a highly active one. By the spring of 1970, orchestrated by the Liaison Office in Tel Aviv, mass protest rallies against the Soviet emigration ban were conducted in Buenos Aires, Melbourne, Johannesburg, Rome, New York, and in other major centers of Jewish population. On April 26, tens of thousands of Jews shared in a Passover "Exodus March" that began at the Soviet mission to the United Nations.

Appalled by this offensive, and by the upsurge of Jewish applications for vyzovs, particularly in the Baltic and Caucasus republics, the Soviet leadership determined to react even more punitively to the emigration campaign. Moreover, in June 1970, it believed that it had found a matchless opportunity. In that month, a group of Russian Jews set out to hijack a Soviet airliner en route from Leningrad to Murmansk, and to force its crew to land in Sweden. There the hijackers would request sanctuary and later travel on to Israel. But the Soviet KGB managed to penetrate the plot and interdicted it at the last moment, just as the aircraft was about to depart from Leningrad. In its subsequent investigations, the KGB rounded up fully 232 Jews who had been involved in the conspiracy, although the lead plotters were identified as Mark Dymshits, Edvard Kuznetsov, and Kuznetsov's wife, Sylva Zalmanson. In the first wave of trials, conducted in Leningrad in December 1970, Dymshits and Kuznetsov were sentenced to death. Others of the conspirators received prison sentences ranging from fifteen years to life.

Instantly, news of the Leningrad sentences evoked record protest rallies among Jewish communities throughout the world. Mercy appeals also poured in from non-Jewish religious and political leaders, even from the Communist parties of France, Italy, and five other European countries. At the behest of the Liaison Office in Tel Aviv, governments of twenty-four nations intervened diplomatically on behalf of the Leningrad defendants—who after all had only conspired to abduct an airliner but had not actually carried out their plot. Taken aback by the international reaction, the Leningrad tribunal then commuted the death sentences to life imprisonment and reduced the other sentences. But even the reductions were hardly mild. The convicted defendants were dispatched to Siberia to serve long prison terms. Altogether, the Leningrad trials (there would be two others) evoked the harshest condemnation of the Soviet regime since the 1968 invasion of Czechoslovakia. At the same time, they generated a frenzy of renewed Jewish applications for emigration.

By then, fulfilling the worst of Soviet anxieties, the "infection" of the Jewish emigration campaign had spread to Moscow itself. Here lived some 340,000 Jews, a population far more acculturated than the Jews of the "hinterland" Baltic and Caucasus republics. Indeed, the upsurge of emigration sentiment among these Russianized elements was less an expression of Zionist conviction than of concern for their threatened status as an intellectual elite. That threat was becoming more a reality with every passing year. In the aftermath of the 1967 War, for the first time in Soviet history, the number of Jews admitted to universities began to decline in absolute numbers as well as in proportions—from 112,000 in 1968 to 88,000 in 1972. The number of Jews entering the scientific community during 1972–73 fell to 1,000, compared to an average of 2,000 to 3,000 between 1955 and 1971. It was above all else this atrophy in educational opportunity that became the compelling inducement for Jewish emigration, and now directly from the heartland republics at the Soviet Union's very core. From the spring of 1971 on, hardly a month went by without Soviet-Jewish intellectuals, in Moscow, Leningrad, Minsk, and Kiev, as well as in Vilnius or Tbilisi, undertaking some form of public protest, whether demonstrations, sit-ins, or hunger strikes at government and party offices.

The Kremlin responded to the threat with characteristic Russian ambivalence. On the one hand, the avalanche of "anti-Zionist" denunciation continued, in books, press editorials, and broadcasts. Yuri Ivanov's incendiary *Beware Zionism* (p. 722) was reprinted and distributed in tens of thousands of copies. Indeed, the malevolence of the campaign resembled that of the last years of Stalin or Nicholas II. Arrests and trials of activists mounted. Innovative new measures were introduced to negate the torrent of vyzov requests. One of these was a crippling "diploma tax." Applicants who had completed their studies at technical institutes were required to pay the equivalent of $7,700 before becoming eligible to move on to subsequent stages of processing. For those who had completed university programs, the tax was raised to $12,000; for those who held a medical degree, to $18,000. The diploma taxes were far more than the Jewish Agency could provide, even with its access to Western Jewish funds.

Yet if harsh retribution and diploma taxes represented one approach to the Jewish emigration movement, it was not the only one. Beginning as early as 1971, the government had also begun quietly increasing its issuance of vyzovs. By the end of 1971, nearly 15,000 Jews had been allowed to depart for Israel. The number more than doubled throughout 1972, notwithstanding the diploma taxes, and reached nearly 32,000 by the end of the year. Between January 1968 and June 1973, no fewer than 62,600 Soviet Jews arrived in Israel, an exodus that dwarfed the emigration permitted any other Soviet minority. In 1972–73 alone, more Jews left the Soviet Union than had all other Soviet citizens of all nationalities during the entire previous forty-five years of Communist rule.

In Tel Aviv, Levanon and his colleagues in the Liaison Office understood precisely the strategy behind Moscow's new approach. In its rather confused and ambivalent effort to deal with the Jewish emigration issue, the Soviet leadership was determined not only to "cauterize" the Jewish activist leadership, but to propitiate American opinion, which discerned analogies between the diploma taxes and the Nazi ransom demands for Jews in the 1930s. If the role of American opinion, in turn, had come to figure mightily in Soviet planning, it reflected an unanticipated new phase that lately had opened in the Israel-Diaspora campaign in behalf of Soviet Jewry. This was the Jews' success in harnessing the diplomatic leverage of the United States government itself.

THE SEARCH FOR AN AMERICAN-SOVIET ACCOMMODATION

The notion of politicizing the Soviet-Jewish issue had not earlier evoked much interest in Congress, even among legislators traditionally responsive to the Jewish lobby. In the late 1960s, however, the National Conference on Soviet Jewry sensed Moscow's growing eagerness to achieve détente with Washington. The Soviets, it was known, were acutely concerned about the evolving rapprochement between the United States and Communist China. Even more significantly, Moscow's need for access to American technology was becoming urgent, particularly on a most-favored-nation basis. For its part, the Nixon administration favored this dispensation, regarding it as a vital emollient for improved Soviet-American relations. In 1971, therefore, at the president's request, Congress approved a new trade treaty with the USSR, setting higher quotas for purchases and sales between the two nations.

Yet, in one respect, the Soviet-American diplomatic courtship was potentially dangerous for Moscow. It raised the issue of Jewish emigration. Here it was that the Jewish lobby's years of cultivation among American congressional leaders began to pay off. The road to legislative approval of most-favored-nation privileges happened to run through the office of Henry Jackson, an influential Democratic senator. Like many a political figure before him, Jackson was persuaded that Jewish influence in the media and financial community could make an important difference in his ardent quest for the 1972 Democratic presidential nomination. Thus, early in 1972, meeting with officials of the National Conference on Soviet Jewry, Jackson devised a strategy that jelled in response to the Kremlin's new diploma taxes. It took the form of a proposed amendment to the most-favored-nation agreement. Under the terms of this draft amendment, which was co-sponsored by Congressman Charles Vanik in the House of Representatives, any nation within the Communist Bloc would be denied participation in Washington's most-favored-nation program "unless that country permits its citizens the opportunity to emigrate to the country of their choice."

This "trade-for-freedom" draft amendment set in motion two and a half years of complex diplomatic maneuvering between Washington and Moscow; and, within Washington, between the White House and Congress. President Nixon and his national security adviser, Henry Kissinger, were dismayed by the proposed Jackson-Vanik Amendment, regarding it as a gratuitous obstacle to normalized relations with the Soviet Union. Yet the document soon won commitments from 270 representatives, including Congressman Wilbur Mills, the powerful chairman of the House Ways and Means Committee, who agreed to lend his name and prestige as a co-sponsor. Negotiations on the amendment continued for months, and agreement was reached only on October 18, 1974, in an exchange of letters between Kissinger (by then secretary of state) and Senator Henry Jackson.

The accord reflected a parallel understanding that first had been reached between the two governments. Under its terms, as outlined in Kissinger's letter to the senator, the Soviets in effect agreed to end all impediments to applicants seeking emigration. In his reply to Kissinger, Jackson indicated that "we understand that the actual number of emigrants will rise promptly from the 1973 level [of thirty-four thousand] to about sixty thousand," a figure that the

Senate henceforth would use as a "benchmark." The House of Representatives then overwhelmingly approved the Senate version. On January 3, 1975, President Gerald Ford signed the Trade Reform Act, with its incorporated Jackson-Vanik-Mills Amendment. The Jewish lobby was thrilled. It had brought the mighty Soviet Union to terms. For a tiny American minority, that accomplishment, too, was a major "benchmark."

It was about to be ambushed. The National Conference on Soviet Jewry had assumed that United States credits to Moscow would be sufficiently generous to encourage the Soviets to fulfill their part of the bargain on Jewish emigration. At almost the same moment, however, before the Senate vote on the bill, Senator Adlai Stevenson III of Illinois added a new qualification, in the form of an amendment to a routine extension of the Export-Import Bank of the United States. Its most important feature placed a ceiling of a relatively meager $300 million in credits to the Soviets over a four-year period. Additional terms obliged the president to extend the credit ceiling only on specific conditions. These included not only Moscow's forbearance on Jewish emigration, but a moderation of its stance on Middle Eastern questions, and its good-faith negotiations on arms control and military force reduction.

Before the Jewish lobby or the White House quite realized what was afoot, the Export-Import Bank bill, with its Stevenson Amendment, passed the Senate on January 5, 1975, only two days after President Ford signed the Trade Reform Act, with its included Jackson-Vanik-Mills Amendment. In effect, the former canceled out the latter. Five days later, humiliated and outraged, the Kremlin decided that the game was not worth the candle. While the most-favored-nation provision of the Trade Reform Act remained on the books, the Soviets declared that it would not be activated—or with it the obligation to permit Jewish emigration. At the moment of the Jews' greatest triumph, their intensive and unrelenting diplomatic effort of the past half-decade now apparently had gone down the drain.

In fact, it had not. The incontrovertible muscularity of Jewish political influence had registered on the Kremlin. Eventually, belatedly, it would take its effect (p. 733). Even in the short term, Soviet policy appeared to waver. In 1972, 31,681 Jews were allowed to depart the USSR. In 1973, the number rose to 34,733. In 1974, the figure sank back to 20,628; and in 1975, to 13,221. Then, in the mid- and late 1970s, the number of emigrants suddenly began to rise again, as Moscow sought to test the goodwill of the new Carter administration. In 1976, the rate of emigration rose to 14,251; in 1977, to 16,173. Moreover, in 1978, Washington's ratification of the Strategic Arms Limitation Treaty (SALT II) seemed an augury of better relations. So, in the same year, did Senator Adlai Stevenson's intimated willingness to raise the ceiling on Soviet credits to $2 billion. Accordingly, the Kremlin authorized a further increase in Jewish emigration: to 28,865 by the end of 1978, then to an unprecedented 51,333 in 1979!

The very next year, however, the promising upsurge was sharply reversed: in 1980, to 21,471; in 1981, to 9,443; in 1982, to 2,688; in 1983, to 1,314; in 1984, to 896—in effect, to the vanishing point. Indeed, all the punitive features that the Jackson-Vanik-Mills Amendment had promised to eradicate were apparent again in full force, even intensified. In Washington and Tel Aviv, American and Israeli experts struggled to assess Moscow's evident decision to revert to form and throttle Jewish emigration. One factor may have been the growing likelihood of a "brain drain." The Soviets had not anticipated so far-reaching an exodus of physicists, mathematicians, engineers, doctors, and other Jewish professionals. Possibly another influence was a renewed strain in Soviet-American relations. President Jimmy Carter's boycott of the Moscow Olympics following the Soviet occupation of Afghanistan, and then President-elect Ronald Reagan's tough anti-Soviet denunciations, prefigured a harsh chill again between the two governments.

But still another factor helped shape Soviet policy, and in the end it proved the most decisive of all. Soviet Jews were applying for departure on the basis ostensibly of invitations from "relatives" in Israel. "Reunification of families" had served as Moscow's face-saving rationale for acceptance of Jewish emigration in the first place. On that basis of "reunification," after all, limited numbers of other non-Russian minorities occasionally had been allowed to depart over the years: Volga Germans to (East) Germany, Poles to Poland, Serbs to Yugoslavia. Inasmuch as Israel was the self-proclaimed homeland for the Jews, it also fitted into a convenient pattern of recognized homelands for the USSR's plurality of races and peoples. Israel manifestly was an embarrassment in Moscow's dealings with the Arabs, but Jewish immigration there at least presented no serious threat to the Leninist concept of national homelands. On the other hand, immigration to countries other than national homelands would indeed present a threat—for example, departure to the United States. Such a development would represent an intolerable precedent for millions of Soviet citizens of all backgrounds, with their own dreams of an easier life in the West. By the mid- and late 1970s, however, it was becoming clear that tens of thousands of Soviet-Jewish vyzov applicants had in mind precisely that alternate new destination.

THE SEARCH FOR AN ISRAELI-AMERICAN ACCOMMODATION

As early as April 1973, Israel's Liaison Office acknowledged that many immigrants who received their vyzovs for Israel actually were turning elsewhere. The altered Jewish emigration pattern in turn reflected the altered Jewish population pattern of the postwar period. Unlike their predecessors of the 1960s, these new Jewish émigrés were acculturated veterans of the Slavic heartland republics. With their purpose in departure unrelated to Zionist idealism, they would seize upon whichever destination offered them better economic or professional opportunities. It was thus in response to these tangible inducements that the proportion of Jews who "defected" en route to Israel climbed to 19 percent in 1974, to 37 percent in 1975, to 49 percent in 1976. For the Israeli government, the transformation in the emigration pattern was more than unsettling. It was shattering, devastating. The initial influx of Soviet Jews had seemed to betoken a revitalization of Israeli demographic and economic growth, and above all of military-manpower security. Now, apparently, that renaissance was in danger of guttering out.

The diversion of Soviet Jews from Israel could not have occurred without the availability of alternatives. Of these, the United States was incomparably the most important. Even under the tough postwar immigration rules, the United States attorney general was authorized to admit refugees from communism on a priority basis. That authority was broadened under the Kennedy administration. Indeed, over the years, Washington actually came to display a preference for Soviet Jews. Without them, it would have to fill its refugee "quota" with semiliterate and often crime-prone immigrants from Cuba or Africa. Soviet Jews at least were educated and hardworking. For this reason, throughout the 1970s, the United States Bureau of Immigration routinely admitted them under the category of "political refugees." Apprised of this fascinating new development, Jews exiting the Soviet Union with their Israeli visas in hand learned to reapply to the United States the moment their trains brought them to their initial transit station in Vienna.

Once in Vienna, the emigrants' first stop traditionally was at the office of HIAS (Hebrew Immigrant Aid Society) and the Joint, both located with the Jewish Agency in a building on the Brahmsplatz. The two American-Jewish philanthropies were more than prepared to accommodate the newcomers. In the 1950s, following the initial surge of displaced-persons immigration to the United States, HIAS and the Joint had entered a fallow period, with the brief exception of 1956–57, when several thousand Hungarian and Polish Jews departed for the United States, following the political uprisings in their countries (pp. 608–10). But the influx of Soviet Jews after 1973 was a very different phenomenon. Indeed, for the two American-Jewish refugee organizations, it was a new lease on life for their professional and fund-raising staffs. Without delay, HIAS-Joint set about ensuring that the new émigrés were provided with a full array of medical and dental services, and with classes in English and civics. All was taken care of, with an efficiency perfected in coping with earlier Jewish crises of destitution and departure.

Moreover, the inducement of an alternate choice for Soviet Jews was further enhanced by a major American-Jewish political coup. During 1976–77, Jewish lobbying groups petitioned Washington to help underwrite the cost of Soviet-Jewish settlement in the United States. President Jimmy Carter, anxious to ensure Jewish goodwill for his Middle East diplomacy, endorsed the request in 1978, and Congress then appropriated a generous subvention. Henceforth, Jewish federation expenses for absorbing Soviet-Jewish immigrants would be matched dollar for dollar by the United States government. Thus, in 1979, Congress awarded $140 million to the federations, and more would follow. If an open door to wealthy America was itself a boon that Israel could not begin to match, the additional inducement of subsidization within the United States merely gilded the lily for Soviet Jews. Accordingly, in 1977, of 16,173 Soviet-Jewish emigrants, 8,347 chose the United States; in 1978, of 28,865 emigrants, 16,167 chose the United States; in 1979, 33,706 of 51,333; in 1980, 16,012 of 21,471; in 1981, 7,689 of 9,443.

More than heartbreaking, the HIAS-Joint offer of a "free choice" to Soviet Jews was intolerable to the Israelis. They insisted that the vast American-Jewish machinery of relocation and absorption in effect precluded a "free choice," for it was an offer no mere mortal could refuse. Well beyond HIAS-Joint vested interests, in fact, the "free choice" also bespoke the guilt feelings of American Jews, who themselves were largely of East European descent. No one had inhibited the departure to America of their own parents and grandparents, after all. Could they now deny the identical right to their Soviet kin? Interestingly enough, this was not a question that had been asked during the 1950s and 1960s, when American-Jewish leaders gave unquestioned priority of immigration to Israel's urgent population needs. But the majority of refugees then had been dark-skinned Jews from North Africa and the Middle East. Often they were culturally deprived. Even more so were the Ethiopian Jews who in recent years were carried off to Israel, with the eager cooperation of American Jewry. It was far more convenient, even antiseptic, to allow beleaguered little Israel to cope with these backward elements.

The statistics told the rest of the story. Between 1969 and 1980, two-thirds of all immigrating Soviet Jews had gone to Israel, the rest to the United States. Between 1980 and 1987, the ratio was almost precisely reversed, and the asymmetry in favor of the United States was steadily widening, in tandem with declining Jewish emigration from the Soviet Union altogether. No responsible Jewish organization suggested that the Soviet-Jewish rescue campaign had been other than worthwhile. By 1988, no fewer than 250,000 of these people had been delivered from the gray aridity of the Communist empire. Yet 125,000 of them, a potential critical mass for Israel's economy and security, were resettled in the United States. The latter figure exceeded the totality of Central European Jews rescued from Hitler between 1933 and 1940. With few exceptions, the newcomers—monitored, subsidized, even cosseted by Jewish federation and United States government funding—adjusted comfortably in New York's Brighton Beach and other American-Jewish communities. But their potential for the Israeli economy and defense forces was lost.

A SOVIET REVOLUTION

Entirely unexpectedly, in the late 1980s and early 1990s, a silent revolution shook the Soviet Union, and the consequences for the nation's Jewish population were profound. The upheaval related intimately to Mikhail Gorbachev's rise to political leadership of the USSR in 1985 and the introduction soon afterward of *perestroika,* a far-reaching structural liberalization throughout the entirety of the USSR. At first, Soviet Jews shared in the heady new atmosphere. Once again, they were admitted to the better universities and allowed employment in their favored academic teaching and research positions. Synagogues were reopened. Jewish books and newspapers were published, and affiliation was permitted with the World Jewish Congress and B'nai B'rith (which actually opened several branches in Moscow and Leningrad).

But the reverse side of liberalization was the collapse of the Soviet economy. That free fall alone was enough to unsettle Jews and impel them into an urgent new campaign for departure. Worse yet, from the Baltic to the Caucasus, the Soviet Union soon found itself mired in ethnic upheavals and nationalist unrest. Fearful of losing control over their far-flung empire, xenophobic groups of Great Russians made their appearance, bearing such names as Fidelity, Renewal, Fatherland, and Memory (Pamyat). As always, Jews were the initial, exposed targets for their chauvinism. Jewish cemeteries were desecrated. Antisemitic graffiti were sprayed on walls. In 1990, a gang of Pamyat hooligans broke into a meeting of the liberal Writers' Union in Moscow, shouting antisemitic epithets, distributing leaflets warning of imminent pogroms. The government's reaction to these episodes was curiously benign. Gorbachev personally was the farthest thing from an antisemite, but he was uninterested in alienating Russian nationalists at a time when political irredentism was suppurating from Lithuania to Chechnya. For the Jews, the economic and political dangers of the late 1980s soon outweighed the vocational and cultural advantages of liberalization.

In growing numbers, they availed themselves of the one feature of perestroika that offered the cleanest solution to their future. It was emigration. And, for his part, Gorbachev was prepared to allow it. The Soviet president was quite desperate to relieve his economy of the burden of the armaments race, and to open out far wider access to American trade and technology on a most-favored-nation basis. From his predecessors, he had learned well the value of cultivating American-Jewish goodwill, and the price of forfeiting it. Here it was that the 1972–1975 struggle over the Jackson-Vanik-Mills Amendment began to pay its belated dividends. A decade and a half had gone by, but in the late 1980s the gates for Jewish departure almost miraculously were opening again. Indeed, they were opening wide. In 1987, after six fallow years,

18,155 Jews were permitted to leave. In 1988, the number rose to 18,965; in 1989, to 71,000. In 1990, it swelled to 200,000!—a figure that was comparable to the earlier turn-of-the-century tidal wave of East European emigration. Meanwhile, Gorbachev's diplomatic strategy met with comparable success. In December 1990, the Bush administration proposed extending most-favored-nation credits to the Soviet Union for urgent food purchases in the United States. This time, America's Jewish leadership heartily approved the move. Sixteen years after passage of the Jackson-Vanik-Mills Amendment, it was apparent that Soviet Jews were departing in numbers exceeding the dreams even of the most committed Jewish activists.

Initially, the mounting torrent followed the usual route westward. Its sheer size caught American Jews by surprise. The United Jewish Appeal's projected theme for its 1989 campaign, "Operation Passage to Freedom," already in place, had focused on improved housing for Soviet and other immigrants already congregated in Israel. But with a new avalanche evidently flooding out of the USSR, the housing campaign for Israel was dropped in favor of a $75 million emergency drive that concentrated exclusively on Jewish migration to the United States. At this point, Israel's government leaders all but exploded in outrage. So did their partisans among American Jews. " 'Free choice' is not the issue," warned Eric Rozenman, writing in *Moment* magazine. "Israel as a refuge for only some Jews may not endure as a homeland for all Jews. For American Jews, the question of the destination of Soviet-Jewish emigrants is awkward. For Israel, it may be crucial."

It was. The UJA emergency drive fell dramatically short of its goal. Nor were the reasons ideological ones alone. The campaign's failure reflected a confrontation with hard economic realities, and specifically with a United States budgetary deficit. Until that moment, Soviet Jews had enjoyed a special dispensation as "political or religious refugees." In view of the long history of Soviet antisemitism, they were not obliged to document their applications for refugee status on the basis of personal oppression. They were simply ushered in, virtually en bloc (p. 731). By the opening of 1989, however, the Immigration Bureau finally altered its approach and began handling applications on just such a case-by-case basis. It rejected those Soviet Jews who could not demonstrate a "well-founded fear of persecution." These were the majority. Most Jews were fugitives less from government oppression or popular xenophobia than from the economic malaise that afflicted all Soviet citizens (although they would not acknowledge the fact).

For American Jewry's federation leadership, the shock of the Immigration Bureau's volte-face was a severe one. For years it had ardently supported, defended, and rationalized "freedom of choice" between Israel and the United States. But "freedom of choice" had been a useful slogan as long as someone else, the American taxpayer, was helping foot the bill. The financial prospect now of coping with a half-million or more immigrants was as unacceptable to Jewish communal officials as to the United States Immigration Bureau. It would be preferable, after all, if Soviet Jews settled in Israel.

For their part, the government and people of Israel raised no objections whatever to a new wave of immigrants. From the autumn of 1989 on, as they coped with the deluge of Soviet newcomers, they moved as forthrightly and stoically as in the original Soviet influx of the 1970s to provide for the immigrants' initial needs: for their food, lodging, clothing, medical care, and the education of their children. In the process, Israel flouted all orthodox fiscal restraints, disregarded the already crushing burdens of military preparedness. It wanted these people. It needed these people. Nothing would be allowed to impede or delay their immigration. And immigrate they did. From 1989 to 2002, no fewer than 800,000 new Soviet Jews arrived in Israel, raising their presence in the little country to approximately 1.1 million. It was the single largest ethnic infusion in Israel's history, and the largest of any kind since the earliest years of the state's independence.

Nor was the demographic revolution less profound for the Jews of the former Soviet Union. As late as 1959, even after the Holocaust, the Jews' presence on Soviet soil was officially recorded as 2.268 million. By 2002, the figure had dropped to 420,000, that is, to one-eleventh the density of Russian Jewry as measured in the last tsarist census of 1897, and to one-fifth the size of the Jewish population even in the earliest post–Congress of Vienna years. For all their vicissitudes as stepchildren of the Russian Empire, the Jews of this mighty eastern terrain had produced a vibrant and historic culture, and had nurtured a web of Jewish communities throughout the world, in Europe and the Americas alike. Once the largest community in the annals of the Diaspora, they now were in the process of translating no less than their life's essence to the Land of Israel.

Afterword

ISRAEL AS BELEAGUERED SURROGATE

In the first decades of its struggle for survival, Israel enjoyed a unique status as the "adopted child" of Western Europe. The recipient of billions of dollars of Western economic aid, the little Zionist republic also became the first non-European nation to be granted a semiofficial membership in the European Common Market. Its exports often were given priority consideration in European governmental contracts. Awarded a plenitude of grants and fellowships, its scientists, academicians, students, and artists shared in a uniquely fraternal partnership with their European colleagues.

If Israel was "special," its relationship to Europe and the United States above all else reflected the afflicted conscience of the Western liberal community. Even where this community had not actively collaborated in the Holocaust, its political leadership acknowledged that it had not bestirred itself sufficiently to save Jews, let alone to eradicate the racism that had made the Final Solution possible. That spasm of conscience was evident perhaps most graphically on November 6, 1995, two days after Israel's Prime Minister Yitzak Rabin was assassinated by a right-wing Israeli fanatic. Rabin's funeral in Jerusalem was attended by leading statesmen from virtually all the countries of Europe and North and South America, including the presidents of the United States, Russia, and the European Union nations. No prime minister of so minuscule a nation had ever been so honored, in life or death.

But if the Jewish state was unique in the imperative it imposed on the Western conscience, its own obligation evidently was to fulfill its idealized surrogate role of heroic Jewish rebirth. That curiously reciprocal afflatus, and the cost of abdicating it, first became evident in the summer of 1982 when Prime Minister Menahem Begin launched Israel's army in a sustained military offensive against Palestinian guerrilla bases in neighboring Lebanon. Throughout Europe, press and television reportage of Israel's bombardment of PLO encampments was harshly critical, even hostile. In Western media accounts, the numbers of Lebanese victims were demonstrably exaggerated.

The fate of West Beirut under Israeli attack was equated with the fate of the Warsaw ghetto during the Nazi Final Solution. Whether in Paris, Rome, London, or other European capitals, the most frequently invoked analogy of Israel's campaign was one of "genocide."

By the end of the twentieth century, the backlash widened and intensified as Israel's Prime Minister Ariel Sharon responded to Arab terror bombings with punitive military incursions into the Palestinian West Bank and Gaza. Condemnation approached quasi-official status when the United Nations Conference on Racism in Durban in August 2001 indicted Israel as the world's single most culpable practitioner of "racist" discrimination. The accusation by then was gaining popular resonance, as well, both on the European continent and in England. Several months earlier, the Portuguese novelist José Saramago, a Nobel laureate, joined an international delegation of writers who traveled to Ramallah, on the Palestine West Bank, to observe Israel's siege of Yasser Arafat's compound. Writing afterward in *El País,* the widely read Madrid newspaper, Saramago described Israel's actions as "a crime comparable to Auschwitz." The denunciation was further underscored by Thomas Paul, an Oxford literature professor, who suggested in an interview with the Egyptian newspaper *al-Ahram* that American-Jewish settlers on the West Bank and Gaza were "Nazis" who should be "shot dead."

One of the consequences of this ongoing demonization was an academic boycott of Israel. In April 2002, an open letter to Britain's left-liberal *Guardian,* signed by 120 university academics and researchers across Europe, cited Israel's "widespread repression of the Palestinian people" in asking the European Union and the European Science Foundation to impose a moratorium on grants and contracts to Israeli researchers. Subsequent petitions urged a European termination of all cultural links with Israel. In Amsterdam, Greta Duisenberg, wife of European Central Bank President Wim Duisenberg, attached a large placard to her family home denouncing Israel as a "fascist" state. At a private dinner in London, Daniel Bernard, the former French ambassador to Britain, alluded to Israel as "that sh——tty little country"; while the renowned Greek composer Mikis Theodorakis publicly characterized Israel as "the root of all evil." In the late spring of 2003, an EU poll of 7,500 Europeans determined that 59 percent of them considered Israel the single gravest threat to world peace, a higher percentage of respondents than those who bestowed this award on Iran or North Korea.

It was the EU survey that impelled Polly Toynbee, diplomatic columnist for *The Guardian,* to observe:

> For the Left, Israel was once Jerusalem the golden, Zionist banners fluttered on peace marches, young idealists worked in socialist kibbutzim, full of all the earnest hopes. . . . Now the Left feels

all the more betrayed by Ariel Sharon, war criminal, igniting the *intifada* by striding into the Al-Aksa mosque and using the trouble he caused to seize power.

Unquestionably, the era had long since passed when Yitzhak Rabin and Golda Meir could address their European counterparts as "comrades" at gatherings of the Socialist International. Polly Toynbee's evaluation was shrewd. For her and other liberal and socialist idealists, Zionism had become a dream denied, and had collapsed into militarism, ethnic chauvinism, and religious extremism. Shamed in the guilt-stricken adoration they had once bestowed on "gallant little Israel," they subscribed now to Theodorakis's execration of the Jewish state. The European conscience would have to seek out another surrogate.

Diaspora Jewry Evaluates Its Balance Sheet

Even as the Jews of Israel initially had experienced their brief moment of international apotheosis, so, in the early decades of Israel's independence, it appeared that the Jews of the Diaspora similarly would experience the blessings of a moral "affirmative action." Both individually and collectively, they too shared in a kind of post factum, compensatory esteem among European political and cultural circles. That achievement was all, and even more, than the ideologists and statesmen of Zionism could have hoped for. From Leo Pinsker to Theodor Herzl to Chaim Weizmann to David Ben-Gurion, the pioneer Zionist visionaries doubtless would have been satisfied with a plain and simple normalization of the Jewish condition. Their dream had been of a Jewish homeland functioning both as a sanctuary for refugees and as a source of dignified security for those Jews who remained behind in Europe. In the early years of Israel's independence, that dream appeared to have been fulfilled.

The virtual collapse of political antisemitism in Europe seemingly was the litmus test of the Jews' normalized status. As late as the 1980s, not a single major party of any significance in a single Western nation dared openly to espouse antisemitic policies. In not a single country outside the Soviet Bloc were the rights of Jews circumscribed in any fashion. In the Western Hemisphere, only the security of Argentine Jewry remained less than assured, and even in Argentina (before its long-delayed free election of 1983), governmental hostility rarely was directed openly and specifically against Jews. Between the two world wars, the Jewish struggle against antisemitism had been conducted essentially against hostile or indifferent governments. In the free world of post-Israeli independence, Jews resisting antisemitism could invariably be assured of warm government support.

Moreover, from the late 1960s to the late 1980s, if there was a serious threat to Jewish security in the West, it was to be identified not with local hate groups but almost exclusively with Arab guerrilla organizations. Frustrated in the Middle East, the Arab campaign against Israel spilled over to Israelis in Europe, whether Israeli athletes at the 1972 Munich Olympics or Israeli diplomats and airline offices in European capitals. Periodically, to be sure, these assaults targeted local Jews, as well. Thus, in July 1980, a grenade attack on a Jewish school in Antwerp left one child dead and thirteen wounded. In January 1982, a bomb destroyed an Israeli restaurant in West Berlin, killing an infant and injuring fourteen adults. In Rome, in October 1982, two masked men threw grenades and machine-gunned a festive Sabbath gathering outside the Great Synagogue, killing a child and wounding thirty-seven others. In France, the objects of Arab attack included synagogues, Jewish schools, student centers, cemeteries, and the Tomb of the Unknown Jewish Martyr. In October 1980, a bomb exploded outside a synagogue on Paris's rue Copernic, killing four people and injuring thirteen.

The violence intensified during the summer of 1982, at the height of Israel's military incursion into Lebanon. Nearly a dozen Jewish targets were hit in Paris, including a popular Jewish restaurant, where 6 people died and 22 were wounded. In September 1986, two Palestinian Arabs burst into Istanbul's stately Neveh Shalom Synagogue during Rosh HaShanah services, raked its sanctuary with automatic fire, and left 22 worshippers dead and twice that many wounded. In Buenos Aires, in July 1994, a car bomb, later traced to the Iranian-based Hizbollah movement, destroyed the Jewish Community Center (AMIA) building, killing 86 people and injuring 250 (two years earlier, a car bomb had destroyed Israel's embassy in Buenos Aires, killing 29 people and wounding 222). For Jews in Israel and the Diaspora alike, the developments were alarming, and at times terrifying.

Throughout the first decades of Israel's existence, therefore, as Diaspora Jews periodically fell victim to Arab terrorism, it appeared relevant to inquire whether the birth of Israel had not exacerbated, rather than mitigated, the Diaspora's historic vulnerability. The answer may well have been implicit in the very structure of Jewish communal life. The political scientist Daniel Elazar incisively defined five major categories of postwar Jewish communal organizations. These included the "subjugated" communities in the Communist and in several Moslem nations; the state-recognized "communities" of continental Western Europe (except France); the state-recognized "religious structures" of France's and Belgium's Consistoire Israélite; the "tacitly recognized" communal organizations of Latin America; and the "voluntary" communal structures of the British Commonwealth and South Africa.

In whichever category these *kehillot* belonged, all except those in the Moslem and Communist blocs, and those of the powerful and secure Jewish populations of North America, had undergone an unofficial but profound "constitutional" metamorphosis after the birth of Israel in 1948. Whether in Latin America, Britain, Italy, or even in France, the Jews' community decision-making processes henceforth were routed increasingly through Jerusalem. The trend became particularly noticeable after the Six-Day War of 1967, when the Israeli government embarked upon a conscious program to shape, strengthen—that is, to Zionize—the institutions of world Jewry by identifying them more closely with the Jewish state. With few exceptions, the attempt was successful. In some instances, notably in Argentina and Brazil, the very party structures of the local federations came to emulate those of the Israeli Knesset (pp. 678, 683). In short, there developed a tacit assumption in nearly every free Diaspora population beyond North America that Israel's greater ability to deal with political matters would allow it to assume the role of protector and spokesman for all Jews everywhere.

By and large, that assumption was borne out. In South Africa, the Afrikaners' subliminal tendency to identify with beleagured Israel offered a certain mantle of protection to an otherwise suspect local Jewish minority. In Argentina, during the outburst of anti-Jewish violence in the 1960s and 1970s, the military junta was deterred from lending antisemitism its "official" approbation when the Israeli ambassador issued a plainspoken warning of diplomatic consequences. In 1982, Israel's Foreign Minister Yitzhak Shamir made a high-profile visit to Buenos Aires on behalf of abducted Jews, and specifically at a time of critical Israeli arms sales to Argentina. Upon arrival, Shamir handed over to the government a list of twenty-eight detainees known to be alive in various prisons. All twenty-eight were released in the next few months. Elsewhere in Latin America—in Brazil, Chile, and Uruguay—the elaborate annual festivities organized for Israel Independence Day served as deliberate reminders to the host governments of the sovereign force that stood behind local Jewish minorities.

So it was, down well into the last years of the twentieth century, that Western Jewry's enhanced legal and physical security, the fortified prestige and political status conferred on Diaspora Jews by Israel, appeared to have more than compensated for Jewish vulnerability to occasional Arab terrorist or right-wing violence. Indeed, it was questionable whether local Jewish minorities were placed in substantially greater peril even in nations overtly hostile to Israel. Was it the rise of Israel alone that doomed the largest number of Jewish communities in the Moslem world, or a more widely diffused Moslem xenophobia that impelled the departure of the European Powers, and thereby of other non-Moslem minorities? Was "anti-Zionism" the animus that terminated the last remnants of organized Jewish life in Eastern Europe, or plain and simple antisemitism thinly disguised and manipulated as "anti-Zionism" for domestic political purposes? If it was the latter, were the Jews of these totalitarian nations ultimately less secure, or more secure, as a consequence of Israel's existence? One must speculate whether, lacking Israeli affidavits and the Israeli-organized network of pressures on the USSR, some 600,000 Soviet, Polish, and Rumanian Jews would have managed to secure emigration vyzovs (as did additional hundreds of thousands of East European Jews after the fall of communism).

In Western nations, too, gentile admiration for Israel ultimately affected the Jews' own sense of identity and self-esteem. The impact of Zionism and the establishment of Jewish statehood dissipated the rather vapid "cultist" approach to Jewish identity that had characterized the prewar leadership of France, Italy, the Netherlands, and in some degree of Britain. The birth of Israel energized Jewish life even in the most thoroughly acculturated Western communities. It was almost exclusively Israeli emissaries who inspired the establishment, and Hebraized the curriculum, of Jewish school systems in Britain, South Africa, Australia, and Scandinavia. Jewish music and drama, Jewish arts and letters, Jewish camps and youth movements, all profited decisively from the stimulus of the Zionist renaissance. Then, for European Jews, as for those in the Western Hemisphere, there appeared little question, in the first half-century of Israel's independence, that the balance sheet of Zionist statehood remained decisively in their favor.

A Twenty-First-Century Prognosis

That affirmative assessment notwithstanding, by the opening of the new century, Jews in Europe, even in the Western Hemisphere, suddenly found themselves confronting a peril that they assumed had been consigned to the dustbin of history. It was the revival of antisemitism. Admittedly, no Diaspora Jew who had survived Europe's totalitarian garden of delights would ever accuse the State of Israel of endangering his basic security. Yet evidence was growing that Israel's blemished image in the West, while far from actively endangering the Jewish presence in Europe, was beginning seriously to complicate it. The first tremors of concern were evoked by a "virus" of antisemitic computer webmail. From 2000 on, moreover, a series of more flagrant and threatening antisemitic incidents, protest marches, desecrations of synagogues and cemeteries, appeared to be gaining momentum.

Thus, in 2001, some 228 antisemitic incidents took place in Europe and Latin America, and for the first time included 56 attacks against individual Jews. In 2002, the number of—listed—attacks against Jewish individuals doubled, to 112, and these were accompanied by some 40 acts of arson against synagogues and Jewish schools. The physical assaults continued in 2003, and among those seriously beaten were rabbis in Vienna and Paris. In Istanbul, in November 2003, the famed Neveh Shalom Synagogue, site of the September 1986 mass murder, was bombed once again, this time killing eleven worshippers. Throughout all of Europe, no comparable wave of antisemitism, and assuredly no comparable acts of violence, had occurred in the more than half-century since the end of World War II.

In January 2004, the Israeli Ministry for Jerusalem and Diaspora Affairs, which closely monitored European-Jewish developments, confirmed that it was France that in 2003 had experienced the highest incidence of antisemitic violence in Western Europe. Indeed, the French government itself had already taken note of the seriousness of the problem. In December 2003, the nation's minister of education acknowledged that the upsurge of anti-semitism had become so grave in his country, and the physical harassment of Jewish schoolchildren so extensive, that many Jewish students were obliged to leave the public education system for private Jewish or even Catholic schools. By then, too, Jewish leaders in Europe took the revived antisemitism seriously enough to engage in a flurry of international congresses, and to press the European Union for an appropriate response.

On December 12, Italy's Prime Minister Silvio Berlusconi, president of the EU, proclaimed the body's "deep concern at the increase in instances of antisemitic intolerance and strongly condemns all manifestations of anti-semitism, including attacks against religious sites and individuals." Virtually every European government expressed the same concern and condemnation, not least of all France's. But Jewish leaders had been pressing for more. It was at their behest, the previous autumn, that the EU finally had agreed to com-mission a research study on European antisemitism. The research group, the Free University of Berlin's highly respected Center for Research on Anti-Semitism (which in fact had been sponsored and funded by the EU itself as far back as 1997), set about conducting its study.

The Center's report, admirably thorough and objective, was completed in November 2003. Yet at first the EU commission hesitated to make the docu-ment public. It was only under heavy Jewish pressure, several weeks later, that the commissioners changed their minds and on December 6 authorized its publication of the report. There were few surprises. Although the document alluded to the growth of rightist and neo-Nazi splinter groups, by intimation it also confirmed an open secret, one that reflected a basic fact of European demography. This was the presence of large, impoverished, and apparently unassimilable Moslem minorities in Europe. In France, there lived nearly 6 million Moslems, most of these from North Africa, and representing the single largest Moslem population anywhere in Europe. However the Research Center sought to cosmeticize the data, its own statistics could not disguise the fact that as many as 80 percent of all episodes of anti-Jewish violence were car-ried out by these undereducated and underemployed Moslem slum-dwellers.

While first and foremost an expression of displaced rage against Israel, the wrath of these North African expatriates was profoundly intensified by their own second-class status in Europe. Given these conclusions, it was understandable that the EU commissioners originally had hesitated to release the report. Antipathy toward Moslem immigrants was itself a widespread fact of life in Europe, particularly in France, Spain, Belgium, and Italy, with their huge North African minority populations. Indeed, the animus was growing every year, and evoking a marked political reaction in country after country, even in Germany, with its 3 million Moslem *Gastarbeiter*. For this reason, the EU commissioners were uninterested in fueling the flames of one variety of xenophobia in the process of evaluating another.

Jewish analysts empathized with the commissioners' ambivalence, and with European insecurities. Nevertheless, in their own historic exposure to Europe's shifting moods, they also grasped the rapidity with which fear and suspicion of other peoples could be redirected against them. After all, this had been the pattern of Jewish vulnerability in earlier eras of their history: when Jew-hatred in Crusader Europe or in Spain in the period of *reconquista* flared up essentially as a by-product of Christian-Moslem rivalries. Did the Jews need to be whipsawed still again between Moslem hatreds and Christian fears? More ominously yet, a time might come when political parties in Europe, and perhaps even in the United States, would reevaluate their nations' burgeoning Moslem minorities and redefine them as objects not merely of fear and suspicion but of potential electoral support. Where then would the Jews be left in the West's social configuration?

But in the end, the most gnawing Jewish preoccupation of all was one that in earlier years no Zionist ideologue, neither Pinsker nor Herzl nor Weizmann nor Ben-Gurion, had ever faintly anticipated. Granted, Israel was a special case in the European psyche, and if Europe's admiration could soar exponentially for Israel as a poster child of the Western conscience, so, too, that admiration could plummet with equal rapidity the moment Israel ceased to fulfill its surrogate role. But whether Israel was a model state or an imperfect state (so the Zionist argument went), whether it was the object of praise or obloquy, Jews living in the Diaspora at least would have achieved the normalized status of other peoples and nations. Their phantom image at long last would have been exorcised by the sheer reality of a Jewish mother state, a sovereign political entity, whether good or bad, conducting the routine governmental functions of other independent nations. If by chance the Republic of Israel proved to be heroic and visionary in its accomplishments, then so much the better for Jews elsewhere.

It was, alas, the reverse side of the equation that had never been contemplated. If Israel fell short in its behavior, if a Jewish state were perceived (whether accurately or groundlessly) as a delinquent, a rogue, a militaristic or an oppressive state, then so much the worse for Jews elsewhere. And now, belatedly, at the onset of the twenty-first century, it was specifically the reverse side of the equation that had to be confronted, pondered, and internalized. If the Jews throughout their long Diaspora experience had functioned as hostages of gentile political and diplomatic behavior, were they to function now as hostages of Israeli political and diplomatic behavior? Was that to be their fate even in bountiful and pluralistic America, where nearly all vocational and political doors appeared to be opening? The prognosis was uncertain.

Nevertheless, if the eccentric lot of this little people seemed altogether to be one of ongoing uncertainty, that ordination, too, was not without a certain mordant compensation. The Jews had long since developed the musculature to cope with uncertainty. The Almighty, so decreed the wisdom of the Sages, had shrewdly prescribed the cure at the moment of dispensing the affliction. In the early twentieth century, Sigmund Freud may have discerned that corrective as incisively as any of his rabbinical forebears, when he adjured his colleague Dr. Max Graf to relinquish any expedient notions of severing his son's links with the Jewish people, of depriving his son of that unique source of Jewish energy (p. 461). "Do not deprive him of that advantage," Freud counseled. And the old prophet could as well have added: do not deprive society at large of that advantage. Possibly more than any people in history, the fate and fortune of the Jews prefigured the fate and fortune of the nations among whom they lived and interacted. In the future, as in the past, with or without a state of their own, that synergy appears all but certain to remain the Jews' immemorial destiny.

Bibliography

This compendium is intended principally for Western readers. Some titles are listed, as relevant, in more than one chapter. For the extensive material dealing with Europe between the French Revolution and World War II, David Vital's magisterial *A People Apart: A Political History of the Jews of Europe, 1789–1939* (Oxford, Eng., 1999) is warmly recommended, as is the supplemental reader compiled by Paul Mendes-Flohr and Jehuda Reinharz, *The Jew in the Modern World: A Documentary History*, 2nd ed. (New York, 1995). The eighteen-volume *Encyclopedia Judaica* (Jerusalem, 2002) continues to serve as a valuable reference work for the entirety of Jewish history. For Israel-Diaspora relations, the author has made extensive use of Israeli newspapers, including, for many years, the weekend edition of *Ma'ariv*, and, more recently, the daily edition of *HaAretz*, available electronically through the Web.

I. *The Jew as Non-European*

Baron, Salo. "Ghetto and Emancipation." *Menorah Journal,* June 1928.

Breuer, Mordechai. "The Early Modern Period," in Michael Meyer, ed. *German Jewish History in Modern Times.* New York, 1996.

Eisenbach, Artur, et al., eds. *The Emancipation of the Jews in Poland, 1780–1870.* Oxford, Eng., 1991.

Engelman, Uria Z. *The Rise of the Jew in the Western World.* New York, 1944.

Gitelman, Zvi. *A Century of Two Peoples: The Jews of Russia and the Soviet Union.* New York, 1988.

Hundert, Gershon D. *Jews in Poland-Lithuania in the Eighteenth Century.* Berkeley, Calif., 2004.

Israel, Jonathan. *European Jewry in the Age of Mercantilism 1550–1750.* 3rd ed. Oxford, Eng., 1965.

Katz, Jacob. *Out of the Ghetto: The Social Background of Jewish Emancipation, 1770–1860.* Cambridge, Mass., 1973.

Kazis, Israel J. "Hasidism." Unpublished Ph.D. dissertation, Harvard University, 1939.

Levine, Hillel. *Economic Origins of Antisemitism: Poland and Its Jews in the Early Modern Period.* New Haven, Conn., 1991.

Lowenthal, Marvin. *A World Passed By.* New York, 1933.

Marcus, Jacob. *The Jew in the Medieval World.* Cincinnati, 1939.

Meyer, Michael A. *The Origins of the Modern Jew: Jewish Identity and European Culture in Germany, 1749–1924.* Detroit, 1967.

Mosse, Werner E. "From Schutzjuden to 'Deutsche Staatsbürger jüdischen Glaubens': The Long and Bumpy Road of Jewish Emancipation in Germany," in Pierre Birnbaum and Ira Katznelson, eds. *Paths of Emancipation: Jews, States, and Citizenship.* Princeton, N.J., 1995.

Oelsner, Toni. "The Jewish Ghetto of the Past." *Yivo Annual of Jewish Science,* Vol. I (1946).

Poliakov, Léon. *The History of Anti-Semitism.* Vol. 1: *From Voltaire to Wagner.* New York, 1965.

Teimanas, D. B. *L'Autonomie des communautés juives en Pologne aux XVIe et XVIIe siècles.* Paris, 1933.

Wistrich, Robert S. *Antisemitism: The Longest Hatred.* New York, 1991.

Yerushalmi, Yosef H. *From Spanish Court to Italian Ghetto.* New York, 1971.

II. *A Glimmering of Dawn in the West*

Altmann, Alexander. *Moses Mendelsshon: A Biographical Study.* Tuscaloosa, Ala., 1973.

Anschel, R. "Les Juifs à Paris au XVIIIe siècle." *Bulletin de la société de l'histoire de Paris,* Vol. 19 (1932).

Arendt, Hannah. "Privileged Jews." *Jewish Social Studies,* Vol. 8 (1946).

———. *Rahel Varnhagen: The Life of a Jewess.* London, 1957.

Baron, Salo W. *An Economic History of the Jews.* Jerusalem, 1975.

———. "Ghetto and Emancipation." *Menorah Journal,* June 1928.

Barzilay, Isaac E. "The Jew in the Literature of the Enlightenment." *Jewish Social Studies,* October 1956.

Berkovitz, Jay R. *The Shaping of Jewish Identity in Nineteenth-Century France.* Detroit, 1989.

Bloom, Herbert I. *The Economic Activities of the Jews of Amsterdam in the Seventeenth and Eighteenth Centuries.* Williamsport, Pa., 1937.

Bourgin, G. "Le Problème de fonction économique des juifs." *Souvenir et Science,* Vol. III (1932).

Breuer, Mordechai. "The Early Modern Period," in Michael Meyer, ed. *German Jewish History in Modern Times.* New York, 1996.

Eisenbach, Artur, et al., eds. *The Emancipation of the Jews in Poland, 1780–1870.* Oxford, Eng., 1991.

Emmerich, H. *Das Judentum bei Voltaire.* Breslau, 1930.

Endelman, Todd M. *Jewish Apostasy in the Modern World.* New York, 1957.

Feiner, Shmuel. *The Jewish Enlightenment.* Philadelphia, 2004.

Hadas, Moses, ed. *Solomon Maimon: An Autobiography.* New York, 1967.

Hertzberg, Arthur. *The French Enlightenment and the Jews.* New York, 1970.

Israel, Jonathan. *European Jewry in the Age of Mercantilism 1550–1750.* 3rd ed. Oxford, Eng., 1965.

Katz, Jacob. *Out of the Ghetto: The Social Background of Jewish Emancipation, 1770–1860.* Cambridge, Mass., 1973.

Kopald, Louis J. "The Friendship of Lessing and Mendelssohn in Relation to the Good-Will Movement Between Christian and Jew." *Yearbook of the Central Conference of American Rabbis,* Vol. 39 (1929).

Lohrmann, Klaus. *Zwischen Finanz und Toleranz: das Haus Habsburg und die Juden.* Graz, Aust., 2000.

Lowenstein, Steven M. *The Berlin Jewish Community: Enlightenment, Family, and Crisis, 1770–1830.* New York, 1994.

Malino, Frances, and Bernard Wasserstein, eds. *The Jews in Modern France.* Hanover, N.H., 1985.

McCagg, William O. *A History of Habsburg Jews, 1670–1918.* Bloomington, Ind., 1989.

Meyer, Michael A. *The Origins of the Modern Jew: Jewish Identity and European Culture in Germany, 1749–1924.* Detroit, 1967.

———. *Response to Modernity: A History of the Reform Movement in Judaism.* New York, 1988.

———. "Where Does Modern Jewish History Begin?" *Judaism,* Vol. 24 (Summer 1975).

———, ed. *German-Jewish History in Modern Times.* Vol. 2. New York, 1996.

Mosse, Werner E. "From Schutzjuden to 'Deutsche Staatsbürger jüdischen Glaubens': The Long and Bumpy Road of Jewish Emancipation in Germany," in Pierre Birnbaum and Ira Katznelson, eds. *Paths of Emancipation: Jews, State, and Citizenship.* Princeton, N.J., 1995.

Patai, Raphael. *The Jews of Hungary: History, Culture, Psychology.* Detroit, 1996.

Rachel, H. "Die Juden im Berliner Wirtschaftsleben zur Zeit des Merkantilismus." *Zeitschrift für die Geschichte der Juden in Deutschland,* Vol. 2 (1930).

Ruderman, David B. *Jewish Enlightenment in an English Key: Anglo-Jewry's Construction of Modern Jewish Thought.* Princeton, N.J., 2000.

Sachar, Howard M. *Farewell España: The World of the Sephardim Remembered.* New York, 1994.

Sänger, Hermann. *Juden und Altes Testament bei Diderot.* Wertheim, Ger., 1933.

Schubert, Kurt. *Österreichen Hofjuden und ihre Zeit.* Eisenstadt, Aust., 1991.

Sée, Henri. "Dans quelle mesure puritains et juifs ont-ils contribué au progrès du capitalisme moderne?" *Revue économique internationale,* Vol. 34 (1927).

Sorkin, David. *Moses Mendelssohn and the Religious Enlightenment.* London, 1996.

Spiel, H. *Fanny von Arnstein: oder die Emanzipation.* Vienna, 1975.

Springer, A. "Enlightened Absolutism and Jewish Reform: Prussia, Austria, and Russia." *California Slavic Studies,* Vol. 2 (1980).

Stern Taubler, Selma. *The Court Jew.* Philadelphia, 1950.

———. "The Jews in the Economic Policy of Frederick the Great." *Jewish Social Studies,* Vol. 10 (1949).

Strauss, Herbert. "Pre-Emancipation Prussian Policies Towards the Jews, 1815–1847." *Leo Baeck Institute Yearbook,* Vol. 2 (1966).

Toaff, Ariel, and Simon Schwarzfuchs, eds. *The Mediterranean and Jewish Banking, Finance, and International Trade (XVI–XVIII Siècles).* Ramat Gan, Isr., 1989.

Wijler, J. S. *Isaac de Pinto, sa vie et ses oeuvres.* Apeldoorn, Neth., 1923.

III. *An Ambivalent Emancipation in the West*

Albert, Phyllis Cohen. *The Jewish Oath in Nineteenth-Century France.* Tel Aviv, 1982.

———. *Les Juifs de France.* Paris, 1946.

———. *The Modernization of French Jewry.* Hanover, N.H., 1977.

Anchel, Robert. *Napoléon et les Juifs.* Paris, 1938.

Berkovitz, Jay L. *The Shaping of Jewish Identity in Nineteenth-Century France.* Detroit, 1989.

Blumenkranz, Bernhard. *Histoire des Juifs en France.* Toulouse, 1972.

Blumenkranz, Bernhard, and André Soboul, eds. *Le Grand Sanhedrin de Napoléon.* Toulouse, 1979.

———, eds. *Les Juifs et la révolution française.* Toulouse, 1976.

Cesarani, David. *Port Jews: Jewish Communities in Cosmopolitan Maritime Trading Centers, 1550–1950.* London, 2002.

Cohen, Yerachmiel, ed. *HaMahapechah haTzarfatit v'Rishuma* [The French Revolution and Its Cause]. Jerusalem, 1991.

Daalder, Hans. "Dutch Jews in a Segmented Society," in Pierre Birnbaum and Ira Katznelson, eds. *Paths of Emancipation: Jews, States, and Citizenship.* Princeton, N.J., 1993.

Emden, Paul H. "The Brothers Goldsmid and the Financing of the Napoleonic Wars." *Transactions of the Jewish Historical Society of England,* Vol. 14 (1940).

Ettinger, Shmuel. "The Beginnings of the Change in the Attitude of European Society Towards the Jews." *Scripta Hierosolymitana,* Vol. 7 (1961).

Graetz, Michael. *Les Juifs en France au 19ième siècle: de la Révolution française à l'Alliance Israélite Universelle.* Paris, 1989.

Hallphen, A. E., ed. *Recueil des lois . . . concernant les Israélites depuis la révolution de 1789.* Paris, 1851.

Hamburger, Ernest. "One Hundred Years of Emancipation." *Leo Baeck Institute Yearbook,* Vol. 14 (1969).

Hyman, Paula. *The Jews of Modern France.* Berkeley, Calif., 1998.

Jersch-Wenzel, Stefi. "Legal Status and Emancipation," in Michael A. Meyer, ed. *German-Jewish History in Modern Times.* Vol. 2. New York, 1996.

Katz, Jacob. *Out of the Ghetto: The Social Background of Jewish Emancipation, 1770–1860.* Cambridge, Mass., 1973.

Malino, Frances. *A Jew in the French Revolution: The Life of Zalkind Hourwitz.* Oxford, Eng., 1996.

———. *The Sephardic Jews of Bordeaux: Assimilation and Emancipation in Revolutionary and Napoleonic France.* University, Ala., 1978.

Mevorach, B., ed. *Napoleon u'T'kufato* [Napoleon and His Era]. Jerusalem, 1968.

Meyer, Michael A. *The Origins of the Modern Jew: Jewish Identity and European Culture in Germany, 1749–1824.* Detroit, 1967.

Morgenstern, Friedrich. "Hardenberg and the Emancipation of Franconian Jewry." *Jewish Social Studies,* Vol. 5 (1943).

Oelsner, Toni. "Three Jewish Families in Modern Germany." *Jewish Social Studies,* Vol. 4 (1942).

Offenburg, Berthold. *Das Erwachen des deutschen Nationalbewusstseins in der preussischen Judenheit.* Hamburg, 1933.

Posener, S. "The Immediate Economic and Social Effects of the Emancipation of the Jews in France." *Jewish Social Studies,* Vol. 1 (1939).

———. "Les Juifs sous le premier empire." *Revue des études juives,* Vol. 90 (1932).

Reissner, H. "Mirabeau's Judenpolitik," *Der Morgen,* Vol. 8 (1932).

Sachar, Howard M. *Farewell España: The World of the Sephardim Remembered.* New York, 1994.

Sagnac, Philippe. "Les Juifs et Napoléon (1806–1808)." *Revue d'histoire moderne et contemporaine,* Vol. 2 (1900–1901); Vol. 3 (1901–1902).

Schwarzfuchs, Simon. *Napoleon, the Jews, and the Sanhedrin.* London, 1979.

Segre, Dan V. "The Emancipation of the Jews in Italy," in Pierre Birnbaum and Ira Katznelson, eds. *Paths of Emancipation: Jews, States, and Citizenship.* Princeton, N.J., 1995.

Strauss, Herbert. "Pre-Emancipation Prussian Policies Towards the Jews." *Leo Baeck Institute Yearbook,* Vol. 11 (1966).

Szajkowski, Zosa. "Jewish Participation in the Sale of National Property during the French Revolution." *Jewish Social Studies,* Vol. 14 (1952).

———. *Jews and the French Revolutions of 1789, 1830, and 1848.* New York, 1970.

———. "Population Problems of Marranos and Sephardim in France, from the Sixteenth to the Twentieth Century." *Proceedings of the American Academy for Jewish Research* (1958).

Waldman, Morris. *Goethe and the Jews.* New York, 1934.

Weber, Eugen. "Reflections on the Jews in France," in Frances Malino and Bernard Wasserstein, eds. *The Jews in Modern France.* Hanover, N.H., 1985.

IV. *Incarceration: The Jews of Tsarist Russia*

Baron, Salo W. *The Russian Jew under Tsars and Soviets.* 2nd ed. New York, 1976.

Bartoszewski, W. T., and Abraham Polonsky, eds. *The Jews of Warsaw.* Oxford, Eng., 1991.

Domnitch, Larry. *The Cantonists: The Jewish Children's Army of the Czar.* Jerusalem, 2004.

Eisenbach, Artur, et al., eds. *The Emancipation of the Jews in Poland, 1780–1870.* Oxford, Eng., 1991.

Ginsburg, Saul M. "Max Lilienthal's Activities in Russia: New Documents." *Publications of the American Jewish Historical Society,* Vol. 35 (1939).

Greenberg, Louis. *The Jews in Russia: The Struggle for Emancipation.* Vol. I. New York, 1976.

Herzen, Alexander. *My Past and Thoughts.* New York, 1974.

Klier, John D. *Russia Gathers Her Jews: The Origin of the Jewish Question in Russia.* DeKalb, Ill., 1986.

Levine, Hillel. *Economic Origins of Antisemitism: Poland and Its Jews in the Early Modern Period.* New Haven, Conn., 1991.

Levitats, Isaac. *The Jewish Community in Russia, 1772–1844.* New York, 1943.

Mahler, Raphael. *Hasidism and the Jewish Enlightenment: Their Confrontation in Galicia and Poland in the First Half of the Nineteeenth Century.* Philadelphia, 1985.

Pipes, Richard. "Catherine II and the Jews: The Origins of the Pale of Settlement." *Soviet Jewish Affairs,* Vol. 5 (1975).

Poliakov, Léon. *The History of Anti-Semitism.* Vol. I: *From the Time of Christ to the Court Jew.* New York, 1965.

Rogger, Hans. *Jewish Policies and Right-Wing Politics in Imperial Russia.* Berkeley, Calif., 1986.

Rosman, M. J. *The Lord's Jews: Magnate-Jewish Relations in the Polish-Lithuanian Commonwealth During the Eighteenth Century.* Cambridge, Mass., 1990.

Shatzky, Jacob. "Warsaw Jews in the Polish Cultural Life of the Early Nineteenth Century." *YIVO Annual of Jewish Social Science,* Vol. 21 (1950).

Stanislawski, Michael. "Russian Jewry, the Russian State, and the Dynamism of Jewish Emancipation," in Pierre Birnbaum and Ira Katznelson, eds. *Paths of Emancipation: Jews, States, and Citizenship.* Princeton, N.J., 1995.

———. *Tsar Nicholas I and the Jews: The Transformation of Jewish Society in Russia 1825–1855.* Philadelphia, 1983.

V. *The Triumph of Emancipation in the West*

Alderman, Geoffrey. *Modern British Jewry.* Oxford, Eng., 1992.

Alon, Amos. *The Pity of It All: A History of Jews in Germany, 1743–1933.* New York, 2002.

Barnett, R. D. "A Diary That Survived: Damascus 1940," in Sonia Lipman and V. D. Lipman, eds. *The Century of Moses Montefiore.* Oxford, Eng., 1985.

Baron, Salo W. "The Impact of the Revolution of 1848 on Jewish Emancipation." *Jewish Social Studies,* Vol. 11 (1949).

———, and F. Kobler. *Der Judenfrage auf dem Wiener Kongress.* Vienna, 1920.

Beller, Steven. *Vienna and the Jews.* Cambridge, Eng., 1989.

Berkovitz, Jay L. *The Shaping of Jewish Identity in Nineteenth-Century France.* Detroit, 1989.

Berlin, Isaiah. "Benjamin Disraeli, Karl Marx, and the Search for Identity." *Transactions of the Jewish Historical Society* [of England], Vol. 22 (1968–69).

Bermant, Chaim. *The Cousinhood.* London, 1971.

Braham, Randolph L., ed. *Hungarian Jewish Studies.* 2 vols. New York, 1968–69.

Ferguson, Niall. *The House of Rothschild.* Vol. I: *Money's Prophets, 1798–1848.* New York, 1998.

Frankel, Jonathan. *The Damascus Affair.* Cambridge, Eng., 1997.

Freund, Ismar. *Die Emanzipation der Juden in Preussen.* Vol. 2. Berlin, 1912.

Friedländer, Fritz. *Das Leben Gabriel Riessers.* Berlin, 1927.

Goodman, Philip. *Moses Montefiore.* London, 1925.

Graetz, Michael. *Les Juifs en France au 19ième siècle: de la Révolution française à l'Alliance Israélite Universelle.* Paris, 1989.

Grilli, Marcel. "The Role of the Jews in Modern Italy." *Menorah Journal,* Autumn 1939.

Hamburger, Ernest. "Jews in the Public Service under the German Monarchy." *Leo Baeck Institute Yearbook,* Vol. 9 (1964).

———. "One Hundred Years of Emancipation." *Leo Baeck Institute Yearbook,* Vol. 14 (1969).

Hughes, H. Stuart. *Prisoners of Hope: The Silver Age of the Italian Jews.* Cambridge, Mass., 1983.

Jersch-Wenzel, Stefi. "Legal Status and Emancipation," in Michael A. Meyer, ed. *German-Jewish History in Modern Times.* Vol. 2. New York, 1996.

Kastner, David. *Der Rheinische Provinziallandtag und die Emanzipation der Juden im Rheinland, 1825–1845.* Cologne, 1989.

Katz, Jacob. *Out of the Ghetto: The Social Background of Jewish Emancipation, 1770–1860.* Cambridge, Mass., 1973.

Kertzer, David I. *The Kidnapping of Edgardo Mortara.* New York, 1997.

———. *The Popes Against the Jews: The Vatican's Role in the Rise of Modern Anti-Semitism.* New York, 2001.

Kober, Adolf. "Jews in the Revolution of 1848 in Germany." *Jewish Social Studies,* Vol. 20 (1949).

Kohler, Max. "Jewish Rights at the Congresses of Vienna (1814–1815) and Aix-la-Chapelle (1818)." *Publications of the American Jewish Historical Society,* Vol. 21 (1918).

Liebeschütz, H., and A. Paucker, eds. *Das Judentum in der deutschen Umwelt, 1800–1850.* Tübingen, Ger., 1977.

Lipman, V. D. *A History of the Jews in Britain Since 1858.* London, 1996.

———, and Sonia Lipman, eds. *The Century of Moses Montefiore.* Oxford, Eng., 1985.

Loewe, Louis. *The Damascus Affair.* Ramsgate, Eng., 1940.

Marrus, Michael R. *The Politics of Assimilation: A Study of the French Jewish Community at the Time of the Dreyfus Affair.* Oxford, Eng., 1971.

Mayer, Gustav. "Early German Socialism and Jewish Emancipation." *Jewish Social Studies,* Vol. 1 (1939).

McCagg, William O., Jr. *A History of Habsburg Jews, 1670–1918.* Bloomington, Ind., 1989.

Meyer, Michael A. *The Origins of the Modern Jew: Jewish Identity and European Culture in Germany, 1749–1824.* Detroit, 1967.

Moldenhauer, R. "Jewish Petitions to the German National Assembly in Frankfurt 1848–49." *Leo Baeck Institute Yearbook,* Vol. 16 (1971).

Mosse, Werner E. "From Schutzjuden to 'Deutsche Staatsbürger jüdischen Glaubens': The Long and Bumpy Road of Jewish Emancipation in Germany," in Pierre Birnbaum and Ira Katznelson, eds. *Paths of Emancipation: Jews, States, and Citizenship.* Princeton, N.J., 1995.

———. *The German Jewish Economic Elite, 1820–1935.* New York, 1989.

———, Arnold Paucker, and Reinhard Rürup, eds. *Revolution and Evolution: 1848 in German-Jewish History.* Tübingen, Ger., 1981.

Neher-Bernheim, R. *Documents inédits sur l'entrée des juifs dans la société française (1750–1850).* Tel Aviv, 1977.

Olivier, Georges. *L'Alliance Israélite Universelle.* Paris, 1959.

Patai, Raphael. *The Jews of Hungary: History, Culture, Psychology.* Detroit, 1996.

Poliakov, Léon. *The History of Anti-Semitism.* Vol. 3: *From Voltaire to Wagner.* New York, 1975.

Posener, S. *Adolphe Crémieux.* 2 vols. Paris, 1933.

———. "The Immediate Economic and Social Effects of the Emancipation of the Jews in France." *Jewish Social Studies,* Vol. 1 (1939).

Richarz, Monika, ed. *Jewish Life in Germany: Memoirs of Three Centuries.* Bloomington, Ind., 1991.

Rose, P. L. *Revolutionary Antisemitism in Germany from Kant to Wagner.* Princeton, N.J., 1990.

Rossi, Mario. "Emancipation of the Jews in Italy." *Jewish Social Studies,* Vol. 4 (1943).

Roth, Cecil. *Benjamin Disraeli: Earl of Beaconsfield.* Philadelphia, 1952.

———. *The History of the Jews of Italy.* Philadelphia, 1946.

Roubik, F. "Zur Geschichte der Juden in Böhmen in der ersten Hälfte des 19. Jahrhunderts." *Jahrbuch für Geschichte in der tschechoslovakischen Republik,* Vol. 6 (1934).

Rubinstein, William D., and Hilary Rubinstein. *Philosemitism: Admiration and Support in the English-Speaking World for Jews, 1840–1939.* New York, 1939.

Rürup, Reinhard. "Jewish Emancipation and Bourgeois Society." *Leo Baeck Institute Yearbook,* Vol. 31 (1986).

Sachar, Abram L. "The Jew Enters Parliament." *Menorah Journal,* September–October 1924.

Sachar, Howard M. *Farewell España: The World of the Sephardim Remembered.* New York, 1994.

Salbstein, M. C. N. *The Emancipation of the Jews in Britain: The Question of the Admission of the Jews to Parliament.* East Brunswick, N.J., 1982.

Segre, Dan V. "The Emancipation of the Jews in Italy," in Pierre Birnbaum and Ira Katznelson, eds. *Paths of Emancipation: Jews, States, and Citizenship.* Princeton, N.J., 1995.

Sterling, Eleonore O. "Anti-Jewish Riots in Germany in 1819: A Displacement of Social Protest." *Historia Judaica,* Vol. 12 (1950).

———. *Judenhass: Die Anfänge des politischen Antisemitismus in Deutschland (1815–1850).* Frankfurt a/M, 1969.

Strauss, Herbert. "Pre-Emancipation Prussian Policies Towards the Jews, 1815–1847." *Leo Baeck Institute Yearbook,* Vol. 11 (1966).

Szajkowski, Zosa. *Jews and the French Revolutions of 1789, 1830, and 1848.* New York, 1970.

Toury, Jacob. *Soziale und politische Geschichte der Juden in Deutschland, 1847–1871.* Düsseldorf, 1977.

Wistrich, Robert S. *Revolutionary Jews from Marx to Trotsky.* New York, 1976.

VI. *Jews in an Emancipated Economy*

Alon, Amos. *The Pity of It All: A History of the Jews in Germany, 1743–1933.* New York, 2002.

Arkin, Marcus. *Aspects of Jewish Economic History.* Philadelphia, 1975.

Birnbaum, Pierre. "Between Social and Political Assimilation: Remarks on the History of the Jews in France," in Pierre Birnbaum and Ira Katznelson, eds. *Paths of Emancipation: Jews, States, and Citizenship.* Princeton, N.J., 1995.

Black, Eugene. *The Social Politics of Anglo-Jewry, 1880–1920.* Oxford, Eng., 1988.

Braham, Randolph L., ed. *Hungarian Jewish Studies.* 2 vols. New York, 1968–69.

Einzig, Paul. "The Jews and German Finance." *Jewish Review,* June–September 1933.

Feldman, David. *Englishmen and Jews: Social Relations and Political Culture, 1840–1914.* New Haven, Conn., 1994.

Ferguson, Niall. *The House of Rothschild.* Vol. 2: *The World's Banker, 1849–1999.* New York, 1999.

Footman, David. *The Primrose Path: A Life of Ferdinand Lassalle.* London, 1961.

Frischer, Dominique. *La Moïse des Amérique: vies et oeuvres du munificent baron de Hirsch.* Paris, 2002.

Gelber, N. M. "The Intervention of German Jews at the Berlin Congress of 1878." *Leo Baeck Institute Yearbook,* Vol. 5 (1960).

Gille, Bertrand. *Histoire de la Maison Rothschild.* Vol. 1. Geneva, 1965.

Grunwald, Kurt. *Turkenhirsch: A Study of Baron Maurice de Hirsch: Entrepreneur and Philanthropist.* Jerusalem, 1966.

Jersch-Wenzel, Stefi. "Population Shifts and Occupational Structure," in Michael A. Meyer, ed. *German-Jewish History in Modern Times.* Vol. 2. New York, 1996.

Jöhlinger, Otto. *Bismarck und die Juden.* Berlin, 1921.

Kober, Adolf. "Emancipation's Impact on the Educational and Vocational Training of German Jewry." *Jewish Social Studies,* Vol. 15 (1954).

Lipman, V. D. *A History of the Jews in Britain Since 1858.* London, 1996.

Marrus, Michael R. *The Politics of Assimilation: A Study of the French Jewish Community at the Time of the Dreyfus Affair.* Oxford, Eng., 1971.

Mayer, Eugen. *Die Frankfurter Juden.* Frankfurt a/M, 1966.

McCagg, William O., Jr. *A History of Habsburg Jews, 1670–1918.* Bloomington, Ind., 1989.

Mosse, Werner E. "From Schutzjuden to 'Deutsche Staatsbürger jüdischen Glaubens': The Long and Bumpy Road of Jewish Emancipation in Germany," in Pierre Birnbaum and Ira Katznelson, eds. *Paths of Emancipation: Jews, States, and Citizenship.* Princeton, N.J., 1995.

———. *The German Jewish Economic Elite, 1820–1935.* New York, 1989.

Patai, Raphael. *The Jews of Hungary: History, Culture, Psychology.* Detroit, 1996.

Rollins, Harold. "The Jews' Role in the Early British Railways." *Jewish Social Studies,* Vol. 4 (1943).

Silbergleit, Heinrich. *Die Bevölkerungs- und Berufsverhältnisse der Juden im deutschen Reich.* Berlin, 1930.

Silberner, Edmund. "Friedrich Engels and the Jews." *Jewish Social Studies,* Vol. 20 (1949).

Stern, Fritz. *Gold and Iron: Bismarck, Bleichröder, and the Building of the German Empire.* New York, 1979.

Straus, Raphael. "The Jews in the Economic Evolution of Central Europe." *Jewish Social Studies,* Vol. 3 (1941).

Theilhaber, Felix A. *Der Untergang der deutschen Juden: Eine volkswirtschaftliche Studie.* Munich, 1911.

Weber, Eugen. "Reflections on the Jews in France," in Frances Malino and Bernard Wasserstein, eds. *The Jews in Modern France.* Hanover, N.H., 1985.

Wistrich, Robert S. *Revolutionary Jews from Marx to Trotsky.* New York, 1976.

———. *Socialism and the Jews: The Dilemmas of Assimilation in Germany and Austria-Hungary.* East Brunswick, N.J., 1982.

VII. *The Impact of Western Culture on Jewish Life*

Agus, Jacob B. *Modern Philosophies of Judaism.* New York, 1941.

Albert, Phyllis Cohen. *The Modernization of French Jewry.* Hanover, N.H., 1977.

Alon, Amos. *The Pity of It All: A History of Jews in Germany, 1743–1933.* New York, 2002.

Altmann, Alexander. *Essays on Jewish Intellectual History.* Hanover, N.H., 1981.

Arendt, Hannah. "Privileged Jews." *Jewish Social Studies,* Vol. 8 (1946).

———. *Rahel Varnhagen: The Life of a Jewess.* London, 1957.

Baron, Salo W. "I. M. Jost, the Historian." *Publications of the American Academy for Jewish Research.* Vol. 1 (1930).

Berkovitz, Jay L. *The Shaping of Jewish Identity in Nineteenth-Century France.* Detroit, 1989.

Black, Eugene. *The Social Politics of Anglo-Jewry 1880–1920.* Oxford, Eng., 1988.

Endelman, Todd. M., ed. *Jewish Apostasy in the Modern World.* New York, 1987.

———, and Tony Kushner, eds. *Disraeli's Jewishness.* London, 2002.

Ginzberg, Louis. *Students, Scholars, and Saints.* Philadelphia, 1943.

Glassman, Bernard. *Benjamin Disraeli: The Fabricated Jew in Myth and Memory.* Lanham, Md., 2003.

Glatzer, Nahum N., ed. *Leopold and Adelheid Zunz: An Account in Letters, 1815–1885.* London, 1958.

———. *Leopold Zunz: Jude-Deutscher-Europäer.* Tübingen, Ger., 1964.

Herz, Henrietta. "A Salonist Remembers," in Leo W. Schwarz, ed. *Memoirs of My People.* Philadelphia, 1943.

Katz, Jacob. *Out of the Ghetto: The Social Background of Jewish Emancipation, 1770–1860.* Cambridge, Mass., 1973.

Liptzin, Sol. *Germany's Stepchildren.* Philadelphia, 1944.

Lowenstein, Steven M. *The Berlin Jewish Community: Enlightenment, Family, and Crisis, 1770–1830.* New York, 1994.

Marcuse, Ludwig. *Revolutionär und Patriot: Das Leben Ludwig Börnes.* Leipzig, 1929.

Marrus, Michael R. *The Politics of Assimilation: A Study of the French Jewish Community at the Time of the Dreyfus Affair.* Oxford, 1971.

Massey, Irving. *Philo-Semitism in Nineteenth-Century German Literature.* Tübingen, Ger., 2000.

Meyer, Michael A. "Abraham Geiger's Historical Judaism," in Jakob J. Petuchowski, ed. *New Perspectives on Abraham Geiger.* New York, 1975.

———. "Jewish Religious Reform and Wissenschaft des Judentums." *Leo Baeck Institute Yearbook,* Vol. 16 (1971).

———. *The Origins of the Modern Jew: Jewish Identity and European Culture in Germany, 1749–1824.* Detroit, 1967.

———. *Response to Modernity: A History of the Reform Movement in Judaism.* New York, 1988.

———, ed. *German-Jewish History in Modern Times.* Vol. II. New York, 1996.

Mosse, Werner E. "From Schutzjuden to 'Deutsche Staatsbürger jüdischen Glaubens': The Long and Bumpy Road of Jewish Emancipation in Germany," in Pierre Birnbaum and Ira Katznelson, eds. *Paths of Emancipation: Jews, States, and Citizenship.* Princeton, N.J., 1995.

Patai, Raphael. *The Jewish Mind.* New York, 1977.

Reissner, H. G. *Eduard Gans: Ein Leben im Vörmarz*. Tübingen, Ger., 1965.

Richarz, Monika, ed. *Jewish Life in Germany: Memoirs of Three Centuries*. Bloomington, Ind., 1991.

Schatzberg, Walter, and Jehuda Reinharz, eds. *The Jewish Response to German Culture: From the Enlightenment to the Second World War*. Hanover, N.H., 1985.

Schorsch, Ismar. *From Text to Context: The Turn to History in Modern Judaism*. Hanover, N.H., 1994.

———. "Zacharias Frankel and the European Origins of Conservative Judaism," *Judaism*, Vol. 30 (1981).

Stahl, F. J. *Der christliche Staat und sein Verhältnis zu Deismus und Judenthum*. Berlin, 1847.

Untermeyer, Louis. *Heinrich Heine: Paradox and Poet*. 2 vols. New York, 1937.

Wallach, L. "The Beginnings of the Science of Judaism in the Nineteenth Century." *Historia Judaica*, April 1946.

VIII. *A Sephardic-Oriental Diaspora*

Abitrol, Michel. "The Encounter Between French Jewry and the Jews of North Africa," in Frances Malino and Bernard Wasserstein, eds. *The Jews in Modern France*. Hanover, N.H., 1985.

Ansky, Michael. *Les Juifs d'Algérie du décret Crémieux à la libération*. Paris, 1960.

———. *Yehudei Algeria* [The Jews of Algeria]. Jerusalem, 1968.

Ashkenazi, Tova. *Salonika HaYehudit* [Jewish Salonika]. Jerusalem, 1960.

Barnett, R. D., and W. M. Schwab, eds. *The Sephardic Heritage: The Western Sephardim*. Vol. 2. Grendon, Eng., 1989.

Beinart, Haim, ed. *The Sephardi Legacy*. Vol. 2. Jerusalem, 1992.

Ben-Ami, Issachar. *Yehudei Maroc* [The Jews of Morocco]. Jerusalem, 1975.

Bensimon-Donath, Doris. *L'Évolution du judaïsme marocain sous le protectorat français: 1921–1956*. Paris, 1968.

Ben-Zvi, Yitzchak. *The Exiled and the Redeemed*. Jerusalem, 1957.

Bodian, Miriam. "Amsterdam, Venice and the Marrano Diaspora in the Seventeenth Century," in Joseph Michman, ed. *Dutch Jewish History*. Jerusalem, 1989.

Bornstein-Makovetsky, Leah. "Sephardic Communities in the Ottoman Empire from the Sixteenth to the Eighteenth Centuries," in R. D. Barnett and W. M. Schwab, eds. *The Sephardic Heritage*. Vol. 2. Grendon, Eng., 1989.

Braude, Benjamin, and Bernard Lewis, eds. *Christians and Jews in the Ottoman Empire*. Vol. 2. New York, 1982.

Chouraqui, André. *L'Alliance Israélite Universelle et la renaissance juive contemporaine*. Paris, 1965.

———. *La saga des Juifs en Afrique du Nord*. Paris, 1972.

Cohen, Hayyim J. *The Jews of the Middle East, 1860-1972*. New York, 1973.

Cohen, Martin A., ed. *The Jewish Experience in Colonial Latin America*. 2 vols. Waltham, Mass., 1971.

Corcos, David. *The History of the Jews of Morocco*. Jerusalem, 1976.

Coubage, Youssef, and Philippe Fargues. *Chrétiens et juifs dans l'Islam arabe et turc*. Paris, 1955.

Emmanuel, I. S. *Histoire des Israélites de Salonique*. Paris, 1936.

Fischel, Walter J. "The Jews of Persia, 1795–1940." *Jewish Social Studies*, Vol. 13 (1950).

Galanté, Abraham. *Histoire des Juifs d'Anatolie*. Vol. 2. Istanbul, 1939.

Hacker, Joseph. "The Sephardim in the Ottoman Empire in the Seventeenth and Eighteenth Centuries," in Haim Beinart, ed. *The Sephardi Legacy*. Vol. 2. Jerusalem, 1992.

Haddad, Hezkel M. *Yehudei Artzot Arav v'Islam* [The Jews of Arab and Islamic Lands]. Tel Aviv, 1983.

Harari, Yosef. *Toldot Yehudei al-Magreb* [History of the Jews of the Maghreb]. Tel Aviv, 1973.

Heyd, Uriel. "The Jewish Communities of Istanbul in the XVII Century." *Orient,* Autumn 1951.

Israel, Jonathan I. "The Sephardi Contribution to Economic Life and Colonization in Europe and the New World: Sixteenth–Eighteenth Centuries," in Haim Beinart, ed. *The Sephardi Legacy.* Vol. 2. Jerusalem, 1992.

Juhasz, Esther, ed. *Sephardic Jews in the Ottoman Empire.* Jerusalem, 1966.

Landau, Jacob. *Jews in Nineteenth-Century Egypt.* New York, 1969.

Lewis, Bernard. *The Jews of Islam.* Princeton, N.J., 1984.

Liebman, Seymour B. *Jews in New Spain: Faith, Flame, and the Inquisition.* Coral Gables, Fla., 1970.

Martin, Claude. *Les Israélites algériens de 1830 à 1902.* Paris, 1936.

Masters, Bruce. *Christians and Jews in the Ottoman Arab World: The Roots of Sectarianism.* Cambridge, Eng., 2001.

Mazur, Belle D. *Studies on Jewry in Greece.* Athens, 1935.

Mézan, S. *Juifs espagnols en Bulgarie.* Paris, 1925.

Nathan, Naphtali. "Notes on the Jews of Turkey." *Jewish Social Studies,* Vol. 27 (1964).

Olivier, Georges. *L'Alliance Israélite Universelle.* Paris, 1959.

Patai, Raphael. *The Vanished Worlds of Jewry.* New York, 1980.

Rapaport, Louis. *The Lost Jews.* New York, 1980.

Rodrigue, Aron. *French Jews, Turkish Jews: The Alliance Israélite Universelle and the Politics of Jewish Schooling in Turkey, 1860–1925.* Bloomington, Ind., 1990.

———. *Jews and Moslems: Images of Sephardi and Eastern Jewries in Modern Times.* Seattle, 2003.

———, and Esther Benbassa. *The Jews of the Balkans: The Judeo-Spanish Community, Fifteenth to Twentieth Centuries.* Cambridge, Mass., 1995.

Sachar, Howard M. *Farewell España: The World of the Sephardim Remembered.* New York, 1994.

Sciaky, Leon. *Farewell to Salonica.* London, 1946.

Shmuelevitz, Abraham. *The Jews of the Ottoman Empire.* Leiden, 1984.

Simon, Reeva S., Michael M. Laskier, and Sara Reguer, eds. *The Jews of the Middle East and North Africa in Modern Times.* New York, 2003.

Stahl, Avraham. *Toldot Yehudei Maroc* [The History of Moroccan Jewry]. Jerusalem, 1966.

Stillman, Norman. *The Jews of Arab Lands in the Modern Period.* Philadelphia, 1991.

Tamir, Vicki. *Bulgaria and Her Jews.* New York, 1979.

Weiker, Walter F. *Ottomans, Turks, and the Jewish Polity: A History of the Jews of Turkey.* Lanham, Md., 1992.

Zafrani, Haim. *Les Juifs du Maroc: Vie sociale, économique et religieuse.* Paris, 1972.

IX. *The Rise of Jewish Life in America*

Arbell, Mordechai. *The Jewish Nation of the Caribbean: The Spanish-Jewish Settlements in the Caribbean and the Guianas.* Jerusalem, 2002.

Borden, Morton. *Jews, Turks, and Infidels.* Chapel Hill, N.C., 1984.

Buchler, Joseph. "The Struggle for Unity: Attempts at Union in American Jewish Life, 1654–1868." *American Jewish Archives,* June 1949.

Carosso, Vincent P. "A Financial Elite: New York's German-Jewish Investment Bankers." *American Jewish Historical Quarterly,* September 1976.

Chyet, Stanley. "The Political Rights of the Jews in the United States, 1776–1840." *American Jewish Archives,* April 1958.

Cohen, Martin A., ed. *The Jewish Experience in Colonial Latin America.* 2 vols. Waltham, Mass., 1971.

Cohen, Naomi W. *Encounter with Emancipation: The German Jews in the United States, 1830–1914.* Philadelphia, 1984.

Cohon, Samuel. "Reform Judaism in America," in Theodore Friedman and Robert Gordis, eds. *Jewish Life in America.* New York, 1951.

Daniels, Doris G. "Colonial Jewry: Religion, Domestic and Social Relations." *American Jewish Historical Quarterly,* March 1977.

Díaz, Adolfo S. "Spain's Wandering Jews." *America,* July 1951.

Feldman, Egal. "Jews in the Early Growth of New York City's Men's Clothing Trade." *American Jewish Archives,* April 1960.

Friedman, Lee M. *Pilgrims in a New Land.* Philadelphia, 1948.

Glanz, Rudolf. *The German Jewish Mass Emigration, 1820–1880. American Jewish Archives,* April 1970.

———. *Jews in Relation to the Cultural Milieu of the Germans in America.* New York, 1947.

Goodman, Abram V. *American Overture: Jewish Rights in Colonial Times.* Philadelphia, 1947.

Grinstein, Hyman B. *The Rise of the Jewish Community of New York, 1654–1860.* Philadelphia, 1945.

Hyman, Paula, Charlotte Baum, and Sonya Michel, eds. *The Jewish Woman in America.* New York, 1976.

Israel, Jonathan I. "The Sephardi Contribution to Economic Life and Colonization in Europe and the New World, Sixteenth–Eighteenth Centuries," in Haim Beinart, ed. *The Sephardi Legacy.* Vol. 2. Jerusalem, 1992.

Jick, Leon A. *The Americanization of the Synagogue, 1820–1870.* Hanover, N.H., 1976.

Karner, Frances P. *The Sephardics of Curaçao.* Assen, Neth., 1969.

Karp, Abraham. *Beginnings: Early American Judaica.* Philadelphia, 1975.

Korn, Bertram K. *American Jewry and the Civil War.* New York, 1961.

———. *Eventful Years and Experiences: Studies in Nineteenth-Century American Jewish History.* Cincinnati, 1954.

Lebeson, Anita. *Jewish Pioneers in America, 1492–1848.* New York, 1931.

Liebman, Seymour B. *The Jews in New Spain.* Coral Gables, Fla., 1970.

Marcus, Jacob R. *The Colonial American Jew, 1492–1776.* 3 vols. Detroit, 1970.

———. *Studies in American Jewish History.* Cincinnati, 1969.

Metz, Allan. " 'Those of the Hebrew Nation . . .': The Sephardic Experience in Colonial Latin America." *American Jewish Archives,* Spring–Summer 1992.

Pool, David de Sola. *Portraits Etched in Stone: Early Jewish Settlers, 1682–1831.* New York, 1952.

Sachar, Howard M. *A History of the Jews in America.* New York, 1992.

Sarna, Jonathan D. *American Jews and Church–State Relations.* New York, 1989.

———. *American Judaism: A History.* New Haven, Conn., 2004.

Schappes, Morris U., ed. *A Documentary History of the Jews in the United States, 1654–1875.* 3rd ed. New York, 1971.

Scharfman, I. Harold. *Jews on the Frontier.* Chicago, 1977.

Supple, Barry E. "A Business Elite: German-Jewish Financiers in Nineteenth-Century New York." *Business History Review,* Summer 1957.

Volkman, Ernest. *A Legacy of Hate: Anti-Semitism in America.* New York, 1982.

Wiznitzer, Arnold. *Jews in Colonial Brazil.* New York, 1960.

Yerushalmi, Yosef H. "Curaçao and the Caribbean in Early Modern Jewish History." *American Jewish History,* December 1982.

X. *False Dawn in the East: Alexander II and the Era of "Enlightenment"*

Aronsfeld, C. C. "Jewish Bankers and the Tsar." *Jewish Social Studies,* Vol. 35 (1973).

Eisenbach, Artur, et al., eds. *The Emancipation of the Jews in Poland, 1780–1870.* Oxford, Eng., 1991.

Finer, Shmuel. *Haskalah and History: The Emergence of a Modern Historical Consciousness.* Portland, Ore., 2002.

Freundlich, Charles H. *Peretz Smolenskin: His Life and Thought.* New York, 1966.

Graham, S. *Tsar of Freedom: The Life and Reign of Alexander II.* New Haven, Conn., 1935.

Greenberg, Louis. *The Jews in Russia: The Struggle for Emancipation.* Vol. II. New York, 1976.

Katsch, Abraham I. "Nachman Krochmal and the German Idealists." *Jewish Social Studies,* Vol. 8 (1946).

Klier, J. D. *Imperial Russia's Jewish Question, 1855–1881.* Cambridge, Eng., 1985.

Levin, Nora. *While the Messiah Tarried: Jewish Socialist Movements, 1871–1917.* New York, 1977.

Levitats, Isaac. *The Jewish Community in Russia, 1844–1917.* Jerusalem, 1981.

Mahler, Raphael. *Hasidism and the Jewish Enlightenment.* Philadelphia, 1985.

———. "The Social and Political Aspects of the Haskalah in Galicia." *YIVO Annual of Jewish Science,* Vol. 1 (1946).

Meisl, Josef. *Haskalah.* Berlin, 1919.

Nathans, Benjamin. *Beyond the Pale: The Jewish Encounter with Late Imperial Russia.* Berkeley, Calif., 2002.

Pelli, Moshe. *The Age of Haskalah.* Leiden, 1979.

Polish, David. "Perez Smolenskin's Contribution to Jewish Thought." *Reconstructionist,* June 11, 1943.

Rawidowicz, Simon. "Nachman Krochmal als Historiker." *Dubnow Festschrift.* Berlin, 1930.

Riasanovsky, Nicholas V. *A History of Russia.* 5th ed. Oxford, 1993.

Rogger, Hans. *Jewish Policies and Right-Wing Politics in Imperial Russia.* Berkeley, Calif., 1986.

———. "The Jewish Policy of Late Tsarism: A Reappraisal." *Wiener Library Bulletin,* Vol. 25 (1971).

Slouschz, Nahum. *The Renascence of Hebrew Literature, 1743–1885.* Philadelphia, 1909.

Spiegel, Shalom. *Hebrew Reborn.* New York, 1930.

Stanislawski, Michael. *For Whom Do I Toil? Judah Leib Gordon and the Crisis of Russian Jewry.* New York, 1988.

———. "Russian Jewry, the Russian State, and the Dynamics of Jewish Emancipation," in Pierre Birnbaum and Ira Katznelson, eds. *Paths of Emancipation: Jews, States, and Citizenship.* Princeton, N.J., 1995.

Zborowski, Mark, and Elizabeth Herzog, eds. *Life Is with People: The Jewish Little-Town of Eastern Europe.* New York, 1952.

Zipperstein, Steven J. "Jewish Enlightenment in Odessa: Cultural Characteristics, 1794–1871," *Jewish Social Studies,* Vol. 43 (1982).

XI. *Russian Twilight: The Era of Pogroms and May Laws*

Aronson, I. Michael. *Troubled Waters: The Origins of the 1881 Anti-Jewish Pogroms in Russia.* Pittsburgh, 1990.

Butnaru, I. C. *The Silent Holocaust: Romania and Its Jews.* New York, 1992.

Charques, Richard. *The Twilight of Imperial Russia.* Oxford, 1958.

Frankel, Jonathan. *Prophecy and Politics: Socialism, Nationalism, and the Russian Jews, 1862–1917.* Cambridge, Eng., 1981.

Gitelman, Zvi. *A Century of Two Peoples: The Jews of Russia and the Soviet Union.* New York, 1988.

Greenberg, Louis. *The Jews in Russia: The Struggle for Emancipation.* Vol. II. New York, 1976.

Henriques, U. R. Q. "Journey to Romania, 1867," in Sonia Lipman and V. D. Lipman, eds. *The Century of Moses Montefiore.* Oxford, Eng., 1985.

Iancu, Carol. "Adolphe Crémieux, l'Alliance Israélite Universelle et les Juifs de Roumanie." *Revue d'Études Juives,* Vol. 133 (1974).

———. *Les Juifs en Roumanie (1866–1919).* Aix-en-Provence, 1978.

Klier, John D. *Imperial Russia's Jewish Question, 1855–1881.* Cambridge, Mass., 1985.

————, and S. Lambroza, eds. *Pogroms: Anti-Jewish Violence in Modern Russian History.* Cambridge, Mass., 1992.

Kohn, Hans. *Prophets and People.* New York, 1946.

Pinson, Koppel, ed. *Essays on Antisemitism.* New York, 1946.

Riasanovsky, Nicholas V. *A History of Russia.* 5th ed. Oxford, Eng., 1993.

Rogger, Hans. *Jewish Policies and Right-Wing Politics in Imperial Russia.* Berkeley, Calif., 1986.

————. "The Jewish Policy of Late Tsarism: A Reappraisal." *Wiener Library Bulletin,* Vol. 25 (1971).

Stanislawski, Michael. *For Whom Do I Toil? Judah Leib Gordon and the Crisis of Russian Jewry.* New York, 1988.

————. "Russian Jewry, the Russian State, and the Dynamics of Jewish Emancipation," in Pierre Birnbaum and Ira Katznelson, eds. *Paths of Emancipation: Jews, States, and Citizenship.* Princeton, N.J., 1995.

Starr, Joshua. "Jewish Citizenship in Rumania (1878–1940)." *Jewish Social Studies,* Vol. 3 (1941).

Stern, Fritz. *Gold and Iron: Bismarck, Bleichröder, and the Building of the German Empire.* New York, 1979.

Wistrich, Robert S. *Socialism and the Jews: The Dilemmas of Assimilation in Germany and Austria-Hungary.* East Brunswick, N.J., 1982.

Zborowski, Mark, and Elizabeth Herzog, eds. *Life Is with People: The Jewish Little-Town of Eastern Europe.* New York, 1952.

XII. *A Migration of Eastern European Jewry, 1881–1914*

Adler, Cyrus. *Jacob Henry Schiff.* New York, 1921.

Alderman, Geoffrey. *Modern British Jewry.* Oxford, Eng., 1992.

Berkow, Ira. *Maxwell Street: Survival in a Bazaar.* Garden City, N.Y., 1977.

Berman, Myron. *The Attitude of American Jewry Towards East European Jewish Immigration, 1881–1914.* New York, 1980.

Black, Eugene. *The Social Politics of Anglo-Jewry 1880–1920.* Oxford, Eng., 1988.

Bristow, Edward J. *Prostitution and Prejudice: The Jewish Fight Against White Slavery, 1870–1939.* New York, 1983.

Cesarini, David, ed. *The Making of Modern Anglo-Jewry.* New York, 1990.

Feldman, David. *Englishmen and Jews: Social Relations and Political Culture, 1840–1914.* New Haven, Conn., 1994.

Frankel, Jonathan. *Prophecy and Politics: Socialism, Nationalism, and the Russian Jews, 1862–1917.* Cambridge, Eng., 1981.

Gartner, Lloyd. *The Jewish Immigrant in England, 1870–1914.* London, 1973.

Gassenschmidt, Christoph. *Jewish Liberal Politics in Tsarist Russia, 1900–1914.* New York, 1995.

Goren, Aryeh, and Yosef Wenkert, eds. *The Jewish Mass Immigration to the United States and the Growth of American Jewry: A Reader.* Jerusalem, 1976.

Handlin, Oscar. *The Uprooted.* Boston, 1951.

Hansen, Marcus L. *The Atlantic Migration.* Cambridge, Mass., 1940.

Howe, Irving. *World of Our Fathers: The Journey of the East European Jews to America and the Life They Found and Made.* New York, 1976.

Karp, Abraham. *Golden Door to America: The Jewish Immigrant Experience.* New York, 1976.

Katzenelenbogen, S. *L'Émigration juive.* Brussels, 1918.

Kissman, Joseph. "The Immigration of Rumanian Jews up to 1914." *YIVO Annual of Jewish Social Science,* Vol. 8 (1947–48).

Lee, Samuel J. *Moses of the New World: The Work of Baron de Hirsch.* New York, 1970.

Lipman, V. D. *A History of the Jews in Britain Since 1858.* London, 1996.

Marrus, Michael R. *The Unwanted: European Refugees in the Twentieth Century.* New York, 1985.

Nadell, Pamela S. "The Journey to America by Steam: The Jews of Eastern Europe in Transition." *American Jewish History,* December 1981.

Riis, Jacob. *How the Other Half Lives.* New York, 1902.

Rischin, Moses. *The Promised City: New York's Jews, 1870–1914.* New York, 1970.

Sachar, Howard M. *A History of the Jews in America.* New York, 1992.

Sanders, Ronald. *The Downtown Jews.* New York, 1969.

———. *Shores of Refuge: A Hundred Years of Jewish Emigration.* New York, 1988.

Seidman, Joel. *The Needle Trades.* New York, 1942.

Szajkowski, Zosa. "How the Mass Migration to America Began." *Jewish Social Studies,* Spring–Summer 1975.

Troen, S. I., and B. Pinkus, eds. *Organizing Rescue: National Jewish Solidarity in the Modern Period.* London, 1992.

Weisser, Michael R. *A Brotherhood of Memory: Jewish Landsmanshaftn in the New World.* New York, 1985.

Wischnitzer, Mark. *To Dwell in Safety: The Story of Jewish Migration Since 1800.* Philadelphia, 1948.

XIII, XIV. *The Onset of Modern Antisemitism; The Mutation of Racism*

Adams, Mark B., ed. *The Wellborn Science: Eugenics in Germany, France, Brazil, and Russia.* New York, 1990.

Alderman, Geoffrey. *Modern British Jewry.* Oxford, Eng., 1992.

Beller, Steven. *Vienna and the Jews.* Cambridge, Eng., 1989.

———. "Why Was the Viennese Liberal *Bildungsbürgertum* Jewish," in Yehuda Don and Victor Karady, eds. *A Social and Economic History of Central European Jewry.* New Brunswick, N.J., 1990.

Benda, Julien. *La Trahison des clercs.* Paris, 1938.

Berding, Helmut. *Moderner Antisemitismus in Deutschland.* Frankfurt a/M, 1988.

Bernasconi, Robert, and Sybil Cook, eds. *Race and Racism in Continental Philosophy.* Bloomington, Ind., 2003.

Birnbaum, Pierre. "Between Social and Political Assimilation: Remarks on the History of the Jews in France," in Pierre Birnbaum and Ira Katznelson, eds. *Paths of Emancipation: Jews, States, and Citizenship.* Princeton, N.J., 1995.

Black, Eugene. *The Social Politics of Anglo-Jewry, 1880–1920.* Oxford, Eng., 1988.

Blacker, C. P. *Eugenics: Galton and After.* Cambridge, Mass., 1952.

Bölich, Walter, ed. *Der Berliner Antisemitismusstreit.* Frankfurt a/M, 1965.

Boudrel, Philippe. *Histoire des Juifs de France.* Paris, 1974.

Boyer, John W. *Political Radicalism in Late Imperial Vienna: Origins of the Christian Social Movement, 1848–1897.* Chicago, 1981.

Bredin, Jean-Denis. *The Affair: The Case of Alfred Dreyfus.* New York, 1986.

Bristow, Edward J. *Prostitution and Prejudice: The Jewish Fight Against White Slavery, 1870–1939.* New York, 1983.

Brustein, William I. *Roots of Hate: Antisemitism in Europe Before the Holocaust.* Cambridge, Eng., 2003.

Burleigh, Michael. *Death and Deliverance: "Euthanasia" in Germany, 1900–1945.* Cambridge, Eng., 1997.

Busi, Frederick. *The Pope of Antisemitism: The Career and Legacy of Edouard-Adolphe Drumont.* Lanham, Md., 1986.

Byrnes, Robert F. *Anti-Semitism in Modern France.* New Brunswick, N.J., 1950.

Carter, William C. *Marcel Proust: A Life.* New Haven, Conn., 2000.

Chant, Colon, ed. *Science, Technology, and Everyday Life, 1870–1950.* London, 1989.

Chapman, Guy. *The Dreyfus Case.* London, 1955.

Cheyette, Bryan. *Constructions of "the Jew" in English Literature and Society*. Cambridge, Eng., 1995.

Cornwell, John. *Hitler's Scientists*. New York, 2003.

Curtis, Michael. *Three Against the Third Republic—Sorel, Barrès, and Maurras*. Princeton, N.J., 1959.

Donaldson, Frances. *The Marconi Scandal*. New York, 1962.

Feldman, David. *Englishmen and Jews: Social Relations and Political Culture, 1840–1914*. New Haven, Conn., 1994.

Ferguson, Niall. *The House of Rothschild*. 2 vols. New York, 1998–99.

Forrest, D. W. *Francis Galton: The Life and Work of a Victorian Genius*. New York, 1974.

Forth, Christopher E. *The Dreyfus Affair and the Crisis of French Manhood*. Baltimore, 2004.

Fraenkel, Joseph, ed. *The Jews of Austria: Essays on Their Life, History, and Destruction*. London, 1967.

Gainer, Bernard. *Alien Invasion: The Origins of the Aliens Act of 1905*. London, 1972.

Galton, Francis. *Inquiries into Human Faculty and Its Development*. New ed. London, 1908.

Gilman, Sander. *The Case of Sigmund Freud: Medicine and Identity at the Fin de Siècle*. Baltimore, 1993.

———. "Jews and Mental Illness: Medical Metaphors, Anti-Semitism, and the Jewish Response." *Journal of the History of the Behavioral Sciences*. Vol. XX (April 1984).

Gutteridge, Richard. *Open Thy Mouth to the Dumb! The German Evangelical Church and the Jews, 1879–1950*. Oxford, Eng., 1976.

Hamburger, Ernest. "Jews in the Public Service under the German Monarchy." *Leo Baeck Institute Yearbook*, Vol. 9 (1964).

Hawkins, Mike. *Social Darwinism in European and American Thought, 1860–1945*. Cambridge, Eng., 1997.

Holmes, Colin. *Anti-Semitism in British Society, 1876–1939*. New York, 1979.

Hyman, Paula E. *From Dreyfus to Vichy: The Remaking of French Jewry, 1906–1939*. New York, 1979.

Jöhlinger, Otto. *Bismarck und die Juden*. Berlin, 1921.

Karbach, Oscar. "The Founder of Political Anti-Semitism: Georg von Schoenerer." *Jewish Social Studies*, Vol. 6 (1945).

Klein, Charlotte. "Damascus to Kiev: *Civiltà cattolica* on Ritual Murder." *Wiener Library Bulletin*, Nos. 28, 32 (1974).

Larkin, Maurice. *Church and State after the Dreyfus Affair: The Separation Issue in France*. London, 1974.

Lebzelter, Cynthia. *Political Anti-Semitism in England 1918–1939*. New York, 1978.

Levy, Richard S. *The Downfall of the Antisemitic Political Parties in Imperial Germany*. New Haven, Conn., 1975.

Lipman, V. D. *A History of the Jews in Britain Since 1858*. London, 1996.

Longee, Robert W. *Paul de Lagarde*. Cambridge, Mass., 1962.

Malino, Frances, and Bernard Wasserstein, eds. *The Jews in Modern France*. Hanover, N.H., 1985.

Mandel, Siegfried. *Nietzsche and the Jews*. Amherst, N.Y., 1998.

Marrus, Michael R. *The Politics of Assimilation: A Study of the French Jewish Community at the Time of the Dreyfus Affair*. Oxford, Eng., 1971.

Massing, Paul. *Rehearsal for Destruction*. New York, 1949.

Maurer, Trude. *Ostjuden in Deutschland, 1918–1933*. Hamburg, 1986.

Mazumdar, Pauline M. H. *Eugenics, Human Genetics, and Human Failings: The Eugenics Society, Its Sources, and Its Critics in Berlin*. London, 1992.

McCagg, William O., Jr. *A History of Habsburg Jews, 1670–1918*. Bloomington, Ind., 1989.

Meyer, Michael A. *German-Jewish History in Modern Times*. Vol. 3. New York, 1996.

———, ed. "Jewish Reaction to New Hostility in Germany, 1879–1881." *Leo Baeck Institute Yearbook*, Vol. 11 (1966).

Mosse, George L. *Toward the Final Solution: A History of European Racism.* London, 1978.

Mosse, Werner E. *The German Jewish Economic Elite, 1820–1935.* New York, 1989.

Oxaal, I., M. Pollak, and G. Botz, eds. *Jews, Antisemitism, and Culture in Vienna.* London, 1987.

Petit, Jacques. *Bernanos, Bloy, Claudel, Péguy: quatre écrivains catholiques face à Israël.* Paris, 1972.

Pinson, Koppel, ed. *Essays on Antisemitism.* New York, 1946.

Ploetz, Alfred. *Die Tüchtigkeit unserer Rasse und der Schutz der Schwachen.* Berlin, 1895.

Poliakov, Léon. *The History of Anti-Semitism.* Vol. 4: *Suicidal Europe, 1870–1933.* Oxford, Eng., 1985.

Pougan, Jacques. *L'Âge d'or du maurrassisme.* Paris, 1971.

Pulzer, Peter. *The Rise of Political Anti-Semitism in Germany and Austria.* Rev. ed. Cambridge, Mass., 1988.

Richarz, Monika, ed. *Jewish Life in Germany: Memoirs from Three Centuries.* Bloomington, Ind., 1991.

Rose, Paul L. *Revolutionary Antisemitism in Germany from Kant to Wagner.* Princeton, N.J., 1990.

Rosenberg, Arthur. "Treitschke und die Juden," *Die Gesellschaft* (Berlin), Vol. 2 (1930).

Rozenblit, Marsha L. *The Jews of Vienna, 1867–1914.* Albany, N.Y., 1983.

Sachar, Howard M. *Dreamland: Europeans and Jews in the Aftermath of the Great War.* New York, 2002.

Schleunes, Karl. *The Twisted Road to Auschwitz: Nazi Policies Toward the Jews, 1933–1939.* Urbana, Ill., 1970.

Schorske, Carl E. *Fin-de-Siècle Vienna: Politics and Culture.* New York, 1980.

Stein, Leo. *The Racial Thinking of Richard Wagner.* New York, 1950.

Stepan, Nancy. "Biological Degeneration: Races and Proper Places," in J. Edward Chamberlin and Sander L. Gilman, eds. *Degeneration: The Dark Side of Progress.* New York, 1985.

———. *The Idea of Race in Science: Great Britain, 1800–1960.* London, 1982.

Thomas, Louis. *Alphonse Toussenel: socialiste national et antisémite.* Paris, 1941.

Waites, Bernard. "Social and Human Engineering," in Colon Chant, ed. *Science, Technology, and Everyday Life, 1870–1950.* London, 1989.

Weber, Eugen. "Reflections on the Jews in France," in Frances Malino and Bernard Wasserstein, eds. *The Jews in Modern France.* Hanover, N.H., 1985.

Weindling, Paul. *Health, Race, and German Politics between National Unification and Nazism, 1870–1945.* Cambridge, Eng., 1993.

Wertheimer, Jack. *Unwelcome Strangers: East European Jews in Imperial Germany.* New York, 1987.

Wilson, Nelly. *Bernard Lazare: Antisemitism and the Problem of Jewish Identity in Late Nineteenth-Century France.* Cambridge, Eng., 1978.

Wistrich, Robert S. *Antisemitism: The Longest Hatred.* New York, 1991.

Wolf, Lucien. *The Myth of the Jewish Menace in World Affairs: or the Truth about the Forged Protocols of the Elders of Zion.* New York, 1921.

Yovel, Yirmiyahu. *Dark Riddle: Hegel, Nietzsche, and the Jews, 1840–1939.* University Park, Pa., 1998.

Zinguer, Ilana Y., and Sam W. Bloom, eds. *L'Antisémitisme éclairé: inclusion et exclusion depuis l'époque des Lumières jusqu'à l'affaire Dreyfus: textes recueillis.* Paris, 2003.

Zucker, S. "Ludwig Bamberger and the Rise of Anti-Semitism in Germany, 1848–1893." *Central European History,* Vol. 3 (1970).

XV. The Rise of Zionism

Avineri, Shlomo. *The Making of Modern Zionism: The Intellectual Origins of the Jewish State.* New York, 1981.

———. *Moses Hess: Prophet of Communism and Zionism.* New York, 1985.

Barney, Jacob. *The Jews in Palestine in the Eighteenth Century.* Tuscaloosa, Ala., 1976.

Bein, Alex. *The Return to the Soil.* Jerusalem, 1952.

———. *Theodor Herzl: A Biography.* Philadelphia, 1956.

Ben-Aryeh, Yehuda. *Eretz Yisrael b'Mea HaYod-Tet* [Palestine in the Nineteenth Century]. Jerusalem, 1970.

Ben-Ehud, Rafael. *Zionismus oder Sozialismus.* Warsaw, 1899.

Ben-Gurion, David. *Israel: A Personal History.* New York, 1971.

———. *Recollections.* London, 1970.

Ben-Zvi, Yitchak. *Eretz Yisrael v'Yishuvah b'Y'mei HaShilton HaOtomani* [Palestine and Its (Jewish) Settlement under Ottoman Rule]. Jerusalem, 1955.

Blumberg, Arnold. *Zion Before Zionism, 1838–1880.* Syracuse, N.Y., 1986.

Blumenfeld, Kurt. *Erlebte Judenfrage: Ein Vierteljahrhundert deutscher Zionismus.* Stuttgart, 1962.

Borochow, Ber. *Nationalism and the Class Struggle.* New York, 1937.

Eisenbach, Artur, et al., eds. *The Emancipation of the Jews in Poland, 1780–1870.* Oxford, Eng., 1991.

Elon, Amos. *Herzl.* New York, 1975.

Epel, Yehuda, ed. *B'toh Reshit HaT'hiyah: Zihronot u'tavim m'Ymei Hovevei Tzion* [At the Beginning of the National Renaissance: Memoirs and Writings from the Days of the Hovevei Zion]. Tel Aviv, 1935.

Fellman, Jack. *The Revival of a Classical Tongue: Eliezer Ben Yehuda and the Modern Hebrew Language.* The Hague, 1973.

Frankel, Jonathan. *Prophecy and Politics: Socialism, Nationalism, and the Russian Jews, 1862–1917.* Cambridge, Eng., 1981.

Gal, Allon. *Socialist-Zionism: Theory and Issues in Contemporary Jewish Nationalism.* Cambridge, Mass., 1983.

Gilbar, Gad G. "The Growing Economic Involvement of Palestine with the West, 1865–1914," in David Kushner, ed. *Palestine in the Late Ottoman Period: Political, Social, and Economic Transformation.* Leiden, 1986.

Grunwald, Kurt. *Turkenhirsch: A Study of Baron Maurice de Hirsch: Entrepreneur and Philanthropist.* Jerusalem, 1966.

Halpern, Ben. *The Idea of the Jewish State.* Cambridge, Mass., 1961.

Hertzberg, Arthur, ed. *The Zionist Idea.* Garden City, N.Y., 1959.

Herzl, Theodor. *The Complete Diaries,* ed. Raphael Patai. English trans. Harry Zohn. 5 vols. New York, 1960.

———. *The Jewish State.* English trans. Marvin Lowenthal. Garden City, N.Y., 1959.

Kushner, David, ed. *Palestine in the Late Ottoman Period: Political, Social, and Economic Transformation.* Leiden, 1986.

Lahover, P. *Bialik: Hayyav v'Yetzirotov* [Bialik: His Life and Works]. Vol. 2. Tel Aviv, 1944.

Lowenthal, Marvin, ed. *The Diaries of Theodor Herzl.* New York, 1962.

Luz, Ehud. *Parallels Meet: Religion and Nationalism in the Early Zionist Movement, 1888–1904.* Philadelphia, 1988.

Margalith, Israel. *Le baron Edmond de Rothschild et la colonisation juive en Palestine, 1882–1899.* Paris, 1957.

Medzini, Moshe. *HaM'diniyut HaZionit m'Reshitah v'ad Moto shel Herzl* [Zionist Diplomacy from Its Origins to the Death of Herzl]. Jerusalem, 1934.

Parfitt, Tudor. *The Jews in Palestine, 1800–1882.* London, 1987.

Patai, Raphael. "Herzl's Sinai Project." *Herzl Year Book,* Vol. 1 (1958).

Pinsker, Leo. *Auto-Emancipation.* New York, 1956.

Rabinowicz, Oskar K. "Herzl and England." *Jewish Social Studies,* Vol. 14 (1951).

Ruppin, Arthur. *Three Decades of Palestine.* Jerusalem, 1936.

Sachar, Howard M. *A History of Israel: From the Rise of Zionism to Our Time.* 2nd ed. New York, 1996.

Schama, Simon. *Two Rothschilds and the Land of Israel.* New York, 1978.

Vital, David. *The Origins of Zionism.* Oxford, Eng., 1975.
———. *Zionism: The Crucial Phase.* Oxford, Eng., 1987.
Weill, Julien. *Zadoc Kahn, 1839–1905.* Paris, 1912.
Weizmann, Chaim. *Trial and Error.* New York, 1949.
Yaari, Avraham. *The Goodly Heritage.* Jerusalem, 1958.
Zipperstein, Steven J. *Elusive Prophet: Ahad Ha'Am and the Origins of Zionism.* London, 1993.

XVI. *The Evolution of Jewish Radicalism: Tsarist Russia*

Aronson, I. Michael. *Troubled Waters: The Origins of the 1881 Anti-Jewish Pogroms in Russia.* Pittsburgh, 1990.
Ascher, Abraham. *Pavel Axelrod and the Development of Menshevism.* Cambridge, Mass., 1972.
———. *The Revolution of 1905.* 2 vols. Stanford, Calif., 1988–92.
Beloff, Max. *Lucien Wolf and the Anglo-Russian Entente, 1907–1914.* London, 1951.
Brym, Robert J. *The Jewish Intelligentsia and Russian Marxism.* London, 1978.
Charques, Richard. *The Twilight of Imperial Russia.* London, 1965.
Cherniavsky, Michael, ed. *Prologue to Revolution.* Englewood Cliffs, N.J., 1967.
Dubnow, Simon. *Nationalism and History: Essays on Old and New Judaism.* Ed. Koppel S. Pinson. Philadelphia, 1958.
Fraenkel, Joseph. *Dubnow, Herzl, and Ahad HaAm.* London, 1963.
Frankel, Jonathan. *Jewish Politics and the Russian Revolution of 1905.* Tel Aviv, 1982.
Gassenschmidt, Christoph. *Jewish Liberal Politics in Tsarist Russia, 1900–1914.* New York, 1995.
Gitelman, Zvi, ed. *The Emergence of Modern Jewish Politics: Bundism and Zionism in Eastern Europe.* Pittsburgh, 2003.
Greenberg, Louis. *The Jews in Russia: The Struggle for Emancipation.* Vol. 2. New York, 1976.
Haberer, Erich. *Jews and Revolution in Nineteenth-Century Russia.* Cambridge, Eng., 1995.
Harcave, Sidney S. *First Blood: The Russian Revolution of 1905.* New York, 1964.
———. "The Jewish Question in the First Russian Duma." *Jewish Social Studies,* Vol. 6 (1944).
Johnpoll, Bernard K. *The Politics of Futility: The General Jewish Workers Bund of Poland, 1917–1943.* Ithaca, N.Y., 1967.
Klier, John D., and S. Lambroza, eds. *Pogroms: Anti-Jewish Violence in Modern Russian History.* Cambridge, Mass., 1992.
Lahover, P. *Bialik: Hayyav v'Yetzirotov* [Bialik: His Life and Works]. Vol. 2. Tel Aviv, 1944.
Lederhendler, Eli. *The Road to Modern Jewish Politics: Political Tradition and Political Reconstruction in the Jewish Community of Tsarist Russia.* New York, 1989.
Levin, Nora. *While the Messiah Tarried: Jewish Socialist Movements, 1871–1917.* London, 1978.
Levin, Shmarya. *The Arena.* New York, 1932.
Levitats, Isaac. *The Jewish Community in Russia, 1844–1917.* Jerusalem, 1981.
Mark, Yudel. "Yiddish Literature," in Louis Finkelstein, ed. *The Jews: Their History, Culture, and Religion.* Vol. 4. New York, 1949.
Mendelsohn, Ezra. *The Class Struggle in the Pale.* London, 1970.
Menes, Abraham. "The Jewish Socialist Movement in Russia and Poland," in Louis Finkelstein, ed. *The Jewish People Past and Present.* Vol. 2. New York, 1948.
Minczeles, Henri. *Histoire générale du Bund: un mouvement révolutionnaire juif.* Paris, 1995.
Mishinsky, Moses. "The Jewish Labor Movement and European Socialism," in H. H. Ben-Sasson and S. Ettinger, eds. *Jewish Society Through the Ages.* New York, 1971.
Orbach, Alexander. "Zionism and the Russian Revolution of 1905: The Commitment to Participate in Domestic Political Life," in *Bar-Ilan Studies in the Humanities,* Nos. 24, 25 (1990).

Pinson, Koppel. "Arkady Kremer, Vladimir Medem, and the Ideology of the Jewish Bund." *Jewish Social Studies,* Vol. 7 (1945).

Portnoy, S. A., trans. and ed. *Vladimir Medem: The Life and Soul of a Legendary Jewish Socialist* [English trans. of V. D. Medem, *Fuhn mayn Leben*]. New York, 1979.

Rawson, Don C. *Russian Rightists and the Revolution of 1905.* Cambridge, Mass., 1995.

Rogger, Hans. *Jewish Policies and Right-Wing Politics in Imperial Russia.* Berkeley, Calif., 1986.

———. "The Jewish Policy of Late Tsarism: A Reappraisal." *Wiener Library Bulletin,* Vol. 25 (1971).

Rubinow, I. M. *Economic Condition of the Jews in Russia.* Washington, D.C., 1907.

Samuel, Maurice. *Blood Accusation: The Strange History of the Beilis Case.* Philadelphia, 1966.

———. *Prince of the Ghetto.* New York, 1948.

———. *The World of Sholom Aleichem.* New York, 1943.

Sapir, Boris. "Liberman et le socialisme russe." *International Review for Social History,* Vol. 3 (1938).

Savickij, N. "P. A. Stolypin." *Le Monde slav,* November–December 1933, December 1934.

Schapiro, Leonard. "The Role of the Jews in the Russian Revolutionary Movement." *Slavonic and East European Review.* Vol. 40 (December 1961).

Sheer, David. *Yiddish and the Creation of Jewish Culture, 1818–1930.* Cambridge, Eng., 2004.

Stanislawski, Michael. "Russian Jewry, the Russian State, and the Dynamics of Jewish Emancipation," in Pierre Birnbaum and Ira Katznelson, eds. *Paths of Emancipation: Jews, States, and Citizenship.* Princeton, N.J., 1995.

Tager, Alexander B. *The Decay of Czarism: The Beilis Trial.* Philadelphia, 1935.

Tobias, Henry J. *The Jewish Bund in Russia: From Its Origins to 1905.* Stanford, Calif., 1972.

Troen, S. I., and B. Pinkus, eds. *Organizing Rescue: National Jewish Solidarity in the Modern Period.* London, 1992.

Wistrich, Robert S. *Revolutionary Jews from Marx to Trotsky.* London, 1976.

Zborowski, Mark, and Elizabeth Herzog, eds. *Life Is with People: The Jewish Little-Town of Eastern Europe.* New York, 1952.

Zimmerman, Joshua D. *Poles, Jews, and the Politics of Nationalism: The Bund and the Polish Socialist Party in Late Tsarist Russia, 1892–1914.* Madison, Wis., 2004.

XVII. Socialist *"Internationalism"* and the Trauma of World War I

Western Europe

Bauer, Otto. *Die Nationalitätenfrage und die Sozialdemokratie.* Vienna, 1907.

Brand, S. K. *Ernst Lissauer.* Stuttgart, 1923.

Braunthal, Julius. *Viktor und Friedrich Adler; Zwei Generationen Arbeiterbewegung.* Vienna, 1965.

Dunker, Ulrich. *Der Reichsbund jüdischer Frontsoldaten 1919–1938.* Düsseldorf, 1977.

Ettinger, Elzbieta. *Rosa Luxemburg: A Life.* Boston, 1986.

Field, Frank. *The Last Days of Mankind: Karl Kraus and His Vienna.* London, 1967.

Geras, Norman. *The Legacy of Rosa Luxemburg.* London, 1976.

Glaser, Ernst. *Im Umfeld des Austromarxismus.* Vienna, 1981.

Lambert, Martin. *Jewish Activism in Imperial Germany.* New Haven, Conn., 1982.

Luxemburg, Rosa. *Der Krise der Sozialdemokratie.* Berlin, 1919.

———. *Selected Works.* New York, 1976.

Mendes-Flohr, P. "The *Kriegserlebnis* and Jewish Consciousness," in W. Benz, ed. *Jews in the Weimar Republic.* Tübingen, Ger., 1998.

Mosse, W. E. *Deutsches Judentum in Krieg und Revolution, 1916–1923.* Tübingen, Ger., 1971.

———, and A. Pauker, eds. *Juden im Wilhelminischen Deutschland, 1890–1914.* Tübingen, Ger., 1998.

Nettl, J. F. *Rosa Luxemburg.* 2 vols. London, 1966.

Rechter, David. *The Jews of Vienna and the First World War.* London, 2001.

Reichsverband jüdischer Frontsaldaten. *Die jüdischen Gefallenen der deutschen Heeres, der deutschen Marine und der deutschen Schutztruppen, 1914–1918: ein Gedenkbuch.* Berlin, 1932.

Rozenblit, Marsha L. *Reconstructing a National Identity: The Jews of Habsburg Austria During World War I.* Oxford, Eng., 2001.

Sachar, Howard M. *Dreamland: Europeans and Jews in the Aftermath of the Great War.* New York, 2002.

Schwarz, Robert. "Antisemitism and Socialism in Austria, 1918–1962," in Joseph Fraenkel, ed. *The Jews of Austria.* London, 1967.

Senekowitsch, Martin. *Gleichberichte in einer grossen Armee: zur Geschichte des Bundes jüdischer Frontsoldaten Österreichs, 1932–38.* Vienna, 1994.

Silberner, Edmund. "Austrian Social Democracy and the Jewish Problem." *Historia Judaica,* Vol. 13 (1951).

Strauss, F. J., ed. *Kriegsbrief gefallener deutschen Juden.* Berlin, 1961.

Theilhaber, Felix A. *Die Juden im Weltkrieg.* Berlin, 1916.

Toury, Jakob. *Die politischen Orientierungen der Juden in Deutschland.* Tübingen, Ger., 1966.

Zechlin, Egmont. *Die deutsche Politik und die Juden im ersten Weltkrieg.* Göttingen, Ger., 1969.

Zucker, S. *Ludwig Bamberger: German Liberal Politician and Social Critic, 1823–1899.* Pittsburgh, 1975.

Eastern Europe

Abramson, Henry. *A Prayer for Government: Ukrainians and Jews in Revolutionary Times, 1917–1920.* Cambridge, Mass., 1999.

Altshuler, Mordechai. "Ukrainian-Jewish Relations in the Soviet Milieu in the Interwar," in Peter J. Potichnyi and Howard Aster, eds. *Ukrainian-Jewish Relations in Historical Perspective.* Edmonton, Can., 1988.

Aster, Howard. *Jewish-Ukrainian Relations: Two Solitudes.* New York, 1983.

Bauer, Yehuda. *My Brother's Keeper: A History of the American Jewish Joint Distribution Committee.* Philadelphia, 1974.

Beloff, Max. *Lucien Wolf and the Anglo-Russian Entente, 1907–1914.* London, 1914.

Charques, Richard B. *The Twilight of Imperial Russia.* Oxford, Eng., 1958.

Chasanowitch, Léon, ed. *Les Pogromes anti-Juifs en Pologne et en Galicie en novembre et décembre 1918.* Stockholm, 1919.

Dubnow, Simon. *Nationalism and History: Essays on Old and New Judaism.* Ed. by Koppel S. Pinson. Philadelphia, 1958.

Gergel, N. "The Pogroms in the Ukraine in 1918–21." *YIVO Annual of Jewish Social Science,* Vol. 12 (1951).

Heifetz, Elias. *The Slaughter of the Jews in the Ukraine in 1919.* New York, 1921.

Hunczak, Taras. *Symon Petlura et les juifs.* Paris, 1987.

Johnpoll, Bernard K. *The Politics of Futility: The General Jewish Workers Bund of Poland, 1917–1943.* Ithaca, N.Y., 1967.

Kenez, Peter. "Pogroms and White Ideology in the Russian Civil War," in John D. Klier and Shlomo Lambrozo, eds. *Pogroms and Anti-Jewish Violence in Modern Russian History.* Cambridge, Mass., 1992.

Lichten, Joseph. "A Study of Ukrainian-Jewish Relations." *Annals of the Ukrainian Academy of Arts and Sciences in the United States,* Vol. 5 (1956).

Marrus, Michael R. *The Unwanted: European Refugees in the Twentieth Century.* New York, 1985.

Potichnyj, Peter J., and Howard Aster, eds. *Ukrainian-Jewish Relations in Historical Perspective.* Edmonton, Alta., 1988.

Schechtman, Joseph B. *The Pogroms in the Ukraine under the Ukrainian Governments, 1917–1920.* London, 1927.

Sieg, Ulrich. *Jüdische Intellektuelle im Ersten Weltkrieg.* Berlin, 2001.

Stone, Norman. *The Eastern Front, 1914–17.* New York, 1917.

Szajkowski, Zosa. "Symon Petliura and Ukrainian-Jewish Relations, 1917–21: A Rebuttal." *Jewish Social Studies,* Vol. 30 (1969).

XVIII. *The Triumph of Bolshevism*

Abramsky, Chimen. "The Biro-Bidzhan Project, 1927–1959," in Lionel Kochan, ed. *The Jews in Soviet Russia Since 1917.* 3rd ed. Oxford, Eng., 1978.

———. *War, Revolution, and the Jewish Dilemma.* London, 1975.

Altshuler, Mordechai. "The Attitude of the Communist Party of Russia to Jewish National Survival, 1918–1930." *YIVO Annual of Jewish Social Science,* Vol. 23 (1969).

———. *Soviet Jewry on the Eve of the Holocaust: A Social and Demographic Profile.* Jerusalem, 1998.

Babel, Isaac. *1920 Diary.* New Haven, Conn., 1995.

Babel, Nathalie, ed. *The Complete Works of Isaac Babel.* New York, 2002.

Barzilai, Yosef. "Sihot im Shimon Dimanshtein" [Conversations with Shimon Dimanshtein]. *HeAvar,* Vol. 15 (1968).

———. *HaTragedia shel HaMahapehah HaSovyetit* [The Tragedy of the Soviet Revolution]. Tel Aviv, 1968.

Deutscher, Isaac. *A Non-Jewish Jew and Other Essays.* New York, 1968.

———. *The Prophet Armed: Trotsky, 1879–1921.* New York, 1954.

———. *The Prophet Unarmed: Trotsky, 1921–1929.* New York, 1959.

Ettinger, Samuel, ed. *Anti-Semitism in the Soviet Union: Its Roots and Consequences.* Jerusalem, 1978.

Friedberg, Maurice. "Jews and Russian Literature," in Lionel Kochan, ed. *The Jews in Soviet Russia since 1917.* 3rd ed. Oxford, Eng., 1978.

Getzler, Israel. *Martov.* Cambridge, Eng., 1967.

Gitelman, Zvi. *A Century of Two Peoples: The Jews of Russia and the Soviet Union.* New York, 1988.

———. *Jewish Nationality and Soviet Politics: The Jewish Sections of the CPSU, 1917–1930.* Princeton, N.J., 1972.

Johnpoll, Bernard K. *The Politics of Futility: The General Jewish Workers Bund of Poland, 1917–1943.* Ithaca, N.Y., 1967.

Kochan, Lionel, ed. *The Jews in Soviet Russia Since 1917.* 3rd ed. Oxford, Eng., 1978.

Levenberg, Samuel. "Soviet Jewry: Some Problems and Perspectives," in Lionel Kochan, ed. *The Jews in Soviet Russia Since 1917.* 3rd ed. Oxford, Eng., 1978.

Levin, Nora. *The Jews in the Soviet Union since 1917: Paradox of Survival.* 2 vols. New York, 1988.

———. *While the Messiah Tarried: Jewish Socialist Movements, 1871–1917.* London, 1978.

Marrus, Michael. *The Unwanted: European Refugees in the Twentieth Century.* New York, 1985.

Miller, Jacob. "Soviet Theory on the Jews," in Lionel Kochan, ed. *The Jews in Soviet Russia since 1917.* 3rd ed. Oxford, Eng., 1978.

Nedava, Joseph. *Trotsky and the Jews.* Philadelphia, 1972.

Nova, Alec, and J. A. Newth. "Jewish Demographic Trends and Occupational Patterns," in Lionel Kochan, ed. *The Jews in Soviet Russia since 1917.* 3rd ed. Oxford, Eng., 1978.

Rothenberg, Joshua. "Jewish Religion in the Soviet Union," in Lionel Kochan, ed. *The Jews in Soviet Russia Since 1917.* 3rd ed. Oxford, Eng., 1978.

Sagedan, Allan L. "American Jews and the Soviet Experiment: The Agro-Joint Project, 1924–1937." *Jewish Social Studies,* Vol. 42 (1981).

Schapiro, Leonard. "The Role of the Jews in the Russian Revolutionary Movement." *Slavonic and East European Review,* Vol. 40 (1961).

Schwarz, Solomon M. *The Jews in the Soviet Union.* Syracuse, N.Y., 1951.

Service, Robert. *Lenin: A Biography*. Cambridge, Mass., 2000.

Weinryb, Bernard. "Antisemitism under the Soviets," in Lionel Kochan, ed. *The Jews in Soviet Russia since 1917.* 3rd ed. Oxford, Eng., 1978.

Wistrich, Robert S. *Revolutionary Jews from Marx to Trotsky.* London, 1976.

XIX. *The Balfour Declaration and the Jewish National Home*

Adler, Selig. "The Palestine Question in the Wilson Era." *Jewish Social Studies*, Vol. 9 (1948).

Bein, Alex. *The Return to the Soil.* Jerusalem, 1952.

Ben-Gurion, David. *Israel: A Personal History.* New York, 1971.

————. *Recollections.* London, 1970.

Brandeis, Louis D. *Brandeis on Zionism.* Washington, D.C., 1942.

Cohen, Naomi W. *American Jews and the Zionist Idea.* New York, 1975.

Darin-Drabkin, Haim. *The Other Society.* New York, 1963.

Ededin, Ben. *Rebuilding Palestine.* New York, 1939.

Eliav, Mordecai. *Die Juden Palästinas in der deutschen Politik, 1842–1914.* Tel Aviv, 1973.

Elon, Amos. *The Israelis: Fathers and Sons.* New York, 1971.

Engel, Anita. *The NILI Spies.* London, 1959.

Friedman, Isaiah. *Germany, Turkey, and Zionism, 1897–1918.* Oxford, Eng., 1977.

————. *The Question of Palestine, 1914–1918: British-Jewish-Arab Relations.* New York, 1973.

Gordon, A. D. *Selected Essays.* New York, 1938.

Hyamson, Albert. *Palestine under the Mandate.* London, 1950.

Jabotinsky, Vladimir. *The Story of the Jewish Legion.* New York, 1945.

Joseph, Bernard (Dov). *British Rule in Palestine.* Washington, D.C., 1948.

Kedourie, Elie. *Britain and the Middle East, 1914–1921.* London, 1956.

Levenberg, Shlomo. *The Jews and Palestine: A Study in Labour Zionism.* London, 1945.

Medzini, Moshe. *Eser Shanim shel M'diniyut Eretz Yisraelit* [Ten Years of Palestinian (Jewish) Diplomacy]. Tel Aviv, 1928.

Pearlman, Moshe. *Ben-Gurion Looks Back.* London, 1965.

Pichon, Jean. *Le partage du Proche-Orient.* Paris, 1938.

Rabinowicz, Oskar K. *Vladimir Jabotinsky's Conception of a New Nation.* New York, 1946.

Reinharz, Jehuda. *Chaim Weizmann: The Making of a Zionist Leader.* New York, 1985.

————. *Chaim Weizmann: The Making of a Statesman.* New York, 1992.

Rose, Herbert H. *The Life and Thought of A. D. Gordon.* New York, 1954.

Ruppin, Arthur. *Building Israel: Selected Essays, 1907–1935.* New York, 1949.

Sachar, Howard M. *Aliyah: The Peoples of Israel.* Cleveland, 1961.

————. *The Emergence of the Middle East, 1914–1924.* New York, 1969.

————. *A History of Israel from the Rise of Zionism to Our Time.* 2nd ed. New York, 1996.

Schechtman, Joseph B. *Vladimir Jabotinsky.* 2 vols. New York, 1956, 1961.

Shapira, Anita. *Berl: The Biography of a Socialist Zionist, Berl Katznelson, 1887–1944.* Cambridge, Eng., 1984.

Starr, Joshua. "Jewish Citizenship in Rumania (1878–1940)." *Jewish Social Studies*, Vol. 3 (1941).

Stein, Leonard. *The Balfour Declaration.* London, 1961.

Sykes, Christopher. *Crossroads to Israel, 1917–1948.* New York, 1956.

Szereszewski, Robert. *Essays on the Structure of the Jewish Economy in Palestine and Israel.* Jerusalem, 1968.

Teller, Judd L. "The Making of the Ideals That Rule Israel." *Commentary*, January–February 1954.

Vereté, Mayir. "The Balfour Declaration and Its Makers." *Middle Eastern Studies*, Vol. 6 (1970).

Vital, David. *Zionism: The Crucial Phase.* Oxford, 1987.

Vlavianos, Basil J., and Feliks Gross, eds. *Struggle for Tomorrow: Modern Political Ideologies of the Jewish People.* New York, 1954.

Wasserstein, Bernard. *Herbert Samuel: A Political Life.* Oxford, Eng., 1992.

Weintraub, D., M. Lissak, and Y. Azmon. *Moshava, Kibbutz, and Moshav.* Ithaca, N.Y., 1969.

Yehuda, Avraham Shalom. *HeHaganah al HaYishuv u'Milhemet HaOlam HaRishonah* [Defense of the Yishuv in World War I]. Jerusalem, 1951.

XX: *The Legacy of Progressivism: Immigrant Jewry in the United States*

Adler, Cyrus, and Aaron Margalith. *With Firmness in the Right: American Diplomatic Action Affecting Jews, 1840–1945.* New York, 1946.

Baker, Leonard. *Brandeis and Frankfurter: A Dual Biography.* New York, 1984.

Berlin, William S. *On the Edge of Politics: The Roots of Jewish Political Thought in America.* Westport, Conn., 1979.

Best, Gary D. *To Free a People: American Jewish Leaders and the Jewish Problem in Eastern Europe, 1890–1914.* Westport, Conn., 1982.

Black, Edwin. *War Against the Weak: Eugenics and America's Campaign to Create a Master Race.* New York, 2003.

Cohen, Naomi W. *Not Free to Desist: The American Jewish Committee, 1906–1966.* Philadelphia, 1969.

Cohen, Sarah Blacher, ed. *From Hester Street to Hollywood: The Jewish-American Stage and Screen.* Bloomington, Ind., 1983.

Courtney, Daria T. "The Minorities Treaties: The Post–World War I Quest for Stability in East-Central Europe." *Maryland Historian,* No. 14 (1983).

Dinnerstein, Leonard, ed. *Antisemitism in the United States.* New York, 1971.

Epstein, Melech. *The Jew and Communism.* New York, 1959.

———. *Jewish Labor in the United States.* Vols. 2, 3. New York, 1950, 1953.

Gabler, Neal. *An Empire of Their Own: How the Jews Invented Hollywood.* New York, 1988.

Gal, Allon. *Brandeis of Boston.* Cambridge, Mass., 1980.

Handlin, Oscar, and Mary Handlin. *Danger in Discord: Origins of Anti-Semitism in the United States.* New York, 1967.

Hardman, J. B. S. "The Jewish Labor Movement in the United States: Jewish and Non-Jewish Influences." *Publications of the American Jewish Historical Society,* September 1962.

Howe, Irving. *World of Our Fathers: The Journey of the East European Jews to America and the Life They Found and Made.* New York, 1976.

Kraut, Alan M. *Silent Travelers: Germs, Genes, and the "Immigrant Menace."* New York, 1994.

Liebman, Arthur. *Jews and the Left.* New York, 1979.

McLaughlin, Robert. *Broadway and Hollywood: A History of Economic Interaction.* New York, 1970.

Menes, Abraham. "The East Side Matrix of the Jewish Labor Movement," in Theodore Friedman and Robert Gordis, eds. *Jewish Life in America.* New York, 1955.

Neuringer, Sheldon M. *American Jewry and United States Immigration Policy, 1881–1953.* New York, 1980.

Ordover, Nancy. *American Eugenics, Queer Anatomy, and the Science of Nationalism.* Minneapolis, 2003.

Quinley, Harold E., and Charles Y. Glock. *Anti-Semitism in America.* New York, 1979.

Rischin, Moses. "The Jews and the Liberal Tradition in America." *Publications of the American Jewish Historical Society,* September 1961.

———. *The Promised City: New York's Jews, 1870–1914.* New York, 1970.

Rosenstock, Morton. *Louis Marshall: Defender of Jewish Rights.* Detroit, 1965.

Ruchames, Louis. "Jewish Radicalism in the United States." In Peter I. Rose, ed. *The Ghetto and Beyond: Essays in Jewish Life in America.* New York, 1969.

Sachar, Howard M. *A History of the Jews in America.* New York, 1995.

Sandrow, Nahma. *Vagabond Stars: A World History of the Yiddish Theater.* New York, 1977.

Singerman, Robert. "The Jew as Racial Alien: The Genetic Component of American Anti-Semitism," in David A. Gerber, ed. *Anti-Semitism in American History.* Urbana, Ill., 1986.

Sorin, Gerald. *The Prophetic Minority: American Jewish Immigrant Radicals, 1880–1920.* Bloomington, Ind., 1985.

Steinberg, Stephen. "How Jewish Quotas Began." *Commentary,* September 1971.

Stolberg, Benjamin. *Tailor's Progress: A History of the International Ladies Garment Workers Union.* New York, 1944.

Tucker, William H. *The Science and Politics of Racial Research.* Urbana, Ill., 1994.

Urofsky, Melvin. *A Mind of One Piece: Brandeis and American Reform.* New York, 1971.

Waites, Bernard. "Social and Human Engineering," in Colon Chant, ed. *Science, Technology, and Everyday Life, 1870–1950.* London, 1989.

XXI, XXII. *Successor States and Minority Guarantees: 1919–1939; The Triumph of East European Fascism*

Abramsky, Chimen. *War, Revolution, and the Jewish Dilemma.* London, 1975.

———, M. Jachimczyk, and A. Polonsky, eds. *The Jews in Poland.* Oxford, Eng., 1986.

Alliance Israélite Universelle. *La Question juive devant la conférence de la paix.* Paris, 1919.

Balogh, Arthur de. *L'Action de la Société des Nations en Matière des Minorités.* Paris, 1937.

Bazany, George. "Magyar Jew or Jewish Magyar," in Bela Vago and George Mosse, eds. *Jews and Non-Jews in Eastern Europe, 1918–1945.* New York, 1974.

Braham, Randolph L., ed. *Hungarian Jewish Studies.* 2 vols. New York, 1968–69.

Butnaru, I. C. *The Silent Holocaust: Romania and Its Jews.* New York, 1992.

Cang, J. "The Opposition Parties in Poland and Their Attitude to the Jews and the Jewish Problem." *Jewish Social Studies,* Vol. I (1939).

Chasanowitch, L., ed. *Les Pogromes anti-juifs en Pologne et en Galicie en novembre et décembre 1918.* Stockholm, 1919.

Comité des Délégations Juives Auprès de la Conférence de la Paix. *Les Droits nationaux des juifs en Europe orientale: Recueil d'études.* Paris, 1919.

Courtney, Daria T. "The Minorities Treaties: The Post–World War I Quest for Stability in East-Central Europe." *Maryland Historian,* No. 14 (1983).

Dobroszycki, Lucjan. "The Fertility of Modern Polish Jewry," in Paul Ritterband, ed. *Modern Jewish Fertility.* Leiden, 1981.

Don, Yehuda, and Victor Karady, eds. *A Social and Economic History of Central European Jewry.* New Brunswick, N.J., 1990.

Drozdowski, Marian M. "The National Minorities in Poland, 1919–1930." *Acta Polonoiae Historica,* No. 22 (1970).

Epstein, Binyamin, ed. *T. G. Masaryk and the Jews: A Collection of Essays.* New York, 1941.

Fishman, Joshua, ed. *Studies in Polish Jewry, 1919–1939.* New York, 1974.

Freidenreich, Harriet P. *The Jews of Yugoslavia.* Philadelphia, 1979.

Gelber, N. M. "The Problem of the Rumanian Jews at the Bucharest Peace Conference, 1918." *Jewish Social Studies,* Vol. 12 (1951).

Greenbaum, Masha. *The Jews of Lithuania, 1916–1945.* Jerusalem, 1995.

Groth, A. J. "Dmowski, Pilsudski, and Ethnic Confict in Pre–1939 Poland." *Canadian Slavic Studies,* Vol. 3 (1969).

Gutman, Yisrael, et al., eds. *The Jews of Poland Between Two World Wars.* London, 1989.

Heller, Celia S. *On the Edge of Destruction: The Jews of Poland Between the Two World Wars.* New York, 1977.

Horak, Stepan. *Poland and Her National Minorities, 1919–1939.* New York, 1961.

Iancu, Carol. *Jews in Roumania, 1866–1919: From Exclusion to Emancipation*. Boulder, Colo., 1996.

Janowsky, Oscar I. *The Jews and Minority Rights, 1898–1919*. New York, 1933.

Joint Foreign Committee of the Board of Deputies of British Jewry and the Anglo-Jewish Association. *The Jewish Minority in Hungary*. London, 1926.

———. *The Jewish Minority in Roumania: Correspondence with the Roumanian Government Respecting the Grievances of the Jews*. London, 1927.

Kahn, Bernhard. *The Jews in Reconstituted Poland*. New York, 1940.

Katzburg, Nathaniel. *Hungary and the Jews: Policy and Legislation, 1920–1943*. Ramat Gan, Isr., 1981.

Kestenberg, Ruth. "The Jews Between Czechs and Germans in the Historical Lands, 1848–1918," in Society for the History of Czechoslovak Jews. *The Jews of Czechoslovakia*. Vol. I. Philadelphia, 1968.

Kieval, Hillel J. *The Making of Czech Jewry: National Conflict and Jewish Society in Bohemia, 1870–1918*. New York, 1988.

———. "Masaryk and Czech Jewry: The Ambiguities of Friendship," in Stanley B. Winters, ed. *T. G. Masaryk*. Vol. I. New York, 1990.

Kohler, Max. "The Peace Conference and the Right of Minorities." *American Jewish Yearbook*, Vol. 22 (1920–21).

Korzec, Pawel. *Juifs en Pologne: la question juive pendant l'entre-deux guerres*. Paris, 1980.

Kovacs, Maria M. "Interwar Antisemitism in the Professions: The Case of the Engineers," in Michael K. Silber, ed. *Jews in the Hungarian Economy, 1760–1945*. Jerusalem, 1992.

Lengyel, Gyorgy. "The Ethnic Composition of the Economic Elite in Hungary in the Interwar Period," in Yehuda Don and Victor Karady, eds. *A Social and Economic History of Central European Jewry*. New Brunswick, N.J., 1990.

Lerski, George W. "Dmowski, Paderewski, and American Jews." *Polin*, Vol. 2 (1987).

Levene, Mark. *War, Jews, and the New Europe: The Diplomacy of Lucien Wolf, 1914–1919*. Oxford, Eng., 1992.

Livezeanu, Ion. *Cultural Politics in Greater Romania*. Ithaca, N.Y., 1955.

Low, Alfred D. *The Soviet Hungarian Republic and the Paris Peace Conference*. Philadelphia, 1963.

Macartney, C. A. *National States and National Minorities*. London, 1934.

Mahler, Raphael. "Jews in the Liberal Professons in Poland, 1920–39." *Jewish Social Studies*, Vol. 6 (1944).

Mair, Lucy P. *The Protection of Minorities: The Working and Scope of the Minorities Treaties under the League of Nations*. London, 1939.

Marrus, Michael R. *The Unwanted: European Refugees in the Twentieth Century*. New York, 1985.

Mendelsohn, Ezra. "The Dilemma of Jewish Politics in Poland: Four Responses," in Bela Vago and George L. Mosse, eds. *Jews and Non-Jews in Eastern Europe, 1918–1945*. Jerusalem, 1974.

———. "German and Jewish Minorities in the European Successor States Between the World Wars," in Ezra Mendelsohn and Chaim Shmeruk, eds. *Studies on Polish Jewry*. Jerusalem, 1987.

———. *The Jews of East Central Europe Between the Wars*. Bloomington, Ind., 1987.

———, et al. *Jews in Independent Poland, 1918–1939*. London, 1994.

Nagy-Talavera, N. *The Green Shirts and Others: A History of Fascism in Hungary and Rumania*. Stanford, Calif., 1970.

Netzer, Shlomo. *Ma'avak yehudei Polin al zechuyoteihem HaEzrachit v'ha'l'umiyot, 1918–1922*. [The Campaign of Polish Jewry for Their Civil and National Rights, 1918–1922]. Tel Aviv, 1980.

Patai, Raphael. *The Jews of Hungary*. Detroit, 1996.

Polonsky, Antony. *Politics in Independent Poland, 1921–1939.* Oxford, 1972.

Robinson, Jacob, Oscar Karbach, et al., eds. *Were the Minority Treaties a Failure?* New York, 1943.

Rosenstock, Morton. *Louis Marshall: Defender of Jewish Rights.* Detroit, 1965.

Sachar, Abram L. *Sufferance Is the Badge: The Jew in the Postwar World.* New York, 1940.

Sachar, Howard M. *Dreamland: Europeans and Jews in the Aftermath of the Great War.* New York, 2002.

———. *Farewell España: The World of the Sephardim Remembered.* New York, 1994.

Silber, Michael K., ed. *Jews in the Hungarian Economy, 1760–1945.* Jerusalem, 1992.

Society for the History of Czechoslovak Jews. *The Jews of Czechoslovakia.* Vols. 2, 3. Philadelphia, 1968–1984.

Starr, Joshua. "Jewish Citizenship in Rumania (1878–1940)." *Jewish Social Studies,* Vol. 3 (1941).

Stern, J. P., ed. *The World of Franz Kafka.* New York, 1981.

Sugar, Peter F. *Native Fascism in the Successor States, 1918–1945.* Oxford, Eng., 1945.

Tokes, Rudolf L. *Bela Kun and the Hungarian Soviet Republic.* New York, 1967.

Ungvari, Tamas. *The "Jewish Question" in Europe: The Case of Hungary.* Boulder, Colo., 2000.

Vago, Bela. *The Shadow of the Swastika: The Rise of Fascism and Anti-Semitism in the Danube Basin, 1936–1939.* New York, 1975.

———, and George L. Mosse, eds. *Jews and Non-Jews in Eastern Europe, 1918–1945.* New York, 1974.

Volovici, Leon. *Nationalist Ideology and Antisemitism: The Case of Romanian Intellectuals in the 1930s.* Oxford, Eng., 1991.

World Jewish Congress. *La Situation des juifs en Roumanie.* Geneva, 1938.

Wynot, Edward D. "The Catholic Church and the Polish State, 1935–1939." *Journal of Church and State,* Vol. 15 (1973).

———. " 'A Necessary Cruelty': The Emergence of Official Anti-Semitism in Poland, 1936–39." *American Historical Review,* Vol. 76 (1971).

XXIII. *A Final Symbiosis of Jewish and Western Culture*

Agus, Jacob. *Modern Philosophies of Judaism.* New York, 1941.

Alon, Amos. *The Pity of It All: A History of Jews in Germany, 1743–1933.* New York, 2002.

Altmann, Alexander. *Essays on Jewish Intellectual History.* Hanover, N.H., 1981.

Arens, Hans. *Stefan Zweig—Der grosse Europäer.* Munich, 1960.

Barker, Richard H. *Marcel Proust: A Biography.* New York, 1968.

Bauer, Johann. *Kafka and Prague.* London, 1971.

Beller, Steven. *Vienna and the Jews.* Cambridge, Eng., 1989.

Botstein, Leon. *Judentum und Modernität: Essays zur Rolle der Juden in der deutschen und österreichischen Kultur, 1848 bis 1938.* Vienna, 1991.

Brenner, Michael. *The Renaissance of Jewish Culture in Weimar Germany.* New Haven, Conn., 1996.

Brod, Max. "The Young Werfel and the Prague Writers," in Paul Raabe, ed. *The Era of German Expressionism.* London, 1974.

Brunner, José. *Freud and the Politics of Psychoanalysis.* Cambridge, Mass., 1995.

Carter, William C. *Marcel Proust: A Life.* New Haven, Conn., 2000.

Clark, Ronald W. *Einstein: The Life and Times.* Cleveland, 1971.

———. *Freud: The Man and the Cause.* London, 1980.

Eisen, Arnold, ed. *Rethinking Modern Judaism.* Chicago, 1998.

Friedman, Morris. *Martin Buber: The Life of Dialogue.* Chicago, 1955.

Gay, Peter. *Freud, Jews, and Other Germans.* New York, 1978.

———. *Weimar Culture.* New York, 1968.

Glatzer, Nahum. *Franz Rosenzweig: His Life and Thought.* New York, 1953.

Goldstein, Moritz. *Begriff und Programm einer jüdischen Nationalliteratur.* Berlin, 1913.

Gradenwitz, Peter. "Jews in Austrian Music," in Joseph Fraenkel, ed. *The Jews of Austria.* London, 1967.

Gregh, Fernand. *L'Âge d'or.* Paris, 1947.

Grunfeld, Frederic. *Prophets Without Honor: A Background to Freud, Kafka, Einstein, and Their World.* New York, 1979.

Hayman, Ronald. *Proust: A Biography.* New York, 1990.

Herz, E. *Before the Fury: Jews and Germans Before Hitler.* New York, 1967.

Hughes, H. Stuart. *Prisoners of Hope: The Silver Age of the Italian Jews.* Cambridge, Mass., 1983.

Hyman, Paula. *From Dreyfus to Vichy: The Remaking of French Jewry, 1906–1939.* New York, 1979.

Karlweiss, M. *Jakob Wassermann.* Amsterdam, 1935.

Katznelson, Siegmund, ed. *Juden im deutschen Kulturbereich.* Rev. ed. Berlin, 1959.

Keegan, Susanne. *The Bride of the Wind: The Life and Times of Alma Mahler-Werfel.* New York, 1992.

Lanouette, William, and Bela Silard. *Genius in the Shadows: A Biography of Leo Szilard.* Chicago, 1994.

Liptzin, Sol. *Germany's Stepchildren.* Philadelphia, 1944.

List, Kurt. "Mahler: Father of Modern Music." *Commentary,* July 1950.

Lorenz, Dagmar, and Gabriele Weinberger, eds. *Insiders and Outsiders: Jewish and Gentile Culture in Germany and Austria.* Detroit, 1994.

Lowenstein, Steven M. "Ideology and Identity," in Michael Meyer, ed. *German-Jewish History in Modern Times.* Vol. 3. New York, 1976.

Melber, Jehuda, ed. *Hermann Cohen's Philosophy of Judaism.* New York, 1968.

Meyer, Michael, ed. *German-Jewish History in Modern Times.* Vol. 3. New York, 1976.

Miller, Justin. "Interpretations of Freud's Jewishness, 1924–1974." *Journal of the History of the Behavioral Sciences.* Vol. 17 (1981).

Nathansen, Henri. *Jude oder Europäer: Portrait von Georg Brandes.* Frankfurt a/M, 1931.

Newlin, Dika. *Bruckner, Mahler, Schoenberg.* New York, 1947.

Niewyk, Donald L. "The Economic and Cultural Role of the Jews in the Weimar Republic." *Leo Baeck Institute Yearbook,* Vol. 16 (1971).

Patai, Raphael. *The Jewish Mind.* New York, 1977.

Pawel, Ernst. *The Nightmare of Reason: Franz Kafka.* New York, 1984.

Poma, Andrea. *The Critical Philosophy of Hermann Cohen.* Albany, N.Y., 1997.

Reichert, H. W., and Herman Salinger, eds. *Studies in Arthur Schnitzler.* Chapel Hill, N.C., 1963.

Robertson, Ritchie. *Kafka: Judaism, Politics, and Literature.* Oxford, Eng., 1985.

Roth, Sigmund. *Juden im ungarischen Kulturleben in der zweiten Hälfte des 19. Jahrhunderts.* Berlin, 1934.

Rozenblit, Marsha L. *The Jews of Vienna, 1867–1914.* Albany, N.Y., 1983.

Sachar, Abram L. *Sufferance Is the Badge: The Jew in the Postwar World.* New York, 1940.

Sachar, Howard M. *Dreamland: Europeans and Jews in the Aftermath of the Great War.* New York, 2002.

Schatzberg, Walter, and Jehuda Reinharz, eds. *The Jewish Response to German Culture: From the Enlightenment to the Second World War.* Hanover, N.H., 1985.

Stern, Fritz. *Einstein's German World.* Princeton, N.J., 1999.

Stern, J. P., ed. *The World of Franz Kafka.* New York, 1981.

Stoltzenberg, Dietrich. *Fritz Haber: Chemiker, Nobelpreisträger, Deutscher, Jude.* Weinheim, Ger., 1998.

Thompson, Bruce. *Schnitzler's Vienna.* New York, 1990.

Wassermann, Jakob. *Mein Weg als Deutscher und Jude.* Amsterdam, 1922.

Winegarten, Renée. "French Culture and the Jews." *Commentary,* January 1968.

Zohn, Harry. "Participation in German Literature," in Society for the History of Czechoslovak Jews. *The Jews of Czechoslovakia.* Vol. I. Philadelphia, 1962.

Zuckerkandl, Berta Szeps. "Three Austrian Jews in German Literature: Schnitzler, Zweig, Herzl," in Joseph Fraenkel, ed. *The Jews of Austria: Essays on Their Life, History, and Destruction.* London, 1967.

Zweig, Stefan. *The World of Yesterday.* New York, 1945.

XXIV. *A Climactic Onslaught of Postwar Antisemitism*

Abramsky, Chimen. *War, Revolution, and the Jewish Dilemma.* London, 1975.

Alderman, Geoffrey. *Modern British Jewry.* Oxford, Eng., 1992.

Anderson, Gerald D. *Fascists, Communists, and the National Government: Civil Liberties in Great Britain, 1931–1937.* Columbia, Mo., 1983.

Andics, H. *Der ewige Jude: Ursachen und Geschichte des Antisemitismus.* Vienna, 1968.

Baker, David. *Ideology of Obsession: A. K. Chesterton and British Fascism.* London, 1996.

Beller, Steven. *Vienna and the Jews.* Cambridge, Eng., 1989.

———. "Why Was the Viennese Liberal *Bildungsbürgertum* Jewish?" in Yehuda Don and Victor Karady, eds. *A Social and Economic History of Central European Jewry.* New Brunswick, N.J., 1990.

Belloc, Hilaire. *The Jews.* London, 1923.

Berkley, George E. *Vienna and Its Jews: The Tragedy of Success, 1880s–1980s.* Lanham, Md., 1988.

Bernard, Philippe, and Henri Dubief. *La Fin d'un monde, 1914–1928; Le Déclin de la IIIe République, 1929–1938.* 2 vols. Paris, 1975–76.

Bernstein, Herman. *The Truth about "The Protocols of Zion": A Complete Exposure.* 2nd ed. New York, 1971.

Birnbaum, Pierre. *Antisemitism in France: A Political History from Léon Blum to the Present.* Oxford, Eng., 1992.

———. *Un Mythe politique: "La République juive."* Paris, 1988.

———, and Ira Katznelson, eds. *Paths of Emancipation: Jews, States, and Citizenship.* Princeton, N.J., 1995.

Black, Eugene. *The Social Politics of Anglo-Jewry 1880–1920.* Oxford, Eng., 1988.

Blumel, André. *Léon Blum: juif et sioniste.* Paris, 1951.

Brustein, William I. *Roots of Hate: Antisemitism in Europe Before the Holocaust.* Cambridge, Eng., 2003.

Bunzl, John, and Bernd Marin. *Antisemitismus in Österreich: sozialhistorische und soziologische Studien.* Innsbruck, Aust., 1983.

Buthmann, William. *The Rise of Integral Nationalism in France.* New York, 1939.

Cohen, Michael. *Churchill and the Jews.* London, 1985.

Cohn, Norman. *Warrant for Genocide: The Myth of the Jewish World Conspiracy and the Protocols of the Elders of Zion.* London, 1996.

Cross, Colin. *The Fascists in Britain.* New York, 1963.

Curtiss, John S. *An Appraisal of the Protocols of Zion.* New York, 1942.

Don, Yehuda, and Victor Karady, eds. *A Social and Economic History of Central European Jewry.* New Brunswick, N.J., 1990.

Favreau, Bertrand. *Georges Mandel.* Paris, 1969.

Feinstein, Wiley. *The Civilization of the Holocaust in Italy: Poets, Artists, Saints, Anti-Semites.* Madison, N.J., 2003.

Fraenkel, Joseph, ed. *The Jews of Austria: Essays on Their Life, History, and Destruction.* London, 1967.

Hamburger, Ernest. "One Hundred Years of Emancipation." *Leo Baeck Institute Yearbook,* Vol. 14 (1969).

Holmes, Colin. *Anti-Semitism in British Society, 1876–1939.* New York, 1979.

Hughes, H. Stuart. *Prisoners of Hope: The Silver Age of the Italian Jews.* Cambridge, Mass., 1983.

Judt, Tony. *The Burden of Responsibility: Blum, Camus, Aron, and the French Twentieth Century.* Chicago, 1998.

Kadish, Sharman. *Bolsheviks and British Jews: The Anglo-Jewish Community, Britain, and the Russian Revolution.* London, 1992.

Kertzer, David I. *The Popes Against the Jews.* New York, 2001.

Kuntz, Dieter, and Susan Bachrach, eds. *Deadly Medicine: Creating the Master Race.* Chapel Hill, N.C., 2004.

Kushner, Tony, and Nadia Vallman, eds. *Remembering Cable Street: Fascism and Anti-Fascism in British History.* London, 2000.

Lebzelter, Cynthia. *Political Anti-Semitism in England 1918–1939.* New York, 1978.

Lunn, Kenneth, and Richard C. Thurlow, eds. *British Fascism.* New York, 1980.

Luxemburg, Rosa. *Der Krise der Sozialdemokratie.* Berlin, 1919.

———. *Selected Works.* New York, 1976.

Machefer, Philippe. *Ligues et fascismes en France, 1918–1939.* Paris, 1974.

Malino, Frances, and Bernard Wasserstein, eds. *The Jews in Modern France.* Hanover, N.H., 1985.

Michaelis, Meir. *Mussolini and the Jews.* Oxford, Eng., 1978.

———. *Toward the Final Solution: A History of European Racism.* London, 1978.

Mosse, George L., and Walter Laqueur, eds. *The Left-Wing Intellectuals Between the Wars, 1919–1939.* New York, 1966.

Mülberger, Detlef, ed. *The Social Basis of European Fascist Movements.* London, 1987.

Oxaal, I., M. Pollak, and G. Botz, eds. *Jews, Antisemitism, and Culture in Vienna.* London, 1987.

Poliakov, Léon. *The History of Anti-Semitism.* Vol. 4: *Suicidal Europe, 1870–1933.* Oxford, Eng., 1985.

Pougan, Jacques. *L'Âge d'or du maurrassisme.* Paris, 1971.

Pulzer, Peter. *The Rise of Political Antisemitism in Germany and Austria.* New York, 1964.

Schwarz, Robert. "Antisemitism and Socialism in Austria, 1918–1962," in Joseph Fraenkel, ed. *The Jews of Austria.* London, 1967.

Silberner, Edmund. "Austrian Social Democracy and the Jewish Problem." *Historia Judaica,* Vol. 13 (1951).

Soucy, Robert J. *French Fascism: The First Wave, 1924–1933.* New Haven, Conn., 1986.

———. *French Fascism: The Second Wave, 1933–1939.* New Haven, Conn., 1995.

Sternhell, Zeev. *Ni droite, ni gauche: L'Idéologie fasciste en France.* Paris, 1983.

Talmon, Jacob. *The Origins of Totalitarian Democracy.* London, 1952.

Tucker, William H. *The Science and Politics of Racial Research.* Urbana, Ill., 1994.

Weber, Eugen. *Action Française: Royalism and Reaction in Twentieth-Century France.* Stanford, Calif., 1962.

———. *Varieties of Fascism.* Princeton, N.J., 1964.

Wistrich, Robert S. *Antisemitism: The Longest Hatred.* New York, 1991.

XXV. *The Triumph of Nazism*

Adams, Mark B., ed. *The Wellborn Science: Eugenics in Germany, France, Brazil, and Russia.* New York, 1990.

Adler-Rudel, S. "The Évian Conference on the Refugee Question." *Leo Baeck Institute Yearbook,* Vol. 13 (1988).

———. *Ostjuden in Deutschland, 1880–1940.* Tübingen, Ger., 1959.

Arendt, Hannah. *The Origins of Totalitarianism.* New York, 1951.

Ascheim, Steven. *Brothers and Strangers.* Madison, Wis., 1982.

Barkai, Avraham. "Exclusion and Persecution: 1933–1938," in Michael Meyer, ed. *German-Jewish History in Modern Times.* Vol. 4. New York, 1976.

———. *From Boycott to Annihilation: The Economic Struggle of German Jews, 1933–1943.* Hanover, N.H., 1989.

Bauer, Yehuda. *The Holocaust in Historical Perspective.* Seattle, 1978.

———. *Jews for Sale? Nazi-Jewish Negotiations, 1933–1945.* New Haven, Conn., 1994.

Beer, Udo. *Die Juden, das Recht und die Republik: Verbandswesen und Rechtsschutz, 1919–1933.* Frankfurt a/M, 1986.

Berglar, Peter. *Walther Rathenau.* Bremen, 1970.

Black, Edwin. *The Transfer Agreement.* New York, 1984.

Boas, Jacob. "German-Jewish Internal Politics under Hitler, 1833–1938." *Leo Baeck Institute Yearbook,* Vol. 29 (1984).

Brecht, Arnold. "Walther Rathenau and the Germans." *Journal of Politics,* Vol. 10 (1948).

Browning, Christopher R. *The Origins of the Final Solution.* New York, 1985.

Deak, Istvan. *Weimar Germany's Left-Wing Intellectuals: A Political History of the Weltbühne Circle.* Berkeley, Calif., 1968.

Dunker, Ulrich. *Der Reichsbund jüdischer Frontsoldaten 1919–1938.* Düsseldorf, 1977.

Eschwege, Helmut. "Resistance of German Jews Against the Nazi Regime." *Leo Baeck Institute Yearbook,* Vol. 15 (1970).

Ettinger, Elzbieta. *Rosa Luxemburg: A Life.* Boston, 1986.

Fishman, Sterling. "The Assassination of Kurt Eisner," in Klaus L. Beghahn, ed. *The German-Jewish Dialogue Reconsidered.* New York, 1996.

Fleming, Gerald. *Hitler and the Final Solution.* Berkeley, Calif., 1984.

Friedlander, Saul. "From Anti-Semitism to Extermination: A Historiographical Study of Nazi Policies Toward the Jews." *Yad vaShem Studies,* Vol. 16 (1984).

Gerlach, Wolfgang. *And the Witnesses Were Silent: The Confessing Church and the Persecution of the Jews.* Lincoln, Nebr., 2000.

Gewirtz, Sharon. "Anglo-Jewish Responses to Nazi Germany 1933–39: The Anti-Nazi Boycott and the Board of Deputies of British Jews." *Journal of Contemporary History,* Vol. 26 (1991).

Grab, Walter, and Julius H. Schoeps, eds. *Juden in der Weimarer Republik.* Stuttgart and Bonn, 1986.

Graham, Loren R. "Science and Values: The Eugenics Movement in Germany and Russia in the 1920s." *American Historical Review.* December 1977.

Grossmann, Kurt. "Deutsche Juden auf der Linken," in Herbert Strauss and Kurt Grossmann, eds. *Gegenwart im Rückblick.* Heidelberg, 1970.

Gruenwald, Max. "The Beginning of the 'Reichsvertretung,'" *Leo Baeck Institute Yearbook,* Vol. 1 (1956).

Guttmann, Theodor. *Dokumentwerk über die jüdische Geschichte in der Zeit des Nazismus.* 2 vols. Jerusalem, 1943, 1945.

Hilberg, Raul. *Perpetrators, Victims, Bystanders: The Jewish Catastrophe, 1933–1945.* New York, 1992.

———, ed. *Documents of Destruction: Germany and Jewry, 1933–1945.* Chicago, 1971.

James, Harold. *The Deutsche Bank and the Nazi Economic War Against the Jews: The Expropriation of Jewish Property.* Cambridge, Eng., 2001.

Jochmann, Werner. "Die Ausbreitung des Antisemitismus," in *Deutscher Judentum in Krieg und Revolution, 1916–1923.* Tübingen, Ger., 1977.

Joll, James. *Walther Rathenau: Prophet Without a Cause.* London, 1960.

Knütter, Hans-Helmuth. *Die Juden und die deutsche Linke in der Weimarer Republik, 1918–1933.* Düsseldorf, 1973.

Maurer, Trude. *Ostjuden in Deutschland, 1918–1933.* Hamburg, 1986.

Milton, Sybil. "The Expulsion of Polish Jews from Germany, October 1938 to July 1939," *Leo Baeck Institute Yearbook,* Vol. 24 (1984).

Mosse, George L. *The Crisis of German Ideology.* New York, 1981.

———. *Germans and Jews: The Right, the Left, and the Search for a "Third Force" in Pre-Nazi Germany.* New York, 1970.

———. "German Socialists and the Jewish Question in the Weimar Republic." *Leo Baeck Institute Yearbook,* Vol. 16 (1971).

Nettl, J. F. *Rosa Luxemburg.* 2 vols. London, 1966.

Niewyk, Donald L. "The Economic and Cultural Role of the Jews in the Weimar Republic." *Leo Baeck Institute Yearbook,* Vol. 16 (1971).

Phayer, Michael. *The Catholic Church and the Holocaust, 1930–1965.* Bloomington, Ind., 2000.

Pois, Robert. "Walther Rathenau's Jewish Quandary." *Leo Baeck Institute Yearbook,* Vol. 13 (1968).

Pulzer, Peter. *The Rise of Political Antisemitism in Germany and Austria.* New York, 1964.

Rheins, Carl J. "Deutscher Vortrupp, Gefolgschaft deutscher Juden, 1933–35." *Leo Baeck Institute Yearbook,* Vol. 26 (1981).

Richarz, Monika, ed. *Jewish Life in Germany: Memoirs from Three Centuries.* Bloomington, Ind., 1991.

Sachar, Abram L. *Sufferance Is the Badge: The Jew in the Postwar World.* New York, 1940.

Sachar, Howard M. *Dreamland: Europeans and Jews in the Aftermath of the Great War.* New York, 2002.

Schleunes, Karl A. *The Twisted Road to Auschwitz: Nazi Policy Toward German Jews.* Urbana, Ill., 1970.

Schulin, Ernst. *Walther Rathenau: Repräsentant, Kritiker, und Opfer seiner Zeit.* Frankfurt a/M, 1979.

Stern, Fritz. *The Politics of Cultural Despair: A Study in the Rise of Germanic Ideology.* Berkeley, Calif., 1961.

Weindling, Paul. *Health, Race, and German Politics Between National Unification and Nazism, 1870–1945.* Cambridge, Eng., 1989.

Weinreich, Max. *Hitler's Professors.* New York, 1946.

Wistrich, Robert S. *Hitler and the Holocaust.* New York, 2001.

Yahil, Leni. *The Holocaust: The Fate of European Jewry, 1932–45.* New York, 1990.

Yisraeli, David. "The Third Reich and the Transfer Agreement." *Journal of Contemporary History,* Vol. 6 (1971).

XXVI. *The Quest for Sanctuary: 1933–1939*

Abella, Irving, and Harold Troper. *"None Is Too Many": Canada and the Jews of Europe, 1933–1948.* Toronto, 1982.

Arab Higher Committee for Palestine. *A Collection of Official Documents Relating to the Palestine Question, 1917–1947.* New York, 1947.

Arad, Gulie N. *America, Its Jews, and the Rise of Nazism.* Bloomington, Ind., 2000.

Avigur, Shaul. *Im Dor HaHaganah* [With the Generation of the Haganah]. Tel Aviv, 1962.

Ben-Gurion, David. *P'gishot im Manhigim Araviyim* [Meetings with Arab Leaders]. Tel Aviv, 1967.

Boyers, Robert, ed. *The Legacy of the German Refugee Intellectuals.* New York, 1972.

Breitman, Richard, and Alan M. Kraut. *American Refugee Policy and European Jewry, 1933–1945.* Bloomington, Ind., 1987.

Brody, David. "American Jewry, the Refugees, and Immigration Restriction, 1932–1942." *Publications of the American Jewish Historical Society,* June 1956.

Caron, Vicki. *Uneasy Asylum: France and the Jewish Refugee Crisis, 1933–1942.* Stanford, Calif., 1999.

Cohen, Michael. *Retreat from the Mandate: The Making of British Policy, 1936–1945.* London, 1978.

Elath, Eliahu. *Haj Mohammed Amin al-Husseini* [in Hebrew]. Jerusalem, 1968.

Esco Foundation for Palestine. *Palestine: A Study of Jewish, Arab, and British Policies.* Vol. 2. New Haven, Conn., 1947.

Feingold, Henry. *The Politics of Rescue: The Roosevelt Administration and the Holocaust.* New Brunswick, N.J., 1970.

Friedman, Saul S. *No Haven for the Oppressed: United States Policy Toward Jewish Refugees.* Detroit, 1973.

Great Britain. *Palestine: Royal Commission Report (Peel Report).* Cmd. 5479. London, 1937.

Grossmann, Kurt R. *Emigration: Geschichte der Hitler-Flüchtlinge 1933–1945.* Frankfurt a/M, 1969.

Kuhl, Stefan. *The Nazi Connection: Eugenics, American Racism, and German National Socialism.* New York, 1994.

London, Louise. *Whitehall and the Jews, 1933–1945.* New York, 2000.

Marrus, Michael R. *The Unwanted: European Refugees in the Twentieth Century.* New York, 1985.

Meinertzhagen, Richard. *Middle East Diary, 1917–1936.* London, 1959.

Naufah, Sayyid. "A Short History of the Arab Opposition to Zionism and Israel." *Islamic Review,* February 1965.

Nicosia, Francis. *The Third Reich and the Palestine Question.* London, 1985.

Reinfelder, Georg. *MS "St Louis": die Irrfahrt nach Kuba: Frühjahr 1939.* Teetz, Ger., 2002.

Reinharz, Jehuda. *Chaim Weizmann: The Making of a Zionist Statesman.* Vol. II. New York, 1993.

Ristaino, Marcia R. *Port of Last Resort: Diaspora Communities in Shanghai.* Stanford, Calif., 2001.

Rose, Norman. "The Debate on Partition, 1937–38: The Anglo-Zionist Aspect—I: The Proposal." *Middle Eastern Studies,* October 1970; "II: The Withdrawal." *Middle Eastern Studies,* January 1971.

Sachar, Howard M. *Europe Leaves the Middle East, 1936–1954.* New York, 1972.

———. *A History of Israel: From the Rise of Zionism to Our Time.* 2nd ed. New York, 1996.

———. *A History of the Jews in America.* New York, 1992.

Sherman, A. J. *Island Refuge: Britain and Refugees from the Third Reich, 1933–1939.* London, 1973.

Stein, Avraham. *HaNoter HaIvri, 1936–1946* [The Hebrew Watchman, 1936–1946]. Tel Aviv, 1949.

Strauss, Herbert A. "Jewish Emigration from Germany: Nazi Policies and Jewish Responses." *Leo Baeck Institute Yearbook,* Vol. 25 (1980).

Strong, Donald B. *Organized Anti-Semitism in America: The Rise of Group Prejudice During the Decade 1930–40.* Washington, D.C., 1941.

Urofsky, Melvin I. *American Zionism from Herzl to the Holocaust.* Garden City, N.Y., 1975.

Wischnitzer, Mark. "Jewish Emigration from Germany, 1933–1938." *Jewish Social Studies,* January 1940.

Wyman, David S. *Paper Walls: America and the Refugee Crisis, 1938–1941.* Amherst, Mass., 1968.

XXVII, XXVIII. *The Holocaust of European Jewry; The* Final Solution *and the Struggle for Jewish Survival*

Albers-Schönberg, Heinz. *Die Schweiz und die jüdischen Flüchtlinge, 1933–1945.* Stäfa, Swit., 2000.

Aly, Götz. *"Final Solution": Nazi Population Policy and the Murder of the European Jews.* London, 1999.

Arad, Yitzhak. *Ghetto in Flames: The Struggle and Destruction of the Jews of Vilna in the Years of Holocaust.* Jerusalem, 1980.

Arcel, Jean. *Transnistria, 1941–1942.* Tel Aviv, 2003.

Arendt, Hannah. *Eichmann in Jerusalem.* New York, 1963.

Avni, Haim. *Spain, the Jews, and Franco.* Philadelphia, 1982.

Barkai, Avraham. "In a Ghetto Without Walls," in Michael Meyer, ed. *German-Jewish History in Modern Times.* Vol. 4. New York, 1976.

Bauer, Yehuda. *A History of the Holocaust.* New York, 1982.

———. *The Holocaust in Historical Perspective.* Seattle, 1978.

———. *Jewish Reactions to the Holocaust.* Jerusalem, 1989.

———. *Jews for Sale? Nazi-Jewish Negotiations, 1933–1945.* New Haven, Conn., 1994.

———. *They Chose Life: Jewish Resistance to the Holocaust.* New York, 1973.

Braham, Randolph L. *The Politics of Genocide: The Holocaust in Hungary.* Rev. ed. New York, 1994.

———. *The Tragedy of Hungarian Jewry.* Boulder, Colo., 1966.

Breitman, Richard. *The Architect of Genocide: Himmler and the Final Solution.* New York, 1985.

Burleigh, Michael. *Ethics and Extermination: Reflections on Nazi Genocide.* Cambridge, Eng., 1997.

Campion, Joan. *In the Lion's Mouth: Gisi Fleischmann and the Jewish Fight for Survival.* New York, 1987.

Centre de Documentation Juive Contemporaine. *Activité des organisations juives en France sous l'occupation.* Paris, 1946.

Cesarani, David, and Paul A. Levine, eds. *Bystanders to the Holocaust.* London, 2002.

Chary, Frederick B. *The Bulgarian Jews and the Final Solution.* Pittsburgh, 1972.

Cornwell, John. *Hitler's Pope: The Secret History of Pius XII.* New York, 1999.

Dean, Martin. *Collaboration in the Holocaust: Crimes of the Local Police in Belorussia and Ukraine, 1941–1944.* New York, 2000.

De Felice, Renzo. *Jews in Fascist Italy.* New York, 2001.

Delpard, Raphaël. *L'Armée juive en France: 1940–1945.* Paris, 2002.

Diamant, David. *Héros juifs de la résistance française.* Paris, 1962.

Feingold, Henry. *Did American Jewry Do Enough During the Holocaust?* Syracuse, N.Y., 1985.

———. *The Politics of Rescue: The Roosevelt Administration and the Holocaust, 1938–1945.* New Brunswick, N.J., 1970.

Fenyvesi, Charles. *When Angels Fooled the World: Rescuers of Jews in Wartime Hungary.* Takoma Park, Md., 2003.

Fleming, Gerald. *Hitler and the Final Solution.* Berkeley, Calif., 1984.

Frantz, Douglas, and Catherine Collins. *Death on the Black Sea: The Untold Story of the* Struma *and World War II's Holocaust at Sea.* New York, 2003.

Friedlander, Saul. *Memory, History, and the Extermination of the Jews of Europe.* Bloomington, Ind., 1993.

———. *The Origins of Nazi Genocide: From Euthanasia to the Final Solution.* Chapel Hill, N.C., 1995.

———. "True Believers: Greed, Ideology, Power and Lust as Motives for the Holocaust." *Times Literary Supplement,* March 2002.

Gaon, Haham S., and M. Mitchell Serels, eds. *Sephardim and the Holocaust.* New York, 1987.

Goitein, S. D. *A Mediterranean Society.* Vol. 2. Berkeley and Los Angeles, 1988.

Gushee, David P. *Righteous Gentiles of the Holocaust.* St. Paul, Minn., 2003.

Gutman, Israel. *Resistance: The Warsaw Ghetto Uprising.* Boston, 1994.

———, ed. *The Encyclopedia of the Holocaust.* New York, 1990.

Haessler, Alfred. *"The Lifeboat Is Full": Switzerland and the Refugees.* New York, 1969.

Hanson, Friedrich. *Biologische Kriegsführung in Dritten Reich.* Frankfurt a/M, 1993.

Hausleitner, Mariana, Brigitte Mihok, and Juliane Wetzel. *Rumänien und der Holocaust: zu den Massenverbrechen in Transnistrien, 1941–1944.* Berlin, 2001.

Higham, John. *Strangers in the Land: Patterns of American Nativism, 1860–1925.* New York, 1968.

Hilberg, Raul. *The Destruction of the European Jews.* Rev. ed. 3 vols. New York, 1985.

———. *Perpetrators, Victims, Bystanders: The Jewish Catastrophe, 1933–1945.* New York, 1992.

———, ed. *Documents of Destruction: Germany and Jewry, 1933–1945.* Chicago, 1971.

Ioanid, Radu. *The Holocaust in Romania: The Destruction of Jews and Gypsies under the Antonescu Regime, 1940–1944.* New York, 2000.

Koblik, Steven. *The Stones Cry Out: Sweden's Response to the Persecution of the Jews, 1933–1945.* New York, 1988.

Koen, Albert. *Le sauvetage des Juifs en Bulgarie, 1941–1944.* Sofia, 1977.

Lazarus, Jacques. *Juifs au Combat.* Paris, 1947.

Levine, Paul A. *From Indifference to Activism: Swedish Diplomacy and the Holocaust, 1938–1944.* Uppsala, Swed., 1998.

Lookstein, Haskel. *Were We Our Brothers' Keepers? The Public Response of American Jews to the Holocaust, 1938–1944.* New York, 1985.

Lubetkin, Z'viah. "The Last Days of the Warsaw Ghetto." *Commentary,* May 1947.

Marrus, Michael R. *The Holocaust in History.* New York, 1987.

———. *The Unwanted: European Refugees in the Twentieth Century.* New York, 1985.

———, and Robert O. Paxton. *Vichy France and the Jews.* New York, 1981.

Mazower, Mark. *Inside Hitler's Greece: The Experience of Occupation, 1941–1944.* New Haven, Conn., 1993.

Michaelis, Meir. *Mussolini and the Jews.* Oxford, 1978.

Molho, M., and J. Nehama. *In memoriam: hommage aux victimes juives des nazis en Grèce.* 3 vols. Salonika, 1948–53.

Morley, John F. *Vatican Diplomacy and the Holocaust, 1939–1943.* New York, 1980.

Oren, Nissan. "The Bulgarian Exception: A Reassessment of the Salvation of the Jewish Community." *Yad VaShem Studies* (1968).

Palgi, Yoel. *Into the Inferno: The Memoir of a Jewish Paratrooper Behind Nazi Lines.* New Brunswick, N.J., 2003.

Penkower, Monty Noam. *The Jews Were Expendable: Free World Diplomacy and the Holocaust.* Urbana, Ill., 1983.

Poliakov, Léon, and Jacques Sabille, eds. *Jews Under the Italian Occupation.* Paris, 1955.

Poznanski, Renée. *Jews in France During World War II.* Hanover, N.H., 2001.

Presser, Jacob. *The Destruction of the Dutch Jews.* New York, 1967.

Rautkillo, Hannu. *Finland and the Holocaust: The Rescue of Finland's Jews.* New York, 1987.

Rodrigue, Aron. "The Mass Destruction of Armenians and Jews in the 20th Century in Historical Perspective," in Hans-Lukas Kieser and Dominik J. Schaller, eds. *Der Völkermord an den Armeniern und die Shoah.* Leiden, 2000.

Sachar, Howard M. *Farewell España: The World of the Sephardim Remembered.* New York, 1994.

Sciaky, Leon. *Farewell to Salonica.* London, 1946.

Sereny, Gita. *Into the Darkness: From Mercy Killing to Mass Murder.* New York, 1974.

Steiner, Frederic. *The Tragedy of Slovak Jewry.* Bratislava, 1949.

Stille, Alexander. *Benevolence and Betrayal: Five Italian-Jewish Families under Fascism.* New York, 2003.

Trunk, Isaiah. *Judenrat: The Jewish Councils in Eastern Europe under Nazi Occupation.* New York, 1972.

Wasserstein, Bernard. *Britain and the Jews of Europe, 1939–1945.* London, 1979.

Weissberg, Alex. *Desperate Mission: Joel Brand's Story.* New York, 1958.

Wistrich, Robert S. *Hitler and the Holocaust.* New York, 2001.

Wyman, David S. *The Abandonment of the Jews: America and the Holocaust, 1941–1945.* New York, 1984.

Yahil, Leni. *The Holocaust: The Fate of European Jewry, 1932–1945.* New York, 1990.

———. *The Rescue of Danish Jewry.* Philadelphia, 1969.

Ysart, Federico. *España y los judíos en la Segunda Guerra Mundial.* Barcelona, 1973.

Ziegler, Jean. *The Swiss, the Gold, and the Dead: How Swiss Bankers Helped Finance the Nazi War Machine.* New York, 1998.

Zucotti, Susan. "Pope Pius XII and the Rescue of the Jews of Italy: Evidence of a Papal Directive?" *Holocaust and Genocide Studies,* Vol. 18 (2004).

———. *Under His Very Window: The Vatican and the Holocaust in Italy.* New Haven, Conn., 2001.

Zweig, Ronald. *Britain and Palestine During the Second World War.* Woodbridge, Eng., 1986.

XXIX. *The Birth of Israel*

Agar, Herbert. *The Saving Remnant.* New York, 1960.

Allon, Yigal. *The Making of Israel's Army.* London, 1970.

Bauer, Yehuda. *Flight and Rescue: Brichah.* New York, 1970.

———. *From Diplomacy to Resistance: A History of Jewish Palestine, 1939–1945.* Philadelphia, 1970.

———. *The Jewish Emergence from Powerlessness.* Toronto, 1979.

———. *My Brother's Keeper: A History of the American Jewish Joint Distribution Committee.* Philadelphia, 1974.

Ben-Avraham, Yehuda. *HaHe'avkut al Tzava Yehudi* [The Battle for a Jewish Army]. Tel Aviv, 1946.

Ben-Gurion, David. *B'Hilachem Yisrael* [In the Struggle for Israel]. Tel Aviv, 1949.

Cana'an, Haviv. *B'Tzet HaBritim* [The Departure of the British]. Tel Aviv, 1958.

Charters, David A. *The British Army and Jewish Insurgency in Palestine, 1945–47.* New York, 1989.

Cohen, Michael. *Churchill and the Jews.* London, 1985.

———. *Truman and Israel.* Berkeley, Calif., 1990.

Elath, Eliahu. *Zionism at the U.N.: A Diary of the First Days.* Philadelphia, 1976.

Ever-Hadani, Aharon. *Am b'Milhamto* [A People at War]. Tel Aviv, 1948.

Feis, Herbert. *The Birth of Israel: The Tousled Diplomatic Bed.* New York, 1969.

Fitzsimons, M. A. *The Foreign Policy of the British Labour Government, 1945–1951.* South Bend, Ind., 1953.

Frister, Roman. *L'Lo P'shara* [Without Reconciliation]. Tel Aviv, 1987.

Ganin, Zvi. *Truman, American Jewry, and Israel, 1945–1948.* New York, 1979.

Glick, Edward B. *Latin America and the Palestine Problem.* New York, 1958.

Gruber, Ruth. *Destination Palestine.* New York, 1948.

Habas, Braha. *The Gate Breakers.* New York, 1963.

Horowitz, David. *State in the Making.* New York, 1953.

Hurewitz, J. C. *The Struggle for Palestine.* New York, 1953.

Karsh, Efraim. *Fabricating Israeli History.* London, 1997.

Katz, Samuel. *Days of Fire.* New York, 1966.

Kimche, Jon, and David Kimche. *Both Sides of the Hill: Britain and the Palestine War.* London, 1960.

———. *The Secret Roads: The "Illegal" Migration of a People, 1938–48.* London, 1954.

Kochavi, Arieh J. *Post-Holocaust Politics: Britain, the United States, and Jewish Refugees, 1945–1948.* Chapel Hill, N.C., 2001.

Krammer, Arnold. *The Forgotten Friendship: Israel and the Soviet Bloc, 1947–53.* Urbana, Ill., 1974.

Lazar, David. *L'opinion français et la naissance de l'État d'Israël, 1945–1949.* Paris, 1972.

Lifshitz, Yehuda., ed. *Sefer HaBrigada* [The Book of the (Jewish) Brigade]. Tel Aviv, 1957.

Marrus, Michael R. *The Unwanted: European Refugees in the Twentieth Century.* New York, 1985.

Parzen, Herbert. "The Roosevelt Palestine Policy, 1943–1945." *American Jewish Archives,* April 1974.

Pearlman, Moshe. *Ben-Gurion Looks Back.* London, 1965.

Rose, Norman. "Weizmann, Ben-Gurion, and the 1946 Crisis in the Zionist Movement." *Studies in Zionism,* No. 1 (1990).

Sachar, Howard M. *A History of Israel: From the Rise of Zionism to Our Time.* 2nd ed. New York, 1996.

———. *A History of the Jews in America.* New York, 1992.

————. *Israel and Europe: An Appraisal in History.* New York, 1998.

Schmorak, Emil. *The Economic Development of Israel.* Tel Aviv, 1943.

Sharett, Moshe. *B'Sh'ar HaUmot, 1946–1949* [On the Threshold of Nationhood, 1946–1949]. Tel Aviv, 1958.

Singer, Mendel. *215 Yamim P'nei Moledatenu* [215 Days Toward Nationhood]. Haifa, 1966.

Stone, I. F. *Underground to Palestine.* New York, 1946.

Tschirgi, Dan. *The Politics of Indecision: Origins and Implications of American Involvement with the Palestine Problem.* New York, 1983.

Weinshall, Ya'akov. *HaDam Asher BaSaf* [The Blood on the Doorstep]. Tel Aviv, 1956.

XXX. *Eastern Jewry in the Postwar: A Failed Convalescence*

The Soviet Bloc

Andreski, S. "Communism and Jewish Eastern Europe." *International Journal of Comparative Sociology,* March–June 1979.

Axelbank, Albert. *Soviet Dissent: Intellectuals, Jews, and Détente.* New York, 1975.

Ben-Ami (Arieh Eliav). *Between Hammer and Sickle.* Philadelphia, 1967.

Brent, Jonathan, and Vladimir P. Naukov. *Stalin's Last Crime: The Plot Against the Jewish Doctors, 1948–1953.* New York, 2003.

Carrère d'Encausse, Hélène. *The Socialist Republic of Romania.* Baltimore, 1969.

Checinski, Michael. *Poland: Communism, Nationalism, Anti-Semitism.* New York, 1982.

Dagan, Avigdor, ed. *The Jews of Czechoslovakia.* Vol. 3. Philadelphia, 1983.

Du Broff, Sidney. "The Jews of Romania." *Jewish Spectator,* August 1968.

Ettinger, Shmuel, ed. *Anti-Semitism in the Soviet Union: Its Roots and Causes.* Jerusalem, 1978.

Fischer-Galati, Stephen. *The Socialist Republic of Romania.* Baltimore, 1969.

Freidenreich, Harriet P. *The Jews of Yugoslavia.* Philadelphia, 1979.

Gilboa, Yehoshua A. *The Black Years of Soviet Jewry.* Boston, 1971.

Goldberg, Itche, and Yuri Suhl. *The End of a Thousand Years: The Recent Exodus of the Jews from Poland.* New York, 1977.

Halévy, Jacob. *Genocide of a Culture: The Execution of the 24.* London, 1972.

Institute of Jewish Affairs. *The Jews of Hungary.* London, 1952.

Jelen, Chrétien. *La purge: chasseau juif en Pologne populaire.* Paris, 1972.

Kochan, Lionel, ed. *Jews in Soviet Russia Since 1917.* 3rd ed. Oxford, Eng., 1978.

Krammer, Arnold. *The Forgotten Friendship: Israel and the Soviet Bloc, 1947–53.* Urbana, Ill., 1974.

Lavi, Theodore. *Yehudei Romania b'Ma'avak al Hatzlatam* [The Jews of Rumania in Their Struggle for Survival]. Jerusalem, 1965.

Lendvai, Paul. *Antisemitism Without Jews.* Garden City, N.Y., 1971.

Levin, Nora. *The Jews in the Soviet Union Since 1917.* Vol. 2. New York, 1988.

Levy, Robert. *Ana Pauker: The Rise and Fall of a Jewish Communist.* Berkeley, Calif., 2001.

Lourie, R. "The Last Jew in Poland." *Dissent,* Autumn 1982.

Lustiger, Arno. *Stalin and the Jews: The Red Book: The Tragedy of the Jewish Anti-Fascist Committee and the Soviet Jews.* New York, 2003.

Meyer, Peter, B. D. Weinryb, E. Duschinsky, and N. Sylvain. *The Jews in the Soviet Satellites.* 2nd ed. Westport, Conn., 1971.

Montefiore, Simon Sebag. *Stalin: The Court of the Red Tsar.* New York, 2004.

Redlich, Shimon. "The Jewish Anti-Fascist Committee in the Soviet Union." *Jewish Social Studies,* Vol. 31 (1969).

Rubinstein, Joshua, and Vladimir P. Naumov, eds. *Stalin's Secret Pogrom: The Postwar Inquisition of the Jewish Anti-Fascist Committee.* New Haven, Conn., 2001.

Sachar, Abram L. *The Redemption of the Unwanted.* New York, 1983.

Sachar, Howard M. *Diaspora: An Inquiry into the Contemporary Jewish World.* New York, 1985.

————. *Israel and Europe: An Appraisal in History.* New York, 1998.

Schroeter, Leonard. *The Last Exodus.* Seattle, 1981.

Szulc, Tad. "Nationalism Is Rampant Again." *Present Tense,* Winter 1977.

Tamir, Vicki. *Bulgaria and Her Jews.* New York, 1979.

Teller, Judd I. *The Kremlin, the Jews, and the Middle East.* Syracuse, N.Y., 1957.

The Moslem World

Abitbol, Michel. *Les Juifs d'Afrique du Nord sous Vichy.* Paris, 1983.

Ansky, Michael. *Les Juifs d'Algérie du décret Crémieux à la libération.* Paris, 1960.

Barer, Shlomo. *The Magic Carpet.* London, 1952.

Bar-Yosef, Yitzhak. *Y'tziat Irak, 1945–50* [Exodus from Iraq, 1945–50]. Jerusalem, 1977.

Benart, Haim, ed. *The Sephardi Legacy.* Vol. 2. Jerusalem, 1992.

Bensimon, Agnès. *Hassan II et les juifs: histoire d'une émigration secrète.* Paris, 1991.

Bensimon-Donath, Doris. *L'Evolution du judaïsme marocain sous le protectorat français: 1921–1956.* Paris, 1968.

Chouraqui, André. *L'Alliance Israélite Universelle et la renaissance juive contemporaine.* Paris, 1965.

————. *La saga des Juifs en Afrique du Nord.* Paris, 1972.

Corcos, David. *The History of the Jews of Morocco.* Jerusalem, 1976.

Derogy, Jacques, and Édouard Saab. *Les deux exodes.* Paris, 1968.

Deshen, Shlomo, and Walter P. Zenner, eds. *Jewish Societies in the Middle East.* Washington, D.C., 1982.

Fischel, Walter J. "The Jews of Persia, 1795–1940." *Jewish Social Studies,* Vol. 2 (1950).

HaCohen, D'vora, and Menachem HaCohen. *One People: The Story of the Eastern Jews.* New York, 1969.

Haddad, Heskel. *Yehudei Artzot Arav v'Islam* [The Jews of Arab and Islamic Countries]. Tel Aviv, 1983.

Hameiri, Yehezkal. *Prisoners of Hate: The Story of Israelis in Syrian Hands.* Jerusalem, 1969.

Hirschberg, Chaim. *M'Eretz m'voh HaShemesh: Im Yehudei Afrika HaTzfonit b'Artzoteihem* [From the Land of the Setting Sun: With North African Jews in Their Own Lands]. Jerusalem, 1957.

Hodes, Lionel. "Jews in Arab Lands." *World Jewry,* April 1968.

Landau, Jacob. "Bittersweet Memories: Memoirs of Jewish Emigrants from Arab Countries." *Middle East Journal,* Vol. 42 (1981).

Laskier, Michael. *The Jews of Egypt, 1920–1970.* New York, 1992.

————. *North African Jewry in the Twentieth Century.* New York, 1993.

Lazar, Moshe. *The Jews of Islam.* Princeton, N.J., 1984.

Levin, Itamar. *The Seizure of Jewish Property in Arab Countries.* Westport, Conn., 2001.

Levy, Habib. *A Comprehensive History of the Jews of Iran.* Costa Mesa, Calif., 1999.

Loeb, Lawrence D. *Outcasts: Jewish Life in Southern Iran.* New York, 1977.

Lottman, Herbert R. "The Last Indian Jews." *Present Tense,* Summer 1976.

Memmi, Albert. *La terre intérieure.* Paris, 1976.

Murad, Emil. *MiBavel b'Mahteret* [From Iraq by Underground]. Tel Aviv, 1972.

Nataf, Félix. *Juif maghrébin.* Paris, 1978.

Raphael, Chaim. *The Road from Babylon.* London, 1985.

Roland, J. G. "Jews of India: Communal Survival or the End of a Sojourn?" *Jewish Social Studies,* Vol. 41 (1980).

Sabille, Jacques. *Les Juifs de Tunisie sous Vichy et l'occupation.* Paris, 1954.

Sachar, Howard M. *Diaspora: An Inquiry into the Contemporary Jewish World.* New York, 1985.

Schechtman, Joseph B. *On Wings of Eagles: The Plight, Exodus, and Homecoming of Oriental Jews.* New York, 1961.

Segev, Shmuel. *"Ma'avak Yakin": HaAliyah HaSodit shel Yehudei Maroc l'Yisrael* ["Operation Yahkin": The Clandestine Emigration of Moroccan Jewry to Israel]. Tel Aviv, 1984.

Simon, Reeva S., Michael M. Laskier, and Sara Reguer, eds. *The Jews of the Middle East and Africa in Modern Times*. New York, 2003.

Sitton, David. *Sephardic Communities Today*. Jerusalem, 1985.

Stillman, Norman. *The Jews of Arab Lands Today*. Philadelphia, 1991.

Taïeb, Jacques. *Être juif au Magheb à la veille de la colonisation*. Paris, 1994.

Tessler, M. A., and L. L. Hawkins. "The Political Culture of Jews in Tunisia and Morocco." *International Journal of Middle Eastern Studies*, February 1980.

Weicker, Walter F. *Ottomans, Turks, and the Jewish Polity: A History of the Jews of Turkey*. Lanham, Md., 1992.

XXXI. *A Precarious Revival in Western Europe*

Amerongen, Martin van. *Deutschland und seine Juden*. Hamburg, 1979.

Ansky, Michael. *Yehudei Algeria* [The Jews of Algeria]. Jerusalem, 1968.

Authers, John, and Richard Wolffe. *The Victim's Fortune: Inside the Epic Battle over the Debts of the Holocaust*. New York, 2002.

Balabkins, Nicholas. *West German Reparations to Israel*. New Brunswick, N.J., 1971.

Benguigui, Georges, Josiane Bijaoui-Rosenfield, and Georges Lévitte. *Aspects of French Jewry*. London, 1969.

Ben-Simon, Doris. *L'intégration des juifs nord-africains en France*. Paris, 1973.

Benvenisti, David. *Kehilot HaYehudim b'Yavan* [Jewish Communities in Greece]. Jerusalem, 1979.

Berghahn, Klaus L., ed. *The German-Jewish Dialogue Reconsidered*. New York, 1996.

Bloch-Michel, J. "Anti-Semitism and the French New Right." *Dissent*, Summer 1980.

Broder, Henryk M., and Michel R. Lang. *Fremd in Eigenem Land—Juden in der Bundesrepublik*. Frankfurt a/M, 1979.

Cohen, Hayyim J. *The Jews of the Middle East, 1860–1972*. New York, 1973.

Della Pergola, Sergio. *Anatomia dell'ebraismo italiano*. Rome, 1976.

Elgraby, Jordan. "The Sephardic Community of Paris." *Present Tense*, Summer 1983.

Fabre-Luce, Alfred. *Pour en finir avec l'antisémitisme*. Paris, 1979.

Fleischmann, Lea. *Dies ist nicht mein Land*. Hamburg, 1980.

Goldmann, Nahum. *Sixty Years of Jewish Life*. New York, 1969.

Greilshammer, Ilan. "The Democratization of a Community: French Jewry and the Fonds Social Juif Unifié." *Jewish Social Studies*, Vol. 40 (1979).

Gutwirth, Jacques. "Antwerp Jewry Today." *Jewish Journal of Sociology*, June 1968.

Harris, André, and Alain de Sédoury. *Juifs et Français*. Paris, 1979.

Hughes, H. Stuart. *Prisoners of Hope: The Silver Age of the Italian Jews*. Cambridge, Mass., 1983.

Joseph, Nadine. "We Feel Like Strangers." *Present Tense*, Summer 1983.

Korkaz, Sylvie. *Les Juifs de France et l'État d'Israël*. Paris, 1969.

Kuschner, Doris. *Die jüdische Minderheit in der Bundesrepublik Deutschland: eine Analyse*. Cologne, 1977.

Laufer, Peter. *Exodus to Berlin: The Return of the Jews to Germany*. Chicago, 2003.

Leboucher, Fernande. *Incredible Mission: Rescue Efforts in France and Italy*. New York, 1969.

Maor, Harry. *Über den Wiederaufbau der jüdischen Gemeinden in Deutschland seit 1945*. Mainz, 1961.

Martin, Malachi. *Three Popes and the Cardinal*. New York, 1972.

Mehlman, J. *Legacies of Anti-Semitism in France*. Minneapolis, 1983.

Memmi, Albert. *La terre intérieure*. Paris, 1976.

Milza, Pierre. *Fascisme français, passé et présent*. Paris, 1987.

Nehama, Andreas, Julius Schöps, and Hermann Simon. *Juden in Berlin*. Berlin, 2001.

Nola, Alfonso Maria di. *Antisemitismo in Italia, 1962–1972*. Florence, 1973.

Phayer, Michael. *The Catholic Church and the Holocaust, 1930–1965*. Bloomington, Ind., 2000.

Roditi, Edouard. "Anti-Semitism in France." *Midstream,* November 1980.

Rosenkranz, Herbert. *Verfolgung und Selbstbehauptung: die Juden in Österreich, 1938–1945.* Vienna, 1978.

Rothschild, Sylvia. "Wien bleibt Wien." *Present Tense,* Spring 1974.

Rovner, Ruth. "Come to Beautiful Switzerland." *Present Tense,* Autumn 1978.

Sachar, Howard M. *Diaspora: An Inquiry into the Contemporary Jewish World.* New York, 1985.

Schmid, Max, ed. *Schalom! Wir werden euch töten! Texte und Dokumente zum Antisemitismus in der Schweiz, 1930–1980.* Zurich, 1980.

Schnapper, Dominique. *Juifs et Israélites.* Paris, 1980.

Walch, Dietmar. *Die jüdischen Bemühungen um die materielle Wiedergutmachung durch die Republik Österreich.* Vienna, 1967.

Wilder-Okladek, F. *The Return Movement of Jews to Austria after the Second World War.* The Hague, 1969.

Wistrich, Robert. "Bruno Kreisky and Simon Wiesenthal." *Midstream,* June–July 1979.

Wolf, Joan B. *The Politics of Memory in France.* Stanford, Calif., 2004.

Zweig, Ronald W. *German Reparations and the Jewish World: A History of the Claims Conference.* London, 2001.

Zweigbaum, Arthur. "Swiss Jewry." *Dispersion and Unity,* Vols. 13, 14 (1971–72).

XXXII. *The Jews of British Commonwealth*

Anctil, Pierre, Ira Robinson, and Gérard Bouchard, eds. *Juifs et canadiens français dans la société québécoise.* Montreal, 2000.

Bermant, Chaim. "Anglo-Jewish Culture." *Present Tense,* Autumn 1976.

Bialystok, Franklin. *Delayed Impact: The Holocaust and the Canadian Jewish Community.* Montreal, 2000.

Bienvenue, Rita M., and Jay E. Goldstein, eds. *Ethnicity and Ethnic Relations in Canada.* Toronto, 1985.

Brasch, Rudolf. *Australian Jews of Today.* Stanmore, Austral., 1972.

Brown, Michael. *Jew or Juif? Jews, French Canadians, and Anglo-Canadians, 1759–1914.* Philadelphia, 1987.

Davies, Alan, ed. *Antisemitism in Canada.* Waterloo, Ont., 1992.

Defries, Harry. *Conservative Party Attitudes to Jews, 1900–1950.* London, 2001.

Elazar, Daniel, and Harold M. Waller. *Maintaining Consensus: The Canadian-Jewish Polity in the Postwar World.* Lanham, Md., 1990.

Goldman, Lazarus M. "The Demography of Australian Jewry." *Jewish Social Studies,* December 1966.

———. *The History of the Jews in New Zealand.* Wellington, N.Z., 1958.

Levi, John S. "The Lucky Country [Australia]?" *Present Tense,* Winter 1975.

———, and G. F. J. Bergman. *Australian Genesis: Jewish Convicts and Settlers, 1788–1860.* 2nd ed. Carlton South, Austral., 1991.

Levine, Stephen I. *The New Zealand Jewish Community.* Lanham, Md., 1999.

Lippmann, Walter M. "The Demography of Australian Jewry." *Jewish Social Studies,* Vol. 28 (1967).

Medding, Peter, ed. *Jews in Australian Society.* Melbourne, 1973.

Moonman, Jane. "The Gilded Ghettos, London Style." *Present Tense,* Spring 1976.

Price, Charles. "Chain Migration and Immigrant Groups, with Special Reference to Australian Jewry." *Jewish Social Studies,* Vol. 25 (1964).

Rosenberg, Stuart. *The Jewish Community in Canada.* 2 vols. Toronto, 1970.

Rosenthal, Odeda. *Not Strictly Kosher: Pioneer Jews in New Zealand (1831–1901).* Wainscott, N.Y., 1991.

Rubinstein, Hilary. *Chosen: The Jews in Australia.* Sydney, 1987.

Rubinstein, William D. "The Australian Left and the Jews." *Midstream,* December 1980.
———. "Jews among Top British Wealth Holders, 1857–1969: Decline of the Golden Age."
    Jewish Social Studies, Vol. 33 (1972).
Rutland, Suzanne D. *Edge of the Diaspora: Two Centuries of Jewish Settlement in Australia.* 2nd
    ed. New York, 2001.
Sachar, Howard M. *Diaspora: An Inquiry into the Contemporary Jewish World.* New York, 1985.
Saron, Gustav, and Louis Hotz, eds. *The Jews in South Africa.* Cape Town, 1955.
Shimoni, Gideon. *Jews and Zionism: The South African Experience, 1910–1949.* London, 1980.
———. *The Jews in Apartheid South Africa.* Hanover, N.H., 2003.
———. "Selig Brodetsky and the Ascendancy of Zionism in Anglo-Jewry, 1939–45." *Jewish
    Social Studies,* Vol. 41 (1980).
Tulchinsky, Gerald. *Taking Root: The Origins of the Canadian Jewish Community.* Toronto, 1992.
Ungar, André. "South African Jews and Apartheid." *Worldview,* August 1973.
Weizmann, Chaim. *Trial and Error.* New York, 1949.

XXXIII. *A Latin Israel in the Southern Hemisphere*

Ansel, Bernard D. *The Beginnings of the Modern Jewish Community in Argentina, 1852–1891.*
    Ann Arbor, Mich., 1978.
Avni, Haim. *Argentina: HaAretz HaYe'udah* [Argentina: The Promised Land]. Tel Aviv, 1973.
Becker, Lavy. "Jews in the Caribbean." *World Jewry,* October 1971.
Beller, Jacob. *Jews in Latin America.* New York, 1969.
Böhm, Gunter. *La Historia de los judíos en Chile.* Santiago, 1984.
Cimet, Adina. *Ashkenazi Jews in Mexico: Ideologies in the Structuring of a Community.* Saratoga
    Springs, N.Y., 1997.
Elkin, Judith L. *The Jews of Latin America.* Rev. ed. New York, 1998.
Emmanuel, Isaac S., and Suzanne A. Emmanuel. *A History of the Jews of the Netherlands
    Antilles.* 2 vols. Cincinnati, 1970.
Grunwald, Kurt. *Turkenhirsch: A Study of Baron Maurice de Hirsch: Entrepreneur and
    Philanthropist.* Jerusalem, 1966.
Herman, Donald. *The Latin-American Community of Israel.* New York, 1984.
Krause, Corinne A. *The Jews in Mexico.* Ann Arbor, Mich., 1974.
Lerner, Natan. *Jewish Organizations in Latin America.* Tel Aviv, 1974.
Lesser, Jeffrey. *Welcoming the Undesirable: Brazil and the Jewish Question.* Berkeley, Calif.,
    1995.
Levine, Robert M. *Tropical Diaspora: The Jewish Experience in Cuba.* Gainesville, Fla., 1993.
Lewin, Boeslao. *Cómo fue la immigración judía a la Argentina.* Buenos Aires, 1971.
———. *La colectividad judía en la Argentina.* Buenos Aires, 1974.
Perera, Victor. "Argentina after Perón." *Present Tense,* Autumn 1975.
Rein, Raanan. *Argentina, Israel, and the Jews: Perón, the Eichmann Capture, and Beyond.*
    Bethesda, Md., 2003.
Rojer, Olga. *Exile in Argentina, 1933–1945.* New York, 1989.
Sachar, Howard M. *Diaspora: An Inquiry into the Contemporary Jewish World.* New York, 1985.
Sadow, Stephen A. "Judíos y gauchos: The Search for Identity in Argentine Jewish Literature."
    Jewish Social Studies, Vol. 43 (1982).
Schers, David, and Hadassah Singer. "The Jewish Communities of Latin America." *Jewish
    Social Studies,* Vol. 38 (1977).
Senkman, Leonardo. *Argentina, la Segunda Guerra Mundial y los refugiados indeseables,
    1933–1945.* Buenos Aires, 1991.
Sofer, Eugene F. *From Pale to Pampa: A Social History of the Jews of Buenos Aires.* New York,
    1982.

Solberg, Carl. *Immigration and Nationalism: Argentina and Chile, 1890–1914.* Austin, Tex., 1970.
Winsberg, Morton D. *Colonia Baron Hirsch: A Jewish Agricultural Colony in Argentina.* Gainesville, Fla., 1964.

XXXIV. *The Efflorescence of American-Jewish Community*

Baer, Jean. *The Self-Chosen: "Our Crowd" Is Dead, Long Live Our Crowd.* New York, 1982.
Bloom, Alexander. *Prodigal Sons: The New York Intellectuals and Their World.* New York, 1986.
Caute, David. *The Great Fear.* New York, 1978.
Danziger, M. Herbert. *Returning to Tradition: The Contemporary Revival of Orthodox Judaism.* New Haven, Conn., 1989.
Dawidowicz, Lucy. *On Equal Terms: Jews in America, 1881–1981.* New York, 1982.
Eckstein, Jerome. "The Holocaust and Jewish Theology." *Midstream,* April 1977.
Ehrlich, Judith Ramsey, and Barry J. Rehfeld. *The New Crowd: The Changing of the Jewish Guard on Wall Street.* Boston, 1989.
Eisen, Arnold. *The Chosen People in America: A Study in Jewish Religious Ideology.* Bloomington, Ind., 1983.
Eisenstein, Ira, and Eugene Kohn. *Mordecai M. Kaplan: An Evaluation.* New York, 1952.
Epstein, Benjamin, and Arnold Forster. *The New Anti-Semitism.* New York, 1974.
Fishkoff, Sue. *The Rebbe's Army: Inside the World of Chabad-Lubavitch.* New York, 2003.
Freedman, Samuel G. *Jew vs. Jew: The Struggle for the Soul of American Jewry.* New York, 2000.
Glazer, Nathan. "The American Jew and the Attainment of Middle-Class Rank," in Marshall Sklare, ed. *The Jews: Social Patterns of an American Group.* Glencoe, Ill., 1958.
Goldstein, Sidney. "American Jewry: A Demographic Analysis," in David Sidorsky, ed. *The Future of the Jewish Community in America.* Philadelphia, 1974.
Goldy, Robert G. *The Emergence of Jewish Theology in America.* Bloomington, Ind., 1990.
Isaacs, Stephen M. *Jews and American Politics.* Garden City, N.Y., 1974.
Kaufman, William E. *Contemporary Jewish Philosophies.* Lanham, Md., 1985.
Kramer, Judith B., and Seymour Levantman. *Children of the Gilded Ghetto.* New Haven, Conn., 1981.
Lavender, Abraham E., ed. *A Coat of Many Colors: Jewish Subcommunities in the United States.* Westport, Conn., 1976.
Levinger, Lee. "The Disappearing Small-Town Jew." *Commentary,* August 1952.
Moore, Debora Dash. *At Home in America: Second-Generation New York Jews.* New York, 1981.
Rosenblum, Herbert. *Conservative Judaism: A Contemporary History.* New York, 1983.
Rosenfeld, Alvin. "The Holocaust in American Popular Culture." *Midstream,* July 1983.
Sachar, Abram L. *A Host at Last: The Story of Brandeis University.* Boston, 1976.
Sachar, Howard M. *A History of the Jews in America.* New York, 1992.
Sklare, Marshall, ed. *The Jews: Social Patterns of an American Group.* Glencoe, Ill., 1958.
Steinberg, Bernard. "Jewish Education in the United States." *Jewish Journal of Sociology,* June 1974.

XXXV, XXXVI. *The Jewish State and World Jewry; Israel, the United States, and the Struggle for Soviet Jewry*

Alexander, Zvi (Netzer). "Immigration to Israel from the USSR." *Israel Yearbook on Human Rights,* Jerusalem, 1977.
Alperson, Myra. "Pro-Israel PACs." *Present Tense,* Spring 1984.
Avi-Hai, Avraham. "Israel-Centrism and Diasporism." *Jewish Journal of Sociology,* June 1976.
Axelbank, Albert. *Soviet Dissent, Intellectuals, Jews, and Détente.* New York, 1975.

Azbel, Mark YA. *Refusenik: Trapped in the Soviet Union.* Boston, 1981.

Ben-Horin. *Ma Koreh Sham: Sipuro shel Yehudei MeBrit HaMoatzot* [What Is Happening There: The Story of Soviet Jewry]. Tel Aviv, 1970.

Brown, Archie, and Michael Kaser, eds. *The Soviet Union Since the Fall of Khrushchev.* New York, 1975.

Carrère d'Encausse, Hélène. *Decline of an Empire.* New York, 1979.

Friedberg, A., and A. Kfir. "Jewish Emigration from Israel." *Jewish Journal of Sociology,* January 1988.

Friedberg, Maurice. "From Moscow to Jerusalem—and Points West." *Commentary,* May 1978.

———. "Moscow and the Soviet Jews: A Parting of the Ways." *Problems of Communism,* January 1980.

Gitelman, Zvi, Musya Glants, and Marshall I. Goldman, eds. *Jewish Life after the USSR.* Bloomington, Ind., 2003.

Goodman, Jerry. *The Jews in the Soviet Union.* New York, 1981.

Gurin, Arnold. "The Impact of Israel on American Jewish Community Organization and Fund-Raising." *Jewish Social Studies,* Vol. 18 (1957).

Heckelman, A. Joseph. *American Volunteers and Israel's War of Independence.* New York, 1974.

Kochan, Lionel, ed. *The Jews in Soviet Russia Since 1917.* 3rd ed. Oxford, Eng., 1980.

Korey, William. *The Soviet Cage.* New York, 1973.

———. "The Story of the Jackson Amendment, 1973–1975." *Midstream,* March 1975.

Lazaris, Vladimir. "The Saga of Jewish Samizdat." *Soviet Jewish Affairs,* Jerusalem, 1979.

Liebman, Charles S. "The Role of Israel in the Ideology of American Jewry." *Dispersion and Unity,* Jerusalem, 1970.

Markish, Esther. *The Long Return.* New York, 1978.

Meerson-Aksenov, Michael. "The Jewish Exodus and Soviet Society." *Midstream,* April 1979.

Naim, Asher. *Saving the Lost Tribe: The Rescue and Redemption of the Ethiopian Jews.* New York, 2003.

Naishtal, Mordechai. *Yehudei Gruziyah* [The Jews of Georgia]. Tel Aviv, 1970.

Orbach, William W. *The American Movement to Aid Soviet Jews.* Amherst, Mass., 1979.

Petuchowski, Jakob J. *Zion Reconsidered.* New York, 1966.

Redlich, Shimon. "Khrushchev and the Jews." *Jewish Social Studies,* Vol. 33 (1972).

Ripp, Victor. *From Moscow to Main Street: Among the Russian Émigrés.* Boston, 1984.

Roi, Yaacov. *The Struggle for Soviet Jewish Emigration, 1948–1967.* Cambridge, Eng., 1991.

Rosenthal, Steven T. *Irreconcilable Differences: The Waning of the American Jewish Love Affair with Israel.* Hanover, N.H., 2001.

Sachar, Howard M. *Diaspora: An Inquiry into the Contemporary Jewish World.* New York, 1985.

———. *A History of the Jews in America.* New York, 1992.

Schmelz, Uri O. "New Evidence on Basic Issues in the Demography of Soviet Jews." *Jewish Journal of Sociology,* December 1974.

Schroeter, Leonard. *The Last Exodus.* Seattle, 1981.

Simon, Rita J., ed. *New Lives: The Adjustment of Soviet Jewish Immigrants in the United States and Israel.* Lexington, Mass., 1985.

Summerfield, Daniel. *From Falashas to Ethiopian Jews: The External Influences for Change, 1860–1960.* London, 2003.

Index

Aaronsohn, Aaron, 355–6, 357
Abd al-Hamid II, of Turkey, 144, 270, 408
Abd al-Majid I, of Turkey, 143
Abdullah I, of Transjordan, 365
Abraham, Karl, 461
Abramovich, Sholem, *see* Mendele Moher
  S'forim
Action française (journal), 476, 478, 479, 480
Action Française (league), 476, 477, 478–9,
  481, 482
Adenauer, Konrad, 629
Adler, Friedrich, 488
Adler, Victor, 313, 487
Africa, *see* individual African nations
Agro-Joint, 332
Ahad Ha'Am, *see* Ginzberg, Asher
Ahlwardt, Hermann, 252, 500
Aksakov, Ivan, 194
Akselrod, Pavel, 287, 293
al-Arish (Egypt), 271–2
Alexander I, of Russia: tentative approach to
  government reforms, Jewish policy, 55–9;
  liberalizes Jewish policy in Congress
  Poland, 60; Jewish policy in perspective, 71;
  had condemned blood libel, 308
Alexander I, of Yugoslavia, 406
Alexander II, of Russia: embarks on major
  reforms, 183; ameliorates Jewish condition,
  184–8; reforms of, produce mixed results,
  193, 194; confronts populist terrorism,
  assassinated, 195; distrusts Pobedonostsev,
  196; Hessia Helfman convicted for
  conspiracy against, 197–8
Alexander III, of Russia: chauvinist in
  temperament, 195–6; Pobedonostsev
  supplies ideology for, 196, 203; shocked by
  pogroms, 199; orders investigation of
  Jewish problem, 200–1; countenances May
  Laws, 202–4
Algeria: Jews ghettoized in, 148–50; impact of
  Crémieux Decree on Jews of, 150; in era of
  Dreyfus Affair, 151, 238; Vichy France
  cancels Crémieux Decree in, 540;

Americans liberate, 626–7; Jews of, fearful
  of nationalist revolt in, 627; with
  independence of, Europeans, Jews depart,
  628; resettlement of Jews from, in France,
  628
Alix, of Russia, 284
Alkalai, Yehuda, 255–6
Allenby, Edmund, 348, 349, 356, 357, 359, 364
Allende, Salvador, 671
Allgemeine Zeitung des Judentum (journal),
  133, 162
Alliance France-Israël, 643
Alliance Israélite Universelle: provides
  schooling for Jews of Near East, Maghreb,
  144–148; denied role in Rumania, 205;
  addresses westward migration of Russian
  Jews, 209–10; in Palestine, provides Jews
  with farm training, 255, school system, 262;
  seeks League of Nations redress of
  Hungary's educational bias, 439–40; funds
  Russian Jews' early travel to Argentina, 673
Almansi, Dante, 541
Altneuland, 272
Amalgamated Clothing Workers, 374
American Council for Judaism, 706
American Federation of Labor, 372, 373, 374
American Jewish Committee: applauds
  Russian Revolution, 378; seeks to defend
  Jewish rights at Paris Peace Conference,
  399; Marshall of, a pioneer of minorities
  treaties 400–1; entreats Washington's help
  on behalf of Polish Jewry, 414; appeals to
  Rumanian government on Minorities
  Treaty, 425; sponsors *Commentary*, 700
American Jewish Congress: reports on
  antisemitism, 394; presses for
  antidiscrimination legislation, 695
American Jewish Joint Distribution
  Committee, *see* Joint Distribution
  Committee
Amery, Leopold, 351, 352, 358
AMIA (Asociación Mutual Israelita
  Argentina), 678, 739

Am Olam (society), 213, 214

Anau, Salvatore, 87

Anglo-American Committee on Refugees, 579–81

Anielewicz, Mordecai, 551

Antabi, Moïse, 82

Anti-Defamation League: reports on antisemitism, 394; presses for antidiscrimination legislation, 693; fears ramifications of Pollard case, 709

Antonelli, Giacomo, Cardinal, 92

Antonescu, Ion, 431, 546, 547, 568–9

Arab Higher Committee, 522, 523, 524, 586, 591

Arab League, 591

Arabia (Saudi Arabia), 347

Arabs (Palestine): pre–World War I, 261; in Herzl's *Altneuland,* 272; early Yishuv wrests control of Jewish self-defense from, 279, 281–2; of Palestine, suffer hardship in World War I, 345; participate in British government in Palestine; 364, 366; mount early riots, 364–5; forced out of Palestine-Jewish economy, 366; growth of population, economy, in mandatory Palestine, 521; mount escalating violence in Palestine, 521–3; 524; royal commissions, hearings on, 522ff.; cautiously satisfied with Woodhead Report), 525; 1939 White Paper gives veto to, on future Jewish immigration, 525; in postwar, Britain maintains policy oriented toward, 576, 577, 580; status of, examined by sequence of investigative committees and commissions, 579–584ff.; partition issue debated, decided by UN, 585–90; British provide military support to, in Israel's War of Independence, 590–1; American Jews concerned by Israel's treatment of, 708; *see also* Palestine (pre-1967)

Arabs (states of), 347–8, 363, 364; in diplomatic crisis on issue of Palestine partition, 577, 578, 585–9, 590; in 1948, armies of, threaten to destroy Israel, 593–4; Ceauşescu plays "honest broker" between Israel and, 613; terrorists of, kidnap Soviet Jews entering Austria, 633; Pope Paul VI fears antagonizing, 636; de Gaulle shifts French policy in favor of, 646; in 1967, armies of, tighten cordon around Israel, 707; warn Libya, on migration of Falashas to Israel, 711–2; USSR shifts to support for, 717; Six-Day War loss of, debacle for

USSR, 722; Soviet-Jewish immigration to Israel embarrasses Soviet relations with, 730; guerrillas from, attack against Israeli, Jewish targets abroad, 739; *see also* individual Arab countries

Arafat, Yasser, 617, 737

Arbeiter Ring (Workmen's Circle), 376, 379

Archives juives (journal), 463

Archiv für Rassen-und Gesellschaftsbiologie (journal), 250, 501

Arco-Valley, Anton von, 495

Arendt, Hannah, 107, 699

Argentina: Jewish refugees from Germany in, 515; Jews from, find political refuge in postwar Spain, 641; government of, solicits Jewish settlers from Russia, 673; Hirsch plans mass transplantation of Russian Jews to, 673–4; growing European-Jewish migration to, 674; immigrant Jews in, as supporters of radicalism, 674–5, of Yiddish culture and communal mutual-help institutions, 675; provides sanctuary for Eichmann, other Nazis, 676; Perón's oscillatinag Jewish policy in, 676; Jews become middle-class community in, 676; political, economic chaos in, 677; revived antisemitism in, 677–8; Israel in Jewish communal life of, 678; Israel as sanctuary from domestic violence in, 678, 679; uncertain Jewish future in, 679–70; Jews in, protest Soviet emigration ban, 725; lingering Jewish insecurity in, 739; Israeli intercession with government of, 740; Jewish communal structure in, remains oriented toward Israel, 740

Arlozorov, Chaim, 519

Arndt, Ernst Moritz, 130

Arnstein (banking house), 102

Aron, Raymond, 642, 646

Arrow-Cross Party, 441–2, 550

Asch, Sholem, 301

Asociación Mutual Israelita Argentina (AMIA), 675, 678

Assad, Hafez al-, 623

Assembly of Jewish Notables, 41–2

Atias, Isaac da Costa, 46

Attlee, Clement: cannot forfeit Middle Eastern oil, Arab goodwill, 575–6; Truman presses, to admit Jews to Palestine, 577; in diplomatic imbroglio with Washington, 578; accepts reality of American-Zionist alliance, 584; abandons historic sphere of British influence, 585

Auerbach, Isaac, 132

Aurore (journal), 237

Australia: admits 2,000 German-Jewish refugees, 515; Jews among early convicts shipped to, 660; in post–World War II, dramatic growth of foreign, Jewish population 660–1; nineteenth-century Jewish immigration to, grows slowly, 661; a frontier society, presents no economic, political barriers to Jews, 661; maintains severe immigration restrictions in Depression, Nazi epoch, 661; parochial Jewish community life in, 662; Jewish school system in, energized by Israel, 741

Austria (post-Habsburg): in Peace Conference "Revolt of the Small Powers," 402; becomes republic, 486–7; Jews prominent in early Social Democratic party, postwar government, public consciousness, 487–8; Christian Socialist backlash against Jews of, 488–9; political polarization, civil conflict, antisemitism mount in, 489–91; Dollfuss establishes rightist government in, 490–1, assassinated, 491; Schuschnigg successor regime in, turns increasingly fascist, antisemitic, 491; Hitler's early career in, 501, 502; Anschluss with, intensifies Hitler's efforts to expel Jews, 511–12, 514; Roosevelt combines immigration quota for, with Germany's, 518; fate of Jews in, during World War II, 535; population of, shares in plunder of Jewish property, 569–70; in postwar, pro-Nazi record of, assessed, 631–2; Israel empties DP camps in, 632; postwar Jewish community in, 632–3; Kreisky's political career in, 633; election of Waldheim, Halder in, 633–4; accepts "moral responsibility" for past deeds, 634; as transit route for emigrating Soviet Jews, 633; recent antisemitic violence in, 741

Auto-da-Fé, 460

"Awake, My People" ("Hakizah Ami"), 189

Axelrod, Tovia, 495

Ba'al Shem Tov, 13–14

Babel, Isaac, 330, 339, 342

Bainville, Jacques de, 475

Balabanov, Angelica, 287

Balfour, Arthur James: remembers Herzl, 276, 283; as foreign secretary, favors pro-Zionist orientation, 357; encourages, formulates pro-Zionist "Declaration," 359, 360, 361; recognizes sovereignty of Czechoslovakia, 402

Balfour Declaration: formulated, 359–60; has little influence on Jews in warring countries, 361; incorporated in Peace Conference award of Palestine mandate to Britain, 364; "redefined," by Peel Report, 524; Attlee denigrates, 576

Balkans, *see* Turkey, Turkish Empire; individual Balkan countries

Ballin, Albert, 251, 315, 458

Bamberger, Ludwig, 87, 245

Bar-Kokhba Society, 462, 466

Barrès, Maurice, 230, 475

Barzilai, Salvatore, 541

Bartels, Adolf, 315

Batshaw, Harry, 657

Bauer, Erwin, 501

Bauer, Otto: ideological theorist of Austrian Social Democrats, 313; in Habsburg army, 314; in postwar Austrian government, 487; spurns political coalition in Depression, 489; flees Austria, 490

Bayezid II, of Turkey, 139, 141

Bea, Augustin, Cardinal, 636

Becher, Kurt, 558, 568

Beck, Jozef, 421

Beck, Karl, 124

Beeley, Harold, 586

Beer, Aaron, 24

Begin, Menahem, 613, 708, 736

Beha-a-Din, 344, 345

Beilis, Mendel: arrested for murder, 305; becomes focus of political trauma in Russia, 305–8; acquitted, 308, departs Russia; 309; Soviet Doctors' Plot reminiscent of, 605

Bejerano, Haim, 410

Belgium: protests Mortara abduction, 93; Final Solution in, 537; postwar Jewish sociology in, 639; Israel airlift of Falashas through, 711; Moslem violence against Jews in, 739

Belinski, Vissarion, 178

Beloff, Max, 650

Belorussia, *see* Poland; Russia (tsarist); Russia (Communist, post-Communist)

Benedict XV (pope), 353

Benes, Eduard, 404, 598

Benigni, Umberto, 484

Ben-Gurion, David: as early immigrant to Palestine, 279; volunteers for Turkish army, 345; returns to Palestine in Jewish Legion, 362; reacts militantly to British White Paper, 525; entreats British to allow Palestinian-Jewish rescue efforts, 553; seeks to protract ransom negotiations on Hungarian Jews, 557; loyal to Britain in World War II, 572; execrates assassination of Lord Moyne, 573; addresses Jewish DPs in Germany, 575; directs Zionist campaign for autonomy, independence: 575–6, 578, 580, 581–82, 584–5, 590, 592ff.; initiates negotiations for German reparations, 629; envisages new, anti-Nazi Germany, 631; maximalist Zionist views of, rejected by most American Jews; 706–7; determines to forge contacts with Soviet Jewry, 717; endorses worldwide campaign on behalf of Soviet Jewry, 719ff.; envisages a Jewish state as source of Jewish normalcy, 738, not Diaspora insecurity, 743

Ben-Yehuda, Eliezer (Perlman): impressed by Pan-Slavism, 257; settles in Palestine, 282–3; creates functional Hebrew language, 283

Berenson, Bernard, 459, 462

Bergelson, David, 336, 342

Bergson, Henri, 361

Berlin, Isaiah, 650

Berlin, Congress, Treaty of, 112–13, 204, 211–12, 422

Berlusconi, Silvio, 742

Bermant, Chaim, 667

Bermuda, Conference of, 567

Bernadotte, Folke, 562

Bernáldes, Andrés, 138

Bernhardt, Sarah, 475

Bernstein, Eduard, 285, 287

Bernstein, Henri, 475

Bernstein, Leonard, 448

Bessarabets (journal), 289

Best & Co., 690

Bethlen, Istvan, 438–9, 440

Bettauer, Hugo, 444–5

Bevin, Ernest: a friend of Zionists in pre–World War II, 576; as foreign secretary, recognizes need for Arab friendship, 576; seeks solution for Jewish refugees in U.S., 576–7; in unsuccessful diplomacy on Palestine, 577–8, 580–1, 584–5

Beware Zionism, 722, 727

Bialik, Chaim Nahman, 290

Biblioteka Warszawska (journal), 71

BILU, 212, 261–2, 278

Biro-Bidzhan, 333–4

Bischoffsheim & Goldschmidt (banking house), 107

Bischoffsheim family, 107, 114

Bismarck, Otto von: presses for Jewish emancipation in Prussia, German Empire, 95; senses Rothschilds' propensity for peace, stability, 105; secures Bleichröder's financial help in building German Empire, 108–10; 111; seeks guarantees for Rumanian Jewry, 112–13, 204–5; as builder of German Empire, legitimizes political antisemitism, 245, 246; "legitimizes" Teutomania, 500

Blair, Frederick, 516

Bleichröder, Gerson von: Bismarck's personal banker, 109–10; helps finance rise of German Empire, 110; ennobled, 111; leads campaign to secure guarantees for Rumanian Jewry, 112–13, 204; funds European industrial development, 113–14; banking house of, remains eminent, 505

Blitzstein, Marc, 393

Bloch, Emanuel, 688

Blum, Léon: active in Dreyfusard cause, 237; favors Balfour Declaration, 361; willing to accept Polish Jews in Madagascar, 421; defends Daladier against rightist mobs, 479; rebuilds Socialist Party after 1920 schism, 480; organizes Popular Front, assumes premiership, 480–1; achieves major reform legislation, 482; government of, collapses, 482–3

B'nai B'rith: founded, 166, becomes largest American-Jewish organization, 171; Freud joins in Vienna, 454; established in Weimar Germany, 463; Anti-Defamation League of, surveys anti-Jewish discrimination in post–War World II, 693; branches of, opened in USSR, 733

Board of Delegates of American Israelites, 167

Board of Deputies of British Jews, 92, 97, 216, 463, 654

Bodenheimer, Max, 275

Börne, Ludwig, 79, 123

Bohemia, Bohemia-Moravia, see Habsburg Empire, Czechoslovakia

Boisdeffre, Raoul de, 234

Bonald, Louis Gabriel de, 39

Bonaparte, Jerome, 46, 128

Bonaparte, Napoleon, see Napoleon Bonaparte

Bopp, Franz, 247

Bor-Komorowski, Tadeusz, 551

Boris III, of Bulgaria, 544, 545–6

Born, Max, 450

Bornemisza, Geza, 441

Borochov, Ber, 278

Bosnia-Herzegovina: Sephardic settlement of, 147–8; clings to Sephardic heritage, 405; Final Solution in, 536; *see also* Yugoslavia

Boulanger, Georges, 230

Bourguiba, Habib, 625–6

Bowman, Isaiah, 517

Brahm, Otto, 448

Brand, Joel, 556–7

Brandeis, Louis: Russian Zionists cool to appeals from, 354; secures Wilson's approval of Balfour Declaration, 359; appeals to Jewish Communists on behalf of Entente, 361; negotiates "Protocol of Peace" for clothing industry, 374; appointed to Supreme Court, 396; influences Roosevelt's New Deal, 396; intercession of, recalled by Masaryk, 404

Brandeis University, 700–1

Brandes, Georg, 456, 458

Bratianu, Ion, 204, 205–6

Bratianu, Ionel, 422, 423, 426, 428, 427, 437

Brazhul-Brushkovski, Boris, 306, 307

Brazil: Sephardic *convertidos* from Portugal prosper in, 156–7; Sephardim in, resume Jewish identity under Dutch rule, 157; flee Portuguese reconquest, 157; refugees from, resettle in Netherlands, in West Indies, 157–8, in Nieuw Amsterdam, 158–9; Jewish refugees from Nazi Germany in, 515; twentieth-century Sephardic revival in, 680; East European–Jewish influx to, 681; in Depression, imposes immigration restrictions on refugee Jews, 681; in post–World War II, varieties of Jewish immigration to, 682; Jews flourish in, 682; centrality of Israel in Jewish communal life of, 683; ongoing Jewish concerns in, 683–4

Brest-Litovsk, Treaty of, 319, 320, 329

Brezhnev, Leonid, 721

British Union of Fascists, 473–4

Brod, Max, 403, 404, 455, 462

Brodetsky, Selig, 654

Brodski, Osip, 339

Bronfman, Samuel, 387

Buber, Martin: influenced by mysticism, develops neo-Hasidic philosophy of Judaism, of Zionism, 465–6; founds Bar-Kohba Society, 466; cooperates with Rosenzweig in Freies jüdische Lehrhaus movement, re-translation of Bible, 466; works of, published by Schocken, 699; attends congress on behalf of Soviet Jewry, 719

Bukharin, Nicholas, 329, 340

Bulgaria: Sephardic settlement in, growth of commercial vitality in, 147; signs Minorities Treaty, 402; nationals of, in post–World War I Yugoslavia, Rumania, 405; as pro-Hitler collaborator, awarded Yugoslav Macedonia, 535; delivers Macedonian, Thracian Jews to Germans for extermination, 544–5; King Boris of, resists further Jewish deportations, 545–6; Jewish survival in, 546; reclaims territory from Rumania, 547; Jewish parachutists dropped into, 553; War Refugee Board provides funds for Jews of, 568; Jews of, destitute in postwar, allowed to depart for Israel, 596–7; remnant Jewry of, not mistreated, 597

Bund (Social Democratic-General Jewish Workers Union): clashes with Zionists in Russia, 277, 298–9; mounts defense against Russian pogroms, 290–1; rise and growth of, 291–2; autonomist aspirations of, 293–4; mounts defense against pogroms, 295; boycotts Duma, 296; fosters prestige of Yiddish language, 299; in malaise during last years of Nicholas I, 309; revives with 1917 February Revolution, 324; maintains identity in early Soviet state, 334; "co-opted" by communism, 334–5; by World War I, more Russian Jews favor, than Zionism, 349; tradition of, carries over to immigrant Jews in U.S., 370, 372ff.

Bureau for Zionist Affairs (Copenhagen), 349, 356

Burton, Montague, 648

Busch, Moritz, 252

Bush, George H. W., 711, 712, 734

Byzantium, 52, 54

Cahan, Abraham: transforms *Forverts* into Americanizing influence, 376; exultant at Russian Revolution, 379

Cairo, Conference of, 365

Calangiano della Sardegna, Tomasso, 81–2

Calé, Walter, 459

Canada: Jews from, in Jewish Legion, 362; maintain immigration restrictions on German-Jewish refugees, 515, 516; supports UN partition resolution, 590; modest nineteenth-century immigration to, 655; expanding twentieth-century Jewish immigration to, 656; Jews achieve middle-class profile in, 656; Jews face complexities of federal structure, Anglo-French kulturkampf in diverse school systems of Quebec province, 657; Depression-era antisemitism in Quebec province, 657; Jews' social, political marginalization in, 657–8; Jews of, dependent on communal resources of United States Jewry, 658; Jewish population in, doubles in post–World War II, 658; Jews in, migrate from Montreal to other cities, 658–9; Jews achieve breakthrough in economic, professional life of, 660; Jews of, contribute volunteers to Israel's war of independence, 702–3, to Israel's population, 704–5

Carol II, of Rumania: installed on Rumanian throne, 427–8; in perennial conflict with Codreanu, Iron Guard, 428–29; crushes Iron Guard, becomes de facto dictator, 429–30; forced into territorial concessions, abdicates, 431, 546

Carr, Wilbur J., 384

Carter, Jimmy, 729, 730, 731

Caskel, Cesar, 167

Cassel, Ernst, 110, 469

Cassirir, Ernst, 446

Castle, The, 455

Catherine I, of Russia, 53

Catherine II, of Russia: an effective "enlightened despot" in Russia, 51–2; inherits Polish-Jewish population, 52–4; ambivalent in policy toward Jews, establishes geographic Pale of Settlement, 54–5; Jewish policy of, in perspective, 55, 71

Cavaignac, Godefroy, 239

Cavour, Camillo di, 78

Ceauşescu, Nicolae: uses Rosen, Jews, to secure trade advantages with U.S., 613; an "honest broker" between Israel, Egypt, 613

Cecil, Robert, 350, 351, 353, 470

Cerfberr, Berr Isaac, 36, 37, 38, 41

Chagall, Marc, 336, 475

Chajzkes, Karl, 87, 90

Chamberlain, Houston Stewart: disciple of Wagner's Aryanism, 250–1; favorite of Wilhelm II, 251; guru of Pan-German League, 254, draws extensively from Aryan mythology, 500

Chamberlain, Joseph: Herzl's diplomatic negotiations with, 271–2, 273–4, 275; Herzl's negotiations with, recalled, 350, fulfilled, 353

Chamberlain, Neville, 515, 525

Chaplinski, District Procurator, 304, 305, 307, 308

Charcot, Jean-Martin, 354

Charles II, of England, 20

Charles Albert, of Sardinia-Piedmont, 86

Chautemps, Camille, 478–9

Cheberiak, Vera, 304, 306, 307, 309

Chernyshevski, Nicholas, 187

Chicherin, Georgi, 499

Chile: Jewish political refugees, in post-Franco Spain, 641; twentieth-century Jewish resettlement in, 670–1; Jews flee Allende, Pinochet regimes in, for Israel, 671–2; Jewish communal structure in, oriented toward Israel, 740

China, 515, 728

Chirac, Jacques, 646, 647

Chmielnicki, Bohdan, 12, 13

Churchill, Randolph, 553

Churchill, Winston: supporter of Zionism, 350, 360; at Cairo Conference, divides Palestine, 365; sees Jews drawn to bolshevism, 471; during World War II, authorizes Jewish rescue attempts, 553; warn Axis collaborators in Holocaust, 567; approves Jewish Brigade, 572; unseated by Labour electoral victory, 575; had maintained White Paper on Palestine, 575; had promised to consult with Arabs on Palestine, 577

Ciechanowski, Jan, 567

Citroën, André-Gustav, 642

City Without Jews, The, 444–5

Civiltà cattolica, La (journal), 227

Clemenceau, Georges, 235, 237, 308

Clermont-Tonnère, Stanislaw de, 36, 38

Clifford, Clark, 589

Codreanu, Cornelius: swept up in Moldavian antisemitism, 426; becomes national hero, 426; leader of Rumanian fascist populism, 427–30; slain, 430

Coelho, Duarte, 156

Cohen, Alexander, 70

Cohen, Benjamin V., 397

Cohen, Elliott, 700

Cohen, Hermann: supports German war

effort, shattered by wartime antisemitism, 316; develops neo-Kantian philosophy of Judaism, 464–5; lectures for Rosenzweig's Lehrhaus, 468

Cohen, John, 648–9

Cohen, Sam, 519

Cohn, Ferdinand, 452

Cohn, Roy, 688

Colombia, 672

Columbus, Christopher, 138

Commentary (journal), 700

Communist Manifesto, 310

Communist Party (United States), 382, 394–5, 687–88

"Conjoint" Committee (Anglo-Jewish): 423, 439

Conservative Judaism (Germany), 136

Conservative Judaism (United States): among "defectors" from Reform, 392; helped by Reform patriarchs, 392; under leadership of Schechter, 392–3; revives, after World War II, 696–7; constituents of, concerned by Orthodox monopoly in Israel, 708

"Constitution of the Jews," 57–8, 60

"Contemporary Jewish Library," 719

Copland, Aaron, 448

Corfu, 636

Costa Rica, 672

Council of Liberal and Reform Congregations (Great Britain), 653

Coughlin, Charles, 517, 689

Coupland, Reginald, 523

Cowen, Zalman, 662

Crémieux, Adolphe, 83–5, 112, 144, 255

Crete, 536

Cristea, Miron, 428–9, 430

Croatia, *see* Yugoslavia

Croce, Benedetto, 464

Croix, La (journal), 238

Croix de Feu, 478, 482

Cromwell, Oliver, 20

Cromwell, Richard, 20

Crossman, Richard, 579, 580, 587

Cuba, 672, 731

Cultusverein deutscher Staatsbürger jüdischen Glaubens, 462–3

Curaçao, 157; *see also* West Indies (Dutch)

Curzon, George, 358, 470, 473

Cuza, Alexandru, 425–6, 429

Cyon, J. F., 197

Cyprus, 583, 587, 614, 628

Czartoryski, Nicholas, 56

Czechoslovakia: Masaryk of, elicits wartime support of Wilson, Allied leaders, 402; protects Jewish rights, 403–4; Jews of, not homogeneous group, 402–3; Jewish intellectuals' careers in, 405; Germany occupies, purges Jews from, 511–12; Jews flee, 514; under Final Solution, 527, 535; Hitler allocates territory from, to Hungary, 548; Slovakia as satellite of Third Reich, 554; only 70,000 Jews survive in, 597; postwar government of, showpiece of Soviet forbearance, 598; provides weapons for Palestine Jewry, Israel, 597; majority of native Jewish survivors in, allowed to depart for Israel, 597–8; helps migrating Polish-Jewish survivors, 598; communized in 1948, experiences Stalinist purge, 605–6; trials of Czech-Jewish officials in, terror campaign against "Zionist conspiracy," 606; *see also* Habsburg Empire; Slovakia

Czerniakow, Adam, 532–3

Daiches, David, 650

Daily Worker (journal), 395

Daladier, Édouard: resigns as premier-designate, supported by Blum in Stavisky crisis, 479; brings Radicals into Popular Front, 480; as premier, leads government rightward, 483; harshly restricts Jewish refugees, explores a transmigration of Jews to Madagascar, 484

Daniel, Yuli, 721

Danilevski, Nicholas, 194–5

Danneker, Theodor, 543–4, 544–5

Daranyi, Kalman, 441

Dassault, Marcel, 642

Daudet, Léon, 476, 477, 480

Davenport, Charles, 381

Dearborn Independent (journal), 383

Debré, Michel, 642

Debs, Eugene, 370

Decken, Josef, 228

de Gaulle, Charles: after returning to power in France, negotiates independence of Algeria, 627; adopts pro-Arab diplomatic stance, 646; Chirac a political loyalist of, 646

Degeneration, 453

Deitch, Lev, 287

De Klerk, F. W. de, 667

De Leon, David Camden, 166

Del Valle, Eric, 672

Denikin, Anton, 321, 322

Denmark: Jewish settlement in, 537; failure of Nazi Final Solution in, 537–8; clergy of, prays for Jews, 562

Derzhavin, Gabriel, 56, 57

Destruction of the European Jews, 551

Dialogue aux Enfers entre Montesquieu et Machiavel, 472

Dictionary of Races, A, 382

Diderot, Denis, 27

Dietrichs, Eugen, 465

Dillingham, William (Commission, Report), 381–2

Dimanshtein, Semyon, 334, 342

Disraeli, Benjamin: secures Suez Canal for Britain, 106; at Congress of Berlin, seeks guarantees for Rumanian Jews, 112, 113; achieves political, diplomatic triumphs, 125–6; transposes Jewish ancestry into political advantage, 126–7

Djemal Pasha, Ahmed, 344, 345, 362

Dmowski, Roman, 412, 413

Doctors' Plot, 605, 712

Documentation catholique (journal), 477

Dohm, Christian Wilhelm von, 28–9

Dollfuss, Engelbert: becomes Austrian chancellor, 490; crushes Social Democrats, 470; outlaws Nazi Party, 490; assassinated, 491

Dominican Republic, 672

Doriot, Jacques, 483

Dostoevsky, Fyodor, 190, 195

Dreyfus Affair: ramifications of, in Algeria, 151; becomes political trauma in France, 235–41ff.; influences Herzl's, Nordau's chimera of assimilation, 241; antisemitism of, utilized for political exploitation in France of 1930s, 481

Dreyfus, Alfred: career of, 233; accused, convicted, imprisoned for alleged treason, 234–5, 237; re-tried, re-convicted, 240; pardoned, promoted, exonerated, 240–1

Droysen, Johann, 242, 250

Drumont, Édouard: author of *La France juive*, 231; editor of *La Libre Parole*, 231–2; exposes Panama Canal scandal, attacks Jewish bankers, "degeneracy," 232–3; exposes Dreyfus putative "treachery," 234; as "pope of antisemitism," 238–9, 453; Maurras as successor of, 475, 476

Dubois, Josiah E., Jr., 567

Dubnow, Simon, 292, 324, 342, 468

Duckwitz, Georg, 538

Duchy of Warsaw, *see* Poland

Dühring, Ernst, 250, 500

Duisenberg, Greta, 737

Dunkelman, Ben, 703

Duplessis, Maurice, 657

Durkheim, Émile, 475

Dymshits, Benyamin, 714

Dymshits, Mark, 726

East Africa Project, 273–5

Ebert, Friedrich, 493, 494, 495, 496, 498, 500

Eckhardt, Dietrich, 504

Eckhardt, Tibor, 441

Eden, Anthony, 557, 575

Educational Alliance, 219

Edward I, of England, 20

Efros (financial house), 185

Egypt: Mehemet Ali rules, 81; threatens to invade Turkey, 82; forced to relinquish rule of Syria, 85; Britain secures Suez Canal in, 106; modern Jewish settlement, embourgoisement in, 152–3; Herzl seeks Jewish charter in al-Arish district of, 271–2; Turks expels Jaffa Jews to, 344; Jewish internees in, volunteer for Zion Mule Corps, 346; British high commissioners in, negotiate with Hashemite Arabs, 347; Egyptian Expeditionary Force launches offensives toward Palestine, 348–9; Aaronsohn as liaison with British in, 355–6; Jewish Legion trained in, 362; Bevin fears antagonizing, on Palestine, 580; Jews in, suffer harassment, violence, during Palestine partition crisis and war with Israel, 621; many Jews in, depart, 621; Sinai-Suez War of 1956, Nasser's vindictiveness in, precipitates ongoing Jewish exodus from, 622; subverts France's rule in Algeria, 643; in 1967, forges noose around Israel, 707; Ethiopia provides Israel buffer against, 709; Israel's military incursion into, alarms Africans, 710; Sadat's assassination in, alarms Numeiri, 711; USSR alarmed at Israel's collaboration with Western nations against, 711; in 1956, Khrushchev alarmed at Israeli defeat of, 716

Ehrlich, Paul, 452

Ehrmann, Sandor, 461

Eichmann, Adolf: purges Jews from Austria, 511, from Germany, 513; given administrative responsibility for Final Solution, 529; gives principal attention to Final Solution in Central-West Europe, 534–5; orders resettlement of French Jews, 540; orders *Judenrazzia* in Italy, 543; presses Rumania for mass Jewish deportations, 547; approves ransom negotiations in Slovakia, 554–5, in Hungary, 555–8; Israel's trial of, opens issues of Christian complicity in Final Solution, 636; Israeli commandos abduct, from Argentina, 677

Einstein, Albert: scientific career, discoveries of, 449–50; seeks help for Weimar Germany, 450; remains identified Jew, Zionist, 461–2; antisemites harass in Vienna, 489, in Germany, 498

Eisenhower, Dwight, 573

Eisner, Kurt, 494–5, 498

Elazar, Daniel, 739

Elbogen, Ismar, 468

Eliav, Arieh, 718–19

Elizabeth, of Belgium, 537

Encyclopedia, 27

Encyclopedia Judaica, 468

Engels, Friedrich, 119

Eotvos, Karl von, 224

Erter, Isaac, 180

Eshkol, Levi, 708

Eskeles (banking house), 102

Essai sur l'inégalité des races humaines, Un, 247

Esterhazy, Walsin, 233–4, 237, 239

Estonia, 530; *see also* Russia (tsarist; Communist, post-Communist)

"Eternal People," 191

Ethiopia: Roosevelt suggests, as possible haven for Jews, 517; supports UN partition resolution, 590; as buffer for Israel's Red Sea route, 709–10; ostensibly terminates relations with Israel, 710; Falashas of, rediscovered, 710, rescued by Israel, 710–12; American Jewry prefers that Falashas settle in Israel, 732

Etzel, 578, 582, 585

Eulenberg, Philip zu, 269

European Common Market, 736

European Economic Community, 651

European Union, 736, 737, 742–3

Evans-Gordon, W., 469

Évian, Conference of, 484, 516

Exodus (vessel), 586–7

Eynigkeit (journal), 595

Fackel (journal), 459

Faitlovich, Jacques, 710

Falashas, *see* Ethiopia

Farewell to Salonika, 146

Farkas, Mihaly, 600, 609

Feisal, al-Hashemi, Emir: leads wartime Arab revolt, 347; in postwar meetings with Weizmann, 364

Feletti, Pier Gaetano, 92, 93

Ferdinand I, of Habsburg Empire, 86, 90

Ferdinand I, of Rumania, 428

Ferdinand II, of Habsburg Empire, 5

Ferdinand II, of Kingdom of Two Sicilies, 86, 90

Ferdinand III, of Habsburg Empire, 4

Fervent Days, 186

Feuchtwanger, Lion, 455

Fichte, Johann Gottlieb von, 130, 242

Filov, Bogdan, 544–5

Finland, 297, 325; *see also* Russia (tsarist)

Finzi, Aldo, 541

Fischer, Eugen, 501

Fischer, Otokar, 405

Fischhof, Adolf, 87

Fitness of Our Race and the Protection of the Weak, The, 250

Fleg, Edmond, 361

Fleischmann, Gisi, 555

Fliess, Wilhelm, 453

Foà, Ugo, 543

"For Whom Do I Toil?" 192

Ford, Gerald, 729

Ford, Henry, 383, 472, 517, 689

Fortune (journal), 386, 690

Forwärts (journal), 494

Forverts (journal), 376–7, 378, 379

Foundations of the Nineteenth Century, The, 251

France: eighteenth-century Jewish population in, 5–6, 18, 20–21; *philosophes'* reaction to Jews, 27–8, 29, 31; revolution of 1789 in, 34; Jews in, on eve of revolution, 34–5; Malesherbes Commission in, 35, 36; popular protests against Alsatian Jews, 35–6; Sephardic, Ashkenazic struggle for emancipation, 36–7; impact of emancipation on Jewish communal structure, 37–8; Napoleon copes with anti-Jewish feeling in, 39; Assembly of Jewish Notables, Sanhedrin, 39–43; Napoleonic conquests bring wider Jewish emancipation, 46–8; restoration of Bourbon dynasty does not doom

France *(continued)*
  liberalism, Jewish emancipation, 73; Jews
  acculturate, complete their emancipation
  in, 73–4; as protector of Catholics in Syria,
  defends Mehemet Ali regime in crisis of
  Damascus Jews, 82–5; Orleanist dynasty
  overthrown in, 86; Jews included in
  Second Republic government, 87; restores
  Pius IX to papal throne in 1848, 90;
  protests papal abduction of Edgardo
  Mortara, 92–3; helps drive Habsburg army
  from Italy, 93; Jews of, thrive under Louis
  Napoleon and Third Republic, 95;
  Rothschilds finance coalition against, in
  Napoleonic wars, 103–4; Rothschilds
  discourage Louis-Philippe government
  from threatening war, 105; Bleichröder
  helps fund Prussian war against, negotiate
  reparations from, 110; Jewish bankers social
  luminaries in, 110; support emancipation of
  Rumanian Jews, 112–13; Jews underwrite
  railroad development in, 114;
  "Gallicization" of Judaism in, 120, 127–8;
  provides cultural inspiration, Alliance
  schools, for Ottoman Jewry, 144, 146;
  occupies North Africa, improves condition
  of native Jews, 150; passes Crémieux
  Decree for Algerian Jewry, 150; Algerian
  colons react to Dreyfus Affair, 151; Jewish
  settlement in West Indies of, 157;
  nineteenth-century Russian exposure to
  culture of, 177; Cyon in, helps lay
  groundwork for Russian treaty, 197;
  Alliance Israélite Universelle of, copes
  with Russian-Jewish emigration, 203;
  veteran Jews of, cool to Russian-Jewish
  refugees, 215; enters alliance with Tsarist
  Russia, 215; fusion of antisemitism, anti-
  republicanism in, 230–1; influence of
  Drumont in, 231–3; Dreyfus Affair in,
  233–9; liquidation of Dreyfus Affair in,
  239–41; separation of Church and State in,
  241; government of, expresses concern over
  Mendel Beilis case, 308; Vaillant of, cofounder of Second International, 311;
  Socialists in, support military effort, in
  World War I, 314; Syrian Arab territory
  reserved for, under Hussein-McMahon
  agreement, 347, under Sykes-Picot
  Agreement, 348; Britain reconsiders role
  of, in Middle East, 348–9; distrusts
  Zionism as Germanophile movement, 349,
  as a British stalking horse, 352–3; includes

  Jewish "advisers" in wartime mission to
  U.S., 354; Jews of, respond mildly to
  Balfour Declaration, 361; Peace
  Conference awards Syria to, 363;
  American-Jewish bankers extend loans to,
  in World War I, 414; loses interest in
  Minority Treaties, 415; Blum of, willing to
  accept Polish Jews in Madagascar, 421; as
  guarantor of Little Entente, 431; Jews in,
  flourish after liquidation of Dreyfus Affair,
  475; patriotic in World War I, 475; growth
  of xenophobia in, 475–7; political structure
  of, fragile in postwar, 477–8; Stavisky Affair
  in, topples government, 478–9; Léon Blum
  and rise of Popular Front, 479, arouses
  frenzied antisemitism, 479, 480–2; fall of
  Popular Front government, 482–3;
  Daladier government harasses Jewish
  refugees, 483–4; clergy disseminates
  Protocols in, 485; occupies German Ruhr,
  500; Grynszpan assassinates German
  diplomat in, 512; Reich Jews flee to, 514;
  Évian Conference on refugees in, 516;
  Syrian revolt against, 521; Nazi Germany
  overruns, 527; operation of Final Solution
  in, 539–41; collaborative pro-Nazi role of,
  later glossed over, 541; role of Jewish
  resistance in, 553; Jewish refugees from, flee
  to Spain, 560–1; Pius XII praises Pétain,
  563–4; heroic wartime role of priests, nuns
  in, 564–5; British, Palestinians, capture
  Lebanon from, 572; in postwar, helps
  Jewish refugee traffic to Palestine, 582–3; in
  UN, votes for Palestine partition, 590;
  provides weapons for Palestine Jewry, 593;
  Jews of North Africa under rule of, 623–4,
  under Vichy rule of, 624–5; negotiates
  independence of Morocco, Tunisia, 624–5;
  is *patrie* for *colons,* Jews, in Algeria, 625–6;
  Algerian Jews in World War II, 626–7;
  Algerian *colons,* Jews depart for, 627; in
  postwar, cancels anti-Jewish laws, opens
  doors to DPs, 642; Claims Conference
  helps revive Jewish life in, 642; Jews regain,
  surpass, former prominence in life of,
  652–3; in military alliance with Israel
  against Nasser's Egypt, 643; impact of
  North African Jews on Jewish communal
  life, 644–6; Mitterand, Chirac, genuflect to
  Jews in, 646–7; birth of Israel, ignites
  Zionism among Jews of, 703; Arab terror
  attacks on Jews in, 739; impact of Israel on
  Jewish communal policies in, Jewish

vitality in, 741; upsurge of antisemitic violence in, evaluated, 742

France juive, La, 231

Franco, Francisco, 560

Frank, Anne, 537

Frank, Hans, 528, 531

Frank, Jacob, 13

Frank, Leonhard, 458

Frankel, Albert, 452

Frankel, Zacharias, 135, 136, 392

Frankfurter, Felix, 396–7

Franklin, Lumby, 655

Franz Ferdinand, of Habsburg Empire, 458

Franz Josef I, of Habsburg Empire, 90, 91, 229, 290

Frederick II, of Prussia, 21–2, 26, 48

Freud, Sigmund: supports Austrian war effort, 314; discerns "Jewish" reasons for his achievements, 451; career of, 452–3; Jewish factors in career of, 453–4; as identified "ethnic" Jew, 460–1; sees Jewish minority status a source of toughness, 744

Friedländer, David, 128–9

Friedmann, Georges, 642

Friedrich, Istvan, 437

Friedrich Wilhelm II, of Prussia, 48

Friedrich Wilhelm III, of Prussia, 48, 49, 50, 76, 111

Friedrich Wilhelm IV, of Prussia, 81, 90, 94

Fuchs, Klaus, 688

Funk, Casimir, 452

Furtado, Abraham, 36, 41

Galicia, *see* Habsburg Empire; Poland

Galton, Francis, 249, 381, 501

Gans, Eduard, 124, 132

Gellert, Christian, 29

Geiger, Abraham: endorses Crown School project in Russia, 67; a scholar of Jewish historicism, pioneer of Reform Judaism, 133–4; as German patriot, 137; influences American Reform Judaism, 172

Gellert, Christian, 29

Gentz, Friedrich von, 108–9

George, Stefan, 465

Georges-Picot, Charles François, 347, 352, 353, 354

German-Jewish Women's League, 220, 463

Germany: ghettoized circumstances of eighteenth-century Jewish life in, 3–4, 5, 6–8; ongoing Jewish settlement in, 5, 7, 8; Jewish autonomy in, 8, 9; Jews of, flee to Poland, 10; shares in partitions of Poland, 15; growth of mercantilism in, 18, improved Jewish conditions in, 21–2, 25; role of *Hofjuden* in, 22–5; evolving Enlightenment attitudes toward Jews in, 26–27, 29; role of Moses Mendelssohn in, 29–32, 33; Jews of, resonate to Sanhedrin, 43; Napoleon liberates Jews in, 46–7; Prussia confronts issue of emancipating Jews in, 48–50; clouded legacy of Jewish emancipation in, 50, 51; at Congress of Vienna, Prussia cedes part of annexed Polish territory to Russia, 60, 61; for Russian Crown school program, Lilienthal secures cooperation of eminent Jews in, 67–9; fate of, in Congress of Vienna, 73; rescission of Jewish emancipation in, 75–7; reactionary romanticism in, 76–7; incremental Jewish emancipation in, 79; Jewish political activism in, 79–81; revolution of 1848 in, 86–7; gradual triumph of liberalism, Jewish emancipation in, 88, 94–5; growth of nineteenth-century Jewish population in, 101; growth of private Jewish merchant banking in, 101–2; growth of House of Rothschild in, 102–3; in Napoleonic wars, funded by Rothschild transfers, 103; role of Rothschilds in state economy, foreign policy of, 106; role of Bleichröder in economy, foreign policy of, 109–10; Hardenberg of, seeks to ease Jewish disabilities, 111; Bismarck of, secures treaty guarantees for Rumanian Jewry, 112–13; ongoing role of Jewish bankers, industrialists in private economy of, 113–14, 116, 117; career of Lassalle in, 118; early career of Marx in, 118–19; eighteenth-century Jews seek acculturation, acceptance in, 120–3; efforts to "Occidentalize" Judaism in, 128–9; rise of modern Jewish scholarship in, 130–3; emergence of "historical" Judaism in, 133–7; Jews from, arrive in colonial America, 161, in post-colonial United States, 162–3; Jews from, maintain Germanic culture in United States, 165; American Jews influenced by Reform Judaism in, 172–3; influence of modernism in, on *Haskalah* in Russia, 177, 178, 179; 205; Jews of, organize Hilfsverein, 209; Russian-Jewish refugees remain in, 214; Schwartzkoppen's espionage on behalf

Germany *(continued)*
of, 233–4; Bismarck creates Wilhelminian
Empire, 242; growth of antisemitism in,
242–7; evolution of Aryan, Pan-German,
racist ideology in, 247–54; Moses Hess's
early career in, 257; Russian-Jewish
university students in, Herzl's earliest
followers, 260, 267; Herzl's conducts
"diplomatic" Zionism through, 267–70;
279; Marx, Engels in, 310; Bernstein's
"revisionist" socialism in, 311; Jews
prominent in Social Democratic Party of,
312–13; Social Democrats in, support war
effort of, 314; in World War I, Jews in,
support war effort, stigmatized, 314–16;
military campaign of, in Russia, 316–17;
"protects" Jews in, 317; Russian army
stigmatizes Jews as spies for, 317; occupies
Ukraine, establishes puppet government
in, 319, 320; Petliura interned in, 320; allows
Lenin train passage through, to Russia,
325, 337; signs Nazi-Soviet Pact in 1939, 343;
Ruppin intercedes with, for Jews in
wartime Palestine, 345; government of,
rejects Zionist overtures for alliance, 349;
includes Jewish "advisers" in its wartime
mission in U.S., 354; Aaronsohn departs
Palestine for, 356; government of, matches
Balfour Declaration offer, 361; most Jews
in, indifferent to Balfour Declaration, 361;
American Jews' changing wartime attitude
to, 361, 378, 381; in 1930s, draws Yugoslavia
into orbit, 406–7; Pilsudski interned in, 411;
loses territory to postwar Poland, 411–12;
nationals of, in postwar Poland, suffer
discrimination, 412–13; nationals of,
face discrimination in Poland, 413; in
World War I, Rumania bargains between,
and Allies, 422; in World War I, Rumania
is duplicitous ally of, 422; nationals of, face
discrimination in post–World War I
Rumania, 424; Rumania drawn into orbit
of, 430–1; forces Rumania to cede back
territory to Hungary, to Russia, 431;
Szalasi, Imredy, seek ingratiation with,
441–2; Jews in cultural life of, 448–55ff.;
efflorescence of Jewish religious thought,
communal life in Weimar Republic, 462–8;
in World War I, British Jews suspected of
loyalty to, 469–70; *Protocols* published in,
471; Jewish refugees from, reach France,
483; French rightists tout, as ideological
model, 482; accuse Jews as seeking war

with, 483; Daladier seeks alternative havens
for Jews from, 484; papacy reproves, for
violating concordat, 485; Dollfuss opposes
Anschluss with, 490, Schuschnigg
genuflects to, 491; Rosa Luxemburg's early
career in, 492; "Spartacist" uprising
crushed in, 493–4; post–World War I
Bavarian radicalism in, 494–6; impact of
Treaty of Versailles on, 496; Jewish leftist-
liberal role in early Weimar politics, 497;
Jewish demographic, economic
circumstances in, during Weimar years,
498; Rathenau's career in, 498–500; Hitler's
wartime, postwar years in, 501–3; Jewish
vulnerability in, 505–6; Hitler achieves
chancellorship, 506–7; Nazi antisemitic
program in, 507–12ff.; Kristallnacht in,
512–13; Jewish refugee emigration from,
before World War II, 514–15; High
Commission for Refugees, Évian
Conference, Roosevelt, seek to address
problem of refugees from, 515–18;
negotiates Ha'avarah agreement with
Jewish Agency, 519–20; encourages Arab
uprising in Palestine, 521–22, 524; overruns
European continent, invades USSR, 527;
slaughters millions of Europeans, 527;
creates administrative structure for Final
Solution, 528–9; embarks on mass Jewish
destruction in USSR, 529–31; systematizes
Jewish extermination in Poland, 531–4;
organizes destruction of Jews in Altreich,
534–5, in Balkans, 534–7, in Lowlands and
Scandinavia, 537–8; operates Polish death
camps, 538–9; seeks to impose Final
Solution in France, 539–41, in Italy, 541–4,
in Bulgaria, 544–6, in Rumania, 546–8, in
Hungary, 548–50; Warsaw ghetto uprising
against, 551–2; other Jewish uprisings
against, 553; Palestinian Jewish parachutists
seek to warn European Jews, 553–4;
Jews in extended ransom negotiations
with, in Italy, 554, in Slovakia, 554–5, in
Hungary, 555–8; Turkey intimidated by,
558–9; sends Jews fleeing from France to
Spain, 560; Switzerland denies sanctuary
to refugees from, 561; knowledge of
Holocaust in, 562; Weiszäcker of, warns
Pius XII, 565; Holocaust plans of, revealed
to Riegner, Allies, 566–7; Roosevelt
authorizes War Refugee Board for rescue
attempts from, 568; final tabulation of
Jewish victims of, 569–560; Holocaust role

of government, people of, evaluated, 570–1; Palestine Jewry mobilizes against, 572; leaves postwar chaos of refugees in Europe, 573; DP camps in, 573–5; Anglo-American Committee visits DP camps in, 579; Zionist training program for DPs in, 579–80; more Jews inundate DP camps of, 581; Palestinian emissaries organize refugee traffic from, to Palestine, 582, 586–7; Operation Barbarossa takes heaviest toll of Jews in Soviet "annexed" territories, 595; Polish-Jewish repatriates occupy lodgings, jobs, once held by, 599; Nagy prepares to renew Hungary's contacts with, 610; in 1941, Iraqi rebels seek help of, 620; Tunisian Jewry threatened by Afrika Korps of, 625; in postwar "atonement" negotiations with Israel, world Jewish organizations, 629–30; revival of Jewish life in, 631; Jews in, develop communal institutions, sense of security, 631; provides half of Austrian restitution money for victims of Nazism, 632; negotiates lump-sum reparations payments to Netherlands, 638, to France, 642; Jews from, early settlers in Latin America, 668ff.; refugees from, settle in Latin America, 668–9ff.; Nazi war criminals from, in Argentina, 676; American Jews belatedly replicate intellectual achievements of kinsmen in, 699; restiveness among nationals of, in USSR, 724, 730; large Moslem population in, 743
Gero, Erno, 600
Gheorghiu-Dej, Gheorghe, 601; seeks greater Rumanian autonomy from USSR, 612; uses Jews to achieve improved trade relations with U.S., 612–13, 614
Ginzberg, Aleksandr, 722
Ginzberg, Asher, 272–3, 274
Ginzberg, Yevgenyi, 722
Giscard d'Estaing, Valéry, 646
Gladstone, William E., 98
Glagau, Otto, 245–6
Glatzer, Norbert (Nahum), 468
Globe (journal), 470
Globocnik, Odilo, 533
Glückel of Hameln, 22, 25
Glueckstein brothers, 649, 650
Gobineau, Arthur de, 247
Godard, Jacques, 37
Gödschke, Hermann, 472

Goebbels, Josef, 570
Göring, Hermann: as early Nazi, 503; manipulates 1933 German election, 507; Hitler's chief policy-maker on Jewish issues, 511–13ff.; instructs Heydrich to prepare Final Solution to Jewish problem, 528
Goethe, Johann Wolfgang von, 120
Goga, Octavian, 426, 429, 430
Gold, Harry, 687, 688
Gold, Michael, 395
Goldberger (family), 116
Goldenson, Leonard, 691
Goldfadden, Abraham, 69
Goldman, Emma, 383
Goldmann, Nahum, 706, 719
Goldschmid (banking house), 102
Goldstein, Moritz, 446
Goldwasser, Michael, 164–5
Gombos, Gyula, 438, 440–1
Gompers, Samuel, 372
Gomulka, Wladyslaw, 607–8
Goodhart, Arthur, 650
Gorbachev, Mikhail, 733, 734
Gorchakov, Alexander, 113
Gordon, Aaron David, 280–1
Gordon, Judah Leib, 188–9, 190, 191, 203
Gorky, Maxim, 289
Gottlober, Abraham Baer, 182
Gottschalk, Andreas, 81
Gottwald, Klement, 606
Goudchaux, Michel, 87
Grabski, Wladyslaw, 415
Grade, Lew, 649
Graetz, Heinrich, 132–3
Graf, Max, 461, 744
Graiver, David, 679
Grand Union Hotel Affair, 170–1
Grant, Ulysses S., 167
Graves, Philip, 472
Great Britain: eighteenth-century population in, 5; religious emotionalism in, 11; Jews achieve right of resettlement in, 20; attitude toward Jews of Enlightenment figures, 28; 60–65, 78; contests imprisonment of Damascus Jews, in diplomatic power struggle with France, 84–5ff.; seeks release of Edgardo Mortara, supports Montefiore mission, 93; growing Jewish population, security and freedom in, 95; growing political liberalization of, Jewish struggle for membership in House

Great Britain *(continued)*
of Commons of, 95–7; supports
Montefiore's efforts on behalf of Jews, 98;
sees liberalism as source of national
greatness, 98–9; early Jewish bankers in,
101; role of Rothschilds in, 102–8ff.;
elevates Jewish financiers to baronetcy,
peerage, 110–11; at Congress of Berlin,
supports cause of Rumanian Jews, 112;
nineteenth-century Judaism remains
traditional in, 120; Disraeli's political,
literary career in, 125–27; Jewish religious
developments in, 127; Sephardic fugitives
settle in West Indies of, 160, in American
mainland colonies, 160; grants
naturalization, equality of status to Jews in
American colonies, 160–1; Jews' role in
American Revolution against, 161; seeks
disentanglement on commitments to
Rumanian Jews, 205; Mansion House
Fund for Russian-Jewish refugees, 209;
thousands of refugees remain in, 216–17;
Galton, Pearson, develop theory of
eugenics in, 249–50; consuls of, give
"capitulatory" protection to Jews in
Palestine, 261; Herzl visits Jewish
businessmen in, 267; Herzl addresses East
European immigrants in, 267, testifies
before parliamentary commission in, 271;
colonial secretary of, explores alternate
settlement sites for Herzl, 273–4; Herzl
establishes vital connection with, 275, 276;
government of, expresses concern over
Mendel Beilis case, 308; Marx's career in,
310; Eduard Bernstein's career in, 311; in
World War I, naval blockade of, imposes
hardships on Palestine inhabitants, 345; in
Gallipoli campaign, organizes Zion Mule
Corps, 346; bases Middle East strategy
around Suez Canal, 347; negotiates with
Hashemite Arabs, sponsors Arab revolt,
347; negotiates Sykes-Picot Agreement on
spheres of influence in Middle East, 347–8;
seeking to "amend" Sykes-Picot
Agreement to its favor, turns to Zionists as
"moralistic" pretext, 348–53ff.; presses
Weizmann to mobilize world Jewry on
behalf of Allied war effort, 354–55;
Aaronson develops spy network on behalf
of, 355–7; Zionists collaborate with, in
formulating Balfour Declaration, 357–8;
authorizes formation of Jewish Legion,
362; forces of, liberate Palestine, 363; Peace
Conference awards Palestine mandate to,
363–4; orchestrates initial Arab-Jewish
cooperation, 364; sets about rejuvenating
public services of Palestine, 364; Churchill
White Paper of redefines Jewish National
Home, 365; revives Palestine economy,
administration, 366; Palestine Jewry gains
depth, to confront later diplomatic
equivocation of, 369; loses interest in
Minority Treaties, 414; in 1930s, uses Ernst
Cassel as peace mediator in 1914, 458;
becomes "Jew-conscious" with pre-1914
influx of immigrants, 469; Jews of, in
World War I, 470; public figures, press,
equate Bolshevik Revolution with Jews,
470–1; impact of *Protocols of Elders of Zion*
in, 471–3; Mosley's incipient fascist
movement in, 473–4; tightens immigration
restrictions against Jews, 474; government
of, warns Blum against intervention in
Spanish Civil War, 483; with France,
sacrifices Czechoslovakia, 483; Jewish
Board of Deputies offers to succor
refugees in, 514; at Évian Conference, bars
discussion of Palestine as Jewish haven,
516; issues Palestine certificates in
Germany through Palästina-Amt, 519;
installs Feisal as ruler of Iraq, 521; appoints
Husseini as Grand Mufti of Palestine,
521–3; MacDonald government vacillates
on Jewish National Home, 522; Germany,
Italy, stir up Arabs against, in Palestine,
522; vainly seeks a diplomatic solution to
Arab restiveness in Palestine, 522–5ff.;
issues 1939 White Paper on Palestine, 525;
Zionists pledge loyalty to, 525–6; army of,
driven from Europe, 527; reacts to German
ransom proposals, 557, to confirmation of
Holocaust, 565; countenances Palestinian-
Jewish rescue effort, 553–4; interns wartime
Jewish refugees, 565; intercepts refugee
ships, 565–6; Churchill joins Roosevelt in
warning collaborationist regimes, 567; in
Bermuda Conference in refugees, 567;
Palestinian Jews in wartime partnership
with, 572; Labour government of, confronts
refugee intransigence, Jewish militance in
Palestine, 573ff.; seeks U.S. cooperation in
resolving refugee issue, 576–81ff; Zionist
counteroffensive against, 581–3; Truman's
adamance against, on refugee issue, 583–4;
refers Palestine question to UN, 585–7;
shamed by *Exodus* episode, 586–7;

UNSCOP majority recommends terminating mandate of, 587; Soviets seek to undermine Middle Eastern influence of, 588; refuses cooperation in implementing Palestine partition, 590–1; abandons Palestine mandate, 594; Iraqi Jews flourish under mandate of, 619; forces of, threatened by pro-Nazi cabal in Iraq, 620; Nasser fans Egyptian resentment against, 621, 622; nationals of, evicted from Egypt, 622; Jews in, achieve wider embourgoisement, political respectability, religio-communal transformation, 648–54; ships from, offer Jewish emigrants cheap passage to North America, 655; Jews in Canada, intent on maintaining ties with Commonwealth of, 659; Jews among convicts from, transported to Australia, 660; Monash honored by government of, 661; social snobbery less common in Australia than in, 662; establish presence in South Africa, leaves internal autonomy to Afrikaners, 663; South African Jews covet connection with, 664; thousands of Jews from, fight for, settle in Israel, 703; Jewish communal structure increasingly oriented toward Israel, 741; Jewish school system in, energized by Israel, 741

Greece: Jews in, during Ottoman Empire, 140; lapsing Jewish fortunes in, 145–6; Sykes envisages, as a British client people, 352; signs Minorities Treaty, 401; in "Revolt of Small Powers," 406; seizes Macedonia in 1912, begins circumscribing Jews in, 407; Venizelist "Hellenization," antisemitism in, 407–8; Smryniot kinsmen of, driven from Turkey into, 409; Salonikan Jews, immigrate extensively to Europe, North and South America, 409; Nazi Final Solution in, 536–7; Jews in, protected in Italian zones of, 536; Soviet postwar pressure on, 576; Britain abdicates protection of, 585; after World War II, government of, neglects, discriminates against Jews, 640; precarious Jewish revival in, 640; *see also* Salonika; Turkey, Turkish Empire

Great Soviet Encylopedia, 604
Greenglass, David, 687, 688
Grégoire, Henri, 27, 28, 29, 35, 36, 38
Gregory XVI, Pope, 75
Grey, Sir Edward, 276
Gringoire (journal), 481
Gromyko, Andrei, 588

Gruenbaum, Yitzhak, 415, 421
Grünwald, Max, 588
Gruzenberg, Oscar, 307
Grynszpan, Herschel, 512
Guardian (journal), 350, 737
Guérin, Jules, 238
Guggenheim, Meyer, 169
Guide to the Perplexed of Our Time, A, 180
Günzberg, Horace de, 185, 199, 207
Günzberg, Joseph, 185

Haas, Wolff, 165
Haase, Hugo, 313, 496, 498
Haase, Otto, 496
Ha'avarah, 419–20
Habad, *see* Hasidism, Hasidim
Haber (banking house), 116
Haber, Fritz: mobilizes German science for war, 315; brings Einstein to Berlin, 449, stands behind Einstein, 450
Habima (theater), 335
Habsburg Empire: erratic settlement of Jews in, 4–5; Jewish self-government in, 8; shares in partition of Poland 15–16; Empress Maria Theresa of, dissuaded from evicting Jews, 18; Jews early "provisioners," financiers for courts of, 21, 22; Joseph II of, enlarges Jewish privileges, 25–6; Jews studying in early universities of, 29; resisting Napoleonic rule, maintains restrictions against Jews, 47–8; at Congress of Vienna, loses some of partitioned Poland to Russia, 60; assisted by Russia's Nicholas I in suppressing Polish uprising, 64; maintains Jewish restrictions intact throughout empire, 77; relaxes Jewish restrictions in Vienna, 78–9; intercedes on behalf of imprisoned Damascus Jews, 84; Jews share in 1848 popular revolution in Austria, 86–7; suppresses revolution in, executes Jewish revolutionaries, 90; eases restrictions on Jews, 91; protests abduction of Edgardo Mortara, 93; rule of, terminated in Italy, 93; following *Ausgleich*, completes imperial emancipation of Jews, 94; growing Jewish population in Prague, Vienna, 100–1; dependent on Jewish bankers for state loans, 101, 103; ennobles Rothschilds, 103; Metternich's foreign policy, supported by Rothschilds, 105; supports Jewish emancipation in Rumania,

Habsburg Empire (continued)
112; Rothschilds, Hirsch, finance railroad construction in, 114, 115; Jews as pioneers of industry, commerce in, 116, 117; Russian elite exposed to science, culture of, 177; maskilim in Galicia urge Russian Jewry to modernize, 178–9, 180; seeks disentanglement from commitments on Rumanian Jews, 205; Galician Jews massively emigrate from, 208; Brody in, first way station for Russian-Jewish departure, 208–9; organizes Israelitische Allianz, 209; thousands of East European Jews remain in, 214, 215; religioethnic xenophobia in, ritual murder indictments in, 222; Tisza-Eszlar, Hilsner blood-libel cases resonate in, 224, 225–6; clerical antisemitism in, 226–8; burgeoning Jewish population, upward mobility in, 227–8; Lueger politically exploits antisemitism in, 228–9; Schönerer develops Pan-German movement in, 251–2; Herzl's education, journalistic career in, 264; political structure of, tolerates Herzl's pluralistic nationalism, 266; Zionist Executive established in, 269; Jews of, in Social Democratic Party, 313; Freud, Zweig support war effort of, 314; in World War I, Galician Jews flee to western Habsburg cities, 316; most Jews of, uninfluenced by Balfour Declaration, 361; Minorities Treaty to protect former subjects of, 400, 401; growth of Bohemian-Jewish population, upward mobility, under late Habsburg Empire, 402–3; Jews of Bohemian, Slovak provinces of, seek treaty guarantees for postwar, 402–3; Jewish population in Bohemian "Crown Lands," 403; Jews become intellectual elite in, 403–4; Peace Conference cedes Galicia of, to postwar Poland, 412; Jews had thrived in post-Ausgleich liberalism of, 432–3; Galician Jews migrate to Hungary, 433; Bettauer's novel portrays antisemitism in, 445–5; Jewish cultural dualism in modern life of, 455–8ff.; "pragmatic" Jewishness in, 460–2; antisemitic clergy, Catholic organizations in, 485; Emperor Karl abdicates throne of, 486; see also Austria; Hungary
Hadassah, 368
Haider, Joerg, 633–4
Haile Selasse I, of Ethiopia, 710
Halévy, Jacques Fromenthal, 475

Halévy, Joseph, 710
Hall, George, 575
Hall, Prescott F., 380
Halutz (movement), 367
Hammerstein, Oscar, 170, 388
Hannson, Per Albin, 538
Hardenberg, Karl August von, 49–50, 75–6, 111
Harrison, Benjamin, 381
Harrison, Earl, 574, 577
Hartmann, Moritz, 124
Hasidism, Hasidim: 13–14, 16, 59, 68–9, 697–8
Hassan II, of Morocco, 624
HaTz'firah, see Tz'firah
Hauptmann, Gerhart, 308
Hebrew Immigrant Aid Society, see HIAS
Hebrew Union College, 273–4, 391
Hegel, Georg W. F., 500
Heine, Heinrich: influential liberal journalist, 79–80; as poet, works through conflicted approach to his Jewish roots, 124–5; 137; Wagner an early friend of, 248
Helena Rubinstein, 387, 690
Helfman, Hessia, 197–8
Henry, Hubert, 233, 239
Herder, Johann Gottfried von, 27, 29, 130, 242
Hereditary Genius, 249
"Heroism and Christendom," 248
Herries, John, 103
Herz, Cornelius, 232
Herz, Henriette (de Lemos), 121–2
Herzen, Alexander, 63, 195
Herzl, Theodor: witnesses degradation of Dreyfus, 241; expatriate Russian-Jewish students as followers of, 260; in meeting with Hirsch, 263; biography of, 264; increasingly preoccupied with antisemitism, 264–5; produces, evokes ambivalent reactions to Der Judenstaat, 265–7; in early diplomacy with German, Turkish leaders, 267–8; organizes Zionist Congress, Zionist Organization, 268–9; resumes diplomacy with German government, 269–70, with Turkish government, 270–1; testifies before British parliamentary commission, 271; meets with Chamberlain, 271; in al-Arish negotiations, 271–2; writes Altneuland, 272–3; evokes skepticism of Asher Ginzberg (Ahad Ha'Am), 272–3; shaken by circumstances of Russian Jewry, 273; East Africa proposal of, creates bitter schism, 273–5; dies, 275; career of, in perspective, 275–6; 295; in World War I, France recalls

Germanophile sympathies of, 349, British public figures recall his negotiations with Chamberlain, 350; envisaged a Jewish state as source of normalcy, 738, a source of Diaspora security, 743

Hess, Moses: as political journalist, 79, 81; as proto-Zionist, 257–8

Heydrich, Reinhardt: directs Reich Main Security Office, 513; ordered to prepare for Final Solution, 528; at Grossen Wannsee conference, 529; allocates General Government as dumping ground for Polish Jewry, 531–2; presses for Final Solution in Slovakia, 554

HIAS (Hebrew Immigrant Aid Society), 731, 732

High Commission for Refugees from Germany, 515–16

Hilberg, Raoul, 551

Hilfsverein der deutschen Juden, 209, 283

Hillel Foundation, 700

Hillmar, Josef, 132

Hillquit, Morris, 371, 372, 379

Hilsner, Leopold, 225

Himmler, Heinrich, 528–9, 539, 552, 555, 557, 562

Hindenberg, Paul, 505

Hirsch, David, 23

Hirsch, Jakob de, 114

Hirsch, Moritz de: as railroad tycoon, 114–16, Trans-Balkan Railway of, revives prosperity of Salonika, 146; philanthropism of, helps fund Jewish resettlement projects in United States, 214; rejects Herzl's Zionist vision, 263, 276; launches project to resettle Russian Jews in Argentinian, Brazilian colonies, 473, 673, 680

Hirschorn, Fred, 387

Hirschmann, Ira, 569

History of Jewish Homilectics, The, 131

History of the Jews, A, 133

Hitler, Adolf: grasps potential of linking antisemitism, Pan-Germanism, 254; Stalin authorizes non-aggression pact with, 343; Yugoslavia genuflects to, 406; Rumanian fascists admire, 428, 431, 441; Rumania's King Carol genuflects to, 431; forces territorial concessions from Rumania, 431; a model for French fascists, 472; Dollfuss resists, 490, Schuschnigg reaches "understanding" with, 491; roots of antisemitism of, 501–3; refashions early Nazi Party, formulates antisemitic program, 503; politically adroit, 503–5, is brought "temporarily" to chancellorship, 506; launches antisemitic program, 507–8; introduces Nuremberg racial laws, 508–9; Jewish reaction to program of, 509–10; intensifies pressure on Jews, for emigration, 510–13ff.; launches Operation Barbarossa, 527; invasion of USSR dictates new approach to Jewish Question, 538; approves liquidation of "Jewish Bolsheviks" in USSR, 540; in deference to, Mussolini adopts policy of antisemitism, 542; warns King Boris, Regent Horthy, against protecting Jews, 546, 549; after Stalingrad, informs Goebbels that all Jews to be exterminated, 570; fixated with Jews until last day of life, 570–1; Argentina's military regime admires, 675

Hlond, August, Cardinal, 419

Hoffmann, Max, 319

Hofmannsthal, Hugo von, 458

Hofshtein, David, 342

Holdheim, Samuel, 135

Holy Roman Empire, *see* Austria; Germany; Habsburg Empire

Honest Faith, An, 256

Hoover Directive, 518

Hope-Simpson Commission, Report, 522

Horowitz, Louis, 387

Horthy, Miklos: Allies approve, as regent of Hungary, 437; after Treaty of Trianon, ends White Terror, 438; appoints Gombos prime minister, 440; appoints Daranyi prime minister, 441; appoints Imredy prime minister, 442; signs second "Jewish Bill," 443; role of, during Holocaust, 548–50, 555

Hourani, Albert, 590

Howard, Michael, 652

Howe, Irving, 700

Hoz, Dov, 345

Hrushevski, Mikhail, 319

Hull, Cordell, 557

Humanité (journal), 480

Humboldt, Wilhelm von, 49, 75–6, 121–2

Hungary: early Jewish settlement in, 5–8; impact of Hasidism on Jews of, 14; Joseph II extends *Toleranzpatent* to Jews of, 26; growth of Jewish population, economic strength in, 78–79; Kossuth wins support of Jews in 1848 uprising, 88; revolution's failure in, 89, 90–1; wins full

Hungary *(continued)*
autonomy after *Ausgleich,* Jewish
emancipation completed in, 94; Jewish
energies in, released, 101, 116; Tisza-Eszlar
case in, 222–5; growth of Jewish
population, upward mobility in, 227–8;
Herzl born in, 264; signs Minorities Treaty,
401; Treaty of Trianon imposes major
losses of territory, population on, 422, 423;
Hitler forces Rumania to cede territory to,
431–2; Karolyi offers Kun government
leadership, 432; recent history of Jews in,
432–3; in postwar, Jews largest minority in,
433; Jews eminent in Social Democratic
Party of, 434; Kun's background in, 434–5;
Kun forms Communist regime in, 435–6,
overthrown, 436–7; Horthy "regency"
established in, 437; "White Terror" in,
437–8; diplomatic struggle over Jewish
numerus clausus in universities of, 439;
Jews remain prominent in economy,
professions of, 440; political antisemitism
intensifies, under Gombos, Szalasi, 441–2;
"Jewish Bills" in, 442–3; collaborates with
Germany in invasion of USSR, Yugoslavia,
546; Germany's Vienna Award to, enlarge
Jewish population in, 546–8; Horthy seeks
to confine Jewish "deportations" to Vienna
Award territories, 548; Hitler sends army
into, 549; Jews of, suffer worst genocide in
all "collaborationist" Europe, 550; RAF
drops Palestinian parachutists into, 553–4;
Eichmann presents ransom demand for
Jews of, 555–8; postwar Communist
leadership of, includes many Jews,
599–600; limited postwar Jewish
communal revival in, immigration from, to
Palestine-Israel, West, 600–1; anti-
deviationist campaign in, suppresses Jewish
communal life in, forecloses Jewish
emigration from, 609; revolution brings in
Imre Nagy as prime minister, 609; death of
Stalin undermines Communist leadership
in, 609–10; seeking contacts with West,
Nagy provokes Soviet invasion in, 610;
many Jews flee 1956 Soviet retaliation in,
610, others unexpectedly win renewed
freedom, toleration, prominence in, 610–11;
see also Habsburg Empire
Hussein, al-Hashimi, Sherif, 347, 364
Husseini, Abd al-Qadir al-, 591
Husseini, Muhammad Amin al-, 521–2, 523,
579

Husserl, Edmund, 446
Hutchison, Joseph, 579

I and Thou, 466
Ignatiev, Nicholas, 200, 207
Il Popolo d'Italia (journal), 542
Immigration Restriction League, 382
Industrial Removal Office, 214
Inonu, Ismet, 558
In Search of Zion, 257
Intergovernmental Committee on Refugees,
516
International Jew, The, 383, 472
International Ladies' Garment Workers'
Union, 373, 379
"In the City of Slaughter," 290
In the Name of the Father and the Son, 722
Iorga, Nicolae, 425, 426, 428
Iran: Bevin cites danger of antagonizing, on
Palestine, 576; historically, Jews persecuted
in, 615–16; Jewish circumstances improve
with Pahlavi dynasty, 616; in productive
relationship with Israel, 616; poorer Jews
from, immigrate to Israel, 617; rising
Islamic militance, new Islamic Republic,
places Jews in jeopardy, 617; Jews of,
gradually flee, 617–18; Soviets fear
nationalist infection from, 720
Iraq: Jews in, 153; World War I Allied
diplomacy on, 348; Peace Conference
allocates to Britain, 521; Feisal
subsequently appointed king of, 521;
guerrillas from, in Palestine civil war, 523;
Bevin fears antagonizing, on Palestine, 576;
Britain provides weapons to, after
evacuating Palestine, 591; under "Young
Turk" government, Jews of, had become
equal Ottoman citizens, 619; under British
mandate, Jews flourished, 620; Arab-Israeli
War jeopardize Jews in, 620; Jewish
Agency reaches emigration agreement
with government of, 620; Jewish departure
from, 620–1; Pollard provides Israel with
classified U.S. data on, 708
Isaacs, Isaac, 661
Israel: inherits vulnerable Peace Conference
borders, 363–4; inherits Ottoman, British
mandatory legal systems, 366, 421; Ben-
Gurion proclaims independence of, 594;
USSR supports establishment of, 596;
Soviet Jews moved by birth of, 596;

Bulgarian Jews allowed to depart for, 597; Czechoslovakia provides weapons for, 598; postwar Jewish immigration to, 598; initial Polish-Jewish immigration to, leaves 80,000 Jews at "home," 599; 30,000 postwar Hungarian Jews to, 601; by 1951, over 160,000 postwar Rumanian Jews immigrate to, 602; Stalinist anti-deviationist campaign pillories Soviet Jews as agents of, 603–5; Czechoslovak anti-Zionist campaign against Jews as agents of, 606; Gomulka in Poland "encourages" Jewish immigration to, 607–8; Hungarian-Jewish exodus after 1956 revolution, largely bypasses, 610; Rumania agrees to major increase of Jewish immigration to, 613; maintains diplomatic ties with, 613; Rumanian-Jewish immigration to, exceeds 250,000, 613–14; Ceauşescu of, plays "honest broker" between Arabs and, 614; Turkish Jews immigrate to, 614–15; Iran establishes relations with, 616; 40,000 Iranian Jews immigrate to, 617; Iranian Islamic Republic executes Jews as "spies" for, 617; Operation Magic Carpet transports Yemenite Jews to, 619; two-phase Iraqi-Jewish immigration for, 620–1; between 1948–49, several thousand Egyptian Jews initially depart for, 621; rise of Nasser, Sinai-Suez War with, increases Egyptian-Jewish immigration to, 622; most Lebanese Jews eventually immigrate to, 622–3; Syria blocks Jewish immigration to, then relaxes ban, 623; from Morocco, Tunisia, large-scale Jewish immigration to, 624–6; immigrating Algerian Jews bypass, for France, 627–8; within eight years, Diaspora Jewish immigration triples population of, 628; negotiates Treaty of Luxembourg with Germany, 629–30; some Jews return from, to Germany, 630–1; presses Kreisky to keep open Jewish Agency transit facility, 633; recalls ambassador from Austria, upon Waldheim's election as president, 633; devotion to, is talisman of Italian-Jewish identity, 635; improving record of Vatican to, 635–8; Dutch early supporter of, 638; Belgian Jewry shares in renaissance of, 639; Spain provides facilities for Moroccan immigrants to, 641; Jews from, settle in Spain, 641; Spain establishes diplomatic relations with, 642; in 1950s, France shares strategic interests with, 643; North African Jews strengthen French Jewry's commitment to, 646; Mitterand, Chirac visit, 646; Jews from South Africa settle in, 667; Uruguay first to recognize, 669–70; substantial exodus of Chilean Jews to, 671, 672; commandos from, abduct Eichmann from Argentina, 677; Perón professes friendship for, 677; regarding as safety net, many Argentine Jews flee to, 678, 679; unifying talisman for Brazilian Jewry, 683; birth of, evokes massive support from American Jewry, other Diaspora communities, 703–4; Ben-Gurion rejects intervention of American Zionists in politics of, 705–6; American Jews re-evaluating attitude toward, 706–7; Six-Day War of, consolidates Diaspora commitment to, 707–8; American Jews concerned by religious, settlements policies of, 708; Pollard episode, evokes American Jewish criticism of, 708–9; in rescue effort for Ethiopian Jewry, 709–12; Soviet leadership fears, as silent partner of U.S., NATO, 715–16; launches campaign to arouse Zionist consciousness of Soviet Jewry, 717–18; Six-Day War inspires growing Soviet immigrationist movement to, 718–27ff.; goes public with campaign for Soviet-Jewish immigration to, 725–7; in partnership with U.S. Congress to secure "trade-for-freedom" agreement with White House, Kremlin, 727–9; diversion of Jewish immigrants from, to U.S., 730–2; amended U.S. immigration policy shifts Soviet-Jewish immigration route back to, 734–5; Soviet Jews largest ethnic infusion in history of, 735; in post-independence years, wins special solicitude of free world, 736; by 1980s, military incursions of, evoke harsh international denunciation, 736–8; Diaspora Jews structure communal life around, 740–1, recent blemished image of, ignites new wave of antisemitic attacks worldwide, 741–2; EU commission report reveals displaced anti-Israel rage of European Moslem populations, 742–3; question raised of Diaspora vulnerability to Israel's perceived misbehavior, 743–4

Israelitische Allianz (Austria), 209

Israelite Colonization Association (ICA), 214, 673, 680

Istoczy, Gysl, 222, 224, 224–5

Italy: first ghettos in, 6; Jews of, in Napoleon's Assembly of Jewish Notables, 41, Sanhedrin, 42; Jews of, liberated by Napoleon, 46; anciens regimes of, restored, Jewish emancipation reversed in, 74–5; Jews of, active in political liberalism, in 1848 revolution, 78, 87–90; Mortara Affair in, 91–3; triumph of Risorgimento, full Jewish emancipation in, 93; Sokolow woos, in Anglo-Zionist diplomacy, 352–3; fascism of, a model for French rightists, 478; clergy of, disseminate *Protocols* in, 484–5; Mussolini introduces anti-Jewish laws in, 486; encourages Arab unrest in Palestine, 520, 522, 524; invades Yugoslavia, Greece, awarded zones of, 535, 536; Jews, find wartime protection in zones of, 536; Mussolini's antisemitic laws in, loosely administered, 541–2; Mussolini overthrown in, 543; Final Solution in, 543–4; Palestinian parachutists dropped into, 553; Jewish Brigade serves in, 572; DP traffic to Palestine from, 593; protects Jews in Tunisia, 625; Libyan Jews settle in, 634; in postwar, evinces goodwill to Jews, 634–5; Jewish demographic revival, cultural vitality in, uncertain, 635; in 1930s, Québéquois Catholic hierarchy admires Fascist regime of, 657; Jewish protest rallies in, against Soviet emigration ban, 726; Jewish communal structure in, 740; Berlusconi proclaims EU's concern at rise in antisemitism, 742; large Moslem population in, 743

Itzig, Daniel, 24

Ivan III, of Russia, 53

Ivan IV, of Russia, 54

Ivanov, Yuri, 722, 727

Izvestia, 343

Jabotinsky, Vladimir: role of, in Zion Mule Corps, 346, in Jewish Legion, 354–5, 362; cooperates with Polish government in fostering Jewish immigration to Palestine, 421; opposes Peel partition plan, 523; followers of, seek to bring wartime refugees to Palestine, 566; Etzel is paramilitary wing of Revisionist Party of, 582

Jackson, Henry (Jackson-Vanik-Mills Amendment), 728, 729–30, 733, 734

Jacobson, Israel, 128

Jacoby, Joel, 79, 81, 124

James, Henry, 380

Japan, 515

Jaurès, Jean, 235, 479–80

Jellinek, Adolf, 391

Jellinek, Hermann, 87, 90

Jessner, Leopold, 449

Jeunesses Patriotes, 480

Jewish Agency: functions as quasi-government for Jewish National Home, 366–7; Gruenbaum joins Executive of, 421; negotiates Ha'avarah with Nazi Germany, 519–20; in struggle to win freedom of immigration, 572, 573–5ff.; in struggle for partition, 585–90ff.; in transition to Israeli statehood, 590–3ff.; negotiates emigration of Jews from Bulgaria, 597, from Rumania, 602, from Yemen, 619, from Iraq, 620; Board of Deputies of British Jewry officially affiliates with, 703; Israeli legislation confirms responsibility of, to transport, settle Jews in Israel, 705; Ben-Gurion forces resignation from, of American Zionist leaders, 706; sponsors Conference on Human Needs in wake of Six-Day War, 708; helps in rescue of Ethiopian Jewry, 712

Jewish Antifascist Committee, 595, 603, 604, 713

Jewish Antiquities (journal), 342

Jewish Brigade, 572, 718

Jewish Chronicle (journal), 469

Jewish Claims Conference, 629, 632, 634, 640, 642, 644, 645

Jewish Legion, 361–3

Jewish National Fund, 279–80

Jewish National Home, *see* Palestine; Zionism

"Jewish Question and the Socialist Jew-State, The," 277

Jewish Theological Seminary, 392–3

Jews' College, 653

Joël, Kurt, 497

Joffe, Adolf, 287, 341

Jogiches, Leo, 312

John XXIII, Pope, 635–6

John Paul II, Pope, 637–8

Johnson, Alfred, 384

Johnson, Lyndon, 719

Joint Distribution Committee (American-Jewish): in Eastern Europe during World War I, 322; in Ukraine during "Battle of the Frontiers," 331–2; resumes work in Poland during 1930s Depression, 416; negotiates agreement with Japan on Shanghai Jews, 515; distributes funds to interned Jews in Italy, 542, in Spain, 561; through War Refugee Board, distributes funds to Jews of Hungary, Rumania, Bulgaria, 568; assumes task of caring for Jewish DPs, 574; in Communist Eastern Europe, operations of, labeled "conspiratorial," shut down, 603, 604, 607; allowed to reopen in period of "thaw," 608, 613; in North Africa, 624, 625; active in, in postwar Western Europe, 629; provides facilities for emigrating Soviet Jews, 731–2; *see also* Agro-Joint

Jonge, Jakob de, 81

Joseph II, of Habsburg Empire, 25–6, 48, 78, 403

Joseph, Keith, 652

"Josephine the Songstress," 456

Jost, Isaac, 134

Jouin, Ernest, 484–5

Joynson-Hicks, William, 474

Juan Carlos I, of Spain, 641

"Judaism in Music," 248

Judaism Without Embellishment, 715, 722

Jude (journal), 465

Judenstaat, Der, 265–7, 268

Jüdisches Lexicon, 468

"Junius" (pamphlet), 492

Kadar, Janos, 610, 611

Kadima, 267

Kafka, Franz: family of, opts for German culture, 403; posthumously most renowned Czech writer, 404, 405; mood of estrangement, isolation, in writings of, 455–6; isolation of, as Jew, 456; becomes deeply Jewish, Zionist, 461; evinces a facet of Jewish intellectuals, 462; published in U.S. by Schocken, 699

Kaganovich, Lazar, 604

Kahn, Otto, 170

Kahn, Zadoc, 215, 230, 263

Kalinin, Mikhail, 332, 333

Kalischer, Zvi Hirsch, 256, 257

Kallay, Miklos, 548–9

Kamenev, Lev, 340, 341, 342

Kant, Immanuel, 30, 33, 242

Kantorowicz, Ernst, 446

Kapital, Das, 310–11

Kaplan, Jacob, 482

Kaplan, Mordecai, 699

Kappler, Herbert, 543, 554, 564

Karl Alexander of Württemberg, 24

Karolyi, Mihaly, 432, 434, 435

Karski, Jan, 567

Kasztner, Reszoe (Rudolf), 556, 557, 558

Kaufman, Irving, 688

Kautzky, Karl, 287

Kazin, Alfred, 699

Kemal, Mustafa: leads struggle to defend, transform Turkey, 409–10; launches étatist economy, 410, adopts harshly Turkophile domestic policy, 410; intimidates Jews into forfeiting Minority Treaty communal rights, 410

Kennedy, John, 636, 731

Kerensky, Alexander, protests Mendel Beilis trial, 308; in Prince Lvov provisional government, drives Lenin into hiding, 324–5; prepares to attend Inter-Allied conference, 326; seeks Trotsky's help in quelling right-wing coup, 329; recalls Russian Jewry as anti-Bolshevik, 334

Kerr, Alfred, 456

Kessel, Joseph, 642

Khazaria, 52–3

Khomeini, Ruhollah, Ayatollah, 617

Khrushchev, Nikita: in confrontation with Gomulka, 607; humiliation in Cuban Missiles crisis exploited by Gheorgiu-Dej, 612; ends Stalinist-style terrorism, 712; authorizes "cultural" relaxation, 713; intent upon restoring USSR's "ethnic balance," 713–14; encourages displacement of Jews in public, academic, professional life, 714–15; endorses "cold pogrom" against Soviet Jewry, 719; unseated as Soviet leader, 720–1

Kichko, Trofim, 715, 722

Kievskaya mysl (journal), 306

King, Mackenzie, 516

Kingsley, Sidney, 395

Kiril, Archbishop, 545

Kirov, Sergei, 341

Kisch, Egon, 404, 488

Kiselev, Pavel, 65, 66

Kishinev (pogrom of), 289–90

Kissinger, Henry, 728

Kitchener, Horatio, 347

Kochubei, Victor, 56, 61

Königswarter (banking house, family), 110

Kohler, Kaufmann, 391

Kolb, Victor, 485
Kornilov, Lavr, 329
Korvette, E. J., 690
Korvin-Klein, Otto, 434, 437
Kosciuszko, Thaddeus, 15
Kossuth, Lajos, 78, 88, 89, 90
Kosygin, Alexei, 719, 721
Kraus, Karl, 458, 459–60
Kreisky, Bruno, 633
Kremer, Arkadi, 292
Kristallnacht, 512–13
Krohmal, Nahman, 178
Kronenberg (financial house), 185
Kronenberg, Leopold, 71
Kronenberg, Samuel, 70
Krushevan, P. A., 289
Kuleshov, Anna, 287
Kun, Bela: invited to assume government
    leadership of postwar Hungary, 431–2;
    early career of, 434–5; as POW in Russia,
    435; as Communist agitator in postwar
    Hungary, arrested, jailed, 435; assumes
    leadership of Hungarian Soviet Republic,
    435–6; operates clumsy dictatorship, 436;
    fails to repel Rumanian aggression, 436;
    overthrown, flees, 437; influences postwar
    radicalism in Germany, 495; at end of
    World War II, veteran comrades of, return
    to power in Hungary, 600
Kuhn, Loeb & Company, 168, 169
Kunfi, Zsigmond, 431, 432, 435
Kuznetsov, Edvard, 726

Lacretelle, Jacques de, 455
Laemmle, Carl, 389
Lafargue, Laura, 313
Lagarde, Paul de, 243–4, 245
La Guardia, Fiorello, 574
La Harpe, Frédéric-César, 55
Landauer, Gustav, 465, 495, 496, 498
Landler, Jeno, 434
landsmanshaftn, 375–5
Landsteiner, Karl, 460, 462
Langer, Frantisek, 405
Lanskoi, Sergei, 184–5
Lasker, Eduard, 245
Lasky, Jesse, 389
Lassalle, Ferdinand, 118, 119
Latvia, 15, 530, 595; see also Russia (tsarist;
    Communist, post-Communist)
Lauder, Esther, 690

Laval, Pierre, 340
Lawrence, T. E., 347
Lawson, John Howard, 395
Lazare, Bernard, 475
League of Nations: endorses British
    mandate, Jewish National Home, for
    Palestine, 365; countenances a Jewish
    Agency for Palestine, 365–66; appointed as
    guarantor of Minorities Treaties, 401;
    proves toothless in Poland, 416, 417, in
    Rumania, 424, in Hungary, 439–40; in
    loose relationship with High Commission
    for Refugees from Germany, 515–16
Lebanon: Palestine Jews participate in
    military campaign against Vichy French
    in, 572; after birth of Israel, equable
    circumstances of Jews in, 622; Jews
    gradually depart, 622; Israel sells Soviet
    arms captured in, to Ethiopia, 710; Israel
    military offensive at guerrilla bases in,
    evokes international opprobrium, 736–7
Lech'i, 573, 578, 585
Lectures on Judaism, 465
Leeser, Isaac, 172
Lefcourt, A. E., 387
Lehman, Herbert, 332, 589
Lehmann, Behrend, 24, 25
Leibniz, Gottfried Wilhelm, 30
Lelyveld, Arthur, 589
Lenin, Vladimir: in intramural quarrel with
    Bund, 293; praises Bundist heroism, 295;
    sends Red Army into Ukraine, 319, builds
    Bolshevik faction, 325; orchestrates
    Bolshevik takeover of Russia, 325–6; in
    intimate collaboration with Trotsky, 326,
    328; authorizes New Economic Policy, 331;
    countenances "freedom of [autonomous]
    development" for minorities, 334; distrusts
    Stalin, 340; incapacitated by stroke, dies,
    340; Bela Kun a protégé of, 435; Rosa
    Luxemburg rejects program of, for
    Germany, 493
Lenz, Fritz, 501
Leo XIII, Pope, 93, 226–7, 229
Leo Baeck College, 653
Leopold I, of Belgium, 105
Leopold I, of Habsburg Empire, 24
Leopold III, of Belgium, 537
Lepecki, Mieczyslaw, 421
Le Pen, Jean-Marie, 646–7
Lermontov, Michael, 181
Lesseps, Ferdinand de, 106
Lessing, Gotthold Ephraim, 29, 30

Levanda, Lev, 69, 186, 206
Levanon, Nehemia, 717–18, 719, 725, 727
Lévesque, René, 619
Levi, Paul, 494, 496
Levi-Città, Tullio, 450
Lévi-Strauss, Claude, 475
Levien, Max, 495, 496
Levin, Rachel, 121, 122
Levin, Shmaryahu, 176, 358
Leviné, Eugen, 495, 496
Levinsohn, Abraham Baer, 179, 181
Levinsohn, Isaac Baer, 176, 180–1
Levinsohn, Micah Joseph, 182, 257
Levitt, William, 691
Levitz Brothers, 690
Lévy-Crémieux, Marcel, 232
Lewisohn, Adolf, 169
"Liaison Office," 718, 720, 725, 726, 727, 730
Liberal Judaism (Great Britain), 653
Libre Parole, La (journal), 231–2, 238
Libya, 624, 709
Lieberman, Aaron, 69
Liebermann, Josef, 117
Liebermann, Max, 117
Liebknecht, Karl, 314, 492–3
Ligue Antisémitique, 230, 231, 238
Lilienblum, Moses Leib, 188, 189–90, 258, 259
Lilienthal, David, 397, 689
Lilienthal, Max, 67–9, 70, 165, 187
Limantour, José Yves, 668
Lincoln, Abraham, 166, 167
Lis, Joel, 132
Lissauer, Ernst, 315, 454
"Literature of Small Peoples, The," 461
Literaturnaya Gazeta (journal), 723
Lithuania: as part of Polish Commonwealth, 11, swallowed by Tsarist Russia in 53, 64; swallowed by USSR, 530; militias of, collaborates in genocide of Jews, 530–1, 551; Jewish immigrants from, to South Africa, 663–4; nationalist restiveness in, 721; *see also* Poland, Russia (tsarist; Communist, post-Communist)
Litvinov, Maxim, 287, 721–2
Litvinov, Pavel, 721
Lloyd George, David: prepares charter document for Herzl, 276; favors revision of Sykes-Picot Agreement, 349, 351; favors using Jews as pretext for revision, 354; seeks to push Balfour Declaration through cabinet, 357–8; seeks Washington's endorsement of draft Balfour Declaration, 558; cites purpose, in supporting Zionist effort, 359; authorizes Jewish Legion, 362; appoints Samuel as Palestine high commissioner, 364; rebuffs Rumanians at Peace Conference, 423; Rothschild entreats, to keep Britain neutral in World War I, 469
Locke, John, 28
Loew, Marcus, 389
London, Meyer, 371, 372, 377, 379
Loos, Adolf, 458
Lopez, Aaron, 161
López, House of (banking), 23
López-Dubec, Salomon, 36
López-Rega, José, 678
L'Osservatore romano (journal), 227, 484
Louis XI, of France, 21
Louis XIII, of France, 157
Louis XIV, of France, 18, 23, 35
Louis XV, of France, 21
Louis XVI, of France, 34, 35, 37
Louis XVIII, of France, 73, 110
Louis Napoleon, of France, 92, 93, 95, 110, 112
Louis-Philippe, of France, 74, 86, 105, 110
Love of Zion, The, 182
Ludendorff, Erich, 317, 503, 505
Lueger, Karl: politically successful in exploiting antisemitism, 228–9, 244–5; as model for Bettauer book, 444; sets tone for "Christian Socials" in postwar Austria, 487; as influence on Hitler, 503
Lupescu, Magda, 427–8, 429, 430
Luxembourg, Treaty of, 630
Luxemburg, Rosa: as radical "purist" in German Social Democratic Party, opposes Germany's entrance into war, 313–14, 492–3; helps organize Spartacist (Communist) Party, 493; in revolt against postwar Ebert government, 493–4; Germans identify all Jews with, 496; murdered, 498
Luzzatti, Luigi, 541
Luzzatto, Samuel David, 67
Lvov, Georgi, 323

Macaulay, Thomas, 96
Machado, Antonio Alvarez, 23
MacDonald, Ramsay, 473, 522
Macedonia, 406, 408
MacMichael, Harold, 557
Macmillan, Gordon, 591
Macy's (company), 170
Madagascar, 421, 484, 528
Magnes, Judah, 221

Mahal, 702–3
Mahler, Gustav, 447, 448, 451, 458
Mahmud II, of Turkey, 141, 143
Maimon, Solomon, 32–3
Makhalov, Basil, 307
Malan, Daniel, 664, 665
Malesherbes, Chrétien, 35, 36
Mandelshtam, Leon, 69
Mandelshtam, Osip, 339, 342
Manhattan Project, 689
Manin, Daniele, 87
Maniu, Iliu, 427
Mann, Thomas, 308
Mannheim, Karl, 446
Mannheimer, Hirsch, 91
Mansion House Fund (Great Britain), 209, 216
Mapu, Abraham, 182, 256
Maria Theresa, of Habsburg Empire, 18, 25, 403
Marin, Gheorghe Gaston, 612
Maritain, Jacques, 464
Markish, Peretz, 336, 342
Marks, Michael, 649
Marks, Samuel, 663
Marks, Simon, 650
Marr, Wilhelm, 249, 252
Marshall, George, 588, 589, 591, 593
Marshall, Louis: favors Agro-Joint project, 332; supports Entente following Russian Revolution, 378; seeks U.S. intercession, develops peace conference strategy for protecting Jews, 399–401; hails formulation of minorities treaties, 401; fails to secure intercession of Republican administrations on behalf of Jews, 414; appeals to Rumanian government on minorities treaty, 425
Martov, Uri, 287, 291, 293, 328
Marx, Karl: early career of, 118–19; denigrates Jewish role in history, 119; in early association with Moses Hess, 257; ideas of, take root in Russia, 285; writes *Das Kapital, Communist Manifesto*, 310–11; strategy of, rejected by Bernstein, 311; internationalism of, remains seemingly intact, 311; two-stage revolutionary formula of, challenged by Lenin, 325
Masaryk, Jan, 598
Masaryk, Tomas: Czech scholar, liberal nationalist, 225; a hero of Czech, Slavic nationalism, 225; in Hilsner trial, denounces blood libel, 225–6; protests

Mendel Beilis trial, 308; wins support of Wilson, other Allied leaders for Czech freedom, 402; as president of Czechoslovakia, assures Jews of security and freedom, 402–3; recalls help of Brandeis, other American Jews, 404; signs, enforces Minorities Treaty, 404–5
Maurogonato, Isaaco Pesaro, 87
Maurras, Charles-Marie: early career of, 475; organizes Action Française, 476; mobilizes postwar French xenophobia against Germans, Jews, 476–7; inspires other rightist leagues, 478; exploits Stavisky Affair, 478–9; leads campaign against Blum, 480–1; accuses Jews of warmongering, 483
May Laws, 201–2, 203
Mayer, Daniel, 642
Mayer, Gustav, 446
Mayer, Louis B., 389–90
Mayer, René, 642, 719
Mayer, Saly, 558, 568
Mazzini, Giuseppe, 78, 87, 257
McClelland, Roswell, 558
McDonald, James, 516, 579
McMahon, Henry, 347
Me'assef (journal), 32
Meschcherski, V. P., 284
Medem, Vladimir, 292–3
Mehmet II, of Turkey, 139
Mehemet Ali, of Egypt, 82, 84, 85, 353
Mein Kampf, 502
Meinville, Julio, 677
Meir, Golda (Meirson): as Israel's envoy to USSR, receives tumultuous Jewish welcome, 596; Ceaușescu tenders banquet to, 613; intercedes with Kreisky, 633; 717, 718; agrees to support Soviet-Jewish emigration campaign, 725; no longer can rely on comradeship of European Socialists, 738
Melchior, Marcus, 538
Melitz (journal), 189
Mendele Moher S'forim, 299–30
Mendelssohn, Abraham (Bartholdy), 123
Mendelssohn, Brendel, 122
Mendelssohn, Erich, 468
Mendelssohn, Henriette, 122
Mendelssohn, Josef, 123
Mendelssohn, Moses: as a young man in Berlin, 29–30; early philosophical publications, widening reputation of, 30–1; translates Torah with Wessely, 31–2; *maskilim* as disciples of, 32; children of,

depart Jewish tradition of, 122; Friedländer an early disciple of, 128–9

Mendelssohn, Recha, 122–3

Mendelssohn (banking house), 102, 505

Mendelssohn-Bartholdy, Felix, 123

Mendès-France, Pierre: negotiates independence for Morocco, Tunisia, 624; negotiates end to Indochina war, 643; beloved political figure, 643; active on behalf of Israel, 646

Menezes, Francisco Barreto de, 157

Mengistu, Haile Mariam, 710, 711

Mercier, Auguste, 233, 240

Meshcherski, V. P., 284

Metternich, Clements von: dominates Congress of Vienna, ensures restoration of "legitimacy" in Europe, 75, endorses easing of Jewish constraints in Europe, not in Habsburg Empire, 77; intercedes on behalf of imprisoned Damascus Jews, 84; overthrown by 1848 revolution, 86; recommends titles, decorations for Rothschilds, 108–9, 111; favors relaxation of Jewish living conditions in Vienna, 111–12

Meyerhoff, Harvey, 690

Meyerhoff, Joseph, 690

Mexico, 18, 668

Michelson, Albert Abraham, 450

Mikhailovski, Nicholas, 195

Mikhoels, Solomon, 595, 603

Miliukov, Pavel, 323

Mills, Wilbur, 729–30, 733, 734

Milner, Alfred, 358

Minkowski, Hermann, 449, 450

Minorities Treaties: Stalin's "cultural" genuflection to, 335; Marshall's diplomacy secures, at Peace Conference, 400–1; "Revolt of Small Powers" against, 402; Czechoslovakia honors, 404–5; Yugoslavia honors, 406; Greece does not honor, 407; Turkey does not honor, 410–11; Poland does not honor, 413ff.; Poland formally repudiates, 417; Rumania spurns, 424ff.; Hungary circumvents, 439–444ff.

Mirabeau, Honoré Riqueti, Comte de, 28, 29, 35

Mitshiuk, Chief Detective, 305

Mitterand, François, 646

Moczar, Miczlyslaw, 608

Modigliani, Amadeo, 475

Mohilever, Shmuel, 227

Molé, Louis Mathieu de, 40, 41, 42, 44, 45

Molotov, Vyacheslav, 605

Monash, John, 661

Mond, Alfred, 469

Montagu (banking house), 102

Montagu, Edwin, 357–8, 359

Montefiore, Moses: on behalf of Jews, intercedes with Nicholas I, 65, with Mehemet Ali, 84, with Abd al-Mejjid I, 85, with Vatican, 93, 97, with Moroccan sultan, 98; apotheosized by nineteenth-century Jews, 98; honored by British government, 98–9; appeals to Bismarck for Rumanian Jewry, 112; sees progress of Russian Jewry under Alexander II, 186; prods Rumania on anti-Jewish policy, 204; role of, cited by Alkalai, 255

Montesquieu, Charles de Secondat de, 28, 51

Montini, Giovanni, Cardinal, 635; *see also* Paul VI, Pope

Morgenstern, Julian, 391

Morgenthau, Henry, 345, 358

Morgenthau, Henry, Jr., 567–8

Morgn Djurnal (journal), 376

Morning Post (journal), 470

Morning Press (journal), 470

Morocco: Montefiore visits, obtains sultan's promise of Jewish security, 97–8; early Jews of, under Berber rule, 148–9; Sephardim settle in, 149; Jews under French rule in, 623–4; Jews in, suffer persecution under Vichy rule, 624; rise of Israel evokes riots against Jews in, beginning of Jewish departure for Israel, 624; Mendès-France negotiates independence for, 624; government of, promises Jews full security, 624–5; most Jews of, depart for Israel, France, 625; Jewish influx into France from, 628; Spain offers transit facilities to emigrating Jews from, 641

Morrison-Grady Plan, 583–4

Mortara Affair, *see* Italy; Vatican

Mortara, Edgardo, 92, 93, 94

Mortara, Ludovico, 541

Moser, Moses, 132

Mosley, Oswald, 473–4

Mosse Verlag (publishing house), 505

Motta, Ion, 428

Moyne, Walter Guinness, Lord, 573, 582

Mühsam, Erich, 495–6, 498

Munk, Salomon, 134

Murad IV, of Turkey, 139

Murray, Archibald, 348

Mussolini, Benito: seeks to undermine Yugoslavia, 406; Rumania's Carol II

Mussolini, Benito *(continued)*
 admires, 428; Hungary's Gyula Gombos
 admires, 441; Mosley admires, 473; a model
 for French fascists, 482; Austria dependent
 upon protection of, 490; Dollfuss,
 Schuschnigg adopt rightist policies of, 491;
 isolated from Allies, turns to Hitler, 491;
 Hitler emulates, 507; upon assuming
 power, does not embrace governmental
 antisemitism, 541; shifts to governmental
 antisemitism, 541–2; anti-Jewish policy of,
 porous, 542; overthrown in coup, "rescued"
 by German troops, 543; Avraham Stern
 admires, 573; Argentine military cabal
 admires, 675
My Career as German and Jew, 455

Nagy, Imre, 609, 610
Napoleon Bonaparte: assumes power in
 France, addresses Jewish issue, 39–40;
 "religious" policy of, 40; authorizes
 Assembly of Jewish Notables, 40–2, 44,
 convenes Sanhedrin, 42, 44; issues
 "organic" regulations on Jews, 44–6; Jews
 apotheosize, 45–6; liberates Jews of
 Europe, 46–7; victories of, over Prussia, 49,
 over Russia, 58–9; establishes Duchy of
 Warsaw, 59; invading Russia, receives little
 help from Russian Jews, 59; French Jews
 liberated from Infamous Decree of, 73;
 Jews no longer passive beneficiaries of, 91;
 aftermath of, leaves ruination in Europe,
 101; Rothschilds finance allied coalition
 against, 103–4; Jewish National
 Affirmation to, re-evaluated, 571
Narodnaya Volya, *see* People's Will
Nasser, Gamal Abd al-: seizes power in
 Egypt, cultivates anti-European, anti-
 Jewish xenophobia in, 622; supports Berber
 nationalists in Algeria, 727; France,
 England, Israel, become allies against, 643;
 in 1967, tightens cordon around Israel, 707;
 Israel sees Ethiopia as barrier against, 710
Natanson, Jakob, 71
Natanson, Ludwik, 71
Nathan, Sara Levi, 78
Nathanson (financial house), 185
Nathan the Wise, 29
National Broadcasting Company, 691
National Conference on Soviet Jewry, 720,
 727, 729

National Council of Jewish Women, 220
National Review (journal), 470
National Workers Alliance (*Farband*), 376,
 379
"National Question and the Class Struggle,
 The," 278
Nationalities Issue and Social Democracy, The,
 313, 487
Nazi-Soviet (Ribbentrop-Molotov) Pact, 343,
 431, 528, 530, 546
Netherlands (Dutch): growth of Jewish
 population in, 5; Jews in trade of, 19–20;
 Jews of, win qualified right of settlement
 in England, 20; Jews of, trade extensively
 with Central European merchants, 21; role
 of Jewish provisioners, financiers in, 23;
 Jews in, during Batavian Republic, 46,
 during Napoleonic rule, 46; restoration of
 House of Orange does not affect Jews in,
 74; Rothschilds warn Belgian government
 against intervening in, 105; West India
 Company of, captures Bahía, protects
 Jews, 157; loses Bahía to Portugal, 157;
 Jewish refugees settle in West Indian
 colonies of, 157–8, 159; reach Nieuw
 Amsterdam outpost, win right of
 settlement in, 158–9, but soon depart, 159;
 British capture, transform Nieuw
 Amsterdam into New York, 160; Nazi
 Germany overruns, 527; operation of Nazi
 Final Solution in, 537; Jews of, shipped to
 Auschwitz, 538–9; ambivalent role of
 clergy in, during Jewish deportations, 563;
 in postwar, Jews of, a well-treated but
 aging population, 638
Netter, Charles, 219, 210
Neue Freie Presse (journal), 241, 264, 488
Neumann, Emanuel, 706
Neurath, Konstantin von, 508, 511
Nevlinski, Philip de, 267
New Economic Policy, 331, 336
New Ghetto, The, 264
Nicaragua, 672
Nicholas I, of Russia: committed to
 autocracy, 61; brings punitive approach to
 Jews, 62; initiates cantonal conscription
 program for Jews, 62–4; plans program for
 massive Jewish relocations, 65; abolishes
 kahals, 63–4; approves Uvarov's Crown
 School program, 66; does not learn lesson
 of Congress Poland, 71–2; as "policeman of
 Europe," helps suppress Hungarian revolt,
 90; Montefiore visits, persuades to modify

Jewish relocation, 97; reign of, coincides with Russian literary romanticism, 181; reign of, leaves hollow legacy, 183, 185

Nicholas II, of Russia: ascends throne, 284; detests Jews, gives Plehve free rein against, 288; foreign governments protest to, on Kishinev pogrom, 290; confronts 1905 uprising, 294, issues October Manifesto, 294–5, 296; "re-interprets" October Manifesto, 296; dissolves Second Duma, 302; refuses to loosen restrictions on Jews, 302–3; embraces Union of the Russian People, 303; takes personal interest in Beilis case, 305, rewards Mendel Beilis prosecutors, 308; Russian Jewry sees no hope under, 309; inept as war leader, 323; abdicates, 324; Soviet antisemitic campaign, resembles last years of, 727

Nicolay, Nicholas de, 140

Niebuhr, Barthold, 130

Niemerower, Jacob, 430

Nietzsche, Friedrich, 243, 500

Nilus, Sergei, 472

Nister, Dov, 336

Nixon, Richard, 686, 728

Nordau, Max, 264–5, 274, 453

North Africa: Judaized Berbers in, backward, persecuted, 148; flight of Sephardim to, 149; area comes under Ottoman rule, 149; Jews of, ghettoized, terrorized, 149–50; under French rule, improved Jewish conditions in, 150; memory of Zion among Jews of, 255; wartime refugee camp established for Jews in, following Bermuda Conference, 657; Jews from, settle in France, 625ff.; American Jews prefer that Israel cope with Jews from, 732; *see also* Algeria; Libya; Morocco; Tunisia

Northcliffe, Albert Harmsworth, Lord, 469

Norway, 527, 538

Noske, Gustav, 495

Novoe Vremie (journal), 194

Novosiltsev, Nicholas, 56

Numeiri, Ja'afar al-, 711

Nuremberg Laws, 508–9, 510

Odets, Clifford, 395

Offenbach, Jacques, 475

Old World and the New, The, 380

Olsen, Stig, 568

Ongania, Juan, 677

Opatoshu, Joseph, 301

Opinión (journal), 679

Oppenheim, Dagobert, 79

Oppenheim, Henry, 106

Oppenheimer, David, 655

Oppenheimer, Franz, 446

Oppenheimer, Joseph Süss, 24

Oppenheimer, J. Robert, 689

Oppenheimer, Samuel, 22–3, 24

Oppenheimer (banking house), 102

Orgelbrand, Samuel, 71

Ormsby-Gore, William, 351, 357

Orthodox Judaism (United States): suffers economic, cultural attrition in early twentieth century, 391; post–World War II revival of, 697–8

Osztereicher, Sandor, 434

Ottolenghi, Guiseppe, 541

Ottoman Empire, *see* Turkey, Turkish Empire

OZET, 332

Pacelli, Eugenio (Pius XII): as papal nuncio, negotiates concordat with Nazi Germany, 485; evinces thinly veiled antipathy to Jews, opposes criticism of German antisemitic policies, 486; *see also* Pius XII, Pope

Paderewski, Ignacy, 401, 402, 419

Pahlavi, Mohammed Reza, of Iran, 616

Pahlavi, Reza, of Iran, 616

Pahlen, Konstantin, 200

País, El (journal), 737

Palestine (pre-1967): Montefiore's efforts for Jews of, 97, 98; BILU migration to, paralleled by Am Olam migration to U.S., 213; sacred in Jewish collective memory, 255; Alkalai's, Kalischer's redemptionist vision for, 255–6; Haskalah evokes idealized memories of, 256; European nationalist movements revive Jewish hopes for, 257; Moses Hess's views on, 257–8; Smolenskin's, Lilienblum's altered vision of, 258–9; Hovevei Zion focuses on immigration to, 260; fitful Jewish migration to, 260; as factor in nineteenth-century diplomacy, 261; modest nineteenth-century Jewish settlement in, 261; BILU settlers in, 261–2; Rothschild support of Jewish agriculture in, 262; not crucial to Herzl's Zionist vision, 263; Hirsch takes dim view of, as Jewish

Palestine (pre-1967) *(continued)*
homeland, 263; *Der Judenstaat* lays no
emphasis on, 265; Herzl seeks Turkish
charter for Jewish settlement in, 269–71; al-
Arish explored, as alternative to, 271–2;
Altneuland's vision of Zionist homeland in,
272; Ahad Ha'Am's vision for, 272–3; Herzl
explores East African alternative to, 273–4;
Zionist Congress splits on issue of
alternative to, 274–5; growing Zionist fund-
raising for, 276–7; Labor Zionist visions for,
277–8; Second *Aliyah* to, 278; harsh realities
of Jewish life in, 278–9; JNF role in,
facilitates kibbutz experiment, 279–80; role
of A. D. Gordon in, 280–1; role of
Hashomer watchmen in, 282; Ben-Yehuda
revives Hebrew language in, 282–3;
pre–World War I Jewish settlement in,
evaluated, 283; Agro-Joint puts more Jews
on soil than in, 332; Habima staff decamps
from Soviet Russia to, 335; in 1914, Jewish
settlement in, juridically, demographically
still vulnerable, 344; fate of Jews in, when
Turkey enters World War I, 344–5;
American, German philanthropies help
succor Jews in, 345; Jews exiles from, in
Zion Mule Corps, 346; in early British
military, diplomatic strategy, 346; projected
disposition of, under Sykes-Picot
Agreement, 348; Allenby prepares to
invade, 348; altered British intentions for,
349; emergence of collaborative Anglo-
Zionist diplomacy on, 350–3, 354–5;
Aaronsohn spy plot in, 355–7; formulation
of Balfour Declaration for, 357–61; creation
of Jewish Legion for campaign in, 361;
wartime fate of Jews in, 362; Allenby's
liberation of, 362–3; Paris Peace Conference
authorizes British mandate in, 363–4; early
Arab-Zionist diplomacy on, 364–5; Cairo
Conference and Churchill White Paper on,
365; operation of British mandate in, 365–6;
political, economic, social development of
Jewish National Home in, 366–9; Polish
government favors, as destination for
"surplus" Jews, 421; substantial Polish-
Jewish immigration to, between wars, 421;
Nazi Germany cooperates in fostering
Jewish immigration to, 510; British
maintain categories for immigration to, 519;
Ha'avarah agreement between Germany
and Jewish Agency of, 519–20; German-
Jewish immigration to, 520; growth of

Jewish National Home in, 521; growth of
Arab population, economy in, 521; Arab
nationalist unrest shifts from Syria to,
521–2; 1929 Arab uprising in, 522; British
royal commissions to, Passfield White
Paper on, 522; Germany, Italy, encourage
Arab unrest in, 522; 1936 Arab rebellion in,
522; Britain dispatches royal commissions
to evaluate, resolve unrest in, 523–5ff.;
Chamberlain White Paper forecloses
Jewish National Home in, 525; Eichmann
visits, 534; Jewish Agency persuades British
to drop Jewish parachutists into Europe,
553–4; Brand meets with Jewish Agency
leaders from, 557; Ben-Gurion in, seeks to
prolong ransom negotiations on
Hungarian Jewry, 557; Turkey limits entry
to Jews with immigration certificates for,
559; Britain imposes limits on Jewish
immigration to, 565, turns back refugee
ships, 565–6; Jews sabotage *Patria* in, 566;
British ease immigration restrictions for,
566; Jews of, support British war effort, 572;
Jewish extremist underground in, 573;
emissaries from, encourage Jewish DPs'
hopes of reaching, 574; Zionist struggle for
Jewish immigration to, 574–77ff.; U.S.
supports Zionist demands for admission of
refugees to, 577–81ff.; Zionist uprising in,
refugee traffic to 581–5; Britain refers issue
of, to UN, 585–9; UN votes partition plan
for, 589–90; Zionists organize government
in, 590; escalating Jewish-Arab military
struggle for, 592, 593; Zionists declare
independence of Israel in, 592–3
Palestine (post-1967): mounting American-
Jewish criticism of Israeli settlement policy
in, treatment of Arabs in, 708; European
criticism of Sharon's military incursions
into, 737
Palestine Liberation Organization, 736
Paley, William, 691
Palmer, A. Mitchell, 382
Palmerston, Henry, 84, 354
Panama, 672
"Panama Canal Scandal," 232
Pan-German League, 253–4
Panofsky, Erwin, 446
Papal States, *see* Italy; Vatican
Papen, Franz von, 506
Pappenheim, Bertha, 220, 468
Passfield, Sidney Webb, Lord (Commission,
Report), 522

Pasternak, Boris, 339
Patria (vessel), 566
Pauker, Anna, 601, 602
Paul I, of Russia, 55, 56
Paul IV, Pope, 6
Paul VI, Pope, 636, 637
Paul, Randolph, 567, 568
Pavelic, Ante, 535, 536, 563
Pearson, Karl, 249–50, 381
Pecherski, Alexander, 553
Peel, Robert (Commission, Report), 523–4
Péguy, Charles, 237, 309
Pehle, John W., 567, 568
Pèlerin, Le (journal), 238
Pelley, William Dudley, 517
People's Will (movement), 285
Pepys, Samuel, 25
Pereira, Jacob, 23
Pereira (banking house, family), 116
Peres, Shimon, 708
Peretz, Yehuda Leib, 300–1
Perl, Joseph, 178, 179, 180
Perles, Rosalie, 463
Perlman, Eliezer, *see* Ben-Yehuda, Eliezer
Perón, Juan: seizes power in Argentina,
    676–7; creates populist regime; tolerates,
    then reverses harassment of Jews, 676;
    unseated, 676–7; restored to power, dies,
    677; in chaotic aftermath of, thousands of
    Jews flee to Israel, 678–9, overspill of Arab
    terrorism in, 679; uncertain economic,
    political future in, 679
Perot, Franz, 246
Peru, 18
Pesari, Abraham, 87
Pétain, Henri-Philippe, 540
Peter I, of Russia, 51
Peter II, of Russia, 51, 53
Peter, Gabor, 600, 609
Petliura, Simon: proclaimed *ataman* of
    independent Ukraine, 320; forces of,
    crushed by Russian, Polish armies, 320;
    army of, inflict massacres on Jews, 320;
    battles Denikin's White Army, Russia's
    Red Army, Pilsudski's Polish army 320–1;
    Jews flee, to protection of Red Army, 330
Philippines, 590
Phillips, Lionel, 663
Phillips, Nathan, 657
Philippson, Ludwig, 67, 133, 162
PICA (Palestine Jewish Colonization
    Organization), 262, 280
Picquart, Georges, 236–7, 241

Pilsudski, Jozef: battles Red Army, 321;
    becomes postwar Poland's "head of state,"
    411; launches "War of the Frontiers" in
    Ukraine, 412; inherits heterogeneous new
    nation, 412; often "outflanked" by
    chauvinist Endek party, 412, 413; briefly
    retires, leads coup to regain control of
    Poland, 416; is superseded by right-wing
    officers, 416; sympathetic to Zionism, 421
Pincherle, Leone, 87
Pinero, Arthur Wing, 454
Pinochet, Augusto, 671–2
Pinsker, Leo (Yehuda Leib): endorses
    Lilienthal's Crown School project in
    Russia, 69; publishes *Self-Emancipation*,
    259; as chairman of Hoveve Zion, 260;
    envisages Jewish state as source of
    normalcy, 738, of Diaspora security, 743
Pinski, David, 301
Pinto, Isaac de, 36
Pisarev, Dmitri, 187
Pissarro, Camille, 475
Pius IX, Pope, 90, 226
Pius X, Pope, 241
Pius XI, Pope, 485, 563
Pius XII, Pope: issues no criticism of
    Mussolini's anti-Jewish measures, 486;
    authorizes emergency loan to Rome Jewry,
    543; refuses to issue warning,
    condemnation, of Nazi Final Solution,
    563–4ff.; record of, contrasted with heroism
    of numerous Catholic priests, nuns, 564–5;
    fends off postwar Jewish appeals to
    repudiate antisemitism, 635; *see also* Pacelli,
    Eugenio
Pleasant Paths, 254
Plehve, Vyacheslav von, 273, 274, 289
Plekhanov, Georgi, 285, 28
Plötz, Alfred, 250, 501
Pobedonostsev, Konstantin: supplies Pan-
    Slavist ideology for Alexander III, 196–7;
    favors harsh policy toward Jews, 197;
    anticipates gradual disappearance of Jews
    in Russia, 203; remains adviser to Nicho-
    las II, 284
Pösch, Theodor, 247
Poincaré, Raymond, 353
Poland: Jewish flight from Western Europe
    to, 4, 9–10; Jewish economic role, self-
    government in, 10–12; Ukrainian uprising
    against, and Jews, 11–12, rise of Jewish
    mysticism, false messianism in, 13; growth
    of Hasidism in, 13–14; politically

Poland *(continued)*
dysfunctional, undergoes successive
territorial partitions, 15–16; deteriorating
condition of Jews during partitions of,
16–17; Napoleon's Duchy of Warsaw, and
Jews in, 47; Russia's Catherine II
attenuates, inherits bulk of Jewish
population in, 52, 54; Russia's Alexander I
annexes Kingdom of Poland (Congress
Poland), 56; uprising of, crushed by
Nicholas I, 64; role of Jews in Congress
Poland, 70–72; Jewish population statistics
in, 175; role of Habsburg Galicia, on
Russian-Jewish Haskalah, 178; historic
Ukrainian uprisings against, 319; in
campaign to reclaim Ukraine, 321;
territorially redivided by Nazi-
Soviet Pact, 343; Jews from, in
post–World War I Palestine, 367; Congress
forecloses postwar Jewish emigration from,
384; signs Minorities Treaty, 401; Minority
Treaty guarantees for Jews in, 402;
Pilsudski's prewar efforts to liberate, 411;
wins independence, 411–12, launches into
"War of the Frontiers," inherits minority
populations, 412; fails to meet political,
educational guarantees to minorities, 413;
harsh antisemitic discrimination in, 413–14;
Allied governments, League, unwilling to
enforce Minorities Treaty on, 414; failure
of Jewish "minorities bloc," *ugoda,* in, 415;
Pilsudski returns to power in, 416;
economic circumstances of, 416; Jews suffer
"cold pogrom" in, 416; repudiates
Minorities Treaty, 417; Jewish question
main domestic issue in, 418–20ff.;
government seeks immigration sites for
Jews, 420–1; some Jews emigrate from, 432;
in Austria, Nazis hound émigré Jews from,
back to, 512; Nazi Germany overruns
western sector of, 527; with beginning of
Operation Barbarossa, USSR evacuates
many Jews in eastern sector of, 529–30;
Germany liquidates remaining Jews in
Soviet sector of, 531; Judenrat in, 532–3;
death camps in, 533–4; antisemitism of,
compounds Jewish helplessness in
Holocaust, 551; Warsaw ghetto uprising in,
551–2; Jewish escape efforts, guerrilla
activities, in, 552–3; mass Jewish
deportations to, no secret to German
people, 562; emissaries of, inform
Roosevelt of Holocaust, 567; collaborative
role of, in Holocaust, 570; Jews returning
to, in postwar, encounter pogroms, flee
westward, 581; Jews from, arrive in newly
established Israel, 598–9; Communist
regime of, seals exits for Jews, closes down
Jewish communal institutions, 607;
"illegal" Jewish emigration continues from,
607; Gomulka government of, wrests
partial autonomy from Soviet Union,
607–8; Gomulka government, successor
regimes, do not suppress antisemitism,
609, encourage further Jewish emigration
from, 608–9; political upheaval in, inspires
uprising in Hungary, 610; Jews from, in
postwar Germany, 631; in postwar Austria,
632; 637; Jews from, settle in Latin
America, 668–84ff.; as minority in USSR,
allowed "family reunions," 724, 730; Jews
of, better off, due to Israel, 741; *see also*
Austria; Russia (tsarist); Ukraine
Poliakov, Samuel, 185
Politzer, Adam, 452
Pollard, Jonathan, 708–9
Pompidou, Georges, 646
Popolo d'Italia, Il (journal), 542
Portalis, Jean-Étienne-Marie, 40, 43
Portugal: Jews from, settle in France, 21, in
Turkish Empire, 139, in Spanish America,
155–6, in Brazil, 156–7; Jews from, flee
Brazil, many to settle in West Indies, 157–8;
during World War II, WRB staffers
operate in, 568; Jews fearful of Latin
American reconquest by, 668; first
Venezuelan Jews, fugitives from
Inquisition of, 669; Vargas in Brazil,
admires fascism of, 681
Pott, August, 247
Pranaitis, Justin, 303, 307–8, 309
Pravda (journal), 604
Preuss, Hugo, 497
Preussische Jahrbuch, Das (journal), 244
Protocols of the Elders of Zion, The: circulated
in U.S. by White Russians, Henry Ford,
383; ostensibly lays out plan for Jewish
control of the world, 471; translated,
circulated worldwide, 418; exposed as
forgery, 471–2; influence of, fades slowly,
472–3; clergy in Italy, France, active in
promoting, 484; Hitler cites, 504; Ivanov's
book replicates, 722
Proust, Marcel, 237, 447
Provisional Zionist Executive Committee
(New York), 358

Prussia, *see* Germany
Pulitzer, Joseph, 169
Pushkin, Alexander, 178, 181

Quandt, Magda, 519
Qawukji, Fawzi al-, 591

Rabin, Yitzhak, 736, 738
Rabinovich, Sholem, *see* Sholem Aleichem
Races of Europe, The, 381
Radek, Karl, 329, 341, 342
Rafalovich (financial house), 185
Rakosi, Matyas, 600, 609, 610
Rampolla, Mariano, Cardinal, 229
Ranke, Leopold von, 130, 242
Rankin, John, 685–6
Rapallo, Treaty of, 499
Rapoport, Solomon, 180
Rasputin, Grigori, 321
Rastsvet (journal), 200, 206, 207, 259
Rathenau, Walther: consulted by kaiser, 251;
    as wartime industrial "tsar," 315, 498; object
    of wartime antisemitism, 315; expresses
    devotion to Germany, 447, 454; as postwar
    statesman, 498–9, negotiates Rapallo
    Treaty, 499; excrated, assassinated,
    499–500
Ratti-Menton, Benoît Laurent-François de,
    81–2, 83
Rawidowicz, Simon, 468
Reagan, Ronald, 709, 730
Reconstructionist Judaism, 699
Red Cavalry, 342
Rée, Paul, 459
Reform Judaism (Germany): decorous,
    modernist prefigurations of, 127–8; impact
    of historicism on, 133; role of Geiger in
    growth of, 134–6
Reform Judaism (Great Britain), 653
Reform Judaism (United States): early
    growth, 272–4, continues growth in early
    twentieth century, 391–2; faces post–World
    War II "competition" from Conservative
    Judaism, 696, 697; concerned by Orthodox
    monopoly of Israel's religious life, 708
Régis, Max, 238
Reik, Haviva, 553
Reinach, Jacques de, 232
Reinhardt, Max, 448–9, 451

Religion of Reason from the Sources of Judaism,
    464
Renner, Karl, 487
Revai, Jozsef, 600, 609
Revai, Sandor, 449
Reventlow, Klaus, 315
Revere, Giuseppe, 87
Revue du monde catholique (journal), 231
Revue internationale des sociétés sécrètes
    (journal), 485
Rhodes, 536
Rhodesia, 667
Ribbentrop, Joachim von, 343
Riegner, Gerhart: receives authenticated
    account of Final Solution, transmits
    information to Stephen Wise, 566; State
    Department verifies information of, 566–7;
    impels Roosevelt's and Churchill's public
    warning to Axis collaborators, 567; presses
    Vatican for encyclical against
    antisemitism, 635
Riesser, Gabriel, 80, 87, 88–9
Rifkind, Malcolm, 652
Ripley, William Z., 381
Road to the Open, The, 460
Roca, Julio, 673
Rochefort, Henri de, 230
Rocque, Casimir de la, 478
Rodriguez, Jacob, 36
Röhm, Ernst, 508
Rohling, August, 226, 228
Rome and Jerusalem, 257
Roncalli, Angelo, Cardinal, 568
Rooey, van, Cardinal, 537
Roosevelt, Eleanor, 537, 589
Roosevelt, Franklin D.: launches New Deal
    program, recruits Jews for his
    administration, 395–7; social activism of,
    shifts Jewish radicalism to liberal
    mainstream, 397–8; expresses concern at
    Rumanian antisemitism, 429; sponsors
    Évian Conference on refugees, 516; seeks
    foreign havens for German-Jewish
    refugees, 516–17; politically inhibited from
    admitting refugees to U.S., 517–18; acts
    decisively on refugees following
    Kristallnacht, 518; co-sponsors Bermuda
    Conference, 567; with Churchill, issues
    warning to genocide collaborators, 567;
    authorizes establishment of War Refugee
    Board, 568; Truman lacks prestige of, 577;
    Attlee recalls promise of, to Arabs, 577
Roosevelt, Theodore, 290

Rosen, Joseph, 332
Rosen, Matthias, 71
Rosen, Moses, 612, 613–14
Rosenberg, Anna, 688
Rosenberg, Ethel, 687, 688
Rosenberg, Julius: active in American
    Communist Party, engages in espionage on
    behalf of wartime USSR, 687–8; tried,
    convicted, executed, 688
Rosenfeld, Kurt, 313
Rosenman, Samuel, 518
Rosenstiel, Lewis, 387
Rosenwald, Julius, 355
Rosenzweig, Franz: drawn back to Judaism,
    467; encouraged by Cohen, Buber,
    develops modern philosophy of Judaism,
    467; writes *Star of Redemption*, 467;
    develops Lehrhaus movement, 468; co-
    translates Bible with Buber, 468; tradition
    of, revived by American-Jewish
    intellectuals, 699; works of, published by
    Schocken, 699
Ross, Edward A., 380
Rotfeld, Lukasz, 533
Rothmund, Heinrich, 561
Rothschild, Anselm von, 114
Rothschild, Edmond de: subsidizes Zionist
    farm colonies, 262; rejects Herzl's Zionist
    vision, 267–8; subsidizes Ben-Yehuda's
    Hebraization efforts, 283; subsidizes
    schools for Ethiopian Falashas, 710
Rothschild, Evelyn de, 108
Rothschild, Lionel, 96–7, 106, 111
Rothschild, Lionel Walter, 359
Rothschild, James, 103, 105, 112
Rothschild, Karl von, 102
Rothschild, Mayer Amschel, 102–3
Rothschild, Mayer Karl von, 116
Rothschild, Nathaniel de, 97, 107
Rothschild, Nathan Mayer: father of Lionel,
    96; establishes family business in England,
    102–3; as financier of allied coalition
    against Napoleon, 103–5; enlarges family
    fortune, 104; shares in intra-family
    marriage arrangements, 107
Rothschild, Salomon von, 75, 105, 108, 114
Rothschild, Wilhelm Karl von, 107
Rothschild (family, banking house): seeks
    Jewish emancipation at Congress of
    Vienna, 77; seeks diplomatic intercession
    on behalf of Damascus Jewish prisoners,
    84; originates in Frankfurt, 102; establishes
    branches in European capitals, 103; family

ennobled, 103; "sixth dynasty of Europe,"
    104; uses influence to maintain European
    peace, 105, to secure intelligence on
    European affairs, 106; promotes intra-
    family marriages, 107; creates legend of
    international power, 107–8; ceases to be
    international firm, 108; remains close to
    conservative governments, 108–9; much
    decorated, 111; as intercessors on behalf of
    Jews, 111, 112; shifts investments to private
    sector, 114; Frankfurt branch of, liquidated,
    116; as favored target of antisemites, 117,
    228; prods Rumania on anti-Jewish policy,
    204; seeks British neutrality in World
    War I, 469; as private bankers in post–
    World War II France, 642; in England,
    belatedly come to Zionism, 654; *see also*
    individual Rothschilds
Rothstein, Arnold, 221
Round Table Conference (London), 525
Rubin, Reuven, 602
Rubinstein, Helena, *see* Helena Rubinstein
Rumania: Louis Napoleon intercedes for
    Jews of, 113; at Congress of Berlin, under
    diplomatic pressure to provide guarantees
    for Jews, 112–13; growth of Jewish
    population in, 203–4; gravely mistreats
    Jews, 204; Congress of Berlin
    commitments of, prove worthless, 204–6;
    persecution by, forces disproportionate
    Jewish immigration to U.S., 211–12; U.S.
    Congress forecloses Jewish emigration
    from, 384; signs Minorities Treaty at Paris
    Peace Conference, 401, 404; plays
    opportunistic role in World War I, 422;
    doubles territory, population, at Peace
    Conference, 422–3; acquires half-million
    Jews with postwar annexations, 423; deals
    harshly with Jews, 424–5; fends off League
    of Nations intervention, 425–6; growth of
    "ideological" antisemitism in, 425–6;
    Codreanu develops chauvinist-populist
    political movement, 426–7; Carol returns
    to, seeks dictatorial power in, 427–8; in
    1930s, Jews become targets of renewed
    chauvinism in, 428–9; Goga, Cristea
    governments embark on anti-Jewish
    "administrative" measures in, 429–30;
    drawn increasingly into German orbit, 431;
    forced to return territory to Hungary,
    Russia, and Bulgaria, 431; pro-German
    government installed in, King Carol
    abdicates, 431; sends army into Hungary at

end of World War I, 432, installs puppet premier, 436–7; under Treaty of Trianon, awarded Hungarian territory, many thousands of additional Jews, 438–9; under second Vienna Award, restores much land to Hungary, 546; as ally of Nazi Germany, invades USSR, 546; rules Transnistria, slaughters Jews, 546–7; in Regat, cruelly mistreats Jews, 547; Germany presses, for mass Jewish deportations, 547–9; 380,000 Jews of, perish, 548; Palestinian parachutists in rescue effort for Jews of, 553; Antonescu of, seeks negotiations through WRB, 568–9; in spite of decimation, Jews of, largest surviving Jewish community in Europe, 601; veteran Communists dominate postwar government in, 601; Jewish economic ruin in, completed during early postwar, 601; heavily Zionist, Jews from, allowed substantial early immigration to Israel, 602; in anti-deviationist campaign, Jewish communal life closed down, 602; in secret deal, Pauker allows quiet Jewish immigration to Israel, 602; in post-Stalin era, government adopts "independent Socialist policy," seeks new ties with West, 611; expediently allows revival of Jewish communal life, use Chief Rabbi Rosen to promote Rumanian image in U.S., 612–13; to win American trade ties, allows near-total Jewish emigration from, 613–14; Jews from, among earliest to arrive in newly established Israel, 628; some Jews from, in postwar Germany and Austria, 631–2; settle in Latin America, 668, 671ff.

Rumkowski, Chaim, 532

Ruppin, Arthur, 279–80, 345

Russell, John, Lord, 96

Russia (tsarist): evangelical sects in, 12; shares in eighteenth-century partitions of Poland, 15–16; Catherine II's rule in, 51–52; early Jewish settlement in, 52–4; inherits Jews of partitioned Poland, 54; Catherine II's ambivalent approach to Jews of, 54–5; Alexander I, explores Jewish issue in, 55–7; "Constitution of the Jews" established in, 57–58; struggle of, with Napoleon, influences Jewish policy, 58–9; unbridgeable barrier between Jews and Russians, 60–1; Nicholas I imposes harsh policies for Jews of, 61–2; impact of cantonal conscription on Jews of, 62–4;

Nicholas I of, as "policeman of Europe," 64; impact of Kiselev Committee report on Jews of, 65–6; Uvarov Crown School program in, 66–70; Jews in Congress Poland, as potential model for Russian tsars, 70–2; Britain protects Turkey against, 82; consuls of, condemn imprisonment of Damascus Jews, 84; helps suppress Hungarian revolution, 90; recipient of Rothschild funding in war against Napoleon, 103; decorates members of Rothschild family, 111; at Congress of Berlin, supports guarantees for Rumanian Jews, 113; Hirsch, Bischofsheim build railroads in, 114; sociology of Jews in, 175–7; influence of European culture on, 177–8; exposure of Jews in, to Western influences, 178–9; growth of Jewish scholarship, secular humanism among Jews of, 179–81; Alexander I inaugurates reforms in, 183–4, alleviates many disabilities on Jews, 184–5; responding to "new era," Jewish maskilim favor "positivist" enlightenment in, 185–7; growth of secular Jewish education in, 187–8; impact of J. L. Gordon and M. L. Lilienblum, 188–90, of Smolenskin, 190–2; mixed consequences of Alexander II's reforms in, 193–4; rise of Slavophilism, populist terrorism in, 194–5; under Alexander III, Pan-Slavist chauvininism, anti-Jewish pogroms in, 195–9; government commissions investigate pogroms, new approach to Jews, 200; May Laws in, 201–3; efflux of Jews from, to Rumania, 203–4; "inner migration" of Jews in Pale, 207, new Jewish migration from Pale, 208; Western Jews oppose Jewish migration wave, 208–10; Jews in Brody way station sent back to, 210; Jewish emigration from, becomes flood tide, 210–11; trauma of Galician, Rumanian Jewry in, 211; Am Olam *narodniki* depart, for America, 213; Jews from, settle in Germany and Austria, 214–15, in France, 215–16, in England, 216–17; major Jewish emigration from, to United States, 217; memory of Zion among Jews of, 255; Haskalah fosters early Zionism in, 256; Hess early ideologue of Zionism in, 257–8; after pogroms, May Laws in, Smolenskin, Lilienblum, Pinsker re-evalute Haskalah optimism, 258–60; Hovevei Zion movement in, 260; émigré

Russia (tsarist) *(continued)*
Jewish students from, as first Zionists, 260;
early BILU pioneers from, 261–2; Herzl
learns of Zionist renaissance in, 267;
Zionist Congress takes cognizance of
Jewish circumstances in, 269; Herzl
affected by torment of Jews in, 272, 283;
Bundist-Zionist clashes among Jews of,
277; pre-1914 immigration to Palestine
from, 278; under Nicholas II, reactionaries
control, 284; industrialization, social and
political radicalism in, 285; Jewish social,
political radicalism develops in, 288–91;
Jews of, mount defense against pogroms in,
295–6; failure of 1905 Revolution, Jewish
emancipation in, 296–8; development of
Yiddish literature in, 298–301; Stolypin era
of reaction, Jewish persecution in, 301–4;
Mendel Beilis case in, 304–9; experiences
shifting military fortunes, in World War I,
316–17; loses vast areas to German conquest,
316–17; Jews of, under brief German rule,
317; tsarist government directs civilian
evacuation as German army advances,
317–18, Jews in, dealt with punitively, 317–8;
in Palestine, Jewish nationals of, expelled
from Jaffa at beginning of World War I,
344; Trumpeldor's military career in, 346;
allocated Middle Eastern territory under
Sykes-Picot-Sazonov treaty, 347, 348; Jews
of, not yet committed to Zionism by 1914,
349; regime of, hostile to Zionism, 349;
Pope Benedict XV fears presence of, in
Jerusalem, 353; Britain hopes Jews will
influence, to stay in war, 354; hostile to
Zionist legion, 354–5; in World War I,
American Jews initially oppose fighting
enemies of, 378, later relent following
revolution in, 378–9; Joint personnel report
on horrors in, 399; Ottoman Jews support
war effort against, 408; Pilsudski organizes
wartime legion against, 411; Rumanian
claims on territory of, 422; in World War I,
Jews from, in England, ambivalent about
military service, 470; French Jewry
embarrassed by World War I alliance with,
475; Jews from, settle in Latin America,
668–81ff.; Argentina seeks Jewish settlers
from, 673; Hirsch's abortive plan to resettle
Jews in, 673; Jews from, bring radical
tradition to Argentina, 673–5; Jews from,
had nurtured American Jewry, 735; *see also*
Poland; Ukraine

Russia (Communist, post-Communist):
Ukraine declares independence of, 319;
Denikin's White Army of, inflicts horrors
on Jews of, 320, 321; February Revolution
in, 321–2; "Joint" describes catastrophe, 322;
enthusiastic Jewish reaction to, 324;
progressive Bolshevik takeover of, 324–6;
majority of Jews in, unsympathetic to
Bolshevism, 326–7; prominent role of
Jewish Bolsheviks in early Communist,
Soviet bureaucracy, 327–30; trauma of early
Communism in, 330–31; NEP breathing
space in, 331; vocational transformation of
Jews in, 331; Agro-Joint project in, 331–3;
Biro-Bidzhan project in, 333–4;
Communization campaign among Jews of,
334–5; ambivalent cultural autonomy of
Jews in, 335–6; accelerated Jewish
"amalgamation" in, 336–9; campaign
against antisemitism in, 339; Stalin
consolidates power in, 340; in purge of
enemies, Stalin exploits antisemitism,
340–2; signs Nazi-Soviet Pact, 342–3;
Jewish Bolsheviks uninterested in Balfour
Declaration, 361; Poland's "War of the
Frontiers" against, 412; in post–World
War I, Rumania awarded Bessarabian
territories of, 422; nationals of, in
post–World War I Rumania, 423; influx of
Jews from, into Rumania, 425; at Hitler's
orders, Rumania returns Bessarabia to, 431;
Kun's career as POW in, 432; many Jews
from, migrate to Hungary, 432–3,
influenced by Bolshevik Revolution in,
433–4; British press, officials, see Jews as
responsible for Bolshevik Revolution in,
470–2; *Protocols* revealed as fraudulent, but
disseminated by White enemies of, 471–3;
French rightists accuse Jews of
identification with, 477; authorizes
Communist participation in French
Popular Front, 480; Nazi-Soviet Pact as
Daladier's pretext for political reaction,
482; floods Austria with Bolshevik
propaganda, 488; Lenin dispatches agents
from, to Bavaria, 495; signs Treaty of
Rapallo with Germany, 499; Hitler's
invasion of, 527–9; SS liquidation of Jews
in, 529–31, 535–6; Rumania obliged to cede
Bessarabia to, collaborates with Germany
in invasion of, 546; Germans, Rumanians,
slaughter Jews in occupied territory of, 547;
Rumania surrenders to, 547; Hungary

collaborates in German invasion of, 548–8;
Horthy signs armistice with, 549; Red
Army of, liberates Budapest, 550; Jews in
Red Army, in partisan bands of, 551; Allied
leaders fearful of antagonizing, by
countenancing ransom negotiations for
Hungarian Jewry, 557; applies postwar
pressure on Turkey, Greece, Iran, 576;
British envisage Arab world as defensive
shield against, 576; shifts position on
Palestine, supports partition, 588, 590;
World War II sees postwar Jewish
population of, reduced by one-third, 595;
extends diplomatic recogntion,
countenances military aid to Israel, 596;
Jews of, moved by birth of Israel, arrival of
Israeli emissary, 596; Jewish evacuees,
veteran Jewish Communists return to
Poland from interior of, 598; Hungarian-
Jewish veteran Communists, Rumanian-
Jewish Communists returned from, 600,
601; wartime nationalism in, had already
fostered antisemitism, 602; upon break
with Tito, Stalin launches anti-Zionist,
anti-Jewish reign of terror campaign, as
feature of anti-Zionist reign of terror,
603–5; death of Stalin, produces "thaw" in,
606; Polish Communists win degree of
autonomy from, 607–8; crushes 1956
Hungarian uprising, but permits gradual
liberalization in, 610; Rumania negotiates
freedom of action in foreign policy, 612;
emigrating Jews from, abducted in Austria,
633; in U.S., Rosenbergs, Gold,
Greenglass, transmit U.S. atomic secrets
to, 687–9; following death of Stalin, Jewish
prisoners in, released, returned to
respectability, 712; non-Russian peoples in,
allowed wider cultural self-expression, 713;
cultural relaxation in, a camouflage for
Great Russian political control, 713–14;
Khrushchev seeks to purge Jews from state
bureaucracies, from professional life, 715;
Khrushchev allows campaign of
calumniation against, 715; Jews in, still
feared as outpost of Western powers, as
internationalists with kin in West, in
Israel, 715–16; Ben-Gurion seeks to reach
out to Jews of, 717; Israeli diplomats
conduct discreet propaganda campaign in,
717–18; Israel organizes oblique campaign
against Jewish "cultural strangulation" in,
719–20; after Six-Day War debacle,
Kremlin anathematizes Jews in, 720–1;
samizdat, ethnic restiveness, fortifies
antisemitic vindictiveness of Kremlin,
721–3; Jews in border provinces of, takes
offensive in struggle for emigration, 723–5;
Israel decides to support Jewish emigration
campaign in, 725; Leningrad hijacking
episode in, 725–6; Jewish emigration
campaign in, spreads to "heartland"
republics, 726; cautiously allows selective
emigration of Jews, 726–8; Senator
Jackson, other U.S. legislators, seek "trade-
for-freedom of emigration" agreement,
728–9; Jackson Amendment deal hangs in
diplomatic balance, 729–30; Jewish
emigration from, veers away from Israel,
730–2; Gorbachev allows expanded Jewish
emigration from, 733; U.S. responds to,
with most-favored-nation trade benefits,
733–4; Jewish emigration from, shifts back
to Israel, 734; atrophy of Jewish population
in, 734
Russia and Europe, 195
Rybachenko, Mikhail, 289
Rydz-Smigly, Edward, 416–16, 419
Ryumin, Mikhail, 712–13

Sachar, Abram L., 700
Sacher, Harry, 350, 355, 654
Sadat, Anwar al-, 613, 711
Ste. Catherine (vessel), 158
Saint-Germain, Treaty of, 486
Sakharov, Andrei, 721
Salmon, Barnett, 649, 650
Salomon, Chaim, 161
Salomon, Fred (Friedrich), 164
Salomons, David, 95–6
Salonika: rise, decline, revival of Jewish life
in, 145–6, 407–8, Jewish emigration from,
408; Nazi Final Solution in, 536–7; *see also*
Greece; Turkey, Turkish Empire
Salvador (vessel), 545
Samuel, Harold, 649–650
Samuel, Herbert, 350, 357, 521
Samuel, Maurice, 177
Sandherr, Jean, 233, 236
Sanhedrin (Napoleonic), 42–45
Saramago, José, 737
Sarfatti, Margherita, 541
Sarnoff, David, 691–3
Saudi Arabia, 709

Sazonov, Sergei, 348

Scazzocchio, Sabatino, 92

Schacht, Hjalmar, 510–11

Schechter, Solomon: as European scholar, 393; accepts presidency of Jewish Theological Seminary, formulates ideology of "catholic Israel," 393; Conservative Judaism languishes following death of, 394

Schema (papal), 636–7

Scheurer-Kestner, Auguste, 237

Schiff, Jacob: as American financier, 169; organizes philanthropies, institutions, for Russian-Jewish immigrants, 213, 214; presses for labor settlement in clothing industry, 374; after Russian Revolution, supports Allied war effort, 378–9; helps establish Jewish Theological Seminary, 393; Maecenas of American Jewish Committee, 399

Schiff, Moritz, 452

Schiller, Friedrich von, 130

Schliermacher, Friedrich, 122

Schneerson, Joseph Isaac, 697

Schneerson, Menahem Mendel, 697–8

Schneiderman, Rose, 374

Schneur, Zalman, 59

Schnitzler, Arthur, 460

Schocken (publishing house), 699

Schönberg, Arnold, 447–8, 451

Schönerer, Georg von: popularizes notion of Pan-German Empire, of Jewish "degeneracy," 252, 253; ideology of, influences Pan-German League, 253, influences Hitler, 254, 502

Schreiber, Moses, 87

Schrötter, Friedrich von, 49

Schulte, Eduard, 566

Schuschnigg, Kurt von, 490–1

Schwartzkoppen, Maximilian von, 233–4

Schwarz-Bart, André, 642

Sciaky, Leon, 146

Scientific Journal for Jewish Theology (journal), 134

Scott, Charles P., 350, 353

Seipel, Ignaz, 488, 489

Self-Emancipation, 259

Selassie, Haile, 710

Seligman(n), Joseph, 162, 168, 170

Selim I, of Turkey, 139, 141

Selim II, of Turkey, 139, 141

Serbia: Jewish settlement in, 148; signs Minorities Treaty, 401–2; Jews well treated in, 406; nationals of, in USSR, have right of "reunification" in Yugoslavia, 730; see also Yugoslavia

Shabbtai Zvi, 13

Shaftsbury, Ashley Cooper, Lord, 98

Shahar (journal), 191

Shamir, Yitzhak, 740

Sharon, Ariel, 737, 738

Shaw, Walter (Commission, Report), 522

Shcheglovitov, Ivan, 304, 306, 309

Shertok, Moshe, 584

Sholem Aleichem, 300

Shomer (HaShomer), 282

Shubert, Samuel, 389

Shubert Company, 389

Shulman, Kalman, 182, 256

Sieff, Israel, 649, 650

"Silbermann," 455

Silver, Abba Hillel, 589, 706

Simon, Ernst, 316, 468

Singer, I. J., 301

Singleton, John, 579

Sinzheim, David, 41, 43

Slansky, Richard, 606

Slansky, Rudolf, 606

Slawoj-Skladkowski, Prime Minister, 420

Slovakia: collaborates in Final Solution, 539; RAF drops Palestinian Jews into, 553; SS ransom negotiations on Jews in, 554–5; see also Habsburg Empire; Czechoslovakia

Skrzynski, Aleksander, 415, 416

Smith, Charles E., 690

Smolenskin, Peretz: role of, in Haskalah, 190–2; spiritual father of Am Olam movement, 213, of early Zionism, 258, 259, 266

Smuts, Jan Christian, 359, 664, 666

Social Democratic Union (Jewish), see Bund

Sokolnikov, Grigori, 327, 341

Sokolow, Nahum, 276, 352–3, 355

Solomon Seligman Society, 379

Solymossy, Esther, 222–4

Sonnino, Sidney, 541

South Africa: admits 5,000 German-Jewish refugees, 515; Britain interns wartime Jewish refugees in, 565; early nineteenth-century Jewish prospectors in, 663; growth of Lithuanian-Jewish immigration, 663–4; Jews in Transvaal Republic, identify with British Empire in Boer War, 664; Jews of, attain swift middle-class status, 664; election of Afrikaner Nationalist government alarms Jews of, 664;

Nationalists in, drop antisemitism from political agenda, 664–5; Jewish political-social progressivism in, 665, political expediency in, 665–6; Jews flourish economically in, 666; ethnocentric Jewish community life in, 666–7; with black political supremacy in, headlong Jewish departure from, 667; many Jews of, fight for, settle, invest in Israel, 703–4, 708; Jewish community structure, school system, energized by Israel, 739–40, 741

South African Jewish Board of Deputies, 665, 666

Sovietish Heymland (journal), 713

Spain: Jews request separate enclaves in, 6; flight of Jews from to North Africa, 10; Jewish exodus produces Kabbalistic apocalypticism, 13; role of Sephardim in international trade of, 19; condemns imprisonment of Damascus Jews, 84; trauma of Jewish exodus, 138ff.; Morocco a hinterland of, 149; builds empire in South America, 155; initially lax on admitting "New Christians" into empire, 155–6; introduces Inquisition, wipes out Jewish presence in overseas empire, 156; in Jamaica, seizes Recife Jewish refugees, 158; Jews from, settle in Dutch, British colonies in Caribbean, 160; Civil War in, helps doom French Popular Front, 482; by 1936, 6,000 Jews had returned to, 560; during Civil War in, Jews flee, driven underground, 560; in World War II, allows 30,000 Jews transit passage, 560; closes doors to Jews, 561, consigns Jewish refugees to internment camps, Joint keeps Jews alive in, 561; in postwar, Franco's government in, eases laws against Jews, 640–1; offers transit facilities for North African Jews, 641; Jewish settlement in, revives, 641; Argentinian, Chilean Jews flee to, 641; King Juan Carlos solicitous of Jews, 641; establishes diplomatic relations with Israel, 641; in 1930s, Québéquois Catholic hierarchy admires fascist regime of, 657; Jews fear reconquest of Latin America by, 668; Venezuela wins freedom from, 670; inquisition of, lingers in Chile, 671; Perón regime admires fascism of, 675; Perón flees to, 676–7; large Moslem population in, 679

Speyer, Edgar, 110, 469

Spire, André, 475

Spirit of the Laws, 51

Stalin, Joseph: promotes Five-Year plans, 333; favors "freedom of [cultural] development," 334, 335; launches Five-Year Plans, 336–7; initially condemns antisemitism, 339–40; exploits antisemitism in power struggle with Trotsky, 340–1; crushes Jewish cultural expression, 342; enters into pact with Hitler, 343; has Trotsky hunted down, murdered, 343; Soviet Jewry optimistic about future under, 595; in postwar, distrusts Jews of annexed territories, 602–3; shifts focus of campaign against "Titoist deviationism" to Jews, 604; launches "anti-Zionist" purge in satellite regimes, parties, 605–608ff.; death of, allows "thaw" in Soviet empire, 606, 609, 712

Stanislaus Augustus, of Poland, 16

Star of Redemption, 467

Stavisky, Serge, 478

Steed, Charles Wickham, 350

Stein, H. F. Karl von, 49, 75

Steinschneider, Moritz, 132

Stern, Avraham, 573

Stern, Sigismund, 87

Stevenson, Adlai, III, 729

Stöcker, Adolf, 244, 245, 246, 251–2

Stolypin, Pyotr, 301, 302, 303, 305

Stratz, Carl, 250

Straus, Isidor, 170

Straus, Lazarus, 170

Straus, Oscar, 170

Strauss, Leo, 468

Strauss, Levi, 165

Streicher, Julius, 508

Stroganov, Pavel, 56

Stroop, Jürgen, 552

Struma (vessel), 559

Studies in Rabbinical Literature, 131

Stürmer, Der (journal), 508

Stuyvesant, Pieter, 158, 159

Suarez, Georges, 48

Sudan, 711

Sue, Eugene, 182

Suez Canal, 106, 345, 346, 347, 348, 352, 356

Suleiman I, of Turkey, 141

Sumner, William Graham, 380

Sutro, Adolph, 165

Suzman, Helen, 665

Sweden: equivocal role in World War II, 538; offers asylum to Danish Jewry, 538;

Sweden *(continued)*
dispatches Wallenberg to help rescue Budapest Jews, 562; last-moment Himmler-Bernadotte negotiations on surviving refugees, 562; WRB operates in, 568

Swig, Benjamin, 690

Switzerland: site of Zionist Congresses, 268; Lenin, Trotsky, other Russian émigré radicals in, 285, 325, 328, 329; Zimmerwald Manifesto formulated in, 329; Luxemburg educated in, 492; Eichmann allows group of Hungarian Jews to entrain for, 557; ongoing rescue negotiations conducted between SS, WRB, and Saly Mayer from, 558; adopts immigration restrictions against refugee Jews, 561; eases restrictions, 561; in postwar, resists releasing bank accounts of murdered Jews, of Nazi plundered assets, 561; Riegner in, first learns of Holocaust, 566; in postwar, belatedly agrees release unclaimed Jewish bank accounts, sheltered Nazi plunder, 634

Sybel, Heinrich von, 250

Sykes, Mark (Agreement), 347–8, 352, 357

Sykes-Picot Agreement, 347–8, 349, 351, 352, 353

Syria: Capuchin monk disappears in, 81; Damascus Jews in, accused, imprisoned, tortured for death of monk, 82; France protects reputation of Mehemet Ali, ruler of, 82–3; international pressure on Mehemet Ali to release imprisoned Jews of, 82–4; Crémieux-Montefiore mission on behalf of imprisoned Jews, 83–5; releases Damascus Jewish prisoners, 85; circumstances of Jews in, not substantially changed, 85; ruled by Turkish Empire, 151; French influence, Alliance school system in, 151–2; Arabs of, suffer in World War I, 345; allocation of, under McMahon-Hussein correspondence, 347, under Sykes-Picot Agreement, 348; allocated to France by Peace Conference, 363; French dethrone Feisal as king in, 521; guerrillas from, in Palestine civil war, 523; Palestinian Jews in military campaign against Vichy French in, 572; dire circumstances of Jews in, following rise of Israel, 1967 War, 623; U.S. persuades Assad to allow emigration of Jews in, 623; Jews from, settle in modern Brazil, 680; Pollard transmits to Israel classified U.S. data on, 708

Syrkin, Nahum, 277

Szabo, Erwin, 434

Szalasi, Ferenc, 441–42, 550

Szamuely, Tibor, 436, 437

Szechenyi, Istvan, 78

Szenes, Hannah, 553–4

Sztojay, Dome, 549

Taft, William Howard, 382

Taittinger, Pierre, 478

Talaat Pasha, Mehmet, 361

Taliano, Emilo, Cardinal, 229

Talmudjude, Der, 226

Tausenau, Karl, 87, 90

Tchlenow, Yehiel, 274–5

Testimony in Israel, 181

Tekoah, Yosef, 720

Thatcher, Margaret, 652

Theodorakis, Mikis, 737

Thiers, Adolphe, 83, 84, 85

Thomas, Norman, 398

Thomson, Basil, 356

"Those Who Weep," 275

Thus Spoke Zarathustra, 243

Thyssen, Fritz, 504

Timerman, Jacobo, 679

Times (journal), 350, 469, 472

Tishman, Julius, 690

Tiso, Jozef, 554

Tisza, Istvan, 431–2

Tisza-Eszlar case, 222–4

Tito, Josip (Broz): Jews in partisans of, 553; allows Jewish immigration to Israel, 597; breaks with Moscow, sets off massive Soviet anti-deviationist campaign, 597ff.

Tizenket Ropirat (journal), 224

Tog (journal), 376

Toller, Ernst, 455, 496

Tolstoy, Leo, 190

Toynbee, Polly, 737–8

Transjordan: 365, 523, 585, 591

Transmigration of the Soul, The, 180

Trebitsch, Arthur, 459

Treitschke, Heinrich von, 243–4, 245, 500

Trial, 455

Triangle Shirtwaist Company, 373, 374

Trianon, Treaty of: drastically amputates Hungarian territory, 438

Tribune juive Strasbourg-Paris, La (journal), 481

Trilling, Lionel, 699

Trotsky, Leon: Akselrod influences, 287; denounces Bund for "deviationism," 293; as student, caught up in revolutionary fervor, exiled to Siberia, 327; escapes, settles in Europe, 327–8; returns to Russia in 1905 Revolution, convicted, sentenced to Siberia, escapes again to Europe, 328; in Switzerland during World War I, helps write Zimmerwald Manifesto, 329; departs with family to U.S., 329; after February Revolution, returns to Russia, becomes Lenin's alter ego in Bolshevik Revolution, 329; as commissar for war, builds Red Army, saves Soviet regime, 329–30; persuades Lenin to adopt New Economic Policy, 331; outflanked by Stalin in Communist Party, stripped of power, exiled to Alma Ata, 340–1; exiled from Russia, driven from one country to another, 341–3; murdered, 343; Stalin likens "Titoist deviationism" to threat of, 603ff.

Truman, Harry: responds to Harrison recommendations on DPs, 574, 577; under conflicting pressures on Palestine issue, 577; recommends admittance of 100,000 Jewish DPs into Palestine, 577, 580, 581ff; approves joint committees with Britain, 579, 583; rejects Morrison-Grady report, 585; endorses Palestine partition, 588–9; establishes commissions on equal rights, for nondiscrimination in armed forces, employment, housing, education, 693

Trumpeldor, Joseph, 346, 365

Truth and Faith, 181

Tunisia: under Ottoman rule, Jews continue to be marginalized, 149–50; French protectorate provides incremental protection for Jews, 150; wins independence from France, 623; Bourguiba of, assures Jews of protection, equality, 625; in World War II, Jews in, endangered by presence of German Afrika Korps, 625; painful Jewish economic recovery in postwar, 625; economic upheavals in, precipitates Jewish departure to France, Israel, 626; Pollard provides Israel with classified data on, 709

Turgenev, Ivan, 190

Turkey, Turkish (Ottoman) Empire: Sufism in, influences Hasidism, 12; Britain seeks to evict Mehemet Ali from Syrian province of, 85; Sultan Abd al-Majjid I issues *firman* on behalf of Jews, 85; war of, with Russia, precipitates Congress of Berlin, 112; Hirsch negotiates Trans-Balkan Railroad project with, 114–15; first destination of Sephardic exiles, 138–9; *Romaniote* minority in, 139; Jews of, number 200,000 by seventeenth century, 139; Sephardim rapidly rebuild lives, flourish in, 139–41; conquers Arab lands, North Africa, 141; slow deterioration of Jewish security, economic, political, cultural life in, 141–3; tentative promise of *Tanzimat* era in, 143–4; Jews seek revival with Alliance school system, 143–5; role of, in Jewish history, 153–4; conquers Palestine, 160; nineteenth-century diplomatic crises of, focuses attention on Palestine, 261; allows European "capitulatory" protection of Palestine Jews, 261, but raises bureaucratic obstacles to Jewish settlement, 262; Hirsch warns against Jewish dealings with, 263; Hirsch envisages no future for Palestine under rule of, 263; Herzl's preliminary diplomacy with, 267; Herzl seeks German "avenue" to, 269–70, resumes direct diplomacy with, 270–1; continues to obstruct Jewish settlement in Palestine, 276; "Young Turk" Revolution offers initial hope for Zionists, 279, loosens authority in Palestine, 282; with outbreak of war, adopts brutal measures against Palestine Jewry, 344–5; permits American, U.S., German remittances to Palestine, 345; Zion Mule Corps fights against, 345–6; Suez Canal central to British war against, 346; Britain seeks to mobilize Arabs against, 347; Sykes-Picot Agreement for partition of territories of, 347–8; Sykes sees Zionists as logical clients against, 349; Aaronsohn spy ring operates against, 355–7; U.S. officially neutral against, 358; counters Balfour Declaration with pro-Zionist assurances, 361; Jewish Legion organized to capture Palestine from, 361–3; Palestine Jews vulnerable to, 362; Palestine left in ruins by, 365–6; signs Minorities Treaty, 401; nationals of, in postwar Yugoslavia, 405; Greeks capture Macedonia from, 407; overthrows Abdul Hamid II, 408; Jews experience backlash of new nationalism of, in World War I, 408–9; prewar, postwar Jewish emigration from, 409; rise of Kemalist quasi-

Turkey, Turkish (Ottoman) Empire *(continued)* dictatorship, 409–10; impact of étatist economy on Jews in, 410; Jews of, intimidated into abandoning "protected" minority status, 410; *Times* correspondent in, reveals *Protocols* a forgery, 471–2; in 1944, Brand meets with Jewish Agency representatives in, 557; had offered limited sanctuary to Jewish refugees during 1930s, 558; seeks to placate Nazi Germany in World War II, 558–9; limits Jewish transit opportunities through, 559, forces *Struma* to depart, 559; inflicts Varlik Vergisi on Jews, other minorities, 559; allows Joint, WRB, to conduct activities in, 559–60; Soviets apply heavy postwar pressure on, 576; Bevin fears antagonizing, on Palestine, 580; British abandon military, financial commitments to, 585; in postwar, many Jews of, depart for Israel, 614–15; Arab terror attacks in, 615; Jewish cultural vitality in, waning, 615; Jews from, and Balkans, settle in Mexico, 668, in Uruguay, 669, in Brazil, 680; Soviets fear nationalist infection from, 720; renewed Arab terrorism against Jews in, 739; *see also* individual Balkan nations; Salonika

Turner, Frederick Jackson, 380

Tz'firah (journal), 207

"Uganda" scheme, *see* East Africa Project

Ujejski, Jozef, 420

Ukraine: Jewish settlement in, 10; Chmielnicki uprising, slaughter of Jews in, 11–12; rise of Hasidism in, 12–13; territory, population of, acquired by Catherine II, 55; Nicholas I's policy of Russification in, 64; intermittent anti-Jewish pogroms in, 198–9; proclaims autonomy from Russia, in World War I, 319; grants Jews pluralistic rights in autonomous regime, 319; under wartime German occupation, Jews protected in, 319; under Petliura, proclaims full independence, 319; army of, in retreat, wreaks havoc on Jews, 320–1; Denikin's White Army in, inflicts unprecedented losses on Jews, 320–2; Joint's personnel describe Jewish catastrophe in, 322; Poland's "War of the Frontiers" in, 399; nationals of, in post–World War I Poland, 412–13, remain implacably antisemitic, 415;

militias of, collaborate in Nazi Final Solution, 531, 551, 553; *see also* Poland; Russia (tsarist)

Ulff, Levi, 23

Ullstein (publishing house), 505

Union of American Hebrew Congregations, 212, 391, 588–9, 696

Union of the Russian People, 303, 306

United Hebrew Charities (New York), 219

United Hebrew Trades, 371–2

United Jewish Appeal, 703, 707, 708, 734

United Nations: establishes UNRRA for DPs, 574; Britain turns over Palestine issue to, 585; UNSCOP hearings, reports on Palestine, 585–8; Soviet Union supports Palestine partition in, 588; United States supports Palestine partition in, 588–9; votes for Palestine partition, 589–90, 596; Britain refuses cooperation with, in Palestine, 590; Rumania abstains on anti-Israel resolutions in, 613; Jews in Lebanese delegation to, 623; conference of, on racism, indicts Israel for racist discrimination, 737

United Nobility Party, 303, 306

United States: impact of Napoleonic Sanhedrin on Jews of, 43; reimposition of *matrikel* in Germany impels Jewish immigration to, 76; Jewish mass meetings in, protest imprisonment of Damascus Jews, 83; outrage in, at Mortara abduction, 92; early Jewish settlement in Dutch colonies, 157–8; Jews under British colonial rule in, during Revolution in, Jews achieve full legal equality in, 161; influx of Central European Jews to, 162–3; Central European Jews achieve economic security in, 163–4; impact of frontier society upon, 164–6; Jews of, during Civil War, 166–7; German-Jewish economic breakthrough in, 167–70; emergence of postbellum anti-Jewish prejudice in, 170–1; growth of Reform Judaism in, 171–4; Russian-Jewish fugitives depart for, 208, 209; Western Jewish philanthropies encourage Jewish transmigration to, 209; Jewish "veterans" in, uneager to receive Russian Jews, 210; migrating Jews experience shock of voyage, arrival in, 211; Secretary of State Hay protests Rumanian treatment of Jews, 212; Rumanian-Jewish immigration in, 212; Jewish efforts to become agriculturists in, 212–13; American-Jewish "veterans" dispatch immigrants to smaller, inland communities, 213–14; since 1881, 2 million Jews reach, 214; Jewish immigrant population growth in cities of, 217, in New York, 217–18; Jews congregate in needle trades of, 218–19; Jewish "veterans" in, organize philanthropies, training programs for immigrants, 219–20; early Jewish crime, in, 220–1; sends delegates to Zionist Congress, 268; Jewish leadership of, hostile to Zionism, 271; Congress of, protests Kishinev pogrom, 308; Jews of, anticipate Paris Peace Conference will remedy plight of East European kinsmen, 322; Jews of, fund Soviet Agro-Joint colonies, 332; in World War I, Ambassador Morgenthau helps succor Palestine Jews, 345; by 1917, Allies urgently need military resources of, 354; helps fund Aaronsohn research station in Palestine, 355; Zionist emergency office established in, 358–9; approves draft of Balfour Declaration, 359; Jews of, enlist in Jewish Legion, 361–2; immigrant Jews of early twentieth century support Socialist candidates for Congress, 370–2; East European immigrants struggle for union protection in garment industry, 371–4; religiosity in, superseded by secular welfare activities, 375; role of Yiddish culture in, 376–7; ambivalent Jewish attitude in, toward World War I, 378; immigrant community swiftly adjusting to ambience of, 378; rise of anti-immigration, antisemitic restrictionist movement in, 380–3ff.; influence of *Protocols of the Elders of Zion* in, 383; Congress passes anti-immigration laws, 383–4; widening post–World War I restrictions against Jews of, 384–6; tentative lower middle class emerging among immigrant community, 386–8; Jews shape popular entertainment in, 388–90; decline of Yiddish, 390, growth of Reform Judaism, 391–2, of Conservative Judaism, 392–4; reacting to Depression, many young Jews veer again to radicalism, 394–5; New Deal channels Jewish loyalties into liberalism, 395–8; in World War I, Jews of, launch relief program for kinsmen in Eastern European battle zones, 399; Marshall, at Paris Peace Conference, leads successful diplomatic effort of, for minorities treaties, 400–1; Masaryk wins diplomatic support of, for Czech cause,

402; Ottoman Sephardim settle in, 409; Harding, Coolidge administrations uninterested in European-Jewish issues, 414; Poland's foreign minister seeks Jewish investment funds in, 415; Paderewski a key Polish liaison with Jews of, 412; mistreatment of Rumanian Jews evokes "query" from Roosevelt in, 429; France vainly seeks funding of, to relocate refugees on Madagascar, 484; in Depression era, rejects large-scale admission of refugees, 516–18; in World II, closes off European immigration, 527; vetoes Hungarian-Jewish ransom negotiations with Eichmann, 557; French Jews seek Spanish transit visas for, 560; presses Swiss government to release unclaimed Jewish bank accounts, 562; Riegner conveys news of Holocaust to, 566; Roosevelt issues warning to Nazi collaborationist governments, 567; co-sponsors Bermuda Conference on refugees, 567; Morgenthau committee exposes State Department obstruction on Jewish rescue, 567–8; Roosevelt approves establishment of War Refugee Board, 568; establishes DP camps in occupied Germany, Austria, 573–4; Harrison Report on treatment of DPs, 574; Britain seeks DP immigration to, 576–7; evolving role of Truman administration in DP, Palestine issues, 577, 578, 579–81, 583ff.; ambivalent attitude of, toward UNSCOP partition recommendation, 588–9; supports partition recommendation in UN, 589–90; equivocates on partition, 591–2; 594; USSR dispatches Mikhoels to lecture in, 595; Soviet anti-Jewish campaign accuses Jews, Israel as agents of, 603ff.; Czech Jews put on trial, convicted as agents of, 606; Rumanian Communist leadership conducts public-relations campaign in, 612, 614; Jews flee Iran for, 618; army of, liberates Algeria, from Vichy rule, 626, 627; presses Austria on its "moral responsibility" to Jews, 634; liberal Catholics in, press for Vatican condemnation of antisemitism, 636; Franco's Spain uses Jews to cultivate goodwill in, 640; Johnson Act in, diverts Jewish immigrants to Canada, 656; Bronfman distillers thrive during Prohibition in, 656; Canadian Jewry dependent upon cultural resources of Jews

United States (continued)
in, 658; South African Jews immigrate to, 667; closing doors to immigration, diverts Polish, Rumanian Jews to Latin America, 668–81ff.; seeking goodwill of, Perón eases treatment of Argentinian Jews, 675; Washington, D.C., secures respite in Argentinian antisemitism, 677, 679; Brazil's military regime covets goodwill of, 682; Brazil threatens to default on loans from, 684; Jews of, in World War II armed forces, 685; Jews of, confront postwar anti-Communist witch-hunt, 685–6, endure trauma of Rosenberg trial and accompanying anti-Jewish suspicion, 687–9; Jews of, no longer confront fascist-style prewar antisemitism, 689; major postwar Jewish economic breakthrough in, discount merchandising, 690, real estate development, 690–1, radio and television industry, 691–3; Jews in, begin to overcome housing, academic numerus clausus, 693, professional and academic restrictions, 693, in legal, medical, teaching professions, 693–5; Jews of, share in movement to suburbia in, 695; changes in American-Jewish religious affiliations in postwar, 695–7; revival of Orthodoxy, Hasidism in, 697–8; growth of Jewish day-school movement in, 698–9; Reconstructionist movement in, 699; intellectuals' revived interest in Jewish culture, 699–700; Jews establish universities in, 700–1; Jews of, react to birth of Israel, 702, participate in Israel's War of Independence, 702–3, contribute financially to Israel, 703; many Jews of, and Canada, settle in Israel, 704–5; Ben-Gurion rejects political role for Zionist leadership of, 705–6; some Jews in, question centrality of Israel in American-Jewish life, 706–7; commitment of Jews in, to Israel, decisively galvanized by Six-Day War, 707–8; growing post-1967 immigration of Jews from, to Israel, 708; many Jews in, troubled by Israeli religious, settlement policies, 708; Jews of, shocked by Jonathan Pollard espionage episode, 708–9; government of, helpful in Israeli rescue of Ethiopian Jewry, 711, 712; Israel's "Liaison Office" mobilizes support for Soviet Jewry among Jews of, 719; Lyndon Johnson intercedes on behalf of Soviet Jews, 719; National Conference on Soviet Jewry in, Jewish vigils, demonstrations in, on behalf of Soviet Jewry, 720, 725; Soviets seek "most-favored-nation" trade agreement with, 728; Jewish lobby, congressional leaders in, secure agreement on "trade-for-freedom" amendment, 727–9; amendment in suspension, 729; diplomatic retaliation by Carter, Reagan further limits Soviet-Jewish immigration, 730; Soviets threatened by diversion of Soviet-Jewish immigration to, 730–1; as Gorbachev opens gates of departure, Soviet Jews immigration to, widens, 733–4; government of, reverses attitude toward Soviet-Jewish immigrants, 734; growing Moslem population in, a threat to Jews' political influence in, 743

United Synagogue (Great Britain), 652
Univers israélite (journal), 481
Uriburu, José, 675
Uruguay, 669
Ussishkin, Menahem, 354, 355
Ustasha, 406, 536
Uvarov, Sergei, 66–70, 187

Vallat, Xavier, 481
Valle, Eric del, 672
Vambery, Arminius, 270
Vanik, Charles, 728, 729–30, 733, 734
Vargas, Getúlio, 681, 682
Varnhagen, Karl August, 121–2
Vatican: signs Concordat with Napoleon, 40, 44; post-Napoleonic era sees restoration of papal government in, Jewish ghettoization in Rome, 74–5; ousted from political rule of Rome in 1848; rule restored, reimposes Roman ghetto, 90; role of, in Mortara Affair, 92–3; disgraced, loses rule over Papal States, city of Rome, 93–4; endorses antisemitism as weapon against political liberalism, 226–7, 228; supports Lueger in Austria, 229, stance of anti-republicanism, anti-Dreyfusardism, in France, 230, 235, 238; France severs diplomatic relations with, 241; in inter-war period, adopts thinly veiled antisemitic stance, 484–6; Germany violates concordat with, Pius XI issues encyclical of reproval against, 485; La Civiltà cattolica in, resumes antisemitic policy, 486; Mussolini invokes approbation of, in introducing anti-Jewish laws, 486;

does not oppose Italy's anti-Jewish laws, 486; willing to lend ransom money to Rome Jewry, 543; evinces moral failure in era of Holocaust, 564ff.; world Jewish leaders press, for encyclical repudiating antisemitism, 635; Pope John XXIII agrees, 635; issues *Schema* condemning antisemitism, 636; under John Paul II, warm relationship established with Jews, Israel, 637–8; *see also* individual popes

Veit, Johann Emmanuel, 123

Venezuela, 669–70

Venizelos, Eleutherios, 407

Verein für Kultur und Wissenschaft der Juden, 124, 132

Versailles, Treaty of, 496

Victor Emmanuel II, of Italy, 93

Victoria I, of Great Britain, 98, 106, 126, 127

Vienna, Congress, Treaty of: conservatism the mood of 1814–15, 73; restores Austrian hegemony over German-speaking Europe, 75; fails to liberate Jews, 76

Vinaver, Maxim, 296–7, 299

Vipper, Yevgeni, 307, 308, 309

Vitalevi, Giuseppe, 78

Voltaire, François-Marie (Arouet), 27, 29, 31, 36

Wagner, Richard: seeks "new" Christianity, untainted by Jewish associations, 248; friend of Heine, 248; adopts racial stereotype for his operas, 248; denounces "Judaism in Music," 248; rabid racist, becomes German cultural icon, 248–9, H. S. Chamberlain a disciple of, 250

Waldeck-Rousseau, René, 239, 240, 241

Waldheim, Kurt, 633

Wallenberg, Raoul, 562, 568

War Refugee Board: Roosevelt establishes, 568; permitted to operate in Turkey, 559; distributes Joint funds for Jews in Italy, Spain, North Africa, 568; in negotiations with Antonescu, saves thousands of Jews, 568–9

Warburg (banking house), 102, 251

Warburg, Max, 505

Warburg, Otto, 332

Warner Bros., 390

Warsaw, Grand Duchy of, *see* Poland

Washington Post (journal), 723

Wasserman, August von, 315

Wasserman, Jakob (family, banking house), 315, 447, 455

Weber, John B., 381

Weil, Simone, 460, 462

Weininger, Otto, 459

Weinstock, Arnold, 648

Weissmandel, Michael, 554–5

Weizmann, Chaim: in initial reaction to Herzl, 268; impact of Asher Ginzberg's writings on, 273; Herzl bequeaths precept, contacts to, 276; sees growth of *Yishuv* as preparation for Balfour Declaration, 283; deplores young Jews' involvement in Russian revolutionary movement, 295; in Manchester, becomes leader of Anglo-Zionism, 350; as wartime scientist, develops important government connections, 350–1; role of, in securing Balfour Declaration, 352–9ff.; cables friends in Russia on behalf of Entente cause, 361; meets Feisal, assured of Arab collaboration, 364; embarks on fund-raising for Jewish National Home, 367; in joint fund-raising trip with Einstein, 462; rallies Zionist leadership to support of Britain in 1939, 525–6; testifies before Anglo-American Committee, 580; achievement of, makes Zionism fashionable among Anglo-Jewry, 654, 703; envisaged a Jewish state as source of Diaspora normalization, 738, not a threat to Diaspora Jewry, 743

Welles, Sumner, 483, 484, 516, 566–7

Wellington, Arthur Wellesley, Duke of, 96

Werfel, Franz, 404, 457, 458

Wertheim, Alexander, 70

Wertheimer, Samson, 23–4, 25

Wessely, Naphtali Herz, 31–2

West Indies (British), 160

West Indies (Dutch), 157–8

West Indies (French), 157

Wigand, Otto, 247

Wilhelm, of Hesse-Cassel, 102

Wilhelm I, of Prussia, Germany, 242, 244

Wilhelm II, of Germany: dismisses Stöcker, 246; admires Houston Stewart Chamberlain, 251; correct to eminent Jews, privately antisemitic, 251; approves of Pan-Germanism, 253; meets with Herzl, fails to help, 269–70; protests Kishinev pogrom, 290; decorates Lissauer, 315

Wilhelm, prince of Hesse-Kassel, 102–3

Willem III, of the Netherlands, 23

William IV, of Great Britain, 98
Will to Power, 243
Wilser, Ludwig, 250
Wilson, Woodrow: approves draft of Balfour
Declaration, 358–9; vetoes restrictive
immigration legislation, 382; allows his
attorney general to arrest, deport suspected
radicals, 382; appoints Brandeis to
Supreme Court, 396; Marshall successfully
importunes, for minority guarantees,
400–1; receives Masaryk, recognizes
Czechoslovakia, 402; firm with Rumanians
at Peace Conference, 423
Wise, Isaac Mayer: exponent of German
culture in U.S., 165; seeks to preserve
Jewish loyalties in U.S., 165; denounces
abolitionists, 166; mobilizes support
against General Grant's Order No. 11, 167;
organizes Union of American Hebrew
Congregations, Hebrew Union College,
172–4; opposes Russian-Jewish
immigration, 210; organizes agricultural
projects for East European Jews, 213
Wise, Stephen S.: as rabbi, develops stance of
liberal activism, 391–2; learns of Final
Solution from Riegner, notifies Sumner
Welles, 566–7; mounts campaign on behalf
of Zionist cause, 589
Wisliceny, Dieter, 554–5
Witte, Sergei, 294, 303
WIZO, 368
Wolf, Lucien, 425
Wolff, Heinrich, 519
Wolfson, Isaac, 649, 650
Wolfssohn, David, 276
Woodhead, John (Commission, Report),
524–5
Workmen's Circle (Arbeiter Ring), 376, 379
World Jewish Congress, 566–7, 634, 635, 733
Wulff, Benjamin Elias, 23
Wyzanski, Charles, 397

Yakir, Piotr, 722
Yemen: ancient Jewish population in, reduced
to *dhimmi* status, 618; Jews of, among
earliest to return to Zion, 618–19; in
1948–49, en masse Jewish immigration
from, to Israel, 619
Yeshiva University, 700
Yevsektsya, 334–5
Yiddish culture, literature: in Tsarist Russia,

299–31; in post-Tsarist Russia, 336; in
United States, 370, 376–7; in Argentina,
675
Yiddische Folks Bibliotek, Die, 300
Yiddishe Volk (journal), 379
Young Men's Hebrew Association, 171, 219
Yugoslavia: Serbia becomes part of, 405; Jews
in, treated well, 406; irredentism,
antisemitism grow in non-Serb regions of,
406; under German pressure, circumscribes
Jewish rights, 406–7; Treaty of Trianon
awards Hungarian territory, thousands of
Jews, to, 438, 439; human losses of, to
Germany, 527; Nazi Final Solution in,
535–6; Jews of, fight in Tito's partisans, 553;
Pius XII does not intercede with Ustashe
regime, 563; in postwar, Jewish survivors
depart for DP camps, 597; after Tito-Stalin
break, Jews allowed revived communal life
in, 597; shrunken Jewish population in, 597
Yustschinski, Andrei, 304, 305

Zalmanson, Sylva, 726
Zand, Mikhail, 722
Zeckendorff, William, 690
Zemurray, Samuel, 387–8
Zhdanov, Andrei, 342, 603, 604, 605
Zhitlowski, Chaim, 292
Ziegfeld, Florenz, 389
Zimmermann, Arthur von, 345
Zimmerwald Manifesto, 329
Zinoviev, Grigori, 327, 340, 341, 342
"Zinoviev Letter," 473
Zion Mule Corps, 346
Zionism, Zionists, Zionist Organization: in
Russia, Crown School graduates
influential in, 69; early Alkalai, Kalischer
visions of, 255–6; role of Haskalah in, 256;
Hess's formulation of, 257–8; Pinsker's
rationale for, 259–60; Hovevei Zion
movement, 260; early trickle of BILU
idealists to Palestine, 261–2; Herzl
discusses vision of, with Hirsch, 263;
Herzl's *Judenstaat* vision of, 264–6; Herzl
belatedly learns of, in Russia, 267; First
Congress of, establishes organizational
structure, 268–9; Herzl's diplomacy for,
269–71; Herzl's vision of, as seen in
Altneuland, 272; Ginzberg's (Ahad
Ha'Am's) vision of, 272; Sixth Congress of,
in crisis on East Africa issue, 274–5;

pragmatic activities of, following Herzl's
death, 276–7; in ideological battle with
Bund, 277; formulation of Labor Zionism,
277–9; funds kibbutz experiment in
Palestine, 279–81; A. D. Gordon's vision of,
280–1; Ben-Yehuda's role in, 282–3;
pragmatic accomplishments of, by 1914,
283; briefly flourishes under Provisional
Government in Russia, 324; suppressed in
Soviet Russia, 335; with outbreak of war,
Turks suppress public institutions of, in
Palestine, 345; Zion Mule Corps an
expression of, 346; still weak among Jews
worldwide, 349–50; wartime development
of British diplomatic relationship with,
350–4; British draft, win American support
for, issue Balfour Declaration, 357–60;
impact of Balfour Declaration on world
Jewry, 360–1; Feisal promises collaboration
with, 364; organizes Jewish Agency,
launches fund-raising campaign for
Palestine Jewry, 367; organization of, used
for German peace overtures, 458; Kafka's
interest in, 461; Einstein's interest in, 462;
Buber's neo-mystical version of, 466; in
Nazi Germany, office of, directs Jewish
immigration to Palestine, 510; leadership
of, reacts cautiously to Peel Report, 524;
leadership of, despairs at 1939 British
White Paper, 525; Eichmann an admirer
of, 534; in Warsaw, organizes ghetto
uprising against Nazis, 551–2; in postwar
struggle for admission of DPs, 572ff.;
campaign of, on behalf of Palestine
partition, 586ff.; outlawed in USSR, 596;
strong in Bulgaria, 597, in Rumania, 602; in
Eastern Bloc, suddenly equated with
"deviationism," 602; Soviet Jews accused of
treason on behalf of, undergo reign of
terror, 603–5, in satellite nations, 605–6ff.;
Yemenite Jews, animated by messianic
version of, 618–19; in Iraq, capital
punishment decreed for, 620; in Egypt,
during Palestine war, Jews terrorized for
loyalty to, 621; North African Jews in
France, committed to, 646; achieves wide
acceptance among British Jews, 654,
among Canadian Jews, 658, among
Australian Jews, 662, among South African
Jews, 665–6; unifying force, in Latin
America, 668ff.; in France, grows slowly,
703; following Israel's birth, Ben-Gurion
redefines, rejects participation of Diaspora
leaders in Israeli political life, 704–6;
American Council for Judaism, "New
Left," reject, 706; criticized by some
American-Jewish intellectuals, 706–7;
Israel as sanctuary for beleaguered
Diaspora Jews meets hope of, 709; remains
strong among Jews of Soviet-annexed
territories, 717–18, 722; Soviet campaign
against, 722–3; underground of, swells
into Soviet-Jewish struggle for emigration,
723–6ff.; in heartland Soviet republics,
not preeminent in Jewish emigrationist
movement, 730; ideologists of, had
anticipated as source of Jewish
normalization, 738; in Eastern Europe
antisemitism disguised as stance against,
740–1; renaissance of, in Diaspora
communities, 741; ideologues of, had not
anticipated risks, as well as benefits, to
Diaspora Jewry, 743–4

Zola, Émile, 237–8
Zondek, Bernard, 452
Zuckerman, Boris, 723, 724
Zukor, Adolf, 389
Zunz, Leopold: endorses Lilienthal's
educational effort in Russia, 67; founder of
modern Jewish scholarship, 130–2; Geiger
a disciple of, 134
Zweig, Arnold, 455, 459
Zweig, Stefan: recalls cool reaction to Herzl's
Judenstaat, 267; recalls Herzl's funeral, 275;
supports Austrian war effort, 314; sees
Jewish intellectuals drawn by "radiant
power of fame," 447; confirms role of Jews
as patrons of culture, 456; doyen of
littérateurs, quintessential internationalist,
457–8; commits suicide, 682
Zworykin, Vladimir, 692
Zygelboim, Szmuel, 552

A Note About the Author

Born in St. Louis, Missouri, and reared in Champaign, Illinois, Howard Morley Sachar received his undergraduate education at Swarthmore and took his graduate degrees at Harvard. He has taught extensively in the fields of Modern European, Jewish, and Middle Eastern history, and lived in the Middle East for six years, two of them on fellowship, the rest as founder-director of Brandeis University's Hiatt Institute in Jerusalem. Dr. Sachar has contributed to many scholarly journals and is the author of a number of previous books: *The Course of Modern Jewish History* (1958), *Aliyah* (1961), *From the Ends of the Earth* (1964), *The Emergence of the Middle East, 1914–1924* (1969), *Europe Leaves the Middle East, 1936–1954* (1972), *A History of Israel from the Rise of Zionism to Our Time* (1976), *The Man on the Camel* (1980), *Egypt and Israel* (1981), *Diaspora* (1985), *A History of Israel from the Aftermath of the Yom Kippur War* (1987), *A History of the Jews in America* (1992), *Farewell España* (1994), *A History of Israel from the Rise of Zionism to Our Time*, revised and updated (1996), and *Israel and Europe: An Appraisal in History* (1999). He is also the editor of the thirty-nine volume *The Rise of Israel: A Documentary History*. Based in Washington, D.C., where he serves as Charles E. Smith Professor of History Emeritus at George Washington University, Dr. Sachar is a consultant and lecturer on Middle Eastern affairs for numerous governmental bodies, and lectures widely throughout the United States and abroad. He and his family live in Kensington, Maryland.

A Note on the Type

This book was set in a modern adaptation of a type designed by the first William Caslon (1692–1766). The Caslon face, an artistic, easily read type, has enjoyed over two centuries of popularity in our own country. It is of interest to note that the first copies of the Declaration of Independence and the first paper currency distributed to the citizens of the new-born nation were printed in this typeface.

Composed by Creative Graphics,
Allentown, Pennsylvania
Printed and bound by Berryville Graphics,
Berryville, Virginia